BEGINNERS GUIDE TO MUSLIM PRAYERS: A COMPREHENSIVE STEP BY STEP GUIDE WITH 33 FULL SACRED PRAYERS FOR EVERY MUSLIM

With Arabic and English

Sayed al-Siddiq

CONTENTS

Title Page
Chapter 1: Fajr Fard Prayer — 1
Chapter 2: Fajr Sunnah Prayer — 9
Chapter 3: Dhuhr Fard Prayer — 17
Chapter 4: Dhuhr Sunnah (Pre) Prayer — 30
Chapter 5: Dhuhr Sunnah (Post) Prayer — 38
Chapter 6: Asr Fard Prayer — 46
Chapter 7: Maghrib Fard Prayer — 58
Chapter 8: Maghrib Sunnah Prayer — 68
Chapter 9: Isha Fard Prayer — 76
Chapter 10: Isha Sunnah Prayer — 90
Chapter 11: Witr Prayer — 98
Chapter 12: Tahajjud Prayer — 109
Chapter 13: Tarawih Prayer — 117
Chapter 14: Duha Prayer — 136
Chapter 15: Ishraq Prayer — 144
Chapter 16: Salatul Istikhara — 152
Chapter 17: Salatul Janazah — 161
Chapter 18: Salatul Tasbih — 165
Chapter 19: Salatul Istisqa — 171
Chapter 20: Salatul Hajah — 178

Chapter 21: Salatul Tawbah	186
Chapter 22: Jumu'ah Prayer	193
Chapter 23: Eid Prayer	203
Chapter 24: Salatul Shukr	212
Chapter 25: Salatul Awwabin	219
Chapter 26: Qasr Prayer	227
Chapter 27: Salatul Dhikr	235
Chapter 28: Qunut Nazilah	244
Chapter 29: Salatul Shifa	247
Chapter 30: Salatul Rizq	256
Chapter 31: Dua Kumayl	263
Chapter 32: Dua Jawshan Kabir	266
Chapter 33: Burdah Prayer	272

CHAPTER 1: FAJR FARD PRAYER

STEP-BY-STEP Fajr Fard Prayer

The Fajr Fard Prayer, the blessed dawn worship, marks the beginning of a new day. As the first obligatory act of daily worship, it invites the believer to renew their connection with Allah, set their intentions for the day, and embrace spiritual discipline. Please ensure you are in a state of wudu (ablution) and have centered your heart with sincere niyyah (intention).

Before You Begin:
• Form your niyyah in your heart: "I intend to perform two rak'ahs of the Fajr Prayer solely for the sake of Allah."

Rak'ah 1:

1. Opening Takbīr (Start of the Prayer):
   الله أكبر
   (Allāhu Akbar) (Allah is the Greatest)

2. Recite al-Fātiha (The Opening Chapter):
   a. بِسْمِ اللَّهِ الرَّحْمَٰنِ الرَّحِيمِ
   (Bismillaahir Rahmaanir Raheem) (In the name of Allah, the Most Gracious, the Most Merciful)

b. اَلْحَمْدُ لِلّٰهِ رَبِّ الْعَالَمِين

(Alhamdu lillahi rabbil 'aalameen) (All praise is due to Allah, Lord of all the worlds)

c. اِلرَّحْمٰنِ الرَّحِيم

(Ar-Rahmaanir Raheem) (The Most Gracious, the Most Merciful)

d. مَالِكِ يَوْمِ الدِّين

(Maaliki yawmid-deen) (Master of the Day of Judgment)

e. إِيَّاكَ نَعْبُدُ وَإِيَّاكَ نَسْتَعِين

(Iyyaka na'budu wa iyyaka nasta'een) (You alone we worship, and You alone we ask for help)

f. اهْدِنَا الصِّرَاطَ الْمُسْتَقِيم

(Ihdinas-siraatal mustaqeem) (Guide us to the straight path)

g. صِرَاطَ الَّذِينَ أَنْعَمْتَ عَلَيْهِم

(Siraatal ladheena an'amta 'alayhim) (The path of those upon whom You have bestowed favor)

غَيْرِ الْمَغْضُوبِ عَلَيْهِمْ وَلَا الضَّالِّين

(ghayril maghdoobi 'alayhim wa lad-daalleen) (not [the path] of those who have earned Your anger or gone astray)

3. Recite a Short Sūrah – Sūrah al-Kāfirūn:

a. قُلْ يَا أَيُّهَا الْكَافِرُون

(Qul ya ayyuhal kaafirun) (Say, "O disbelievers,")

b. لَا أَعْبُدُ مَا تَعْبُدُون

(Laa a'budu maa ta'budoon) (I do not worship what you worship)

c. وَلَا أَنْتُمْ عَابِدُونَ مَا أَعْبُد

(Wa laa antum 'aabidoon maa a'bud) (Nor are you worshippers of what I worship)

d. وَلَا أَنَا عَابِدٌ مَا عَبَدتُّم

(Wa laa ana 'aabidun maa 'abadtum) (And I will not be a worshipper of that which you worship)

e. وَلَا أَنتُمْ عَابِدُونَ مَا أَعْبُدُ

(Wa laa antum 'aabidoon maa a'bud) (Nor will you be worshippers of what I worship)

f. لَكُمْ دِينُكُمْ وَلِيَ دِينِ

(Lakum deenkum wa liya deen) (For you is your religion, and for me is mine)

4. Rukū' (Bowing):
   As you bow, say "الله أكبر"
   (Allāhu Akbar) (Allah is the Greatest)
   Then recite:
   سُبْحَانَ رَبِّيَ الْعَظِيمِ
   (Subhana rabbiyal 'adheem) (Glory be to my Lord, the Most Great)
   [Repeat at least three times]

5. Rising from Rukū':
   While rising, say:
   سَمِعَ اللَّهُ لِمَنْ حَمِدَه
   (Sami' Allāhu liman hamidah) (Allah hears those who praise Him)
   Then, as you stand upright, say:
   رَبَّنَا وَلَكَ الْحَمْدُ
   (Rabbana wa laka al-hamd) (Our Lord, to You be all praise)

6. Sujūd (First Prostration):
   Go down into prostration saying "الله أكبر"
   Then recite:
   سُبْحَانَ رَبِّيَ الْأَعْلَى
   (Subhana rabbiyal a'la) (Glory be to my Lord, the Most High)
   [Repeat at least three times]

7. **Brief Sitting (Jalsa):**
   While sitting briefly between the prostrations, supplicate:

   رَبِّ اغْفِرْ لِي

   (Rabbi ighfir li) (O my Lord, forgive me)

8. **Sujūd (Second Prostration):**
   Say "الله أكبر" as you move into the second prostration
   Then recite:

   سُبْحَانَ رَبِّيَ الأَعْلَى

   (Subhana rabbiyal a'la) (Glory be to my Lord, the Most High)

   [Repeat at least three times]

9. **Rising for the Next Rak'ah:**
   Say "الله أكبر" and stand to begin the second rak'ah.

Rak'ah 2:

---

1. **Opening Takbīr:**

   الله أكبر

   (Allāhu Akbar) (Allah is the Greatest)

2. **Recite al-Fātiha (Repeat as in Rak'ah 1):**

   a. بِسْمِ اللهِ الرَّحْمَنِ الرَّحِيمِ

   (Bismillaahir Rahmaanir Raheem) (In the name of Allah, the Most Gracious, the Most Merciful)

   b. اَلْحَمْدُ لِلَّهِ رَبِّ الْعَالَمِينَ

   (Alhamdu lillahi rabbil 'aalameen) (All praise is due to Allah, Lord of all the worlds)

   c. اِلرَّحْمَنِ الرَّحِيمِ

   (Ar-Rahmaanir Raheem) (The Most Gracious, the Most Merciful)

d. مَالِكِ يَوْمِ الدِّينِ

(Maaliki yawmid-deen) (Master of the Day of Judgment)

e. إِيَّاكَ نَعْبُدُ وَإِيَّاكَ نَسْتَعِينُ

(Iyyaka na'budu wa iyyaka nasta'een) (You alone we worship, and You alone we ask for help)

f. اهْدِنَا الصِّرَاطَ الْمُسْتَقِيمَ

(Ihdinas-siraatal mustaqeem) (Guide us to the straight path)

g. صِرَاطَ الَّذِينَ أَنْعَمْتَ عَلَيْهِمْ

(Siraatal ladheena an'amta 'alayhim) (The path of those upon whom You have bestowed favor)

غَيْرِ الْمَغْضُوبِ عَلَيْهِمْ وَلَا الضَّالِّينَ

(ghayril maghdoobi 'alayhim wa lad-daalleen) (not [the path] of those who have earned Your anger or gone astray)

3. Recite a Short Sūrah – Sūrah al-Ikhlās:

a. قُلْ هُوَ اللَّهُ أَحَدٌ

(Qul huwa Allāhu 'ahad) (Say, "He is Allah, [Who is] One")

b. اللَّهُ الصَّمَدُ

(Allāhu as-samad) (Allah, the Eternal Refuge)

c. لَمْ يَلِدْ وَلَمْ يُولَدْ

(Lam yalid wa lam yoolad) (He neither begets nor is born)

d. وَلَمْ يَكُنْ لَهُ كُفُوًا أَحَدٌ

(Wa lam yakun lahu kufuwan ahad) (Nor is there to Him any equivalent)

4. Rukū' (Bowing):

While bowing, say "الله أكبر"

(Allāhu Akbar) (Allah is the Greatest)

Then recite:

سُبْحَانَ رَبِّيَ الْعَظِيمِ

(Subhana rabbiyal 'adheem) (Glory be to my Lord, the Most Great)

[Repeat at least three times]

5. Rising from Rukū':
    Rise while saying:
    سَمِعَ اللَّهُ لِمَنْ حَمِدَه

    (Sami' Allāhu liman hamidah) (Allah hears those who praise Him)

    Then, as you stand, say:
    رَبَّنَا وَلَكَ الْحَمْد

    (Rabbana wa laka al-hamd) (Our Lord, to You be all praise)

6. Sujūd (First Prostration):
    Descend into prostration saying "الله أكبر"
    Then recite:
    سُبْحَانَ رَبِّيَ الْأَعْلَى

    (Subhana rabbiyal a'la) (Glory be to my Lord, the Most High)

    [Repeat at least three times]

7. Brief Sitting (Jalsa):
    While seated briefly, supplicate:
    رَبِّ اغْفِرْ لِي

    (Rabbi ighfir li) (O my Lord, forgive me)

8. Sujūd (Second Prostration):
    Say "الله أكبر" as you enter the second prostration
    Then recite:
    سُبْحَانَ رَبِّيَ الْأَعْلَى

    (Subhana rabbiyal a'la) (Glory be to my Lord, the Most High)

    [Repeat at least three times]

9. Final Tashahhud (Testimony):
    Sit comfortably and recite the Tashahhud:

ٱلتَّحِيَّاتُ لِلَّهِ وَالصَّلَوَاتُ وَالطَّيِّبَاتُ

(At-tahiyyatu lillahi was-salawatu wat-tayyibatu)
(All greetings, prayers, and pure words are for Allah)

ٱلسَّلَامُ عَلَيْكَ أَيُّهَا النَّبِيُّ

(As-salamu 'alayka ayyuha an-nabiyyu) (Peace be upon you, O Prophet)

وَرَحْمَةُ اللَّهِ وَبَرَكَاتُهُ

(Wa rahmatullahi wa barakatuhu) (And the mercy and blessings of Allah)

ٱلسَّلَامُ عَلَيْنَا وَعَلَىٰ عِبَادِ اللَّهِ الصَّالِحِين

(As-salamu 'alayna wa 'ala 'ibaadil-lahi as-saaliheen)
(Peace be upon us and upon the righteous servants of Allah)

أَشْهَدُ أَنْ لَا إِلَهَ إِلَّا اللَّهُ

(Ash-hadu an la ilaha illallahu) (I bear witness that there is no deity except Allah)

وَأَشْهَدُ أَنَّ مُحَمَّدًا رَسُولُ اللَّهِ

(Wa ash-hadu anna Muhammadan Rasool Allah)
(And I bear witness that Muhammad is the Messenger of Allah)

10. Taslīm (Concluding the Prayer):

   Turn your head to the right and say:

   ٱلسَّلَامُ عَلَيْكُمْ وَرَحْمَةُ اللَّهِ

   (As-salamu 'alaykum wa rahmatullahi) (Peace and mercy of Allah be upon you)

   Then turn to the left and repeat:

   ٱلسَّلَامُ عَلَيْكُمْ وَرَحْمَةُ اللَّهِ

   (As-salamu 'alaykum wa rahmatullahi) (Peace and mercy of Allah be upon you)

Notes:
- At every transition—be it standing, bowing, prostrating, or sitting—remember to recite "الله أكبر" with sincerity.

- The repetition of "سُبْحَانَ رَبِّيَ الْأَعْلَى" and "سُبْحَانَ رَبِّيَ الْعَظِيمِ" (at least three times in each posture) follows the Prophetic tradition and nourishes the soul with remembrance.
- Feel free to add short personal supplications (duʿā) during the sitting (jalsa) if time and concentration allow.

May this detailed guide serve as a means of spiritual elevation and sincere communion with Allah as you begin your day in devotion.

CHAPTER 2: FAJR SUNNAH PRAYER

STEP-BY-STEP Fajr Sunnah Prayer

Below is an in-depth guide to the Fajr Sunnah (voluntary) prayer – an act performed before the obligatory Fajr prayer that refines one's spiritual focus and deepens the connection with the Divine as the day unfolds. Before you begin, ensure you are in a state of ritual purity (wudu) and set your heart with sincere niyyah.

Before You Begin:
• Form your niyyah in your heart: "I intend to perform two rak'ahs of the Fajr Sunnah prayer for the sake of Allah."

—————— Rak'ah 1: ——————

1. Opening Takbīr (Start of the Prayer): الله أكبر
   (Allāhu Akbar)
   (Allah is the Greatest)

2. Recite al-Fātiha (The Opening Chapter):

a. بِسْمِ اللَّهِ الرَّحْمَٰنِ الرَّحِيمِ
   (Bismillaahir Rahmaanir Raheem)
   (In the name of Allah, the Most Gracious, the Most Merciful)

b. اَلْحَمْدُ لِلَّهِ رَبِّ الْعَالَمِين

(Alhamdu lillahi rabbil 'aalameen)
(All praise is due to Allah, Lord of all the worlds)

c. اِلرَّحْمٰنِ الرَّحِيمِ

(Ar-Rahmaanir Raheem)
(The Most Gracious, the Most Merciful)

d. مَالِكِ يَوْمِ الدِّينِ

(Maaliki yawmid-deen)
(Master of the Day of Judgment)

e. إِيَّاكَ نَعْبُدُ وَإِيَّاكَ نَسْتَعِينُ

(Iyyaka na'budu wa iyyaka nasta'een)
(You alone we worship, and You alone we ask for help)

f. اهْدِنَا الصِّرَاطَ الْمُسْتَقِيمَ

(Ihdinas-siraatal mustaqeem)
(Guide us to the straight path)

g. صِرَاطَ الَّذِينَ أَنْعَمْتَ عَلَيْهِمْ

(Siraatal ladheena an'amta 'alayhim)
(The path of those upon whom You have bestowed favor)

غَيْرِ الْمَغْضُوبِ عَلَيْهِمْ وَلَا الضَّالِّينَ

(ghayril maghdoobi 'alayhim wa lad-daalleen)
(not of those who have incurred Your anger nor of those who go astray)

3. Recite a Short Sūrah – Sūrah al-Kāfirūn:

a. قُلْ يَا أَيُّهَا الْكَافِرُونَ

(Qul ya ayyuhal kaafirun)
(Say, "O disbelievers,")

b. لَا أَعْبُدُ مَا تَعْبُدُونَ

(Laa a'budu maa ta'budoon)
(I do not worship what you worship)

c. وَلَا أَنتُمْ عَابِدُونَ مَا أَعْبُدُ

(Wa laa antum 'aabidoon maa a'bud)
(Nor are you worshippers of what I worship)

d. وَلَا أَنَا عَابِدٌ مَا عَبَدتُّم
(Wa laa ana 'aabidun maa 'abadtum)
(And I will not be a worshipper of what you have worshipped)

e. وَلَا أَنتُم عَابِدُونَ مَا أَعْبُد
(Wa laa antum 'aabidoon maa a'bud)
(Nor will you be worshippers of what I worship)

f. لَكُم دِينُكُم وَلِيَ دِين
(Lakum deenkum wa liya deen)
(For you is your religion, and for me is mine)

4. Rukū' (Bowing):
   - As you move into the bowing position, say "الله أكبر"
     (Allāhu Akbar)
     (Allah is the Greatest)
   - Then recite:
     سُبْحَانَ رَبِّيَ الْعَظِيم
     (Subhana rabbiyal 'adheem)
     (Glory be to my Lord, the Most Great)
     [Repeat at least three times]

5. Rising from Rukū':
   - Rise while saying:
     سَمِعَ اللَّهُ لِمَنْ حَمِدَه
     (Sami' Allāhu liman hamidah)
     (Allah hears those who praise Him)
   - Then, while standing, say:
     رَبَّنَا وَلَكَ الْحَمْد
     (Rabbana wa laka al-hamd)
     (Our Lord, to You be all praise)

6. Sujūd (First Prostration):
   - As you descend into prostration, say "الله أكبر"
     (Allāhu Akbar)
     (Allah is the Greatest)

- Then recite:

  سُبْحَانَ رَبِّيَ الأَعْلَى

  (Subhana rabbiyal a'la)
  (Glory be to my Lord, the Most High)
  [Repeat at least three times]

7. **Brief Sitting (Jalsa):**
   - Sit briefly and supplicate, for example:

   رَبِّ اغْفِرْ لِي

   (Rabbi ighfir li)
   (O my Lord, forgive me)

8. **Sujūd (Second Prostration):**
   - Say "الله أكبر" as you perform the second prostration
     (Allāhu Akbar)
     (Allah is the Greatest)
   - Then recite:

   سُبْحَانَ رَبِّيَ الأَعْلَى

   (Subhana rabbiyal a'la)
   (Glory be to my Lord, the Most High)
   [Repeat at least three times]

9. **Rising for the Next Rak'ah:**
   - Say "الله أكبر" as you stand to begin Rak'ah 2
     (Allāhu Akbar)
     (Allah is the Greatest)

—————— Rak'ah 2: ——————

1. **Opening Takbīr:** الله أكبر
   (Allāhu Akbar)
   (Allah is the Greatest)

2. **Recite al-Fātiha:**

   a. بِسْمِ اللَّهِ الرَّحْمَٰنِ الرَّحِيمِ
   (Bismillaahir Rahmaanir Raheem)
   (In the name of Allah, the Most Gracious, the Most Merciful)

b. اَلْحَمْدُ لِلَّهِ رَبِّ الْعَالَمِين
(Alhamdu lillahi rabbil 'aalameen)
(All praise is due to Allah, Lord of all the worlds)

c. اِلرَّحْمَٰنِ الرَّحِيم
(Ar-Rahmaanir Raheem)
(The Most Gracious, the Most Merciful)

d. مَالِكِ يَوْمِ الدِّين
(Maaliki yawmid-deen)
(Master of the Day of Judgment)

e. إِيَّاكَ نَعْبُدُ وَإِيَّاكَ نَسْتَعِين
(Iyyaka na'budu wa iyyaka nasta'een)
(You alone we worship, and You alone we ask for help)

f. اهْدِنَا الصِّرَاطَ الْمُسْتَقِيم
(Ihdinas-siraatal mustaqeem)
(Guide us to the straight path)

g. صِرَاطَ الَّذِينَ أَنْعَمْتَ عَلَيْهِم
(Siraatal ladheena an'amta 'alayhim)
(The path of those upon whom You have bestowed favor)
غَيْرِ الْمَغْضُوبِ عَلَيْهِمْ وَلَا الضَّالِّين
(ghayril maghdoobi 'alayhim wa lad-daalleen)
(not of those who have incurred Your anger nor of those who go astray)

3. Recite a Short Sūrah – Sūrah al-Ikhlās:

a. قُلْ هُوَ اللَّهُ أَحَد
(Qul huwa Allāhu 'ahad)
(Say, "He is Allah, [Who is] One")

b. اللَّهُ الصَّمَد
(Allāhu as-samad)
(Allah, the Eternal Refuge)

c. لَمْ يَلِدْ وَلَمْ يُولَد

(Lam yalid wa lam yoolad)
(He neither begets nor is born)

d. وَلَمْ يَكُن لَّهُ كُفُوًا أَحَدٌ
(Wa lam yakun lahu kufuwan ahad)
(Nor is there to Him any equivalent)

4. Rukū' (Bowing):
   - As you bow, say "الله أكبر"
     (Allāhu Akbar)
     (Allah is the Greatest)
   - Then recite:
     سُبْحَانَ رَبِّيَ الْعَظِيم
     (Subhana rabbiyal 'adheem)
     (Glory be to my Lord, the Most Great)
     [Repeat at least three times]

5. Rising from Rukū':
   - Rise while saying:
     سَمِعَ اللَّهُ لِمَنْ حَمِدَه
     (Sami' Allāhu liman hamidah)
     (Allah hears those who praise Him)
   - Then, while standing, say:
     رَبَّنَا وَلَكَ الْحَمْد
     (Rabbana wa laka al-hamd)
     (Our Lord, to You be all praise)

6. Sujūd (First Prostration):
   - As you prostrate, say "الله أكبر"
     (Allāhu Akbar)
     (Allah is the Greatest)
   - Then recite in Sujūd:
     سُبْحَانَ رَبِّيَ الْأَعْلَى
     (Subhana rabbiyal a'la)
     (Glory be to my Lord, the Most High)
     [Repeat at least three times]

7. Brief Sitting (Jalsa):

- Sit briefly and recite:

رَبِّ اغْفِرْ لِي

(Rabbi ighfir li)

(O my Lord, forgive me)

8. Sujūd (Second Prostration):
   - Say "الله أكبر" as you perform the second prostration

     (Allāhu Akbar)

     (Allah is the Greatest)

   - Then recite:

   سُبْحَانَ رَبِّيَ الأَعْلَى

   (Subhana rabbiyal a'la)

   (Glory be to my Lord, the Most High)

   [Repeat at least three times]

9. Final Tashahhud (Sitting for the Testimony):
   - After the second prostration, sit and recite: التَّحِيَّاتُ

   لِلَّهِ وَالصَّلَوَاتُ وَالطَّيِّبَاتُ

   (At-tahiyyatu lillahi was-salawatu wat-tayyibatu)

   (All greetings, prayers, and pure words are for Allah)

   اَلسَّلَامُ عَلَيْكَ أَيُّهَا النَّبِيُّ

   (As-salamu 'alayka ayyuha an-nabiyyu)

   (Peace be upon you, O Prophet)

   وَرَحْمَةُ اللَّهِ وَبَرَكَاتُهُ

   (Wa rahmatullahi wa barakatuhu)

   (And the mercy and blessings of Allah)

   اَلسَّلَامُ عَلَيْنَا وَعَلَى عِبَادِ اللَّهِ الصَّالِحِينَ

   (As-salamu 'alayna wa 'ala 'ibaadil-lahi as-saaliheen)

   (Peace be upon us and upon the righteous servants of Allah)

   أَشْهَدُ أَنْ لَا إِلَهَ إِلَّا اللَّهُ

   (Ash-hadu an la ilaha illallahu)

   (I bear witness that there is no deity except Allah)

وَأَشْهَدُ أَنَّ مُحَمَّدًا رَسُولُ اللّٰه

(Wa ash-hadu anna Muhammadan Rasool Allah)

(And I bear witness that Muhammad is the Messenger of Allah)

10. Taslīm (Concluding the Prayer):
- To finish the prayer, first turn your head to the right and say:

اِلسَّلَامُ عَلَيْكُمْ وَرَحْمَةُ اللّٰه

(As-salamu 'alaykum wa rahmatullahi)

(Peace and mercy of Allah be upon you)

- Then turn your head to the left and repeat:

اِلسَّلَامُ عَلَيْكُمْ وَرَحْمَةُ اللّٰه

(As-salamu 'alaykum wa rahmatullahi)

(Peace and mercy of Allah be upon you)

Notes:

- The Fajr Sunnah prayer, though voluntary, is a cherished practice of the Prophet Muhammad (peace and blessings be upon him). It enriches your spiritual preparation and infuses the early hours with divine blessings.
- As you transition between positions (standing, bowing, prostrating, and sitting), remember to say "اللهُ أَكْبَر" with mindfulness of Allah's supreme greatness.
- You are encouraged to add personal supplications (du'ā) during the brief sittings to further seek benefit and guidance from Allah.

May this Sunnah prayer enrich your connection with Allah and set a blessed tone for your day.

CHAPTER 3: DHUHR FARD PRAYER

─────────── STEP-BY-STEP Dhuhr Fard Prayer
───────────

Below is an in-depth guide to the Dhuhr Fard (obligatory) prayer, performed after the sun passes its zenith. This mid-day prayer offers a spiritual break from daily activities, reinforcing discipline, mindfulness, and reconnection with Allah. Before you begin, ensure you are in a state of wudu and have prepared your heart for sincere worship.

───────────────────
Before You Begin:
• Form your niyyah in your heart: "I intend to perform four rak'ahs of the Dhuhr prayer for the sake of Allah."

─────────── Rak'ah 1: ───────────

1. Opening Takbīr (Start of the Prayer):　الله أكبر
    (Allāhu Akbar)
    (Allah is the Greatest)

2. Recite al-Fātiha (The Opening Chapter):

    a. بِسْمِ اللَّهِ الرَّحْمَٰنِ الرَّحِيمِ
    (Bismillaahir Rahmaanir Raheem)
    (In the name of Allah, the Most Gracious, the Most Merciful)

b. اَلْحَمْدُ لِلّٰهِ رَبِّ الْعَالَمِين
(Alhamdu lillahi rabbil 'aalameen)
(All praise is due to Allah, Lord of all the worlds)

c. اِلرَّحْمٰنِ الرَّحِيم
(Ar-Rahmaanir Raheem)
(The Most Gracious, the Most Merciful)

d. مَالِكِ يَوْمِ الدِّين
(Maaliki yawmid-deen)
(Master of the Day of Judgment)

e. اِيَّاكَ نَعْبُدُ وَإِيَّاكَ نَسْتَعِين
(Iyyaka na'budu wa iyyaka nasta'een)
(You alone we worship, and You alone we ask for help)

f. اهْدِنَا الصِّرَاطَ الْمُسْتَقِيم
(Ihdinas-siraatal mustaqeem)
(Guide us to the straight path)

g. صِرَاطَ الَّذِينَ أَنْعَمْتَ عَلَيْهِمْ، غَيْرِ الْمَغْضُوبِ عَلَيْهِمْ وَلَا الضَّالِّين
(Siraatal ladheena an'amta 'alayhim, ghayril maghdoobi 'alayhim wa lad-daalleen)
(The path of those upon whom You have bestowed favor, not of those who have incurred Your wrath nor of those who have gone astray)

3. Recite a Short Sūrah – Sūrah al-Ikhlās:

a. قُلْ هُوَ اللَّهُ أَحَد
(Qul huwa Allāhu 'ahad)
(Say, "He is Allah, [Who is] One")

b. اللَّهُ الصَّمَد
(Allāhu as-samad)
(Allah, the Eternal Refuge)

c. لَمْ يَلِدْ وَلَمْ يُولَد
(Lam yalid wa lam yoolad)

(He neither begets nor is born)

d. وَلَمْ يَكُن لَّهُ كُفُوًا أَحَدٌ

(Wa lam yakun lahu kufuwan ahad)
(Nor is there any equivalent to Him)

4. Rukū' (Bowing):

- As you move into the bowing position, say "الله أكبر"
  (Allāhu Akbar)
  (Allah is the Greatest)
- Then recite:
  سُبْحَانَ رَبِّيَ الْعَظِيمِ
  (Subhana rabbiyal 'adheem)
  (Glory be to my Lord, the Most Great)
  [Repeat at least three times]

5. Rising from Rukū':

- Rise while saying:
  سَمِعَ اللَّهُ لِمَنْ حَمِدَه
  (Sami' Allāhu liman hamidah)
  (Allah hears those who praise Him)
- Then, while standing straight, say:
  رَبَّنَا وَلَكَ الْحَمْدُ
  (Rabbana wa laka al-hamd)
  (Our Lord, to You be all praise)

6. Sujūd (First Prostration):

- As you go down into prostration, say "الله أكبر"
  (Allāhu Akbar)
  (Allah is the Greatest)
- Then recite:
  سُبْحَانَ رَبِّيَ الْأَعْلَى
  (Subhana rabbiyal a'la)
  (Glory be to my Lord, the Most High)
  [Repeat at least three times]

7. Brief Sitting (Jalsa):

- Sit briefly and supplicate; for example, recite:
  رَبِّ اغْفِرْ لِي
  (Rabbi ighfir li)
  (O my Lord, forgive me)

8. Sujūd (Second Prostration):

- Say "الله أكبر" as you prostrate again
  (Allāhu Akbar)
  (Allah is the Greatest)
- Then recite:
  سُبْحَانَ رَبِّيَ الأَعْلَى
  (Subhana rabbiyal a'la)
  (Glory be to my Lord, the Most High)
  [Repeat at least three times]

9. Rising for the Next Rak'ah:
   - Stand up while saying "الله أكبر"
     (Allāhu Akbar)
     (Allah is the Greatest)

——————— Rak'ah 2: ———————

1. Opening Takbīr: الله أكبر
   (Allāhu Akbar)
   (Allah is the Greatest)

2. Recite al-Fātiha:

a. بِسْمِ اللَّهِ الرَّحْمَٰنِ الرَّحِيمِ
   (Bismillaahir Rahmaanir Raheem)
   (In the name of Allah, the Most Gracious, the Most Merciful)

b. اَلْحَمْدُ لِلَّهِ رَبِّ الْعَالَمِينَ
   (Alhamdu lillahi rabbil 'aalameen)
   (All praise is due to Allah, Lord of all the worlds)

c. الرَّحْمَٰنِ الرَّحِيمِ

(Ar-Rahmaanir Raheem)
(The Most Gracious, the Most Merciful)

d. مَالِكِ يَوْمِ الدِّين

(Maaliki yawmid-deen)
(Master of the Day of Judgment)

e. إِيَّاكَ نَعْبُدُ وَإِيَّاكَ نَسْتَعِين

(Iyyaka na'budu wa iyyaka nasta'een)
(You alone we worship, and You alone we ask for help)

f. اَهْدِنَا الصِّرَاطَ الْمُسْتَقِيم

(Ihdinas-siraatal mustaqeem)
(Guide us to the straight path)

g. صِرَاطَ الَّذِينَ أَنْعَمْتَ عَلَيْهِمْ، غَيْرِ الْمَغْضُوبِ عَلَيْهِمْ وَلَا الضَّالِّين

(Siraatal ladheena an'amta 'alayhim, ghayril maghdoobi 'alayhim wa lad-daalleen)
(The path of those upon whom You have bestowed favor, not of those who have incurred Your wrath nor of those who have gone astray)

3. Recite a Short Sūrah – Sūrah al-Falaq:

a. قُلْ أَعُوذُ بِرَبِّ الْفَلَق

(Qul a'udhu birabbil falaq)
(Say, "I seek refuge in the Lord of daybreak")

b. مِن شَرِّ مَا خَلَق

(Min sharri ma khalaq)
(From the evil of what He has created)

c. وَمِن شَرِّ غَاسِقٍ إِذَا وَقَب

(Wa min sharri ghaasiqin idhaa waqab)
(And from the evil of darkness when it settles)

d. وَمِن شَرِّ النَّفَّاثَاتِ فِي الْعُقَد

(Wa min sharri n-naffathati fil 'uqad)
(And from the evil of those who blow on knots)

e. وَمِن شَرِّ حَاسِدٍ إِذَا حَسَد
(Wa min sharri haasidin idhaa hasad)
(And from the evil of the envier when he envies)

4. Rukū' (Bowing):

- Bow saying "الله أكبر"
  (Allāhu Akbar)
  (Allah is the Greatest)
- Then recite:
  سُبْحَانَ رَبِّيَ الْعَظِيم
  (Subhana rabbiyal 'adheem)
  (Glory be to my Lord, the Most Great)
     [Repeat at least three times]

5. Rising from Rukū':

- Rise while saying:
  سَمِعَ اللَّهُ لِمَنْ حَمِدَه
  (Sami' Allāhu liman hamidah)
  (Allah hears those who praise Him)
- Then, while standing, say:
  رَبَّنَا وَلَكَ الْحَمْد
  (Rabbana wa laka al-hamd)
  (Our Lord, to You be all praise)

6. Sujūd (First Prostration):

- As you go down, say "الله أكبر"
  (Allāhu Akbar)
  (Allah is the Greatest)
- Then recite:
  سُبْحَانَ رَبِّيَ الْأَعْلَى
  (Subhana rabbiyal a'la)
  (Glory be to my Lord, the Most High)
     [Repeat at least three times]

7. Brief Sitting (Jalsa):

- Sit and recite:
  رَبِّ اغْفِرْ لِي
  (Rabbi ighfir li)
  (O my Lord, forgive me)

8. Sujūd (Second Prostration):

- Prostrate saying "الله أكبر"
  (Allāhu Akbar)
  (Allah is the Greatest)
- Then recite:
  سُبْحَانَ رَبِّيَ الْأَعْلَى
  (Subhana rabbiyal a'la)
  (Glory be to my Lord, the Most High)
  [Repeat at least three times]

9. After completing the second rak'ah, remain seated and recite the First Tashahhud:

- التَّحِيَّاتُ لِلَّهِ وَالصَّلَوَاتُ وَالطَّيِّبَاتُ
  (At-tahiyyatu lillahi was-salawatu wat-tayyibatu)
  (All greetings, prayers, and pure words are for Allah)

- السَّلَامُ عَلَيْكَ أَيُّهَا النَّبِيُّ
  (As-salamu 'alayka ayyuha an-nabiyyu)
  (Peace be upon you, O Prophet)

- وَرَحْمَةُ اللَّهِ وَبَرَكَاتُهُ
  (Wa rahmatullahi wa barakatuhu)
  (And the mercy and blessings of Allah)

- أَشْهَدُ أَنْ لَا إِلَهَ إِلَّا اللَّهُ
  (Ash-hadu an la ilaha illallahu)
  (I bear witness that there is no deity except Allah)

──────────── Rak'ah 3: ────────────

1. Stand up for the third rak'ah, saying:
   الله أكبر

(Allāhu Akbar)
(Allah is the Greatest)

2. Recite al-Fātiha:

a. بِسْمِ اللهِ الرَّحْمٰنِ الرَّحِيمِ
(Bismillaahir Rahmaanir Raheem)
(In the name of Allah, the Most Gracious, the Most Merciful)

b. اَلْحَمْدُ لِلّٰهِ رَبِّ الْعَالَمِين
(Alhamdu lillahi rabbil 'aalameen)
(All praise is due to Allah, Lord of all the worlds)

c. اِلرَّحْمٰنِ الرَّحِيم
(Ar-Rahmaanir Raheem)
(The Most Gracious, the Most Merciful)

d. مَالِكِ يَوْمِ الدِّين
(Maaliki yawmid-deen)
(Master of the Day of Judgment)

e. اِيَّاكَ نَعْبُدُ وَإِيَّاكَ نَسْتَعِين
(Iyyaka na'budu wa iyyaka nasta'een)
(You alone we worship, and You alone we ask for help)

f. اَهْدِنَا الصِّرَاطَ الْمُسْتَقِيم
(Ihdinas-siraatal mustaqeem)
(Guide us to the straight path)

g. صِرَاطَ الَّذِينَ أَنْعَمْتَ عَلَيْهِمْ، غَيْرِ الْمَغْضُوبِ عَلَيْهِمْ وَلَا الضَّالِّين
(Siraatal ladheena an'amta 'alayhim, ghayril maghdoobi 'alayhim wa lad-daalleen)
(The path of those upon whom You have bestowed favor, not of those who have incurred Your wrath nor of those who have gone astray)

3. (In the third rak'ah, it is customary to recite only al-Fātiha without an additional surah.)

4. Rukū' (Bowing):

- Bow saying "الله أكبر"
  (Allāhu Akbar)
  (Allah is the Greatest)
- Then recite:
  سُبْحَانَ رَبِّيَ الْعَظِيم
  (Subhana rabbiyal 'adheem)
  (Glory be to my Lord, the Most Great)
  [Repeat at least three times]

5. Rising from Rukū':

- Say:
  سَمِعَ اللَّهُ لِمَنْ حَمِدَه
  (Sami' Allāhu liman hamidah)
  (Allah hears those who praise Him)
- Then, while standing, say:
  رَبَّنَا وَلَكَ الْحَمْد
  (Rabbana wa laka al-hamd)
  (Our Lord, to You be all praise)

6. Sujūd (First Prostration):

- Say "الله أكبر"
  (Allāhu Akbar)
  (Allah is the Greatest)
- Then recite:
  سُبْحَانَ رَبِّيَ الْأَعْلَى
  (Subhana rabbiyal a'la)
  (Glory be to my Lord, the Most High)
  [Repeat at least three times]

7. Brief Sitting (Jalsa):

- Sit briefly and recite:
  رَبِّ اغْفِرْ لِي
  (Rabbi ighfir li)
  (O my Lord, forgive me)

8. **Sujūd (Second Prostration):**

- Prostrate saying "الله أكبَر"
  (Allāhu Akbar)
  (Allah is the Greatest)
- Then recite:
  سُبْحَانَ رَبِّيَ الأَعْلَى
  (Subhana rabbiyal a'la)
  (Glory be to my Lord, the Most High)
  [Repeat at least three times]

9. **Rising for the Next Rak'ah:**
   - Stand up saying "الله أكبَر"
     (Allāhu Akbar)
     (Allah is the Greatest)

──────────── Rak'ah 4: ────────────

1. **Opening Takbīr:** الله أكبَر
   (Allāhu Akbar)
   (Allah is the Greatest)

2. **Recite al-Fātiha:**

a. بِسْمِ اللَّهِ الرَّحْمَٰنِ الرَّحِيمِ
   (Bismillaahir Rahmaanir Raheem)
   (In the name of Allah, the Most Gracious, the Most Merciful)

b. اَلْحَمْدُ لِلَّهِ رَبِّ الْعَالَمِين
   (Alhamdu lillahi rabbil 'aalameen)
   (All praise is due to Allah, Lord of all the worlds)

c. الرَّحْمَٰنِ الرَّحِيمِ
   (Ar-Rahmaanir Raheem)
   (The Most Gracious, the Most Merciful)

d. مَالِكِ يَوْمِ الدِّين
   (Maaliki yawmid-deen)
   (Master of the Day of Judgment)

e. إِيَّاكَ نَعْبُدُ وَإِيَّاكَ نَسْتَعِينُ
(Iyyaka na'budu wa iyyaka nasta'een)
(You alone we worship, and You alone we ask for help)

f. اهْدِنَا الصِّرَاطَ الْمُسْتَقِيمَ
(Ihdinas-siraatal mustaqeem)
(Guide us to the straight path)

g. صِرَاطَ الَّذِينَ أَنْعَمْتَ عَلَيْهِمْ، غَيْرِ الْمَغْضُوبِ عَلَيْهِمْ وَلَا الضَّالِّينَ
(Siraatal ladheena an'amta 'alayhim, ghayril maghdoobi 'alayhim wa lad-daalleen)
(The path of those upon whom You have bestowed favor, not of those who have incurred Your wrath nor of those who have gone astray)

3. (In the fourth rak'ah, after al-Fātiha, do not recite an additional surah.)

4. Rukū' (Bowing):

- Bow saying "الله أكبر"
  (Allāhu Akbar)
  (Allah is the Greatest)
- Then recite:
  سُبْحَانَ رَبِّيَ الْعَظِيمِ
  (Subhana rabbiyal 'adheem)
  (Glory be to my Lord, the Most Great)
  [Repeat at least three times]

5. Rising from Rukū':

- Say:
  سَمِعَ اللَّهُ لِمَنْ حَمِدَه
  (Sami' Allāhu liman hamidah)
  (Allah hears those who praise Him)
- Then, while standing, recite:
  رَبَّنَا وَلَكَ الْحَمْدُ
  (Rabbana wa laka al-hamd)

(Our Lord, to You be all praise)

6. Sujūd (First Prostration):

- Prostrate saying "الله أكبر"
  (Allāhu Akbar)
  (Allah is the Greatest)   • Then recite:
  سُبْحَانَ رَبِّيَ الأَعْلَى
  (Subhana rabbiyal a'la)
  (Glory be to my Lord, the Most High)
  [Repeat at least three times]

7. Brief Sitting (Jalsa):

- Sit briefly and recite:
  رَبِّ اغْفِرْ لِي
  (Rabbi ighfir li)
  (O my Lord, forgive me)

8. Sujūd (Second Prostration):

- Again, say "الله أكبر"
  (Allāhu Akbar)
  (Allah is the Greatest)
- Then recite:
  سُبْحَانَ رَبِّيَ الأَعْلَى
  (Subhana rabbiyal a'la)
  (Glory be to my Lord, the Most High)
  [Repeat at least three times]

9. Final Tashahhud (Sitting for the Testimony):

- After the second sujūd, sit and recite: التَّحِيَّاتُ لِلَّهِ وَالصَّلَوَاتُ وَالطَّيِّبَاتُ
  (At-tahiyyatu lillahi was-salawatu wat-tayyibatu)
  (All greetings, prayers, and pure words are for Allah)

  السَّلَامُ عَلَيْكَ أَيُّهَا النَّبِيُّ
  (As-salamu 'alayka ayyuha an-nabiyyu)
  (Peace be upon you, O Prophet)

وَرَحْمَةُ اللَّهِ وَبَرَك

CHAPTER 4: DHUHR SUNNAH (PRE) PRAYER

STEP-BY-STEP Dhuhr Sunnah (Pre) Prayer

Below is an in-depth guide to the pre-obligatory Sunnah rak'ahs observed before the Dhuhr Fard prayer. These voluntary prayers gently prepare your heart and mind for the fulfillment of the obligatory duty. Before you begin, ensure you are in a state of ritual purity (wudu) and have centered your intentions.

Before You Begin:
• Form your niyyah in your heart: "I intend to perform two rak'ahs of the Dhuhr Sunnah (Pre) prayer for the sake of Allah."

Rak'ah 1:

1. Opening Takbīr (Start of the Prayer):
   الله أكبر
   (Allāhu Akbar)
   (Allah is the Greatest)

2. Recite al-Fātiha (The Opening Chapter):
   a. بِسْمِ اللَّهِ الرَّحْمَٰنِ الرَّحِيمِ
   (Bismillaahir Rahmaanir Raheem)

(In the name of Allah, the Most Gracious, the Most Merciful)

b. اَلْحَمْدُ لِلَّهِ رَبِّ الْعَالَمِينَ

(Alhamdu lillahi rabbil 'aalameen)

(All praise is due to Allah, Lord of all the worlds)

c. الرَّحْمَٰنِ الرَّحِيمِ

(Ar-Rahmaanir Raheem)

(The Most Gracious, the Most Merciful)

d. مَالِكِ يَوْمِ الدِّينِ

(Maaliki yawmid-deen)

(Master of the Day of Judgment)

e. إِيَّاكَ نَعْبُدُ وَإِيَّاكَ نَسْتَعِينُ

(Iyyaka na'budu wa iyyaka nasta'een)

(You alone we worship, and You alone we ask for help)

f. اهْدِنَا الصِّرَاطَ الْمُسْتَقِيمَ

(Ihdinas-siraatal mustaqeem)

(Guide us to the straight path)

g. صِرَاطَ الَّذِينَ أَنْعَمْتَ عَلَيْهِمْ غَيْرِ الْمَغْضُوبِ عَلَيْهِمْ وَلَا الضَّالِّينَ

(Siraatal ladheena an'amta 'alayhim ghayril maghdoobi 'alayhim wa lad-daalleen)

(The path of those upon whom You have bestowed favor, not of those who have earned Your anger nor of those who go astray)

3. Recite a Short Sūrah – Sūrah al-Kāfirūn:

a. قُلْ يَا أَيُّهَا الْكَافِرُونَ

(Qul ya ayyuhal kaafirun)

(Say, "O disbelievers,")

b. لَا أَعْبُدُ مَا تَعْبُدُونَ

(Laa a'budu maa ta'budoon)

(I do not worship what you worship)

c. وَلَا أَنْتُمْ عَابِدُونَ مَا أَعْبُدُ

(Wa laa antum 'aabidoon maa a'bud)

(Nor are you worshippers of what I worship)

d. وَلَا أَنَا عَابِدٌ مَا عَبَدْتُمْ

(Wa laa ana 'aabidun maa 'abadtum)
(And I will not be a worshipper of what you worship)

e. لَا أَنتُمْ عَابِدُونَ مَا أَعْبُدُ
(Wa laa antum 'aabidoon maa a'bud)
(Nor will you be worshippers of what I worship)

f. لَكُمْ دِينُكُمْ وَلِيَ دِينِ
(Lakum deenkum wa liya deen)
(For you is your religion, and for me is mine)

4. Rukū' (Bowing):
   - As you move into the bowing position, say "الله أكبر"
     (Allāhu Akbar)
     (Allah is the Greatest)
   - Then recite:
     سُبْحَانَ رَبِّيَ الْعَظِيم
     (Subhana rabbiyal 'adheem)
     (Glory be to my Lord, the Most Great)
     [Repeat at least three times]

5. Rising from Rukū':
   - Rise while saying:
     سَمِعَ اللَّهُ لِمَنْ حَمِدَه
     (Sami' Allāhu liman hamidah)
     (Allah hears those who praise Him)
   - Then, while standing straight, say:
     رَبَّنَا وَلَكَ الْحَمْد
     (Rabbana wa laka al-hamd)
     (Our Lord, to You be all praise)

6. Sujūd (First Prostration):
   - As you go down into prostration, say "الله أكبر"
     (Allāhu Akbar)
     (Allah is the Greatest)
   - Then recite in Sujūd:
     سُبْحَانَ رَبِّيَ الْأَعْلَى
     (Subhana rabbiyal a'la)

(Glory be to my Lord, the Most High)
[Repeat at least three times]

7. **Brief Sitting (Jalsa):**
   - Sit briefly between the two prostrations.
   - You may supplicate; for example, recite:

   رَبِّ اغْفِرْ لِي

   (Rabbi ighfir li)

   (O my Lord, forgive me)

8. **Sujūd (Second Prostration):**
   - Say "الله أكبر" as you move for the second prostration.
   (Allāhu Akbar)
   (Allah is the Greatest)
   - Then recite:

   سُبْحَانَ رَبِّيَ الأَعْلَى

   (Subhana rabbiyal a'la)

   (Glory be to my Lord, the Most High)
   [Repeat at least three times]

9. **Rising for the Next Rak'ah:**
   - Say "الله أكبر"
   (Allāhu Akbar)
   (Allah is the Greatest)
   - Then stand up to begin Rak'ah 2.

Rak'ah 2:

---

1. **Opening Takbīr:**

   الله أكبر

   (Allāhu Akbar)
   (Allah is the Greatest)

2. **Recite al-Fātiha:**

   a. بِسْمِ اللهِ الرَّحْمَٰنِ الرَّحِيمِ

   (Bismillaahir Rahmaanir Raheem)

(In the name of Allah, the Most Gracious, the Most Merciful)

b. اَلْحَمْدُ لِلَّهِ رَبِّ الْعَالَمِينَ

(Alhamdu lillahi rabbil 'aalameen)

(All praise is due to Allah, Lord of all the worlds)

c. الرَّحْمَنِ الرَّحِيمِ

(Ar-Rahmaanir Raheem)

(The Most Gracious, the Most Merciful)

d. مَالِكِ يَوْمِ الدِّينِ

(Maaliki yawmid-deen)

(Master of the Day of Judgment)

e. إِيَّاكَ نَعْبُدُ وَإِيَّاكَ نَسْتَعِينُ

(Iyyaka na'budu wa iyyaka nasta'een)

(You alone we worship, and You alone we ask for help)

f. اهْدِنَا الصِّرَاطَ الْمُسْتَقِيمَ

(Ihdinas-siraatal mustaqeem)

(Guide us to the straight path)

g. صِرَاطَ الَّذِينَ أَنْعَمْتَ عَلَيْهِمْ غَيْرِ الْمَغْضُوبِ عَلَيْهِمْ وَلَا الضَّالِّينَ

(Siraatal ladheena an'amta 'alayhim ghayril maghdoobi 'alayhim wa lad-daalleen)

(The path of those upon whom You have bestowed favor, not of those who have earned Your anger nor of those who go astray)

3. Recite a Short Sūrah – Sūrah al-Ikhlās:

a. قُلْ هُوَ اللَّهُ أَحَدٌ

(Qul huwa Allāhu 'ahad)

(Say, "He is Allah, [Who is] One")

b. اللَّهُ الصَّمَدُ

(Allāhu as-samad)

(Allah, the Eternal Refuge)

c. لَمْ يَلِدْ وَلَمْ يُولَدْ

(Lam yalid wa lam yoolad)

(He neither begets nor is born)

d. وَلَمْ يَكُنْ لَهُ كُفُوًا أَحَدٌ

(Wa lam yakun lahu kufuwan ahad)
(Nor is there to Him any equivalent)

4. Rukū' (Bowing):
   - As you bow, say "الله أكبر"
     (Allāhu Akbar)
     (Allah is the Greatest)
   - Then recite:
     سُبْحَانَ رَبِّيَ الْعَظِيم
     (Subhana rabbiyal 'adheem)
     (Glory be to my Lord, the Most Great)
     [Repeat at least three times]

5. Rising from Rukū':
   - While rising, say:
     سَمِعَ اللَّهُ لِمَنْ حَمِدَه
     (Sami' Allāhu liman hamidah)
     (Allah hears those who praise Him)
   - Then, while standing, say:
     رَبَّنَا وَلَكَ الْحَمد
     (Rabbana wa laka al-hamd)
     (Our Lord, to You be all praise)

6. Sujūd (First Prostration):
   - Descend into prostration saying "الله أكبر"
     (Allāhu Akbar)
     (Allah is the Greatest)
   - Then recite:
     سُبْحَانَ رَبِّيَ الْأَعْلَى
     (Subhana rabbiyal a'la)
     (Glory be to my Lord, the Most High)
     [Repeat at least three times]

7. Brief Sitting (Jalsa):
   - Sit briefly and, if you wish, recite:
     رَبِّ اغْفِرْ لِي
     (Rabbi ighfir li)

(O my Lord, forgive me)

8. Sujūd (Second Prostration):
    - Say "الله أكبر" as you perform the second prostration.
    (Allāhu Akbar)
    (Allah is the Greatest)
    - Then recite:
    سُبْحَانَ رَبِّيَ الْأَعْلَى
    (Subhana rabbiyal a'la)
    (Glory be to my Lord, the Most High)
    [Repeat at least three times]

9. Final Tashahhud (Sitting for the Testimony):
    - After the second prostration, sit and recite:
    اَلتَّحِيَّاتُ لِلَّهِ وَالصَّلَوَاتُ وَالطَّيِّبَاتُ
    (At-tahiyyatu lillahi was-salawatu wat-tayyibatu)
    (All greetings, prayers, and pure words are for Allah)
    اَلسَّلَامُ عَلَيْكَ أَيُّهَا النَّبِيُّ
    (As-salamu 'alayka ayyuha an-nabiyyu)
    (Peace be upon you, O Prophet)
    وَرَحْمَةُ اللَّهِ وَبَرَكَاتُهُ
    (Wa rahmatullahi wa barakatuhu)
    (And the mercy and blessings of Allah)
    اَلسَّلَامُ عَلَيْنَا وَعَلَى عِبَادِ اللَّهِ الصَّالِحِينَ
    (As-salamu 'alayna wa 'ala 'ibaadil-lahi as-saaliheen)
    (Peace be upon us and upon the righteous servants of Allah)
    أَشْهَدُ أَنْ لَا إِلَهَ إِلَّا اللَّهُ
    (Ash-hadu an la ilaha illallahu)
    (I bear witness that there is no deity except Allah)
    وَأَشْهَدُ أَنَّ مُحَمَّدًا رَسُولُ اللَّهِ
    (Wa ash-hadu anna Muhammadan Rasool Allah)
    (And I bear witness that Muhammad is the Messenger of Allah)

10. Taslīm (Concluding the Prayer):
- To conclude the prayer, first turn your head to the right and say:

اِلسَّلَامُ عَلَيْكُمْ وَرَحْمَةُ اللّٰه

(As-salamu 'alaykum wa rahmatullahi)
(Peace and mercy of Allah be upon you)

- Then turn your head to the left and repeat:

السَّلَامُ عَلَيْكُمْ وَرَحْمَةُ اللّٰه

(As-salamu 'alaykum wa rahmatullahi)
(Peace and mercy of Allah be upon you)

Notes:
- At each transitional movement—standing, bowing, prostrating, and sitting—it is customary to say "اﷲ أكبر" (Allāhu Akbar) (Allah is the Greatest).
- The pre-obligatory Dhuhr Sunnah prayer serves as a gentle spiritual preparation for the Dhuhr Fard prayer. Use this time to align your heart and mind with Allah before fulfilling the obligatory act of worship.
- You may add any personal supplications (du'ā) during your brief sitting (Jalsa) to seek further closeness to Allah.

May your prayer bring tranquility, focus, and a deep connection with the Divine.

CHAPTER 5: DHUHR SUNNAH (POST) PRAYER

────────── STEP-BY-STEP Dhuhr Sunnah (Post) Prayer ──────────

Below is an in-depth guide to the Dhuhr Sunnah (Post) Prayer —a voluntary set of two rak'ahs performed after the obligatory Dhuhr prayer. This prayer deepens one's spiritual experience and extends the moments of reflection and connection with Allah after the midday prayer. Before you begin, ensure you are in a state of ritual purity (wudu) and have set your intention (niyyah) with sincerity.

Before You Begin: • Form your niyyah in your heart: "I intend to perform two rak'ahs of the Dhuhr Sunnah (Post) Prayer for the sake of Allah."

────────── Rak'ah 1: ──────────

1. Opening Takbīr (Start of the Prayer): الله أكبر
   (Allāhu Akbar)
   (Allah is the Greatest)

2. Recite al-Fātiha (The Opening Chapter):
   a. بِسْمِ اللهِ الرَّحْمٰنِ الرَّحِيم
   (Bismillaahir Rahmaanir Raheem)

(In the name of Allah, the Most Gracious, the Most Merciful)

b. اَلْحَمْدُ لِلّٰهِ رَبِّ الْعَالَمِين
(Alhamdu lillahi rabbil 'aalameen)
(All praise is due to Allah, Lord of all the worlds)

c. الرَّحْمٰنِ الرَّحِيم
(Ar-Rahmaanir Raheem)
(The Most Gracious, the Most Merciful)

d. مَالِكِ يَوْمِ الدِّين
(Maaliki yawmid-deen)
(Master of the Day of Judgment)

e. إِيَّاكَ نَعْبُدُ وَإِيَّاكَ نَسْتَعِين
(Iyyaka na'budu wa iyyaka nasta'een)
(You alone we worship, and You alone we ask for help)

f. اَهْدِنَا الصِّرَاطَ الْمُسْتَقِيم
(Ihdinas-siraatal mustaqeem)
(Guide us to the straight path)

g. (Optionally, continue with the full verse by adding:)
صِرَاطَ الَّذِينَ أَنْعَمْتَ عَلَيْهِم
(Siraatal ladheena an'amta 'alayhim)
(The path of those upon whom You have bestowed favor)
  [Optionally include: غَيْرِ الْمَغْضُوبِ عَلَيْهِمْ وَلَا الضَّالِّين
  (Ghayril maghdoobi 'alayhim wa lad-daalleen)
  (Not of those who have incurred Your anger, nor of those who go astray)]

3. Recite a Short Sūrah – Sūrah al-Ikhlās:

a. قُلْ هُوَ اللّٰهُ أَحَد
(Qul huwa Allāhu 'ahad)
(Say, "He is Allah, the One")

b. اَللّٰهُ الصَّمَد
(Allāhu as-samad)
(Allah, the Eternal Refuge)

c. لَمْ يَلِدْ وَلَمْ يُولَدْ
   (Lam yalid wa lam yoolad)
   (He neither begets nor is born)

d. وَلَمْ يَكُنْ لَهُ كُفُوًا أَحَدٌ
   (Wa lam yakun lahu kufuwan ahad)
   (Nor is there any equivalent to Him)

4. Rukū' (Bowing):

• As you move into the bowing position, say "Allāhu Akbar."
• Then recite:
   سُبْحَانَ رَبِّيَ الْعَظِيم
   (Subhana rabbiyal 'adheem)
   (Glory be to my Lord, the Most Great)
      [Repeat at least three times]

5. Rising from Rukū':

• Rise while saying:
   سَمِعَ اللَّهُ لِمَنْ حَمِدَه
   (Sami' Allāhu liman hamidah)
   (Allah hears those who praise Him)
• Then, standing upright, say:
   رَبَّنَا وَلَكَ الْحَمْد
   (Rabbana wa laka al-hamd)
   (Our Lord, unto You is all praise)

6. Sujūd (First Prostration):

• As you lower into prostration, say "Allāhu Akbar."
• Then recite:
   سُبْحَانَ رَبِّيَ الْأَعْلَى
   (Subhana rabbiyal a'la)
   (Glory be to my Lord, the Most High)
      [Repeat at least three times]

7. Brief Sitting (Jalsa):

- Sit briefly between the two prostrations.
- Recite a supplication of reflection, for example:

رَبِّ اغْفِرْ لِي وَارْحَمْنِي

(Rabbi ighfir li warhamni)

(O my Lord, forgive me and have mercy on me)

8. Sujūd (Second Prostration):

- Move into your second prostration while saying "Allāhu Akbar."
- Then recite:

سُبْحَانَ رَبِّيَ الأَعْلَى

(Subhana rabbiyal a'la)

(Glory be to my Lord, the Most High)

[Repeat at least three times]

9. Rising for the Next Rak'ah:
   - Say "Allāhu Akbar" and stand up to begin Rak'ah 2.

——————— Rak'ah 2: ———————

1. Opening Takbīr: الله أكبر

   (Allāhu Akbar)

   (Allah is the Greatest)

2. Recite al-Fātiha (The Opening Chapter):

a. بِسْمِ اللَّهِ الرَّحْمَٰنِ الرَّحِيمِ

(Bismillaahir Rahmaanir Raheem)

(In the name of Allah, the Most Gracious, the Most Merciful)

b. اَلْحَمْدُ لِلَّهِ رَبِّ الْعَالَمِين

(Alhamdu lillahi rabbil 'aalameen)

(All praise is due to Allah, Lord of all the worlds)

c. الرَّحْمَٰنِ الرَّحِيمِ

(Ar-Rahmaanir Raheem)

(The Most Gracious, the Most Merciful)

d. مَالِكِ يَوْمِ الدِّين

(Maaliki yawmid-deen)
(Master of the Day of Judgment)

e. اِيَّاكَ نَعْبُدُ وَإِيَّاكَ نَسْتَعِين
(Iyyaka na'budu wa iyyaka nasta'een)
(You alone we worship, and You alone we ask for help)

f. اَهْدِنَا الصِّرَاطَ الْمُسْتَقِيم
(Ihdinas-siraatal mustaqeem)
(Guide us to the straight path)

3. Recite a Short Sūrah – Sūrah al-Falaq:

a. قُلْ أَعُوذُ بِرَبِّ الْفَلَق
(Qul a'udhu birabbi al-falaq)
(Say, "I seek refuge in the Lord of daybreak")

b. مِن شَرِّ مَا خَلَق
(Min sharri ma khalaq)
(From the evil of that which He created)

c. وَمِن شَرِّ غَاسِقٍ إِذَا وَقَب
(Wa min sharri ghaasiqin idha waqab)
(And from the evil of darkness when it descends)

d. وَمِن شَرِّ النَّفَّاثَاتِ فِي الْعُقَد
(Wa min sharri an-naffaa-thaati fil 'uqad)
(And from the evil of those who practice secret arts)

e. وَمِن شَرِّ حَاسِدٍ إِذَا حَسَد
(Wa min sharri haasidin idha hasad)
(And from the evil of an envier when he envies)

4. Rukū' (Bowing):

• As you bow, say "Allāhu Akbar."   • Then recite:
سُبْحَانَ رَبِّيَ الْعَظِيم
(Subhana rabbiyal 'adheem)
(Glory be to my Lord, the Most Great)
   [Repeat at least three times]

5. **Rising from Rukū':**

- Rise while saying:

سَمِعَ اللَّهُ لِمَنْ حَمِدَه

(Sami' Allāhu liman hamidah)

(Allah hears those who praise Him)

- Then, while standing, say:

رَبَّنَا وَلَكَ الْحَمْد

(Rabbana wa laka al-hamd)

(Our Lord, unto You is all praise)

6. **Sujūd (First Prostration):**

- As you lower into prostration, say "Allāhu Akbar."
- Then recite:

سُبْحَانَ رَبِّيَ الأَعْلَى

(Subhana rabbiyal a'la)

(Glory be to my Lord, the Most High)

　　　[Repeat at least three times]

7. **Brief Sitting (Jalsa):**

- Sit briefly and, in deep reflection, supplicate:

اللَّهُمَّ اغْفِرْ لِي وَارْحَمْنِي

(Allahumma ighfir li warhamni)

(O Allah, forgive me and have mercy on me)

8. **Sujūd (Second Prostration):**

- As you perform the second prostration, say "Allāhu Akbar."
- Then recite:

سُبْحَانَ رَبِّيَ الأَعْلَى

(Subhana rabbiyal a'la)

(Glory be to my Lord, the Most High)

　　　[Repeat at least three times]

9. **Final Tashahhud (Sitting for the Testimony):**

- After the second sujūd, sit and recite the Tashahhud:

اَلتَّحِيَّاتُ لِلَّهِ وَالصَّلَوَاتُ وَالطَّيِّبَات

(At-tahiyyatu lillahi was-salawatu wat-tayyibatu)
(All greetings, prayers, and pure words are for Allah)

اَلسَّلَامُ عَلَيْكَ أَيُّهَا النَّبِي

(As-salamu 'alayka ayyuha an-nabiyyu)
(Peace be upon you, O Prophet)

وَرَحْمَةُ اللَّهِ وَبَرَكَاتُه

(Wa rahmatullahi wa barakatuhu)
(And the mercy and blessings of Allah)

اَلسَّلَامُ عَلَيْنَا وَعَلَى عِبَادِ اللَّهِ الصَّالِحِين

(As-salamu 'alayna wa 'ala 'ibaadil-lahi as-saaliheen)
(Peace be upon us and upon the righteous servants of Allah)

أَشْهَدُ أَنْ لَا إِلَهَ إِلَّا اللَّه

(Ash-hadu an la ilaha illallahu)
(I bear witness that there is no deity except Allah)

وَأَشْهَدُ أَنَّ مُحَمَّدًا رَسُولُ اللَّه

(Wa ash-hadu anna Muhammadan Rasool Allah)
(And I bear witness that Muhammad is the Messenger of Allah)

10. Taslīm (Concluding the Prayer):

• To conclude, first turn your head to the right and say:
اَلسَّلَامُ عَلَيْكُمْ وَرَحْمَةُ اللَّه
(As-salamu 'alaykum wa rahmatullahi)
(Peace and mercy of Allah be upon you)
• Then turn your head to the left and repeat:
اَلسَّلَامُ عَلَيْكُمْ وَرَحْمَةُ اللَّه
(As-salamu 'alaykum wa rahmatullahi)
(Peace and mercy of Allah be upon you)

Notes:
• At every movement—standing, bowing, prostrating, and

sitting—remember to say "Allāhu Akbar." • Although the Dhuhr Sunnah (Post) Prayer is optional, it is highly recommended to use these extra rak'ahs to engage in deeper supplication and reflection.

• Feel free to include additional du'ā (supplications) during your sitting (Jalsa) to nurture a more profound connection with Allah.

May your prayer be performed with full concentration and sincerity, drawing you ever closer to the divine presence of Allah.

CHAPTER 6: ASR FARD PRAYER

STEP-BY-STEP Asr Fard Prayer

Below is an in-depth guide to the Asr Fard (obligatory) prayer—a sacred act that reminds believers to seek solace and guidance during the challenges of the day. It serves as a spiritual checkpoint, emphasizing reliance on Allah during life's routine struggles. Before you perform the prayer, ensure you are in a state of ritual purity (wudu) and have prepared your heart and mind for sincere worship.

Before You Begin:
• Form your niyyah in your heart: "I intend to perform four rak'ahs of the Asr prayer for the sake of Allah."

Rak'ah 1:

---

1. Opening Takbīr (Start of the Prayer):
   الله أكبر
   (Allāhu Akbar)
   (Allah is the Greatest)

2. Recite al-Fātiha (The Opening Chapter):

a. بِسْمِ اللَّهِ الرَّحْمَٰنِ الرَّحِيمِ
(Bismillaahir Rahmaanir Raheem)
(In the name of Allah, the Most Gracious, the Most Merciful)

b. الْحَمْدُ لِلَّهِ رَبِّ الْعَالَمِينَ
(Alhamdu lillahi rabbil 'aalameen)
(All praise is due to Allah, Lord of all the worlds)

c. الرَّحْمَٰنِ الرَّحِيمِ
(Ar-Rahmaanir Raheem)
(The Most Gracious, the Most Merciful)

d. مَالِكِ يَوْمِ الدِّينِ
(Maaliki yawmid-deen)
(Master of the Day of Judgment)

e. إِيَّاكَ نَعْبُدُ وَإِيَّاكَ نَسْتَعِينُ
(Iyyaka na'budu wa iyyaka nasta'een)
(You alone we worship, and You alone we ask for help)

f. اهْدِنَا الصِّرَاطَ الْمُسْتَقِيمَ
(Ihdinas-siraatal mustaqeem)
(Guide us to the straight path)

g. صِرَاطَ الَّذِينَ أَنْعَمْتَ عَلَيْهِمْ غَيْرِ الْمَغْضُوبِ عَلَيْهِمْ وَلَا الضَّالِّينَ
(Siraatal ladheena an'amta 'alayhim ghayril maghdoobi 'alayhim wa lad-daalleen)
(The path of those upon whom You have bestowed favor, not of those who have earned Your anger nor of those who go astray)

3. Recite a Short Sūrā – Sūrā al-Kāfirūn:

a. قُلْ يَا أَيُّهَا الْكَافِرُونَ
(Qul ya ayyuhal kaafirun)
(Say, "O disbelievers,")

b. لَا أَعْبُدُ مَا تَعْبُدُونَ
(Laa a'budu maa ta'budoon)

(I do not worship what you worship)

c. وَلَا أَنتُمْ عَابِدُونَ مَا أَعْبُدُ
(Wa laa antum 'aabidoon maa a'bud)
(Nor are you worshippers of what I worship)

d. وَلَا أَنَا عَابِدٌ مَا عَبَدتُّمْ
(Wa laa ana 'aabidun maa 'abadtum)
(And I will not be a worshipper of what you have worshipped)

e. وَلَا أَنتُمْ عَابِدُونَ مَا أَعْبُدُ
(Wa laa antum 'aabidoon maa a'bud)
(Nor will you be worshippers of what I worship)

f. لَكُمْ دِينُكُمْ وَلِيَ دِينِ
(Lakum deenkum wa liya deen)
(For you is your religion, and for me is mine)

4. Rukū' (Bowing):

- As you bow, say "الله أكبر"
  (Allāhu Akbar)
  (Allah is the Greatest)
- Then recite:
  سُبْحَانَ رَبِّيَ الْعَظِيمِ
  (Subhana rabbiyal 'adheem)
  (Glory be to my Lord, the Most Great)
  [Repeat at least three times]

5. Rising from Rukū':

- Rise while saying:
  سَمِعَ اللَّهُ لِمَنْ حَمِدَهُ
  (Sami' Allāhu liman hamidah)
  (Allah hears those who praise Him)
- Then, while standing, say:
  رَبَّنَا وَلَكَ الْحَمْدُ
  (Rabbana wa laka al-hamd)

(Our Lord, to You be all praise)

6. Sujūd (First Prostration):

- As you prostrate, say "الله أكبر"
  (Allāhu Akbar)
  (Allah is the Greatest)
- Then recite:
  سُبْحَانَ رَبِّيَ الأَعْلَى
  (Subhana rabbiyal a'la)
  (Glory be to my Lord, the Most High)
  [Repeat at least three times]

7. Brief Sitting (Jalsa):

- Sit and recite a supplication, for example:
  رَبِّ اغْفِرْ لِي
  (Rabbi ighfir li)
  (O my Lord, forgive me)

8. Sujūd (Second Prostration):

- Prostrate again saying "الله أكبر"
  (Allāhu Akbar)
  (Allah is the Greatest)
- Then recite:
  سُبْحَانَ رَبِّيَ الأَعْلَى
  (Subhana rabbiyal a'la)
  (Glory be to my Lord, the Most High)
  [Repeat at least three times]

9. Rising for the Next Rak'ah:
   - Stand up with "الله أكبر"
     (Allāhu Akbar)
     (Allah is the Greatest)

Rak'ah 2:

---

1. Opening Takbīr:

    الله أكبر

    (Allāhu Akbar)
    (Allah is the Greatest)

2. Recite al-Fātiha:

    a. بِسْمِ اللَّهِ الرَّحْمَٰنِ الرَّحِيمِ

    (Bismillaahir Rahmaanir Raheem)
    (In the name of Allah, the Most Gracious, the Most Merciful)

    b. اَلْحَمْدُ لِلَّهِ رَبِّ الْعَالَمِينَ

    (Alhamdu lillahi rabbil 'aalameen)
    (All praise is due to Allah, Lord of all the worlds)

    c. الرَّحْمَٰنِ الرَّحِيمِ

    (Ar-Rahmaanir Raheem)
    (The Most Gracious, the Most Merciful)

    d. مَالِكِ يَوْمِ الدِّينِ

    (Maaliki yawmid-deen)
    (Master of the Day of Judgment)

    e. إِيَّاكَ نَعْبُدُ وَإِيَّاكَ نَسْتَعِينُ

    (Iyyaka na'budu wa iyyaka nasta'een)
    (You alone we worship, and You alone we ask for help)

    f. اهْدِنَا الصِّرَاطَ الْمُسْتَقِيمَ

    (Ihdinas-siraatal mustaqeem)
    (Guide us to the straight path)

    g. صِرَاطَ الَّذِينَ أَنْعَمْتَ عَلَيْهِمْ غَيْرِ الْمَغْضُوبِ عَلَيْهِمْ وَلَا الضَّالِّينَ

    (Siraatal ladheena an'amta 'alayhim ghayril maghdoobi 'alayhim wa lad-daalleen)
    (The path of those upon whom You have bestowed favor, not of those who have earned Your anger nor of those who go astray)

3. Recite a Short Sūrā – Sūrā al-Ikhlās:

    a. قُلْ هُوَ اللَّهُ أَحَدٌ

(Qul huwa Allāhu 'ahad)
(Say, "He is Allah, [Who is] One")

b. اللَّهُ الصَّمَد
(Allāhu as-samad)
(Allah, the Eternal Refuge)

c. لَمْ يَلِدْ وَلَمْ يُولَد
(Lam yalid wa lam yoolad)
(He neither begets nor is born)

d. وَلَمْ يَكُن لَّهُ كُفُوًا أَحَد
(Wa lam yakun lahu kufuwan ahad)
(Nor is there to Him any equivalent)

4. Rukū' (Bowing):

- As you bow, say "الله أكبر"
  (Allāhu Akbar)
  (Allah is the Greatest)
- Then recite:
  سُبْحَانَ رَبِّيَ الْعَظِيم
  (Subhana rabbiyal 'adheem)
  (Glory be to my Lord, the Most Great)
  [Repeat at least three times]

5. Rising from Rukū':

- Rise while saying:
  سَمِعَ اللَّهُ لِمَنْ حَمِدَه
  (Sami' Allāhu liman hamidah)
  (Allah hears those who praise Him)
- Then, while standing, say:
  رَبَّنَا وَلَكَ الْحَمْد
  (Rabbana wa laka al-hamd)
  (Our Lord, to You be all praise)

6. Sujūd (First Prostration):

- Prostrate saying "الله أكبر"

(Allāhu Akbar)
(Allah is the Greatest)
- Then recite:

سُبْحَانَ رَبِّيَ الْأَعْلَى

(Subhana rabbiyal a'la)
(Glory be to my Lord, the Most High)
   [Repeat at least three times]

7. Brief Sitting (Jalsa):

- Sit and recite:

رَبِّ اغْفِرْ لِي

(Rabbi ighfir li)
(O my Lord, forgive me)

8. Sujūd (Second Prostration):

- Prostrate again saying "الله أكبر"
(Allāhu Akbar)
(Allah is the Greatest)
- Then recite:

سُبْحَانَ رَبِّيَ الْأَعْلَى

(Subhana rabbiyal a'la)
(Glory be to my Lord, the Most High)
   [Repeat at least three times]

9. Rising for the Next Rak'ah:
- Stand up with "الله أكبر"
(Allāhu Akbar)
(Allah is the Greatest)

Rak'ah 3:

---

1. Opening Takbīr:

الله أكبر

(Allāhu Akbar)
(Allah is the Greatest)

2. Recite al-Fātiha:

a. بِسْمِ اللَّهِ الرَّحْمَٰنِ الرَّحِيمِ
(Bismillaahir Rahmaanir Raheem)
(In the name of Allah, the Most Gracious, the Most Merciful)

b. اَلْحَمْدُ لِلَّهِ رَبِّ الْعَالَمِينَ
(Alhamdu lillahi rabbil 'aalameen)
(All praise is due to Allah, Lord of all the worlds)

c. الرَّحْمَٰنِ الرَّحِيمِ
(Ar-Rahmaanir Raheem)
(The Most Gracious, the Most Merciful)

d. مَالِكِ يَوْمِ الدِّينِ
(Maaliki yawmid-deen)
(Master of the Day of Judgment)

e. إِيَّاكَ نَعْبُدُ وَإِيَّاكَ نَسْتَعِينُ
(Iyyaka na'budu wa iyyaka nasta'een)
(You alone we worship, and You alone we ask for help)

f. اهْدِنَا الصِّرَاطَ الْمُسْتَقِيمَ
(Ihdinas-siraatal mustaqeem)
(Guide us to the straight path)

g. صِرَاطَ الَّذِينَ أَنْعَمْتَ عَلَيْهِمْ غَيْرِ الْمَغْضُوبِ عَلَيْهِمْ وَلَا الضَّالِّينَ
(Siraatal ladheena an'amta 'alayhim ghayril maghdoobi 'alayhim wa lad-daalleen)
(The path of those upon whom You have bestowed favor, not of those who have earned Your anger nor of those who go astray)

3. Rukū' (Bowing):

- Bow saying "الله أكبر"
(Allāhu Akbar)
(Allah is the Greatest)
- Then recite:
سُبْحَانَ رَبِّيَ الْعَظِيمِ

(Subhana rabbiyal 'adheem)
(Glory be to my Lord, the Most Great)
[Repeat at least three times]

4. Rising from Rukū':

- Rise while saying:
  سَمِعَ اللَّهُ لِمَنْ حَمِدَه
  (Sami' Allāhu liman hamidah)
  (Allah hears those who praise Him)
- Then, while standing, say:
  رَبَّنَا وَلَكَ الْحَمْد
  (Rabbana wa laka al-hamd)
  (Our Lord, to You be all praise)

5. Sujūd (First Prostration):

- Prostrate saying "الله أكبر"
  (Allāhu Akbar)
  (Allah is the Greatest)
- Then recite:
  سُبْحَانَ رَبِّيَ الْأَعْلَى
  (Subhana rabbiyal a'la)
  (Glory be to my Lord, the Most High)
  [Repeat at least three times]

6. Brief Sitting (Jalsa):

- Sit and recite:
  رَبِّ اغْفِرْ لِي
  (Rabbi ighfir li)
  (O my Lord, forgive me)

7. Sujūd (Second Prostration):

- Prostrate again saying "الله أكبر"
  (Allāhu Akbar)
  (Allah is the Greatest)
- Then recite:

سُبْحَانَ رَبِّيَ الأَعْلَى

(Subhana rabbiyal a'la)
(Glory be to my Lord, the Most High)
  [Repeat at least three times]

8. Rising for the Next Rak'ah:
   - Stand up with "الله أكبر"
     (Allāhu Akbar)
     (Allah is the Greatest)

Rak'ah 4:

---

1. Opening Takbīr:
   الله أكبر
   (Allāhu Akbar)
   (Allah is the Greatest)

2. Recite al-Fātiha:

   a. بِسْمِ اللَّهِ الرَّحْمَٰنِ الرَّحِيمِ
   (Bismillaahir Rahmaanir Raheem)
   (In the name of Allah, the Most Gracious, the Most Merciful)

   b. الْحَمْدُ لِلَّهِ رَبِّ الْعَالَمِينَ
   (Alhamdu lillahi rabbil 'aalameen)
   (All praise is due to Allah, Lord of all the worlds)

   c. الرَّحْمَٰنِ الرَّحِيمِ
   (Ar-Rahmaanir Raheem)
   (The Most Gracious, the Most Merciful)

   d. مَالِكِ يَوْمِ الدِّينِ
   (Maaliki yawmid-deen)
   (Master of the Day of Judgment)

   e. إِيَّاكَ نَعْبُدُ وَإِيَّاكَ نَسْتَعِينُ
   (Iyyaka na'budu wa iyyaka nasta'een)
   (You alone we worship, and You alone we ask for help)

f. اَهْدِنَا الصِّرَاطَ الْمُسْتَقِيم

(Ihdinas-siraatal mustaqeem)
(Guide us to the straight path)

g. صِرَاطَ الَّذِينَ أَنْعَمْتَ عَلَيْهِمْ غَيْرِ الْمَغْضُوبِ عَلَيْهِمْ وَلَا الضَّالِّين

(Siraatal ladheena an'amta 'alayhim ghayril maghdoobi 'alayhim wa lad-daalleen)
(The path of those upon whom You have bestowed favor, not of those who have earned Your anger nor of those who go astray)

3. Rukū' (Bowing):

- Bow saying "الله أكبر"
  (Allāhu Akbar)
  (Allah is the Greatest)
- Then recite:
  سُبْحَانَ رَبِّيَ الْعَظِيم
  (Subhana rabbiyal 'adheem)
  (Glory be to my Lord, the Most Great)
  [Repeat at least three times]

4. Rising from Rukū':

- Rise while saying:
  سَمِعَ اللَّهُ لِمَنْ حَمِدَه
  (Sami' Allāhu liman hamidah)
  (Allah hears those who praise Him)
- Then, while standing, say:
  رَبَّنَا وَلَكَ الْحَمْد
  (Rabbana wa laka al-hamd)
  (Our Lord, to You be all praise)

5. Sujūd (First Prostration):

- Prostrate saying "الله أكبر"
  (Allāhu Akbar)
  (Allah is the Greatest)
- Then recite:

سُبْحَانَ رَبِّيَ الْأَعْلَى
(Subhana rabbiyal a'la)
(Glory be to my Lord, the Most High)
   [Repeat at least three times]

6. Brief Sitting (Jalsa – Tashahhud):

- Sit and recite the Tashahhud: ٱلتَّحِيَّاتُ لِلَّهِ وَالصَّلَوَاتُ وَالطَّيِّبَاتُ
(At-tahiyyatu lillahi was-salawatu wat-tayyibatu)
(All greetings, prayers, and pure words are for Allah)

ٱلسَّلَامُ عَلَيْكَ أَيُّهَا النَّبِيُّ
(As-salamu 'alayka ayyuha an-nabiyyu)
(Peace be upon you, O Prophet)

وَرَحْمَةُ اللَّهِ وَبَرَكَاتُهُ
(Wa rahmatullahi wa barakatuhu)
(And the mercy and blessings of Allah)

ٱلسَّلَامُ عَلَيْنَا وَعَلَى عِبَادِ اللَّهِ الصَّالِحِين
(As-salamu 'alayna wa 'ala 'ibaadil-lahi as-saaliheen)
(Peace be upon us and upon the righteous servants of Allah)

أَشْهَدُ أَنْ لَا إِلَهَ إِلَّا اللَّه
(Ash-hadu an la ilaha illallahu)
(I bear witness that there is no deity except Allah)

وَأَشْهَدُ أَنَّ مُحَمَّدًا رَسُولُ اللَّه
(Wa ash-hadu anna Muhammadan Rasool Allah)
(

CHAPTER 7: MAGHRIB FARD PRAYER

STEP-BY-STEP Maghrib Fard Prayer

Below is an in-depth guide to the Maghrib fard (obligatory) prayer—a sacred act performed shortly after sunset as daylight gives way to night. This prayer calls upon the believer to pause, reflect on the blessings of the day, and seek Allah's divine assistance and mercy for the hours ahead. Before you begin, ensure you have performed wudu (ritual purity) and quieted your heart for sincere worship.

Before You Begin:
• Form your niyyah in your heart: "I intend to perform three rak'ahs of the Maghrib prayer for the sake of Allah."

Rak'ah 1:

1. Opening Takbīr (Start of the Prayer):
   الله أكبر
   (Allāhu Akbar)
   (Allah is the Greatest)

2. Recite al-Fātiha (The Opening Chapter):
   a. بِسْمِ اللَّهِ الرَّحْمَٰنِ الرَّحِيمِ

(Bismillaahir Rahmaanir Raheem)
(In the name of Allah, the Most Gracious, the Most Merciful)

b. اَلْحَمْدُ لِلَّهِ رَبِّ الْعَالَمِين
(Alhamdu lillahi rabbil 'aalameen)
(All praise is due to Allah, Lord of all the worlds)

c. اِلرَّحْمَٰنِ الرَّحِيم
(Ar-Rahmaanir Raheem)
(The Most Gracious, the Most Merciful)

d. مَالِكِ يَوْمِ الدِّين
(Maaliki yawmid-deen)
(Master of the Day of Judgment)

e. اْيَّاكَ نَعْبُدُ وَإِيَّاكَ نَسْتَعِين
(Iyyaka na'budu wa iyyaka nasta'een)
(You alone we worship, and You alone we ask for help)

f. اَهْدِنَا الصِّرَاطَ الْمُسْتَقِيم
(Ihdinas-siraatal mustaqeem)
(Guide us to the straight path)

g. صِرَاطَ الَّذِينَ أَنْعَمْتَ عَلَيْهِمْ غَيْرِ الْمَغْضُوبِ عَلَيْهِمْ وَلَا الضَّالِّين
(Siraatal ladheena an'amta 'alayhim ghayril maghdoobi 'alayhim wa lad-daalleen)
(The path of those upon whom You have bestowed favor, not of those who have earned Your anger nor of those who go astray)

3. Recite a Short Sūrah – Sūrah al-Kāfirūn:

a. َقُلْ يَا أَيُّهَا الْكَافِرُون
(Qul ya ayyuhal kaafirun)
(Say, "O disbelievers,")

b. َلَا أَعْبُدُ مَا تَعْبُدُون
(Laa a'budu maa ta'budoon)
(I do not worship what you worship)

c. ُوَلَا أَنْتُمْ عَابِدُونَ مَا أَعْبُد

(Wa laa antum 'aabidoon maa a'bud)
(Nor are you worshippers of what I worship)

d. وَلَا أَنَا عَابِدٌ مَا عَبَدتُّم

(Wa laa ana 'aabidun maa 'abadtum)
(And I will not be a worshipper of what you have worshipped)

e. وَلَا أَنتُمْ عَابِدُونَ مَا أَعْبُد

(Wa laa antum 'aabidoon maa a'bud)
(Nor will you be worshippers of what I worship)

f. لَكُمْ دِينُكُمْ وَلِيَ دِين

(Lakum deenkum wa liya deen)
(For you is your religion, and for me is mine)

4. Rukū' (Bowing):
   - As you move into the bowing position, say "الله أكبر"
     (Allāhu Akbar)
     (Allah is the Greatest)
   Then recite:
   سُبْحَانَ رَبِّيَ الْعَظِيم
   (Subhana rabbiyal 'adheem)
   (Glory be to my Lord, the Most Great)   [Repeat at least three times]

5. Rising from Rukū':
   - Rise while saying:
     سَمِعَ اللَّهُ لِمَنْ حَمِدَه
     (Sami' Allāhu liman hamidah)
     (Allah hears those who praise Him)
   - Then, while standing straight, say:
     رَبَّنَا وَلَكَ الْحَمْد
     (Rabbana wa laka al-hamd)
     (Our Lord, to You be all praise)

6. Sujūd (First Prostration):
   - As you descend into prostration, say "الله أكبر"

(Allāhu Akbar)
(Allah is the Greatest)
- Then recite:

سُبْحَانَ رَبِّيَ الأَعْلَى

(Subhana rabbiyal a'la)
(Glory be to my Lord, the Most High)   [Repeat at least three times]

7. Brief Sitting (Jalsa):
   - Sit briefly and supplicate; for example, recite:

   رَبِّ اغْفِرْ لِي

   (Rabbi ighfir li)
   (O my Lord, forgive me)

8. Sujūd (Second Prostration):
   - Say "الله أكبر" as you move into the second prostration.
   - Then recite:

   سُبْحَانَ رَبِّيَ الأَعْلَى

   (Subhana rabbiyal a'la)
   (Glory be to my Lord, the Most High)   [Repeat at least three times]

9. Rising for the Next Rak'ah:
   - Say "الله أكبر" and then stand up to begin Rak'ah 2.

Rak'ah 2:

---

1. Opening Takbīr:

   الله أكبر

   (Allāhu Akbar)
   (Allah is the Greatest)

2. Recite al-Fātiha:

   a. بِسْمِ اللَّهِ الرَّحْمَٰنِ الرَّحِيمِ
   (Bismillaahir Rahmaanir Raheem)
   (In the name of Allah, the Most Gracious, the Most Merciful)

b. ‎الْحَمْدُ لِلَّهِ رَبِّ الْعَالَمِين
(Alhamdu lillahi rabbil 'aalameen)
(All praise is due to Allah, Lord of all the worlds)

c. ‎الرَّحْمَٰنِ الرَّحِيم
(Ar-Rahmaanir Raheem)
(The Most Gracious, the Most Merciful)

d. ‎مَالِكِ يَوْمِ الدِّين
(Maaliki yawmid-deen)
(Master of the Day of Judgment)

e. ‎إِيَّاكَ نَعْبُدُ وَإِيَّاكَ نَسْتَعِين
(Iyyaka na'budu wa iyyaka nasta'een)
(You alone we worship, and You alone we ask for help)

f. ‎اهْدِنَا الصِّرَاطَ الْمُسْتَقِيم
(Ihdinas-siraatal mustaqeem)
(Guide us to the straight path)

g. ‎صِرَاطَ الَّذِينَ أَنْعَمْتَ عَلَيْهِمْ غَيْرِ الْمَغْضُوبِ عَلَيْهِمْ وَلَا الضَّالِّين
(Siraatal ladheena an'amta 'alayhim ghayril maghdoobi 'alayhim wa lad-daalleen)
(The path of those upon whom You have bestowed favor, not of those who have earned Your anger nor of those who go astray)

3. Recite a Short Sūrah – Sūrah al-Ikhlās:

a. ‎قُلْ هُوَ اللَّهُ أَحَد
(Qul huwa Allāhu 'ahad)
(Say, "He is Allah, [Who is] One")

b. ‎اللَّهُ الصَّمَد
(Allāhu as-samad)
(Allah, the Eternal Refuge)

c. ‎لَمْ يَلِدْ وَلَمْ يُولَد
(Lam yalid wa lam yoolad)
(He neither begets nor is born)

d. وَلَمْ يَكُنْ لَهُ كُفُوًا أَحَدٌ

(Wa lam yakun lahu kufuwan ahad)
(Nor is there to Him any equivalent)

4. Rukū' (Bowing):
    - As you bow, say "الله أكبر"
       (Allāhu Akbar)
       (Allah is the Greatest)
    Then recite:
    سُبْحَانَ رَبِّيَ الْعَظِيم
    (Subhana rabbiyal 'adheem)
    (Glory be to my Lord, the Most Great)   [Repeat at least three times]

5. Rising from Rukū':
    - Rise saying:
    سَمِعَ اللَّهُ لِمَنْ حَمِدَه
    (Sami' Allāhu liman hamidah)
    (Allah hears those who praise Him)
    - Then, while standing, say:
    رَبَّنَا وَلَكَ الْحَمْد
    (Rabbana wa laka al-hamd)
    (Our Lord, to You be all praise)

6. Sujūd (First Prostration):
    - Say "الله أكبر" as you enter prostration.
    - Then recite:
    سُبْحَانَ رَبِّيَ الْأَعْلَى
    (Subhana rabbiyal a'la)
    (Glory be to my Lord, the Most High)   [Repeat at least three times]

7. Brief Sitting (Jalsa):
    - Sit briefly and supplicate; for example, recite:
    رَبِّ اغْفِرْ لِي
    (Rabbi ighfir li)
    (O my Lord, forgive me)

8. Sujūd (Second Prostration):
   - Say "الله أكبر" as you move into the second prostration.
   - Then recite:

   سُبْحَانَ رَبِّيَ الأَعْلَى

   (Subhana rabbiyal a'la)
   (Glory be to my Lord, the Most High)   [Repeat at least three times]

9. Rising for the Next Rak'ah:
   - Say "الله أكبر" and stand up to begin Rak'ah 3.

Rak'ah 3:

---

1. Opening Takbīr:

   الله أكبر

   (Allāhu Akbar)
   (Allah is the Greatest)

2. Recite al-Fātiha:

   a. بِسْمِ اللَّهِ الرَّحْمَٰنِ الرَّحِيمِ
   (Bismillaahir Rahmaanir Raheem)
   (In the name of Allah, the Most Gracious, the Most Merciful)

   b. الْحَمْدُ لِلَّهِ رَبِّ الْعَالَمِينَ
   (Alhamdu lillahi rabbil 'aalameen)
   (All praise is due to Allah, Lord of all the worlds)

   c. الرَّحْمَٰنِ الرَّحِيمِ
   (Ar-Rahmaanir Raheem)
   (The Most Gracious, the Most Merciful)

   d. مَالِكِ يَوْمِ الدِّينِ
   (Maaliki yawmid-deen)
   (Master of the Day of Judgment)

   e. إِيَّاكَ نَعْبُدُ وَإِيَّاكَ نَسْتَعِينُ

(Iyyaka na'budu wa iyyaka nasta'een)
(You alone we worship, and You alone we ask for help)

f. اهِدِنَا الصِّرَاطَ الْمُسْتَقِيمَ

(Ihdinas-siraatal mustaqeem)
(Guide us to the straight path)

g. صِرَاطَ الَّذِينَ أَنْعَمْتَ عَلَيْهِمْ غَيْرِ الْمَغْضُوبِ عَلَيْهِمْ وَلَا الضَّالِّينَ

(Siraatal ladheena an'amta 'alayhim ghayril maghdoobi 'alayhim wa lad-daalleen)
(The path of those upon whom You have bestowed favor, not of those who have earned Your anger nor of those who go astray)

3. [No additional surah is recited in Rak'ah 3.]

4. Rukū' (Bowing):
   - As you bow, say "الله أكبر"
     (Allāhu Akbar)
     (Allah is the Greatest)
   Then recite:
   سُبْحَانَ رَبِّيَ الْعَظِيمِ
   (Subhana rabbiyal 'adheem)
   (Glory be to my Lord, the Most Great)   [Repeat at least three times]

5. Rising from Rukū':
   - Rise saying:
   سَمِعَ اللَّهُ لِمَنْ حَمِدَه
   (Sami' Allāhu liman hamidah)
   (Allah hears those who praise Him)
   - Then, while standing, say:
   رَبَّنَا وَلَكَ الْحَمْدُ
   (Rabbana wa laka al-hamd)
   (Our Lord, to You be all praise)

6. Sujūd (First Prostration):
   - Say "الله أكبر" as you prostrate.
   - Then recite:

سُبْحَانَ رَبِّيَ الْأَعْلَى

(Subhana rabbiyal a'la)

(Glory be to my Lord, the Most High)   [Repeat at least three times]

7. Brief Sitting (Jalsa):
   - Sit briefly and, if you wish, recite a supplication such as:

   رَبِّ اغْفِرْ لِي

   (Rabbi ighfir li)

   (O my Lord, forgive me)

8. Sujūd (Second Prostration):
   - Say "الله أكبر" as you perform the second prostration.
   - Then recite:

   سُبْحَانَ رَبِّيَ الْأَعْلَى

   (Subhana rabbiyal a'la)

   (Glory be to my Lord, the Most High)   [Repeat at least three times]

9. Final Tashahhud (Sitting for the Testimony):
   - After the second sujūd, sit and recite:

   اَلتَّحِيَّاتُ لِلَّهِ وَالصَّلَوَاتُ وَالطَّيِّبَاتُ

   (At-tahiyyatu lillahi was-salawatu wat-tayyibatu)

   (All greetings, prayers, and pure words are for Allah)

اَلسَّلَامُ عَلَيْكَ أَيُّهَا النَّبِيُّ

(As-salamu 'alayka ayyuha an-nabiyyu)

(Peace be upon you, O Prophet)

وَرَحْمَةُ اللَّهِ وَبَرَكَاتُهُ

(Wa rahmatullahi wa barakatuhu)

(And the mercy and blessings of Allah)

اَلسَّلَامُ عَلَيْنَا وَعَلَى عِبَادِ اللَّهِ الصَّالِحِين

(As-salamu 'alayna wa 'ala 'ibaadi allahi as-saaliheen)

(Peace be upon us and upon the righteous servants of Allah)

أَشْهَدُ أَنْ لَا إِلَهَ إِلَّا اللَّهُ

(Ash-hadu an la ilaha illallahu)

(I bear witness that there is no deity except Allah)

وَأَشْهَدُ أَنَّ مُحَمَّدًا رَسُولُ اللَّه

(Wa ash-hadu anna Muhammadan Rasool Allah)

(And I bear witness that Muhammad is the Messenger of Allah)

10. Taslīm (Concluding the Prayer):
   - Turn your head to the right and say:

   اِلسَّلَامُ عَلَيْكُم وَرَحمَةُ اللَّه

   (As-salamu 'alaykum wa rahmatullahi)

   (Peace and mercy of Allah be upon you)

   - Then turn your head to the left and repeat:

   ِّلَامُ عَلَيْكُم وَرَحمَةُ اللَّهاِلس

   (As-salamu 'alaykum wa rahmatullahi)

   (Peace and mercy of Allah be upon you)

Notes:

- At each transition (standing, bowing, prostrating, and sitting), it is customary to say "الله أكبر" (Allāhu Akbar) (Allah is the Greatest).
- The recommended repetitions in Rukū' and Sujūd follow the Sunnah of the Prophet (peace and blessings be upon him).
- You may include additional du'ā (supplications) during your sitting (Jalsa) as desired.

This completes the Maghrib Fard Prayer.

CHAPTER 8: MAGHRIB SUNNAH PRAYER

STEP-BY-STEP Maghrib Sunnah Prayer

Below is an in-depth guide to the Maghrib Sunnah prayer—a voluntary act performed after the obligatory Maghrib prayer. This extra set of rak'ahs enhances spiritual satisfaction and provides additional moments of gratitude as you wind down your day. Approach this prayer with a sincere heart and a calm spirit, ready to embrace the blessings of extra remembrance of Allah.

Before You Begin:
• Form your niyyah in your heart: "I intend to perform two rak'ahs of the Maghrib Sunnah prayer for the sake of Allah."

Rak'ah 1:

1. Opening Takbīr (Start of the Prayer):
   الله أكبر
   (Allāhu Akbar)
   (Allah is the Greatest)

2. Recite al-Fātiha (The Opening Chapter):

a. بِسْمِ اللَّهِ الرَّحْمَٰنِ الرَّحِيمِ
   (Bismillaahir Rahmaanir Raheem)

(In the name of Allah, the Most Gracious, the Most Merciful)

b. اَلْحَمْدُ لِلَّهِ رَبِّ الْعَالَمِين
(Alhamdu lillahi rabbil 'aalameen)
(All praise is due to Allah, Lord of all the worlds)

c. اِلرَّحْمَنِ الرَّحِيم
(Ar-Rahmaanir Raheem)
(The Most Gracious, the Most Merciful)

d. مَالِكِ يَوْمِ الدِّين
(Maaliki yawmid-deen)
(Master of the Day of Judgment)

e. إِيَّاكَ نَعْبُدُ وَإِيَّاكَ نَسْتَعِين
(Iyyaka na'budu wa iyyaka nasta'een)
(You alone we worship, and You alone we ask for help)

f. اهْدِنَا الصِّرَاطَ الْمُسْتَقِيم
(Ihdinas-siraatal mustaqeem)
(Guide us to the straight path)

g. صِرَاطَ الَّذِينَ أَنْعَمْتَ عَلَيْهِم
(Siraat alladheena an'amta 'alayhim)
(The path of those upon whom You have bestowed favor)

3. Recite a Short Sūrah – Sūrah al-Kāfirūn:

a. قُلْ يَا أَيُّهَا الْكَافِرُون
(Qul ya ayyuhal kaafirun)
(Say, "O disbelievers,")

b. لَا أَعْبُدُ مَا تَعْبُدُون
(Laa a'budu maa ta'budoon)
(I do not worship what you worship)

c. وَلَا أَنْتُمْ عَابِدُونَ مَا أَعْبُد
(Wa laa antum 'aabidoon maa a'bud)
(Nor are you worshippers of what I worship)

d. وَلَا أَنَا عَابِدٌ مَا عَبَدتُّم

(Wa laa ana 'aabidun maa 'abadtum)
(And I will not be a worshipper of what you have worshipped)

e. وَلَا أَنتُمْ عَابِدُونَ مَا أَعْبُد
(Wa laa antum 'aabidoon maa a'bud)
(Nor will you be worshippers of what I worship)

f. لَكُمْ دِينُكُمْ وَلِيَ دِين
(Lakum deenkum wa liya deen)
(For you is your religion, and for me is mine)

4. Rukū' (Bowing):
   - As you bow, say "Allāhu Akbar."
   الله أكبر
   (Allāhu Akbar)
   (Allah is the Greatest)
   - Then recite:
   سِبْحَانَ رَبِّيَ الْعَظِيم
   (Subhana rabbiyal 'adheem)
   (Glory be to my Lord, the Most Great)
   [Repeat at least three times]

5. Rising from Rukū':
   - Rise while saying:
   سَمِعَ اللَّهُ لِمَنْ حَمِدَه
   (Sami' Allāhu liman hamidah)
   (Allah hears those who praise Him)
   - Then, while standing, say:
   رَبَّنَا وَلَكَ الْحَمْد
   (Rabbana wa laka al-hamd)
   (Our Lord, to You be all praise)

6. Sujūd (First Prostration):
   - Lower into prostration saying "Allāhu Akbar."
   الله أكبر
   (Allāhu Akbar)
   (Allah is the Greatest)

- In sujūd, recite:

  سُبْحَانَ رَبِّيَ الْأَعْلَى

  (Subhana rabbiyal a'la)

  (Glory be to my Lord, the Most High)

  [Repeat at least three times]

7. Brief Sitting (Jalsa):
   - Sit briefly and supplicate; for example, say:

   رَبِّ اغْفِرْ لِي

   (Rabbi ighfir li)

   (O my Lord, forgive me)

8. Sujūd (Second Prostration):
   - Move into the second prostration saying "Allāhu Akbar."

   الله أكبر

   (Allāhu Akbar)

   (Allah is the Greatest)

   - Then recite:

   سُبْحَانَ رَبِّيَ الْأَعْلَى

   (Subhana rabbiyal a'la)

   (Glory be to my Lord, the Most High)

   [Repeat at least three times]

9. Rising for the Next Rak'ah:
   - Stand up by saying "Allāhu Akbar" to begin Rak'ah 2.

   الله أكبر

   (Allāhu Akbar)

   (Allah is the Greatest)

Rak'ah 2:

---

1. Opening Takbīr:

   الله أكبر

   (Allāhu Akbar)

   (Allah is the Greatest)

2. Recite al-Fātiha:

a. بِسْمِ اللَّهِ الرَّحْمَٰنِ الرَّحِيمِ
(Bismillaahir Rahmaanir Raheem)
(In the name of Allah, the Most Gracious, the Most Merciful)

b. اَلْحَمْدُ لِلَّهِ رَبِّ الْعَالَمِينَ
(Alhamdu lillahi rabbil 'aalameen)
(All praise is due to Allah, Lord of all the worlds)

c. الرَّحْمَٰنِ الرَّحِيمِ
(Ar-Rahmaanir Raheem)
(The Most Gracious, the Most Merciful)

d. مَالِكِ يَوْمِ الدِّينِ
(Maaliki yawmid-deen)
(Master of the Day of Judgment)

e. إِيَّاكَ نَعْبُدُ وَإِيَّاكَ نَسْتَعِينُ
(Iyyaka na'budu wa iyyaka nasta'een)
(You alone we worship, and You alone we ask for help)

f. اهْدِنَا الصِّرَاطَ الْمُسْتَقِيمَ
(Ihdinas-siraatal mustaqeem)
(Guide us to the straight path)

g. صِرَاطَ الَّذِينَ أَنْعَمْتَ عَلَيْهِمْ
(Siraat alladheena an'amta 'alayhim)
(The path of those upon whom You have bestowed favor)

3. Recite a Short Sūrah – Sūrah al-Ikhlās:

a. قُلْ هُوَ اللَّهُ أَحَدٌ
(Qul huwa Allāhu 'ahad)
(Say, "He is Allah, the One")

b. اللَّهُ الصَّمَدُ
(Allāhu as-samad)
(Allah, the Eternal Refuge)

c. لَمْ يَلِدْ وَلَمْ يُولَدْ

(Lam yalid wa lam yoolad)

(He neither begets nor is born)

d. وَلَمْ يَكُنْ لَهُ كُفُوًا أَحَدٌ

(Wa lam yakun lahu kufuwan ahad)

(Nor is there to Him any equivalent)

4. Rukū' (Bowing):
   - As you bow, say "Allāhu Akbar."
     الله أكبر
     (Allāhu Akbar)
     (Allah is the Greatest)
   - Then recite:
     سُبْحَانَ رَبِّيَ الْعَظِيمِ
     (Subhana rabbiyal 'adheem)
     (Glory be to my Lord, the Most Great)
     [Repeat at least three times]

5. Rising from Rukū':
   - Stand up while saying:
     سَمِعَ اللَّهُ لِمَنْ حَمِدَه
     (Sami' Allāhu liman hamidah)
     (Allah hears those who praise Him)
   - Then recite:
     رَبَّنَا وَلَكَ الْحَمْدُ
     (Rabbana wa laka al-hamd)
     (Our Lord, to You be all praise)

6. Sujūd (First Prostration):
   - Descend into prostration with "Allāhu Akbar."
     الله أكبر
     (Allāhu Akbar)
     (Allah is the Greatest)
   - In sujūd, recite:
     سُبْحَانَ رَبِّيَ الْأَعْلَى
     (Subhana rabbiyal a'la)

(Glory be to my Lord, the Most High)
[Repeat at least three times]

7. Brief Sitting (Jalsa):
    - Sit briefly and make a supplication; for example, say:
    رَبِّ اغْفِرْ لِي
    (Rabbi ighfir li)
    (O my Lord, forgive me)

8. Sujūd (Second Prostration):
    - Enter your second prostration saying "Allāhu Akbar."
    الله أكبر
    (Allāhu Akbar)
    (Allah is the Greatest)
    - Then recite:
    سُبْحَانَ رَبِّيَ الْأَعْلَى
    (Subhana rabbiyal a'la)
    (Glory be to my Lord, the Most High)
    [Repeat at least three times]

9. Final Tashahhud (Sitting for the Testimony):
    - After the second sujūd, sit and recite:
    التَّحِيَّاتُ لِلَّهِ وَالصَّلَوَاتُ وَالطَّيِّبَاتُ
    (At-tahiyyatu lillahi was-salawatu wat-tayyibatu)
    (All greetings, prayers, and pure words are for Allah)
    السَّلَامُ عَلَيْكَ أَيُّهَا النَّبِيُّ
    (As-salamu 'alayka ayyuha an-nabiyyu)
    (Peace be upon you, O Prophet)
    وَرَحْمَةُ اللَّهِ وَبَرَكَاتُهُ
    (Wa rahmatullahi wa barakatuhu)
    (And the mercy and blessings of Allah)
    السَّلَامُ عَلَيْنَا
    (As-salamu 'alayna)
    (Peace be upon us)
    أَشْهَدُ أَنْ لَا إِلَهَ إِلَّا اللَّهُ
    (Ash-hadu an la ilaha illallahu)
    (I bear witness that there is no deity except Allah)

اَشْهَدُ أَنَّ مُحَمَّدًا رَسُولُ اللَّهِ

(Wa ash-hadu anna Muhammadan Rasool Allah)

(And I bear witness that Muhammad is the Messenger of Allah)

10. Taslīm (Concluding the Prayer):
    - To finish the prayer, turn your head to the right and say:
    السَّلَامُ عَلَيْكُمْ وَرَحْمَةُ اللَّهِ

    (As-salamu 'alaykum wa rahmatullahi)

    (Peace and mercy of Allah be upon you)
    - Then turn your head to the left and repeat:
    السَّلَامُ عَلَيْكُمْ وَرَحْمَةُ اللَّهِ

    (As-salamu 'alaykum wa rahmatullahi)

    (Peace and mercy of Allah be upon you)

Notes:

- This Maghrib Sunnah prayer is an optional act that follows the obligatory Maghrib prayer, offering a precious opportunity for extra reflection and gratitude.
- The additional rak'ah serves to deepen your connection with Allah, complementing your daily worship with renewed spiritual energy.
- Feel free to include personal supplications (du'ā) during the brief sitting (Jalsa) in both rak'ahs to express your heartfelt requests and thanks.
- Maintain mindfulness and sincerity in every posture and verbal recitation, inviting Allah's mercy and blessings as you conclude your day.

CHAPTER 9: ISHA FARD PRAYER

STEP-BY-STEP Isha Fard Prayer

Below is an in-depth guide to the Isha fard (obligatory) prayer—a sacred act performed after the twilight has disappeared. This prayer offers believers the opportunity to wind down their day, engage in sincere reflection, and renew their commitment to Allah. Before you begin, ensure you are in a state of ritual purity (wudu) and have centered your heart for sincere worship.

Before You Begin:
- Form your niyyah in your heart: "I intend to perform four rak'ahs of the Isha prayer for the sake of Allah."

Rak'ah 1:

---

1. Opening Takbīr (Start of the Prayer):
   الله أكبر
   (Allāhu Akbar)
   (Allah is the Greatest)

2. Recite al-Fātiha (The Opening Chapter):

a. بِسْمِ اللهِ الرَّحْمٰنِ الرَّحِيمِ
(Bismillaahir Rahmaanir Raheem)
(In the name of Allah, the Most Gracious, the Most Merciful)

b. اَلْحَمْدُ لِلّٰهِ رَبِّ الْعَالَمِينَ
(Alhamdu lillahi rabbil 'aalameen)
(All praise is due to Allah, Lord of all the worlds)

c. الرَّحْمٰنِ الرَّحِيمِ
(Ar-Rahmaanir Raheem)
(The Most Gracious, the Most Merciful)

d. مَالِكِ يَوْمِ الدِّينِ
(Maaliki yawmid-deen)
(Master of the Day of Judgment)

e. إِيَّاكَ نَعْبُدُ وَإِيَّاكَ نَسْتَعِينُ
(Iyyaka na'budu wa iyyaka nasta'een)
(You alone we worship, and You alone we ask for help)

f. اهْدِنَا الصِّرَاطَ الْمُسْتَقِيمَ
(Ihdinas-siraatal mustaqeem)
(Guide us to the straight path)

g. صِرَاطَ الَّذِينَ أَنْعَمْتَ عَلَيْهِمْ, غَيْرِ الْمَغْضُوبِ عَلَيْهِمْ وَلَا الضَّالِّينَ
(Siraatal ladheena an'amta 'alayhim, ghayril-maghdhoobi 'alayhim wa lad-daalleen)
(The path of those upon whom You have bestowed favor, not of those who have earned Your anger nor of those who go astray)

3. Recite a Short Sūrah – Surah Al-Ikhlās:

a. قُلْ هُوَ اللَّهُ أَحَدٌ
(Qul huwa Allāhu 'ahad)
(Say, "He is Allah, One")

b. اللَّهُ الصَّمَدُ
(Allāhu as-samad)
(Allah, the Eternal Refuge)

c. لَمْ يَلِدْ وَلَمْ يُولَدْ
(Lam yalid wa lam yoolad)
(He neither begets nor is born)

d. وَلَمْ يَكُنْ لَهُ كُفُوًا أَحَدٌ
(Wa lam yakun lahu kufuwan ahad)
(Nor is there to Him any equivalent)

4. Rukū' (Bowing):

• As you bow, say "الله أكبر."
• Then recite:
سُبْحَانَ رَبِّيَ الْعَظِيمِ
(Subhana rabbiyal 'adheem)
(Glory be to my Lord, the Most Great)   [Repeat at least three times]

5. Rising from Rukū':

• Rise while saying:
سَمِعَ اللَّهُ لِمَنْ حَمِدَهُ
(Sami' Allāhu liman hamidah)
(Allah hears those who praise Him)
• Then, while standing straight, say:
رَبَّنَا وَلَكَ الْحَمْدُ
(Rabbana wa laka al-hamd)
(Our Lord, to You be all praise)

6. Sujūd (First Prostration):

• As you lower into prostration, say "الله أكبر."
• Then recite:
سُبْحَانَ رَبِّيَ الْأَعْلَى
(Subhana rabbiyal a'la)
(Glory be to my Lord, the Most High)   [Repeat at least three times]

7. Brief Sitting (Jalsa):

- Sit briefly; you may supplicate, for example:

  رَبِّ اغْفِرْ لِي

  (Rabbi ighfir li)

  (O my Lord, forgive me)

8. Sujūd (Second Prostration):

- Say "الله أكبر" as you move into your second prostration.
- Then recite:

  سُبْحَانَ رَبِّيَ الْأَعْلَى

  (Subhana rabbiyal a'la)

  (Glory be to my Lord, the Most High)   [Repeat at least three times]

9. Rising for the Next Rak'ah:

- Say "الله أكبر" and stand to begin Rak'ah 2.

Rak'ah 2:

---

1. Opening Takbīr:

   الله أكبر

   (Allāhu Akbar)

   (Allah is the Greatest)

2. Recite al-Fātiha (Repeat as in Rak'ah 1):

a. بِسْمِ اللَّهِ الرَّحْمَنِ الرَّحِيمِ

   (Bismillaahir Rahmaanir Raheem)

   (In the name of Allah, the Most Gracious, the Most Merciful)

b. اَلْحَمْدُ لِلَّهِ رَبِّ الْعَالَمِين

   (Alhamdu lillahi rabbil 'aalameen)

   (All praise is due to Allah, Lord of all the worlds)

c. الرَّحْمَنِ الرَّحِيمِ

   (Ar-Rahmaanir Raheem)

   (The Most Gracious, the Most Merciful)

d. مَالِكِ يَوْمِ الدِّينِ

(Maaliki yawmid-deen)
(Master of the Day of Judgment)

e. إِيَّاكَ نَعْبُدُ وَإِيَّاكَ نَسْتَعِينُ

(Iyyaka na'budu wa iyyaka nasta'een)
(You alone we worship, and You alone we ask for help)

f. اهْدِنَا الصِّرَاطَ الْمُسْتَقِيمَ

(Ihdinas-siraatal mustaqeem)
(Guide us to the straight path)

g. صِرَاطَ الَّذِينَ أَنْعَمْتَ عَلَيْهِمْ, غَيْرِ الْمَغْضُوبِ عَلَيْهِمْ وَلَا الضَّالِّينَ

(Siraatal ladheena an'amta 'alayhim, ghayril-maghdhoobi 'alayhim wa lad-daalleen)

(The path of those upon whom You have bestowed favor, not of those who have earned Your anger nor of those who go astray)

3. Recite a Short Sūrah – Surah Al-Falaq:

a. قُلْ أَعُوذُ بِرَبِّ الْفَلَقِ

(Qul a'udhu birabbi al-falaq)
(Say, "I seek refuge in the Lord of daybreak")

b. مِن شَرِّ مَا خَلَقَ

(Min sharri ma khalaq)
(From the evil of that which He created)

c. وَمِن شَرِّ غَاسِقٍ إِذَا وَقَبَ

(Wa min sharri ghaasiqin idha waqab)
(And from the evil of darkness when it settles)

d. وَمِن شَرِّ النَّفَّاثَاتِ فِي الْعُقَدِ

(Wa min sharri an-naffaasaat fil 'uqad)
(And from the evil of those who practice sorcery)

e. وَمِن شَرِّ حَاسِدٍ إِذَا حَسَدَ

(Wa min sharri haasidin idha hasad)
(And from the evil of an envier when he envies)

4. Rukū' (Bowing):

- As you bow, say "الله أكبر."
- Then recite:

سُبْحَانَ رَبِّيَ الْعَظِيم

(Subhana rabbiyal 'adheem)

(Glory be to my Lord, the Most Great)   [Repeat at least three times]

5. Rising from Rukū':

- Say:

سَمِعَ اللَّهُ لِمَنْ حَمِدَه

(Sami' Allāhu liman hamidah)

(Allah hears those who praise Him)

- Then say:

رَبَّنَا وَلَكَ الْحَمْد

(Rabbana wa laka al-hamd)

(Our Lord, to You be all praise)

6. Sujūd (First Prostration):

- Say "الله أكبر" as you prostrate.
- Then recite:

سُبْحَانَ رَبِّيَ الْأَعْلَى

(Subhana rabbiyal a'la)

(Glory be to my Lord, the Most High)   [Repeat at least three times]

7. Brief Sitting (Jalsa):

- Sit briefly; you may say:

رَبِّ اغْفِرْ لِي

(Rabbi ighfir li)

(O my Lord, forgive me)

8. Sujūd (Second Prostration):

- Say "الله أكبر" and perform your second prostration.

- Then recite:

سُبْحَانَ رَبِّيَ الْأَعْلَى

(Subhana rabbiyal a'la)

(Glory be to my Lord, the Most High) [Repeat at least three times]

9. Tashahhud (Sitting for the Testimony):

After completing the second sujūd, remain seated and recite:

اَلتَّحِيَّاتُ لِلَّهِ وَالصَّلَوَاتُ وَالطَّيِّبَات

(At-tahiyyatu lillahi was-salawatu wat-tayyibatu)
(All greetings, prayers, and pure words are for Allah)

اَلسَّلَامُ عَلَيْكَ أَيُّهَا النَّبِي

(As-salamu 'alayka ayyuha an-nabiyyu)
(Peace be upon you, O Prophet)

وَرَحْمَةُ اللَّهِ وَبَرَكَاتُه

(Wa rahmatullahi wa barakatuhu)
(And the mercy and blessings of Allah)

أَشْهَدُ أَنْ لَا إِلَهَ إِلَّا اللَّه

(Ash-hadu an la ilaha illallahu)
(I bear witness that there is no deity except Allah)

وَأَشْهَدُ أَنَّ مُحَمَّدًا رَسُولُ اللَّه

(Wa ash-hadu anna Muhammadan Rasool Allah)
(And I bear witness that Muhammad is the Messenger of Allah)

- Then, after a brief pause, say "الله أكبر" and stand to begin Rak'ah 3.

Rak'ah 3:

---

1. Opening Takbīr:

الله أكبر

(Allāhu Akbar)
(Allah is the Greatest)

2. Recite al-Fātiha:

a. بِسْمِ اللهِ الرَّحْمٰنِ الرَّحِيم
(Bismillaahir Rahmaanir Raheem)
(In the name of Allah, the Most Gracious, the Most Merciful)

b. اَلْحَمْدُ لِلّٰهِ رَبِّ الْعَالَمِين
(Alhamdu lillahi rabbil 'aalameen)
(All praise is due to Allah, Lord of all the worlds)

c. اِلرَّحْمٰنِ الرَّحِيم
(Ar-Rahmaanir Raheem)
(The Most Gracious, the Most Merciful)

d. مَالِكِ يَوْمِ الدِّين
(Maaliki yawmid-deen)
(Master of the Day of Judgment)

e. اِيَّاكَ نَعْبُدُ وَإِيَّاكَ نَسْتَعِين
(Iyyaka na'budu wa iyyaka nasta'een)
(You alone we worship, and You alone we ask for help)

f. اَهْدِنَا الصِّرَاطَ الْمُسْتَقِيم
(Ihdinas-siraatal mustaqeem)
(Guide us to the straight path)

g. صِرَاطَ الَّذِينَ أَنْعَمْتَ عَلَيْهِمْ, غَيْرِ الْمَغْضُوبِ عَلَيْهِمْ وَلَا الضَّالِّين
(Siraatal ladheena an'amta 'alayhim, ghayril-maghdhoobi 'alayhim wa lad-daalleen)
(The path of those upon whom You have bestowed favor, not of those who have earned Your anger nor of those who go astray)

3. Recite a Short Sūrah – Surah an-Nās:

a. قُلْ أَعُوذُ بِرَبِّ النَّاس
(Qul a'udhu birabbi an-naas)
(Say, "I seek refuge in the Lord of mankind")

b. مَلِكِ النَّاسِ
   (Maliki an-naas)
   (The Sovereign of mankind)

c. إِلَٰهِ النَّاسِ
   (Ilahi an-naas)
   (The God of mankind)

d. مِن شَرِّ الْوَسْوَاسِ الْخَنَّاسِ
   (Min sharri al-waswaasil khannaas)
   (From the evil of the whisperer who withdraws)

e. الَّذِي يُوَسْوِسُ فِي صُدُورِ النَّاسِ
   (Allathee yuwaswis fee sudoori an-naas)
   (Who whispers evil into the breasts of mankind)

f. مِنَ الْجِنَّةِ وَالنَّاسِ
   (Mina al-jinnati wan-naas)
   (Among jinn and among men)

4. Rukū' (Bowing):

• As you enter bowing, say "الله أكبر."
• Then recite:
   سُبْحَانَ رَبِّيَ الْعَظِيمِ
   (Subhana rabbiyal 'adheem)
   (Glory be to my Lord, the Most Great)   [Repeat at least three times]

5. Rising from Rukū':

• Say:
   سَمِعَ اللَّهُ لِمَنْ حَمِدَه
   (Sami' Allāhu liman hamidah)
   (Allah hears those who praise Him)
• Then say:
   رَبَّنَا وَلَكَ الْحَمْدُ
   (Rabbana wa laka al-hamd)
   (Our Lord, to You be all praise)

6. Sujūd (First Prostration):
   - Say "الله أكبر" as you prostrate.
   - Then recite:
   سُبْحَانَ رَبِّيَ الأَعْلَى
   (Subhana rabbiyal a'la)
   (Glory be to my Lord, the Most High)   [Repeat at least three times]

7. Brief Sitting (Jalsa):
   - Sit briefly; you may recite:
   رَبِّ اغْفِرْ لِي
   (Rabbi ighfir li)
   (O my Lord, forgive me)

8. Sujūd (Second Prostration):
   - Say "الله أكبر" and perform your second prostration.
   - Then recite:
   سُبْحَانَ رَبِّيَ الأَعْلَى
   (Subhana rabbiyal a'la)
   (Glory be to my Lord, the Most High)   [Repeat at least three times]

9. Rising for Rak'ah 4:
   - Say "الله أكبر" and stand to begin Rak'ah 4.

Rak'ah 4:

---

1. Opening Takbīr:
   الله أكبر
   (Allāhu Akbar)
   (Allah is the Greatest)

2. Recite al-Fātiha:
   a. بِسْمِ اللَّهِ الرَّحْمَنِ الرَّحِيمِ

(Bismillaahir Rahmaanir Raheem)
(In the name of Allah, the Most Gracious, the Most Merciful)

b. اَلْحَمْدُ لِلَّهِ رَبِّ الْعَالَمِين
(Alhamdu lillahi rabbil 'aalameen)
(All praise is due to Allah, Lord of all the worlds)

c. اِلرَّحْمَٰنِ الرَّحِيم
(Ar-Rahmaanir Raheem)
(The Most Gracious, the Most Merciful)

d. مَالِكِ يَوْمِ الدِّين
(Maaliki yawmid-deen)
(Master of the Day of Judgment)

e. إِيَّاكَ نَعْبُدُ وَإِيَّاكَ نَسْتَعِين
(Iyyaka na'budu wa iyyaka nasta'een)
(You alone we worship, and You alone we ask for help)

f. اِهْدِنَا الصِّرَاطَ الْمُسْتَقِيم
(Ihdinas-siraatal mustaqeem)
(Guide us to the straight path)

g. صِرَاطَ الَّذِينَ أَنْعَمْتَ عَلَيْهِمْ, غَيْرِ الْمَغْضُوبِ عَلَيْهِمْ وَلَا الضَّالِّين
(Siraatal ladheena an'amta 'alayhim, ghayril-maghdhoobi 'alayhim wa lad-daalleen)
(The path of those upon whom You have bestowed favor, not of those who have earned Your anger nor of those who go astray)

3. Recite a Short Sūrah – Surah Al-Ikhlās:

a. قُلْ هُوَ اللَّهُ أَحَد
(Qul huwa Allāhu 'ahad)
(Say, "He is Allah, One")

b. اَللَّهُ الصَّمَد
(Allāhu as-samad)
(Allah, the Eternal Refuge)

c. لَمْ يَلِدْ وَلَمْ يُولَد

(Lam yalid wa lam yoolad)
(He neither begets nor is born)

d. وَلَم يَكُن لَهُ كُفُوًا أَحَد

(Wa lam yakun lahu kufuwan ahad)
(Nor is there to Him any equivalent)

4. Rukū' (Bowing):

- As you bow, say "الله أكبر."
- Then recite:

سُبْحَانَ رَبِّيَ الْعَظِيم

(Subhana rabbiyal 'adheem)
(Glory be to my Lord, the Most Great)   [Repeat at least three times]

5. Rising from Rukū':

- Say:

سَمِعَ اللَّهُ لِمَنْ حَمِدَه

(Sami' Allāhu liman hamidah)
(Allah hears those who praise Him)

- Then say:

رَبَّنَا وَلَكَ الْحَمد

(Rabbana wa laka al-hamd)
(Our Lord, to You be all praise)

6. Sujūd (First Prostration):

- Say "الله أكبر" and prostrate.
- Then recite:

سُبْحَانَ رَبِّيَ الْأَعْلَى

(Subhana rabbiyal a'la)
(Glory be to my Lord, the Most High)   [Repeat at least three times]

7. Brief Sitting (Jalsa):

- Sit briefly; you may recite:

رَبِّ اغْفِرْ لِي

(Rabbi ighfir li)
(O my Lord, forgive me)

8. Sujūd (Second Prostration):

- Say "الله أكبر" and perform your second prostration.
- Then recite:

سُبْحَانَ رَبِّيَ الْأَعْلَى

(Subhana rabbiyal a'la)
(Glory be to my Lord, the Most High)   [Repeat at least three times]

Final Tashahhud and Taslīm:

After the second sujūd of Rak'ah 4, sit for the final Tashahhud and recite:

اَلتَّحِيَّاتُ لِلَّهِ وَالصَّلَوَاتُ وَالطَّيِّبَاتُ

(At-tahiyyatu lillahi was-salawatu wat-tayyibatu)
(All greetings, prayers, and pure words are for Allah)

اَلسَّلَامُ عَلَيْكَ أَيُّهَا النَّبِيُّ وَرَحْمَةُ اللَّهِ وَبَرَكَاتُهُ

(As-salamu 'alayka ayyuha an-nabiyyu wa rahmatullahi wa barakatuhu)
(Peace be upon you, O Prophet, and the mercy and blessings of Allah)

اَلسَّلَامُ عَلَيْنَا وَعَلَى عِبَادِ اللَّهِ الصَّالِحِينَ

(As-salamu 'alayna wa 'ala 'ibaadil-lahi as-saaliheen)
(Peace be upon us and upon the righteous servants of Allah)

أَشْهَدُ أَنْ لَا إِلَهَ إِلَّا اللَّهُ

(Ash-hadu an la ilaha illallahu)
(I bear witness that there is no deity except Allah)

وَأَشْهَدُ أَنَّ مُحَمَّدًا رَسُولُ اللَّهِ

(Wa ash-hadu anna Muhammadan Rasool Allah)
(I bear witness that Muhammad is the Messenger of Allah)

To Conclude the Prayer (Taslīm):

- Turn your head to the right and say:
  اِلسَّلَامُ عَلَيْكُمْ وَرَحْمَةُ اللّٰه
  (As-salamu 'alaykum wa rahmatullah)
  (Peace and mercy of Allah be upon you)

- Then turn your head to the left and say:
  اِلسَّلَامُ عَلَيْكُمْ وَرَحْمَةُ اللّٰه
  (As-salamu 'alaykum wa rahmatullah)
  (Peace and mercy of Allah be upon you)

CHAPTER 10: ISHA SUNNAH PRAYER

STEP-BY-STEP Isha Sunnah Prayer

Below is an in-depth guide to the Isha Sunnah (voluntary) prayer—a supplementary act of worship performed after the obligatory Isha prayer. This prayer brings spiritual tranquility, deep reflection, and prepares the heart for a peaceful rest while nurturing a closer relationship with the Creator. Before you begin, ensure that you have performed wudu and that your heart is filled with sincere intention.

Before You Begin:
• Form your niyyah in your heart: "I intend to perform two rak'ahs of the Isha Sunnah prayer for the sake of Allah."

Rak'ah 1:

1. Opening Takbīr (Start of the Prayer):
    الله أكبر
    (Allāhu Akbar)
    (Allah is the Greatest)

2. Recite al-Fātiha (The Opening Chapter):

a. بِسْمِ اللَّهِ الرَّحْمَٰنِ الرَّحِيمِ
   (Bismillaahir Rahmaanir Raheem)

(In the name of Allah, the Most Gracious, the Most Merciful)

b. اَلْحَمْدُ لِلَّهِ رَبِّ الْعَالَمِين
(Alhamdu lillahi rabbil 'aalameen)
(All praise is due to Allah, Lord of all the worlds)

c. اِلرَّحْمٰنِ الرَّحِيم
(Ar-Rahmaanir Raheem)
(The Most Gracious, the Most Merciful)

d. مَالِكِ يَوْمِ الدِّين
(Maaliki yawmid-deen)
(Master of the Day of Judgment)

e. إِيَّاكَ نَعْبُدُ وَإِيَّاكَ نَسْتَعِين
(Iyyaka na'budu wa iyyaka nasta'een)
(You alone we worship, and You alone we ask for help)

f. اهْدِنَا الصِّرَاطَ الْمُسْتَقِيم
(Ihdinas-siraatal mustaqeem)
(Guide us to the straight path)

g. صِرَاطَ الَّذِينَ أَنْعَمْتَ عَلَيْهِمْ غَيْرِ الْمَغْضُوبِ عَلَيْهِمْ وَلَا الضَّالِّين
(Siraatal ladheena an'amta 'alayhim ghayril maghdoobi 'alayhim wa lad-daalleen)
(The path of those upon whom You have bestowed favor, not of those who have earned Your anger nor of those who go astray)

3. Recite a Short Sūrah – Sūrah al-Ikhlās:

a. قُلْ هُوَ اللَّهُ أَحَد
(Qul huwa Allāhu 'ahad)
(Say, "He is Allah, [Who is] One")

b. اللَّهُ الصَّمَد
(Allāhu as-samad)
(Allah, the Eternal Refuge)

c. لَمْ يَلِدْ وَلَمْ يُولَد
(Lam yalid wa lam yoolad)

(He neither begets nor is born)

d. وَلَمْ يَكُن لَّهُ كُفُوًا أَحَدٌ
(Wa lam yakun lahu kufuwan ahad)
(Nor is there to Him any equivalent)

4. Rukū' (Bowing):
   • As you move into the bowing position, say "Allāhu Akbar."
   • Then recite:
   سُبْحَانَ رَبِّيَ الْعَظِيمِ
   (Subhana rabbiyal 'adheem)
   (Glory be to my Lord, the Most Great)
   [Repeat at least three times]

5. Rising from Rukū':
   • Rise while saying:
   سَمِعَ اللَّهُ لِمَنْ حَمِدَه
   (Sami' Allāhu liman hamidah)
   (Allah hears those who praise Him)
   • Then, while standing straight, say:
   رَبَّنَا وَلَكَ الْحَمْدُ
   (Rabbana wa laka al-hamd)
   (Our Lord, to You be all praise)

6. Sujūd (First Prostration):
   • As you descend into prostration, say "Allāhu Akbar."
   • Then recite:
   سُبْحَانَ رَبِّيَ الْأَعْلَى
   (Subhana rabbiyal a'la)
   (Glory be to my Lord, the Most High)
   [Repeat at least three times]

7. Brief Sitting (Jalsa):
   • Sit briefly between the two prostrations and supplicate; for example:
   رَبِّ اغْفِرْ لِي
   (Rabbi ighfir li)

(O my Lord, forgive me)

8. Sujūd (Second Prostration):
   - Say "Allāhu Akbar" as you move into the second prostration.
   - Then recite:

   سُبْحَانَ رَبِّيَ الأَعْلَى

   (Subhana rabbiyal a'la)
   (Glory be to my Lord, the Most High)
   [Repeat at least three times]

9. Rising for the Next Rak'ah:
   - Say "Allāhu Akbar" and stand up to begin Rak'ah 2.

Rak'ah 2:

---

1. Opening Takbīr:

   الله أكبر

   (Allāhu Akbar)
   (Allah is the Greatest)

2. Recite al-Fātiha (The Opening Chapter):

   a. بِسْمِ اللَّهِ الرَّحْمَٰنِ الرَّحِيمِ
   (Bismillaahir Rahmaanir Raheem)
   (In the name of Allah, the Most Gracious, the Most Merciful)

   b. الْحَمْدُ لِلَّهِ رَبِّ الْعَالَمِينَ
   (Alhamdu lillahi rabbil 'aalameen)
   (All praise is due to Allah, Lord of all the worlds)

   c. الرَّحْمَٰنِ الرَّحِيمِ
   (Ar-Rahmaanir Raheem)
   (The Most Gracious, the Most Merciful)

   d. مَالِكِ يَوْمِ الدِّينِ
   (Maaliki yawmid-deen)
   (Master of the Day of Judgment)

e. اِيَّاكَ نَعْبُدُ وَإِيَّاكَ نَسْتَعِينُ
(Iyyaka na'budu wa iyyaka nasta'een)
(You alone we worship, and You alone we ask for help)

f. اَهْدِنَا الصِّرَاطَ الْمُسْتَقِيمَ
(Ihdinas-siraatal mustaqeem)
(Guide us to the straight path)

g. صِرَاطَ الَّذِينَ أَنْعَمْتَ عَلَيْهِمْ غَيْرِ الْمَغْضُوبِ عَلَيْهِمْ وَلَا الضَّالِّينَ
(Siraatal ladheena an'amta 'alayhim ghayril maghdoobi 'alayhim wa lad-daalleen)
(The path of those upon whom You have bestowed favor, not of those who have earned Your anger nor of those who go astray)

3. Recite a Short Sūrah – Sūrah al-Falaq:

a. قُلْ أَعُوذُ بِرَبِّ الْفَلَقِ
(Qul a'oodhu birabbi al-falaq)
(Say, "I seek refuge in the Lord of the daybreak")

b. مِن شَرِّ مَا خَلَقَ
(Min sharri ma khalaq)
(From the evil of that which He created)

c. وَمِن شَرِّ غَاسِقٍ إِذَا وَقَبَ
(Wa min sharri ghaasiqin idha waqab)
(And from the evil of darkness when it settles)

d. وَمِن شَرِّ النَّفَّاثَاتِ فِي الْعُقَدِ
(Wa min sharri an-naffathati fil 'uqad)
(And from the evil of those who blow on knots)

e. وَمِن شَرِّ حَاسِدٍ إِذَا حَسَدَ
(Wa min sharri haasidin idha hasad)
(And from the evil of an envier when he envies)

4. Rukū' (Bowing):
   - As you bow, say "Allāhu Akbar."
   - Then recite:

سُبْحَانَ رَبِّيَ الْعَظِيم
(Subhana rabbiyal 'adheem)
(Glory be to my Lord, the Most Great)
[Repeat at least three times]

5. Rising from Rukū':
   - While rising, say:
   سَمِعَ اللَّهُ لِمَنْ حَمِدَه
   (Sami' Allāhu liman hamidah)
   (Allah hears those who praise Him)
   - Then, while standing, say:
   رَبَّنَا وَلَكَ الْحَمْد
   (Rabbana wa laka al-hamd)
   (Our Lord, to You be all praise)

6. Sujūd (First Prostration):
   - As you descend into prostration, say "Allāhu Akbar."
   - Then recite:
   سُبْحَانَ رَبِّيَ الْأَعْلَى
   (Subhana rabbiyal a'la)
   (Glory be to my Lord, the Most High)
   [Repeat at least three times]

7. Brief Sitting (Jalsa):
   - Sit briefly and, if you wish, recite a supplication such as:
   رَبِّ اغْفِرْ لِي
   (Rabbi ighfir li)
   (O my Lord, forgive me)

8. Sujūd (Second Prostration):
   - Say "Allāhu Akbar" as you move into the second prostration.
   - Then recite:
   سُبْحَانَ رَبِّيَ الْأَعْلَى
   (Subhana rabbiyal a'la)
   (Glory be to my Lord, the Most High)
   [Repeat at least three times]

9. Final Tashahhud (Sitting for the Testimony):
   • After the second sujūd, sit and recite the Tashahhud:

اَلتَّحِيَّاتُ لِلَّهِ وَالصَّلَوَاتُ وَالطَّيِّبَاتُ
(At-tahiyyatu lillahi was-salawatu wat-tayyibatu)
(All greetings, prayers, and pure words are for Allah)

اَلسَّلَامُ عَلَيْكَ أَيُّهَا النَّبِيُّ
(As-salamu 'alayka ayyuha an-nabiyyu)
(Peace be upon you, O Prophet)

وَرَحْمَةُ اللَّهِ وَبَرَكَاتُهُ
(Wa rahmatullahi wa barakatuhu)
(And the mercy and blessings of Allah)

اَلسَّلَامُ عَلَيْنَا وَعَلَى عِبَادِ اللَّهِ الصَّالِحِينَ
(As-salamu 'alayna wa 'ala 'ibaadil-lahi as-saaliheen)
(Peace be upon us and upon the righteous servants of Allah)

أَشْهَدُ أَنْ لَا إِلَهَ إِلَّا اللَّهُ
(Ash-hadu an la ilaha illallahu)
(I bear witness that there is no deity except Allah)

وَأَشْهَدُ أَنَّ مُحَمَّدًا رَسُولُ اللَّهِ
(Wa ash-hadu anna Muhammadan Rasool Allah)
(And I bear witness that Muhammad is the Messenger of Allah)

10. Taslīm (Concluding the Prayer):
   • To conclude, turn your head to the right and say:
   اَلسَّلَامُ عَلَيْكُمْ وَرَحْمَةُ اللَّهِ
   (As-salamu 'alaykum wa rahmatullahi)
   (Peace and mercy of Allah be upon you)
   • Then turn your head to the left and repeat:
   اَلسَّلَامُ عَلَيْكُمْ وَرَحْمَةُ اللَّهِ
   (As-salamu 'alaykum wa rahmatullahi)
   (Peace and mercy of Allah be upon you)

Notes:
- At each transition (standing, bowing, prostrating, and sitting), it is recommended to say "Allāhu Akbar."
- The recitations in Rukū' and Sujūd are to be repeated at least three times, following the Sunnah of the Prophet.
- Additional supplications (du'ā) may be offered during the brief sitting (Jalsa) at your discretion.

CHAPTER 11: WITR PRAYER

STEP-BY-STEP Witr Prayer

Below is an in-depth guide to the Witr prayer—a final, odd-numbered prayer performed after Isha that provides a spiritual closure to your night's worship. This unique prayer marks the last intimate moment of supplication, inviting you to pour your heart out to Allah before the day concludes. Before you begin, ensure you are in a state of ritual purity (wudu) and have set your heart for sincere devotion.

Before You Begin:
• Form your niyyah in your heart: "I intend to perform the Witr prayer for the sake of Allah."

Rak'ah 1:

1. Opening Takbīr (Start of the Prayer):
   الله أكبر
   (Allāhu Akbar) (Allah is the Greatest)

2. Recite al-Fātiha (The Opening Chapter):

   a. بِسْمِ اللَّهِ الرَّحْمَٰنِ الرَّحِيمِ
   (Bismillaahir Rahmaanir Raheem) (In the name of Allah, the

Most Gracious, the Most Merciful)

b. اَلْحَمْدُ لِلَّهِ رَبِّ الْعَالَمِين

(Alhamdu lillahi rabbil 'aalameen) (All praise is due to Allah, Lord of all the worlds)

c. اِلرَّحْمَنِ الرَّحِيم

(Ar-Rahmaanir Raheem) (The Most Gracious, the Most Merciful)

d. مَالِكِ يَوْمِ الدِّين

(Maaliki yawmid-deen) (Master of the Day of Judgment)

e. إِيَّاكَ نَعْبُدُ وَإِيَّاكَ نَسْتَعِين

(Iyyaka na'budu wa iyyaka nasta'een) (You alone we worship, and You alone we ask for help)

f. اهْدِنَا الصِّرَاطَ الْمُسْتَقِيم

(Ihdinas-siraatal mustaqeem) (Guide us to the straight path)

g. صِرَاطَ الَّذِينَ أَنْعَمْتَ عَلَيْهِمْ غَيْرِ الْمَغْضُوبِ عَلَيْهِمْ وَلَا الضَّالِّين

(Siraatal ladheena an'amta 'alayhim ghayril maghdoobi 'alayhim wa lad-daalleen) (The path of those upon whom You have bestowed favor – not of those who have incurred Your anger nor of those who go astray)

3. Recite a Short Sūrah – Sūrah al-Kafirūn:

a. قُلْ يَا أَيُّهَا الْكَافِرُون

(Qul ya ayyuhal kaafirun) (Say, "O disbelievers,")

b. لَا أَعْبُدُ مَا تَعْبُدُون

(Laa a'budu maa ta'budoon) (I do not worship what you worship)

c. وَلَا أَنْتُمْ عَابِدُونَ مَا أَعْبُد

(Wa la antum 'abidoon maa a'bud) (Nor are you worshipers of what I worship)

d. وَلَا أَنَا عَابِدٌ مَا عَبَدتُّم

(Wa la ana 'abidun maa 'abadtum) (And I will not be a

worshipper of what you have worshipped)

e. وَلَا أَنتُمْ عَابِدُونَ مَا أَعْبُدُ

(Wa la antum 'abidoon maa a'bud) (Nor will you be worshipers of what I worship)

f. لَكُمْ دِينُكُمْ وَلِيَ دِينِ

(Lakum deenukum wa liya deen) (For you is your religion, and for me is mine)

4. Rukū' (Bowing):
   - As you move into Rukū', say "الله أكبر"
     (Allāhu Akbar) (Allah is the Greatest)
   - Then recite:
     سُبْحَانَ رَبِّيَ الْعَظِيمِ
     (Subhana rabbiyal 'adheem) (Glory be to my Lord, the Most Great)
     [Repeat at least three times]

5. Rising from Rukū':
   - As you rise, say:
     سَمِعَ اللَّهُ لِمَنْ حَمِدَهُ
     (Sami' Allāhu liman hamidah) (Allah hears those who praise Him)
   - Then, while standing, say:
     رَبَّنَا وَلَكَ الْحَمْدُ
     (Rabbana wa laka al-hamd) (Our Lord, to You be all praise)

6. Sujūd (First Prostration):
   - While going into Sujūd, say "الله أكبر"
     (Allāhu Akbar) (Allah is the Greatest)
   - Then recite:
     سُبْحَانَ رَبِّيَ الْأَعْلَى
     (Subhana rabbiyal a'la) (Glory be to my Lord, the Most High)
     [Repeat at least three times]

7. **Brief Sitting (Jalsa):**
   - Sit briefly and supplicate, for example:

   رَبِّ اغْفِرْ لِي

   (Rabbi ighfir li) (O my Lord, forgive me)

8. **Sujūd (Second Prostration):**
   - Go into Sujūd, saying "الله أكبر"

   (Allāhu Akbar) (Allah is the Greatest)
   - Then recite:

   سُبْحَانَ رَبِّيَ الأَعْلَى

   (Subhana rabbiyal a'la) (Glory be to my Lord, the Most High)

   [Repeat at least three times]

9. **Rising for the Next Rak'ah:**
   - Say "الله أكبر"

   (Allāhu Akbar) (Allah is the Greatest) and stand for Rak'ah 2.

Rak'ah 2:

---

1. **Opening Takbīr:**

   الله أكبر

   (Allāhu Akbar) (Allah is the Greatest)

2. **Recite al-Fātiha:**

   a. بِسْمِ اللهِ الرَّحْمَٰنِ الرَّحِيمِ

   (Bismillaahir Rahmaanir Raheem) (In the name of Allah, the Most Gracious, the Most Merciful)

   b. الْحَمْدُ لِلَّهِ رَبِّ الْعَالَمِينَ

   (Alhamdu lillahi rabbil 'aalameen) (All praise is due to Allah, Lord of all the worlds)

   c. الرَّحْمَٰنِ الرَّحِيمِ

   (Ar-Rahmaanir Raheem) (The Most Gracious, the Most

Merciful)

d. مَالِكِ يَوْمِ الدِّينِ

(Maaliki yawmid-deen) (Master of the Day of Judgment)

e. إِيَّاكَ نَعْبُدُ وَإِيَّاكَ نَسْتَعِينُ

(Iyyaka na'budu wa iyyaka nasta'een) (You alone we worship, and You alone we ask for help)

f. اهْدِنَا الصِّرَاطَ الْمُسْتَقِيمَ

(Ihdinas-siraatal mustaqeem) (Guide us to the straight path)

g. صِرَاطَ الَّذِينَ أَنْعَمْتَ عَلَيْهِمْ غَيْرِ الْمَغْضُوبِ عَلَيْهِمْ وَلَا الضَّالِّينَ

(Siraatal ladheena an'amta 'alayhim ghayril maghdoobi 'alayhim wa lad-daalleen) (The path of those upon whom You have bestowed favor – not of those who have incurred Your anger nor of those who go astray)

3. Recite a Short Sūrah – Sūrah al-Ikhlās:

a. قُلْ هُوَ اللَّهُ أَحَدٌ

(Qul huwa Allāhu 'ahad) (Say, "He is Allah, [Who is] One")

b. اللَّهُ الصَّمَدُ

(Allāhu as-samad) (Allah, the Eternal Refuge)

c. لَمْ يَلِدْ وَلَمْ يُولَدْ

(Lam yalid wa lam yoolad) (He neither begets nor is born)

d. وَلَمْ يَكُن لَّهُ كُفُوًا أَحَدٌ

(Wa lam yakun lahu kufuwan ahad) (Nor is there any equivalent to Him)

4. Rukū' (Bowing):
   - As you bow, say "الله أكبر"
     (Allāhu Akbar) (Allah is the Greatest)
   - Then recite:
     سُبْحَانَ رَبِّيَ الْعَظِيمِ
     (Subhana rabbiyal 'adheem) (Glory be to my Lord, the Most Great)

[Repeat at least three times]

5. Rising from Rukū':
   • Stand while saying:
   سَمِعَ اللَّهُ لِمَنْ حَمِدَه
   (Sami' Allāhu liman hamidah) (Allah hears those who praise Him)
   • Then say:
   رَبَّنَا وَلَكَ الْحَمْد
   (Rabbana wa laka al-hamd) (Our Lord, to You be all praise)

6. Sujūd (First Prostration):
   • Say "الله أكبر" as you descend into Sujūd
   (Allāhu Akbar) (Allah is the Greatest)
   • Recite:
   سُبْحَانَ رَبِّيَ الأَعْلَى
   (Subhana rabbiyal a'la) (Glory be to my Lord, the Most High)
   [Repeat at least three times]

7. Brief Sitting (Jalsa):
   • Sit briefly and supplicate:
   رَبِّ اغْفِرْ لِي
   (Rabbi ighfir li) (O my Lord, forgive me)

8. Sujūd (Second Prostration):
   • Say "الله أكبر" while entering Sujūd
   (Allāhu Akbar) (Allah is the Greatest)
   • Recite:
   سُبْحَانَ رَبِّيَ الأَعْلَى
   (Subhana rabbiyal a'la) (Glory be to my Lord, the Most High)
   [Repeat at least three times]

9. Rising for Rak'ah 3:
   • Say "الله أكبر"
   (Allāhu Akbar) (Allah is the Greatest) and stand for

Rak'ah 3.

Rak'ah 3 (With Qunoot):

---

1. Opening Takbīr:
   الله أكبر
   (Allāhu Akbar) (Allah is the Greatest)

2. Recite al-Fātiha:

   a. بِسْمِ اللَّهِ الرَّحْمَٰنِ الرَّحِيمِ
   (Bismillaahir Rahmaanir Raheem) (In the name of Allah, the Most Gracious, the Most Merciful)

   b. الْحَمْدُ لِلَّهِ رَبِّ الْعَالَمِين
   (Alhamdu lillahi rabbil 'aalameen) (All praise is due to Allah, Lord of all the worlds)

   c. الرَّحْمَٰنِ الرَّحِيم
   (Ar-Rahmaanir Raheem) (The Most Gracious, the Most Merciful)

   d. مَالِكِ يَوْمِ الدِّين
   (Maaliki yawmid-deen) (Master of the Day of Judgment)

   e. إِيَّاكَ نَعْبُدُ وَإِيَّاكَ نَسْتَعِين
   (Iyyaka na'budu wa iyyaka nasta'een) (You alone we worship, and You alone we ask for help)

   f. اهْدِنَا الصِّرَاطَ الْمُسْتَقِيم
   (Ihdinas-siraatal mustaqeem) (Guide us to the straight path)

   g. صِرَاطَ الَّذِينَ أَنْعَمْتَ عَلَيْهِمْ غَيْرِ الْمَغْضُوبِ عَلَيْهِمْ وَلَا الضَّالِّين
   (Siraatal ladheena an'amta 'alayhim ghayril maghdoobi 'alayhim wa lad-daalleen) (The path of those upon whom You have bestowed favor – not of those who have incurred Your anger nor of those who go astray)

3. Recite a Short Sūrah – Sūrah al-Falaq:

a. قُلْ أَعُوذُ بِرَبِّ الْفَلَقِ

(Qul a'udhu bi rabbil-falaq) (Say, "I seek refuge in the Lord of daybreak")

b. مِن شَرِّ مَا خَلَقَ

(Min sharri ma khalaq) (From the evil of that which He created)

c. وَمِن شَرِّ غَاسِقٍ إِذَا وَقَبَ

(Wa min sharri ghasiqin idha waqab) (And from the evil of darkness when it settles)

d. وَمِن شَرِّ النَّفَّاثَاتِ فِي الْعُقَدِ

(Wa min sharri an-naffathati fil 'uqad) (And from the evil of those who blow on knots)

e. وَمِن شَرِّ حَاسِدٍ إِذَا حَسَدَ

(Wa min sharri hasidin idha hasad) (And from the evil of an envier when he envies)

4. Qunoot Supplication:
   • Before proceeding to Rukū', raise your hands and recite the Qunoot:

ألَّلهُمَّ اهْدِنِي فِيمَنْ هَدَيْتَ

(Allahumma ihdini fiman hadait) (O Allah, guide me among those You have guided)

وَعَافِنِي فِيمَنْ عَافَيْتَ

(Wa 'afini fiman 'afait) (and grant me well-being among those You have granted well-being)

وَتَوَلَّنِي فِيمَنْ تَوَلَّيْتَ

(Wa tawallani fiman tawallait) (and take me into Your care among those You have taken into Your care)

وَبَارِكْ لِي فِيمَا أَعْطَيْتَ

(Wa barik li fima a'thait) (and bless me in what You have given me)

وَقِنِي شَرَّ مَا قَضَيْت

(Wa qini sharra ma qadait) (and protect me from the evil of what You have decreed)

5. Rukū' (Bowing):
    - As you bow, say "الله أكبر"
        (Allāhu Akbar) (Allah is the Greatest)
    - Then recite:
        سُبْحَانَ رَبِّيَ الْعَظِيم
        (Subhana rabbiyal 'adheem) (Glory be to my Lord, the Most Great)
        [Repeat at least three times]

6. Rising from Rukū':
    - Stand while saying:
        سَمِعَ اللَّهُ لِمَنْ حَمِدَه
        (Sami' Allāhu liman hamidah) (Allah hears those who praise Him)
    - Then say:
        رَبَّنَا وَلَكَ الْحَمْد
        (Rabbana wa laka al-hamd) (Our Lord, to You be all praise)

7. Sujūd (First Prostration):
    - Say "الله أكبر" as you go into Sujūd
        (Allāhu Akbar) (Allah is the Greatest)
    - Recite:
        سُبْحَانَ رَبِّيَ الْأَعْلَى
        (Subhana rabbiyal a'la) (Glory be to my Lord, the Most High)
        [Repeat at least three times]

8. Brief Sitting (Jalsa):
    - Sit briefly and supplicate:
        رَبِّ اغْفِرْ لِي
        (Rabbi ighfir li) (O my Lord, forgive me)

9. Sujūd (Second Prostration):
   - Say "الله أكبَر" as you descend into Sujūd
     (Allāhu Akbar) (Allah is the Greatest)
   - Recite:
     سُبْحَانَ رَبِّيَ الأَعْلَى
     (Subhana rabbiyal a'la) (Glory be to my Lord, the Most High)
     [Repeat at least three times]

10. Final Tashahhud (Sitting for the Testimony):
    - After the second Sujūd, sit and recite:

    اَلتَّحِيَّاتُ لِلَّهِ وَالصَّلَوَاتُ وَالطَّيِّبَاتُ
    (At-tahiyyatu lillahi was-salawatu wat-tayyibatu) (All greetings, prayers, and pure words belong to Allah)

    اَلسَّلَامُ عَلَيْكَ أَيُّهَا النَّبِي
    (As-salamu 'alayka ayyuha an-nabiyyu) (Peace be upon you, O Prophet)

    وَرَحْمَةُ اللَّهِ وَبَرَكَاتُهُ
    (Wa rahmatullahi wa barakatuhu) (And the mercy and blessings of Allah)

    اَلسَّلَامُ عَلَيْنَا وَعَلَى عِبَادِ اللَّهِ الصَّالِحِين
    (As-salamu 'alayna wa 'ala 'ibaadil-lahi as-saaliheen) (Peace be upon us and upon the righteous servants of Allah)

    أَشْهَدُ أَنْ لَا إِلَهَ إِلَّا اللَّه
    (Ash-hadu an la ilaha illallahu) (I bear witness that there is no deity except Allah)

    وَأَشْهَدُ أَنَّ مُحَمَّدًا رَسُولُ اللَّه
    (Wa ash-hadu anna Muhammadan Rasool Allah) (And I bear witness that Muhammad is the Messenger of Allah)

11. Taslīm (Concluding the Prayer):
    - Turn your head to the right and say:
      اِلسَّلَامُ عَلَيْكُمْ وَرَحْمَةُ اللَّه

(As-salamu 'alaykum wa rahmatullahi) (Peace and mercy of Allah be upon you)
- Then turn your head to the left and repeat:

ﺍﻟﺴَّﻼَمُ عَلَيْكُمْ وَرَحْمَةُ اللهِ

(As-salamu 'alaykum wa rahmatullahi) (Peace and mercy of Allah be upon you)

Notes:
- The Witr prayer offers a final, reflective dialogue with Allah and is a means to end your nightly worship with heartfelt supplication.
- You may choose different short surahs for variety in each Rak'ah while maintaining focus and sincerity.
- The Qunoot supplication in the third Rak'ah is especially recommended to ask Allah for guidance, blessings, and protection.
- Throughout the prayer, observe calm and reflective composure, embracing the profound intimacy with Allah as you conclude your worship.

CHAPTER 12: TAHAJJUD PRAYER

--------- STEP-BY-STEP Tahajjud Prayer ---------

Below is an in-depth guide to the Tahajjud (voluntary night vigil) prayer—a sacred act performed in the deepest hours of the night that fosters introspection, elevates spiritual consciousness, and offers a quiet moment to seek Allah's guidance in solitude. This prayer is marked by a calm, reflective recitation and a heartfelt supplication, inviting you to draw nearer to Allah during the stillness of the night. Ensure you are in a state of ritual purity (wudu), have set a peaceful atmosphere, and form your sincere niyyah before you begin.

Before You Begin:
• Form your niyyah in your heart: "I intend to perform the Tahajjud prayer for the sake of Allah." ---------

For this example, we present a two Rak'ah Tahajjud prayer. (Additional sets of two Rak'ahs may be prayed as desired.)

--------- Rak'ah 1: ---------

1. Opening Takbīr (Start of the Prayer): الله أكبر
   (Allāhu Akbar)
   (Allah is the Greatest)

2. Recite al-Fātiha (The Opening Chapter):

a. بِسْمِ اللَّهِ الرَّحْمَٰنِ الرَّحِيمِ
(Bismillaahir Rahmaanir Raheem)
(In the name of Allah, the Most Gracious, the Most Merciful)

b. اَلْحَمْدُ لِلَّهِ رَبِّ الْعَالَمِينَ
(Alhamdu lillahi rabbil 'aalameen)
(All praise is due to Allah, Lord of all the worlds)

c. الرَّحْمَٰنِ الرَّحِيمِ
(Ar-Rahmaanir Raheem)
(The Most Gracious, the Most Merciful)

d. مَالِكِ يَوْمِ الدِّينِ
(Maaliki yawmid-deen)
(Master of the Day of Judgment)

e. إِيَّاكَ نَعْبُدُ وَإِيَّاكَ نَسْتَعِينُ
(Iyyaka na'budu wa iyyaka nasta'een)
(You alone we worship, and You alone we ask for help)

f. اهْدِنَا الصِّرَاطَ الْمُسْتَقِيمَ
(Ihdinas-siraatal mustaqeem)
(Guide us to the straight path)

g. صِرَاطَ الَّذِينَ أَنْعَمْتَ عَلَيْهِمْ
(Siraatal ladheena an'amta 'alayhim)
(The path of those upon whom You have bestowed favor)
[End with the supplication as a humble acknowledgment of Allah's guidance]

3. Recite an Additional Sūrah (Recommended Reflection Passage): For Tahajjud, a reflective recitation is encouraged. Here, recite Surah al-Ikhlās:

a. قُلْ هُوَ اللَّهُ أَحَدٌ
(Qul huwa Allāhu 'ahad)
(Say, "He is Allah, [Who is] One")

b. اْللَّهُ الصَّمَد
(Allāhu as-samad)
(Allah, the Eternal Refuge)

c. لَمْ يَلِدْ وَلَمْ يُولَد
(Lam yalid wa lam yoolad)
(He neither begets nor is born)

d. وَلَمْ يَكُنْ لَّهُ كُفُوًا أَحَد
(Wa lam yakun lahu kufuwan ahad)
(Nor is there to Him any equivalent)

4. Rukū' (Bowing): • As you gently bow, say "Allāhu Akbar."
   • Then recite:
   سُبْحَانَ رَبِّيَ الْعَظِيم
   (Subhana rabbiyal 'adheem)
   (Glory be to my Lord, the Most Great)
   [Repeat at least three times]

5. Rising from Rukū': • Rise while saying:
   سَمِعَ اللَّهُ لِمَنْ حَمِدَه
   (Sami' Allāhu liman hamidah)
   (Allah hears those who praise Him) • Then, while standing straight, say:
   رَبَّنَا وَلَكَ الْحَمْد
   (Rabbana wa laka al-hamd)
   (Our Lord, to You be all praise)

6. Sujūd (First Prostration): • As you descend into prostration, say "Allāhu Akbar." • Then recite:
   سُبْحَانَ رَبِّيَ الْأَعْلَى
   (Subhana rabbiyal a'la)
   (Glory be to my Lord, the Most High)
   [Repeat at least three times]

7. Brief Sitting (Jalsa): • Sit briefly between the two prostrations. • Supplicate softly; for example, recite:
   رَبِّ اغْفِرْ لِي

(Rabbi ighfir li)
(O my Lord, forgive me)

8. Sujūd (Second Prostration):
   • Say "Allāhu Akbar" as you move into the second prostration.   • Then recite again:
   سُبْحَانَ رَبِّيَ الْأَعْلَى
   (Subhana rabbiyal a'la)
   (Glory be to my Lord, the Most High)
   [Repeat at least three times]

9. Rising for the Next Rak'ah:
   • Say "Allāhu Akbar" and then stand up to begin Rak'ah 2.

——————— Rak'ah 2: ———————

1. Opening Takbīr: الله أكبر
   (Allāhu Akbar)
   (Allah is the Greatest)

2. Recite al-Fātiha:

a. بِسْمِ اللَّهِ الرَّحْمَنِ الرَّحِيمِ
   (Bismillaahir Rahmaanir Raheem)
   (In the name of Allah, the Most Gracious, the Most Merciful)

b. الْحَمْدُ لِلَّهِ رَبِّ الْعَالَمِينَ
   (Alhamdu lillahi rabbil 'aalameen)
   (All praise is due to Allah, Lord of all the worlds)

c. الرَّحْمَنِ الرَّحِيمِ
   (Ar-Rahmaanir Raheem)
   (The Most Gracious, the Most Merciful)

d. مَالِكِ يَوْمِ الدِّينِ
   (Maaliki yawmid-deen)
   (Master of the Day of Judgment)

e. إِيَّاكَ نَعْبُدُ وَإِيَّاكَ نَسْتَعِينُ
   (Iyyaka na'budu wa iyyaka nasta'een)

(You alone we worship, and You alone we ask for help)

f. اَهْدِنَا الصِّرَاطَ الْمُسْتَقِيمَ
(Ihdinas-siraatal mustaqeem)
(Guide us to the straight path)

g. صِرَاطَ الَّذِينَ أَنْعَمْتَ عَلَيْهِم
(Siraatal ladheena an'amta 'alayhim)
(The path of those upon whom You have bestowed favor)

3. **Recite an Additional Sūrah:** For the second Rak'ah, recite Surah al-Falaq to invoke protection and seek refuge from all harm:

a. قُلْ أَعُوذُ بِرَبِّ الْفَلَقِ
(Qul a'udhu bi rabbil falaq)
(Say, "I seek refuge in the Lord of daybreak")

b. مِن شَرِّ مَا خَلَقَ
(Min sharri ma khalaq)
(From the evil of that which He created)

c. وَمِن شَرِّ غَاسِقٍ إِذَا وَقَبَ
(Wa min sharri ghaasiqin idha waqab)
(And from the evil of darkness as it intensifies)

d. وَمِن شَرِّ النَّفَّاثَاتِ فِي الْعُقَدِ
(Wa min sharri an-naffathati fil 'uqad)
(And from the evil of those who practice secret arts)

e. وَمِن شَرِّ حَاسِدٍ إِذَا حَسَدَ
(Wa min sharri haasidin idha hasad)
(And from the evil of an envier when he envies)

4. **Rukū' (Bowing):** • As you bow, say "Allāhu Akbar."
• Then recite:
سُبْحَانَ رَبِّيَ الْعَظِيمِ
(Subhana rabbiyal 'adheem)
(Glory be to my Lord, the Most Great)
[Repeat at least three times]

5. **Rising from Rukū':** • While rising, say:

   سَمِعَ اللَّهُ لِمَنْ حَمِدَه

   (Sami' Allāhu liman hamidah)
   (Allah hears those who praise Him)
   • Then, standing upright, say:

   رَبَّنَا وَلَكَ الْحَمْد

   (Rabbana wa laka al-hamd)
   (Our Lord, to You be all praise)

6. **Sujūd (First Prostration):** • Say "Allāhu Akbar" as you lower into prostration.
   • Then recite:

   سُبْحَانَ رَبِّيَ الْأَعْلَى

   (Subhana rabbiyal a'la)
   (Glory be to my Lord, the Most High)
      [Repeat at least three times]

7. **Brief Sitting (Jalsa):**
   • Sit briefly and make a humble supplication, for example:

   رَبِّ اغْفِرْ لِي

   (Rabbi ighfir li)
   (O my Lord, forgive me)

8. **Sujūd (Second Prostration):**
   • Say "Allāhu Akbar" as you perform the second prostration.
   • Then recite:

   سُبْحَانَ رَبِّيَ الْأَعْلَى

   (Subhana rabbiyal a'la)
   (Glory be to my Lord, the Most High)
      [Repeat at least three times]

9. **Final Tashahhud (Sitting for the Testimony):**
   • After the second sujūd, sit and recite the Tashahhud:

   اَلتَّحِيَّاتُ لِلَّهِ وَالصَّلَوَاتُ وَالطَّيِّبَاتُ

   (At-tahiyyatu lillahi was-salawatu wat-tayyibatu)
   (All greetings, prayers, and pure words are for Allah)

ٱلسَّلَامُ عَلَيْكَ أَيُّهَا النَّبِيِّ
(As-salamu 'alayka ayyuha an-nabiyyu)
(Peace be upon you, O Prophet)

وَرَحْمَةُ اللَّهِ وَبَرَكَاتُهُ
(Wa rahmatullahi wa barakatuhu)
(And the mercy and blessings of Allah)

السَّلَامُ عَلَيْنَا
(As-salamu 'alayna)
(Peace be upon us)

أَشْهَدُ أَنْ لَا إِلَهَ إِلَّا اللَّه
(Ash-hadu an la ilaha illallah)
(I bear witness that there is no deity except Allah)

وَأَشْهَدُ أَنَّ مُحَمَّدًا رَسُولُ اللَّه
(Wa ash-hadu anna Muhammadan Rasool Allah)
(And I bear witness that Muhammad is the Messenger of Allah)

10. Taslīm (Concluding the Prayer):
   - To end the prayer, first turn your head to the right and say:
     السَّلَامُ عَلَيْكُمْ وَرَحْمَةُ اللَّه
     (As-salamu 'alaykum wa rahmatullahi)
     (Peace and mercy of Allah be upon you)
   - Then turn your head to the left and repeat:
     السَّلَامُ عَلَيْكُمْ وَرَحْمَةُ اللَّه
     (As-salamu 'alaykum wa rahmatullahi)
     (Peace and mercy of Allah be upon you)

Notes:
- At each transition—standing, bowing, prostrating, and sitting—it is customary to say "Allāhu Akbar."
- In Tahajjud, take time for deep reflection and longer recitations; choose passages from the Qur'an that speak to your heart.

- This prayer, offered in the quiet hours of the night, is an opportunity to renew your connection with Allah and seek His guidance in solitude.

May your Tahajjud prayer elevate your spirit and bring tranquility to your soul.

CHAPTER 13: TARAWIH PRAYER

STEP-BY-STEP Tarawih Prayer

Below is an in-depth guide to the Tarawih prayer—a special set of extended prayers performed during the month of Ramadan after Isha. This sacred worship deepens one's immersion in the recitation of the Quran, nurtures spiritual reflection, and fosters a sense of communal unity in this blessed month. Before you begin, ensure that you are in a state of ritual purity (wudu), have prepared your chosen portions of the Quran, and clear your heart for sincere devotion.

Before You Begin:
• Form your niyyah in your heart: "I intend to perform eight (8) rak'ahs of the Tarawih prayer for the sake of Allah."

Rak'ah 1:

1. Opening Takbīr (Start of the Prayer):
   الله أكبر
   (Allāhu Akbar)
   (Allah is the Greatest)

2. Recite al-Fātiha (The Opening Chapter):
   a. بِسْمِ اللَّهِ الرَّحْمَٰنِ الرَّحِيمِ
   (Bismillaahir Rahmaanir Raheem)

(In the name of Allah, the Most Gracious, the Most Merciful)

b. اَلْحَمْدُ لِلَّهِ رَبِّ الْعَالَمِينَ

(Alhamdu lillahi rabbil 'aalameen)

(All praise is due to Allah, Lord of all the worlds)

c. الرَّحْمَنِ الرَّحِيمِ

(Ar-Rahmaanir Raheem)

(The Most Gracious, the Most Merciful)

d. مَالِكِ يَوْمِ الدِّينِ

(Maaliki yawmid-deen)

(Master of the Day of Judgment)

e. إِيَّاكَ نَعْبُدُ وَإِيَّاكَ نَسْتَعِينُ

(Iyyaka na'budu wa iyyaka nasta'een)

(You alone we worship, and You alone we ask for help)

f. اهْدِنَا الصِّرَاطَ الْمُسْتَقِيمَ

(Ihdinas-siraatal mustaqeem)

(Guide us to the straight path)

g. صِرَاطَ الَّذِينَ أَنْعَمْتَ عَلَيْهِمْ غَيْرِ الْمَغْضُوبِ عَلَيْهِمْ وَلَا الضَّالِّينَ

(Siraatal ladheena an'amta 'alayhim ghayril maghdoobi 'alayhim wa lad-daalleen)

(The path of those upon whom You have bestowed favor, not of those who have incurred Your anger nor of those who go astray)

3. Recite a Selected Passage from the Qur'ān (a lengthy recitation):

a. تَبَارَكَ الَّذِي بِيَدِهِ الْمُلْكُ

(Tabaaraka allathee biyadihil mulku)

(Blessed is He in whose hand is the dominion)

b. وَهُوَ عَلَى كُلِّ شَيْءٍ قَدِيرٌ

(Wa huwa 'ala kulli shay'in qadeer)

(And He is over all things competent)

4. Rukū' (Bowing):
   - As you bend forward, say "الله أكبر"
   (Allāhu Akbar)

(Allah is the Greatest)
- Then recite:

  سُبْحَانَ رَبِّيَ الْعَظِيم

  (Subhana rabbiyal 'adheem)
  (Glory be to my Lord, the Most Great)
  [Repeat at least three times]

5. Rising from Rukū':
   - While rising, say:

     سَمِعَ اللَّهُ لِمَنْ حَمِدَه

     (Sami' Allāhu liman hamidah)
     (Allah hears those who praise Him)
   - Then, standing upright, say:

     رَبَّنَا وَلَكَ الْحَمد

     (Rabbana wa laka al-hamd)
     (Our Lord, to You be all praise)

6. Sujūd (First Prostration):
   - As you lower into prostration, say "الله أكبر"
     (Allāhu Akbar)
     (Allah is the Greatest)
   - In Sujūd, recite:

     سُبْحَانَ رَبِّيَ الْأَعْلَى

     (Subhana rabbiyal a'la)
     (Glory be to my Lord, the Most High)
     [Repeat at least three times]

7. Brief Sitting (Jalsa):
   - Sit briefly and make a supplication; for example, recite:

     رَبِّ اغْفِرْ لِي

     (Rabbi ighfir li)
     (O my Lord, forgive me)

8. Sujūd (Second Prostration):
   - Say "الله أكبر" as you move into your second prostration
     (Allāhu Akbar)
     (Allah is the Greatest)

- Then recite:

  سُبْحَانَ رَبِّيَ الْأَعْلَى

  (Subhana rabbiyal a'la)

  (Glory be to my Lord, the Most High)

  [Repeat at least three times]

9. Rising for the Next Rak'ah:
   - Say "أَكْبَر الله" and stand up to begin your next rak'ah

     (Allāhu Akbar)

     (Allah is the Greatest)

Rak'ah 2:

---

1. Opening Takbīr:

   الله أكبر

   (Allāhu Akbar)

   (Allah is the Greatest)

2. Recite al-Fātiha:

   a. بِسْمِ اللَّهِ الرَّحْمَٰنِ الرَّحِيمِ

   (Bismillaahir Rahmaanir Raheem)

   (In the name of Allah, the Most Gracious, the Most Merciful)

   b. الْحَمْدُ لِلَّهِ رَبِّ الْعَالَمِينَ

   (Alhamdu lillahi rabbil 'aalameen)

   (All praise is due to Allah, Lord of all the worlds)

   c. الرَّحْمَٰنِ الرَّحِيمِ

   (Ar-Rahmaanir Raheem)

   (The Most Gracious, the Most Merciful)

   d. مَالِكِ يَوْمِ الدِّينِ

   (Maaliki yawmid-deen)

   (Master of the Day of Judgment)

   e. إِيَّاكَ نَعْبُدُ وَإِيَّاكَ نَسْتَعِينُ

   (Iyyaka na'budu wa iyyaka nasta'een)

   (You alone we worship, and You alone we ask for help)

f. اهدِنَا الصِّرَاطَ الْمُسْتَقِيمَ
(Ihdinas-siraatal mustaqeem)
(Guide us to the straight path)

g. صِرَاطَ الَّذِينَ أَنْعَمْتَ عَلَيْهِمْ غَيْرِ الْمَغْضُوبِ عَلَيْهِمْ وَلَا الضَّالِّينَ
(Siraatal ladheena an'amta 'alayhim ghayril maghdoobi 'alayhim wa lad-daalleen)
(The path of those upon whom You have bestowed favor, not of those who have incurred Your anger nor of those who go astray)

3. Recite a Selected Passage from the Qur'ān – Surah Al-Ikhlās:
   a. قُلْ هُوَ اللَّهُ أَحَدٌ
   (Qul huwa Allāhu 'ahad)
   (Say, "He is Allah, [Who is] One")

   b. اللَّهُ الصَّمَدُ
   (Allāhu as-samad)
   (Allah, the Eternal Refuge)

   c. لَمْ يَلِدْ وَلَمْ يُولَدْ
   (Lam yalid wa lam yoolad)
   (He neither begets nor is born)

   d. وَلَمْ يَكُنْ لَهُ كُفُوًا أَحَدٌ
   (Wa lam yakun lahu kufuwan ahad)
   (Nor is there to Him any equivalent)

4. Rukū' (Bowing):
   • As you bow, say "الله أكبر"
   (Allāhu Akbar)
   (Allah is the Greatest)
   • Then recite:
   سُبْحَانَ رَبِّيَ الْعَظِيمِ
   (Subhana rabbiyal 'adheem)
   (Glory be to my Lord, the Most Great)
   [Repeat at least three times]

5. Rising from Rukū':
   • Say:
   سَمِعَ اللَّهُ لِمَنْ حَمِدَه

(Sami' Allāhu liman hamidah)
(Allah hears those who praise Him)
- Then, standing upright, say:
رَبَّنَا وَلَكَ الْحَمْدُ
(Rabbana wa laka al-hamd)
(Our Lord, to You be all praise)

6. Sujūd (First Prostration):
   - As you enter prostration, say "الله أكبر"
   (Allāhu Akbar)
   (Allah is the Greatest)
   - Then recite:
   سُبْحَانَ رَبِّيَ الْأَعْلَى
   (Subhana rabbiyal a'la)
   (Glory be to my Lord, the Most High)
   [Repeat at least three times]

7. Brief Sitting (Jalsa):
   - Sit and supplicate, for example:
   رَبِّ اغْفِرْ لِي
   (Rabbi ighfir li)
   (O my Lord, forgive me)

8. Sujūd (Second Prostration):
   - Say "الله أكبر" as you prostrate again
   (Allāhu Akbar)
   (Allah is the Greatest)
   - Then recite:
   سُبْحَانَ رَبِّيَ الْأَعْلَى
   (Subhana rabbiyal a'la)
   (Glory be to my Lord, the Most High)
   [Repeat at least three times]

9. Rising for the Next Rak'ah:
   - Say "الله أكبر" and stand up
   (Allāhu Akbar)
   (Allah is the Greatest)

Rak'ah 3:

1. Opening Takbīr:
   الله أكبر
   (Allāhu Akbar)
   (Allah is the Greatest)

2. Recite al-Fātiha:
   [Repeat the full al-Fātiha recitation as in Rak'ah 1]

3. Recite a Selected Passage from the Qur'ān – Surah Al-Falaq:
   a. قُلْ أَعُوذُ بِرَبِّ الْفَلَقِ
   (Qul a'udhu bi rabbil falaq)
   (Say, "I seek refuge in the Lord of daybreak")
   b. مِن شَرِّ مَا خَلَقَ
   (Min sharri ma khalaq)
   (From the evil of that which He created)
   c. وَمِن شَرِّ غَاسِقٍ إِذَا وَقَبَ
   (Wa min sharri ghaasiqin idha waqab)
   (And from the evil of darkness when it settles)
   d. وَمِن شَرِّ النَّفَّاثَاتِ فِي الْعُقَدِ
   (Wa min sharri n-naffathaati fil 'uqad)
   (And from the evil of those who practice witchcraft)
   e. وَمِن شَرِّ حَاسِدٍ إِذَا حَسَدَ
   (Wa min sharri haasidin idha hasad)
   (And from the evil of an envier when he envies)

4. Rukū' (Bowing):
   - Say "الله أكبر" as you enter Rukū'
     (Allāhu Akbar)
     (Allah is the Greatest)
   - Then recite:
     سُبْحَانَ رَبِّيَ الْعَظِيمِ
     (Subhana rabbiyal 'adheem)
     (Glory be to my Lord, the Most Great)

[Repeat at least three times]

5. Rising from Rukū':
   - Recite:

   سَمِعَ اللَّهُ لِمَنْ حَمِدَه

   (Sami' Allāhu liman hamidah)
   (Allah hears those who praise Him)

   - Then say:

   رَبَّنَا وَلَكَ الْحَمْدِ

   (Rabbana wa laka al-hamd)
   (Our Lord, to You be all praise)

6. Sujūd (First Prostration):
   - Say "الله أكبر" before prostrating
   (Allāhu Akbar)
   (Allah is the Greatest)
   - Recite:

   سُبْحَانَ رَبِّيَ الْأَعْلَى

   (Subhana rabbiyal a'la)
   (Glory be to my Lord, the Most High)
   [Repeat at least three times]

7. Brief Sitting (Jalsa):
   - Sit briefly and supplicate:

   رَبِّ اغْفِرْ لِي

   (Rabbi ighfir li)
   (O my Lord, forgive me)

8. Sujūd (Second Prostration):
   - Say "الله أكبر" as you move into the second sujūd
   (Allāhu Akbar)
   (Allah is the Greatest)
   - Recite:

   سُبْحَانَ رَبِّيَ الْأَعْلَى

   (Subhana rabbiyal a'la)
   (Glory be to my Lord, the Most High)
   [Repeat at least three times]

9. Rising for the Next Rak'ah:
   - Say "الله أكبر" and stand
   (Allāhu Akbar)
   (Allah is the Greatest)

Rak'ah 4:

---

1. Opening Takbīr:
   الله أكبر
   (Allāhu Akbar)
   (Allah is the Greatest)

2. Recite al-Fātiha:
   [Repeat the full al-Fātiha recitation as before]

3. Recite a Selected Passage from the Qur'ān – Surah An-Nās:
   a. قُلْ أَعُوذُ بِرَبِّ النَّاسِ
   (Qul a'udhu bi rabbin-naas)
   (Say, "I seek refuge in the Lord of mankind")
   b. مَلِكِ النَّاسِ
   (Malikin-naas)
   (The Sovereign of mankind)
   c. إِلَٰهِ النَّاسِ
   (Ilaahin-naas)
   (The God of mankind)
   d. مِنْ شَرِّ الْوَسْوَاسِ الْخَنَّاسِ
   (Min sharri al-waswaas al-khannas)
   (From the evil of the whisperer who withdraws)
   e. الَّذِي يُوَسْوِسُ فِي صُدُورِ النَّاسِ
   (Allathee yuwaswis fee sudoorin-naas)
   (Who whispers in the breasts of mankind)
   f. مِنَ الْجِنَّةِ وَالنَّاسِ
   (Mina al-jinnati wan-naas)
   (Of both jinn and mankind)

4. Rukū' (Bowing):
   - Say "الله أكبر" as you bow
     (Allāhu Akbar)
     (Allah is the Greatest)
   - Then recite:
     سُبْحَانَ رَبِّيَ الْعَظِيم
     (Subhana rabbiyal 'adheem)
     (Glory be to my Lord, the Most Great)
     [Repeat at least three times]

5. Rising from Rukū':
   - Recite:
     سَمِعَ اللَّهُ لِمَنْ حَمِدَه
     (Sami' Allāhu liman hamidah)
     (Allah hears those who praise Him)
   - Then say:
     رَبَّنَا وَلَكَ الْحَمْد
     (Rabbana wa laka al-hamd)
     (Our Lord, to You be all praise)

6. Sujūd (First Prostration):
   - Say "الله أكبر" before prostrating
     (Allāhu Akbar)
     (Allah is the Greatest)
   - Recite:
     سُبْحَانَ رَبِّيَ الأَعْلَى
     (Subhana rabbiyal a'la)
     (Glory be to my Lord, the Most High)
     [Repeat at least three times]

7. Brief Sitting (Jalsa):
   - Sit and supplicate:
     رَبِّ اغْفِرْ لِي
     (Rabbi ighfir li)
     (O my Lord, forgive me)

8. Sujūd (Second Prostration):

- Say "الله أكبر" as you prostrate again
  (Allāhu Akbar)
  (Allah is the Greatest)
- Recite:
  سُبْحَانَ رَبِّيَ الأَعْلَى
  (Subhana rabbiyal a'la)
  (Glory be to my Lord, the Most High)
  [Repeat at least three times]

9. Rising for the Next Rak'ah:
   - Say "الله أكبر" and stand
     (Allāhu Akbar)
     (Allah is the Greatest)

Rak'ah 5:

---

1. Opening Takbīr:
   الله أكبر
   (Allāhu Akbar)
   (Allah is the Greatest)

2. Recite al-Fātiha:
   [Repeat the full al-Fātiha recitation]

3. Recite a Selected Passage from the Qur'ān – (Repeat of Surah Al-Mulk excerpt):
   a. تَبَارَكَ الَّذِي بِيَدِهِ الْمُلْكُ
      (Tabaaraka allathee biyadihil mulku)
      (Blessed is He in whose hand is the dominion)
   b. هُوَ عَلَىٰ كُلِّ شَيْءٍ قَدِيرٌ
      (Wa huwa 'ala kulli shay'in qadeer)
      (And He is over all things competent)

4. Rukū' (Bowing):
   - Say "الله أكبر" and then recite:
     سُبْحَانَ رَبِّيَ الْعَظِيمِ

(Subhana rabbiyal 'adheem)
(Glory be to my Lord, the Most Great)
[Repeat at least three times]

5. Rising from Rukū':
   - Recite:
   سَمِعَ اللَّهُ لِمَنْ حَمِدَه
   (Sami' Allāhu liman hamidah)
   (Allah hears those who praise Him)
   - Then say:
   رَبَّنَا وَلَكَ الْحَمْد
   (Rabbana wa laka al-hamd)
   (Our Lord, to You be all praise)

6. Sujūd (First Prostration):
   - Say "الله أكبر" before prostration
   (Allāhu Akbar)
   (Allah is the Greatest)
   - Recite:
   سُبْحَانَ رَبِّيَ الأَعْلَى
   (Subhana rabbiyal a'la)
   (Glory be to my Lord, the Most High)
   [Repeat at least three times]

7. Brief Sitting (Jalsa):
   - Sit and supplicate:
   رَبِّ اغْفِرْ لِي
   (Rabbi ighfir li)
   (O my Lord, forgive me)

8. Sujūd (Second Prostration):
   - Say "الله أكبر" as you prostrate
   (Allāhu Akbar)
   (Allah is the Greatest)
   - Recite:
   سُبْحَانَ رَبِّيَ الأَعْلَى
   (Subhana rabbiyal a'la)

(Glory be to my Lord, the Most High)
[Repeat at least three times]

9. Rising for the Next Rak'ah:
   • Say "الله أكبر" and stand
   (Allāhu Akbar)
   (Allah is the Greatest)

Rak'ah 6:

---

1. Opening Takbīr:
   الله أكبر
   (Allāhu Akbar)
   (Allah is the Greatest)

2. Recite al-Fātiha:
   [Repeat the full al-Fātiha recitation]

3. Recite a Selected Passage from the Qur'ān – (Repeat of Surah Al-Ikhlās):
   a. قُلْ هُوَ اللَّهُ أَحَدٌ
   (Qul huwa Allāhu 'ahad)
   (Say, "He is Allah, [Who is] One")
   b. اللَّهُ الصَّمَدُ
   (Allāhu as-samad)
   (Allah, the Eternal Refuge)
   c. لَمْ يَلِدْ وَلَمْ يُولَدْ
   (Lam yalid wa lam yoolad)
   (He neither begets nor is born)
   d. وَلَمْ يَكُن لَّهُ كُفُوًا أَحَدٌ
   (Wa lam yakun lahu kufuwan ahad)
   (Nor is there to Him any equivalent)

4. Rukū' (Bowing):
   • Say "الله أكبر" and then recite:
   سُبْحَانَ رَبِّيَ الْعَظِيمِ

(Subhana rabbiyal 'adheem)
(Glory be to my Lord, the Most Great)
[Repeat at least three times]

5. Rising from Rukū':
    - Recite:
    سَمِعَ اللَّهُ لِمَنْ حَمِدَه
    (Sami' Allāhu liman hamidah)
    (Allah hears those who praise Him)
    - Then say:
    رَبَّنَا وَلَكَ الْحَمْدِ
    (Rabbana wa laka al-hamd)
    (Our Lord, to You be all praise)

6. Sujūd (First Prostration):
    - Say "الله أكبر" before prostration
    (Allāhu Akbar)
    (Allah is the Greatest)
    - Recite:
    سُبْحَانَ رَبِّيَ الْأَعْلَى
    (Subhana rabbiyal a'la)
    (Glory be to my Lord, the Most High)
    [Repeat at least three times]

7. Brief Sitting (Jalsa):
    - Sit and supplicate:
    رَبِّ اغْفِرْ لِي
    (Rabbi ighfir li)
    (O my Lord, forgive me)

8. Sujūd (Second Prostration):
    - Say "الله أكبر" as you prostrate
    (Allāhu Akbar)
    (Allah is the Greatest)
    - Recite:
    سُبْحَانَ رَبِّيَ الْأَعْلَى
    (Subhana rabbiyal a'la)

(Glory be to my Lord, the Most High)
[Repeat at least three times]

9. Rising for the Next Rak'ah:
   - Say "الله أكبر" and stand up
   (Allāhu Akbar)
   (Allah is the Greatest)

Rak'ah 7:

---

1. Opening Takbīr:
   الله أكبر
   (Allāhu Akbar)
   (Allah is the Greatest)

2. Recite al-Fātiha:
   [Repeat the full al-Fātiha recitation]

3. Recite a Selected Passage from the Qur'ān – (Repeat of Surah Al-Falaq):
   [Repeat the complete Surah Al-Falaq recitation as in Rak'ah 3]

4. Rukū' (Bowing):
   - Say "الله أكبر" and then recite:
   سُبْحَانَ رَبِّيَ الْعَظِيم
   (Subhana rabbiyal 'adheem)
   (Glory be to my Lord, the Most Great)
   [Repeat at least three times]

5. Rising from Rukū':
   - Recite:
   سَمِعَ اللَّهُ لِمَنْ حَمِدَه
   (Sami' Allāhu liman hamidah)
   (Allah hears those who praise Him)
   - Then say:
   رَبَّنَا وَلَكَ الْحَمْد

(Rabbana wa laka al-hamd)
(Our Lord, to You be all praise)

6. Sujūd (First Prostration):
   - Say "الله أكبر" before prostration
   (Allāhu Akbar)
   (Allah is the Greatest)
   - Recite:
   سُبْحَانَ رَبِّيَ الْأَعْلَى
   (Subhana rabbiyal a'la)
   (Glory be to my Lord, the Most High)
   [Repeat at least three times]

7. Brief Sitting (Jalsa):
   - Sit and supplicate:
   رَبِّ اغْفِرْ لِي
   (Rabbi ighfir li)
   (O my Lord, forgive me)

8. Sujūd (Second Prostration):
   - Say "الله أكبر" as you prostrate
   (Allāhu Akbar)
   (Allah is the Greatest)
   - Recite:
   سُبْحَانَ رَبِّيَ الْأَعْلَى
   (Subhana rabbiyal a'la)
   (Glory be to my Lord, the Most High)
   [Repeat at least three times]

9. Rising for the Next Rak'ah:
   - Say "الله أكبر" and stand up
   (Allāhu Akbar)
   (Allah is the Greatest)

Rak'ah 8 (Final Rak'ah):
---

1. Opening Takbīr:
   الله أكبر
   (Allāhu Akbar)
   (Allah is the Greatest)

2. Recite al-Fātiha:
   [Repeat the full al-Fātiha recitation]

3. Recite a Selected Passage from the Qur'ān – (Repeat of Surah An-Nās):
   [Repeat the complete Surah An-Nās recitation as in Rak'ah 4]

4. Rukū' (Bowing):
   - Say "الله أكبر" and bow:
   (Allāhu Akbar)
   (Allah is the Greatest)
   - Then recite:
   سِبْحَانَ رَبِّيَ الْعَظِيم
   (Subhana rabbiyal 'adheem)
   (Glory be to my Lord, the Most Great)
   [Repeat at least three times]

5. Rising from Rukū':
   - Recite:
   سَمِعَ اللَّهُ لِمَنْ حَمِدَه
   (Sami' Allāhu liman hamidah)
   (Allah hears those who praise Him)
   - Then say:
   رَبَّنَا وَلَكَ الْحَمْدر
   (Rabbana wa laka al-hamd)
   (Our Lord, to You be all praise)

6. Sujūd (First Prostration):
   - Say "الله أكبر" before prostration
   (Allāhu Akbar)
   (Allah is the Greatest)

- Recite:

  سُبْحَانَ رَبِّيَ الأَعْلَى

  (Subhana rabbiyal a'la)
  (Glory be to my Lord, the Most High)
    [Repeat at least three times]

7. Brief Sitting (Jalsa):
   - Sit and make your supplication:

     رَبِّ اغْفِرْ لِي

     (Rabbi ighfir li)
     (O my Lord, forgive me)

8. Sujūd (Second Prostration):
   - Say "الله أكبر" as you prostrate for the final time
     (Allāhu Akbar)
     (Allah is the Greatest)
   - Recite:

     سُبْحَانَ رَبِّيَ الأَعْلَى

     (Subhana rabbiyal a'la)
     (Glory be to my Lord, the Most High)
       [Repeat at least three times]

Final Tashahhud and Taslīm:

After completing the eighth rak'ah, remain seated and recite the Tashahhud:

التَّحِيَّاتُ لِلَّهِ وَالصَّلَوَاتُ وَالطَّيِّبَاتُ

(At-tahiyyatu lillahi was-salawatu wat-tayyibatu)
(All greetings, prayers, and pure words are for Allah)

السَّلَامُ عَلَيْكَ أَيُّهَا النَّبِيُّ

(As-salamu 'alayka ayyuha an-nabiyyu)
(Peace be upon you, O Prophet)

وَرَحْمَةُ اللَّهِ وَبَرَكَاتُهُ

(Wa rahmatullahi wa barakatuhu)

(And the mercy and blessings of Allah)

اَلسَّلَامُ عَلَيْنَا وَعَلَىٰ عِب

CHAPTER 14: DUHA PRAYER

STEP-BY-STEP Duha Prayer

Below is an in-depth guide to the Duha (forenoon) prayer— a sacred act to express gratitude for a new day and to seek additional blessings, energizing the believer for the day ahead. The Duha prayer is observed after sunrise and before the midday Dhuhr prayer. Before you perform the prayer, ensure you are in a state of ritual purity (wudu) and have prepared your heart for sincere worship.

Before You Begin:
• Form your niyyah in your heart: "I intend to perform two rak'ahs of the Duha prayer for the sake of Allah."

Rak'ah 1:

1. Opening Takbīr (Start of the Prayer):
   الله أكبر
   (Allāhu Akbar)
   (Allah is the Greatest)

2. Recite al-Fātiha (The Opening Chapter):

   a. بِسْمِ اللَّهِ الرَّحْمَٰنِ الرَّحِيمِ
   (Bismillaahir Rahmaanir Raheem)

(In the name of Allah, the Most Gracious, the Most Merciful)

b. اَلْحَمْدُ لِلَّهِ رَبِّ الْعَالَمِين

(Alhamdu lillahi rabbil 'aalameen)

(All praise is due to Allah, Lord of all the worlds)

c. اِلرَّحْمَنِ الرَّحِيم

(Ar-Rahmaanir Raheem)

(The Most Gracious, the Most Merciful)

d. مَالِكِ يَوْمِ الدِّين

(Maaliki yawmid-deen)

(Master of the Day of Judgment)

e. إِيَّاكَ نَعْبُدُ وَإِيَّاكَ نَسْتَعِين

(Iyyaka na'budu wa iyyaka nasta'een)

(You alone we worship, and You alone we ask for help)

f. اَهْدِنَا الصِّرَاطَ الْمُسْتَقِيم

(Ihdinas-siraatal mustaqeem)

(Guide us to the straight path)

g. صِرَاطَ الَّذِينَ أَنْعَمْتَ عَلَيْهِمْ غَيْرِ الْمَغْضُوبِ عَلَيْهِمْ وَلَا الضَّالِّين

(Siraatal ladheena an'amta 'alayhim ghayril maghdoobi 'alayhim wa lad-daalleen)

(The path of those upon whom You have bestowed favor, not of those who have earned Your anger nor of those who go astray)

3. Recite a Short Sūrah – Surah ad-Duḥā:

a. وَالضُّحَى

(Wa ad-Duḥā)

(By the forenoon)

b. وَاللَّيْلِ إِذَا سَجَى

(Wa al-layli idha saja)

(And by the night when it covers)

c. مَا وَدَّعَكَ رَبُّكَ وَمَا قَلَى

(Ma waddaa ka rabbuka wa ma qala)

(Your Lord has not forsaken you, nor has He expressed dislike)

d. وَلَلْآخِرَةُ خَيْرٌ لَكَ مِنَ الْأُولَىٰ
(Wa la lil-akhirati khayrun laka minal-oola)
(And the Hereafter is better for you than the first)

e. وَلَسَوْفَ يُعْطِيكَ رَبُّكَ فَتَرْضَىٰ
(Wa la sawfa yu'teeka rabbuka fatarda)
(And your Lord will grant you so that you are satisfied)

f. أَلَمْ يَجِدْكَ يَتِيمًا فَآوَىٰ
(Alam yajidka yateeman fa awa)
(Did He not find you an orphan and give you shelter?)

g. وَوَجَدَكَ ضَالًّا فَهَدَىٰ
(Wa wajadaka daallan fahada)
(And did He not find you astray and guide you?)

h. وَوَجَدَكَ عَائِلًا فَآوَىٰ
(Wa wajadaka 'aa'ilan fa awa)
(And did He not find you in need and provide for you?)

i. وَأَحْسَنَكَ فَأَحْسَن
(Wa ahsanaka fa ahsana)
(And He has improved your condition, so He will continue to do so)

4. Rukū' (Bowing):

• As you move into the bowing position, say "Allāhu Akbar."
• Then recite:
سُبْحَانَ رَبِّيَ الْعَظِيم
(Subhana rabbiyal 'adheem)
(Glory be to my Lord, the Most Great)
 [Repeat at least three times]

5. Rising from Rukū':

• Rise while saying:

سَمِعَ اللَّهُ لِمَنْ حَمِدَه

(Sami' Allāhu liman hamidah)

(Allah hears those who praise Him)

- Then, while standing, say:

رَبَّنَا وَلَكَ الْحَمْد

(Rabbana wa laka al-hamd)

(Our Lord, to You be all praise)

6. Sujūd (First Prostration):

- As you enter prostration, say "Allāhu Akbar."
- Then recite in Sujūd:

سُبْحَانَ رَبِّيَ الْأَعْلَى

(Subhana rabbiyal a'la)

(Glory be to my Lord, the Most High)

   [Repeat at least three times]

7. Brief Sitting (Jalsa):

- Sit briefly between the two prostrations.
- You may supplicate; for example, recite:

رَبِّ اغْفِرْ لِي

(Rabbi ighfir li)

(O my Lord, forgive me)

8. Sujūd (Second Prostration):

- Say "Allāhu Akbar" as you move into the second prostration.
- Then recite:

سُبْحَانَ رَبِّيَ الْأَعْلَى

(Subhana rabbiyal a'la)

(Glory be to my Lord, the Most High)

   [Repeat at least three times]

9. Rising for the Next Rak'ah:
   - Say "Allāhu Akbar" and stand up to begin Rak'ah 2.

Rak'ah 2:

1. Opening Takbīr:

    الله أكبر

    (Allāhu Akbar)

    (Allah is the Greatest)

2. Recite al-Fātiha:

a. بِسْمِ اللّٰهِ الرَّحْمٰنِ الرَّحِيمِ

(Bismillaahir Rahmaanir Raheem)

(In the name of Allah, the Most Gracious, the Most Merciful)

b. اَلْحَمْدُ لِلّٰهِ رَبِّ الْعَالَمِينَ

(Alhamdu lillahi rabbil 'aalameen)

(All praise is due to Allah, Lord of all the worlds)

c. الرَّحْمٰنِ الرَّحِيمِ

(Ar-Rahmaanir Raheem)

(The Most Gracious, the Most Merciful)

d. مَالِكِ يَوْمِ الدِّينِ

(Maaliki yawmid-deen)

(Master of the Day of Judgment)

e. إِيَّاكَ نَعْبُدُ وَإِيَّاكَ نَسْتَعِينُ

(Iyyaka na'budu wa iyyaka nasta'een)

(You alone we worship, and You alone we ask for help)

f. اهْدِنَا الصِّرَاطَ الْمُسْتَقِيمَ

(Ihdinas-siraatal mustaqeem)

(Guide us to the straight path)

g. صِرَاطَ الَّذِينَ أَنْعَمْتَ عَلَيْهِمْ غَيْرِ الْمَغْضُوبِ عَلَيْهِمْ وَلَا الضَّالِّينَ

(Siraatal ladheena an'amta 'alayhim ghayril maghdoobi 'alayhim wa lad-daalleen)

(The path of those upon whom You have bestowed favor, not of those who have earned Your anger nor of those who go astray)

3. Recite a Short Sūrah – Surah al-Ikhlās:

a. قُلْ هُوَ اللَّهُ أَحَدٌ
   (Qul huwa Allāhu 'ahad)
   (Say, "He is Allah, [Who is] One")

b. اللَّهُ الصَّمَدُ
   (Allāhu as-samad)
   (Allah, the Eternal Refuge)

c. لَمْ يَلِدْ وَلَمْ يُولَدْ
   (Lam yalid wa lam yoolad)
   (He neither begets nor is born)

d. وَلَمْ يَكُنْ لَهُ كُفُوًا أَحَدٌ
   (Wa lam yakun lahu kufuwan ahad)
   (Nor is there to Him any equivalent)

4. Rukū' (Bowing):

- As you bow, say "Allāhu Akbar."
- Then recite:
  سُبْحَانَ رَبِّيَ الْعَظِيم
  (Subhana rabbiyal 'adheem)
  (Glory be to my Lord, the Most Great)
      [Repeat at least three times]

5. Rising from Rukū':

- While rising, say:
  سَمِعَ اللَّهُ لِمَنْ حَمِدَه
  (Sami' Allāhu liman hamidah)
  (Allah hears those who praise Him)
- Then, while standing, say:
  رَبَّنَا وَلَكَ الْحَمْد
  (Rabbana wa laka al-hamd)
  (Our Lord, to You be all praise)

6. Sujūd (First Prostration):

- As you enter prostration, say "Allāhu Akbar."

- Then recite in Sujūd:

  سُبْحَانَ رَبِّيَ الْأَعْلَى

  (Subhana rabbiyal a'la)
  (Glory be to my Lord, the Most High)
  [Repeat at least three times]

7. **Brief Sitting (Jalsa):**

- Sit briefly and supplicate; for example, recite:

  رَبِّ اغْفِرْ لِي

  (Rabbi ighfir li)
  (O my Lord, forgive me)

8. **Sujūd (Second Prostration):**

- Say "Allāhu Akbar" as you perform the second prostration.
- Then recite:

  سُبْحَانَ رَبِّيَ الْأَعْلَى

  (Subhana rabbiyal a'la)
  (Glory be to my Lord, the Most High)
  [Repeat at least three times]

9. **Final Tashahhud (Sitting for the Testimony):**

- After the second sujūd, sit and recite the Tashahhud:

  التَّحِيَّاتُ لِلَّهِ وَالصَّلَوَاتُ وَالطَّيِّبَاتُ

  (At-tahiyyatu lillahi was-salawatu wat-tayyibatu)
  (All greetings, prayers, and pure words are for Allah)

  السَّلَامُ عَلَيْكَ أَيُّهَا النَّبِيُّ

  (As-salamu 'alayka ayyuha an-nabiyyu)
  (Peace be upon you, O Prophet)

  وَرَحْمَةُ اللَّهِ وَبَرَكَاتُهُ

  (Wa rahmatullahi wa barakatuhu)
  (And the mercy and blessings of Allah)

  السَّلَامُ عَلَيْنَا وَعَلَى عِبَادِ اللَّهِ الصَّالِحِينَ

  (As-salamu 'alayna wa 'ala 'ibaadil-lahi as-saaliheen)
  (Peace be upon us and upon the righteous servants of Allah)

أَشْهَدُ أَنْ لَا إِلَهَ إِلَّا اللَّه

(Ash-hadu an la ilaha illallahu)
(I bear witness that there is no deity except Allah)

وَأَشْهَدُ أَنَّ مُحَمَّدًا رَسُولُ اللَّه

(Wa ash-hadu anna Muhammadan Rasool Allah)
(And I bear witness that Muhammad is the Messenger of Allah)

10. Taslīm (Concluding the Prayer):

• To conclude the prayer, first turn your head to the right and say:

اَلسَّلَامُ عَلَيْكُمْ وَرَحْمَةُ اللَّه

(As-salamu 'alaykum wa rahmatullahi)
(Peace and mercy of Allah be upon you)

• Then turn your head to the left and repeat:

اَلسَّلَامُ عَلَيْكُمْ وَرَحْمَةُ اللَّه

(As-salamu 'alaykum wa rahmatullahi)
(Peace and mercy of Allah be upon you)

Notes:
• At each transition (standing, bowing, prostrating, and sitting), it is customary to say "Allāhu Akbar."
• The recommended repetitions (for example, repeating the Rukū' and Sujūd recitations three times) follow the Sunnah of the Prophet.
• You may add additional supplications (du'ā) during your sitting (Jalsa) as desired.

CHAPTER 15: ISHRAQ PRAYER

STEP-BY-STEP Ishraq Prayer

Below is an in-depth guide to the Ishraq prayer—a gentle, post-sunrise prayer performed approximately fifteen to twenty minutes after the sun has risen. This prayer is celebrated for its invocation of divine mercy, its power to purify the spirit, and its ability to energize the body. Before you begin, ensure you are in a state of ritual purity (wudu) and have prepared your heart for sincere worship.

Before You Begin:
• Form your niyyah in your heart: "I intend to perform two rak'ahs of the Ishraq prayer for the sake of Allah."

Rak'ah 1:
---

1. Opening Takbīr (Start of the Prayer):
   اللَّهُ أَكْبَر
   (Allāhu Akbar)
   (Allah is the Greatest)

2. Recite al-Fātiha (The Opening Chapter):

a. بِسْمِ اللَّهِ الرَّحْمَٰنِ الرَّحِيمِ
(Bismillaahir Rahmaanir Raheem)
(In the name of Allah, the Most Gracious, the Most Merciful)

b. اَلْحَمْدُ لِلَّهِ رَبِّ الْعَالَمِينَ
(Alhamdu lillahi rabbil 'aalameen)
(All praise is due to Allah, Lord of all the worlds)

c. الرَّحْمَٰنِ الرَّحِيمِ
(Ar-Rahmaanir Raheem)
(The Most Gracious, the Most Merciful)

d. مَالِكِ يَوْمِ الدِّينِ
(Maaliki yawmid-deen)
(Master of the Day of Judgment)

e. إِيَّاكَ نَعْبُدُ وَإِيَّاكَ نَسْتَعِينُ
(Iyyaka na'budu wa iyyaka nasta'een)
(You alone we worship, and You alone we ask for help)

f. اهْدِنَا الصِّرَاطَ الْمُسْتَقِيمَ
(Ihdinas-siraatal mustaqeem)
(Guide us to the straight path)

g. صِرَاطَ الَّذِينَ أَنْعَمْتَ عَلَيْهِمْ غَيْرِ الْمَغْضُوبِ عَلَيْهِمْ وَلَا الضَّالِّينَ
(Siraatal ladheena an'amta 'alayhim ghayril maghdoobi 'alayhim wa lad-daalleen)
(The path of those upon whom You have bestowed favor, not of those who have earned Your anger nor of those who go astray)

3. Recite a Short Sūrah – Surah Al-Inshirah:

a. أَلَمْ نَشْرَحْ لَكَ صَدْرَكَ
(Alam nashrah laka sadrak)
(Did We not expand for you your breast?)

b. وَوَضَعْنَا عَنْكَ وِزْرَكَ
(Wa wada'na 'anka wizrak)

(And removed from you your burden?)

c. اَلَّذِي أنقَضَ ظَهْرَكَ
(Alladhī anqada zahrak)
(And loosened for you your back?)

d. وَرَفَعْنَا لَكَ ذِكْرَكَ
(Wa rafa'na laka dhikrak)
(And exalted for you your renown?)

e. فَإِنَّ مَعَ الْعُسْرِ يُسْرًا
(Fa inna ma'al 'usri yusra)
(Indeed, with hardship comes ease.)

f. إِنَّ مَعَ الْعُسْرِ يُسْرًا
(Inna ma'al 'usri yusra)
(Indeed, with hardship comes ease.)

g. فَإِذَا فَرَغْتَ فَانصَبْ
(Fa idha faraghta fansab)
(So when you have finished, then stand up [to worship].)

h. وَإِلَى رَبِّكَ فَارْغَب
(Wa ila rabbika farghab)
(And to your Lord, direct [your] desire.)

4. Rukū' (Bowing):
   • As you move into the bowing position, say "Allāhu Akbar."
   • Then recite:
   سُبْحَانَ رَبِّيَ الْعَظِيمِ
   (Subhana rabbiyal 'adheem)
   (Glory be to my Lord, the Most Great)
   [Repeat at least three times]

5. Rising from Rukū':
   • While rising, say:
   سَمِعَ اللَّهُ لِمَنْ حَمِدَه
   (Sami' Allāhu liman hamidah)

(Allah hears those who praise Him)
- Then, while standing straight, say:

رَبَّنَا وَلَكَ الْحَمْدُ

(Rabbana wa laka al-hamd)
(Our Lord, to You be all praise)

6. Sujūd (First Prostration):
   - As you go down into prostration, say "Allāhu Akbar."
   - Then recite:

   سُبْحَانَ رَبِّيَ الْأَعْلَى

   (Subhana rabbiyal a'la)
   (Glory be to my Lord, the Most High)
   [Repeat at least three times]

7. Brief Sitting (Jalsa):
   - Sit briefly between the two prostrations. You may supplicate; for example, recite:

   رَبِّ اغْفِرْ لِي

   (Rabbi ighfir li)
   (O my Lord, forgive me)

8. Sujūd (Second Prostration):
   - Say "Allāhu Akbar" as you move for the second prostration.
   - Then recite:

   سُبْحَانَ رَبِّيَ الْأَعْلَى

   (Subhana rabbiyal a'la)
   (Glory be to my Lord, the Most High)
   [Repeat at least three times]

9. Rising for the Next Rak'ah:
   - Say "Allāhu Akbar" and then stand up to begin Rak'ah 2.

Rak'ah 2:

---

1. Opening Takbīr:

اللَّهُ أَكْبَر

(Allāhu Akbar)

(Allah is the Greatest)

2. Recite al-Fātiha:

a. بِسْمِ اللَّهِ الرَّحْمَنِ الرَّحِيمِ

(Bismillaahir Rahmaanir Raheem)

(In the name of Allah, the Most Gracious, the Most Merciful)

b. اَلْحَمْدُ لِلَّهِ رَبِّ الْعَالَمِين

(Alhamdu lillahi rabbil 'aalameen)

(All praise is due to Allah, Lord of all the worlds)

c. اِلرَّحْمَنِ الرَّحِيم

(Ar-Rahmaanir Raheem)

(The Most Gracious, the Most Merciful)

d. مَالِكِ يَوْمِ الدِّين

(Maaliki yawmid-deen)

(Master of the Day of Judgment)

e. إِيَّاكَ نَعْبُدُ وَإِيَّاكَ نَسْتَعِين

(Iyyaka na'budu wa iyyaka nasta'een)

(You alone we worship, and You alone we ask for help)

f. اَهْدِنَا الصِّرَاطَ الْمُسْتَقِيم

(Ihdinas-siraatal mustaqeem)

(Guide us to the straight path)

g. صِرَاطَ الَّذِينَ أَنْعَمْتَ عَلَيْهِمْ غَيْرِ الْمَغْضُوبِ عَلَيْهِمْ وَلَا الضَّالِّين

(Siraatal ladheena an'amta 'alayhim ghayril maghdoobi 'alayhim wa lad-daalleen)

(The path of those upon whom You have bestowed favor, not of those who have earned Your anger nor of those who go astray)

3. Recite a Short Sūrah – Surah Al-Falaq:

a. قُلْ أَعُوذُ بِرَبِّ الْفَلَق

(Qul a'oodhu bi-rabbi al-falaq)

(Say, "I seek refuge in the Lord of daybreak")

b. مِن شَرِّ مَا خَلَقَ
(Min sharri ma khalaq)
(From the evil of that which He created)

c. وَمِن شَرِّ غَاسِقٍ إِذَا وَقَبَ
(Wa min sharri ghaasiqin iza waqab)
(And from the evil of the darkening night)

d. وَمِن شَرِّ النَّفَّاثَاتِ فِي الْعُقَدِ
(Wa min sharri nnaffathaati fil 'uqad)
(And from the evil of those who practice witchcraft)

e. وَمِن شَرِّ حَاسِدٍ إِذَا حَسَدَ
(Wa min sharri haasidin iza hasad)
(And from the evil of an envier when he envies)

4. Rukū' (Bowing):
   - As you bow, say "Allāhu Akbar."
   - Then recite:
     سُبْحَانَ رَبِّيَ الْعَظِيم
     (Subhana rabbiyal 'adheem)
     (Glory be to my Lord, the Most Great)
     [Repeat at least three times]

5. Rising from Rukū':
   - While rising, say:
     سَمِعَ اللَّهُ لِمَنْ حَمِدَه
     (Sami' Allāhu liman hamidah)
     (Allah hears those who praise Him)
   - Then, while standing, say:
     رَبَّنَا وَلَكَ الْحَمْدُ
     (Rabbana wa laka al-hamd)
     (Our Lord, to You be all praise)

6. Sujūd (First Prostration):
   - As you go down into prostration, say "Allāhu Akbar."
   - Then recite:

سُبْحَانَ رَبِّيَ الْأَعْلَى
(Subhana rabbiyal a'la)
(Glory be to my Lord, the Most High)
[Repeat at least three times]

7. Brief Sitting (Jalsa):
   • Sit briefly and, if you wish, supplicate; for example, recite:
   رَبِّ اغْفِرْ لِي
   (Rabbi ighfir li)
   (O my Lord, forgive me)

8. Sujūd (Second Prostration):
   • As you move for the second prostration, say "Allāhu Akbar."
   • Then recite:
   سُبْحَانَ رَبِّيَ الْأَعْلَى
   (Subhana rabbiyal a'la)
   (Glory be to my Lord, the Most High)
   [Repeat at least three times]

9. Final Tashahhud (Sitting for the Testimony):

After the second sujūd, sit and recite:

اَلتَّحِيَّاتُ لِلَّهِ وَالصَّلَوَاتُ وَالطَّيِّبَاتُ
(At-tahiyyatu lillahi was-salawatu wat-tayyibatu)
(All greetings, prayers, and pure words are for Allah)

اَلسَّلَامُ عَلَيْكَ أَيُّهَا النَّبِيُّ
(As-salamu 'alayka ayyuha an-nabiyyu)
(Peace be upon you, O Prophet)

وَرَحْمَةُ اللَّهِ وَبَرَكَاتُهُ
(Wa rahmatullahi wa barakatuhu)
(And the mercy and blessings of Allah)

اَلسَّلَامُ عَلَيْنَا وَعَلَى عِبَادِ اللَّهِ الصَّالِحِينَ
(As-salamu 'alayna wa 'ala 'ibaadil-lahi as-saaliheen)

(Peace be upon us and upon the righteous servants of Allah)

أَشْهَدُ أَنْ لَا إِلَهَ إِلَّا اللَّه

(Ash-hadu an la ilaha illallahu)

(I bear witness that there is no deity except Allah)

وَأَشْهَدُ أَنَّ مُحَمَّدًا رَسُولُ اللَّه

(Wa ash-hadu anna Muhammadan Rasool Allah)

(And I bear witness that Muhammad is the Messenger of Allah)

10. Taslīm (Concluding the Prayer):

• To conclude the prayer, first turn your head to the right and say:

السَّلَامُ عَلَيْكُمْ وَرَحْمَةُ اللَّه

(As-salamu 'alaykum wa rahmatullah)

(Peace and mercy of Allah be upon you)

• Then turn your head to the left and repeat:

السَّلَامُ عَلَيْكُمْ وَرَحْمَةُ اللَّه

(As-salamu 'alaykum wa rahmatullah)

(Peace and mercy of Allah be upon you)

Notes:
• At each transition—standing, bowing, prostrating, and sitting—it is customary to say "Allāhu Akbar."
• The recommended repetitions (for example, repeating the Rukū' and Sujūd recitations three times) reflect the Sunnah of the Prophet.
• You may add personal supplications (du'ā) during your sitting (Jalsa) as desired.

CHAPTER 16: SALATUL ISTIKHARA

STEP-BY-STEP Salatul Istikhara

Below is an in-depth guide to performing Salatul Istikhara—the prayer for seeking divine guidance when decisions need to be made. In times of uncertainty, this prayer helps to invite clarity and the wisdom of Allah into your life. Follow the steps below with a sincere heart and focused intention.

Before You Begin:
• Ensure you are in a state of ritual purity (wudu).
• Form your niyyah in your heart: "I intend to perform Salatul Istikhara for Allah's guidance regarding my decision."

Rak'ah 1:

1. Opening Takbīr (Start of the Prayer):
   الله أكبر
   (Allāhu Akbar)
   (Allah is the Greatest)

2. Recite al-Fātiha (The Opening Chapter):

a. بِسْمِ اللهِ الرَّحْمٰنِ الرَّحِيْمِ
(Bismillaahir Rahmaanir Raheem)
(In the name of Allah, the Most Gracious, the Most Merciful)

b. اَلْحَمْدُ لِلّٰهِ رَبِّ الْعَالَمِيْنَ
(Alhamdu lillahi rabbil 'aalameen)
(All praise is due to Allah, Lord of all the worlds)

c. اِلرَّحْمٰنِ الرَّحِيْمِ
(Ar-Rahmaanir Raheem)
(The Most Gracious, the Most Merciful)

d. مَالِكِ يَوْمِ الدِّيْنِ
(Maaliki yawmid-deen)
(Master of the Day of Judgment)

e. اِيَّاكَ نَعْبُدُ وَإِيَّاكَ نَسْتَعِيْنُ
(Iyyaka na'budu wa iyyaka nasta'een)
(You alone we worship, and You alone we ask for help)

f. اهْدِنَا الصِّرَاطَ الْمُسْتَقِيْمَ
(Ihdinas-siraatal mustaqeem)
(Guide us to the straight path)

g. [Optional: You may complete with the remaining verse if preferred.]

3. Recite a Short Sūrah – Sūrah al-Kāfirūn:

a. قُلْ يَا أَيُّهَا الْكَافِرُوْنَ
(Qul ya ayyuhal kaafirun)
(Say, "O disbelievers,")

b. لَا أَعْبُدُ مَا تَعْبُدُوْنَ
(Laa a'budu maa ta'budoon)
(I do not worship what you worship)

c. وَلَا أَنْتُمْ عَابِدُوْنَ مَا أَعْبُدُ
(Wa laa antum 'aabidoon maa a'bud)
(Nor are you worshippers of what I worship)

d. وَلَا أَنَا عَابِدٌ مَا عَبَدتُّم۟
(Wa laa ana 'aabidun maa 'abadtum)
(And I will not be a worshipper of what you have worshipped)

e. وَلَا أَنتُمْ عَابِدُونَ مَا أَعْبُد
(Wa laa antum 'aabidoon maa a'bud)
(Nor will you be worshippers of what I worship)

f. لَكُمْ دِينُكُمْ وَلِيَ دِين
(Lakum deenkum wa liya deen)
(For you is your religion, and for me is mine)

4. Rukū' (Bowing):
   • As you move into the bowing position, say "Allāhu Akbar."
   • Then recite:
   سُبْحَانَ رَبِّيَ الْعَظِيم
   (Subhana rabbiyal 'adheem)
   (Glory be to my Lord, the Most Great)
   [Repeat at least three times]

5. Rising from Rukū':
   • While rising, say:
   سَمِعَ اللَّهُ لِمَنْ حَمِدَه
   (Sami' Allāhu liman hamidah)
   (Allah hears those who praise Him)
   • Then, while standing straight, say:
   رَبَّنَا وَلَكَ الْحَمْد
   (Rabbana wa laka al-hamd)
   (Our Lord, to You be all praise)

6. Sujūd (First Prostration):
   • Say "Allāhu Akbar" as you go into prostration.
   • Then recite:
   سُبْحَانَ رَبِّيَ الْأَعْلَى
   (Subhana rabbiyal a'la)

(Glory be to my Lord, the Most High)
[Repeat at least three times]

7. Brief Sitting (Jalsa):
   - Sit briefly and supplicate; for example, recite:
   رَبِّ اغْفِرْ لِي
   (Rabbi ighfir li)
   (O my Lord, forgive me)

8. Sujūd (Second Prostration):
   - Say "Allāhu Akbar" as you prostrate again.
   - Then recite:
   سُبْحَانَ رَبِّيَ الْأَعْلَى
   (Subhana rabbiyal a'la)
   (Glory be to my Lord, the Most High)
   [Repeat at least three times]

9. Rising for the Next Rak'ah:
   - Say "Allāhu Akbar" as you stand up to continue with Rak'ah 2.

Rak'ah 2:

---

1. Opening Takbīr:
   الله أكبر
   (Allāhu Akbar)
   (Allah is the Greatest)

2. Recite al-Fātiha:

a. بِسْمِ اللَّهِ الرَّحْمَنِ الرَّحِيمِ
(Bismillaahir Rahmaanir Raheem)
(In the name of Allah, the Most Gracious, the Most Merciful)

b. اَلْحَمْدُ لِلَّهِ رَبِّ الْعَالَمِينَ
(Alhamdu lillahi rabbil 'aalameen)
(All praise is due to Allah, Lord of all the worlds)

c. الرَّحْمَنِ الرَّحِيمِ
(Ar-Rahmaanir Raheem)
(The Most Gracious, the Most Merciful)

d. مَالِكِ يَوْمِ الدِّينِ
(Maaliki yawmid-deen)
(Master of the Day of Judgment)

e. إِيَّاكَ نَعْبُدُ وَإِيَّاكَ نَسْتَعِينُ
(Iyyaka na'budu wa iyyaka nasta'een)
(You alone we worship, and You alone we ask for help)

f. اهْدِنَا الصِّرَاطَ الْمُسْتَقِيمَ
(Ihdinas-siraatal mustaqeem)
(Guide us to the straight path)

3. Recite a Short Sūrah – Sūrah al-Ikhlās:

a. قُلْ هُوَ اللَّهُ أَحَدٌ
(Qul huwa Allāhu 'ahad)
(Say, "He is Allah, [Who is] One")

b. اللَّهُ الصَّمَدُ
(Allāhu as-samad)
(Allah, the Eternal Refuge)

c. لَمْ يَلِدْ وَلَمْ يُولَدْ
(Lam yalid wa lam yoolad)
(He neither begets nor is born)

d. وَلَمْ يَكُنْ لَهُ كُفُوًا أَحَدٌ
(Wa lam yakun lahu kufuwan ahad)
(Nor is there any equivalent to Him)

4. Rukū' (Bowing):
    - Say "Allāhu Akbar" as you bow.
    - Then recite:
    سُبْحَانَ رَبِّيَ الْعَظِيمِ
    (Subhana rabbiyal 'adheem)

(Glory be to my Lord, the Most Great)
[Repeat at least three times]

5. Rising from Rukū':
   - While rising, say:
   سَمِعَ اللَّهُ لِمَنْ حَمِدَه
   (Sami' Allāhu liman hamidah)
   (Allah hears those who praise Him)
   - Then stand straight and say:
   رَبَّنَا وَلَكَ الْحَمْدُ
   (Rabbana wa laka al-hamd)
   (Our Lord, to You be all praise)

6. Sujūd (First Prostration):
   - Say "Allāhu Akbar" and prostrate.
   - Then recite:
   سُبْحَانَ رَبِّيَ الْأَعْلَى
   (Subhana rabbiyal a'la)
   (Glory be to my Lord, the Most High)
   [Repeat at least three times]

7. Brief Sitting (Jalsa):
   - Sit briefly and supplicate:
   رَبِّ اغْفِرْ لِي
   (Rabbi ighfir li)
   (O my Lord, forgive me)

8. Sujūd (Second Prostration):
   - Say "Allāhu Akbar" and prostrate.
   - Then recite:
   سُبْحَانَ رَبِّيَ الْأَعْلَى
   (Subhana rabbiyal a'la)
   (Glory be to my Lord, the Most High)
   [Repeat at least three times]

9. Final Tashahhud (Sitting for the Testimony):
   - After the second prostration, sit and recite:
   التَّحِيَّاتُ لِلَّهِ وَالصَّلَوَاتُ وَالطَّيِّبَاتُ

ٱلسَّلَامُ عَلَيْكَ أَيُّهَا النَّبِيُّ
(As-salamu 'alayka ayyuha an-nabiyyu)
(Peace be upon you, O Prophet)

وَرَحْمَةُ اللَّهِ وَبَرَكَاتُهُ
(Wa rahmatullahi wa barakatuhu)
(And the mercy and blessings of Allah)

أَشْهَدُ أَنْ لَا إِلَهَ إِلَّا اللَّهُ
(Ash-hadu an la ilaha illallahu)
(I bear witness that there is no deity except Allah)

وَأَشْهَدُ أَنَّ مُحَمَّدًا رَسُولُ اللَّهِ
(Wa ash-hadu anna Muhammadan Rasool Allah)
(And I bear witness that Muhammad is the Messenger of Allah)

Istikhara Supplication:

Before concluding the prayer, remain seated and recite the following supplication with a sincere heart:

1. اللَّهُمَّ إِنِّي أَسْتَخِيرُكَ بِعِلْمِكَ
   (Allahumma inni astakhiruka bi'ilmika)
   (O Allah, I seek guidance through Your knowledge)

2. وَأَسْتَقْدِرُكَ بِقُدْرَتِكَ
   (wa astaqdiruka biqudratika)
   (And I seek ability through Your power)

3. وَأَسْأَلُكَ مِنْ فَضْلِكَ الْعَظِيمِ
   (wa as'aluka min fadlika al-'azheem)
   (And I ask You from Your tremendous bounty)

4. فَإِنَّكَ تَقْدِرُ وَلَا أَقْدِرُ

(fa innaka taqdiru wa la aqdiru)
(For indeed You have power while I have none)

5. وَتَعْلَمُ وَلَا أَعْلَمُ
   (wa ta'lamu wa la a'lamu)
   (And You know, while I do not know)

6. وَأَنْتَ عَلَّامُ الْغُيُوبِ
   (wa anta 'allamul ghuyub)
   (And You are the Knower of the unseen)

7. اللَّهُمَّ إِنْ كُنْتَ تَعْلَمُ أَنَّ هَذَا الْأَمْرَ
   (Allahumma in kunta ta'lamu anna hadha al-amra)
   (O Allah, if You know that this matter)

8. خَيْرٌ لِي فِي دِينِي وَمَعَاشِي وَعَاقِبَةِ أَمْرِي
   (khayrun li fi deeni wa ma'ashi wa 'aqibati amri)
   (is good for me in my religion, my livelihood, and the outcome of my affairs)

9. فَاقْدُرْهُ لِي وَيَسِّرْهُ لِي وَبَارِكْ لِي فِيهِ
   (faqdurhu li wa yassirhu li wa barik li fihi)
   (Then decree it for me, make it easy for me, and bless it for me)

10. وَإِنْ كُنْتَ تَعْلَمُ أَنَّ هَذَا الْأَمْرَ
    (wa in kunta ta'lamu anna hadha al-amra)
    (And if You know that this matter)

11. شَرٌّ لِي فِي دِينِي وَمَعَاشِي وَعَاقِبَةِ أَمْرِي
    (sharrun li fi deeni wa ma'ashi wa 'aqibati amri)
    (is detrimental for me in my religion, my livelihood, and the outcome of my affairs)

12. فَاصْرِفْهُ عَنِّي وَاصْرِفْنِي عَنْهُ
    (fasrifhu 'anni wa-srifni 'anhu)
    (Then turn it away from me, and turn me away from it)

13. وَاقْدُرْ لِي الْخَيْرَ حَيْثُ كَانَ
    (waqdur li al-khayra haythu kana)

(And decree for me what is good wherever it may be)

14. ثُمَّ أَرْضِنِي
(thumma ardini)
(Then make me satisfied with it)

Taslīm (Concluding the Prayer):

- To conclude, turn your head to the right and say:
  اِلسَّلَامُ عَلَيْكُمْ وَرَحْمَةُ اللَّه
  (As-salamu 'alaykum wa rahmatullahi)
  (Peace and mercy of Allah be upon you)

- Then turn your head to the left and repeat:
  اِلسَّلَامُ عَلَيْكُمْ وَرَحْمَةُ اللَّه
  (As-salamu 'alaykum wa rahmatullahi)
  (Peace and mercy of Allah be upon you)

Notes:
- Perform Salatul Istikhara with full sincerity and concentration.
- Maintain a clear heart and mind, and trust in Allah's wisdom and guidance.
- This special prayer is a means to seek divine clarity in every decision you face.

CHAPTER 17: SALATUL JANAZAH

─────────── STEP-BY-STEP Salatul Janazah Prayer

Before You Begin: • Form your niyyah in your heart: "I intend to perform the Salatul Janazah prayer for the sake of Allah."

─────────── Step 1: First Takbīr and Recitation of al-Fātiha

1. Opening Takbīr:
   • Say: الله أكبر
   (Allāhu Akbar)
   (Allah is the Greatest)

2. Recite al-Fātiha: a. بِسْمِ اللَّهِ الرَّحْمَٰنِ الرَّحِيمِ
   (Bismillaahir Rahmaanir Raheem)
   (In the name of Allah, the Most Gracious, the Most Merciful)

   b. اَلْحَمْدُ لِلَّهِ رَبِّ الْعَالَمِينَ
   (Alhamdu lillahi rabbil 'aalameen)
   (All praise is due to Allah, Lord of all the worlds)

   c. اِلرَّحْمَٰنِ الرَّحِيمِ
   (Ar-Rahmaanir Raheem)

(The Most Gracious, the Most Merciful)

d. مَالِكِ يَوْمِ الدِّينِ

(Maaliki yawmid-deen)
(Master of the Day of Judgment)

e. إِيَّاكَ نَعْبُدُ وَإِيَّاكَ نَسْتَعِينُ

(Iyyaka na'budu wa iyyaka nasta'een)
(You alone we worship, and You alone we ask for help)

f. اهْدِنَا الصِّرَاطَ الْمُسْتَقِيمَ

(Ihdinas-siraatal mustaqeem)
(Guide us to the straight path)

g. صِرَاطَ الَّذِينَ أَنْعَمْتَ عَلَيْهِمْ

(Siraatal ladheena an'amta 'alayhim)
(The path of those upon whom You have bestowed favor)

h. غَيْرِ الْمَغْضُوبِ عَلَيْهِمْ وَلَا الضَّالِّينَ

(Ghayril maghdoobi 'alayhim wa lad-daalleen)
(Not of those who have incurred Your anger nor of those who go astray)

——————— Step 2: Second Takbīr and Salawat upon the Prophet ———————

1. Second Takbīr:
   - Say: الله أكبر
     (Allāhu Akbar)
     (Allah is the Greatest)

2. Recite Salawat on the Prophet:
   - Say: اللَّهُمَّ صَلِّ عَلَى مُحَمَّدٍ وَعَلَى آلِ مُحَمَّدٍ
     (Allahumma salli 'ala Muhammadin wa 'ala ali Muhammadin)
     (O Allah, send Your blessings upon Muhammad and upon the family of Muhammad)

——————— Step 3: Third Takbīr and Supplication for the

Deceased ——————

1. **Third Takbīr:**
   - Say: الله أكبر
     (Allāhu Akbar)
     (Allah is the Greatest)

2. **Supplicate for the deceased:**
   - Recite: اللَّهُمَّ اغْفِرْ لِمَيِّتِنَا، وَلِحَيِّنَا، وَلِشَاهِدِنَا، وَلِغَائِبِنَا
     (Allahumma ighfir li mayyitina, wa li hayyina, wa li shahidina, wa li gha'ibina)
     (O Allah, forgive our deceased, our living, those present and those absent)

   - Then add: وَاجْمَعْ بَيْنَا فِي جَنَّاتِ النَّعِيمِ
     (Wa ajma' baynana fee jannaatin na'eem)
     (And unite us in the Gardens of Bliss)

—————————— Step 4: Fourth Takbīr and Final Supplication ——————————

1. **Fourth Takbīr:**
   - Say: الله أكبر
     (Allāhu Akbar)
     (Allah is the Greatest)

2. **Conclude with a general supplication:**
   - Recite: اللَّهُمَّ اغْفِرْ لِجَمِيعِ المُسْلِمِينَ وَالمُسْلِمَاتِ
     (Allahumma ighfir lijamee'il-muslimeena wal-muslimaat)
     (O Allah, forgive all the Muslim men and women)

   - Then add: وَاسْتُرْ عَوْرَاتِنَا، وَتَقَبَّلْ دُعَاءَنَا
     (Wa astur 'awraatinaa, wa taqabbal du'aanaa)
     (And conceal our faults, and accept our supplications)

—————————— Step 5: Taslīm (Concluding the Prayer) ——————————

1. To conclude, turn your head to the right and say:

- Recite: اِلسَّلَامُ عَلَيْكُمْ وَرَحْمَةُ اللَّهِ
  (As-salamu 'alaykum wa rahmatullah)
  (Peace and mercy of Allah be upon you)

2. Optionally, turn your head to the left and repeat:
   - Recite: اِلسَّلَامُ عَلَيْكُمْ وَرَحْمَةُ اللَّهِ
     (As-salamu 'alaykum wa rahmatullah)
     (Peace and mercy of Allah be upon you)

Notes:
- Salatul Janazah is performed while standing and does not include bowing (rukū') or prostration (sujūd).
- Maintain solemnity and humility throughout this sacred ritual, mindful of the transient nature of life and the eternal mercy of Allah.
- It is highly recommended to perform this prayer in congregation, reinforcing the unity and compassion of the Muslim community.

CHAPTER 18: SALATUL TASBIH

STEP-BY-STEP Salatul Tasbih Prayer

Salatul Tasbih is a unique voluntary prayer devoted to the continuous glorification of Allah. Its repeated recitations of His exalted attributes purify the heart and mind, allowing the worshiper to immerse in the infinite greatness of the Creator. Before you begin, ensure that you are in a state of ritual purity (wudu) and have centered your heart with sincere niyyah:
- "I intend to perform Salatul Tasbih for the sole purpose of glorifying Allah."

Rak'ah 1:

---

1. Opening Takbīr (Start of the Prayer):
    - Say:
    الله أكبر
    (Allāhu Akbar)
    (Allah is the Greatest)
    - Immediately after the opening takbīr, recite the Tasbīh 15 times:

سُبْحَانَ اللَّهِ وَالْحَمْدُ لِلَّهِ وَلَا إِلَهَ إِلَّا اللَّهُ وَاللَّهُ أَكْبَرُ

(Subhanallahi wal hamdulillahi wa la ilaha illallah, wallahu akbar)

(Glory be to Allah, all praise is for Allah, there is no deity except Allah, and Allah is the Greatest)

2. Recite al-Fātiha:

a. بِسْمِ اللَّهِ الرَّحْمَٰنِ الرَّحِيمِ

(Bismillaahir Rahmaanir Raheem)

(In the name of Allah, the Most Gracious, the Most Merciful)

b. الْحَمْدُ لِلَّهِ رَبِّ الْعَالَمِينَ

(Alhamdu lillahi rabbil 'aalameen)

(All praise is due to Allah, Lord of all the worlds)

c. الرَّحْمَٰنِ الرَّحِيمِ

(Ar-Rahmaanir Raheem)

(The Most Gracious, the Most Merciful)

d. مَالِكِ يَوْمِ الدِّينِ

(Maaliki yawmid-deen)

(Master of the Day of Judgment)

e. إِيَّاكَ نَعْبُدُ وَإِيَّاكَ نَسْتَعِينُ

(Iyyaka na'budu wa iyyaka nasta'een)

(You alone we worship, and You alone we ask for help)

f. اهْدِنَا الصِّرَاطَ الْمُسْتَقِيمَ

(Ihdinas-siraatal mustaqeem)

(Guide us to the straight path)

g. صِرَاطَ الَّذِينَ أَنْعَمْتَ عَلَيْهِمْ غَيْرِ الْمَغْضُوبِ عَلَيْهِمْ وَلَا الضَّالِّينَ

(Siraatal ladheena an'amta 'alayhim ghayril maghdoobi 'alayhim wa lad-daalleen)

(The path of those upon whom You have bestowed favor, not of those who have earned Your anger nor of those who go astray)

• Immediately after completing al-Fātiha, recite the Tasbīh 15 times (same as above).

3. Rukū' (Bowing):
   - Say "Allāhu Akbar" and bow gracefully.
   - In the rukū', recite the Tasbīh 15 times:

   سُبْحَانَ اللَّهِ وَالْحَمْدُ لِلَّهِ وَلَا إِلَهَ إِلَّا اللَّهُ وَاللَّهُ أَكْبَرُ

   (Subhanallahi wal hamdulillahi wa la ilaha illallah, wallahu akbar)

   (Glory be to Allah, all praise is for Allah, there is no deity except Allah, and Allah is the Greatest)

4. Rising from Rukū':
   - Rise from bowing while saying "Allāhu Akbar."
   - As you stand, recite the Tasbīh 15 times:

   سُبْحَانَ اللَّهِ وَالْحَمْدُ لِلَّهِ وَلَا إِلَهَ إِلَّا اللَّهُ وَاللَّهُ أَكْبَرُ

   (Subhanallahi wal hamdulillahi wa la ilaha illallah, wallahu akbar)

   (Glory be to Allah, all praise is for Allah, there is no deity except Allah, and Allah is the Greatest)

5. Sujūd (First Prostration):
   - Exclaim "Allāhu Akbar" and enter prostration.
   - In the first sujūd, recite the Tasbīh 15 times:

   سُبْحَانَ اللَّهِ وَالْحَمْدُ لِلَّهِ وَلَا إِلَهَ إِلَّا اللَّهُ وَاللَّهُ أَكْبَرُ

   (Subhanallahi wal hamdulillahi wa la ilaha illallah, wallahu akbar)

   (Glory be to Allah, all praise is for Allah, there is no deity except Allah, and Allah is the Greatest)

6. Brief Sitting (Jalsa) Between Sujūd:
   - Sit briefly and, while seated, recite the Tasbīh 15 times:

   سُبْحَانَ اللَّهِ وَالْحَمْدُ لِلَّهِ وَلَا إِلَهَ إِلَّا اللَّهُ وَاللَّهُ أَكْبَرُ

   (Subhanallahi wal hamdulillahi wa la ilaha illallah, wallahu akbar)

   (Glory be to Allah, all praise is for Allah, there is no deity except Allah, and Allah is the Greatest)

7. Sujūd (Second Prostration):

- Say "Allāhu Akbar" as you move into the second prostration.
- In the second sujūd, recite the Tasbīḥ 15 times:

سُبْحَانَ اللَّهِ وَالْحَمْدُ لِلَّهِ وَلَا إِلَهَ إِلَّا اللَّهُ وَاللَّهُ أَكْبَرُ

(Subhanallahi wal hamdulillahi wa la ilaha illallah, wallahu akbar)

(Glory be to Allah, all praise is for Allah, there is no deity except Allah, and Allah is the Greatest)

8. Rising for the Next Rak'ah:
   - While rising, say "Allāhu Akbar" and as you stand, recite the Tasbīḥ 15 times:

سُبْحَانَ اللَّهِ وَالْحَمْدُ لِلَّهِ وَلَا إِلَهَ إِلَّا اللَّهُ وَاللَّهُ أَكْبَرُ

(Subhanallahi wal hamdulillahi wa la ilaha illallah, wallahu akbar)

(Glory be to Allah, all praise is for Allah, there is no deity except Allah, and Allah is the Greatest)

Rak'ah 2 & Rak'ah 3:

Repeat the identical sequence of actions and Tasbīḥ recitations (steps 1 through 8 as in Rak'ah 1) for Rak'ah 2 and Rak'ah 3.

Rak'ah 4:

Follow the same steps as in Rak'ah 1 through 7:

1. Opening Takbīr
   – Say "Allāhu Akbar" and recite the Tasbīḥ 15 times.

2. Recite al-Fātiha and then recite the Tasbīḥ 15 times.

3. Rukū' with 15 Tasbīḥ recitations.

4. Rising from Rukū' with 15 Tasbīḥ recitations.

5. First Sujūd with 15 Tasbīh recitations.
6. Brief Sitting (Jalsa) with 15 Tasbīh recitations.
7. Second Sujūd with 15 Tasbīh recitations.
8. Final Tashahhud:
    • After the second sujūd of Rak'ah 4, rise into the final sitting position and recite the Tashahhud:

اَلتَّحِيَّاتُ لِلَّهِ وَالصَّلَوَاتُ وَالطَّيِّبَات
(At-tahiyyatu lillahi was-salawatu wat-tayyibatu)
(All greetings, prayers, and pure words are for Allah)

اَلسَّلَامُ عَلَيْكَ أَيُّهَا النَّبِي
(As-salamu 'alayka ayyuha an-nabiyyu)
(Peace be upon you, O Prophet)

وَرَحْمَةُ اللَّهِ وَبَرَكَاتُه
(Wa rahmatullahi wa barakatuhu)
(And the mercy and blessings of Allah)

اَلسَّلَامُ عَلَيْنَا وَعَلَى عِبَادِ اللَّهِ الصَّالِحِين
(As-salamu 'alayna wa 'ala 'ibaadil-lahi as-saaliheen)
(Peace be upon us and upon the righteous servants of Allah)

أَشْهَدُ أَنْ لَا إِلَهَ إِلَّا اللَّه
(Ash-hadu an la ilaha illallahu)
(I bear witness that there is no deity except Allah)

وَأَشْهَدُ أَنَّ مُحَمَّدًا رَسُولُ اللَّه
(Wa ash-hadu anna Muhammadan Rasool Allah)
(And I bear witness that Muhammad is the Messenger of Allah)

9. Taslīm (Concluding the Prayer):
    • Turn your head to the right and say:
    اَلسَّلَامُ عَلَيْكُمْ وَرَحْمَةُ اللَّه
    (As-salamu 'alaykum wa rahmatullahi)
    (Peace and mercy of Allah be upon you)

- Then turn to the left and repeat:
  ﺍﻟﺴَّﻼَمُ عَلَيْكُمْ وَرَحْمَةُ اللّٰهِ
  (As-salamu 'alaykum wa rahmatullahi)
  (Peace and mercy of Allah be upon you)

Notes on Salatul Tasbih:

- In each of the 4 rak'ahs, the special Tasbīh is recited 15 times at eight key positions:
    - Immediately after the opening takbīr
    - Immediately after reciting al-Fātiha
    - In the rukū' (bowing)
    - When rising from rukū'
    - In the first sujūd (prostration)
    - In the sitting (jalsa) between the two sujūd
    - In the second sujūd
    - When rising to stand for the next rak'ah (or before concluding the prayer in the fourth rak'ah)

  These repetitions collectively serve to immerse your heart in the remembrance of Allah's perfection.

- While performing Salatul Tasbih, maintain a demeanor of complete khushu' (humility and concentration), allowing the rhythmic glorification to cleanse and elevate your spirit.

May this prayer draw you closer to Allah and illuminate your path with His infinite mercy and grace.

CHAPTER 19: SALATUL ISTISQA

STEP-BY-STEP Salatul Istisqa Prayer

Below is an in-depth guide to Salatul Istisqa—the supplicatory prayer for rain invoked in times of drought or hardship. This prayer unites the community in a humble plea for Allah's mercy and underscores our total reliance on His providence. Before you begin, ensure you are in a state of ritual purity (wudu) and that your heart is sincere in seeking relief and blessing.

Before You Begin:
• Form your niyyah in your heart: "I intend to perform Salatul Istisqa seeking Allah's mercy and asking for beneficial rain."
• Ensure you have a clean space and, if possible, perform this prayer in congregation as a united community.

Rak'ah 1:

1. Opening Takbīr (Start of the Prayer):
   الله أكبر
   (Allāhu Akbar)   (Allah is the Greatest)

2. Recite al-Fātiha (The Opening Chapter):
   a. بِسْمِ اللَّهِ الرَّحْمَٰنِ الرَّحِيمِ

(Bismillaahir Rahmaanir Raheem)   (In the name of Allah, the Most Gracious, the Most Merciful)

b. اَلْحَمْدُ لِلَّهِ رَبِّ الْعَالَمِين
(Alhamdu lillahi rabbil 'aalameen)   (All praise is due to Allah, Lord of all the worlds)

c. الرَّحْمَٰنِ الرَّحِيم
(Ar-Rahmaanir Raheem)   (The Most Gracious, the Most Merciful)

d. مَالِكِ يَوْمِ الدِّين
(Maaliki yawmid-deen)   (Master of the Day of Judgment)

e. إِيَّاكَ نَعْبُدُ وَإِيَّاكَ نَسْتَعِين
(Iyyaka na'budu wa iyyaka nasta'een)   (You alone we worship, and You alone we ask for help)

f. اهْدِنَا الصِّرَاطَ الْمُسْتَقِيم
(Ihdinas-siraatal mustaqeem)   (Guide us to the straight path)

3. Recite a Supplicatory Verse for Rain:
   After al-Fātiha, recite the following verses which invoke Allah's mercy and the blessing of needed rain:

اللَّهُمَّ صَيِّبًا نَافِعًا
(Allahumma Sayyiban naafi'an)   (O Allah, send down beneficial rain)

وَارْزُقْنَا غَيْثَكَ الْمُهَيْمِن
(Wa arzuqna ghaythaka al-muhaymin)   (And provide us with Your sovereign rain)

4. Rukū' (Bowing):
   • As you bow, say "الله أكبر"
      (Allāhu Akbar)   (Allah is the Greatest)
   • Then recite:
      سُبْحَانَ رَبِّيَ الْعَظِيم
      (Subhana rabbiyal 'adheem)   (Glory be to my Lord,

the Most Great)

　　　[Repeat at least three times]

5. Rising from Rukū':
    - Rise while saying:

    سَمِعَ اللهُ لِمَنْ حَمِدَه

    (Sami' Allāhu liman hamidah)　　(Allah hears those who praise Him)
    - Then, while standing straight, say:

    رَبَّنَا وَلَكَ الْحَمْد

    (Rabbana wa laka al-hamd)　　(Our Lord, to You be all praise)

6. Sujūd (First Prostration):
    - As you move into prostration, say "الله أكبر"

    (Allāhu Akbar)　　(Allah is the Greatest)
    - Then recite in Sujūd:

    سُبْحَانَ رَبِّيَ الأَعْلَى

    (Subhana rabbiyal a'la)　　(Glory be to my Lord, the Most High)

    [Repeat at least three times]

7. Brief Sitting (Jalsa):
    - Sit briefly and supplicate; for example, recite:

    رَبِّ اغْفِرْ لِي

    (Rabbi ighfir li)　　(O my Lord, forgive me)

8. Sujūd (Second Prostration):
    - Say "الله أكبر" as you move into the second prostration.
    - Then recite:

    سُبْحَانَ رَبِّيَ الأَعْلَى

    (Subhana rabbiyal a'la)　　(Glory be to my Lord, the Most High)

    [Repeat at least three times]

9. Rising for the Next Rak'ah:
    - Say "الله أكبر" as you rise to commence Rak'ah 2.

Rak'ah 2:

1. Opening Takbīr:
   الله أكبر
   (Allāhu Akbar)   (Allah is the Greatest)

2. Recite al-Fātiha:

   a. بِسْمِ اللَّهِ الرَّحْمَٰنِ الرَّحِيمِ
   (Bismillaahir Rahmaanir Raheem)   (In the name of Allah, the Most Gracious, the Most Merciful)

   b. اَلْحَمْدُ لِلَّهِ رَبِّ الْعَالَمِينَ
   (Alhamdu lillahi rabbil 'aalameen)   (All praise is due to Allah, Lord of all the worlds)

   c. الرَّحْمَٰنِ الرَّحِيمِ
   (Ar-Rahmaanir Raheem)   (The Most Gracious, the Most Merciful)

   d. مَالِكِ يَوْمِ الدِّينِ
   (Maaliki yawmid-deen)   (Master of the Day of Judgment)

   e. إِيَّاكَ نَعْبُدُ وَإِيَّاكَ نَسْتَعِينُ
   (Iyyaka na'budu wa iyyaka nasta'een)   (You alone we worship, and You alone we ask for help)

   f. اهْدِنَا الصِّرَاطَ الْمُسْتَقِيمَ
   (Ihdinas-siraatal mustaqeem)   (Guide us to the straight path)

3. Recite the Supplicatory Verses for Rain Again:
   اللَّهُمَّ صَيِّبًا نَافِعًا
   (Allahumma Sayyiban naafi'an)   (O Allah, send down beneficial rain)

   وَارْزُقْنَا غَيْثَكَ الْمُهَيْمِن
   (Wa arzuqna ghaythaka al-muhaymin)   (And provide us

with Your sovereign rain)

4. Rukū' (Bowing):
   - Upon bowing, say "الله أكبر"
     (Allāhu Akbar)   (Allah is the Greatest)
   - Recite:
     سُبْحَانَ رَبِّيَ الْعَظِيم
     (Subhana rabbiyal 'adheem)   (Glory be to my Lord, the Most Great)
     [Repeat at least three times]

5. Rising from Rukū':
   - While rising, say:
     سَمِعَ اللَّهُ لِمَنْ حَمِدَه
     (Sami' Allāhu liman hamidah)   (Allah hears those who praise Him)
   - Then, while standing, say:
     رَبَّنَا وَلَكَ الْحَمْد
     (Rabbana wa laka al-hamd)   (Our Lord, to You be all praise)

6. Sujūd (First Prostration):
   - As you lower into prostration, say "الله أكبر"
     (Allāhu Akbar)   (Allah is the Greatest)
   - Recite:
     سُبْحَانَ رَبِّيَ الْأَعْلَى
     (Subhana rabbiyal a'la)   (Glory be to my Lord, the Most High)
     [Repeat at least three times]

7. Brief Sitting (Jalsa):
   - Sit and recite:
     رَبِّ اغْفِرْ لِي
     (Rabbi ighfir li)   (O my Lord, forgive me)

8. Sujūd (Second Prostration):
   - Move into the second prostration saying "الله أكبر"
   - Then recite:

سُبْحَانَ رَبِّيَ الأَعْلَى

(Subhana rabbiyal a'la)   (Glory be to my Lord, the Most High)

[Repeat at least three times]

9. Final Tashahhud (Sitting for the Testimony):
After the second sujūd, sit and recite the Tashahhud:

اَلتَّحِيَّاتُ لِلَّهِ وَالصَّلَوَاتُ وَالطَّيِّبَاتُ

(At-tahiyyatu lillahi was-salawatu wat-tayyibatu)   (All greetings, prayers, and pure words are for Allah)

اَلسَّلَامُ عَلَيْكَ أَيُّهَا النَّبِيُّ

(As-salamu 'alayka ayyuha an-nabiyyu)   (Peace be upon you, O Prophet)

وَرَحْمَةُ اللَّهِ وَبَرَكَاتُهُ

(Wa rahmatullahi wa barakatuhu)   (And the mercy and blessings of Allah)

اَلسَّلَامُ عَلَيْنَا وَعَلَى عِبَادِ اللَّهِ الصَّالِحِينَ

(As-salamu 'alayna wa 'ala 'ibaadil-lahi as-saaliheen) (Peace be upon us and upon the righteous servants of Allah)

أَشْهَدُ أَنْ لَا إِلَهَ إِلَّا اللَّهُ

(Ash-hadu an la ilaha illallahu)   (I bear witness that there is no deity except Allah)

وَأَشْهَدُ أَنَّ مُحَمَّدًا رَسُولُ اللَّهِ

(Wa ash-hadu anna Muhammadan Rasool Allah)   (And I bear witness that Muhammad is the Messenger of Allah)

10. Taslīm (Concluding the Prayer):
- To conclude, turn your head to the right and say:

اَلسَّلَامُ عَلَيْكُمْ وَرَحْمَةُ اللَّهِ

(As-salamu 'alaykum wa rahmatullahi)   (Peace and mercy of Allah be upon you)

- Then turn to the left and repeat:

اَلسَّلَامُ عَلَيْكُمْ وَرَحْمَةُ اللَّهِ

(As-salamu 'alaykum wa rahmatullahi) (Peace and mercy of Allah be upon you)

Post-Prayer Supplication for Rain:

After completing Salatul Istisqa, raise your hands in heartfelt supplication and recite:

اَللَّهُمَّ أَنْزِلْ عَلَيْنَا غَيْثَكَ الْمُبَارَكَ، وَاجْعَلْ أَرْضَنَا طَيِّبَةً، وَأَمْنَحْنَا رَحْمَتَكَ يَا أَرْحَمَ الرَّاحِمِين

(Allahumma anzil 'alayna ghaythaka al-mubarak, wa ij'al ardana tayyibah, wa amnahna rahmataka ya arham ar-rahimeen)

(O Allah, send upon us Your blessed rain, make our land wholesome, and bestow upon us Your mercy, O Most Merciful of the merciful.)

Notes:
• At every stage of transition—standing, bowing, prostrating, and sitting—remember to say "اللہ أكبر" (Allāhu Akbar).
• The supplications for rain are drawn from prophetic traditions, emphasizing our humble reliance on Allah for sustenance and mercy.
• Let the unity of the congregation and your sincere invocation be a means for relief and divine blessing upon the community.

May this supplicatory prayer for rain bring relief, prosperity, and the abundant mercy of Allah to all in need.

CHAPTER 20: SALATUL HAJAH

────────── STEP-BY-STEP Salatul Hajah Prayer
──────────

This chapter outlines the complete prayer for Salatul Hajah —a two-rak'ah prayer performed in moments of urgent need or hardship. Salatul Hajah is a heartfelt invocation where the believer turns to Allah, seeking His assistance and mercy when faced with difficulties. Before you begin, ensure you are in a state of ritual purity (wudu) and have cleared your heart to ask for divine help.

──────────

Before You Begin:
• Form your niyyah in your heart: "I intend to perform two rak'ahs of Salatul Hajah to seek Allah's assistance and relief in my time of need."

────────── Rak'ah 1: ──────────

1. Opening Takbīr (Start of the Prayer):   الله أكبر
   (Allāhu Akbar)
   (Allah is the Greatest)

2. Recite al-Fātiha (The Opening Chapter):

a. بِسْمِ اللَّهِ الرَّحْمَنِ الرَّحِيمِ
(Bismillaahir Rahmaanir Raheem)
(In the name of Allah, the Most Gracious, the Most Merciful)

b. الْحَمْدُ لِلَّهِ رَبِّ الْعَالَمِينَ
(Alhamdu lillahi rabbil 'aalameen)
(All praise is due to Allah, Lord of all the worlds)

c. الرَّحْمَنِ الرَّحِيمِ
(Ar-Rahmaanir Raheem)
(The Most Gracious, the Most Merciful)

d. مَالِكِ يَوْمِ الدِّينِ
(Maaliki yawmid-deen)
(Master of the Day of Judgment)

e. إِيَّاكَ نَعْبُدُ وَإِيَّاكَ نَسْتَعِينُ
(Iyyaka na'budu wa iyyaka nasta'een)
(You alone we worship, and You alone we ask for help)

f. اهْدِنَا الصِّرَاطَ الْمُسْتَقِيمَ
(Ihdinas-siraatal mustaqeem)
(Guide us to the straight path)

g. صِرَاطَ الَّذِينَ أَنْعَمْتَ عَلَيْهِمْ
(Siraatal ladheena an'amta 'alayhim)
(The path of those upon whom You have bestowed favor)

3. Recite a Short Sūrah – Sūrah al-Falaq:

a. قُلْ أَعُوذُ بِرَبِّ الْفَلَقِ
(Qul a'udhu bi rabbil-falaq)
(Say, "I seek refuge in the Lord of daybreak")

b. مِنْ شَرِّ مَا خَلَقَ
(Min sharri ma khalaq)
(From the evil of that which He created)

c. وَمِنْ شَرِّ غَاسِقٍ إِذَا وَقَبَ
(Wa min sharri ghasiqin idha waqab)

(And from the evil of darkness when it settles)

d. وَمِن شَرِّ النَّفَّاثَاتِ فِي الْعُقَدِ
(Wa min sharri an-naffathati fil 'uqad)
(And from the evil of those who practice witchcraft)

e. وَمِن شَرِّ حَاسِدٍ إِذَا حَسَدَ
(Wa min sharri hasidin idha hasad)
(And from the evil of an envier when he envies)

4. Rukū' (Bowing):   • As you move into bowing, say "Allāhu Akbar."
   • Then recite: سُبْحَانَ رَبِّيَ الْعَظِيمِ
      (Subhana rabbiyal 'adheem)
      (Glory be to my Lord, the Most Great)   [Repeat at least three times]

5. Rising from Rukū':   • Rise saying "Allāhu Akbar."
   • Then recite: سَمِعَ اللَّهُ لِمَنْ حَمِدَه
      (Sami' Allāhu liman hamidah)
      (Allah hears those who praise Him)
   • And then say: رَبَّنَا وَلَكَ الْحَمْد
      (Rabbana wa laka al-hamd)
      (Our Lord, to You be all praise)

6. Sujūd (First Prostration):   • As you enter prostration, say "Allāhu Akbar."
   • Then recite: سُبْحَانَ رَبِّيَ الْأَعْلَى
      (Subhana rabbiyal a'la)
      (Glory be to my Lord, the Most High)   [Repeat at least three times]

7. Brief Sitting (Jalsa):
   • Sit briefly between the prostrations.
   • Optionally, supplicate by saying: رَبِّ اغْفِرْ لِي
      (Rabbi ighfir li)
      (O my Lord, forgive me)

8. Sujūd (Second Prostration):

- Say "Allāhu Akbar" as you perform the second prostration.
- Then recite: سُبْحَانَ رَبِّيَ الْأَعْلَى

    (Subhana rabbiyal a'la)

    (Glory be to my Lord, the Most High)   [Repeat at least three times]

9. Rising for the Next Rak'ah:
   - Say "Allāhu Akbar" and stand to begin the second rak'ah.

──────────── Rak'ah 2: ────────────

1. Opening Takbīr: الله أكبر

    (Allāhu Akbar)

    (Allah is the Greatest)

2. Recite al-Fātiha (The Opening Chapter):

a. بِسْمِ اللَّهِ الرَّحْمَٰنِ الرَّحِيمِ

    (Bismillaahir Rahmaanir Raheem)

    (In the name of Allah, the Most Gracious, the Most Merciful)

b. الْحَمْدُ لِلَّهِ رَبِّ الْعَالَمِينَ

    (Alhamdu lillahi rabbil 'aalameen)

    (All praise is due to Allah, Lord of all the worlds)

c. الرَّحْمَٰنِ الرَّحِيمِ

    (Ar-Rahmaanir Raheem)

    (The Most Gracious, the Most Merciful)

d. مَالِكِ يَوْمِ الدِّينِ

    (Maaliki yawmid-deen)

    (Master of the Day of Judgment)

e. إِيَّاكَ نَعْبُدُ وَإِيَّاكَ نَسْتَعِينُ

    (Iyyaka na'budu wa iyyaka nasta'een)

    (You alone we worship, and You alone we ask for help)

f. اهْدِنَا الصِّرَاطَ الْمُسْتَقِيمَ

    (Ihdinas-siraatal mustaqeem)

    (Guide us to the straight path)

g. صِرَاطَ الَّذِينَ أَنْعَمْتَ عَلَيْهِمْ
(Siraatal ladheena an'amta 'alayhim)
(The path of those upon whom You have bestowed favor)

3. Recite a Short Sūrah – Sūrah an-Nās:

a. قُلْ أَعُوذُ بِرَبِّ النَّاسِ
(Qul a'udhu bi rabbin-naas)
(Say, "I seek refuge in the Lord of mankind")

b. مَلِكِ النَّاسِ
(Malikin-naas)
(The Sovereign of mankind)

c. إِلَهِ النَّاسِ
(Ilahin-naas)
(The God of mankind)

d. مِنْ شَرِّ الْوَسْوَاسِ الْخَنَّاسِ
(Min sharri al-waswaasil khannaas)
(From the evil of the whisperer who withdraws)

e. الَّذِي يُوَسْوِسُ فِي صُدُورِ النَّاسِ
(Allathee yuwaswisu fee sudoorin-naas)
(Who whispers into the breasts of mankind)

f. مِنَ الْجِنَّةِ وَالنَّاسِ
(Mina al-jinnati wan-naas)
(Among jinn and among men)

4. Rukū' (Bowing): • As you bow, say "Allāhu Akbar."
   • Then recite: سُبْحَانَ رَبِّيَ الْعَظِيمِ
      (Subhana rabbiyal 'adheem)
      (Glory be to my Lord, the Most Great)   [Repeat at least three times]

5. Rising from Rukū': • Rise saying "Allāhu Akbar."
   • Then recite: سَمِعَ اللَّهُ لِمَنْ حَمِدَه
      (Sami' Allāhu liman hamidah)

(Allah hears those who praise Him)
   - And then say: رَبَّنَا وَلَكَ الْحَمْد
      (Rabbana wa laka al-hamd)
      (Our Lord, to You be all praise)

6. Sujūd (First Prostration):
   - As you enter prostration, say "Allāhu Akbar."
   - Then recite: سُبْحَانَ رَبِّيَ الْأَعْلَى
      (Subhana rabbiyal a'la)
      (Glory be to my Lord, the Most High)   [Repeat at least three times]

7. Brief Sitting (Jalsa):
   - Sit briefly between the prostrations.
   - Optionally, recite: رَبِّ اغْفِرْ لِي
      (Rabbi ighfir li)
      (O my Lord, forgive me)

8. Sujūd (Second Prostration):
   - Say "Allāhu Akbar" as you perform the second prostration.
   - Then recite: سُبْحَانَ رَبِّيَ الْأَعْلَى
      (Subhana rabbiyal a'la)
      (Glory be to my Lord, the Most High)   [Repeat at least three times]

9. Final Tashahhud (Sitting for the Testimony):
   - Sit and recite: اَلتَّحِيَّاتُ لِلَّهِ وَالصَّلَوَاتُ وَالطَّيِّبَاتُ
      (At-tahiyyatu lillahi was-salawatu wat-tayyibatu)
      (All greetings, prayers, and pure words are for Allah)

اَلسَّلَامُ عَلَيْكَ أَيُّهَا النَّبِيُّ
(As-salamu 'alayka ayyuha an-nabiyyu)
(Peace be upon you, O Prophet)

وَرَحْمَةُ اللَّهِ وَبَرَكَاتُهُ
(Wa rahmatullahi wa barakatuhu)
(And the mercy and blessings of Allah)

اَلسَّلَامُ عَلَيْنَا وَعَلَى عِبَادِ اللَّهِ الصَّالِحِينَ

(As-salamu 'alayna wa 'ala 'ibaadil-lahi as-saaliheen)
(Peace be upon us and upon the righteous servants of Allah)

10. Special Dua for Salatul Hajah:
    • While still seated, raise your hands and supplicate: اللَّهُمَّ إِنِّي عَاجِزٌ عَن نَفْسِي، وَأَسْتَجِيرُ بِكَ مِن كُلِّ هَمٍّ وَضِيقٍ

    (Allahumma innee 'aajizun 'an nafsee, wa astajeeru bika min kulli hammin wa diiq)

    (O Allah, I am helpless without You and seek refuge in You from every worry and distress)

    فَانْظُرْ إِلَيَّ بِنَظَرِ رَحْمَتِكَ، وَافْتَحْ لِي بَابَ خَيْرِكَ

    (Fandhur ilayya binaZari rahmatika, wa iftah li baaba khayrika)

    (Look upon me with the vision of Your mercy, and open for me the door to Your blessings)

    إِنَّكَ عَلَىٰ كُلِّ شَيْءٍ قَدِيرٌ

    (Innaka 'ala kulli shay'in qadeer)
    (Indeed, You are capable of all things)

11. Taslīm (Concluding the Prayer):
    • To conclude the prayer, first turn your head to the right and say: اَلسَّلَامُ عَلَيْكُمْ وَرَحْمَةُ اللَّهِ

    (As-salamu 'alaykum wa rahmatullahi)
    (Peace and mercy of Allah be upon you)

    • Then turn your head to the left and repeat: السَّلَامُ عَلَيْكُمْ وَرَحْمَةُ اللَّهِ

    (As-salamu 'alaykum wa rahmatullahi)
    (Peace and mercy of Allah be upon you)

Notes:
• Recite each section with sincerity and focus, for Salatul Hajah is offered in times of personal hardship and urgent need.
• While the above structure follows the Sunnah in its movements and recitations, you may also add personal supplications (du'ā) during the brief sitting (Jalsa) if your heart

moves you.
• Trust in Allah's mercy and know that He is the Best of Helpers in all affairs.

CHAPTER 21: SALATUL TAWBAH

STEP-BY-STEP Salatul Tawbah Prayer

Below is an in-depth guide to Salatul Tawbah, the Prayer of Repentance, through which believers seek forgiveness for their sins, cleanse their spiritual slate, and reaffirm their commitment to a righteous path. Approach this prayer with sincere humility and a contrite heart. Before you begin, ensure you are in a state of ritual purity (wudu) and have prepared your heart for genuine repentance.

Before You Begin:
• Form your niyyah in your heart: "I intend to perform two rak'ahs of Salatul Tawbah to seek repentance and forgiveness from Allah."

Rak'ah 1:

1. Opening Takbīr (Start of the Prayer): الله أكبر
   (Allāhu Akbar)
   (Allah is the Greatest)

2. Recite al-Fātiha (The Opening Chapter):

   a. بِسْمِ اللَّهِ الرَّحْمَٰنِ الرَّحِيمِ
   (Bismillaahir Rahmaanir Raheem)
   (In the name of Allah, the Most Gracious, the Most Merciful)

b. اَلْحَمْدُ لِلَّهِ رَبِّ الْعَالَمِين
(Alhamdu lillahi rabbil 'aalameen)
(All praise is due to Allah, Lord of all the worlds)

c. اِلرَّحْمَنِ الرَّحِيم
(Ar-Rahmaanir Raheem)
(The Most Gracious, the Most Merciful)

d. مَالِكِ يَوْمِ الدِّين
(Maaliki yawmid-deen)
(Master of the Day of Judgment)

e. اْيَّاكَ نَعْبُدُ وَإِيَّاكَ نَسْتَعِين
(Iyyaka na'budu wa iyyaka nasta'een)
(You alone we worship, and You alone we ask for help)

f. اَهْدِنَا الصِّرَاطَ الْمُسْتَقِيم
(Ihdinas-siraatal mustaqeem)
(Guide us to the straight path)

g. ْصِرَاطَ الَّذِينَ أَنْعَمْتَ عَلَيْهِم
(Siraatal ladheena an'amta 'alayhim)
(The path of those upon whom You have bestowed favor)

3. Recite the Repentance Invocation (Du'ā Tawbah): لا إله إلا أنت سبحانك إني كنت من الظالمين

(La ilaha illa Anta, subhanaka, innee kuntu min al-zalimīn)
(There is no deity except You; Glory be to You; indeed I was among the wrongdoers)

4. Rukū' (Bowing): • As you bow, say "Allāhu Akbar." • Then recite:
   سِبْحَانَ رَبِّيَ الْعَظِيم
   (Subhana rabbiyal 'adheem)
   (Glory be to my Lord, the Most Great)
   [Repeat at least three times]

5. Rising from Rukū': • Rise while saying:

سَمِعَ اللَّهُ لِمَنْ حَمِدَه

(Sami' Allāhu liman hamidah)
(Allah hears those who praise Him)
- Then, while standing, say:

رَبَّنَا وَلَكَ الْحَمْد

(Rabbana wa laka al-hamd)
(Our Lord, to You be all praise)

6. Sujūd (First Prostration):
   - As you enter prostration, say "Allāhu Akbar."
   - Then recite:

   سُبْحَانَ رَبِّيَ الْأَعْلَى

   (Subhana rabbiyal a'la)
   (Glory be to my Lord, the Most High)
   [Repeat at least three times]

7. Brief Sitting (Jalsa):
   - Sit and supplicate with:

   رَبِّ اغْفِرْ لِي

   (Rabbi ighfir li)
   (O my Lord, forgive me)

8. Sujūd (Second Prostration):
   - Say "Allāhu Akbar" as you perform the second prostration.
   - Then recite:

   سُبْحَانَ رَبِّيَ الْأَعْلَى

   (Subhana rabbiyal a'la)
   (Glory be to my Lord, the Most High)
   [Repeat at least three times]

9. Rising for the Next Rak'ah:
   - Say "Allāhu Akbar" and stand to begin Rak'ah 2.

——————— Rak'ah 2: ———————

1. Opening Takbīr: الله أكبر
   (Allāhu Akbar)
   (Allah is the Greatest)

2. Recite al-Fātiha:

a. بِسْمِ اللهِ الرَّحْمٰنِ الرَّحِيم
(Bismillaahir Rahmaanir Raheem)
(In the name of Allah, the Most Gracious, the Most Merciful)

b. اَلْحَمْدُ لِلّٰهِ رَبِّ الْعَالَمِين
(Alhamdu lillahi rabbil 'aalameen)
(All praise is due to Allah, Lord of all the worlds)

c. اِلرَّحْمٰنِ الرَّحِيم
(Ar-Rahmaanir Raheem)
(The Most Gracious, the Most Merciful)

d. مَالِكِ يَوْمِ الدِّين
(Maaliki yawmid-deen)
(Master of the Day of Judgment)

e. اِيَّاكَ نَعْبُدُ وَإِيَّاكَ نَسْتَعِين
(Iyyaka na'budu wa iyyaka nasta'een)
(You alone we worship, and You alone we ask for help)

f. اَهْدِنَا الصِّرَاطَ الْمُسْتَقِيم
(Ihdinas-siraatal mustaqeem)
(Guide us to the straight path)

g. ْصِرَاطَ الَّذِينَ أَنْعَمْتَ عَلَيْهِم
(Siraatal ladheena an'amta 'alayhim)
(The path of those upon whom You have bestowed favor)

3. Recite the Repentance Invocation: لا إله إلا أنت سبحانك إني كنت من الظالمين

(La ilaha illa Anta, subhanaka, innee kuntu min al-zalimīn)

(There is no deity except You; Glory be to You; indeed I was among the wrongdoers)

4. Rukū' (Bowing): • Bow while saying "Allāhu Akbar."
• Then recite:

سِبْحَانَ رَبِّيَ الْعَظِيم
(Subhana rabbiyal 'adheem)
(Glory be to my Lord, the Most Great)
[Repeat at least three times]

5. Rising from Rukū':
   • Rise with:
   سَمِعَ اللَّهُ لِمَنْ حَمِدَه
   (Sami' Allāhu liman hamidah)
   (Allah hears those who praise Him)
   • Then stand while saying:
   رَبَّنَا وَلَكَ الْحَمْد
   (Rabbana wa laka al-hamd)
   (Our Lord, to You be all praise)

6. Sujūd (First Prostration):
   • In prostration, say "Allāhu Akbar."
   • Recite:
   سُبْحَانَ رَبِّيَ الْأَعْلَى
   (Subhana rabbiyal a'la)
   (Glory be to my Lord, the Most High)
   [Repeat at least three times]

7. Brief Sitting (Jalsa):
   • Sit and supplicate earnestly with:
   رَبِّ اغْفِرْ لِي وَتُبْ عَلَيَّ
   (Rabbi ighfir li wa tub 'alayya)
   (O my Lord, forgive me and grant me sincere repentance)

8. Sujūd (Second Prostration):
   • Say "Allāhu Akbar" as you perform the second prostration.
   • Then recite:
   سُبْحَانَ رَبِّيَ الْأَعْلَى
   (Subhana rabbiyal a'la)
   (Glory be to my Lord, the Most High)
   [Repeat at least three times]

9. **Final Tashahhud (Sitting for the Testimony):**
   • After the second sujūd, sit and recite:

اَلتَّحِيَّاتُ لِلَّهِ وَالصَّلَوَاتُ وَالطَّيِّبَاتُ
(At-tahiyyatu lillahi was-salawatu wat-tayyibatu)
(All greetings, prayers, and pure words are for Allah)

اَلسَّلَامُ عَلَيْكَ أَيُّهَا النَّبِي
(As-salamu 'alayka ayyuha an-nabiyyu)
(Peace be upon you, O Prophet)

وَرَحْمَةُ اللَّهِ وَبَرَكَاتُهُ
(Wa rahmatullahi wa barakatuhu)
(And the mercy and blessings of Allah)

اَلسَّلَامُ عَلَيْنَا وَعَلَى عِبَادِ اللَّهِ الصَّالِحِين
(As-salamu 'alayna wa 'ala 'ibaadil-lahi as-saaliheen)
(Peace be upon us and upon the righteous servants of Allah)

أَشْهَدُ أَنْ لَا إِلَهَ إِلَّا اللَّه
(Ash-hadu an la ilaha illallahu)
(I bear witness that there is no deity except Allah)

وَأَشْهَدُ أَنَّ مُحَمَّدًا رَسُولُ اللَّه
(Wa ash-hadu anna Muhammadan Rasool Allah)
(And I bear witness that Muhammad is the Messenger of Allah)

10. **Taslīm (Concluding the Prayer):**
    • To conclude the prayer, turn your head to the right and say:

اَلسَّلَامُ عَلَيْكُمْ وَرَحْمَةُ اللَّه
(As-salamu 'alaykum wa rahmatullahi)
(Peace and mercy of Allah be upon you)

   • Then turn your head to the left and repeat:

اَلسَّلَامُ عَلَيْكُمْ وَرَحْمَةُ اللَّه
(As-salamu 'alaykum wa rahmatullahi)
(Peace and mercy of Allah be upon you)

Notes:
• Approach Salatul Tawbah with sincere remorse and mindfulness, truly resolving to turn away from sin.
• Recite each supplication with a heart full of humility as you ask Allah for His boundless forgiveness.
• Let this prayer serve as a means to purify your soul and renew your commitment to following the path of righteousness.

CHAPTER 22: JUMU'AH PRAYER

--- STEP-BY-STEP Jumu'ah Prayer ---

Before You Begin:
• Ensure you are in a state of ritual purity (wudu) and have arrived at the mosque early.
• Sit quietly and prepare your heart to listen attentively to the Khutbah (sermon), a vital element of the Jumu'ah gathering.
• Remind yourself that this congregational prayer is not only an act of worship but also an opportunity for collective reflection and guidance.

--- Khutbah (Sermon) – Part 1: ---

1. The Imam stands before the congregation and begins by praising Allah: الحمد لله رب العالمين

    (Alhamdu lillahi rabbil 'alameen)
    (All praise is due to Allah, the Lord of all the worlds)
    ونستغفره نستعينه
    (Nasta'eenuhu wa nastaghfiruh)
    (We seek His help and forgiveness)
    وأشهد أن لا إله إلا الله وحده لا شريك له
    (Wa ash-hadu alla ilaha illa Allahu, wahdahu la sharika lahu)
    (And I bear witness that there is no deity except Allah, Alone without partner)

2. The Imam then admonishes and reminds: يا أيها الناس اتقوا الله

(Yā ayyuhā al-nāsu, ittaqū Allāh)
(O people, fear Allah)
فاتقوا الله عباد الله
(Fattaqū Allāh, 'ibād Allāh)
(So fear Allah, O servants of Allah)

3. The Imam briefly emphasizes the importance of righteous conduct and the imminence of the Hour, inviting the hearts of the congregation to sincere reflection.

——————————— Brief Sitting Between Khutbahs: ———————————

After concluding Part 1, the Imam sits silently for a short interval. The congregation remains seated in respectful quietude, reflecting on the words heard.

——————————— Khutbah (Sermon) – Part 2: ———————————

1. The Imam rises again saying: الله أكبر
  (Allāhu Akbar)
  (Allah is the Greatest)

2. He continues with further testimony and supplication:
أشهد أن لا إله إلا الله الثابت في السماوات والأرض
(Ash-hadu alla ilaha illa Allāhu, al-thābit fi al-samāwāti wal-arḍ)
(I bear witness that there is no deity except Allah, who is firm in the heavens and on the earth)

اللهم اهدنا فيمَن هديت
(Allahumma ihdinā fiman hadayta)
(O Allah, guide us among those whom You have guided)

وتولنا فيمن توليت
(Wa tawallānā fiman tawallayta)
(And take us into Your care among those You have

taken into Your care)

لنا من لدنك سلطاناً ونصراواجعل

(Wa ja'al lanā min ladunka sultānan wa naṣran)

(And grant us from Yourself authority and victory)

أن ساعة قيامتكم أقرب مما تعتقدوناعلموا

(I'lamū anna sā'ata qiyāmatikum aqrab mimmā ta'taqīdūn)

(Know that the hour of your resurrection is nearer than you think)

3. The Imam concludes the Khutbah with a final supplication for the congregation: اللهم اغفر للمسلمين، والمسلمات، والمؤمنين والمؤمنات

(Allahumma ighfir lil-muslimīn, wal-muslimaāt, wal-mu'minīn wal-mu'mināt)

(O Allah, forgive the Muslim men and women, and the male and female believers)

——————— Transition to Prayer: ———————

After the second Khutbah, the Imam declares: فَانتَقِلُوا إلى الصلاة

(Fa'tanqilū ilā as-salāh)

(Then proceed to the prayer) The congregation rises in unison, ready to perform the Jumu'ah Fard prayer.

——————— Rak'ah 1: ———————

1. Opening Takbīr (Start of the Prayer): الله أكبر
   (Allāhu Akbar)
   (Allah is the Greatest)

2. Recite al-Fātiha (The Opening Chapter):

   a. بِسمِ اللَّهِ الرَّحْمَنِ الرَّحِيمِ
   (Bismillaahir Rahmaanir Raheem)
   (In the name of Allah, the Most Gracious, the Most Merciful)

   b. اَلْحَمْدُ لِلَّهِ رَبِّ الْعَالَمِين
   (Alhamdu lillahi rabbil 'alameen)

(All praise is due to Allah, Lord of all the worlds)

c. اِلرَّحْمٰنِ الرَّحِيمِ

(Ar-Rahmaanir Raheem)
(The Most Gracious, the Most Merciful)

d. مَالِكِ يَوْمِ الدِّينِ

(Maaliki yawmid-deen)
(Master of the Day of Judgment)

e. إِيَّاكَ نَعْبُدُ وَإِيَّاكَ نَسْتَعِينُ

(Iyyaka na'budu wa iyyaka nasta'een)
(You alone we worship, and You alone we ask for help)

f. اهْدِنَا الصِّرَاطَ الْمُسْتَقِيمَ

(Ihdinas-siraatal mustaqeem)
(Guide us to the straight path)

g. صِرَاطَ الَّذِينَ أَنْعَمْتَ عَلَيْهِمْ

(Siraatal ladheena an'amta 'alayhim)
(The path of those upon whom You have bestowed favor)

غَيْرِ الْمَغْضُوبِ عَلَيْهِمْ وَلَا الضَّالِّينَ

(Ghayril maghdoobi 'alayhim wa lad-daalleen)
(Not of those who have earned Your anger nor of those who go astray)

3. Recite a Short Sūrah – Sūrah al-Kāfirūn:

a. قُلْ يَا أَيُّهَا الْكَافِرُونَ

(Qul ya ayyuhal kaafirun)
(Say, "O disbelievers,")

b. لَا أَعْبُدُ مَا تَعْبُدُونَ

(Lā a'budu mā ta'budoon)
(I do not worship what you worship)

c. وَلَا أَنْتُمْ عَابِدُونَ مَا أَعْبُدُ

(Wa lā antum 'ābidūn mā a'bud)
(Nor are you worshippers of what I worship)

d. وَلَا أَنَا عَابِدٌ مَا عَبَدتُّم

(Wa lā anā 'ābidun mā 'abadtum)

(And I will not be a worshipper of what you have worshipped)

e. وَلَا أَنتُم عَابِدُونَ مَا أَعْبُد

(Wa lā antum 'ābidūn mā a'bud)

(Nor will you be worshippers of what I worship)

f. لَكُم دِينُكُم وَلِيَ دِين

(Lakum deenu-kum wa liyā deeni)

(For you is your religion, and for me is mine)

4. Rukū' (Bowing):
   - As you bow, say "الله أكبر"

     (Allāhu Akbar)

     (Allah is the Greatest)
   - Then recite: سُبْحَانَ رَبِّيَ الْعَظِيم

     (Subḥāna rabbiyal 'azeem)

     (Glory be to my Lord, the Most Great)

   [Repeat at least three times]

5. Rising from Rukū':
   - While rising, say: سَمِعَ اللَّهُ لِمَنْ حَمِدَه

     (Sami' Allāhu liman ḥamidah)

     (Allah hears those who praise Him)
   - Then, while standing, recite: رَبَّنَا وَلَكَ الْحَمْد

     (Rabbana wa laka al-ḥamd)

     (Our Lord, to You be all praise)

6. Sujūd (First Prostration):
   - As you descend, say "الله أكبر"

     (Allāhu Akbar)

     (Allah is the Greatest)
   - In prostration, recite: سُبْحَانَ رَبِّيَ الْأَعْلَى

     (Subḥāna rabbiyal a'la)

     (Glory be to my Lord, the Most High)

[Repeat at least three times]

7. Brief Sitting (Jalsa):
   - Sit briefly and supplicate: رَبِّ اغْفِرْ لِي
     (Rabbi ighfir li)
     (O my Lord, forgive me)

8. Sujūd (Second Prostration):
   - Again, say "الله أكبر" as you enter prostration.
   - Recite: سُبْحَانَ رَبِّيَ الْأَعْلَى
     (Subḥāna rabbiyal a'la)
     (Glory be to my Lord, the Most High)
   [Repeat at least three times]

9. Rising for the Next Rak'ah:
   - Stand up, saying "الله أكبر" and prepare for Rak'ah 2.

———————— Rak'ah 2: ————————

1. Opening Takbīr: الله أكبر
   (Allāhu Akbar)
   (Allah is the Greatest)

2. Recite al-Fātiha:

   a. بِسْمِ اللَّهِ الرَّحْمَٰنِ الرَّحِيمِ
   (Bismillaahir Rahmaanir Raheem)
   (In the name of Allah, the Most Gracious, the Most Merciful)

   b. الْحَمْدُ لِلَّهِ رَبِّ الْعَالَمِينَ
   (Alhamdu lillahi rabbil 'alameen)
   (All praise is due to Allah, Lord of all the worlds)

   c. الرَّحْمَٰنِ الرَّحِيمِ
   (Ar-Rahmaanir Raheem)
   (The Most Gracious, the Most Merciful)

   d. مَالِكِ يَوْمِ الدِّينِ
   (Maaliki yawmid-deen)

(Master of the Day of Judgment)

e. اِيَّاكَ نَعْبُدُ وَاِيَّاكَ نَسْتَعِينُ

(Iyyaka na'budu wa iyyaka nasta'een)
(You alone we worship, and You alone we ask for help)

f. اَهْدِنَا الصِّرَاطَ الْمُسْتَقِيمَ

(Ihdinas-siraatal mustaqeem)
(Guide us to the straight path)

g. صِرَاطَ الَّذِينَ أَنْعَمْتَ عَلَيْهِمْ

(Siraatal ladheena an'amta 'alayhim)
(The path of those upon whom You have bestowed favor)

غَيْرِ الْمَغْضُوبِ عَلَيْهِمْ وَلَا الضَّالِّينَ

(Ghayril maghdoobi 'alayhim wa lad-daalleen)
(Not of those who have earned Your anger nor of those who go astray)

3. Recite a Short Sūrah – Sūrah al-Ikhlās:

a. قُلْ هُوَ اللَّهُ أَحَدٌ

(Qul huwa Allāhu ahad)
(Say, "He is Allah, [Who is] One")

b. اللَّهُ الصَّمَدُ

(Allāhu as-samad)
(Allah, the Eternal Refuge)

c. لَمْ يَلِدْ وَلَمْ يُولَدْ

(Lam yalid wa lam yoolad)
(He neither begets nor is born)

d. وَلَمْ يَكُنْ لَهُ كُفُوًا أَحَدٌ

(Wa lam yakun lahu kufuwan ahad)
(Nor is there to Him any equivalent)

4. Rukū' (Bowing):
   - Bow by saying "الله أكبر."
   - Then recite: سُبْحَانَ رَبِّيَ الْعَظِيمِ
     (Subhāna rabbiyal 'azeem)

(Glory be to my Lord, the Most Great)
[Repeat at least three times]

5. Rising from Rukū':
    - Rise while saying: سَمِعَ اللّٰهُ لِمَنْ حَمِدَه
        (Sami' Allāhu liman ḥamidah)
        (Allah hears those who praise Him)
    - Then, while standing, recite: رَبَّنَا وَلَكَ الْحَمْد
        (Rabbana wa laka al-ḥamd)
        (Our Lord, to You be all praise)

6. Sujūd (First Prostration):
    - Descend saying "الله أكبر."
    - In prostration, recite: سُبْحَانَ رَبِّيَ الْأَعْلَى
        (Subḥāna rabbiyal a'la)
        (Glory be to my Lord, the Most High)
    [Repeat at least three times]

7. Brief Sitting (Jalsa):
    - Sit briefly and supplicate: رَبِّ اغْفِرْ لِي
        (Rabbi ighfir li)
        (O my Lord, forgive me)

8. Sujūd (Second Prostration):   • Again, say "الله أكبر" as you perform the second prostration.
    - Recite: سُبْحَانَ رَبِّيَ الْأَعْلَى
        (Subḥāna rabbiyal a'la)
        (Glory be to my Lord, the Most High)
    [Repeat at least three times]

9. Final Tashahhud (Sitting for the Testimony):
    - After the second prostration, sit and recite: التَّحِيَّاتُ
    لِلّٰهِ وَالصَّلَوَاتُ وَالطَّيِّبَات
        (At-tahiyyatu lillahi was-salawatu wat-tayyibatu)
        (All greetings, prayers, and pure words are for Allah)
    السَّلَامُ عَلَيْكَ أَيُّهَا النَّبِيُّ
        (As-salāmu 'alayka ayyuhā an-nabiyyu)

(Peace be upon you, O Prophet)

رَحْمَةُ اللّٰهِ وَبَرَكَاتُهُ

(Wa raḥmatullāhi wa barakātuhu)

(And the mercy and blessings of Allah)

السَّلَامُ عَلَيْنَا وَعَلَىٰ عِبَادِ اللّٰهِ الصَّالِحِينَ

(As-salāmu 'alaynā wa 'alā 'ibādillāhi aṣ-ṣāliḥīn)

(Peace be upon us and upon the righteous servants of Allah)

أَشْهَدُ أَنْ لَا إِلَٰهَ إِلَّا اللّٰهُ

(Ash-hadu an lā ilaha illallāhu)

(I bear witness that there is no deity except Allah)

أَشْهَدُ أَنَّ مُحَمَّدًا رَسُولُ اللّٰهِ

(Wa ash-hadu anna Muḥammadān Rasūlullāh)

(And I bear witness that Muhammad is the Messenger of Allah)

10. Taslīm (Concluding the Prayer):

• To conclude the prayer, turn your head to the right and say: السَّلَامُ عَلَيْكُمْ وَرَحْمَةُ اللّٰهِ

(As-salāmu 'alaykum wa raḥmatullāh)

(Peace and mercy of Allah be upon you)

• Then turn your head to the left and repeat: السَّلَامُ عَلَيْكُمْ وَرَحْمَةُ اللّٰهِ

(As-salāmu 'alaykum wa raḥmatullāh)

(Peace and mercy of Allah be upon you)

Notes:

• The Jumu'ah prayer uniquely incorporates the Khutbah, which is essential for communal guidance and reflection; listening attentively is a significant act of worship.

• Arriving early to benefit from the sermon and maintaining silence during the Khutbah are highly recommended.

• The above prayer text for the two rak'ahs follows the established pattern of the obligatory prayer, led by the Imam in unison with the congregation.

CHAPTER 23: EID PRAYER

---------- STEP-BY-STEP Eid Prayer ----------

Below is an in-depth guide to the Eid prayer—a jubilant, congregational act performed during Eid al-Fitr and Eid al-Adha. This prayer marks a time of celebration, unity, and gratitude, bringing the community together in joyous worship and festive spirit. Before you begin, ensure you are in a state of ritual purity (wudu) and form your niyyah in your heart: "I intend to perform two rak'ahs of the Eid prayer for the sake of Allah."

---------- Rak'ah 1: ----------

1. Opening Takbīr (Takbīr al-Ihram):
   Arabic: الله أكبر
   (Allāhu Akbar)
   (Allah is the Greatest)

2. Additional Takbeers:
   It is Sunnah in the Eid prayer to recite six additional takbeers before commencing al-Fātiha. With each additional takbīr, raise your hands slightly and say the following:

Takbīr 2:
   Arabic: الله أكبر
   (Allāhu Akbar)
   (Allah is the Greatest)

Takbīr 3:
   Arabic: الله أكبر
   (Allāhu Akbar)
   (Allah is the Greatest)

Takbīr 4:
   Arabic: الله أكبر
   (Allāhu Akbar)
   (Allah is the Greatest)

Takbīr 5:
   Arabic: الله أكبر
   (Allāhu Akbar)
   (Allah is the Greatest)

Takbīr 6:
   Arabic: الله أكبر
   (Allāhu Akbar)
   (Allah is the Greatest)

Takbīr 7:
   Arabic: الله أكبر
   (Allāhu Akbar)
   (Allah is the Greatest)

3. Recite al-Fātiha (The Opening Chapter):
   a. Arabic: بِسْمِ اللهِ الرَّحْمَنِ الرَّحِيمِ
      (Bismillaahir Rahmaanir Raheem)
      (In the name of Allah, the Most Gracious, the Most Merciful)

   b. Arabic: اَلْحَمْدُ لِلَّهِ رَبِّ الْعَالَمِين
      (Alhamdu lillahi rabbil 'aalameen)
      (All praise is due to Allah, Lord of all the worlds)

   c. Arabic: الرَّحْمَنِ الرَّحِيم
      (Ar-Rahmaanir Raheem)
      (The Most Gracious, the Most Merciful)

d. Arabic: مَالِكِ يَوْمِ الدِّين
   (Maaliki yawmid-deen)
   (Master of the Day of Judgment)

e. Arabic: إِيَّاكَ نَعْبُدُ وَإِيَّاكَ نَسْتَعِين
   (Iyyaka na'budu wa iyyaka nasta'een)
   (You alone we worship, and You alone we ask for help)

f. Arabic: اهْدِنَا الصِّرَاطَ الْمُسْتَقِيم
   (Ihdinas-siraatal mustaqeem)
   (Guide us to the straight path)

g. Arabic: صِرَاطَ الَّذِينَ أَنْعَمْتَ عَلَيْهِمْ غَيْرِ الْمَغْضُوبِ عَلَيْهِمْ وَلَا الضَّالِّين
   (Siraatal ladheena an'amta 'alayhim ghayril-maghdoobi 'alayhim wa lad-daalleen)
   (The path of those upon whom You have bestowed favor, not of those who have earned Your anger, nor of those who go astray)

4. Recite a Short Sūrah – Sūrah al-A'lā:
   This Sūrah celebrates the majesty of Allah and the bounties of creation, reflecting the joy of Eid.

a. Arabic: سَبِّحِ اسْمَ رَبِّكَ الْأَعْلَى
   (Sabbiḥ isma rabbika al-a'lā)
   (Glorify the name of your Lord, the Most High)

b. Arabic: الَّذِي خَلَقَ فَسَوَّى
   (Alladhī khalaqa fasawwā)
   ([He] who created and proportioned)

c. Arabic: وَالَّذِي قَدَّرَ فَهَدَى
   (Wa-alladhī qaddara fahadā)
   (And who destined and guided)

d. Arabic: وَالَّذِي أَخْرَجَ الْمَرْعَى
   (Wa-alladhī akh-raja al-mar'ā)
   (And who brings forth [springs] in abundance)

e. Arabic: فَجَعَلَهُ غُثَاءً أَحْوَى

(Fa-ja'alahu ghuthā'an ahwā)
(And made it as a barren mound)

5. Rukū' (Bowing):
   • As you move into the bowing position, say "Allāhu Akbar."
   • Then recite:
   Arabic: سُبْحَانَ رَبِّيَ الْعَظِيم

   (Subhana rabbiyal 'adheem)
   (Glory be to my Lord, the Most Great)
   [Repeat at least three times]

6. Rising from Rukū':
   • Rise while saying:
   Arabic: سَمِعَ اللَّهُ لِمَنْ حَمِدَه

   (Sami' Allāhu liman hamidah)
   (Allah hears those who praise Him)
   • Then, while standing, say:
   Arabic: رَبَّنَا وَلَكَ الْحَمْد

   (Rabbana wa laka al-hamd)
   (Our Lord, to You be all praise)

7. Sujūd (First Prostration):
   • As you go down into prostration, say "Allāhu Akbar."
   • Then recite in sujūd:
   Arabic: سُبْحَانَ رَبِّيَ الْأَعْلَى

   (Subhana rabbiyal a'la)
   (Glory be to my Lord, the Most High)
   [Repeat at least three times]

8. Brief Sitting (Jalsa):
   • Sit briefly between the two prostrations.
   • Offer a simple supplication, for example:
   Arabic: رَبِّ اغْفِرْ لِي

   (Rabbi ighfir li)
   (O my Lord, forgive me)

9. Sujūd (Second Prostration):
   - Say "Allāhu Akbar" as you move into the second prostration.
   - Then recite:
     Arabic: سُبْحَانَ رَبِّيَ الْأَعْلَى
     (Subhana rabbiyal a'la)
     (Glory be to my Lord, the Most High)
     [Repeat at least three times]

10. Rising for the Next Rak'ah:
    - Say "Allāhu Akbar" and then stand up to begin Rak'ah 2.

──────────── Rak'ah 2: ────────────

1. Opening Takbīr:
   Arabic: الله أكبر
   (Allāhu Akbar)
   (Allah is the Greatest)

2. Recite al-Fātiha (The Opening Chapter):
   a. Arabic: بِسْمِ اللَّهِ الرَّحْمَٰنِ الرَّحِيم
      (Bismillaahir Rahmaanir Raheem)
      (In the name of Allah, the Most Gracious, the Most Merciful)

   b. Arabic: الْحَمْدُ لِلَّهِ رَبِّ الْعَالَمِين
      (Alhamdu lillahi rabbil 'aalameen)
      (All praise is due to Allah, Lord of all the worlds)

   c. Arabic: الرَّحْمَٰنِ الرَّحِيم
      (Ar-Rahmaanir Raheem)
      (The Most Gracious, the Most Merciful)

   d. Arabic: مَالِكِ يَوْمِ الدِّين
      (Maaliki yawmid-deen)
      (Master of the Day of Judgment)

   e. Arabic: إِيَّاكَ نَعْبُدُ وَإِيَّاكَ نَسْتَعِين
      (Iyyaka na'budu wa iyyaka nasta'een)

(You alone we worship, and You alone we ask for help)

f. Arabic: اهْدِنَا الصِّرَاطَ الْمُسْتَقِيمَ

(Ihdinas-siraatal mustaqeem)

(Guide us to the straight path)

g. Arabic: صِرَاطَ الَّذِينَ أَنْعَمْتَ عَلَيْهِمْ غَيْرِ الْمَغْضُوبِ عَلَيْهِمْ وَلَا الضَّالِّينَ

(Siraatal ladheena an'amta 'alayhim ghayril-maghdoobi 'alayhim wa lad-daalleen)

(The path of those upon whom You have bestowed favor, not of those who have earned Your anger, nor of those who go astray)

3. Recite a Short Sūrah – Sūrah al-Ikhlās:

   a. Arabic: قُلْ هُوَ اللَّهُ أَحَدٌ

   (Qul huwa Allāhu 'ahad)

   (Say, "He is Allah, [Who is] One")

   b. Arabic: اللَّهُ الصَّمَدُ

   (Allāhu as-samad)

   (Allah, the Eternal Refuge)

   c. Arabic: لَمْ يَلِدْ وَلَمْ يُولَدْ

   (Lam yalid wa lam yoolad)

   (He neither begets nor is born)

   d. Arabic: وَلَمْ يَكُنْ لَهُ كُفُوًا أَحَدٌ

   (Wa lam yakun lahu kufuwan ahad)

   (Nor is there to Him any equivalent)

4. Rukū' (Bowing):
   - As you bow, say "Allāhu Akbar."
   - Then recite:

     Arabic: سُبْحَانَ رَبِّيَ الْعَظِيمِ

     (Subhana rabbiyal 'adheem)

     (Glory be to my Lord, the Most Great)

     [Repeat at least three times]

5. Rising from Rukū':

- While rising, say:

  Arabic: سَمِعَ اللَّهُ لِمَنْ حَمِدَه

  (Sami' Allāhu liman hamidah)

  (Allah hears those who praise Him)

- Then, while standing, say:

  Arabic: رَبَّنَا وَلَكَ الْحَمْد

  (Rabbana wa laka al-hamd)

  (Our Lord, to You be all praise)

6. **Sujūd (First Prostration):**
   - Say "Allāhu Akbar" and lower into prostration.
   - Then recite:

     Arabic: سُبْحَانَ رَبِّيَ الْأَعْلَى

     (Subhana rabbiyal a'la)

     (Glory be to my Lord, the Most High)

     [Repeat at least three times]

7. **Brief Sitting (Jalsa):**
   - Sit briefly and, if desired, recite a supplication such as:

     Arabic: رَبِّ اغْفِرْ لِي

     (Rabbi ighfir li)

     (O my Lord, forgive me)

8. **Sujūd (Second Prostration):**
   - Say "Allāhu Akbar" as you move into the second prostration.
   - Then recite:

     Arabic: سُبْحَانَ رَبِّيَ الْأَعْلَى

     (Subhana rabbiyal a'la)

     (Glory be to my Lord, the Most High)

     [Repeat at least three times]

9. **Final Tashahhud (Sitting for the Testimony):**
   - After the second sujūd, sit and recite the Tashahhud:

     Arabic: التَّحِيَّاتُ لِلَّهِ وَالصَّلَوَاتُ وَالطَّيِّبَاتُ

     (At-tahiyyatu lillahi was-salawatu wat-tayyibatu)

     (All greetings, prayers, and pure words are for

Allah)

Arabic: اَلسَّلَامُ عَلَيْكَ أَيُّهَا النَّبِي
(As-salamu 'alayka ayyuha an-nabiyyu)
(Peace be upon you, O Prophet)

Arabic: وَرَحْمَةُ اللّٰهِ وَبَرَكَاتُهُ
(Wa rahmatullahi wa barakatuhu)
(And the mercy and blessings of Allah)

Arabic: اَلسَّلَامُ عَلَيْنَا وَعَلَىٰ عِبَادِ اللّٰهِ الصَّالِحِين
(As-salamu 'alayna wa 'ala 'ibaadil-lahi as-saaliheen)
(Peace be upon us and upon the righteous servants of Allah)

Arabic: أَشْهَدُ أَنْ لَا إِلَهَ إِلَّا اللّٰه
(Ash-hadu an la ilaha illallahu)
(I bear witness that there is no deity except Allah)

Arabic: وَأَشْهَدُ أَنَّ مُحَمَّدًا رَسُولُ اللّٰه
(Wa ash-hadu anna Muhammadan Rasool Allah)
(And I bear witness that Muhammad is the Messenger of Allah)

10. Taslīm (Concluding the Prayer):
   • To end the prayer, first turn your head to the right and recite:
   Arabic: اَلسَّلَامُ عَلَيْكُمْ وَرَحْمَةُ اللّٰه
   (As-salamu 'alaykum wa rahmatullahi)
   (Peace and mercy of Allah be upon you)
   • Then turn your head to the left and repeat:
   Arabic: اَلسَّلَامُ عَلَيْكُمْ وَرَحْمَةُ اللّٰه
   (As-salamu 'alaykum wa rahmatullahi)
   (Peace and mercy of Allah be upon you)

Notes:
• The additional takbeers in the first rak'ah are a distinctive feature of the Eid Prayer, emphasizing the exaltation and joy of

this blessed day.
• Reflect on the unity and gratitude of the community as you join together in this congregational worship.
• You may add personal du'ā (supplications) during the brief sitting (jalsa) to express your heartfelt thanks and ask for Allah's continued guidance.

May your Eid be filled with peace, unity, and abundant blessings.

CHAPTER 24: SALATUL SHUKR

-------- STEP-BY-STEP Salatul Shukr Prayer

Below is an in-depth guide to Salatul Shukr—the prayer of gratitude offered to thank Allah for His countless blessings. This special prayer encourages believers to reflect on their fortunes and cultivate a spirit of thankfulness in every area of life. In this guide, Salatul Shukr is presented in two rak'ahs Before you begin, ensure you have performed wudu and formed the sincere niyyah in your heart.

Before You Begin:
• Form your niyyah: "I intend to perform Salatul Shukr to express my gratitude for Allah's blessings."

-------- Rak'ah 1: --------

1. Opening Takbīr (Start of the Prayer): الله أكبر
   (Allāhu Akbar)
   (Allah is the Greatest)

2. Recite al-Fātiha (The Opening Chapter):

   a. بِسْمِ اللَّهِ الرَّحْمٰنِ الرَّحِيمِ

(Bismillaahir Rahmaanir Raheem)
(In the name of Allah, the Most Gracious, the Most Merciful)

b. اَلْحَمْدُ لِلَّهِ رَبِّ الْعَالَمِين
(Alhamdu lillahi rabbil 'aalameen)
(All praise is due to Allah, Lord of all the worlds)

c. اِلرَّحْمَٰنِ الرَّحِيم
(Ar-Rahmaanir Raheem)
(The Most Gracious, the Most Merciful)

d. مَالِكِ يَوْمِ الدِّين
(Maaliki yawmid-deen)
(Master of the Day of Judgment)

e. اِيَّاكَ نَعْبُدُ وَإِيَّاكَ نَسْتَعِين
(Iyyaka na'budu wa iyyaka nasta'een)
(You alone we worship, and You alone we ask for help)

f. اَهْدِنَا الصِّرَاطَ الْمُسْتَقِيم
(Ihdinas-siraatal mustaqeem)
(Guide us to the straight path)

g. صِرَاطَ الَّذِينَ أَنْعَمْتَ عَلَيْهِم
(Siraatal-ladheena an'amta 'alayhim)
(The path of those upon whom You have bestowed favor)

3. Recite a Short Supplication of Gratitude: اللَّهُمَّ إِنِّي أَشْكُرُكَ نِعَمَكَ الَّتِي لَا تُعَدُّ وَلَا تُحْصَى

(Allahumma inni ashkuruka ni'amaka allatee la tu'add wa la tuhsa)

(O Allah, I thank You for Your blessings that are countless and beyond measure)

4. Rukū' (Bowing):
   • As you bow, say "Allāhu Akbar."
   • Then recite:
   سُبْحَانَ رَبِّيَ الْعَظِيم
   (Subhana rabbiyal 'adheem)

(Glory be to my Lord, the Most Great)
[Repeat at least three times]

5. Rising from Rukū':
   - Rise while saying:
   سَمِعَ اللّهُ لِمَنْ حَمِدَه
   (Sami' Allāhu liman hamidah)
   (Allah hears those who praise Him)
   - Then, while standing, say:
   رَبَّنَا وَلَكَ الْحَمْد
   (Rabbana wa laka al-hamd)
   (Our Lord, to You be all praise)

6. Sujūd (First Prostration):
   - As you enter prostration, say "Allāhu Akbar."
   - Then recite:
   سُبْحَانَ رَبِّيَ الْأَعْلَى
   (Subhana rabbiyal a'la)
   (Glory be to my Lord, the Most High)
   [Repeat at least three times]

7. Brief Sitting (Jalsa):
   - Sit briefly and recite the supplication:
   رَبِّ اجْعَلْنِي مِنَ الشَّاكِرِين
   (Rabbi ij'alni mina ash-shakireen)
   (O my Lord, make me among the thankful)

8. Sujūd (Second Prostration):
   - Say "Allāhu Akbar" and prostrate again.
   - Then recite:
   سُبْحَانَ رَبِّيَ الْأَعْلَى
   (Subhana rabbiyal a'la)
   (Glory be to my Lord, the Most High)
   [Repeat at least three times]

9. Rising for the Next Rak'ah:
   - Say "Allāhu Akbar" and stand to begin Rak'ah 2.

―――――――――― Rak'ah 2: ――――――――――

1. Opening Takbīr: الله أكبر
    (Allāhu Akbar)
    (Allah is the Greatest)

2. Recite al-Fātiha:

a. بِسْمِ اللَّهِ الرَّحْمَنِ الرَّحِيمِ
(Bismillaahir Rahmaanir Raheem)
(In the name of Allah, the Most Gracious, the Most Merciful)

b. اَلْحَمْدُ لِلَّهِ رَبِّ الْعَالَمِينَ
(Alhamdu lillahi rabbil 'aalameen)
(All praise is due to Allah, Lord of all the worlds)

c. الرَّحْمَنِ الرَّحِيمِ
(Ar-Rahmaanir Raheem)
(The Most Gracious, the Most Merciful)

d. مَالِكِ يَوْمِ الدِّينِ
(Maaliki yawmid-deen)
(Master of the Day of Judgment)

e. إِيَّاكَ نَعْبُدُ وَإِيَّاكَ نَسْتَعِينُ
(Iyyaka na'budu wa iyyaka nasta'een)
(You alone we worship, and You alone we ask for help)

f. اهْدِنَا الصِّرَاطَ الْمُسْتَقِيمَ
(Ihdinas-siraatal mustaqeem)
(Guide us to the straight path)

g. صِرَاطَ الَّذِينَ أَنْعَمْتَ عَلَيْهِمْ
(Siraatal-ladheena an'amta 'alayhim)
(The path of those upon whom You have bestowed favor)

3. Recite a Short Supplication of Gratitude: اللَّهُمَّ زِدْنِي شُكْرًا وَبَرَكَةً
    (Allahumma zidni shukran wa barakata)
    (O Allah, increase me in thankfulness and blessings)

4. Rukū' (Bowing): • As you bow, say "Allāhu Akbar."
   • Then recite:
   سُبْحَانَ رَبِّيَ الْعَظِيم
   (Subhana rabbiyal 'adheem)
   (Glory be to my Lord, the Most Great)
   [Repeat at least three times]

5. Rising from Rukū':
   • Rise while saying:
   سَمِعَ اللَّهُ لِمَنْ حَمِدَه
   (Sami' Allāhu liman hamidah)
   (Allah hears those who praise Him)
   • Then, while standing, say:
   رَبَّنَا وَلَكَ الْحَمْد
   (Rabbana wa laka al-hamd)
   (Our Lord, to You be all praise)

6. Sujūd (Prostration):
   • As you prostrate, say "Allāhu Akbar."
   • Then recite:
   سُبْحَانَ رَبِّيَ الْأَعْلَى
   (Subhana rabbiyal a'la)
   (Glory be to my Lord, the Most High)
   [Repeat at least three times]

7. Brief Sitting (Jalsa):
   • Sit briefly and recite the supplication:
   رَبِّ اجْعَلْنِي مِنَ الشَّاكِرِين
   (Rabbi ij'alni mina ash-shakireen)
   (O my Lord, make me among the thankful)

8. Sujūd (Second Prostration):
   • Say "Allāhu Akbar" and prostrate again.
   • Then recite:
   سُبْحَانَ رَبِّيَ الْأَعْلَى
   (Subhana rabbiyal a'la)
   (Glory be to my Lord, the Most High)

[Repeat at least three times]

9. Final Tashahhud (Sitting for the Testimony):

- Sit and recite: اَلتَّحِيَّاتُ لِلَّهِ وَالصَّلَوَاتُ وَالطَّيِّبَاتُ
  (At-tahiyyatu lillahi was-salawatu wat-tayyibatu)
  (All greetings, prayers, and pure words are for Allah)

  اَلسَّلَامُ عَلَيْكَ أَيُّهَا النَّبِيُّ
  (As-salamu 'alayka ayyuha an-nabiyyu)
  (Peace be upon you, O Prophet)

  وَرَحْمَةُ اللَّهِ وَبَرَكَاتُهُ
  (Wa rahmatullahi wa barakatuhu)
  (And the mercy and blessings of Allah)

  اَلسَّلَامُ عَلَيْنَا وَعَلَى عِبَادِ اللَّهِ الصَّالِحِينَ
  (As-salamu 'alayna wa 'ala 'ibaadil-lahi as-saaliheen)
  (Peace be upon us and upon the righteous servants of Allah)

  أَشْهَدُ أَنْ لَا إِلَهَ إِلَّا اللَّهُ
  (Ash-hadu an la ilaha illallahu)
  (I bear witness that there is no deity except Allah)

  وَأَشْهَدُ أَنَّ مُحَمَّدًا رَسُولُ اللَّهِ
  (Wa ash-hadu anna Muhammadan Rasool Allah)
  (And I bear witness that Muhammad is the Messenger of Allah)

10. Taslīm (Concluding the Prayer):

- Turn your head to the right and say:
  اَلسَّلَامُ عَلَيْكُمْ وَرَحْمَةُ اللَّهِ
  (As-salamu 'alaykum wa rahmatullahi)
  (Peace and mercy of Allah be upon you)
- Then turn your head to the left and repeat:
  اَلسَّلَامُ عَلَيْكُمْ وَرَحْمَةُ اللَّهِ
  (As-salamu 'alaykum wa rahmatullahi)
  (Peace and mercy of Allah be upon you)

Notes:
• Salatul Shukr is a voluntary prayer that serves as a heartfelt expression of gratitude for Allah's innumerable blessings.
• You may add personal supplications (du'ā) during the brief sittings (Jalsa) to further manifest your thankfulness.

CHAPTER 25: SALATUL AWWABIN

STEP-BY-STEP Salatul Awwabin Prayer

Salatul Awwabin is known as the prayer of the penitent—a voluntary act of worship that offers the believer an exquisite opportunity to turn back to Allah in humility. Through this dua-filled prayer, one seeks Allah's forgiveness, mercy, and compassionate grace. May your heart be sincere in repentance as you perform these two rak'ahs of extra supplication.

Before You Begin: • Form your niyyah in your heart: "I intend to perform two rak'ahs of Salatul Awwabin, the prayer of the penitent, seeking Allah's forgiveness and mercy."

---------- Rak'ah 1: ----------

1. Opening Takbīr (Start of the Prayer): الله أكبر
   (Allāhu Akbar)
   (Allah is the Greatest)

2. Recite al-Fātiha (The Opening Chapter):

a. بِسْمِ اللَّهِ الرَّحْمَٰنِ الرَّحِيمِ
   (Bismillaahir Rahmaanir Raheem)
   (In the name of Allah, the Most Gracious, the Most Merciful)

b. اَلْحَمْدُ لِلَّهِ رَبِّ الْعَالَمِين
   (Alhamdu lillahi rabbil 'aalameen)
   (All praise is due to Allah, Lord of all the worlds)

c. اِلرَّحْمَنِ الرَّحِيم
   (Ar-Rahmaanir Raheem)
   (The Most Gracious, the Most Merciful)

d. مَالِكِ يَوْمِ الدِّين
   (Maaliki yawmid-deen)
   (Master of the Day of Judgment)

e. إِيَّاكَ نَعْبُدُ وَإِيَّاكَ نَسْتَعِين
   (Iyyaka na'budu wa iyyaka nasta'een)
   (You alone we worship, and You alone we ask for help)

f. اهْدِنَا الصِّرَاطَ الْمُسْتَقِيم
   (Ihdinas-siraatal mustaqeem)
   (Guide us to the straight path)

g. صِرَاطَ الَّذِينَ أَنْعَمْتَ عَلَيْهِمْ غَيْرِ الْمَغْضُوبِ عَلَيْهِمْ وَلَا الضَّالِّين
   (Siraatal ladheena an'amta 'alayhim ghayril maghdoobi 'alayhim wa lad-daalleen)
   (The path of those upon whom You have bestowed favor, not of those who have earned Your anger nor of those who go astray)

3. Recite a Short Sūrah – Surah al-Ikhlās:

a. قُلْ هُوَ اللَّهُ أَحَد
   (Qul huwa Allāhu 'ahad)
   (Say, "He is Allah, [Who is] One")

b. اَللَّهُ الصَّمَد
   (Allāhu as-samad)
   (Allah, the Eternal Refuge)

c. لَمْ يَلِدْ وَلَمْ يُولَد
   (Lam yalid wa lam yoolad)
   (He neither begets nor is born)

d. وَلَمْ يَكُن لَّهُ كُفُوًا أَحَدٌ

(Wa lam yakun lahu kufuwan ahad)
(Nor is there to Him any equivalent)

4. Rukū' (Bowing):
   - As you move into the bowing position, say "الله أكبر"
     - Then recite:
       سُبْحَانَ رَبِّيَ الْعَظِيم
       (Subhana rabbiyal 'adheem)
       (Glory be to my Lord, the Most Great)
       [Repeat at least three times]

5. Rising from Rukū':
   - Rise while saying:
     سَمِعَ اللَّهُ لِمَنْ حَمِدَه
     (Sami' Allāhu liman hamidah)
     (Allah hears those who praise Him)
   - Then, while standing, say:
     رَبَّنَا وَلَكَ الْحَمْد
     (Rabbana wa laka al-hamd)
     (Our Lord, to You be all praise)

6. Sujūd (First Prostration):
   - As you go down into prostration, say "الله أكبر"
     - Then recite:
       سُبْحَانَ رَبِّيَ الْأَعْلَى
       (Subhana rabbiyal a'la)
       (Glory be to my Lord, the Most High)
       [Repeat at least three times]

7. Brief Sitting (Jalsa):
   - Sit briefly between the two prostrations.
     - Recite the supplication:
       رَبِّ اغْفِرْ لِي وَارْحَمْنِي
       (Rabbi ighfir li wa irhamni)
       (My Lord, forgive me and have mercy on me)

8. Sujūd (Second Prostration):
   - Say "الله أكبر" as you move into the second prostration.
     - Then recite:
       سُبْحَانَ رَبِّيَ الأَعْلَى
       (Subhana rabbiyal a'la)
       (Glory be to my Lord, the Most High)
       [Repeat at least three times]

9. Rising for the Next Rak'ah:
   - Say "الله أكبر" and then stand up to begin Rak'ah 2.

──────────── Rak'ah 2: ────────────

1. Opening Takbīr: الله أكبر
   (Allāhu Akbar)
   (Allah is the Greatest)

2. Recite al-Fātiha:

a. بِسْمِ اللَّهِ الرَّحْمَٰنِ الرَّحِيمِ
   (Bismillaahir Rahmaanir Raheem)
   (In the name of Allah, the Most Gracious, the Most Merciful)

b. اَلْحَمْدُ لِلَّهِ رَبِّ الْعَالَمِينَ
   (Alhamdu lillahi rabbil 'aalameen)
   (All praise is due to Allah, Lord of all the worlds)

c. الرَّحْمَٰنِ الرَّحِيمِ
   (Ar-Rahmaanir Raheem)
   (The Most Gracious, the Most Merciful)

d. مَالِكِ يَوْمِ الدِّينِ
   (Maaliki yawmid-deen)
   (Master of the Day of Judgment)

e. إِيَّاكَ نَعْبُدُ وَإِيَّاكَ نَسْتَعِينُ
   (Iyyaka na'budu wa iyyaka nasta'een)
   (You alone we worship, and You alone we ask for help)

f. اهْدِنَا الصِّرَاطَ الْمُسْتَقِيمَ

(Ihdinas-siraatal mustaqeem)
(Guide us to the straight path)

g. صِرَاطَ الَّذِينَ أَنْعَمْتَ عَلَيْهِمْ غَيْرِ الْمَغْضُوبِ عَلَيْهِمْ وَلَا الضَّالِّينَ

(Siraatal ladheena an'amta 'alayhim ghayril maghdoobi 'alayhim wa lad-daalleen)

(The path of those upon whom You have bestowed favor, not of those who have earned Your anger nor of those who go astray)

3. Recite a Short Sūrah – Surah al-Ikhlās:

a. قُلْ هُوَ اللَّهُ أَحَدٌ
(Qul huwa Allāhu 'ahad)
(Say, "He is Allah, [Who is] One")

b. اللَّهُ الصَّمَدُ
(Allāhu as-samad)
(Allah, the Eternal Refuge)

c. لَمْ يَلِدْ وَلَمْ يُولَدْ
(Lam yalid wa lam yoolad)
(He neither begets nor is born)

d. وَلَمْ يَكُنْ لَهُ كُفُوًا أَحَدٌ
(Wa lam yakun lahu kufuwan ahad)
(Nor is there to Him any equivalent)

4. Rukū' (Bowing):
   - As you bow, say "الله أكبر"
     - Then recite:
       سُبْحَانَ رَبِّيَ الْعَظِيمِ
       (Subhana rabbiyal 'adheem)
       (Glory be to my Lord, the Most Great)
       [Repeat at least three times]

5. Rising from Rukū':
   - While rising, say:
     سَمِعَ اللَّهُ لِمَنْ حَمِدَه
     (Sami' Allāhu liman hamidah)

(Allah hears those who praise Him)
- Then, while standing, say:

رَبَّنَا وَلَكَ الْحَمْد

(Rabbana wa laka al-hamd)
(Our Lord, to You be all praise)

6. Sujūd (First Prostration):
   - As you go down, say "الله أكبر"
     - Then recite:

   سُبْحَانَ رَبِّيَ الْأَعْلَى

   (Subhana rabbiyal a'la)
   (Glory be to my Lord, the Most High)
   [Repeat at least three times]

7. Brief Sitting (Jalsa):
   - Sit briefly and recite the supplication:

   رَبِّ اغْفِرْ لِي وَارْحَمْنِي وَثُبْ عَلَي

   (Rabbi ighfir li wa irhamni wa tub 'alayya)
   (My Lord, forgive me, have mercy on me, and accept my repentance)

8. Sujūd (Second Prostration):
   - Say "الله أكبر" as you perform the second prostration.
     - Then recite:

   سُبْحَانَ رَبِّيَ الْأَعْلَى

   (Subhana rabbiyal a'la)
   (Glory be to my Lord, the Most High)
   [Repeat at least three times]

9. Final Tashahhud (Sitting for the Testimony):
   - After the second sujūd, sit and recite: التَّحِيَّاتُ لِلَّهِ وَالصَّلَوَاتُ وَالطَّيِّبَات

   (At-tahiyyatu lillahi was-salawatu wat-tayyibatu)
   (All greetings, prayers, and pure words are for Allah)

السَّلَامُ عَلَيْكَ أَيُّهَا النَّبِي

(As-salamu 'alayka ayyuha an-nabiyyu)
(Peace be upon you, O Prophet)

وَرَحْمَةُ اللّهِ وَبَرَكَاتُه
(Wa rahmatullahi wa barakatuhu)
(And the mercy and blessings of Allah)

اَلسَّلَامُ عَلَيْنَا وَعَلَى عِبَادِ اللّهِ الصَّالِحِين
(As-salamu 'alayna wa 'ala 'ibaadil-lahi as-saaliheen)
(Peace be upon us and upon the righteous servants of Allah)

أَشْهَدُ أَنْ لَا إِلَهَ إِلَّا اللّه
(Ash-hadu an la ilaha illallahu)
(I bear witness that there is no deity except Allah)

وَأَشْهَدُ أَنَّ مُحَمَّدًا رَسُولُ اللّه
(Wa ash-hadu anna Muhammadan Rasool Allah)
(And I bear witness that Muhammad is the Messenger of Allah)

10. Taslīm (Concluding the Prayer):
  • To conclude the prayer, first turn your head to the right and say:
    اِلسَّلَامُ عَلَيْكُمْ وَرَحْمَةُ اللّه
    (As-salamu 'alaykum wa rahmatullahi)
    (Peace and mercy of Allah be upon you)
  • Then turn your head to the left and repeat:
    اِلسَّلَامُ عَلَيْكُمْ وَرَحْمَةُ اللّه
    (As-salamu 'alaykum wa rahmatullahi)
    (Peace and mercy of Allah be upon you)

Notes:
• This prayer, known as Salatul Awwabin, is a heartfelt means of seeking forgiveness and turning to Allah in sincere repentance.
• At every movement—standing, bowing, prostrating, and sitting—remember to utter "الله أكبر" with mindfulness of its profound meaning.
• Supplement the prayer during your brief sittings (Jalsa) with personal du'ā for repentance and renewal.

May this prayer of the penitent bring you closer to Allah's infinite mercy and forgiveness.

CHAPTER 26: QASR PRAYER

STEP-BY-STEP QASR PRAYER

Below is an in-depth guide to the Qasr Prayer—a shortened version of the obligatory prayers granted to travelers. This concession reflects the flexibility and compassion of Islamic law, ensuring that even while on the move, you maintain your essential connection with Allah. The Qasr Prayer condenses what would normally be four rak'ahs into two, offering ease without compromising the spirit of worship.

Before You Begin: • Ensure you are in a state of ritual purity (wudu) and have prepared your heart for sincere worship. • Form your niyyah in your heart: "I intend to perform the Qasr Prayer (shortened obligatory prayer) for the sake of Allah."

Rak'ah 1:
---

1. Opening Takbīr (Start of the Prayer):
   الله أكبر
   (Allāhu Akbar)
   (Allah is the Greatest)

2. Recite al-Fātiha (The Opening Chapter):

a. بِسْمِ اللهِ الرَّحْمٰنِ الرَّحِيمِ
 (Bismillaahir Rahmaanir Raheem)
 (In the name of Allah, the Most Gracious, the Most Merciful)

b. اَلْحَمْدُ لِلّٰهِ رَبِّ الْعَالَمِين
 (Alhamdu lillahi rabbil 'aalameen)
 (All praise is due to Allah, Lord of all the worlds)

c. اِلرَّحْمٰنِ الرَّحِيم
 (Ar-Rahmaanir Raheem)
 (The Most Gracious, the Most Merciful)

d. مَالِكِ يَوْمِ الدِّين
 (Maaliki yawmid-deen)
 (Master of the Day of Judgment)

e. اِيَّاكَ نَعْبُدُ وَإِيَّاكَ نَسْتَعِين
 (Iyyaka na'budu wa iyyaka nasta'een)
 (You alone we worship, and You alone we ask for help)

f. اَهْدِنَا الصِّرَاطَ الْمُسْتَقِيم
 (Ihdinas-siraatal mustaqeem)
 (Guide us to the straight path)

g. صِرَاطَ الَّذِينَ أَنْعَمْتَ عَلَيْهِمْ غَيْرِ الْمَغْضُوبِ عَلَيْهِمْ وَلَا الضَّالِّين
 (Siraatal ladheena an'amta 'alayhim ghayril maghdoobi 'alayhim wa lad-daalleen)
 (The path of those upon whom You have bestowed favor, not of those who have earned Your anger nor of those who go astray)

3. Recite a Short Sūrah – Sūrah al-Kāfirūn:

a. قُلْ يَا أَيُّهَا الْكَافِرُون
 (Qul ya ayyuhal kaafirun)
 (Say, "O disbelievers,")

b. لَا أَعْبُدُ مَا تَعْبُدُون
 (Laa a'budu maa ta'budoon)
 (I do not worship what you worship)

c. وَلَا أَنتُمْ عَابِدُونَ مَا أَعْبُدُ

(Wa laa antum 'aabidoon maa a'bud)

(Nor are you worshippers of what I worship)

d. وَلَا أَنَا عَابِدٌ مَا عَبَدتُّمْ

(Wa laa ana 'aabidun maa 'abadtum)

(And I will not be a worshipper of what you have worshipped)

e. وَلَا أَنتُمْ عَابِدُونَ مَا أَعْبُدُ

(Wa laa antum 'aabidoon maa a'bud)

(Nor will you be worshippers of what I worship)

f. لَكُمْ دِينُكُمْ وَلِيَ دِينِ

(Lakum deenkum wa liya deen)

(For you is your religion, and for me is mine)

4. Rukū' (Bowing):

- As you move into the bowing position, say:
  الله أكبر
  (Allāhu Akbar)
  (Allah is the Greatest)
- Then recite:
  سُبْحَانَ رَبِّيَ الْعَظِيمِ
  (Subhana rabbiyal 'adheem)
  (Glory be to my Lord, the Most Great)
  [Repeat at least three times]

5. Rising from Rukū':

- Rise while saying:
  سَمِعَ اللَّهُ لِمَنْ حَمِدَه
  (Sami' Allāhu liman hamidah)
  (Allah hears those who praise Him)
- Then, while standing straight, say:
  رَبَّنَا وَلَكَ الْحَمْدُ
  (Rabbana wa laka al-hamd)

(Our Lord, to You be all praise)

6. Sujūd (First Prostration):

- As you go down into prostration, say:
  الله أكبر
  (Allāhu Akbar)
  (Allah is the Greatest)
- Then recite:
  سُبْحَانَ رَبِّيَ الْأَعْلَى
  (Subhana rabbiyal a'la)
  (Glory be to my Lord, the Most High)
  [Repeat at least three times]

7. Brief Sitting (Jalsa):

- Sit briefly between the two prostrations.
- You may supplicate by reciting:
  رَبِّ اغْفِرْ لِي
  (Rabbi ighfir li)
  (O my Lord, forgive me)

8. Sujūd (Second Prostration):

- Say "الله أكبر"
  (Allāhu Akbar)
  (Allah is the Greatest)
- Then recite:
  سُبْحَانَ رَبِّيَ الْأَعْلَى
  (Subhana rabbiyal a'la)
  (Glory be to my Lord, the Most High)
  [Repeat at least three times]

9. Rising for the Next Rak'ah:
   - Say "الله أكبر" and then stand up to begin Rak'ah 2.

Rak'ah 2:
---

1. Opening Takbīr: الله أكبر
    (Allāhu Akbar)
    (Allah is the Greatest)

2. Recite al-Fātiha:

a. بِسْمِ اللهِ الرَّحْمٰنِ الرَّحِيمِ
(Bismillaahir Rahmaanir Raheem)
(In the name of Allah, the Most Gracious, the Most Merciful)

b. اَلْحَمْدُ لِلّٰهِ رَبِّ الْعَالَمِينَ
(Alhamdu lillahi rabbil 'aalameen)
(All praise is due to Allah, Lord of all the worlds)

c. اِلرَّحْمٰنِ الرَّحِيمِ
(Ar-Rahmaanir Raheem)
(The Most Gracious, the Most Merciful)

d. مَالِكِ يَوْمِ الدِّينِ
(Maaliki yawmid-deen)
(Master of the Day of Judgment)

e. إِيَّاكَ نَعْبُدُ وَإِيَّاكَ نَسْتَعِينُ
(Iyyaka na'budu wa iyyaka nasta'een)
(You alone we worship, and You alone we ask for help)

f. اَهْدِنَا الصِّرَاطَ الْمُسْتَقِيمَ
(Ihdinas-siraatal mustaqeem)
(Guide us to the straight path)

g. صِرَاطَ الَّذِينَ أَنْعَمْتَ عَلَيْهِمْ غَيْرِ الْمَغْضُوبِ عَلَيْهِمْ وَلَا الضَّالِّينَ
(Siraatal ladheena an'amta 'alayhim ghayril maghdoobi 'alayhim wa lad-daalleen)
(The path of those upon whom You have bestowed favor, not of those who have earned Your anger nor of those who go astray)

3. Recite a Short Sūrah – Sūrah al-Ikhlās:

a. قُلْ هُوَ اللهُ أَحَدٌ
(Qul huwa Allāhu 'ahad)

(Say, "He is Allah, [Who is] One")

b. اَللَّهُ الصَّمَدُ
(Allāhu as-samad)
(Allah, the Eternal Refuge)

c. لَمْ يَلِدْ وَلَمْ يُولَدْ
(Lam yalid wa lam yoolad)
(He neither begets nor is born)

d. وَلَمْ يَكُنْ لَهُ كُفُوًا أَحَدٌ
(Wa lam yakun lahu kufuwan ahad)
(Nor is there to Him any equivalent)

4. Rukū' (Bowing):

- As you bow, say "الله أكبر"
  (Allāhu Akbar)
  (Allah is the Greatest)
- Then recite:
  سُبْحَانَ رَبِّيَ الْعَظِيمِ
  (Subhana rabbiyal 'adheem)
  (Glory be to my Lord, the Most Great)
  [Repeat at least three times]

5. Rising from Rukū':

- While rising, say:
  سَمِعَ اللَّهُ لِمَنْ حَمِدَه
  (Sami' Allāhu liman hamidah)
  (Allah hears those who praise Him)
- Then, while standing, say:
  رَبَّنَا وَلَكَ الْحَمْدُ
  (Rabbana wa laka al-hamd)
  (Our Lord, to You be all praise)

6. Sujūd (First Prostration):

- As you go down, say "الله أكبر"
  (Allāhu Akbar)

(Allah is the Greatest)
- Then recite:

سُبْحَانَ رَبِّيَ الْأَعْلَى

(Subhana rabbiyal a'la)
(Glory be to my Lord, the Most High)
   [Repeat at least three times]

7. Brief Sitting (Jalsa):

- Sit briefly and, if you wish, recite a supplication such as:

رَبِّ اغْفِرْ لِي

(Rabbi ighfir li)
(O my Lord, forgive me)

8. Sujūd (Second Prostration):

- Say "الله أكبر" as you perform the second prostration.
(Allāhu Akbar)
(Allah is the Greatest)
- Then recite:

سُبْحَانَ رَبِّيَ الْأَعْلَى

(Subhana rabbiyal a'la)
(Glory be to my Lord, the Most High)
   [Repeat at least three times]

9. Final Tashahhud (Sitting for the Testimony):

- After the second sujūd, sit and recite the Tashahhud:

التَّحِيَّاتُ لِلَّهِ وَالصَّلَوَاتُ وَالطَّيِّبَاتُ

(At-tahiyyatu lillahi was-salawatu wat-tayyibatu)
(All greetings, prayers, and pure words are for Allah)

السَّلَامُ عَلَيْكَ أَيُّهَا النَّبِيُّ

(As-salamu 'alayka ayyuha an-nabiyyu)
(Peace be upon you, O Prophet)

وَرَحْمَةُ اللَّهِ وَبَرَكَاتُهُ

(Wa rahmatullahi wa barakatuhu)
(And the mercy and blessings of Allah)

اَلسَّلَامُ عَلَيْنَا وَعَلَى عِبَادِ اللَّهِ الصَّالِحِينَ

(As-salamu 'alayna wa 'ala 'ibaadil-lahi as-saaliheen)
(Peace be upon us and upon the righteous servants of Allah)

أَشْهَدُ أَنْ لَا إِلَهَ إِلَّا اللَّهُ

(Ash-hadu an la ilaha illallahu)
(I bear witness that there is no deity except Allah)

وَأَشْهَدُ أَنَّ مُحَمَّدًا رَسُولُ اللَّهِ

(Wa ash-hadu anna Muhammadan Rasool Allah)
(And I bear witness that Muhammad is the Messenger of Allah)

10. Taslīm (Concluding the Prayer):

- To conclude, turn your head to the right and say:
  اِلسَّلَامُ عَلَيْكُمْ وَرَحْمَةُ اللَّهِ
  (As-salamu 'alaykum wa rahmatullahi)
  (Peace and mercy of Allah be upon you)

- Then turn your head to the left and repeat:
  اِلسَّلَامُ عَلَيْكُمْ وَرَحْمَةُ اللَّهِ
  (As-salamu 'alaykum wa rahmatullahi)
  (Peace and mercy of Allah be upon you)

Notes:
- This Qasr Prayer is performed by travelers as a shortening of the standard four-rak'ah obligatory prayer, reducing it to two rak'ahs while preserving the essential components of worship.
- At each transition (standing, bowing, prostrating, and sitting), it is customary to say "اللهُ أَكْبَر" (Allāhu Akbar) – (Allah is the Greatest).
- You are encouraged to add personal supplications (du'ā) during sitting (Jalsa) if you wish.

May this Qasr Prayer serve as a means to keep you connected with Allah even on your journeys.

CHAPTER 27: SALATUL DHIKR

STEP-BY-STEP Salatul Dhikr Prayer

Below is an in-depth guide to Salatul Dhikr—a dedicated prayer designed to immerse the believer in the remembrance of Allah through the recitation of His beautiful names and praises. This meditative practice nurtures mindfulness, gratitude, and spiritual awareness. Before you begin, ensure that you are in a state of ritual purity (wudu) and have calmed your heart for sincere dhikr.

Before You Begin:
• Form your niyyah in your heart: "I intend to perform two rak'ahs of Salatul Dhikr for the remembrance of Allah."

Rak'ah 1:

1. Opening Takbīr (Start of the Prayer):
   الله أكبر
   (Allāhu Akbar)
   (Allah is the Greatest)

2. Recite al-Fātiha (The Opening Chapter):

a. بِسْمِ اللَّهِ الرَّحْمَٰنِ الرَّجِيم
   (Bismillaahir Rahmaanir Raheem)

(In the name of Allah, the Most Gracious, the Most Merciful)

b. اَلْحَمْدُ لِلَّهِ رَبِّ الْعَالَمِين
(Alhamdu lillahi rabbil 'aalameen)
(All praise is due to Allah, Lord of all the worlds)

c. اِلرَّحْمَنِ الرَّحِيم
(Ar-Rahmaanir Raheem)
(The Most Gracious, the Most Merciful)

d. مَالِكِ يَوْمِ الدِّين
(Maaliki yawmid-deen)
(Master of the Day of Judgment)

e. إِيَّاكَ نَعْبُدُ وَإِيَّاكَ نَسْتَعِين
(Iyyaka na'budu wa iyyaka nasta'een)
(You alone we worship, and You alone we ask for help)

f. اهْدِنَا الصِّرَاطَ الْمُسْتَقِيم
(Ihdinas-siraatal mustaqeem)
(Guide us to the straight path)

g. صِرَاطَ الَّذِينَ أَنْعَمْتَ عَلَيْهِمْ غَيْرِ الْمَغْضُوبِ عَلَيْهِمْ وَلَا الضَّالِّين
(Siraatal ladheena an'amta 'alayhim ghayril maghdoobi 'alayhim wa lad-daalleen)
(The path of those upon whom You have bestowed favor, not of those who have earned Your anger nor of those who go astray)

3. Dedicated Dhikr Recitations:
    a. Recite:
    سِبْحَانَ اللَّهِ وَبِحَمْدِه
    (SubhanAllahi wa bihamdih)
    (Glory be to Allah and praise Him)
        [Repeat at least three times]

    b. Recite:
    لَا إِلَهَ إِلَّا اللَّه
    (La ilaha illallah)
    (There is no deity except Allah)

[Repeat at least three times]

c. Then, in a slow and reflective manner, recite the following Most Beautiful Names of Allah:

- اْلرَّحْمَان
  (Ar-Rahman)
  (The Most Gracious)

- اْلرَّحِيم
  (Ar-Rahim)
  (The Most Merciful)

- اْلمَلِك
  (Al-Malik)
  (The King)

- اْلقُدُّوس
  (Al-Quddus)
  (The Most Holy)

- اْلسَّلَام
  (As-Salam)
  (The Source of Peace)

- اْلمُؤْمِن
  (Al-Mu'min)
  (The Granter of Security)

- اْلمُهَيْمِن
  (Al-Muhaymin)
  (The Protector)

[Recite each name once with heartfelt reflection on its meaning.]

4. Rukū' (Bowing):
   • As you move into the bowing position, say "Allāhu Akbar."
   • Then recite:

سِبْحَانَ رَبِّيَ الْعَظِيم

(Subhana rabbiyal 'adheem)
(Glory be to my Lord, the Most Great)
   [Repeat at least three times]

5. Rising from Rukū':
   - While rising, say:
   سَمِعَ اللَّهُ لِمَنْ حَمِدَه

   (Sami' Allāhu liman hamidah)
   (Allah hears those who praise Him)
   - Then, while standing upright, say:
   رَبَّنَا وَلَكَ الْحَمد

   (Rabbana wa laka al-hamd)
   (Our Lord, to You be all praise)

6. Sujūd (First Prostration):
   - As you descend into prostration, say "Allāhu Akbar."
   - Then recite:
   سُبْحَانَ رَبِّيَ الْأَعْلَى

   (Subhana rabbiyal a'la)
   (Glory be to my Lord, the Most High)
      [Repeat at least three times]

7. Brief Sitting (Jalsa):
   - Sit briefly between the two prostrations and recite:
   رَبِّ اغْفِرْ لِي

   (Rabbi ighfir li)
   (O my Lord, forgive me)

8. Sujūd (Second Prostration):
   - Say "Allāhu Akbar" as you move into the second prostration.
   - Then recite:
   سُبْحَانَ رَبِّيَ الْأَعْلَى

   (Subhana rabbiyal a'la)
   (Glory be to my Lord, the Most High)
      [Repeat at least three times]

9. Rising for the Next Rak'ah:
   - Say "Allāhu Akbar" and stand to begin Rak'ah 2.

Rak'ah 2:

---

1. Opening Takbīr:
   الله أكبر
   (Allāhu Akbar)
   (Allah is the Greatest)

2. Recite al-Fātiha:

   a. بِسْمِ اللَّهِ الرَّحْمَٰنِ الرَّحِيمِ
   (Bismillaahir Rahmaanir Raheem)
   (In the name of Allah, the Most Gracious, the Most Merciful)

   b. اَلْحَمْدُ لِلَّهِ رَبِّ الْعَالَمِين
   (Alhamdu lillahi rabbil 'aalameen)
   (All praise is due to Allah, Lord of all the worlds)

   c. الرَّحْمَٰنِ الرَّحِيمِ
   (Ar-Rahmaanir Raheem)
   (The Most Gracious, the Most Merciful)

   d. مَالِكِ يَوْمِ الدِّين
   (Maaliki yawmid-deen)
   (Master of the Day of Judgment)

   e. إِيَّاكَ نَعْبُدُ وَإِيَّاكَ نَسْتَعِين
   (Iyyaka na'budu wa iyyaka nasta'een)
   (You alone we worship, and You alone we ask for help)

   f. اهْدِنَا الصِّرَاطَ الْمُسْتَقِيم
   (Ihdinas-siraatal mustaqeem)
   (Guide us to the straight path)

   g. صِرَاطَ الَّذِينَ أَنْعَمْتَ عَلَيْهِمْ غَيْرِ الْمَغْضُوبِ عَلَيْهِمْ وَلَا الضَّالِّين
   (Siraatal ladheena an'amta 'alayhim ghayril maghdoobi

'alayhim wa lad-daalleen)
(The path of those upon whom You have bestowed favor, not of those who have earned Your anger nor of those who go astray)

3. Supplementary Dhikr Recitations:
    a. Recite once again:
    سِبْحَانَ اللَّهِ وَبِحَمْدِه
    (SubhanAllahi wa bihamdih)
    (Glory be to Allah and praise Him)
    [Repeat at least three times]

b. Recite:
   لَا إِلَهَ إِلَّا اللَّه
   (La ilaha illallah)
   (There is no deity except Allah)
   [Repeat at least three times]

c. Then invoke a supplication of remembrance:
   اللَّهُمَّ ذَكِّرْنِي بِذِكْرِكِ
   (Allahumma dhakkirni bithikrika)
   (O Allah, remind me with Your remembrance)
   [Reflect on this plea as you continue.]

d. Conclude this segment by slowly reciting the same sequence of Allah's beautiful names as in Rak'ah 1:
   - الرَّحْمَان (Ar-Rahman) (The Most Gracious)
   - الرَّحِيم (Ar-Rahim) (The Most Merciful)
   - المَالِك (Al-Malik) (The King)
   - القُدُّوس (Al-Quddus) (The Most Holy)
   - السَّلَام (As-Salam) (The Source of Peace)
   - المُؤْمِن (Al-Mu'min) (The Granter of Security)
   - المُهَيْمِن (Al-Muhaymin) (The Protector)

4. Rukū' (Bowing):
    - As you bow, say "Allāhu Akbar."
    - Then recite:
    سُبْحَانَ رَبِّيَ الْعَظِيم
    (Subhana rabbiyal 'adheem)

(Glory be to my Lord, the Most Great)
[Repeat at least three times]

5. Rising from Rukū':
   - While rising, say:
   سَمِعَ اللَّهُ لِمَنْ حَمِدَه
   (Sami' Allāhu liman hamidah)
   (Allah hears those who praise Him)
   - Then, while standing, say:
   رَبَّنَا وَلَكَ الْحَمْدِ
   (Rabbana wa laka al-hamd)
   (Our Lord, to You be all praise)

6. Sujūd (First Prostration):
   - As you descend, say "Allāhu Akbar."
   - Then recite in prostration:
   سُبْحَانَ رَبِّيَ الْأَعْلَى
   (Subhana rabbiyal a'la)
   (Glory be to my Lord, the Most High)
   [Repeat at least three times]

7. Brief Sitting (Jalsa):
   - Sit briefly and recite a humble supplication:
   رَبِّ اغْفِرْ لِي
   (Rabbi ighfir li)
   (O my Lord, forgive me)

8. Sujūd (Second Prostration):
   - Say "Allāhu Akbar" as you perform the second prostration.
   - Then recite:
   سُبْحَانَ رَبِّيَ الْأَعْلَى
   (Subhana rabbiyal a'la)
   (Glory be to my Lord, the Most High)
   [Repeat at least three times]

9. Final Tashahhud (Sitting for the Testimony):

- After the second sujūd, sit and recite the Tashahhud:

اَلتَّحِيَّاتُ لِلَّهِ وَالصَّلَوَاتُ وَالطَّيِّبَاتُ
(At-tahiyyatu lillahi was-salawatu wat-tayyibatu)
(All greetings, prayers, and pure words are for Allah)

اَلسَّلَامُ عَلَيْكَ أَيُّهَا النَّبِيُّ
(As-salamu 'alayka ayyuha an-nabiyyu)
(Peace be upon you, O Prophet)

وَرَحْمَةُ اللَّهِ وَبَرَكَاتُهُ
(Wa rahmatullahi wa barakatuhu)
(And the mercy and blessings of Allah)

اَلسَّلَامُ عَلَيْنَا وَعَلَى عِبَادِ اللَّهِ الصَّالِحِينَ
(As-salamu 'alayna wa 'ala 'ibaadil-lahi as-saaliheen)
(Peace be upon us and upon the righteous servants of Allah)

أَشْهَدُ أَنْ لَا إِلَهَ إِلَّا اللَّهُ
(Ash-hadu an la ilaha illallahu)
(I bear witness that there is no deity except Allah)

وَأَشْهَدُ أَنَّ مُحَمَّدًا رَسُولُ اللَّهِ
(Wa ash-hadu anna Muhammadan Rasool Allah)
(And I bear witness that Muhammad is the Messenger of Allah)

10. Taslīm (Concluding the Prayer):
    - To conclude, turn your head to the right and say:
      اَلسَّلَامُ عَلَيْكُمْ وَرَحْمَةُ اللَّهِ
      (As-salamu 'alaykum wa rahmatullahi)
      (Peace and mercy of Allah be upon you)
    - Then turn your head to the left and repeat:
      اَلسَّلَامُ عَلَيْكُمْ وَرَحْمَةُ اللَّهِ
      (As-salamu 'alaykum wa rahmatullahi)
      (Peace and mercy of Allah be upon you)

Notes:

- The recitations within Salatul Dhikr are meant to foster deep contemplation and spiritual mindfulness.
- As you articulate each phrase and reflect on the meanings of Allah's names, allow your heart to be fully present in His remembrance.
- This prayer can be performed in a quiet, undisturbed environment to enhance your connection with the Divine.

CHAPTER 28: QUNUT NAZILAH

STEP-BY-STEP Qunut Nazilah Prayer

Below is the full text of the Qunut Nazilah supplication—a heartfelt plea recited during times of calamity or communal distress. Through this supplication, believers seek Allah's mercy, protection, and guidance in moments of hardship. Ensure that you are in a state of ritual purity (wudu) and that your heart is calm and sincere before reciting this supplication.

Before You Begin: • Form your niyyah in your heart: "I intend to recite the Qunut Nazilah supplication for the sake of Allah during this time of distress."

1. اَللّٰهُمَّ إِنَّكَ أَنْتَ الْحَكِيمُ الْخَبِيرُ
   (Allahumma innaka anta al-hakīm al-khabīr)
   (O Allah, indeed You are the All-Wise, All-Aware)

2. اَللّٰهُمَّ يَا ذُو الْجَلَالِ وَالْإِكْرَامِ، أَسْتُرْ عَلَيْنَا حِلْمَتَكَ وَرَحْمَتَكَ
   (Allahumma yā dhū al-jalāl wa al-ikrām, astur 'alaynā hilmataka wa rahmataka)
   (O Allah, Possessor of Majesty and Honor, cover us with Your protection and mercy)

3. اِللّٰهُمَّ إِنَّ هَذَا الزَّمَانَ مَحْشُورٌ بِالْفَوَاحِشِ وَالْمِحَنِ

(Allahumma inna hādhā az-zamān mashūrun bil-fawāḥish wal-miḥan)

(O Allah, this time is overwhelmed with immorality and trials)

4. فَأَنْقِذْنَا مِنْ كُلِّ دَابَّةِ السُّوءِ، وَاقْضِ عَنَّا هَذَا الْبَلَاءِ

(Fa anqidhnā min kulli dābbati as-suw', wa aqdi 'annā hādhā al-balā')

(So, save us from every source of evil and alleviate this calamity from us)

5. اللَّهُمَّ أَنْزِلْ ضِيَاءَ رَحْمَتِكَ عَلَيْنَا وَطَهِّرْ قُلُوبَنَا

(Allahumma anzil ḍiyā'a raḥmatika 'alaynā wa ṭahhir qulūbanā)

(O Allah, send down the light of Your mercy upon us and purify our hearts)

6. وَارْزُقْنَا الثَّبَاتَ فِي كُلِّ خُطُوَاتِنَا، وَاجْعَلْ أَمْرَنَا فَرَجًا وَخَلَاصًا

(Wa arzuqnā ath-thibāta fī kulli khuṭuwātinā, wa ij'al amranā farajan wa khalāṣan)

(Grant us steadfastness in every step and make our affairs a means of relief and deliverance)

7. اللَّهُمَّ صَلِّ عَلَى مُحَمَّدٍ وَأَصْحَابِهِ

(Allahumma ṣalli 'alā Muḥammadin wa aṣḥābihi)

(O Allah, send blessings upon Muhammad and his companions)

8. وَاجْعَلْ شِفَاءَ قُلُوبِنَا مِنْ جَمِيعِ آثَامِنَا

(Wa ij'al shifā'a qulūbinā min jamī' āthāminā)

(And grant healing to our hearts from all our sins)

9. رَبَّنَا آمَنَّا بِكَ، وَتَوَكَّلْنَا عَلَيْكَ

(Rabbana amanna bika, wa tawakkalnā 'alayka)

(Our Lord, we have believed in You and placed our trust in You)

10. فَأَنْجِنَا مِنْ كُلِّ كَرْبٍ، وَامْنَحْنَا فَرَجًا وَهُدًى

(Fa anjunā min kulli karbin, wa amnaḥnā farajan wa

hudan)

(So save us from every distress, and grant us relief and guidance)

11. سِبْحَانَكَ اللَّهُمَّ، إِنَّكَ رَبُّ الْعَظِيم

(Subḥānak Allahumma, innaka rabbul 'aẓīm)

(Glory be to You, O Allah, indeed You are the Lord of the Almighty)

12. آمِين

(Āmīn)

(Ameen)

——————— End of Qunut Nazilah Prayer ———————

CHAPTER 29: SALATUL SHIFA

STEP-BY-STEP Salatul Shifa (Prayer for Healing)

Below is an in-depth guide to Salatul Shifa – the Prayer for Healing – a sacred supplication intended to seek both physical and spiritual restoration from Allah. This prayer offers solace in times of illness and distress and serves as a reminder of the Divine Power to restore and renew the spirit. Before you begin, ensure you are in a state of wudu (ritual purity) and have prepared your heart and mind for sincere supplication.

Before You Begin:
• Form your niyyah in your heart: "I intend to perform two rak'ahs of Salatul Shifa, seeking healing and renewal from Allah."

Rak'ah 1:

1. Opening Takbīr (Start of the Prayer):
   الله أكبر
   (Allāhu Akbar)
   (Allah is the Greatest)

2. Recite al-Fātiha (The Opening Chapter):
   a. بِسْمِ اللَّهِ الرَّحْمَٰنِ الرَّحِيمِ

(Bismillaahir Rahmaanir Raheem)
(In the name of Allah, the Most Gracious, the Most Merciful)

b. اَلْحَمْدُ لِلَّهِ رَبِّ الْعَالَمِين

(Alhamdu lillahi rabbil 'aalameen)
(All praise is due to Allah, Lord of all the worlds)

c. اِلرَّحْمَٰنِ الرَّحِيم

(Ar-Rahmaanir Raheem)
(The Most Gracious, the Most Merciful)

d. مَالِكِ يَوْمِ الدِّين

(Maaliki yawmid-deen)
(Master of the Day of Judgment)

e. إِيَّاكَ نَعْبُدُ وَإِيَّاكَ نَسْتَعِين

(Iyyaka na'budu wa iyyaka nasta'een)
(You alone we worship, and You alone we ask for help)

f. اهْدِنَا الصِّرَاطَ الْمُسْتَقِيم

(Ihdinas-siraatal mustaqeem)
(Guide us to the straight path)

g. صِرَاطَ الَّذِينَ أَنْعَمْتَ عَلَيْهِم

(Siraatal ladheena an'amta 'alayhim)
(The path of those upon whom You have bestowed favor)

غَيْرِ الْمَغْضُوبِ عَلَيْهِمْ وَلَا الضَّالِّين

(ghayril maghdoobi 'alayhim wa lad-daalleen)
(not of those who have earned Your anger nor of those who go astray)

3. Recite the Healing Supplication:

اللَّهُمَّ رَبَّ النَّاسِ، أَذْهِبِ الْبَأْسَ، اشْفِ أَنْتَ الشَّافِي،

(Allahumma Rabb an-naas, adhhibil ba'sa, ishfi, anta ash-shafi)
(O Allah, Lord of humankind, remove the affliction and heal, for You are the Healer)

لَا شِفَاءَ إِلَّا شِفَاؤُكَ، شِفَاءً لَا يُغَادِرُ سَقَمًا

(la shifa'a illa shifa'uka, shifa'an la yughadiru saqaman)
(There is no cure except Your cure, a healing that leaves no illness behind)

4. Recite a Short Sūrah – Sūrah al-Ikhlās:

a. قُلْ هُوَ اللَّهُ أَحَدٌ
(Qul huwa Allāhu 'ahad)
(Say, "He is Allah, [Who is] One")

b. اللَّهُ الصَّمَدُ
(Allāhu as-samad)
(Allah is the Eternal Refuge)

c. لَمْ يَلِدْ وَلَمْ يُولَدْ
(Lam yalid wa lam yoolad)
(He neither begets nor is born)

d. وَلَمْ يَكُنْ لَهُ كُفُوًا أَحَدٌ
(Wa lam yakun lahu kufuwan ahad)
(And there is none comparable to Him)

5. Rukū' (Bowing):

• As you move into the bowing position, say "Allāhu Akbar."
• Then recite:
سُبْحَانَ رَبِّيَ الْعَظِيم
(Subhana rabbiyal 'adheem)
(Glory be to my Lord, the Most Great)   [Repeat at least three times]

6. Rising from Rukū':

• Rise while saying:
سَمِعَ اللَّهُ لِمَنْ حَمِدَه
(Sami' Allāhu liman hamidah)
(Allah hears those who praise Him)
• Then, while standing, say:

رَبَّنَا وَلَكَ الْحَمْدُ

(Rabbana wa laka al-hamd)
(Our Lord, to You be all praise)

7. Sujūd (First Prostration):

• As you descend into prostration, say "Allāhu Akbar."
• Then recite:

سُبْحَانَ رَبِّيَ الْأَعْلَى

(Subhana rabbiyal a'la)
(Glory be to my Lord, the Most High)   [Repeat at least three times]

• In this intimate moment, make an additional supplication for healing:

اللَّهُمَّ اشْفِنِي وَاشْفِ كُلَّ مَرَضٍ

(Allahumma ishfi ni wa ishfi kulla maradin)
(O Allah, heal me and heal every illness)

8. Brief Sitting (Jalsa):

• Sit briefly between the two prostrations.
• Supplicate, for example:

رَبِّ اغْفِرْ لِي

(Rabbi ighfir li)
(O my Lord, forgive me)

• And add:

اللَّهُمَّ رَحْمَتُكَ تُحْيِي قَلْبِي

(Allahumma rahmatuka tuhyee qalbi)
(O Allah, Your mercy enlivens my heart)

9. Sujūd (Second Prostration):

• Say "Allāhu Akbar" as you perform the second prostration.
• Then recite:

سُبْحَانَ رَبِّيَ الْأَعْلَى

(Subhana rabbiyal a'la)
(Glory be to my Lord, the Most High)   [Repeat at least three times]

- Optionally, repeat the healing supplication:

   اللّٰهُمَّ اشْفِني وَاشْفِ مَرْضَانَا

   (Allahumma ishfi ni wa ishfi mardanā)

   (O Allah, heal me and heal our sick)

10. Rising for the Next Rak'ah:
    - Say "Allāhu Akbar" and stand to begin Rak'ah 2.

Rak'ah 2:

---

1. Opening Takbīr:

   الله أكبر

   (Allāhu Akbar)

   (Allah is the Greatest)

2. Recite al-Fātiha:

   a. بِسْمِ اللَّهِ الرَّحْمَٰنِ الرَّحِيمِ

   (Bismillaahir Rahmaanir Raheem)

   (In the name of Allah, the Most Gracious, the Most Merciful)

   b. اَلْحَمْدُ لِلَّهِ رَبِّ الْعَالَمِينَ

   (Alhamdu lillahi rabbil 'aalameen)

   (All praise is due to Allah, Lord of all the worlds)

   c. الرَّحْمَٰنِ الرَّحِيمِ

   (Ar-Rahmaanir Raheem)

   (The Most Gracious, the Most Merciful)

   d. مَالِكِ يَوْمِ الدِّينِ

   (Maaliki yawmid-deen)

   (Master of the Day of Judgment)

   e. إِيَّاكَ نَعْبُدُ وَإِيَّاكَ نَسْتَعِينُ

   (Iyyaka na'budu wa iyyaka nasta'een)

   (You alone we worship, and You alone we ask for help)

   f. اهْدِنَا الصِّرَاطَ الْمُسْتَقِيمَ

(Ihdinas-siraatal mustaqeem)
(Guide us to the straight path)

g. صِرَاطَ الَّذِينَ أَنْعَمْتَ عَلَيْهِم
(Siraatal ladheena an'amta 'alayhim)
(The path of those upon whom You have bestowed favor)

غَيْرِ الْمَغْضُوبِ عَلَيْهِمْ وَلَا الضَّالِّين
(ghayril maghdoobi 'alayhim wa lad-daalleen)
(not of those who have earned Your anger nor of those who go astray)

3. Recite the Healing Supplication for the Second Rak'ah:

اَللَّهُمَّ إِنِّي أَسْأَلُكَ شِفَاءً عَاجِلًا، وَرَاحَةً دَائِمَة
(Allahumma inni as'aluka shifa'an 'ajilan, wa rahatan da'imatan)
(O Allah, I ask You for swift healing and constant solace)

وَتَجَدُّدًا لِرُوحِي وَجَسَدِي
(wa tajaddudan li ruhi wa jasadi)
(and renewal for my soul and body)

4. Recite a Short Sūrah – Sūrah al-Ikhlās:

a. قُلْ هُوَ اللَّهُ أَحَد
(Qul huwa Allāhu 'ahad)
(Say, "He is Allah, [Who is] One")

b. اللَّهُ الصَّمَد
(Allāhu as-samad)
(Allah is the Eternal Refuge)

c. لَمْ يَلِدْ وَلَمْ يُولَد
(Lam yalid wa lam yoolad)
(He neither begets nor is born)

d. وَلَمْ يَكُنْ لَهُ كُفُوًا أَحَد
(Wa lam yakun lahu kufuwan ahad)
(And there is none comparable to Him)

5. Rukū' (Bowing):

- As you bow, say "Allāhu Akbar."
- Recite:

سُبْحَانَ رَبِّيَ الْعَظِيم

(Subhana rabbiyal 'adheem)

(Glory be to my Lord, the Most Great)   [Repeat at least three times]

6. Rising from Rukū':

- While rising, say:

سَمِعَ اللَّهُ لِمَنْ حَمِدَه

(Sami' Allāhu liman hamidah)

(Allah hears those who praise Him)

- Then, while standing, say:

رَبَّنَا وَلَكَ الْحَمْد

(Rabbana wa laka al-hamd)

(Our Lord, to You be all praise)

7. Sujūd (First Prostration):

- Descend into prostration with "Allāhu Akbar."
- Recite:

سُبْحَانَ رَبِّيَ الْأَعْلَى

(Subhana rabbiyal a'la)

(Glory be to my Lord, the Most High)   [Repeat at least three times]

- Invoke healing:

اللَّهُمَّ اشْفِني وَاشْفِ مَرْضَانَا

(Allahumma ishfi ni wa ishfi mardanā)

(O Allah, heal me and heal our sick)

8. Brief Sitting (Jalsa):

- Sit briefly and recite:

رَبِّ اغْفِرْ لِي

(Rabbi ighfir li)

(O my Lord, forgive me)

9. Sujūd (Second Prostration):

• Perform the second prostration saying "Allāhu Akbar."
• Recite:
سُبْحَانَ رَبِّيَ الْأَعْلَى
(Subhana rabbiyal a'la)
(Glory be to my Lord, the Most High)   [Repeat at least three times]

• Optionally, repeat the healing plea:
هُمَّ اشْفِنِي وَاشْفِ مَرْضَانَاالل
(Allahumma ishfi ni wa ishfi mardanā)
(O Allah, heal me and heal our sick)

10. Final Tashahhud (Sitting for the Testimony):

• After the second sujūd, sit and recite:
التَّحِيَّاتُ لِلَّهِ وَالصَّلَوَاتُ وَالطَّيِّبَاتُ
(At-tahiyyatu lillahi was-salawatu wat-tayyibatu)
(All greetings, prayers, and pure words are for Allah)

السَّلَامُ عَلَيْكَ أَيُّهَا النَّبِيُّ
(As-salamu 'alayka ayyuha an-nabiyyu)
(Peace be upon you, O Prophet)

وَرَحْمَةُ اللَّهِ وَبَرَكَاتُهُ
(Wa rahmatullahi wa barakatuhu)
(And the mercy and blessings of Allah)

السَّلَامُ عَلَيْنَا وَعَلَى عِبَادِ اللَّهِ الصَّالِحِينَ
(As-salamu 'alayna wa 'ala 'ibaadil-lahi as-saaliheen)
(Peace be upon us and upon the righteous servants of Allah)

أَشْهَدُ أَنْ لَا إِلَهَ إِلَّا اللَّهُ
(Ash-hadu an la ilaha illallahu)
(I bear witness that there is no deity except Allah)

وَأَشْهَدُ أَنَّ مُحَمَّدًا رَسُولُ اللَّهِ
(Wa ash-hadu anna Muhammadan Rasool Allah)

(And I bear witness that Muhammad is the Messenger of Allah)

11. Concluding Healing Supplication:

- In your final sitting, supplicate for comprehensive healing:

اَللَّهُمَّ اشْفِ جَمِيعَ مَرْضَانَا وَمَرْضَى الْمُسْلِمِين

(Allahumma ishfi jami'a mardanā wa marda al-muslimeen)
(O Allah, heal all our sick and the sick among the Muslims)

اِللَّهُمَّ ارْزُقْنَا الْعَافِيَةَ فِي الدُّنْيَا وَالآخِرَة

(Allahumma arzuqna al-'afiyah fid-dunya wal-akhirah)
(O Allah, grant us well-being in this world and in the Hereafter)

12. Taslīm (Concluding the Prayer):

- To conclude, turn your head to the right and say:

اِلسَّلَامُ عَلَيْكُمْ وَرَحْمَةُ اللّٰه

(As-salamu 'alaykum wa rahmatullahi)
(Peace and mercy of Allah be upon you)

- Then turn your head to the left and repeat:

اِلسَّلَامُ عَلَيْكُمْ وَرَحْمَةُ اللّٰه

(As-salamu 'alaykum wa rahmatullahi)
(Peace and mercy of Allah be upon you)

Notes:
- At every transition—standing, bowing, prostrating, and sitting—recite "Allāhu Akbar."
- The repeated supplications and healing invocations reflect the Sunnah and the believer's constant reliance on Allah for both physical and spiritual renewal.
- Feel free to add personal du'ā during sitting (Jalsa) to invoke additional comfort and healing.

May Salatul Shifa bring you restoration, solace, and a renewed spirit through the mercy of Allah.

CHAPTER 30: SALATUL RIZQ

STEP-BY-STEP Salatul Rizq (Prayer for Sustenance)

Below is an in-depth guide to Salatul Rizq—a sacred voluntary prayer performed to seek Allah's provision and blessings in one's livelihood. This prayer reaffirms a believer's trust in divine sustenance, encourages ethical earning, and nurtures gratitude for every blessing received. May Allah grant abundance in halal sustenance to all who recite it with sincerity.

Before You Begin:
- Ensure you are in a state of ritual purity (wudu).
- Form your niyyah in your heart: "I intend to perform two rak'ahs of Salatul Rizq for the sake of Allah, seeking His provision and blessings in my sustenance."

Rak'ah 1:
---

1. Opening Takbīr (Start of the Prayer):
   الله أكبر
   (Allāhu Akbar)
   (Allah is the Greatest)

2. Recite al-Fātiha (The Opening Chapter):

a. بِسْمِ اللهِ الرَّحْمٰنِ الرَّحِيم
(Bismillaahir Rahmaanir Raheem)
(In the name of Allah, the Most Gracious, the Most Merciful)

b. اَلْحَمْدُ لِلّٰهِ رَبِّ الْعَالَمِين
(Alhamdu lillahi rabbil 'aalameen)
(All praise is due to Allah, Lord of all the worlds)

c. الرَّحْمٰنِ الرَّحِيم
(Ar-Rahmaanir Raheem)
(The Most Gracious, the Most Merciful)

d. مَالِكِ يَوْمِ الدِّين
(Maaliki yawmid-deen)
(Master of the Day of Judgment)

e. إِيَّاكَ نَعْبُدُ وَإِيَّاكَ نَسْتَعِين
(Iyyaka na'budu wa iyyaka nasta'een)
(You alone we worship, and You alone we ask for help)

f. اهْدِنَا الصِّرَاطَ الْمُسْتَقِيم
(Ihdinas-siraatal mustaqeem)
(Guide us to the straight path)

g. صِرَاطَ الَّذِينَ أَنْعَمْتَ عَلَيْهِم
(Siraatal ladheena an'amta 'alayhim)
(The path of those upon whom You have bestowed favor)

3. Recite the Special Supplication for Rizq:

اَللّٰهُمَّ ارْزُقْنِي رِزْقاً حَلَالاً طَيِّبًا
(Allahumma arzuqni rizqan halalun tayyiban)
(O Allah, grant me lawful and pure sustenance)

وَافْتَحْ لِي أَبْوَابَ رِزْقِك
(Waftah li abwaaba rizqika)
(Open for me the doors of Your provision)

4. Rukū' (Bowing):

- Say "Allāhu Akbar" as you bow.
- Then recite:

    سُبْحَانَ رَبِّيَ الْعَظِيم

    (Subhana rabbiyal 'adheem)
    (Glory be to my Lord, the Most Great)
    [Repeat at least three times]

5. Rising from Rukū':
   - While rising, say:

     سَمِعَ اللَّهُ لِمَنْ حَمِدَه

     (Sami' Allāhu liman hamidah)
     (Allah hears those who praise Him)
   - Then, standing upright, say:

     رَبَّنَا وَلَكَ الْحَمْد

     (Rabbana wa laka al-hamd)
     (Our Lord, to You be all praise)

6. Sujūd (First Prostration):
   - Say "Allāhu Akbar" and go into prostration.
   - Then recite:

     سُبْحَانَ رَبِّيَ الْأَعْلَى

     (Subhana rabbiyal a'la)
     (Glory be to my Lord, the Most High)
     [Repeat at least three times]

7. Brief Sitting (Jalsa):
   - Sit briefly between the two prostrations.
   - You may supplicate, for example:

     رَبِّ اغْفِرْ لِي وَارْزُقْنِي

     (Rabbi ighfir li warzuqni)
     (My Lord, forgive me and grant me sustenance)

8. Sujūd (Second Prostration):
   - Say "Allāhu Akbar" as you lower into the second prostration.
   - Then recite:

     سُبْحَانَ رَبِّيَ الْأَعْلَى

(Subhana rabbiyal a'la)
(Glory be to my Lord, the Most High)
[Repeat at least three times]

9. Rising for the Next Rak'ah:
   - Say "Allāhu Akbar" and stand up to begin Rak'ah 2.

Rak'ah 2:

---

1. Opening Takbīr:
   الله أكبر
   (Allāhu Akbar)
   (Allah is the Greatest)

2. Recite al-Fātiha:

a. بِسْمِ اللَّهِ الرَّحْمَٰنِ الرَّحِيمِ
   (Bismillaahir Rahmaanir Raheem)
   (In the name of Allah, the Most Gracious, the Most Merciful)

b. اَلْحَمْدُ لِلَّهِ رَبِّ الْعَالَمِين
   (Alhamdu lillahi rabbil 'aalameen)
   (All praise is due to Allah, Lord of all the worlds)

c. الرَّحْمَٰنِ الرَّحِيم
   (Ar-Rahmaanir Raheem)
   (The Most Gracious, the Most Merciful)

d. مَالِكِ يَوْمِ الدِّين
   (Maaliki yawmid-deen)
   (Master of the Day of Judgment)

e. إِيَّاكَ نَعْبُدُ وَإِيَّاكَ نَسْتَعِين
   (Iyyaka na'budu wa iyyaka nasta'een)
   (You alone we worship, and You alone we ask for help)

f. اَهْدِنَا الصِّرَاطَ الْمُسْتَقِيم
   (Ihdinas-siraatal mustaqeem)

(Guide us to the straight path)

g. صِرَاطَ الَّذِينَ أَنْعَمْتَ عَلَيْهِمْ
(Siraatal ladheena an'amta 'alayhim)
(The path of those upon whom You have bestowed favor)

3. Recite the Special Supplication for Rizq:
اللَّهُمَّ بَارِكْ لِي فِي رِزْقِي
(Allahumma baarik li fi rizqi)
(O Allah, bless me in my sustenance)

وَاجْعَلْهُ وَاسِعاً وَكَافِيًا
(Waj'alhu wasi'an wa kaafiyan)
(And make it abundant and sufficient)

4. Rukū' (Bowing):
   - Bow while saying "Allāhu Akbar."
   - Then recite:
   سُبْحَانَ رَبِّيَ الْعَظِيم
   (Subhana rabbiyal 'adheem)
   (Glory be to my Lord, the Most Great)
   [Repeat at least three times]

5. Rising from Rukū':
   - While rising, say:
   سَمِعَ اللَّهُ لِمَنْ حَمِدَه
   (Sami' Allāhu liman hamidah)
   (Allah hears those who praise Him)
   - Then, standing upright, say:
   رَبَّنَا وَلَكَ الْحَمْدُ
   (Rabbana wa laka al-hamd)
   (Our Lord, to You be all praise)

6. Sujūd (First Prostration):
   - Say "Allāhu Akbar" and lower into prostration.
   - Then recite:
   سُبْحَانَ رَبِّيَ الْأَعْلَى
   (Subhana rabbiyal a'la)

(Glory be to my Lord, the Most High)
[Repeat at least three times]

7. Brief Sitting (Jalsa):
   - Sit briefly and supplicate, for instance:

   رَبِّ، اجْعَلْ رِزْقِي نُورًا لِقَلْبِي

   (Rabbi, ij'al rizqi nooran liqalbi)
   (My Lord, make my sustenance a light for my heart)

8. Sujūd (Second Prostration):
   - Say "Allāhu Akbar" as you perform the second prostration.
   - Then recite:

   سُبْحَانَ رَبِّيَ الْأَعْلَى

   (Subhana rabbiyal a'la)
   (Glory be to my Lord, the Most High)
   [Repeat at least three times]

9. Final Tashahhud (Sitting for the Testimony):

- After the second sujūd, sit and recite:

اَلتَّحِيَّاتُ لِلَّهِ وَالصَّلَوَاتُ وَالطَّيِّبَاتُ

(At-tahiyyatu lillahi was-salawatu wat-tayyibatu)
(All greetings, prayers, and pure words belong to Allah)

اَلسَّلَامُ عَلَيْكَ أَيُّهَا النَّبِيُّ

(As-salamu 'alayka ayyuha an-nabiyyu)
(Peace be upon you, O Prophet)

وَرَحْمَةُ اللَّهِ وَبَرَكَاتُهُ

(Wa rahmatullahi wa barakatuhu)
(And the mercy and blessings of Allah)

اَلسَّلَامُ عَلَيْنَا وَعَلَى عِبَادِ اللَّهِ الصَّالِحِين

(As-salamu 'alayna wa 'ala 'ibaadil-lahi as-saaliheen)
(Peace be upon us and upon the righteous servants of Allah)

أَشْهَدُ أَنْ لَا إِلَهَ إِلَّا اللَّه

(Ash-hadu an la ilaha illallahu)

(I bear witness that there is no deity except Allah)

وَأَشْهَدُ أَنَّ مُحَمَّدًا رَسُولُ اللَّه

(Wa ash-hadu anna Muhammadan Rasool Allah)

(And I bear witness that Muhammad is the Messenger of Allah)

10. Taslīm (Concluding the Prayer):

- To finish, first turn your head to the right and say:

اِلسَّلَامُ عَلَيْكُمْ وَرَحْمَةُ اللَّه

(As-salamu 'alaykum wa rahmatullahi)

(Peace and mercy of Allah be upon you)

- Then turn your head to the left and repeat:

ِلَامُ عَلَيْكُمْ وَرَحْمَةُ اللَّهالس

(As-salamu 'alaykum wa rahmatullahi)

(Peace and mercy of Allah be upon you)

Notes:

- Salatul Rizq is a means to seek Allah's provision and express gratitude for His blessings.
- Reciting this prayer with sincerity reinforces trust in divine sustenance and promotes ethical earning.
- Feel free to include additional personal supplications during the brief sittings.

CHAPTER 31: DUA KUMAYL

STEP-BY-STEP Dua Kumayl Supplication

Below is an in-depth supplicatory prayer text for Dua Kumayl —a revered invocation traditionally recited in the quiet hours of the night. This prayer, filled with deep spiritual insights and emotional resonance, calls upon Allah's mercy, guidance, and the illumination of the soul. Before you begin, ensure you are in a state of spiritual readiness and that your heart is opened to sincere reflection.

Before You Begin:
• Sit in a quiet place with a pure heart and focused intention.
• Take a moment to clear your mind and seek closeness to Allah.

Dua Kumayl Prayer Text:

---

1. Invocation of Divine Mercy
   اللَّهُمَّ إِنِّي أَسْأَلُكَ بِرَحْمَتِكَ الَّتِي وَسِعَتِ الْكَوْن

   (Allahumma inni as'aluka bi rahmatika allati wasi'at al-kawn)

   (O Allah, I ask You by Your mercy that encompasses all existence)

2. Praise and Acknowledgment of His Oneness
   اللَّهُمَّ أَنْتَ الَّذِي لَا إِلَهَ إِلَّا أَنْتَ، الْوَاحِدُ الْقَهَّار

(Allahumma anta alladhī la ilaha illā anta, al-wāhid al-qahhār)

(O Allah, You are the One besides whom there is no deity—the Unique, the Conqueror)

3. Supplication for Guidance and Illumination

اَهْدِنِي وَأَنِرْ قَلْبِي، وَاجْعَلْنِي مِنْ أُولِي الْأَمْرِ

(Ihdinī wa anir qalbi, wa aj'alnī min ulī al-umūr)

(Guide me and illuminate my heart, and make me among those endowed with favor)

4. Seeking Forgiveness and Mercy

اَللَّهُمَّ اغْفِرْ لِي ذُنُوبِي وَآثَامِي، وَتُبْ عَلَيَّ بِرَحْمَتِكَ

(Allahumma ighfir lī dhunūbī wa athāmī, wa tub 'alayya bi rahmatika)

(O Allah, forgive my sins and transgressions, and envelop me in Your mercy)

5. Acknowledgment of Servitude

إِنِّي عَبْدُكَ، وَابْنُ عَبْدِكَ، وَابْنُ أَمَتِكَ

(Innī 'abduka, wa ibn 'abduka, wa ibn amatika)

(Indeed, I am Your servant, the son of Your servant, and the son of Your maid)

6. Petition for Enlightenment and Elevated Station

اَللَّهُمَّ انْشُرْ عَلَيَّ نُورَ عِلْمِكَ، وَارْفَعْ قَدْرِي فِي قَضَائِكَ

(Allahumma anshur 'alayya nūr 'ilmika, wa arfā' qadri fī qadā'ika)

(O Allah, bestow upon me the light of Your knowledge, and elevate my station in Your decree)

7. Reliance on the Sustainer of All

أَنْتَ الْمُقَوِّمُ لِلْكَوْنِ، فَاجْعَلْنِي مِنَ الْمُتَوَكِّلِينَ عَلَيْكَ

(Anta al-muqawwimu lil-kawn, faj'alnī min al-mutawakilīn 'alayka)

(You are the supporter of all creation; make me among those who place complete trust in You)

8. Request for Tranquility and Merciful Light

اللَّهُمَّ أَنْزِلْ سَكِينَتَكَ عَلَيَّ، وَغَرِسْ نُورَ رَحْمَتِكَ فِي قَلْبِي

(Allahumma anzil sakeenataka 'alayya, wa gharis nūr rahmatika fī qalbī)

(O Allah, send down Your tranquility upon me and embed the light of Your mercy in my heart)

9. Entreaty for the Prophet's Intercession

اللَّهُمَّ بَشِّرْنِي بِشَفَاعَةِ نَبِيِّكَ الأَكْرَمِ، وَاجْعَلْنِي مِنْ أُولِي الْعَظَمَةِ

(Allahumma bashshirnī bi shafā'ati nabiyyika al-akram, wa aj'alnī min ulī al-'azamah)

(O Allah, give me glad tidings through the intercession of Your Noble Prophet, and make me among those granted greatness)

10. Affirmation of Allah's Omnipotence

اللَّهُمَّ إِنَّكَ عَلَى كُلِّ شَيْءٍ قَدِيرٌ، وَبِرَحْمَتِكَ نَلْتَمِسُ النُّورَ فِي ظُلُمَاتِ الدُّنْيَا

(Allahumma innaka 'alā kulli shay'in qadīr, wa bi rahmatika nalta-misu an-nūr fī zhulmāt ad-dunyā)

(O Allah, You have power over all things, and by Your mercy we seek to emerge into the light from the darkness of this world)

11. Final Supplication and Affirmation

رَبِّ اغْفِرْ لِي، وَارْحَمْنِي، وَاهْدِنِي، فَإِنَّكَ أَنْتَ الْوَهَّابُ

(Rabbi ighfir lī, warhamnī, wahdīnī, fa innaka anta al-wahhāb)

(My Lord, forgive me, have mercy upon me, and guide me, for indeed You are the Bestower)

ءَامِينَ يَا رَبَّ الْعَالَمِينَ

(Ameen ya rabba al-'ālamīn)

(Amen, O Lord of all worlds)

CHAPTER 32: DUA JAWSHAN KABIR

STEP-BY-STEP Dua Jawshan Kabir Supplication

Below is an in-depth guide to reciting the Dua Jawshan Kabir, also called the Great Shield Supplication. This extensive prayer for protection and relief features rich, poetic verses that invoke Allah's mercy and serve as a spiritual armor in times of adversity. Recite this supplication with a sincere heart and focused mind, seeking refuge and divine safeguarding.

Before You Begin:
• Purify your heart and make your intention clear: "I supplicate to You, O Allah, for protection, mercy, and relief."

——————— Dua Jawshan Kabir: ———————

1. بِسْمِ اللَّهِ الرَّحْمَنِ الرَّحِيمِ
    (Bismillahir Rahmanir Raheem)
    (In the Name of Allah, the Most Gracious, the Most Merciful)

2. يَا حَيُّ يَا قَيُّوم
    (Ya Hayyu Ya Qayyum)
    (O Ever-Living, O Sustainer)

3. بِرَحْمَتِكَ أَسْتَغِيث
    (Birahmatika astaghithu)

(In Your mercy, I seek refuge)

4. اللَّهُمَّ أَنْقِذْنِي مِنْ جَمِيعِ أَعْنَاقِ أَعْدَائِي

(Allahumma anqithni min jami'i a'naaqi a'daaa'i)

(O Allah, rescue me from the clutches of all my enemies)

5. وَاجْعَلْنِي مِنْ أَوْلِيَائِكَ

(Waj'alni min aawliya'ika)

(And include me among Your devoted allies)

6. أَنْتَ السَّمِيعُ الْعَلِيمُ

(Anta as-Sami'ul 'Aleem)

(You are the All-Hearing, the All-Knowing)

7. يَا مَنْ لَا شَرِيكَ لَهُ

(Ya man la shareeka lahu)

(O You who have no partner)

8. لَا إِلَهَ إِلَّا هُوَ الْحَكِيمُ الْعَظِيمُ

(La ilaha illa Huwa al-Hakeem al-Azeem)

(There is no deity except Him, the Most Wise, the Most Great)

9. اِحْفَظْنِي بِعِزَّتِكَ وَنَجِّنِي مِنْ فِتْنَةِ الدُّنْيَا

(Ihfazni bi 'izzatika wa najjini min fitnat ad-dunya)

(Protect me with Your might, and save me from the trials of this world)

10. اللَّهُمَّ اجْعَلْ ذِكْرَكَ يَنْشُرُ فِي قُلُوبِنَا

(Allahumma ij'al dhikrika yanshuru fi quloobina)

(O Allah, let Your remembrance spread in our hearts)

11. وَأَنْوِرْ أَبْصَارَنَا بِحُضُورِكَ

(Wa anawwir absaarana bihudoorika)

(And illuminate our eyes with the light of Your presence)

12. اللَّهُمَّ أَرِنِي نُورَكَ فِي ظُلُمَاتِ اللَّيْلِ

(Allahumma arini nooraka fi dhulumat al-layl)

(O Allah, reveal Your light amid the darkness of night)

13. ‏وَأَسْقِنِي رِزْقَ الطُّمَأْنِينَة
(Wa asqini rizqa at-tuma'ninah)
(And grant me the sustenance of tranquility)

14. ‏أَمِّنِّي مِنْ بَطْشِ الدَّهْرِ وَآفَاتِ الزَّهْق
(Aminni min batshi ad-dahr wa afaat az-zahq)
(O Allah, shield me from the blows of time and the calamities of life)

15. ‏اللَّهُمَّ انْتَصِرْنِي عَلَى كُلِّ ضَغْطٍ وَبَلَاء
(Allahumma intasirni 'ala kulli daghtin wa bala'in)
(O Allah, grant me victory over every oppression and affliction)

16. ‏بِرَحْمَتِكَ الْوَاسِعَةِ، تَجَمَّعَتِ الْمَسَاوِي
(Birahmatika al-wasi'ah, tajamma'at al-masaawee)
(By Your boundless mercy, may all extremes converge in Your favor)

17. ‏أَسْتَغْفِرُكَ يَا مَنْ تَغْفِرُ الذُّنُوبَ جَمِيعًا
(Astaghfiruka ya man taghfiru adh-dhunooba jamee'an)
(I seek Your forgiveness, O You who forgives all sins)

18. ‏وَأَتُوبُ إِلَيْكَ مِمَّا نَثَرَتْهُ شَوَادِقُ قَلْبِي
(Wa atubu ilayka mimma natharat-hu shuwadiqu qalbi)
(And I repent to You for the blemishes that have marred my heart)

19. ‏اللَّهُمَّ اكْرِمْنِي بِكَرَمِكَ الَّذِي لَا يُضَاهِيهِ كَرَم
(Allahumma akrimni bikaramika alladhi la yudahaheeh karam)
(O Allah, honor me with Your unparalleled generosity)

20. ‏وَوَسِّعْ لِي رِزْقِي وَبَصِّرْنِي فِي شُؤُونِ حَيَاتِي
(Wa wassi' li rizqi wa bassirni fi shu'oon hayati)

(And expand my provision, granting me insight in all my affairs)

21. إِنِّي فِي فِتْنَةِ الدُّنْيَا وَظَلَمَاتِ اللَّيَالِي

(Inni fi fitnat ad-dunya wa zulumat al-layali)

(I am immersed in the trials of this world and the darkness of nights)

22. أَلْجَأُ إِلَيْكَ يَا رَزَّاقُ، إِذَا ضَاقَتِ المَصَائِبِ

(Alja'u ilayka ya Razzaaq, idha daaqat al-masaaa'ibu)

(I take refuge in You, O Provider, when calamities prevail)

23. اللَّهُمَّ قُنْ عَنِّي عَذَابَكَ بِيَدِكَ القَدِيرَةِ

(Allahumma qun 'anni 'adhabaka biyadika al-qadeerah)

(O Allah, shield me from Your punishment with Your mighty hand)

24. وَاجْمَعْ شُرُورَ الدُّنْيَا وَأَعْدَاءَ الإِيمَانِ

(Wajma' shuroor ad-dunya wa a'da'a al-eemaan)

(And gather the evils of this world and the foes of faith)

25. أَصْبِحْنَا بِنُورِكَ، وَحُلَّتْ ظِلَالُكَ عَنْهَا

(AsbiHna binurika, wa hullah talilaluka 'anhaa)

(May we arise in Your light, and may Your shadows vanish from our lives)

26. وَسَتِّرْ عَنَّا سَوَادَ الدُّنْيَا وَفِتْنَةَ الشَّهَوَاتِ

(Wa sattir 'anna suwaada ad-dunya wa fitnat ash-shahawaat)

(And conceal from us the darkness of this world and the enticement of desires)

27. يَا رَبَّ العَالَمِينَ، صَفِّ قُلُوبَنَا بِطِيبِ الإِيمَانِ

(Ya Rabb al-'aalameen, saffi quloobana bateeb al-eemaan)

(O Lord of the Worlds, purify our hearts with the fragrance of faith)

28. وَاجْعَلْ مَحَبَّتَكَ رَايَةَ نُورٍ فِي جُنُودِ دُعَائِنَا

(Waj'al mahabbataka rayaata noor fi junoood duaa'ina)

(And make Your love the banner of light among the ranks of our supplications)

29. أَرْسِلْ عَلَيْنَا سَلَامَكَ وَأَفْرِشْ لَنَا رِضَاكَ

(Arsil 'alayna salaamaka wa afrish lana ridaaka)

(O Allah, send upon us Your peace and spread Your pleasure over us)

30. وَاخْتِمْ دُعَاءَنَا بِالدُّخُولِ فِي مَلَاذِكَ الْمُبَارَكِ

(Wa akhtim duaa'ana bid-dukhool fi malaadhika al-mubarak)

(And conclude our supplication with admittance into Your blessed refuge)

31. إِنَّكَ عَلَى كُلِّ شَيْءٍ قَدِيرٌ

(Innaka 'ala kulli shay'in qadeer)

(Verily, You are capable of all things)

32. تَجَبَّرْ عَنَّا شُرُورَ الزَّمَانِ وَفِخَاخَ الرَّغْبَةِ

(Tajabbir 'anna shuroor az-zamaan wa fikhakh ar-raghbah)

(O Exalted, remove from us the evils of time and the snares of desire)

33. اِطْمِئِنَّ قُلُوبَنَا بِثِقَتِكَ وَآمِنْ بِوَجْهِكَ الْكَرِيمِ

(Atmi'inna quloobana bithiqatika wa aamin bi wajhika al-kareem)

(Reassure our hearts with the confidence of Your promise and grant us security through Your noble countenance)

34. يَا مَنْ تَبَسَّمَتِ السَّمَاوَاتُ لِحُسْنِ مَجْدِكَ

(Ya man tabassamat as-samaawatu li husni majdika)

(O One whose glory illuminates the heavens with splendor)

35. وَيَا مَنْ أَرْسَلَ فِي دُرُوبِ الحَيَاةِ عِلْمَ الرُّخْصَة

(Wa ya man arsal fi duroob al-hayaat 'ilm ar-rukhsah)

(O One who granted the knowledge of ease along the paths of life)

36. آمِينَ، آمِينَ، آمِين

(Aameen, Aameen, Aameen)

(Amen, Amen, Amen)

Notes:

• Reflect on each verse as you recite it, allowing its meaning to envelop your heart.

• Embrace the supplication as a spiritual shield that defends you against the adversities of both this world and the Hereafter.

• Recite with sincerity and trust in Allah's boundless mercy and protection.

CHAPTER 33: BURDAH PRAYER

STEP-BY-STEP Burdah Prayer

Below is an in-depth guide to the Burdah Prayer—a devotional recitation inspired by the famous Burdah poem. This prayer encapsulates love and reverence for the Prophet Muhammad (peace and blessings be upon him), weaving together lyrical praises and deep emotional expression to guide your heart toward divine grace and a profound spiritual connection.

Before You Begin:
• Ensure you are in a state of ritual purity (wudu) and settle your heart in sincere love and remembrance of the Prophet.

Step 1: Opening Invocation

1. بِسْمِ اللهِ الرَّحْمٰنِ الرَّحِيم

   (Bismillaahir Rahmaanir Raheem)
   (In the name of Allah, the Most Gracious, the Most Merciful)

Step 2: Salutations upon the Prophet 2. يَا رَسُولَ اللهِ، صَلَّى اللهُ عَلَيْكَ وَسَلَّم

(Ya Rasool Allah, Sallallahu 'alayka wa sallam)

(O Messenger of Allah, peace and blessings be upon you)

Step 3: Reciting the Verses of Reverence 3.1. أَنْتَ سِرُّ الْهُدَى وَمِفْتَاحُ الْبَرَكَاتِ

(Anta sirru al-huda wa miftahu al-barakaat)

(You are the secret of guidance and the key to blessings)

3.2. فِي ظِلِّ حُبِّكَ تَتَجَلَّى رَحْمَةُ اللَّهِ عَلَى الْعَالَمِين

(Fi dhilli hubbika tatajalla rahmatullah 'ala al-'aalameen)

(In the shade of your love, Allah's mercy shines upon the worlds)

3.3. قُلُوبُنَا تَخْشَعُ لِسَلَامِكَ وَتَفْرَحُ بِأَنْوَارِ هَدَايَتِك

(Qulubuna takhsha'u lisalamika wa tafrahu bi anwaar hidayatika)

(Our hearts humble before your peace and rejoice in the lights of your guidance)

3.4. سَكَّنْتَ الْمَحَبَّةَ فِي قُلُوبِنَا، وَبَثَثْتَ النُّورَ فِي كُلِّ زَاوِيَة

(Sakkanta al-mahabba fi qulubina, wa bathatha an-noora fi kulli zaa'wiya)

(You have instilled love in our hearts and spread light in every corner)

3.5. تَجْرِي بِحُبِّكَ أَنْهَارُ الرَّحْمَةِ وَالْمَغْفِرَة

(Tajree bihubbika anhru ar-rahma wa al-maghfirah)

(By your love, the rivers of mercy and forgiveness flow)

Step 4: Concluding Supplication for Blessings 4. اللَّهُمَّ صَلِّ عَلَى مُحَمَّدٍ وَعَلَى آلِهِ وَصَحْبِهِ

(Allāhumma salli 'ala Muhammadin wa 'ala aalihi wa sahbihi)

(O Allah, send blessings upon Muhammad and upon his family and companions)

4.1. إِنِّي أَسْأَلُكَ بِنُورِ وَجْهِهِ الْعَظِيمِ، أَنْ تُنِيرَ قُلُوبَنَا بِمَحَبَّتِه

(Innee as'aluka binuri wajhihi al-'azeem, an tunira qulubana bimuhabbatihi)

(I ask You, by the light of his noble countenance, to illuminate our hearts with his love)

Step 5: Taslīm (Concluding the Recitation) 5. السَّلَامُ عَلَيْكُمْ وَرَحْمَةُ اللَّهِ وَبَرَكَاتُهُ

(As-salamu 'alaykum wa rahmatullahi wa barakatuh)
(Peace, mercy, and blessings of Allah be upon you)

Notes:
- Recite each verse slowly and reflectively, allowing every word to resonate within your heart.
- You may repeat any section or pause for additional personal supplication (du'ā) to deepen your spiritual connection with the Prophet Muhammad (peace be upon him).

Printed in Great Britain
by Amazon

The Life and Death of Abercrombie Lyle

Also by Stephen Small

Non-fiction

Political Thought in Ireland 1776-1798:
Republicanism, Patriotism, and Radicalism

An Irish Century 1845-1945: From the Famine to
World War II

Stephen Small

The Life and Death of Abercrombie Lyle

Palatine Publishing

Copyright © Stephen Small 2025

Stephen Small has asserted his right to be identified as the author of this Work in accordance with the Copyright, Designs and Patents Act 1988

www.stephensmall.co.uk

ISBN 978-1-9192258-1-4

Palatine Publishing

'Without friends no one would choose to live,
though he had all other goods.'

Aristotle, *Nicomachean Ethics*, Book VIII

PROLOGUE

Paestum, Southern Italy, 31 August 1926

I always knew it couldn't last. The idyllic eighteen months among the Greek temples and turquoise waters were too perfect, and for such happiness the gods would exact a price. One might argue an extortionate one. When I arrived in Paestum after fleeing south from Milan, I sensed something cold and hard beneath the silent heat and ancient beauty. It felt like a place that would demand a sacrifice for protecting us; a *quid pro quo* for keeping the demons of the modern world away. Or perhaps there was just something in that dry Campania soil that needed a little blood now and then.

We saw them coming from a long way off. Three small clouds of dust, rising above the parched earth and growing ever closer. Once the clouds were attached to black specks on the old road from Salerno, it could only mean one thing. There were barely any motor cars in Paestum in those days, never mind a convoy of three. It could only be authority of some kind, and authority of any kind was bad news for us in fascist Italy. Living quietly and treading softly among the ghosts of Magna Grecia, we imagined ourselves invisible to that world, but we had been seen. We probably had time to flee, but where to? This was our haven, our heaven, and who willingly flees that. Besides, we had nowhere else to go.

As the vehicles approached, we decided to greet our guests in the courtyard of the decaying farmhouse. There was no point putting them to the trouble of breaking down doors we had recently repaired: a task they would no doubt have enjoyed. Small victories must be taken when they can. We had plenty of time to compose ourselves in the white August heat. Carla, Louisa, Enrico and I stood in a line, as if on parade, though not a parade that would impress our guests. Carla moved to my side and took my hand. It was the last time I remember touching her.

A dirty silver Lancia roared through the open, rusted gates and came to an abrupt halt in front of us. Its violent braking sent our chickens into a frenzy and the stench of exhaust fumes felt like a violation of our sanctuary. Cerberus embraced his name with a deep growl I had never heard him make before. I ruffled his soft golden ears to calm him, but he was no fool and knew danger when he saw it, even if the humans were behaving as if old family friends were arriving for tea. Prepared for our fate, whatever that might be, I felt strangely calm. But the calm shattered when *he* stepped down from the running board of the Lancia. There, with shiny black boots, jodhpurs, and absurdly tasselled hat, stood my former friend, Brio, as darkly handsome as ever. Carla dropped my hand, but too late. Her husband had clearly seen.

I remember his sad smile, and a momentary, pathetic lurch of hope that memories of happier times would prompt a spontaneous re-write of the pre-ordained scene. They didn't.

The rest was a blur of brutal chaos. Perhaps it would have gone differently without her touch, but I doubt it. He would have seen the looks we had exchanged as his car approached, and no doubt had known about our betrayal for some time.

*

Years later, I had a memory of her in the rear window of his car as it drove away. Her delicate hands clenched and pounding on the glass. Her normally calm face flushed and plastered with strands of long black hair, contorted in rage and silently screaming 'Abercrombie!' In this memory, she became the tragic heroine of a Greek myth. A doomed goddess or mortal beauty in a tale of rape or abduction. There were plenty of them to embellish my memory if I chose to indulge such thoughts. But in the end, it didn't matter if Brio was dragging her into the underworld or carrying her away as a spoil of victory. She was always leaving me.

In any case, I knew that image must be false, for I could not have seen it. When I came to, from the rifle butt to my forehead, it was dark, and Brio and his thugs had gone. They had left me nothing. Enrico and Louisa were gone. Carla was gone. And Cerberus was lying in a pool of his own blood, a single shot through his single, dear head.

Would I have that time again, knowing the price in advance? It's hard to say, but I think yes, despite what came after.

PART I

1

Naples, 30 August 1945

It was a wonder there were any books left to burn. I sometimes thought they must be printing them just to fuel the spectacle. At least I hoped so. It made my compulsion to witness their destruction less painful. Of course, I didn't really imagine such insanity could be true. So, every Sunday, for over a year, I had emerged from Naples's claustrophobic *centro storico*, passing the few remaining booksellers on Port'Alba, to join the crowds that flowed into Piazza Dante. I took comfort from the fact that the mob seemed to shrink as the months went by, despite the entreaties of the priests after mass, and even Il Duce himself. It was three years since Britain had surrendered after the fall of Cairo, and some people clearly found it hard to keep hating their enemies for that long. I wasn't one of them.

I shuffled toward the unlit pyre in the centre of the square. The huge statue of Dante had turned his back on it. I fantasized that eventually the great poet must shed a tear, but he never did. Mussolini had once been a writer himself, but his increasing subservience to Hitler had brought degradations and humiliations to Italy that shocked even old cynics like me. Looking back to the early days of fascism, the young thugs with clubs and a taste for dressing up now seemed almost quaint, like a few unruly drunks at a village fete, compared to the last few years. The unspeakable gassing of the Abyssinians. The disappearance of the Jews, apart from a few well-connected converts who miraculously found their mother's rosary beads in the attic. The endless march of young men to the Eastern front: a tribute for our generous overlord's protection, like Athens sending its youth to feed the Minotaur at the behest of Minos. Compared to these, burning books was small beer, but somehow it depressed me even more. I'd been teaching Ancient History at the University of Naples for fifteen years now, and its students had slowly lost the ability to think for themselves. If they kept burning books, they would never find a way out of their labyrinth, or even realise they were in one.

I came as close to the pile as I could to pick out a title I recognised and try to remember a moment from the book. This might be the last time that it lived in my mind, and if I could recall a passage, it would live a little longer. Scanning the pile for my act of silent rescue, my eye was caught by a pristine cream dust jacket fluttering in the hot breeze on top of the ripped and abused books. When I glimpsed the flickering title, I stopped and stared for several seconds to make sure my eyes were not playing tricks on me. But as the breeze died and the cover settled, I could see that it read:

The Life and Death of Abercrombie Lyle

I stood in disbelief, trying to make sense of a book bearing my name that I had neither written nor heard of. I reached into the pile and grasped it. The title filled the front cover, printed blood red in a large font. The book had been torn apart, and the back was missing.

'Hey, what are you doing?' The guard, in a black cape, shouted from his seat beneath Dante. He rose and started toward me. I knew it was madness, but couldn't stop myself. I reached deeper into the pile and started rooting around like a parent looking for a child in the rubble of a collapsed building. The stench of kerosene heightened my desperation as I searched for the rest of the book.

'Stop. Stop that now!'

I could hear boots breaking into a run and getting closer. I only had a few seconds. I glimpsed what might have been the back of the book, lower in the pile, but before I could dig the other books away, I was wrenched backward by my jacket collar and thrown to the ground. I scrambled to my feet and stood before a brutish, middle-aged man with a shaven head. Without stopping to think, I swung my boot into his groin with all the force I could muster, catching him by surprise. He fell to the ground with a cry. I was drawn back to the pyre but, reluctantly, turned and ran.

There was shouting behind me, and then a single gunshot, but once I had passed through the archway into Port'Alba, the *centro storico* embraced me. At the next corner, I slowed to a brisk walk – the cobbles and crowds made running both impractical and conspicuous. I took a few random turns and for a moment almost lost myself. But I would never be lost for long in here. I knew these dark, narrow streets and alleyways too well. Soon, I found myself opposite the splintered door and ancient ochre plaster of Caffè Giordano. The bells of Santa Chiara began to strike noon. The bonfires would be lit on the final peel. Then the cheering would start, and the harsh tinny sound of the loudspeakers would boom off the crumbling walls of the old city. I knew, almost to the word, what the old Duce would say. He'd been saying much the same thing every week since 1942. My grey flannel shirt was drenched with sweat beneath my jacket. I took slow, deep breaths to calm myself, but the smell of rotting food and sewage rising from the hot gutters almost made me retch. I decided to get off the street. The sun was barely over the yardarm, as my Da would no doubt have reminded me, but I really needed a drink.

2

Milan, 1 March 1919

Brio noticed the young foreigner as soon as he walked into the cramped back room at Marchesi and sat at the table next to him. Tall, thin and sandy-haired, with pale, freckled skin, he was still a boy, perhaps nineteen or twenty. His wide mouth was delicate, almost feminine, and wore a subtle smile, as if he were in a state of constant amusement. On a woman, he would not have minded kissing it. The boy also had a distant look that Brio had seen many times. He was no Italian, perhaps German or English, but he would wager his last lira he was a brother in all that really mattered.

There had been a time when Brio thought there were only two types of men: those that worked hard and were still poor, and those that hardly worked and had more than they needed. Since returning from the front, he still considered himself a socialist. His father had worked on the railways and had been a union organiser since he was a small boy. Socialism was in his bones. But he realised that the war had changed everything. A new division was clear to him, if often invisible to others. He could see it in their eyes when they walked the gilded arcades of the Galleria or watched whatever nonsense La Scala regurgitated. Some observed from behind an invisible veil, detached from the spectacle, a part of them forever somewhere else. Others, usually older men, could still marvel at a glittering shop window, or listen, enraptured, to a strutting aristocrat in wig and breeches lamenting the fate of a beloved. But there was nothing in that shop or on that stage that could delight those who had been in hell. In the new world, there were still two sorts of men, but what divided them had changed. Now, there were those who had fought and those who hadn't, and there was no doubt in Brio's mind. This young man from the north had seen what he had seen.

Brio let him settle and look at the menu. The nervous smile he gave the waitress persuaded Brio that English was a better bet than German. Brio then called across to him, in English. 'Try the pistachio pastry. It is exquisite.' He reinforced the recommendation with his dazzling trademark smile, as he delicately brushed a crumb off the corner of his moustache with his napkin. An immediate look of recognition, and nod of gratitude, confirmed that he had guessed the nationality correctly. This pleased Brio. He saw himself as the kind of man who could read people and understand what they needed.

After a moment of hesitation, the young man replied. 'Thank you. I will.' He stared at the menu, as if struggling to identify the item. The waitress returned and the young man ordered, in halting, but comprehensible, Italian.

Brio reached across and offered his hand. 'Brio Salvatore.' The young man shook it, more firmly than Brio had expected. He noticed a small scar on his left cheek and the unmistakable inky powder burns on hands that belonged to an older man.

'Abercrombie Lyle. It's a pleasure to meet you.'

Brio turned his chair to face Abercrombie. 'What brings you to Milan, Mr Lyle?' Brio watched as Abercrombie paused, looking away to his left for a few seconds, as if considering the question for the first time, or perhaps deciding how much he wanted to reveal to a stranger. Eventually, he replied.

'I wanted to see Da Vinci's *Last Supper*. I believe it's in a church not far from here.'

Brio looked at him with even greater interest. 'It is indeed. Santa Maria Della Grazie. About a ten-minute walk.'

'It must be a magnificent sight. I've only ever seen photographs.'

Brio was thrown off kilter. 'You know, I'm ashamed to say, I've never seen it in the flesh myself.'

Abercrombie looked shocked. 'Why don't you come with me?'

His enthusiasm was unexpected, like a small boy transfigured by a surprise birthday present. Looking back, that was the moment he had fallen a little in love with this odd young man from the north. Perhaps love was the wrong word. There was no sexual attraction. It was more like a glimpse of what it would be like to have a younger brother instead of three older sisters. Brio had introduced himself with the assurance of a sophisticated man about town on his home turf, offering a little guidance to a bewildered comrade in an unfamiliar city; and here he was, being invited out to play by the new boy in the neighbourhood. He would soon realise that this was Abercrombie's special gift. Floating above layers of grief and trauma that Brio did not yet know, was a capacity for infectious good humour that had somehow survived the horror. Rather than leading Abercrombie, perhaps Abercrombie could help him find something that he had lost. Without his usual calculations, Brio replied, 'Why not!' surprising himself with his spontaneity. He would be late back to the newspaper, but they could survive without him for an hour.

Brio settled the bill, and as they stepped onto Via Meravigli into the cool, bright afternoon, he tried again to assume the role of guide, but Abercrombie clearly knew which way to go. So they walked side by side, while Abercrombie chatted with an ease that disarmed Brio. Few veterans that Brio met wanted to discuss their experiences. But Abercrombie was quite candid, at least about where and when he had seen action, even if he revealed nothing very personal. By the time they reached the church, Brio had learned that they had a deeper connection. Before Abercrombie had served on the Western Front, they had both fought the Bulgarians in Salonika in 1917. They had even been in Greece at the same time. They were truly brothers in arms. Brio was not normally superstitious or impressed by coincidences, but this seemed like some sort of sign.

At the church, Brio noticed Abercrombie crossing himself before approaching an old monk in a dark habit standing near the entrance. He dropped a coin in a wooden box, and they were directed through the riot of colourful renaissance paintings and frescos that covered the walls and vaulted ceilings. It was too much for Brio. He felt overwhelmed by the confusion of colour and imagery, which to him felt closer to hell than heaven. He was relieved to enter the much plainer refectory that housed the Last Supper, and when he looked up to the end wall, covered by the huge fresco, he felt small and humbled. It was a sensation he had not experienced since he had been taken to the Duomo as a boy.

Everything he had seen in the war had convinced him that there could be no God, or at least no God that deserved his allegiance or respect. But something about the scene began to speak to him. Initially, he was taken by the serenity of Jesus in full knowledge of the excruciating pain he would soon suffer, and by the gentle features of John, who Brio thought bore a faint resemblance to Abercrombie. But the longer he looked, it was the apostles' reaction to Jesus's betrayal that most caught his interest. He put himself in their place and felt the full range of their emotions: shock, incomprehension, anger. He thought of the consequences radiating from this moment, first to the crucifixion but then beyond, to the grief and confusion of the apostles before the resurrection, and after that to the persecution and humiliation they would suffer for their faith.

At this point, Brio had a sort of epiphany. These comrades of Jesus, he realised, had themselves been betrayed by a man who had led them to catastrophe. He scanned the apostles and racked his brain for recollections of their fates. Some he was unsure of, but most, he was certain, were martyrs. Fragments of bible stories from his Jesuit teachers emerged. Peter, crucified upside down. Paul, beheaded in Rome. Andrew, crucified on a diagonal cross. One of them sawn in half, and another flayed alive, if he remembered correctly. It wasn't just Christ who had suffered. He had led his men to agonies he must have foreseen. In their own way, these men had suffered as much, if not more, than Jesus. He, at least, knew that in a few days he would ascend to a heavenly seat beside his father. The apostles would face a long, uncertain journey of struggle, doubt and rejection, ending in agonising death, often alone, in a foreign land. What kind of leader would knowingly do that to his most loyal followers? He looked again at the downcast eyes of Jesus, passively accepting his fate, and thereby committing his apostles to a fate even worse than his. Where was the outrage at his betrayal? The demand for justice and punishment? Jesus was no saviour. He was leading his lambs to their slaughter. Brio's eye was drawn to Peter, gripping a knife that he was clearly ready to use. His was the natural response. The *correct* response. Later, in Gethsemane, he had at least tried to fight, until his useless master had stayed his hand.

He glanced across to Abercrombie, who appeared to be having a more sublime reaction to the painting. He looked sad, but calm.

'Incredible, isn't it?' Abercrombie said, still facing the fresco.

'Yes, it is . . . Thank you for bringing me here, Mr Lyle, it has been a most . . . illuminating experience.'

Abercrombie turned to Brio. Something in his tone seemed to have broken the spell the picture had cast on him. 'What is it? What's wrong?'

'Nothing. Or rather, everything,' replied Brio.

Abercrombie looked at him quizzically. 'Is everything all right?'

'No. But it will be. One day, perhaps.' Brio turned and walked away. 'Come. Let's get out of this musty pile of stones and get some fresh air.'

*

In the weeks that followed, Brio adopted Abercrombie and initiated him into his circle of friends. Abercrombie was plunged into a maelstrom of crowded cafés and noisy bars, of political arguments fuelled by cheap wine and strong passions. Brio worried that this new life would overwhelm Abercrombie, but he could not leave him alone for more than a few days at a time. On the surface, this was an act of pure benevolence and hospitality, but Brio realised that he needed his new friend as much as Abercrombie needed him. There was something about the Englishman that kept the anger at bay – that kept him tethered to a hope of normality and happiness.

Within two weeks of their meeting, Brio had found Abercrombie more affordable accommodation, in the spare room of a friend from his old regiment, and a job teaching English at a local college for working men run by a union. It didn't pay much, but Abercrombie didn't seem to need much. He spent his days learning Italian, wandering the streets, and reading, and his early evenings teaching. After class, once the next day's issue of *Avanti!* had gone to the presses, they would often meet at the bar down the road.

One night in late March, Brio asked Abercrombie to meet him at a different location as he had a surprise for him. He wanted to introduce him to not one, but two, very memorable people. Brio took great pleasure in the look of anticipation on Abercrombie's face but would not indulge his protégé's desire to know who they were. It was to be a surprise.

Looking back on that night, many years later, he had not oversold the evening. The two individuals, in their very different ways, would have the most profound impact on Abercrombie's life, and on his own.

Brio often wished that the evening had never happened.

3

Naples, 30 August 1945

I ordered a beer and sat in the darkest corner of Caffè Giordano, staring at the cover of the book that bore my name. I had never heard of another Abercrombie Lyle, and even if a few were dotted about back in Britain, or some corner of the crumbling empire, I knew it must be an uncommon, even rare, name.

I opened the cover with a mixture of dread and anticipation. From the first page, I knew that whatever this was, it was not the biography of a coincidental namesake. The first chapter transported me back to my childhood in Liverpool before the first war. The detail was incredible and accurate. I scanned the first few pages and saw references to my father, a merchant seaman from Scotland, and my Irish-born mother, who worked in service in the grand Georgian house of a local ship owner. Images of my youth were conjured with alarming clarity. Great steamships, busy docks and the overhead railway. Masses of recent and not so recent Irish immigrants. Damp, windy, soot-caked streets off Scotland Road. They were all brought vividly to life. My school, the Lord Nelson pub on our street corner, and even *my neighbours* were described – as if I had written about them myself.

Whoever the author was, they knew almost as much about my past as I did, and some that I had forgotten. I looked at the author's name. Elsa Carivali. I had never known or heard of an Elsa Carivali, but something about the name bothered me. There was no biography or any information about her, so I plunged back into the book, not quite knowing whether to carry on reading from the start or go straight to the end. I went to the end first, or rather, the end of what was left. The final surviving paragraph made me shiver.

Abercrombie was attending his pitiful weekly pilgrimage in Piazza Dante, furtively scrutinizing the pile of prohibited literature, when his attention was caught by a cream dust jacket on top of the pyre. He thought he must be hallucinating, but there, on the cover, was his name. He stared, uncomprehending, looking like the village idiot to anyone observing; but he was not hallucinating. The book's title was clear, and it read: The Life and Death of Abercrombie Lyle.

My beer arrived and I touched the cool bottle to my forehead. Perhaps I was hallucinating, perhaps my lonely existence, and two decades of grief for Carla, had finally unhinged me. I looked at the tiled floor and tapped it with my worn boot. I scanned the whitewashed walls, noticed a few regulars and nodded to one, who nodded back. A stocky, middle-aged man I didn't recognize, with grey, slicked-back hair, was sitting in the far corner watching me, but that was not so unusual. It sometimes felt like everyone was watching everyone these days. Pinching my leg produced reassuring pain. My hands were trembling, which was to be expected, but they were certainly mine, with the crooked little finger that had never been properly set after that day in Paestum. The memory sent my fingers to the scar on my forehead. Everything seemed as real and normal as it could be, except for the book.

 I closed it, took a deep breath and drank half of my beer in one draught. Questions competed chaotically in my mind. How could there be a book about my life that I didn't know about? Who could have written it? Did *I* write it? Had I written it and gone insane, or had some sort of amnesiac event that had erased it from my memory? This explanation seemed impossible, given that the events had just occurred. But if I did not write it, then who else could have? There were things in there that very few people, if anyone, could have known about me. Perhaps most disturbingly, it was written in a way that felt like the author could read my mind.

 I could not think clearly, but through the cacophony of questions a few began to emerge more powerfully than others. Most eerily of all, how could it contain something that had only happened a few minutes ago? And how could this page not be the end of the book? What could be in the final pages, and how could they even exist if they described the future? Then another thought struck me with even greater force, pushing all the other crazy questions into the background, at least for now. Whatever the origin or purpose of the book, perhaps it could provide a clue to the question that had driven or distracted me for nineteen years.

What had happened to Carla?

4

Milan, 23 March 1919

'Carla!' She heard her name called from across Piazza San Sepolcro and turned to see her darling Brio striding toward her, arms outstretched. She couldn't help but break into a smile as he closed the last few steps. She braced for what she knew was coming. Scooping her up into his strong arms, he twirled her in the air with ease, as if she were a doll. The big idiot. Then he pulled her close and kissed her in a way that made her weak. Despite the very public space, she was absorbed in a world that only contained the two of them. He set her down to wolf whistles from the crowds of young men also waiting in the piazza, and she felt herself blush. She punched him playfully in the chest.

'Will you never grow up, Brio?' she laughed.

'Only when you marry me.'

He really was a handsome beast, and as she looked into his dark eyes, and felt the soft bristles of his moustache on her lips once again, she knew she might have said yes, there and then, if he had asked.

'All in good time,' she whispered, and he finally set her free from his vice-like embrace. She straightened her hat and scanned the square to check they hadn't made too much of a spectacle of themselves. Sullen-looking men were staring at them hungrily. They were obviously veterans and mostly dressed shabbily, even those in uniform. One was missing a leg and on crutches. Another had a hideous metal mask covering half of his face. She suddenly felt ashamed of her happiness and glanced at Brio sternly to remind him to behave himself. She felt an undercurrent of menace in the crowd, and tried not to make eye contact with anyone, as if she were walking alone on a dark street late at night.

'What is this place? Why are we here? ... And why were you late!' She had only recently arrived herself but remembered he should have been here ten minutes ago. 'Fancy letting me wait here with these ... men hanging around. Who are they? What are they waiting for?'

'The same thing as us, my dear. Enlightenment! Or, failing that, some entertainment.'

She was about to ask for an explanation when she noticed a tall, sandy-haired young man standing a few metres behind Brio, smiling at them indulgently. Aside from his colouring and clothing – he was formally dressed in a dark grey suit and moss green necktie – he looked different from the others. She didn't feel threatened. He actually looked quite pleasant, even if he was behaving oddly. But given his proximity and the focus of his gaze, Carla felt she should alert Brio. She whispered in his ear. 'There's a strange man behind you staring at us in a peculiar way, as if he knows us.'

Brio turned to look and broke into his own, more extravagant, smile. Carla noticed that he looked almost as happy as when he'd called out to her. She was intrigued. Brio winked at Carla then gestured for the young man to join them, giving no explanation until he stood in front of them to form a close triangle.

'Carla, meet Mr. Abercrombie Lyle.' Brio gestured theatrically to Abercrombie with one hand. 'Abercrombie, I present the most beautiful woman in Milan. Carla Cellini.' Brio completed the gesture with his other hand, as if he were a conductor presenting two performers on stage for a round of applause from the audience.

Abercrombie reached out and took Carla's hand. She thought he was about to kiss it, but he merely shook it and said, in rather poor Italian: 'For the first time, I think you lie to me, Brio. Miss Cellini is not the most beautiful woman in Milan.' He paused, just long enough to create a moment of awkwardness. 'She is surely the most beautiful woman in all of Italy.' Then he blushed, as did Carla. There was a brief embarrassed silence before Brio roared with laughter and clapped Abercrombie on the back.

'Come, let's go inside,' said Brio, ushering them toward the door of a large building behind them, as if he were the owner, and Carla and Abercrombie his guests for a dinner party.

Inside the hall, Carla felt even more self-conscious than in the piazza. She couldn't tell for sure, but she felt like the only woman in a room of perhaps a hundred men. Few looked older than thirty, apart from some of the meeting organisers, who sat in cane-backed chairs on a low stage. Most of the men were in military uniform of varied kinds, and several were dressed oddly in black shirts and grey riding breeches with polished black boots. The smell of stale sweat and fresh beer on the breath of those closest to her did nothing to lift her mood, and she was subjected to a few rather unpleasant stares. They found an inconspicuous corner at the back of the large meeting room. She took her hat off and stood sandwiched between Brio and Abercrombie for protection.

Carla gave Brio a dig in the ribs. 'You beast, what sort of date is this? Why have you brought me to one of your dreadful political meetings?'

Brio bent down and replied in a whisper, 'I wouldn't call this one of *my* political meetings.' She felt a tingle from his breath on her ear. How infuriating that he could arouse her when she was trying to be annoyed. 'And I apologise for the . . . ambiance. But I think you will both find this interesting. Or at least you will find *him* interesting.' Brio looked at her playfully, as if refusing to acknowledge her discomfort would make it disappear.

'Who is this mystery man?' Carla retorted. On cue, and before Brio could offer more than a glance in response, the hall erupted in applause as a line of suited or uniformed men walked onto the stage. At their head was a bull of a man with dark hair receding from a huge forehead and staring eyes. As he stood before the crowd, he thrust his prominent jaw upward, like a boxer daring his opponent to punch it, and raised his arm to accept the adulation of the audience.

'That,' said Brio, 'is my old boss at *Avanti!* Benito Mussolini.'

She had to admit, she was intrigued. Although she did not take an active role in the *Partito Socialista Italiano*, she was interested in politics and had heard quite a lot about Mussolini. It would be hard not to in the world she inhabited. He had been the most prominent socialist in Milan until he denounced the PSI's neutral stance on the war. This was all long before she had arrived in the city last year as a volunteer nurse, but she had vague recollections of Brio speaking fondly of Mussolini for having given him his first job in journalism when he took him on as a junior reporter. Since then, Mussolini had been ejected from the party, and the newspaper, and she had never given him much thought, but looking at him now, she could see that he had something about him. Whether she liked that something was another matter.

'I thought you said he was yesterday's man when he was kicked off the newspaper,' she shouted in Brio's ear to cut through the din of applause.

'He was, but I'm curious to see what yesterday's man's idea of tomorrow looks like.'

They were evidently watching the birth of a new movement of some sort and had to endure some tedious procedural motions along with the election of the organisation's officers, some of whom seemed to have been picked at random from the front row of the audience. Thank God they were hidden away at the back. But there *was* something fascinating about the energy in the room, even if Carla found it disturbing. When Mussolini finally rose to speak, she struggled to make sense of the mishmash of ideas and promises he offered.

The members of this new movement would be both aristocrats *and* democrats, conservatives *and* liberals, reactionaries *and* revolutionaries. They would follow the constitution or ignore it, depending on the circumstances. He warned against the reactionary right and the destructive left. At times, he sounded like a socialist, promising to get rid of the monarchy, reduce the working day and create a republic. He called for votes for women and the abolition of all titles. He called for liberty for everyone, even for his enemies, and proclaimed freedom of thought and speech as the highest expression of human civilization. At other times he sounded like an old imperialist, with a list of lands and cities that Italy must claim, or a conventional conservative, as he stressed the need for industry and commerce to play a leading role in the new

Italy. They were a party, and yet not a party. They were an 'anti-party.' There was talk of betrayal by Britain and France in the post-war settlement, and beneath it all was an undercurrent of violence. If they didn't get what they wanted, whatever that was, they would take it: a threat implicit in their name, the *Fascio Italiano di Combattimento*.

As if reading her mind, she heard Abercrombie mutter in English: 'Sounds like he wants to have his cake *and* eat it,' which made Carla smile for the first time since they had entered the hall. She hadn't heard the expression before, but it summed up proceedings perfectly. Brio shot her a quick warning glance and she put on a more serious face.

If there was a consistent theme, it was not so much *what* the new party stood for, as *who* it stood for. Mussolini repeatedly saluted the wounded soldiers that had done their duty to Italy, and he expressed a reverence bordering on worship for the sons of Italy who had died to secure greatness and freedom for the fatherland. Only through their blood sacrifice, and more of it when needed, would the new Italy be born.

Brio was clearly transfixed, whether because of professional interest, as an aficionado of politics, or an affinity with the aims of the new group, she could not yet tell. Normally, Carla could confidently predict Brio's views, which were solidly socialist and consistently critical of the revolving administrations he felt offered no meaningful solutions to Italy's ills. She felt that Brio must reject much of what Mussolini had said, even if only on the grounds of consistency. But as she scrutinized his face, it was hard to tell what he was thinking.

After a while, Carla had had enough. There was undoubtedly something powerful about his oratory, but it was more performance than substance. She nudged Brio and asked if they could leave, but he gently gripped her arm without looking at her, in a gesture which clearly meant 'not yet.' When Mussolini finally finished, he raised his hand once again to accept the rapturous applause. The outstretched arm looked like he was trying to quieten the crowd, but he seemed to have no interest in stopping the acclaim, as he nodded at the room pompously in recognition of the adulation. Taking their opportunity, Brio took Carla's hand and edged his party toward a door at the back. When they reached it, two large black-shirted men with clubs seemed reluctant to let them pass, reviewing them sceptically, as if they couldn't understand why they would want to leave the performance when the maestro may be about to deliver an encore. As the applause subsided, Carla noticed that many of the men nearby were looking at them. Then, to her horror, she heard Mussolini call out from the stage.

'What's the matter, Brio? Was it something I said?' Mussolini was standing, feet apart and hands on hips, staring at Brio. The attention of the entire crowd turned to them. For once, Brio was speechless as Mussolini addressed the room. 'We are honoured, comrades, by the presence of a journalist from *Avanti!* Here, no doubt, to mock our historic gathering in his column tomorrow.' The mood in the room turned septic and jeers rang out. Those closest to the trio moved even closer. Carla had never been more frightened in her life. Mussolini let his dogs growl and strain on their leashes for a moment, before transforming his stern face into a huge grin. 'Or perhaps you are here to join us, old friend?'

Brio finally found his tongue. 'Who knows, Benito?' he shouted across the room. 'I hear all the best fascists start out at *Avanti!*' Brio gave a little bow, and Mussolini roared with laughter. Most of the veterans got the joke and joined in, but the mood in the room seemed fragile to Carla and the brutal-looking men on the doors looked unsure of what to do. She couldn't help herself from scanning the men closest to her and one lewdly ran his tongue around his lips as their eyes met. She turned away and tightened her grip on Brio's hand. She felt someone brush against her back and glanced round in horror, but was relieved to see that it was Abercrombie stepping between her and the leering man.

'Let our socialist friends go in peace,' commanded Mussolini, with an expansive wave of his arm and his own bow.

'The socialists are no friends of ours!' someone heckled from the front.

'Yes, yes, we have many friends in the socialist movement, comrades,' retorted Mussolini. 'They just don't know it yet!'

As more laughter rang around the room, Carla felt Brio pull on her hand while Abercrombie gently pushed her between the two guards, who parted to let them through with obvious reluctance. Together, Brio and Abercrombie kept her moving out the door and into the chilly March air.

5

Naples, 30 August 1945

Once I realised the book could contain clues about what had happened to Carla, I brought *The Life and Death of Abercrombie Lyle* to my face and kissed it, tasting a hint of the fuel that would have incinerated its secrets in seconds if still on that pile. For while I sensed something inhuman and evil about it, the book had also given me something precious and joyous. The flame of hope, so nearly extinguished, had been rekindled. I had been given another chance to find her. Strangely, it didn't occur to me at the time to worry about the title. But if I ever found the end of 'my' biography, it didn't sound like it would be a happy one.

After Paestum, I had searched for Carla for almost a decade. I had travelled across Italy and returned to our old haunts in Milan many times. I had tailed Brio around Rome in the vain hope he might lead me to her, and I had scoured Paestum again and again. But the trail had gone cold quickly. I never admitted it to myself at the time, but by the first anniversary of her abduction from Paestum my quest had become perfunctory and ritualistic. I couldn't stop looking, but in my heart, I didn't expect to find her.

For several years after that, as funds from my meagre teaching salary allowed, I searched in small towns in the deep south of Italy – in Basilicata, Puglia, Calabria – where I knew undesirables of the new regime had been exiled, but I could find no trace of her, nor of Louisa or Enrico. In 1935, I had met a former communist in Naples who told me of a woman he had seen when exiled to the island of Lipari in 1928. His description sounded as if it could have been Carla, or it could just as easily have been someone else. I managed to track down others who had been in *confino* on Lipari, but no one had seen her, and, as far as anyone could tell, she had never been there.

After that, with no hint of her fate one way or another for ten years, I stopped looking. The small voice of reason that had long told me she must be dead grew shrill. *She is gone, Abercrombie. You must accept this. If she were still alive, she would have found a way to let you know, even if she were rotting in a prison. She was resourceful and kind. She would not leave you in this purgatory, even if she were in hell.*

In the following years, this voice had grown stronger, but it could never completely extinguish the hope that smouldered behind the cold facade of my new life. Sometimes this hope was the one thing that prevented my world from freezing over. To assuage my guilt at giving up the search, I made a promise to Carla, and to myself, that I would not leave Italy until I found her, or at least discovered her fate, whether she was living or not.

When the new war started, I at least had a distraction. I never really expected to see Carla again, but if Italy were defeated and the fascists toppled, I might discover what had happened to her, buried in some archive, or even from Brio himself if he were captured. I followed the progress of the war avidly, seeking news from soldiers returning from Libya and people I knew with connections to the port. I became skilled at filleting the propaganda and layering in my own sources. It was a strange time. I welcomed the British bombs that once came close to killing me when they strayed from the railway sidings a mile away, and I felt a perverse satisfaction when rations were introduced and I had to nail another hole in my belt.

By February 1941, the Italian army in Libya was clearly in disarray, but I took no pleasure in the many merchant ships that never returned, nor the bewildered, wounded peasants that haunted the city in bedraggled uniforms too big for their stunted bodies. I had brief hope that Italy might capitulate and Mussolini be forced out by the Army or the King if Libya fell, but the British advance stalled and the arrival of Rommel turned the tide in the spring.

Then came an event that crushed my hopes. I had never liked Churchill. His colossal arrogance and boy-scout jingoism had grated ever since the shambolic and suicidal Gallipoli campaign, and I never forgot his role in creating the Black and Tans – those peculiar British cousins of the fascist *squadristi*, recruited from a similar set of damaged old soldiers and allowed to run amok in Ireland. For Churchill, politics was a game, and ordinary people just pawns on his chessboard. Anyone so profligate with the lives of others couldn't be trusted.

But he'd been right about Hitler, and his surprising return to grace as prime minister in 1940 had certainly stiffened spines back home. I remembered well his 1940 Christmas address to the Italian people after their cowardly and humiliating failure in Greece. It had been an unexpected tonic. *Italians, this is the point to which one man alone has brought you; one man alone!* This wasn't the kind of thing Italians were used to hearing about their infallible Duce, but after the debacle in Greece, I began to hear mutterings of agreement.

When news broke that Churchill had gone down with the *Prince of Wales* in August 1941 off Scapa Flow *en route* to meet Roosevelt, my very lonely sense of grief, amid the public celebrations, took me by surprise. Inevitably it summoned memories of my own father's death at sea, and I feared for Britain's resolve to go on fighting alone. America's entry to the war in December briefly raised my hopes, but they seemed more interested in the Pacific than the Mediterranean.

In 1942 the news just kept getting worse. Crippling losses of shipping in the Atlantic. The fall of Singapore. Then Malta in May. I was no military genius, but everyone in Naples knew that capturing Malta removed a major obstacle to supplying the troops in North Africa. It was the beginning of the end for the British in Egypt, and the end came quickly. Without Churchill, morale seemed to collapse. The new prime minister, Anthony Eden, struggled to hold the government together amid a series of confidence votes that were gleefully reported in the Italian press, and when Tobruk fell in June, demoralised British forces fell back on Cairo. Auchinleck surrendered to Rommel in early July. The game was clearly up for the British in India as well, unless the war could be brought to a swift conclusion. Eden resigned, ushering in Halifax with a mandate to seek an armistice. I can still see the photographs of him smiling in his silly bowler hat and old-fashioned civilian clothes on the seafront at Biarritz, surrounded by Hitler, Mussolini and Petain – all in military uniform. The gormless bastard. Britain was allowed to keep India, for the time being, but was forced to surrender Burma to Japan and all of its African colonies to Italy or Germany. Italy now had control of the Mediterranean, with colonies stretching from Libya to Palestine and bases in Malta and Crete. Mussolini's dream of *Mare Nostrum* had been achieved.

The government hastily printed maps that looked like a new Roman Empire, and this one would never need to defend itself from barbarians at the gates. This time they'd opened the gates at the beginning and invited the barbarians in to build the empire for them. Mussolini had to be the luckiest man alive. Then again, Faust probably thought he'd hit the jackpot at the beginning.

When the armistice came, I briefly wondered if I should return to Liverpool. But there was nothing for me there, so I decided to keep my promise to Carla and stay in Naples. Perversely, the faint breath that kindled embers of hope across the years, even after the British surrender, was Brio's.

I knew Brio was still alive. Everyone knew that Brio was alive, for he was now one of the most powerful men in Italy. I had seen how Carla and Brio had been together when we were young. I knew how much he loved her and had seen what he would do to protect her. Despite what happened between the three of us, my instinct told me he couldn't hurt a hair on her head. But I couldn't be sure. Love and hate are such close bedfellows. I had once loved Brio, too, but now hated him with an intensity that made me ache when I thought of him. Sometimes the irony was almost too much to bear. My scintilla of hope was the knowledge that the monster I despised had enough love for Carla to have kept her alive.

6

Milan, 19 March, 1919

After their escape from Mussolini's meeting, Brio had never seen Carla so angry. She was on her second Mi-To at Bar Magenta but still wouldn't speak to him. At first, he had tried to pass it off as an amusing adventure they would all laugh about in a few days, but she wasn't having that, responding with a series of glares that seemed to strengthen rather than diminish over time.

When she went to powder her nose, Abercrombie turned to him and said: 'She's had a shock. She'll be fine, but she needs time to calm herself.' Then he gave Brio a friendly nudge. 'A bit of grovelling wouldn't go amiss, as well.'

Brio nodded. Abercrombie was right. He needed a different strategy.

'One day, when I was six or seven,' Abercrombie continued, 'a wee bairn, as my Da would say, he'd taken me on a march through town on St Patrick's Day, and we were pelted with bricks and stones by Orangemen. When he got me home, blood pouring from this little beauty.' Abercrombie pointed to his cheek. 'Ma turned into a Whirling Dervish and started whacking him with a ladle. Looking back, it was quite funny, but not at the time.'

Brio turned to Abercrombie. 'I sense some sage advice emerging from this heart-warming tale of domestic serenity.'

'The point is, it was the angriest I ever saw my mother, and no amount of bluster about "little scratches" or "making a man of him" would settle her. It was only when Da got down on his knees and begged her forgiveness that she let him off the hook. The whiskey helped as well. It was the only time I ever saw him on his knees outside of St Anthony's Church.'

'Point taken. And who are these Orangemen?' asked Brio.

'Another time. She's on her way back.'

When she reached the table, before she had time to glare at him again, Brio took her hand and looked her in the eyes. 'I am so sorry my darling. That was foolish and reckless of me. I put you in danger, and the thought of someone hurting you is so terrible that I pretended the danger wasn't real. But it was real. I know what some of those men are capable of. Can you forgive me? I swear, I will never put you in danger again.'

Carla took another sip of her drink, and as if Brio had laced it with a magical calming elixir in an absurd comic opera, her face softened.

'Yes, I can forgive you. But what were you thinking! That was a very stupid thing to do. We could have been beaten . . . or worse.' Carla wasn't quite ready to absolve him yet.

'I know, I know.' Brio's eyes were downcast, and his hands clasped on his lap like an altar boy accepting his punishment after being caught drinking the communion wine. Then his eyes flashed up to Carla and there was a hint of a grin on his sensuous lips. 'But wasn't it fascinating?'

Carla looked at him sceptically. 'At times, but some of those men were vile. Some of them . . .' her voice trailed off, as if she were imagining what might have come next. 'And your friend is a pompous peacock. His speech made no sense! Please don't tell me you agree with what he said.'

'Pure gobbledygook,' Abercrombie interjected, 'even accounting for the parts my poor Italian might have missed.'

'Yes, of course, much of it was nonsense,' replied Brio, testily. 'He's obviously still working it all out, but did you see how he spoke, and how they reacted?'

'I did, and I didn't much like it, if I'm honest,' said Carla.

There was something about Carla's attitude that irritated Brio. He understood her reaction, but he didn't like the way she was judging these men without any idea of what they had experienced. To be fair, how could she? In the last months of the war, she had seen some of the damage it could inflict on a human body as a nurse, but this had been in Milan, far from the front. He decided to take a different tack.

'But didn't you feel the energy? There was something new and powerful in the way he spoke, don't you think? Those men are desperate for a better Italy after what they've been through. He understands their anger. He might be the one who can ride the wounded beast, control it, give it what it needs and deserves.'

'I'm not sure he was trying to control it,' replied Abercrombie. 'More like merrily digging his spurs into its belly. I saw their faces. Some of those men haven't come back from the front yet, and we both know what men did there. It all felt a bit dangerous to me.' He gave Brio a meaningful look. 'Apart from the very silly hats,' continued Abercrombie. 'Some of them were wearing a sort of Stetson covered in feathers. It's quite hard to be frightened of a man with half a dead bird on his head.'

Brio looked at his friend. It was the first time he had alluded so directly to the horror of the war. The first time he had gone beyond sanitized anecdotes and the mundane practicalities of army life. He also found it hard to believe that Abercrombie was unaware that the headgear he was referring to belonged to the Arditi, the Italian shock troops, who most certainly were men that one should be frightened of. Then he noticed Carla shooting Abercrombie a sly grin and realised what he was up to. 'Perhaps you're right,' Brio offered in a conciliatory tone. 'And perhaps this *Fascio di Combattimento* will go nowhere. But we should keep an eye on him. He might still be a useful ally for the Left. I knew him well before the war. He's a brilliant man. A force of nature.'

'Flatulence is also a force of nature,' replied Abercrombie, 'I usually try to ignore it, or blame it on the nearest dog.' At this, Carla burst out laughing and sprayed some of her orange Mi-To onto Abercrombie's face. He nodded at her as if she had paid him a compliment, before theatrically removing an imaginary pair of spectacles. He used his handkerchief to mime cleaning them before wiping his face. With that, Brio shrugged and joined in the laughter.

7

Naples, 30 August 1945

I needed a quiet, safe place to read the book from start to finish, with pens, paper and space to think. That place wasn't Caffè Giordano, which was filling up and getting noisy. So, I left some change on the table and was rising to leave when a familiar voice called out to me.

'Michael, wait. I need to talk to you.' Although I had gone by the name of Michael for the last nineteen years, it still occasionally failed to register, if I was tired or distracted. It took me a second to realise that Luigi, a neighbour from my apartment building, had spotted me and was making his way across the room. I liked Luigi but wasn't in the mood for local gossip.

'How are you, Luigi?' I asked.

'Much better now that you've stopped ignoring me,' he smiled. I looked at him quizzically. I had no idea what he was talking about.

'Friday, on the landing. You came out of your apartment and turned away from me, as if I didn't exist. Very rude, Michael. I thought the Irish were a friendly people, not like your "stiff upper lip" English neighbours.'

'I apologise. In my own little world again, no doubt. I'm never at my best in the mornings. I was probably still half asleep,' I offered by way of excuse.

'Half crazy, you mean. It was the middle of the day, and if that's you half asleep, I'd like to see you wide awake. I've never seen anyone skip down those stairs so fast. When I shouted your name, you started running like you were late for your own funeral.' Luigi seemed more confused than angry, but not as confused as me. I hadn't left my office in the university since arriving at nine that morning, except to eat lunch in the faculty dining room.

'What time did you say this was?' I asked.

'About two o'clock. Don't you remember?' Luigi looked at me like I had gone insane.

'Are you sure it was me?'

'Well, I wouldn't swear on my firstborn's life, but it looked like you, from the back at least. I'd recognise those skinny legs anywhere.'

I began to feel woozy, as if I were disconnecting from myself.

Luigi carried on, oblivious to the impact of his news. 'That's a terrible suit, by the way.' He felt my collar. 'You need a new one, if you don't mind my saying, and the cut makes you look so "English," which is never a good thing. How old is this? Let me send you to my cousin. He'll sort you out. He's very reasonable.'

I ignored the offer and apologised again, making an excuse about rushing to give a class, which I realised later would hardly reassure Luigi on my sanity, given that it was Sunday. I raced back to my rooms, a few hundred yards away on a street three yards wide off Via dei Tribunali called Vico del Fica Al Purgatorio. The tall, decaying buildings were tied together by washing lines that blocked out the light. I hated it down there, trapped in the bottom of a dark trench, no matter how hard the sun battered the terracotta tiles on the rooftops above. When I'd moved in fifteen years ago, the dark humour of my new address had, for some reason, appealed, but I hadn't considered the daily reminder of my state of limbo that the street sign would provide. I really should have moved somewhere else.

I fumbled with my keys, eventually unlocking the heavy wooden doors to the courtyard, and ran up to my little apartment on the fifth floor. Inside, I opened the windows and shutters, to let some light and air into the stuffy room, and took deep breaths to calm myself. I scanned my bedroom, sitting room and tiny kitchen. They looked as I had left them. In the sitting room I checked my old oak desk and unlocked the narrow central drawer. My meagre savings and letters of employment from the university as an assistant professor in the Department of History were undisturbed. Nothing seemed to be missing or out of place. Luigi must have made a mistake. He'd seen someone of similar size and shape running down the stairs and assumed it was me.

I slumped in my cracked leather armchair, staring at Enrico's drawings of the three temples of Paestum that hung over my desk, doubting once again if having them on my walls was wise. They kept dragging me into the past when I didn't want to go there. But I couldn't bear to take them down. It was all I had left of the time we'd spent together. Well, almost all.

I stared at the Temple of Neptune and pictured the four of us clustered before the six enormous Doric columns of its entrance, the biscuit-coloured stone glowing in the setting sun. I closed my eyes and let myself wallow in the imagined din of the crickets under 'our' oak tree, lying on the old picnic blanket, strewn with half-eaten plates of tomatoes, bread and mozzarella. Enrico, with a sketch pad, was squinting, a pencil held horizontally at the end of an outstretched arm. Louisa had her eyes closed in concentration and was humming softly, perhaps working on her next composition, perhaps just amusing herself. Carla's head was on my lap, sleepy in the heat, trying to read a book. I was simply watching her face and gently twirling her thick black hair in my fingers. When she was distracted like this, I could gaze indefinitely into her eyes. Their ice blue irises with contrasting dark edges gave them an otherworldly quality. I used to tell her she looked more Irish than Italian, a fantasy her inventive mind embraced with gusto. When the fancy took her, she would play a game, creating episodes of an ever more lavish history for our ancestors, and a fantastical, adventurous future for us.

The stories stretched back in time to her romantic forebears – a gallant Gaelic lord, dispossessed by Cromwell and shipwrecked off the Amalfi coast in the service of some old Bourbon king, and a Piedmontese princess, whose offspring would now rule Italy had she not absconded with said Gaelic lord. They had many grand adventures, and there were many grand adventures to come for us in a future that made Phileas Fogg seem like an agoraphobic. But the ending was fixed upon early. The two of us in our dotage in Arran jumpers, scribbling away in a whitewashed cottage on the wild Connemara coast. I was happy to go along, adding decorations and details, often inspired by my mother's tales, to the ever-growing Baroque cathedral of our future. There were moments, when she was in full flight, those eyes alight with mischief, when I would wonder how an ordinary boy from Liverpool had been admitted to this particular paradise. I knew some sort of cosmic mistake had been made but hoped that if I kept quiet, with my head below the parapet, it would be a while before anyone noticed.

I opened my eyes and now saw that Enrico's sketch was slightly askew. With a pulse of nausea, I realised that it was the sketch directly above my hiding place. I went to the desk and saw a small, new scratch on a floorboard by one of its legs. I panicked and dragged the desk across the floor. Snatching the old knife I used for a letter opener off the desk, I prised up the floorboard and reached in for Carla's old jewellery box that she had left behind in Paestum. It was still there, and relief flowed through me. But when I took it out to check inside, I had my second shattering shock of the day. My old British passport, in my real name, was still at the bottom in its envelope, but my fake Irish Free State passport in my new name, Michael Lynch, was missing.

This discovery untethered me. I hadn't known how valuable it would be when I'd got it, but that Irish passport had been a godsend. As a citizen of a fellow Catholic country that had also suffered at the hands of the selfish, plutocratic, imperialist British, I was tolerated by the university authorities. But without my 'proof' that I was Irish and not British, I would never have been allowed to teach and would likely have been interned.

Even as an Irishman, my teaching had been subjected to intense scrutiny. During the war I had been careful. It was easy to keep a low profile teaching ancient Greek and Roman history if you stuck to the classics and occasionally waxed lyrical about the glories of Rome. But since the Armistice I had become reckless, taking risks to get my students to think for themselves.

I had given a class on Greek philosophy for many years but this year I'd clearly ruffled the little eaglets' feathers with my lecture on Plato's allegory of the cave. Some of the students evidently hadn't appreciated my joke that perhaps they were all chained in their own dark cave watching shadows cast by a puppet master, rather than looking at the real world. Someone had slipped an anonymous 'thank you' note in my pocket, but several had complained, and I knew, after my dressing down by the Dean, that I was likely in some sort of black book.

Part of me didn't really care if I was sacked. I had begun to despise teaching this new generation of Italians. Their transubstantiation into the body and blood of fascism was almost complete, and my occasional acts of petty classroom rebellion felt pointless. But the missing passport was different. If they knew I was a British national posing as Irish, I would almost certainly be arrested, and might even be shot as a spy.

I continued to root through Carla's jewellery box and noticed that the poems she had written for me were also gone. As was my old handkerchief with the orange Mi-To stains, and worst of all, my only photograph of Carla had been taken. Or rather, it had been replaced by another picture. The woman in this new picture was still Carla. She had her eyes. But something was off. It took me longer than it should have to recognise the anomaly, but when I did, I fell to my knees and threw up. There was no doubt. In the new picture, Carla was much older than the last time I had seen her in Paestum.

8

Milan, 11 April 1919

Brio and Abercrombie sat in the warm, early evening sun outside one of Brio's favourite bars. There was something about Abercrombie's company that Brio found so – uplifting. An evening with Abercrombie was like a short trip in a hot air balloon. He could leave his politics and anxieties below and, for a few hours, forget the daily struggle to forge a better future for his beloved and unfortunate country. Looking down from their basket, Abercrombie might make a wry observation about Italy, or the world beyond, that no one else he knew could make, and together, they could soar through the clouds and scan the horizon to explore what the future might bring.

Abercrombie had his own demons, which Brio sometimes glimpsed, but his detachment from Italy's recent trauma, the poverty of Milan's streets, and the neuroses of her politics, gave him a lightness that Brio clung to whenever he could. Together, they would float above the city and say what they wanted, as long as it made one of them feel better or the other one laugh. Brio wasn't sure how Abercrombie did it, if what he'd been through had been anything like his experience, but he was a tonic, and if he could put him in a bottle and sell him, he would be a millionaire in these dark times.

Part of Abercrombie's appeal was that he was beyond the fray. With Abercrombie, he didn't have to worry about transgressing a socialist orthodoxy, or accusations of reformism, or syndicalism, or nationalism, or whatever 'ism' he wasn't supposed to espouse. Abercrombie would talk about politics but always managed to slip through his fingers before he could pin a label on him. *An 'ism' is like a prism,* Abercrombie would say, *turn it around and you get another interesting view.* Of course, this made no sense if you thought about it too hard. But it was the kind of thing Abercrombie might drop into a conversation without a care for whatever deeply held beliefs he might be trampling over. Brio wondered what it must be like to float above the world like this, and while he liked the temporary feeling of liberation Abercrombie gave him, he worried that his friend might have become untethered from reality. After a while, Brio was always ready to return to the noisy and troubled soil of Italy, even if the landing came with a bump.

Their bar was on a small square behind the Pinacoteca Brera. After their visit to the Last Supper, Brio had felt compelled to show Abercrombie the other artistic treasures of his city, and he was gratified to know that, like many tourists, Abercrombie was unaware of the gallery's existence. It seemed like foreigners thought that all the art produced in Italy over the centuries had ended up in Florence, Venice or Rome. Abercrombie had been delighted by the Pinacoteca, and Brio felt like he had given him a small gift, a partial re-payment for the joy he'd brought him in the few weeks of their acquaintance.

'It's my birthday on Tuesday,' observed Abercrombie. 'I'd almost forgotten.'

'We must celebrate!' replied Brio.

'How old do you think I am?'

'Now that I know you a little, I would wager twelve, or maybe thirteen?' replied Brio.

'If only that were true,' Abercrombie gave him a rueful smile. 'I will be twenty-one.'

'Then we most certainly will celebrate.' Although Brio knew this age must be correct, he found it hard to accept. To him, Abercrombie often behaved like he was either much younger or much older.

'There's no need to go to any trouble.'

'No, please. I insist. Carla wants to see you again, and we have some friends you should meet . . . And you're so far from home. We can't let you sit all alone in your little room with only your books for company.'

Abercrombie laughed. 'I don't think you know me very well if that's what you think I'd be doing on my twenty-first birthday.'

'So, what would you be doing?'

Abercrombie went silent for a short while. 'I'm not sure what I would do here, but if I were home, there would be an obscene amount of beer and whiskey, no food worth speaking of, and a racket of Irish music, some of it songs of a rather dubious nature encouraging acts of violence against anyone wearing a British uniform.'

'That sounds like fun, if rather barbaric. A party with no food!'

'Yes, Liverpool can be a bit barbaric.'

Brio realised that he knew very little about his friend's former life beyond a few wartime anecdotes, and almost nothing about his life before the war. He wanted to ask him why he was here and not there. What he was hoping to find, or what he was running away from. But he didn't feel it was his place to interrogate him, yet. Abercrombie would no doubt tell him more when he was ready. He also didn't like to think of him having to run away from anything, and, for selfish reasons, he worried that scratching the surface of Abercrombie's past might prick the balloon and let the air escape. He wasn't ready for this phase of their friendship to end, and so he satisfied himself with a simpler question.

'Do you miss Liverpool?'

'Only the beer and the whiskey. There's not much else left to miss.' Abercrombie scanned the piazza, his face soft and serene as the low evening sun burnished his pale, freckled face. 'I think I prefer it here.'

He seemed on the verge of saying more but didn't.

After a pause that Brio sensed Abercrombie would not break, he asked, light-heartedly, 'So there was no sweetheart left behind?'

'No, at least no one I really cared for. Not like you and Carla.'

'Yes, I'm very lucky. She's a good girl.'

'A good girl! Is that the best you can do?'

'You're right, of course. She is exquisite. I don't know what I would do without her.'

'Then don't dilly dally, Brio, or some other fellow might march in, and you'll get to find out.' Abercrombie scrutinized Brio in a way that made him uneasy, as if he had somehow said the wrong thing about Carla. 'She's clearly head over heels in love with you, for some inexplicable reason. So, what are you waiting for? If I were you, I'd be down on one knee with a ring in my pocket before the night was out.'

Brio wanted to change the subject.

'And why would there be singing about shooting British soldiers? That doesn't seem very patriotic, and rather ungrateful after all they must have suffered in the war.'

Abercrombie laughed, with a sarcastic edge Brio hadn't heard before. 'Oh, it's *very* patriotic. You couldn't get more patriotic than some of the fellows I know.'

'Sometimes you speak in riddles, my friend. I'm not sure I'll ever understand how the mind of an Englishman works.'

'Me neither,' replied Abercrombie, as he turned to look for the waiter and called him over to order two more whiskeys. 'And whatever made you think I was English?'

9

Naples, 30 August 1945

Sitting on my apartment floor with my back against the desk, I looked again at the new picture of Carla. I turned it over and saw '1933' written on the back. The handwriting looked familiar, but I couldn't be sure it was hers based on so few characters. I scrutinized the image for any clues that might shed light on her new life or reveal where the photograph had been taken. The most obvious feature was that it was only part of a picture. It had been cut down the middle to make an oddly narrow portrait. Someone had clearly been excised.

She is standing on a garden lawn with mature trees in the background and looking at the camera. She is wearing a pale silk blouse and a checked tweed skirt with a tartan-like pattern. Her hair is shorter, an unruly bob. She is as beautiful as ever, perhaps more so with some of the youthful softness sharpened by age. If the date is correct, she is 35 or 36. The arm nearest the cut is held straight and vertical in a way that looks unnatural until I realise that her hand is being held. The cut is precise at the edge of her right hand, but it can't remove the curled fingers of another hand passing through it. The fingers are small and their height from the ground hits me hard. She is holding the hand of a child.

I feverishly started filling in the rest of the picture in my mind. An idyllic, yet awful, domestic scene of a mother in her garden, with her son or daughter. The most disturbing part was that she looked happy. My mind ran wild with the possibilities of her life after Paestum. Who else had been cut from the picture? More children? Their father? I don't know what I expected her life to be like if she were still alive, but it wasn't this. I should have been happy that she wasn't rotting in a cell on Lipari or banished to some godforsaken, dried-up mountain village in the south, but I was disorientated by the image. Over the years, I had beatified Carla in my memory. She had become an icon of female perfection, a Platonic ideal. I had spent many years surreptitiously searching for her, refusing to believe she was dead but having no clue as to her whereabouts, and all along, there she was, having an ordinary, contented life – a life that did not contain me. I struggled to push the negative thoughts from my mind, to focus on the proof of her survival and the hope that I might still find her, but I couldn't. I felt betrayed.

*

I'm not sure how long I sat on the floor of my apartment but eventually the sun dipped low enough for it to reach deep into the room and shine uncomfortably in my eyes. Then I noticed the smell of my vomit, which roused me like a dose of smelling salts. My new life, such as it was, had been blown apart. The revelation that Carla might be alive and happy had ripped away the stale bandages concealing my old, wounded identity, pulling off strips of diseased flesh. I knew I was in danger from some incomprehensible, diabolical force and should leave immediately – that I couldn't sit here inert, as day became night, in the shell hole of my false existence – but I was unable to get up.

Only when I was about to wet my pants, did I struggle to my feet and go to relieve myself like an automaton. In the communal bathroom down the hall, I cleaned myself up as best I could and looked at my haggard face in the small, broken mirror. It didn't really matter what I looked like. The events of the day had opened a trap door beneath me. I had been in a version of purgatory that could barely be tolerated, and now I was somewhere else. If not yet hell, then somewhere close, and not a place where I cared if my shirt was stained with my own vomit. Whatever came next, I could not go back to what I had been a few hours ago. That life, if life it could be called, was gone. So, I returned to my rooms and packed my rucksack with some bare essentials: a few clothes, what money I had, and, after a moment of hesitation, my old British passport. I added the fragments of Carla, my sacred relics, and, of course, the partial copy of *The Life and Death of Abercrombie Lyle*. There was only one way to go now, and that was down, into whatever hell lay in store for me. Whether I would come back up again seemed almost irrelevant.

10

Milan, 1 April 1919

Carla stood on the platform hoping that the train bearing her father would never arrive. She had not seen him since returning home to Asti for Christmas three months ago. But there had been plenty of letters. Letters that she now only skimmed, in case her mother was ill or there was some news of her nephew, Francesco. They contained little of interest, beyond the odd reminder of how much they all missed her. She had barely read the last few. She didn't need to. They all said the same thing, with minor variations. *The War is over. You must come home!* That last Christmas had been a visit to forget from the moment she stepped off the train. She remembered the look of disappointment on her mother's face when she couldn't see the trunk they had packed her off with, and she had realised that she wasn't coming home, just visiting.

Her parents had reluctantly allowed her to volunteer as a nurse in the last year of the war, though they hated the idea of their beautiful, unmarried daughter, barely twenty and alone in Milan with all those young soldiers and no one to protect her. Under normal circumstances, it would have been out of the question for her to leave home unmarried. But they were so proud of Paolo, away at the front, serving his country. So zealous in their support for the war. So convinced of the justice of the cause. It was hard for her father, with his lawyer's mind, to make the case against her. Especially as he had pronounced on the need for all Italians to play their part so many times around the dinner table. Carla had deployed her arguments well, appealing to the heart as well as the head. *I must help our brave soldiers, Papa. Imagine Paolo lying wounded in a hospital bed with no one to nurse him. If all of Italy's daughters were locked away at home, who would be there for Paolo?*

In the end, it was easier for Carla to persuade them, or rather him, than she had expected. Her father was a logical man. He knew when a case had been won or lost. And when he gave in, there was even a rare moment of good humour. He patted her cheek and told her she might make a brilliant lawyer herself one day, before giving her an indulgent smile that she hadn't seen for many years. At the time she had been so pleased. She had hugged him and showered his face in kisses like a little girl. Only later did she recall the self-satisfied reference to his own greatness, and after that, she wondered if the smile was only good-humoured acquiescence. Did it also contain a hint of condescension at the very idea of a woman being able to do what he could do, even one as clever as his beloved Carla?

The realisation of Carla's parents that she was returning to Milan after Christmas wasn't the reason for the horror of that visit, however. It was the gaping, silent, Paolo-shaped vacuum opposite her at the dinner table, and the tears of her mother that could not have filled that void had they flowed for eternity. There were several reasons why Carla didn't want to go back to Asti: the desire to protect her new freedom, the boredom she would feel if she returned, the pressure to marry some son of her father's respectable business friends and settle into a middle-class provincial life. And, of course, there was Brio. But there was only one reason why she *couldn't* go back. She could not bear to be in that house knowing that her twin brother Paolo would never be there with her.

There were many small things that made this unthinkable. The photographs of her brother in uniform above the fireplace on the dining room mantelpiece. How could she ask for them to be removed? The sight of her mother's shuddering shoulders when she caught her quietly sobbing in the kitchen. The solemn demeanour that now fixed her father's face in marble.

The realisation that she could never live in that house again had come suddenly. She was sitting alone, late in the evening, reading in the parlour to fill the hours before she was exhausted enough to sleep, and she had noticed the impression left by Paolo beside her on the old velvet sofa with the tired gold braid and tassels. She had sat with him there so many times, reading her latest story to keep him amused on long winter days, until he became restless, and his heels kicked against the heavy clawed feet of the uncomplaining beast. She had knelt before the sofa and stroked the depression left by her twin. When she touched the little gouges made by the heels of his swinging boots, the grief broke on her like a wave she had foolishly turned her back on. For a moment, she wailed, hard, like a siren, and no matter how much she had tried to stop, for fear of waking her mother, it wouldn't let her go until it was spent. She knew then, this permanent presence of his absence, signifying how he would always be beside her, and yet never there, could not be borne.

The steam of the slowing train wrapped her in warm, dirty air, before rising and dissipating against the iron arches of the station roof. Screeching brakes took an age to bring her father's train to a stop beside her. He emerged from the smoke, and they embraced, awkwardly, almost formally. His gaunt, bearded face was even sterner than she had remembered, as if he were bearing more bad news, or perhaps he was steeling himself for a task he did not wish to perform.

'Hello Papa. Are you well?'

Her father removed his hat before he replied, as if he were an undertaker.

'As well as can be expected . . . in the circumstances.'

An awkward silence followed and became excruciating for Carla amid the bustle and bonhomie surrounding them. Other passengers were greeted with warm embraces of reunion or hearty handshakes and laughter. She noticed two young lovers kissing.

'Will you not ask if I, too, am in good health?'

'I would not need to ask if you were at home, where I could see for myself.'

Carla felt her spirits sink even lower. 'Let us not quarrel, Papa. Come, we will have a pleasant lunch, and you can tell me how Mamma is. And Francesco, is he doing well at school?'

'They are both mere shadows compared to their former selves. But I have not come to Milan to relay news of our family. Nor to take you out to lunch. I have come to bring you home.'

'But Papa—'

'This has gone on long enough, Carla. We will take a carriage to your lodgings. You will pack your belongings, and we will return to the station to take the last train home to Asti. Tonight.' Her father held her firmly by the shoulders and stared at her. 'Is this clear, Carla?'

Carla met his gaze. 'Oh Papa, I am sorry. I know I have neglected mother. I promise I will visit soon. Perhaps I could come home for Easter, in a couple of weeks, but I cannot live at home again. I have a life here now.'

'Your life is where I say it is! With your family, until we find you a suitable husband and you are married—'

He suddenly released her and took a step back, as if an electric shock had passed between them.

'Of course. How could I have been so blind? There is already a man. You have a man, here in Milan. That is why you will not do as I bid.'

'Papa, no, no. That is not the reason. I can't—'

'Do not lie to me, Carla!' He took her chin and forced her to look at him. His beard was long and unkempt. 'Look me in the eye and tell me there is no man.'

Carla hesitated.

'What a fool I have been! Sending you money each month, praying and begging for you to come home, before your reputation, your honour, is tarnished, and all the while you are already ruined!'

'Papa, no. It is not like that. There is a man that I am . . .'

'Say it, you are in love with this man. You are in love with him!'

'Yes, I think I am. But he, we, have behaved honourably. I swear it.'

'Who is he?'

'His name is Brio.'

'What does he do?'

'He is a journalist for . . .' Carla hesitated again.

'For what. What rag does he write for?'

Carla looked at the ground and realised that the next word she must utter would seal her fate. Then she looked her father in the eye and decided to say it with pride. 'He works for *Avanti!* Papa, and yes, he is a socialist.'

He looked at her in horror. She could see that he was trembling, as if struggling to contain his rage. She had never seen him this angry. For a horrible moment, she feared he would launch into a diatribe about how she had sullied the memory of her brother and all the men who had died for Italy. But his words, when they came, were as calm as a frozen lake.

'If, as you say, you have behaved . . . honourably, then all is not lost. I will forgive you, on the condition that you break it off and return with me to Asti today.' He said this as if he were offering his final word on a legal contract.

Carla did not need to consider his offer. She knew it simply was not possible for her to agree.

'I'm sorry Papa, but no. I will not do that.'

Her father closed his eyes, his head sank forward and his whole body sagged.

'Then you leave me with no choice.'

Carla felt a chill pass through her.

'Until you break it off with this Brio, you are no longer welcome at our home. Your allowance will cease with immediate effect, and you will have no further communication with your mother or nephew.'

'You cannot stop me seeing mother, or Francesco!'

Her father continued, as if she had not spoken.

'I hope you come to your senses. But let me warn you now. If you were to marry this, Brio, we . . . we would no longer consider you our daughter.'

'Papa, you do not mean this? You cannot mean this!'

Carla took the thick collar of her father's black frock coat in her hands. She was torn between trying to shake some sense into him and begging him to reconsider, but before she could do either, and without saying a word, he removed her hands with a grip so hard that it hurt her wrists. Then he slowly walked away down the platform without turning. Carla sunk to her knees and sobbed.

11

Milan, 15 April 1919

To celebrate my twenty-first birthday, it had been arranged that I would meet Carla at the bar down the street from *Avanti!* Brio would escape as soon as he could, and we would head to a local osteria for a late dinner with some of their friends. He said I would be doing him a favour. He had arranged with the editor to leave early, but it was never easy to get away and I could keep Carla amused instead of having to wait alone for him, which seemed to be a regular feature of their relationship, and, as far as I could tell, the only source of tension between them. From my perspective, the favour went the other way. I was very much looking forward to seeing Carla again, if a little nervous about being on my own with her. My Italian was improving but still far from perfect.

I arrived early and sat facing the door at what, by now, was our regular table. To my surprise, Carla and Brio arrived together a few minutes later. I rose and this time kissed her hand, before giving Brio his now customary kiss on both cheeks.

'He thinks you are a Contessa, or a Princess,' Brio said, which made her smile.

I blushed.

'Don't listen to him,' said Carla. 'He's a brute. He's just jealous of your fine English manners.' Carla looked me in the eye, and something went awry in my guts.

'Ah, but he's not really English,' replied Brio. Carla looked perplexed.

'It's complicated,' I said, not wanting to explain my Celtic soup of ancestry at this point.

'Anyway, slight change of plan,' said Brio. 'I can't get away for another hour, but I have arranged for you to be shown around the print shop.'

I could see that Carla was excited. Now that the war was over, she was training to be a teacher, but she was also an aspiring writer.

"Thank you, darling.' She kissed him on the cheek, then turned to me. 'He's been promising to show me the print shop ever since I met him, but the beast is always too busy.'

'If you think I'm a beast, you should see some of the dirty devils who work down there. They are literally filthy, by the way. I'll be amazed if your blouse escapes unblemished.' Brio gave Carla the merest hint of a raised eyebrow.

Carla's eyes glanced down at her pristine white bosom, as if she were having second thoughts. My eyes could not help but follow hers. I pulled them away quickly, feeling slightly ashamed of myself.

'But you have this fine English gentleman to protect your honour from the dirty devils,' Brio continued, 'so you will be fine.'

Carla stuck her tongue out playfully at Brio. It was just a tongue, but it felt like I had seen something I shouldn't. I was disappointed at not having Carla to myself but tried not to show it.

'Won't it be very noisy?' I asked.

'No, not very, they're still setting the type and waiting on a few late articles. The noisy stuff happens later when they start printing,' replied Brio.

'What are we waiting for then?' Carla sounded like we were setting off an adventure. I downed my drink, left coins on the table and followed the two lovers out of the bar.

*

We entered the old brick building on Via San Damiano via large wooden double doors overhung by a small first-floor balcony that gave out onto the street. The *Avanti!* office formed a section of one long, unbroken three storey façade that gave the impression of a modest fortress. Inside, a high-ceilinged but gloomy room stretched back from the street. An oily, inky smell pervaded the space, and there were only two front windows, either side of the main door, to break the monotony of the bare brick walls and cast-iron pillars.

We were greeted by a middle-aged, balding man called Michele, who in youth had probably been as tall as me but whose hunched shoulders diminished to more average size. He wore a filthy brown, deep-pocketed, leather apron and an enormous, upturned moustache that looked capable of getting caught in the bewildering and dangerous looking machinery arrayed behind him.

'Salve, Signorina Cellini,' Michele kissed her hand with archaic courtesy, then turned and nodded to me, 'Signor Lyle.' He swept his arm across the print shop. 'Let me show you where the real work happens at *Avanti!* We will let Signor Salvatore go sharpen his pencils, or whatever he does up there.' Michele, shooed Brio away with a dismissive gesture and took Carla gently by her elbow to begin the tour. Brio smiled at Carla, patted me on the shoulder and disappeared off into the print shop.

A dozen or so men were busily setting the type and checking equipment, but Michele was a model of unruffled charm and patience, as he explained the processes and machinery to Carla. I recognised my place as a tolerated appendage to a rare jewel, the like of which was no doubt rarely seen in the print shop. I happily tagged along behind as they toured each machine, stopping to talk to some of the men. I had never been in a printing press before and found it fascinating, though I struggled to comprehend all of Carla and Michele's conversation. To the evident delight of Michele, Carla asked detailed technical and business questions about the mechanics of the typesetting, the size of the print run, and the cost of printing. She seemed especially taken with the huge rotary printing press with its circular drums that could print and fold 20,000 pages an hour from continuous rolls of paper. When our tour was over, Michele, graciously explained that he had some proofs to check but we were welcome to stay and observe the start of the printing, as long as we were careful not to get too close to any moving parts.

Just as I was thanking Michele, I heard some shouting from the street outside and Michele excused himself to see what was going on. A few seconds later there was banging on the door. I could see through the machinery that two printers had put their shoulders to it and were being buffeted by an unseen force from the outside. Above us, along the side of the print shop, an internal door flew open at the top of a steep set of stairs. I saw a frantic bearded man lean over the wooden balustrade and shout: 'Bolt the doors, there's a mob outside trying to get in.' Two nearby printers ran past and bolted the large double doors to our left at the back of the workshop. It was just in time, as a few seconds later there was also banging on these rear doors. Then came a crash of broken glass as something flew through a window at the front of the shop.

I could hear shouts and a horrific scream. The front door had been forced, and fights were breaking out at the front of the shop as the mob poured in. I realised we were in danger of being trapped. I grabbed Carla's hand. 'We need to go, now.' She nodded and we started toward the staircase across the print shop. Another window smashed somewhere behind us, and Carla screamed as a flaming torch flew in, landing near a huge roll of paper, which instantly caught fire. As we reached the foot of the stairs a tall man with a club appeared and took a swing at me. I ducked, and as the arc of his swing flew over my head, I took my chance and threw my shoulder hard into his chest, sending him into the brick wall at the foot of the staircase. As the man tried to stand, I kicked the side of his head with all the force I could muster, then I stamped on his wrist, which lay across the edge of the second step. The crunch of broken bone felt horrible. I just had time to claim the club before two more men were almost upon me.

'Brio!' Carla screamed. I followed her gaze upward. The image would imprint on my memory. Charging down the stairs, coat flying, eyes ablaze, and wielding a full-length hat stand above his head, Brio launched himself at the two men. I just had time to get out of his way as Brio's momentum, fury and multi-pronged weapon had a devastating effect on the nearest assailant, his face exploding in a bloody mess as he fell back into his comrade. I dragged the first thug off the staircase and

Carla didn't hesitate to skip over him and dash up the stairs. I followed her and turned at the top to check on Brio. He was a few steps below, hat stand pointing down at another man about to ascend the stairs. The man was dark-haired, wiry and carrying a long dagger. I noticed he was wearing a black shirt, like most of the other intruders. From my elevated position, I could now see twenty or so of these black-shirted men setting about the presses, smashing and breaking what they could. Then a man in full Bersaglieri officer's uniform put his hand on the shoulder of the dagger-wielding man facing Brio and shouted something in his ear. The man tried to start up the stairs but was pulled back and pushed in the direction of the printing presses.

'Brio, come now!' Carla shouted.

I saw Brio hesitate, as if he really wanted to charge down the stairs and back into the heat of the battle, but he followed us up the stairs and turned to Carla.

'You know the way to the back stairway?' She nodded. 'Both of you go, now. I'll meet you at the bar.'

'Where are you going?' Carla asked, panic clear in her voice.

'I can't leave now,' replied Brio.

I was torn between helping my friend and ensuring Carla's escape.

As if reading my mind, Brio pushed us through the doorway. 'This isn't your fight. Get her out of here!'

I looked beyond Brio and saw several small fires burning and blackshirts attacking printers across the shop. A few were fighting back with whatever tools they had to hand but it was a mismatch of weaponry and numbers. Other blackshirts were smashing the rotary presses with sledge hammers. It was a scene of chaos that could have been painted by Hieronymus Bosch. My instinct was to close the door on Carla and follow Brio down the stairs, but when I saw the imploring look in his eyes I nodded, took Carla's hand and pulled her into the office. She struggled and screamed at Brio to come with them. I caught a last glimpse of Brio running down the stairs with the hat stand held before him like a pike. I grabbed Carla round the waist and half lifted, half dragged her further into the office. A few young *Avanti!* men ran past toward the stairs to join the fray. I shouted 'where's the exit?' One pointed to a door at the far end of the room past two rows of desks. Then Carla finally acquiesced. She took my hand and led me through a door, onto a flight of dingy wooden stairs. We ran down and out into a large courtyard shared with the surrounding buildings to form an enclosed rectangle. I realised that it must be the same courtyard that gave access to the rear of the print shop. To my left I saw two printers staggering out of the rear entrance. One of them was bleeding from his head and helping an older man, who was dragging a leg and barely conscious. I noticed with horror that the older man was Michele. We immediately went to help. We each put one of the lame printer's arms over our shoulders and guided him toward an arched passageway that led onto a side street. The other printer followed, pressing a rag to his head. Then the sound of smashing and shouting was broken by a muffled whump as something exploded inside the print shop. A shower of shattered glass flew from a ground-floor window onto the courtyard where we had stood moments earlier. I could feel the heat on my back and an awful cry chased us across the courtyard. Then came sporadic gun shots.

'We must go back for Brio!' shouted Carla, struggling with Michele. But I knew I had to get Carla out of the courtyard.

'We'll get them somewhere safe, and I'll go back,' I replied.

Exiting via the stone archway, we turned left on the side street, away from Via Damiano, toward the imposing brick pillars and large iron railings of an elegant urban villa. We dragged Michele through the gates and into the garden, which had a large glass conservatory to the right. I tried the door, but it was locked. I kicked at the lock with my heel, and it gave way onto an improbable miniature paradise of lush foliage and exotic flowers in bold, primary colours. It seemed as safe as anywhere in the immediate vicinity, although the expanse of glass surrounding us made me nervous after what I'd just seen.

'Help Michele. His leg is bleeding. I'll be back,' I said, and before Carla could object or follow me, I placed the groaning printer on an ornamental wrought-iron bench and ran out.

Re-entering the courtyard, it was a battle scene. Men were staggering or being carried out the rear door of the print shop. Smoke and flames were now gushing from the first-floor windows. As I got closer to the rear door, I could feel the crunch of glass underfoot. Two blackshirts came running out. The first one, laughing, despite a huge gash across his face, looked around, and ran, club held high, toward a printer cowering in the far corner of the courtyard. The second had a pistol and fired random shots back into the building until he seemed to run out of ammunition. He turned and stared at me from five yards away. He slowly pointed the gun at my chest. The blackshirt's face was sweaty and crazed, as if drunk, or lost to some other high. His hair shone slick in the flickering light of the flames. He pulled the trigger and shouted 'bang!' while flipping up the barrel of the gun to mimic the retort. Then he laughed maniacally and turned away to follow his comrade across the courtyard. Something inside me flipped and I charged at the man, who didn't seem to realise the danger until I was almost on him. I flew into him with a hip-high rugby tackle that took us crashing to the ground. The gun skittered away, and I had him face down on the flagstones. The blackshirt reached for a club on his belt but I put a knee on his wrist to pin it. As I straddled the man, I realised that I was holding a bizarre, dandyish tail of hair on the top of his head. Instinctively, I used it to pull his head back before using the heels of my hands to slam his face into the flagstones, with the kind of force that only rage can generate. I heard the crunch of his pulverised nose, and the man went limp.

For a moment, I was paralysed by what I had done. Was he dead? Before I had time to find out, a vicious thud across the back of my head knocked me off the prone blackshirt. Dazed, I stared up at another blackshirt standing over me, just in time to see him knocked to the ground by a long, pole-like object with broken bits of wood hanging from the end. The wielder swung the pole again, this time crashing it down with tremendous force onto the top of the man's head as he tried, and failed, to get to his feet. The blackshirt went down again and I now saw my saviour. Wild-haired, panting, with blood dripping from his fingers, a god of vengeance and fury stood over me, his clean hand reaching down to pull me from the underworld.

The Carabinieri were finally entering the courtyard from the print shop, blowing whistles, shouting, and somehow adding to the insanity. I felt myself rising to my feet and being held around the waist.

'Where is Carla?' Brio shouted into my ear, cutting through the chaos.

'Safe.' I felt detached from the mayhem, as if it were happening on a stage and I was safely up in the gods. 'Garden,' I managed to point toward the archway.

I allowed Brio to half lead and half carry me out of the courtyard. On the street, I felt sleepy and disorientated but somehow stayed upright and directed Brio to the conservatory with a series of hand gestures.

We entered a surreal world of natural wonder. It smelled of sweet, flowery perfume and damp, musty death. I saw Carla, her blouse, pristine and virginal an hour ago, now torn and bloodied. I saw a look of horror on Brio's face and heard Carla's, *I'm fine, I'm fine,* as if it came from another world a whole universe away. I felt myself placed down gently, padded and numb, on the welcoming softness of the paved floor. I stared up at huge green fronds framed by a blackness of flickering crimson and gold, reflecting and dancing above me. The concerned, filthy faces of two familiar people looked down on me. I realised in a microcosm of clarity that these were the two people I loved most dearly in the world. The *only* people I loved in the world. I was calm, but their faces were contorted, desperate and shouting silently from the other world. They were beautiful and ghastly at the same time. I thought perhaps this other world could be heaven, or it could be hell, or perhaps it was both. And then I didn't care which it was, as I submerged into the simple truth of pure blackness.

12

Naples, 30 August 1945

The only place I could think of to take stock of my situation was the old reading room of the university library. I knew it wasn't the best place to hide from someone who knew my movements, but it wasn't the worst. It was secluded and quiet – very quiet on a Sunday evening, as it was only accessible to a handful of faculty and staff who had a key. I needed somewhere to read and make sense of my situation. It seemed as good a place as any. And if they did find me, whoever they were, I might at least get some answers, even if they were answers I didn't want to hear.

I waited until it was almost fully dark to leave my apartment and slipped down the central stairwell to the ground floor, checking that no one was peering out from their front doors as I passed. My building was not an especially private place, but the residents seemed preoccupied with Sunday night family dinners and their doors were all closed. On one door I noticed a small *curniciello*, the curled red horn one saw everywhere in Naples to ward off the evil eye. I touched it and thought that perhaps I should finally start wearing one like everyone else.

As I descended, I wondered if I would ever see my neighbours again. I had lived here for over ten years and was fond of them, despite the fact that they couldn't seem to ask for the salt without shaking the foundations of our building. There are only two types of communication in Naples: shouting and laughing. They made the Milanese sound positively English. But for once, the clamour of their percussive domestic lives was welcome as it masked my progress to the ground floor.

Unfortunately, there was only one way out to the street: through the main door into the courtyard. I quietly lifted the latch and waited for a noise or commotion. One usually didn't have to wait long, and when I heard a loud greeting from a window above, I slid out and down our narrow alleyway, hoping this would serve as a distraction if I were being watched. I walked briskly north, in the opposite direction to the university. After three or four random turns, I stopped and hid in the dark recess of a doorway. I thought I heard footsteps stop abruptly in the direction I had come from, but there were many distant footsteps on the hard stone streets. I waited for several minutes and didn't see anyone pass. It didn't seem like I was being followed, but I couldn't be sure.

I headed south on Vico San Nicola a Nilo, then west on Via San Biagio del Librai to pick up Via Giovanni Paladino, which took me to the entrance of the library. I quietly opened the huge wooden door using keys that the head librarian, my friend Borromeo, had made for me a few years ago when he grew tired of having to kick me out every night. I stepped into the colonnaded courtyard of statues, keeping to the shadows of the arcade, and then softly climbed the marble staircase to the first-floor gallery. The keys also gave me access to the old library reading room and I went to my usual desk in the far corner. After a moment's hesitation I decided to stay there. I needed something familiar, some calm and normality, while I planned my next step, and if they were looking for me here, sitting in another seat wouldn't make any difference.

The fresh air had cleared my mind a little, and I tried to hold my anger at Carla in check, at least until I had read the book. There was so much I didn't know about what had happened to her after Paestum, and so much that she may not have known about me. I had no idea what conditions may have been placed on her liberty, or what lies she might have been told. She could believe that I was dead. She might have waited and searched for years herself, before deciding that her life must go on. I made the best effort I could to suspend judgement until I knew more. I owed her that, at least. Pushing the new image of her domestic contentment away, I removed the torn book from my rucksack and picked up where I had left off in 'my' biography.

13

Milan, 17 April 1919

I was dragged from a desperate and confusing dream by a strident chorus of birdsong. Emerging into a grey half-light I could see a faint, distorted cross. It took me a moment to identify it as a silhouette of a window frame on the wall opposite, rather than a symbol of the afterlife. I felt the presence of another person next to me. I tried to turn my head and gasped at the stab of excruciating pain at the back of my skull.

'Don't try to move, old man,' a familiar voice advised, as I felt a large hand fall on my forearm.

'What happened?' I asked.

'A large manganello happened,' Brio replied, referring to the ungainly club that was a favoured weapon of the *squadristi*. The events of the previous evening slowly emerged in my fuzzy mind.

'Is that one of your filthy Italian aperitivos? You must remind me never to drink them again.'

Brio laughed. 'You see. I told you he'd be fine.'

'Carla, where's Carla?'

'I'm fine. Don't try to talk,' she replied unseen. A much softer hand alighted on my other arm.

'And you, Brio?'

'A few cuts and bruises. Nothing a few whiskeys couldn't cure,' he replied.

'By which he means two broken ribs, a broken knuckle, a deep cut to his left forearm that nearly severed an artery, and a body mostly the colour of an aubergine,' said Carla.

'Why aren't you lying in a hospital bed as well?' I asked.

'Why indeed!' answered Carla.

'I will lie down again presently. I wanted to be here when our English socialist hero woke up.' Brio sounded genuinely proud.

'I don't think any of those descriptors are true,' I replied. 'Especially not the hero. If I remember rightly, it was you who saved me.'

'And so modest, too. How very English! But don't try to talk any more. You must rest. And have some water. You must be very thirsty.'

'Not very—'

'Yes, yes. The doctor said you must drink some water when you wake up.' Brio, his back turned to Carla, leaned into my field of vision, wincing with the effort, and gave me an exaggerated wink. 'Carla, would you be a dear and get him some water?'

'Are you sure the doctor said that?' Carla sounded sceptical.

'Yes, yes, be a good girl. I can see from his cracked lips. He's parched.'

I felt her hand leave my arm and heard the rustle of her skirts as she left the room.

'Listen, don't talk, we don't have much time.' Brio was suddenly urgent and serious. 'The man you . . . fought with . . . is dead. No one else saw. No one else knows. Say nothing about it. If the carabinieri—'

'Carabinieri?'

'Quiet. If they ask. Tell it exactly as it happened except that when you came back into the courtyard looking for me, you were hit on the head from behind and saw nothing. I saw you on the ground and helped you escape. You know nothing about what happened in the courtyard. Understand?'

'I understand. But Carla?'

'She knows nothing, and she wasn't there. It will all be fine if we stick to the story.'

Carla returned with a glass of water and Brio helped to raise me so I could take a sip. Pain seared through my head and down my neck.

'Now you must rest, my friend,' said Brio.

'Well, that was a twenty-first birthday to remember.' I said.

'Not really,' replied Brio. 'You were unconscious for much of it.'

As I lay back down and waited for the wave of pain to subside, I was almost grateful for its intensity. It helped to block out the thought of what I had done. This rage had never been there before the war, and after the war I hoped never to feel it again. But perhaps it would always be a part of me now, a demon that may have lain dormant if not roused by the insults of battle and misfortune. Perhaps it would never sleep deeply again, but merely doze, ready to lash out at the slightest provocation, never fully soothed by my desperate pilgrimage for delights and distractions.

'Let him sleep,' said Carla, as she reached over and kissed my cheek. I now saw her for the first time since waking up. She looked astoundingly beautiful. I guiltily inhaled the perfume-infused air that enveloped me and felt a few of her stray hairs almost imperceptibly brush my cheek. The genuine affection in her ice-blue eyes made me feel even weaker. She stroked my cheek with the back of her hand, and, along with the soft, warm flesh, I felt something cold. I took her hand and felt the simple band on her third finger. My eyes flashed to hers and then to Brio, who couldn't help unleashing one of his expansive smiles.

'You don't get much past him, even with a fractured skull,' beamed Brio. I ignored the diagnosis, which was the first I'd heard of it, and glanced again at Carla. She looked bashful but very happy.

'We were going to wait until you felt better before we told you,' she said. 'He proposed to me last night.' Carla looked across to Brio and took his hand as well, creating an open chain between us.

'And you were crazy enough to say yes?' I said, with as much of a smile as I could muster.

'I save your life, and this is the thanks I get?' Brio replied in mock protest.

'I'm very happy for both of you,' I said. And I meant it. I was happy for them, but there were other things I was feeling that were harder to name. I reached out with my other hand to take hold of Brio's free hand and close the circle.

'It's like we're getting the blessing of the family priest on his death bed,' said Brio.

'I do give you my blessing. But I don't think you need it. I think you are both already blessed. I think you are both wonderful.'

'Jesu!' mocked Brio, 'I think that bang on the head did more damage than we thought.'

And, in truth, I did feel strangely confused and disorientated. The pain, the exhaustion, the self-loathing for what I had done, and the intense emotions I felt for Brio and Carla, swirled in my mind. It was almost too much to bear.

'Go to sleep, dear boy,' said Carla, releasing my hand and stroking it as she laid it down. 'We'll come back later to see how you're doing.' She smiled at Brio with such contentment it almost made me cry. Brio winked at me and reached a strong protective bear paw across her back. I watched them leave, their hands joined again, and mine empty.

14

Naples, 30 August 1945

I settled in my corner of the old library, with its familiar dusty smells and walls of ancient books. The dim light of my desk lamp enclosed me in a protective halo while the library lay dark and silent around me. I stroked my hand across the polished oak of the desk and let the smooth, cool sensation soothe me, like the fragment of silk trim from my old baby blanket had done in the trenches. When I felt calmer, I took the book from my rucksack and placed it carefully at precise right angles to the desk, as if this could help order and make sense of what it contained. I opened it and started to read chapter 2, which charted my war years.

The Life and Death of Abercrombie Lyle was an increasingly strange and disorienting book. It was uneven, in that some events of trivial importance were recounted in detail while some of great significance were glossed over. And it was schizophrenic. It was written in the third person, but the tone shifted. It felt like the biography of two different people. Sometimes it read like I was writing about myself, with recollections aligned to my memories and interpretations of events. Other passages described a very different Abercrombie, interpreting my actions in cruel and unfavourable ways. As I progressed, I had to remind myself that, unless I had suffered some sort of amnesia, both 'Abercrombies' were imposters, but I began to recognise two very different narratives. One was kinder, sometimes too kind, ascribing more altruism and purity to my motivations and behaviours than they deserved. The other was critical, sometimes to the point of outright condemnation. I labelled my two selves 'the Saint' and 'the Doppelgänger.'

I could feel these two voices at play throughout the text, tossing it back and forth and sometimes fighting over it. Teasing them apart precisely was impossible. They were intertwined, often in the same paragraph, in a Manichean struggle for my story that made me doubt my own memories and even my sanity. Then I arrived at a passage that felt as if a surgeon had sliced to the core of my brain and emerged with a dark pearl of regret that I had thought buried safely beyond even my own reach.

When Michael went off to his war, there were no marching bands and pretty girls waving scarfs at Lime Street station. He left at night, alone, in the hold of the cattle boat to Dun Laoghaire. He had told Abercrombie to meet him before last orders in the Lord Nelson, without the other fellows. Abercrombie knew something was afoot but had no idea what it was. He supposed Michael might be up to no good with stolen goods from the docks and was trying to rope him in. He had rehearsed excuses to get out of it without sounding like a snivelling coward. But he was barking up the wrong tree.

His twin brother always told him everything, and, after a few pints, he would add a few implausible additions. Michael was only just the right side of a braggart, but he could tell a good yarn, and Abercrombie hung on every word of them. Girls, drink, escapades at the docks. They were born together but Michael was always ahead of Abercrombie in so many ways. 'How come you're twins and he's already a man' was the kind of comment they often got. Abercrombie rarely made it beyond 'we're not identical' before some Smart Alec chirped up with 'too bloody right you're not' and he gave up on biological explanations.

So, when Abercrombie found him staring into his pint, he knew something was wrong. 'I'm off to Dublin. Tonight.' he said. 'I can't tell Ma. You'll have to do it.' Abercrombie asked why he was going and for how long, and all the other things a twin brother would ask when his other half says he is leaving home at no notice. But he could hardly get another word out of him. Abercrombie remembered the ferocity with which Michael said he couldn't *tell him, as if it were beyond his control; and when he said that there were moments in life when a fellow gets sick of talking and wants to do something, Abercrombie was certain he was in danger. He knew that he should have stopped him. He tried, but in a weak and pitiful manner, and he realised later that Michael was telling him, rather than Ma,* because *he was weak and pitiful, because he knew Abercrombie wouldn't and couldn't stop him. Ma would have whacked him with a hairbrush. She'd have reduced him to his ten-year-old self, told him to stop being an eejit and sent him off to bed; and he'd have probably taken it. Abercrombie merely begged him pathetically not to go and then cried like a girl when he left. If he'd been a man, a man like his brother, he'd have beaten some sense into him, and he would still be alive.*

The memory of that night, the night I had last seen my twin brother, nearly unravelled me. For years I had pushed him so far down and away from me to a place where I couldn't even hear his voice. At odd times, faint echoes reached me, usually late at night. Sometimes in my dreams, he was bleeding and crying to me for help in the cellar of some shitty Dublin slum. Sometimes he just wanted a chat down the pub. But I always ignored him. It was too painful to listen. It was easier to endure my shame and regret as an abstract emotion. Real and hard, but simple, hidden at the bottom of my pocket, and as small as I could make it. My black pearl.

15

Milan, 18 April 1919

Later that day, or it could have been the next, I woke again, emerging from a febrile dream of distorted, charcoal-smeared faces, golden fires and flowing blood. The dream lingered briefly, somewhere between an image and a feeling, eluding understanding as the real world regained supremacy. I smelt, rather than saw, that there were flowers in the room and then realised that someone was holding my hand. I didn't need to look to know it was Carla.

'How are you feeling?' she asked.

'Like someone's been using my head as a football . . . but better for having you here.'

'You know, you don't have to make a joke of everything. Not all of life is a joke.'

'I think the last few days prove you wrong.' I turned my head to see her and, despite the vision I was rewarded with, an ice pick of pain made me instantly regret it. 'I came all the way here to see some beautiful things and forget about the war, only to end up in a fight with a bunch of crazy Italians, who, last time I checked, were meant to be on our side.' I paused to let the pain subside. 'I think I saw one of them hitting someone with some sort of stiffened fish. You must admit, that is quite funny.'

'You can't help yourself, can you? Give that head of yours a rest.' She spoke to me with a tone of irritation that I had only heard her use with Brio.

I lay back down, hating that I couldn't see her. 'How is Brio? And what about Michele and the others?'

'Brio will be fine, apart from some numbness in his hand that might never go. Michele is not so good. They saved his leg, but he'll never walk properly again. Three printers, and one fascist, are dead. But I won't be shedding any tears for him. I hope the bastard is burning in hell.'

Her curse and its vehemence shocked me, but also knocked some sense into me. Earlier, in moments of lucidity, I had tortured myself for killing the blackshirt, even to the point of considering whether I should turn myself in to the Carabinieri. Her tone reminded me that the blackshirt would have shot me had he not run out of bullets. Killing him may even have saved someone else. But the fury of my assault on him still disturbed me.

'When you were unconscious, we realised that we knew almost nothing about you. About who you really are, and who would miss you if you had . . .'

'I don't think anyone would miss me,' I replied.

'First the clown, now self-pity. You are incorrigible. You must have some family, or friends, back in England, that we should tell . . . if anything happened.'

'It's not self-pity. I just don't think I would be missed.'

'There's no one?'

'No. Ma died of Spanish flu in January. Da went shortly before her. His ship sunk by a U-boat in the last weeks of the war. The news of that nearly finished her off before she even got the flu.'

'I'm so sorry. I had no idea.'

My mind drifted back to my mother, lying in a hospital bed much like the one I was in, feverish and weak in her final hours.

'You've had a horrible time.'

'No worse than many others.' There was a long silence. I had no idea what time of day it was, or even what day it was. The half-light in the room could have been dawn or twilight.

'No brothers or sisters?' She asked.

I didn't want to talk about my brother.

'There's an alcoholic uncle, a few old school friends, and about a hundred cousins. Oh, they'd have a good old drink, and tell each other what a grand fellow I was, but I'm not sure they'd really *miss* me.'

'That's very sad, not to have a family that cares about what happens to you.' Carla's tone made me feel like an object of pity. Of all the things I wanted Carla to feel for me, pity was the last. 'Are you sure there isn't anyone you've forgotten? The doctor said a concussion like that could affect your memory.'

'I'm sure.'

'No sweetheart, back in Liverpool? No wild Irish Colleen, fresh off the boat, staring out to sea, pining for her soldier boy who returned from the war only to fly away, like a wild goose . . . or should it be swan? To break her heart again?' Carla's voice had risen in mock romantic declamation. I appreciated the attempt to amuse me. It was like she could feel my mood and ride it, gently but firmly, in the direction it needed to go.

'No. Unless you count Kitty O'Halloran. She was pretty wild, but I doubt a fumble or two behind the Lord Nelson has driven her to keep a vigil for my return at the Pier Head. By the way, that's an impressive cocktail of clichés you've thrown together there. Your bedside table must be groaning under romantic novels and tomes of Irish history.'

'As a matter of fact, I have been reading some Irish history, and some Yeats. I found them in your room. I'm trying to understand what goes on in that strange head of yours.'

'You've been in my room?' For a moment, I felt uneasy and slightly ashamed, but then I saw it as a sign of a greater intimacy developing between us.

'Well, someone had to. How do you think that pile of clothes made its way here, and your cigarettes?'

'I'd assumed, Brio . . .'

'Ha! All he's brought you is whiskey . . . which I have taken away on doctor's orders,' Carla quickly added.

'So there's no one we should tell, if something happened to you?'

'There's my grandmother, in Scotland. She was kind to me when Da died. She gave me some money that she was hoping to leave to him. I suppose she'd want to know what had happened to the last of the Lyles. But we were never close.'

'And who is Michael?' asked Carla.

The unexpected mention of my brother's name caused my face to twitch. How could she possibly know about Michael? Then I remembered the inscription in the volume of Irish history he'd given me before he left.

Eventually I replied, 'no one who cares about me now.'

We were both silent for a long time. At some point she must have let go of my hand, as I now I felt it rest again on top of mine.

'I see now why you wanted to leave, but what brought you here?'

There were many answers to that question. One was simple and the others more complicated, but they all led eventually to the simple one. I was broken by everything I had seen in the war and everything I had lost at home. I had come to Italy to find whatever solace I could in its beauty and, without any great expectations, to find a way to start my life again. My sojourn in Italy was a quest for my own renaissance in the only place I could think to find it. I was a walking cliché, and too embarrassed to admit this to Carla. It was easier to give her a more complicated answer.

'I suppose I'd have to say that it was a book.'

'A book?' Carla looked at me, intrigued. 'Which one?'

'I don't know. I never knew what it was called. I only remember reading it. No, it was more like falling into it. My mother had brought me to work one day in the Big House, as she called it. I must have been eleven or twelve. I sneaked out of the kitchen, desperate to explore. It was like a palace compared to our tiny terrace. I found my way into Mr Tyrer's study, and open, on his desk, was an enormous leather-bound book. It looked so old and so heavy. I didn't dare to close it to look at the cover. But I did turn the pages, very carefully. There were sketches of Roman ruins and drawings of fine sculptures, Renaissance palazzos, maps of Italian cities, coloured plates of exotic birds and flowers. It was another world. I didn't know then, but later I realised the author must have been on the Grand Tour. I promised myself that one day, I would travel to Italy to see it all for myself. When my parents died, there was nothing for me to stay for. So here I am. If I hadn't met you and Brio, I'd probably be in some hovel in Florence or Rome, with no money, and wondering what to do next with my life.'

There was another long silence. I had no more to say. I hadn't told any of this to another soul, not even Brio. It was like speaking a language I had just started to learn, and my vocabulary was exhausted. I suddenly felt very tired, as if my two months in Milan had been one extraordinarily long day that had kept me awake with a wild array of distractions and stimulants. I now realised that I desperately needed to sleep. A wave of exhaustion swept over me and, for once, in Carla's presence, I let my mind go blank. I stopped trying to think of the next thing to say to amuse her and started to drift.

Before I floated off, I felt her lips on my forehead and heard her say: 'In that case, you must stay here with us, and we will be your new family, Mr Abercrombie Lyle.'

16

Naples, 30 August 1945

I struggled on with the next chapter, which covered the end of the war and my decision to leave for Italy in early 1919. Toward the end, I felt that I might have had gone a little mad. The two voices were still there, but I began to wonder if they might both be mine. In the final words of the chapter, the duet between Saint and Doppelgänger achieved a stark dissonance.

> *When news reached their little house that his father's ship had gone down in the Atlantic, a week before Armistice Day, it hit them like one of the autumn gales that Ma used to march the family into on Formby sands; but where* they *revived her soul with memories of the wild Connemara coast, this cruel wind knocked her down. Abercrombie saw her strong and vivid presence transform into something fragile and insubstantial, like dead marram grass loosed from the dunes, and sent tumbling into the sandy wilderness. The loss of Michael two years before bent her flat. This broke her; and when Abercrombie saw that she had no will to go on, it nearly broke him, too.*
>
> *However, he knew, even then, that in the end he would let her blow away into nothingness and save himself. His roots had also been ripped out, but he sensed that they could survive elsewhere. He had already abandoned his Ma once, when he had joined up to fight with Michael barely cold in his coffin, and now he decided that he would leave Liverpool again, even though he knew it might kill her.*
>
> *As he later found, his fickle roots were destined to insinuate themselves into the welcoming soil of warmer climes; and in that soil,*

he thrived. To his great surprise and good fortune, he would chance upon a delightful garden. He was cultivated and protected, mistaken for an exotic, foreign flower that needed particular care. Too late, his gardeners realised that what had initially delighted with its difference, was no more than a common weed that would choke and destroy the native species in the garden.

I closed the book and forced myself to step back from the explosion of emotions it had sparked. I felt drained and needed a break before I could go on. To distract myself from my memories, I reflected on the puzzle the book presented, and the more I considered the events it recounted – events that had occurred before my arrival in Italy, it seemed impossible that Brio or Carla could have written what I had read so far. Unbelievable as it was to me, the only plausible conclusion was that I *had* written this book, or at least part of it. I had spent many hours at the Front relieving the tedium by re-reading a treasured volume of Sherlock Holmes that Ma had given me as a boy. As Holmes would have put it, when you have eliminated the impossible, whatever remains, however improbable, must be the truth. *I* must have written these pages and then had a breakdown or neurasthenic crisis that had erased my memory.

The dual nature of the narrative was troubling and difficult to comprehend, but not all the lacerating observations were crazy. There had been plenty of regret and self-doubt over the years, and many passages contained elements of truth. I wondered what my ability to abandon my mother and go to war within weeks of Michael's death said about me as a son, and I had felt unending guilt about my failure to stop Michael leaving. Perhaps these had driven me to write a confessional, and it had sent me mad in the process, with the madness emerging on the pages in ever more vicious self-flagellation.

As this possibility sank in, I looked at the book with renewed horror. What depths of despair and self-hatred would it reveal in the chapters to come? If there were moments of darkness in these chapters, what might I have committed to the page in later chapters? The ones that inevitably must cover the obsidian-black years after Paestum.

I stared at my watch. It had been given to me by my Scottish grandmother and had once been my grandfather's. I watched the steady progress of the hands and heard the inexorable ticking of time passing. The effect was hypnotic, and I was so tired that it took a few seconds for my eyes to focus and my brain to translate the position of the hands into a time. It was past two o'clock in the morning and the only thing I knew about myself for certain was that I was spent. All I wanted was sleep, and, once I recognized this, my body took over and my head dropped. Like a survivor of a shipwreck tossed for so long in a storm that he no longer cares what happens, I lay my head on the desk, as if it were my life raft, and gave in to my exhaustion.

17

Milan, 20 December 1919

On the eve of Brio and Carla's wedding, it seemed to me that Italy was heading toward some sort of cataclysm. In Milan, strikes and factory occupations were regular events. A worker's council formed, and new huddles of unemployed men seemed to emerge on street corners every day – most of them former soldiers who knew how to fight. I had seen extreme poverty and violent strikes in Liverpool before the war, but this felt different. I remembered my home city grinding to a halt for an entire summer when I was thirteen. There were endless open-air meetings of striking dockers, railwaymen and seamen on the plateau outside St George's Hall. Michael would persuade me to sneak away from school to savour the chaos. I had been young, so it was hard to compare, but looking back, that had felt like a long, unexpected school holiday. What was happening in Milan felt like the end of school altogether. I realised later that when the wealth and power of Liverpool's elite had really been threatened, it was clear who was in charge. I remembered Da raging about Churchill sending a gunboat down the Mersey, *as if we were bloody Africans or Chinamen*. I remembered soldiers marching down Scotland Road, past the end of our street, behind armoured motor wagons. When the police had had enough, they charged the massive crowds on St George's Plateau with batons, injuring hundreds, and the army had shot two people dead. But what was happening in Milan felt like no one was in charge, or rather, the people who were supposed to be in charge either didn't know what to do or didn't have the will to do it.

'This isn't like England,' Brio reminded me as we sat in a noisy bar with his best man, Enrico, and a few other friends, the night before his wedding. 'You have your ancient constitution, your king and your parliament. Your aristocrats know how to hold on to power even when there's mayhem on the streets. They bend a little here, invite a few more people to join the club if they have to, but they know when to tighten their grip on the workers' balls. When to stamp on their necks!' With this Brio had slammed his glass down on the table, splashing some of the precious amber fluid onto the back of his hairy hand, which he licked from wrist to knuckles. I wasn't sure I'd ever seen such a huge tongue emerge from a human mouth. There was something grotesque about it, and my mind wandered to the whole calf's tongue that had repulsed me when Ma had brought it home from the butcher's. Once my mind had turned to offal, there were more recent images that inevitably clamoured for attention.

Thankfully, the waiter put another glass in front of me and I realised that Brio was still speaking.

'The English have been doing it for centuries, all over the world. Generations of the same families with their hands around the necks of the workers. They loosen their grip a little now and then to let the people gasp a few desperate breaths, but not for long.' Brio's hands shook in an open clasp before my face before he snapped them shut. 'No one expects them to lose their grip, maybe some don't even want them to, as long as there's enough bread on the table.'

Enrico interjected. 'Brio, there's nothing special about the English milords. As a patriotic Italian, I resent your impudent slander on the ability of our aristocracy to stamp on the necks of our own workers just as viciously.' He swept a long fringe from his flushed forehead. 'It's a matter of national pride. I have complete confidence that they can stamp as hard as any Englishman – and probably with more style!' he added, wagging a finger at Brio. 'Don't you agree, Abercrombie?'

'What you assert is undoubtedly, incontrovertibly, indisputably true,' I said. No one could prick Brio's bubble when he was in full flow better than Enrico, even if it sometimes took Brio a little while to realise it.

'Rest assured, comrade,' Enrico slapped Brio on the back. 'I'm quite certain that our own King and Parliament will not bring shame on our great nation with any hint of moderation. Let no man say that our glorious masters are less proficient in the arts of oppression than the English! They will surely reassert their authority any day now with as much brutality and cruelty as any rulers known to the annals of history!' Enrico raised his glass high and then drained it in one. 'As soon as they run out of champagne and work out how to button up their trousers.'

The table burst into laughter and Brio looked at Enrico as if he were a simpleton.

'Abercrombie, don't listen to him. They couldn't find a fanny in a Neapolitan whorehouse. Weak, clueless, imbeciles to a man. Our Parliament is a joke compared to yours. But – and here is why we have hope, when your country, dear friend, does not,' he tapped his nose conspiratorially, 'they are so useless, they won't be around much longer.'

'You can't be sure of that.' I replied.

'I can feel it in my bones. I can smell it on the streets. Nature abhors a vacuum. Look what happened in Russia, what's happening in Germany. Some sort of revolution is coming. It's inevitable.' Brio took another swig of whiskey. 'Maybe not in England. Your aristocrats and capitalists know what they're doing, and if they ever get into trouble, they can wave the flag and send your hot-blooded young men off to find glory or fortune elsewhere. We have to make the best of it here.'

'Yes, Brio, and we will!' Enrico interrupted. 'We Italians may not have bread, but we have art! Only today, at the Pinacoteca, a veteran told me he hadn't eaten for days. And yet, he could still swoon in ecstasy before Bellini's Madonna and Child. He was so overcome with emotion, he collapsed right in front of me! With such sensibility, there is always hope!'

This time Brio merely acknowledged Enrico's comment with a confused shake of his head, before ploughing on. 'But we're a poor country compared to England. Something will break, and I think soon. Italy feels like a dam that's about to burst.'

'I know the feeling,' I lurched to my feet in response to this unfortunate metaphor and staggered off in search of a privy.

18

Naples, 30 August 1945

From chapter four of *The Life and Death of Abercrombie Lyle*, which started with my arrival in Milan, the book took on a new character. It became more detailed and the emotional reflections more subtle. The accounts of how I met Brio and Carla, the nights when we witnessed the birth of fascism, and the awful attack on *Avanti!* were vivid and fine grained. I was in the meeting room with Mussolini. I re-lived the pain of my fractured skull and the days I spent recovering in hospital. The narrator's reactions and fears were my reactions and fears. As I read on, it became clear that, implausible though it was, either Brio or Carla *could* have written this part of the book, or at least provided the information. Knowing that Brio and Carla were both skilled writers, in their own very different ways, it was possible that one of them had had a hand in it.

At this point, I knew that there were only three possible authors of this book: Brio, Carla or myself, or some combination of the three of us. I suppose I had known this since I had first picked it up. But this knowledge did not solve the puzzle. For the more I read, the more questions it raised. Even if Carla, or Brio, could, in theory, have written some of the book, aside from the incredible creative achievement of recounting my life with such psychological accuracy, surely there were aspects of my life before Milan they could not possibly have known about. I *must* have written at least part of the book myself, and if so, the most plausible explanation, or the 'smart money' as Ma would have said, was on me having written the whole thing, which meant that I must have gone mad, or that a breakdown of sorts had erased part of my memory, perhaps to protect myself from some trauma. But I didn't *feel* insane or deranged. Depressed, distraught, even overwrought, at times, but not mad. I forced myself to read on, hoping to find some clue that would make more sense of the book. And then I did.

> *Everyone said that Carla had never looked more beautiful than on her wedding day, but Abercrombie disagreed. For though she certainly was beautiful, the overall effect of the jewellery and white satin, of her wild hair contained and shrouded by a veil, seemed contrived. Conventionally she was the perfect bride, but she was too perfect for his taste. Or perhaps this judgement was his first, unconscious, attempt to protect himself from Carla, and her effect on him. He remembered that day as bittersweet. For while he was happy for both of them, the finality of their union forced him to admit to himself that he would never have her. When they both held that knife, he saw the depth of their love for each other in their eyes. When he watched them plunge the knife into the huge millefoglie wedding cake, it felt like they had also plunged it into his heart. He knew from that moment, as much as he loved them both, his friendship would be vulnerable to the worm of jealousy.*

When I read 'my' recollections of Brio and Carla's wedding reception, I knew for certain that some of the book could not have been written by me. There were events described that I couldn't have just forgotten. They were events I could not have experienced, *because I hadn't been present*. However this book had come about, one of either Brio or Carla had definitely had a hand in it, and whichever one it was, they had made a big mistake.

I had never seen them cut the cake. I knew for certain that I hadn't. For while they had been doing that, I had been outside on the street doing something I could never forget. I had been having a cigarette with Benito Mussolini.

19

Milan, 21 December 1919

Brio and Carla's wedding was a small but joyous occasion. It took place on the Sunday before Christmas, which gave it a festive spirit, and, I felt, a sense of possibility and new beginnings. From the darkest day of the year, surely new light and hope would follow, despite the increasing chaos on the streets and in the factories.

The high spirits among their circle of friends also reflected the warm afterglow of the November election. Brio had worked tirelessly, writing and campaigning, and the Socialist party had achieved its best ever result, with 32 percent of the vote and 156 seats in parliament. They were now the largest single party in Italy. Brio had even received a personal letter from party leader, Nicola Bombacci, to thank him for his efforts in helping to secure such an impressive victory in Milan. Perhaps equally satisfying was the fact that the fascists had performed very badly. Not a single fascist was elected to office of any kind, and in Milan they received less than 5,000 votes to the socialists 190,000. So poorly had they fared that Milan's socialists had felt compelled to gloat. They staged a mock funeral for Mussolini, parading a coffin with his name on the side through the city's streets. The fascist threat seemed to have been a damp squib.

At the reception, Brio had given a mesmerising speech. He began with glowing tributes to Carla's beauty and high moral character, comparing it favourably to his own, with a few self-deprecating jokes. Then he skilfully slipped into an almost ecstatic vision of the bright future ahead for them all, and for their beloved Italy, in the wake of the socialist's success. Toward the end, there was a toast to the friends, sons, husbands and brothers who had fallen in the war, and he concluded with a pledge that he and Carla would work every day, stronger in their love for each other than either could be alone, to build a better future for Italy. He ended with a call to everyone present to join them in their mission and was given a rousing ovation.

When Brio sat down to a chorus of clinking glasses, Carla's musician friend, Louisa, put her hand on my shoulder and shouted above the din into my ear. 'I'm confused. Is he marrying Carla or Italy?'

I gave her a wry smile. She had a point. Impressive though it was as a piece of oratory, perhaps there was a little too much politics for the occasion.

'I'm not sure,' I replied, 'but it looks like Carla's going to be a busy woman, whether she likes it or not.'

'It's like he's just introduced her to his crazy stepchild from a former marriage on his wedding day.' Louisa adopted a gruff, mannish tone. 'By the way, darling, did I mention that as well as all the cooking and cleaning, you'll be helping me knock this young reprobate called Italy into shape for the rest of your life?' Louisa smiled wickedly.

'I see a very bright future for them, filled with long, winter evenings spent in political meetings.' I raised my glass to the happy couple across the room and almost lost my balance, nudging into Louisa's arm. The sight of Carla gazing adoringly at Brio made me feel a little nauseous.

'I bet *you* could think of better things to do with Carla on long winter evenings than take her to political meetings.' Louisa took a deep pull on her cigarette and gave me a look. Her hand had made its way to my thigh. She had clearly become interested in more than my rudimentary knowledge of Irish reels and jigs. I returned the look. I had always thought Louisa attractive. Short, unruly auburn hair and a slightly upturned nose gave her a mischievous face that she inhabited with vigour. Then again, when I was this drunk, I found most Italian women attractive. They had a way of handling cigarettes I had never encountered in Liverpool.

Louisa looked as blotto as I was, and I realised, in a diminishing window of clarity, that I was in danger of doing something I might regret. Then again, it wasn't as if there was any point in saving myself for Carla. The thought crossed my mind that perhaps Carla had sat us next to each other in an attempt to play matchmaker. I wasn't sure I liked that thought. Tempting though it was, I was in no mood to settle for a consolation prize on this, of all evenings. I needed some fresh air. Excusing myself to Louisa, I went outside for a cigarette.

*

On the street it was crisp, with a bright moon that was almost full. I stared for a long time at the silver disc and tried, unsuccessfully, to work out if it was waxing or waning. I let the cool air chill me, relishing its freshness after the clamour and fug of the wedding. I recalled that this had been our intended destination on the night we had been attacked at *Avanti!* Whether it was the cold or the recollection, a shiver ran through me, and I savoured the sensation. Then I remembered why I was standing outside and reached into my jacket for my cigarettes. I put one in my mouth but couldn't find my matchbook. I patted all my pockets, several times, before sensing a presence beside me.

'Let me help you.' The stranger struck a match and cupped it with the other hand as he leaned into me.

I sucked hard for the light to catch. 'Thanks,' I said, in English, as I glanced toward the man's face. He was still holding the match, which cast its light up onto a strong jaw and staring eyes. The effect of the single source of light from below the face reminded me of a trick Da used to do with a torch to frighten me in the dark.

'Don't I know you from somewhere?' I asked, hearing a slur in my question.

'I imagine you do. I certainly remember you.' The stranger pinched the match slowly between his fingers to put out the light.

'You're one of Brio's friends,' I stated.

'You could say that.'

'I'm afraid I can't remember where we met.'

'San Sepolcro, on the 23rd of March,' replied the stranger, his flat wide mouth curling a little in amusement.

The light from the moon glistened off the stranger's eyeballs, which seemed to have an abnormal expanse of white around the dark irises, but I couldn't tell if this was because his eyes opened wider than most people's or if his irises were small in relation to the rest of the eyeball. I stared at the stranger's eyes, mesmerized for several seconds, pondering this conundrum. Then I remembered where I'd seen him before and realised how drunk I must be.

'Benito Mussolini.' He held out his hand just as recognition dawned, and before I knew it, I was shaking it.

'Aber—'

'I know who you are.'

A deep drag on my cigarette, and the identification of the stranger, had a sudden sobering effect, as the idea that Mussolini knew who I was sank in.

'What are you doing here?' was all I could think of to say. I felt like an idiot.

'I wanted to offer my congratulations to the happy couple . . . and to give them a little gift.'

'Please go right ahead. I'm sure Brio and his guests would be delighted to see you.' I felt better about this riposte. 'But watch out, he might be armed this time. I think they're about to cut the cake.'

Mussolini smiled. 'I think not, but perhaps you would be so kind as to give this to Brio.' He handed me a small parcel, beautifully wrapped in black tissue paper.' It looked like a miniature coffin.

'I suppose it's too small for a club. But how do I know it's not a bomb, or some such thing?' As soon as the words left my mouth, I felt like an idiot again, and Mussolini started to laugh.

'My dear English friend, do you think if I wanted Brio dead, I would need to resort to such fanciful methods?'

'It seemed like your thugs wanted him dead not so long ago.'

Mussolini's eyebrows scrunched and his bottom lip thrust out in a theatrical expression of exaggerated pity, as if he were speaking to an annoying and rather stupid child.

'I know,' he said, nodding his head, 'sometimes the *squadristi* get a little . . . carried away in their patriotic zeal. But we Italians are a civilised people, Mr Lyle. We are not thugs. We built an empire that survived for 800 years, the glory of which has never been surpassed. When my ancestors were building the Coliseum, yours were shivering in mud huts and painting themselves blue to frighten us away. It didn't work, by the way.'

'No, we had to wait for some bloody Germans to come over and do that for us. I wonder why they've always been so good at fighting?' As I said this, I noticed that there was something very annoying about Mussolini's nose. I began to develop a strong conviction that it needed smashing.

'In any case,' continued Mussolini, 'Brio was in no real danger. I have plans for him.'

I tried to grasp what Mussolini was implying but was distracted by a growing desire to hit him. I had reservations about the jaw. That looked like it could break your knuckles, while remaining entirely unscathed, but the nose, that would smash quite beautifully.

'Did you never wonder why he escaped with only a few scratches?' asked Mussolini.

I could feel my anger growing. 'I *was* there, you know. It all looked pretty dangerous to me.' One swift blow would do it.

'Indeed, it was dangerous. For you. And even more so for the poor patriot you . . . *encountered* in the courtyard.' Mussolini's eyes widened even further, and he jutted his head toward me to emphasize his point. 'You should be more careful, and not get involved in other people's fights, Mr Lyle.'

I swayed backward, as the implication of what Mussolini knew sank in.

'But for my friend Brio,' Mussolini continued, 'it was less dangerous. My men had their orders.'

My desire to strike Mussolini became almost unbearable. Whether he sensed this, or he simply felt that his lesson had been delivered, I would never know. With this last comment, Mussolini tipped his hat and turned to walk away, seemingly oblivious to how close his nose had come to obliteration by a drunken Liverpudlian.

I had a momentary urge to tackle him to the ground but then remembered that I was holding Mussolini's wedding gift. I was confused about how to tackle him to the ground while still holding the present. I located a safe perch for the gift on a nearby wall, but somehow the moment had passed, and my rage slowly subsided as I watched Mussolini strut briskly into the shadows. I suddenly felt very cold and began to shiver. I put the gift to my ear to check it wasn't ticking, just in case, and returned, unsteadily, to the party.

PART II

20

Paestum, 10 September 1926

After the abduction of Carla, I stayed on at the farmhouse for a while in case, through some miracle, Carla, Louisa or Enrico turned up, and because I didn't know what else to do. For a week I clung to the hope that they might be released, or escape, and return, but I knew this was unlikely, for when I staggered back into the kitchen after Brio's thugs had left me unconscious in the yard, I found an envelope propped against a bottle of Jameson's whiskey. It contained a ticket for a one-way passage from Naples to Liverpool via Marseille on a steamer, leaving in two weeks' time. It also contained a letter from Brio.

Abercrombie,

When you stole Carla from me, you broke my heart and nearly broke my will to live. The day we first met, when we saw the Last Supper together, I thought I had found the brother I never had. That day, I knew God was dead, but we were alive and better off without him. We were new men, forged in the furnace of war. I dreamt of what we could do with the broken world the old men had left us. I thought we could do great things together. I admired your ability to see beauty where others see ugliness, your ability to laugh when others cry. When my boots were full of lead, you could float above the chaos, as if the laws of gravity had no hold on you; and so I clung to you to stop me falling into despair; but I realise now that you float because you have no substance, and you laugh because you cannot feel the pain of others. You have slipped every knot that should hold a man in place. Your country, your family, your friends were all left behind as you soared away from reality, carrying away Carla, like a rare jewel, to amuse you.

Wake up Abercrombie! Your world is not real. A new world is being built. You could have helped make this world better for the people all around us who are in pain and hungry, that are lost and need help. Instead, you lie in the sun and listen to ghosts.

That day we met, when I looked at the disciples above me on the wall, I thought you were John, but you were Judas. You betrayed me. I should shoot you in the back like a coward fleeing from the front. Yet even now, I find it hard to hate you, for a part of me still loves my little brother, and inside I am still keening, yes, keening.

I will always remember the night you told me what happened to your brother, and how, on hearing the news, your mother made a sound you had never heard her make before, as if her soul were being torn from her throat. I made that sound when realised that you had left me to go to Carla, for I knew our friendship was dead.

But I have Carla back. Her place is with me, at my side, as we join our comrades in the sacrifices it will take to build the new Italy. I will forgive her, and in time we will be happy again. You, Abercrombie, should grow up and go home. For the memory of our friendship, I wish you what happiness you can find, but you must find it elsewhere. Build something, fight for something, die for something back home. You have no life here. Don't look for her. Leave Italy. I will be watching. I have many eyes now; and know this. If you contact Carla, or even try to find her, I will put that bullet in your back.

21

Naples, 31 August 1945

I awoke hunched over the desk, my left arm numb from where I had been resting my head. After a moment of disorientation, I remembered why I was in the Old Library, and though I still felt exhausted, remembering that one of Brio or Carla must have been involved in writing *The Life and Death of Abercrombie Lyle* quickly woke me up. Questions remained about the origins of the chapters on my youth, but the fact that I knew another hand had been involved in the chapter on Milan restored some faith in my sanity. Perhaps the voice of the 'Doppelgänger' was not my own deranged, guilty conscience.

But this immediately raised more questions: which one of them had written it, and, of course, *why*? And why had it fallen into my hands now? There was no obvious explanation, but it must be an attempt to communicate with me in some way. It couldn't have been carefully placed at the top of that pyre by chance, and if it had been placed there for me to find, whoever did it must know my habits intimately. But what were they trying to achieve? Was I being warned? Or even helped? Or toyed with in some cruel way I couldn't yet fathom? Was it an attempt to frighten or intimidate me? Perhaps it had been put there to hook me – bait to draw me out of hiding? But they clearly knew where I lived. Why not just knock on my door, or send someone to arrest me, or slip a stiletto under my ribs on a dark walk home from the library? Why go to these elaborate lengths?

I opened the source of my torment once more and read the next chapter as fast as I could, searching for more clues or slips. I was no longer poring over every word, amazed at the audacity, the improbability, the very existence of the book in my hands. I was scanning for irregularities.

I didn't know what game was being played, what the rules were, or what I might win, or lose, by playing. And I didn't know how much time I had to work all this out. But some sort of game was afoot. I had to start thinking like a detective, rather than a bewildered, pitiful fool.

My mind turned to Holmes. How would he react? What would he do? I knew I was no Holmes. I was barely a Watson. No doubt I had already missed many clues that he would have spotted, but I needed a guide through this dark labyrinth and could think of no one better. This was a puzzle to solve, and I'd be damned if I'd let whoever was playing with me lead me along like a kitten following a ball of wool.

I ploughed through the next chapter, but, almost as if the book had sensed my new resolve, my tormentor was again a step ahead of me. My biography brought back vivid memories of early 1920s Milan, but it yielded no new answers. The narrator, more Saint than Doppelgänger, settled into a stable voice and described my life with my new friends. The first years of Brio and Carla's marriage were happy ones, despite the unhappy times. There was the excitement and chaos of the strikes of 1920, joyful marches on summer days, and friends quickly made in heady moments of brotherly love. I remembered the sense of hope and expectation among Brio's circle. They were on the brink of something momentous. When the workers occupied factories, I recalled the panic in the press. The revolution was imminent, but its leaders dithered, and even before the Socialist's success in the local elections in late 1920, there had been a sense of sand slipping through fingers. Then there was the rapid metastasis of fascism after a brief period of dormancy. Their vicious attacks on the newly elected Socialist town halls revealed the impotence of a mass movement that wasn't prepared for a fight when their enemy used any excuse to pick one. The government was content that the fascists were doing their dirty work for them, and I remembered Brio's anger at comrades who were unwilling to organise their own militias and fight as hard as the fascists.

But the text offered no further clues to the author's identity, and it began to read like a diary that someone had promised to keep but had lost interest in. I could not recall writing any of it, but the information could have come from me. I remembered all the experiences. But it could also have come from Brio or Carla, or even one of our close friends, and if someone else had written it, they had been careful only to include events and conversations that I had been present at. I was getting nowhere.

22

Milan, 23 March 1921

When I heard that the new *Avanti!* office had been attacked, again, by fascist *squadristi,* I raced over in a cab I couldn't afford to find Brio, unscathed, tending to injured colleagues. He was helping a man with horrific burns on his hands and arms into an ambulance. I saw a body lying under a sheet on the street and through the broken windows could see small fires still burning inside. It was less than a year since the new office had opened, and though I was relieved that Brio was safe, I knew he would be devastated after all the fundraising and hard work that had gone into setting up the new premises.

Brio acknowledged me with a nod, but didn't stop to talk. I knew he wouldn't leave until all the wounded had been seen to and the fires extinguished. I preferred the smell of burnt building to burnt flesh, so I inserted myself into a line of men passing buckets of water down a chain from a water hydrant someone had smashed the top off.

'Where's the fire brigade?' I asked the soot-smeared man next to me. 'And the carabinieri?'

'Probably having a drink with the bastards who did this.' The man shrugged. The other men in the line seemed more resigned than angry.

When the fires were out and the injured on their way home or to hospital, I persuaded Brio to go home to Carla, who I knew would be worried sick. We took a tram back and sat in silence as it bumped and screeched along. I could tell Brio was furious, but I was reluctant to open his floodgates in such a public place. I noticed he had cut the fleshy side of his right hand below his little finger. I could see a small piece of glass still in the wound and pointed it out to Brio, but he waved his hand, as if entirely indifferent to it.

We got off the tram at the corner of Brio's street, but he was reluctant to go home. He seemed too tightly wound, and, after something closer to an order than a request, I agreed to go for a drink in his local bar. The owner was about to close up, but when he saw Brio's thunderous face, he let us in. He had no whiskey, so Brio ordered four grappas, which I had never cared for. Brio knocked two back and twirled the third in his fingers. I realised that only one of them was for me. I sensed a tirade was coming and thought it better that Brio get it out of his system in the bar than at home with Carla. When it came, I was surprised at its target.

'There are men at *Avanti!* that fought like lions at Caporetto and Piave. I know they are brave, but most of them won't fight the fascists. They are an army, and we are boy scouts. A few have pistols in their desk drawers, but they won't organise. They won't mobilize. All they do is repeat idiotic slogans about "not succumbing to provocations" and "rising from the ashes no matter how often the Fascists burn our buildings down". But I'm sick of shovelling broken glass from ruined buildings. If we won't fight, we're fucked. Simple as that.'

'Surely you don't want a civil war? Italians killing Italians.' I asked.

Brio looked at me like I was a child. 'We're already in a fucking civil war, and we're losing, in case you hadn't noticed!' He knocked back the third grappa. I could see him eyeing mine, which I hadn't yet touched. 'You drinking that?' I pushed it across the bar, and he twirled it nervously in his fingers. 'And as for those sons of whores in our parliamentary party, they're as bad as the rest of them. Corrupt, frightened old men. I'm not sure they even want a revolution.'

'Do *you* really want one?' For all his fine talk, I was never sure that Brio was prepared for the consequences of what he campaigned for. 'A lot of things get broken, and a lot of people get hurt in revolutions.'

Brio looked at me like I was not just a child, but a particularly stupid one that hadn't been paying attention in class. 'It doesn't matter if I want a revolution or not. We're getting one. The question is, what kind? At the moment, it looks like we're getting a fascist one.'

'Things must calm down soon,' I replied. 'This chaos can't go on forever. The government will have to do something.'

'The war has driven Italy mad, Abercrombie. She is like a crazy, hysterical woman who won't stop thrashing and screaming. Someone needs to slap her face and take control of her. I don't think we're capable of doing that.'

'I'm not sure I like the metaphor.' I looked at my friend and glimpsed something in his eyes that made me uneasy. The exhaustion and anger seemed to have stripped away his usual urbanity and self-control. 'Perhaps your old friend Mussolini is the only one man enough to slap Italy around and calm her down. Is that what you're saying?'

Brio downed the last grappa and slammed the empty glass down on the table. He winced as he banged the cut on his hand. He lifted it to look at the cut properly for the first time and finally plucked the glass out. A small trickle of blood ran down his hand. I offered Brio my handkerchief, but he just stared at me and raised his hand to my face, so I could more clearly see the trail of blood. A drop fell on the bar.

'It's just blood, Abercrombie. Don't look so scared. We've both seen plenty of it, and we'll both see plenty more before this is all over.'

'I've seen enough blood to last me a lifetime. I don't want to see any more. Especially not the blood of my friends.' With that, Brio smiled sadly and took my handkerchief, wrapping his weeping hand in the clean, white linen.

'Nothing worthwhile was ever built without blood. It's just a matter of whose blood and how much will be needed.'

I had grown tired of the conversation. I got up from my stool and started toward the door. I stopped at the threshold and watched my friend, hunched over the bar. 'Go home, Brio. Get some rest. I think the day has sent you a little crazy.' The bell tinkled as I opened the door to the street, letting the cool evening air in. 'And have Carla clean and bind that wound properly, before it turns septic.' Brio waved dismissively with his back to me, then called the barman over for another drink. The barman looked at Brio sourly. He had a towelled fist in a glass and was drying it vigorously, but he stopped and poured him another drink. Brio was a difficult man to say no to.

23

Naples, 31 August 1945

Frustrated by the lack of clues in the first Milan chapter, I stared at the books all around me as if they could give me an answer. Dawn was peering into the Old Library from the clerestory windows above. It was now nearly seven in the morning, and the librarians would start arriving in about an hour. I looked toward the front desk and the shelves of returned books to one side. On the other side were huge leather-bound catalogues for the rare volumes and rows of little oak drawers with card indexes for the more recent collections. A thought struck me. It seemed unlikely, but could there be other copies of my book? If someone had gone to the trouble of printing it, perhaps they had printed more than one, and if they had, perhaps there was a copy sitting in this very library – a copy that did not have the final pages torn away. I knew it was a long shot, but I grabbed my copy and walked over to the banks of drawers that contained the index cards. I thought I heard a faint noise from the room behind the librarian's desk and stood frozen for a few seconds, listening hard, but it was not repeated, and I supposed I had imagined it. I looked for authors beginning with C and found a drawer for 'Car to Cas' written on a small piece of cream card slotted into a brass holder on the front. Opening it quietly, in case someone was here early, I flicked through the card index and there it was.

Carivali, Elsa
The Life and Death of Abercrombie Lyle
Pub: Rome, 1945
pp. 333
Call no. 3118121-919-1129225

I couldn't believe it. There *was* another copy, and it was here. I saw the page extent and looked at the last page of my copy, numbered 313. There were 20 pages of the book that I didn't have.

I looked through the adjacent cards in the index, but there were no other books by Elsa Carivali. Who could she be? In all likelihood, she didn't exist. It was probably a symbolic name or sick joke of some sort. I played with the letters of her name in my mind and quickly realised that they contained 'Carla.' I wrote the remaining letters in my notepad: *i, v, i, e, l, s, a.* It didn't take long for a pattern to emerge. This was not a puzzle that required advanced cryptology skills. Rather than a breadcrumb, Elsa Carivali had placed a freshly baked loaf at the start of the trail, to make sure I couldn't head off in the wrong direction. 'Elsa Carivali' was an anagram of 'Carla is alive.'

I felt light-headed and realised that I hadn't eaten since breakfast the previous day, most of which was now on the floor of my apartment. My mouth was dry and foul tasting. I needed some water, a coffee and some food, if I was going to think straight. I scribbled the details on a call slip, and was about to put it in the slot at the front desk, but realised that I would get it quicker if I came back as the library opened and asked the librarian to retrieve it personally. For the first time since I had discovered that Carla's photograph had been switched, I saw a hint of light in the bottom of the pit I had fallen into. Whatever the origin or purpose of this grotesque biography, I felt one step closer to discovering Carla's fate.

24

Milan, 21 December 1924

I heard the tinkle of the bell over the door and looked up to see Carla's flushed, startled face as she passed from the crisp evening street into the bright, fuggy bar. I watched as she scanned the room, savouring her beauty for a moment before she saw me. I could have called out to her. We had nothing to conceal. But I wanted her recognition to be more intimate. When our eyes met, she gave the faint smile of an old friend who need do no more to show she is delighted to see me.

Seeing Carla was always a bittersweet experience. I knew I was in love with her, perhaps I had been from the first night we had met, but I had locked that love in a box and cushioned it with so much friendship and joy that the sharp edges hurt less and less as the years went by. And I owed so much to both Brio and Carla, who clearly loved each other deeply, that I had thrown away the key to the box several years ago. I rose to greet her and felt the delicious cold of her cheeks as I kissed them. Taking her hands, I stepped back a little to look at her properly. She held my gaze a fraction longer than normal, and I detected a hint of sadness. Or was it something else? I cocked my head, asking the silent question.

'Let's get a drink first,' she answered. I released her hands and pulled a chair out for her. She took off her coat and gloves and sat down. I ordered a whisky and soda and she her usual Mi-To. I restrained my curiosity until they arrived. We had always been comfortable together in silence whenever Brio wasn't with us. Love him as I did, sometimes it was a relief not to be buffeted by his relentless energy. I wondered if Carla ever felt the same and knew that she must, at least sometimes. The drinks arrived.

'Well?' I asked.

'Do you know what day it is?' she asked, evidently annoyed but trying to look amused.

'How could I forget? It's the fifth anniversary of the day you broke my heart and married your brute of a husband.'

'Stop it. I'm in no mood for jokes.'

'Who said I'm joking?' I looked at her with more directness than I normally allowed myself. 'Where is he, by the way? And why am I the lucky beneficiary of an evening at La Scala with the most beautiful woman in Milan, on her wedding anniversary, no less?' Carla took a drink and couldn't meet my eyes for a moment. She looked as if she were struggling for words. For a few long seconds, she stared at the table, somewhere else entirely. She took another drink and forced a smile.

'You once said I was the most beautiful woman in Italy, not just Milan?'

'Well, I hadn't been in Italy very long then, and I've since been to Rome—' I was interrupted by a sharp kick to the shin.

'Ow, that hurt.'

'You're as bad as he is. Always joking, never serious. Unless it's politics. He's as serious as you like about politics, and the glorious future that awaits his beloved Italy, if only it would listen to him.'

'Point taken. In all seriousness, where is he?'

'He's on a train to Rome.'

'Why?'

'Il Duce clicks his fingers and off he trots.'

'Now, surely *you're* joking?' I said.

'I'm not.'

I could see that she wasn't. She looked furious. 'But I thought he hated Mussolini?'

'Keep your voice down,' hissed Carla.

I raised my hands in silent apology and leaned in closer. 'What's going on?' I whispered. 'Is he in trouble?'

'He's in trouble with me, but no, not as far as I know.'

'Well?'

'I haven't told you because . . . I didn't know what to say, and I don't think he's told me everything yet.' She seemed reluctant to talk, as if struggling with how much to reveal. She looked embarrassed.

'It started a few months ago,' she began.

'What started? What's going on?'

'You know he was so down after the election, but ever since the Matteotti affair, he's been acting . . . strange.'

'What do you mean?'

'When he heard that the socialist MPs had walked out of parliament, he flew into a rage and started marching around the apartment, shouting and swearing.'

'And?' I raised my eyebrows.

'Oh, you know, "that's exactly what he wants . . . he's literally got away with murder," that sort of thing. Then one night he was sitting in his armchair reading the newspaper. He suddenly stood up, threw his glass of whisky in the fireplace, and stormed out. I didn't see him for two days. I still don't know where he went, but he stank like a distillery when he came back. I blame you, by the way. He never drank whisky until you taught him how. Then, when the senate backed Mussolini in June, he went sort of limp, disinterested in everything. "That's it," he said. "It's all over. We may as well give up,"'

'That doesn't sound like Brio?' I knew my friend to be passionate, even erratic, but I had never seen him apathetic.

'He's changed. He's calmer, but not in a good way. He didn't talk about politics for weeks, so I knew something was wrong. Things seemed to get better for a while, but the spark had gone. He talked of leaving the paper and doing something else: writing a novel, becoming a teacher, anything but *Avanti!* He stopped going to party meetings. Said it was pointless. They'd missed their moment and had failed.'

Carla took a sip of her drink and sat back in her chair. Brio had told me none of this, and I was struggling to make sense of the news.

'Then in October, he started leaving the house late at night without saying a word. I thought he must be having an affair. I confronted him, but he denied it. I believed him, eventually. I know he still loves me, but he wouldn't say where he'd been. One night he didn't come back until the early hours. I'd waited up. I told him I was leaving him if he didn't tell me what was going on – and then it all came out.' Carla couldn't look me in the eye and seemed, for a moment, unwilling to go on, as if saying whatever she was about to say would be stepping into a place she could never return from.

I reached across the table and took her hands, which were squeezing the life out of a tightly balled handkerchief. 'It's OK,' I said gently. 'You don't have to tell me.'

She looked at me and seemed to draw strength from my gaze. 'No, I want to . . . You deserve to know.' She regained her composure and continued. 'Apparently Mussolini contacted him via an old friend in May, before Matteotti's murder. It seems he was secretly putting feelers out to a few socialists he thought he could work with. Brio ignored him, at first. Then it all blew up with the Matteotti affair.'

'So what changed his mind?'

'Mussolini contacted him, personally, a few weeks ago. He'd heard Brio had given up on the party and offered him a job in his press office or editing one of his rags. He said he needed help to "keep socialism at the heart of fascism." I'm sure there was a healthy dose of flattery involved.'

I released her hands. I couldn't comprehend what Carla had just told me. 'What about Matteotti?'

'Brio doesn't believe Mussolini ordered his murder. It doesn't make sense, he says, given how it's almost brought him down. He says he may have known his thugs would give him a beating for his speech in Parliament, but he's not stupid enough to have ordered his murder. It probably just got out of hand.'

'What did you say?'

'We had a horrible row. The only truly horrible row we've ever had. The kind that, when you both run out of steam, you think you may have broken something that can't be fixed.' Carla finished her drink in one large draught. She looked a little lost, but calmer now that she had revealed her secret. It was a while before she could go on.

'So what happens now?'

'He says he hasn't decided yet. He might do something else, but he's resigned from *Avanti!* Then, yesterday, he tells me he has to go to Rome. On our wedding anniversary. Just like that!'

I was in shock. Aside from the disturbing description of the row, I couldn't fathom Brio's political transformation. I had known of his previous admiration for Mussolini, as a young socialist journalist just starting out, but I thought their politics were poles apart now, and after what had happened at *Avanti!*, when Brio had nearly been killed – and more of their friends had been hurt since – it didn't seem credible that he would throw his lot in with the fascists.

'The thing you never understand about Brio,' continued Carla, as if reading my mind, 'is that what he really cares about is making a new and better Italy. The socialism was a means to an end. That comes from his family, like being brought up a Catholic. But if it can't make an Italy fit for the new Italian, can't give Italians what they deserve after the war, can't make sense of the sacrifice, he was always going to look for something else. Now he thinks this is the only way left.'

'But all the violence and thuggery. He's lost friends at the paper. He's been in the office when they attacked *Avanti!* – in the new place and the old one. It's a miracle he's not been killed himself.'

Carla shrugged her shoulders, as if to say, I've been through this in my own mind a thousand times. It was shocking to see her state of acceptance while my mind was lashing out wildly.

'All that ridiculous posturing, and the crazy ideas about a new Roman empire. The man is a buffoon!'

'You *must* be more careful what you say,' Carla whispered, as she leaned toward me and glanced at the people on either side. She took my hands again and spoke quietly, looking me in the eye. 'Mussolini acts like a buffoon, but he's not. He's been very clever. Parliament and the King have already underestimated him. It was hanging by a thread, but Brio's convinced he'll weather this. He thinks he's here to stay.'

We were both silent for a moment. Carla broke the silence first. 'I can't bear to think about Brio working for *him*. Or us moving to Rome and having to be with *his* people. Going to their parties. Laughing at their jokes . . . having them in our home. When I know what they are, and what they've done.'

I shared Carla's distaste, but there was a violence to the contempt in her voice that surprised me. I had a lot of news to make sense of, but the implications of Carla's revelation slowly and painfully slotted into place. I realised, among other things, that Brio and Carla might leave Milan. The dual suns I had circled for the last five years were wobbling on their axes and I might be slung into a much colder, darker orbit. Then another thought struck me. What if they broke up? I had sometimes worried that my happiness was too tightly bound to theirs, and that perhaps I should tread a more independent path, but I had never considered what I would do if they parted, because it was not possible by the laws of nature as I understood them. I had other friends in Milan, but I suddenly felt very alone. Perhaps I might manage without one of them, but I wasn't sure I could survive in the darkness without either. And if my two suns were to pull in different directions, which would I follow?

'What will you do?' I asked Carla, and perhaps also myself.

'I don't know yet. He says we'll have to move to Rome. But I'm not sure I can do that. I'm not sure I can be that person.' She looked at her watch. 'But right now we're going to the opera. Curtain's up in fifteen minutes.'

I had forgotten about the opera. Normally, a night at the opera with Carla would be as close as I could imagine to heaven without actually dying. It was the last thing I wanted to do now. But I willed myself to put a brave face on.

'What are we seeing? I don't think you said.'

'*La Bohème*,' Carla reminded me.

'Wonderful. That ought to cheer us up.' I crossed my eyes, cocked my head and made a gesture with my hand as if I were hanging myself. She smiled indulgently. 'And don't forget to put your gloves back on. I don't want your tiny hand to be—'

'Yes, yes, silly man. Come on, we'll be late.' And with that, Carla appeared, for the time being, to have returned to a more familiar version of herself.

*

They walked in silence to the theatre. Carla knew that Abercrombie's attempt to lighten the mood as they were leaving the bar was as much an effort to distract himself as it was to cheer her up. But she was happy to drop the subject for now. He would need time to come to terms with what she had told him.

As they entered the gilded brilliance of the grand foyer of La Scala, he seemed to Carla to be lost in thought. He would normally be intrigued and excited by the haute bourgeois Milanese glamour on display, his quick, maddeningly glib mind crafting humorous or disparaging observations. But when she cast a glance at his fine, almost feminine features, he seemed more troubled than she had ever seen him before. His mind was clearly spiralling, trying to make sense of Brio's apostasy, searching for clues or comments that he had missed. Most tellingly, he was paying no attention to her at all. Carla felt a stab of guilt. To this point, she had only thought of the impact of Brio's transformation on their lives, but now she saw the waves rippling outwards. Abercrombie had said nothing since leaving the bar, but she knew she was watching the first step of an inexorable journey toward the death of a friendship. She chided herself for throwing the news at him so carelessly, like an indifferent doctor telling a patient they had terminal cancer before they had even sat down. As they climbed the steps toward their cheap seats at the back of the prima galleria, she took his hand and squeezed it. He glanced at her and tried to conceal a tear with his handkerchief.

'You poor thing. I know this must be a shock. I should have broken the news more gently.'

'Crying before it even *starts*. That's not good. I'll be a bloody mess by the time Mimi warbles her last.' Abercrombie looked down at the well-dressed throng in the foyer below them. 'I suppose that will be your new world. Hob-nobbing with captains of industry and government ministers. No more cheap seats for you.' As he said this, something in his tone disturbed Carla. She didn't mind the playful dig at her, and it wasn't said with any bitterness. That was an emotion she had never heard him express, even though he'd had as rough a time of it in the war as Brio – and *he* splashed his bitterness around liberally: on Parliament, the Church, the Populari, the British, the French, the supine idiots in his own party. What shocked her was that it was the first time she had ever heard Abercrombie feel sorry for himself.

'I'm sorry,' he said. That was unfair of me. I know you don't care about that sort of thing.'

She nodded, but his words had struck home. As well as the pain they revealed, they forced her to think more deeply about what her friends would say if she followed Brio to Rome. Aside from the difficulty of surviving, alone in Milan, on her meagre teacher's salary, she had been viewing her impending decision as a struggle between love and principle, between duty and independence, and perhaps she worried a little about the shame she would be subjected to for abandoning her husband. But what about the shame of being seen by her friends as a fascist convert? She considered what the people that mattered to her, like Louisa and Enrico, might think of her decision. They would assume that she had made the same ideological transition as Brio, or worse still, that she was cynically going along with it – jumping on *fortuna's* wheel at an opportune moment to carry her up in the world.

'No, that will not be my new world,' she said decisively, looking Abercrombie in the eye. 'I prefer it in the cheap seats.'

'The last time we came, we could only see half the stage.'

'But we could still hear all the music.'

'Probably more of the music,' replied Abercrombie.

'How so?'

'There's less snoring up in the Gods.'

She gave him a peck on the cheek.

'What was that for?'

Carla shrugged. 'I don't know. I just wanted to.'

*

Inside the auditorium, Abercrombie did not cry, but Carla and many others did, even though in this performance Mimi never died. Well before the final act, the singers and orchestra unexpectedly stopped upon some invisible signal from the wings. The curtain came down and a man in a black suit appeared on stage to announce that they had received word that maestro Puccini had tragically died in Brussels. The effect on the audience was devastating. Carla heard gasps of shock and uncontrolled weeping. As the orchestra struck up Chopin's Funeral March, Carla took Abercrombie's hand. She could feel him looking at her, but she didn't look at him. Tears flowed down both her cheeks as she stared straight ahead. She felt like she was at the bedside of a loved one who had passed away after a long illness.

25

Naples, 31 August 1945

I sat in a quiet corner of Caffè Giordano and devoured two custard filled sfogliatellas, washing them down with a double espresso and a large glass of water. I was exhausted, but soon felt the surge of sugar and caffeine revive me. Feeling a little more human, I rolled my shoulders back and massaged the familiar knots in the muscles behind my neck. Young Alfredo, the owner's son, was looking at me from behind his cracked marble-topped counter. He didn't greet me, which I thought rather odd, given his friendly nature and addiction to local gossip. When he saw he had my attention, he gave a nod in the direction of the bathroom and held up two fingers, before turning away to dry some glasses. I checked the second hand of my old watch and waited for two minutes before leaving some coins on the table and gathering my belongings. As I was about to enter the toilet, I was pulled into the tiny storeroom behind the bar.

'Are you in some sort of trouble, Michael?' Alfredo whispered, once the door was closed. Before I could answer, he looked me up and down and sniffed at me with his long, convex nose. I had never noticed before how hairy his nostrils were. Then again, I had never been this close to him. 'You look terrible, and smell worse. What's going on?'

'What do you mean?' I answered. I wanted to hear what he knew before offering any information of my own.

'You look like you've been up all night. Your clothes are filthy, and you smell of vomit.'

'A rather late night, perhaps a hair of the dog would be in order . . .'

Alfredo waved a hand and gave me a look that eloquently dismissed my attempt to treat him like an idiot. 'Someone has been in here asking about you.'

I was shocked but not surprised. My pastries felt less secure in my guts, and I dropped the pretence. 'When? What did he say?'

'I'm not sure if he was a policeman, at least he wasn't in uniform, and he wasn't local. Not *Camorra*, either. But somehow official. He had . . . authority, if you know what I mean. I have a nose for these things.'

'What did he say?'

'He was young, very young actually, but something about him scared the shit out of me, if I'm honest.' Alfredo kissed the tiny red horn that hung from his neck.

'What did he say, Alfredo!' I realised I was gripping Alfredo's arm tightly and let go, smoothing his jacket. 'I'm sorry. Please. What did he say?'

Alfredo now looked at me like I was a stranger, or perhaps worse. 'Not very much. That was the frightening part. I'm used to threats and bluster about what someone is going to do to some other person if they don't get something they want. But he just asked if I knew a Michael Lynch.'

'And you said?'

'Yes, of course. He comes in here all the time. I didn't want to mess around with this one.'

'And then?'

'He looked at me, for a very long time. He had these strange, ice-cold eyes.' Alfredo seemed to drift away for a moment, and not to a good place.

'And?' I pressed.

'He said to give you this the next time I saw you.' Alfredo handed me a buff A4 envelope. Typed on the front was the name, Abercrombie Lyle, and nothing else. 'Who is this Abercrombie?' asked Alfredo. I ignored him and tore open the envelope. Inside was a large print of the photograph of Carla that I had first seen yesterday. It was larger, not only because it had been printed at a larger size, but because it contained part of the image that had previously been excised. Now there were two smiling faces – Carla's and that of a small boy, aged perhaps six or seven, who was holding her hand. The boy stared at me through the camera and across the years. It was uncanny, but I felt instantly that the boy was my son.

26

Milan, 23 December 1924

Brio had agreed to meet Abercrombie at Marchesi, where they had first met over five years ago. He thought Abercrombie's choice of venue rather touching. Perhaps he thought the memory would somehow bring him to his senses. He would probably order the same pistachio pastry, as if it were some fucking madeleine that could transport them back in time. Brio knew what was coming. Carla had told Abercrombie about Rome, and he was here to knock some sense into his old friend. He was surprised it had taken her so long.

Brio arrived early and went through to the back room beyond the long glass counter gleaming with a kaleidoscope of cakes and other delicacies. It was busy, with the noisy chorus of conversation punctuated by percussive clinking of china. He couldn't help smiling as he noticed that the table Abercrombie had sat at when they had first met was the only one free. He claimed it and ordered two cappuccinos and two pistachio pastries. He would indulge his old friend, up to a point.

Abercrombie arrived and waved to Brio as he strode toward him. Brio considered giving him a Roman salute, but even Abercrombie's expansive sense of humour would have baulked at that. Instead, he rose and embraced Abercrombie with genuine warmth.

'How are you, old friend? It's been a while,' said Brio.

'I've been better,' replied Abercrombie. There was nothing in his demeanour to suggest any hostility, but he seemed unusually sombre.

'What's the matter? Did you catch a cold on the way back from the opera? I hear it was a rather upsetting evening.'

'No, I'm fine, but one of my dearest friends seems to have gone completely insane. It's rather concerning.'

Brio laughed. No matter the circumstance, the weapon was always humour. He took it as a mark of respect for their friendship, but Abercrombie would have trouble piercing his thick hide with such a flimsy foil.

'Oh dear, that is a worry. And what exactly has this poor soul done to concern you so?' Brio made a comedic sad face.

'He's betrayed his friends, abandoned his principles and run off with a lunatic whore with a penchant for sado-masochism. You know, clubs and knives, that sort of thing. But I expect he'll come to his senses soon enough, once the dirty little thrill of his treachery no longer titillates.'

Brio tried his best to conceal the point scored and reset his guard.

'Well, that is a concern. So, this friend is married?'

'Oh yes, very happily. Or so I'd thought.'

'That's terrible,' Brio replied, 'How is his wife taking it?'

'Badly. Her world has fallen apart. You see, deep down, she's still madly in love with him, but he doesn't seem to care. Perhaps he thinks he can keep his whore and carry on with her as if nothing has changed, but I don't think that's going to wash.'

'Perhaps she'll get used to it in time,' Brio replied. 'Lots of happily married men have a "bit on the side" as you say in English.'

'I don't think so. She's not that kind of girl.'

'And she told you this herself, did she? This wife of the dear friend.'

'Yes.'

Brio had never seen Abercrombie this earnest. He knew that Abercrombie's anger was genuine and heartfelt, but it was irritating and presumptuous, nonetheless. He had tolerated a closeness between Abercrombie and Carla that he would never have permitted his other male friends, even though he had long suspected that Abercrombie was a little in love with Carla. This connection had never troubled Brio. He had always been confident that Abercrombie's sense of honour and gratitude precluded any chance of infidelity, and he never worried about Carla being attracted to him in that way, despite how fond she was of him. He was their little brother, after all. He also never saw him as a threat, in a physical sense. His Englishness also played a part, for some reason. God knows he would never have allowed any of his Italian friends to take Carla to the opera unaccompanied. Perhaps he had made a mistake to trust him with his wife so freely.

'I can see that you care for her deeply, as well as for your friend. You must be very close.'

'We are,' replied Abercrombie.

Brio stared at Abercrombie as he might at a junior reporter whose piece had failed to meet his expectations. 'Perhaps, if things don't work out for your friends. She will appreciate having you around to comfort her.' Abercrombie's eye twitched. Brio smiled. 'The winter nights are chilly in Milan. Perhaps you can keep her warm when this fool runs off with his new whore.'

'She's not that kind of friend,' replied Abercrombie, looking down at his untouched pastry. And Brio could see that he meant it. Or at least that he thought he did.

'Well then, that is sad for you . . . and perhaps for her,' Brio replied in a more conciliatory tone, feeling a pang of guilt. 'But maybe it won't come to that.'

'I'm hoping it won't. I know she would be ecstatic if her husband, who I believe to be a fine, brilliant, loving man, came to his senses and left this . . . other person, and came home.' Abercrombie lifted his head to Brio. A tiny sniff and a single tear escaped Abercrombie's eye. 'She's a very forgiving person. A remarkable woman.'

Damn this crazy Englishman, thought Brio. This was not 'cricket,' as Abercrombie would say. He had sometimes wondered how a nation of Abercrombies could hold off the Germans, somehow put up with the fucking French for four years, and hoodwink the Italians into fighting on their side before palming them off with a few baubles at the peace talks. But now he knew. They didn't fight fair. They were slippery. Brio stood up, took Abercrombie's head in both hands and planted a sloppy kiss on his forehead.

'Eat your pastry and try to cheer up, old man. I think I know who these mutual friends are. I'll speak to them and see what can be done.' And with that, he patted Abercrombie on the shoulder and left.

27

Naples, 31 August 1945

I left Caffé Giordano in a daze. My mind tumbling and churning over the photograph I had just seen. Where was the boy now? Did he know I was his father? Did he even know I existed? I tried to let the thought that I might have a son settle in my mind as I walked back to the library, but it was such an unfamiliar concept that I struggled to make sense of it. It wouldn't bed in, and my mind kept spiralling with questions.

I stopped and pulled the photo from the envelope again, staring at the boy's face. I knew, logically, that I couldn't be certain he was my son. He had Carla's eyes, and the hair looked dark, rather than sandy, but something about the way he held himself. The way he cocked his head. The hint of smugness on his wide mouth, smiling at the camera, as if enjoying a private joke, as if he were teasing me across the years. *I bet you never expected this*. People say they know these things in their bones, but that isn't right. Bones are hard and cold things. What I felt was warm, spreading through me, and if it came from anywhere physical, it flowed from my bowels not my bones. It was joy, and hope, and, I realised, it was love. Though I had never seen him in the flesh, never touched or held him, I felt he was a part of me. I just knew he was mine. There was no other way to describe it. Mine and hers.

I looked at the street around me and felt refreshed. The sun had not yet risen above the rooflines and the shaded canyons of the *centro storico* were crisp and cool ahead of the inevitable furnace of the day. My skulking the previous evening felt pointless. They knew where I lived, where I went, and who I was. I was probably being watched right now. I turned a full circle but could see no strange men lurking on corners or hiding behind copies of *Il Popolo d'Italia*, just the ordinary life of the city waking up. Sellers and hawkers opening the shutters of tiny shops or setting out stalls of fruit and vegetables. There was a faint smell of bread, and skinny cats were making the most of the morning to scavenge in gutters before seeking shade to pass the day in. There was no point in concealing my movements, so I decided to return to the Old Library using my key to the main entrance. The first set of church bells started to strike eight a few minutes early. Mussolini may have made the trains more punctual, but he had no power over the ill-timed chorus of the old city's churches, erratically framing the hour. The library would open in ten minutes.

Back in its musty gloom, my moment of joy slunk away, and anxiety crept into its place. The reality of my situation had not fundamentally changed. If anything, it had become more perilous as there was more at stake. I was now looking for two people, not one. At the issue desk, the deputy librarian, Marco, looked surprised to see me. 'Professore, I didn't see you come in.' I forced a smile and handed him the call slip I had written earlier.

'Would it be possible to retrieve this yourself, Marco? I'm in a rush today.'

'Of course, Professore,' the librarian lowered half-moon spectacles from his balding head to his narrow nose and read the slip. He looked puzzled, his brows furrowing beneath a smooth, shiny dome. 'This is strange,' he said.

'In what way?'

'The call number is . . . unusual.' He flashed a brief, nervous glance at me, over the top of his glasses. 'Please, take a seat, Professore. This won't take long.'

I sat down at a desk a few yards away and started on the next chapter, but I was too distracted by the anticipation of getting my hands on the entire book to concentrate. Flicking from the start to the end of the chapter it appeared to cover the later Milan years when things turned sour. The first section recalled the evening of the attack on the new *Avanti!* office. I remembered the strange conversation I'd had with Brio. I could still see the jagged cut on his hand. The blood dripping onto the bar. At the time, I had assumed it was just wild talk, stoked by his frustration and anger at the fascist attack, and a few rapid grappas, but in retrospect it felt like the first step to what came next.

I skimmed over the section, trying to focus on the account of the conversation between me and Brio. From the room behind the librarian's desk, I heard a faint, muffled conversation. I couldn't hear what was being said, but the long pauses made me realise that someone in the conversation was either speaking very quietly or on the other end of a telephone. At one point the voice became raised. I was pretty sure it was Marco, and he didn't sound happy, but I couldn't hear what he said. The conversation went on for a while and I sensed strong disagreement. I heard the phone return to the receiver with what must have been considerable force. I felt a deep unease. I could not recall ever hearing a librarian talking on the phone before in all the years I had been in the library, and I had never heard what sounded like an argument, albeit a quiet one.

The following few minutes were excruciating. I couldn't see or hear any activity in the room behind the desk. I was almost certain that the room contained no exit other than out onto the library floor. What was Marco doing in there? Instinctively, I put my copy of the book back in my rucksack and approached the desk. As I did, Marco appeared from the room holding a book. *The* book. I could already tell from the cream dust jacket. We met at the desk. He looked at me, as if wrestling with some emotion or decision. After a few seconds he handed me the book. He looked rather sad.

'Professore, you might find it more convenient to read this at your leisure away from the library.' He raised an eyebrow and glanced toward the door. When I did not immediately head for the exit, he continued. 'In fact, I insist you leave now. The library is closing temporarily, and you must leave now!' I did not need a third hint. I nodded my thanks and shoved the precious object in my rucksack. As I did, I heard footsteps bounding up the marble staircase that led to the library entrance. I turned and ran away from the entrance toward a rear door. I looked across the floor of the library and saw two men in dark suits run to the issue desk.

'Where is he!' one shouted in Marco's face.

Before he had time to answer, the other one pointed toward me. 'Over there!'

For a moment I watched, horrified, as the first man slapped Marco viciously, sending his glasses flying from his face. I turned and ran through the back entrance. I didn't have much of a head start, but I did have a key. I raced around the first-floor arcaded gallery of the open courtyard and down the steps toward the main entrance. My instinct screamed at me to keep running through it, but I knew my only chance lay in locking the door and hoping that they didn't have a key themselves. Once through, I closed the ancient hunk of wood behind me, pulling on the rusted iron handle ring. It took a few seconds for my shaky hand to get the thick barrel of the heavy key in the lock. It was an old lock, and not the smoothest. I jiggled the key home and remembered that I needed to pull the door toward me with some force for the bolt to align with the slot. I could hear pounding steps now from the other side. I had perhaps three or four seconds. I couldn't get the key to turn. I put my foot against the other, closed half of the door and heaved on the ring with all my weight. The key finally turned, metal scrapping on metal, as the bolt slid home. A moment later I heard the soft but powerful thud of somebody crashing against the door, causing the wood to creak, followed by a frantic tugging and twisting at the handle from the other side. I pulled out the key and was about to keep running, but stopped when I heard one of them shout from the other side.

'You won't get away, Abercrombie. It's only a matter of time.'

Being addressed by my real name for the first time in over a decade dislocated something inside me. The voice wasn't local. The accent was Roman. The tone amused, despite the panting, as if this was all just a game of hide and seek at a posh house party. I knew I should be running. There were other keys. Marco would have a set, and it would only take a fit man a minute at most to run up the stairs to get them and come back down.

'I can see you through the keyhole, Abercrombie. I know you're still there. There's nowhere to hide. Make it easy on yourself.'

Like hell I would. I didn't recognise the voice, but he spoke as if he knew me. There was something irritating about it, like he'd agreed to play with the kids, got bored, and wanted to get back to the adults for a drink. The idea came to me in a flash. Without stopping to let myself think, I took a pencil from my jacket pocket and slammed it though the keyhole with the base of my hand. The scream was horrific, but I had heard worse sounds come from a human mouth. Bizarrely, a childhood memory of Ma calling me a Peeping Tom and shouting at me never to spy through keyholes popped into my head. I turned and ran through the arched passageway out of the courtyard and straight down Vico San Marcellino. The screaming only stopped, for me at least, once I was a long way down the street, with the thick baroque walls of the university between me and my pursuers.

28

Milan, 24 December 1924

'I can't stay with him,' said Carla. 'I've thought it through from every perspective and I have to leave him.'

We walked side by side in the dank winter morning. Tired, rusty leaves clung to the trees of Parco Simpione, destined shortly to join their brothers on the ground. A few evergreens provided solid clumps of dark, living colour. I had no idea what type of trees they were. There hadn't been many trees on Scotland Road, and none of them looked like these. The slate sky was on the verge of rain that would add to the puddles we skirted as we ambled along the wide gravelled path.

'What will you do?' I asked.

'Go away somewhere. I can't stay here.'

'Why? You have a job here. He will be in Rome. You can just stay, and he can leave.'

'That won't work.'

'Why?' I asked, perplexed.

She looked at me with pity. 'You know what he's like. He'll never allow that.'

'He won't have a choice. He can't make you go with him.'

'Oh, Abercrombie.' She rarely used my name. 'For all your cleverness, you are such an innocent.' She said it tenderly, almost like a mother. Her condescension rankled.

'Just tell him you're staying put, and if he ever comes to his senses, he'll know where to find you. He'll probably hate it in Rome, realise he's made a mistake, and be back in a few weeks.'

'I don't think so.'

'This is just a . . . temporary infatuation. Like a fling – perhaps not the best analogy. He'll come to his senses, realise what he's lost and come back. I'm sure of it. Then we can carry on, as if none of this ever happened.'

Carla stopped walking and turned to me. 'Is that what you want? For all this to keep going on forever, like we're . . . Peter Pan and Wendy?' There was something in her tone that bothered me. I was finding it hard to look her in the eye, and when I did it felt like trying to push the same poles of two magnets together.

She started to walk again, and I resumed my place beside her. We didn't speak for a long while as we headed slowly toward the grand triumphal Arco Della Pace, looming ahead in the mist.

'Perhaps this will be a good thing for you,' Carla said, breaking the silence. 'Perhaps it's time you found . . . someone else to love. Someone you can *be* with.'

'What do you mean?' I felt like she'd punched me in the stomach. She had broken an unwritten rule that was all the more powerful for never having been agreed or acknowledged.

'You know what I mean . . . And I love you, too, but not like you want me to. Perhaps it's best for everyone if I just disappear.'

'That's madness. It doesn't make sense. You simply can't do that!' Precious, tiny jewels were slipping through my fingers at a speed I couldn't grasp.

'Can't? Oh dear, is it that bad?' I couldn't speak. After a long pause, Carla continued. 'I'm sorry, I should have been more careful with you. I've been unfair. It seemed like you had everything . . . under control.'

There was no point denying my feelings for her.

'I do. I did. When everything was ticking along normally. But things have changed.'

'Yes.'

'I still don't see why you have to leave Milan.'

'He's not like you. He'll never leave me in peace. You must see that.' She reached out and stroked my cheek with the back of her gloved hand. The unexpected touch of the soft suede almost dissolved me. 'You know what he's like. He'll pester and charm and pester and charm until I weaken, and I don't want to weaken. I'd be like an old drunk sitting in a bar with a soda water and expecting to be sober by the end of the night.'

I hated to admit it, but she was probably right. I also hated the inference that I might be the soda water and Brio the whiskey.

'Where will you go?'

'I don't know yet.'

'Don't know or won't tell me?'

Carla looked at me as if weighing up something important. 'Don't know yet, but not sure if I can tell you when I do.'

'Why!'

'You know why. He'll get it out of you.'

'He'd have to torture me first.'

'That's what I'm worried about,' Carla shot back.

'Oh, come now, you're being melodramatic. We're not in some shabby verismo shocker at the opera. He's not a monster.'

'Not yet. But he's becoming one of them. And we both know what they can do.'

We walked on in silence, reaching the shelter of the triumphal arch as the threatened rain finally began to fall. I was annoyed at Carla. It was an emotion I was entirely unfamiliar with. This was nothing, however, compared with the surge of anger I felt for Brio. For the first time since we had met, I could imagine hurting him. I allowed myself to wallow in this thought for a moment then pushed it away. I couldn't yet bring myself to see Brio as irredeemable – as one of them. I would give him one last chance to explain what he had done and to see if he could be persuaded out of it. But even if I succeeded, I knew that something had shifted in the unstable set of forces that had held our love and friendship together. That shift might break us apart forever, or perhaps we might settle back into a new pattern, but I knew we could never again be what we were.

29

Naples, 31 August 1945

After my escape from the library, I needed to find a safe place to read the damn thing from cover to cover before making my next move. I'd been running around like a madman for the last twenty-four hours and was barely halfway through it. I hadn't even finished the second Milan chapter, which surely promised some revelations, given how violently our little triangle had exploded. There was also the unexpected matter of my son. I tried to let the idea of fatherhood settle in my mind as I walked briskly into the heart of the old city.

But where to go? I couldn't go back to my apartment, and the library was now out of bounds. I needed a new sanctuary. As the thought crossed my mind, I was walking past Chiesa dei Santi Marcellino e Festo on my right and Chiesa dei Santi Severino a Sossio was coming up on my left. I didn't think that entering a church and invoking the medieval idea of sanctuary would provide much protection from whoever was pursuing me. If it was Brio, or some agent of his, he would likely laugh at the quaintness of such a desperate move, but I *was* desperate. Both churches seemed too close to what I'd just done at the library. I scoured my mind for a small, secluded church that would serve my purpose, but couldn't think of one that wouldn't trap me in a dead end if I were found. I needed somewhere big, dark and confusing, with multiple exits and places to hide. It had to be the Duomo. I was already striding toward the Cattedrale di San Gennaro and quickened my pace.

Inside the Duomo, I wet my finger in the holy water and instinctively made the sign of the cross on my forehead. It had been many years since I had done that, and a long while since I had been inside this gloomy, irrational mongrel of Gothic, Romanesque and Baroque. I had never much liked it, if I was honest. Although Naples had been my home for nineteen years, and I had slowly become fond of its cramped chaos of architectural styles, the Duomo was a mess, albeit one with dark jewels and odd places of beauty. I stared down the nave at the enormous, marble Mary amid an explosion of golden rays, surrounded by a maelstrom of angels, and ecstatic at the moment of impregnation by the Holy Spirit. She looked less troubled by her unexpected parenthood than I was.

I thought about heading into the crypt, which although small and subterranean, somehow felt light and serene compared to the bombast of the cathedral itself, but I knew I could be cornered there. The Chapel of San Gennaro had too many people. So, I plumped for the first tiny side chapel on the right. I sat on the floor, my back against the wall and hidden from view of the main entrance, but able to see anyone coming down the nave. I was alone apart from an old woman in many layers of black, head down in another world of prayer or pain, or both. I lit a candle in a tiny red glass vessel and placed it on a small brass rack with several others, dropping the smallest coin I had through the slot in the box. For what it was worth, I said a silent prayer for Carla, for my son, if that is what he was, and then for myself. The words felt odd, like I was struggling for some half-remembered schoolboy French, and they opened a door to my childhood. As if from nowhere, in mumbling Latin, I heard myself saying the Hail Mary. *Ave Maria, gratia plena* . . . I finished it in English . . . *pray for us sinners, now and at the hour of our death. Amen.* I had said those words a thousand times as a boy, but, as far as I could remember, not since leaving Liverpool – apart from a few desperate incantations in the War. Those had made me feel dirty and hypocritical once the crisis had passed, but now the words calmed me.

The new copy of the book looked and smelled pristine when I took it from my rucksack. I turned to the end, and it gave with a slight crack, as if it had never been opened. But once again, it wasn't the end. It had more pages than my original copy, but they only went up to 323. The last ten pages looked to have been neatly excised with a sharp blade.

Pages 313 to 323 read as though the Doppelgänger had looked into dark crevasses in my mind that even I had not explored. There was almost nothing solid in this section. No places, actions, or narrative to speak of. Time itself had no place there. It was a rambling psychological exploration of my state of mind. If there were coherent themes, they were regret and failure. Some of it rang true, but I was looking at myself in a dark, distorted mirror. The pages described a journey of self-flagellation that was taking me down to the gates of hell itself. Apparently, I had reviewed my life and found it wanting in almost every respect. I had been too weak-minded to save my brother, and then I had abandoned my mother in her time of greatest need. I had left Liverpool to find solace and diversion after the war, and had miraculously found it in the friendship of Brio and Carla. Then I had thrown it away with my treachery and ingratitude. In the years since, I had lived a life of denial and conscious forgetfulness, hiding in mouldy archives and ancient stories, trying to postpone the inevitable penance I must pay. It felt like the mother of all confessions. The outpouring of an ocean of sins too vast for a few Hail Marys to absolve.

Then, incredibly, it included a reference to the picture of Carla and the boy. What omnipotent power, what all-seeing eye, could be the author of this apocalyptic biography? It felt like I was being controlled, as if I were a mere puppet with strings being pulled from so far above me that I could not see my master. There was an intelligence at work that seemed beyond mine. Perhaps I should resign myself to its will and accept my fate. For a moment, my mind seized with incomprehension. I couldn't think.

I took some deep breaths, and the aroma of the burning candles mixed with the stale sweat of the old woman brought me back to the present. I started to read the section again, forcing myself to read it for clues like a detective novel, albeit one with myself as the . . . what exactly was I? The hero? The villain? The victim? Perhaps all three?

As I forced myself to take a more detached perspective, I saw that these final passages were strangely generic and vague, denuded of any context or specificity. The voice was now firmly that of the Doppelgänger, full of anxiety and loathing, and as I read again 'my' thoughts on opening the envelope with the photograph, one line was simply wrong.

Abercrombie came into the possession of an envelope addressed to him in his real name. When he nervously pulled out a large glossy photograph, he stared in bewilderment at the picture of Carla holding the hand of a small dark-haired boy that must be her son, and just as clearly, the son of Brio.

The Doppelgänger assumed that the boy was Brio's son. This thought had not entered my mind when I first looked at the photograph. But my moment of triumph at finding this flaw was short-lived. What if I had been wrong? What if the boy *was* Brio's son, and if he was, what did that say about Carla and Brio?

I took the picture out and scrutinized it again. Carla looks happy. And there was something else that I hadn't noticed in my initial shock: the oddly square shape of the print. The first had been a narrow portrait, printed up the edge but clearly cropped. This too was printed to the edge with mother and child centred in the square, but who prints square photos? I ran my finger softly down both vertical edges of the print and they felt different. The one to the right of Carla felt like the edge of a new print usually does. They one to the left of the boy had the faintest trace of roughness, like it may have been cut by a sharp blade or scalpel. I couldn't be sure, but it seemed likely that the master version had contained something or someone else, and I could not stop from making the inevitable leap. I filled in the blank with a dark, handsome man, perhaps a little more thickset than when I knew him, but possibly even more dashing with a touch of grey in his black mane, dressed in a more expensive, better-cut suit, beaming with the good fortune of a man in possession of all the things that are supposed to make a man happy: wealth, power, a beautiful wife . . . and a son.

30

Milan, 25 December 1924

As soon as I heard the pounding on the door of my apartment, I knew it was Brio. There was no one else I knew well enough to demand admittance so violently, and when I heard him shouting through the door, I also knew that Brio was drunk.

'Open the door, Abercrombie. I know you're in there.'

I opened the door just as Brio had finished shouting and rather surprised him. He seemed to be expecting resistance. I looked my friend over while tying the belt of my dressing gown. His clothes and hair were in disarray and his eyes red rimmed and moist. He looked wild.

'Is she in there, Englishman?' Brio would sometimes call me 'Englishman' playfully. This time there was an edge to it.

'By, "she," I assume you mean Carla, and no, she isn't. But you'd better come in before you wake up the next street as well.' I stood back from the doorway to let him pass. He looked suspicious as I gestured toward my modest sitting room like the doorman of a grand hotel.

'You had better not be hiding her.'

'Take a look, Brio. My apartment is tiny. You'll have your answer in a few seconds if you don't trust me.' To my disappointment, Brio brushed passed me and started to search the apartment. He even went into my bedroom. I watched passively as he threw open the wardrobe and knelt to look under the bed. My apartment was beginning to smell of whiskey from Brio's breath. It was seven o'clock in the morning.

'Would you like some coffee?' I asked.

Brio glared at me. 'Do I look like I want some fucking coffee?'

'No, but you look like you need some.' I went into the kitchen and lit the stove, leaving Brio standing in my small sitting room like a boxer whose opponent had inexplicably left the ring.

'Sit down, Brio,' I shouted from the kitchen, 'before you fall over.'

'Where is she? And don't lie to me.'

'I'm not talking to you until you're sitting down with a cup of coffee in your hand.'

'I don't want coffee. Give me a fucking drink!'

I ignored him and busied myself with the coffee pot, hoping Brio's storm would blow itself out with no one in the room to shout at. I heard him rummaging around and then a roar of triumph above the sound of breaking glass.

'Found it! I knew you'd have whiskey somewhere.'

I was annoyed that Brio must have broken one of my three remaining whiskey glasses. But the discovery at least seemed to have momentarily placated him. When I returned to the room with two cups of coffee, he was sitting in my only armchair drinking from the bottle. I tried to hand him a cup, but he wouldn't take it. He merely glowered and took another swig of whiskey. I turned my desk chair around to face Brio and sat.

'Where is she? I know you know. She tells you everything.'

I looked at my friend and felt a stab of genuine pity pierce my irritation. I waited and counted to three.

'I'm only going to say this once, so don't ask me again. I don't know where she is, and even if I did, I wouldn't tell you.'

Brio rose from his chair, unsteadily, and stood towering over me. He seemed on the verge of violence. He swayed slightly, his huge hands clenching and unclenching. I starred up at him but remained seated. I had seen Brio's fury at close quarters and knew what he was capable of but had never felt the fury turned on me. I was afraid, but I stared my friend down, and after a few seconds of indecision, Brio slumped back into the armchair. It felt like the worst of the storm had passed but it had washed away another brick in the crumbling wall of our friendship.

'If I find out that you're lying to me, I'll—'

'What? Beat me with your new manganello? I'm disappointed by the melodrama, Brio. It can't have come as a surprise that she left you.'

Brio looked at me with unconcealed anger. I could feel my own irritation rising.

'This is entirely your own fault,' I continued. 'A self-inflicted injury. You had the most wonderful woman in the world. You had her in the palm of your hand. She worshipped you. And you've cast her aside like an old newspaper.'

'Don't taunt me, Abercrombie.'

'Or what?' My irritation was maturing into something stronger. I took a sip of my coffee and burnt my tongue. Looking around my normally tidy sitting room I saw books shoved to the floor, all the drawers of the desk wide open and broken glass beneath them.

'You are the one taunting *me*, Brio. All this false outrage. I'm not that stupid, and neither are you. *You* are the only person you should be angry at, and if you're not, then I'm angry enough for both of us. *You* are the one who has pushed her away. What did you expect? And now neither of us can have her!' I instantly regretted his last utterance as Brio exploded with vicious laughter.

'Ah, the truth. At last! Of course, I've known all along that you're in love with her, but I never thought you had the balls to say it to my face.' Brio slapped the arm of the chair with glee. 'And you thought that one day you might "have her"?' Brio threw his head back and laughed, almost maniacally. 'You're a funny man, Abercrombie, but that might be the funniest thing you've ever said. Bravo, Bravo!'

I opened my mouth to deny it but stopped myself.

'Yes, I love her. I've loved her—'

'From the moment I first laid eyes on her,' completed Brio, in a wistful, high-pitched tone.

'No.' I hesitated, staring into the vibrating surface of my coffee, but there seemed to be no good reason to hold back. 'It was at your wedding that it hit me. Hearing her vows. It all sounded so permanent. Knowing she could never be with me brought it home how much I loved her.' I raised my eyes to fix Brio, 'but I suppose we now know that nothing is really permanent, don't we?'

Brio slid down further in his seat so he could stretch his foot out far enough to nudge my leg. 'Hey, I bet you're secretly hoping she'll come running back in a few days, so you can comfort her.' He kicked my leg again, harder. 'You must be thinking that you're in with a chance now, eh?' Another nudge. 'You're probably glad I'm going to work for Mussolini. This is a huge stroke of luck for you. Yes?'

I stared out of the window, trying to ignore Brio's little kicks. I couldn't look at my friend, if that was what he still was. I could not comprehend how he could be so cruel.

'Yes, it's a huge stroke of luck for you. A *deus ex machina*. Other than dying, Brio going off to work for Mussolini is probably the only thing that could break up the happy couple and give you a sniff of a chance. You've been sniffing around her for years. Sniff, sniff, sniffing like a little lap dog in heat.'

'Why did you do it, Brio?'

'What, take the job?'

'Become a fascist.'

Brio laughed again. I had once lapped that laughter up. Drunk it deep. Now it made me sick.

'I'm not a fascist. Well, technically, I suppose I am. I had to join the party to get the job. But I'm not really a fascist. Whatever that even means. I'm not sure anyone knows yet, not even Mussolini.' Brio took another swig. 'Of course, as we both know, many of them are vile psychopaths.' Brio paused. 'You really don't understand, do you?'

'No.'

Brio cocked his head, as if reappraising his friend of five years. He took another swig of whiskey. 'They have power, you fool. They have power and know how to use it.' More whiskey. 'And you know what else?'

'Enlighten me.'

'Most of the people *want* them to use it. They don't care if a few heads get broken when they don't have enough bread to eat and the country is in chaos. Something had to change. Italy has been left behind. Our people have been left behind. You've seen the poverty, the ignorance. And that's Milan! You've never been south of Rome. It's like the fucking Middle Ages down there. Feudal lords and people living like animals. It's the only way I can make a difference now. I can't bury my head in a book like you. I have to *do* something.'

It was a while before either of us spoke again.

'Please leave.' I spoke softly and did not look at Brio.

'Not yet, old friend. I'm quite comfy now, and I'm enjoying our conversation. These are things we should have got off our chests a while ago.'

I turned to face Brio. 'Get out of my home, now.'

Brio shook his head and drained the rest of the whiskey. He wiped his mouth on the sleeve of his overcoat and started swinging the empty bottle like a pendulum between his thumb and forefinger. It was the absolute assurance of his manner that did it. He was practically horizontal and extremely drunk, but it was clearly inconceivable to him that I could make him leave. Before he had time to react, I leapt from my chair, snatched the bottle from his hand and slapped him hard across the face.

'I said, get out!'

Brio was shocked, momentarily, then he roared with more laughter. I grabbed him by his lapels and tried to heave him to his feet, but the dead weight of a drunken Brio wouldn't cooperate, and we tipped over the armchair, sending us both into a heap on the floor. He seemed to find this hilarious and wrapped his arms around me.

'Perhaps we should both forget about Carla. Perhaps *we* should get married. You've always been a little in love with me, as well, I think?'

I tried to push myself out of Brio's embrace and get to my feet, but I couldn't. Despite his state, Brio was still stronger than me, and now he was planting sloppy, bristly kisses on my face.

'We still have her wedding dress in the wardrobe. It would probably fit you, you're so skinny.'

As Brio came in for another kiss, which looked like it was aimed for my lips, I used the limited gap between our faces to plant a sharp head butt on his nose. It wasn't hard enough to break it, but it startled him enough to release his grip. I sprang to my feet and Brio pushed himself across the floor so that his back was up against the armchair. He put his hand to his nose. Blood trickled down between his fingers.

I stood over him, fists clenched. A flood of fear and elation coursed through me.

'Get out, now!'

'We both know that I could beat you to a pulp, Englishman.' Brio seemed to have sobered up. It even crossed my mind that he might have been exaggerating his drunkenness.

'In a fair fight, perhaps. But this isn't a fair fight.'

'I thought the English always fought fair?' Brio dabbed his nose with a filthy handkerchief.

'We both know they don't.' I picked up the empty whisky bottle, the dregs running down my wrist as I held it by the neck like a glass club. 'And for the last time, I'm not a bloody Englishman!'

'What are you then, Abercrombie?'

'Fuck knows. Irish, Scottish, Scouser. It doesn't matter. We all know how to fight dirty. We had good teachers.'

Abercrombie felt like another version of himself, a person he had known for fleeting moments in the war but rarely since.

Brio grinned. 'Ok, *Scouser*, you win. I'll go. I'll leave you to your books and your daydreams of Carla.' He struggled stiffly to his feet like an old man, using the armchair for leverage. He rose to his full height and stretched like a bear emerging from hibernation. Then he shot out his left hand and clamped my wrist. His right leg hooked around my calf and sent me spinning to the floor. Somehow the bottle emerged in Brio's right hand, which he then brought down hard on the edge of the desk, sending shards flying across the room. He fell on top of me before I could rise from my hands and knees and used his considerable weight to pin me, face down, on the threadbare rug of my sitting room floor. I struggled and bucked but couldn't throw him off.

Then I felt the sharp sting of jagged glass press into my neck and stopped thrashing. His moustache brushed my ear, and his foul breath was almost as overpowering as his body, which pushed me hard into the floor.

'Don't worry, Abercrombie. I'm not going to kill you. But you should be more careful. Look. I think you may have cut yourself shaving.'

'Fuck you, Brio.' I bucked again and felt the glass go a little deeper into my neck.

Then Brio lifted the bottle away and threw it across the room, where it smashed on the wall. His panting, heavy mass was still on top of me. There was a moment of strangely intimate calm.

'You know, I think I like this new Abercrombie.' Brio whispered in my ear. I could feel its tiny hairs tingle. 'I think we could be friends.' And with that, he rolled himself off me, rose to his feet, and left the apartment without looking back.

31

Naples, 31 August 1945

Abercrombie knew that he must find the final part of The Life and Death of Abercrombie Lyle. *Despite his shame and remorse, he knew he must follow his story to the inevitable conclusion. He also knew that he needed to see Carla one last time, though he did not know what he would say to her. To find Carla, he had to find the end of his book, and he knew of only one man who could help him find it. Borromeo.*

As I sat in the side chapel of the Duomo, reading this last, surviving line of my new copy of the book, I felt disembodied. It felt as though it had seen into my mind. Even before I read that line, I had come, independently, to the same conclusion on my inevitable next step. There was one person who could help, and that was my old friend, the chief librarian, Borromeo. He was the only person I knew who had the access, connections and knowledge to potentially find a complete copy of my book. Now that I saw his name in black and white, I could see no alternative course of action, even if Borromeo was being used in some way as a breadcrumb on my path.

A host of questions and concerns jostled at the edges of my thoughts. How could I contact him without putting him in danger? Should I be following the path laid out for me? Surely, I should be trying to confound my Doppelgänger, not doing what he wanted or expected. It seemed impossible that Borromeo was not being watched, and probable that I was walking deeper into a trap, but I could see no path that didn't go through Borromeo. To bastardize the mantra of my new guide, Holmes, when all other paths are impossible, the one remaining, however, inadvisable, must be taken.

There was some work to do first, however. I still had half the book to read, and I wanted to take my next step armed with whatever knowledge I could glean from it. I pushed myself as far back into the gloom of the side chapel as I could and carried on from where I left off, pencil in hand to dissect and connect what I could. I read of my sparring with Brio in Marchesi, my winter walk in the park with Carla, and my fight with Brio in my apartment. I reflected that while the detonator of our friendship had been Brio's apostasy, perhaps the admission of my love for Carla, first to Carla and then to Brio, had also shaped the explosion. It seemed to have precipitated Carla's rapid exodus from Milan without telling me where she was going, and it certainly ended my friendship with Brio.

The book's narrative now created fresh problems, reaching across two decades to confound and confuse me. For Brio had not been present when I strolled with Carla in the park and Carla had not been present when I met Brio in Marchesi, nor when I had fought with him in my apartment – and I had never told her about this last episode. This led to an improbable but inevitable conclusion. One way or another, knowingly or unwittingly, freely or under duress, *both* of them must have been involved in the creation of the *Life and Death of Abercrombie Lyle*. The logic of my conclusion needed no further support, but the final section of the chapter on the later Milan years confirmed Carla's involvement, for it contained a reference to a letter she had sent me from Paestum that Brio could not have known about unless Carla had told him. It was a letter that changed my life.

32

Milan, 24 March 1925

Unusually, I had not thought of Carla once that morning. It was a bright spring day, and I had risen early to take a stroll in Parco Simpione before heading into the university, where I now taught English and sat in on any course related to ancient Rome and Greece that I could in a pitiful attempt to fill her absence. On my return, as I pushed open the door to my apartment, I felt it wedge on something and saw the corner of an envelope sticking out from under it. Sliding in and closing the half-open door from the inside, I saw my name on the unstamped envelope and recognised the handwriting instantly. I tore the envelope open and had the letter in my hand within a couple of seconds.

My Dear Abercrombie,

I am sorry I left without saying goodbye. I couldn't put either of us through that, nor risk that I would weaken and tell you where I was going.

When I left Milan, I needed time to think, without you or Brio telling me what I could or couldn't do. I needed stillness and silence to listen to my own heart, without either of you drowning it out. You men, you always know what is best for us women, even when you have no idea what is best for yourselves.

I needed to think about what I had done to Brio and whether I could forgive Brio for what he had done to me. I also needed time to see if I could imagine a life without him, and I needed to do that without you as a constant reminder of him – and of another possible future.

Hollow thumps replaced my chest, and my legs felt weak.

You should know that I sent him a letter, about a month after I left. I decided he deserved one last chance. He is my husband, and I hoped that my absence, and the threat of its permanence, might have changed his mind. I told him that I would come back to him if he would leave his new job and return to Milan. I told him that if he wanted me back, he could post a notice in the personal columns of La Stampa *on my birthday. It should read:*

Recent widower B - - -, aged 29, warm, handsome and kind-hearted, seeks recent widow of similar age for happy married life in Milan.

He posted the following:

Recent widower B - - -, aged 29, warm, handsome and passionate, seeks recent widow of similar age as wife and partner for a life of virtue and duty in the service of Italy. Must be willing to reside in Rome.

I knew then that our marriage was over. For a while I mourned for Brio, as he was. But I cannot grieve for ever, and I have another life to live now – a life I want you to be a part of, if you still want that.

I was dizzy with joy.

Abercrombie, I am lonely, and I miss you, my dear friend. I cannot pretend to love you in the way that I loved Brio. But I have examined my heart fiercely in the long, silent nights and know that I want you here with me. 'Love' is such a short and simple word. We ask far too much of it, and it asks too much of us.

My feelings for you are not a light bulb that must be on or off. We will have light of many kinds: bright, hopeful dawns, the soft glories of twilight, and, perhaps, one day, the glare of a midday sun. I will not let the tyranny of such a little word as 'love' destroy what chance of happiness we have left because I cannot give you the certainty it demands. So let us not use it for what we may create together. We will use different words or invent a new word, or many, if we like. Perhaps, one day, 'love' will be one of them.

So, I am sending this very personal notice to you, and only to you. Recent widow C - - - -, aged 27, warm, beautiful (so you tell me) and hopeful, seeks dear friend of similar age as her partner for a life of happy uncertainty. Must be willing to reside in Villa Hera, Paestum, Campania.

33

Naples, 31 August 1945

Remembering Carla's letter from twenty years ago transported me to a time of such iridescent happiness that I began to cry. The old lady in black, my companion in the side chapel, must have heard or sensed something and turned to look at me. She seemed puzzled by the smile I gave her, then she smiled back at me, cracking her wrinkled face to reveal a glimmer of the young girl she had once been. She rose stiffly from her kneeling position and approached me. It took an age. She knelt in front of me, took my hand, and kissed it. I still don't understand what happened next, but for some reason I cupped her cheeks with my hands, and we starred into each other's eyes for a moment. Something passed between us, and I swear the hint of a blush forced its way into her grey skin. She rose again, this time a little more freely, and crossed herself. She gave me another, almost bashful, smile and shuffled out of the side chapel, into the nave, and toward the entrance of the Duomo.

    I felt serene. It seemed as if one of us had been blessed, but it wasn't clear who had given and who had received this blessing. For a moment I forgot why I was in the Duomo. Then my eyes rested on the open book on my lap. I was at the start of the chapter on Paestum, but I didn't want to read on yet. I wanted to remember. I wanted to remember how I had felt on the day I received my invitation to heaven, not to be told how I had felt by my malevolent biographer. I allowed myself, for the first time in many years, to re-live what was undoubtedly the happiest day of my life.

34

Milan, 24 March 1925

I didn't bother to write back to Carla, or to leave a message for anyone else. That would simply delay the moment when I might see her again. I went to my room and packed a case and rucksack with the few things that I would miss and couldn't replace. It didn't cross my mind that I might not go to her. It was the only thing I could do.

The train journey took most of the day. Milan to Rome, Rome to Naples, Naples to Paestum. I spoke to no one and barely noticed that there were other people sharing my journey. I was carried by a strong current that I neither wanted, nor was able, to resist. Only when I was deposited, the sole passenger to alight, at the small brick station at Paestum, with the light fading and the air cooling, did I begin to feel nervous. I passed through a huge arch in the thick stone walls and walked toward the centre of the ancient city. Soon, a small road cut across my path and beyond to my left I saw two Greek temples ahead of me, the setting sun shining through the enormous Doric columns of the largest and nearest. Both temples appeared remarkably intact. It was a magical sight. An old man gave me directions to Villa Hera. I struggled to understand his dialect but understood enough. I turned left and walked for a while but needed more directions after passing out of the old city walls on the southern side of Paestum. These were given reluctantly, suspiciously, by an old woman at a decrepit farmhouse. A rough track took me into fertile, open country, past low stone walls and a small herd of buffalo. It was almost dark when a larger stone wall appeared in the distance with the bulk of a house behind it. Closer, I saw a gap in the wall that became a metal gate as I neared it. Through it I could see a single lit window on the ground floor. I pushed the gate, which was rusty, and a loud grating announced my presence. A few seconds later, before I had reached the front door, it opened.

Although the journey had been inevitable, I had been uncertain about the nature of my reception. Would there be awkwardness, or simple joy at my arrival? Would we be friends at first, and only lovers, perhaps, later?

Carla stood holding a candle in one hand. A coarse scarlet shawl was clasped at her throat by the other. She seemed older and her hair was loose and long. I had never seen it that way before, and I had never seen her more beautiful than in the light of that candle. She placed it calmly on the floor and came to me.

There were no words and no hesitation. The directness of her gaze was almost too much to bear, and any doubts as to my new status were dispelled with that first look. I saw that Carla had already consummated our relationship in her heart. Now that I had arrived in Paestum, the physical enactment was preordained, and Carla was wise enough not to delay a moment of beauty when neither of us knew how much time we would have. She took my cheeks in her hands and kissed me softly on the lips. When she broke the kiss, I couldn't have spoken had I wanted to, and I sensed that words were neither wanted nor needed. She picked up the candle and led me by the hand inside the house. She led me up the stairs and did not let go until we had entered her bedroom and the door was closed behind us.

PART III

35

Paestum / Naples, 10 September 1926

I finally left Paestum ten days after Carla's abduction. I wasn't sure if I intended to use Brio's ticket and get on the boat home, but there was nothing to keep me at the farmhouse. They weren't coming back.

I set off at dawn for the station at Paestum. When I arrived, the station was closed. There was a notice pasted on the door that the only trains to Naples were from Battipaglia, over twenty kilometres away. I couldn't face going back and so set out on foot, hoping to hitch a ride for some of the way. It was still cool, but the heat rose steadily to a crescendo as the morning wore on, and the one car that passed failed to stop. By the time I arrived, I had run out of water and was a little lightheaded. At Battipaglia, I caught the FS train to Naples via Salerno. The journey was hot, sweaty and slow, with sporadic, inexplicable stops. My fellow passengers appeared to prefer livestock to baggage. There were several chickens, a goose, and the old woman next to me had a baby goat on her lap. It was hard being crammed in among so many smells, and so much life, after ten days of numb, silent solitude. Normally, I would have been entertained by the people around me, listening hard to decipher the local dialect, but I saw them from behind a veil. At one point, a dog barked, and the instant memory of Cerberus, buried in his shallow grave behind the house, was too much. To my shame, I started to cry. A wizened, walnut-faced man with a coarse-whiskered white moustache offered me some roasted pumpkin seeds, and I could barely force a *grazie mille* from my throat. It was the first time I'd heard my own voice since Carla's abduction. It sounded like someone else's.

As we approached the city, the cratered bulk of Vesuvius glowered over us, somehow managing to deepen my gloom. I got off the train and the chaos on the station forecourt, and beyond in Piazza Garibaldi, was overwhelming. The sheer number of people was disorienting after Paestum, and I felt like I had woken from an anxious dream only to find myself actually on the stage of a music hall in mid performance with an instrument I didn't know how to play. But the shock was also a tonic. The dormant street urchin inside me sensed the threat, the hustlers and hawkers, and he woke up and took charge of my body in self-preservation. Despite my recent rural life, I was a city boy and knew how to survive in a city. Don't catch anyone's eye. Don't get into conversation. And don't stop. I was disembodied, but I walked with purpose and a hint of swagger. I headed down Corso Umberto I toward an address near the port given to me all those years ago before I departed for Italy by Ma's old boss, Mr Tyrer, from the Big House on Shaw Street. Skirting the *Centro Storico* to my right, I heard the chaotic chorus of innumerable churches striking six o'clock.

As I approached the grand nineteenth-century office building on Piazza Giovanni Bovio, I could see slices of brilliant blue from the Bay of Naples to the south. A delicious breeze off the bay cooled my face. At the entrance, a small brass plate identified the office of Charles Price, Shipping Agent. I paused to catch my breath, then climbed the staircase to the fifth floor. I rang the bell and a very tall young man with black, slicked hair, thin moustache and a noticeable limp opened the door. His pallor and general air of elongation made him look like he had emerged from a painting by El Greco. I asked for Mr Price and told him my name, adding that I was an acquaintance of Henry Tyrer. He ushered me in and asked me to wait in a small lobby while he disappeared behind a heavy mahogany door. I sat down and a scruffy mongrel of indeterminate lineage raised its head from a basket in the corner to run the rule over me. Satisfied that I was no immediate threat, it curled back down to sleep.

A few seconds later, a flabby, late middle-aged man emerged. He had thinning, wavy hair, mostly grey with remnants of black, and pale skin with pores that were struggling to cope with the heat of a southern Italian summer. Charles Price was one of those Englishmen abroad who seemed genuinely indifferent to the display of perspiration. Perhaps he was incapable of preventing its flow and had simply given up, happy to allow large oval stains to radiate from his armpits. Everything about him looked soft, except for the small, dark eyes, which were disconcertingly intense.

'You know Henry, you say?'

'Yes,' I replied, realising that I had given no thought to what I might say to Price, or even what I wanted from him. In a moment of self-awareness, it struck me that I must look no better than a common tramp, and I had the aroma to match. Price looked at me, his faintly jaundiced eyes wide open, expecting further elaboration on my relationship to Tyrer, but I had nothing more to say. There was so much to be explained that I didn't know where to start. Then he seemed to relax, and his face softened in an expression of pity.

'You'd better come in then.' There was a note of reluctance in his voice, but also kindness. He led me into his office and motioned for me to sit in a deep leather armchair. It may have been the most comfortable chair I had ever sat in. Exhaustion embraced me. Without asking any more questions, Price handed me a glass of water, which I drained in one long draught. Then he took that glass from my hand and replaced it with a fine, heavy, cut-glass tumbler with a very generous measure of whiskey. I smelled the peat, and though it was Scottish, and of much better quality than the stuff I was used to, I was back in the Lord Nelson sipping a cheaper Irish version with my Da and my brother. I closed my eyes and drifted away for a moment, enjoying the finest single malt I had ever tasted.

'So, how do you know Henry?' he said softly. Price was now sitting behind his large desk, holding his own glass.

'He employed my mother, in the Big House.' I reached into my jacket and handed him the letter of introduction I'd been given over seven years ago. 'He gave me this when I left England after the War and said that I should give it to you if I ever needed help in Naples.' There was one for Charles Price and one for another friend in the shipping trade in Genoa

– in case I ever got myself into a jam, as Henry had put it. I felt my current circumstances qualified as rather a sticky sort of jam.

The letter was still sealed, and Price sliced it open. As he read, he cast occasional glances at me. Then he neatly folded the letter, slid it back into its envelope and put it in his desk.

'Mr Lyle, how may I be of service?'

I looked at him and answered, truthfully, 'I'm not sure I know.'

'Then why are you here, Mr Lyle?' Price asked.

'I'm not sure I know that either.' I felt very tired.

Price cocked his head and stared at me intensely for several seconds. It felt as if he were burrowing deep into my soul. Then he rang a bell on his desk and the tall young man with the limp came in.

'Pietro, please take Mr Lyle to The Grand Hotel de Londres and ask Theresa to give him a room and dinner on my account. Then find him some new clothes. Something a little less . . . rustic. He looks about your size, if a little shorter.' Pietro smoothed his moustache by parting the finger and thumb of his right hand along his upper lip, then nodded in a way that suggested Price's request was a triviality that had already been taken care of.

'Mr Lyle, I shall collect you in the morning, rested, refreshed and ready to tell me your story. For I can tell when a man has a story, and I sense that yours is best served with coffee, not whiskey.' He took the empty glass from my hand and nodded to Pietro, who helped me from the armchair and led me out of his office. I was clearly now Pietro's responsibility until the morning. I mumbled something approximating to a thank you, for I was by now almost overcome with exhaustion and the whiskey had gone straight to my head. Pietro gracefully took my elbow and helped me down the five flights of stairs. As we got to the bottom, I noticed that he was no longer limping. He caught me looking at his gait. I looked at him quizzically.

'Mr Price is very kind to orphans and stray animals.' The remark seemed cryptic, but once I grew to know Naples, it was the sort of thing one heard all the time.

*

The following morning, I awoke to the sound of a gentle but persistent knocking on the door. After a moment of disorientation, I opened my eyes and took in the room around me. Bright light filleted through the partly closed Venetian blinds, telling me it must be mid-morning already. I had slept for a long time. I ran my hand across the smooth linen sheets and remembered where I was. Last night, Pietro had run a bath for me and ordered room service. Some sort of firm meaty fish poached in white wine with clams, tomatoes and black olives, followed by hazelnut gelato. I hadn't eaten so well since leaving Milan.

'Mr Lyle, are you awake?' Pietro's voice was soft. 'Mr Price wishes to see you for breakfast.'

'Thank you, Pietro. I'll be down as soon as I can.' As I said this, I was dismayed at the thought of meeting Price in my rancid old suit, but when I raised my head from the pillow, I saw a new double-breasted navy suit hanging from the handle of the wardrobe, and on the cane-backed chair by the window lay a new, collared white shirt, underwear, socks and a burgundy tie patterned with little silver diamonds. Beneath the chair was a pair of polished black brogues. On the writing table, a new grey fedora. My old clothes were nowhere to be seen. In the bathroom, a comb, toothbrush, razor and shaving cream had been laid out on a thick white cotton towel. After I had made use of them and dressed, I looked in the full-length mirror on the wardrobe door and hardly recognised myself. I had never worn a tie in Paestum and the only hat that had been on my head was a battered straw thing to keep off the sun. I looked like a smart young gentleman of leisure, or would have if not for the tanned skin of a farmer and the eyes of an older, sadder man staring back at me.

*

Price sat at a table in the empty dining room reading an old copy of *The Times* and pouring coffee from a large silver pot. He glanced up as I approached.

'That's more like it.' He folded his paper and poured me some coffee. 'You look like a proper Englishman, instead of . . .' His voice trailed away.

'Mr Price, you've been so generous. I don't know what to say.'

'You don't need to say anything. If one of my oldest friends asks me to do someone a favour, it is done. But you can thank me if you like.' He beamed at me with such warmth that I felt a little embarrassed.

'Thank you.'

'*Prego*. Now, sit down and start at the beginning. Take your time. I want to hear everything.'

And so he did. I told him all that had happened to me since I had left Liverpool. Price had the sort of face that instantly disarmed. He would have made a wonderful priest, and as my story spun out it had the feel of a long confession, but with a more comfortable chair, coffee and delicious pastries – and without the undertow of shame. Price was a good listener. I hadn't talked so much in a long time and had never revealed myself so fully to anyone but Carla. Occasionally, he asked a question for clarification. Mostly, he just let me talk.

When my story arrived at his office on the previous evening, he leaned back in his chair and looked troubled for the first time since I had met him.

'That is a remarkable and tragic story, Mr Lyle.'

'Please, call me Abercrombie.'

'Indeed, Abercrombie,' he gave a little smile and stressed my name as if it had some significance that I couldn't fathom.

I expected him to ask me what I planned to do next, or for the conversation to flow into what help I required. But he took me back to the very beginning and questioned me about my time in Liverpool. He seemed particularly interested in my mother, her work as the housekeeper at the Big House, and how long she had worked for Tyrer. He also wanted to know how well I knew Tyrer myself. I thought, at first, he was testing whether my story was genuine before deciding whether to help me, in case I was some sort of fraud. But I soon realized that wasn't it. His questions became detailed and surgical. His eyes were reaching into my soul, looking for something I may not have realised was there.

He pressed me for memories of Tyrer, and I had to admit, rather embarrassingly, that I didn't know Tyrer very well. I had been in his house many times, and had often caught brief glimpses of him, somehow always on the edge of my vision – a presence that was never fully present. Most of what I knew about him had come from Ma or from what I had deduced from the books and prints in his study. I told Price how the huge, illustrated book I found there as a child had changed the course of my life, and for a moment, I felt that perhaps I had told him too much, but his indulgent smile washed that thought from my mind almost before it had entered. I admitted I had only spoken to him twice.

'And what did he say to you? Please, tell me everything you can remember?'

So, I did. It seemed impossible not to, under those dark eyes, and as I trawled for memories of my encounters with Tyrer, I brought things up from the deep that I hadn't thought about for many years.

'The first time, he'd caught me in his study, looking at his big book of Italy, as I came to know it. He seemed to appear from nowhere. I was petrified, but he looked amused. I remember he had a peculiar way of talking, as if I were another grown up, rather than some snot-nosed urchin. He asked me if I liked his book. I said yes, very much. He asked why. I barely had the words to explain. I could only have been ten or eleven, but I told him that his book was like a door to another world. A world of amazing things, with temples so old that they had crumbled to ruins, and palaces that made his huge house look tiny, and statues of beautiful gods and goddesses, and stories of heroes, and mythical creatures, and great battles (some of them with elephants!), and maps that could guide you through this other world.'

'So, he wasn't angry to have found you in his study?' asked Price.

'No. Not that I can remember. Quite the opposite. He behaved like some sort of uncle I'd never met who was trying hard to take an interest. Rather like you are now.' I smiled at Price, in case he misinterpreted my last remark as a criticism. 'Then I remember telling him that what I'd said before wasn't right. Opening his book was more like opening a door within a door, as the door to his study was already a door to another world, and this was another world within another world.'

'And what did he say to that?' asked Price. He was leaning forward in his chair, as if I had reached a moment of importance in my tale.

'He laughed and ruffled my hair. I remember worrying that it was greasy, and he might be repulsed. But he told me I could come back and visit his Other World, the first one, in his study, if it was all right with Mary. It took me a moment to realise he was talking about Ma. And that one day, perhaps, I would visit the other, other world when I became a man. After that, Ma brought me to the house sometimes during the school holidays. He let me take books from his study and read them in the kitchen or the garden. I read all sorts of stuff. I learned more in that house than I did at school, and if the book wasn't valuable, he might let me take it home. I must have read every Sherlock Holmes story and a lot of Dickens. Occasionally, I was allowed to stay in the study to look at the Big Book of Italy. Ma would lock me in and tell me to be quiet as she didn't want the other staff to know I was there, and then she would come back for me an hour or so later. They were some of the happiest hours of my life. At least, until I met Carla.'

Price looked at me, as if weighing something up, then asked about my other conversation with Tyrer. Something was stirring behind those eyes, but I couldn't yet tell what it was.

'He wrote to me after Ma died and asked to see me at the Big House. It was strange seeing him after the war. He seemed much older than I remembered, though it was only four years since I'd last seen him. I stopped going to the house when the war started. I don't know why. It seemed as if only half of him was in the room with me. He must have still been grieving for his son. He was killed in Italy, ironically, up on the Asiago less than a year before. I was in a bad way myself. Ma had been gone a couple of months. Da not long before her. I needed money badly and was lucky if I got one or two days a week at the docks. The foreman always picked older, bigger fellows, or men he knew, unless there were a lot of ships in. I was close to being evicted from the only home I'd ever known, though it wasn't much of a home anymore. Needless to say, I was rather surprised when he handed me a small leather suitcase. He told me not to open it there and to keep it in a safe place until I was ready. "Ready for what?" I had asked. "To open the door to the other, other world," he replied. On the front of the suitcase, on a card slotted into a brass holder, he had written, *Una porta un altro mundo*. When I got home, inside was an envelope with £200, and a small library of books: a Baedeker for Italy and an Italian primer, translations of *The Divine Comedy*, *The Aeneid*, and Vasari's *Lives of the Artists*. Gibbon's *Rise and Fall of the Roman Empire* – and two sealed letters, one of them addressed to you and one to another contact in Genoa. "In case I ever got myself into a jam and needed help," as he put it.'

'And was there no letter for you? No explanation for this generous gift?' asked Price.

'No. I've often thought about that. He even told me that there was no need to come back to thank him, almost as if he didn't want me to visit again, although he was perfectly pleasant. I suppose he felt sorry for me. Ma had worked for him for twenty years. Perhaps he felt some obligation to her. Perhaps he saw it as a patriotic duty to help an under-employed old soldier. To the world, I was a grown man. I'd been to war. But I was still a boy, really, and now I was an orphan. Perhaps he realised that and somehow knew that I needed to get away from Liverpool for a while, away from all the memories. Perhaps it also had something to do with his son dying so recently. He had no other children.'

'Did you ever meet his wife?'

'No.'

'And you haven't opened either of the letters?'

'Of course not. They weren't addressed to me. To be honest, I've not thought about them until . . . recent events. I wrote to thank him once I had an address in Milan, but he never wrote back.'

Price looked at me for a long time. I began to feel queasy. Something wasn't right about the turn the conversation had taken. But I couldn't put my finger on what it was.

'Your name is rather unusual for a working-class lad from Liverpool, don't you think?' Something about the way Price asked this made me uncomfortable.

'My Da was Scottish. I believe it's a Scottish name.'

'Yes, it undoubtedly is.' Price drummed his fingers on the table and looked distracted. He had broken eye contact with me, which was a relief, and was staring off out of a window to a partial view of the bay. 'Henry's family was originally from Scotland too, you know.'

I wasn't sure how to respond. I felt like I was back at school and Brother Davitt was trying to tease the answer to an impenetrable maths problem out of me.

'Abercrombie, I think you should look at this.' Price took a photograph from his pocket and handed it to me. It contained two young men about my age, both in white trousers, striped blazers and odd little matching striped caps. By the look of their large moustaches, it had been taken before I had been born. They were standing on a lawn holding tennis rackets. I instantly recognised Price, with curly hair struggling to free itself from under the cap, and those dark eyes. The other man also looked familiar. Then it hit me in the chest like both barrels of a shotgun fired in quick succession.

The other man was Tyrer.

And he bore an uncanny resemblance to me.

Written at the bottom right of the photograph was: Abercrombie Hall, Anstruther, Scotland, 1886.

'I know this must come as a bit of a shock, but I think there's a very simple explanation for Henry's generous gift.'

I felt like I was sinking into a circle of hell that I hadn't known existed.

'You see, I don't believe you are an orphan after all.'

36

Paestum, 10 September 1926

Carla stood in the abandoned kitchen of the farmhouse, sweating and dirty, trying to make sense of what could have happened to Abercrombie after Brio had carried her off. It was clear that he had left. She had checked their room. His rucksack and battered old suitcase were gone. But where to? The initial dismay at not finding him soon gave way to annoyance. Why had he not waited for her? Did he have so little faith that he thought she wouldn't try to find him? She remembered the advice she gave her nephew in the park in case they were ever separated: to wait where they had last been together, and she would find him. But Abercrombie was no child, and she soon realised that he was probably doing the same thing she was: looking for his lover. If he was still alive.

On that nightmare car journey to Rome, Brio had assured her that he had not killed Abercrombie. He had merely sent him packing. He had told her, calmly, that he had given him a one-way passage back to Liverpool by sea via Naples (he wanted him off Italian soil as soon as possible). He had told him that he would kill him if he ever set foot in Italy again. Of course, he could have had him killed already, but out of respect for their former friendship, and mindful of her feelings for him, he had let him go, despite his betrayal. Brio had always been a good liar, and she couldn't be sure he was telling the truth. Carla found the matter-of-fact way he spoke about killing the man who had recently been his best friend chilling, but when she had asked him how she could know if he was telling the truth, he had looked genuinely upset. *How could you even think that of me?* And she had believed him – just about.

Now, at the farmhouse, a nagging doubt wheedled away at her. What if Brio *had* killed Abercrombie, or perhaps he had told his men to give him a beating and they had got carried away? It wouldn't have been the first time. They could even have taken some of his things to make it look like he had left of his own accord, in case anyone came to look for him. She felt compelled to search the house and grounds. After checking all the rooms, she went out into the garden behind the house and saw recently turned earth beneath the largest orange tree. She felt nauseous. She went into the outbuilding to get the spade, almost hoping she wouldn't find it. After a few shovels into the dry, loose soil, she saw a glimpse of golden fur. Relief and exhaustion overwhelmed her. If Cerberus had been buried, Abercrombie had probably been alive to do it. Then she remembered that this had been Cerberus' favourite spot of shade to hide from the harsh southern sun and was overcome with sorrow. She knelt before the grave and sobbed, like she hadn't done since her visit home for Christmas after Paolo had died. So many emotions wove and weft their way through her. She didn't know whether she was crying for Cerberus, Abercrombie, or herself. She decided it didn't matter. She just needed to cry.

The day had begun in Rome full of purpose, and even pride, at how she had persuaded Brio to let her out of the apartment to go shopping for some 'feminine needs.' He had even been generous, giving her money to buy new clothes to replace the ones left behind in Paestum. It was more than she earned as a schoolteacher in three months, and she had wondered how he had so much money to throw around. Giving Brio's goon the slip with a costume change in the dressing room of a department store, she had timed her manoeuvre perfectly, with just enough leeway to catch the last train that would get her to Naples in time for the last train of the day from Naples to Paestum. How clever she had thought herself, when the train had pulled out of Rome with her minder nowhere to be seen. Now she felt stupid and defeated. It had taken so much effort and deceit to escape Brio, and it seemed all for nought.

Carla willed herself to stop crying and took some deep, steadying breaths. She pushed the earth back over Cerberus with her hands and considered her next step. She knew she didn't have much time. The best case was that her minder would be too embarrassed to tell Brio immediately and would waste an hour or two looking for her before raising the alarm. This, combined with Brio's complacency, might give her until mid-morning tomorrow before his men would turn up at the farmhouse, or worse still, Brio himself, to drag her back to Rome in the same silver Lancia, down the same dusty roads as he had ten days ago. She couldn't bear that. The worst case was that he was on his way now, perhaps only a couple of hours behind her.

For a few minutes, she was unable to move. She stared away into the west. The sun always set so fast in Paestum. A pink glow radiated from the stone walls of the house. Above her, so many stars, and a bright, nearly full moon had emerged from a vast sea of cerulean sky. She noticed that the air was cooler than when she had arrived and carried a hint of salt. She rubbed her hand across the damp grit on her neck and felt tired enough to sleep right there on the ground, but she knew she couldn't and hauled herself up.

After slaking her thirst with water from the well, she inspected her ruined mint green silk dress. Brio had bought it, along with several other expensive dresses chosen more for him than her. He had hung them neatly inside a mirrored closet in the expensively furnished art deco apartment he had imprisoned her in. It was the very latest style, he had assured her, fresh from Paris, as if this somehow compensated for her abduction and rape. It had a low waist, slanted fussy hemline at the calf, and no shape to speak of. It felt like a useless sack and looked ridiculous on the farm in Paestum. She hated it. On an impulse, she pulled it roughly over her head and threw it to the ground. It felt so fresh, standing in the cool in her undergarments. Then she stripped naked and poured bucket after bucket of cool water over her head. Refreshed, she looked around at the parched countryside beyond the farm walls and toward the mountains of the Cilento darkening in the east. She saw almost no traces of civilisation and felt like she had stepped back in time. Goosebumps rose on her bare thighs and belly. She headed back to the house.

Standing in the kitchen, naked and dripping, she realised she was ravenous. She dried herself as best she could with a rag and foraged for food. There wasn't much left to eat, but she found some hard cheese in the larder that looked edible and a few overripe tomatoes. She sat at the table and ate like an animal, the juice of the tomatoes running down her chin and onto her breasts. It was only then that she noticed the empty bottle of whiskey sitting on a letter. The light had almost gone, so she lit a candle. She read the letter from Brio to Abercrombie, then read it again. She couldn't believe that Abercrombie would simply slink back to England, with his tail between his legs, despite the violence of Brio's threat. But Abercrombie wasn't here, and she had no idea where he had gone. He may have gone to Rome to look for her there, which would be incredibly dangerous. Or perhaps back to Milan, in case she had somehow made her way there to hide out with one of their old friends. Or he may have decided to head back to England. She wanted to believe that he was looking for her, but Brio's letter had disturbed her and planted a seed of doubt.

She wanted more time to think, but knew she didn't have it. Then she realised that whatever his plan, if he had a plan, all roads led through Naples. She decided that her best option was to follow him there and see if she could pick up his trail. Perhaps she could work out likely sailings and intercept him before he got on the boat. Though what she would say to him, if that was indeed his plan, she wasn't sure. For the first time since she left Rome, she had a moment of doubt about the wisdom of her quest.

She wearily climbed the stairs to their bedroom and stared longingly at the unmade bed. All she wanted was to fall into it and wrap herself in the sheets. She might inhale a last vestige of his scent as she fell into a deep, delicious sleep. But she might also wake to see Brio standing over her, disappointed. She opened the wardrobe, and all her old clothes were still there. She looked through them for something practical, but nothing seemed right. Some of Abercrombie's clothes were there, too. She took his old grey flannel suit jacket off its hangar and pressed it into her face. Then she put it on and stared at herself in the mirror on the dresser. She held her hair up in a rough bun above her head, and in the flickering light of her candle saw a different person. A new person. The open jacket just covered her nipples, and she was still naked from the waist down, her dark pubic hair exposed. She struggled to reconcile the image with who she was meant to be. But she felt no shame in her near nakedness. Brio had already stripped her of more important things than clothes. She felt free.

Finding the matching suit trousers, she put them on. They were tight across her buttocks and felt strange, but comforting, like she imagined a baby might feel wrapped tight in swaddling clothes. She wondered what Abercrombie would think if he happened to walk in at that moment. She thought he would probably laugh, and then try to climb into one of her dresses. Then she wondered what Brio would think and thought he'd probably be disgusted. If he even recognised her.

If he even recognised her.

She ran downstairs to the kitchen and found a pair of blunt scissors. Then she ran back up the stairs and sat at the dressing table mirror. She started to hack away at her hair. Long clumps fell to the floor. Yesterday, such a loss would have been a disaster. She had seen women with bobbed hair from her window in Rome and thought they looked odd. She couldn't understand then why they wanted to look so mannish. Now she shed her locks without a trace of remorse. She left a little length on the front but cut the rest short, trying to mimic Abercrombie's hair. It was rough, but she liked that she could see the shape of her head and her exposed neck without the corona of hair to frame it, and constantly remind her, and others, of her sex. Now she was just a head, with eyes, a mouth and a brain: not so different from a man.

She rooted through the rest of his abandoned clothes and found a pale blue shirt that was loose enough to not feel too tight across her chest. The trousers were too long, but the safety pins in her sewing box could fix that. Shoes were a problem. She couldn't wear her own, which were horrible for walking in anyway. She thought about going barefoot, but that was impractical for the stony earth of the Campania. She found Abercrombie's battered old black shoes. He must have taken his boots. They were at least three sizes too big and there was a small hole in the right sole, but she had no choice. She wore two pairs of his old socks and stuffed a handkerchief in the toe end of each shoe. She looked at herself in the mirror and was excited by her transformation. Her thoughts turned to a quick departure before Brio could catch her at the farmhouse. She found her old brown leather Gladstone-hinged portmanteau, which was masculine enough to not draw attention, and hastily packed anything of practical use. A spare shirt, underwear and socks from Abercrombie's drawer, an old cable knit green cardigan, a blanket, some basic toiletries, pen and paper. She took the money that Brio had given her and split it up, hiding notes in different places: bag, shoes and various pockets. It felt good sliding bank notes directly into a pocket. She threw her purse in the bottom of the wardrobe.

Back in the kitchen, she added matches, a water bottle, the sharpest knife she could find, leftover cheese wrapped in a cloth, and the letter from Brio. Hair from her new fringe flopped annoyingly in her eyes as she packed her bag, so she slicked it back with water and then with some olive oil. She caught her reflection, flickering in the black glass of the now dark kitchen window, and liked it.

If she had looked a little lower, she would have noticed an envelope on the windowsill behind the sink with her name written in familiar handwriting. But she didn't.

A few minutes later, she was out of the farmhouse and walking by the light of the moon across the hard earth of Paestum toward the temples that felt like an extension of the home she was leaving behind. She passed between the temples of Neptune and Hera, and when she reached their far side, she put the blanket down and sat with her back against *their* oak tree, with its view, framed by the two temples, of the mountains beyond. They had spent so much time in this sacred spot that she could feel the weight of Abercrombie's head on her lap and see his face staring up at her, with that look of quiet joy, so powerful that it commanded the gods to stop time, just for them. She then looked west toward the sea that she could smell just beyond the narrow strip of pines that ran along the shoreline. Then up at the moon and the silver sea of stars above her.

Where was he? And why wasn't he here with her now?

37

Naples, 11 September 1926

'I'm so sorry, Abercrombie. Perhaps I shouldn't have said anything, but I thought you deserved to know the truth.' Price fiddled with a bread roll and looked unsure of himself for the first time since we had met. I stared at him, numb and unable to talk.

'If your parents had been alive, I might not have mentioned it, but I thought you might want to know who you really are, and that you still have . . . a father.'

'No. I *had* a father. He's at the bottom of the Atlantic, and his name wasn't Henry.' I said this with more vehemence than Price deserved.

'I'm sorry. It's . . . a lot to digest.'

'Of course, and after all you've gone through. I don't know what I was thinking.' Price looked like he was regretting his candour. 'You must feel like your world has turned upside down.'

In truth, it felt more like it had shattered. You can only turn something upside down if it's still in one piece. My life was in fragments. *Who was I?* I was not the son I thought I was. My Da was not my real father. Could Michael have been a half-brother? Or, more likely, he was Tyrer's son too. And who had Ma really been? How long had she been with Tyrer? Was it a brief passion? A long-standing affair? Had my Da known? What had been real and what had been false from my childhood? My family had already been taken from me in body, and now my memory of them was disintegrating. It felt like a second set of bereavements. *Who was I?* I had the story I told myself, and now another story, revealed by a stranger, that had more truth to it than my own. My life was a shower of shrapnel, slowly exploding before my eyes, engulfing me, obliterating whatever I had once been.

38

Paestum, 11 September 1926

Carla had been sitting under the oak tree for over an hour, staring at the temples and unable to leave. She felt at peace for the first time since her abduction, but she knew she should keep moving to put as much distance between her and the farmhouse as she could before Brio arrived. She *felt* safe, but she knew she wasn't. He may have brought men to look for her. He may have brought dogs. After what she had seen in Rome, she knew that Brio had resources.

The tiny train station at Paestum was out of the question, even with her disguise. If she could get to the larger, busier station at Salerno she might risk taking a train to Naples, but he might be watching there or even have men on the trains. She knew she should stay away from the main road north. The last thing she wanted was to walk straight into the headlights of his Lancia coming the other way, so she headed toward the sea through the pine forest that stretched down to the beach below Paestum. Her plan was to walk north along the beach for a while, to keep off the roads, and then join the old coast road hoping to hitch some sort of ride to Salerno. But when she reached the beach and saw the silver moonlight beckoning her toward the sea, a new plan emerged. Brio would expect her to set off north, whether her destination was Naples, Rome or Milan, and he would expect her to travel by road or by rail. The moon and the sea whispered another idea to her. She saw a few lights visible from the small port of Agropoli, about 10 kilometres to the south. There would be boats, and she had some money. She should be able to get to Naples from there, one way or another, even if it took a little longer. Based on the timings in Brio's letter, she still had a couple of days before Abercrombie's ship sailed, and once she was out to sea, she would be safe from Brio, for now.

At the beach, she allowed herself a couple of hours of uncomfortable half-sleep, wrapped in her blanket and hidden in the pines. Well before dawn, she started trudging south along the coast, just within the tree line. There was no danger of getting lost with the sound of the waves to her right and the moonlight filtering through the trees, but she had to pick her way carefully and tripped more than once, clumsy in Abercrombie's shoes. After half an hour, frustrated at her slow progress, she made her way down to the sea's edge, took off her shoes and socks, rolled up her trousers, and walked barefoot along the thin strip of sand made flat by the sea, which washed her feet in delicious, cool intervals.

Near Torre San Marco, the stony shore and approaching headland forced Carla to put her shoes back on and cut up to the coast road. The stars faded into the grey daylight of dawn, taking the excitement of her night-time adventure with them. Her arms ached from carrying her bag, and she still had about an hour of walking to reach Agropoli. She trudged on, up over the headland, and emerged at the harbour shortly after seven o'clock, according to a church clock. She made her way to a bakery she knew from previous visits and bought some bread. Sitting on the harbour wall, she tore off chunks and ate them, scanning the boats bobbing listlessly on the water. She knew nothing of boats, but they looked tired and ill kept to her amateur eye. She wondered if any were capable of taking her all the way to Naples, even if their captain was willing. Along the harbour she saw a group of old men sitting motionless outside a bar, as if time meant nothing to them, despite how little they had left of it. One sipped a coffee. A pair were picking something from a fishing net stretched between them. The rest starred out to sea. No one seemed to be talking. She buttoned her jacket and smoothed her hair back (how strange it felt to have so little of it). She approached the group, rehearsing in her mind what to say.

When she reached the first table, no one looked up.

'Good morning.' A few heads turned toward her, but no one returned her greeting. She had tried for a lower version of her own voice rather than a masculine gruffness. It sounded odd, and she cursed herself for not practicing it beforehand, but there was no turning back now.

'Does anyone know of a boat I might hire?' Glances were exchanged.

'There are no boats here. Can anyone see a boat?' The voice came from a gaunt, balding man, in his middle years, leaning back on his chair against the stone of the wall. The depth of his voice shamed her duplicity. He didn't look at her but kept staring out to the harbour.

'I have an aeroplane you can borrow.'

Carla didn't see where this offer came from, but it brought low chuckles from the group.

'Hey, Gino, lend him your Bugatti, you mean old bastard.' The laughter grew as the men warmed to their theme. This was probably the most fun they had had in a decade.

'I train the Duke d'Aosta's racehorses. Would you like one of those?

Carla found the owner of the last remark and fixed him with a glare. 'Thank you for your kind offer, sir, but I'm more in the mood for sailing than horse riding today.' Then she took a 100 lira note from her pocket and held it in front of her, staring at the balding man who had spoken first.

'I suppose you also can't see any money here. Can anyone see any money here?' This brought more laughter from group, and a sly smile from the famous racehorse trainer.

'And where is it that the young, *gentleman,* wants to sail today?' This from the purported owner of the Bugatti, who looked like he had been wearing the same shirt since the invention of the motor car.

'Naples,' said Carla.

'That is rather a long journey. But I'll take you for 200.'

'I will take you for 180.' Cried a voice from inside the bar.

'160,' called another. Carla had inadvertently initiated a reverse auction.

The gaunt man unfurled himself from his seat and drew himself up close to Carla. He was taller than he had seemed when seated and towered over her. He took the money she still held in her hand, giving her a look of contempt.

'He offered it to me for 100 first and I accept. We leave now.' He took her elbow firmly and led her away from the crowd outside the bar, which seemed to Carla to have magically grown since her arrival, and not all of the men looked so old to her now. Carla wasn't sure whether to be grateful or afraid, but she let him lead her away. Once they were out of earshot of the bar, he loosened his grip and whispered, 'that was possibly the most stupid thing I have ever seen.'

'What do you mean?'

'You could have drowned today. Or worse. Probably after a whack on the head or knife in the ribs.'

Carla was dumbstruck.

'Or if you were lucky, Gino might have just turned you in to his brother in the Carabinieri. After he had robbed you, of course.'

They had stopped now at the edge of the harbour wall, overlooking a small, single-masted sailboat with flaking white and blue paint.

'Get in.' He pushed her roughly toward the boat.

'I'll do no such thing. Who on earth do you think you are, manhandling me like this?' Carla realised that she had spoken in her normal voice.

The tall man smiled, sarcastically. 'I apologise. *Please* get in . . . Signora Salvatore.'

At the sound of her name, Carla's resistance seeped away, and she did as she was told. Glancing back toward the bar, she saw that a few of the younger men had broken away from the group and were ambling toward them. They managed to appear both casual and threatening, like a school of bored sharks.

Her rescuer, if that was what he was, untied the painter and skipped into the boat more nimbly than Carla expected, given his age and gangly physique. He sat on a cross bench and slipped a pair of oars into the rowlocks, using them to push the boat backwards into clear water before turning the boat around. Then he began to pull away into the harbour. His strokes were unhurried, but Carla could see that he was putting real force into them.

'How did you know my name?'

Before he could reply, there were wolf whistles and shouts from the men at the harbour wall.

'Domenico, look after the *young gentleman*. He may not be able to swim if he falls overboard.'

'Don't worry,' cried another, 'He'll be safe with Domenico. He has a strong *breast*stroke.' Sat in the stern, Carla couldn't now see the men and didn't want to. But she could hear their howls of laughter. She caught Domenico's eye, who joined in the laughter and waved at them. She felt herself blushing. When they were further out, he stopped smiling.

'Did you seriously think that the beautiful, widowed schoolteacher from Paestum, living with her "brother," could simply put on a suit, cut her hair, and pass herself off as a man?'

Carla didn't know what to say, but Domenico's question was clearly rhetorical.

'Get in the front of the boat. I need to put the sails up.' He slid the oars down the side of the gunnels and offered her a sinewy, tawny hand. His strong grip helped her exchange places as they both ducked under the boom. With remarkable dexterity he removed the rope fastening the gaff to the boom and hoisted the mainsail. He settled in the stern like he was part of the boat, with one hand on the tiller and the other controlling the main sheet.

The boat picked up speed in the breeze, which was stronger out of the harbour, and Carla twisted her body toward the open sea to avoid his stare. A fine spray caressed her face at regular intervals as they moved through the waves. She had never been on the sea before, and she was enraptured. She closed her eyes and thrust her face into the wind, feeling the sea move beneath and around her, carrying them in elongated spirals, up and down, slower and faster, always forward, but never in a straight line. She'd never felt anything quite like it. Well, perhaps one thing. She listened to the ever-changing, shimmering sounds, as the boat was forced and caressed through the swell by the invisible power that filled taught curves in the dirty canvas above her. It was a paradox: relaxing and exhilarating, rhythmical and irregular, all at the same time. The gentle, reassuring surge, followed by the pull of the undertow, always with a hint of danger. The slap of a wave a reminder that you were at the whim of an unfathomable authority that could turn from sublime to malevolent in a moment. There were so many subtly changing forces at play, but she felt a stillness she had never felt on land. She was struck by how different a life lived on the sea must be and understood for the first time why ancient lore and superstition had such a hold on sailors. She was insignificant, yet part of something immense. If this were all his doing, Neptune was surely the most powerful of the gods.

'You've never been on the sea before?' Carla didn't turn to face Domenico and didn't feel the need to respond. 'You can feel him. I can tell.'

'Feel who?'

'Him. It. Whatever you wish to call your god.' Although he was shouting to cut through the wind, Domenico's voice was softer now. It was hard to tell which direction it was coming from. 'This is where I find *my* god, not in a church, or anywhere man can make dirty.'

Carla stared into the infinite indigo depths and wondered what it might be like to become one with them.

'He is more powerful here,' Domenico continued. 'He is *only* power here.'

'And beauty,' replied Carla.

'Yes, and beauty.'

For a while, there was only the sound of the boat and the sea.

'Why are you here, Signora?'

'Because you marched me onto your boat a little while back. Don't you remember?'

'No, *why* are you here? Who are you running from, or to?'

Carla did not turn to Domenico. It seemed easier that way. Easier to confide, or confess, as if Domenico were some seafaring priest from the ancient past. She was already at his mercy, what was the point of hiding anything out here. This was no place for subterfuge.

'I'm running from a man who won't let me go . . . to another who may not want me. I am running from a fire into . . . thin air.' She forced a laugh. 'But all I can see is water.'

'You are a poet, Signora?'

'Actually, I am, but not a very good one, I think.'

'Then perhaps you should tell me a simple story in plain prose. I like a good story, and we have a lot of time. So, I ask again. Why are you here?'

'You may find my story a little tawdry. Perhaps it will sully your sacred sea.'

Now Domenico laughed. 'There is not enough sin in the world to do that, and he hardly notices when tears fall into him.'

'Perhaps the sea will not like my story and punish me with a storm.'

'The sea does not judge. The sea merely listens.'

Carla saw that he was right. Her concerns were a ripple in this vastness and would be gone, soon enough, one way or another.

And so Carla told him her story, plainly and without artifice. She didn't hide her infidelity to her husband, or her life with Abercrombie. She related her distaste, and sadness, for what Brio, and Italy, had become. And she told him what Brio had done to her the night he had brought her back to Rome. She surprised herself with her honesty. Such admissions to a stranger were dangerous, life-threatening even. But the terrestrial world held no fears out here. It was powerless and puny, despite Mussolini's best efforts to prove otherwise back on land. She imagined Neptune, looking on, amused, at the latest pretender to Roman glory.

She also told Domenico of the beloved brother, Paolo, that she had lost in the war, and of the small boy he had left behind; of her disappointment in her parents, who worried more about the shame she had brought on them by leaving home unmarried, than the shame they had brought on themselves by abandoning their only living child; and of her despair at how the division and violence of the war had unleashed even more division and violence after it ended, when it was supposed to bring unity and peace. It were as if Italy were in the grip of a fever that came and went and came again, like the malaria from Campania's swamps, each time demanding more blood, with no sign of a cure. And she asked him what was it about blood that so obsessed these men? And why did they think that spilling it could be 'cleansing'? If something was spilled it needed cleaning up, *it* didn't do the cleaning. And none of these men could explain how *her* blood, every month, made her dirty, yet the blood they shed could purify a nation. She knew that nothing good had come from shedding that blood. At least her blood, along with all the mess and the pain, could bring new life.

Then it struck her. She calculated the days and laughed, bitterly. She had always been very regular. She should have shed her blood a few days ago, perhaps a week.

'What is it, Signora? Why do you laugh?'

Carla turned to face Domenico for the first time since he had unfurled the sail that had taken them out into this shifting, magnificent wilderness.

'I think I may be pregnant.'

Domenico smiled. 'That is wonderful news, Signora. Something joyful has come from this tale of woe.' Then a look of uncertainty crossed his face. He opened his mouth as if to speak and stopped.

'I don't know,' pre-empted Carla. 'It could be either of them.' A cloud seemed to pass over Domenico's face. For a while, he was silent and there was only the sea and the wind. He glanced toward the shore, then at the tiny flag at the top of the mast. They were quite far out to sea now, well out of sight of the harbour, and the wind had picked up. The troughs between the peaks of the waves were longer and deeper. Domenico's expression became stern again. He adjusted course a little and pulled the mainsail toward him. The boat picked up speed.

'Hold on tight,' he shouted. Carla gripped the bench as Domenico pushed the tiller away from him and ducked under the boom as it swung above his head. He settled into the other side of the stern as the boat took a right-angled turn to starboard and back toward land.

'Why did you change course?'

'I haven't. I'm tacking.'

'But we're heading back to land. We should be going over there.' Carla pointed to the tip of the Sorrento peninsula and the Island of Capri far across the wide Gulf of Salerno.

Domenico laughed. 'She's never been to sea, but she's a great navigator.'

'What's going on? Where are you taking me?'

'We were never going to Naples. It's too far and too dangerous in a boat this size, and we'd never make it in a day with this northerly wind.'

Carla began to panic. 'You took my money and said you would take me to Naples. I insist you take me to Naples!'

Domenico laughed again. 'You can insist all you like, but unless Neptune emerges from the sea and carries us on his back, we wouldn't make it. Besides, in case you hadn't noticed, we have no food or water on board. We're going back to land.'

'But I don't want to go back!'

'Don't worry. I'm not taking you back to Agropoli. We're going to Salerno. We should make it there by early afternoon. You can take a train to Naples from there. It is safer, and faster. With luck, you'll be in Naples tonight.

Carla relaxed a little and looked back toward the coastline, where she thought she could just make out the Temple of Neptune and the town of Paestum,

'Besides, a small boat in the open sea is no place for a woman with child.'

39

Naples, 11 September 1926

After Price's revelation about Ma, I excused myself and left the hotel in what I can only describe as an altered state. I felt, and indeed looked, like another man. The sun gleamed off the polished shoes that I now realised were stiff and uncomfortable. I wore a hat and suit that another man had bought, at the behest of yet another man. Neither of them quite fitted me. I wanted to rip them off, but I had nothing else to wear. I didn't even know what Pietro had done with my old clothes. He had probably thrown them away, which is what they deserved, but now that felt like an insult, as if I were to be allowed nothing of my former self.

I walked aimlessly, passing through the glass-roofed arcade of a grand galleria and across the façade an old opera house. The crowded streets buffeted me, and their clamour soon became unbearable. I needed space around me, not other people. I headed toward the bay and soon found myself in a large, open piazza in front of a disintegrating, red-and-ochre eighteenth century block that must have been the Royal Palace. Ahead to the right was a brutal, bulky stone fortress, exposed and alone, guarding the entrance to the port. Given my mood, it seemed as good a destination as anywhere. After a short, painful walk, I reached a stone bridge and headed across to a set of gates that led into the fortress. They were locked, but a narrow lane to the left allowed me onto the promontory and skirted the walls of the fort. I kept walking until I reached its tip and could go no further. I looked out to sea and wondered where I should go from here. There was nowhere *to* go, unless I wished to throw myself into the water lapping against the rocks below the fortified harbour wall. Perhaps that wasn't such a bad idea. I looked back across the port behind me and saw several large steamships. One of them was probably the *SS Patria*, headed to Marseilles the day after tomorrow, and for which I had a ticket back at the hotel, courtesy of Brio. For a fleeting moment, it crossed my mind to just get on it and go home. But what to? I didn't even have my memories to return to. I would be going home to nothing. Worse, I would be going home to a memory of something that had never truly existed.

I spotted a seagull sitting on some rocks about ten yards away, staring at me. It took off and flew toward me, landing on the wall just beyond arms reach. I had never liked seagulls. At the docks back home, they would swoop and scavenge, like white sea vultures. This one looked at me with a cold eye, as if challenging me in some obscure way. They are always larger and more menacing close up than when flying. Its proud, pristine chest was puffed out and I could see that strange drop of red on its beak that looks like blood. It appeared entirely unconcerned that I could react in any way that could do it harm. I lunged at it, full of rage, but it had been right, effortlessly launching itself up and away. I felt the tip of its wing brush my nose as it took flight, as if mocking me.

'Fuck you, Brio!' I roared after it, causing several of its fellow felons to take flight as well. I watched them soar and wheel above me, before heading out to sea. But I wouldn't follow them. I vowed silently to Carla that I wouldn't leave Italy until I had found her. She was the only thing I had left, and I was the only person who could save her from Brio, though I did not yet know how to do that, or even where she was. No matter. I couldn't and wouldn't just piss off back to Liverpool. Some deep instinct animated my right arm, and I crossed myself, as if to sanctify my pledge.

From down the street, I saw Pietro approaching with a look of concern on his narrow face and no trace of a limp. He must have followed me at Price's request to keep an eye on me. Or maybe it had been his own initiative. Perhaps my sign of the cross had sparked him into action, thinking that I might be about to hurl myself of the wall and into the sea. When he reached me, he placed his hand on my shoulder.

'Come, Mr Lyle, let us return to the hotel.'

I felt embarrassed. He must have heard my outburst and be thinking that I had lost my grip on reality. Perhaps he was right.

'Mr Lyle, do not judge Mr Price too harshly. He is a good man.'

I nodded.

'Whatever path lays before you, Mr Lyle, let us help you take the first step.'

I nodded again. If I were ever to find Carla, I would need all the help I could get. So together, we started back into the city and away from the sea.

40

Naples, 13 September 1926

Carla sat by the window of an upstairs table in a bar across the street from the dockside. She sipped the dregs of her second espresso, forgetting how cold it would be, and shuddered at the sourness. She was attracting suspicious looks from the waiter, having been there since they had opened at eight o'clock. It was now after ten. She had a decent view of the *SS Patria,* which was berthed a short distance away and was taking on final provisions and luggage for its departure at noon. Porters hauled large portmanteaus or carried smaller suitcases up one gangplank, while dockworkers trudged stoically up another with improbably large bundles or crates bending their backs or balanced on their heads. Hundreds of passengers had already embarked, and Carla had watched every one of them. She would have preferred a closer spot but didn't want to risk being seen by one of Brio's men checking whether Abercrombie had boarded the ship. Nevertheless, she felt confident that she would recognise him, even from this distance.

Time dragged, and she felt her concentration wander. She ordered another coffee, but that was a mistake. It made her jittery, and she worried that she might get distracted and miss him. The rate at which passengers were boarding increased as it approached eleven o'clock, and a sizeable crowd of passengers, and people to see them off, had now gathered on the dock below her. She couldn't take a chance on missing him in the crowd of late boarders and decided to get nearer to the ship, even if that risked being recognised. She nodded to the waiter who sauntered over and stood in front of her, blocking her line of sight.

'Another coffee, perhaps?' His sarcasm was lost on Carla who was trying to look around him.

'No, the bill please.'

As she said this, half leaning out of her chair, she spotted him. Or was it him? The waiter had adjusted his position, as if deliberately trying to obscure her view. She leant the other way and briefly caught Abercrombie's distinctive profile among the growing mass of people congregating on the dockside. But the clothes were those of another man: a wealthy, well-dressed, young man in a navy suit of the latest cut and a grey fedora, which hid any sign of his sandy hair. A seed of doubt was planted. Carla rose and placed a 10 lira note on the table, not even bothering to glance at the waiter. She grabbed her bag, ran down the stairs and out of the bar. But this was another mistake. She was now on the same level as everyone else, and as she ran toward the gangplank, scanning the tops of the heads for a grey fedora, she bumped into a porter who was pulling a trolley loaded with cases. This sent her sprawling to the floor. She scrambled to her feet with the porter's coarse Neapolitan curses showering down on her. She was now perhaps fifty meters away from the foot of the gangplank and the density of passengers had slowed her pace. Looking up she saw the fedora on top of a head climbing up to the ship. She couldn't be sure it was him and cursed her overconfidence. She scrutinised his movement as he walked up and away from her. Surely it was him. But where had he got those clothes? A horrible thought insinuated itself into her mind. Perhaps Brio had bribed him to leave. Perhaps he was walking up that gangway with notes peeled from the same bankroll Brio had given her money from. As he reached the top he stopped and turned, removing his hat and scanning the crowd below, almost as if looking for her. In her bones she felt it was him, but he was some distance away now, and a part of her didn't want it to be true. Before she could make up her mind, he disappeared into the ship.

Carla withdrew to a less exposed place beside some wooden crates to consider her next step. She had her ticket to Marseilles and her instinct told her that if she didn't get on the ship, she would never see Abercrombie again. But she also didn't want to embark on a wild goose chase if Abercrombie was still in Naples, or even in Rome, looking for her. She watched the line of people boarding, which was getting shorter.

There was no one who remotely looked like Abercrombie, and when the last person made their way up the gangway, she decided to play her last card.

With the crowd now dispersed, she could see that the foot of the gangway was guarded by a very tall young man with a narrow face and a rather absurd white nautical uniform. His jacket dripped with enough gold braid to put him command of the entire Italian navy. As she approached, he blew a whistle, before shouting a final call for boarding. Carla walked up to him and showed him her ticket.

'You've cut that rather fine, Sir. We were about to pull up the gangplank.'

'I've been waiting for my friend, but he doesn't seem to have arrived. I'm hoping he's already on board and I've somehow missed him. Can you tell me if a Mr. Abercrombie Lyle has boarded?'

Carla noticed a sly grin. 'We're not supposed to give out that information, Sir.'

'I would be most obliged if you can make an exception. I don't want to leave without him. Or even worse, for him to leave without me.'

The official gave her a knowing look and smoothed his fine, dark moustache with finger and thumb, subtly rubbing them together as he finished. The gesture was accompanied by a direct, and, to Carla's thinking, rather impertinent, stare.

'Of course, I understand you have an obligation of confidentiality,' Carla reached into Abercrombie's jacket pocket, 'but when you give your passenger list a final check, if someone were to look over your shoulder . . .' Carla produced a 50 lira note and passed it with her ticket to the young man, who nodded graciously. He turned the pages of his passenger list languidly, pausing when he had found what she wanted.

And there he was. Abercrombie Lyle, with a tick next to his name.

'Will Sir be boarding?'

Carla hesitated. Disappointment that Abercrombie had chosen to leave swirled with the excitement of finding him. She felt a moment of panic that she wouldn't know what to say when she tracked him down on board. Perhaps it would be different between them now, with this worm of betrayal inside her. Perhaps he didn't even want to be found and just wanted to go home to England to put the horror of that last day in Paestum behind him. But she had come this far and needed to know for certain, one way or the other, if he still wanted her.

A bellow erupted from the ships horn.

'Sir, are you boarding? You must decide now.'

Carla stepped onto the gangplank and walked up to the ship.

41

Naples, 13 September 1926

Price and Pietro were in exceptionally good spirits. Price had closed his office for the day, a little earlier than usual, and we were on our second large whiskey. He was perched on his desk smoking a cigar. Pietro and I were sitting in his heavenly armchairs. I was still wearing the porter's uniform I had used to leave the ship before it sailed. The alcohol seemed to have dissolved the hierarchy between employer and employee. As Pietro recounted the day's escapade, Price looked on indulgently, as if he were a well-loved rascal of a son that he almost disapproved of. But he could not disapprove too strongly, given that he had been the mastermind behind the sleight of hand that had thrown Brio off my trail. Pietro was into his stride now and, to my surprise, this previously sombre young man was a rather good, and amusing, storyteller.

'So, there he was, this young pup, not even able to grow a moustache yet. A pretty young fellow.' Pietro flicked a glance at Price. 'I almost felt sorry for him. He was so desperate to find out if you were on the ship. He must have fallen asleep on the job and thought he was in for a beating from this Brio of yours. So, I thought I'd have some fun with him.'

'What did you do?' Price leaned forward from his desk in eager anticipation.

Pietro pulled out a 50 Lira note from his breast pocket with the flourish of a magician. 'I thought I'd let the fool offer me a little . . . inducement to check the passenger list.'

Price burst out laughing. 'Brilliant!'

'The young chap must be half blind. Abercrombie practically did a pirouette and blew him a kiss at the top of the gangway. Even after he saw your name on the passenger list, the poor boy didn't quite know what to do. In the end, he got on the ship to make sure.'

'Bravo, Pietro!' Price clapped his hands together then reached across to give Pietro a hearty slap on the knee. 'I can picture him now, roaming the ship, wondering how you've vanished into thin air! He must be terrified what Brio will say when he gets off empty handed in Marseille!'

'I imagine he'll lie and tell Brio that you've been safely packed off back to Liverpool,' replied Pietro.

'Or that you've fallen overboard!' suggested Price.

'If that is the quality of henchman you are up against, Abercrombie, or should I say, Michael,' Pietro gave me a sly wink, 'we should have no trouble finding Carla and re-uniting the two of you.'

I was not so sure. I couldn't deny that, for the first time since Brio's arrival in Paestum, my mood had lifted a little. Having executed a clever plan to get one over on Brio felt good, but I was no closer to Carla than I'd been this morning when I boarded the ship. The prank had given me some breathing room, but it was a baby step on what could be a long and treacherous path to Carla.

Price chortled and refilled our glasses. He looked like he hadn't had this much fun since he'd been a young man dressed in his funny little stripped cap with Henry Tyrer.

'Ah, before I forget.' Price reached into his desk and handed me what looked like a small, green book. The cover was embossed with a golden harp and the words Saorstát Éireann. My Gaelic was minimal, but I knew enough to translate this into 'Irish Free State.' It looked almost new. I opened it and saw my photograph staring back at me. My new name was Michael Lynch. Must I now go by my brother's name? That seemed a cruel twist, but I could hardly ask them to change it. I also had a new birthday to remember that made me three years older. I could have carried off more. Apparently, I had been born in Limerick.

'I can't believe how quickly you got hold of this. How did you manage it?'

'One of the many wonderful things about this strange city,' Price eulogised, 'there is very little one can't acquire, if you know the right people.'

'And are able to pay,' added Pietro.

'And don't enquire into the provenance,' completed Price.

'I'm not sure how I can ever repay you for this. Both of you.'

'You can start by taking us out to dinner.' Price reached over and took the 50 Lira note from Pietro's hand. 'Abercrombie–, sorry, *Michael*, your first meal as a new man will be paid for by your arch enemy!' He handed the note to me, beaming, as if it were the winning raffle ticket at a prize draw. Pietro looked disappointed, then rearranged his long face into an enormous grin.

Price raised his glass. 'To Michael and Carla!'

'To Michael and Carla!' Pietro joined in.

I raised my glass as well but felt less 'gung-ho' than my companions. Neither of them had met Brio, and neither of them knew what he was capable of – although Pietro was about to find out. We were borrowing Price's car and driving to Rome tomorrow afternoon to look for Carla.

42

En route to Marseille, 14 September 1926

It was as if he had vanished into thin air. Where could he have gone? The ship was enormous, but Carla had prowled every deck, bar and dining room, in ever more desperate loops, and there was not a glimpse of anyone who looked like Abercrombie. After a few hours, the sun sank low in the west, and she could glimpse the coast of Sardinia off the port bow. She circumnavigated the deck yet again. She couldn't believe that she hadn't seen him. In more rational moments she knew it was feasible. Perhaps she had just been unlucky. Perhaps he had holed himself up in a cabin, morose and licking his wounds, regretting leaving her behind with Brio. Perhaps he had thrown himself overboard. No, she didn't think he had that in him. Nevertheless, she felt a rising sense of panic. It was maddening that he was so close, but they were not together. She patrolled the corridors knowing that he could be behind any of the cabin doors she passed. She wanted to knock on every one and shout his name, but knowing how deranged and pathetic that would look, she couldn't bring herself to do it.

She tracked down the purser, a fussy looking middle-aged man with a Hapsburg chin, antique pre-war moustache, and slicked blond hair greying at the temples. She asked him what cabin Abercrombie was in and was greeted with disdain bordering on contempt. *Je ne sais autorisées à dévoiler cette information . . . Monsieur.* His manner was so frosty that she didn't even try a bribe this time. And again, there was that pause, even a hint of sarcasm, before the *Monsieur*, or was she imagining it? She wondered what a strange fish she must appear, and sound: neither man nor woman. She had initially delighted in the novelty and freedom of her transformation, but now she was regretting it. She was sure she could have charmed the information out of the pompous French ass in less than a minute in her normal guise. But dressed like this, she couldn't even flirt with him. Defeated, she retired to her cabin and decided that she was becoming a woman again in Marseille, whether she found Abercrombie or not.

The next morning, she resumed her search with increasing desperation. After more than a day at sea a rugged headland appeared off their starboard bow, and she realised it was now unlikely she would find him before they docked. But he *must* be on board somewhere, and if he was on board, he had to get off when they arrived in Marseille. Before the ship docked, she would position herself where the passengers disembarked. She knew, as a matter of logic, that he would have to funnel past her at some point. She forced herself to accept this truth and reject the possibility of any other outcome.

Details of the French coast came into sharper focus as they approached the headland. She could make out small sandy coves and pastel-hued fishing villages. It looked idyllic. More rugged yet somehow softer, more domestic, than the coast she had left. She wondered what Abercrombie would make of it. Then she wondered what he would make of her. The thought of his reaction when he saw her, in his old clothes and hair shorn, made her laugh. She imagined the slow-dawning joy of his recognition, and how he would embrace her. Then she imagined the scene they would present to their fellow passengers, two 'men' in a passionate kiss as the ship disgorged its human cargo beside them. She laughed again. It wouldn't be long now. Perhaps an hour or so, two at most, and they would be together. She still had a decent amount of Brio's money, and they would be in France, beyond his reach. They would be free. Truly free for the first time in their lives. They could find a quiet, pretty hotel in one of the little seaside towns she could see – it would be like a honeymoon – and they could plan their new life together. They could go anywhere. Do anything. They were young, and strong, and clever. They could find a small village and live quietly by the sea. They could go to Paris, or England. They could disappear together. She felt almost giddy with happiness. Their new life would begin before the setting sun hit the sea. She was Mrs Abercrombie Lyle. No one would know that they weren't married, and when the baby came . . . *when the baby came.*

A shadow fell across her sunlit future. What if it wasn't his? It would be obvious enough, eventually, maybe even from the moment of birth. How would he react if it was clearly Brio's? Even if he was prepared to call it his own and become the father, the child would be a constant reminder of Brio, and what he had done to her.

43

Rome, 15 September 1926

Even through the filthy windscreen and from fifty yards away, as soon as I saw him emerge from the entrance to the Press Office of the Head of Government, I had no doubt it was Brio. He stood for a moment at the top of the steps and tugged on both sleeves of his dark suit. Brio always faced the world as elegantly as he could, but the gesture looked a little forced, as if he was making it easy for us to spot him. Something about it took me back to my performance at the top of the gangplank of the *SS Patria*. Could he know that I was watching him, as I had hoped that he had been watching me? Even his suit looked similar to mine, although rather more impressively filled. Was he playing some sort of game? I tried to push the thought from my mind. There was no way he could know that I was here.

He trotted down the steps, as ever, remarkably nimble for his size. Seeing him again, I felt sick. I touched the soft leather briefcase on my lap and felt the hard outline of Pierce's old Webley service revolver, but that didn't give me the reassurance I had sought. If anything, I felt worse.

'Is that him?' Pietro nudged my arm.

'Yes.'

'Bellisimo!' Pietro gave me a wink, but I was in no mood for levity. I hadn't done anything this dangerous since the war, or at least since the night of the attack on *Avanti!* I was a little out of practice on casual heroics. Pietro, on the other hand, was in fine fettle. On the long drive to Rome he became more talkative and now he seemed excited by our 'little adventure,' as he called it.

Ahead, at the gates that led onto the street, Brio nodded to the two carabinieri on duty, looked both ways, and started to walk straight towards us. I felt completely exposed and realised that we hadn't properly thought this through. If he spotted me here, it was all over. I tipped my hat down and bent forward as if looking for something on the floor. I could hear his footsteps on the pavement as he passed the car on my side. A few seconds later I felt Pietro nudge me again.

'He's gone,' said Pietro.

'Do you think he saw us?' I asked.

'I don't think he could have seen you, but he had a good look at me as he passed. I see what you mean. He's a handsome devil.'

Pietro seemed unconcerned by the danger I had put him in. As he was a stranger to Brio, the risk for him was minimal, for now. But that could change in an instant. I sneaked a glance behind us and saw Brio step off the pavement and cross the street, breaking into a trot to skip ahead of a car. Pietro waited for a few more seconds and then started the engine.

'Don't let him out of your sight,' ordered Pietro. 'Tell me what he's doing.'

Pietro seemed much more comfortable with our mission than I was. It seemed like he might have done this kind of thing before.

'He's walking away. I'm losing him . . . wait. He's stopped . . .' Leaning out the window and craning my neck, I saw him in the distance standing next to his silver Lancia, and that day in Paestum came flooding back. I was dreading what we had planned, but now the dread was infused with anger.

'What's he doing?'

'He's getting into his car.'

I felt the Fiat shudder as Pietro yanked on the gear stick and pressed his foot on the accelerator. He pulled away then glanced behind him through the tiny clear panel in the black hood behind us. As he swung around 180 degrees, he nearly hit a bicyclist that he hadn't seen passing alongside, eliciting some vile obscenities regarding his mother's profession, which I later learned were more or less true. This provoked a honk from another car, held up by our manoeuvre. I cringed at the attention we were drawing but Pietro remained calm. Now facing toward Brio's Lancia, about 100 yards ahead, we saw it pull away and began to follow, as close as we dared, balancing the risk of losing him with the danger of being spotted.

We were in the heart of official Rome and had to snake through the busy Piazza d'Aracoeli and into an oval of mayhem in front of the bombastic, colonnaded Monumento a Vittorio Emmanuel II. For a few seconds, we couldn't see him, but there weren't many cars as large and as shiny as Brio's. I glimpsed it slipping right, several cars ahead, and from there it was a simple task to stay on his tail, even for amateur sleuths like us.

About ten minutes later Brio turned off Via Cavour onto a small side street. I was wary of following him down it. If he was onto us, it could be a trap, if not, there was a good chance that this was his destination. I told Pietro to drop me on the corner and wait until I signalled. For a moment he looked unwilling but then nodded and stopped at the junction with a line of sight up the street. I grabbed the gun from the briefcase, jumped out and shoved it down the back of my waistband. When I saw the street sign, Via Sforza, it didn't surprise me that Brio had chosen a street named after the most powerful dynasty to have ruled his home city of Milan. I felt confident this was where he lived, and if this was where he lived, perhaps it was also where Carla was.

Via Sforza ran steeply uphill, with a high, ancient embankment to the left, before turning sharply around it at the top. I saw no sign of the Lancia and started running up the hill, wondering if I'd made a huge mistake. When I got to the bend I was out of breath and slowed to walking pace before peering round the corner. Bingo! The Lancia was parked up ahead on the right, almost blocking the street, and there was Brio, approaching a butter-coloured, stuccoed apartment building. It had a had a fortress-like air, with a solid wooden door, Roman arched windows on the ground floor, and more austere, shuttered windows on the three floors above. I felt the urge to run up the street, Webley in hand, and demand to know what he had done with Carla, but I retreated and waved to Pietro to join me. As I peered round the corner again, I saw Brio disappear into the building. The flat, plain façade felt very public, and very exposed for what we needed to do next, but we didn't have much choice. Pietro pulled up in the Fiat before the corner and out of sight of Brio's building.

'He's gone into the third building round the corner, up on the right. The yellow one. This won't be easy. The whole street will see us.' As I said this, an old man came round the corner and eyed us suspiciously.

'What the fuck are you looking at?' Pietro hissed in his face in full Neapolitan. The man scurried by, taking us, in our smart suits with mysterious bulges, either for undercover police of some sort, or worse. Then I realised that even if somebody did see us, who would try to stop us? We needed to stay focused on Brio.

'Let's stick to the plan and make it quick,' said Pietro, looking me in the eye and putting his hand on my shoulder. I nodded.

'And if the plan goes wrong?'

He waved his little Beretta in my face. 'We have these. It's easy to improvise with a gun in your hand.' I was grateful to have Pietro with me, but I was beginning see him in a new light that wasn't altogether flattering.

We ran to the door of the apartment building. To the left of the door was a brass plate with buttons and names. The button at the top was labelled B. Salvatore. I took a deep breath and pushed it. After a slight delay, somewhere high above, I heard a coarse ringing. I stood with my back against the wall to the side of the door and Pietro stood directly in front of it, his hand in his pocket, gripping his Beretta. We had decided that his anonymity would give him a momentary advantage. We waited for sounds of footsteps coming down to let us in. Instead, after a few seconds, there was a loud buzz and a click from the door.

'I suppose we'll be improvising then,' Pietro said, and pushed it open. Inside, we saw an open staircase with iron bannisters ascending around a square central stairwell. If Brio was expecting us, we would be sitting ducks on that staircase. Standing in the stairwell, in a metal cage, was a brand-new elevator that emerged from the basement and rose the full height of the building.

Pietro hadn't let the outside door shut. He put a finger to his lips and said, in the deep, gravelly voice of a much older man. 'Hold the door, please.' Then, in his own voice, 'Of course, signor.' He gestured me toward the elevator. I got the hint and walked over to push the button. Pietro let the door close and replied to Brio's imaginary neighbour, 'my pleasure. Let me get the elevator for you, I'm going up as well.' He even managed a distinct note of sarcasm, as if to cover the imaginary neighbour's rudeness for not thanking him. The elevator rumbled into life, then Pietro removed his shoes and began to spring silently up the stairs, shoes in one hand, Beretta in the other. If Brio was on to us, he would at least have to deal with two angles of attack.

The lift clunked into place, and I noisily slid back the collapsible metal door. I got in and pushed the button for the fourth floor. There was more racket from the closing door and then I began to ascend. It felt like a slowly moving prison cell. I was both trapped and vulnerable. The lift took an age to get to the fourth floor, and as it climbed, I had plenty of time to imagine what might await me. Brio might be sitting in his flat, sipping a whiskey after a hard day at the office, musing over the next set of lies about wheat production. Or he might be waiting for me at the top with his own weapon drawn. Before the elevator had come to a stop, I could see through the criss-crossed confusion of metal and wire that it was the latter. Brio was standing above me with a handgun tracking my head.

44

Marseille, 15 September 1926

It was a sparkling afternoon when the vast bulk of the *SS Patria* gently touched the dockside, somehow combining the inevitability of enormous inertia with improbable delicacy. Carla watched the dockhands make figures of eight with ropes of huge girth on the cast iron bollards and settled against the railings to watch the passengers disembark. She felt something was wrong from the moment the first passengers descended the gangplank, as if a small part of her knew he wasn't, and never had been, on the ship. From this initial unease, a creeping anxiety enveloped her with every person who wasn't Abercrombie that left the ship. Her mind circled around his most likely order of departure. Surely, he would be keen to get off and among the first to do so. Or perhaps a reluctance to leave her behind would make him cling to the ship till the last moment, as if stepping foot on French soil symbolized a rupture from her he sought to delay?

The passengers continued to pass before her in small groups, or one by one. She scrutinized them all but did not see Abercrombie. When the last stragglers departed, she sank to her knees on the deck, too drained and disappointed to even cry. It had been the most dispiriting experience of her life. What could have happened to him? She had seen his name on the passenger list. Could she have missed him getting off? It was possible, with all the chaos of baggage and occasional clusters of passengers blocking her view, especially if he was trying not to be seen, or like her, in disguise, but it seemed unlikely. A harsh snort escaped her as she imagined a tragi-comic scenario of her failing to recognise Abercrombie dressed as a woman while he failed to recognise her dressed as a man. Could he still be on board? Perhaps he was hiding and planning to return to Naples as a stowaway. Perhaps this was all an elaborate ruse to convince Brio's men that he had actually gone?

She had kept her eyes on the point of egress, in case he was a late leaver, and now noticed the prissy purser staring at her. Still on her knees, she joined her hands in prayer and then crossed herself to cover her embarrassment, before standing up. He approached her, the look on his face even more contemptuous than the previous evening.

'I, too, thank God whenever I return to the sacred soil of France, but I did not think you were French, Monsieur?'

Carla gave a forced smile and did not attempt an explanation.

'Did . . . *Monsieur* find his friend?' He asked in a tone that implied expectation of a negative response.

'I'm afraid I did not.' Carla attempted the most casually male tone she could muster. 'Tell me, purser, is this ship going straight back to Naples?'

'Non, Monsieur. It will remain her for two weeks before heading directly to New York.'

'Is there any chance my friend may still be on board?'

'Absolutely none, Monsieur. We inspect our ships very thoroughly on arrival to check for stowaways.' He pushed his glasses up his large, curving nose and smiled for the first time. 'Unless he is very good at playing hide and seek.'

An awkward silence followed. Then the purser reprised his smile and extended his arm toward the gangplank. With this silent, elegant gesture, Carla knew he was telling her, *now fuck off my ship*. Having no good reason to hang around, she meekly complied.

45

Rome, 15 September 1926

As the clattering elevator shuddered to a halt, I saw two things in quick succession. First, Brio's obvious shock when, from under my hat, enough of my face became visible for him to recognise me. Second, the spider-like figure of Pietro silently advancing on him from behind. Brio had just enough time to utter, 'Oh, Abercrombie,' in a disappointed tone, before the butt of Pietro's pistol came down with sickening force on the back of his head, dropping him to the floor.

*

'Where is she?' Brio was regaining consciousness, with the help of the hardest slap across the face I could muster. It had felt good, for a moment. We had put him on a dining room chair and tied his hands behind his back. His feet were also tied to the legs of the chair. Pietro, who now had a black scarf over his nose and mouth, stood behind him, with the muzzle of his pistol pressed into the back of Brio's neck. As he came round, he started struggling against his bonds and almost toppled over.

Pietro yanked the back of his collar to keep him upright, half throttling Brio, and then roughly pushed the gun into his temple. He whispered in his ear. 'Stay still, and answer his question, or I'll splatter your filthy fascist brain across the walls of your beautiful apartment.'

And it was a beautiful apartment, in a rather cold way. We were at the top of the building, and white walls, glass and gleaming mirrors created an impression of endless light. Behind Brio, an angular, futuristic clock and a stylized bronze nude sat on a huge square fireplace of grey marble that clearly wasn't original to the building. The place must have been gutted and re-made, almost erasing any trace of its past. I hadn't seen anything like it before. In the rest of the building, each level had four apartments. Brio's seemed to take up the entire top floor. It had three bedrooms, large study, dining room, kitchen, bathroom, and the large sitting room we were now in. We had seen it all in great detail looking for Carla, or for signs of her. She wasn't there but she had been. In the master bedroom the mirrored closet had several dresses that still smelt of her, and I found a shopping list in her handwriting on a dressing table. The banal domesticity of the items: talcum powder, stockings, hairbrush, had disturbed me. It seemed like she was settling back into a life with Brio.

In the sitting room I stood before her husband. We had placed him in the centre of the room on a huge rug that dominated the space. The rug's crazy angles of overlapping rust and cream shards, and off-kilter sequences of turquoise waving parallel lines, were disorienting and made me feel queasy. As Pietro eased the pressure on Brio's throat, Brio managed a smile.

'I must congratulate you, Abercrombie,' he said, huskily.

I looked at Brio with a blank face, trying not to react to whatever taunts or bluster he might throw at me. I was expecting an attempt to rile or distract me and had promised myself not to get caught up in his games.

'Two weeks ago, I left you half dead, reeking of chicken shit in a godforsaken, rustic backwater, and now here you are,' he nodded his head back, 'with a genuine *Camorrista* as a side kick. And look at you, all spruced up, in a very stylish suit, at least by your standards. And pointing a gun in my face. Bravo! I didn't think you had it in you.'

'Where is she?' I repeated.

'I'm impressed,' continued Brio, 'but a little confused. Tell me. What's in it for him? The lanky Neapolitan sodomite who got such a thrill out of throttling—' Pietro punched Brio in the side of his head, sending him crashing to the floor.

From his horizontal position Brio coughed and laughed at the same time. He twisted his head to glance at Pietro. 'I see I've touched a nerve, but surely he's not your . . . Oh, Abercrombie, I always thought there was something a little . . . peculiar about you, but that's fast work. Your bed must still be warm from Carla.'

Pietro kicked Brio hard in the balls, which at least shut him up. His face screwed into an awful grimace. I didn't like the way this conversation was going. Pietro looked like he was gearing up for another kick.

'Stop!' I shouted at Pietro, whose eyes radiated with fury. 'Leave him be.'

Pietro was full of surprises today.

As Brio's accusations settled in my mind, they connected other parts of a picture that I had struggled to put together. Pietro's hatred of the fascists. The ease with which they had acquired a passport. His connections at the docks. Probably his relationship with Price. His willingness to help me now made more sense but made me feel far less comfortable.

'You can take the mask off, *Camorrista*.' Brio groaned. 'I never forget a face, and I've already seen you, parked in a brown Fiat 503 outside my office. That's a horrible car, by the way. It was a struggle driving slowly enough to let you keep up with me.'

'Maybe when I kill you, I'll take your beautiful silver Lancia, instead,' replied Pietro, 'but I'll need to scrub the seats with bleach before I sit in them.' The normally calm and reserved Pietro looked like he was barely in control of his emotions. He had become another person.

'Of course, you know what your brotherhood will do to you when they find out you're a sodomite.'

I knew what Brio was up to. He had a poor hand to play and seemed to think that goading Pietro might create an opportunity for him. 'So, if you're finding this exciting, I recommend you get your cock out and tug on it now, while you still have it.'

Pietro went for Brio again, and I had to wrestle with him to hold him back. He was stronger than I expected, and I wasn't sure I could hold him. Then he went limp, and I was no longer holding him back but holding him up. Something had cracked inside him, and he was shuddering with silent sobs. I eased him into an armchair.

'What a touching scene,' Brio was still horizontal on the floor, tied to the chair. He was grinning and looked a little crazy, with one cheek bright red and his hair a mess. A trickle of blood had escaped his nostril, and his nose looked like it might be broken, though it was hard to tell from my upright angle.

An unexpected wave of pity overcame me, followed by an undertow of nostalgia that pulled me hard into the past. Brio's disarray, and undoubted courage, took me back to the aftermath of the battle with the fascists at *Avanti!* I saw him, for a moment, as he had once been. Apart from my brother, he was the only true friend I had ever had. I tried to push the emotion away but couldn't. I began to well up.

I knelt in front of him, then, not quite knowing why, I lay on my side, facing Brio, with my head on the soft woollen rug, about a foot from his, the broken geometric shapes of the carpet connecting and fracturing the space between us. I looked at him. I hadn't realised it until now, but there was so much I wanted to say. I didn't know where to start but knew I may never get another chance.

'You want to kiss me, don't you?' Brio said, gently. I couldn't tell if he was mocking me or not. I thought probably not, and it nearly undid me. For a part of me did want to kiss him, but not in the way he was implying. I wanted to kiss him as one might kiss a dear friend who had disappeared for many years and returned. I wanted to forgive him, and for him to forgive me. And in that moment, despite what had passed between us, and what he had taken from me, if that kiss could have erased the last few years and returned all three of us to Milan, and what we had been there, I would have done it.

We lay, looking at each other, and for a moment, as he smiled at me wryly, I glimpsed the old Brio. I was probably deluding myself, but I wanted to believe that it was still possible for us to be friends again. That we would both suddenly burst out laughing at the absurdity of our situation and somehow turn the clock back.

'What happened, Brio? How did all this happen?' There was a glimmer of sorrow in his swollen face, before it hardened.

'There are much bigger things than the three of us, Abercrombie.' Brio closed his eyes and moved his jaw from side to side as if trying to put it back in place. 'The world was broken. My country was broken. You know this but have chosen to hide from it. I couldn't do that. I had to do something to fix it, or at least try.'

'But you hated them. How could you join them? How could you become a mouthpiece for that strutting ass?'

He exhaled through his nose in a sort of sigh and looked at me again. 'Tell me, Abercrombie. Is there nothing bigger than you and Carla in your world? Does nothing else matter? Is the universe empty, beyond your desire for her?'

I had not expected this question, but an answer gushed from somewhere deep inside me. 'No. The universe is full of wonder, Brio, if we let ourselves see it. A world of beauty and love, of laughter and joy, of kindness and friendship. Do you not remember these things? *They* are bigger than us. But also part of us. We create them, and nurture them, into something magnificent.'

Brio closed his eyes and grimaced in pain 'They are not real. Not in these times. If they ever were. They are an illusion. A distraction.' Then he opened his eyes and stared at me. '*You* were a distraction.'

'That's not true, Brio. I know they are real, because we shared them. In the end, they are the *only* things that are real. These other things – like Italy, or Ireland, glory or honour, they are fabrications and lies. Lies that seduce us because they seem powerful and noble. But they ruin our lives. They kill and maim, and make us act like animals, if we give ourselves over to them. You must have seen this in the War.'

'I saw friends lose limbs, or half their faces, only to come home and have the half they had left spat on by strangers in the street – and then be left there to rot like rubbish. We have to make an Italy that is better than that. I thought we could do it with socialism, but I was wrong. That wasn't strong enough for Italians. Or we weren't strong enough for it.

We are so sick we need more powerful medicine. We need big leaders and big ideas to bang our heads together and make us do big things.'

'I saw friends butchered like animals as well, for what? For big ideas that meant nothing to them in the end.'

Brio now turned his face to the carpet, as if he didn't want to look at me.

'You know how I know this?' I continued. 'Because some could still talk at the end, and you know what? Not one of them said a word about their country, or their king, or the glory and honour of dying for them. Not one of them had anything to say about an *idea*. They talked about their wives and girlfriends, their children, and their mothers, and the pain they knew they would have to live with when they were gone. Ordinary people, who they loved, and who loved them. That's the only thing that matters.'

Brio was facing me again now and his face was set hard. 'Have you finished your sermon?'

'No. I have one last thing to say to you, Brio. You are an even bigger idiot than most, because you had so much love. It flowed all around and through you. In your heart, you know this. But you threw it all away for an idea! What a fool you are.'

Brio gave a bitter laugh. 'Perhaps you are an even bigger fool, Abercrombie. I may have lost Carla, for now, but I still have my ideas. What do you have? You have nothing!' He spat something hard and wet at me. Brio's remark hit me more forcefully than the tooth. We were both silent for a while.

'Where is she, Brio?'

The unmistakable sound of a pistol being cocked reminded me that I was not alone with Brio. I turned my head toward the ceiling and saw Pietro standing over us with his weapon pointing at Brio's knee. He seemed to have regained his composure.

'Answer his question now or I'll put a bullet in your knee.'

Brio glanced at Pietro, then back at me. 'She's not here.'

'We know that. Where is she?' I asked.

'She must have gone out shopping.'

Pietro stomped on Brio's hand with his heal. Brio let out a short scream before controlling himself. Pietro shoved the pistol into Brio's knee.

'She left three days ago,' Brio conceded.

'Where did she go?' I asked.

Brio somehow managed a grin. 'I've no idea, but she won't be looking for you, if that's what you're thinking.'

That was exactly what I had been thinking. I had begun to swell with hope that Carla was back at the farmhouse waiting for me to come home.

'Why do you say that?'

'There's something in my desk that will answer your question.'

'What are you talking about? What have you done to her?'

'It's in the top drawer on the left in a buff folder. You'll need the key though. It's in my right trouser pocket.' Brio glanced up at Pietro. 'Perhaps your friend would enjoy fishing it out?'

I saw Brio grimace again and noticed that Pietro's heel was still pressing down hard on his hand. 'Pietro. Stop, please.' Pietro lifted his foot and took a step back, still covering Brio with his pistol. I rose to my knees and reached into Brio's pocket. It felt disturbingly intimate. I had never had to put my hand in another man's pocket before. I removed the key and headed straight for Brio's study. The key turned smoothly and underneath some papers was a thin buff folder. I placed it on the desk and flipped it open. The folder contained the most disturbing photographs I had ever seen.

'See anyone you recognise?' I heard Brio shout from the sitting room.

I did. The photographs were of me, and I was dead. Or at least that was how I looked. I was lying on my side in the yard at Paestum, in a position not dissimilar to Brio's. I was still and pale with blood covering much of my face, and the side of my head was a congealed mess of matted hair.

'Not a pretty sight, are they?'

I returned to the sitting room holding a close up of my dead head, which I flashed at Pietro.

'I didn't want to upset her, but she wouldn't believe that you were dead. Rather touchingly, she didn't think I had it in me to kill you. Of course, I told her it was all a terrible accident, I had asked the boys to give you a beating, to teach you a lesson, but, well, you know how they can get carried away.'

I was transfixed by the evidence of my death. If I didn't know better, I would have thought I was dead myself.

'I even shed a few tears,' continued Brio. 'I was so very sorry to have caused, accidentally of course, the death of my best friend, even if he had betrayed me. Yes, we both had a good cry, and you know how Carla needs to be comforted when she gets upset. It was a very tender moment. Just like old times. After I had . . . very thoroughly comforted her . . . we both lay in bed and raised a glass of whiskey in your memory.'

I stared at Brio, in a state of shock and incomprehension.

'I don't know where she is, Abercrombie, but I know she's not looking for you. When she comes to her senses. She'll come back to me. Deep down, I know she still loves me. She just needs a little time to adjust to her new reality. And besides, she has no money and nowhere else to go.'

This time it was my foot that launched itself into Brio's groin. As he groaned, I yanked the chair upright, which took all my strength. I pulled the Webley from my waistband, cocked it and pointed it at his head. For a moment, I thought I might actually do it, but in my heart, I knew that I could never kill him like this, tied to a chair and in cold blood, like I was executing a deserter.

'Would you like *me* to finish him?' Pietro offered softly. I had no doubt that even the slightest nod would see Brio's brains splattered across his pristine walls. I think Brio knew this too. He opened his mouth, as if to say something clever, but closed it without saying anything. For the first time since I had met him, I saw real fear in his eyes.

46

Liverpool, 19 September 1926

From her elevated position outside Lime Street station, Carla looked across a magnificent vista of imperial grandeur and commercial bustle. To her right, bronze lions and martial heroes on horseback protected a large plaza and huge classical temple. It was larger than any temple she knew from Paestum, or even Rome, but of more recent origin and intact. There were more classically inspired buildings and a tall column beyond. To her left, office buildings, department stores and churches sprawled chaotically. Ahead she caught a glimpse of slate-grey river, barely delineated from the afternoon sky. The map she had bought in the station told her to head down toward the river and then turn right behind the colossal temple, which was labelled as St. George's Hall. In her last days with Brio, he had talked about building a new Rome. The people of Liverpool, it seemed, had beaten him to it.

She considered a cab but wanted to see some of Abercrombie's city and decided to walk. She passed a busy square, with shops, a theatre and several pubs. The public gardens behind St George's Hall were full of office workers eating lunch or strolling the broad paths. She felt Abercrombie had been a little unkind to his native city, which seemed a fine, vibrant place, if a little shabby beneath the grandeur. But then what big city didn't have its dark corners. She headed north up Byrom Street and then Scotland Road, which began to reveal a different Liverpool, beyond the central island of commerce, where the tide of wealth receded. It was busy and thriving on the surface, but there were fewer fine suits, and the faces were pinched and pale. It felt a little like Naples in monochrome, although it smelt altogether different. Rotting food and bad sewers were replaced with coal smoke and horseshit, and the cool, damp wind that blew up the side streets running west down to the river made her shiver like she never had in Naples.

She passed a large open market and noticed a young man, younger than herself, selling ice cream from a handcart with the name Capaldi written on the side. She stopped to check that she wasn't hallucinating, but he was real. The cart was decorated with a crude painting of the Amalfi coast, a gaudy splash of pink, sand, and blue amid the blackened brick and dull grey pavement. He caught her eye and burst into song. She stood, staring, as the popular Neapolitan tune, *Torna a Surriente*, rose above the other market sounds. The song was almost a cliché back home, but still beautiful. The young man, who was directing the song to her, became the abandoned lover, looking out across an imaginary sea and imploring his heartbreaker to return to Sorrento. She knew it was flirtation disguised as salesmanship. He was even smiling through the most melancholy lines, as if he didn't understand lyrics he must have sung a hundred times. But his voice was a pleasant, light baritone, and hearing Italian in this alien place, was strangely moving. She couldn't help herself and started to cry.

Suddenly he was in front of her, offering her a pink gelato in a cone. 'Non piangere, per favore.'

Carla forced a smile and brushed away her tears with a handkerchief. He offered the gelato again, and she took it. It was remarkably good. By far the best thing she had tasted since arriving on the boat train from Calais yesterday, and the sweet strawberry taste did make her feel better.

'Grazie.' She fumbled in her new French purse for a coin, but he waved her away.

'You are missing your family back home?' he asked.

Carla, thought about her dead brother and the parents she hadn't seen since they had disowned her for leaving home before she had married.

'No . . . I have no family back home. But there is someone I miss.'

'And he is back in Italy?' Carla thought she detected a note of hope in his voice and couldn't help herself smiling again as she sniffed and wiped her nose. He was handsome enough, but a mere boy.

'I don't know. I don't think so. But I don't know where he is. I'm hoping he's here.' She licked her ice cream. 'Do you know the Lyle family? They live in St Martin's Street.'

'I don't know them.' He sounded disappointed. 'But St Martin's Street is up Scottie Road on the left, a short walk.'

'Thank you,' Carla replied, after a moment to work out that 'Scottie Road' must be Scotland Road. She graced him with a final heartfelt smile that was also intended as a farewell.

'If you don't find him, I'll be here for a while.' He positioned himself in her path and extended his hand. 'My name is Leandro. If you need help, you can find me at 82 Gerard Street.' Carla shook his hand. Then, his face brightened, as if he'd just had a divine revelation. 'And my parents run a lodging house there, if you need somewhere to stay!'

'Thank you, Leandro, you've been very kind.' Carla released his grip and started to move away.

'Wait. I don't know your name.'

Carla hesitated and then replied, 'Carla . . . Carla Lyle.' She saw the tragic look of disappointment cross his face as the nature of her search dawned on him. Then he became stern.

'If I may say, your English husband is a fool. He should be the one weeping and chasing after you. Not the other way around.'

Carla opened her mouth to reply, but realised that she either had nothing, or too much, to say. She merely nodded and carried on her way.

*

Carla could not believe that the narrow, terraced houses of St Martin's Street were only a mile from the splendour of St George's Hall. The faces of the children playing in the street were mottled and smeared with dirt, as if to mark them out as another tribe. She didn't know which house Abercrombie's family had lived in but felt that this was the sort of place where people would know each other's business. It would be hard not to. The meagre two-storey houses faced onto a narrow pavement and then a cobbled street, which seemed to serve more as a space for children to release energy that couldn't be contained in their homes, than any sort of thoroughfare. A few women, some chatting in pairs, stood in doorways, not so much watching the children as existing in a parallel world. Those on their own stared into space, as if imagining another place they should be. The pairs were animated and loud, breaking into occasional cackles of laughter. Carla couldn't understand most of what they said. Abercrombie would sometimes affectionately mimic the Irish accents of his older family members, but those softly modulating tones hadn't prepared her for the raucous scouse version that clattered around this dirty urban gorge.

Carla walked the length of the street, looking for likely candidates for her enquiries. She was attracting bold glances from everyone she passed. In her new, pale blue French dress, close cropped hair and cloche hat, she stood out like a peacock in a hen house, but she thought that no bad thing. Perhaps their curiosity would loosen their tongues. She reached the end of the road and turned back up the street, a manoeuvre which guaranteed that all eyes were on her for the return journey. She picked on a pair of young women, one with a baby on her hip, the other heavily pregnant. They looked about Abercrombie's age. She hoped they might remember him from childhood.

In broken English she asked, 'Good afternoon, I look for the house of the Lyle family.'

'And who might you be?' asked the pregnant woman. She had black hair tied in a bun and a still-pretty face, but hard dark eyes that scrutinized Carla beneath full, furrowed brows. Carla guessed they were of similar age, but the soon-to-be mother already had the air of a fearsome matriarch in the making.

'I look for Abercrombie Lyle. Do you know him?'

'Sure, or at least I did. What's it to you?'

'Ah, leave off Kitty. She looks harmless enough.' The other woman, fair with freckles, shifted the baby on her hip. 'They used to live four houses up at number 22, but . . . that was a wee while ago. The Hegertys live there now.'

'Has he been here, recently?' Carla asked as pleasantly as she could.

'Nobody's seen him for years,' replied the fair one. 'He upped and left, without so much as a bye your leave, a few months after the end of the war.'

'Does he have family or friends here? If he returns, where would he go?'

The mother with babe gave Kitty a sly nudge with her hip. 'Probably to see this one here. Didn't you have a thing going with Abercrombie?'

Kitty looked irritated. 'That was nothin' Annie, just the odd a cuddle behind the pub at closing time.'

'Sure, it was the other one you had a thing for, now I remember. What was his name?'

'Michael,' replied Kitty, who now looked a little less fierce.

'I'm sorry,' said Carla. 'Abercrombie spoke of his brother many times. He said he was a very brave young man.'

'He was that,' replied Kitty, wistfully, before snapping back. 'Too bloody brave. And who the hell are you, anyway, with yer fancy dress and funny accent, acting like you knew Michael?'

Carla hesitated, then held out her hand to Kitty. 'I'm sorry. My name is Carla, I'm . . . I'm Abercrombie's wife.'

*

A few minutes later, Carla was sitting at a small table, covered with a red and white checked oilcloth, in the tiny back room of Abercrombie's old house, holding a hot cup of muddy liquid and surrounded by a dozen women of various ages. They pressed around her, bombarding her with questions.

He went to Italy, you say? . . . What on earth did he go there for? . . . And how long did you say you've been married? . . . Have you any little ones? . . . And where is he now? . . . So, he ran off on you as well, did he? . . . The little bugger!

They were fascinated by her, and incredulous that Abercrombie had married this 'beautiful Italian princess.' With all the questions and interruptions, it took a while for Carla to tell the story of their life in

Italy, or at least an edited version of it. Carla asked if anyone had seen him since his disappearance, but it was soon clear that no one had seen or heard from him since the day he left in 1919. Piecing together the comments she could understand, and helped by the dramatic facial expressions and meaningful looks the women exchanged, she realised that Abercrombie was something of a local legend in St Martin's Street. His disappearance was an unsolved mystery, made all the more intriguing by the tragic circumstances. The consensus was that Abercrombie had been a gentle, well-liked lad, with a touch of the faerie about him, according to one old woman. He was happier with his head in a book, or on his own, staring out at the Mersey, than he was mucking about in the street with the other boys. Everyone agreed he had never quite been the same after his brother was killed in the Easter Rising. He had then returned from the war a distant, 'queer fella,' to find his father dead. His mother then got the Spanish Flu and quickly followed him. They all agreed that he then 'went a bit funny in the head,' before vanishing.

Despite the initial fascination with Carla, the women soon took to arguing with each other about what happened to Abercrombie. There had, it seemed, been much speculation at the time, which was now recapitulated with varying degrees of confidence and rejected with vehemence by those that now knew better. The mood shifted from initial amazement and relief that he was still alive, or at least had been recently, to confusion and condemnation of yet another flit. Those who thought he had taken his own life were perplexed, and then annoyed. It was unclear to Carla if they were annoyed that he had left without a word of farewell or because their theories had been discredited and their mourning wasted. One insisted on his suicide, as if Carla didn't exist. A few were openly sceptical of Carla's story. She began to feel like an inconvenient distraction for those attached to alternative explanations for Abercrombie's disappearance.

Well, I heard, from a very reliable source, I might add, that he went to join 'the boys'. A cousin of Johnny's from Cork swears he saw him at the ambush of Michael Collins, God rest his soul. Plugged him right between the eyes! . . . Nonsense, they found the poor bastard floating in Bramley Moore dock with an empty bottle of whiskey still in his hand! . . . Utter rubbish! Now, how could he have passed out from the drink and still be holding on to a bottle of whiskey? . . . Ah, that one sees her husband do it every Friday night! . . . Well, have you never heard of rigor mortis you eejit! . . .

Carla felt overwhelmed, and then lightheaded, as if all the air was being sucked from the cloying room by these women. She was no longer the centre of attention but alone, in an eye of indifference, surrounded by a storm of debate and recrimination. She remembered that, apart from the gelato, she hadn't eaten all day. She sipped the tepid liquid. It was tea of some sort but milky and sweet. She needed the sustenance and drank it down, but it tasted awful.

Well, whatever happened to the slippery bastard, I know for a fact that the day before his flit, our Bridget saw him up at that big house on the Brow where his Ma, Mary used to work . . . He did spend an awful lot of time up there as a lad . . . Aye, and so did Mary . . . You shut your filthy mouth, Winnie. I'll not hear a word against Mary. She was a good woman!

Carla suddenly felt very sick. The voices became indistinguishable in the dark room.

The poor thing has gone white as a sheet . . . you don't suppose she's carryin' his baby, do you? . . . Course she is. Why else would she go traipsing halfway across the world after that soft lad?

Her vision began to diminish within a constricting circle of black, and, just as it was too late to do anything about it, she realised she was fainting. Before she went, she caught a few more words from a voice she thought she recognised.

Well, I was fond of Mary myself, she was like a mother to me, but let's just say that Abercrombie wasn't at all like his brother, Michael . . . And no one would know that better than you, Kitty O'Halloran!

As Carla heard the room roar into laughter, it swirled and turned to black.

47

Milan, 19 September 1926

We left Brio gagged and tied to the chair. There were many times in later years when I wondered if I should have just killed him. Occasionally, I even pretended to myself that I regretted not killing him. But I knew I could never have done it, at least not like that, and I knew that if I had shot him in cold blood, I would have regretted that more.

Now that Carla thought I was dead, there was no hope of her trying to find me. I would have to find her. Milan was the obvious next breadcrumb on the trail but, of course, Brio knew that, too. So, if she had gone there, it wouldn't be easy to find her. She would be hiding from Brio, and he would be looking for her, and looking for me, looking for her. I had no doubt that if he found me, this time he would put a bullet in me, or worse.

I had persuaded Pietro to return to Naples without me, by promising that I would follow him there by the end of the month if I couldn't find Carla in Milan. I knew where to look and how to hide in Milan. There were old places and acquaintances I would need to haunt, and it would be a lot easier without a six-foot three Neapolitan following me around. I was immensely grateful for his help, but I was also relieved to see him drive away. He had revealed a cruelty I found disturbing, and if by some miracle I found Carla, I felt that his presence would somehow taint the moment.

On my first day in Milan, I had a sniff of a clue, or at least what might have been a clue. I was sitting in the back corner of a bar near the old *Avanti!* office when I recognised the unmistakable profile of the old head of the print shop, Michele. He limped in with a walking stick and was a pitiful sight. He looked like an old man of eighty, though I knew he was in his early sixties. I waited until he settled at a table and quietly sat next to him. He didn't recognise me, and I had to remind him of my connection to Brio, which immediately made him jumpy. It took a few moments to calm him and convince him I had not also become a fascist. When I mentioned Carla, his face brightened, for a moment, and then a quiet fury overcame him.

'How could Brio have done that to us?' I couldn't explain and didn't want to try. I would not be an apologist for Brio. I told him that Carla and I had been living in Campania and that Brio had found us and taken her a few weeks ago. Michele seemed far away, in a state of incomprehension, as if he hadn't understood me.

'I heard she disappeared when Brio went to Rome,' he eventually replied, 'but I haven't heard anything about her since.' We sat in silence for a while and then I asked if he had known our friends Louisa or Enrico. Again, he seemed not to have heard me, but then he leaned in close and whispered. 'You know, there are others who have . . . disappeared. I've heard of people being sent to an island off Sicily called Lipari. To get them,' his voice became almost inaudible, 'out of the way.'

I asked how he knew this.

'An old *Avanti!* journalist was sent there and escaped. He told me he had seen people there he recognised from Milan.' Then he grabbed my arm, as if just remembering something. 'He said he thought he saw Enrico arrive on a boat the day before he got away, although he couldn't be sure as his face was all bashed up. Didn't Enrico know Carla? Were you not all friends?' He looked at me with intense, watery eyes. 'Perhaps he sent her there as well? Yes, yes, that's what he must have done, the bastard.' He spat on the floor with surprising vehemence, narrowly missing my boot.

After that I got no more sense out him. His outburst seemed to have taken the sting out of his anger, and he became distant. He sipped his grappa, and I bought him another. I tried asking more questions about Enrico, and if he could put me in touch with his journalist friend, but all I got in response was wistful muttering about 'that poor, poor girl.' After a while, it was clear that he knew nothing more about Enrico, and when he asked who I was for the third time, I left him alone.

I spent the next three days looking for Enrico and Louisa. If Michele's journalist friend was correct, Enrico, and probably Louisa, were imprisoned on a tiny island hundreds of miles away. But I prayed that he had been mistaken, and that they were here, keeping a low profile in Milan. If I could find them, there may be a chance they could lead me to Carla. I stalked their former apartments and all their usual watering holes. There was no trace of them. Few of their old neighbours wanted to talk to me, and those that would had not seen them since they had left Milan over eighteen months ago. They had no idea where they might be, and I had no idea if the journalist's story was credible or not. I wanted to help Enrico and Louisa but could think of no plausible way to spring them from a gaol they may, or may not, be in, on a remote, guarded island without getting myself pointlessly killed. My frustration and guilt were exacerbated by the fact that I had been so riled by Brio, and so preoccupied by Carla's fate, that I hadn't even asked Brio about Enrico and Louisa, not that I could have trusted a word he would have said.

I had a lot of time to think in Milan. Too much time. Standing in the shadows outside the apartment buildings of old friends or sitting in the corners of cafés and bars we used to frequent. It was an uncomfortable experience. I would sit for hours at a stretch, and each time I heard the jingle of the door as someone entered, there was an excruciating moment. Would it be an old friend, or one of Brio's henchmen, or Brio himself, or even Carla? It felt like I was sitting in a trench again, endlessly waiting for something to happen, then hearing the sound of a shell and wondering if that vicious sucking whistle would be the last thing I would hear.

I had spent many happy hours in these places, but they failed to conjure many fond memories. The more I reflected, I realised that in all of those hours they had been a couple, and I had wished they weren't. They had been married and in love, and I had been – well, what had I been? At best an indulged appendage, at worst, a rather pitiful gooseberry. Milan reminded me that Carla had been with Brio for much longer than she had been with me, and for most of that time she had been happy. The longer I was in Milan, the more Paestum seemed like a dream, or an aberration. *This* had been Carla's real life. Our time in Paestum had been a fantasy, forced on Carla by Brio's pig headedness. In my heart, I knew we would never have been together if Brio had not had his metamorphosis. It had been love by default. And could I ever be sure it *was* love, not just friendship, moulded and mutated into a copy of the real thing?

As the fruitless days passed, my thoughts darkened. I knew that political exile on Lipari had not been Carla's fate but I had no idea where she was. I had hit a dead end. After another week of drifting across Milan like a vagrant ghost, wild ideas filled with jealousy and betrayal drove me a little insane. What if Carla had tired of me and had colluded in her abduction to get rid of me? What if she was glad to be back where she belonged – with Brio? Perhaps she really had popped out for some shopping and had returned to Brio's apartment to witness the mess we had left him in? Brio would have a field day with that. Perhaps I was the monster now and he was her saviour? For the most part I knew this was crazy, but at times I slipped my moorings and drifted from reality.

In the many hours I spent drinking espressos, or cheap grappa instead of whiskey to preserve my diminishing funds, I also had the time to wrestle with the fact that I was really the child of Ma and Tyrer, not my Da. I was not who I thought I was, and *Ma* was not who I thought *she* was. I worried obsessively about Ma, and what she had done with Tyrer – perhaps for many years. If my own mother, the best woman in the world, was capable of such duplicity, why not Carla? And even if Carla had loved me, perhaps Brio was right. Perhaps she would 'come to her senses' and realise that she should return to him. He was still her husband, after all, and what was I? A dead man.

48

Liverpool, 19 September 1926

Carla was out of breath by the time she had climbed Everton Brow. Dusk was gathering, and it had started to drizzle as she stood before the large Georgian terraced house she had been directed to by the women of St Martin's Street. Number 17 Shaw Street had a glossy black door and a brass knocker in the shape of a cupped hand holding a ball, or was it the world? It looked like it had come from an Italian palazzo, and while the house was grand enough, it was not quite grand enough for this. She stood on the doorstep wondering what sort of reception she would get, when a light came on inside the house, shinning weakly through the fanlight above the door. She rapped the heavy hand on the knocker plate three times. After a long wait the door opened and a plump, tired-looking, middle-aged woman in a grubby maid's uniform stood before her. Dark hair escaped from her dishevelled white cap, and she held a filthy rag in her hand. Carla couldn't help herself stare at a disfiguring mole on her chin that sprouted two wiry black hairs.

'Can I help you?' She gave Carla a look of unconcealed suspicion.

'May I speak to Mr Tyrer?'

'Is he expecting you?'

'No, but I need his help.'

The maid was unmoved. 'Mr Tyrer is unwell and is not receiving visitors.'

'Please. I must see him!' Carla replied, with more desperation than she had intended.

The maid seemed taken aback by Carla's display of emotion but did not soften. 'He gave strict instructions that he was not to be disturbed. Perhaps you could come back tomorrow. Goodbye!'

The maid started to close the door in Carla's face, but Carla threw her Gladstone bag into the gap to stop it shutting. The maid looked like she'd been slapped in the face.

'Take your bag out of the doorway and leave this instant, or I'll call the police!'

'Please, I beg you. I look for Abercrombie Lyle. I must find him. Have you seen him? Has he been here? Please!'

At the mention of Abercrombie's name, the maid looked shocked. 'You know Abercrombie?'

'Yes, yes, is he here?'

'How do you know him?' The maid looked like she had seen a ghost and was now clutching the dirty cloth to her breast.

Carla composed herself. She had pierced the maid's armour and needed to drive home her advantage. 'He is my husband.'

The maid shrieked and made the sign of the cross, as if the devil himself was trying to gain entry. From somewhere inside the house a man's voice growled: 'Sheila, who is it? What on God's earth is going on out there?' The maid was quivering, as if unable to speak. It took her a few seconds to summon a response.

'It's a lady, sir. She, she . . .'

'What does she want?'

'She says she's Mr Abercrombie's . . . *wife*, sir.' The maid was staring at Carla, her eyes beginning to glisten with tears. The silence that followed was excruciating. It felt as if something momentous was happening, but Carla did not know what. An initial surge of hope at the maid's recognition of Abercrombie's name was displaced by a sense of unease. She hung on the response of the growling voice as if her entire future depended on it. When it came, something in its tone of resignation filled her with dread.

'Tell her she had better come in.'

*

Carla sat in an armchair in Tyrer's study, holding a large glass of brandy, and staring in disbelief at a notice in this morning's *Liverpool Post*. She was shaking. She read it again, for the third time, desperately hoping that her modest command of English had led her to misunderstand its message.

A DEATH AT SEA

With great sadness we report that Abercrombie Lyle, a native of Liverpool, was reported missing, presumed dead, this Wednesday last, after failing to disembark the SS Patria *on arrival in Marseille from Naples. The circumstances of his death are unknown, and it is thought that he fell overboard. The French authorities have no reason to suspect foul play.*

Mr Lyle served with distinction in The Kings' Lancashire Regiment in the Great War, attaining the rank of Lance Corporal and receiving the Military Cross in 1918 for his courageous actions in the Salonika campaign. It is understood that Mr Lyle was returning to England after a long sojourn in Italy. He has no surviving relatives in the city.

'I'm so sorry, Mrs Lyle.' Tyrer was standing over her, offering her a handkerchief. His presence, blocking the light from the lamp on his desk, broke Carla's trance. She looked up at a tall man, supporting himself with a cane and peering down at her. His unruly beard, grey with a hint of ginger, partly concealed his sunken cheeks, but couldn't disguise an unusually wide mouth, whose subtly upturned ends made him look both sad and amused at the same time. He scrutinized her, not unkindly, with rheumy grey-blue eyes. Eyes that could have been Abercrombie's in forty years' time.

'I can't believe it. I saw him getting on the boat. He, he looked fine.'
'But surely you were with him, on board the ship?'
'No.'
Tyrer stroked his beard, as if confused. 'Did you see him disembark?'

'No.'

'So, you never actually saw or spoke to him on the ship?'

'No.'

'But you say you are his wife?'

'Yes, but . . .'

There was a long silence. Carla could sense that Tyrer was expecting more from her by way of explanation. When it didn't come, he shuffled to an armchair on the other side of his study at an angle to Carla's. Both faced a large, Georgian fireplace with egg and dart decoration beneath the mantel and a Greek funerary urn as the centrepiece of the relief. The smouldering coals were in danger of going out. He lowered himself gingerly into the armchair and Carla noticed how heavily he was breathing.

'Are you alright, Mr Tyrer?' Carla asked. Tyrer took a sip of clear liquid from a tiny glass bottle on a silver tray beside the chair and did not answer. Carla noticed the room around her for the first time since she had been ushered in by the maid and realised that this must be the room Abercrombie had told her about. Tyrer's study. The *porta un altro mundo*. Ancient maps and bookcases lined the walls, which were filled with leather bound books. On a table near the door sat a marble bust of Marcus Aurelius and one that could have been Aristotle, or maybe Plato. On the desk she saw a huge, tan, leather-bound book. The spine was as wide as her hand and the whole thing was the size of a small child. It was open but from her seated position she couldn't see what was on the page.

'He loved that book,' said Tyrer, noticing her interest. 'He spent hours alone in here with it. He must have known every plate and drawing like his own skin.' Tyrer fell silent again and stared at the fireplace for so long that Carla suspected he may have forgotten she was there. Eventually, he turned to her again. 'Do you think he may have . . .'

'No. He would not do that. It is not in his nature,' replied Carla, but she knew she was saying this, in part, to convince herself. Coming on top of all the trauma of the War, and his last few years in Liverpool, she had to admit that recent events may have just been too much to bear. Suicide was a possibility. But in her heart, she didn't believe it to be true.

Tyrer didn't press the point and smiled at her. There was such sadness and kindness in his eyes, that a sort of catharsis overwhelmed her. It was a look she knew so well. It were as if Abercrombie himself was trying to comfort her from beyond the grave. She made no sound, but the tears flowed down her face and would not stop until she had no more.

'I'm so sorry, Mrs Lyle.'

Carla managed a small nod. 'Carla, please, call me Carla.'

'I'm so sorry, Carla.'

'I am sorry for you, too, Sir.'

Tyrer looked at her quizzically.

'I have lost a husband. You have lost a son.'

Tyrer opened his mouth, as if to reply, then gave her that melancholic, amused smile. 'Yes.'

They sat in silence again for a while.

'It is hard enough to lose one son. Now I have lost two. This one I hardly knew and could not even own as mine. I thought about writing to him in Milan, after he left, but it seemed wrong. I felt I should let him go and be his own man, with whatever happy memories of his family he still had. After my wife, Annabelle, died, I considered contacting him. I have thought of him a lot this past year, especially since–' Tyrer was seized by a bout of coughing. When it finished, he seemed to have lost the thread of his monologue. 'Of course, it's all too late now. Everything seems so very . . . late.'

'He spoke of you fondly, several times, but I don't think he had any idea about . . .'

'No, he wouldn't have. He adored his mother. It wouldn't have crossed his mind that she could have . . .' Tyrer did not finish the sentence. 'The thing about Abercrombie is . . . he was always rather naïve. In a good way, mostly. Mary told me he was almost incapable of seeing the bad in people. She worried he wasn't tough enough for the real world.' Tyrer stared into the dying fire. 'She told me a story once. He was six or seven. She had been watching his brother from a distance throwing stones at a tin can on a wall. He had been trying and missing for a long time, until Abercrombie came along, picked up a stone, and hit it with his first throw. He ran to collect the can as a trophy, and when he turned to bring it back, his brother, out of frustration, threw a stone at Abercrombie and hit him on the head.'

'That's awful. I thought they were close.'

'They were, mostly, but that's not the point. It was Abercrombie's reaction that worried her. Any other boy in the street would have thrown one back or chased after his brother for a fight. But Abercrombie just looked at Michael with incomprehension, as if he couldn't understand how he could have done such a thing, or even what it might mean.'

Tyrer fell silent again and drifted off somewhere else. After what seemed like an eternity, he startled Carla by ringing a small bell on the tray beside him. Eventually, the maid knocked and entered the room.

'Shelia, please prepare a room for Mrs Lyle. She will be staying with us for . . .' He looked across at Carla and gave her that strange smile again, 'for as long as she needs to.' Shelia nodded and turned to leave. 'And some food. Please bring her something to eat. She's had a terrible shock and should eat something.'

'And would you like some supper, sir? You've not eaten all day.'

'No, I'm not hungry. But she must eat.'

After Sheila left, Carla said, 'if you are ill, Mr Tyrer. You must eat.'

'I am more than ill, Carla. I am dying, as you are no doubt astute enough to have realised, and the one slim hope that I may have something to live for has now departed. I am ready to go and have no desire for Sheila's awful cooking to prolong my existence.'

Somehow Carla managed a rueful smile. Tyrer even shared Abercrombie's ability to make a joke at the most unlikely moment.

'As I said, you are welcome to stay for as long as you want, although I'll wager it won't be too long before the company of a dying bore and Shelia's cooking will induce your return to Italy.'

'Thank you. That is kind. But you are wrong, Mr Tyrer.'

'I don't think so. The mere sight of her steak and kidney pudding has made hardened sea captains blanch with fear.'

'About having nothing to live for.'
'How so?'
'I may be carrying your grandchild, Sir.'

PART IV

49

Rome, 2 July 1945

Brio stood on his balcony at the top of the Ministry of Communications, looking out on the fresh blue dawn that still held a faint trace of the night to the west. He surveyed the litter-strewn street below with deep satisfaction. The celebrations for *Mare Nostrum* had been smaller this year, but he was not concerned. It was three years since the British surrender in North Africa had given Italy control of the Mediterranean, and there was bound to be a diminution of intensity. No, this was a moment to savour, for this was *his* day. He had created it. The rituals and the rites, the music and the marching. They were all his. It was undoubtedly his greatest achievement. He was the chief storyteller and choreographer of the new Italy. The Praetor of a new Roman Empire.

Few of last night's revellers knew that the Italians had played only a minor part in the victory. They could never have driven the British Army into the sea at El Alamein without Rommel's Afrika Korps. But what were facts? The people of Italy knew the *truth* about their glorious victory, and they knew it in their guts, where it mattered. They had sung stirring songs; thrown flowers at the smiling parades of military men – helmets and gun barrels flashing in the midsummer sun; then revelled like Bacchus through the wildest night in the new Roman calendar. They didn't need facts. They had truth, and only an idiot now believed these to be the same thing. Thankfully, there were very few of those left in Italy.

Now, the city was still. Brio felt like the only person awake in the world, and the quiet dawn roared triumphantly in his ears. There were few men that could silence Rome, and he was one of them.

An irritating triple knock on the door to his office broke his reverie. How many times had he told Alfano to only knock twice!

'Come in.' Brio did not turn to greet his secretary. He remained on the balcony, his back to the open French windows. He wanted to savour his silent triumph a little longer before admitting the frantic day ahead. While the city slept away its collective hangover, he must be busy. For the day after the celebration was as important as the day itself. The stories, sounds and images he would lay before the nation were all part of a tapestry he would weave. There would be a lot to do today. Making myths was hard work.

'The photographs of Il Duce's visit to Naples have arrived, Sir.'

Brio turned to see Alfano standing in the open doorway and a buff folder sitting on the gilded, marble Second Empire table he used as a desk. Brio dismissed him with a flick of his forefinger and sat down to review the prints. His staff did not understand why he bothered himself which such details. Any number of seasoned editors could have selected a striking image for the front page of the evening papers. But Brio knew that these seeming details were not mere ornamentations on the façade of fascist Italy, they were the foundations, and very few could be trusted with their upkeep. He scanned the photographs, swiftly separating possibles from rejects. A few were good enough for a normal day, but they weren't quite what he needed today.

He had not wanted Il Duce to celebrate the day in Naples, a place he despised. It was the only major city in Italy they had not completely tamed. The tentacles of the Camorra were long and had tangled with a flotsam of communists, anarchists and socialists who refused to accept that Italy had sailed into the future. Naples was not a major threat to the state, but an irritating rag-tag underground movement had given him some concerns about Il Duce's safety, which was why Mussolini had insisted on going, to show the nation that there was nowhere in Italy that he wasn't loved. And so Brio needed the perfect picture to prove it.

The last photograph caught his eye. It was a glorious image. Taken from slightly above Il Duce, who was standing in a moving, open-top car, it captured the great man's smiling profile, and below him an adoring crowd. He was among the people, yet still over them. His adherents were brilliantly lit in the low sunlight, which seemed to emanate from their ecstatic faces, and all of them had their arms raised in salute – except for one.

Brio could feel a fury rising within him. This lone dissenter had ruined by far the best photograph. Otherwise, this was the perfect image, but it was unusable, unless he could somehow crop him out. It would make it an oddly square-shaped picture, but he was quite near the edge. Yes, perhaps it could still work. He imagined a vertical line and his eye followed it up from the bottom, past the man's unsmiling face.

It was him.

He hadn't seen that face for almost 20 years, and he had aged badly, but he had no doubts. The man who would not salute was Abercrombie Lyle.

50

Naples, 31 August 1945

After the old woman in black had left, I sat alone in the side chapel of the Duomo. I scanned the nave and risked a quick look around the corner of the chapel back to the main entrance of the cathedral. I could see no suspicious men loitering behind pillars, so I settled back into a dark corner and opened my biography where I had left off, at my arrival in Paestum.

The chapter began ecstatically, recounting with sunny brilliance the happiness that had overwhelmed me. The opening lines reminded me how the love for Carla that I'd sealed away for years in Milan, under more pressure than I realised, had exploded like champagne and bathed us both in its bliss. Carla, surprised and intoxicated by its force, had allowed my joy to wash us away. We swam in a sea of giddiness. Our love was an ocean to explore, and we had only begun to splash about in the shallows. What remained beyond this sunlit beach would be deep and inexhaustible.

But clouds appeared quickly in the text. Mere hints at first. Odd inflexions of events that were not quite how I had remembered them. The arrival of Louisa and Enrico was a blessed day to my recollection, a widening of our circle of love to our best friends. Yet the book hinted at reservations on Carla's part and jealousy on mine. Was that how it had been?

The rest of the chapter bore a rapidly diminishing relationship to my memory of the time we had in Paestum and sent me spiralling into paranoia. There were increasing hints that Carla was unhappy, and even that she had regretted her decision to invite me to the farmhouse. I was compared, unfavourably, to our dog, Cerberus, who at least had the grace to find a spot of shade to sleep in and leave Carla alone for a few hours a day, whereas I would trail along beside her like a needy lap dog. Then there was this.

There came a day in late August 1926 when the enervating heat finally burned away Carla's remaining reservoir of forbearance. She realised that she was repelled by the smells and sounds of their impoverished, rustic exile. More pressingly, she decided she could no longer tolerate Abercrombie's constant presence. She knew she must escape, but she feared that Abercrombie would be crushed. She feared for his sanity if she simply abandoned him, and she wanted to leave in a manner that left him some dignity and fond memories of their time together.

Over the next few days, she dreamt of a clean, city life. Of fine restaurants and chic cafés. Of food that hadn't been killed, cleaned and cooked by her own hands. Of fashionable shops and new dresses, not the filthy clothes that were mended many times and no better than rags.

She wondered about Brio's new life in Rome, and the glamour and comfort that could be hers within a day with the briefest of telegrams. When she thought of Brio's cool, strong hands, the clammy pawing of Abercrombie in those sweaty nights became unbearable. She cast her mind back to the way she had felt when Brio had first wrapped her in his arms on a magical winter's night in Milan. The world could storm and rage around her, but she would not be touched. She had been a fool and should never have left him for this disgusting prison, with Abercrombie as her gaoler.

She agonised about what to do, but not for long. One day, she took an early morning walk to the sea, as Abercrombie slept and before dawn had awoken. On the deserted beach, she stripped naked and plunged into the cool Tyrrhenian Sea to wash away any traces of Abercrombie from the night before. She emerged from the waves reborn and knew with absolute clarity that she must return to Brio. Any delay would only prolong the suffering for all three of them.

From there, it was easy. She had dressed and returned to the farmhouse. She took a few lira from the terracotta jar on the kitchen counter and walked into Paestum while Abercrombie was still sleeping. She tried not to think about him in case her gentle nature took pity on him and weakened her resolve. She arrived at Paestum's post office as it opened and sent a telegraph addressed to Brio Salvatore at the Ministry of Communications, Rome. She had no doubt that it would find its way to him within a day or two. It simply read:

I want to come home.
Carla.
Villa Hera, Paestum, Campania.

51

Rome, 3 July 1945

The Abercrombie Problem, as Brio had begun to call it, was a distraction that he knew he should solve quickly and quietly. It would be easy enough to alert the local authorities, give them his picture, and have him arrested. He didn't even need to trump up a charge. There was the murdered blackshirt from 26 years ago. Although that might subject his own actions that day to scrutiny he didn't want. It would be cleaner to have him shot and dumped somewhere he would never be found. But a full day later, he had not yet given the order. The reason for his prevarication was opaque and troubling. Perhaps the shock of Abercrombie's resurrection had paralysed him. Abercrombie was supposed to be rotting in the ground. When he had instructed a contact in Naples all those years ago, it had only taken a few days for the message to come back that his problem had gone away. He still had the telegram. *Missing item found. Returned to manufacturer.*

Fucking Naples.

He knew he should have gone there himself to see the body. But he hadn't wanted to raise questions about why he had such a close interest in the death of a British subject. It was a different world back then. He was still clambering up the blood-slicked pole, not sitting on top of it. Britain, a recent ally, was still a major power that Mussolini was wary of. The last thing Mussolini would have wanted was a diplomatic scandal over a murdered ex-serviceman, and if his prints were found on the murder weapon, it would be career ending. It would also have run the risk of publicly connecting Abercrombie to Carla. His mission then was to rehabilitate his wife as a paragon of Italian womanhood, not alert the piranhas he swam with to the fact that she was a slut who had left him for another man.

On the surface, his mission had succeeded. He had Carla back, and he had his beautiful son, Virgilio, who he loved dearly. But this success was superficial at best. Carla hated him and their marriage was a sham. She had locked herself away in their villa, rarely leaving and refusing to be seen in public with him. The stories he used to tell his colleagues to explain her absence at official events were laughable, and he gave up even trying many years ago. In 1930 he had been invited, with a select group of the Party's rising stars, to join Mussolini at the Adriatic resort of Riccione for the Ferragosto weekend. One wag had asked him if Miss Havisham would be joining them. It still rankled. He was now too powerful for anyone to comment on Carla's behaviour to his face, but he had no doubt it was a source of ridicule for anyone brave enough to gossip behind his back. Most of his younger colleagues probably didn't even know Carla existed.

She had at least kept her side of the bargain with Virgilio. He saw him every weekend he wanted to, but that had become less frequent after the War began. His role as Minister of Propaganda was unrelenting, and it was even more demanding after Italy's victory. Creating gods and heroes was easy when they had monsters to fight. It was hard to make record rice yields in Piedmont get the blood pumping, even for him. And though he hated to admit it, Virgilio had been something of a disappointment. He was smart as a whip, but bookish and quiet. He was respectful, and occasionally awestruck by his Papa's achievements, but there was a spark missing from their relationship. He blamed Carla. She had so smothered and coddled him that he had become a mummy's boy. Now that he was eighteen, he really must do something about that.

Brio opened the folder on his desk and stared at the picture of Abercrombie's deceptively gentle face. Seeing it again, after all these years, had opened a tomb and set loose a demon he'd thought long dead – a demon that was scratching at his scars till they bled. Abercrombie's resurrection had released a truth back into his world that he had long ago walled up. A truth he had tried to ignore for nineteen years. Ultimately,

Abercrombie was to blame for his dead marriage and disappointing son. If he'd never taken him under his wing, Carla would still be his. Truly his. And Virgilio would have a full-time father guiding him to manhood, not a part-time Papa unable to prevent the whispers of a bitter woman making him soft. Brio could mould the minds of forty-four million Italians but could barely persuade his own son to attend military school. The irony of this public success and private failure was excruciating. The corruption and decomposition of his marriage, and the emasculation of his son, had a single cause: Abercrombie Lyle. But his 'death' had placed him beyond punishment for his crimes. Now the situation had changed. With this revelation, a wave of clarity and purpose surged through Brio. If the urges and feelings that nearly overwhelmed him had not been so dark, he might have described them as joy. This picture on his desk had given him something that he now realised he had needed for nearly two decades – an opportunity for justice.

Of course, he had already known that ignoring Abercrombie's resurrection was impossible. That would be like walking around with a piece of broken glass in your shoe. He knew he would have to be eliminated, but now he knew why he had prevaricated. A swift death was simply insufficient recompense for the pain he had caused and the lives he had ruined. He needed something more satisfying. He needed something that would hurt Abercrombie, and not just physically. Something commensurate with the psychological and spiritual trauma he had inflicted on him and his family over many years. Something which forced Abercrombie to recognise the consequences of his treachery. He needed him to go to hell, and to take his time getting there.

There came a triple rap on the office door.

'How many fucking times must I tell you, Alfano? Twice, only twice!'

The door didn't open.

'Come in, come in! For god's sake.'

The door opened tentatively, and Brio knew it wasn't Alfano, even before the head of Virgilio appeared.

'I'm sorry, Papa, I didn't mean to disturb you, I was in Rome and . . . thought I'd–'

'Virgilio, my boy! Ignore Papa's foul mouth. Come here!' Brio leapt from the seat behind his desk and had his arms wrapped around the boy before he was over the threshold. 'What are you doing here? Does your mother know you're in Rome? You know how worried she gets.'

'No, but I'm so bored, cooped up at the villa. I can't stay there for another two months until military school.'

'You know she'll be furious with me if she knows you're here.'

'I don't care. And she's always furious with you anyway. Even when she pretends she isn't.'

Brio smiled. Virgilio was often naïve, but he had always been quick to pick up on people's emotions, especially his mother's.

'I swear, when she put the phone down on you the other day, she looked like she wanted to kill you!'

Brio laughed. 'I know that look. Believe me, if looks could kill, your mother would have done for me years ago!'

'C'mon Papa. I need something to do! There must be something I can do here. I'll do anything. File papers, scrub the floor, make you coffee, just how you like it! Come on, let me stay in Rome for the summer.'

'Most people want to get out of Rome for the summer.' Brio now held his son by the shoulders at arm's length, scrutinizing his face. 'Wait, how long have you been in Rome? Don't tell me you were here for the celebrations?'

'No, worse luck. I came down this morning. The pictures looked amazing in the newspapers, though. I'm definitely coming next year.'

Brio scrunched his brows and held his son in a sceptical glare. He knew Virgilio was an open book and would crumble quickly if he was lying.

'I'm not lying, Papa. Look, I've brought you fresh strawberries from the garden. Smell them. I picked them myself this morning. They'd never look like that if they'd been sitting in my rucksack for two days.'

Brio could see he was telling the truth. What a sweet boy he was. Too sweet. Too protected. He blamed Carla, again, but he knew part of the blame was also his. It was time to cut the apron strings and toughen him up. Then again, there would be time enough for that at officer training.

Perhaps he should enjoy one last summer with his boy before he had to become a man, with all that meant in the new Italy.

'Well, that's very thoughtful of you. And in return, I'm going to take you for a magnificent lunch. We can talk about all the adventures you'll have very soon in Milan. You know that's where I met your mother?'

'Of course, you've told me all about it a million times, Papa!' Virgilio rolled his eyes indulgently.

Not quite all, thought Brio. 'And then I'm going to pack you off on the train back to your mother.'

'Papa, please. I'm not a child anymore. I'm eighteen, in case you've forgotten. I'm a man. I need something . . . manly to do. I'm going crazy up there!'

Brio pinched Virgilio's check and ruffled his hair. He *was* becoming a man. He seemed taller than when he'd last seen him only five weeks ago at his birthday party – almost as tall as him, and while he would never have his brute strength, he was making the transition from gangly youth to the sort of rangy athlete that might one day command respect from his men. He also noticed a few days' growth on his upper lip. It had an oddly reddish tinge.

'What's this? Growing a moustache to show me what a man you are?' Brio ran his thumb across the wispy stubble, meaning it affectionately, but Virgilio pulled away and Brio realised that he had gone too far.

'I'm serious. I won't be treated like a boy anymore. I'll be a soldier in a few months. If I'm old enough to kill a man and die for my country, I'm old enough to do something more useful than read books and help Mamma in the garden!'

Brio began to see Virgilio in a new light. His nostrils were flared and his jaw was set with determination. He actually looked quite fierce. There was a fire in his eyes Brio had never seen before, and he liked it. He'd had his doubts about sending him to the Teulié military school, and Carla had been dead against it, but for the first time, he thought he might do okay, or even more than okay.

'Please Papa, there must be something you need help with. You're always so busy. There must be something I can do for you?'

An idea began to form in Brio's mind. There was something he needed help with, and it wasn't something he wished to trust to his usual coterie of willing thugs. He still wasn't sure what to do about Abercrombie, but once he had worked it out, an eager, unquestioning helper he could trust absolutely, with no connection to the apparatus of the state, could be useful. Whatever it was, there was bound to be something relatively easy and safe for Virgilio to do, running messages or keeping tabs on Abercrombie and reporting back on his movements. As he thought about it more, Brio smiled. It could be the greatest gift he had ever given him. He would feel like he had been plucked from the tedium of the villa and placed on the pages of one of those adventure or detective stories he was always reading. Brio had recently given him a set of John Buchan novels that he had devoured. The lad was clearly straining on his leash, desperate for excitement and adventure. A plan began to form in his mind. Virgilio would love it.

'Well, as you seem so keen, perhaps there is something you can do for me.' Brio stared into his son's pale eyes. He had his rapt attention. 'A sort of secret mission that I can only trust my own flesh and blood with.'

'Yes, yes, what is it? What is it?'

'All in good time. There are things I need to arrange that may take a few weeks. But first you must promise me two things, and then I'll take you for that lunch.'

'Anything, anything!' Virgilio was vibrating with excitement.

'First. You will go back to the villa this afternoon, without complaining, and wait until I send for you.' Virgilio looked a little crestfallen but nodded obediently.

'Second. Whatever you do, don't tell your mother!' Brio tapped his nose, and Virgilio gave him the biggest smile he had seen from him in years. Brio clapped him, hard, on the shoulder. 'Or this time, she might *actually* kill me.'

52

Naples, 31 August 1945

I left the Duomo in shock. A version of the truth that I had held to for nearly twenty years was crumbling. Could it be true? Could Carla have tired of me so completely that she had conspired with Brio to leave Paestum? I didn't trust this evil book, but a worm of doubt was squirming in my mind. Even if she had tired of me, would she really have gone back to him, after everything he had done? It seemed incomprehensible. The memory of Cerberus, lying in his own blood, drifted back to me. And what about the disappearance of Enrico and Louisa? Surely Carla could not have been party to any plan that would harm them, even if she had become bored of me. I decided that this version of events could not be true. It was simply too outlandish. But that had been my first reaction to the revelations about Ma and Tyrer, and that *had* been true.

I recalled the image of Carla screaming and pounding on the rear window of Brio's Lancia as they left me in Paestum all those years ago. It was as vivid as the old man hawking fried fish from a tiny shop front right in front of me across the small plaza outside the Duomo. But I knew this image of Carla to be false. So, what other memories might also be false? Perhaps I had imagined more of a struggle than I had really witnessed. The rifle butt to the face was real enough. I still had the scar. But it had all happened so fast. Maybe Carla had initially gone along with the pretence to save my feelings. Perhaps Brio had let his thugs off the leash to teach me a lesson, and Carla's angry protests were about that. Maybe that hadn't been part of the plan, but she *had* still sent the telegram. She may have known nothing of Cerberus' fate, or that of Enrico and Louisa. It didn't feel like something Carla would do. Such an elaborate subterfuge to put the blame on Brio and leave me with the comforting delusion that she had loved me until the end. I could still almost feel that last squeeze of her hand as we stood in the courtyard. It was a memento more real to me than the Mi-To stained handkerchief. A pure, wordless affirmation of her love. Or perhaps it was really an apology.

There was one short chapter of my incomplete book that I had not yet read – the chapter after Carla's abduction, or was it flight? I was almost past caring now if I was being followed, and for a moment I sat on the steps of the entrance to the Duomo to finish it in the full glare of the late afternoon sun. But a scintilla of self-preservation moved me toward a bar across the plaza. Trauma always tasted better with a beer. I ordered one and sat in a back corner, glancing toward the bright open doorway as a tall young man poked his head in and caught my eye. He did his best to keep his eyes moving, as if looking for someone else, then he walked on, as if he hadn't seen what he was looking for. But I was convinced that he had. Yesterday, this would have sent me into a panic and a hurried search for a rear exit. But I was strangely indifferent. They knew where I was. Perhaps they had always known where I was. I resolved to stop trying to run from them, whoever they were. And somehow the face, caught for a moment in the doorframe, like an amateur photograph shot into the sun, actually calmed me. It did not look sinister. It was beatific, lit from behind with rays of sunlight searching into the dark bar and illuminating previously invisible motes floating in the air. He looked oddly familiar. But most strikingly, he looked as uncertain about what was happening as I was.

I returned to the last extant chapter. The title made me laugh out loud at the insanity: *Et in Arcadia Ego*. But my mood darkened as I read on.

On the journey back from Paestum, Carla was torn between anger at Brio for treating Abercrombie so roughly and relief at being rid of him. Brio had sat in the back seat with Carla to comfort and reassure her. He understood her concern. Carla was a kind soul, as befits a true Italian woman. She did not want to see Abercrombie suffer and did not understand what Brio had done. She had been hoping for a prompt reply to her telegram with an invitation to join Brio, an address in Rome, and perhaps a first-class train ticket, not a rescue party that she didn't need. The whole affair had been an unnecessary surprise, and badly done, to her thinking.

But when Brio had explained, she could see that he was right. He had assumed responsibility for them both. She had not needed a painful conversation with Abercrombie, or a difficult letter. She had not needed to plan and worry, or to slink away at midnight or daybreak, fearing discovery and a scene. Brio had acted with decision and élan. He had responded to her call for help and rescued her from her misery, like a man who wanted, above all, to protect her.
Abercrombie would see that Brio had reclaimed what was rightfully his. He would see that there was no point in looking for her, for he could never take her away from a man like Brio. She was free and back where she belonged.

As Carla had sunk into Brio's reassuring chest. It struck her that Brio had uttered no word of reproach for her betrayal – and he never did in all the happy years they would spend together. He had acted like a true and forgiving husband. His magnanimity made her feel ashamed of what she had done.

When they arrived in Rome, any lingering doubts about her decision were soon dispelled. What a magical evening that had been. Brio's new apartment was magnificent, like a modern-day palace, spacious, and gleaming, with a rooftop terrace surrounded by the seven hills. Carla had taken a long, luxurious bath. She felt truly clean for the first time since she had left Milan. Brio had hired a chef, and they had dined amid the stars. Later, Brio had kissed her as only he could. She felt whole again and gave herself to him more fully than she had even on their wedding night. She knew that something special had passed between them that evening. For deep in her soul, she knew that was the night that God had given them their beautiful son, Virgilio.

The rest of the chapter would have been tedious for any other reader, but this book was written for only one person, and for me, it was excruciating. It described an idyllic life of bland, domestic happiness for Brio and Carla. A beautiful baby boy, Virgilio, was born. Carla was serene, cared for and cosseted, with time to write her poetry and for jaunts to the city with Brio for opera and dinners with their new, powerful friends. Brio's effortless ascent to the higher realms of power was alluded to, as was his increasing intimacy with Mussolini, but obliquely, as if the author did not wish to dwell on anything that might cast shadows on the tableau of bliss. There was even a stern but loveable old nanny (some distant relative of Brio's from Milan) to ensure that Virgilio flourished without being spoiled, along with adoring servants, an old married couple called Emilio and Sofia, to ensure that the model young family lived in a household that ran effortlessly. And what a lovely household it was. The secluded, rural Villa La Quercia had been purchased by Brio near Frascati in the hills outside of Rome, with a rambling garden in the English style and views across the distant city.

It tortured me to read these pages, and as I turned them, it felt like I was turning the wheel of my own rack. But I sensed something false about the chapter. The house and gardens seemed more like a film set than a real home, created for an idealised bourgeois family. What a shallow and banal existence for someone like Carla. I felt myself being pulled in two. Part of me clinging desperately to another, earlier truth, while a new voice was telling me to accept this new one. *Don't fight it. Give in and accept the fact that Carla betrayed you.* But the first truth would not be silenced. There was something about this chapter I just didn't believe. It was all too perfect.

At the end of the chapter, there was an additional, very short chapter I had not noticed before, called 'Judas in exsilium.' It described my search for Carla and my 'wilderness years' in Naples. It was sketchy and lacerating.

Abercrombie was crushed by Carla's departure. After some cursory efforts to find her, more to delude himself that he was a man worthy of her affection, than any real expectation of being reunited, he slunk into the nearest rat hole he could find to lick his wounds. Naples. To inoculate Carla against any future outbreak of affection for Abercrombie, unlikely as that was, Brio realised that it was necessary to kill him off. Not literally, of course, but to prevent Carla from seeking him out, from a sense of pity, or to reassure herself of his wellbeing, she must believe him to be dead. This was a simple enough affair to manage for Brio. As the editor of a national newspaper, he was able to place a notice of him being lost at sea on his journey back to England. Naturally, Carla was upset for a few days, and felt responsible for his probable suicide, but Brio reassured her that it was inevitable, given his weak mind and melancholic disposition. Carla, practical and optimistic by nature, did not take long to put Abercrombie behind her. That life was gone, and a new, more important one was growing within her.

Despite his betrayal and ingratitude, they both retained a residue of affection for Abercrombie, and each year, on the anniversary of their meeting at the birth of fascism, on 23 March, they would raise a glass to the Abercrombie they had first known. They chose, generously, to remember that *Abercrombie: amusing, innocent and loyal, like the best of puppies, before his inexplicable transformation to the cynical and treacherous rat who had come so close to destroying their lives.*

Of course, Brio knew all along that Abercrombie was alive. He knew he was extruding a pitiful, lonely existence in the squalid slums of Naples' Centro Storico. *Over the years, he had become a wraith, lost in obscure studies of the distant past. He had inveigled his way into that city's ancient university by befriending the head librarian, Borromeo, and through his auspices had been admitted to a degree in classical history. Eventually, this Borromeo even secured him a junior teaching post, and he began to style himself 'Professore,' though he was more like a parasite than a professor. Periodically, Brio considered plucking him from his host and crushing him between his fingers, but he seemed so harmless that he thought it best to leave him in this half-life. Until one day, it became clear to Brio that Abercrombie was not quite as harmless as he had thought. Abercrombie's time in purgatory had come to an end.*

I turned the next page and was back at the end of the penultimate section, which I had already read. It described my familiar routines in Naples, right up to my discovery of *The Life and Death of Abercrombie Lyle* on the unlit pyre. There was nothing else new to read in this version, but I knew that there was a final section still missing.

I didn't know what to believe at this point. I tried to step back from the insanity to see if I could place my feet on solid foundations. Think. I had to find a path through this confection of truth and lies. What did I know? First, that this book was slippery. It shifted tone and sympathies. It pulled me around like a marionette. It was not stable. It could not be trusted or taken as read. Second, I was confident that I could finally dispel all doubts about my involvement. Despite earlier concerns that I might have written part of it myself and somehow forgotten, I was convinced that I had not gone mad. I had never been to Villa La Quercia. I could not have written this section, and I did not believe that I had written any of it. I slapped myself on the cheek, eliciting a worried look from the fish seller. Come on, Sherlock, lay out the options.

One: Brio has written it alone, with the help of some minions. This was possible but extremely unlikely given the early chapters on Liverpool, unless he had sent people there to dig up my history, which would have been an extraordinary effort, and I wasn't sure that I had ever told him enough that he would know where to start.

Two: Carla had written it alone, which was also highly implausible if not impossible. I had told her much more about my childhood than I had Brio. She would have known where to look for more information, but surely she would not have been able to conduct that level of investigation into my past, and the hostility and cruelty made it hard to believe (or perhaps I just didn't want to believe) that it was all her work.

Three: they had written it together. A flush of nausea swept over me. This was such a preposterous notion that it didn't make sense, but in terms of means, if not motive, it made more sense than the other options. Together, they had more knowledge, access to more information, and the resources to find what they didn't know. It was a horrible explanation, but if I stripped away what I *wanted* to be true, this explanation made more sense than the others. It still seemed unlikely, but it was the least unlikely, even if their collaboration was difficult to contemplate. As my fictional mentor would say: *When you have eliminated the impossible, whatever remains, however improbable, must be the truth.*

So, was this it? Brio and Carla had, together, written a book that would raise my hopes and dash them. A book that would let me believe that Carla was alive and then lead me to the realisation that she must despise me. A book designed to punish me, and send me mad in the process.

It felt like I was making some progress on the origins of the book, but I hadn't touched on the biggest question of all. *Why?* Why go to all this trouble to punish me for something I had done twenty years ago? *And why now?* There was only one way to find out. The book itself had laid out my path, and it led through Borromeo. I was being dragged by the nose on a strange journey, and possibly one with a sacrificial altar at the end of it. I felt a surge of rage for both of them. Let the bastards drag me. I'd be buggered if I would turn back now. I was determined to find out what the hell was going on. I needed to go back into the heart of the *Centro Storico*. Back to the scene of the crime I had recently fled from. To the old library. To Borromeo.

I left the bar deep in thought. The smells from the fried fish seller cut through them and I realized how hungry I was. I bought some and started to stuff the assorted pieces of fish and calamari into my mouth. They were too hot, but I kept on eating. The pain of my burning mouth was somehow reassuring.

Initially, I sensed, rather than saw, someone following me. With a quick glance to my right, as I turned off Via Duomo onto Via dei Tribunali, I saw the same radiant young man who was looking for me in the bar. I only captured a glimpse, but I was sure it was him. I slowed my pace to make it easy for him. Rather than feeling threatened, I was oddly reassured that there was at least one person left in the world who cared enough to be following me. Rather than feeling pursued, it was almost as if I were being watched over.

53

Villa La Quercia, Frascati, 3 July 1945

Carla was sick with worry. When she had woken and peered into Virgilio's room around eight o'clock, his absence had immediately disturbed her. She rose early, but Virgilio, like his father, was not an early riser, and recently it had been difficult to get him up before 10am. The empty room, with the bed made and the desk tidy, had struck her as unusual. She had looked in his wardrobe. His rucksack was missing. Then she saw the note on his desk. A folded piece of paper with 'Mamma' on the front. Inside, in his boyish and rather messy hand, it read:

I've gone out for the day. I'll be back late. Don't worry.
Virgilio

She had smiled on reading it. He had at least tried to put her mind at rest when other boys might have just gone. But she had worried all day, and now it was getting dark. The secrecy, or at least the economy of information, was not like him. He was up to something, or keeping something from her, and as the day had worn on, she convinced herself that Brio must be involved. She had no evidence for this, but a certain restlessness in Virgilio since he had finished secondary school, and more frequent questions about Brio and his work, made her suspicious. A part of her knew he was in Rome with Brio.

Soon he would leave home for good, but at least he wouldn't be with him. She hated the idea of him going to military school, but she hated the idea of him moving to Rome as Brio's apprentice even more. She wanted to cast a spell that would keep him within the bounds of the villa, but she knew he was getting bored and needed to leave. She had wanted the university in Bologna, which no doubt Brio could have arranged. But Brio had insisted on military school in Milan. Virgilio seemed indifferent, or rather undecided, as if he were afraid of upsetting either of them and so could choose neither. When Brio had suggested, as a compromise, that he could find him a junior reporter job in Rome on one of his papers, so he could follow in his footsteps, she had relented on the military school. In many ways, journalism was a better option for Virgilio, who was a studious boy and a good writer, but this was out of the question. At least in military school he would be in Milan, and outside the immediate orbit of Brio. So she gave in. But when she saw the sly smile on Brio's mouth, she realised she had been manipulated into the choice that he had always wanted. Brio had promised that he could secure Virgilio a safe posting in Greece or Abyssinia on graduation, but she knew that eventually he might be sent to the endless war on the Russian steppes – and that Brio didn't always keep his promises.

She walked outside and down the gravelled path to the gate, hoping to see Virgilio, tired but cheerful, tramping up the dusty road from the station. Shades of pink sank in the west over the city. 'The gloaming,' Abercrombie would have called it. A time of day they had both treasured, sitting under 'their' oak tree at Paestum, with a glass of rough red wine, wringing out the last drops of the day, not one of which could be wasted, as if they both knew, beneath their joy, each one could be their last.

The way her love for Abercrombie had flowered in Paestum was unexpected. Before he arrived, she worried that her deep affection and friendship might be too sisterly. A love for her brother that could not be staunched had been poured over Abercrombie. This had nourished a friendship that was strong, but was it supple enough for them to form something new, or might it snap in the attempt? She worried she might never love him in the way she loved Brio. And she didn't. But she needn't have worried. Their love was different, but still glorious. She learned that love is not one way of being with someone, or something that is cut away from one man and re-stitched to another. Love plays many melodies in many ways. She loved Brio as an adored, pampered soloist might love a handsome, charismatic conductor. With Abercrombie, she played simple duets, only looking at each other to make their music. It was the love of earthly mortals, rather than the seduction of a god, which she knew had rarely ended well.

There was still no sign of Virgilio. She stood in the cooling air and shivered, watching the bats circle and loop, manic yet graceful, around the eaves and among the ancient oaks. They sent her into a hypnotic state. She cast her mind back to the day Brio had brought her to the house on their seventh wedding anniversary on 21 December 1926. She would never have believed it possible, but that Christmas was even more horrible than the one she had spent with her parents, and without Paulo, at the family home in Asti the year before her marriage. She could still picture the enormous, lavishly decorated Christmas tree that must have taken decades to grow in the mountain air of an alpine valley, severed and dead in their living room. And the gifts. Perfume, jewellery and furs. Enough cut flowers to stock a florist. Even toys and clothes for the unborn child, all of them for a boy, of course.

In his arrogance, he had actually believed that they would, in time, become a happy family. He was persistent, and surprisingly patient, but ultimately disappointed. For the first few years she barely spoke to him and never left the grounds. As Virgilio grew, she occasionally ventured into the outside world to create a semblance of a normal life for her son, walking with Virgilio in the wooded hills above the house, and later on occasional trips to the museums and monuments of Rome, but she never allowed herself to be seen in public with Brio, refusing absolutely to accompany him on any official events. Despite his obvious frustration at the embarrassment this initially caused, it was a stance he soon accepted, no doubt worried about the 'mad woman' creating a scene in front of his colleagues, many of whom probably didn't even know she existed.

They led separate lives. Brio maintained a succession of mistresses in his apartment in Rome, and on Sundays he would arrive in the Lancia to take Virgilio out for one of their 'adventures.' He got to share Virgilio with her, and that was it. She had realised many years ago that she had still given him far too much. But she'd had a weak hand when she returned to Italy after Tyrer's death. She turned up at his apartment on Via Sforza, visibly pregnant and in a bad way. She could still recall the faint but brutal electric ringing when she had finally summoned the willpower to push the buzzer to his apartment.

The faint sound of the telephone briefly merged with her memories then brought her back to this world. She ran to the house. The ringing stopped as she opened the door. She heard the housemaid, Sofia, speaking to Brio. *Si, Signore Salvatore, she is right here.* Sofia handed her the phone with a serene smile. It always sickened Carla that Sofia responded to any interaction with Brio as if she were being blessed by the Pope.

'Is he with you?' Carla asked brusquely. She caught a scowl from Sofia as she retreated down the hall.

'It's so lovely to hear your voice, darling,' answered Brio.

It never failed to amaze Carla how he managed to keep it up after all these years.

'Is he with you?' There was a long pause on the line, followed by a sigh.

'He was. I put him on the train twenty minutes ago. He should be with you in half an hour.'

Carla knew she should put the phone down at this point, but she couldn't help herself. The worry had eroded her usual self-control. 'Why was he with you? What are you up to, Brio?'

'Can't a boy come and see his Papa when he wants to? He was missing me.'

'That's not the deal, Brio. You can't just summon him down to Rome whenever you feel like it.'

'There was no summons. He just turned up. He's bored up at the villa.'

Carla considered her next words. She knew there shouldn't be any. She should hang up now that she knew he was safe. She had all the information she needed.

'You do know that he's desperate to leave you, don't you?' Brio always knew how to twist the knife. 'He's a man now, Carla. He doesn't need his Mamma anymore. He simply can't wait to get to Milan, and away from you.'

His words hurt her more than usual, as she knew they were partly true. She couldn't think of anything to say in response.

'But I've sent him home, like a good father, even though he begged me to let him stay for the rest of the summer.'

Carla wanted to smash the phone against the wall to shut him up.

'Unlike some people, I understand how important it is to keep a promise, and how hurtful it can be when you don't.'

Why couldn't she just put the phone down?

'By the way, we shared a couple of bottles of exceptional Barolo, so go easy on him. He may be a little blotto.'

He had ended the conversation on a word they both knew to be one of Abercrombie's calling cards. Then she heard him hang up before she could beat him to it.

By the time Virgilio arrived home, the darkness was almost complete. Carla lay on the sofa in the sitting room, staring out the open French windows into her garden. She had a crushing headache but felt incapable of getting up for her pills, or even to turn the light on. She could have called for Sofia but couldn't face her unspoken contempt. So, she lay in the pitch-dark room, her eyes adjusting to the point where she could discern the outline of the black trees that separated her sanctuary from the deep indigo sky beyond. She could have closed her eyes and still seen the ragged profile of the oaks and sweet chestnuts just as clearly in her mind's eye. Aside from Virgilio, her garden was the one thing left in the world that she cared about.

She had expected to feel angry with him, but when she heard the quiet click as he turned the latch on the front door, she felt only relief. She sensed his presence at the threshold to the sitting room a couple of metres behind her. She could hear him, a little out of breath from the climb up the hill. A faint aroma of wine floated toward her. He hadn't come blustering in, turning on the light, oblivious to the rest of the world. She was sure that he knew she was in the room, and that he knew that *she* knew he was standing behind her. She wanted to pause that moment for eternity. That silent acknowledgement of their love for each other. Of their kindness to each other. No recriminations from the mother. Only gentle solicitude from the son. Then she was overwhelmed with an emotion she could not comprehend, and tears rolled down her cheeks, her silence finally broken by a sharp involuntary sniff.

'Mamma,' whispered Virgilio, 'what's the matter?' He approached the sofa and lay his hand on her shoulder. She reached up to clasp it. 'You're cold, Mamma. Shall I close the windows?'

'No. I want to see my garden.'

'But it's so dark out there. You can't see a thing.'

'I can see everything.'

'Mamma, I'm sorry I went to see—'

'Shh,' Carla squeezed his hand to forestall the confession. 'It's okay. I know where you've been.'

'I should have asked you, but . . .'

'But I would have said no, and we would have argued. And I know how much you hate arguing with anyone, especially me. And if you had gone, I would have called Brio and had a row with him. And if you hadn't gone, you would have moped around all day pretending you weren't sulking. But we would both have known you were. And we would both have been miserable all day. So, you thought it would be easier for everyone if you just left.'

'Yes.'

'And you we're right.'

'I was?'

'Yes, I have no right to keep you cooped up here all summer. You were right. And I have been selfish.' Carla felt his other warm hand placed softly on her cheek, like his father would have done. The smell of the wine on his warm breath was stronger now.

'You're really cold, Mamma.' Can I at least get you a blanket?

'You are a dear boy. I love you so much.' She kissed the back of his hand and felt a tiny involuntary twitch. She was embarrassing him, but he was too kind to pull his hand away.

'Please Mamma, can I get you something?'

Carla heard a note of discomfort. He wanted to do something for her. He wanted to show his love in a practical way. She had been too sentimental. Again. She was expecting too much of him. She loved them both so much, but it wasn't fair to expect Virgilio to fill his place as well.

'Yes, go get Mamma a blanket from my room.' She aimed for a brisker tone. 'And while you're there, bring me one of my headache pills from my dressing table.' He withdrew, silently, probably relieved. Her request had signalled a return to normality from the heightened emotions. A few seconds later, the hallway light went on and she heard his big shoes skip up the stone staircase to the first floor. Carla shuddered, realizing how cold she was. She should get up and close the windows, but she still couldn't move from the sofa. He would be back soon. She would let him place the blanket on her and she would ask him to tuck her in, as if she were the child and he were the parent. She would laugh and make a little game of it. He would be relieved that her good humour had returned. She smiled at the comforting thought and then had a happy realisation. His growing up was not a separation to be mourned, but a flourishing to embrace. It would mean there was at least one adult in the world that cared for her and could even look after her as *she* grew old. She let her mind conjure her future son: an impressive, handsome, middle-aged man, bringing her flowers and stories of the outside world, pouring tea for the two of them in the garden beyond the French windows, as she sat in her chair, blanket tucked around her knees. In this imagined future she was not happy, but she was content.

After a while, it seemed like that future world might come and go before Virgilio brought her a blanket in this present one. What was taking him so long? 'Dozy' was the word Abercrombie would have used. She was very cold now and was about to shout up to him when she heard his footsteps coming down the staircase, more slowly than on the way up. The light above her head came on and she was blinded by the glare.

She pushed herself up and twisted to look over the back of the sofa. Virgilio was standing in the doorway. His face was white.

'Mamma, what's this?' He thrust his hand toward her, holding a thick, green, leather-backed journal.

Carla stared at the journal and then up at her son. The cold she had felt was a warm summer's day compared to the ice that now ran through her.

'And who is Abercrombie Lyle?'

54

Naples, 31 August 1945

I retraced my steps from this morning. It was early evening now and the *centro storico* was lively. The afternoon heat had subsided, and the streets had filled with people. In Liverpool, loitering was a furtive activity for the downtrodden. In Naples, it was elevated to an art form, and somehow infused with its own purpose. On a warm evening such as this, the whole city vibrated with aimless energy. I envied the people around me. It felt like I was the only man in Naples with somewhere to go, and certainly the only one in a hurry to get there.

I could have made it hard for anyone following me. There are no end of narrow alleyways or archways to duck into, but I couldn't see the point. If they wanted to kill or abduct me, they could have done so easily by now, and whoever had written this damned book clearly intended me to visit Borromeo. I knew they had set a trap of some sort, but the only way to discover its nature was to step into it, and they were unlikely to spring it before I had contacted the librarian. So, I walked straight down Via dei Tribunali and turned left on Via Nilo. I passed calmly through the grey baroque archway, into the courtyard, up the marble steps, and into the library, as if this morning's violent chase had never happened. Once inside, however, I was less comfortable. The librarian on duty this morning had been replaced by an unfamiliar face. I knew all the librarians, and he wasn't one of them. He was young, with sallow, sunken cheeks and dark, overgrown eyebrows that didn't quite conceal the glances he cast my way as he lifted his nose from a book. He reminded me of a crow.

I strode down the central aisle and through the tired blue curtains covering the plain Palladian arch at the end, which separated the public from the private spaces of the old library. I half expected him not to be there, but as the old brass curtain rings slid across the rail, I saw Borromeo's face rise to meet mine. His huge smile brightened the dingy back room. Borromeo had been bald and obese ever since we had been introduced by Price, and he had set me on my new path nineteen years ago. These features gave him an ageless quality that seemed both close to death and newly born. When he smiled, you felt blessed, but by some sort of pagan, rather than Christian, priest. It was too mischievous for a Catholic smile. Maybe Italian priests could smile like this. I hadn't known many since I'd been here. But not the ones back home. Except for old Father Sullivan, who I was sure had never been much of a Catholic in any case.

'Michael! I'd like to say, what a beautiful surprise, but it isn't.' His mouth was smiling, but his eyes creased a little, either in scrutiny or concern. I couldn't read his expression.

'It's good to see you, too,' I replied. 'It's been too long.'

Borromeo gestured to an old, upholstered armchair opposite his desk. It looked comfortable but wasn't. It had lost most of its stuffing and I could feel the springs pressing into my bony backside like a medieval torture device, or perhaps a precursor for sinners of modest transgressions: a hint that a quick confession would have them out of that chair and back in the bosom of the Church, while a failure to acknowledge errors would lead to something infinitely more painful. Or perhaps Borromeo just hadn't realised how awful it was. His backside didn't need the stuffing.

'Are you well, Michael? You look . . . less elegant than usual.'

I laughed. Even in my Sunday best, 'elegant' was a compliment I rarely received. 'I've had better days, old friend.'

'Can I get you a drink? You look like you need one.'

I didn't say 'no' and with surprising dexterity, he reached into his desk, produced a dark bottle and two small glasses, which looked like they had already been used. He poured deftly. As I reached over to claim mine, I could hear him wheezing, as if the effort had taken its toll. I sipped Marsala. Not my favourite, but it would do.

'I need your help,' I said.

Borromeo spread his hands wide. 'Name it, and, if it is within my power, it is yours.'

'I'm looking for . . . a rather unusual book. I was hoping you might have a copy in the library.'

'We have many books, and a very efficient catalogue, but you know that already.' He gave me that concerned look again, as if to say: *come now, are we not old friends? Tell me why you are* really *here.*

I hesitated, wondering what, if anything, he already knew, and how to protect him as much as possible. It felt like the less he knew the better.

'Naturally, I am at your disposal,' he continued. 'However, I am curious as to why you have come to me personally. Is the book you seek not in the catalogue?'

'Actually, yes, it is, and I already have a copy, but I was hoping you might have another. The one I have . . . has some pages missing.'

'That is, indeed, most unfortunate.' Borromeo pursed his lips, as if the very idea of a damaged book, especially one under his care, caused him pain.

'And these missing pages are important to you?'

'Yes, very important.'

Borromeo leaned forward in his chair with his fingers steepled under his chin. 'Now I am intrigued. What, may I ask, is the nature of this "rather unusual book"?' He had a salty look in his eye that I don't think I had seen before. I shifted in the chair to move the annoying spring to another part of my backside. I had no reason to mistrust Borromeo, but something about his questions unnerved me. I should have expected curiosity, given the rather mysterious nature of my request, but it felt like he was toying with me for his own amusement, which wasn't like him.

'It is called, *The Life and Death of Abercrombie Lyle*.'

'It is not a title I am familiar with. Is it old?'

'No, it is new. I would say it could not be any newer.' I paused again, weighing how much to tell him about this cursed book. 'In fact, it may even describe events that have not yet happened.'

Borromeo's eyes widened in surprise. 'That is most interesting! So, it contains a prophecy of some sort?'

'Perhaps. I'm not sure yet. I will know when I find a complete version.' I could hear the wheezing distinctly now, as if all this talk of prophetic books was exciting him.

'We do have some . . . special collections. For material that . . . let us say, may not correlate with current tastes.' Borromeo gave me an intense glare and brought his index finger to his lips. I had never seen his eyes bulge quite so extravagantly. He continued in a whisper. 'They are held deep beneath the old library, in an ancient catacomb, and only I have the key to enter.' He theatrically pulled out a bunch of old keys, connected by a chain to his belt, and held them up to me. 'Would you like me to take you down, into the darkness, to search for it?'

A long pause stretched between us. Then, as I was about to answer, he exploded into laughter, which precipitated a violent coughing fit. He produced a grubby handkerchief to help muffle the aftershocks and dabbed his eyes as the convulsions diminished.

'Oh, Michael. I shouldn't have, but the look on your face.' He was seized by more coughing.

I was shocked that he could choose this moment to make a joke at my expense, but then I caught myself. He could have no idea what this book meant to me, nor of the trauma of my last two days. He was just having some fun – and perhaps this was not his first Marsala of the evening. Nevertheless, his antics disturbed me. Borromeo had a sly sense of humour, but this had an undercurrent of cruelty.

'There will be no need to descend into the hellish caves and rummage for your book among the Roman skulls.' He was still chuckling to himself and now blew his nose like a tuba. 'Your book is on my desk. Or at least I assume that's what is in the envelope. It is addressed to you.' His last words, thrown out casually, nearly passed me by. At the corner of his desk and within arms-reach was a bulky Manilla envelope. I grabbed it and saw Michael Lynch written on the front in a rather poor hand. I tore it open and snatched out the book. My third copy.

'Where did this come from? How did you get this?'

'It was hand delivered late this afternoon.'

'By whom? Did he leave a name?'

'No, not that I remember. He just walked through the same curtains you came through and handed it to me. He said you would be along shortly and would I mind giving it to you.'

'Did that not seem strange? What did he look like?' I realised that my tone was more aggressive than I had intended, and Borromeo seemed a bit put out.

'Young. Tall. Rather frightening, if truth be told.'

'And he left no name or message?'

'No.'

I opened the book and went straight to the back. This one was complete, ending on page 333. As I flicked past the last page something fell out. A photograph. Before it hit the floor, I knew what it would contain. Three faces stared back up at me. Two I had seen before. Carla and the boy. My son. Their identical images were on a print in my pocket. The third, of course, was Brio.

'Michael. Michael! Is everything alright? You look like you have seen a ghost. You're trembling.'

I looked up at Borromeo, whose face had transformed into a caricature of concern.

'What is it? What is that book?'

'It is called *The Life and Death of Abercrombie Lyle*.'

'Yes, I can see that. But *what* is it? Why is it so important?' he stared at me. 'Who is this Abercrombie Lyle?'

I bent down to pick up the photograph.

'Who are those people?' Borromeo asked. Is one of them Abercrombie Lyle?'

'No.'

'Then who is he?'

'I need you to think very carefully,' I said, showing Borromeo the picture. 'Imagine this boy is a young man. Imagine he is the same age as the man who gave you this envelope.'

'What is going on, Michael?'

I ignored his question. 'Think and look. You are a clever man, Borromeo. An observant man. And I need you to answer a very important question.'

Borromeo looked frightened.

'Could the man who gave you the envelope have been *this* boy when he was young?' I pointed at the boy I believed to be my son. 'Could they be the same person?'

'I, I'm not sure. The boy is a *lot* younger.'

'Look hard. Could it be the same person?'

'Well, yes. I can't be sure, but it could be. There is a certain, similarity. The wide mouth. The smirk. Yes, I think it possibly is him.'

I looked at my old friend's worried face and felt a sense of profound detachment. It was like those moments of unexpected clarity when one is very drunk. When you see the world for what it really is. When you have understood a deep truth, and yet know that you could never describe it to anyone, least of all oneself.

'Michael, what is going on? Are you in trouble?'

I stared across the desk at him as if was he were calling out to me from a life raft that I already knew was beyond reach. He looked very worried now. He reminded me of the way Carla and Brio had looked in the greenhouse behind *Avanti!* as I had slipped out of consciousness, battered and bruised, all those years ago.

'Michael, what is happening? Who is this Abercrombie Lyle?'

Faintly, I heard myself say, '*I* am Abercrombie Lyle.'

55

Naples, 31 August 1945

Borromeo's mouth was open, and his expression bewildered. He seemed incapable of speech, which was a first. I also had nothing to say. I didn't have the time or inclination to construct any sort of explanation. I'm not sure I would have known where to start if I had, and despite our long friendship, the only thing that mattered to me now was to finish reading the book and to follow its directions. I turned to leave, and Borromeo finally found his voice.

'Be careful, Michael. No book has yet been written that can predict the future.'

'What about the Book of Revelation?'

Borromeo laughed. 'Sadistic fairy tales, written by a lunatic.'

'Well, this one is doing a bloody good job so far.' As I opened the curtain and looked back into the reading room, I heard him reply.

'We make our own future, Michael. No one else can make it for us.'

I wasn't convinced.

The library was quiet but not empty. I wanted to be on my own with the final pages and felt the urge to get away from Borromeo. So I left the library. I did not know what to expect from those last few pages, whether they would reveal the fate of Carla, whether they would show her to be dead or alive, or what they might tell me about the boy who was surely my son. I placed my hand on the pristine cream dust jacket of the book and reflected that the last hand to touch it before mine was likely my own flesh and blood. If so, what was his part in all this? Did he know I was his father? From my brief glimpse he looked benign, and a little confused, but both descriptions I had of him from Alfredo and Borromeo painted a dark picture of an intimidating young man with authority beyond his years. If he *was* my son, what the hell had they done to him to turn an eighteen-year-old into that?

The only thing I felt confident about was that the final pages would contain an account of my death, and even if Borromeo was right about being masters of our own destiny, that's not something anyone can take lightly.

I made the short journey to Basilica Santuario del Gesù Vecchio, a baroque masterpiece next door to the library. If I was about to discover how, where, and when, I would die, a church seemed as good a place as any to read about it. As Borromeo had alluded, sadistic fairy tales written by lunatics were its stock-in-trade. I could even light a candle for myself when I was done. I walked down the nave of the empty church, as I had many times before, and sat in the middle, directly underneath the rotunda. I'd had enough of hiding in side chapels.

56

Rome, 31 August 1945

Brio picked up the handset of the black, British-made Bakelite telephone on his desk. He dialled '0' and asked his secretary, Alfano, to make a call to Naples. Of all the plunder he had embellished his office with since his elevation to Minister of Propaganda, this humble, mass-produced telephone was the most precious. It had been taken from General Auchinleck's personal office in British GHQ after the fall of Cairo and was given to him as a gift from Il Duce himself, with an inscription on its base: *To my friend Brio, my direct line to the soul of the Italian people.* Coming from the great man, this was no small compliment.

Through this mouthpiece, with the hairline crack, and down this grubby cord, the last, futile entreaties would have passed between the general and Prime Minister Anthony Eden, back in his bunker in London. In his more poetic moments, Brio imagined echoes of these messages still trapped, bouncing around in the wires, screaming their ghostly chorus of desperation for all eternity. It gave Brio immense pleasure that they had been set in motion by Eden himself. It was like having a tiny piece of your enemy captive but still alive on your desk as a reminder of the triumph. He would have preferred it to be a piece of Churchill, but then if Churchill hadn't drowned in the North Atlantic *en route* to a rendezvous with Roosevelt, he might not have the phone at all. Of course, he knew it couldn't be true that these echoes still existed in any real, physical sense, but then he didn't much care about that sort of truth.

He *had* cared about the sort of truth that British Intelligence had sent into the world during the war. That had been of great interest to Brio when its full extent was revealed in 1942. He had to hand it to the British, despite their arrogance and decadence, or perhaps because of it, they had always been capable of surprising moments of brilliance, even as their empire crumbled before their eyes. In a way, he owed them a debt of gratitude. For this phone was not a mere trophy of victory, it symbolised a final step in the perfection of his own thinking – an evolution that had driven his recent progress through the upper echelons of the fascist party. The creativity of British Intelligence, and especially their deceptions, had inspired him. He had realised that the adage of truth being the first casualty of war was wrong. Truth flourished in war. It grew and multiplied, limited only by the imagination of the storyteller. Truth was liberated by war, allowed to soar above the petty, mundane realities of peacetime. In war, truth was not a casualty, it was whatever you wanted it to be.

'Borromeo is on the line, sir.' The voice of his secretary broke his reverie and brought him back to the task at hand.

'Put him through.' There was a click and then faint static. Above it he could hear Borromeo breathing. It was his most annoying feature. Borromeo could have been sitting at his desk all day, his only exertion turning the pages of his precious books, and you could still hear his breathing.

'You wished to speak to me, Minister?' There was an old-fashioned formality to Borromeo that irritated Brio. Not once had Borromeo said anything that could be defined in a transcript as an insult, but Brio knew that Borromeo's impeccable, courtly manners were a shield for his infinite contempt. Even when Brio had threatened him with punishment for collaborating with a foreign spy, if he didn't do his bidding, Borromeo had behaved as if he were doing Brio a favour, when he should have been shitting his pants. Brio also suspected that Borromeo was, for some incomprehensible reason, actually fond of Abercrombie. But he was too much of a coward, and too comfortable in his ivory tower, to do anything to help him in his hour of need. He was bourgeois at heart, with noble manners but lacking nobility of spirit. Yet another despicable adherent of *la vita comoda*. One day, soon, he would punish Borromeo, but not yet. He might still need him.

'Has he made contact?' asked Brio.

'He has.'

'Did you give it to him?' asked Brio. An irritating moment of silence ensued.

'Of course.'

'Has he read it?' The annoyance in Brio's tone seemed to lengthen the gaps between Borromeo's responses. What he would do to that man one day.

'It is impossible to say.'

'Hazard a guess, you useless lump of lard!' The next pause was even longer. He could hear the drumming of fingernails on a desk down the line.

'I would say, by now, he probably has.'

'Then I shall expect him tonight?' asked Brio. He listened to Borromeo's breathing for a few more seconds. The anticipation of making it stop calmed him.

'What we expect and what we receive . . .'

Brio waited for Borromeo's pregnant aphorism to deliver but was disappointed.

'Did he seem . . . ready?' asked Brio. This time there was no delayed response.

'My good man, he's been *ready* for nearly twenty years!' Brio could hear laughter mixed with asphyxiation at the end of the line and slammed the phone down, an action he instantly regretted as the hairline crack in the handset now seemed slightly wider.

57

Naples, 31 August 1945

Everything seemed much simpler now that I knew what the fates, or at least my biography, had in store for me. I closed the book and sat calmly in my pew, but I knew this calm was the precursor to something quite different. I felt a premonition of fury, so focussed and pure, like shimmering, barely audible strings in the first bars of an overture Verdi might have written after selling his soul to the devil. I gazed around at the space where I had sought solace over many years and sometimes found it. But I wasn't finding any now. Looking down the nave to the altarpiece, all I saw was a chaos of gold and contorted angels. Crowns surrounding Corinthian columns that supported nothing. For the first time, they failed to impress me. I had a sort of epiphany. I realised how incredibly ugly it all was. Trinkets for the credulous. I couldn't believe that I had once been overwhelmed by its beauty. Then again, it's easy to be impressed by such things when you've been brought up on Scottie Road.

I could feel Naples slipping away from me. Whatever the next few hours held, this may be the last time I would see this church. I stood and stared up into the rotunda, where the setting sun cast crimson across the frescos. Christ wore robes that seemed to be soaked in blood. His head emitted four broad rays of its own sunlight as he blessed a woman, probably one of the Marys. I couldn't tell if it was the Magdalene or his mother. It was all a long way above me and the light was fading. Whoever it was, she looked anxious. Christ just looked bored.

I heard a faint, polite cough echo across the church from behind me. It was the cough of a museum caretaker as closing time approached. I turned and saw the partial outline of a tall young man standing behind a pillar near the entrance. He had his back to me.

'Bravo!' I commented. He was playing his part to perfection. I had said it *sotto voce* to myself, but it echoed across the empty space. I noticed him straighten his back and walk purposefully out of the church, as if my response had unsettled him and he was trying to reassert his authority. I felt guilty. I had no idea what lies he had been told to prepare him for this role, but there was every chance that the young man was my son, whether he knew it or not, and I had not intended to humiliate him.

Of course, I followed. On the street, I saw him standing to my right behind a set of iron railings with a gate into the university that was usually locked. It was now wide open. Again, he had his back to me. I let my boots clatter on the narrow, cobbled street and he began to walk away from me again. After the gate, the street ran steeply downhill and doubled back on itself twice. It then widened and doglegged to become Via Antonio Tari. This led south to the broad boulevard of Corso Umberto I, which marked the boundary of the *centro storico*. And there it was, as had been prophesied, parked on the street ahead and pointing toward the boulevard for a quick getaway. The huge silver Lancia was a museum piece now, and it stood out magnificently from the small, drab wartime Fiats that passed on the road ahead. I couldn't help but smile. Whether it was Brio's original car, or a similar model sourced specifically for this charade, I couldn't tell, but the sight of the rear window instantly conjured that image of Carla pounding and screaming: an image of something I knew I hadn't seen, but it was as vivid as the day I had invented it.

The young man got into the front passenger seat. The right rear door was already open for me. This was my best, and possibly last, chance to escape. I was still on my own turf. It was getting dark, and the men who would transport me to my destiny had the disadvantage of being sat in a car almost 50 yards away. If I wanted to run back in the labyrinth of the *centro storico*, there was a good chance I could have lost them. But I never seriously considered doing it.

The final section of the book had contained two chapters. The penultimate had been called *Ludus*. Well, I had always liked a good game, as both Brio and Carla knew. The stakes in this one were higher than I was used to, but this was a game I had waited to play for nineteen years. So, I would go along with it for now. Especially as I knew I had a card up my sleeve that the author, or authors, of my biography were unaware of.

It was the last chapter I was more worried about. *Iudicum* was much less playful. I had no doubt that a judgement of some sort would be cast on someone, and in all probability, it would be me. But, for now, I had a few hours on the well-worn back seat of an old Lancia, which was ample time to consider my next move, and I had it on good authority that also sitting on the back seat would be a bottle of Jameson's. A nice touch, I thought. Only a half pint, mind. I was not to be ushered out of existence insensible. *The game's afoot!* I thought to myself and walked to the car with a grin that I hoped would be interpreted as insouciant. If I was going to play, I would put on a good show. No trembling and pissing on the back seat of Brio's beloved Lancia.

I got into the car and was greeted by a sturdy-looking man in his forties with a two-day growth, slicked grey hair and an eye patch. He had a pistol pointed at me and was fidgety.

'Give me any excuse, and I would take great pleasure in putting a bullet through your eye,' the man hissed, enveloping me in a stench of whiskey.

The idea of driving on bumpy roads for three hours, next to a man I'd recently maimed, while he was holding a gun to my head, made me less sanguine about the journey. I noticed that the bottle of whiskey on the seat beside him had been opened.

'I'm not sure Brio would be pleased to know that you're drinking my whiskey.'

'Who the fuck is Brio?' he asked.

I directed my reply to the man in the driving seat. 'Do I have to sit next to a one-eyed drunk pointing a gun at me all the way to Rome? Wouldn't it be safer if you swapped places and let him drive instead?'

A felt a jab to my gut that shut me up. Luckily, he had to deliver it with his left hand and the confines of the car limited its force, but it still winded me.

'I suppose you think that's funny?' Spittled fumes sprayed my cheek, and I tensed for another blow. Pain radiated across my stomach and into my groin. I felt nauseous, but I knew it would pass. I wasn't seriously hurt.

Then, from the front passenger seat: 'Give him the whiskey and put the gun away.' The voice was youthful but commanding. There can't be many fathers who've heard such first words from their son. Ordering an arsehole twice his age to give me a drink and not kill me in a single sentence. I liked him already. I thought about replying, but before I could think of anything, he followed with, 'and not another word from you until we arrive, or I'll shoot you myself.' His threat was a relief of sorts. He was clearly in charge and his task was to get me safely to the villa. In any case, I wasn't much in the mood talking, and this wasn't the right time for my revelation. I just hoped I'd get a chance to deliver it, at a moment he might believe me. I snatched the bottle of whiskey and took a swig. Just one. Then put the stopper back in and clutched it tight in my right hand, away from the Cyclops. You never knew when a bottle of whiskey might come in handy. I knew from my days in Liverpool that there were more ways than one for such a thing to incapacitate a man.

The outskirts of Naples soon gave way to parched farmland, and I had a clear view of Vesuvius to my right before the road bent left and headed north to Rome. I determined not to even look at Cyclops for the rest of the journey. My comment had been stupid, and I could have had my head blown off before the game had even started, which would have proven Borromeo's point about self-determination, I suppose, but in an entirely pointless manner. In a way, I'd already proved his point, as the journey so far had born little relation to the skeleton narrative of the chapter. So, I decided to resume my allotted role and settled down for a few hours of silent anxiety. My only goal was to make sure that I didn't get myself killed before arriving at the villa. After nineteen years of waiting to see Carla again, a few hours more didn't seem like much. What kind of Carla

I would see, and what she would make of me, was impossible to know, but if the book was to be believed, it would not be a happy reunion.

58

Villa La Quercia, 31 August 1945

It was approaching midnight when we pulled off the country lane and into the driveway of Villa La Quercia. My back was sticky from the hot ride, and I was getting close to breaking my vow not to piss on Brio's back seat. I was regretting not asking the driver to pull over an hour or so back, but I hadn't wanted to give Cyclops any opportunity to misinterpret a toilet break for an attempt to escape. A bullet in the back with my cock hanging out in a country layby was not the alternative ending I wanted for *The Life and Death of Abercrombie Lyle*.

The driver cut the engine, and for a moment all was peaceful, apart from the chirruping of insects. It was pitch dark. The young man in front of me got out and opened my door. I was given a sharp jab in the ribs by something hard, which must have been Cyclops' gun. I nearly made a joke about it being too late for foreplay but bit my tongue and did as I was bid, slipping the snug little whiskey bottle in my hip pocket as I got out. The young man had stepped back into the shadows. But as I glanced his way, we were both suddenly illuminated by light that flooded from the front door as it opened. We stood staring at each other from no more than three yards. It was the first time I had seen him properly, and it dispelled all doubt. I felt blessed, like Mary at the annunciation. Something in my expression must have conveyed this, as my son's face transformed. The flat, hostile glare softened into puzzlement, and perhaps was on its way to some other emotion.

'Hello, Abercrombie,' Brio's deep voice shattered the moment. I turned to see my old friend standing at the top of the steps, backlit in the doorframe, casting his shadow onto the gravelled drive. It reached all the way into the space between me and my son. He had lost none of his flair for the dramatic.

I turned to face him. 'Hello, Brio.'

He stood, legs apart, with his hands on his hips, and scrutinized me for several seconds. Something about the silhouette looked familiar, and yet unlike my memory of Brio. It was posed, rather than imposing. Brio had a natural authority that flowed from his animal power and grace. He had always reminded me of a bear, but this bear looked stuffed. Then the penny dropped. It was his mentor that had sprung to mind, not the old Brio. He stood back and to the side, gesturing expansively for me to enter his cave. I obliged, passing close to him and inhaling his expensive aftershave. I took a few steps down the hallway, dumped my old rucksack, and made a show of looking around.

'What, no Carla? Has she nipped out to the shops for a fatted calf?' I half expected a hearty laugh and a violent clap on the shoulder from behind, but merely received a dark grin when I turned back to face him.

'I see you haven't changed, Abercrombie.' He was, of course, completely wrong, but for tonight I would do my best to conjure the old Abercrombie and sprinkle it with as much cocky scouser as I could muster. Brio had his arm across the doorway and was barring entry to my son. It was an image I didn't like. It was also the first sign that what he, or they, had planned for this evening, would not mirror what had been written. There was a sharp exchange of looks on the threshold and a hint of youthful rebellion on my son's face. He wanted to come in, and according to the script he would have. Brio clearly had other plans. I hadn't expected this, and the thought flashed through my mind that if he left now, I might never see him again. But this wasn't the moment to shout out that I was his real father.

'Why don't you let him in, Brio? This is supposed to be a family gathering, after all.'

Brio whispered something in my son's ear and tried to close the door in his face.

'How ungrateful, and after all he's done for you.' Brio seemed to be meeting some resistance. I didn't want to play my joker so early, but blurted: 'He just wants to spend some time with his father.'

The door finally slammed shut. Brio briefly leaned with his forehead on the door and took a moment to compose himself before turning to face me. I noticed his left eye twitch and his right hand clench, then open. I sensed it was taking all of his self-control to refrain from launching himself down the hallway at me. Outside, I heard the car start and the crunch of its wheels on the gravel as it left the driveway. It seemed like this was not going quite to plan for either of us.

Brio pointed for me to proceed through a door to the right at the end of the hall. Was this it? The moment I would finally see Carla again. I hesitated, feeling my shield of bravado softening. What if she was sitting there, smiling knowingly and clearly a co-author of this madness? Even if she hadn't connived in its writing, the book had laid out an appalling scene of domestic bliss through that door. If it was to be believed, she would be sitting, immaculate, on the arm of a sofa, in a powder blue cardigan and pearls, commanding her tastefully decorated room. She would greet me with a whiskey soda and pitying indifference. She would ask after my health, offer a brief allusion to the regret she felt for 'how things turned out,' and then stand beside her husband. She would take his hand and gaze up adoringly at his big, handsome face to tell me everything I needed to know about her future, and mine, without needing to say a word, before leaving to let the boys have a little chat. I had played this scene in my mind many times in the Lancia, and it hadn't got any easier to watch. Even if she wasn't in on the farce, she might view me as an embarrassment. An old flame dragged to dinner to satisfy the inexplicable whim of a boorish husband. She might be indulging Brio in an evening to be tolerated and quickly forgotten. I think I preferred her as co-conspirator. According to the book, she would play no part in the final chapter, *Iudicum*. She didn't need to. She would already have passed her judgement with that look.

As if sensing my unwillingness to step into the footlights, Brio waved brusquely toward the sitting room like the director of a school play encouraging a nervous lead, and I obeyed. I had no other choice. I opened the door and stepped into the room as if I were stepping off a cliff.

She wasn't there.

'Did you really think I'd let you see her again?' Brio was standing behind me with a gun pointed at my back. 'You're welcome to a whiskey. But you'll have to help yourself.' He waved the gun in the direction of a drinks tray to my right. 'It won't be served to you by my wife.'

I had, of course, known that Carla might not be there, but it was still a shock. I saw no harm in fixing a drink. It would buy me some time to think and move me further away from Brio.

'Some host you are.' I waved the cut-glass decanter, offering Brio a drink as well. He shook his head. 'So, the wife is out and you're trying to get me drunk. Anyone would think you had ulterior motives.' This elicited a snort of genuine mirth. Perhaps half a point to me, but I was starting with a big handicap. He had a gun, and I didn't.

As I poured myself a generous measure, I noticed a larger, silver framed version of the photograph that had dropped out of my book. The three of them did look extraordinarily happy, almost to the point of smugness, but it still struck me as a little off.

'You see, I couldn't do anything to jeopardise the happiness we've built together.' Brio explained. 'She has no interest in you, of course, but why upset her by dredging that ... *episode* up again.'

I took a sip of my whiskey and let him continue. He clearly wasn't finished with his opening monologue.

'It would be like jumping down into a latrine. You remember those?' I nodded. 'It would be like jumping in, putting my hand into the piss and the shit, and throwing it in her face. Don't you agree?'

He had an amused, controlled air, but something wasn't right. No one talks about throwing shit in the face of a woman he loves. Unless he hates her as well.

'So where is she?'

'She'll be out. All night. Staying with one of her friends in Rome.'

'So she has no idea I'm here?'

'She knows you're here but didn't wish to see you.'

'She's got better things to do?'

'Yes. She's at the opera. *Manon Lescaut*, I think.'

I laughed.

'What's so funny?'

'You must have had to work pretty hard to get Carla out of the way with that. She's always hated Manon.' Brio looked nonplussed. 'She's a gold-digging tart... Manon, that is, not Carla.' I looked around the room ostentatiously. 'Then again, people change.' Brio rolled his neck a little as if trying to release some tension. Thankfully, he didn't clench his fist again. It was still holding a pistol pointed at my chest.

'So, I'm supposed to believe that Carla knows I'm here but had no interest in seeing me?'

'Yes. She never mentions you. Probably barely remembers you.'

'Really? So how did that conversation go? "By the way darling, that pitiful fool you once ran away with. What was his name? Abercrombie, yes, that's it. Anyway, he's coming over for a drink and a bit of a chat. I think it would be better if you popped out to avoid a scene." "What a bore. Yes, perhaps you're right, darling. I think I'll go to see that opera I've been meaning to see. The one that I hate."'

Brio was smiling, but it seemed a little forced.

'I suppose I'm also to believe she had no hand in this ridiculous pantomime?'

Brio regained his poise.

'Whatever gave you that idea? I could never have done this without Carla. This is all her work. Well, most of it.'

I was confused, again, but not surprised. I did my best to hide it by taking a sip of whiskey. It was very good, the best I'd tasted since my last drink with Price before he returned to England just before the war.

'I was a little disappointed with her work, at first,' continued Brio. 'But I now think *The Life and Death of Abercrombie Lyle* is her masterpiece – or perhaps *our* masterpiece.'

I knew the most likely explanation for this unlikely situation required some involvement from Carla. But what exactly had that been? And most importantly, why had she done it? I couldn't see how her piece fit into the puzzle.

'Look around you, Abercrombie. Look at what we have created here, despite your efforts.' Brio swept his pistol arm around the room, like an estate agent who is a little too desperate to make the sale. I never responded well to a hard sell.

'We have created a perfect family, in this beautiful, idyllic house. A perfect triangle of love that you will never break . . . and will never know yourself.'

He had a point, on the surface. The room was magnificent. Relaxed, stylish and elegant – expensive looking, but only when you looked hard. It lacked any pretension. It was large enough to be quite grand, but nothing was there to impress, only to enjoy. It was the antithesis of Brio's flat in Rome, and it had Carla stamped all over it. I sipped more whiskey and realised how tense I was. I had unsettled Brio, but I was unsettled myself. I didn't feel any closer to the truth, and that frustration was fuelling anger, with both of them.

I tried to slow my breathing and relax a little. There was something I was missing. I took another sip of whiskey, letting the familiar warmth open my mind, more in anticipation of its effect than the reality. I was still sober but tried to let myself feel a little drunk. I scoured the room. *Come on. Observe. Think. Ignore Brio. What's the reality behind the game?*

I was at the back of the room. Ahead of me, and behind Brio, French windows opened out onto the blackness of what I presumed to be a huge garden. Probably the one the photograph had been taken in. One of the doors was slightly ajar to allow some air in after the long hot day. To my left, beyond the door I had entered, was a wall of books. Close to the wall a chaise longue in faded green velvet lay next to a low coffee table piled with more books. The opposite wall had a large fireplace. A single armchair, upholstered in a pattern of sage and pale pinks, sat at an angle to the fireplace. It had a table beside it, with a smaller, neater, pile of books and a phonograph. I could see a record sleeve with a picture of Jussi Björling. The table also had a small photograph. I wasn't quite close enough to see it well, so I walked over and picked it up. It nearly undid me. A young Carla, almost as I remembered her from Paestum, stared at me with my boy, as a toddler, sitting on her shoulders. He was holding her much shorter hair as if he was riding a horse without a bridle. She was smiling at the camera but looked more proud than happy. I glanced at Brio, who seemed to be taking great pleasure in my examination of the photograph. Then I looked around for more images of the happy family but couldn't see any. To the right of the French windows, beside its own floor-to-ceiling window, was a small writing desk and a chair, which would have allowed a view into the garden. I saw nothing that looked like it had ever belonged to Brio.

The more I perused the room, the more I liked it. I knew that with the right books and the right music, and the occasional stroll in the gardens, it was the kind of room she could have spent her whole life in. I imagined what it would be like to share this life with her, in this room, but couldn't quite make the image work in my mind's eye. I also couldn't place Brio in this room, despite, or perhaps due to, the way he was standing there, so cocksure. He was ruining the aesthetic, and somehow, despite its size, the room was designed for only one person.

Then it struck me. This wasn't her domestic heaven. This was her prison cell.

'It's a shame I had to bring you here at night,' Brio commented. 'It's a house to be enjoyed in the daytime. The gardens are magnificent. It's a pity you won't get to see them at their best . . . Or at all, for that matter.'

'It certainly is a lovely room. You must have enjoyed many happy hours here with your wonderful family.'

'I have. Many, many hours, over many years, in the warm bosom of the two people I love most.' I knew Brio was trying to taunt me. I also knew he was lying.

I gestured to the framed picture I still held in my hand.

'What's his name?'

'You mean my son?'

'The boy. What's he called?'

Brio squinted at me. It had been a long time since I had seen him, but I still knew him. I'd have placed good money on what was going through his head at that moment. A part of him would want to have done with it and just put a bullet in me now, but I knew he wouldn't. He couldn't tolerate me goading him into an early resolution. That would be a form of defeat, like taking his new football home in a huff because he wasn't winning as easily as he'd expected. It would also leave a horrible mess on the expensive-looking arts and crafts wallpaper behind me. Whatever their arrangement was, I couldn't imagine Carla would be very happy with that.

'Have you forgotten his name? Some dad you are . . . But then . . .' I trailed off and canted my head to the side, wincing sceptically. I was pushing my luck but fuck him. I knew he wouldn't do it here. There was a whole chapter still to go, albeit a very short one.

'You know his name,' Brio replied.

'You mean he's *actually* called Virgilio? The poor boy. I thought that was some sort of symbolic nonsense cooked up for my biography. You're crueller than I thought. Did he get horribly bullied at school?'

I felt uneasy using my son like this, but I needed to play all the cards in my hand. I still had my wild card, but he had his pistol, which was a royal flush to my high pair. I put the picture of Carla and my young son down and walked back to the drinks tray.

'Are you sure you won't join me for a drink? For old time's sake?' He shook his head. I poured myself a good measure but didn't drink any. I casually picked up the larger photograph of the three of them. The frame felt heavy and must have been expensive, even if the silver was only plate.

'Enjoy your drink, Abercrombie. I don't wish to sound melodramatic, but it will be your last.' Brio still sounded supremely confident, but I could tell he was a little shaken. I was more than a little shaken myself. I could feel the adrenaline coursing through me. Like it used to in that moment of quiet between the end of the barrage and the shrill call to death of the captain's whistle. I knew I should be scared, and I was, but I was mainly angry, and impatient to get on with it.

I peered at the photograph, affecting a puzzled look, and moved closer to Brio. What lies lay behind that image? What living death had Carla been subjected to here. And what had they done to my son to turn him into someone who could handle himself like a mobster at the age of eighteen?

'This is a lovely photo.' I gestured at the image. 'I can see the resemblance . . . to Carla that is. Perhaps less so to you.' I smiled up at him. 'I'm not sure he'll ever be as handsome as you, Brio. He's very skinny.'

'See, here.' I held the picture out and moved toward him, as if inviting his opinion on the image. 'He has a rather unusual, long mouth. Not at all like yours, or Carla's.'

'Keep your distance, Abercrombie.' I was now about three yards from him.

'Are they freckles on his face?'

Brio laughed. 'Is this the best you can do?'

'Are you sure he's really yours, Brio? I mean, we both know she's got form.'

Brio shifted the angle of the gun down to my crotch. 'One more word and I'll start there. I've never liked this carpet anyway.'

A wave of pure hatred overcame me. I looked him in the eye and decided that I wasn't interested in the last chapter. That one didn't have Carla or my son in it, in any case.

'Who is this performance for, Brio? It can't be for me anymore. You know I don't believe a word of it. I don't know what sort of arrangement you have with Carla, but we both know the happy family act is complete bollocks.'

'Be quiet.'

'Perhaps it's for *you*, to convince yourself how happy you all are? To convince yourself it's all been worth it.'

'I said, quiet!'

'If it's for Virgilio,' I gestured with my head to the French windows behind him, 'by the look on his face, he's not enjoying it either.'

Brio couldn't help himself glance over his shoulder. As he did, I threw the picture frame into his face with a backhanded flick and launched myself at him. The frame caught him in the mouth, and I was on top of him before he could react, sending him crashing to the floor. His pistol flew under the chaise longue, and I pinned his hand to the carpet. He was older and slower now. I'd surprised him. But I only had a few seconds. I needed the gun before his greater strength turned the scales. Our faces were close, and his open mouth was bleeding. I could feel his hot breath on my face as he tensed beneath me like a volcano about to erupt. The face of the young, mud-caked German boy came to me unbidden, and I bit down on Brio's lower lip like a wild animal, as I had done to him. My teeth tore into his flesh and his scream deafened me. Then the sound of a gunshot crashed through the room. We both froze, and I felt something hard press against the top of my head.

59

Villa La Quercia, 31 August 1945

'Don't move.'

I couldn't see him, but I knew it was my son. I could see Brio. His ghastly face was six inches from mine. I noticed for the first time that there was more grey hair in his moustache than black. Blood ran from his mutilated mouth down both cheeks to the floor. It looked like he was smiling but it was hard to tell. He started to push me off.

'I said don't move. Either of you.'

The pressure of the muzzle on the back of my head had gone, and a confused look came over Brio's face. A strong hand grabbed my shoulder and dragged me off Brio, flipping me onto my back. We lay together staring up at Virgilio, who stood over us, the gun now pointing at Brio.

Brio gestured toward Virgilio with a grasping hand. 'Give it me.' He was hard to understand. Virgilio showed no sign of obeying and then took a couple of steps back to be out of reach of any sudden lunges. He was young but clearly no idiot.

'How long. Outside?' asked Brio.

'Long enough,' replied Virgilio, who looked calm but must have been struggling to contain his emotions.

'Don't trust him.' Brio tilted his head toward me. 'Don't believe a word he says.' Brio was having difficulty speaking. He leaned up on one elbow and spat blood on the carpet.

'I'm not sure I can believe a word you say, either, Papa, after what I've just heard.'

I knew that timing would be everything. If I went too hard with the truth, I might panic the boy. It might be too much for him to take in. If I waited too long, he might crumble and give Brio his gun. Despite the hint of recognition I hoped I had seen on the driveway, it may not have crossed his mind until a few moments ago that Brio may not be his father. He had likely been following his orders his whole life. It would be easy for him to resolve this mess by putting his trust in his 'Papa.' He was only eighteen, after all. Then again, I was only eighteen when I first killed a man. I thought back to how angry and confused I had been when I learned from Price that my Da was not my father. I hadn't shot the messenger, but I hadn't had a gun in my hand. It was not clear how this would play out, and I sensed I would need to lead him gently to his own conclusion.

Virgilio stood casting glances at each of us in turn, as if trying to make his mind up about something.

'This is how it's going to work,' Virgilio said.

There was something familiar about his intonation and facial expression. Then I remembered. He reminded me of Carla when she'd had enough of Brio's rowdy, drunken friends and had decided that the evening must come to an end. Virgilio took a clean handkerchief out of his pocket and threw it at Brio. 'I will ask the questions, to each of you in turn. You will stay silent until addressed, and if I *know* you are lying, I will shoot you in the leg. Understand?'

'Yes.' I replied.

'If you tell a second lie, I will shoot you in the other leg.' I nodded. 'And if there is a third lie . . .'

'We understand.' I answered.

'Good.'

'Virgilio. I can explain.' Brio stretched his hand out while grasping with his fingers. 'Give me the gun, son.'

'Do you understand, Papa?'

Brio began to struggle up from the floor, shouting. 'This isn't a fucking game. Give me the gun, now!'

With remarkable athleticism, Virgilio leapt forward and gave Brio a ferocious slap across the face, sending him back to the floor. Then he sprang back to his well-judged spot about five yards away. I realised in that moment that the balance of power in the room wasn't as fragile as I'd thought. Virgilio wasn't 'only eighteen' he was nearing his physical peak and smart as a whip, while Brio was nearly fifty, and I wasn't far behind. Brio looked like he still had most of his old strength, but we were both middle-aged men on our way to becoming old. Brio probably hadn't been in a fight for over twenty years. We were both slower and maybe weaker than Virgilio.

And he had a gun.

'I agree, this is no game, Papa. Or rather, we're playing a new game. My rules. Not the ridiculous game I've been playing for you. Do you understand, Papa? . . . If that is who you are.'

I looked across at Brio and could feel the rage emanate from his prone body like heat from a fire. He rubbed his cheek and gave a nod. But he didn't have the look of a willing participant. He coughed and spat more blood on the carpet.

'You can both sit with your backs against the chaise longue,' continued Virgilio. But don't get up. Shuffle across on your arses. Slowly.'

Virgilio waited patiently until we were in position, with Brio pressing the handkerchief against his mouth to stem the bleeding.

'You.' Virgilio waved the gun at me. 'Are you my father?'

I hadn't expected such a direct first question. I took a moment to think about my response.

'I believe that I am, yes.' I replied softly.

Virgilio stared at me, scrutinizing me, judging me, then nodded, as if satisfied with my answer. For now.

'Papa, is it possible that this man is my father?'

Brio could no longer constrain himself. 'How can you even think that? After all I've done for you. I've given you everything!'

'Answer my question, Papa.' Virgilio replied. 'Is it *possible* that this man is my father?'

'No! You are *my* son!'

Virgilio walked toward Brio and pointed the gun toward his leg. Brio stared up in disbelief and then another deafening roar ripped through my head. Brio reached down to his leg and then looked up at Virgilio in relief once he realised he had shot into the floor.

'You are forgetting, Papa, that I read Mamma's journal before I gave it to you. All of it.' Virgilio took a step closer and pointed the gun at Brio's knee. 'I will also remind you that I graduated top of my class in mathematics and second in biology. I will give you one last chance. Could he be my father?'

Brio cast me a glance of pure hatred. He couldn't look at his son as he gave his answer and stared at the hole Virgilio had made in the rug next to his leg.

'It is possible.' Brio exhaled, as if a part of his soul were escaping his body.

The phrase 'Mamma's journal' fizzed in my brain. What did that mean? Had she kept some sort of diary? What had she written? What did Virgilio know? Or think he knew?

'You,' Virgilio pointed the gun at me. 'Why did you betray Papa? He was your best friend.'

Again, the question threw me. Had this accusation come from Brio or Carla? I needed to choose my words very carefully. I'd been more confident traversing minefields. Potential answers raced through my mind, but I decided this game was too complicated for any strategy I could devise in the next few seconds. The truth might blow up in my face, but I could only tell the truth, as I had seen it, as gently as I could.

'I don't know what you've read or been told, but I did not believe that I was betraying Brio. I believed he had betrayed us.' Brio snorted with derision and shuffled around, as if the truth made him uncomfortable.

'Who is this "us"?' asked Virgilio.

'Your mother, and me, and all our friends.'

'And how did *he* betray *you*?'

I was in a court martial without a lawyer, or even a clear idea what the charge was, and I knew my testimony might not go down well with a young man raised by one of the most powerful men in Italy – a young man who had never known an Italy before fascism.

'How did *he* betray *you*!'

'It is hard to explain if you weren't there.' This time I had the slap across the face.

'Try!'

I rubbed my jaw and took a moment to compose myself, but my head was ringing.

'Times were different back then.'

'I know that the Socialists and the Jews were trying to destroy our country,' replied Virgilio. My heart sank as he uttered these words, and I felt my anger rise again at Brio – and Carla. 'You don't look like a Jew. Are you a socialist?'

'I am neither. But I have sympathy for the Jews.' Virgilio looked uncomfortable. 'Perhaps, back then, I believed in socialism, but not in the way Brio did.'

Virgilio cast a confused look at Brio.

'Ah, I see. Something else he hasn't told you . . . But since the war, the last war, I don't believe in any "ism."'

Virgilio seemed perplexed by my answer. 'What does that mean?'

'It means he's a traitor.' Brio interjected. Virgilio ignored him. 'He's never believed in anything!'

'Quiet!' roared Virgilio.

'I didn't say I don't believe in anything. I just don't believe there is only one way to make sense of the world. When people think there is, they start killing each other.'

'So, what *do* you believe in, *father*?' It was the first time Virgilio had called me that. It was twisted with sarcasm and sounded horrible.

Again, this was not a question I was expecting. I did not have an answer to hand, but as I looked up at my son, sneering at me, I was overwhelmed by sadness and pity, not just for him, but for Carla, for myself, for Ma and Da, for Michael, for Louisa and Enrico, and even for Brio. Then words fell out of my mouth that I had never said before and had never consciously thought.

'I believe in my family and my friends, and in being kind to them. I believe in love and in the people we love. In the end, that is all there is, and soon enough, even that is gone, except, perhaps, for the memory of our love in those that are left behind.' I was looking at my son and realised that tears were beginning to obscure my view of him. 'We had so much love and friendship, for a few years, and then he took it away. That is how he betrayed me and your mother. He betrayed us by throwing all that away for an "ism." It didn't matter which one.'

Virgilio looked puzzled. He seemed younger and less sure of himself. He had one more question but asked it without conviction.

'Why did you steal my mother away from Papa?'

'I did not "steal" your mother. People are not possessions. Especially not Carla. She is not the kind of person who *can* be stolen. At least not her soul.' I glanced at Brio, who had sunk lower and was squirming. He was almost horizontal again. 'She is the most incredible person I have ever met. She left your father reluctantly because he went to Rome to work for Mussolini, which was a betrayal of everything *she* believed in.'

Virgilio now looked very confused. I let the confusion settle into a mind that must have been close to bursting.

'Later, she asked me to be with her. So, I went, because I loved her more than I can explain, and there was nothing that could have stopped me, short of a bullet. It was the most amazing and beautiful thing that ever happened to me.' I paused to judge the effect on my son of my declaration of love for his mother. I noticed a tear escape his eye that was quickly wiped away.

'Even if you choose to shoot me, son. I will die content, because of what my time with your mother has produced.' I looked him in the eye. 'You are a remarkable young man, despite what they have done to you, and my one regret, apart from not spending the last nineteen years with your mother, is that I have not spent those years with you.'

'Have you finished?' Brio mumbled to my right. I looked at the blood-soaked handkerchief he held to his mouth with his left hand, then noticed that his right hand held his pistol discretely on his lap. It was pointed in my direction. I looked back at Virgilio to see if he had noticed and what his reaction would be, but he was staring, slack-jawed, at something off to his left and behind me.

'Mamma?'

I twisted to look behind the sofa, and there she was, standing in the doorway, in a sparkling black evening gown, staring at me. She looked like she'd seen a ghost, which in a way, I suppose she had.

60

Villa La Quercia, 31 August 1945

'Virgilio.' Brio addressed his son sternly. 'It's time to put the gun down.'

'Papa is right, Virgilio,' Carla said softly. She glided toward her son. 'Give it to me, before you hurt someone.' Virgilio was swinging the gun erratically between me and Brio. His earlier control was slipping. 'Please, Virgilio, give me the gun.' She was next to him now, gently stroking his shoulder while her other hand lay open below Virgilio's hand to receive the weapon.

'I don't trust any of you! You've all lied to me!' Virgilio looked on the edge of some sort of breakdown. 'I'm not giving anyone the gun until someone tells me the truth!'

'Your father has already told you the truth, my darling boy,' answered Carla. 'Now give me the gun and I promise I'll tell you anything you want to know.'

Brio looked quizzically at Carla, and I caught Carla subtly shaking her head at him with wide eyes, as if to say. *Please don't shoot Abercrombie here. Not in front of the boy.* Virgilio may not have noticed that Brio had retrieved his pistol, but Carla had clearly seen it.

'Virgilio.' Her voice was warm and creamy. 'I know you don't want to hurt anyone.'

I wasn't so sure. A few minutes ago he had seemed more than capable of shooting someone. But Carla must know our son better than me. In any case, he was not the one most likely to send me to my maker now that Brio had his gun back. I could only hope that he wouldn't shoot me here, in cold blood, in front of his family. My fate was entirely in their hands.

'You lied to me, too, Mamma.' Virgilio looked reproachfully at Carla.

'That's not true. I have never lied to you.' Carla now cradled his gun hand with one of hers. 'But there are things I've never told you that perhaps I should have.'

'That book. That horrible journal!'

'Give me the gun, Virgilio, and I promise, on my life, that your father and I will tell you everything you want to know.'

Virgilio stared at her, and she smiled at him with such love that I could see his resolve collapsing.

'Cross my heart and hope to die.' She licked a forefinger and made a cross on her chest. It was a gesture that my Ma had made to me, and that she must have made many times to Virgilio. For he became her little boy again before my eyes. He sank his head into her chest and let her take the gun from him. She held his face tight against her bosom and he began to sob.

'There, there. I could never let you shoot Papa.'

Carla held the gun in her other, outstretched, arm, and Brio began to rise from the floor to take the weapon she was handing him for safekeeping. Then the look on his face changed abruptly.

'That is something *I* should have done many years ago.'

The third almighty crash of the evening knocked Brio back to the floor. He lay beside me once again, blood welling from the centre of his chest. Instinctively, I knelt over him, pressing my hands down on the wound to staunch the flow. I pressed with all my strength as the blood slipped, unstoppable, through my fingers, covering them in crimson. But I knew he was already dead.

61

Villa La Quercia, 31 August 1945

I eventually gave up on Brio. His face had made the transformation into lifeless facsimile that I had seen so many times before. A force of nature that had once been boundless simply evaporated, contradicting any sense of science or religion that I could comprehend. How could such brutal strength slip away with no sign of struggle? I put two fingers to his jugular but knew I would find no pulse. I just needed to give myself permission to stop trying to keep him alive. My two bloody fingers left marks on his neck, as if I had performed some sort of macabre benediction. I closed his eyes, which left more grotesque smears on his eyelids. I should have left them open.

Carla and Virgilio were staring in shock at Brio's body. I let them stare while I gathered my thoughts. There were so many questions, but they must wait. In the end, none of them made much difference now. Carla could have shot either, or neither, of us. But choosing neither was tantamount to shooting me, after a short stay of execution. She had chosen that I should live, and Brio should die. Her choice had answered the only question that really mattered. There might be time to understand why later, if we were lucky and made the right decisions in the next few minutes.

The simplest solution would be for me to take the gun from Carla and leave. Carla and Virgilio could say that they had arrived and found Brio dead. They could give me a small head start but not much of one. If I were caught, as I likely would be. I would say I had shot Brio. There were witnesses to testify that they had brought me to the house. No one would suspect Carla and Virgilio. They could carry on as best they could without him, or me. But would Virgilio play along? Or Carla, for that matter? I had my doubts. If she was anything like the Carla I had known, she would rather admit to what she had done than lie about it and expect her son to lie to protect her. That would mean both Carla and I would be arrested and almost certainly executed, leaving Virgilio an orphan. I knew what that felt like at his age and wouldn't wish it on anyone, least of all my own son.

Carla and I could flee and abandon Virgilio, but I knew that was not possible for either of us, and not much better for Virgilio than the first option. The only other choice was immediate flight for all of us, if Virgilio could be persuaded. I decided that this was what we must do. I would not deprive Virgilio of three parents in one evening.

'We have to leave. Now.' I said.

Carla looked at me and slowly came back to her senses. She scanned the room as if seeing it for the first time, though she must have spent many, many hours here. Then she took Virgilio's cheeks in her hands and brought his startled face close to hers.

'Virgilio. Listen to me. You must trust me now and do as I say.'

Virgilio was still in shock. 'You killed Papa.'

'I had no choice. I will explain everything in the car.'

'You killed Papa!' Virgilio screamed in his mother's face. Carla slapped him.

'I killed Papa to stop him killing your *real* father.' Carla gripped Virgilio's chin and turned it roughly to face me. '*He* is your father. Not Brio.'

Virgilio looked at me and then at his dead Papa. He sank to his knees and clasped Brio's hand, kissing it and pressing it to his cheek. He began to sob.

Carla knelt beside Virgilio and took Brio's hand from her son's.

'I know you loved your Papa, but people aren't always what they seem.'

'Papa was the best man in Italy.'

'No, my darling. Papa was a brute, and a bully. I should never have let him be your Papa.'

'But you did, and now you've killed him!'

'Yes. And I should have killed him before you were born, so he could never have infected you with his hatred and lies!' Carla had her son's face in her hands again, but he would not look her in the eyes.

'Look at me. Look at me!' Virgilio's face was contorted with horror and incomprehension as he stared at his mother. 'I have been the prisoner of a man who kidnapped and *raped* me. A man who let me believe for nineteen years that your father was dead when he was alive all this time.'

'If this is true, then I hate you, for you are a coward!'

At this, Carla crumpled.

'You are right. I should never have returned to him. But I was pregnant and penniless. I didn't know what to do or where to go. And I thought your real father was dead. I had no one else.' Carla's head slumped in a way I had never seen before. She looked up at me. 'I never let him touch me again after the day he took me away from you.' Then her head dropped. 'But I should never have agreed to live in this house and raise our son here.'

'Why didn't you leave?' Virgilio sneered. 'You could have walked out anytime you wanted.' Something about him reminded me of my brother, Michael, when he used to taunt me. It struck me that he was almost the same age as Michael had been the last time I had seen him.

'I stayed for you, Virgilio. For you! To give you all this.' Carla waved her arm around the room. 'Would you rather we had begged beside a road!'

I touched her shoulder gently. 'We must leave.' Carla leaned her face down to rest her cheek on my hand, and I felt the world come alive again.

Virgilio was staring at me now. He looked lost, as if his world had collapsed.

Carla rose and went to her writing desk. She threw some keys at me.

'My car is in the garage. Take Virgilio and bring it round the front.'

'Where are you going?' Having just found her after nineteen years apart, I had a moment of panic at the thought of even a momentary separation.

'I'll join you in a few minutes. I have something to do.'

I nodded and looked at Virgilio. He seemed calmer, or perhaps just numb with confusion and shock. I took one last look at Brio and barely recognised my old friend. His face was already grey with death and his open, blood-caked mouth looked like a portal to hell. Virgilio was also staring at his Papa's face and had begun to shake. I had to get him out of the house.

'C'mon,' I said, lifting him by the elbows. 'Let's go.'

*

Carla was as good as her word. We had not waited long on the driveway when she appeared from the house, dressed more comfortably in slacks and a cardigan, and carrying her old portmanteau. She got in the back with her son, and I saw her cuddle him to her and slip something in his mouth, which he swallowed compliantly. She clearly had no plan beyond getting out of the house, with whatever was in the bag, after whatever she had felt compelled to do. Our destination was up to me.

'How do I get onto the road to Naples from here?'

'Turn left out the drive and follow the road down the hill to Frascati. There will be signs from there.'

I pulled away and noticed a strong smell of whiskey from the back seat. It could have come from my earlier bottle, but it was intense and seemed to be coming from Carla herself. Perhaps she had needed something to fortify her, or perhaps she had brought a bottle to sedate Virgilio. I didn't ask. A few minutes later, we turned a hairpin bend and were facing almost back in the direction we had come from. An orange glow rose from where I estimated the villa should be. A few seconds later an unmistakable tongue of fire flickered in the forest. I caught Carla's eye in the rear-view mirror and the stench of whiskey now made sense.

'I wanted him to burn in hell,' she said. 'But that was the best I could do.'

EPILOGUE

For a long while on the drive to Naples we were silent. There was so much to say, so many years of absence to fill, that I didn't know where to start. Eventually, Carla told me that Virgilio was asleep. She had given him a sleeping pill, and I saw that his head was resting on her lap like a small boy exhausted after a long day at the seaside.

'Where have you been, Abercrombie?' Her tone was soft but held a note of reproach. In the darkness of the car, with the endless empty road, I now couldn't even see Carla's eyes when I looked in the mirror. It felt like I was in a confessional.

'I looked for you. I looked for a long time,' I replied. 'I went to Brio's flat in Rome. I knew you had been there, but Brio told me you had gone. He told me you thought I was dead.'

'I did, although a small part of me never quite believed it.'

'I went to Milan,' I continued, 'and back to Paestum, and Rome again, and Milan again. I looked for you for years but could find no trace. I followed Brio several times, but he never led me to you. And then, I'm ashamed to say, I gave up. After many years went by, I even thought that perhaps you might prefer to be left unfound, even if you knew I was still alive.'

Carla did not respond immediately.

'How could you think that?'

I felt ashamed of my inconstancy.

'I looked for you, too. Until I knew, or believed, you were dead. It was . . . the most horrible day. I saw it in a newspaper, in Liverpool.'

'You went to Liverpool?'

'I went to a lot of places looking for you. I spoke to all your old neighbours . . . and Mr. Tyrer.'

'You spoke to Tyrer?'

'Yes. I stayed with him, for a short while.'

'Why?'

After a pause, Carla said. 'Because he was your father. Did you never suspect it?'

'Actually, I didn't. Not in Paestum. But I've known for many years now.'

'I thought he might have had some contact with you. I was desperate.'

Carla's visit to Liverpool. Her journal, found by Virgilio and no doubt given to Brio. My son watching me in Naples and reporting my movements back to Brio. I didn't quite have all the pieces of the puzzle yet, but I had enough to guess how *The Life and Death of Abercrombie Lyle* may have come about – how it could have contained so much detail about my past before Milan and such intimate knowledge of my life in Naples. I had no energy, or desire, to imagine the missing pieces right now, nor to probe her further on her search for me. I had a deep sense of guilt that I had given up on her, even though I had devoted so many years to the quest. I lapsed into silence and tried not to think about the last few days.

We drove on into the night and toward an uncertain future, the possibilities and dangers of which were almost too much for my tired soul to contemplate. What awaited us in Naples? A door shut in our faces by my old friend Pietro, who I hadn't seen since Price had left for England before the war? The Carabinieri searching for us across the city? Or Brio's men in dark suits with vengeance in their hearts and guns in their hands? Long days cowering in a scorching attic until the inevitable tip off did for us? Perhaps, if we were lucky, Pietro would smuggle us on board a ship to America or Ireland, where we could build a new future. Part of me wanted to keep driving south for a swansong in Paestum. Returning to our old life, even for a few days, would be a bliss I had never thought possible. Although I knew that if we did, a new set of dust clouds would approach along the road from Salerno to carry us away at some point.

I hoped that dawn would never come, for everything I wanted in the world, everything I needed, was safe and unseen in this car. I savoured the quiet growl of our tyres on the road and the soft snoring of my son. I decided not to think of the day ahead. I tried not to think at all. We passed through a village with a single streetlamp alight in the centre of a small piazza. I stopped the car under it and looked at my son in the rear-view mirror, his head cradled on Carla's lap. She had been silent for a long time, and I thought she might be sleeping, too. But her eyes were fixed on mine, and she was smiling. All the chaos of the last few days, and all the pain of the years before, were silenced in that gaze. I knew that dawn must come, with light that would bring shape to our future and cast shadows upon it. But for now, the night was a blank canvas that could be illuminated with any future I chose. In that moment, I was content with the possibilities it held.

ACKNOWLEDGEMENTS

I would like to thank my wife, Millicent, my children, Hillary and Bertie, and my brother, Andrew, for indulging my interest in Italian history and enduring many holiday detours while I 'popped my head' down an interesting street or into an old church.

I would also like to thank the writers, editors and beta readers who read drafts or offered invaluable guidance, especially Karen Kendrick, James Aitcheson, Steve Connor, Kath Buckley, Liz Hedgecock, Chris Vick and Sara Hunt, but there are many others. Thank you all for your support.

Finally, thank you to the friends who listened patiently to my political and historical ramblings as the book evolved. A novel may have only one writer, but there are many who contribute, whether they realise it or not. Any errors, of course, are all mine.

AFTERWORD

This book emerged from three sources: a fascinating tour of Italy in 2022 (and subsequent trips); an idea that popped into my head during a creative writing exercise (Abercrombie finding the book bearing his name on the unlit pyre); and my concerns over the rise of neo-fascist, authoritarian leaders in countries that should know better, which sent me back to interwar Italy to understand one of their influential role models. Mussolini plays only a bit part in the novel, but his shadow lurks throughout, as I believe it now does for us all.

Stephen Small has a DPhil in Modern History and a BA (Hons) in Philosophy, Politics & Economics from Oxford University, and an MA in History from the University of Michigan. He has taught history and political thought in several US and UK universities, including UC Berkeley, Boston College, San Francisco State University and St. Mary's University Twickenham. He has written fiction and non-fiction for many years alongside careers in academia, book publishing, communications and consulting. Originally a native of Liverpool, Stephen now lives in nearby Warrington with his wife, Millicent, and their dog, Sebastian. This is his first novel.

www.stephensmall.co.uk

Printed in Dunstable, United Kingdom

This is for everyone who r up, to persist as your true self, always growing and never quitting, to finally become who you are meant to be.

This is also for anyone who has ever faced grief, and they had to find the people, the methods, and determination to make it through. But know this: we will make it and it can strengthen us, especially when we persist and find those who love us, and we can always do what we believe to be just, even if the world tries to pull us into the dark.

The strongest light always shines brightest in the blackest dark. Choose your next chapter for yourself. Be bright. Never fade. Be golden. If nothing else, escape to a magical world in these words. Then keep going. I'm with you. So are all these characters.

Ve harron!

THE NEXT
GOLDLIGHTER

This is a work of fiction. All characters, places, names, and concepts herein are either a work of the author's imagination or used fictitiously.

No part of this work may be reproduced, altered, or sold in any form or by any means, mechanical or electronic, without prior written permission from the author.

The Next Goldlighter

Text copyright ©2025 R. Cozander.
Characters, names, and all other intellectual property copyright ©2024 R. Cozander and Cozander Creative. All rights reserved.

A WORLD AWAY

"My king," said the man in a brown, hooded cloak. He kept his face concealed by the hood, even as he took a bow toward the armored man seated on a white marble throne. "The golden Keeper, Samuel Narion, is dead." His voice was timid and low, though he enunciated.

"Heran," said the man in gold plate armor embossed with a lion's head. His deep voice projected throughout the stone-walled space, as if he spoke to a full audience instead of one man. "You are certain of his death?"

"It has been confirmed by multiple sources, Majesty... including the nuisance who also plans to take the weapon for himself. He sent out a hunting party of Shirrkki."

The king chuckled. "He is nothing to us unless he acquires the weapon. Send them. They will arrive well before his forces manage anything significant, I'm sure. Even if he were to arrive first, our plans and resources exceed his in every way. I will have it."

"What of the boy who is next in line as Keeper?"

"You told me your sources place him out of our realm, in a place without our magic. He is barely of age, and he will not have learned anything of its real power beyond what seems like stories when it cannot be demonstrated."

"That is what I expect as well." Heran tapped his foot for a moment. "What is *their* goal?"

"They must *not* kill the boy until after he is brought here."

The king stood from his white throne and stepped down to Heran's level. The lion of a man's yellow eyes pierced through Heran as he stared down at the smaller hooded advisor. "Lure him here, to our realm. After the weapon is within our reach, without the possibility of floating between realms if he dies, retrieve it, or get him to come to us. That sphere is our top priority. If there are any mistakes, I will hold you accountable and will kill your creatures myself, no matter how useful they have become."

"You have your mission, then." Heran glanced to the doorway to the hall on his right where two tall silhouettes with orange eyes stood concealed by the shadows. "Use what is necessary to ensure the boy is in our realm with the sphere first, then to take it or bring him here."

"Correct." The king nodded once. "But keep to minimal citizenry losses where possible." He jabbed a finger toward the same doorway where the orange-eyed creatures waited, before turning back to Heran. "I do need a kingdom to rule. Now send them off to do their work. I have another matter to attend to; and *he* will want this news."

Heran gave a theatrical bow at the waist, straightened, then delivered a sharp wave to the eyes in the shadows. After the creatures hissed a "yes, sir", Heran uttered a strange word to produce a transparent gaseous disk. A clawed hand reached out to grab the disk as it floated to the figures. Then the two tall silhouettes moved from their place in the darkness to leave the palace in a blur of black and faded green.

The king walked out of the throne room and down a spiral staircase, across the courtyard, and into an adjacent tower of the palace. He entered through two twenty-foot polished white-wood doors into a room with a massive glossy black shard levitating in the center. The front was smooth, flat, similar in appearance to a fifteen-foot high mirror broken from its frame, but not made of the usual material, more like a polished black crystal so the reflections were shadows of the true images. The dark surface moved in ripples like black oil as the king got closer.

"Well?" came a deep voice from the black ripples. It reverberated and, while it was not a yell in volume, it filled the entire empty space with anger and hatred. The king halted his steps as it spoke.

"Samuel Narion, the golden Keeper, is dead," said the king. "My right hand sent the hunters and provided them with means to travel between realms temporarily."

"Then it is nearly time for my return," said the harsh, echoing voice. "We will begin the next phase. And you will be far more useful now than ever."

The king attempted to speak, but he was paralyzed, his eyes filled with gray, and he uttered, "Very well, Master. Thank you for this power." He could move again after a moment and took a knee, head bowed to the rippling black shard.

"*Finally*," the voice growled with venomous satisfaction.

1

Not being aware can cause problems, especially when coveted magic is involved. At times, tragedy just happens anyway, and all one can do is respond. How it shapes someone is the question: what kind of person do they want to be? What actions would define them when the choice of their response is in their own hands?

Opren Saphren discovered these notions when he transcended from a small-town butcher's son with no knowledge of real magic, to something beyond a natural human, all due to the possession of a small artifact that, unbeknownst to him, held otherworldly magic. Even just a day before his change began, his only pressing concern was his opponent for an unsanctioned kickboxing match as he earned experience prior to attempting a professional path in mixed martial arts. He knew nothing of what occurred a world away, nor his potential fate, only that a fist was about to collide with his head.

Opren stepped left to dodge the right hook, moving completely to his opponent's right side, toward the ropes of the boxing ring. The other man swore. *He caught me but knows what my stance switch means.* At the current angle, his opponent was completely vulnerable to his strikes. He delivered two heavy punches into the other's ribs, then saw his opportunity and took it, exhaling sharply as he hit his shaken and unguarded opponent in the face to knock him down.

It was five minutes into the kickboxing match and the other young man did not get up during the count to ten. After a moment, his opponent regained the ability to sit up and Opren approached him.

"Are you good?" Opren extended a hand to help the black-haired man to his feet. The other took his hand and stood, clearly still hazy and off-balance, but he seemed coherent enough to speak.

"Good as I can be," the man replied between breaths as he rubbed his jaw. "You are really good. What's your name?"

"Opren. And before you ask, I don't know where it comes from either." He gave a half-smile.

"Jerry. Not quite as interesting as your name, but I do know where it's from." Jerry breathed deeply and blinked to recover his senses.

Opren laughed. He invited Jerry to have coffee with him as they exited the ring and offered to buy to make amends for the bruises he caused. Jerry accepted. After they both changed in a locker room attached to the warehouse where the fight took place, Opren cashed out his winnings. Then the two met at a café called *Coffeefull* a few places down the street.

"Even though we hadn't met til today, I recalled seeing your name before," said Jerry when they were settled at a two-seater table. "I thought I could take you when I saw you in your corner, before I knew you're the one beating the hell out of everyone locally. How many wins in a row is that now?"

"Fourteen." Opren almost grimaced while trying to smile. "I'm not trying to be noticed for it, yet, but you're the second person this week to recognize my name. I thought joining the fights without an announcement of the participants would stop that, but winners still get posted."

"It is easy to pick out from a group," said Jerry with a shrug.

"Maybe I should change my name to John. That's common," said Opren, and Jerry chuckled. "I enter the underground matches for experience prior to going pro and having a noted record, and I preferred the initial anonymity. I guess that's no longer possible."

"Not really. Even with unofficial stuff, sometimes especially, that kind of record still speaks for you, John or Opren. You just need to stop winning."

"It's just great how working hard to be good at some things ends up earning dislike from others."

"Seems backwards, huh?"

Opren nodded. "Thanks for choosing coffee over spite, even right after the result of our match. It's good to know someone who can win or lose without it affecting their respect for someone."

"You too, Opren. You could have just gloated and left me there."

"My mother would have knocked me out instead if she heard I had done that." Both laughed.

After coffee, they said their farewells, added "good luck in other matches", and Opren returned to his parents' house: a small single-story with stained-wood outer walls and a charcoal roof, a rustic interior, and a front and back porch, designed amongst several trees by his late grandfather to look like a cabin combined with a modern home. It fit well in their small-town area of the North Carolina mountains.

As he walked up, his mother was sweeping pine needles off the porch. She looked up and smiled.

Loria Saphren was a rather short and slender woman with shoulder-length light brown hair. Her smile always radiated throughout a room, and her voice and blue eyes were more powerful than her size suggested she could be. She could give him one look that would stop him in his tracks, or she could say something to comfort him quickly. Even though he was grown now, half a foot taller than she was, she could still have the same effect.

"Welcome back," said his mother, standing straight and halting her sweeping. "How did it go?"

"Two rounds. I won in about five minutes. His name was Jerry and we got coffee afterward. He was a much better loser than the guy last week who ran out yelling."

"The one you told me broke a chair against the wall?" She rolled her eyes.

"Yeah, him." Opren laughed.

"I'm glad people like Jerry are in this sport too, but the man who stormed out is proof of why I wish you would stop fighting people in underground matches. You work enough with your father to pay fees for better matches and a real gym membership by now, even if we have to take you to one of the bigger areas for a good one. Why not get started on your next steps? You know you have the talent."

"We have already talked about this," said Opren. "I use what money I feel like on the gear and membership for the wooden weapons tournaments, and I want a certain level of real experience before I have an official record in MMA. It'll help my career start better. Kickboxing or MMA is easier to find, especially since there is not much in this area as it is, and underground bets can help earn extra money, instead of just paying it. I've learned more by fighting people from other backgrounds. Without restrictions, people can do more interesting things."

"You say that like it is a good aspect, but that is what concerns me. Some of those matches might not even be legal, and the betting certainly is not, so be careful. I am glad you continue to win, though. Congratulations on your... fourteenth, isn't it?"

"Yeah." He nodded. She always kept track and the recognition from her meant more than the public every time. "My goal is twenty in a row before moving to official stuff, but I'm starting to worry about ruining my chance to make fight friends with how much my name is going around the community as someone who never loses. I think I'm making social enemies without the publicity a pro might get from that. But I guess I have to get used to it once I enter the bigger stuff. Some professionals have plenty of haters."

"While I don't like the underground fighting, as in *any* sport or competition, it is not your fault they haven't practiced as hard as you do," she said. "Whoever works hardest deserves to win. I know many of those men only use their natural brute strength and that's why they can't participate in the official events, due to lack of skill. Besides, you aren't taking away from their wins by winning yourself, unless they lose to you. Everyone else is just being negative for no reason."

"I guess you're right."

"I know I am." She smiled and he couldn't help but return a smile. "There is stew inside with some of the meat from the shop as well as the last of the meat from you hunting with your father. He should be home in a half hour, and we will eat then."

"Sounds good! I'll wash up while waiting."

After Opren showered, he relaxed in his room until his father returned from the butcher's shop and deli he owned in town. He lay on his bed as he looked at a picture of himself, his father, Beram, and his maternal grandfather, Samuel. They were all smiling while they stood in front of a lake, with Opren to Beram's left, Grandfather Sam to Beram's right. Beram's broad-shouldered, six-foot-two figure made younger Opren and even Samuel look smaller. Opren had Beram's brown eyes and dark brown hair, so he was much like a miniature version of his father in the picture. Grown, he had reached an average 5' 10" and his face took on a bit of his mother's features as well, but he did have the broader shoulders of his father for his own frame, if not the bulk and height.

He set down the picture and picked up a piece of parchment-style paper with the title: The Last Will and Testament of Samuel Narion– Imitation Print for Opren Saphren. He read it for the eighth time in two weeks:

To my grandson, Opren Saphren, I leave my golden orb. I regret to be dead before your birthday to adulthood in Elven eyes, but in time you will learn the truth as I did. I hope it shines for you when things seem darkest. Care for it well until you find its purpose, and your own.

With love,

Grandfather Sam

It was not the original page— the original had been safely stored— but with or without his grandfather's handwriting in green ink, on the imitation parchment or the true parchment on which his grandfather had written his full will, it remained equally appreciated and confusing.

The essentials made sense: he had inherited the family artifact, a plum-sized golden sphere, and his grandfather intended to give it to him for a specific birthday. But the details were cloudy, especially anything to do with what the sphere was or did or required.

Despite eight readings he still felt like he missed something right in front of him. He looked over at the golden sphere on his nightstand. It was the same as he remembered from all the years he had seen it while it still belonged to Grandfather Sam, always the same in the same spot, now on his own nightstand when he went to fight or sleep. It was just sitting there, smooth and golden—but not real gold as far as he knew—and it had no purpose aside from being a special decoration. It was surely sentimental to the family, but it was not a practical object for anything.

And yet… he felt something he could not place whenever he was near the sphere or focused on it, as he felt then while he stared at it. It felt almost like the orb was alive.

The weirdest part of his grandfather's words, even in the parts to his parents or other family or friends, was the mention of "adulthood in Elven eyes". It was the only part of the will that seemed out of place in a formal document. Then again,

Grandfather Sam had an odd sense of humor sometimes.

Maybe he was being funny because of what I like to read. But I've never read about Elven adulthood specifically. What age even is that?

The front door opened to indicate his father had come home, so he stuck the sphere into its soft leather carrying pouch and tied the pouch to his beltloop, then went into the kitchen.

"Hello, Opren! How'd your fight go?" asked his father in his loud voice.

"I won in about five minutes. And he was actually a good opponent and sportsman-like loser. We got coffee after."

"Not as fun as Mr. Chair, huh?" said his father with a chuckle.

He laughed too. "No, not fun like that."

Opren and his parents sat down at their four-seat round table for dinner. His mother had his father and him pass her their bowls so she could ladle out the beef, venison, and vegetable stew to each of them, then herself. All served, they bowed their heads and said grace.

"Are you working tomorrow?" asked his father as they ate.

"I should be asking if you need me to come in. I've already had two days off."

"Well, it's your birthday, so I figured I'd give you a choice. I'll be there until the afternoon, but not too late since it is a Saturday."

"Turning twenty doesn't have much to do. Not like twenty-one. I'll work for a few hours if you will spar with me afterward. I have a weapons tournament in a week. I haven't been getting ready with weapons since I've had multiple MMA-related matches this month."

"You could be focusing on the bigger weapons stuff," said his mother. "You have chosen to sign up for the underground matches and put off other practice."

"She ha' a goo' poind," said his father, mouth full. His

mother shot over a piercing look. His father swallowed and apologized. "She has a good point, Opren. But I will help you practice, whenever I'm not too tired. You just need to bring another deer for home, if you *really* want to help, then come check in at the shop."

"All right, will do. This is delicious, by the way, Mom."

"Thank you," said his mother. "It helps you all provided the quality meat. You make a good team."

Opren practiced some swings and stances with his wooden sword, mostly in Japanese styles, and did bodyweight exercises for about an hour after dinner. Toward the end of his practice, as he pushed himself, he thought he saw a flash come from the pouch tied to his belt loop. He checked on the sphere and it was normal. It was likely just the way the light hit it or his imagination. He was growing worn down from all the physical activity anyway, so he went inside to read until it was time to sleep.

He woke before the sun rose so he could prepare to hunt. He gathered what he would need, packed it in his brown camouflage backpack, and tied the pouch with the golden sphere to his beltloop for luck. He finished breakfast around the same time as the sunrise began.

As Opren left the house with his parents still asleep, the sun started to reveal itself with golds and pastels to break the lingering midnight blue. He preferred to sleep until later, but the sunrise was always worth it in the mountains. The distant skyline of trees and hills was lit with a golden silhouette around the blues of mountains in the distance, while some of the sight was pastel purple at the point where the glow met the mountaintops and faded into the darker parts of the sky.

He slung his pack onto his back, and he grabbed their hunting bow from a closet on the outside of the house before leaving the yard. It was a good morning to hunt silently, rather than with a gun. One of his trainers had told him to use a bow whenever he could to help teach himself patience and precision because "not all fights are won by force alone".

Generally, he felt force with technique was the deciding factor for knocking out someone, but he listened to the "homework assignment" anyway, as it couldn't hurt to see what the experience taught him.

His family lived so near to the forest he never felt the need to take a vehicle, so he just walked to the gathering of trees, then hiked through the trails awhile, until he found one of the usual spots to wait for deer. He set his backpack against a tree, climbed into the tree stand his father had set up a few months before, and waited, scanning the area with his eyes.

It took about two hours to find a deer and manage to take it down, but he returned just as his father was preparing to go to the butcher's shop. The only problem was he had not thought to bring what he needed to get the deer back to the shop for cleaning or the house properly. His father let him use the pick-up truck to make it much easier, and the two of them rode to the spot where the deer had fallen. It took minimal effort with his father helping to get the deer into the truck-bed.

"Did you dye your hair last night?" asked his father as they drove to the shop.

"No." Opren raised an eyebrow. He had only washed his hair as usual.

"Looks lighter than it was at dinner. Or it could just be because I'm still not awake enou—" His father yawned loudly. "Gotta get coffee when we get to the shop."

Opren looked in the side mirror of the truck and it did appear he had highlights in his hair. It was like when people stay awhile in Florida or California, or anywhere with a lot of sunlight hitting their hair and causing it to go from natural brown to lighter. But that did not happen in just one day.

"Maybe." He was unsure of what to say otherwise.

Opren and his father spent the morning cleaning the deer, then chopping and slicing it, before they moved on to some beef. They set out the best beef pieces in the display case, kept two chunks for home, and then Opren made labels for the display as his father prepped and wrapped the several cuts of deer for Opren to take home. Depending on the grade of meat and type of meat, he priced things accordingly. A majority of the case held different grades of beef, with some pork, lamb, or deli meats thrown in, and everything was top quality, even the less expensive grades.

His father never sold the really cheap stuff. He donated any meat he did not intend to use to animal shelters or facilities that produced healthy animal food. It was Opren's job to take the leftovers to those places on weekdays, but they were closed on Saturday. Without the extra runs to make, he finished his tasks around noon.

He received permission from his father to leave, and he cleaned his hands and threw his apron into the designated basket. He reminded his father of the need to spar when finished as he picked up the packages of venison to bring home.

"Thumbs up," expressed his father verbally, hands still covered in raw meat as he continued to remove the less-edible parts of some beef.

Opren walked home, meat in his backpack, as it was only a mile away from the shop. A great thing about a small town was how easily everything could be reached and experienced. The mutually positive and negative thing was everyone knew everything about everyone, or so it seemed, especially if one owned a business. This was pleasant as he could greet familiar faces on his way home, but then a woman he had known since he was five took note of something for which he had no response.

"Good afternoon, Opren," she said with a grin. But her expression turned to concern, and that's when it was clear it was not just his father being sleepy when he thought his hair was different. "Are you feeling all right? Your eyes look strange."

"Hi, Mrs. Greene. I feel great, yeah. Just got off work at the shop. What do you mean?"

"Well, children are known to sometimes have different

eyes at birth than when they are older, or hair too," she replied. "But your eyes have always been brown, the easiest color to be dominant in people's genes. Now, your eyes look like two different colors. One is more like it has amber or something in it, like a golden dog's eye. The other is still brown. Are you sure you are not allergic to something you ate?"

"Do allergies affect eye colors?" His adrenaline rose a bit. Was something wrong with him?

"I'm not sure. But if you feel all right, I suppose I won't worry. Have your mother check or see a doctor if you feel strange, though."

"I will. Have a great day, Mrs. Greene."

"You too, Opren," she said with a smile, as he stepped past her to continue home.

What is going on with me? He increased his pace toward home, determined to check on his appearance before anyone else could see him.

When he reached the house, he immediately went to the bathroom to look in the mirror. His eyes were not quite the way Mrs. Greene had described them, but they were certainly not his normal brown. The outer and inner circles of his irises were golden, causing an amber look to the whole as she had mentioned about his one eye, and when he got close to the mirror he could see flecks of gold between the rings. They were both brown in the majority from a distance, just not as dark. But the sudden appearance of *gold* in his eyes was different from a change to hazel or a person with one blue eye and one green eye from birth.

That was when he felt soft vibrations coming from the golden sphere in its pouch, still tied to his belt loop. He pulled it out and it was glowing softly. He saw nothing but a flash of light for a moment, then it was dark and he felt a rush as if he crested a hill at top speed on a bike. He was no longer sure what he was looking at when he could see again, and he felt heat throughout his body similarly to if someone were pouring warm water over him.

2

Opren stood in a moonlit forest, grasping the golden sphere in his right hand. The sphere released wisps of golden energy, like light fused with smoke, that seeped between his slightly apart fingers.

He was simultaneously certain he had never been there and sure he knew of it, but his head was buzzing and trying to figure out which thought was correct seemed like a low priority. Instead, he looked at the hairy, stocky-yet-six-feet-tall beast-man holding a battle-ax right in front of him. He was breathing heavily, as was the beast-man.

"Are we done?" His voice came out with a force unlike his usual inflection. He wasn't angry, but the voice was firm, commanding.

The words just came out, as if he spoke in a dream but did not actually think the words first, and it was only then he consciously noted they had been fighting. How had he been in a fight with someone so big and not been aware of it? And this beast-man was clearly not even Human. That should make it even easier to recall! How much time had passed? And how was he not dead?

The beast-man laugh-growled. "You make good warrior, shiny boy. Join Shirrkki as ally. We take shiny ball, you make captain."

"I have no interest in being part of your war-band." He held the Shirrkki's gaze as he continued to speak in that other voice. How did he know this "Shirrkki" came from a war group? But he did know without any memory of learning it. "And this ball is a family artifact I won't give away."

When he glanced down as he said "this ball", he realized it was not just the sphere releasing golden light, but his entire body lit the area as well. He emitted a golden energy, which must have been the reason he felt warmth pulsing through him, whatever the energy was and was doing.

"Then we not done!"

The growling voice should have startled him, but he felt unaffected by it, except it gave him a reason to meet the eyes of the Shirrkki with his own again. The time between the Shirrkki speaking and their eyes meeting again seemed slower than it should have felt. His senses were strange, as if they were on high alert to everything and toughened at the same time. Emotions were stable yet sharp, and he felt a drive like any time he was having a great fight, but even more than that. Observations were many in a blink. What normally could have taken a half a minute to analyze took a second or two. Even these observations happened in such a manner he had time to note his hairy opponent's next move.

The Shirrkki lunged, but he moved effortlessly around the beast-man's broad back, causing the Shirrkki's fur to move from the wind of his motion, and the orb changed into a golden longsword. He stabbed the Shirrkki through the ribs on the beast-man's right side, removed the sword, and took a single step away as blood soaked the other's brown fur.

He staggered as the strange energy around him faded and the sword became a solid golden sphere, without any hint of the wisps of light seeping from it a moment ago. He coughed and sweat ran down his face. He staggered again... and all went black as he felt himself fall into a tree...

Opren woke in his own bed in his parents' house. He had the words "Rure Forest" and "Shirrkki" in his mind, along with some word that sounded a bit like "walrus", but it must have been gibberish of a word he couldn't quite recall. The golden sphere was on his nightstand, as he always kept it when he slept, along with the copy of the message from Grandfather Sam's will. He was no longer sweating, but he trembled for a moment as he sat up. He was also no longer wearing a shirt or pants, only undershorts.

He stared at the sphere, thinking about what he could recall of the night's events. Was it just a dream? The sphere was just sitting there in the same spot as always, without any indication of light coming from it, despite the images that flashed through his mind. He must have been reading too many fantasy and epic novels lately to conjure such a thing as the so-called "Shirrkki"–those beastly man-creatures had referred to themselves that way, but it must have been his imagination, based on fictional talking apes or the fairy tale about the girl and the beast in a castle or something. He would just need to work off the strange thoughts.

"What happened, Opren?" his mother's voice broke his trance. She must have been waiting for him to wake because she was at the foot of his bed as she spoke. Her tone held a lot of worry with a little curiosity.

"I had an odd dream...it must have been a dream... I caused something to happen with the orb Grandfather Sam gave to me. There were creatures..."

"Something of what nature? Are you all right now? You have slept for over a day!" spat his mother without a breath.

"Mom, please slow down." He rubbed his temples and blinked three times. "I can only answer one thing at a time, and I just woke up and feel lightheaded like I was sick or knocked out. I'm all right now otherwise, just need to eat." He furrowed his brow as what she said hit him. "I slept for over a day?"

His mother nodded. She took a deep breath before

speaking and said, slower, "Yes, you slept for over a day. I have some soup for you already prepared. I thought you might have a virus, but the nurse I had look at you said you are perfectly all right other than sleeping for too long and a large shoulder bruise, but the bruise is normal like when you fall in your fights. Now what 'something' happened?"

"I'm not entirely sure." He still needed to figure it all out himself, let alone describe it to someone else. His mother pursed her lips as if she disliked the answer. "I think it had, uh, magic. It gave me... power of some sort..." As he trailed off, his jaw tightened and his breathing quickened a bit when he recalled falling into a tree as he fell unconscious. If he had a large bruise without explanation...

So it was not a dream, after all? Then how?!

"Well..." His mother took a long breath and looked out the window. She turned back to him. "What did it cause when you used the power?"

He was taken aback at how genuinely curious and accepting of his story she was, but he wanted her help to sort his thoughts. He continued as he thought through what he could recall as hard as he could:

"I remember flashes of light... and my voice changed. I spoke without meaning to, as if it wasn't me thinking the words I said. It used me more than I used it, or something like that. There was a sword... and Shirrkki– they were these tall beast-men of a sort, like the brutish barbarians in novels and fairy tales, but they looked like animals, like the Minotaur in epics is both man and beast. I killed one, I think. I don't know how I got back..." He trailed off again as he concentrated, trying to think of ways he might have returned to the house if it were somehow real.

"I cannot tell you any more than that, either," said his mother. "I found you in bed already, but you were soaked with sweat and breathing as if you had just finished a fight, despite being unconscious for who knows how long? I was extremely worried until the nurse examined you."

"You still sound worried," he teased with a slight grin. "Although you are taking the weird stuff really well."

"Well, yes, I am still a bit worried! I already worry you will come home with something broken or bleeding when you have sanctioned combat matches, but you were unconscious without an identifiable cause for nearly two days!" She took a long breath and released it at once. "But I am glad to see you are now awake and seem to still be in a good mental state, considering you still like to make light of things that are dangerous." She rolled her eyes and folded her arms.

"It makes pain or tough moments better." He shrugged.

"Go ahead and enjoy the soup in the kitchen for lunch. I told your father you would not be working when you first wake. Just relax."

"I really think I will be fine once I eat and move around a bit, so–"

"No," she interjected. "He agreed with me, so no competition practice or shop work until tomorrow."

Opren reluctantly consented, climbed out of bed and pulled on new pants and a shirt– his mother or the nurse must have removed the ones he had on for his inspection. He placed the golden orb into its leather carrying pouch and tied the string to his belt loop.

"Do you think it is possible this was not just a dream?" he asked. "You don't seem to be entertained or confused by what I said. And I have a new bruise, which would have come from the tree I fell into before I passed out."

She stood silently for a moment, apparently gathering her thoughts. What she said brought no more clarity, but it still seemed like a sort of confirmation.

"You might find fewer things surprise you now that you are twenty, especially in years to come. But you also must discover your own purpose, your own knowledge, through your own experiences. If I give you too much of my perspective too soon, you might be unprepared. Please be alert and cautious as often as you can. It might also be best not to mention these events to anyone else, as a dream or not."

His mother exited the bedroom with an expression that surely included concern, but he could not place the remaining emotion.

Opren spent three hours searching through five books he owned: two from his school days about true history, one book about mythical history, one book about family trees to yet again try to find his name, and a storybook based on the legendary life and adventures of Polaris, a white wizard who would show up with magical knowledge just when others needed him. The information in his books was no help except to confirm the sphere must have a magical property of some sort, and it was likely old, like many enchanted artifacts from lore.

But magic did not exist, right? It was weird to even consider it, as he had learned to catch enough magicians and people who allegedly used witchcraft, in his town and elsewhere. They were really just strange people who did not know how to be a real Wiccan or crazy folks, so they either conned people or practiced weird, uneducated occult rituals. One of them had gotten arrested and everyone talked about it the next day. If magic existed in his town, he and everyone else should certainly know by now. His father heard about everything in the shop.

"Without magic as an explanation, I have nothing to describe what happened," he thought aloud, closing the last book with a thud in frustration.

He went into the kitchen to ask when dinner would be ready, and his parents were talking—well, whispering— in a tense way.

"I have to share what I know with him now," said his mother. It was almost like a yelling whisper due to her emphatic tone.

"I know," said his father softly. "But were we not going to keep him from that path?"

"I know it was my decision, but I knew when my father

gave him that–"

His mother immediately stopped speaking and both his parents turned toward him as he entered the kitchen fully. She pursed her lips and closed her eyes. When she opened her eyes, she spoke.

"What did you hear?"

"Enough to know I have to be right. The events that caused me to end up in bed for so long were real, right?"

"Yes." His mother nodded. She took a seat at the kitchen table and he followed suit, while his father turned toward them silently. She sighed. "And despite what I said earlier, I have concluded I must tell you more of what I know."

"This has to do with Grandfather Sam's golden orb, right?"

"It does," she confirmed. "What you experienced was the first time its magic imbued you with power and–"

"It *is* magic!" He stood with a jolt. "I assumed magic couldn't exist, but I found no other explanation!"

"Yes. Now please sit and let me finish," said his mother. He sat again, and she placed a hand on his forearm. "I know this is tough for someone to take in after knowing nothing about it."

"I know that myself," said his father. "Although, you'll learn I was a bit less unaware than you."

"It is more bizarre and exciting, but not really tough to hear. Like a new world has opened to me."

"It's funny you say it that way, because that is exactly one of the things that has happened," said his mother. "You were not here in our forest or our town for any of the events you recall, right?" Opren nodded. "The magic in the sphere originated somewhere else, in a different version of the world. The land is called Everniot."

"So magic comes from a place called Everniot?" asked Opren.

His mother shook her head. "This particular type of magic seems to, but there is hidden magic and less powerful forms of elemental magic even in this world you would consider the 'normal' world. The most powerful source of magic I know of is either the world with Everniot or the supernatural realm. I don't know what kind of magic the orb contains, but I know it is old and special to our family line."

"*That's* why the orb was so important to Grandfather Sam. So can you do magic?"

"Not much," she said. "Nothing here, and I was never able to wield anything like the orb and its sword. That is something Grandfather Sam had to pass down to a son or grandson in the line. I could have used it if he chose me, but there is something about it that links more powerfully with a man when they reach Elven adulthood. There is other magic that acts the same for women, or for adults instead of children, or children more than adults."

"Elven adulthood…" he recalled the words from his grandfather's will.

"You just turned twenty," said his father. "That's what elves consider to be of age."

"So elves are also real. Why didn't Grandfather Sam just say that?"

"I assume he wanted you to start to seek the answers and ask us," said his mother. "He always did like to do that sort of thing. You remember all his riddles and subtle humor. Well, my original intention was to keep you in the dark about this so you would be safer. The problem is, you were passed the orb at just the right time and its magic can only be controlled by the one who it bonds to as they come of age. So without you being able to control it, it was sure to change you eventually. I just didn't realize it would pull you to Everniot as soon as you discovered the magic. I also had no idea Shirrkki would be there waiting to hunt you. It never did that for my father, but he knew how to control it and we had another limited means of travel to get here. I wasn't even sure the magic in it could do that."

"Have you been there?"

"Everniot is where we are *from*, Opren."

"Wait what?! How have I never known?"

"Your father and I thought if we shared our past with you, you might use your natural need to satisfy curiosity and cause the sphere to activate as a child or teenager. Without your bond to the sphere, the Shirrkki would have killed you as an adult. Think what could have happened as a child if something accidentally occurred. It was too unpredictable."

"But why didn't you tell me once I grew up? Or even a couple weeks ago when I received the sphere? Or what if Grandfather Sam had just trained me to use the power?" He furrowed his brow. "It's not like I'm any more prepared now that this is happening compared to what I would have been then, but if you had told me as soon as the will confused me, I might have been prepared for the sudden magic enough not to feel crazy for thinking it *is* magic! I also could have tried to learn something before the magic just took control, or been ready to wield it."

"I know, and I'm sorry." On top of her tone, his mother expressed guilt with her eyes. "Unfortunately, as far as training, he was too old and the magic drained him too much here, as the energy of this world is different from Everniot. By the time I would allow it, he was dying. We did not realize he needed the magic in our world to live with his prior strength."

"Sorry for yelling." Opren sat, as he had stood again when he got upset. "So you said the sphere has a connection with me now, it has magical power it can give the user, and now my hair and eyes are changing because of that. But how do I make it bring me to the other world, Everniot, intentionally?"

"The magic we were given to bring us here to this version of the world is gone," she replied. "Grandfather Sam used it to check on the status of the other world until about two years ago. That's why we thought the Shirrkki were done searching for it. They aren't the type to look very hard for something. They're just aggressive beast-men without much up here." She tapped her head. "The magic it uses to bring you to the other world seems to be unique to you, and I don't know how to cause it for you."

"Can they get to this 'version' of the world? Why do you say it that way, 'version of the world'?"

"They can't get to this world on their own. There is a sort of barrier of existence. Everniot's world and this world are layers of the larger parts of existence, but they are ultimately both a sort of version of this planet with different names, Earth and Uundular," explained his mother. "Everniot is here by placement too, but the makeup of the land is different there, the people are different, and neither layer knows much about the other, except in unique cases. So it is the same world, a different version, but could also be called a different world. That's as much as I know about how it works. I was never a scholar."

"This *is* getting tougher to take in now," he commented, reviewing everything in his mind for a moment. After the brief pause, he concluded, "So I need to figure out how to go between here and Everniot myself at some point, because I am the only one who can really use the sphere's magic now, and the Shirrkki can't get here so we are safe. Do you think the sphere will keep pulling me to Everniot until I can control it?"

"That's very likely. And if it does, you still need to be careful of the Shirrkki," she warned. "I don't know why they are back to seeking the orb so many years later or how they could know where you shifted into Everniot, but they are dangerous despite being stupid."

"I was a soldier in my younger days in Everniot," said his father. "My four-man team had a hard time dealing with five Shirrkki. That was with full gear and weapons and training. Had they taken us by surprise, it might have been a problem."

"That's why you have no pictures from your time in the military," said Opren. "You weren't in the United States Army. You were in the army in Everniot."

"The Ra' Yana City Soldier Corps," said his father proudly. "For eight years. After I met your mother, I decided to live less intensely so I could have a child. When you were born, she realized what it meant to have a son, and she talked to me about coming here. I had never heard of the kind of magic your grandfather could do– and never saw him do it, even still, but I heard it is in legends– and I had no idea there was another world. When your mother told me, I was shocked, but it was for your safety, so I went along with it and became a regular butcher here. Learning to drive quickly enough to not be suspicious was interesting. There are no motorized cars in Everniot. But learning quickly to accomplish a mission is what a soldier does."

"I'm not sure what to feel right now, but it's like startled and excited at the same time." Opren shook his head. "I definitely want to learn more about the sphere and its magic, enough to control it. I just wish I had known all this sooner. But thank you for keeping me safe when I was little. I was born there, right? That would explain how I knew the forest, maybe."

"Yes," replied his mother. "The Rure Forest and Ravberd are as near to each other as the forest is to town here. You were only two when we left Ravberd in Everniot to come here."

"Going by TV and what you described, this seems like the two worlds mirror each other or something. Because we are in nearly an identical place as the other version."

"I think so," she said. "Maybe your books and TV shows will make everything else you discover easier to absorb too."

"For now, think about all that before we give you more," said his father. "For now, let's eat!"

"So we *can* continue later, though, if I have more questions?" He was hungry but reluctant to stop hearing about the other world and anything else he never even knew to ask.

"Absolutely," said his mother.

His father nodded.

During dinner, Opren said almost nothing. He took his father's suggestion and went over everything he recalled of the events in what turned out to be the Rure Forest in Everniot, everything his parents had shared about their past, and everything he now knew about the orb and its magic.

Despite his astonishment and curiosity, the questions he had forgotten to ask that later seemed important were *why are the Shirrkki hunting the sphere? Why were they ever hunting it or his family? Why would anyone? Who else might?*

3

A week after Opren had learned of Everniot and the reason the golden orb was special, his eyes had maintained their golden color lining the brown, his hair started to appear as light brown as his mother's, with golden strands here and there, and his energy levels were constantly high.

He began to tell people he had dyed his hair when they asked, just to make it easier. As for his eyes, he tried to avoid the subject. Fortunately, most people around his age just assumed he wore contacts to make his eyes that way, but anyone who had known him awhile seemed less contented by that explanation. Contacts were not ideal for fights, and he always had perfect vision.

Between working in the butcher's shop and fight training as usual, Opren started to try different things with the sphere, hoping to make it turn into the golden sword or bring him back to Everniot. But whether he held it tightly and concentrated, threw it up in the air and caught it, held it out with his palm up, it resting there, or he attempted several verbal commands, nothing happened. He even tried to go into Pisgah Forest— if he stood in the forest that lined up with the Rure Forest, it should be easier to "shift" over.

"Mom, I don't understand how I can use the magic in the sphere if I can't even make it do anything once," he said after work the following Monday. "You don't think there is someone who could teach real magic here, do you?"

"There is allegedly a shopkeeper in New York who is powerful in old magics," said his mother. "But even in Everniot, we had little throwaway money, so we can't afford that trip right now."

"Is that the *only* place you have heard about anywhere in the U.S.?"

"Yes, unfortunately. And it is only speculation because finding magical beings here is difficult if they don't want to be found. Most people capable of any kind of real magic don't even know. I know only one person who knows of magic in this state. She is a witch, which is not the same as a more powerful magic user. She uses her talents to make potions as teas, smoothies, and supplements, to aid immunity, speed up hair growth or healing, and other things like that. A witch in Everniot, especially one who works with darker power from the supernatural realm, would be much more powerful. A witch here is only able to make things levitate and mix potions, unless she were to have a spell set from Everniot. My friend doesn't know anything advanced, so she would be just as uncertain as anyone else."

"What should I do without anyone to tell me anything else?" He felt stuck. "I know you and Dad have shared a lot, but I need someone to explain more about the magic to me. It seems like I need to get to Everniot for that, but I can't get to Everniot without more knowledge or magic. It's like a bad cycle."

"I think you should continue to live as you would without the shift to Everniot and, only if the magic pulls you over again, see if you can stay for a few days next time," suggested his mother. "Unless that happens, it may be safer to remain here anyway. The Shirrkki cannot reach you here."

"But how can I protect myself from magical things if I don't learn to use magic, or at least get a real sword and learn to be sure when the magic will take me there? And that won't be likely unless I use knowledge from somewhere over there. I like your suggestion about having the magic pull me over by surprise and checking out the place."

"Why am I not surprised?" She rolled her eyes and sighed. "Just don't try to go somewhere dangerous intentionally, please, and be careful of where you go if you do end up there again."

He reassured her he would be careful if anything else strange happened, especially if he did end up back in Everniot for any reason. He returned to his usual daily activities, including his MMA and weaponry practice– which his mother had figured out were such an interest due to his origin in Everniot combined with his connection to the sphere. Grandfather Sam had always been a fighter as well, and so were Sam's father and grandfather, according to stories. Opren was mostly satisfied living his regular life, albeit with a new sense of eventual purpose and potential. That was until a few days later.

Fourteen days after he had shifted to the Rure Forest the first time, he felt a strange tingling throughout his body, then tension. He never left the house without the sphere tied to his belt or somewhere else on his person anymore, and it seemed to be vibrating in its pouch. He took out the sphere; it was pulsing with soft light. Two minutes later, he felt normal, and the sphere was neither glowing nor vibrating.

He was walking home from a weapons match, so he continued with the intention of mentioning the sensation and pulsing light to his mother. His father should also be home at that point, and he would get both their input as to why it might have done that. But when he reached his street it was severely obvious the evening would be anything but a pleasant satisfaction of curiosity.

Their house was on fire, and the walls were already

crumbling as he ran toward it. He heard his mother scream, before she was cut off by something. It sounded as if she lost her breath. Then he saw why: some sort of tall black and green creature was holding her by the throat, while she hung inches above the ground. He went wide-eyed. *That's nothing like a Shirrkki! What the hell?*

The creature was humanoid in shape and stood on two legs, but its face looked like a skeletal reptile, with cobra-like fangs in place of canines and thin snake-skin all over its skull and body. It was taller than his father, but it was not as broad. Its slender, long-nailed fingers wrapped around his mother's neck too easily, and it almost seemed like it grinned when it looked toward him. It hissed and threw his mother into the wall of the burning, crumbling house. She coughed on her hands and knees and his fear left to be replaced with anger and the urge to protect her.

"Leave!" she strained to yell as he ran toward her. "Avoid them! Leave!"

"No way!" he shouted. The skeletal reptile creature turned its eyes– slits for pupils inside of bright orange– to him again. "Stay away from her!"

He barely dodged a swipe by the creature and slid on his knees to reach his mother.

"Are you all right?"

"Please, honey. I love you. You have to leave now," she begged. "You cannot… fight the No-Prey…" She fell over after a cough, breathing too much of the smoke on top of whatever physical damages she had received.

"I'm not leaving you to burn." He lifted her and turned to carry her out of the growing flames.

"Yesss," hissed the creature, startling him enough to halt.

"You understand me and can speak?"

"Yesss. She will burrnnn," said the creature, voice a loud, projected whisper.

"Why are you doing this? Get off our property!"

"Sssphere, boy," said the creature.

"Are you from Everniot?"

"Yes!" yelled his father, running out of the house with a shotgun in hand. "They are called No-Prey, Opren!" He shot the "No-Prey" as soon as he finished his sentence. "Always hunters and never hunted, or some poetic slogan shit such as that. They have magic and are predators for hire!"

"They want the sphere!" said Opren. "And wait, 'they', meaning more than one–NO!"

He began to shake as he watched another of the creatures shove its hand through his father's back and out through his chest. He did not even see where the creature came from it moved so fast, and he had only managed a single step toward his father.

"You will pay f–" He was cut off when winded by the other No-Prey slamming into his own back, but with its shoulder instead of its claw. He stumbled and dropped his mother, who had just regained consciousness. She coughed and grunted as she thudded and rolled a few feet away.

"There is nothing you can do but save yourself, Opren," said his mother, and tears started to run down her face. "We love you, but you *need to go*."

"Clossse your eyesss, boy," said the creature who had slammed into him, as it walked over to his mother. It lifted her and flung her into the house, then threw a magically produced ball of fire in after her.

Opren charged at the creature, but he was knocked away by a backhand he could not see coming, the force of which made him dizzy even before he hit the remaining railing of the porch. His vision blurred, and he shook his head to find clarity.

When he looked up, his father's dead body lay in what was now a blazing front area that used to be the living room, and his mother was not yet dead but was screaming as she burned. He stood and called to the creatures as they began to walk away from the house. They turned with mutual sickening grins and said something he could not understand. He saw a strange blurred motion in the air around them, then they vanished. They must have returned to Everniot, so he took out the sphere, which was now glowing intently.

"Work, damn you!" he yelled at the golden ball, gripping it tightly and shaking it. "Take me to Everniot, *now*!"

The sphere did nothing else, so Opren ran to the spot the No-Prey had used to disappear. Then, he fell to his knees and yelled at the top of his lungs as he thought only of going after the creatures. Every fiber of his being had only one goal: avenge his parents. Rushing warmth coursed through his body, and he was blinded by golden light. He blinked once and a different town came into focus.

The town he had shifted to had people running away from something, so he assumed the No-Prey must have been there as well, which meant he must have made it to Everniot. A sign said "Ravberd Pub" which confirmed the thought. He looked around to see a few houses in that town were also burning down and unnaturally crumbled. He clenched his teeth and snarled as he continued to search through the place.

"No-Prey! Where are you?" he called.

Suddenly, another flash of light brought him back to his destroyed house in North Carolina. He felt the burn of tears as he sought and found his mother's body under the rubble that had occurred during his time in Ravberd. Firefighters had arrived just as he returned. They entered what was left of the house and one helped him carry his mother's body outside, while two others lifted and brought out his father's body. They told him to remain outside for his safety and to have the EMTs check him.

"I'm so sorry for your loss, Opren," said one firefighter who knew his father from the shop. "You are all great people. What happened?"

"I-I doubt you'd believe it, Chris." He wiped away tears. "It was arson, though."

"It isn't the first case of arson I've seen, son," said the fire chief, Malcolm Rays. "Just the first one around here. This damage sure is unusual, though. Normally, fires alone don't do all this."

"The arson isn't the part you won't believe," said Opren. "It's what caused the fire and killed my parents."

"What did it?" asked Chris. "You mean who?"

"I don't know if who or what is better." He shook his head. Tears started again as he saw his parents get zipped up into body bags by the EMTs who had confirmed them both dead. "But they were not human beings. They are not from this world."

"Son, I think you need to take it easy," said Chief Rays. "You just went through one of the most traumatic experiences anyone could ever– and should never– go through."

"I told you, you wouldn't believe it. But you are correct about the trauma of an unusual experience. I just don't plan to deal with it how you suggest."

He ignored the EMT who tried to check him and left the area, also ignoring calls from Chief Rays and the EMT's to come back. He walked until he reached a familiar spot in the forest, then let out his tears freely, sitting against a tree. He wept for about ten minutes, then reviewed what had happened once in his mind. At the end of his recollection, he cried a bit more before he took out the sphere.

"You *will* work for me," he said with as much emphasis as he could muster, looking down at the golden sphere. "The magic in you will help me kill these things, one way or another. I *need* to get back to *Everniot*."

He woke as the sun spread light through the forest, still against the tree. He looked around and it seemed as though he was not in the same spot, but he was sure he had not moved before unintentionally falling asleep. He stood and walked around until he found a path, about five minutes later. He followed the path and when he reached the end, he realized it was once again Ravberd he had arrived to, not his regular town.

"So, what? I just have to tell you to work and you actually do, except in your own time." He looked at the sphere still in his hand. He placed it into its pouch and walked into Ravberd Pub.

"Welcome!" said the bartender. "We don't get many new faces in here this time of year, but you are the second this afternoon. What can I get you?"

"Thank you. But I need to ask a few questions. I don't need a drink right now."

"Go ahead and ask away." The bartender's brow furrowed as they met eyes. He dropped the cheery voice. "Are you all right, lad?"

"I'm not sure right now, really. My parents were murdered by some creatures called the No-Prey." All twenty or so people in the pub went silent. "I guess you all have heard of them?"

"Rumors say they are what came through town and burned down some houses less than an hour ago. But thank goodness nobody was killed. It was just their idea of harmful fun as they passed through," said the bartender. "Whether or not someone died was of little concern it seemed, but I've heard they only intentionally kill if given a job and, if they are given one, they never fail. I'm so sorry to hear of your loss. Where are you from? Did they kill anyone else in your town?"

"I hope not, but I am not sure. They specifically wanted to steal something from my family. I came from somewhere you wouldn't know about, I'm sure, but I was actually born here. My parents moved us when I was two years old."

"Oh, you must be Samuel's grandson. He used to come in here, and he told me you all were leaving town. That was eighteen years ago, I think, but I last saw him three years ago."

"That's right. My name is Opren. Grandfather Sam also passed a month ago, so he won't be back here, unfortunately."

"I'm Garth. I own this pub." Garth held out a hand and Opren shook it. "Good to meet you, Opren. I do wish it was under better circumstances. Now what would you like to ask?"

Opren spent twenty minutes in the pub and asked Garth several questions, to which Garth had short or vague answers. The only thing he could answer with certainty was where to go to find out more.

"Ra' Yana City is the capital of this sect. It's the biggest city in the nearby area, so you should find their library," said Garth. "They also have all kinds of people to talk to and enough security around the place to keep out trolls or Shirrkki raids. It'll be about a full day's hike through the forest."

"Thank you, Garth. I will be sure to return for a drink once I have my answers and avenge my parents."

He remained in the town so he could find a new backpack and a few supplies for his trip, such as a water bottle and dry food. The only problem was he did not have Everniot money. He returned to Garth's pub a half hour later to ask about how to earn some and Garth was kind enough to give him what he needed to buy the backpack, a cantine, and dry fruit and nut bars. Garth advised him to check the hunting board and other quick-task postings in Ra' Yana when he arrived. Those could sustain him for a good length of time if he did not wish for permanent employment.

When ready, he entered the Rure Forest and followed a path labeled Ra' Yana City. The forest really was nearly identical to the forest near where he was raised, despite being another version of the world. There were many fir and pine trees, other trees with colored needles, and what appeared to be poplar trees and some small-leaf trees he did not recognize.

I need to come up with a plan. And hope the magic doesn't pull me away again. As he walked, he took deep breaths to clear his head and be more aware of his surroundings.

When the sun began to lower, he stopped to relieve himself and to have a snack. He stretched after setting down the backpack, then rinsed his hands before taking out a fruit and nut bar. His face tightened and his eyes watered as he experienced flashes of his parents' murder. He finished the bar, then took the deepest breath he could and expelled the air slowly. Until he found a way to use the orb's magic and hunt down the No-Prey, he would need to be stable and focused. He knew that as a fighter. Although, not getting enraged by being kicked or missing a punch was a lot easier than the current pain accompanied by an emptiness and grief.

Only moonlight provided any sight by the time he stopped again, but he noted he had no trouble seeing and there was a print in the dirt. He saw the same sort of print last he stopped, but he had assumed it to be a bear. Upon further inspection, the print was bigger than a human's foot, but it was not a bear's claw either. He looked over to a pile of brush that rustled. It was not a natural gathering of branches and leaves, especially not for a forest with mostly needled trees.

He took a cautious step forward, then paused, peering into the leaves and large sticks. It was a camouflage that had worked for a while, but something was following him, and he had a pretty good idea as to what.

"You smart human," a rough, deep voice said. "Shirrkki not discovered this way often."

First, the large hairy head with tiny goat-like horns emerged, then the large dark eyes with thick brows and the large jaw, then the massive shoulders and torso. Soon, the entire six and a half feet of the stocky beast-man could be seen as he stepped out of his camouflage into the area dimly lit by the moonlight. He wore a thick hide of a sort reinforced with pieces of wood as armor that could blend with nature.

"Were you waiting for me? How did you know I was coming?"

"Shirrkki don't need you. Need shiny ball for lord."

"Who is this lord?"

"No matter to you. You give shiny ball, Shirrkki get reward and make lord happy. Say no and be killed in dawn sun."

"You might as well try to kill me now. Because the ball was a gift from my grandfather, and it belongs to my family, to me. I'm not giving it to you, just like I didn't give it to your friend." He clenched his teeth with his mouth still closed. Why had he said that? He knew it would provoke the large beast-man.

"He was not friend," said the Shirrkki. "Was weak and you killed him. Killing by dawn sun brings luck but will kill you now like you want." He growled, readying his stance to attack.

Opren did not want to find out if he could brawl with the beast-man unless necessary, so he turned to run. The Shirrkki roared as he ran from the area. Two new Shirrkki responded with roars, and it was clear they were better prepared to capture or kill him and take no chances of losing the sphere again. Their heavy feet thudded from two sides as he sprinted away—though, toward what or where was a mystery.

After running for over ten minutes, he halted to catch his breath. He wished for the sword and power to come from the sphere again. Unfortunately, without even knowing how it happened the first time, he had no idea how to cause it this time. He had read magic was supposedly controlled by will and concentration. He tried concentrating, but nothing happened. He did what he assumed would be willing the sword to appear... still nothing. The rapid thudding of the Shirrkki's steps getting closer made sure he could no longer concentrate.

As he ran again, he hit something solid and swore. He looked up to see an armored, gray-haired Shirrkki holding a battle ax.

"Damn..." He took a few steps back.

"Not fast enough, boy," said the armored Shirrkki. The wood-armored Shirrkki and the other, one with black hair and fur and a single horn, caught up to them just after he spoke. "Give shiny ball now."

"If you Shirrkki would give me some information about the reason you need it, who the lord is who wants it, or anything like that, I might try to help. But I am not going to just hand it over."

"Die thun," said the armored Shirrkki as he swung back his ax. But as he moved forward to strike, the moment seemed to slow.

"*Woffrumdus!*" yelled Opren without thinking. The word just came out and echoed through the area. He was blinded for a second by a flash of light, but then he could see as usual, if not better. As the echo faded, he already held a shining golden longsword. He dodged the ax and spun around the back of the armored Shirrkki.

The Shirrkki growled and spun to face him, while the black-haired Shirrkki drew a large dagger and brought out a chain. The Shirrkki wrapped the chain around Opren's left arm and proceeded to go for the arm holding the golden sword, but Opren flicked his wrist up and the sword broke the chain as if it were not even a rope. The armored Shirrkki lifted his large ax again, while the Shirrkki with the camouflage attempted to hold Opren from behind, likely to prevent him from dodging the way he had before.

"Really?" scoffed Opren. He felt good, but he could not think before he just acted, just spoke...just *did*.

As the ax fell, he flipped over the wood-armored Shirrkki behind him and cut off the arm of the armored Shirrkki that was holding the ax. Instead of into Opren, the ax– and arm– fell to the ground. The now single-armed Shirrkki roared out of what seemed to be pain and anger at once.

The black-haired Shirrkki stabbed at him with the dagger, but he grabbed its arm and forced it upward at the elbow, breaking it and causing the dagger to drop. He stabbed this Shirrkki, dodged a slice from a short-sword held by the wood-armored Shirrkki, and was grabbed by the throat by the Shirrkki that was missing an arm. The Shirrkki threw him against a tree and charged him to headbutt him, winding him, then punched him over and over and over. The brutal punches did not take as much of a toll as expected, but they were making it hard to react or think.

He felt the rushing warmth of the golden energy. Upon a burst of golden light, the Shirrkki was forced back somehow. He took the opportunity and stabbed the Shirrkki between the neck and shoulder. As he did, the wood-armored Shirrkki attempted to strike but Opren spun with the golden sword and slashed the beast-man. With a kick to this last Shirrkki, he stepped back and staggered. All three Shirrkki were in bloody heaps on the ground.

Opren returned to normal as the sword became the

sphere again. He placed the sphere into its pouch shakily. He staggered again as he picked up his bag.

What the hell is going on?

His legs shook as he turned to walk from the area and locate the path. He rocked backward and staggered once again... his head clouded as he felt feverish... then nothing...

4

Emerald rode her silver-gray mare through the Rure Forest.

"This is how we get to Ra' Yana City, Shari," said Emerald to her mare. "We will see many Human people there."

Shari softly huffed in response to indicate she was pleased.

She rode Shari past a lot of similar trees– much smaller and less diverse than the ones at home, but still healthy and tall. The leaves she was most familiar with were replaced with needles, flowers with colored, tiny leaves. The differences of the fauna and flora in the area compared to her home fascinated her. She smiled as a light breeze reached her face and fluffed her hair. She loved that nature always treated her pleasantly.

A couple hours into the trip, they stopped in a small town called Ravberd. She wanted to see what true commoners did in a small place before reaching a large capital like Ra' Yana City. She also felt like having something to drink other than the water she brought along.

When she located the town's pub, she told Shari to wait

by the other horses tied outside. She sniffed and wrinkled her nose as she glanced at the ropes holding the horses close to posts.

As she entered the pub, she was greeted with, "Hello there, gorgeous!" It was a Human man with scruffy facial hair. "I would love to be first to buy you a drink."

"She doesn't need a drink, Jon... a more suitable... outfit," another man forced through heavy slurring.

"Why are you wearing such boring brown leather, miss?" asked the one called Jon. "You would look gorgeous in a green dress."

"I can pay for my own drink, thanks," she said. "And I wear the leather pants and top because it provides a good travel attire, it doesn't show dirt, I'm not usually interested in standing out, and it is less appealing to men who focus on my body before my words." She gave an easily-seen-as-fake smile.

"No need to be rude," said Jon. "I wanted to be helpful."

"You wanted to lure in a young woman you think to be appealing." She rolled her eyes. "Ulterior motives do not make for generosity."

"Buy your own damn drink and wear what you want then, bitch." He shooed her with his hand. He turned to his blatantly drunk friend. "This is why chivalry is pointless, Gav."

She walked up to a stool a few away from the two men and sat down. The barkeep approached.

"Welcome, miss. What would you like?"

She overheard three women whispering as they passed her to reach a table. They did their best to keep their voices low, but despite their obvious awareness–and apparent awe–of her Reiyal Elven birth, they must not have known elves could hear much better than humans.

"You don't have many who look like me in here often, do you?" she asked the barkeep.

He appeared apologetic as he replied, "You are a rarity of looks even compared to the elves, or any women of any kind we have seen. We do have occasional Wood-Elves, but they are not local to us, usually travelers. Where are you from? It can't be too close, I imagine."

"I prefer not to talk about my home freely, but I am not local, that much is true. I'm traveling to experience classes and culture in places outside of my home sect. By the way, those of us you call Wood-Elves are Uundulal, while my tribe is the Reiyal, not Light-Elves. You are describing us rather than using the correct terms. I notice it often outside of the Elven areas, but you might get better tips if you refer to those who come in here properly. Most elves care for detail and thoughtfulness."

"Sorry for our patrons giving you a bad impression, and sorry for the mistake on my part. I'm Hans. Garth over there is the owner if you have any real problem." He thumbed to the other side of the bar, where a gray-haired man with a light goatee was taking an order for a couple. "So have you decided what you would like to drink?"

"I'm called Emerald. And I appreciate the thought, but I am sure I can handle my own quarrels." She flexed an arm and chuckled. "Give me something you would recommend since I'm not from around here. Something to remember you and the place."

"I've got just the thing," said Hans with a twinkle in his eye. Despite his error, his genuine nature was inviting.

He filled a glass mug with a liquid that was somewhere between rosy wine and golden ale in color and passed it to her. She took a sip. There was a warmth and smoothness to the fruit-noted ale.

"This is quite good." She smiled. "Thank you."

After she finished her drink, she left a gold coin on the counter and exited the pub. She turned to see Hans had rushed out after her, and he attempted to hand her back the coin. She shook her head.

"But Emerald, you know the drink was only eight cripes. This is a whole fillot, which is nearly enough to buy the whole damn place a round!" he said with wide eyes. "Nobody has ever left a tip that massive, so was it not accidental?"

"It was not an accident. Just keep it. I can do without it." She turned away and called Shari to follow. "Have a wonderful day, Hans!" She left him to his bewilderment and waved over her shoulder as she continued into town. She caught him muttering, "And you, Emerald the Reiyal." Perhaps not all Humans were rude and ignorant by nature.

A woman ran past her suddenly, yelling about something. Emerald followed the woman's path in reverse with her eyes and saw some charcoal smoke coming from somewhere down the road, to the left. She forgot about blending in at all and broke into a sprint toward the smoke, weaving gracefully through several other people running away from the cause. As she reached the source, her heart sank then beat faster.

A burning house was crumbling in front of her, while another had damage from several minutes earlier. She wanted to help, but she could only heal the wounded or manipulate her own body. The rest of the magic she knew was with nature. She never learned to produce water without a source or put out such a fire. A healer by birth was not as helpful in such a situation.

"At least they got everyone out," said a man. "Some kind of creature did this, as well as another to the other four, but they left before anyone could identify them. The knights from the east of town came, so I suppose they scared it away, for now."

She looked around to observe the other damaged houses she missed during her sprint.

"Do you have intelligent creatures in this sect often?" She brushed some hair away from her face and behind her ear. She did not care at that moment it would bring attention to her pointed ears.

"Oh! You are an elf," said the man, as if she herself had no idea. "Um, no, we don't have anything intelligent enough to intentionally cause such a fire and know to run. But the same creatures came through yesterday. They did not cause this damage the first time."

She thought for a moment. There were few creatures

capable of the act with such precision. The town would need more than its few non-magical routine knights.

"I am going to Ra' Yana City. This was only a short pause to my trip there," she said. "When I arrive, I will inform the military forces they should investigate and find whatever these creatures might have been."

"Thank you miss...er..."

"Emerald."

"Thank you, miss Emerald."

She returned to the horse's area by the pub.

Let's continue, Shari. We have a new task to accomplish." She climbed atop and the two started out of the town and back into the Rure Forest.

As the sky grew dark, only the moon lit the spaces between the trees, but her Elven eyes could see in low light without any trouble. She enjoyed the way things glistened at times in such lighting. The needles on the trees allowed streams of the moonlight to get through in patterns leaves would not present.

A sudden flash of light appeared and a shout like a war cry came from far through the trees.

"That could be another fire by the creature. Shari, go to the light!"

The mare galloped at full speed for around two minutes, until they reached a small clearing between the trees. The light had disappeared, but she saw some bodies on the ground instead, including three Shirrkki and a single smaller body, a human. She jumped off Shari before the horse even slowed, commanding the mare to wait as she dashed to the human. She placed her hand, palm open on the young man's chest. His heart was still beating as it should, just rapidly. She checked that he was breathing; he was.

He must have been knocked out or... did he *cause that flash? Maybe he used too much* Nuuita.

The Shirrkki were clearly dead or dying because they lay in pools of their own blood.

"Thank goodness he is still alive," she said to Shari. *But what actually happened here?*

She checked beneath the human's shirt and found some bruises and scrapes, and his arm had signs of strain against rope or something of the sort– she noticed a chain and considered that a likely source of the damage. She healed all the external wounds and hoped he had no serious internal damage.

"Let's rest a moment and then we will take him to Ra' Yana City with us." Shari huffed and nodded once.

Emerald took out a dagger from a sheathe on her right thigh, reached into a saddlebag on Shari to bring out an apple, and cut the apple in half. She gave the first half to Shari, then she sliced the other into four for herself. A few moments later, as she finished her last bite, she heard a sound...*footsteps?*

She scanned the trees thoroughly. Shari pointed her ears back and fidgeted her hooves.

"Don't worry, girl." She patted the mare. "I have us protected. You just kick them in the face if necessary."

A pair of amber eyes appeared, almost level with her own. Whatever was staring at her was about five feet tall. It was too short to be a Shirrkki, which was good, but it was also too large to be a regular wolf or deer. The answer was found as the eyes moved and out stepped a large, smoky-black-furred, wolf-like creature. A granwolf! She had yet to meet a granwolf, but she knew about the over-sized wolves with close to elf-level intelligence. She had always wondered how it felt to communicate through their thought transference.

Don't worry. I won't eat you, the voice of the granwolf was felt inside her head, as if she had another stream of thoughts that were not her own. It felt both like listening and like thinking. *I won't eat your mare either.*

"I'm not worried. I know granwolves are not small-brained beasts without control for their aggression. I'm called Emerald...you are?"

If you were a human, you would not have that answer, I bet.

I'm Barbosa, Noble Granwolf of the Spine's Caverns. Good to meet you, Emerald. Aside from your mare, are you traveling alone? She isn't great for conversation or protection against nastier creatures.

"I have magic, and I am quite a bit more than I appear. But you are correct about the lack of conversation. Would you like to join us? We are on our way to Ra' Yana, the largest capital city of this sect of the kingdom."

I would be glad to join, said Barbosa. *I'd feel better if I can be your guard, despite you saying you can care for yourself.*

"Well, I appreciate your concern." She smiled. "Welcome to our adventure."

Don't elves usually avoid danger and adventure to focus on skill-building, research, and duty? asked Barbosa.

"I'm atypical." She shrugged. "I prefer to be unlike others expect me to be. While speaking of the unusual, what brings *you* here to Human areas?"

I was hunting this area for deer. It has a lot more than by the Caverns, he replied.

"I will leave you to that when you want. I don't eat meat, and I would rather not kill anything that doesn't attack me."

You'll never be a truly strong fighter without the nutrients in meat, said Barbosa with a chuckle.

"I do well enough without it." She flashed a smirk before a smile.

I've heard elves are stronger than they look, which is good because I think you need more meat on you. *I suppose you don't need to worry about being a target to be food.* He chuckled again.

"You might think that, but many Human and Elven men want me like they are hungry for something."

Are you a good-looking mate for your kind? asked Barbosa.

"Unfortunately, more than I would ask for. Maybe that could change if I meet a decent man, but Elven men who respect me also won't dare to court me, and Human men rarely give me respect during my travels. I dress like a commoner and go only by Emerald, but I'm not common and my proper name is a bit different. I will share when the time comes, but don't tell anyone about the secret, please. Because I pretend to be a commoner, yet I look as I do...I'm sure you have heard and seen how men can be."

I have, said Barbosa. *Lucky for you, you have me around now. They'll be too intimidated.*

She laughed. "Good! I'm going to set up a sleeping spot for the human. Let's rest and make the remaining trip in–"

She stopped her words and held up a hand for silence as she heard the crack of a branch being snapped nearby. She turned her head to the right and out from the shadows stepped a brown-furred Shirrkki without head hair. It carried a jagged broadsword.

"Hello," she greeted politely. *This will go badly if he is here because of the dead three.*

"Move, elf girl," replied the Shirrkki. "Shirrkki won't kill if ball is in hand."

"You won't kill him or me?" She had left her dagger in her bag on Shari after slicing the apple, to make sitting or lying down more comfortable.

"Leave boy and Shirrkki won't kill," said the beast-man.

"Won't kill him or me?" she repeated. She knew not to trust war-bred people who were more animal than person. Their aggressive instincts were fed more violence until they enjoyed the hunt and kill. "You need to be more specific. I don't want to agree to something I misunderstand."

She was stalling as she stepped toward Shari slowly, to grab her dagger from its pouch.

"You, elf girl." He gestured to her with his jagged sword. "If you take boy, you die. You leave boy so Shirrkki can take ball. You go."

"I don't want you to kill him, either," she said sternly. She reached the bag with the dagger.

It was then the Shirrkki realized what she did, and he lunged. She pivoted and dodged the jagged sword the Shirrkki thrust toward her torso, so only her raised outer forearm received the cut. She stabbed the Shirrkki in the thigh, then the gut, then the neck. She leaped up and pressed her feet to the beast-man's chest to do a backflip and landed lightly on her feet as the Shirrkki crashed into a tree to bleed until dead.

Emerald pushed hair from her face with her dagger-less hand as she turned to Barbosa. "As I said, I can take care of myself."

That you can, Miss Emerald, agreed Barbosa with a chuckle. *Well done!*

"*Ve harron*, Noble Barbosa."

I apologize that I do not speak Elvish, said Barbosa.

"*Ve harron* is thank you," she explained.

You're welcome, then, he said.

She re-bound the sheathe to her thigh and stuck the dagger inside in case they encountered another Shirrkki or other threat. As she did, the young man stirred and turned himself over with a groan.

"Are you all right?" She hurried over to him.

"I… Shirrr…" he tried to speak. His eyes were only half open.

"The Shirrkki are all dead. You are going to be all right."

The young man's hand fell to a leather pouch tied to his belt loop, then he drifted into unconsciousness again.

"Just rest. We will get you to safety and I'll make sure you are all right," she said, though it was doubtful he heard her then.

Let's leave these woods before others show up, said Barbosa. *You and Shari have enough stamina to make it if I carry the human, right?*

"We do. Good idea." She climbed on Shari then pushed another misplaced bit of hair behind her ear. "We should move at a steady pace. Ra' Yana should only be a few hours away from here."

Before they departed, she healed her gash. She held her hand about an inch above the large cut, palm down as she concentrated.

Your magic has a pretty glow to it, said Barbosa. *Softer and paler than other green auras I have seen.*

"Healing magic is usually the color of life and natural energy," she said with a smile. "I agree, it is pretty."

When they reached the city, she was required to turn in her dagger for inspection, as it was Elven and not made of common Human materials. It was also not something easily allowed in central cities because they took precautions to anything going in, despite selling weapons and armor inside the city. It was a good, expected precaution and she gave no argument. She could always get it back later or make do with something else. She informed the guards who took the dagger about the houses that were set on fire by some unidentified creature in Ravberd. He agreed to request his officer to send a couple of mage-knights and said a squad of soldiers would surely investigate.

She found a decent inn in the west area of the city, and she reserved a room for the young man whenever he woke. For the time being, she brought him with her to the room she had reserved by letter from the previous city she visited. She put him in the bed next to her own.

"I really hope you are not too badly hurt or sick." She carefully let his head drop to the pillow with her hand. She checked that his heart was still beating steadily and then pulled the cover to his chest. For the first time since she found him, she really took a moment to look at him.

He was neither muscular nor thin for a human, but he appeared sturdy with broad shoulders, maybe built for sport or farming, and his skin was a warm, sandy tone, as though he spent time outdoors. His hair was brown like hers, but his was trimmed and straight and it included some golden strands. His face had an inviting appearance as he slept.

"Even though I would prefer you not to say this at first the other way around, I have to say you are handsome for a human. Good thing you are unable to hear me yet." She laughed at herself quietly. "I do hope you are a good enough person to have helped."

The next morning, Barbosa volunteered to continue to rest in the room and monitor the young man–it was barely sunrise, too early for the granwolf if he had the choice– so Emerald explored the city for a few hours. When she returned, Barbosa informed her the young man had stirred again, but he immediately had gone back to sleep. This time though, the sleep seemed natural, and his pulse and breathing were normal.

She had not changed clothes since she reached the city, so she took out a new outfit and went to shower. By the time she had washed and dressed, she entered the main room to find the human was waking fully.

5

Opren woke lightheaded and disoriented...again. He was in a bed, clearly no longer in the forest.

How did I get here? He lifted his head and looked around to see another bed, a counter with some cabinets and a small gas stove, and a connected bathroom. *This is an inn? I wonder– WHAT THE–*

To the left of the bed lay a large charcoal-furred beast. He flinched, trying to stay silent while it moved. It opened its eyes and seemed to ignore him for the time being as it still lay there.

"Oh good, you're truly awake," said a delightful, feminine voice with a pleasant accent he could not place, as someone entered from the washroom. He turned to see who spoke.

There stood a young woman with a joy-inducing grin, short and slender, with warm-yet-fair, flawless skin and thick brown hair like his was, but hers was beyond shoulder length, wavy, and had streaks of an earthy green that appeared natural. Her hair shone in the sunlight coming through the window and, despite being a bit of a mess, it seemed clean. Her clothing was modest but fitted, shaping her. She had athletic toning, yet a feminine figure and prominent bust.

The sleeveless brown leather she wore helped focus to pull to her vivid violet eyes; the rare color was enthralling, and her sharply arching, thin eyebrows were unique. If it were not rude, he could have stared awhile.

"I was beginning to worry you were in a coma," she said. "I'm called Emerald...and you are?"

"Opren." He sat up straight. "Where are we?"

"Ra' Yana City," said Emerald. She brushed her hair behind her ear with her hand. *Her ears are pointed on top!*

"So I'm definitely still in Everniot," he voiced his thought almost unconsciously. "This is actually where I was headed. Thank you for bringing me from the forest. How did you bring me here? And you're an–"

"A Reiyal elf, yes. And you're a human," said Emerald as if she were simply agreeing the sky was blue that day. He wanted to exclaim, but meeting a beautiful Elven girl was not as strange as the magic in the orb or learning of a whole other world, so he just went with it and let her continue. "You should close your mouth, it's impolite." He closed his mouth with a click and swore at himself inside. He had barely realized he remained slack jawed in surprise and looking like that was such a good first impression. "I did not bring you alone. Barbosa helped me by carrying you. I could have dragged you or put you onto my horse, but he offered." She gestured to the wide-snouted, wolf-like beast. "You might want him as a bodyguard if you plan to fight more Shirrkki. How did you kill three of them at the same time? Do you have training, or did someone help?"

"I'm not really sure what happened. I only know they wanted to take something I recently inherited. It seems to be a goal the Shirrkki and some lord have, according to one of the Shirrkki. I don't know why, but some other monsters killed my parents and burned down my home, so I plan to find out what's special about the thing and learn how to kill the monsters." He gestured to the charcoal-furred wolf-creature. "That thing is called Barbosa?"

This... 'thing'... as you phrased it... is a noble granwolf of the Spine's Caverns. My name is Barbosa, yes, and I will be fine with it if you want me to accompany you... if you show some respect. I am not just a simple beast like some pet dog. Opren felt a new part of his thoughts make these words, but they were not his– they were in a gruff, deeper voice.

"I thought granwolves were only in my mom's stories," said Opren, still to Emerald. "How do you know one?"

I met her while hunting, said Barbosa. *She was in the woods alone and I felt it would be better to watch out for her. And we are a hidden species now, but we're around.*

"I can take care of myself, but it was kind of him to accompany me," said Emerald, smiling at Barbosa. "Did you cause the flash of light?"

"I think...so." He almost choked as he spoke. He must have been dehydrated and the talking took a toll on his throat. "May I have some water?"

"Just a moment." She went into an adjacent room.

Get used to talking to me like another person if you want the company, said Barbosa. *I suggest taking me because you obviously can't handle yourself well.*

"What do you mean by 'obviously can't handle yourself'?" Opren scoffed. Unfortunately, he caused himself to choke again before he could continue. "I killed all three Shirrkki alone and I have only seen them twice in my life, both times recently."

Barbosa gave short, happy growls...was he *laughing*?

I could see that you did. I also saw you passed out and just woke up after two days. Passing out after a temporary victory means death could be close behind.

"Don't act like you are better than me and you can come. I could—" Opren coughed again once. "I could use a companion."

Careful, boy. I am better than you as far as you need to be concerned. Don't be an immature cub to me, and you might earn my respect. You could be in real danger if alone while many

Shirrkki have a reason to hunt you. If that's the case, you need help.

Emerald returned with a large glass of water. Opren took it and drank it quickly.

"I will come too," she said. "I'm already traveling but had no companions before. Don't pretend you would prefer not to have *my* company, and I would prefer the company of someone who is adventuring instead of wanting to get me drunk. Some of the less respectable men even want me to come home with them for 'enjoyable times'." She rolled her eyes and shook her head. "You Human men are worse than Elven men."

"You heard us clearly from the other room?" asked Opren.

"Elf, remember?" She indicated her ears. "I can hear much better than humans. And Barbosa can choose who hears the thoughtspeech he projects, within a range. By the by, maybe you should wait for water before arguing next time."

"That's certainly useful," said Opren. "And while I don't like the disrespect you have received, you are gorgeous, so I am not surprised all the men notice."

"My looks are more a bother than a gift," said Emerald, yawning and stretching her arms, which made her chest expand and brought Opren's eyes to her breasts. "Keep your eyes on mine or somewhere else other than me." She burned into Opren with her gaze for a brief silence. She lightened her expression again and said, "Because of my appearance, I have a hard time enjoying places unbothered. I prefer people notice me for how I act and what I can do, rather than how I look and what they want to do with me. It's a distraction for them from who I really am. I suppose I could be one of those girls who uses attraction to get people to do what I want, but that holds little value and tends to work only because most societies are based on the perspective of males in charge."

"Sorry. I will try to avoid commenting about your looks too often," said Opren. "But I assume a promised kiss from you could be good motivation, so I'm not surprised you could get someone to do what you want, if you wanted."

He would have expected a young woman who appeared as

Emerald did to show off herself, like many online models, but it so far seemed Everniot was different from where he grew up, and she was not a human. Both worlds were his, but it would take some getting used to with the different cultures, knowledge, and customs. Maybe elves did not hold physical attraction in high esteem...or maybe it was just Emerald.

"I'm sure you are hungry." She looked at him sternly. She had not snapped at him, but it was clearly a tone that meant "change the topic or shut your mouth". He had gone too far with his comments and he felt a little ashamed. His recent unconsciousness and his current nervous excitement were not helping him present himself well. It was a bad time to speak first but think later. "Let's go get some food and get to know each other, so we know neither of us wants to kill the other if we are to travel together."

Opren agreed.

At the restaurant, Barbosa sat under the table enjoying a slab of meat silently, while Opren and Emerald talked.

"So what are you in this city for?" asked Opren.

"I'm just traveling, making new friends, and learning as I do," she replied brightly. "I love getting to know other cultures and unbinding myself from everyday tasks for the sake of the previously unknown. What about you?"

Her easy sense of adventure and spontaneous intent were impressive, almost inspiring. He enjoyed new experiences too, but it was as if she were carefree yet craved the thrill of something new simultaneously. Given his current circumstances, he was not sure when his reasons could be that way again. Everything needed to revolve around avenging his parents and learning what he could for that purpose and to protect the sphere.

"I'm gathering stuff for a trip that may take a while. I need to find out about an item my grandfather gave me when he passed away. That's what the Shirrkki wanted." He clenched his teeth as he recalled his parents' murder. "And what the No-Prey wanted."

"The No-Prey?" exclaimed Emerald in a lowered-yet-sharp voice. "You mean a *sleeskax*?"

"What is a, uh, sleeskax?"

"Terrible creatures usually summoned to act as magical assassins or mercenaries," she explained. "They are sometimes even called 'living death', but No-Prey was their most common label long enough no-one really wants to call them by their actual name now out of fear of considering them real instead of a legend. Even one can massacre a town. They are malicious and take pleasure in their kills, which they never fail to execute. And they could easily be described as monsters, since they are said to look like reptilian corpses with fangs and burning eyes, but their flesh does not rot, in fact it heals all wounds, and they are intelligent."

"That sounds right. What does it matter if someone says sleeskax or No-Prey?" It was funny someone would fear something enough not to use its name. "It isn't even a proper name, just what they are."

"No, but it is about admitting such a horror exists," she said. "Denial seems to help soothe fear, even if it is a false solution. I do not agree with it, but I see it work for some. If people are more content, so be it. But you know, magic *can* be attached to names and words. Haven't you heard that before? It is one way we end up with spells and enchantments. Maybe some fear calling their name would summon them."

"I, uh...I'm not from here in the way you are," he admitted. *I think I can trust her enough to share a little. She did save my life and seems genuine, and I need help here.* "I was born in Ravberd, according to my parents just before...before I came back here to figure out about the thing I inherited." Opren looked down and paused, clenched a fist, then released with a sigh. He looked back up. "I was born here, but I have been away while I grew up. I probably don't know about the things in Everniot you might find obvious, if it has to do with the history or magic or anything you would consider a legend."

"Oh," she said in a way that seemed more like pleased

curiosity than the expected confusion or judgment. "Well, I'll teach you what I can." She smiled. "You and Barbosa will give me a party of traveling companions, and I will make sure you know everything you need to about Everniot and its people. And we can learn about new culture types together, since that is what I intend to do as part of my travels. I have not been away from my home except while I was pre-adolescent to learn magic and some other useful skills. Maybe you can teach me something I haven't read about humans in return."

He went wide-eyed. "You know magic?"

"Yes." She giggled as she nodded. "I assume you do not, since you asked that way."

He shook his head. "No, but I have magic somehow, especially with the sphere." He had spoken without thinking, due to his excitement. He furrowed his brow and cursed himself inside again. He could trust her with some things, but *that* was meant to remain a secret for as long as possible since he was already hunted for the thing.

"Why do you look that way?" asked Emerald. "Is it because you keep thinking of your home and what happened?"

"Yes, in part." He looked into her eyes and felt a calming warmth, as if he were in a wonderful blanket. "But I will be all right, I think. I'm not sure, really, but I will make sure they are avenged... my parents, I mean."

"Well, I will help you with that too, if I can," said Emerald. "I do not recommend seeking to kill. Elven culture tends to avoid that sort of act as a whole, especially if out of malice instead of a need to avenge like you have. I agree with the words of wisdom 'needless violence is to be avoided'. That said, I suggest you train on Rhahkmant'e, the Black Stone Mountain. It is a special military and magical training area of the Elven sect border that meets the nearest Human sect to where I live. From what you have said, you plan to fight Shirrkki and might encounter sleeskaxes again— though I really hope you don't go looking for them so you can live longer. They already hunt you so you should prepare to fight them, but please try to avoid them for as long as possible. I'm happy to make a new friend, but I don't want a new dead friend. You will learn spellwielding on the mountain, since you must have the natural ability but lack of control—I assume that's how you survived so far, right? Now, what is the sphere?"

"I was not going to mention it, but since I did and you seem trustworthy, it is the family artifact my grandfather gave to me in his will," he said quietly. "After multiple tries to steal it and kill me for its magic, I thought I should keep it to myself what the thing is. Look under the table."

Opren took the sphere from its pouch carefully and held it beneath the wooden table. Emerald bent sideways to look under the table. She straightened again in her seat after about ten seconds.

"I have never seen that before, nor anything like it that would contain magic. Usually, magical artifacts are covered in Runaic writing or are made of Avarinnium, the elves' metallic mineral that can hold magical energy and spirit energy we call *Nuuita*."

"Well, I'm glad you and I are on the same page as far as not knowing anything about it," he said. Emerald laughed.

"Sorry," she said. "But someone at Rhahkmant'e might be more helpful."

"About that suggestion." He sighed. "How in the world am I supposed to get in there? How am I, a regular butcher's son from a different place, expected to be allowed to train there? I'm nobody, as far as they're concerned, I'm sure. If it is a special magical military training facility, I'm not going to attempt to *make* them teach me."

"*You* might be 'nobody', according to you," said Emerald. She turned around, checked for any onlookers, and lifted the back of her shirt up to her head.

Near her right shoulder-blade was a tattoo of a tulip-shaped shield with a dragon's face on it, an intricately hilted sword behind that, and words encircling the whole thing in what must have been Elvish. It was all done in a deeply saturated emerald green.

"I like your tattoo. But what is that supposed to mean?"

"Wow, you really are not from here." It was not a tone of criticism, but she was clearly amused by his ignorance. He wasn't sure how to take that. "I'm Reiyal, which humans tend to label Light-Elven, and this is the Elven seal of nobility and high-service. Only the highest elves have it in green. Everyone else has it in black, if they are at least special warriors, noble families, or related to the royal family. Commoners would not have such a mark unless granted it as a reward. Certain factions of Luunal, which you might call Dark-Elves, do not use this part of our ceremonies, taking on something else instead, but all Elven and most Human nobility at least recognize this symbol. Elves are the only people to gain favor with dragons, and a millennium or so ago, the first Elven king to establish the bond created this as a means of identifying those closest to his family."

"A *tattoo* is meant to prove all that?" He raised one eyebrow. "I could get a tattoo like that and be permitted to Rhahkmant'e? Is that what you plan to do? But I'm also not an elf." He chuckled, and so did Emerald as she pulled her shirt back down and turned to face him.

"No, silly." She shook her head. "Firstly, the tattoo is enchanted, so if someone shapeshifted into my form, it would not work in Avarinnia. If someone copies the tattoo, when a mage in Avarinnia attempts to bring out the magic, it would do nothing and be proven fake. Mine would glow with the lovely green of life energy, then change to a color that represents my bloodline. And as for getting into Rhahkmant'e, I am going with you. It is where I learned magical combat before I was permitted to use the training grounds in Avarinnia. They must allow you to do what I ask; I have rank there."

"Oh, that's a better plan," he said.

"*Ve harron.*" She smiled. "I know."

"Vay ha—what?"

"It means thank you."

They exchanged some more background about each other over another half hour while they ate, but Emerald was a bit vague or avoidant on some details. She said she did not yet want to freely discuss her home life or how she grew up or he might see her differently too soon. He left out some details about his version of the world, mostly so he might avoid any confusion until he understood the differences better himself. *How would I explain computers if they don't even use electricity the same way?* It was pointless to avoid the truth with her otherwise. She already knew about the sphere, so if she were to be a threat, it would happen anyway. Instead, she seemed eager to help. Outside the restaurant, Barbosa separated from them until later and they walked through the city.

Every once in a while, Emerald would move in such a way that grabbed his attention subconsciously, or she would react to something in such a way that he couldn't help but smile. She had some sort of pull, but he could not place what it was. It was nothing to do with her body or even her facial beauty, but it was something else that he felt made her different and attractive—not physically attractive, though she was, but attracting, like he wanted to bring or follow her anywhere and would be disappointed without her presence now that he had experienced it. He had never felt so natural with a woman so quickly, either, despite his early stumbles with words, despite their cultural differences.

Emerald accompanied him to the library to seek information about the orb. They found nothing there, so they tried two bookstores in different sections of the city. Neither of the shops had anything useful, so Opren chose to find his supplies for the coming journey to Rhahkmant'e instead.

After Opren visited a recommended swordsmith—who, it turned out, his father had visited while serving as a soldier—he had a well-balanced sword and sheathe. He ended up trading the blade in another shop for a wristbow with a mechanism designed to generate the same power as a larger crossbow. The projectile weapon would allow him to keep his distance against any more creatures that were stronger than a human. Emerald explained he could receive a sword from the mountain, so giving that up was not a concern. Then it was time to find a horse...or at least, a horse was the first thought.

Emerald led him to a shop she had seen the previous day, in the northern part of the city. It was called *Harold's Mounts n Gear Discounts*.

"I hope he has some strong horses that can handle long trips," said Opren.

There were actually various types of animals, including one that he would never have expected– a golden-bodied griffin with a dark-brown head and glistening blue eyes. It was the perfect image of an eagle's face, wings, and talons with a large lion's body and back claws.

Harold explained she ended up in his shop after she injured her wing. He took her into his care, hoping to help her heal and then sell her, but she didn't seem to like the second idea. Harold said she rejected—with pecks and swipes—almost anyone who came into her stall, unless it was Harold, his granddaughter, or other "youngsters".

Opren reached out to pet her and hoped for the best, ready to jerk his hand back should she attempt to bite. The griffin first stared at his hand as if waiting...but for what? He lowered his hand and slowly moved toward her neck to pet her like one would pet a horse. She took an abrupt step back but then came forward slowly, allowing her huge beak to contact his hand. She stepped back, growl-squawked, and nodded once.

Harold clapped his hands together. "Amazing!" He smiled. "I get over twenty people in here tryin' to buy this fantastic creature, they have no chance, and you come in here for ten minutes and, already, she's yer friend! I'll sell her to you and only you... since she doesn't care for anyone else, anyway. What's your offer?"

"How much do you sell your finer horses for?" asked Opren.

He was not entirely sure how to bargain over a valuable

animal, since he was still learning exactly how the monetary system worked in Everniot as it was. Emerald had given him plenty of money to use, but he had only purchased things already set at a price until that point. She explained seventy cripes became a sliv and seven of those became a fillot, but that did not help his judgment on pricing of a mount or anything of serious value.

"It ranges from one hundred-thirty to one hundred-eighty fillots," said Harold.

"Then I guess I'll pay you two hundred for her." *A rare animal I assumed was a myth until now must be worth more than a horse.*

"That's an offer I'd take from most men... but not you," said Harold, tapping the air with a finger as he thought. "I'll give her to you for.... one eighty-seven... plus two large saddlebags, free of charge. You seem like a good young man and, as I said, even if you offered me ten cripes and another, experienced rider offered five hundred fillots, it seems she will pick you, whether I say it's fine or not. She also likes your lady, I see." Harold gestured with a nod.

Opren turned. Emerald was petting the griffin without hesitation.

This girl is something.

"Thank you, sir." Opren grinned. "But she isn't my lady. We're just traveling together. She saved my life on the way here."

After they attached the bags to the griffin—which took a little coaxing—Opren and Harold finished with their transaction. Opren named the griffin Ra'ze based on Emerald's suggestions of naming conventions and a list of names he had seen in a book. A griffin was the symbol of Ra' Yana, so it suited her to have Ra in her name. Ra'ze rolling-chirped her approval of the name. Harold pulled Opren to the side, in a corner out of the stall.

"Son, let me give you some wisdom," said Harold, placing his hand on Opren's shoulder. "If that girl could pet the griffin the way she did so easily and you are going on a journey together, you should consider yourself lucky to even have the chance. Don't reject the idea of her being your lady. She's stunning."

"She is stunning," said Opren. "And different. I certainly would be glad to have someone like her as my lady, but I doubt she would be interested... and we did just meet. She saved my life, but I didn't know her until today. But thank you again for the great deal."

Harold waved as Emerald and Opren left with Ra'ze. A little way down the street, Emerald looked at Opren.

"You know I heard you talking with him, right?"

"Of course you did." He sighed. "Does it make you not want to travel with me anymore?"

"No, I'm still going with you." She smiled and shook her head.

Opren caught her glance over with just her eyes and hint at another smile as they walked... more than once. *What's amusing her?* She seemed to be smiling about a thought, not directly at him, but it still felt like it had to do with him. *Maybe she's observing me because I'm Human.*

By the time they gathered everything they needed, the sky was dark blue.

"I suppose I should let you sleep," said Emerald. "If we are to leave in the morning, you need rest. You just recovered, after all. The inn where I am is full, so I found you a room in the one we passed a few shops earlier. Barbosa will join you in case someone gets to you here."

"I like how you worded it 'should let me sleep'," he said with a chuckle. "Do you not sleep? You're an elf, not a vampire, right?"

"Elves sleep about half the amount humans do, and we can rest briefly in a meditative state to give up to a few hours of extra energy each period of rest time, which differs from elf to elf," she replied. Opren raised his eyebrows. "I'm going to sleep, but not for another hour or so. You, on the other hand, should sleep now, so you don't get tired, especially if things are currently hunting you. You may need energy and strength to fight even before Rhahkmant'e."

"Wow, that's convenient. You have a lot of interesting things about you."

"I'm sure my hearing and lack of need for sleep are what you noted most. I've enjoyed the day with you, though. I hope you rest well." She smiled. As she walked away, she tilted her head to say over her shoulder, "See you in the morning!"

He was drawn by the light footsteps and subtle bounce in her walk. No Human girl was ever that interesting to him, yet some were pretty who had liked him. Then again, they did not present a challenge. He laughed quietly at himself.

On the way to the inn, he began to feel the unusual boost of energy he had felt a week after his first accidental use of the orb. He could relax, unlike adrenaline or caffeine-induced energy, but he felt capable of five fights in a row or a sixteen-hour workday without stopping.

Barbosa was already waiting outside when he reached the inn. Opren rented a stall for Ra'ze—and explained to the attendant not to touch her, only to check on her and give her water for their own safety—before going up to the room with Barbosa. To his surprise, they were not required to pay for the key.

Emerald had reserved a much better room than he ever would have requested. It had two comfortable beds, a polished oak table with matching chairs, and a large bathing area. He hoped she did not pay full price, especially after she already gave him money for Ra'ze and his weapon and food.

As he lay down in one of the beds, he had flashes of his parents' murder again, but this time he could bear it just enough to push them out and drift into sleep.

The next morning, as the sun shone through the window, Opren looked out at a table-sized sundial near the inn. It was half past seven o' clock. Emerald had said to meet at nine.

"Wake up, Barbosa," he said, turning to the granwolf, who was curled up like an enormous cat on the other bed. Barbosa grumbled. "We need to get ready to leave before Emerald arrives."

The granwolf yawned and stretched, then went downstairs for a bath in a pond. Opren shaved and washed, then packed what supplies weren't already organized in their bags. By the time he finished, Barbosa had returned. They checked out of the inn.

"We could let Ra'ze stay until midday, so we'll just come back for her after we buy some food to bring with us."

We should buy some cheese to bring, suggested Barbosa. Opren agreed and quickly shopped for what they wanted, walking briskly between shops. He still had unusual energy, despite the time of morning it was and lack of breakfast so far.

After shopping, the pair went to pick up Ra'ze, who greeted them with a rolling chirp. Opren rubbed her with a smile.

"Good to see you, too." He attached the luggage they acquired to a saddle and carrier he purchased the previous day, strapping it all to the griffin. "That feel all right?"

The griffin nodded. Barbosa suggested anything leftover from what Ra'ze was carrying should be tied to him since he was stronger than humans or elves, and Emerald's mare would have enough of her own things to carry. They checked the big sundial. It was well after eight.

"Good thing we're almost ready. It's time to meet Emerald."

Oh, and of course we wouldn't want to keep your lovely lady waiting, would we, Opren? Barbosa laughed. Opren pointed out she wasn't *his lady*.

The group waited outside of the inn where they expected to meet Emerald, until a little after nine. Opren commented on her lateness. He was positive that was where she should show. He groaned and mumbled something not entirely meant to be coherent. *Did I screw up?*

"That's soo articulate." A laugh followed the newly familiar voice behind them.

"Morning, Emerald." He turned to face her. Her hair was brushed and widely curled at the front. *Her hair like that is wonderful! She is too pretty to ignore it in a mirror. She acts as if she doesn't care unless I bring it up, but she* must *feel at least somewhat good about being beautiful when men are not bothering her.* "Your hair is really pretty that way."

"Since we're giving out compliments, you look good cleanly shaven," said Emerald. "We should establish I am pretty even by Elven standards, so the compliment is pointless, and everything should be settled."

"I suppose we can be... 'settled'," said Opren. An uncomfortable silence followed. He broke it, "Well, let's head out, crew!" Barbosa and Emerald laughed at his attempt, and he joined them, glad it broke the tension even if it made him sound like he had no idea how to command.

For the first half of the day, Opren rode Ra'ze and Emerald rode Shari, while Barbosa had the endurance to travel plenty of distance before he needed to stop. While on their mounts, Emerald and Opren had no trouble continuing slowly while eating something small. But after the sky was dark, it became necessary to let the animals rest and to eat something more than the dry food bars or a single piece of fruit.

"Let's set up camp," said Opren. "Be prepared to wake early, though."

"*I'll* wake *you*." Emerald laughed. "Elves need less sleep, remember? I'm always up early compared to your average sleep times."

After forming the camp, the companions decided where to sleep. Barbosa would not fit in the only tent well—which was fine with him as he usually slept outside—but Emerald and Opren could both fit.

"Let me get this straight. You want to sleep in my tent because you forgot one and prefer the shelter?" said Opren. Emerald nodded. "And you want to change in the morning?"

Emerald nodded a second time. "Not gonna work." He shook his head. He did not want to see her reaction to him taking note of her unclothed, considering her responses to any comment of her appearance while fully dressed, even accidentally.

"*Rela*, it's just a tent together. I'm not going to sleep naked or in your sack," said Emerald, one hand raised to near chest-level, as if to receive a better explanation in physical form.

"You– Wait, do you usually sleep naked?" Opren's face felt warmer and his stomach tightened for a second as she laughed, not replying at first.

"I'm going to change before you wake," said Emerald, brushing off his question. "Or else set up a curtain."

"To be safe, just set up a curtain anyway." He gave up trying to argue. It wasn't that he would not enjoy sleeping next to her or watching her change. It was that he was afraid to enjoy it more than she probably wanted him to.

Emerald agreed to do so, then walked toward the darker part of the forest with more trees.

"Where are you going?"

"To find firewood," she replied over her shoulder. "We will need more than what you brought to start a fire."

"All right, but come back soon, please. I'm going to cook. And it's dark." *Now I sound like Mom.*

"I won't be long. I'll also pick some more fruit if I find some," Emerald called back as she disappeared into the shadows.

Twenty minutes later, Opren dished out food to Barbosa and himself. He gave Ra'ze a bowl of meat he cooked with oats and carrots.

"I wonder where Emerald is," he thought aloud.

Probably not finished with finding fruit and wood, offered Barbosa.

He said he agreed to the obvious but inwardly was a little worried after the amount of time. He thought about the Shirrkki and hoped she would not run into more of them. *She saved your life, idiot. She's probably gonna be fine.* He laughed at himself.

Hold on, I hear quick footsteps, Barbosa's next sentence broke his thoughts. *Too small and quiet to be Shirrkki, but not Emerald's– I can't hear her footsteps at a distance.*

"Be ready."

Opren grabbed his new wristbow from a bag on Ra'ze's left, strapping it onto his arm just as an aged-looking man burst from the trees.

"Don't ya shoot me, shoot them!" yelled the man as Opren pointed the wristbow at him.

The man pointed to where he had just run from as two rabid wolves tore through the leaves. He rolled out of the way as one wolf tried to attack him. As it bit at the man's thigh, Opren shot it in the side, which caused it to fall and howl in pain. The second wolf turned its attention to Opren. It leaped on him and bit for his neck. Just as its mouth was going to reach his neck, Barbosa gave it a powerful swipe, knocking it off him.

Barbosa gave a massive howl, stunning the wolves, the man, and Opren alike. Barbosa quickly finished the wolf that bit at Opren.

The first wolf was injured by Opren's arrow, but not dead, and it went for the older man a second time.

"No," Opren grunted as he stood, shooting the wolf another time, hitting its ribs. It howled in pain but still bit at the man. The man managed to dodge it just in time. The wolf opened its mouth for another attempt, but Ra'ze slammed her large sharp beak into its already injured ribs. The wolf yelped and fell to the ground with a whine, barely moving. It tried to snarl, but Ra'ze killed it before it could do anything more.

"Who are you?" Opren pointed the wristbow at the man again.

"M'name's Evaniere Poltis. Most people call me Pole for short, since I always carry one for hiking and another for fishing. Now could ya please point that thing somewhere else?"

The man gestured at the wristbow.

"Well, Pole, it seems this forest is too big of an issue for either of us alone. Would you care to join our group?" Opren lowered his wristbow.

"Seems best for both of us, yeah. If you feel you can trust me enough."

"We don't need to trust you… at first, at least. If you become trouble…" Opren pointed at his wristbow, then at Pole's heart.

"Yeah, yeah. I get it," said Pole, waving his hand as if to knock the thought away like a bug. Opren smiled and nodded once in confirmation.

If you keep adding companions at this rate, you'll be able to have an army to fight the Shirrkki and sleeskaxes, boy, said Barbosa with a chuckle.

After greeting Barbosa, Pole commented on how extraordinary granwolves were. It was a surprise this old man knew what Barbosa was right away. But then, Opren's own judgment on who would know what in Everniot was weakened by not growing up there.

"You haven't happened to see a pretty young woman about my age, have you?" asked Opren. Pole denied seeing any women recently, looking disappointed as he did.

"He's talking about me," said Emerald's voice beside Opren as she walked out of the darkness of the close-together trees. Both men turned to face her.

"Where have you been?" asked Opren, more concern than intended in his voice.

"It was hard to find fruit in this part of the forest," she replied. "But then I heard the wolves and Barbosa and hurried back. I'm glad you managed on your own."

"I see why you described her as pretty." Pole grinned. "Can I have a hug in place of a handshake? I'm Evaniere Poltis, but call me Pole." Emerald consented and hugged him, rolling her eyes as she did.

"See? I told you, men do this type of thing often," she said to Opren as she released. Then to Pole, "Call me Emerald."

"How is it you pop out of nowhere all the time?" asked Opren.

"Elf, remember?" She indicated her ears. "We can train to fool each other when approaching. I had fun with it as a child, so now I do it automatically, and I *can* even fool other elves when I want. No humans could hear me without magic."

Emerald picked up the small branches she brought, grabbed some kindling, and walked over to restart the fire. After she finished serving the remaining food, including a thing she found called a porla—a juicy red fruit that turned out to be delicious—she commented everyone should get some sleep. The others agreed and settled into their respective places. Opren finished setting up the tent as Pole laid out his own blankets and said "good night".

Once both Opren and Emerald were inside of the tent, she set up a thin blanket between them to act as a curtain. The two lay down and said "good night" to each other through the material.

The following three days of travel were incident free, which everyone was pleasantly surprised to note. On the fourth day, the enormous black mountain came into view shortly after noon.

6

As they got closer to Rhahkmant'e, the stone of the massive hills appeared to be like obsidian or something similar, not only regular rocks. It was like a gigantic black gemstone, the largest black stone Opren had ever seen or imagined. None of the mountains back where he grew up were quite so impressive, not that he had seen in person at least; sure, some were taller, but none had such an appearance.

The companions reached a space at the bottom edge of the mountain after another hour. Emerald explained some of the rules and goings-on at Rhahkmant`e, so the group didn't seem like ignorant newcomers. Curiosity grew about how much food and what kinds of sleeping quarters they might be granted, based on her informing them the inn at Ra'Yana was nothing compared to what was at the mountain. Emerald walked up to a wide, tough-looking man with what appeared to be shards and chunks of stone on—no *in or as*—part of his skin, including in place of hair. He had locks made of smooth dark stone (however stone could act like hair).

"*Shle-ca-poneeton-wan-rogth,*" Emerald said to the man.

"*Rutendehg,*" the man replied in a language Emerald

explained was Rhognomarish. She said he had chosen to guard the mountain for the last three decades, as it was the closest thing to his home mountains in the far northern sect.

"*Ve harron*," said Emerald in Elvish. The two gave quarter-bows, and the man slammed his fist into the rock a total of nine times in five different places. The wall opened, like clay remolding quickly into a growing hole, to display a short tunnel.

"You may pass," the Rhognomar said in a heavy accent Opren heard as a blend between Scottish and Russian.

Everyone went through the small tunnel, which suddenly changed size and shape to accomodate as the mare, Ra'ze, and Barbosa climbed through. The man tapped the wall four times after everyone was through, causing it to close behind them as if nothing had happened. A tall woman in full polished silver armor approached them.

"Welcome to Rhahkmant`e!" she said in a dignified, clear voice. "Welcome back, Emerald. Are you here to see your cousin?" Emerald explained the reason for the visit. Then the armored woman instructed the others what to do for the evening and the following morning, introducing herself as Athera, Head Mage-Knight of Rhahkmant'e, as she spoke to each person. The group was then dismissed to find their respective places of rest and learn the layout of the city.

After Opren rested for the night in a beautiful room, about twice the size of the room in Ra'Yana, with a huge bed, redwood table, and elaborate bathing area (which confirmed Emerald's description), he went to see Athera as requested, to begin his new lessons. He started left out of the… "inn" (it was clearly more than an inn, more like a hotel with suites, but that term did not seem to exist in Everniot), spun and started right.

Upon arrival to a fenced-in area, he handed the guard a small bronze card Athera had given him and was permitted to enter the sparring grounds where she trained.

"Welcome, Opren," greeted Athera as he walked near.

She was taller than he remembered from the prior evening and had striking features now visible with her helmet removed. He imagined her in a dress, as she might be at a social gathering, and decided the armor suited her much better. She stood completely straight and her expression exuded wisdom with an air of valor. *I bet she could seem intimidating during battle to most men and women alike.*

"Good morning, Lady Athera."

"No need to address me formally, unless we are in highly honorable company, but thank you for the respect from the start," said Athera. "I need to start you immediately so you might catch up with the other starting trainees as soon as we can manage before I can train you thoroughly. Emerald told me you have a magical artifact you don't understand. If I can, I will help you with that after the basic training is complete. We will begin work on spell-wielding and magic fundamentals today, followed by your initial spell when you have a good grasp on casting. What type of magic would you like to learn first: offensive, defensive, focus, healing, or communication and persuasion?"

"The sooner, the better," said Opren. He smiled to Athera, but he inwardly felt as if he were about to fight in a dangerous tournament. He would enjoy learning, especially anything related to combat as usual, but he had a purpose beyond competition at the end of his training this time, a drive that said he could not fail instead of a regular passion. He had to learn this well enough to avenge his parents. "What's a focus spell?"

"Levitation, improved hearing or concentration, magical camouflage, and the like are focus spells," replied Athera. "All spells require one to focus in some capacity to cast until mastered, but these may take extra time, concentration, and clarity. Unfortunately, that will cause you to take longer to learn anything else at first so, since you seem like someone who doesn't want to wait, I suggest doing that type later."

"Defensive, then." He would not need much offense if the

orb were to continue giving him power. Once he learned some of its magic for his own intentional use, he could simply fight with that.

"That's a good choice." Athera had a smile in her eyes. "Before we begin anything, I will explain how spells work. Please pay close attention and ask any questions you might have during pauses. But do not interrupt. You, the spell-wielder, have stages and so do the spells you want to cast. The stage of magic you use cannot exceed your personal stage as what we call a *Casteri*. If you attempt to use a higher stage spell, you may die or, at the very least, expend an excessive amount of energy to use it, and you will likely be unable to control it. If you grow as a Casteri, the spells you know may follow, but a specific Stage One fire spell, for example, will do nothing more. Only the Stage Two version you may pick up through training will do anything else. That said, most lower stage spells take much less energy to use, once whoever uses them becomes a more experienced Casteri.

"Magical source and spirit energy are often called *Nuuita*, as it is the term for it in Elvish, since the elves tend to be the most gifted in natural magic and elemental spells and have used it the longest. To them, there is life energy and spirit energy. Spirit energy comes from the soul and heart, while life energy is exactly what it says: the living self's energy. Magic comes from the spirit and nature, so it is logical to consider the energy to produce magic the same. Casteri is also from an Elvish term.

"Depending on your proficiency in which elements you use, your stage as a Casteri may increase by certain standards the old mages created to judge one's overall magical power and skill. An example of this is me. Since I can use multiple elements and types of magic masterfully, I am considered a Stage Four Casteri even though every spell I use, save for one, tends to be Stage Three and lower."

"Is Stage Four high?" asked Opren.

"The highest stage spell-wielder you will meet on a

regular basis is Stage Four, but the highest stage ever known is Stage Seven, which happens to include Runaic magic. As far as most historians and mages know today, only Stage Six and below Casteri are living and the few above Stage Five are wizards, beyond any single elemental spell-wielder. All right, now we can get to the experience part of the lesson for today. Before that, any further questions?"

"So do I need to do anything with my body or hands for this or just concentrate?" he asked.

"First, you need to figure out which element is your Birth Element, the elemental source you are most attuned to and likewise most easily able to use and advance. To do this, I will test you with a few things." Athera handed him a scroll to study—it contained full details about the information she had just given him, in the case he needed a refresher or a little more history—and she took some items out of a bag next to her. She placed a large, thin sheet of wood on the ground in front of him to use as a sort of table and placed the various items on top.

"What's the mouse in the jar for? I assumed when you said elements, they were like fire and water."

"You are correct. We will use him to check if your specialty would be with summoning," said Athera. "He has been trained to sense certain things that would indicate you can call him from anywhere or manipulate him against his will. If the mouse comes to you, you are a summoner, which is a subclass of a Casteri. It is properly called Fanucasteri, an animal magic wielder. If he stays away, you are something else. If he is attracted to you before you even open the jar, like this," Athera placed her hand over the jar, and the mouse floated to it, trying to scratch its way out once it reached the top, and fell when she removed her hand, "it means you can already summon something. That's a spell we cast on this mouse for testing, but a Fanucasteri can manage to attract any animal against its will if need be, once they become experienced. I am a Fanucasteri myself, so I can also do this whenever I want with any animal friendly with me or overpowered by my will." She placed her hand over the "table", concentrated for a second, and the mouse disappeared from the jar and instantly appeared beneath her hand.

"Most summoners choose a specific type of animal to work with, but experienced ones may use multiple types of animals, or other beings." She paused. Opren furrowed his brow, unsure what "other beings" meant. "I see that gave you pause. Yes, some Fanucasteri can master a different being other than an animal or insect, even objects imbued with life or, in darker instances, human-like beings. If you don't have the summoner essence, I can still teach you some magic you can use to go along with summoning, but you will never be able to use multiple beings at the same time, and your control will be limited. Now, I want you to place your hand near each of these things one at a time, focusing on the object and whatever you want to do with it, with an otherwise clear mind."

"In case I am a, uh, Fanucasteri, may I try the mouse first?" he asked.

Athera agreed, placing the mouse back inside the jar. Opren placed his hand over the jar as she had done, but nothing happened. He opened the jar and put his hand down to the mouse so it could crawl to him while he focused on it. It stayed where it was, looked at Athera a few times, and ignored him. He grunted. He had enjoyed the thought of summoning as his primary magic type.

Athera instructed him to move on to something else.

He placed his hand over a bowl of water she had placed on the table. Concentrating on making it rise to his hand failed, so he tried to push it into ripples instead. That also failed, so he moved to a lantern with a flame inside and tried to make the flame grow or flicker wildly. Nothing special happened, which was another disappointment because he liked the idea of being a Firecasteri or, as Athera explained it was really called, a Brenicasteri from the spell-word for fire– *Bre`nithe*. Water was Wydrecasteri after the spell-word *Wydre*; lightning was Reiycasteri after *Reiya*; and stone and earth was Uunducasteri after *Uundu*. Athera added that Uundu received its word from the Elvish goddess for nature, Uundulara, like their name for the planet, Uundular. Only elves or fae could be completely true Uunducasteri, because they were able to manipulate nature and plants, as well as combine with nature or receive renewal from nature, in ways humans and other races could not. Even non-Uunducasteri elves could manage some minor nature-based magic. *I wonder what nature magic Emerald can do.*

After trying all the items, Opren seemed to have no Birth Element. He grew discouraged, until Athera explained he had forgotten about one element that needed nothing—more accurately, *anything*—to test. She first made sure there was no breeze and held up a large leaf. He tried to make the leaf move by concentrating on it and willing it to be pushed but, as with everything else, nothing happened.

"Maybe I actually can't learn elemental magic. Clearly, this is not working either." He did not intend to quit training, especially because he needed magic to face the sleeskax, but he wondered if the orb was the only way he would be able to wield magic.

Athera explained his method was incorrect for what they were testing. If he tried to move the *leaf*, he was more accurately trying to be an Uunducasteri or a psychic, not a Hycasteri—which he had called Windcasteri—like she expected him to be. She instructed him to focus on the air itself and make the *air* hit the leaf to move it, as opposed to trying to make the leaf move. He obeyed, but with no success this way either. He tried again at her command and, when he felt a subtle swirling vibration rise in his chest, travel down his arm, and come from his hand, then a slight push against the air, he finally knocked the leaf out of her hand.

"Now I have it! About time. I know what it's supposed to feel like now!"

Athera congratulated him and said, "So you *are* a Hycasteri. That's very convenient, since you should always have air around you. Most Casteri must find and use their element as a source until they practice for some time, but you have your source wherever you need. I'm going to set up some targets of different shapes and sizes and weights, at which I want you to blow the wind until you can move them all. This will take some time but, even if you fail at first, keep going."

"I never intended to quit." *And I damn sure won't now.*

Athera set up the targets, including some leaves that would be no challenge now that he understood what to do, some empty and some full barrels... and *cannonballs...*

How in the hell am I meant to move those with just air?

He managed to hit all the leaves with ease in a matter of minutes and moved on to some thick parchment. He knocked a few marbles off the fence after a few minutes of practicing accuracy, then rocked an apple, but didn't make it fall. He willed the wind to hit harder until the slight push at casting the spell grew in force, which worked and knocked the apple off the fence. He repeated this same strength for a few other fruits and a few small stones. By the time he reached an empty barrel, shooting small bursts of air was simple, and he could aim pretty well at the distance of about ten feet he stood from the targets. Unfortunately, the large barrel gave no indication of being hit by anything. Opren shot air at it five more times, trying to shoot stronger bursts—even a few times in rapid succession—but only managed to make a sound with the strongest he could seem to manage, and not even the smallest movement.

After letting him fail several more times, Athera said, "Try saying *Hyt*, the base spell and Old-Elvish word for air and wind, when you shoot at the barrels. Imbue the act with the spell essence itself, carried by the word to invoke it."

Opren said the spell-word, rocking one of the empty barrels the first time he did, knocking it over on the second time. He continued with the other barrels until all were tipped. Athera set them up and instructed him to do it again, this time while he tried to make the barrel fly backward. He questioned if this would work at his current level, but she assured him that, with the spell-word, it should.

"*Hyt!*" He focused his intention on a barrel, visualizing it lifting off the ground—based on how the air would feel as it flew from him and into it, like picturing a bullet hitting a target while readying for the feel of the gun upon firing and correctly squeezing the trigger—and flying back several feet. This worked for about two feet while the barrel was a couple inches above the ground, yet he didn't make the barrel tip over in the process. A lack of power remained in his shots of wind, and his willpower alone seemed to do nothing, and the spell-word had already boosted his ability (probably tenfold on the first cast).

Athera instructed him to try until he could tip over a full barrel *without* the spell-word. She explained this was an advanced technique, usually not picked up before Stage Two, but she wanted to see what progress he could make by attempting it. He spent over two hours as he practiced on an empty barrel until he could tip it or make it rise a couple inches and fall about a foot from its original spot. Through that, he also learned how to hold things up with the wind, instead of just blasting them into movement.

Athera let him have a break so he could get something to eat before any further training. She ate along with him and explained in further detail the terms and descriptions of specific elements, Casteri and their abilities, non-elemental magics, common familiar animals used by summoners, and the first spell he was going to learn after the basic air and wind control. She explained that every spell could be classified as unclassed, Dark, or Light. Dark spells were commonly used by possessed beings, demons, or those who worked with the dead, like necromages. He assumed that evil beings used Dark magic, but Athera corrected that many Casteri could learn to control all three classes of magic, regardless of morals, ethics, religion, philosophies, race, or otherwise. It mattered whether a Dark or Light spell would control the user more than the other way around, as well as the spell-wielder's intent. Dark could cause a positive outcome, and Light could cause damage, in certain hands.

Opren continued his practice with Hycasting for another few hours, and eventually managed to knock the empty barrels over one at a time, rocking full barrels close to tipping point. Athera dismissed him for the night and told him to meet her at nine in the morning to complete his first true lesson and move on to learning the Stage One defensive spell.

Opren gathered his friends for dinner and found a good place to eat in the near center of the mountain-city. The males, including Barbosa, had a very complete meal that involved fish, steak, vegetables, cake, salad, fruit, pudding, cheeses, and wine. Emerald enjoyed a smaller portion of each side. She mentioned she did not eat meat, other than fish, and gave Barbosa her received meat, which made him ecstatic. Following dinner, the group split again and Opren went to bed early.

Opren hurried to Athera's sparring grounds the next morning, almost late. He lost track of time after waking early to practice on his own.

Athera was sparring with a huge man who had a scruffy beard, one good eye, and a scar over the left eye (possibly blind). He was easily over six and a half feet tall and wore large, hardened-hide boots and thick furs stitched together as a coat. He must have made the items himself from whatever creatures he might have killed. Athera was surprisingly strong to block and parry the man's attacks without even a flinch, dodging others with great agility.

When they saw Opren, the two stopped fighting; both combatants were breathing heavily, so they must have been going awhile. Athera reached and greeted Opren first, the large man coming over behind her.

"Hullo! I am Rutundo!" boomed the man, extending a hand.

"Opren, sir." He took Rutundo's thick hand, unsurprised by the man's firm grip, glad it did not crush his own.

Along with his patched-fur clothing, damaged eye, scruffy appearance and large stature, Rutundo had scars on his hands. The presence he gave off made Opren almost want to take a step back. *No one would doubt this man could fight the way he was with Athera just a moment ago, but I was right about her in battle too.*

"Good to meet ya, Opren! Athera and I have been discussing what you need to learn to be an impressive combatant with magic, bare hands, and weapons. I have agreed to teach ya weapons and weaponless fighting styles while she continues teaching ya spell-wielding. That way, you learn faster. She said you like getting right to things!" Rutundo grinned. His grin was unexpectedly warm and inviting for someone who appeared so tough.

"Good to meet you, too," Opren replied. "Thank you for agreeing to teach me."

"Not a problem! I'll see ya the day after tomorrow to begin with stances!" Rutundo left the area, with a wave as he walked toward the edge of the fighting circle.

Athera set up the same targets as the previous day. Opren was to shoot air at the full barrels until he could knock them over, without the spell-word. He did this for what felt like hours before he managed to tip his first barrel. Once he did, Athera told him to do the same thing to the empty barrels again, trying to make them fly back, *with* the spell-word. This time, all three empty barrels flew back several feet together.

"That was awesome!" Opren grinned.

Athera congratulated him and said he should not even be able to knock back more than two at the same time with his current experience. She explained his practice without the spell-word enabled him to make air push things with enough force so that when he used the spell-word to increase the power, the result was much greater than anything he could do previously. It would always increase by a magnitude, not simply an additional boost. She added his progress was excellent without the spell-word, especially for under a week of practice.

"You are now ready to cast a specific combat spell. Since you want to learn a defensive spell first, you will use the spell-word *hydep*, meaning 'air guard'. It forms a shield of air pressure."

She demonstrated by telling Opren to throw some sticks at her as she held up a hand and said the spell-word. A small movement in the air was visible, as if a large breeze were blowing small dust particles just in front of her, altering how she could be seen, almost like looking at her through rippled glass or vapors. When he threw the sticks at her, they just stopped, knocked back with the transparent breeze. "Now it's your turn," she said, releasing the spell and dropping her hand.

Athera gathered some sticks and pebbles as she commanded him to practice containing the air pressure in a circular shape or between his hands. After he got the hang of it, she told him to try the spell while she threw a stick at him. He almost managed a ball of air but failed to block the stick, which hit him in the shoulder.

"Well done," said Athera.

"How was that 'well done'? I just made a ball of air, not the shield-like disc you made. I didn't even block the stick."

"Most people manage a smaller ball of air the first time they attempt the spell, and many can't hold one as large as you just managed to hold," replied Athera. "You just need to work on the size and shape; and we will work with pressure balls later for offensive techniques, so it's good you happen to already understand the basics of that. Now, try again."

Opren raised his right hand in front of him. "*Hydep.*" He focused on creating the same sort of ball of air– but larger– and immediately willed it to flatten into a paperthin disc. He successfully created a disc of about one foot in diameter, but was only able to hold it for a few seconds before it turned to a small breeze and vanished, missing the chance to block the stick, again resulting in him being hit. After four more attempts, he managed a successful pressure shield of about a foot in diameter and blocked three consecutive sticks thrown at his right shoulder and one at the left of his chest.

"Your natural ability to control the amount of energy you expend during a spell is—whether intentional or not—quite impressive," said Athera. "You also seem to have a drive to better everything you attempt without being told to do so. Assuming you don't intend to take a break anytime soon, we will keep practicing until it is time to eat, and you should attempt a shield of about four times the size of what you have done."

She picked up several sticks and pebbles, allowed him to get ready, then tossed them repeatedly toward different parts of his body. He managed to block most of what was thrown, but he was hit in the foot twice and head once. He bit back a swear at the last one.

After an hour or so, he managed a larger pressure shield and blocked everything Athera threw. She chose to throw larger rocks and sticks since he was making great progress. It would really hurt if he did not cast correctly at that point. *That's one way to motivate me.* Eventually, he was able to block large sticks and stones, and he could form a shield of pressure about three feet in diameter. Soon after he succeeded in the new size and skill, it was time for their late lunch. Athera had brought sandwiches so they did not need to leave the area and could immediately return to practice, as they would still need a lot of time that day for Opren to learn the spell's proper Stage One.

"Normally, we would spend about a week on what you have done in the past two days, and another on just this spell," said Athera as he finished his sandwich. "But because you wish to learn as much as you can in just months- and we normally start training children of twelve or thirteen for a year before they are told to progress to Stage Two—I will go as quickly as possible as long as you can keep up. It seems the two days I had planned for this spell may take one because of your natural reduction of output energy."

He was unsure what she meant when she described his energy output or how much he would use, but he was glad it seemed like he was doing something that would accelerate his progress.

Athera instructed him to continue practice, and she set up a mechanism that shot either stones or small blocks of wood his way. The gear turning the machine was notched with different spacing to randomize the time between each shot. He had to learn to block something for which he needed to have a reflex, not just anticipate the timing, for combat. A new challenge for him was he could no longer observe an opponent's movements either with a machine.

Four hours later, the sun set and Athera allowed him to stop for the day. Rutundo would be his instructor the next day, in the same place and at the same time. With Rutundo, he would learn stances, strikes, blocks and parries with and without a sword; along with some new bow and staff skills. *I should pick up on this part of training easily.* Athera explained his lessons as a physical combatant and as a Casteri would alternate day by day so she would see him again in two days.

The first lesson with Rutundo went well, as did his several consecutive lessons over the next few weeks. His skills in spell-wielding when working with Athera—as well as practicing solo—increased to almost mastery level of Stage One Hycasting.

After the few weeks, Opren enjoyed practice fights with Rutundo a great deal more than when he first began. His stances and blocks were flawless, parries strong and swift, strikes powerful and quick. His strength was nothing close to the large weapons master's, but he was a bit faster than the larger man so could now hold his own for a few blows if they were to really fight.

Athera gave Opren his final lesson in Stage One Hycasting

on this twenty-sixth day of being at Rhahkmant`e. He had managed a five-foot-diameter, square or circular pressure shield; large, rapidly fired pressure spheres (with which he could easily knock back full barrels); wind blades and forms to encase his hands or weapons; and extreme gusts of air (with which he could cause a person to lift from the ground and shoot back several feet). His final Stage One lesson involved casting all of these without the spell-word for any of them, at will, as if in reflexive response to anything someone may try during combat.

Part of his higher-level training involved magical combat with Emerald—which correctly worried him, but not for why he worried. He was afraid to hurt her, whereas the reality was her skills surpassed his. After they were in combat for over ten minutes, Athera stopped them. They were both breathing heavily and Opren was sure he was bruised.

"Emerald, you may leave and go heal that cut on your arm. Thank you for helping today. We will need you to help with full combat soon. I'll send a person to bring you here when it's time," said Athera. Turned to Opren, she said, "Well done. You have completed everything I can teach you about Stage One Hycasting. Review everything tonight and tomorrow. On Luunday, we will begin Stage Two."

Opren said 'good-bye' to Rutundo and Athera and sought Emerald. He eventually found her beneath a willow tree near a pond.

"Hi, there," she said with her bright smile.

"What have you been up to?"

"Just appreciating time here again. I enjoy the beauty of the mountain, and I love combat training. I'm not really supposed to enjoy the combat as much as just need the training for my own protection, but I'm glad my parents allowed me to come here a few years ago."

"Why shouldn't you enjoy it? Besides, you were amazing today! You could have beaten me easily in real combat, I'm sure. Also, you don't really seem like a noble Light-El—Reiyal—

from what I've been hearing. Why do you dislike your beauty and ignore your status until necessary? I'm sure you could do whatever you want if you let people know."

"I would rather just enjoy my life than have duties and be held to a higher standard by strangers. My looks are a gift and a curse alike. Because of them, I can get whatever I want from nearly any male and some females, but I would rather just get those things because of my personality. I'm an elf, so I can put the emotion of attraction or peace into any living creature with any good inside, like vampires can seduce or attract any human or other prey." Emerald braided some vines on the willow as she spoke. "The difference is mine is a more positive ability for both people, but I feel both are useless since it takes no skill of one's self or their character, other than what they do through something almost unfair and magical. For instance, if you feel in love with me, the magic is amazing of that emotion and bond alone, yet if I *made* you want to love me through my abilities, the magic is only magic with nothing special about it."

'The magic is only magic'...not if you were from my world.

"I don't think you would need to cast a spell on me to get me to love you," he said. His stomach fluttered and he tightened his jaw. *Damn. I should have thought before saying that.* He prepared for her to lash out as she did when her physical beauty was given attention.

"What would I need to do then?" she asked. She sounded genuinely curious, maybe entertained, not at all cold or annoyed as expected.

"Huh-what?" he sputtered.

"I know you don't have my hearing, but I know you heard me," said Emerald. She raised her eyebrows and cocked her head slightly. "So?"

"You are lovely just the way you are," he said. "I enjoy talking with you and practicing combat with you. You are extremely generous, helpful, and supportive, but you don't baby me or others you know. You have a presence unlike any other woman I've met. You also don't abuse your rank, whatever power it might come with. Most of the time, I barely remember you are nobility. You are knowledgeable. And you are so b..." He stopped himself before the compliment of her outer appearance. It was that sort of thing that seemed to be the problem, even if she accepted the current exchange.

"Not going to finish?" she asked and folded her arms. "Not that you did not already say enough. You seem to think a lot of me. Thank you for saying all that."

"You won't like the last bit as much. But I do think a lot of you. You are great." He smiled.

"I know what you were going to say. Even without context, you have a habit of not stopping your mouth in time despite silencing your words." She chuckled. "I know you like my face and body, and I am all right with it since you mentioned all the important things first."

"Really? I can tell you you are beautiful without getting slapped now?" He smiled.

"If you are going to be that way about it, I might just smack you anyway." She rolled her eyes. "I prefer *velluu* for pretty or beauty and *velluusa* for beautiful, though."

"Those are Elvish, right?" he asked. She nodded. "All right, you are *velluusa*, Emerald."

"*Ve harron, suuveiy*, Opren," she said, meaning "Thank you, very much".

"What is your opinion of me?"

"I thought you would ask," she said. "You are strong in spirit, despite the obvious hardship you have faced. You are persistent and seem devoted and loyal. You don't take people for granted and even before you said it, I could tell you appreciated my generosity and do not take advantage of others. You are an atypical human, just as I am an atypical elf. You have something about your presence as well. You seem to have a purpose for your power, rather than a want to have power itself. You choose the inner beauty of someone, such as me, even when you very clearly notice the outer."

"Your outer is just a bit outstanding. So using yourself isn't really a fair comparison point."

"It's what makes it matter most that you noticed what's beyond the outside," she said with a grin. "Thank you for being fair and respectful without an ulterior goal."

"You're welcome." He briefly returned the smile. But then his heart sank a bit and he looked down at he thought about why he prioritized what he did. "I was raised well…"

"Yes," said Emerald. She used a finger to raise his chin to make his eyes meet hers. "You were." She moved toward him and kissed his cheek lightly. "You are a good man. Despite your want for revenge, there is velluu inside of your *Nuuita*, in your spirit and heart. Don't lose it."

"I hope I won't." He smiled again, though this one was a bit forced.

Emerald returned a smile. "Good."

His smile became genuine and a bit larger as he lingered on her violet eyes. *Maybe she likes me too. Now I just need to master spell-wielding and swordsmanship so I don't die against the sleeskaxes like she said.*

7

Athera gave Opren time off for a few days and he was, for the first time, genuinely glad for a brief period without training. After all, in only a month he had completed the magical combat curriculum someone would normally take a gradual year to finish. Then again, most people would have begun around age thirteen, not twenty, but his rate of progress still impressed Athera and Emerald...and himself. The accelerated training took its toll without any breaks. Unlike with the orb's magic, while casting wind he did not come back from exhaustion with even more energy than prior to use. It felt like a workout, but of something inside rather than his physical body (though his body also grew tired).

Opren walked through the market strip of Rhahkmant'e with Barbosa and Emerald on his second day off. The strip was a long street near the leftmost-center of the city on the second level of the mountain. It was lined with carts of several shapes and sizes, selling all types of foods and other goods, including some fireworks at two of the stands they passed.

The three found Pole in a pub near the center of the strip and he chose to join them for a bit. The two-legged group enjoyed ice cream after lunch and Barbosa was bought cheese. Emerald purchased a candied apple to bring Ra'ze. Pole chose to depart for the pub again as the others went to deliver the apple, because he was still interested in talking to the woman who was serving drinks and nobody wanted to know how long it would take if they waited.

"Don't get into trouble," said Emerald, shaking her head. "Opren has a reason to be here, but you are just our guest who is not training. I heard one woman already set your cloak on fire for being rude while drunk last week."

"I was *not* rude," said Pole. "I was just trying to flirt. She did not like my age and she is the one who called me a derogatory name. In addition, I had to buy a new cloak." He huffed as he gestured at his outfit.

"That is why you should not approach women solely on their appearance," said Emerald with a false grin.

"Yeah, yeah," said Pole, waving away the comment.

"Just don't get us kicked off the mountain," said Opren. "I need to finish here. I'm not leaving if you get thrown out, but you came with me, so it won't look good for either of us."

Pole agreed to not stand out or cause a problem, though he still tried to argue once more about the woman who set his cloak on fire with a spell when Emerald shot him a stern look. The others turned to walk back through the central area of the strip and a slender-yet-fit young man who appeared the same age as Opren was walking toward them. His platinum hair stood out against the earthy tones of the shops and bricks on the pathways, and he wore a scarlet vest. His eyes seemed to be fixed on Opren. As he came close enough to speak, he paused and smirked.

"Good afternoon," he said. "You must be Opren. I am Rufius. I have heard you train with Athera and seem to be progressing rather quickly. I train with Vallot. Athera's skills and power rival Vallot's, but I've been curious to see if her currently alleged best student can hold their own against me. I doubt it, but let's see if you deserve to train on this mountain like the rest of us."

"Are you asking for a fight?" said Opren.

"Yes," said Rufius. "Do you accept?"

"Opren, don't do what he says," said Emerald in a low voice. She was holding Opren's arm as she pulled close to speak near his ear.

Opren looked Rufius up and down and considered his mannerisms. He seemed like any other cocky opponent, the kind Opren had beaten several times even before magic. There was little chance this lean guy was stronger than him and, even though Opren was new to spell-wielding, he was certainly not inexperienced in combat. There was no reason he could see to avoid the fight.

"Let's fight then," said Opren. Emerald released his arm and folded her arms. He turned to her. "What?"

"Well, you already accepted," she said, gesturing with a hand. "Now you will find out."

"Let's start ten paces away from each other," said Rufius with another irritating smirk.

Opren followed Rufius to the middle of the street that was to the left of the fountain, where few people were walking. The few who were nearby seemed to know what was about to happen and entered their destination shops or moved off the road to watch in a safer spot. Evidently, street duels were not rare on Rhahkmant'e. The two men stood with their backs together and then each took ten steps away before turning to face the other. Opren wanted to laugh at how it reminded him of an old-fashioned duel in history or western films, but he refocused his thoughts since he knew to take a fight seriously.

"Be careful," said Emerald.

Opren found her worry sweet but, like his mother's, it was a bit unnecessary in the case of a one on one fight, or so he thought.

"Ready?" asked Rufius. Opren nodded once. "Begin!"

Rufius moved and then Opren could not see him. Pain lanced through his back. Rufius had appeared behind him and kneed him hard—he realized only after it had happened, and he was usually good at reading opponents, but not any could disappear. Opren grunted and staggered forward, and barely managed to dodge a sword slash as Rufius had flipped over him. The silver of the polished blade and red of gems in the handle flashed by much too close to his face for comfort. He had only just drawn his own sword and had no time to block or make a swing with it. *What the hell?* Maybe Emerald's concern was not misplaced, after all.

Opren managed to parry two other diagonal swings from Rufius' blade, but the power generated by the direction and momentum of twirling the sword was surprising—yeah, he had clearly misjudged Rufius' strength, or at least Rufius' potential to generate as much striking force as himself, and Rufius was *fast*.

"If you don't actually fight back," said Rufius between swings and twirls. He parried one of Opren's attempts at a stab with little effort. "You won't even make this fun."

Of course, Opren *was* fighting back, but it seemed to faze Rufius about as much as if they were playing basketball and Opren were only attempting to grab the ball from him, not even nearly the effort or concern one would expect as a sharpened *sword* came at them. Opren was getting more frustrated by the second, and Rufius must have seen it in his face because the same smirk returned to Rufius' face.

"*Hyt!*" yelled Opren as he flipped his empty palm toward Rufius.

A powerful gust pushed the platinum-haired man back a few paces. Rufius stumbled, but only briefly before he backflipped into a defensive stance with his sword held horizontally in front of his face. The smirk had changed into a look of irritation.

"I had heard you were most gifted in close combat, but if you want to start casting, we can *certainly* do that," said Rufius, a hint of viciousness in his tone. Rufius was not just sparring for fun; he planned to win without question that he was superior. This was a more dangerous game than expected.

Rufius raised a hand above his head with his palm to the sky and faced his other palm toward Opren.

"Don't do—" started Emerald, but it was too late.

A flash dropped out of the sky and into Rufius' raised palm and out of the other towards Opren, and it hit. There was no time to think or move before Opren's whole body burned and tingled. He let out a yell and tried to regain control of his body, but his muscles were slow to respond and it *hurt*. Athera had explained how to use *Nuuita* to protect oneself from the elements and other magical afflictions, but he had yet to perform the technique. In that second, he wished more than anything he had already learned it properly.

Rufius released the lightning and dashed forward as Opren dropped to a knee. Opren attempted to stand, but Rufius had his sword near his throat.

"Work harder," said Rufius. "I want a better fight next time. Otherwise, get off the mountain and quit." He dropped his sword hand so Opren could stand and then spun the sword and sheathed it in one motion. He offered a hand, which Opren took. Opren's pride was miserable, but he was not going to turn down the show of respect.

"I plan to do the first one," said Opren. "I'm not used to being the one who is helped off the ground. I usually get to offer. Quitting is not an option. I have a reason to be here and will beat you if you think that's what is required to keep training here."

"You are inexperienced when it comes to spell-wielding," said Rufius. "But you withstood my lightning longer than most. You need to master aura-warding by cloaking yourself with just a little of your *Nuuita*. I am surprised I had to only help you off your knee instead of completely on the ground in the fetal position without it."

"I don't know whether to take that as a compliment or—"

Before Opren could finish, Emerald had run over with a furious expression to slap Rufius on the cheek hard enough to make his head turn involuntarily.

"You are an arse, Rufius!" she said in a tone Opren had not heard from her before. It was something like the tone she had used when he, or especially anyone else, had mentioned her physical features in any way beyond factual statements when they first met, but it had a new fierceness... and new volume. "He does not even have on armor or anything of the sort. You knew he was not able to match you when it comes to magic and you were winning without difficulty in regular combat. What were you trying to prove there?" She folded her arms and stared at Rufius with her sharp and arched eyebrows angled so that it reminded Opren of an angry viper more than a person. She was much more intimidating when upset than he had imagined.

"I have no armor," said Rufius with a shrug. "And metal would have been as bad once electrified. He could have resisted if he had learned aura-warding. He has learned a lesson, and I have proven I am far better, as expected. I want to see what he can do after this. Besides, I did not use the spell-word intentionally."

"Even the weakest lightning is a problem for anyone without an aura-ward," said Emerald. "Which you know all too well." She shook her head and turned to Opren.

"Why are you looking at me that w—

"Shut up. I told you not to fight him," said Emerald, placing a finger to his lips. Her face had turned back to its normal version of stern, but her tone was still sharp. "Rufius is my cousin. He is a Half-Elf and a gifted Reiycasteri. He is dangerous, as you now know. You were not even close to being ready to face him without specific preparations. We can work on what you need, especially the aura-warding you were meant to learn soon anyway, but you jumped at a fight you had no chance at winning despite my warning. You *need* to *trust* me here."

"I do trust you, Emerald." His body finally stopped tingling and only the spot where the lightning had struck him still burned. "I just assumed I could take him."

"You are both fools who gave into testosterone and pride over cleverness and good judgment, I think," said Emerald. She stepped toward him and he expected a slap as well, but she touched the place on his chest where the lightning hit and after the initial pain of her contact, he felt a cooling and pleasant sensation. When she removed her hand and the soft green glow vanished, he had no marks and felt normal. "I am not going to be your whore for healing so you can fight everyone who instigates you. I'm going to talk to my cousin and then I will meet you and Barbosa at the pub with Pole."

Opren had not decided what he would do next, but he also did not plan to argue with Emerald in her current state. He and Barbosa left the area while Emerald continued to scold Rufius.

Well, you seem to have brought the wolf out from the bright flower Emerald usually is, said Barbosa with a chuckle.

"I don't think it's funny," said Opren.

You were the one in trouble, so that makes sense, said Barbosa.

Opren shot him a look before pushing open the door to the pub. They walked in to see Pole chatting with two women who were clearly not sober—which would probably explain why they both continued to talk to him and hang on him, despite being half his age, and why neither seemed jealous of the other. They did not appear to be the kind of women who would have come from a brothel, as one might expect of such behavior.

"You're back!" greeted Pole with a smile. "Want to have a drink with us?"

Opren walked close enough to the table so he did not need to yell back and said, "Just one, sure. I'm really back because I got my ass handed to me against, turns out, Emerald's cousin. Emerald was angry at us both and sent me back so she could talk to him before rejoining us."

"Well, have a seat," said Pole, gesturing to an empty chair. Opren took the chair and Barbosa lay down beside him.

I said he pulled the wolf out of the flower Emerald usually is, said Barbosa to Pole, allowing Opren to hear. *He doesn't think that's funny.*

"Oh, come, Opren." Pole smiled. "That is a good joke coming from a granwolf."

"She was certainly scary enough to be an angry wolf," said Opren. "I have never seen that side of her."

"Rethinking if you should ever want to be with her?" asked Pole.

"No. But maybe I should wear armor on dates—uh, formal outings together— if she is not in a great mood beforehand."

Pole laughed heartily and one of the women he had been flirting with giggled into a hiccup.

"I'm glad you all are enjoying yourselves so much," said Emerald's voice behind Opren. She had walked up to him without his notice. He hoped she had not heard the entire exchange.

She only just arrived, said Barbosa, guessing the concern.

"I am sorry about being reckless," said Opren as he turned to face her. To his relief, she no longer had an aggressive expression. "Until I am sure of my abilities and I have completed training, I will trust your judgment."

"Thank you," said Emerald with a nod. "Now, let's just truly relax for the next three days. I know you are going to work harder during training now to match Rufius, so you might as well rest and enjoy not being damaged every day."

He agreed, mentally amending her comment from "match Rufius" to *best* Rufius.

They spent the next three days without much thought about training, in part because Emerald kept them all so busy with plans for other things that they had no choice but to focus on everything *but* training. Opren appreciated it even more than he would have before his fight with Rufius, despite his preference to progress constantly until he completed his lessons and could avenge his parents. Most of the women he had met back home would have either stopped spending time with him because he worked too much on combat or would have been too passive and just let him make the decisions. He hated that he was one of the two who upset Emerald, but he was even more attracted to her when her reaction turned into something so direct, assertive, and thought out. Her anger did not make her lose her reasoning. Opren was inspired to control himself better because of it.

At the end of the rest period, Emerald agreed to help him with the aura-warding technique so they could take extra time outside of his usual lessons. He would need to master it, at least at a basic level, if he planned to stand against Rufius' Reiycasting. It turned out Rufius had only cast a Stage One spell to strike him, but Rufius was a Stage *Three* Reiycasteri.

8

The day after Opren's break ended, Emerald demonstrated how to use *Nuuita* to resist damage, particularly against adverse magic and elemental spells. She knew Opren had already learned to raise his output of *Nuuita,* but he needed to learn to hold a small amount of it at all times while in combat.

"Over time, your body will be able to react to do this nearly as reflexively as throwing up your hands for a block," she said. "Did you notice what I did?"

"No," said Opren. He had not learned to recognize changes in spirit energy levels yet, so it would have been a surprise if he had noticed.

"Well, you saw me take a breath as if preparing, right?"

"Yeah, I noticed that. But this must take more than a breathing technique."

"I was using my controlled breath and the second it took to concentrate on the release of just a little of my *Nuuita,*" she explained. "It is meant to be unnoticeable. I am gifted in healing and control of my own body and spirit, so I can do it without thought during a fight as well. But *your* goal is to just do it when you need to, then we can advance further once you master the basic use."

"Is there something I'm meant to feel?" asked Opren.

"It is similar to the sensation of raising your output of *Nuuita*, but instead of letting it out for a spell, just hold it," she said. He was not looking at her directly and she sensed his spirit energy growing and shrinking as she explained, but he was not holding it properly. He had learned to control his output well, but he did not seem to know how to absorb the energy again or how to let it linger. "Wait." She held up a hand and he stopped.

"What?" He looked at her again.

She walked over and stood in front of him. She took a small step forward so they were almost touching and it would be easy to kiss each other.

"Feel the tension?"

"Well, yeah," he replied with a nervous smile. "How could I not?"

"Attempt to get this close to me with your energy, but do not touch my *Nuuita* with yours," she said. "You will feel a push back of a sort if ours collide because I am resisting currently. Think of it as nearly kissing me and holding this tension, but with your *Nuuita*."

"This might be too distracting," said Opren.

"Then close your eyes and do it by your other senses and feeling of your spirit," she said. "Or would you rather never fight Rufius again and just lay with me?"

"That is like a trick question, or it has a catch," he said.

"What about avenging your parents? If you cannot fight Rufius, you will surely die against sleeskaxes." It was harsh, but it would motivate him. He needed the drive he had whenever she was not the one teaching, not the distraction of his lust or infatuation for her.

"You made your point," he replied without a hint of the previous smile. "I understand this is important."

Opren closed his eyes and took a breath. Then, she could

sense his spirit energy expanding. He held it back just enough, as he was meant to do. Unfortunately, it did not linger long enough, but he did manage precise control of his output.

"Great!" she said. "Do the same thing again but forget about me and just hold it there."

Opren took another breath and attempted the technique as Emerald stepped back. He appeared to have it, but she could not read his exact output or if it still lingered while farther than a step away. She asked him what he felt.

"I am holding it," he said. "But now what?"

"Hold it that way indefinitely," she said. "It will barely drain you in comparison to spells or other magic. If you do it properly, you can hold it during any situation unless you are unconscious. This is not really spell-wielding. It is more of a fundamental of magical combat that even non-Casteri can perform. It only requires above-average *Nuuita*, so nearly half of the humans and all of the elves of Everniot could learn to do it."

"How do I block anything with it?" he asked.

"It doesn't work like a shield. It is more like spirit armor. Once you lock it into place, it protects you," she explained. "True spirit armor is more than this, but for the purpose of simplicity just think of it like that. It is the same as light armor against aggressive spells."

As Emerald answered, Athera approached the area of the training grounds where they were practicing. She stood to the left of Emerald and looked at Opren.

"What it actually does is reduce the impact of another Casteri's *Nuuita* on you," said Athera. "It protects you from the initial physical harm of the element and weakens the magic used. Any harmful thing, whether magical or physical, must break through the aura before it can impact your body as usual."

"Which is why we as Casteri can survive being struck by lightning or hit by fire directly, or deal with the impact of rocks and such, as long as the source of the damage was produced or enhanced by magic," said Emerald. "I nearly forgot to explain why that happens. Thank you, Athera."

"But how do I make it do that instead of just releasing it?" asked Opren.

"You have to feel the difference," said Athera. "That seems to work well for you in all other cases."

"Watch us," said Emerald. "Athera, will you please throw a fireball at me?" Athera agreed and Emerald prepared herself by taking a grounded stance that would help her remain balanced even if she were to be hit with a solid blow.

"Are you ready?" asked Athera.

"You know you don't need to ask anymore." Athera had helped train her in this same technique, so the mage-knight knew she could even be hit in the back without preparation and still reflexively protect herself, not to mention heal any damage. Athera said she considered her the most gifted healer she had ever seen when Emerald finished training at sixteen, which was already two years earlier than most who do not become soldiers or instructors.

"I was being polite," said Athera.

Emerald smiled and Athera shifted her stance. She could tell Athera was moving slowly for Opren's sake, because she could see the whole motion and had time to check if Opren was paying attention. A fireball flew at her from Athera's left hand, then another from Athera's right. Both struck and Emerald held her stance. She laughed quietly at Opren's surprised face.

"You didn't get burned at all?" asked Opren, eyes wide.

"Not at all," she said. "That is what I was saying. It takes higher level spells to burn or severely shock someone while using an aura-ward properly. That was just a Stage One without a spell-word."

"But Rufius used Stage One against me without a spell-word," said Opren, brow furrowed. "And the shock hurt like hell."

"Fire is dangerous because it damages over time and, in heavy doses, it can do severe immediate damage, but lightning is faster and more destructive," said Emerald. "Lightning is the most dangerous basic element to wield and to face. That said, I am considered above-average when it comes to preventing or healing damage to my own body."

"If you are above-average, is it supposed to seem that easy when I do it?" he asked.

"Not yet, but yes," she said. "Try it. I am not good with fire because my Birth Element was not an element really; it was healing. I will throw a small and weak fireball at you."

Opren steadied himself and she made sure he was ready before producing a fireball. When she threw the fire, it stopped as it was meant to when it hit his spirit, but he flinched and his shirt was burned through to leave a one-inch hole. His skin was red but not burned away. It occurred to her she might have a misplaced judging-point for how well one should do the first few attempts. After all, she did it right on the first try, but she was neither the norm for students of the mountain nor Human. She was the only one in her class at the time to do it so well, the only one with the gift for healing and body magic.

"Good thing I can heal you if you are going to perform like that." She hoped the tease would make him push harder because he enjoyed challenges and competitions.

"Throw another one," said Opren. His eyes said he was ready this time, truly ready.

She produced a bigger fireball, similar to the ones Athera had thrown at her, and threw it at him with a snap of her wrist. Another fireball flew past her and hit him at the same time as her own. She turned to Athera and the knight grinned.

"What the hell was that?" exclaimed Opren, throwing up his hands.

Emerald turned back to Opren, who had been unharmed and stood breathing heavily due to his spike in adrenaline. He clearly had done the technique well.

"You did it." She smiled. He might not be happy she ignored his actual point to the question, but he would be glad he accomplished the goal.

"It's a good thing, since I had to stop *two*." He held up his fingers to indicate the number. "And they were bigger."

"You needed the extra motivation to succeed," said Athera. "I have noticed the same during our sessions. The more difficult or dire I make the situation, the faster you progress. It is quite impressive."

"True," said Opren. He huffed, but then his look of determination returned. "We should try with lightning now."

"We should go through the other elements first so you can practice before taking severe damage," said Emerald. "But we will work most on lightning. Athera will need to cast that because I have not learned to wield it. It is a difficult and dangerous thing to use if it isn't one's Birth Element."

"You should demonstrate how to break a spell after resisting," said Athera. "He might not be able to use it until later, but it would be good for him to see."

"Good idea." Emerald nodded. She readied herself again. "And lightning would be the best for this demonstration."

Athera raised a hand to the sky and faced her other toward Emerald. Athera said the spell-word, *Reiya,* Rufius had omitted—*at least he didn't attempt to kill Opren upon their first encounter*—charging the lightning to its full potential as it passed through her and struck Emerald. Emerald felt the tingle and a slight burn as Athera held the beam of electricity, but she held her ground. She gritted her teeth and focused on her forearms as she clenched her fists. She sent her *Nuuita* through her body and into her arms as she forced them down similarly to a swiping block downward. The spell broke and the lightning stopped, its effect gone. She could move as usual. She huffed and pushed a misplaced bit of hair behind her ear.

"That was awesome!" exclaimed Opren as he came over to her. "What did you do? You didn't even use a spell-word. The spell just *stopped*?"

"That is the basic result, yes," said Emerald. She could not help but smile at his excitement. He was like she was as a child, but it was funny to see it come from a man. "You must push the energy through you into a point that it can come from in a sort of burst. Combine the burst with physical resistance and, if your *Nuuita* is one with your body the way it should be as you hold it, you will break a spell. Though it only works if you are equal to or more powerful than the spell or the other Casteri."

Emerald had Opren perform the technique just to resist damage from every other element, then finally lightning, as they had discussed, for the next hour. He did fantastic, so she moved on to have him attempt to break the weakest forms of the spells she knew. The spells were nothing more than a child could perform, but she was still impressed that he managed to break three of the five she cast. Rufius' lightning would be a very different story, of course, but Opren was able to progress at a faster rate than anyone she had classes with as a child or adolescent. Considering his Human birth, it was truly special how well he could do everything he had learned in a brief time.

Opren wanted to eat as the sun set and Emerald was glad to allow him a break at his request.

"Oh, you are not compelled to train all day, every day, even in your sleep now," she teased.

Opren lightly pushed her shoulder as they walked, so she shoved him back and he nearly fell. He had seen some of her magic and sword-skill now, so she was no longer concerned about revealing her whole strength and abilities. She had not intended to knock him over, but she laughed as he had to catch himself.

"Are all elves that strong despite your size and weight, or is that just you?" asked Opren, after straightening and continuing his pace. He appeared to be attempting to look as though it didn't bother him, as if she had not just surprised him.

"Both," said Emerald, giggling before holding a smile in amusement. "Most Reiyal women don't train for physical combat, so I am stronger than most. Our culture is against war—starting or causing war, at least—unless it is absolutely required, and the men tend to be the physical combatants while women learn to call upon the earth, the elements, and energies to heal or protect by the granting of Uundulara. But our bodies use our muscle differently in some cases than humans or other races. We are stronger by similar-size comparison."

"I suppose I need to get even stronger than my father was," said Opren. As he finished the words, his eyes lost their intrigue and the new look was one of grief. But it was fleeting, as he immediately brought himself out of the moment with a sigh he seemed to want to hide. He looked at her and said with his usual tone, "That way I can best Rufius in physical combat without a problem."

"Yes." She flashed him a soft smile as she nodded. She truly wanted to reassure him if he had seemed to want it, instead of pretending he was not bothered, but she allowed him to handle his feelings how he chose. Maybe he could win the internal battle and not need to risk facing the sleeskaxes again, or so was her wish.

Opren did not return to the training ground with her after they ate, as he had agreed to meet Pole for a drink; Emerald met with Athera alone, which is what Athera had asked for before training started, so it worked out for the better.

"Are you aware five more assaults and two more infiltrations have had to be prevented on the outer edges of the base since you brought Opren here?" asked Athera.

"I heard someone talking about an attempted assault two days ago," said Emerald. "But I had no idea there were so many already."

"You mentioned his golden sphere has a special magic and Shirrkki have already attempted to kill him or take him for it more than once," said Athera. "I knew we would not have a problem keeping out Shirrkki, but I am concerned this increase in a need for watchfulness means whoever commands them knows he is here, specifically. If that is the case," she took a breath and thought a moment, "we will need to let him know and he will need to train in a way that will allow him to exceed his usual limits. He is already pushing himself, but he does not have the magical prowess to survive against the sleeskaxes... not yet."

"He seems resilient and persistent," said Emerald. "But I don't think a human who is new to being a Casteri is going to be able to learn in a structured way and still progress as quickly as he needs to." She thought through what she had seen of Opren's training. He seemed to need little rest and no amount of pressure stopped him. Something about him kept him going, whether it was his need to avenge his parents or something else, and he was already a fighter before magic and sharp blades were part of the combat. He also seemed to access his greatest power in the most threatening circumstances, including when he was almost killed for his orb. "I am going to send the king and queen a letter of request."

"You mean you want to bring him to Avarinnia?" asked Athera, eyes wide. "I expect they will allow the request from you, but will he be all right to train there?"

"The risk of such intense training will help him unlock what he needs," said Emerald. "I am starting to care for him, but I suppose he will need the danger. He also needs to experience what he truly must face to avenge his parents if he finds the sleeskaxes, like you said. I had hoped it was not inevitable for him to face them, but wishes won't prepare him, nor will they change his mind. I'll be there to heal him even more swiftly than the usual medical mages in the training grounds. He will also be able to learn other magics and non-military histories there better than here. Besides, my parents will not let a trainee die in their city. And he may be safe here from would-be thieves, but few places—maybe Delionyta with the dragons—are more difficult to breach than Avarinnia. Father made sure of it."

"Be careful." Athera smiled softly. "Someone might hear you and know what you really are."

"Enough people on this mountain already know,

unfortunately." Emerald returned the smile. "But it will be interesting to see Opren's reaction to hear the whole truth."

Emerald returned to her room and wrote a letter to King Eeloneus Avaria and Queen Bellavuu of Avarinnia, her parents, to request that they permit her new friends to train there as a special assignment for one of the warriors. She knew they would say yes, but she also knew they would scold her for being gone awhile and then making a special request. They only tolerated her sense of "whimsical adventure" and love of combat, but they did not condone it. She wrote the letter properly, formally, without any indication of her specific relationship with them by blood. It would help protect Opren, as well as herself, while traveling under her commoner's guise. She left out any specifics of Opren's sphere and shared only that it was an old magic the Reiyal Elders should know more about than the people training for war.

Emerald expected she would need to tell Opren everything before they took the journey, but she had about three weeks it would take the next part of his training before it would be relevant. She had enough time to gradually leave hints, or to prepare a way to say it. Knowing him, she might be able to just tell him the news, wait for his reaction to settle, then he would be all right. Then again, he could briefly lose his composure. She smiled at his probable reaction. *Only one way to know for certain. Maybe I should be more concerned what Muumleiy is going to say when I mention I would court a human.*

9

Opren heard from Athera about the attacks on Rhahkmant'e since he had arrived. It was ridiculous he was just learning of them *weeks* after the first few. He probably could have done something about them right as they had occurred.

"Knowing you would have liked to take action is a reason I waited to tell you," said Athera.

"But you told Emerald, right? She seems completely aware of everything, but I'm the *target* and had no knowledge of it until now."

"You needed to have few distractions to train with constant progress so quickly in the beginning," said Emerald. "But now that you have reached the point you have, Athera thought it was better to be open with you."

"You didn't?" he asked. For her expressions of concern, it was odd Emerald would keep something like this from him. He was a bit annoyed everyone else seemed to be aware of things he was ignorant about. He was already in a new place with new cultures and knowledge, but to further be kept in the dark when it involved him was not all right.

"I only learned of how frequent they have been this week as well," said Emerald. "And the guards have had no difficulty stopping the assaults and catching the invaders. One of the reasons this place is so great for training is nobody can access it without permission. You have not needed to know, because you have not needed to take action. You would have gotten in the way. I know that hurts to hear, but it is true. You need to train a bit more before you face real threats to your life."

"I have my grandfather's sphere. If I—

"That is exactly *why* they want to get to you, and you know it," said Emerald. "It would only attract more enemies."

"That is true," he admitted. "I still hate others are now risking themselves when I am able to fight."

"You are able to fight, yes," said Athera. "But the Casteri and even the regular soldiers around our central perimeter have trained for a decade, at minimum. We do not place early warriors as full-time guards. We are secure. That is their job. If we were to experience a true threat, we would have already let you know, and we would assign someone to watch you and protect you and anyone you meet. That said, a real threat to you outside of here is not usually a serious threat to our guards, if enemies can even manage to find and breach the hidden entrances at all. You do not have their experience. Your unique magic is unpredictable, right?" Opren nodded, though frustrated at the reality in her words. "That means you would not help enough with what I have taught you, which means you would be a liability instead of a help, until you learn control."

"But, again, I am the target," said Opren. "Why risk them coming here at all, if I can go out and fight and bring them to just one spot, even as a decoy?"

"There really is no risk to the hidden villages or training grounds based on a threat assessment of what has come," said Athera. "You need to train and not worry about the warriors here. They deal with these threats consistently, as they are here to train just for that sort of thing. It is only a rare thing to have attempts show this frequently in a short time, since most nearby warlords and rulers know we cannot be entered without permission and attacking a military Casteri facility is foolish."

"What if it gets more serious?" he asked. "I should not stay here waiting much longer if they continue. What if they send the No-Prey—the sleeskaxes? I saw what they could do. When they—"

"I have a solution," said Emerald when his voice broke at the thought of his parents' murder. "Please, trust me."

"I do trust you," he said quietly.

"Then I have some things to share with you before our next steps in your training," said Emerald. "And I hope the next part of the training will include information and practice with your orb's magic."

Emerald explained how she sent a letter to the King and Queen of Avarinnia, that the king and queen were, in truth, her father and mother, and that she was actually one of the three Princesses of Avarinnia—triplets. When he inquired about her sisters, she warned of Ruubi, who was said to be interested in most men and women, and said Soferina was the only one of them who really enjoyed being a proper, dutiful princess. Other than that, she said he would need to wait until he met them to know more.

After Emerald described her family, she told of her plan to have him train in Avarinnia in more detail than the letter described. Her parents only needed to know enough to give permission, but she had a goal for him to work with a special warrior and the Elder Mages in the city to discover everything he could about his orb and learn combat with it and further master Hycasting.

"They responded to my letter earlier today and agreed to my request," said Emerald. "They said Rufius' father, the king's brother, my Shela—uncle, in your language—Selios, will train you in Hycasting and combat. He is off from special missions currently, but he is an unusual elf like me and Rufius. He enjoys combat for fun, not simply necessity, which is probably why Rufius enjoys it so much. Rufius strives to be as skilled and powerful as him."

"They agreed to allow a direct relative of the king to train me?" asked Opren, dumbfounded. It would have been generous to request a high-ranking officer to train him as an outsider and commoner, let alone one of royal blood.

"He said he would enjoy it. He sent me a letter at the same time, and Rufius is to train with him, so he chose to train Rufius' new training rival." She smiled.

"Is he aware I intend to kick his son's ass?" Opren raised an eyebrow.

"He is also aware you need more training before that's likely," she said. "And if you two push each other to improve, once you are at that level with your own magic, it can only help you both."

"So elves don't approve of fighting," he said. "But the king's brother likes it and people know?"

"Most elves hate war, the damage and loss elevated conflict can cause, and unnecessary aggression, but fighting without the intent to kill is not a problem, unless out of foolish anger," corrected Emerald. "We are one of the most powerful races when it comes to magical combat, which helps to prevent brutality during needless conflict and win during greater struggles. It is how we stay peaceful, with a balance of strength and diplomacy that prevents attacks."

"What about you?"

"I enjoy adventure and the combat is a sport," said Emerald. "You fought as a sport without trying to kill before you came here, right? It is most likely like that. I certainly do not enjoy harming anyone and would prefer to protect and prevent wounds."

"Well, you are a healer." He smiled. "That makes sense. Anyway, that plan is good going forward, but it does not fix things right now."

"Yes," she said. "But I am also more than that. I have an

idea. If you can beat me right now, I will let you go fight at the perimeter next time there is an attack. But if I win, you don't ask again, like I know you will otherwise, and you allow the soldiers to do their jobs without question. I won't use elemental spell-wielding, but I may use the other magic I can do. Primarily, it should be sword and hand combat. What do you think?"

"If you were not a princess, I would probably just go fight anyway." He smirked. "But I like your idea."

"I'm going to hit you harder for saying that," said Emerald as she took a few paces away. "Get ready."

Emerald took a ready stance and Opren followed. He barely had time to nod before she flew at him in a sprint faster than he had seen during their practice sessions. She did not vanish from sight like Rufius had done, but she was nearly as difficult to see between movements. She reached him and elbowed him in the gut—*hard*. He coughed as he lost all the air in his lungs.

I guess she wasn't joking.

She had not started with a sword but, as she twirled away from him, she reached out her right hand and a sword flew from one of the many weapons barrels, zipped past his left ear and landed in Emerald's grasp. She completed spinning a second later, swiping the blade around as she did.

"Now, have you learned your lesson?" asked Emerald with a smirk. She was enjoying the fight already, more than he expected.

He tried to laugh between coughs, which hurt, but he managed to say, "Tough teacher."

Emerald pulled a pink ribbon from her pocket and tied it to the hilt of the sword, then around her own wrist. She wrapped it up to keep the six feet or so of slack out of the way. He thought it was a good idea to be sure he could not disarm her, but then it was clear there was more to it. She spun and threw the sword at him, sliced his right upper arm before he could think to react, whipped the ribbon back and caught the sword again. Then he felt the warmth and cooling sensation of Emerald's healing magic on his arm as she paused and held up her left hand. *She can heal at a distance, too!*

"That would have been a deeper gash on your trapezius had we been fighting to the death. You aren't doing very well." She had to know that would tick him off, but he assumed that was the idea.

Opren readied himself and raised his sword before charging her, which she dodged with ease to dance behind him, but he was ready for that to happen this time. She attempted to wrap the long ribbon around his neck, but he flicked his wrist so the blade could turn and slice the ribbon. Emerald flipped far enough away she was out of striking range and mended the ribbon with magic.

"That's better," she said.

Emerald was the one who charged this time, and he had to deflect the sword coming at him through the air twice before she even reached him to clash blades together. When she did reach him, she flipped over him and he barely blocked a slash to his shoulder. The blow threw him off balance and she took the opportunity to knock him down with her body. She placed her sword point to his throat and winked.

"But not quite enough."

"Dammit," he grumbled. She threw her sword perfectly into the barrel from which she had magically pulled it. Then she offered a hand. He took it and shook his head as she helped him to his feet. "Is Rufius going to be this bad when we fight for real?"

"I'm faster than he is without casting," she said. "But he will be using lightning, so he will be worse. But you see now why I don't want you to recklessly head into combat with unknown attackers. If they are not simple Shirrkki, they could have magic or skill that will make them a real threat."

"Well, what do I do in that case, if it is not in a place like this or with someone who cares to hold back like you?" He placed more anger in his tone than he had intended, but he still let it out. "My parents didn't have a choice! At least I have the chance at activating some special magic and a golden sword to kill whatever comes at me. They had no way! I need to do *something*! I can't just be useless and wait— can't ju—" His eyes burned as tears of anger and memory and grief all hit in waves that rocked him before the drops fell down his cheeks.

Emerald moved closer to him and put both her hands on his shoulders, and said, "Opren Saphren. Look at me." He took a breath to steady himself but let the tears continue as he lifted his head to meet her eyes with his own. "You are not waiting as a useless person. In fact, you are doing the opposite of waiting by training your arse off nearly every day, even outside of official sessions. You have progressed to a point most trainees don't reach until they train for a year, and you have done that in only several weeks. You have a special magic, and you will learn to use it. For now, it might be better if you can let out this emotion and give yourself another moment. You have resisted the feelings every time I see you struggle to accept your parents' passing. You need to let it happen before you can move past it."

"They didn't just pass away, Emerald." He wiped the remaining tears from his eyes. He took another breath to stabilize his voice. "They were murdered in front of me... brutally murdered as if for fun. I need to avenge them, not just cry for them."

"You are a true fighter, Opren," said Athera as she came closer to them. "But even the toughest, most hardened soldiers need time to grieve some days."

"I am here with you and will not leave you, because you are my friend now," said Emerald. "And I will gladly help you become stronger and more skillful until you are truly ready to make the choice of how you want to avenge your parents or do anything else. But please do not rush to your own death unprepared."

"You are right," said Opren. "Your words remind me of my mother; she would say something similar." He hugged Emerald without thinking, and she returned the embrace. "*Ve harron.* Let's do this your way, so only the sleeskaxes have to die next."

10

Over the next week, Emerald exchanged two more letters with her parents, until all was prepared for Rufius, Opren, Ra'ze, Barbosa, and—to Emerald's mild distaste but Opren's request—Pole. Rufius and Opren were equally grumpy about having to train together as "partners", as it turned out Selios had planned for some coming sessions. Unlike with any other teacher, Rufius could not request anything against his own father, the king's brother. Both young men would just need to tough it out, Emerald said.

Opren tried to see it as a challenge to overcome, but Rufius always had that smug air of superiority that made him want to hit Rufius, not cooperatively train with him.

Athera explained how the outer area of the mountain was to be traveled through and explored when they were ready to head out. There were certain plants to avoid because one kind ate mammals like a giant fly trap, and the other few were poisonous if ingested. Otherwise, it was to be a beautiful place and generally the same as any other mountain woods in terrain and fauna.

Pole showed up late to the gathering to leave; he said he

needed to say farewell to one of the bartenders who had just arrived at her bar before the group needed to meet. Opren had already picked up Ra'ze during the wait so, with Pole present, everyone was ready.

Emerald fed the griffin an apple for waiting patiently for Pole despite it being clear Ra'ze was ready to stretch her wings and legs after being stuck in a stall for a majority of the last several weeks. Emerald explained Ra'ze could explore freely in Avarinnia without concern for her safety or the elves being afraid the way some humans could be, and the griffin seemed to understand because she responded with a happy deep, rolling chirp.

The group set off down the path Athera said to take, and immediately Emerald voiced her recollection of where they were in relation to the edge of the mountains and the beginning of the sect ruled by Avarinnia.

"I want to show you one area I remember is beautiful in particular before we leave."

Everyone followed Emerald for about a half hour, until they reached a small clearing. On the other side of the clearing were some plants and trees showing a mix of vivid colors, from blues to purples to reds to yellows and gorgeous shades of green. Some of the leaves glistened in the sunlight as if they were reflective. *There wasn't anything quite like this back home.*

"This is truly amazing." Opren smiled. He walked up and touched a sparkling leaf. It was soft and felt like one would expect, but it gave the appearance of something glossy. "These plants are like stained-glass art. They always grow this way?"

"In Human Evernish they are called Crystal Rainbow," said Emerald. "They are one of my favorite plants. I would prefer these over the usual flowers as a gift."

Opren noted if he felt like giving Emerald flowers, he should instead find some Crystal Rainbow to create a bouquet. They really were more fascinating than simple red roses or white lilies.

Emerald allowed Opren to lead once they saw some of the

scenery she had mentioned, and she handed him a map. He seemed to be going the correct way, according to her judgment of their progress toward Avarinnia, but then Barbosa felt and smelled something strange.

The air has a feeling the way it does when any of you cast magic near me, projected Barbosa to everyone. *And I smell rock, the way you might notice it if a stone was crushed and made dust.*

"Also, while on the topic of things that are out of place," said Rufius, "I think you have us lost, Opren. What fool gets lost with a map in hand? I thought you grew up in a mountain forest area? *That* tree and *that* particular stone wall are the same as an hour ago." Rufius pointed at a tan stone wall on one part of the mountain. It did appear familiar. But Opren knew not to go in circles, of all things. He had learned to navigate in the woods as a child from his father.

"I know I was going straight east like Emerald said to," said Opren, resisting the urge to yell out frustration at the situation and irritation at Rufius. "Don't just assume—"

"The rock is doing something," said Pole urgently.

The others looked at the stone wall Pole was pointing at, the same one Rufius had first indicated. The wall was moving —not in a simple downward pattern like a rockslide, but truly *adjusting* itself. It turned and shifted until a shape like a fat body formed. The body itself was like a boulder and the arms and legs were multiple large shards of rock. The thing was like a ten-foot tall person made of stone.

"It's a golem," said Rufius before Opren could ask.

"Are they dangerous?" asked Opren. "Or could we just avoid it?"

"They are puppets, like a summon but without actual life, in most cases," said Rufius. "It is not a natural creature. Someone put it here."

"You think it is the same person who made us go in circles with magic?" asked Pole.

"Very likely," said Emerald.

How do we kill it if it attacks? I can't bite through stone, said

Barbosa.

The golem walked slowly toward the group, its head —really a smaller rock with eyeholes and no actual face— directing what would be its gaze on Opren.

"It definitely sees us, if that's possible," he said. "Maybe it is meant to take my orb for whoever made it."

The golem began to pick up pace as it passed the halfway point between the wall on which it was previously camouflaged and the group. It broke into a stumbling charge as it was only twenty feet away.

"Dodge!" yelled Rufius.

As Opren leaped out of the way in time to let the large stone creature pass, he saw Rufius cast lightning at the main boulder that would be its body. The lightning seemed to give it an extra shove into the trees it was already tripping into at the end of its charge, but no damage seemed to occur and it must have felt nothing. It tumbled and curled itself into a ball, rolled in a circle and expanded into the shape of a body again as it faced them.

"That was Stage Two and clearly had no effect," said Rufius sharply. "Too bad we don't have an Uunducasteri who specializes in stone. They might be able to control it since it is not really alive."

"Then what now, since you are supposed to be the best?" Opren jabbed verbally, but he also genuinely hoped for an answer. Rufius glared at him, but the Half-Elf admitted he had never specifically trained against puppet-summons without flesh so was not sure. "Great."

The golem lifted one of its bulky arms and the extra rocks around it clustered together to turn what would be a fist into a club of debris. It went for Barbosa, but the granwolf dodged easily. Emerald was turned the other way when it struck at her, but she was so swift she managed to roll away and its club-hand got stuck in the dirt for a moment.

"I have an idea," said Rufius.

Rufius concentrated on the golem and moved his hand

in the air as if to direct someone. To Opren's happy surprise, the golem moved slowly toward the direction Rufius gestured. Rufius took several steps away and gestured for the golem to come to him. As it got nearer, he jumped into the nearby river. It followed again and tumbled into the rushing water, at which second Rufius leaped out and electrocuted the entire area of the river in one fluid motion. He landed on the bank, shivering.

"Damn, it is *cold*, even for only seconds under," he exclaimed.

Opren laughed. "Well, you saved us, so good job. How did you do that? Where I am from, we would say you have a thing called 'the Force' as a joke, but I assume you don't know what that means."

"No," said Rufius, rubbing his chest and arms for warmth. "What I did was manipulate the energy around it through intense concentration. It can be used to suggest and persuade against lower-intelligence beings, but I was able to switch its targeting commands to myself by using some spirit energy in this case because it has no real brain to manipulate."

"And obviously it ain't swimming or jumping out like you did because it is made of rocks," said Pole. "Great idea using the water!"

"I guess you are really skilled and clever when you need to be," said Opren. "But I do still plan to beat you soon."

"Well, I appreciate the due credit," said Rufius. "But good luck if you really do intend to beat me anytime soon."

Emerald whipped her head around at a noise, which turned out to be slow clapping when Opren gave the sound his full attention too. The group watched as a six-foot silhouette of a man appeared, darkened, then became a lean man with gray skin and intense red eyes. His irises glowed in the dim light of the trees he appeared between.

"Well done, indeed," he said smoothly. His voice reverberated with a rasp. Opren felt uneasy when the man spoke, and he had never heard such an echo from someone when they spoke at a low volume. The reverberation itself reminded him of his own transformed state when the sphere's magic empowered him, but this man did not have an intensity or strength added to his inflection, rather another presence entirely—something that felt inhuman. "I had intended to test the power Opren can wield, but he failed so far. I must take other steps, it seems."

"Who are you, and how do you know who I am?" Opren furrowed his brow as he did not take his own eyes off the man's glowing red eyes. The thought of this man potentially having to do with his parents' murder was not just a passing one. His presence felt much like the malicious one of the sleeskaxes, but it was also different somehow.

"Forgive my lack of proper introduction. I am Lord Zargunn, Enhanced Half-Demon, Mercenaries' Bounty Never to Be, Hunter of Treasures. You may simply call me Lord Zargunn or 'my lord'. I already know who you are, Opren Saphren, new Keeper of the Goldlight, Boy Between Worlds."

"I'm not one for fancy titles, especially with threats, Zargunn. The only one I ever wanted was Ultimate Fighting Champion. But what do you mean by 'Keeper of the Goldlight'?"

"And here I thought you might want a civil discussion," said Zargunn. The tone sounded like a jab out of spite. "But if you wish to keep it so informal, to each their own. The Goldlight is your magical weapon, so you are its Keeper by ancient to present title."

"You mean the—" Opren started to refer to his sphere, but he caught himself. Unfortunately, Zargunn was quick to catch his glance, or maybe the mysterious man who claimed to be a Half-Demon somehow already knew.

"The golden sphere you inherited," finished Zargunn.

"Well, thank you for helping me know what to call it. Now what do you want and why have you been spying on me?"

"Strictly speaking," said Zargunn. "I have been observing the sphere and its potential, but you became an inevitable piece of that. Now, I wished to see how difficult it might be to take it from you."

"Please correct me if I am wrong, Lord Zargunn," said Emerald in a tone that must have been her way when speaking with other nobility in formal and diplomatic settings. Opren nearly cracked a smile to hear her sound so proper. "You sent a golem to assault our party to test Opren's current abilities and power when wielding this magical weapon called the Goldlight?"

"Indeed," said Zargunn with a slow, single nod.

"Are you not aware the Reiyal crown holds say over this area, Rhahkmant'e, and its trainees and citizens?" continued Emerald. "To make matters less ideal, I am Princess Esmeraldi Avaria of Avarinnia, and you have threatened me and my cousin." She glanced at Opren, likely aware he was surprised to hear her proper name for the first time. She did say she was "called Emerald", not that is her given name *was* Emerald. Clever.

"Did any harm come to you?" asked Zargunn. A hint of annoyance was in Zargunn's voice but not a bit of concern at his mistake.

Emerald denied any harm had come to her, but Rufius said, "I am cold because I had to cause your pet to follow me into the river." He gave Zargunn a stare as if imitating the river's temperature. "But I am also undamaged."

"Well, all is quite well, then," said Zargunn with a slight pleasantness that seemed fake. "Opren is my only target, and I had not intended to threaten his life truly, either."

"What *was* your intent by attacking us?" asked Pole.

"As I said, to test Opren and the magic," said Zargunn. "You all should listen better."

"I listened just fine, Zargunn," said Opren. "And it sounds like you were hoping to threaten me just enough to cause the Goldlight to activate. Now what is your plan? Since you have seen that first one fail, do you want to take it yourself?"

"I won't chance that without seeing your potential," said Zargunn. "But I will bring out the power another way. Here."

Everyone tensed as Zargunn waved his light gray hand in a fluid gesture toward Opren. Opren steadied himself, expecting an offensive spell of some sort to hit him. A few seconds passed and it seemed it was only an empty flourish.

Swirling red and black smoke suddenly circled Opren and he felt uneasy, then dizzy and queasy. The nausea passed and he felt hot. His head was pulsing, thumping lightly and buzzing. The world blurred and when he looked at Zargunn again, the man's glowing red eyes were the only clear sight. Zargunn faded and two similarly built figures replaced him. Sight returned as Opren's head pounded and he began to seethe. At first, it seemed the seething was a false emotion, but then he saw the figures clearly.

The two sleeskaxes moved toward him in similar strides, cackling. Opren drew his sword and his balance returned, but he felt sluggish. As the sleeskaxes got closer, he noted a flash from the golden orb—the Goldlight—at his side. The rage hit him like a waterfall and he opened his mouth...

"*Woffrumdus!*" He yelled the spell-word intentionally for the first time. He changed as usual, but something was different: his aura swirled with red as well as gold and he felt further empowered by the anger.

"Opren! Wait!" cried Emerald, but she sounded far away as he moved to attack the sleeskaxes. "Something is wro..."

Emerald's voice faded, along with everything else but his emotions, blurred visuals, and his targets, as he slashed both his regular sword and the Goldlight blade through the first foe. He felt the impact with the sleeskax's waist just as everything faded to black, as everything fell silent except his own throbbing skull and heartbeat. Then the world spun and... nothing...

Emerald rushed over to Opren after he cut both creatures in half. He was much faster than when they fought. The two Shirrkki fell in two pieces each, bleeding profusely. Opren fell as if struck with a blow to the head by surprise and his red and gold aura faded. Emerald lifted his head; he was trembling, despite his lack of consciousness. What had Lord Zargunn done?

"Opren," she said quietly. "Opren," she tried firmly, but still no response. She shook him and said loudly, "Opren!"

Opren's trembling stopped as he opened his eyes halfway. He saw her, she thought, but it was like he did not fully recognize her at first. She said his name once more and he opened his eyes completely.

"What hap—

"Are you all right?" she asked before he could finish. His state of being was more immediately important than an explanation.

"My head hurts," said Opren groggily, bringing a hand to his temple. "I'm a little tired and feel as if I used all my strength, but I will make it."

"All right." She used some of her *Nuuita* to restore a bit of his, a trick she had learned from her mother the one time she had seen her father use too much of his *Nuuita*. "You scared me."

"I really am fine," said Opren, trying to flash a smile to reassure her. "Other than the headache."

"I mean, you in that state, also," she said. She felt apologetic, but she also needed him to understand there was something wrong with his transformation. The way he had described it was entirely golden and vivid and powerful, but he said he had confidence and an authoritative and charismatic presence. The form in which he had just killed the Shirrkki was red and gold, his eyes were blank until his anger seemed to take over, and his presence felt malicious, not far off from Lord Zargunn's. When she explained all this, Opren seemed confused. "I expect that was caused by Lord Zargunn's corrupt magic, not by the sphere's usual use."

"But wait," said Opren, his brows together, concentrating. "I killed Shirrkki? What happened to the sleeskaxes he summoned?"

"There were no sleeskaxes, Opren," said an approaching Rufius. Rufius kneeled to Opren and Emerald's level. "It must have been an illusion due to whatever Zargunn did to you to force your transformation."

"He harnessed your rage and need for revenge," said Pole from his place some steps away. He was inspecting the area, muttering to himself before—and again after—his comment.

"You have random spurts of wisdom and knowledge," said Opren, regaining his usual vocal strength. He pushed himself up and struggled to his feet, but he kept his balance. He shook his head and rubbed his temples, so Emerald touched his head to relieve his pain. "Thank you." He turned to Pole. "What else do you know about everything?"

"I have heard of the Goldlight," said Pole. "Your magic is a lot more unique than most. Despite my potentially questionable fun habits, I also have a habit of observing people and reading a lot of books. That and life experience help me know things."

"I would like to know more of what you know," said Emerald. "You are still relatively a stranger to us, even though you seem to be an ally."

"Right now," Pole sighed, "I can only tell you we are out of Zargunn's magic. At a later time I might share more of how I know that, but right now we should get moving to Avarinnia."

Something tells me you did not need as much help when we stumbled into you as you let on, said Barbosa to Pole, but so Emerald could hear also. She suspected the same.

Emerald and Opren both had more questions for Pole, but for the time being the old human was correct: they needed to continue so they could arrive as soon as possible to the safety of Avarinnia. Opren confirmed he felt ready to continue the journey, so Emerald told the group to follow her and they headed east—*properly* this time.

Two days after they left the mountain, they passed through a small town with both Human and Elven residents. Emerald had seen it once before, and she remembered it being bright and cheery, with a lot of trading and street athletics going on. This time, it was not busy at all, and she did not hear the sounds of playing.

I smell lingering smoke, said Barbosa.

Emerald wanted to be optimistic, but she was reminded of the burning houses in Ravberd and considered the possibility of a sleeskax being present. She did not have to wonder long, as a dark figure dashed out in front of the group. The creature was tall and slender, with black and green reptilian skin and skeletal features. It bared fangs as it opened its mouth to speak.

"We waited, boy," said the sleeskax, gaze toward Opren. "Give the sssphere." It reached out an open hand.

"Opren, wait!" But her words were too slow, as Opren had already charged toward the sleeskax and cast a gale to knock the creature off balance. He cut the sleeskax's hand off, but the sleeskax used its other palm to strike Opren and knock him back a few feet and onto his buttocks.

"This one is real, right?" said Opren.

"Yes," said Emerald. "But you aren't ready to just fight it alone."

The sleeskax cackled as its severed hand grew back in seconds.

"Let's put it down enough to get away," said Pole.

"Reiya!" Rufius cast a powerful bolt of lightning directly into the chest of the sleeskax, and Opren changed to his golden form, without the extra red aura, and used the golden sword to slice off the creature's legs. When Rufius and Opren worked together, they could be formidable. If they learned to do that, instead of fighting against each other, that would be a great success.

Opren used his regular sword to stab the sleeskax's torso and nail it to the ground.

"I could kill him now," said Opren.

"No! We do not know if it will work, so get more powerful and skilled, then you can face them if you wish," countered

Emerald.

Opren raised his golden blade, but Rufius shocked him with a weak spell to stun him briefly, and Barbosa grabbed him and dragged him away so they could leave.

"I was going to behead it! *That* should work on anything," said Opren angrily. "Why the hell did you stop me?"

"It had begun to heal and was ready to strike you at the same time if Barbosa had not grabbed you," said Rufius. "I thought you learned not to leap into situations you aren't ready for when I beat you."

"It's not the same! Those killed my parents!"

"If you aren't going to face them with a clear head, you need to be strong enough to survive either way," said Emerald.

"I can move again, so let me walk," said Opren, and Barbosa released him so he could stand. "It's just the reason I came here is to avenge my parents and I might have been able to kill one of the two monsters that took them. I didn't look for it, it was just an opportunity in our way."

"I know, Opren," said Emerald. "But we were not prepared, and you need to be sure you won't die along with them, or instead of them. I'm not sure if Rufius or I can even kill them alone, yet. Let's continue as planned in Avarinnia."

"Okay," said Opren. "Sorry for getting angry at you all. I can't help it when around the sleeskaxes."

"Self-mastery is another thing you can learn in Avarinnia," said Emerald.

"It's different somehow than just my anger at what they did, though," said Opren. "But I can't explain it."

"Maybe you can figure that out, too," said Pole.

The remaining three days it took to reach Avarinnia proceeded without another serious incident. Everyone was thankful for that. When they reached the main part of the sect, the part with the city itself, Emerald relaxed a bit. The chances were greatly reduced anyone would attack them there. *And I would love to see them attempt it.* That may not have been the wisest sentiment, but they were safe for a time.

11

Opren estimated it reached an hour before sunset when the group approached the edge of Avarinnia.

He had never seen trees so massive and tall; they must have been centuries old and well-kept. The glow tracing them presented a beautiful picture. There were trees he had never seen; the leaves were broad and intricately shaped on some, vivid like flower petals more than leaves on others (but still shaped like leaves), or petals so big they would have to be some kind of flower unique to that world. Some of the more complex designs in the leaves appeared like one might expect of a painting or design print, but certainly not a natural occurrence growing from the branches of a huge tree. Even a few trunks had bark that had new textures he had never heard about, let alone seen himself. Next, a few plants had huge flowers on them in reds and silvers. Maybe Rufius' style was fashioned after whatever plant they were.

"This is amazing," he said to Emerald as Ra'ze and Shari were in step beside each other with he and Emerald atop.

"Wait until we enter the city." She smiled. There was a

whimsical inflection in her voice.

They reached the gates of Avarinnia—enormous pale pink walls that were nearly see-through but looking through them would be like looking through a thick pink frost or rose quartz. They had the slickness of ice or glass, but the color of pink sea salt, yet they had a slight sheen like metal might have.

"What kind of stone is the gate made of?" he asked.

"You really aren't from here," said Rufius with a single short laugh. Opren shot him a look. "They are Avarinnium."

"It is a stone and metal at the same time; a special crystalline mineral, like diamonds in how hard it is and how rare it is outside of our sect," said Emerald. "It is stronger than any other material we could use without going to the Northland mountains, and it is valuable to trade. It also has a special property to hold or reflect magic. Only Rytherium, mined and used for enchanted smithing by the Rhognomar in the far north, outside of the Human and Elven kingdom, is harder and able to break Avarinnium with physical force. We have to mold it by magic, with precision and patience. It takes a special training course just to work with it."

"I think I saw this on some of the armor at Rhahkmant'e," said Opren. "Now that makes a lot of sense. So even a diamond could not break this gate?"

"The diamond may crack in doing so," said Emerald. "My great-great-great-grandfather founded this city and only magic helped him shape the Avarinnium, which is done now by the Elders and crafter mages. He is the namesake of both, Wellanon Lorn Avaria, Eighth King of the Reiyal of Everniot. Before him, the elves were scattered and could not fortify a barricade of peace, after a civil war."

"'Barricade of peace'?" repeated Opren as a question.

"The royal agreements in this sect, and with rulers of other sects at times, hold a standard of balance and peace that should never falter. War is pointless against our city, our people, so we are a wall against would-be assaults on our areas and other peoples as well."

"That's amazing."

Protecting more than one city, holding agreements with many, preventing outside threats from starting. Any one of those things seemed like a great feat, let alone all of them at once for centuries. Most leaders and politicians could barely decide to take action, let alone do something like that.

"Are you going to say that about everything today?" Emerald laughed.

She got off Shari and approached a guard in full Avarinnium plate armor at the gate. He bowed on a knee, but she told him to rise and gestured to the four guards in towers on either side of the gate, the other two on the ground, and to someone somewhere Opren could not see. The gate began to slide upward silently and smoothly– it must have been a magical seal and not a crank as he had expected. Emerald motioned for everyone to follow her as she walked through the open gate.

Before Opren could say the word "amazing" again, he took note of something else after the first after that next and another. The initial sight was a group of trees higher than the walls he had not realized were *inside* the city when he saw them from the outside at a distance. He also noted the inner city was concealed somehow by the fog that seemed to be suspended above it but was gone to reveal the full view of the clear sky with its setting sun's light to illuminate the city when viewing it from within. The trees were not just impressive in themselves—they were, of course, at such a size and with their unique details—but more fascinating were the elves: both children and adults running or gracefully walking along the extra-thick branches from one tree to the next. They appeared to be working or playing or exercising, depending on where he looked. On the ground were huts of all kinds, some built into trees, some made of gigantic flowers and beautiful polished wood. Aside from the smaller huts, many of the larger and clearly high-class homes were gorgeous wood from smooth and polished to unique textures to simple, naturally white or green like some of the smoother barks of the trees.

The second new sight was a group of regal hooded figures in bright white cloaks traced with green. There were around thirty of them and they were casting and chanting in an area beside a stone wall, weaving all kinds of elements and growing plants and constructing objects. He enjoyed the combat magic he had experienced and learned on Rhahkmant'e, but to see so much magical prowess outside of combat at once was truly astonishing. It was like an artistic show more than someone doing work or going through lessons.

"Some of the Elder Mages," said Emerald. He had not meant to stop walking, but with so much to take in it was automatic. Ra'ze nudged him, evidently eager to get to wherever she could get food and explore her own way.

The third sight was impossible to miss as they approached the innermost area because it was their destination: the palace itself. It was unlike any palace he had ever read about or seen in any film or photograph or painting. It was not sharp and dominating like a gothic castle might be, nor was it soft and simple like a young person might enjoy after reading fairy tales. It had four corners built into the biggest trees of the entire city–from them, rather. The walls were all the soft pink Avarinnium, but they were adorned with gorgeous sapphires and emeralds at any point with a door or window. The windows were stained-glass or simply open holes, and the doors were polished white wood. The two main doors were at least thirty feet tall, decorated in the royal symbol Emerald had tattooed on her right upper back. The carved image was inset with emeralds for the dragon's face on the shield, the shield was Avarinnium, the sword was made of rubies, and the words in Elvish around the whole thing were set with shaped sapphire. He followed a short jutting stone path to the end with his eyes as he looked from the door back to where they stood, then halted his walk when he realized the remaining fifty feet of what should be a bridge over a long drop was empty except for some light.

Opren opened his mouth to ask about a bridge, but Barbosa growled at the light and Emerald answered before either could speak.

"The bridge of light is solidified magical energy. You won't fall; don't worry."

I am not stepping out to some trick to be lost to the abyss beneath, said Barbosa so all could hear. *You two-legged people can go first if it is truly so safe.*

"The bridge is magic so my father, the king, can remove it instantly in the event of an invasion or other unwanted occurrence," said Emerald. "It is much more effective than anything drawbridges or barriers can accomplish, especially with some of the plants Athera warned you about from Rhahkmant'e after the drop. Elves of any kind will be caught in bubbles." She pointed at a man with black hair in a huge bubble of soft light—similar to the magical bridge—and laughed. "Like this fool. He has tried and failed to steal from the palace six times now, maybe even a seventh while I have been gone. Our people are trapped until my parents or my sister decide to do something with them. For non-elves, you would fall to your death. We have only needed that one time since I was born, but most see the point of breaking into the palace nullified. It is also fun to scare newcomers, sometimes." She chuckled.

Not all creatures enjoy heights, Princess Esmeraldi, said Barbosa.

"You don't need to address me formally, Barbosa," said Emerald. "I'm still the same, even here. Unless we are in significant company and it is for show, at least. Now, let's cross. Opren and I will go first to reassure you."

Opren was not sure *he* was reassured considering he was neither Elven nor noble, but Emerald took his hand and pulled him along with her before he could protest. Walking on the light bridge felt like walking on warm glass. It was not hot, just pleasantly warm. He did his best not to look straight down through the mostly transparent substance; he was not afraid of heights, but he was afraid of falling into a dark pit of man-eating venomous plants. Emerald lightly squeezed his hand when his eyes drifted too far, which brought him back to focus on the dazzling palace. He kept his attention there since it was easy to stare at such a sight.

The group followed, with Rufius laughing at Opren's expression upon first stepping out onto the light bridge. Halfway to the palace, Opren grew accustomed to it—though it felt much longer than the time that had really passed—and no longer worried. Besides, he could not fall with Emerald right beside him or they would both be caught in a bubble at worst—unless the magic were actually so selective only Emerald would be grabbed. *No, keep positive. We're fine.*

Barbosa growled quietly for almost the entire fifty feet, but he faced the fear until reaching the palace doors. Pole seemed strangely unbothered and Ra'ze chose to fly to the other side. The guards floating around on their own light platforms watched the griffin, but they said and did nothing.

Emerald let go of Opren's hand when they reached the regular stone ground and called out something in Elvish, her proper name tagged with what sounded like "Ooh-lye-lera", a word that probably meant princess. The doors opened without a sound, which was odd for something so massive but he was beginning to suspect all things could happen in this beautiful, magical city of the elves. To even think that sentence was fantastical and amazing. He laughed at himself when he nearly commented "amazing" aloud…again.

"*Oluu, ne ferli*, Esmeraldi," said the queen, facing Emerald as she stepped down from her throne toward the group. She opened her arms and spoke louder, "Welcome to you all."

The woman was about the same height as Emerald, but she had blonde hair with blue streaks, instead of Emerald's brown with green streaks, and it reached her waist with shining golden waves. Had Opren not had context to know she must be the Queen of Avarinnia, he might have assumed she was in her thirties, but that was impossible with a daughter who was… he realized he did not know Emerald's actual age, but he knew she was of adult age. The woman was enchanting, and her voice had a thicker accent than Emerald's when she switched to the Human common language that was nearly identical to the English he spoke. Her eyes were blue and reminded him of his mother's eyes, but her arching thin eyebrows were a distinct difference. She wore a flowing green dress and an Avarinnium tiara adorned with tiny emeralds.

"*Ve harron, Muumleiy,*" said Emerald. She said something else in Elvish that Opren could not register. Her tone was less pleasant, as was whatever the queen said in return. Emerald brightened again as she switched back to Human English/Evernish. "These are the new friends I mentioned in my letters." She gestured to the group in a slow motion, skipping Rufius.

"Young human, you must be Opren Saphren, correct?" said the queen pleasantly.

"Yes, Your Majesty." He hoped that was the proper title for Elven royalty. He bowed at the waist. "Thank you for allowing us to come here."

"I am Queen Bellavuu of the Reiyal. Glad to meet you. It is no trouble at all. I am glad someone caused Esmeraldi to return home sooner than she might have otherwise." There was a hint of motherly sternness in Queen Bellavuu's voice.

"I am King Eeloneus Avaria of the Reiyal," said the man who sat on the other seat of the throne, in a deep voice as smooth as Bellavuu's, except his pronunciation was flawless. The king was taller than any of the other elves so far once he rose to his feet and stepped down from the throne. King Eeloneus wore a silk shirt that matched Bellavuu's dress, and he had a breastplate and boots of Avarinnium, a crown constructed of Avarinnium as was Bellavuu's tiara. His crown held a single oval diamond with the royal emblem engraved in green in the center, beneath the highest point, and three little emeralds vertically set to each side, followed by two sapphires, followed by a single ruby as one looked further from the center. His hair was brown and shoulder-length, and his eyes were a wonderful green. The only imperfection on his fair skin seemed to be a scar over his left bicep that only showed halfway from beneath his shirt sleeve. Like his wife, he did not look to be whatever his real age must be. Unlike his wife, his arching eyebrows gave him a stern expression, until he smiled when he said, "Welcome!"

As King Eeloneus reached them, Opren felt true strength and peace in his presence. He had never seen a man so handsome and warrior-like in ideal balance. Even fit actors or statues were nothing compared to him. "You must be Pole. Barbosa. Ra'ze." He dipped his head at each of them respectively, then approached Ra'ze as naturally as Emerald had done when upon first encountering the griffin and rubbed her. Ra'ze nuzzled the king, which was a show of affection she had yet to give Opren or Emerald, let alone anyone else. "Strong bird-beast, aren't you?" Ra'ze gave a happy squawk and ruffled her wings. King Eeloneus smiled.

"Your Majesty," said Opren with another bow. He straightened to look Eeloneus in the eyes. "I truly appreciate your welcome."

"Oh, he is polite," said a young woman's voice that made Opren tingle as he had when he first listened to Emerald. Her voice was a bit higher than Emerald's and included a singsong inflection. Her Elvish accent stood out a little more as well, but she was clearly related. The owner of the voice turned out to be nearly identical to Emerald in appearance but for her rose-petal red hair that fell beyond her shoulders, her green eyes to match the king's—though the look in them was nothing like her father's—and her white attire that was clearly intended to show a lot more skin than would be proper, even for a non-royal. She wore a sleeveless top—rather a corset—with tight pants, no shoes, and her pants were open at the side by about two inches down the entire length of each leg with a crisscross lacing to match the back of the corset. Not wearing shoes seemed common among the elves outside, but the outfit was not like anyone else. "Oluu, handsome. I am Ruby." As she stopped to hold out a hand with exaggerated enthusiasm, he reluctantly dropped his eyes to her exposed cleavage as her chest bounced. He immediately snapped back to her face and she giggled. "You are supposed to look, hence the corset and no top." Opren tried to take her hand to shake. "No, silly. You are to kiss it."

"I see you have met the royal whore," said another woman's voice, much less bubbly than Ruby's, lower than Emerald's. This young woman sounded like a royal would be expected to sound, although her tone was biting. The bite was dismissed as she stepped in front of the group and greeted, "Please forgive our sister. I am Princess Soferina Avaria, and it is my pleasure to welcome you to our city." She nodded to each person individually. "You all may address me outside of formal proceedings as Sapphire, if you wish. Ruby, stop flirting with our guests."

As Sapphire's eyes met Opren's, he noted how well the nickname fit, as her eyes were the same vivid deep blue as the gemstone and she had the same blue streaks through her hair as her mother, except her hair was light brown. Her jawline was a bit more pronounced than Emerald or Ruby's and, along with a long blue cold-shoulder dress that reached its coverage to her neck, she seemed a bit more intentionally mature.

"Is there a reason you all have names of gems? What is Ruby's real name?" whispered Opren to Emerald.

"Whispering is irrelevant in the silence," mock-whispered Ruby. "We hear well. Ruubi is my given name, but it is spelled in Elvish, not in your way like the gem." She spoke clearly as she continued. "We called each other the informal names as children and they held. So where are you from, Opren?"

"He is from somewhere far away, so he might not tell the difference well if a princess he is trying to treat respectfully and politely is toying with him or being serious," said Emerald coolly.

"Oh, the aggressive rogue is being proper now, is she?"

said Ruubi with a laugh as she flexed her arm. "I haven't offered to bed him or anything, Emmi."

"He did not ask to see your body on display, either," said Sapphire. "Go put on something more suitable for, well, anywhere outside of your bed chamber." She shook her head and sighed before turning back to the group. "You would think she is an adolescent, but we are truly triplets."

"Excuse me, Shela Eeloneus," said Rufius. "As I do not require introductions, may I go see my father now?" The king nodded once. "Ve harron." Rufius turned to the left of the throne room and exited.

"*Ne ferli*, behave," said Queen Bellavuu. She continued in Elvish too quickly to try to follow, but she was clearly scolding them. Sapphire straightened and pursed her lips as if embarrassed. It seemed the blue-eyed princess was not usually scolded, and it was clear one reprimand must have been for her, specifically. Probably due to her comment about Ruubi being "the royal whore", Opren guessed. "We really do put on a better face for guests when we have more time to plan," Queen Bellavuu spoke to everyone. "It seems our daughters assumed tavern-level informality was an option because you are neither Elven nor royal, but we prefer to treat everyone in our home with equal respect and hospitality. That is meant to include manners that far outweigh sibling teases."

"I'm not much for formalities myself," said Pole with a shooing gesture. "It is no worry."

I am your guest, projected Barbosa. *The way you go about things is your own choice here. As long as I am not personally disrespected, I have no problem with it either.*

"Your Majesty, has Emerald mentioned to you about my origins?" asked Opren. "All I know of royalty and formal proceedings came from books. I am just doing my best to remain respectful, but I have no idea if I am doing anything right or wrong. I would rather remain casual, to be transparent."

"See. Sofi, not everyone has a rose in their buttocks," said

Ruubi.

"That does not dismiss your lack of attempt to be proper and inviting," said King Eeloneus.

"I was friendly and inviting," said Ruubi, folding her arms and turning to the king.

"You were going to be more than friendly, *ne ferli*," said the king. She tried to argue again, but he folded his arms and gave her a hard look.

"I apologize," said Ruubi, unfolding her arms and losing her playful face. "I will go prepare the bed chambers for our guests." She turned to Opren. "Also, would your griffin like to follow me to her quarters so she can then explore outside?"

Opren patted Ra'ze and said he would see her later. Ra'ze energetically followed Ruubi after the two were introduced, and they exited to the same side as Rufius had done.

"I was in the middle of some responsibilities for the new hall renovations myself," said Sapphire. "I will be in the library this evening, or we may be able to chat during dinner. For now, I must return to the task before my helper makes a mess of the arrangements I planned. Good day to you all." She dipped her head once and briskly walked past them to exit the main door to the room.

"Esmeraldi can show you around the city while Ruubi prepares your sleeping chambers," said the queen. "You may explore freely but, as I have heard your situation, I recommend not leaving our city walls. You will be perfectly safe here, but we have only limited ways to protect you elsewhere."

"That said," added Eeloneus. "When you are trained by my brother, Selios, you will be at a level ready for most threats. Please do wait until your first few sessions with him to chance anything. We will see you all for dinner in our West Hall. You are dismissed unless you have any questions at this time."

"Ve harron, King Eeloneus and Queen Bellavuu," said Opren. Barbosa and Pole joined him in a bow. The king and queen nodded and returned to sit at their thrones.

Emerald spoke to her parents for another moment in

Elvish, then she led the others back out and across the bridge of light to the main city area. Beautiful music was coming from two kinds of instruments; one of them was a bit like a polished white cello and the other was a wind instrument. Even the shops appeared to be made of trees and stone mixed in a way that was neat but still natural and nearly untampered. Opren's mountain town might have been near a forest, it might have been rustic, but it was nothing like that city when it came to inclusion of nature. Avarinnia might have been the most beautiful place he had ever seen, in pictures or in person. He briefly felt a peace he had not felt in weeks.

Barbosa and Pole went off to do their own exploration, so Opren agreed to Emerald's idea of a tour led by her. If it had been a date, it was the best date he ever had, and to top it off she just happened to be an actual *princess* enjoying time with a common butcher and fighter. The adamant drive he had felt since his parents were murdered gave way enough to allow genuine awe to sink in and take him for a refreshing ride of wonder, even before the largest feast he had ever joined in attacking later that evening.

12

"Wake up, sleepy," Emerald said for the second time, louder this try. "We will miss breakfast." She pushed into Opren's arm a bit and he finally stirred. "About time. Let's get going!"

"Why am I not wearing clothes?" asked Opren groggily, looking down at himself. He obviously had forgotten some of the night's events. "Did we do anything, um, sexual?"

"No," said Emerald, laughing. "You drank too much mead and whatever else and by the time we went to bed, you were hot and immodest. Why? Do you wish we had?" She folded her arms and raised her eyebrows.

He blinked a few times and said, "I don't know how to answer that without somehow getting in trouble."

"Wise choice. I don't want you to think I'm so free with myself because Ruubi would have taken you to bed to do anything *but* sleep if I were not there. I suppose you don't recall what she did either?"

"Not at the moment…should I?" he asked as he pulled on the pants she had placed on a stool beside the bed.

"I will allow her to bring it up if she happens to." She

rolled her eyes as she recalled her rose-haired sister dancing with Opren while he was intoxicated; it was all right and well until Ruubi placed his hands on her in all the places where she should not have, then kissed him too passionately, after she had helped him to get overly drunk. "But that one we can leave forgotten."

"O...kay?" said Opren. Then his expression changed from confusion as he asked excitedly, "So, is this your bedroom?" He was looking around as if he were a boy searching a new house. Emerald chuckled at the sight of the young man who generally seemed considerably tough and ready to fight or overcome or endure acting so whimsical and surprised.

"Yes. Do you like it?" It was obvious he did as he looked at her bed and touched its surrounding ribbon-like strands of pink and green material hanging from the ceiling, then scanned her dark wood furniture, but she wanted to hear his answer.

"I love it. I see you didn't keep it all prissy and princess-y." Opren smiled. He was indicating her weapon's display, with four kinds of swords set on crystal racks in front of an Elven tulip-shaped shield set with Avarinnium upon the wall. She had set the swords in order from longest at bottom to shortest on top, then a sheathed dagger was above all of it.

She walked over and reached up to take down the dagger and presented it to Opren.

"This is my favorite," said Emerald with a smile. "Shela Selios gifted it to me when I came of age, and I haven't seen its equal in three years." She allowed him to unsheathe the Avirinnium-edged slightly curved nine-inch blade. He examined the emeralds set in the platinum hilt, then let the sun reflect off the blade. He seemed to enjoy its beauty and respect its lethality the same way she did, considering the way he handled it as he looked it over. Then he sheathed it and handed it back to her.

"That's the nicest dagger I've ever seen, let alone held. So you are twenty-three years old?" said Opren. She nodded.

"It was difficult to judge your parents' ages because evidently elves keep their looks. I started to wonder if I'm much younger than you, because I knew you must be of age. I had my twentieth birthday just before coming here."

"We take over twice the time as humans to age in appearance after maturity and longer to deteriorate in health," said Emerald. "My mother is ninety-four and my father is eighty-seven. Opren gained an expression of combined surprise and embarrassment that made her giggle. "Did you expect them not to be that many years of age?"

"It's a bit awkward to say, but your mother is so gorgeous I would have assumed her to be no more than fifty and still look young," said Opren bashfully. "I know some guys my age would have flirted with her, like Pole does, thinking she is a model in her thirties or forties."

"Pole would be much wiser *not* to flirt with my mother," said Emerald, amused by the thought of her mother's possible reaction but annoyed to think of Pole's habits if it were to lead to that. "Elves do not mind sharing many things but, once we marry that bond is permanent, and we do not break commitments. We do not step out of our enjoyment with our spouse to enjoy others. Much of the time once we do find love, we have little interest in others anyway. Ruubi is an exception to be quite so flirtatious. She makes up for Sapphire's uptight nature and my preferences and then more."

"I understand Sapphire's dislike because they seem like opposites, but why do you hate Ruubi's habits so much?" he asked.

"I don't usually hate them," she said. "But I also did not like how she acted with you upon meeting you or while at the dinner feast. And I agree with Sapphire that we are to at least uphold standards of certain things in our own home as the princesses, even if she does equally disagree with my sense of adventure over duty."

"It's funny, you have helped me so much, have invited me to your home palace, let me spend the night in your room, and you seem jealous of Ruubi being improper around me, but we aren't dating," said Opren. She was not sure of the word he used, but she expected the meaning.

"What do you mean by 'dating'? Is that what you call courting?"

"Oh, sorry. I forgot you would probably not have that term here, especially outside of humans," he said. "It is when two people spend time together without anyone else, or with another couple of significant others, and it can lead to what would be more seriously commited dating, which is like courting. So maybe it is 'pre-courting', except I know in some history courting is a requirement to marriage, whereas this is before a commitment or expectation of marriage. I have no idea if I'm explaining this correctly because everyone where I grew up just knows it as a part of culture, and I don't know what it's like here."

"That is a lot of complication," said Emerald, placing a finger on her cheek as she thought. "Why don't you just commit, or go for someone else if you are not sure? Just spend time with people a bit to get to know them and then court or not. Pretend or falsely implied commitments seem chaotic and awkward."

Opren smiled. "I'm glad to hear you say that, because I feel like people where I'm from need to work on it."

"Do you want to 'pre-court' me?" she asked. Opren looked stunned. "What?"

"Is that allowed? I'm not nobility. Definitely not royalty or Elven," he said.

"Unlike some Human royal families, Elven royals and nobles tend to marry who they wish, within reason of character," said Emerald. "We do not arrange marriages. The mix of Human and Elven blood is uncommon in our society and tradition but, if my parents were to argue, I would simply point out the king's own brother married a Human woman who gave birth to Rufius, a talented heir to a warrior's legacy. So, yes or no? I would be glad to pre-court you, if you accept."

"Absolutely," said Opren. His smile was bigger than she had seen. "Does that mean I can compliment your appearance now, or does that require full courtship?"

She rolled her eyes and laughed. "Treat me like you would a Human woman with whom you do that 'dating'."

"I'm not sure how to go about that from much experience," said Opren. He looked down as if embarrassed. "I only had one short teenage relationship in school, nothing as an adult."

"Then just do what naturally works for you," she said. "That is what I always do. Besides, it has worked for you this far." She took a step over to him and lifted his chin lightly and kissed him. She paused and, still near his face, said, "Now Ruubi and I are even." She kissed him again deeply and he fell over onto the bed, obviously not expecting it. She fell on him and laughed. "And now I'm the only one who has kissed you twice because you are mine. I need to teach you how to fall gracefully." She stood and helped him up. They stood facing each other, at just enough distance to comfortably look at the other's face.

"Yeah, you do." He chuckled. "I'm going to assume Ruubi kissed me during the parts I can't remember? But I also assume you are better at it because… wow." He lightly touched his lips. "I don't think I'll forget that."

"She did more to arouse you, but I kissed you for fun and intimate connection now that we are together," she said. "She was trying to get passionate for a different sort of fun than spontaneous elation." She rolled her eyes.

"Well, to be fully open, she is sexy and entertaining, but she is not my type to be with," said Opren. "Can she even fight?"

"You will find out when we start lessons with Selios today," she said. "That is in two hours, don't forget. She is helping, and Sapphire will be there for a few sessions as part of the extra things my father is requiring of them for how they acted when you arrived. But I am better." She winked for playful emphasis.

"I prefer that," said Opren. "Ruubi reminds me of popular girls in school who use their appearance and status to attract boys to do things for them, but you clearly do things yourself."

"Good. Because you are my *Laleiy* and she needs to back off now."

"Lolly?" asked Opren, saying it with the wrong inflection.

Emerald let loose a laugh before she corrected by pronouncing each syllable slowly, "Lah-lay-ee. It is the Elvish term of endearment when romancing someone or courting, or for children who are dear. We have one for marriage as well, but that is the common one for all bonds. Your language might use darling or dear or my love. Female to male is Laleiy. Male to female is Liileiy, lie-lay-ee. Loleiy with the long 'o' is for children."

"Let's see if I get this right," said Opren. "Ve harron, ni velluusa Liileiy."

"Yes." She grinned. He had done well with his pronunciation for being so new to the language, even though his accent was obviously non-Elven.

Emerald led Opren to the West Hall for breakfast. While they ate, he asked about her side conversations with her parents.

"They were bothered I had left without saying something to them directly, then I returned only after I wanted to bring you and the others for a favor," she explained. "But we settled the tension last night, I think." She finished a bite of food and added to reassure him, "It doesn't affect you, if that is a concern."

"I just noticed your tones in Elvish were not pleasant," said Opren. "So I wanted to be sure nothing was seriously wrong. What about Lord Zargunn?"

Emerald reiterated the details of each of Avarinnia's defenses and explained her mother had a special pool of water that would change color if any sort of unwanted being arrived to the edge of the city. It was monitored all hours of the night by two Elder Mages, while during the day two others took the post. Queen Bellavuu checked weekly if nothing was reported.

"And the Uundulal are likely to note something and send word even sooner than our own guards," she added. "The reason my sisters knew to come to the throne room when we arrived is the hidden elves in the trees *we* even have difficulty detecting sent notice to the guards before we reached the gate, and elves can communicate through a sort of long-distance sensory link for a warning of danger or summons. It feels like heat and tingling for danger or a pull to the person or place for summons."

"So, when the guards sent notice to your parents, they were able to summon Sapphire and Ruubi without saying a word?" asked Opren. Emerald nodded. "That is awesome."

They finished their plates just as the servers began to clear the take-your-own set-up. Emerald could have used her status as princess to request an extension for a half hour, but Opren said he had eaten enough, and she was also satisfied.

She then led him to the area outside of the palace where the advanced Reiyal and Uundulal trained for battle and spell-wielding.

13

Opren followed Emerald to a strange wall of a substance that looked like milk had been dropped in water. It was not solid, almost like a fog but more fluid-like, and it floated between a gathering of vines. He touched it cautiously and it rippled, but it barely felt like anything. The spot he touched made a noise—no, the noise came from beyond the spot, from the other side of the strange divider.

"It is a sound barrier," said Emerald. "It won't do anything to us, but it holds the sound inside a dome my father made around the area so none of the noises of training make it to the social and study areas of the city or the palace."

"I thought Rhahkmant'e was impressive, but the magic elves can do is…"

"Amazing?" she finished for him with a chuckle. He nodded. "How could I have guessed? You could also say it in Elvish: *aluneiy*."

"Ha ha," said Opren as if bored, but he genuinely laughed with her after he failed to keep a serious face.

They stepped through the milky sound barrier and, with each step through a short tunnel, there came clearer sounds of metal hitting metal as swords were clashing, grunts and yells of the fighters that were muffled at first but gradually grew in intensity. They stepped out into the area and the full volume of the ringing metal clangs and heavy breathing, groans, and shouts hit his ears and filled his mind.

"*Aluneiy* is right," said Opren as he looked around.

Areas for various training applications were set throughout the area. One group of combat rings looked inspired by traditional boxing rings, except the floor was only raised six inches; there was a polished wood on some and smooth stone on others. The three ropes on each side were regular thick rope instead of the cushioned materials used in most of his matches, and a few of the rings had no rope. *A ring-out must be part of the way to win, like in karate tournaments.* A few larger rings had a pentagon shape to them, instead of the usual square. Adjacent to those constructed rings were simpler shallow pits of dirt with magically illuminated circles around them, about a foot deep at most—enough to differentiate the outside of the ring, but otherwise the illuminated circle would be the only tell these were not natural terrain changes.

Down a slight incline from the fighting rings were targets of several kinds, some floating and mobile, some set on a base. Elven men and women threw knives or darts or fired arrows into them. Reiyal and Uundulal—Emerald explained they were the elves with tan or greenish-hued skin and occasional facial markings, as opposed to the nearer to porcelain or peach of her family and most in Avarinnia—trained simultaneously. Some of the projectiles were set aflame or charged with lightning as the warriors threw them, while a few designated training units over one black-haired woman was catching the arrows shot at her before gripping them tightly to burn them to ash. *I need to learn that!*

Up the hill farther than the traditional fighting rings were platforms made of polished white stone, some set with Avarinnium, and a few of the platforms moved slowly, magically floating in the air while people trained atop. On one of these floating platforms—a still one—was Rufius fighting with a man who looked like him if two decades aged, with shoulder-length platinum hair and a forehead scar that stopped just before his eye.

"That's Shela Selios," said Emerald when she noticed Opren watching.

Selios' agility was unbelievable as he moved nearly as gracefully as Emerald yet generated such force in his hits that anything Rufius could not dodge—more than Opren would have expected as fast as Rufius seemed to be—would push Rufius a foot or two upon impact. Rufius was in a full Avarinnium breastplate and boots, along with pants studded with the magic-absorbing pink gem-metal. Suddenly, Rufius was hit with a gust that threw him from the platform. He was caught by the light from one of the magic circles around the ring and lowered to the ground gently.

"I thought we agreed no ring-out wins!" Rufius snapped at his father.

Emerald brought Opren closer, and he noted the same smirk on Selios' face he had seen on Rufius' face many times in the past couple months. Selios was obviously pleased with himself.

That's where he gets it from.

"You need to always prepare for your opponent to do the unexpected," said Selios in a voice that held the sharpness of Rufius' tone but with a smooth accent nearer to the king and queen's, and deeper. Where Rufius sounded like a top student and proud titleholder, Selios sounded like a victorious soldier who had superior training and experience. "And I did expect you to prevent it somehow. You failed to anticipate it simply because you *assumed* I would not cast something to knock you out." He walked over to the very edge of the floating ring and gestured for Rufius to come up. "Again?" He looked over to see Opren and Emerald. "Oh, welcome! A few minutes early, too, Emerald. Well done! And you must be Opren."

"Yes, sir," said Opren. "And you are Selios Avaria." Opren

moved to give a quick bow but Selios jumped down and placed a hand on his shoulder while reaching out his other hand to shake. Opren took it in a state of slight confusion.

"I'm a *warrior* first, royal family second," said Selios. "I don't prefer people to bow to me or go by custom that is outside of the respect I demand as an officer and instructor."

"Good to meet you, sir," said Opren. "And it'll be much easier for me to stick to general respect than try to stand by ceremony. I struggle with the customs here, honestly."

"Battles don't give much time for ceremony or formality," said Selios. "It has become a bit…er… awkward at this point, to be considered a royal. I have been a special warrior here for over two decades."

"Something tells me he had an influence on you." Opren turned to Emerald. She thumped his arm and smiled. He turned back to Selios, "What do you have for us to do today?"

"First, you need to get full training armor like my son," said Selios, gesturing to Rufius with his thumb. "He wears it against me for the same reason you will need it against any of us, Opren: you are able to aura-ward, but you are not conditioned to the level required for this amount and kind of training. Rufius was always better at attacking and dodging than preventing and enduring so it is still advisable, even at his level, against what I cast."

"Thank you for telling him how to go against me, Father," said Rufius sarcastically. "I thought he is meant to improve until we match, but not with extra tips."

"It is irrelevant once you two train together," said Selios. "You will need to become equal as quickly as possible to learn the Unity Magic I wish to teach you. You should know each other's strengths and weaknesses to fight well against *and* alongside the other without flaws."

"Do you know anything about the Goldlight?" asked Opren. Selios gained a surprised look.

"Is *that* the special magic you have?" asked Selios.

"According to someone called Lord Zargunn, yeah."

"I have heard about him. It is likely accurate, and I am glad you are still alive if you met him. There is someone you may want to speak to after some of your training," said Selios. "She is an oracle from a special line and once told me something about that sort of magic in a convoluted poem. It seems someone held the magic before you. She might be able to give you more information than I can, but I can train you to use the magic at will, at least. Beyond that, you will need to train yourself or find other mentors. What I can do for you is provide the kinds of training you will need to practice with the Goldlight magic, and I am an advanced Hycasteri. I will bring you to Rufius' and Emerald's level in natural spell-wielding as soon as you are capable, and all of you will learn something new by the end."

"Did *Darmleiy* give you permission to teach us Stage Four finally?" asked Emerald excitedly. Selios smiled and gave a nod. "*Ias!*" Emerald pumped her fist and jumped once with a clap.

"Is *Darmleiy*... father?" asked Opren, trying to use context. Emerald nodded. Opren turned to Selios, concerned as he recalled how easily Emerald had beaten him on Rhahkmant'e, even without distance casting. "But I am only a Stage Two spell-wielder, sir."

"You have learned the fundamentals, and I have heard you are a quick student," said Selios. "By next week, you will begin Stage Three training. I just need to assess your current combat level. The magic itself will be the easier part if your *Nuuita* can handle it, but how and when to use it takes practice. You will need to train more to refine your skill and effectiveness. I have brought Stage One Casteri into the special program and taken them to Stage Three in only one moon phase before. You are more gifted than them, I think, based on what Emerald has written to me. But let's see. You will be fitted with armor inside there." Selios pointed behind the others to a small hut built into a wide tree. "Then come back to fight. You will all fight each other while I observe and assess you."

Opren retrieved his Avarinnium-covered training attire

and waited for Emerald to exit the hut with hers. The process only took five minutes for each of them—the attendants for suiting trainees were obviously good at their jobs; it was just another thing to add to how well everything ran in Avarinnia. *I wish Mom and Dad could have seen this place.* Grief hit briefly as he missed his parents, but he set his thoughts on how well he had to do during the next level of training to be capable of avenging them.

"Are you all right, Laleiy?" asked Emerald as she came outside while he stood with his eyes closed.

"I was just focusing my mind before combat." He wanted to tell her he thought of his parents and wished they could be there, but her extra concern for his feelings would not help him during the fights. It was not a lie, just a partial truth; he was re-focusing his mind.

Selios had them jump up to the floating ring without any aid. At first, Opren was blatantly unsuccessful, as it was a ten-foot leap. Emerald hopped down in her light way to demonstrate slowly and explained how to use just enough of his *Nuuita* to aid him in his leap. Opren slammed against the stone platform and Emerald had to ease the pain and remove the bruise the first time doing it this way, but the second time he managed to rise *over* the platform and landed on his feet —with a bit of a stumble, but he did not fall. Progress. Rufius laughed and Opren shot him a look.

"Well done," said Emerald, then she turned to her cousin. "Rufius, it took you eight attempts when we were young, so hush." She leaned toward Opren and whispered, "He hates that I was the only one to get it the first time as children." Rufius flared his nostrils but said nothing and Opren smirked.

"We're heeeere!" sang a young woman from the direction of the entrance to the training grounds. Opren turned toward the voice. Ruubi walked toward them with Sapphire behind her a couple of strides. When Ruubi reached the floating platform, she flipped onto it and blew hair from her face as she landed. "How is everyone?" She smiled as she looked around at the group. She was wearing a tight scarlet one-piece that lacked any coverage for her legs or arms, but it did cover everything on her torso, albeit while shaping her form.

"Well, we have yet to fight," said Rufius. "So all right for now."

"Good," said Opren. "I understand that's a non-restrictive outfit for a fight, but do you ever wear more? That has no protection."

"This is just to go under my armor pieces," said Ruubi. "But I don't wear a lot because of how I fight. This is less about gaining interested looks than my regular outfits."

"Not that she disliked the stares as we walked over here," said Sapphire, rolling her eyes. The blue-eyed princess wore the same dress she had worn the previous evening. Unless she intended to cast at a distance with absolutely no physical combat involved, without the need to dodge, a long, fitted dress would be a hindrance and would get damaged.

"Are you going to fight in *that*?" asked Opren.

"No, silly boy. That would be impractical." Sapphire spun and her dress bottom reformed into leggings that reminded Opren of decorated Samurai hakama, while her top became a fitted half-sleeve shirt; it was like watching a tailor change a garment completely in two seconds, only the threads did it all themselves. "I do not always have time to change my clothing between tasks and types of things on my schedule, so I learned this spell."

"Is there anything you all *can't* do with magic?" asked Opren, fascinated at the possibilities.

"Bring back the dead as truly living again," said Selios. "But there are certainly ways to prolong life and delay the need." Emerald whispered something to Selios and Selios looked at Opren. "I'm sorry, Opren. As a warrior who has seen battle and served as a special agent, I sometimes forget to be wary of my words."

"It is all right, sir," said Opren. Emerald must have told Selios about his parents' murder. "Just teach me to avenge the dead without fail."

"That I can do," said Selios with the familiar smirk. "On that note, let's begin the assessment. Ruubi will fight Emerald and Soferina will fight Opren. The victors will fight, then the winner of that match will fight Rufius. For now, Rufius needs a break after his training with me."

Ruubi and Sapphire received armor from the outfitting hut while the others waited. When they returned, Ruubi and Emerald stepped to the center of the ring while Selios commanded everyone else to move to a platform next to the one on which the fight was to take place. When all non-combatants were seated on the extra platform, Selios raised his fist and counted down in Elvish. Sapphire translated for Opren by holding up her own hand and counting off fingers from three to two to one. Selios opened his fist and swiped downward with his hand.

Ruubi moved her hand through the air in a circle and a large metal ring appeared. It was like a bladed dancing hoop, with several handle-like spaces around the center. Emerald summoned a sword as her rose-haired sister danced toward her and tied a thick ribbon to the sword and her wrist as she had done when Opren fought her on Rhahkmant'e. Ruubi built momentum during fluid motions each step she took toward Emerald, each time she spun the dancing hoop-blade around her body or twirled it with her hand.

Opren had never seen someone appear so beautifully fierce and aggressively sensual during a fight. He had never learned how to defend against a weapon or fight-style such as Ruubi's either—which meant he was in trouble whoever won this match because he had already lost to Emerald on Rhahkmant'e.

"Ooh, Emmi, Opren's watching me," teased Ruubi.

"You are going to regret antagonizing me after what you already did last night," said Emerald.

"What did *he* think?" asked Ruubi as she stepped into striking distance. Emerald's ribbon and the size of Ruubi's ring-blade made them nearly even in weapons reach.

"He forgot because you helped him get even more drunk," said Emerald with a happy smirk. "Too bad he can't recall if he enjoyed it, but he did enjoy when I kissed him today." She ducked as Ruubi swiped the hoop in a wide, horizontal arc. Emerald took the opportunity during the lengthy attack to rise in the same motion and knocked Ruubi off-balance with her body. "We are together now." Emerald spun and landed a rounding kick to Ruubi's side.

Ruubi grunted and fell into a roll to regain her balance as she stood. "Lucky you. Or really, lucky him, I suppose."

"Finding another man to amuse you hasn't been a problem before, anyway," said Emerald. "So please remain platonic with him."

"I suppose he is the first boy who has kept *your* interest in a while," said Ruubi. "I won't complicate things." She jumped and twirled the ring-blade in another wide arc as she came down toward Emerald.

"Thank you." Emerald rolled backward to avoid the lethal hoop.

Emerald sprung off the ground as soon as she regained her footing, tossed the sword around Ruubi and had it return to her hand as the long sash rapped around her sister once, pulled to force Ruubi closer, and kicked into a backflip to knock the bladed ring from Ruubi's hands. Ruubi moved to summon the weapon back to her, but Emerald had forced Ruubi to the edge of the platform. Emerald raised her empty hand, and a small flame burst to life in front of Ruubi's face. Ruubi staggered back and fell from the ring. The magic light helped her to the ground as she said something in Elvish that must have been a swear.

"I still did not intend to lose." Emerald smiled.

Ruubi folded her arms and said, "I'll try harder next time."

"Well done, Emerald," said Selios. "Now for Soferina and Opren."

Opren hopped over to the combat platform with ease

now that he knew better how to control the technique with his *Nuuita*. Sapphire seemed as though she had used no more effort than to take a regular step when she followed. Opren shook his head.

"I don't know if I'll ever get the hang of things so gracefully as you."

"Well, if you have other ways to make up for it, it might be all right," said Sapphire. "I do hope you can protect yourself well, at least."

She summoned two curved daggers with wide blades set with blue gems and held them in a reverse grip, blades pointing behind her. Opren smiled at the thought of Sapphire using sapphires to mark her weapons. His smile did not last once she moved after Selios said *"alo!"*—the word Sapphire said meant "begin". He could not keep track of her movements well enough to predict where or how she would strike.

Opren managed to raise his sword in time to deflect her first slash, but she quickly adjusted and caught his forearm with the other dagger before hopping back several feet in one smooth motion.

"Not quite enough," said Sapphire.

Was she teasing him or just being critical? In either case, it irritated him in the same way as when he fought Rufius. He moved in before she could take the initiative again and struck at her body with his sword, while delivering a kick to her knee. He succeeded in catching her and knocked her off-balance. Unfortunately, that might have been a mistake.

As one of her daggers slid away, Sapphire dropped the other and raised both hands and said, "*Wydrefn*."

Before Opren could move again, he felt his sweat come off his body as liquid rushed up and grew around him. It surrounded him and formed a massive ball of swirling, pressurized water. He could not breathe and even flailing was a struggle. He tried to look for an opening, frantic, but there was no airhole. He began to feel weak against the weight of the spherical current and lack of oxygen did not help. His eyes began to close as he was near to running out of oxygen completely, then a golden flash appeared.

As Opren finished struggle-yelling the spell-word for the Goldlight magic, the water was forced open and away from him. He grabbed the golden longsword that hovered beside him in the air, and he landed on the ground in a ready stance. He could feel the magical energy in the area and sensed each person's presence without looking at them. It seemed they had a certain impact on his senses depending on how strong their *Nuuita* must be. Selios was the highest, which was obvious, but he was surprised to feel Emerald more strongly than Rufius or her sisters and in contention with Selios. This was not something he recalled coming from the Shirrkki, probably because they had no magic, or because he had yet to learn what *Nuuita* felt like.

"You were supposed to lose consciousness just as I released the spell," said Sapphire. She seemed surprised, as did everyone else, but she still took a ready stance. "I was not aware you can become the Goldlighter."

"Yeah. It will take more than that," said Opren without thinking the words. He felt in control of his actions this time, but he still seemed to have a lack of self-control of his words and emotions while transformed.

He charged Sapphire, and she vanished as he reached her. He sensed her presence as she reappeared and sprayed water at him, turning it to icicles as it got near, but he swiped his regular sword through them as he tossed his golden sword toward her and willed it to return to him the way Emerald had with her sword—it worked. Sapphire was distracted enough by the false attack that Opren could charge again and he hit her in the gut with the hilt of his sword, then front-kicked her to knock her through the air several feet and out of the ring.

Opren walked over to the edge of the platform. "Your turn, Emerald." He pivoted to walk back to the center while she hopped atop, but he felt dizzy and lost balance. Emerald caught his hand as he fell backward off the platform and the dizziness left. She pulled him fully onto the platform as his golden aura disappeared, and he felt himself return to normal. "Thanks."

"The Goldlight form clearly takes a lot out of you," said Emerald. "It must be a higher stage spell than anything else you have learned. Sit down for a bit." He sat as told and she touched his head, which removed all lightheadedness and restored some of his strength. It was like he had not eaten all day then had a great meal and his strength was restored, all in a few seconds.

"Considering Zargunn and others seem to think it's special enough to steal, I assume it is powerful," said Opren. "And that's why I know I can use it against them once I learn to control it."

"Be careful not to overuse it until you increase your *Nuuita* and mastery," said Emerald. "If you expend all your *Nuuita*, it might take life energy. If that is gone, you die."

Selios instructed Rufius and Emerald to return the next day to continue. He said Opren should rest before his assessment and the test needed to happen outside of the Goldlighter form. Once all were dismissed, Sapphire and Ruubi returned to other tasks until Selios would need them again. Before departing the area, Sapphire told Opren she had a book for him in the royal library—which she managed—that included some of the accounts of the Goldlighter.

Later that evening, Sapphire summoned Opren to the beautiful and enormous Avarinnia library to give him the book.

"Now you will not be ignorant of what your own power might accomplish," she said as she presented him the book. "If you really are this person," she turned to page 40 and pointed at a picture that really did remind Opren of himself when transformed (which must have been how Sapphire recognized what to call him so quickly), "or destined to become them, you did well to learn from Shela Selios and others here. You have such a power that it must be controlled properly but, if you can, this elusive man has been a force throughout history and you could be as well." She handed him the book.

The following day, Opren's assessment went smoothly and Selios graded him as they both expected. Opren also lost to Emerald…again. But knowing her true capability only made Opren want to train harder to beat her *and* Rufius.

Selios stopped the match between Rufius and Emerald after he judged their required effort to fight each other would only waste the stamina they needed to help train Opren. And by "train" Opren learned Selios meant to beat the hell out of him and heal him and repeat, until he figured out how to prevent, dodge, or counter whatever they did. It was much more intense than anything Athera had him go through, but there was something like a challenge in it, which he enjoyed—between the pain and frustration.

Opren began to discover something about himself that did seem innate and instinctual before, but he needed the correct circumstances to really reveal it. When he fought as hard as he could, it gave him a passion and determination he rarely had any other time. Selios' conditioning and forced combat experience brought it out like never before and, when Opren felt it the most, the Goldlight sphere would glow brighter in its pouch as he pushed harder—he could feel that occur too, even when he didn't look at it. He felt like his connection to the Goldlight increased with every use, as well as each fight even without its magic.

14

Opren trained for another fortnight under Selios' guidance—which sometimes felt more like taking orders than being taught but, considering Selios was a special operative in the Avarinnia military, it was not surprising. It was like being coached when training for boxing, his training with Athera, and what he would expect from a drill sergeant blended together. Outside of combat, Selios had a dry and gritty sense of humor compared to any other elves Opren encountered, but he was sociable.

At the end of the two weeks, Opren was capable of some Stage Three casting with minimal control despite his affinity for power generation. The force of his wind was higher than average, according to Selios, but he needed to learn to focus it better in small or large castings at will, and he needed to control his output of *Nuuita*. For Hycasting, the *Nuuita* control was only of minor importance, but if Opren were to learn anything outside of his Birth Element—especially when he was to train with the Goldlight magic next—he would need better concentration and proper energy management.

"Think of it this way," said Selios on day twelve. "You are

sprinting, and you are great at sprinting, even sprinting into a wall to knock it down. I need you to train for a marathon, a run of long distance, a race that requires stamina to be maintained through to the end like pushing over ten consecutive walls."

The analogy was similar to one Opren had heard from an instructor back home. It made sense, especially then because they were discussing a martial arts or boxing match, but it was less obvious how it could be applied to spell-wielding. The feeling of casting something was clear enough, but to hold back and cast simultaneously made it confusing. All he had done so far was make sure he could cast more powerfully, hold magic for longer, or resist more intently. Holding in his energy or focusing on a pinpoint with precision almost seemed like the opposite of what was needed to make a spell effective in combat, like pulling punches in a magical sense. But Selios explained he did not need to hold back so much as effectively generate the preferred amount of power in proper moderation to outlast, like conserving physical stamina to last all rounds of a long fight while allowing the foe to get fatigued. Like waiting until the opponent could not throw a strong punch, in casting it was waiting until the opponent could not cast a powerful enough spell to retaliate, but in both cases being sure one could still attack and defend effectively.

Selios required Opren to focus solely on his spirit energy manipulation for the third week. They could move on to actual combat training with Rufius again once he had control at an expert level. It was also vital to the Unity Magic he and Rufius were meant to learn and to his gradual release that would be necessary to take full control of the magic of the sphere.

It was all a good challenge with the promise of enough power and skill to combat sleeskaxes in a relatively short time —short when compared to the usual trainees, but to Opren on days he swelled and burned with the thoughts and grief of his parents' murder, their killers, and his need to avenge them, it was *not* soon enough. The intense training did do well to distract him from negative emotions that were not directly related to practice or hindrances during the sessions, but some days, even just some moments, the emotions were sharp and the memories lingered through every activity.

All of that was drowned out in a combination of anger and shock when a silhouette with familiar red eyes appeared on his twentieth day in Avarinnia, right in the center of the common areas. He and Emerald had started back to the training grounds after lunch when it happened and immediately all the elves and few others in the area panicked—after all, according to Emerald it should be impossible for someone to invade the Reiyal capital city so easily, but Lord Zargunn had done it in merely a second, without warning.

"What the hell?" exclaimed Opren, turning to Emerald. "Didn't you say he would be detected by the Uundulal or stopped before he could enter?"

"She was not wrong, Opren," said Zargunn in his double-presence voice.

Pole happened to be exiting the pub in the area that had become his favorite place to spend his days while in Avarinnia, unless he was fishing in their beautiful ponds. He saw the demonic man and went wide-eyed.

Zargunn continued, "I am not able to walk into the city, nor am I able to pass through the forest without detection, even with magical camouflage. I performed a true vanish and reappearance, which, as you may not know, is a rare feat for most Casteri. It is not a repositioning technique such as the ones you all might use in combat, but a dematerialization and reconstruction of self at a greater distance. If done poorly, one can dismember oneself. The usual security probably does not take the most advanced Casteri, wizards, or those like myself into account because of our rarity."

"I suppose you wish to see how Opren has grown while here, what the Goldlight magic can do," said Pole, not taking his eyes off Zargunn. He sounded a bit different.

Several Reiyal and Uundulal warriors in armor rushed into the square. Some shielded those who were still standing around but were not capable of combat, while the others drew blades and faced Zargunn with the apparent intent to strike at any second.

"I have learned something," said Zargunn, slowly looking around at the warriors but seemingly unfazed by the threat to his presence and life. "Opren, the negative emotions I brought out of you last we met took a different turn than I expected. They also provided me with clarity. I have since found out you connect me in some way with your parents' death. I want you to know that I will not hesitate in the slightest to kill, but I am in no way responsible for those sleeskaxes who murdered your parents."

"How do you know about that so thoroughly?" asked Opren, heat rising in him alongside curiosity.

"Well, you already—no."

An Uundulal warrior came at Zargunn with a spear before he could explain, so the Half-Demon whipped out his arm and the spear followed his hand, wrenching itself from the man's grip—or rather, Zargunn used his will to wrench the spear away. The spear caught fire—*green* fire.

Zargunn resumed his previous stance and conversational tone as he continued, "You already are aware I have observed you while observing the Goldlight orb. That began when you were in the other realm, but my scrying spell was blinded by whatever the sleeskaxes brought with them. They seem to have access to magic I do not yet possess, such as the ability to travel between realms for a time. That fog over my scrying window at the time was the only point at which I missed anything important. When I looked into it further, I was able to discover what occurred that day."

"So, if you had nothing to do with their murder," said Opren, trying to breathe steadily to calm his rising anger. "Who did? If you are a Half-Demon with advanced magic, who could have access to magic beyond you, aside from maybe these elves? Or who commands creatures you can't?"

Zargunn sighed. "I do not know. If I were aware of that,

I would be talking to them with far fewer words, instead of talking to you. They must be powerful or have great influence, or both. As it stands, I n—I *said no!*"

Zargunn spun so quickly as two more warriors attempted to lance him that Opren only knew it was a turn by reading the first and last part of the movement and making the assumption. The two Reiyal were flung away, both with their own spears in their torsos through the parts of their armor that were not Avarinnium, and they were held to a tree, hanging on the spearshafts and groaning in pain as blood began to run from their wounds. Four other elves rushed to aid them, while another warrior cast flames at Zargunn; the Half-Demon just waved a hand to extinguish the flames without taking damage.

How did he move so quickly and still accurately stab them?

"Now, this is getting irritating." All attempted friendliness dropped from Zargunn's tone. The second, rougher presence stood out much more than when he was calm. "I will kill you all if required. I am simply having a chat with this boy." Zargunn gestured lazily to Opren, but his expression was not nearly so nonchalant at that point. His threat was not just a threat but a promise.

"You want to kill Opren and steal the Goldlight orb," said Emerald. "That is not simply a chat without consequence. As you are in our sect of the kingdom and do not belong here in our city without permission, we will escort you out or remove you by force."

"You see what force gets you," said Zargunn, his voice biting. He gestured to the critically injured warriors. "And I think you know green flames mean I am more than a match for a few warriors."

"I don't give a damn," said Opren. He did not have a logical reason as to why his anger burned so strongly at that moment, but he also did not care enough to stop himself. He charged Zargunn. "*Woffrumdus!*"

As Opren took his fourth step toward the Half-Demon he

had already changed to his form conjured by the Goldlight, and the golden sword was in his hand. He felt the rush and felt in control. It was different this time because he had done it on command, not in critical desperation—though he had no idea what he did differently; but it was not the time to care, it was time to fight.

Zargunn grinned and moved to spin—but this time Opren could see him throughout the entire motion. Zargunn's coat came off and he reached out and produced two green fireballs. Zargunn threw the fireballs, but Opren managed to dodge. Unfortunately, a nearby market stand was set ablaze instead. Two of the elves tried to put it out with water spells, but it only grew.

"You can't douse Green Flames of Darkness," said Zargunn. "They only burn for a short time and grow and bend to my intent while they do. Only the caster can remove them before they finish."

"Then put them out before I kill you," said Opren. His voice did not reverberate, though he felt stronger than he would have outside of Goldlight form when he said it. He did choose the words, but his air of command and inflections were due to the Goldlight essence within him. He was not afraid, not even slightly, but he was aware he should not have threatened the Half-Demon lord without being sure he could hold the form. His brain said this could end like his first encounter with Rufius, or worse, but everything else in his being wanted the fight. It was as if the Goldlight essence also wanted the fight. He was not sure how he knew, but he just sensed the spirit within the power.

"Right now, *nobody* else needs to die," said Pole with an adamant expression Opren had not yet seen on him. His voice and his demeanor did not fit the lazy old man they knew. "*I will stop this.*"

Opren watched, in possibly more awe but equal shock compared to the others in the area, as Pole straightened his back and a white light burst from him and slowly radiated outward. His eyes changed from brown to blue and his beard thickened and became white, as did his hair. A polished white staff with a crystal set atop appeared in his left hand as he finished the change.

"Polaris!" exclaimed one of the warriors.

"Indeed," said Pole—Polaris, the man in white who no longer appeared as an old traveler, now almost majestic in comparison. He was not only from a story after all, but a man from Everniot. Opren sensed some sort of vibration emanating from Polaris—it must have been the feeling of Polaris' spirit energy. As powerfully malicious as the sleeskaxes or Zargunn felt, Polaris felt twice as powerfully bright and pure. "Opren and Emerald, I owe you two an explanation. For now, let me handle this corrupt man."

Emerald nodded once, and Opren could tell she understood exactly what was going to happen. Opren also nodded and held a guarded stance, but he did not move toward Zargunn again while he waited. Polaris stepped forward, deflecting a few green fireballs with a sharp flick of his staff as he moved; the movements were dexterous and sharp and much more fluid than any of Pole's movements, like the difference of watching a drunken brawler compared to a skilled fighter monk. Pole was only an act, that was clear.

"Zargunn," said Polaris firmly. "Or should I say, Zacharia?"

"How do you know?" asked a wide-eyed Zargunn. "I am no longer that man, so it really does not matter. Die, old man!"

The Half-Demon threw several fireballs so rapidly Opren might have had difficulty defending against them even while in Goldlighter form. But Polaris closed his eyes and calmly muttered a quick word, which caused all the green flames to shake and disappear before they reached him.

"You cannot harm me with Demonic magic," said Polaris, opening his eyes. "Have you not realized I am a White Wizard with holy magic? With all your knowledge and magical expertise, have you not heard my legends? I will exorcise you, Zacharia. But you must fight the demon of your own will once

I remove it."

"No!" screamed Zargunn, the rough voice cracking as it fully took over, much like if Zargunn were being choked.

Polaris raised his staff and took a breath to say something, but Zargunn suddenly vanished.

Opren felt dizzy and exhausted as he released the Goldlight essence, realizing he had held it for much too long. It was good he did not lose consciousness, all things considered, but he would have preferred not to feel so off-balance and weak every time he returned to normal.

Emerald came over and touched Opren on the chest, restoring some of his energy and stabilizing his equilibrium.

"Thank you, Liileiy."

"You're welcome," said Emerald. She turned to the wizard in white and grew a stern look. "What is going on here, Polaris?" She folded her arms as she waited for the answer.

"Where to begin..." Polaris looked off into the distance as he contemplated his response. After about twenty long seconds, he said, "I have been observing events surrounding the Goldlight sphere for a time, in order to aid the Keeper should he need it, and I have simultaneously been gathering information about Lord Zargunn, formerly a cursed man named Zacharia, even before he was truly possessed by a demon as he is now. My goals turned out to align. Unfortunately, I knew he would come for Opren and the Goldlight at some point soon, but I never predicted his infiltration of Avarinnia, of all places."

"If Zargunn was possessed, why does he call himself a Half-Demon?" asked Opren. He assumed a half-being meant born in part, like Rufius was a Half-Elf because of his Human mother and Elven father.

"Unlike when a normal person is possessed, the demon could not fully take over," said Polaris. "Zacharia was already cursed in a special way nobody quite understands, hence Ergunus who possessed him has only influence over him and not total control. Zacharia is aware of everything he does, tends to make decisions—albeit toward temptations and cruelty in ways the original man would have avoided, with a greater lust for power—and he is capable of everything he could do before his possession. He already suspects he was fused with a demon as a baby and that is why he is cursed, so it was fitting, particularly now, to call himself a Half-Demon. The proper term would be Fusion Half-Demon, which makes him fully Human and fully Demonic with the ability to switch between the two. Currently, he is only in his corrupted state at all times because of the possession he gives in to."

"Why does he suspect he was fused with a demon? Who would do such a thing?" asked Opren, brow furrowed in a sum of distaste, concern, and confusion as he shook his head.

"He was going to die as a baby," said Polaris. He took a breath with his eyes closed during a pause. "His mother already died during childbirth, so his father made a deal with one called Herraegunnus that could save him and make him stronger than before. Unfortunately, the magic used was not of this world and the giver of the enhancement was something not human or elf-like at all. After the fusion was complete, the alleged savior, who turned out to be anything but altruistic, vanished, leaving Zacharia cursed and fused with a Demonic being. Something about that is why I think demons are attracted to him, or he has some relation to them. It is clearly why he was possessed by Ergunus, though I am unsure why the demon fights for a host so passionately; most demons would simply take over another if removed until destroyed."

"I suppose he chose to gain power later in life after facing a lot of pain as a child?" said Emerald. "Now he can flaunt his power instead of be shamed for his curse."

"Actually, no," said Polaris, shaking his head. "He kept to himself and I was tasked with observing him for his wellbeing, until he became possessed and I needed to find a time I could get to him and remove the demon inside. The fused being can never be removed or it would result in Zacharia's death, but the unwanted possessor can be, as long as Zacharia wills him away before being re-possessed."

"Do you think he wants the Goldlighter to grow more powerful or for another reason?" asked Opren. "He already seems formidable without it."

"His abundance of power, as he is now, has its limits," said Polaris. "What he does not seem to know is he cannot wield something bound to a family line like the Goldlight unless he kills you. While that would not be a problem for him to attempt, a magical artifact like the Goldlight sphere will most often be so linked to its user, its Keeper in this case, it will not yield to a master who has harmed the Keeper. That said, I know of spells that might rebind it if he has enough supernatural energy. Uniquely, your Goldlight magic can prevent its own use but still empower a caster of other spells. The irony is I have reason to believe corrupt and Demonic beings may not be able to use the kind of power in that magic at all. I don't know why yet, but I heard stories about your grandfather and earlier Keepers of what could only be that sphere and the Goldlight. Also, the sphere and magic are not the Goldlighter, Opren, *you* are...or rather, you will be if you ascend from just being the artifact's Keeper to someone bound with the magic."

Opren considered how Zargunn could use the Goldlight essence to enhance himself without the use of the Goldlighter transformation, and how he could use the power to cast other spells, even if the Goldlight itself was just an energy source that could not be wielded by a demon. Then, a thrilling idea hit.

"Could I also use the Goldlight energy to power myself?"

"You are its Keeper, so you certainly can," said Polaris.

"I could speed up my training by enhancing my other spells, like my Hycasting, with the Goldlight!" Opren grinned. "If I do that, I might be able to match Zargunn in combat, right? The Goldlight is clearly powerful enough if Zargunn needs it with the power he already has, but I don't have time to keep training at a planned rate. If Zargunn or anyone—the sleeskaxes even—could possibly just teleport into here...no, I won't stand by and wait." He changed to a stern expression as his excitement became a resolve. "I need to learn and improve as much as possible in only days, not weeks or months anymore. I never wanted to take this long anyway. I need to do something almost immediately, even if I have to risk using too much spirit or stamina."

Emerald was observing the conversation, but she had not reacted, until she gained the look of someone who wanted to speak, then thought, then seemed to have an idea, then thought, then she finally spoke:

"There may be a way, if I can convince my parents to allow it." She appeared to be forming a plan in her mind as she continued. "The *Leiyuum Spe'we*—the Elder Mages—have a ritual Unity spell that requires a group of them to cast and hold in an enchanted room in a tower of the palace. When they use it, one can step within the magic to be transported to a sort of spiritual existence within the mind, between regular life and realms and something separate from this existence. Anything experienced or learned there remains with you and affects you, but time passes differently. It is like lucid dreaming while awake, but you can also have others in that spirit plane. It is usually used to quickly train specific magic to the Elders, or to royalty and military when in dire need, but, if you are permitted, you could train in that place. The one problem will be conditioning your body."

"You know I prefer to just go for things," said Opren. "But in your genuine opinion, do you think I can handle that at my current level?"

"I hope so," said Emerald. "If you are not ready, Zargunn or the sleeskaxes would kill you and use the Goldlight power for something else anyway, so we might as well try it. This is now too dire if they can even get to you here. I'm not stopping you from the path of battle anymore but do be prepared. Isn't that what you would suggest?"

Opren laughed once and grinned. "Yeah, it is. Let's go request permission."

While Emerald led everyone to the palace, Polaris explained why she and her parents could not even know his objectives or his specific disguise during his missions—despite being commonly asked by the Reiyal crown to do things anyway, it turned out. When they reached the huge palace doors, Emerald said the request was particularly rare and special, so she should be the one to present it. She took a breath and displayed what must have been her face of diplomatic royalty, then walked into the palace with the others in tow.

Opren waited while Emerald explained what happened in the square, most of the details not new to the king and queen. They already heard the story from a guard who came to report. Had Polaris not been successful in driving out the Half-Demon, other measures could have been taken, such as bringing in Selios or King Eeloneus himself. As those were unnecessary measures, Queen Bellavuu had chosen to wait and convinced King Eeloneus to allow the wizard to handle things. After all, Polaris had proven in the past he was a valuable ally for battle or infiltration—the latter of which was reinforced by his success in getting past even *their* detection of disguises in the city while he was Pole, which they mentioned more than once to drive home their dissatisfaction of the occurrence yet admission of his abilities. At the end of the explanation and return commentary, the queen declined to allow Opren to train with the Elders' magic.

"We have been glad to have Opren here," said Queen Bellavuu. "But we cannot allow outside battles to be lured into our city further. And we never allow outsiders to train in that place, especially one who is not Elven or in service to the crown for the good of elves. While the Avaria family has been one of progress and freedom, we still cannot break laws or endanger our people simply due to a request. We also cannot be generous without limits to a young human with an unpredictable magic, especially one so powerful as legends make the Goldlighter to be. Tell us, Opren, what would you like to say to change my mind? I will give you one opportunity to respond. If I am satisfied, I may further consider the request."

"I would rather give my life to protect your city, for you and Emerald and everyone, than sit back and do nothing," said Opren. "I do not expect any further generosity on your part. You have already shown me more than I would ever ask for, and I never expected to come to a place like this when I started out to learn magic and avenge my parents. But that does not change that I will be far more effective of an ally if I know how to wield and really control the power I inherited. If everyone dangerous in this world wants this power, it's obviously significant. That means I could use it to fight them. It also means I can do more than just avenge my parents. I do not want any other violence to come to this wonderful place, and if I cannot train here with the Elders' magic, I will leave. The target is me, and I never wanted to involve anyone else in the danger. I don't expect to change your mind, Your Grace, but now you know what I think and feel about this."

After an uncomfortably long tense silence, Queen Bellavuu stood and approached Opren.

"Look into my eyes, Opren Saphren," said the queen, placing her hands on the sides of his face.

As their eyes met, Queen Bellavuu's gaze caused something in him he could not explain, but it felt like he was floating while the world was moving slowly. He did not know how much time passed before she broke the contact of their stares, but it felt like an hour, and he felt heavy at the end.

"Do you understand the risks involved in training your mind and spirit before your body has an opportunity to be conditioned, before mastery over your own energy control is reached?" asked the queen. Unlike during her greeting or while socializing during the feasts they had each week, her eyes were not bright and glistening, they held the wisdom and experience of her age even while she had changed from her prior stern expression. She was asking in a way that was kind, but there was clearly a concern.

"I do." Opren gave a single nod. He did not know what

she saw in his eyes, or if his words might have helped, but it seemed she would allow him to train in the Elders' spirit plane. "I need to be successful, otherwise my body could break, or I could be fatigued or worse. I just won't fail. I need to do this to be sure *nobody* else dies for me. I need to do this so I can avenge my parents. I've been discovering I don't break or stop as easily as most humans. I truly appreciate the opportunity to use this special magic, Your Majesty." He bowed at the waist.

"Do not overload yourself to the point of loss of life," advised King Eeloneus. "*Ne ferli*—my daughter—holds you as someone special enough to make a rare request more than once now, and I will not see her in pain because you took a foolish route. She cannot heal you if your spirit breaks during this, either. It is magic of the mind and spirit, only. Some of her advanced spells affect restoration of *Nuuita* in minor but sacrificial amounts, while her usual magic only heals the body, not the mind or the core source of natural energy, the true *Nuuita*. If you break, you will remain magically or mentally limited at best, permanently hindered."

"I understand, Your Majesty," said Opren. He did understand and accept it, but he was a bit uncertain how well he could truly overcome the trials ahead without experience with the kind of training he planned to undertake, or the kind of magical plane he would use. Regardless, he needed to get started and go from there, if he ever hoped to avenge his mother and father. And being passive was *never* an option.

Upon dismissal from the throne room, Opren followed Emerald to the northeast part of the palace, into an octagonal room with vaulted ceilings and stained-glass windows. It was a special chamber for the Elder Mages of Avarinnia, one of four they had in different places in the palace for unique purposes. Ten mages in green-vine-pattern-trimmed white cloaks stood in formation when Opren and Emerald entered.

"Do you all have the full instructions?" asked Emerald. Her voice had remained steady and firm and she kept that "royal posture" for all moments from the time they entered the palace, but when she turned to Opren now, her voice was not as steady and she nearly whispered, "Are you certain this is how you want to do this? I *do* believe in you, but I am concerned, especially after seeing how much the Goldlight takes from you during the transformation."

"We told your parents this is the only way I can train quickly enough, and they even agreed nothing else would work as well because we have less time before something must be done, based on Zargunn now being involved so directly and more reports of problems," said Opren. "And it took convincing; that's pointless if I back down now. You know I have some sort of special thing when I need to use Nuuita, so I will be all right. Your concern gives me more motivation to succeed."

In truth, he was not entirely sure he would be all right as easily as his regular training, but he wanted her to feel comfortable with the decision. He did not want to be distracted by her feelings while he was in a dream-state or astral plane or whatever the spell caused; he had enough on his mind and heart.

"Be safe and do well, Laleiy," said Emerald kindly but firmly. She touched her forehead to his while holding him and he returned the embrace, then she released and commanded the Elders to begin the spell.

"When will—"

In answer to his incomplete question, Selios, his mentor for that training as well, arrived. Selios greeted Emerald and Opren and nodded to the Elder Mages. Then he instructed Opren to step into a two-foot circle of light on the floor while he stepped into another. Opren obeyed and when they both held their positions, light flooded throughout an Elvish rune-web in the floor, connecting his circle to Selios'. The mages muttered some spell-words Opren had yet to hear, then everything changed...

Transferring into the mental-spiritual plane of existence was similar in a way to shifting between worlds, but the difference was Opren could tell he was not fully there. His body was a bit detached as if he had gone to sleep, despite having a seemingly solid and sensory-capable body like in a dream. Selios looked exactly the same as he did outside of the plane as he stepped forward and spoke. The other man speaking was the core indicator this was not a dream, despite how much it felt like one. As they discussed the plan for the training, Opren felt more and more as though he genuinely existed in this dream-plane, this spell-place. Selios explained the experience would be as though he were training outside, with the only difference being his true body would need to catch up later.

Their first goal was to increase Opren's Hycasting power by combining his energy with the Goldlight essence as he cast a combat spell while transformed. Opren acknowledged his understanding of how to do it, shifted to Goldlighter form, and they began.

15

Opren enjoyed training in the mental-spiritual spell-plane, which the elves called *Na Esoluunspe*, meaning something like "altered time magic". Opren dubbed it the Time-Altering Plane. He realized after a few hours that things such as hunger or thirst or temperature did not bother him there, even though all his senses remained in all other ways. Sleep was also unnecessary, Emerald had explained. That made it ideal for learning, working, training. By the end of his twelve-hour training session that was to be a test period before the real, full length of training, he had managed to perfect his spell-enhancement technique that added the Goldlight energy to anything else—such as wind spells—while transformed.

Selios told Opren to stand in the same position as they were when they entered the plane when they completed the twelve hours. Opren was thankful for similar light circles in the place required because he would have forgotten the exact position. They exited that state of consciousness and Opren's body was glowing. He looked down and was still in Goldlighter form. Surprise hit, but then he recalled it was explained certain physical things would be affected once he exited the plane. The good thing was twelve hours inside the magic meant just under two hours in actual life. Goldlighter form wore on Opren's body but, because he had only used the power in the unique dreamlike state in the magical plane, his toll was reduced—still noticeable but not fatiguing.

"Hi," said Opren. Emerald stood to his right, observing him. *Has she been watching me the entire time?*

"Oluu," said Emerald. "How do you feel?"

"Good for twelve hours of straight training," said Opren. He released the Goldlighter form and stepped toward her. His balance was a bit off, but he did not stagger or fall. "Have I been in Goldlighter form the whole time out here?"

"No," said Emerald. "But for much of the time, yes. The time you were in the form totaled nearly one hour here. You were in the Time-Altering Plane about an hour and a half. The timeframe as it translates for you is not precise, but one and a half to two hours equals twelve hours, obviously. Our measurements come from knowing a full twenty-four hours requires up to four hours, and a week requires a full day and night."

"I noticed it took only three of the mages to cast the spell for that length with us both," said Opren. "What if all ten cast it?"

"We don't do that for fewer than six people, ever." Emerald's face dropped to a serious look. "You are strong, but we do this test to be certain you can even survive the toll and going in and out, how it affects your real body. A toll on your mind would also start to take effect if all ten Elder Mages were to cast it. Ideally, we use seven members to create a perfect Unity Magic circle. This is advanced Unity Magic—like the sort of thing you are supposed to learn with Rufius, but at a higher level. I expect you will cover that after the essentials of wielding the Goldlight now."

"I want to do the full week with all seven Elders then, please."

Opren knew there was a greater risk than going in and

out in daily sessions, but the less time in the regular realms he used while still inept, the better toward his mastery. The concentrated dose of training he had just experienced proved how much more he could accomplish in the Time-Altering Plane.

"Shela Selios, are *you*," Emerald pointed at Selios, "all right with staying inside that plane for so long?"

"I can manage," said Selios with a smirk. "I have used this before, for five days inside."

"While you are doing this, I am going to go to Rhahkmant'e to request Athera and Vallot come help with your Unity Magic training and to deliver them a message from my parents," said Emerald. "The other Elders will observe your state and inform my parents if anything strange occurs. *Please* be careful, Opren. I know you will want to train constantly, but this accelerates your training so much, it is both all right and recommended to take a half-day break out here between multiple-day sessions inside. No self-training inside without someone to monitor you. Practice out here if you must, to condition yourself properly. That's progress too, don't forget."

"That's true," said Opren. "You made such a good point, I suppose I have to listen." He smiled and she punched him lightly in the arm before returning the smile.

"I am not supposed to tell you this, but I want you to know the serious nature here," her face became stern as it had when Opren mentioned using all ten Elders for the spell, "King Eeloneus' father, my grandfather, used that most powerful casting and, when he returned to our true time, he nearly died. It was a time of war and he needed to harness a spell nobody could perform with only a few days, or even weeks, of training. That is why we do not use it; it is dangerous. Seven days with seven Elder Mages is enough for anyone in one period. That toll may surprise you."

Emerald instructed the Elder Mages on what to do before she said her farewell to Opren. It did not occur to him initially, but her leave would be for nearly a month in his experience, due to three weeks total inside the Time-Altering Plane over the true days he would train with Selios while she was gone. She would really be gone for two weeks at most but, while the Time-Altering Plane made things like learning or doing much more efficient compared to training in true time, waiting in want or missing someone would be made worse.

Opren ate a satisfying meal before returning to the tower. Barbosa joined him while he sat in the standard palace dining hall, the one that was not used for larger feasts but for regular lunches and dinners. The king and queen had permitted use of any part of the palace and they expected he would be safer while pushing his limits if he remained within the place with the greatest defenses. Even supernatural magic could not breach the spell barriers around there, and there was a constantly vigilant guard force in and around the place, as well as the king and queen themselves if anyone did somehow breach the defenses.

The granwolf related he had managed to explore the entire city and its borders, had learned all its exits and entrances, and had learned of all the best places to relax, eat, or watch people. That meant Barbosa needed new entertainment, in his own opinion.

I thought now I would come watch you train for parts of each day, said Barbosa.

"Where were you when Zargunn showed up?"

I heard about that, and I am glad you all survived, said Barbosa. *I was too far away to get to you to be of much help had Zargunn decided to try harder to kill you, based on the stories I heard. I only do well in physical, non-magical battle.*

"Probably right. Have you met the real Polaris yet? Pole turned out to be a disguise."

I haven't. I thought something smelled off about him before, and it wasn't the scent of drinks or dirty lies, just not fully appropriate for the person in front of me, said Barbosa. *I will need to stick around more often, it seems. You are magnetic to danger and sudden occurrences even while not on the road.* The granwolf chuckled.

"I wish I weren't. This family artifact has begun to feel like a family curse. My parents..." Opren paused and recomposed his emotions. "They might still be alive if not for this damn ball being coveted. A power like this is only good once I learn to use it. It's a problem if others keep getting hurt instead, especially if the bad guys get it and deal more damage. I can't allow that. I won't. Speaking of which, I need to go train more. Selios said we had a half hour break."

Opren pushed back his chair and Barbosa made to follow him as he left the hall, but he explained how his new training worked and that Barbosa would only be able to observe his sleep-like state from the outside, unless the granwolf actually wanted to try going to the Time-Altering Plane with him and Selios.

That sounds very unpleasant to experience, said Barbosa. *I'll pass. I will observe your training for Unity Magic when Emerald returns with Athera and Vallot, assuming they do agree to come. I have never seen what sorts of things Unity Magic can do.*

Opren told Barbosa to have a good evening and returned to the chamber where the Elder Mages cast the spell for the Time-Altering Plane. Selios had already returned from eating and informing Rufius what was to happen—Rufius would need to train with someone else for a true-time week while Selios worked with Opren. At the end of the Time-Altering Plane training, Rufius was expected to meet Opren and Selios for the regular training schedule, to begin Unity magic training.

Selios gestured for Opren to step onto his spot to enter the Time-Altering Plane and simultaneously took his own place. Opren did so, closed his eyes, and took a deep breath as the mages began the spell. He opened his eyes a few seconds later to see they were in the spell-place.

Selios required Opren to fight him for the first two hours inside the plane. Opren was to use everything he had learned to that point, combined with the Goldlight essence, to manage against Selios for over five minutes without being knocked unconscious, knocked down for longer than ten seconds, or knocked out of the fighting ring Selios drew.

The ground was sand that time, where it had been firmer dirt the first time. Opren asked why it had changed.

"The *Leiyuum Spe'we* can see into our minds in this state," said Selios. "Whatever I require the place to be, they make it to be. Unfortunately, we cannot bring external objects into here in most cases. That means Ruubi could not summon her ring-blade in here, for example. The reason you can use the Goldlight is you are using its energy only, not a physical material."

"But what about the sword?" asked Opren. "I need to learn to use the spell to its full."

"I have a theory about that." Selios grinned. "Activate the Goldlight magic as you would to make the sword, if you can."

Opren readied himself and pulled on the Goldlight energy and said the spell-word. He was successful, but the orb was not around to transform into a sword so, as expected, he did not hold one.

"So that doesn't work," said Opren, disappointed. He had hoped he could perfect everything while in the Time-Altering Plane, instead of using real time.

"Now *summon* a sword," said Selios as if Opren were missing the obvious answer.

Opren willed a sword to come to him. Nothing happened. Then he pulled on the Goldlight essence as he would to add it to a wind spell. A bright golden blade formed from the energy right next to his hand. The sword was not solid—not physical material anyway—but it looked just like the longsword that usually came from the orb (minus the metal core). It was a blade and hilt of pure magical golden light—a Goldlight sword. He grabbed it and was able to hold it like a solid object that was perfectly comfortable for his hand. The difference was this sword felt nearly weightless, not a heavy material the way a regular sword might be.

"This is awesome," said Opren, swinging and slashing the

sword around. "But can I cut—"

Opren reflexively evaded and sliced through a large rock that flew his way, that Selios had thrown. The rock was split smoothly down the middle and the blade had no resistance placed on it as it passed through. The magically produced sword seemed even more effective than the other one at going through solids.

"I suppose that answers your question?" said Selios with an amused smirk. "Want to try more to see how well you can really defend in that form?"

"Let me try something first."

Opren attempted to summon another Goldlight energy sword and, to his delight, it worked. Then, he transformed the image in his mind of the blades and resummoned them as katanas. That also worked. He had full control over what blade he summoned and could use more than one at will. *This is going to be fun.* He nodded at Selios once to begin, and the platinum-haired elf began to summon stones.

"Conveniently, natural things like plants and water still may exist here when we need them," said Selios. "Rocks included."

Opren had to block a stone and dodge two others before he had a chance to ask how natural things could be used, but weapons and such could not. Selios spared no time talking pointlessly. Opren appreciated the heavy focus on the goal to get as much training done as soon as possible.

Opren and Selios spent three days inside the Time-Altering Plane...until Opren somehow broke the hold and ended up outside of the spell. He immediately re-entered, but he was not even sure how he did it. He spent only a moment outside, but he did see one of the Elder Mages express just a hint of shock when he regained consciousness before the spell was even halfway finished.

"What the hell?" thought Opren aloud when he re-entered and staggered for a moment. "How did that happen?"

"I don't know," said Selios. "Were you tired out there?"

"No. I felt energized, actually. It's nearly the opposite of what I would expect."

"You are starting to control the Goldlight," said Selios. "It gives you power and, if you are primarily absorbing and outputting its essence energy, not your own *Nuuita*, you must not be tiring as a result. That is extraordinary!"

"It really is." Opren smiled. "That doesn't explain my jump out of here, but it means I can handle the entire week without a problem, I think."

"Good." Selios nodded once. "Now let's continue!"

Another two days of training and Opren was able to activate and deactivate the Goldlight magic with no problems. He could hold the form for as long as he liked, and he began to feel more driven and more empowered, not worn down or less energetic. No matter how many spells he cast, he could keep going. No matter how long he remained in Goldlighter form, he did not need to rest. Selios warned it could be due to the Time-Altering Plane experience, but they both hoped it was due to the magic Opren could wield or some special case with Opren himself.

It was the final day inside, the seventh day, that came with its problems. Opren felt challenged by Selios when the experienced warrior started to push harder to win in combat, and Opren finally began to feel the wear and tear of constant training and spell-wielding. Opren pushed harder as well and attempted to summon swords after setting a few in the air to act as obstacles for Selios. When he materialized a sixth blade, he flashed and left the Time-Altering Plane again, but he did not end up back in the palace chamber. This time, he was not in Avarinnia at all...

16

Opren looked around at the two buildings in front of him, noted a streetlight—a streetlight! He was back in the world where he grew up. Somehow, it seemed the Goldlight magic had teleported him back without his intent. He wracked his brain—he had been thinking heavily of his parents and home as he pushed himself.

"Did I think too much about returning here?" he thought aloud as he stepped out of the road. "I can't be here, though. I need to finish training. I need to get back and avenge Mom and Dad. Goldlight, take me back to Everniot!" He looked down at the sphere in his hand and shook it. "Come on, dammit! *Please*."

He closed his eyes and took a few deep breaths to calm himself, then focused on Avarinnia and the palace and his training. He kept concentrating on where he wanted to go while he shifted back to regular form and then back into Goldlighter form. After about five minutes of this back and forth, a flash happened. When he opened his eyes, he had returned to Everniot, to Avarinnia, to the palace…but he was not in the Elders' chamber; he had transported back to the balcony outside the chamber windows because of how he had moved before coming back.

"Opren!" called a man from the ground. Opren looked down and Polaris said, "Hop on this."

The wizard produced what looked like a small cloud and floated it up to Opren's level. Opren stepped carefully onto it and it floated to the ground with him along for the ride, before vanishing when he stepped off.

"What happened to cause you to be there?" asked Polaris. "You know, I think it is more effective to train *inside* the room."

"Very funny," said Opren, still breathing heavily and trying to gather his thoughts. "I somehow transported back to the realm I came from, then back to here. I forgot if I move in one realm, I probably end up in a different place in the other too."

"When you say 'realm', you mean you aren't from here at all, don't you?" asked Polaris. "You don't only mean you aren't from this kingdom or this continent. I suspected something of the sort when I realized the Goldlight artifact seemed to be missing entirely, then returned."

"You're right," said Opren. "It's a different world or different version of the world, according to what my mother told me before she was killed."

"That explains why you say some things differently and why you are ignorant of this world's ways," said Polaris. He thought for a moment, scratching his beard. "So, the Goldlight magic has the power to take you between realms. Did you mean to return or was that also an accident? Are you able to control it?"

"I put in a ton of effort and yelled at the sphere and the magic," said Opren. "It finally worked when I shifted between forms enough. I don't know if I can always make it happen, but I am meant to learn eventually, I think. My grandfather could travel between at will, so maybe it was the Goldlight magic that allowed him to do it. I don't really know, because my mother said they couldn't return anymore once he used too much of the magic."

"I don't know if Zargunn or anyone else who wants it would know that much," said Polaris. "But I recommend keeping that bit of information to yourself outside of this city."

"Yeah, I didn't plan to tell anyone as it is. But you found me after this incident and Selios will need to know. Damn, I need to go back up there and explain!"

Opren ran back into the palace and up the stairs to the Elder Mages' chamber. When he got there, Selios was tense, his jaw clenched.

"Are you all right?" asked Opren, not expecting to find his instructor in that state.

"You vanished, and I thought maybe you had left the spell again," said Selios quickly. "Thus, I used the Elders' ability to see my thoughts to have them pull me out. But then you were just *gone*! Even they could not sense your presence. I thought maybe you had vanished the way Zargunn can, but they could have sensed where you vanished from if that were true. Then you returned outside the window somehow, and I am glad you are unharmed."

"So what's wr–"

"If the Goldlighter is able to do that and it lines up with a mission I have been working, the information is both vital and dangerous!" said Selios in a tone that held more anxiety than Opren had so far heard from the hardened soldier. "Zargunn is not the only one who wants your orb, nor is he the most dangerous."

"I know he isn't, since he claims not to have sent the sleeskaxes," said Opren. "But the sleeskaxes can already travel between realms, which they did to kill my parents. Why is it more dangerous for them to do it with the Goldlight magic?"

"I don't know what the full extent of the power of the Goldlighter is, but I understand the magic is to be wielded as a weapon," said Selios. "The kind of magic the sleeskaxes must have used was supernatural and limited. The Goldlight might not have limits to how often it can transport the user. A magical weapon in the hands of someone who plans to conquer is dangerous, but to add the ability to travel between realms at-will would make them a threat to more than even our world's kingdoms."

Selios punched a wall and Opren was surprised his fist cracked the pale, polished stone. It made more sense once the soft white aura around Selios' fist was visible, but it was still impressive.

"Should we continue training after a longer break?" asked Opren, now starting to feel concerned about Selios.

"Yes." Selios ran a hand through his hair and let out a sigh. "I apologize for my overreaction. I must go see the oracle. Get some rest and eat again, as it has been many hours out here. I will be back in a day."

Polaris finally entered the chamber after catching up to Opren as Selios left the chamber in a hurry. Polaris gave Opren an inquisitive look.

"What I just did with traveling between realms has him concerned about something with a mission and the Goldlight magic," said Opren. "I wish he had told me more details about what the mission is and what scared him. He only said it is about someone dangerous controlling a weapon that can also help them conquer other realms."

"I assume he is going to the oracle," said Polaris. Opren widened his eyes in surprise. "I know quite a bit and I have been an aid in many places, as I mentioned. I first came here when Selios was your age, so I learned his habits well. I also specialize in knowing and observing."

"I've noticed."

Opren had not realized he was still in Goldlighter form until that moment, and he shifted back to normal. Exhaustion hit him like an anvil. The time training had taken a toll, but not as badly as it could have, but holding the Goldlighter form even outside the magical plane for such prolonged periods had taken its own price. It was still better than passing out, but he had overdone it slightly. He said a weary "good night" to Polaris and forced himself to cross the palace and climb the steps to his bedroom, then crashed onto his bed and slept.

17

Emerald had no trouble reaching Rhahkmant'e, which was a welcome relief from the recent threatening events, even to include Lord Zargunn showing himself inside her *home* city, of all places. She hated the idea it was still possible for certain kinds of advanced Casteri or other magic users to get in and harm her people. She might not care for daily royal duties like Sapphire, but she certainly *did* care about protecting the people, just as she would have had she been born a commoner among them.

She had already notified Athera she would be returning for a day by letter, and the knight was waiting for her near the entrance as usual.

"You seem to have made good time," said Athera with a subtle smile. "I trust you did not run into any major threats?"

"*Aharron Uundulara*, I did not," said Emerald. "Have you had an opportunity to speak to Vallot about what I mentioned in the letter?"

As if in answer to her question, Vallot could be seen approaching them, his purple-gray skin standing out in the sunlight of the bright, cloudless day. He reached speaking distance and greeted her with a nod.

"Are you sure your city wants me there?" asked Vallot.

"Even the most traditional and close-minded Reiyal have come to accept we are no longer at war," said Emerald. "And besides, you are a rogue Luunal, which means you are not supported or obligated by any decisions your former people might make or oppose, even if the political battle still continued."

"A rogue tends not to be welcome in most places," said Vallot. His smooth voice held a bitterness. His tone brightened as he said, "But I appreciate your request to have me. Rufius is a fantastic student and gifted Reiycasteri, and helping he and Opren progress once more will be a wonderful experience."

"And you know we have both helped train enough of their adolescents and soldiers and allies, they would be hard-pressed to refuse us," said Athera. "After all, I need you for Unity Magic. With Emerald making the request and me requiring your partnership, they would have already turned down the whole thing if you were *that* unwanted."

"I do suppose my merits outweigh my history," said Vallot. "I have placed another teacher as a substitute while I am away, so I am ready to leave whenever it is time."

"I would like to rest before we travel back, but we should leave early in the morning," said Emerald. "Opren has begun to train in the *Na Esoluunspe*—the Time-Altering Plane, he has called it—so it might seem to him that I am gone for weeks instead of days. I also want to be sure he is all right."

"The king and queen actually allowed him to train that way?" exclaimed Vallot. His usual chill composure was completely discarded, which must have meant he knew more about the specific kind of Unity Magic than Emerald realized. Luunal elves were much more focused on mind-related spells, protective enchantments, and curses than they were on nature-bonding, spiritual planes, and Unity Magic as it related to anything but the sort of fighting duet Rufius and Opren were to learn. Vallot must have learned of the *Leiyuum* chamber and spells of his own accord. Then again, Luunal did tend to know surprisingly more than they should be expected to know.

"The Half-Demon, Lord Zargunn, showed himself in the center of one of our squares and killed some of our warriors while attempting to talk to and possibly threaten Opren," said Emerald. "The man who was with us called Pole was actually Polaris, the White Wizard, so when he revealed himself and attempted to exorcise the demon possessing Zargunn—really, a man named Zacharia controlled by a demon named Ergunus—Zargunn vanished as quickly as he came into the city. The level of threat he poses to Opren and anyone around Opren means the Goldlight sphere is not going to be safe unless Opren learns to use it sooner than would be possible in regular time." She paused before adding less intently, "And my mother used her ability to Soulgaze before she would allow it. She won't tell me what she saw in him, but it helped change her mind even though he is not an elf or long-term ally."

"The Goldlight?" asked Athera, eyes wide. "Is *that* the golden orb Opren carries? The artifact of the Goldlighter?"

"Yes," said Emerald. "I had heard of it in stories, but I didn't know that's what he had until it was identified by Lord Zargunn."

"The letter you have from your parents," said Athera. "Do you know what it is about?"

"I did not ask." Emerald shook her head. "Do you already know? They did say it was an additional brief of some sort."

Athera thought for a moment, appearing to struggle with how to say her next thought. She sighed.

"I suppose it will only benefit you to know." She looked Emerald in the eyes. "Lord Zargunn is not the only one who wants the Goldlight artifact. Your parents and I have communicated about it since just before you brought Opren here, which is part of the reason all his training has easily been set-up, just in case what turns out to be true was accurate. The sources say towns are being razed by corrupt magic and what seem to be demons. Whenever someone survives, they tell of someone requesting a gold weapon or golden ball or golden fighter. Opren will be in much more danger and the threat is a problem to multiple sects now, somehow starting near the Royal Sect."

"So you and my parents have been planning how to prevent more damages, particularly when the corrupt beings arrive in this sect, I assume?" said Emerald.

"Correct." Athera nodded. "If Opren does master the Goldlight, he can fight. It was only a thought by your parents and their council before, but now we know."

"That must be part of why they allowed him to train in the Time-Altering Plane without a greater argument or longer consideration," said Emerald, realizing the practical aspect of it but worrying for Opren. Then again, Opren would want to fight, and it was time to stop withholding any information from him, even if things became life-threatening.

"It seems to me the best thing we can do is continue Opren's training as planned," said Vallot. "He is in danger either way. He seems like the type to want to fight for himself."

"That's why I am worried," said Emerald. "I know he will."

"If he is meant to be the Goldlighter, his path is not a safe one, but he may be the one with the power to overcome it all," said Athera.

As Emerald lay down to rest for the night, she repeated Athera's words in her mind. But if towns were being destroyed by demons or sleeskaxes, could Opren really face that? He was not from the realm and he was unfamiliar with magic when he arrived. Of course, he was also the most resilient and fast-learning human she had ever met when it came to combat or spell-wielding, so there was hope. Telling him not to fight would only make him fight harder to prove he could anyway. She sighed but smiled to herself. Persistence and a willful nature pulled them both. *I hope those will be enough.*

The following morning, Emerald waited with Shari near the entrance to Rhahkmant'e for her former Human mentor and Luunal ally. When Athera and Vallot arrived on their own horses, Emerald climbed onto Shari and lead the way out.

The return to Avarinnia took only the same amount of time as when Emerald had traveled alone, thanks to Vallot's Elven heritage and Athera's military experience; neither of the other two had to rest for long, either. While journeys were usually better if exploration was involved, the current circumstances did not permit that kind of relaxation. She only wished she had known how serious the situation really was when it came to Opren's sphere.

"I will need to have a conversation with my parents when we arrive," said Emerald as Avarinnia came into view. "I don't think Opren will want to discover we have kept this from him, unless we tell him directly."

"I suppose not, based on his reactions to us withholding information about the attacks on Rhahkmant'e," said Athera.

"We will meet with Selios and cover what needs to occur during training while you do," said Vallot.

Vallot received a glare from one of the guards as they reached the gate, but Emerald was not questioned. Not everyone in the city would be aware of who Vallot was or why he was there, and some of the Reiyal were taught as children not to trust Luunal, but she hoped it would become clear he was an ally since she, the princess, was the one leading him and Athera into the city; it was one of the rare occasions she was glad for her royal status. Most of the people would recognize the special knight who regularly served their king and queen and their military; Athera had visited Avarinnia before.

Athera led Vallot to the training grounds while Emerald entered the palace.

Emerald's boot-heels clacked loudly on the floor as she marched more than walked to the throne. A guard attempted to ask if she needed anything, while a palace maid greeted her, but she just denied the guard and waved dismissal at the woman as she continued. She also ignored a noble known for traditional thinking who was the fourth to recently question her about Opren using their "sacred" magic as an outsider, but the comment was still heard and added to her determination for open clarity. Her parents looked toward her as she neared.

"You managed to make the trip in good time," said her father. As he stood to greet her properly, he lost his royal air and presentation, and his brow creased in the middle once he took in her body language and expression.

"Do you intend to allow Opren to master the Goldlight magic primarily so he can *leave* and go fight the corrupt beings in other cities?" asked Emerald. She did not raise her voice or snap at him, but she was stern with emphatic intent.

18

Opren had been dreaming of his parents, of the shop and helping his father, of his mother watching him fight in a tournament, and of their time together during their last visit to the beach. He had been content, but a voice broke through his dream-state and woke him, even though he was not fully sure what was real yet or who was yelling—well, not yelling, but too loud for morning.

"Opren! Wake up! Are you all right?" called the young woman's voice. It was familiar, but the owner did not immediately register to him.

Opren opened his still-drowsy eyes to see a wave of rose-petal red hair falling over bare porcelain-skin shoulders and a bouncing person as she began to call again then stopped—she must have noticed she successfully woke him. He looked into Ruubi's green eyes and saw a concern he had not yet seen from her. It reminded him of Emerald's expression when he overtrained, save for Emerald's entrancing violet eyes. Ruubi's eyes were beautiful, and he could be happy to wake to eyes like that and was sure anyone would be, especially as happy as Ruubi usually was or feigned to be; but he would never get lost in her eyes as he had Emerald's.

He looked past Ruubi to the window and a sudden spike of adrenaline hit. The sun was too low for morning—his window was not to the east. He shot out of bed and Ruubi exclaimed.

"Are you feeling well?" she asked, barely remaining out of the way but following him closely while he pulled on a shirt and grabbed his armor for training. "*What* are you doing?"

"I'm extremely late and I haven't had enough time to train today so—"

"Did you forget Shela Selios went to the oracle? You can train on your own if you are up to it, but I came to check on you after so much sleep because I heard you had an incident and Emerald hasn't been here," said Ruubi. "Maybe you shouldn't tell her I came in while you were not fully clothed, or she might get the wrong idea. I'm not going to seduce you or anything anymore. I like my fun, but I keep my promises and respect commitments between others. This might look bad."

"Wait...how long was I asleep?" He turned back to face her. His head felt a bit heavy in the way it might if he drank too much but did not get a full hangover.

"Over sixteen hours," said Ruubi, indicating the wall clock with her finger. "But you feel all right now, right? I don't have the gift of healing like Emmi, but I can recommend to a healer to come look at you or I can bring you food. I really don't know if training is a good idea so soon after that kind of exhaustion."

"I'm fine," said Opren. In truth, he could have been glad to rest a bit longer, he wished his head would feel less pressure, and he needed a meal and water, but he was not in the mood for someone to be concerned about him in that way when there were more serious circumstances surrounding them than whether or not he was comfortable and in ideal condition, especially anyone other than Emerald. "Thanks for checking, though."

"You're welcome," said Ruubi in her usual bubbly tone. "Please let me know if you need anything."

"Will do. Thanks, Ruubi," said Opren as he headed for the

door again.

He would not be able to use the Time-Altering Plane, but he could practice what he now knew to do out in the true world. His body already took the toll of holding the Goldlighter form, so maybe he could adapt in a way like martial artists do when they get punched enough and can take the hit, or how muscles could strain but get stronger in the aftermath of heavy activity. If not, he might really need Ruubi and healers to help, but he hoped otherwise.

"*Ariayi*," said Ruubi as she left the room but headed in the opposite direction down the hall, which he had come to know meant something like "see you later" in Elvish. Emerald had said to avoid ever saying *aranoi* instead, as it was a permanent goodbye, such as when one is to leave with no plan of return, one is dead, or something else expected to be permanent. *Ariayi* was the most common farewell.

Opren headed to the regular training grounds and considered throwing the Goldlight blades into the targets, to see if he could do so accurately and if the blades would keep their form and remain solid—or whatever they were that *seemed* solid—once he released them. His training plan came to a pause in his head as he passed through the entry hall to the palace and heard voices from the throne, including Emerald's voice.

Opren entered. Emerald was in a state that was neither fiery anger nor cold bitterness, but her tone held something between the two in its bite, and she did not even raise her vocal volume. Somehow, she also managed to add the inflection of concern. He doubted his control of his own tone would be nearly so perfect for what he might want to express.

"Do you intend to allow Opren to master the Goldlight magic primarily so he can *leave* and go fight the corrupt beings in other cities?" Emerald added some things in Elvish that Opren had yet to learn.

As Opren approached, Emerald and the king and queen all turned their heads to him. King Eeloneus had not responded, but now Opren had a question of his own.

"King Eeloneous," greeted Opren with a dip of his head. "What corrupt beings does Emerald mean?" He turned to Emerald. "What are you talking about?"

The determined look in Emerald's eyes and forehead eased a bit as she said, "I brought Athera and Vallot back to help you train as planned. Athera informed me what the letters between her and my parents have been about. How are you?"

"Confused at the moment," said Opren, the crease between his eyes bringing the heaviness to focus there, while his head grew hazy overall. "But I was doing well in training, until a, uh, minor incident."

"Then let's trade answers because I am curious about that, and I knew you would want to know about what I learned," said Emerald. She sighed. "I apologize. I was going to discuss this with my parents before you, to have all the clarity and truth of it ahead of time and then tell you. I suppose now we will learn together."

"It is best this way," said King Eeloneus.

Queen Bellavuu had remained mostly still and quiet to this point, but she stood and stepped over to the right of her husband. She looked at Opren, then Emerald.

"I agree," said the queen. "All transparency can now occur to you both at once. What would you like to know first?"

"I would appreciate more information on the 'corrupt beings' and why I might want to fight them," said Opren. He hoped his tone was not demanding, as he did want to remain respectful toward the king and queen, even while he became lightheaded and had his parents and Zargunn on his mind. The surprise of yet another threat was not welcome at the time, especially as his training was incomplete. "Please," he added, hoping to soften the statement and turn it to a more pleasant request.

"Beginning at the Royal Sect, the most established and wealthy part of the kingdoms as run by humans, where the High-King of Humans, Lariat Rykeron, resides, there have been reports of monsters and Demonic creatures and the undead, as well as even more outlandish tales of what must be exaggeration," said King Eeloneus. "The descriptions from witnesses of the corrupt beings or the destruction and survivors of the attacks have described them similarly in five towns and one city outside of the sect so far. Nearly all reports mention a sleeskax or a so-called 'monster' leader that can somewhat speak. Every time one of the sleeskaxes speaks, it requests the location of 'the golden ball of power', 'the golden weapon', 'gold fighter', or simply 'sphere boy'. After you came with Emerald to our city and it was clear you were to be the new Keeper of the Goldlight artifact, possibly even to become the Goldlighter of legend, I had strong suspicions it is you they seek."

"Lord Zargunn showing in our own home reinforced the problem," said Queen Bellavuu. "I believed you would be quite safe here, but if he can show himself, it is a problem. The wider threat is likely a coordinated group of corrupt beings, and sleeskaxes could pose a threat to our people. You were to train regardless of the new circumstances and developing critical threats, so Eeloneus and I felt it best for you to do exactly what you requested, as long as my sight into your soul's nature proved you are worthy, as occurred. In return, we also thought it might be best to allow you to fight—even ask it of you—when you have adept control over the Goldlight. You would then become an obvious target—in the way a sword could be a target; you could deal damage in return."

"And that is the reason you so easily permitted us to use the spell, without heavier resistance or time to consider it further," said Emerald. "I did find it out of place for you to not even discuss it before giving us a final 'yes'. You already had a goal, and our request suited that goal."

"Correct," said Queen Bellavuu. "Furthermore, Opren will be safer as threats come for him, and he could battle the threats outside of here, as you also expected. If he is a target, it is likely he would be followed when he leaves, but only after he is prepared would that be requested. That would save any other deaths to our citizens."

"I will," said Opren. He had taken in all the news he needed to commit to his decision. There was no choice because Zargunn would reach him, or the new monsters would, or he would reach the sleeskaxes as he had planned from the time of his parents' murder. It was an easy thing to agree with someone who asked for what you already meant to give or do.

"You cannot simply fight without—" started Emerald.

"I cannot simply wait while doing nothing," said Opren before she could finish. He immediately felt remorse for the mistake and her eyes regained their earlier purposeful intensity. Unlike usual, he did not get lost in her violet eyes. Instead, they pierced him and held him to the spot. Was it her expression and his feelings that held him, or her ability to entice or persuade through eye contact as an elf? Either way, all his fight temporarily disappeared.

"Without being as prepared as the short time will allow and without others," said Emerald firmly, not breaking her stare into his eyes, into him. "I want to help you. I knew you would be too damn stubborn not to fight, especially if this were the truth as it is. But do not interrupt me during a serious conversation again, or I will not be such a nice traveling companion or anything else. You may have a special magic, but you are not to the level to boast that power yet. I will let you fight whatever you want if you can beat me. First, you must spend time in the Time-Altering Plane with Rufius; I know it will take too long for you two to match spirits out here, even after Athera and Vallot train you. Then, you will fight me. Every time you lose, you will train another day in the Time-Altering Plane, then fight me again."

"What if—"

"I am giving you this order as Princess Esmeraldi of Avarinnia," she said, this time talking over him. "Do you accept, or do you wish to dispute this matter formerly?"

Opren wanted to be angry, but he did not want to anger

her any further. He wanted to ignore her warnings and train his own way and go hunt down the sleeskaxes who killed his parents before they killed anyone else, but he knew preparing would be what his parents would want. He wanted to leave while she was asleep the next night, but he knew and felt already he would miss her too much. He knew from his training back home that rushing to danger would be sloppy and lead to a fool's defeat, but he was restless, and every new threat meant the problem was growing. He did not want anyone else in places he did not even know to die because of a search for him, but he did need to complete the training if he wished to protect them. And he would find no better way to accelerate his training against true time than with the magic available in the Elven city.

"Forgive my disrespect, Princess," said Opren, pushing all hints of sarcasm from his tone and keeping only the slight shame and genuine apology. He bowed then straightened but kept his head down. "I gladly accept your suggestion and command."

Emerald reached out a hand and lightly pressed his chin upward to have his eyes meet hers. She just looked at him sternly for a moment that seemed too long, then she softly smiled.

"That must have been painful to force," she said. "Ve harron."

"Could I have said anything else, given how you made it an order?" He attempted to sound lighthearted.

"I certainly would not have recommended it," interjected King Eeloneus. "That righteous temper and her usual patience come from her mother. My strength is in charisma and even I feel small when Bellavuu makes a point with infallible logic. Beware an Elven lady's angry glare." He smiled.

Opren appreciated the king's use of mild humor to break the lingering tension. He was not sure if he could do it himself at that point otherwise. He had already pushed too hard in the presence of royalty and did not want to be the one to do it again.

"Your turn to explain," said Emerald. "What incident?"

Opren told her about his accidental flash back to his realm and his return to the balcony of the Elders' chamber window by mistake. She did not react immediately, but she asked the king and queen if it was a concern.

"Magic such as that tends to be tethered to its home or the caster's point of interest," said King Eeloneous. He turned to Opren. "It must be due to *your* perceived home being out of this realm but *its* home being here. There is no magic we know of, even in the legends of the Goldlighter, that should allow unlimited travel between dimensions. It would be something at or beyond the level of the Goldlighter, certainly, and the Goldlighter is meant to be a living weapon as I understand the history and your abilities."

"My mother said my grandfather could sometimes travel back and forth," said Opren. "And it seemed to be intentional. How would that be?"

"He used a tether point and likely portal spells," said Queen Bellavuu. "But those are never permanent when talking of dimensions, or you risk a dimensional tear. If the corrupt beings are demons, a dimensional tear would be their way of arrival to all dimensions with any numbers. There is a great deal of danger in that and only the most powerful wielders of magic in history could cause one intentionally. Did your grandfather frequently leave and return?"

"Maybe once a year."

"I suspect he spent a great deal of energy each time he did," said Queen Bellavuu. "And it was only possible because the magic knew he had an attachment to two homes. In your case, you are dealing with magical instability in yourself and in what you are casting. Because you also have some emotional trauma and confusion, the Goldlight essence is likely trying to accept your will, even if you do not consciously intend to go between worlds."

"What about the sleeskaxes?" asked Opren. "They

traveled at will."

"They only traveled to your home and immediately returned, correct?" said King Eeloneus. Opren nodded. "They must have used a temporary realm-transportation spell from a supernatural source. I will need to investigate how they received one. Sleeskaxes cannot do magic like that on their own. That may be connected to a mission I gave to Selios."

Opren remembered how quickly the magic space—a portal between versions of the world, evidently—disappeared behind the sleeskaxes. Thinking of the event stirred his anger and longing for more time with his parents, as well as his want to find the sleeskaxes anew, but he pushed away most of that once again so he could focus until he was ready to face them *and win.*

"With that mostly resolved," said a familiar woman's voice behind Opren. Opren turned to see the tall figure, thickly braided brown hair, and strong face of Athera. Seeing his first spell-wielding mentor lifted the weight from his emotions just a little. "We should begin training as soon as possible."

19

At the Avarinnia training grounds, on one of the floating stone fighting rings, Athera watched—studied—as Vallot gave Opren his pre-assessment of everything Opren could do at that point, magically and combatively.

Athera knew Opren as her trainee and knew what he could do before he left Rhahkmant'e under her training and Rutundo's, so she did not need to assess him as directly. Observing while Vallot fought him was more educational, until she knew what to expect to help him improve where he might need work. To her delight, Opren had become skilled enough to hold his own against Vallot, until Vallot began to fight with greater effort as if the fight were real instead of practice.

"He never takes it easy on anyone," said Athera to Emerald. She looked back at Rufius, who was summoned by Vallot while Athera had retrieved Opren and Emerald from the palace. "As you well know." Rufius nodded. "But he has never had a bad student, other than those who could not handle him and quit."

"You have also never produced a bad trainee," said Rufius.

"When I taunted Opren before, it was based on his lack of experience and skill and probable lack of strength—which I now see was a mistake—but I always knew your talent and capabilities."

"Is that a way of sucking up or an attempt to remain in good standing despite how you act toward my trainee?" said Athera with a brow raised.

"I—" tried Rufius.

"I'm joking, Rufius," said Athera, quirking the corner of her mouth between a smile and a smirk. "I'm aware you mean no disrespect. You are direct and sometimes harsh like your mentor, but you are a gifted warrior in every way. Opren is as well, despite his lack of experience over a greater time. That is why Vallot and I suggested you two work together for Unity magic, and why we agreed to help."

Athera looked back at the fight between Vallot and Opren on the ring floating about five feet from the one where she, Emerald, and Rufius were spectating. Opren yelled his unique spell-word and shifted into his golden form. Athera had heard stories of the Goldlighter, and Emerald had described what the change did, but to see how Opren glowed and moved now that he was in control was a wonder. She had personally trained several men and women to summon weapons from a box or from the other side of a battlefield, but she had never seen someone produce pure magical energy in the shape of a blade. Vallot managed to break through the first—Opren must have been holding the magic with a weak attempt—but Opren produced another and allowed his orb to change into a golden longsword as well. It was clear the longsword was truly solid, as it had started as a solid and changed form, but the golden energy blades had their own advantages and, if Opren could learn to keep them intact as well, he would have something no other Casteri or warrior could wield.

Another three minutes of combat occurred between Vallot and Opren before Vallot stopped the match with a hand raised.

"Enough," said Vallot, tying his not-quite-shoulder-length white hair back. He took a deep breath and composed himself. "Well done."

Opren shifted back to regular form and was breathing heavily, but he nodded and smiled as he thanked Vallot for the praise. The two men stepped to the edge of the ring to face the others.

"That magic is truly unique," said Athera.

"Indeed." Vallot nodded.

"Are you aware there are no spells to create instantly out of pure magical energy like the Goldlight?" Athera asked Opren. "Most take time, and even those are advanced magic."

"Not until now," said Opren. "But that explains more of why Zargunn and whoever else want it, despite being powerful already. If it is the only magical thing that can allow that, anyone who wants to be the most powerful would probably seek it."

"Correct," said Vallot. "And it seems to enhance you whether you are already so skilled or not."

"That would mean anyone with access to the Goldlight magic is more capable than they would be without it," said Athera. "It even turns the inept into a warrior, but it would be much more powerful in already gifted or terrible hands."

Vallot looked at her, which she knew was because she finished his thought before him. She rarely did it on Rhahkmant'e, but it was not new for them to know what the other was to say. They had trained together and fought together and taught together for over a decade. She gave him a light smile and he turned away.

"I suppose it is the only reason I am strong enough to fight Vallot," said Opren, looking a bit disappointed.

Athera smiled. "Not entirely. You have a special trait to be able to expend massive amounts of *Nuuita* without hurting yourself. You are the Keeper of the Goldlight, so it would bend to your will properly and easily after practice and nobody else will be as powerful as the true Goldlighter, I expect. That tends to be how linked magic works. Until you die, you are the one who has the most potential to wield it. Without it, you may be an average Casteri, but you are still a true warrior at heart and in talent and skill."

"It did take some time while I fought you to force your change," said Vallot. "You would lose without the Goldlight magic, but you would not die against me in a real fight, unless I truly wanted to kill you."

Opren appeared to consider their words for a moment before expressing his agreement and asking what was to come next. Athera told him to take a half hour to recover after his fight. He was, unsurprisingly, not happy with such a short session that did not include anything new before a break, but he agreed to do as she said once she explained her plan was to use the Time-Altering Plane next.

"The three of you are to meet us in the chamber with the Elders after your break," said Athera.

After Opren, Emerald, and Rufius had left the area, Athera turned to Vallot.

"What is it?" asked Vallot.

"Being off the mountain and back to working together, does it remind you of old times, Val?"

"A bit." Vallot looked around at the training area. "But this place is something. Our training was never in such a nice, well-assorted arena. Even before my exile, we trained in other ways, not as beautiful as this place but just as efficient."

"True," said Athera. "Do you think you will struggle with the Unity? It has been a while, after all."

"You have noticed my distance, then?" Vallot sighed.

"We were something once," said Athera. "How could I not? I'm a knight and a teacher. Being perceptive is a necessary trait. Not that I needed skill to tell how connected or distant you were."

"Some of those battles changed me, Athera. I have been harsh without remorse, cold without discontentment. You know until a year ago they had me do interrogations because the Reiyal and some of the humans feel too 'pure', or whatever they want to call it. They assumed a rogue Luunal would do better anyway, as if we have any greater enjoyment of pain or fear. Very few subscribe to that way."

"Well, you can be brutal when you need to be." Athera gave a wry smile. "But I suppose it is *my* fault you are thought of as a rogue, isn't it?" She looked at him with an apologetic expression, but she also felt a sadness.

"The exile I face is not your fault," said Vallot, a deeper crease between his brows as he shook his head. "I chose you while my people—my former people, that is—chose prejudice and made a judgment."

"Busyness and duty have been in the way, but I would like to be as we were again soon, if possible," said Athera. "Can you remember it enough in your heart as well as your mind to do the Unity without hindrance?"

"I would like that as well," said Vallot. His grin was so brief she nearly missed it, but there was a longing in his deep green eyes. "I can always do what is necessary to set an example for those I help train, but for how you asked, I think it is possible."

"We will find out soon. I believe only the shell of your heart has hardened, Val; not the entire thing."

Athera led Vallot to the palace so they could wait in the room where the Elders would cast the Time-Altering Plane. Vallot hesitated before he stepped inside. She knew he felt unworthy to face the Reiyal royals in their own capital, particularly their own palace.

"If you were not welcome, the guards would have stopped us by now," said Athera.

"Would the same be true if I were not with you so closely?" asked Vallot. All of his positive inflection from their recent talk in the training area was gone. Vallot again sounded like a strict man with many scars from life. He did not snap at her—he knew she would not allow it—but he held the emotion of the hate of his people in his voice.

"Does it scare you or anger you more to think about it?" asked Athera.

"I would only be afraid of how much I would need to hurt them," said Vallot.

"You used to smirk when you said that," said Athera. "I suspect now you are serious and not so amused by it. In any case, this city and its people will mostly accept you. In the last few years, many people have changed their attitudes. King Eeloneus and Queen Bellavuu are not like some of the royals of the past."

"The Avaria line has been good, in truth," said Vallot. "But the family Queen Bellavuu comes from might have other ways of seeing our differences, and I know even the Avarias have had disagreements, even a battle a century and a half ago, with the Luunal royals."

"Queen Bellavuu is a patient, wise woman," said Athera. "And—

Before Athera could finish and urge Vallot to enter, the doors opened and out stepped the blue-eyed princess friends called Sapphire. She softly smiled and greeted them when she noticed them.

"Are you going in to see the king and queen?" asked Sapphire.

"Yes," said Athera. "It is good to see you, too. It has been a few years."

"Yes, it has," said Sapphire. "I would have liked to visit the mountain, but I have been busy here. I am glad you were able to come here again, even if parts of the circumstances are not ideal."

"I was born for battle," said Athera. "Vallot was a special operative. *Ideal* is not what we expect at any time, really. The goal is to overcome, regardless of preferences."

"Well, I hope you enjoy your time here as much as possible," said Sapphire. "Good to make your acquaintance, Vallot. I have heard about you, and you seem like a skilled mentor and fierce warrior. I must get back to my duties, but I do wish you all a good day. *Ariayi*."

Princess Sapphire walked past them with two assistants and a guard following her. Athera gestured for Vallot to enter the open doorway and he did, finally. They walked into the throne area and knelt before the king and queen.

"Vallot Kressor, welcome to Avarinnia," said King Eeloneus. "Lady Athera Sarwind, glad to see you again. You both may stand comfortably."

Vallot looked up, a subtle expression of surprise on his face, one that Athera could only pick up due to years around the man. Vallot was always good at hiding his emotions; it was part of the skillset that made him good for interrogations. Athera knew his surprise was due to the unlikely sort of greeting. For a Reiyal royal of any rank to welcome Vallot by full name directly and individually, it was an honor, especially when it came from the king himself. The same would be true if a non-royal Reiyal were to visit the Luunal city, but that would be much less likely to happen due to the risk.

"Ve harron, King Eeloneus," said Vallot.

"I would ask why you did not immediately come to greet us," said King Eeloneus. "But I suspect I know."

"We are not our ancestors or your former people," said Queen Bellavuu, standing from her seat. She walked to them and placed a hand on Vallot's chest. "If your *Nuuita* and heart are for our people, for elves of all kind, we are glad to accept you as any other great elf. It is likewise the reason we shall allow you to use the Time-Altering Plane to train your students as Selios and Emerald have requested. In Selios' brief absence, we can think of few better warriors in our sect, and none with your experience in training star pupils and soldiers alike. If we felt otherwise, we would not have allowed Rufius to train with you."

Athera smiled and Vallot reflexively almost returned the smile when he glanced at her, but he still held in the emotion. In any case, Athera at least knew he was grateful and elated, even if he refused to show enthusiasm to the king and queen.

"We would like to wait for our trainees inside the chamber in which the Elders cast the Time-Altering Plane, please," said Athera.

Queen Bellavuu nodded. "You are both welcome to explore the palace and eat in the dining hall as well. I expect you are too focused on the training currently, but for later you are free to do as you wish. I trust you both do understand the risks involved in using the magical plane?"

"We do, Queen Bellavuu," said Athera with a dip of her head. "Ve harron."

"Good," said Queen Bellavuu. "You are dismissed. Enjoy your time in Avarinnia."

"Ve harron, suuveiy," said Vallot, emphasizing his thanks.

Athera guided Vallot to where she recalled the Elders to be. Unfortunately, she made a wrong turn when they reached the second corridor at the top of the stairs, but she corrected herself and they made it to the room without further confusion. It was not a bad mistake for four years since the last time she had visited Avarinnia.

Vallot meditated while Athera planned out in her mind how to handle any group assaults on Rhahkmant'e or Avarinnia. It made the ten minutes until Opren, Rufius, and Emerald met them pass without much notice.

20

Opren had to admit his interactions with Rufius were beginning to seem less confrontational. Rufius had remained with them for the half-hour break and walked with them back to the palace, and Opren talked to him about their training goals. It felt like talking to someone who also wanted to work hard, who wanted to win, but who did not seem as stuck-up and cocky as the Half-Elf had when they first met. There was still a healthy amount of competitive nature in them both, but it was out of an allied rivalry.

As they reached the corridor of the palace that had the Elder Mages ready to cast the Time-Altering Plane, Opren recalled a question he had intended to ask Emerald but thought Rufius might know even better.

"Why is Vallot a rogue exile? Do you know?"

"He fell in love with a Human woman and chose to ally with humans continually," said Rufius. "I would refrain from bringing it up to him."

"Why should that matter? You are a Half-Elf with a Human mother, right?"

"Old royalty among the elves—in the case of all Elven

people, not just Uundulal, Luunal, or Reiyal exclusively—frowned upon mixing blood," said Rufius. "My father is actually the first known royal descendant to be with a human and have a child. That only tends to happen among the commoners, the people who travel most, and occasionally the soldiers who remain away, or when a bastard child occurs nobody will admit to. Without war, it is uncommon for soldiers because their aim is to guard the city and train, not go elsewhere. My father did not meet my mother during a war, as we have had none in this century. The Avaria family has done a lot for Reiyal and Uundulal—really trying to improve life for all elves and all people—but the Luunal tend to hold to old law and old rituals with strict judgment."

"So past traditions breed hate among the old-style thinking," said Opren. "And was exile always the way for an elf who fell in love with a human?"

"Yes," said Rufius. "Our grandfather changed that for our sect, but not *all* elves in the world agree. Some Elven lords remain convinced a Half-Elf has tarnished blood." His eyes revealed a pain Opren had not seen in him before. "We are neither a pure human nor a pure elf. Luunal still believe loving outside of the Elven bloodlines will create weakness, either in our minds or our magic. They exiled Vallot for that reason. At one time, if a Luunal loved outside of Luunal, they would exile them too."

"That seems ridiculous," said Opren. He furrowed his brow as he related disagreements and prejudice where he was raised to the ideas the elves had even among each other and towards others who were, in truth, nearly the same as them. Maybe humans did not have such potential in magic in the same way, or as long a lifespan, but otherwise they were nearly identical to elves. He considered how Emerald spontaneously accepted him and chose to pre-court him and vice-versa. She might like combat and adventure more than the average elf, but she would have done something much bigger just by accepting him as more than a travel ally, it turned out. "Who was the human anyway?"

Opren did not receive an answer as they entered the Elders' chamber and saw Athera and Vallot waiting for them. Vallot was meditating to the right of the room, while Athera seemed to be pacing prior to their entry.

"On time. Well done," said Athera. She turned to her left. "Val. They have arrived."

Opren felt like he had an epiphany when he heard her speak. *Val?* He knew they had served in combat together, but was Athera the human that caused Vallot to be dismissed permanently from his own people? He had not seen them as romantically involved before, but he also had rarely seen them together to be able to judge. Based on how Unity magic was described to him, Opren thought it might be fitting people in love could do it well—but then why was Rufius his partner for the training?

Vallot opened his eyes and rose to his feet.

"Rufius and Opren will enter the Time-Altering Plane first, then we will join."

"After we are all inside, except Emerald who will monitor us from here, Vallot and I will demonstrate how to match our *Nuuita*," said Athera. "The goal is for you two to do the same thing."

Emerald turned to the Elder Mages. "We will need eight or nine of you to cast a week-long Time-Altering Plane, please. Unless you can do it with fewer for four people. I do not want to overwork their minds and bodies."

One of the Elders replied in a low voice in Elvish, most of which Opren could not understand, but the Elder nodded and the others began to chant the spell. The Elvish symbols on the floor began to glow softly, this time with lines of the light extending out to eight of the hooded mages. The spell was visually more impressive as new patterns appeared on the floor, which must have been a representation of how strong the spell was going to be.

"This spell seems to work by levels of magnitude, rather

than simple addition per extra caster," observed Vallot aloud.

"Something like that," said Emerald. "My parents explained it in detail one day, but I expect Sapphire took in the information better than I did. I was always more interested in how it affected those inside and what it was for over exactly how it worked."

One of the two Elders who were not involved in the casting of the spell indicated it was time for Opren and Rufius to step into their respective light circles. He gestured for Vallot and Athera to follow as Opren and Rufius entered theirs.

The octagonal Avarinnium room with its stained-glass windows vanished and was replaced by a sandy ground and low hills. Opren turned to his left to see the ocean. He must have entered first with the beach on his mind. When he had entered with Selios, Selios would control how the place would be, but now it must have worked subconsciously. Rufius appeared to Opren's right, but a bit farther than when they were in the palace chamber.

"A coast?" asked Rufius. Opren shrugged. "It is a pleasant change from the dirt of the mountain and stone of the training grounds. Not enough green, though."

"Which of you chose the setting?" asked Athera as she appeared fifteen feet in front of them. Rufius thumbed at Opren and Athera smiled. "Is this an attempt at a holiday vacation or ocean travel?"

"No," said Opren with a laugh. "It was on my mind and just happened."

"Well, it will do," said Vallot as he appeared beside Athera.

"Watch us and try to sense our energy," said Athera. "Based on my understanding of our mental-spiritual state, it should be easier in here."

Athera and Vallot held each other's gaze and took a simultaneous breath. As they exhaled, their auras were dimly visible.

Opren closed his eyes and noted a sensation like the one he had in Zargunn's presence but without the anger or fear.

It was softer, but it was like a humming without the noise. He opened his eyes and linked his sense of the energy with his view of the auras. He watched for a few moments before he became confident that he could tell what they were doing. When he felt comfortable observing their energy, he told Rufius he had figured it out.

"I have it as well," said Rufius. "Have you noticed when they align their *Nuuita*?"

"I think so. The vibration is stronger, and their auras seem to change nearer to white."

Rufius nodded.

Athera and Vallot stopped and confirmed with Opren and Rufius their observations were correct. It was time to demonstrate what the Unity could do. The instructors took a few breaths and their eyes met.

"Ready, Val?" asked Athera.

"I am," said Vallot.

Both gained a brighter, white aura as their spirit energy levels increased greatly and in unison. When they stopped staring at each other, their auras remained. Vallot moved suddenly and he was like a blur. It reminded Opren of how swiftly Zargunn had spun when he killed the Elven warriors in the square. Vallot appeared right in front of Rufius.

"Cast an offensive spell at me," said Vallot. "Something powerful."

Rufius did as instructed and several bolts of lightning blasted Vallot in the chest, knocking him back with a grunt. Rufius looked concerned, but Athera only smiled as her aura faded for a second with a shake. Athera's aura shook again and returned to its stable state as Vallot stood, unharmed.

"That is one of the greatest things possible with Unity Magic in combat," said Athera. "I gave some of my spirit energy to Vallot and it restored him. Outside of here, he might be a bit tired after the lightning strike, he might even require a healer, but he would never die or run out of spirit energy as long as I am alive and my energy is stable. It works both ways."

"If you learn to match each other in technique and *Nuuita*, you will be able to fight many opponents with only the two of you, if necessary," said Vallot. "The goal of this training is to have you do precisely that. After the week in here is done, you will use it in the training grounds."

"Opren, do not use the Goldlight during this," said Athera. "I think it would boost your energy too much. It might also make your Unity with Rufius unstable and even dangerous. The goal is to *match*, not to overpower or even to raise your energy levels high at first. The Unity will allow you to cast spells without expending your *Nuuita*, even if you would be unable to otherwise or alone. That is how *this* powerful spell works, in part." She gestured broadly to indicate where they were.

"I assume some spells, like this one, are only possible if done through Unity Magic?" said Rufius.

"Correct," said Vallot.

Three days passed inside the Time-Altering Plane as Opren and Rufius practiced solo and duet manipulation of their spirit energy. Opren began to grow impatient with the tedious nature of the training since there was no combat to it, no casting, and no new knowledge since they had discovered how Unity Magic could be done. But just before he voiced his dull frustration, he and Rufius happened to match their *Nuuita*.

"Do you feel that?"

"Oh, yes," said Rufius. "And you must have more potential than I realized because this new energy is intense."

"Thanks for saying so. I wouldn't think you would want to admit that." Opren chuckled.

"I never said I would lose to you because of it. But you are clearly strong." Rufius presented his usual smirk.

"I guess it would be pointless to hide anything, even due credit, now that we need to work together and match each other," said Opren. It would be even more interesting to fight Rufius once they were so closely matched, too, since Vallot and

Athera required them to learn to fight as a unit.

By the end of their week in the Time-Altering Plane, Opren and Rufius had successfully used the Unity technique over ten times, Opren had learned to anticipate Rufius' movements, and Rufius had figured out a way to help Opren release more of his innate *Nuuita* that was usually in reserve. Opren's extra energy caused them both to cast more powerful versions of their usual spells, effectively making all spells a stage higher. It was similar to how the Goldlight essence could charge Opren's wind but, with the Unity, they could trade energy between themselves without any stamina toll the Goldlight might take. The two rival allies even began to enjoy training together and, the more they got to know the other, the more powerful their Unity casting seemed to become.

Emerald was waiting with a look of anticipation when the four in training returned to what had been dubbed the True Plane.

"How did it go?" she asked.

"We did it." Opren smiled. Emerald returned an even bigger smile.

"Now we just need to do it out here, in the training grounds," said Rufius.

"Did we forget to mention you will need to fight us this time?" said Vallot.

Opren lost his smile as he turned to Vallot with a solid "yes".

"We need to be sure you can really fight, as opposed to cast in the air alone," said Athera. "At least you know you cannot die unless you both were to be killed, and I won't allow Vallot to try that hard to test it."

Vallot gave Athera a look Opren could not determine, but Athera grinned and Vallot shook his head with a lighter expression. After a week of constant training and learning with Rufius, Opren could read some of his rival-partner's immediate thoughts and moods the same way too, so he understood they had a kind of connection. That would be even greater if they were really in love and spent years in battles together.

"Do you want to fight me after that or tomorrow?" asked Emerald.

Despite Opren's urgency, it would not go well if he attempted to fight anyone else after the constant training and a fight with their mentors. He would need to rest before he could beat Emerald for his chance to leave and find the sleeskaxes with her continued approval and assistance.

"Tomorrow."

"Wise choice, Laleiy." Emerald smiled. "You are learning."

"Was that a compliment or a hidden insult?" asked Opren as they exited the room to move to the training grounds.

"I'll let you figure it out," said Emerald with a laugh, bumping his shoulder with her own.

Somehow, Emerald's teasing made Opren find her more interesting whenever she did it, but it also motivated him out of mild irritation; it meant he still was not as strong and capable as he would prefer to be. He was further attracted to her because he was attracted to a challenge, but maybe he enjoyed the challenge even more because she was part of it. It was like a love-hate relationship with her ability to beat him, until he proved otherwise.

The final test for Opren and Rufius while using their Unity went even better than expected. Their bodies had no problem responding to what they already knew to do after their time-altered training. Due to the essential aspects being of the mind, emotions, and spirit control, they lacked nothing while inside the Time-Altering Plane.

Opren registered the physical sensations even more clearly in the True Plane, and Rufius seemed more comfortable outside of the spell plane. They were able to match Athera and Vallot's speed and strength consistently. They also never got tired—Opren had assumed that was because of the Time-Altering Plane effects, but it was true outside too—and they were able to fight at full intensity for over five minutes straight. The only problem was when his aura faded simultaneously with Rufius' aura.

"Wait," said Opren and Rufius at the same time.

"They changed too," said Rufius, pointing at Athera and Vallot, who were now back to normal and beside each other on the other side of the floating stone platform.

"Unlike when we were inside the spell plane," said Vallot. "Unity Magic has its limits, or it will pull from your life energy. It is the same reason the Elders cannot hold their spell too long without adding another member."

"The basic combat Unity lasts only ten minutes at most," said Athera. "The test was to see if you could match us for the whole time, which you knew. But it was also to see if you could hold the change as long as possible, which you did." She smiled and clapped her hands a few times. "Congratulations. You passed this training."

Opren realized Unity Magic was not used more often due to the specific requirements and limitations. That aside, he and Rufius could certainly change a battle on their own in the brief time it would last. The Goldlight enhancement of his own spells might be more effective over a whole battle or in random situations but, the more he could accomplish, the better. Besides, he could now match Rufius in many ways and they had become genuine, formidable allies when not competing for fun.

"Somehow, I feel Rufius and I becoming friends was an ulterior motive with this," Opren said to Emerald.

"I consider it more of a positive extra occurrence," said Emerald.

"I still intend to beat you again when the corrupt beings have been killed and we find out what is going on," said Rufius. "I highly doubt you can best me yet. And I consider us partners, maybe not quite friends."

"We'll see, partner." Opren smirked. Rufius returned a happy smirk.

A guard ran up to the floating rings and asked for Rufius'

attention.

"Sir, your father has returned from the oracle. He thought you would want to know."

"Thank you," said Rufius with a nod. "This was a good time to complete training."

"Later," said Opren.

Rufius left the area.

"Now we should go eat," said Athera. "Time may pass differently in that spell plane, but my stomach still knows it has been over a true day since a good meal."

Opren thoroughly agreed. The remaining four headed to the palace dining hall.

21

Opren fought Emerald as planned the next afternoon, but when she revealed she had been keeping a technique she learned from Selios a secret—the same one Selios could use to deal immense damage while enhanced by an aura—she ended up the victor. Opren had tried to use the Goldlighter form to match her speed and strength, but she still gracefully dodged without mistakes while he barely managed to catch her—thinking he had finally caught her off guard multiple times, but that was always wrong.

"Back to the Time-Altering Plane for now," she said after they both caught their breath and took a few sips of water.

"I was close, though." He was not sure if he meant it as confidently as he voiced it or if his use of the Goldlight was altering his senses and emotions again, but he was all right with either.

"That is true," said Emerald. "But you could be close to laying with me, too. Does that mean we already did and don't need to? Close is not always enough."

"Hilarious," said Opren. His thoughts wandered for a moment, to how she might look at him if she did want to have sex, but then he snapped himself back to the present, real moment. "I will manage the day after tomorrow."

Opren remained at the training grounds for an hour while Emerald went to meet with Ruubi for something. He threw his Goldlight energy blades into the targets in one of the lower training sections designated for archery and thrown weapons. More accurately, he threw them *through* the targets—they never slowed due to the friction of inserting into solid wood and just passed to the other side. He accidentally destroyed one of the targets by throwing several in rapid succession. His accuracy was spot on, and he could hold the energy at least until it passed through the target.

When Opren finished his thrown-blades practice, he changed back to normal. To his delight, he was not overly tired. His body and spirit were truly adapting to the Goldlighter form. He noted his training with Rufius must have helped, especially once Rufius helped him unlock his potential with his great reserve of *Nuuita*. He wished it had happened sooner, but he liked his progress and current abilities. All that was left was to beat Emerald, then he could use the Goldlight to stop any additional killing, once they discovered exactly what was going on near the Royal Sect. And when he next met the sleeskaxes, he would make them look like the shredded target. He could not use the power to stop the monsters from killing his parents or to reverse anything that had happened, but he had kept his promise to learn to use it to become able to avenge them.

Opren spent four days inside the Time-Altering Plane specifically training with the Goldlight. He had no partner or instructor this time, but he no longer needed one for what he was doing, and Emerald had approved it as long as he did not exceed five days inside alone. He only needed targets and the adjustment to the passing of time versus the True Plane. He finished by the weekly feast in true time. He met with Emerald near the throne to head together to the grand dining hall.

Barbosa joined them as they reached the door, which was

odd.

"How did you get to join the feast?" asked Opren.

I made a request to the king and queen, said Barbosa. *Unlike humans, these elves don't treat me like some sort of wild beast or a pet. I am nobility in my pack, remember?*

"Why did you wait weeks to make the request?" asked Emerald with a laugh.

I was originally under the impression only Opren was allowed despite being non-royal, said Barbosa. *But as I explored and noted how the citizens treated me nearly the same as each other once they knew I'm a granwolf and not a simple beast, I thought I would be welcome everywhere. Then I saw Polaris join one of the weeks, instead of his usual trips to the pub and decided to ask.*

"Good to have the extra company," said Opren. "I have several things to catch you up on since we spoke last."

During the meal, Opren explained to Barbosa his training progress status and described the new threats occurring around the Royal Sect, with Emerald helping to fill in some details he had not learned but she had discussed with her parents and Athera. He also explained how the Time-Altering Plane helped him learn much more quickly than any other way he could train.

I don't think I will ever join you in that Time-Altering Plane, said Barbosa. *Sometimes, certain magic is too unusual for me. I trust what I can smell, hear, eat, or paw. I would like to come to observe the remainder of your training sessions in the regular plane.*

"You can paw the light-bridge," teased Opren.

That is still barely trustworthy, and I like to avoid it, said Barbosa with a low growl. *That is one of the reasons I took extra time to request permission to feast with you, but don't tell anyone else that.*

"We won't," said Emerald. "Like Opren and Rufius, your pride about bravery is too important."

"What are you trying to say?" said Opren, jaw slack and brow furrowed.

"I said exactly what I meant." Emerald smiled. "But you all do have true courage, too. I would not be pre-courting you otherwise."

I was not aware you are to mate now, but I am not surprised, said Barbosa.

"We're not yet," said Opren. "This is like we are interested in mating, but we are testing the possibility of staying with one another in marriage beforehand, except with what we are calling pre-courting we are testing if we want to officially court each other to the public, I guess."

"Courting is not about mating, really," said Emerald. "It is the thing some people do before they marry. Marriage is more of a commitment than an act of mating. Mating can happen at any point."

Humans and elves have complicated love lives, said Barbosa. *Either commit and mate and remain loyal, or don't do any of it. It seems so much simpler. When I find a mate, I intend to stay with her for life and protect her and our cubs.*

"I thought you had simplified it when I mentioned dating," said Opren to Emerald. "But he makes it even more direct and simplified. Why do humans and elves complicate it?"

"Well," said Emerald. "If you want to mate with me tonight, we could. But is that really what you want?"

"Are you serious?" asked Opren. He was shocked by her spontaneous prompting. She might have suddenly kissed him on a whim, but to have sex was something else, something he might expect to be brought up so nonchalantly by Ruubi, but not by Emerald. He even had rarely considered having sex with her because he was so busy training and appreciated her company in general. He loved being around her and enjoyed the rare couple of times they kissed, but he assumed she was not ready to think about sex, so he would not have prompted it yet himself.

"What do you want to do?" she asked again.

"I want to have sex with you when you are ready, but after

we resolve the problems," he replied. "You already know you have an amazing face and body, and I have wondered what you would look like naked and assume if I see you naked I will want sex, but what do you want?"

"I want *you*," said Emerald. "Because you respect my choice, and it has nothing to do with my rank. I only pulled the princess card on you because I was tense and wanted to see your reaction. You are so much better than most people because you only care about time with Emerald, if you made Emerald happy, if you can beat Emerald. Nothing you do is for Princess Esmeraldi."

"You do have an attractive strength as a princess, though," said Opren. "I want to be good for you in both roles."

"Your interest in me and being good for me regardless of where I come from is what matters," said Emerald. "So, you may court me publicly and officially, if you wish when you have faced what you need to face. We can be committed to each other and, at some point, lay together. I did not really want to do anything sexual tonight, though."

"I absolutely would like that." Opren smiled. "And I didn't think you would. You surprised me by saying it at all."

"Oh, it is not because of lack of interest. But you need to be focused tomorrow for our fight. I don't want an amazing night with me to distract you." She winked.

Don't want to throw your sword up too high during battle, right Opren? said Barbosa with a chuckle, and Opren felt warm.

"I'm going to grab more steak." He stood to escape the topic. "Do you two need anything?"

Barbosa asked for another piece of steak as well, but Emerald had eaten her fill of nearly every non-meat at the feast. Opren returned a moment later and gave the top slice of beef from his plate to the granwolf. Barbosa thanked him and began to eat silently. Opren realized there was an awkward silence now and felt the need to fill it.

"What time do you want to fight tomorrow?"

"An hour or so after lunch should be a good time," said

Emerald.

The following day, Opren had lunch with Polaris and told the wizard everything that had happened since they last spoke, like he had the night before with Barbosa. Polaris still managed to disappear and return without notice regularly, but at least it was clear why he did at that point. The wizard shared his latest news and, to Opren's disgust, it turned out two more places had been attacked by something inhuman, one of which reported a sleeskax.

"I really need to beat Emerald today," said Opren. "Will you be coming with us to the Royal Sect?"

"You two are planning to go there?" asked Polaris.

"I am. Emerald said if I beat her, she will not stop me and will help," said Opren. "The king and queen believe I will be able to prevent more damage since I'll be the target and out in the open, and I will be able to kill the danger now."

"Kill the sleeskaxes, you mean," said Polaris.

"I want to kill any of the corrupt beings, but especially the sleeskaxes."

"I will come along again," said Polaris. "I might need to be sure you don't get yourself killed in the process. And if demons or other corruption are causing problems, I can help with that as well as protect innocents."

"Great! Thank you. I will let you know when we are going to leave, assuming you are around."

"I will know," said Polaris. "I'll meet you all at the gate when you leave."

Opren headed to the training grounds for what he hoped would be the final time until he helped end the sleeskaxes' damage to towns and families like his own. When he arrived, he found Athera there. She intended to watch as he and Emerald fought. She inquired about his goals after winning and, when he explained, she too wanted to come along. She was already involved and said she felt a mild responsibility to guard her former trainees.

"Vallot has seen little action recently," said Athera. "I am going to ask if he would like to join us. I have a feeling he will be glad to cut down corrupt beings and to discover what is really going on."

"Before you go," said a man behind Opren. He turned to see Selios. "You should go speak with my oracle friend. She told me of another prophecy. She also might be able to give you some advice for what you will face, though she does speak in riddles. I intend to send some soldiers to help clean up the towns farthest from the Royal Sect that have been hit while you all go to the inner sect and the capital, Ivorite Province. So do not worry about those, unless passing through. If necessary, I may go assist those squads but, for now, I will be going with you."

"All right," said Opren. "That is a relief to know. I'm honestly not sure how to go about this, but with you both helping, I am sure we have a high chance to do some good. I never imagined this would become something bigger when I came to learn and avenge my parents."

"None of us could have," said Selios. "Nothing like this has happened for over a century, and reports told us the magic you hold had disappeared."

"Planning is always helpful," said Emerald from one of the floating platforms. "But you still need to beat me before it matters."

"Right," said Opren. He turned and walked over to the levitating flat-topped stones and leaped up onto the one where Emerald was waiting.

"Oluu, Laleiy. Ready?"

"That seems like an ironic greeting before we fight." Opren smiled.

"I wanted to be sweet before I get aggressive," said Emerald. "I will assume you are ready."

As soon as Emerald finished speaking, she dashed at him and used the spell Selios taught her to make her body stronger and even faster, able to land hits with an impact that would be impossible for a human or elf without magic. Opren successfully moved away from her first punch, her spinning elbow, and her backhand—barely in time for the backhand. He was caught with a kick as she continued to spin—it knocked the wind out of him. She used the opportunity to uppercut him and knock him into the air. She was not holding back anything anymore, it seemed. As Opren landed on his back, she summoned her sword and tied the sash around her wrist as usual.

Opren's mind raced, but she leaped up to bring her foot down and he instinctively blasted her with a major gale. She flipped backward in the air and barely managed to catch herself in time to roll-tumble back into a standing position with her sword ready. Opren stood, drawing his own sword. He pulled some of the Goldlight essence into himself without changing, one of the new tricks he learned while inside the Time-Altering Plane the day before. It would allow him to cast empowered bursts of wind and strong enough vacuums to cut through flesh with little effort.

"Something new happened just now, right?" asked Emerald. "What did you do? I felt a change and saw the Goldlight glow."

"I learned how to use its power a bit, even when not in Goldlighter form."

Emerald smiled before she vanished. Opren attempted to sense her, but he had not learned to do that outside of Goldlighter form. He searched for her, but he could not see any indication. Suddenly, something grabbed his ankle and Emerald jumped out from the rock while pulling him along to cause him to fall back, then the stone closed itself over his feet.

"I learned a new spell too," she said as she landed. "Selios had taught me to blend and merge with nature, but I wanted to be able to do it with other things. I had the idea of using it for stone after we saw the golem, and I realized the rings here would be useful like the ground."

Opren could not pull out his feet, no matter how he twisted, pushed, pulled, or kicked—well, kicking was impossible anyway. But he was not going to let her end this, not yet. As Emerald walked over to place her blade next to his throat and claim victory, he said the spell-word for the Goldlight and changed. The golden flash included a burst of energy that broke the stone trappings around his feet and pushed Emerald back a few paces. He wondered if he had achieved a more powerful change while inside the Time-Altering Plane, but now he was certain he had done it. He flipped into a ready position, the physical golden blade in his right hand after the orb transformed into it, a blade of golden energy in his left hand.

Emerald blew a strand of hair from her face and leaped at him quickly, but he was able to match her movements with ease. This transformation not only sent out a more powerful aura when he activated the magic, it made him better, stronger, more alert, more agile than the prior change. He felt in control of himself and in control of the fight. He stopped Emerald's stab at him and parried fluidly, almost as gracefully as she could do and with even more force in his movements. She was knocked off balance by the sudden circular push and twist and dropped her sword. She managed to whip her ribbon and regain hold of the weapon, but Opren anticipated her next kick and swipe and slash, all before they happened as if he knew exactly how to fight like her—which he did, but he did not know it because he learned it, rather because the Goldlight gave him a kind of "combat foresight".

The foresight combined with his new level of speed and grace allowed him to counter five more attacks while she tried her hardest, even while she used Selios' body enhancement spell. She threw the sword and whipped it back, but Opren sliced through the sash before it could fly past him—of course not into him as would be the intent, because he was too swift for that now, and he had seen her use the technique more than once even if the Goldlight had not given him a special foresight. Emerald's sword fell to the ground a foot behind him. He stabbed his energy blade into the stone in front of the sword, then summoned two more to place at points to form a triangular shape around her sword—that way she could not retrieve it.

"*Relista,*" swore Emerald in Elvish.

Despite the obvious disadvantage Emerald now had, she still attempted to summon the sword, and it did disappear from beneath the triangle of golden energy blades, but just as it reached her hand, Opren swiped his golden sword down through it and it broke as it fell to the ground. He then grabbed her arm before she could dodge, allowed the longsword to change back into the sphere, pulled her close and kissed her quickly before letting go. He re-summoned a golden energy blade, tripped her, and placed the blade near her throat, then moved to point at her heart.

"I win, finally, Liileiy." He grinned.

"Did you kiss me to be sweet or to trick me?" Emerald looked up at him with a mix of defiance and interest.

"I just felt like it, and the Goldlight essence seems to make me more spontaneous and boldly confident. But I clearly have the potential to back up the confidence. And I thought you have surprised me enough, it's my turn."

"I'm not sure whether to be more frustrated or aroused," said Emerald. "But you did win. Congratulations."

Opren dissipated the energy blade and changed back to regular form. He extended a hand to help Emerald up, but she did not need it and stood before he finished offering. She stepped toward him and punched him in the gut, then healed his bruises and removed the pain. Then she kissed him deeply. He lost track of the amount of real time that passed, but it was a long moment and a wonderful one where all he was focused on was Emerald, her eyes the few times they both opened theirs, her flowery scent, her lips, and her hands as she played in his hair with her one hand and ran the other along his back as he did with her. When she finished, she pulled away and smiled, and he returned the smile.

"I suppose you deserved a better kiss than the quick one

you stole, since you worked so hard and did manage to truly kick my arse," said Emerald.

"I still have to beat the sleeskaxes and find out what's going on that's starting to affect the kingdom, all for the Goldlight or whatever else," said Opren, letting his smile fade as he thought of the real reason he needed to train, to beat her, to leave. He would have loved to introduce her to his parents, but they were dead. He would have enjoyed staying in Avarinnia, but even the gorgeous and prepared Elven city was no longer completely safe. He would have preferred to involve fewer people, but he could not have faced what he needed to alone, not before training. He wanted to have more moments like the current one, a fight as a challenge he would need to overcome like he used to, especially with Rufius and Emerald. But that would need to wait until he was safe, until the kingdom was safe, until he finished every part of each of the problems that involved him or the Goldlight, directly or by default or by the choice of the sleeskaxes and the other corrupt beings. His brow furrowed as he thought harder about what was still to come.

Emerald must have noticed because she asked, "What is it? Thinking of what you need to do next? Or I should say, what *we* need to do next?"

"Yes." Opren nodded. "All I wanted when I was home just months ago was to be the best fighter I could be, maybe join a competition for martial arts called UFC, the Ultimate Fighting Championship, and win someday, and continue to help my father take care of his business. Now, this thing, this orb with the Goldlight, has caused me to become a magical warrior. That's awesome, except I never could have predicted something passed from my grandfather would be so coveted, even to the point of people being killed for it, my parents being killed for it. Now, I suppose I must use it for more than revenge. All I originally wanted the first month I came here was to learn this world, learn enough magic to wield it in combat, then kill the sleeskaxes for what they did."

"And now you don't want that?" asked Emerald, running her hands lightly up and down his arms and looking into his eyes.

"Well, I want to be with you as much as I want to avenge my parents, especially in this moment. And I still want to kill the sleeskaxes, but even more because they are hurting people I don't even know, just to find me and the Goldlight sphere."

"So now you can be Sir Shiny Hero," said Emerald, feigning an announcer's tone with a smile. "I think ending the sleeskaxes because they are hurting and killing more people than you personally know and learning about the corruption with the intent to stop it is heroic. A hero is better than a champion. I think your goals have improved, even if it is through harsh necessity."

"My mother really would have liked you," said Opren. "And my father would have liked how you challenge me, rather than just follow me."

"Well, now that you have official permission to leave and aid from the princess, let's take this evening to rest and prepare, then go make your parents proud."

22

Opren, Emerald, Ruubi, Rufius, Barbosa, Polaris, and a royal guard named Alcorn, who happened to be Rufius' childhood training partner, followed Selios to the oracle's mountain the following day.

After Opren had heard the oracle's prophecy as Selios suggested, they would ask any questions she might be able to answer. Then, they would send word to Athera so she and Vallot could join as requested, to all head to the nearest town with a recent attack by so-called monsters and demons. For the time, Athera was busy discussing defensive measures with the king and queen, should anything go awry, and she felt no need to see the oracle; she would be satisfied with a summary from the others.

Ruubi had come along for fun, despite Selios and Emerald both protesting the idea. It was less that Ruubi might be a distraction because she was not likely to take things seriously enough and more that she would get hurt if she tried to have too much fun at the wrong time, instead of approach any danger with the correct attitude. Emerald had been on enough explorations to know the difference, but Ruubi had only traveled outside Avarinnia four times in their lives and never to dangerous places. When Sapphire also tried to argue, Ruubi told her to come along too, but the dutiful princess said she needed to remain behind, especially with both her sisters "off on some grand quest to find death".

Barbosa had come along for the journey more than anything, as he was tired of being in the same place every day, despite how beautiful it was in the city. He intended to help in battle any way he could, but he said he expected the others were able to do better than him at that point; his greatest contribution would be his senses of smell and hearing to warn them of anything strange.

Alcorn had come out of formality, as Ruubi was not allowed to leave the city without a protective escort—and watchful eye. He also brought Ra'ze for Opren. Opren had expected to go pick her up himself, but he appreciated Alcorn's willingness to help with more than his basic orders required. Opren hoped the other man did not get himself into any bad situations, as Alcorn did not have the level of magic the others possessed, but he was not going to argue with a royal decision unless it was truly a problem; he had already pushed his limit with royalty as it was.

It took until sunset to reach the oracle's small mountain. Once they did, Selios informed them it required a climb to the top, there was no path.

"I'm too old for mountain climbing," said Polaris, giving the wall of earth a distasteful look. "I will meet you all atop. I will travel by magic." Polaris raised his staff but Selios grabbed the wizard's wrist and shook his head.

"I wouldn't try that, Polaris," said Selios. "She has wards so magic does not work the same up there. You might only half reappear, even with your abilities. It is how she prevents people like Zargunn doing what he did in our city to her home."

"Well, you all give me the summary when you return, then," said Polaris. "I will wait down here, maybe find a spot to fish."

"At least it is a small mountain, compared to most," said Alcorn. "They made us climb a higher one toward the end of training."

"You always did find the brighter side of things, Alcorn," said Rufius. "I suppose we might as well begin the climb."

Rufius stepped up to the natural wall and placed his hands and feet in small holes that had already been made. Evidently, someone had the good idea to create a recurring path so not everyone who wanted to make the climb would need to do it completely from scratch. As Rufius started to climb, Alcorn followed his lead. Then Ra'ze flew upward and never descended, so she must have made it to the top her way while the others had to do it the long way.

Opren had an idea and shifted to Goldlighter form. He produced golden energy blades and stabbed the wall. It worked, as the blades met little resistance the same way they had when he threw them through the targets in the training grounds. He used the Goldlighter form's enhancement to his strength, speed, and stamina to scale the mountain at twice the rate of the others—which translated to fifteen minutes until the top. While the remainder of the group continued to climb, with Rufius yelling how it was unfair to do the climb the way Opren had done, Opren relaxed with Ra'ze at the top edge, petting the griffin. There was still a small hill to climb, but this one had a path to the right of where he and Ra'ze sat.

After another fifteen minutes, Rufius and Emerald reached the top, with Selios just behind. It took two more minutes for Alcorn, and Ruubi was the last another moment later. Barbosa was not with any of them and Opren looked around. Somehow, the granwolf had reached the top from the other side.

"Why did you go that way?" asked Opren.

It had more uneven terrain that worked for my claws better than it would have for your hands, said Barbosa. *I was up here shortly after you but wanted to see if you would notice.* He chuckled.

"Just this path left," said Selios, nodding to the curving dirt incline with flat stones to step on that led up the hill. "I expect she only wants Opren at first."

Opren nodded and walked toward the path, then saw a woman who appeared to be in her mid-twenties walking down the path. The woman had large hazel eyes and curly brown hair that reached the top of her shoulders in a sort of long bob. This must have been the oracle's assistant or something of an apprentice. She took note of Opren and the others and waved.

"Hello, there," said the woman. Her voice was almost girlish, like Ruubi when she was happy. "How are you?"

"This one is cute," said Ruubi. She turned and said louder, sweeter, "Oluu, cute lady. How are you?"

"We are not here to flirt, Ruubi," said Selios. "Be respectful."

"I am being nice," said Ruubi, hands on her hips as she turned to Selios. "I'm sure the oracle won't mind if I socialize with her helper."

"That is not the oracle's helper," said Selios in a hushed tone, the mid-twenties woman getting close enough to hear—Elven or Human ears.

"Oluu, lusty girl," said the woman, matching Ruubi's flirtatious tone as she matched the sort of wording. Her expression remained inviting and playful, matching Ruubi's energy, but her voice lowered slightly and contained more maturity as she continued. "You are Ruubi Avaria, the Royal Rose, promiscuous princess and, according at least to Soferina, the 'royal whore'." The woman laughed once as she said the offensive title.

"Oh, I like you," said Ruubi. "You already know about me, too." Ruubi seemed to have been hit with a physical thought as she nearly jumped. "Oh! *You* are the oracle."

"Indeed," said the hazel-eyed, mid-twenties-looking woman. "I am Oracle Kimmie. I know you came seeking answers, especially *you*," she turned to Opren and got closer to his face than he was comfortable with, "Opren Saphren of two worlds, Keeper of the Goldlight and new Goldlighter...well, theoretically."

"What?" asked Selios and Opren in unison. Only Selios continued with, "You told me we are correct, that he is to be the Goldlighter."

"I told you he is *meant* to be," corrected Kimmie. "I did not share more because that is for him. Opren, I need you to follow me to my house. The two things I must share with you are for you to hear. After I share them, you may do as you wish with the information, but I am bound by oath to share the prophecy I have for you with only you at this time. That is why I required Selios to bring you here, instead of bringing the message and prophecy with him."

Kimmie turned and started toward the path up the small hill. Opren followed. Emerald attempted to follow, but Kimmie held up a hand.

"I am—" tried Emerald.

"I know who and what you are, Esmeraldi Avaria with the violet eyes," said Kimmie, cutting off Emerald's protest. Opren knew that could go badly, but Emerald simply pursed her lips and remained where she was. "You have a special aspect about you as well, Princess. Perhaps you would like to know your potential next?"

"I will reveal it myself when appropriate," said Emerald. "But I already know. Shela Selios passed that information to me when I was a child, from the previous oracle."

"New choices and new paths lead to new endings," said Kimmie. Opren had no idea what the vague statement meant, but the way the oracle said it, entirely in her mature voice, it felt important. "Well, let's complete this prophecy business." Kimmie waved for him to follow again as she turned back toward the house and walked up the path.

"This young oracle is odd. And not in the mysterious wisdom sort of way," Rufius said just before he was out of ear's reach.

Opren entered Oracle Kimmie's house and saw what

might be described as a laboratory for a bibliophile, a medium, and a fortune teller all at once. The first table in the small entry hall was covered in a few things that reminded Opren of mirrors and crystal balls, while the shelves all around the place, even in the entry were covered in thick tomes and single-page scrolls and sheets alike. She led him into a room with higher ceilings and every wall was a bookshelf. The tables in what must have been her study—or personal library, really—were covered with packs of fortune cards, other heptagonal cards, small gems and other stones, several notebooks, two scales, a few jars of he knew not what, and a group of crystalline gourds. There also floated a huge crystal ball in the center of the room.

"I have been observing you some since you have arrived, but not through scrying," said Kimmie. Her voice was light and retained the tone that resembled a teenage girl, not a formally educated and mature woman. But as she stared into his eyes, her expression and inflections changed. "I knew you would come here, but I knew not when. Now I shall share the prophecy of the legacy you carry on as Keeper and Goldlighter."

Opren initially thought of Kimmie as cute, a bit eccentric, and likely wise for one so youthful. Now, he was not sure if the person inside a twenty-something woman's shell matched her years, but he did know she was intimidating in a way that had nothing to do with her appearance, rather something about her presence.

Kimmie took a slow, deep breath with her eyes closed. She opened her eyes and began the prophecy with a ghostly addition to her voice, and her face became stoic while her eyes focused on everything and nothing at once. It was as though she saw something he did not, outside of the physical realm, as she spoke the words:

> "A boy turned man must find his way
> The light he holds like Golden light of day
> As it has been in past and present

It will be again in future however distant
The Dark with the Light
It cannot survive after Time
But the light in the dark
May not occur if not for a heart
One must surely seek
To find what he can be
A will beyond all alive
In where death should lie
While at that time unleash
To spark what can really be
Another will overcome
Tasks seemingly cumbersome
With a mind like no other
So worlds apart they can find the other
This Seeker traveling within light
Will come around at a proper time
Between the two a task will do
To satisfy their connection
When myth is truth there should be two
To manage a beautiful correction
But worsened still is the pain of worlds
If not for one with Silver holds
Together walking hand in hand
Against the evil forces planned"

When Kimmie finished, Opren was intrigued but confused. He waited for her face to return to its prior look that held more life before he spoke.

"If this is about me, it sounds like you are saying I'm meant to defeat some kind of evil, but am I also meant to meet someone? My grandfather enjoyed riddles, but I was never as good at them."

"A prophecy comes *through* me, not from me really, but I wrote the words and notes on this scroll from what I could retain and figure out," said Kimmie. She picked up a scroll of handwritten words in blue ink and rolled it, inserting it into a metal tube before handing it to Opren.

"Thanks," said Opren as he took it. "Who are the people, and what is the evil?"

"I do not know details that specific," said Kimmie. "I apologize. But I can tell you High King Rykeron has never commanded armies like the creatures ravaging his towns now. Something is imbalanced in our world, and the signs point to the Royal Sect. I also know King Rykeron wants to obtain your Goldlight artifact. Selios' missions and the current state of things have confirmed my predictions and visions. Though, I have never been wrong in my foresight, so I am not surprised. Additionally, there may be more to come, but it is unclear what the darkness is that I have seen."

"High King Rykeron? Is he the one ruling from the Royal Sect?"

"Indeed." Kimmie nodded. "Why would a powerful king who has ruled for a decade without war suddenly destroy his own sect, slaughter his own citizens, and hunt down an ancient magical object that seemed lost to our realm?"

"You seem to know enough to know I'm not from Everniot," said Opren. "Not from here as far as my memories, anyway. I was born here, but my family left before I had memories of anything significant. I didn't even know until this year. I have no idea who the king is or what his motives would be. I was hoping to find answers from you."

"I was asking the question because *you* need to ask it yourself. If you read my notes, the text version of the prophecy I have left for you, and discover the meanings as your life progresses, it will guide you," said Kimmie. "And I have given a major hint as to what you could do next. I recommend avoiding High King Rykeron for your safety, but you should follow your heart and will. There is a part of you that needs to face whatever dark power has arrived to this kingdom. Transcendence may surprise you in days to come; but further pain may be better off avoided."

"I came here to avenge my parents murder," said Opren. "Emergency workers advised I take time to grieve or whatever, but I did not intend to be passive then. I still need to find the sleeskaxes that burned down my house and murdered my parents right in front of me. If this King Rykeron has anything to do with it, or even if he is victimizing his own people just to get to me and my artifact and cause some kind of fear, I am not going to hide from him."

"It was only my recommendation," said Kimmie. "I see a struggle to your future if you meet the king, and not only due to him. It is unclear what or why, but I read in the cards and crystals…further pain and loss. Then chaos." She met his eyes again and this time hers seemed to drown his thoughts in something heavy.

"I already lost everything that matters most," said Opren, clenching his fists. He furrowed his brow and intended to pierce her entrancing gaze with the anger boiling to the surface, to get the point across. "I am no longer helpless. I will find the sleeskaxes. I will confront High King Rykeron and find out what the hell is really going on."

"You might find much more accuracy to that way to word your quest than you will prefer," said Kimmie. "Hell might be exactly what you find."

"I suppose I will know when I get to it," said Opren. "Thank you for the insight and the prophecy. I know what I am going to do, instead of aimlessly killing every sleeskax I find. I am going to head directly to the palace of the Royal Sect and start by confronting High King Rykeron himself."

Opren left the house and returned to the group waiting for him down the pathway. Emerald approached first, but Rufius spoke first.

"Now what? Did you learn anything useful?"

Opren shared the scroll of notes and what he recalled of the prophecy. He told them of his plan to head straight to the Royal Sect, to the palace itself, rather than to the random towns being attacked near it. They would pass through at least one town that needed help anyway, but he needed his answer: Was King Rykeron the real master behind his parents' death? If so, the sleeskaxes might not be the only targets for his retaliation. He knew he should be concerned about whether fighting or killing a king was a good idea, but he also felt a bit of the Goldlight seeping into him by subconscious intent, and it made him want to continue the path of aggression, of revenge, justice, or punishment—whether good or not. The pain he experienced should not be experienced by others, so he knew he was at least somewhat justified in his want to rid the world of the cause, whoever or whatever might be that cause.

"Are you sure you want to do this?" asked Emerald. "If you are wrong about the High King of Humans, he could execute you for treason due to the accusation."

"Well, if he is behind this, I am already wanted, probably dead or alive, just for inheriting the Goldlight sphere that he wants," said Opren. "But he might not expect me to wield it well enough to go against his wishes. If I'm dead either way, maybe running toward the danger is the best idea. At least I have a choice. I've never stood down from a fight and this one matters too much."

"You will need me to gain an audience," said Emerald. "Non-royals may not speak to him in person without an appointment set by a royal or the attendance of a royal is required."

"I didn't expect any of you—well, maybe Ruubi—to sit out of this, but I also won't mind if you want to," said Opren. "This is your kingdom, not mine, and I know I wouldn't sit out if the roles were reversed. I don't know if I will have an impact on your kingdom and never expected the scale of my goal to grow so far beyond learning about the Goldlight and how to use it to find and kill the monsters that murdered my parents."

"It is not your responsibility," said Ruubi in an authoritative tone that had none of its usual playful nature. Everyone turned to her with surprised expressions. Opren really did not expect her to respond first or in a tone more befitting to Emerald or Sapphire. "You have your own goals and your power is yours to do with what you wish. It is this kingdom's nobility—my family and the other royals especially—who need to rise up if the High King of Humans is causing corruption. You are right about that. I may enjoy myself, but I do not intend to sit out of such a serious matter either. I am going with you. It was all curiosity and whim until now, but I want to be of assistance."

"So much for you teasing me about living dangerously," said Emerald with a smirk. Then she smiled. "Just don't flirt with the king."

"I have never met him, but is he truly handsome? I have only seen paintings," said Ruubi. Emerald, Rufius, and Selios gave her a look and she giggled. "I am joking."

Emerald shook her head. "At least you will bring more light to a potentially dark situation."

I have avoided the Royal Sect because of the blasting weapons, said Barbosa. *I have seen what they can do. Humans are geniuses when it comes to destruction, even of living things. Are you able to heal me if I am shot, Miss Emerald?*

"What?" asked Opren, brows raised, eyes wide in surprise. "Your realm has guns? Is that what he means?"

"If you mean mechanical or ignited handheld projectile shooters, what made you think we had none?" asked Rufius. "We train with swords and magic, but Elven people are much more apt to have an affinity for magic than humans. Everyone was equal once, but as elves and humans chose separate paths, the elves remained linked with nature and the humans did not. Humans turned to technology, especially on the other continent. Is that the same or different in your realm?"

"My realm had only humans, that I knew of," said Opren. "But guns were common and very dangerous."

"Most of the time, magic makes the need for anything other than throwing projectiles or arrows needless," said Selios. "I have encountered some men with guns, which we call cannonsticks. I summon their weapons to me before they know of my presence, then I strike. But in recent encounters, some of the weapons have anti-enchantments which block any external magic. As militaristic as the king has always been in his thinking, we will need to prepare to be unable to summon the weapons there."

"In answer to Barbosa's question," said Emerald before the discussion could continue. Opren's sudden tension made him forget she still had to reply. "I have never healed a wound from a gun, but I have learned enough medical techniques to remove an arrow or a bullet. I also doubt there will be much difference. Don't get shot in the head or the heart, though." She looked at Opren, then Rufius, sternly.

"I hope not to be shot at all," said Opren with a small laugh, trying to alleviate the thoughts of the consequences.

The group descended the small mountain to meet with Polaris. After they updated the wizard on their discussion and the prophecy, he confirmed his observed evidence and the rumors he heard lined up with the oracle's words about King Rykeron. He also confirmed the thought all the Royal Sect's weapons were anti-enchanted, as he had been there before.

The group started their return to Avarinnia to rest and gather supplies. They would leave in the morning, heading south to the Royal Sect. As they passed through the denser part of the forest, everyone heard something at nearly the same second. Barbosa gave a low growl.

"What is it?" asked Opren.

Groundwyrm, said Barbosa.

"What's a—"

Opren did not need to finish his question as a massive snake-like creature came out of the ground, spinning its body of hundreds of jagged tan scales. It was four times the size of an anaconda in width and likely double the length from what Opren could see as it drilled back into the ground. It passed through the dirt with as much ease as if it were thick liquid. It shot back out and knocked Polaris into the air.

Polaris swore as he thudded into a tree during his

uncontrolled landing. He placed a magical bubble around himself before the groundwyrm could open its mouth to reveal hundreds of pointed teeth. The groundwyrm struck, but Polaris' translucent white bubble protected him from harm. The creature turned its head to Emerald.

Emerald had already drawn her dagger and took a ready stance. The groundwyrm darted toward her like a cobra striking prey, but she managed to dodge. She struck its side with the dagger as she rolled and returned to a standing positon. No damage was done to the rough scales and the creature only whipped its head around to face her again.

Barbosa leaped at the creature and slashed it with his large claws, but he barely managed to chip a scale either.

These are nearly impossible to kill, said Barbosa. *A pack of granwolves lost two and, of the four that returned, one was missing a leg before they could bring one of these down.*

"Not impossible, then," said a familiar voice. Something was different, but the voice was familiar enough and Opren turned to see Zargunn emerge from the shadows of three trees behind them. "Only difficult. I am going to help." His voice had none of the sickening reverberation.

Zargunn's skin was light brown, not gray when he stepped into enough light to be seen clearly. Something was certainly different about the Half-Demon or whatever he was. Also, the man's eyes were not glowing, only bright red in iris color.

"If you think I'll give you the Goldlight sphere because you helped us kill this thing." Opren gave Zargunn a harsh look.

"I am holding back the one possessing me, Opren," said Zargunn. "This is me, Zacharia. But I cannot do this for long. I will not lie and say I never wanted the power of the Goldlight, but I have learned I cannot use it because its magic will not respond to Demonic power. I am going to help in the hope you will give me some answers, as I could not scry you while you spoke with the oracle. Her mountain has powerful psychic protection."

"I will kill you if you turn on us again," said Opren. He

swore as he had to dodge a swing of the groundwyrm's head. He rolled under the sharp scales just as the groundwyrm cracked a few treebranches. The branches landed in the place Ruubi had been just a second before, but she had managed to dodge as well.

"Understood," said Zargunn who was currently Zacharia. The man's skin changed between random patterns of gray and tan and he was sweating.

"You can do this, Zacharia!" said Polaris. "Resist Ergunus!"

Zacharia called the groundwyrm to him and as the creature opened its mouth of razor-sharp teeth, he flung several fireballs into the massive snake's mouth. The groundwyrm screeched and hissed as it burrowed underground again. Zacharia barely rolled out of the way as the groundwyrm returned to the surface with the same force as it had used to knock Polaris into the air. Zacharia was holding his head as he stood again, barely able to keep his balance.

"What is going on?" asked Rufius. "Is he not able to use his power while holding back the demon?"

"Not exactly," said Polaris. "But he is in no condition to fight while Ergunus wants control."

"I can't do this," said Zacharia, all charisma and arrogance lost from his tone. He sounded like a sick beggar more than the Half-Demon who had killed multiple warriors in Avarinnia while having a mild-mannered conversation. He must have been suffering.

"Yes, you can!" said Polaris. "You have power without that wretched possession!"

Opren shifted into Goldlighter form and lunged as the groundwyrm went for Zacharia. He knew after seeing the speed of the rough-scaled creature Zacharia was not in a condition where he could dodge again. Opren did not not know if he wanted to help Zacharia or Zargunn or whoever the man or Half-Demon was, but he also did not feel good about letting the groundwyrm eat him. Opren summoned two Goldlight blades and stabbed the groundwyrm. The creature stopped just before it reached the struggling Zacharia. It whipped its head back to Opren and hissed. Opren changed the orb into the solid sword and readied himself.

As the groundwyrm struck, Opren spun to the left and rammed the blade through the groundwyrm's throat in one fluid motion. He then flipped over the creature as he threw two more energy blades into its eyes. The groundwyrm collapsed with a final screech and twitched twice before lying still. It was dead.

Opren shifted back to normal and took a deep breath to steady his equilibrium. He approached Zacharia.

"Are you—"

"Get back!" exclaimed Zacharia as he flailed a hand through the air. His skin was all gray again and the echo to his voice crept back in for a piece of the words. "I can't!"

"Demon and Vessel: Holy Severance!" yelled Polaris. A burst of white light hit Zargunn who was Zacharia in the chest and Zacharia screamed in pain—no, the demon voice screamed while Zacharia yelled.

"*OUT!*" forced Zacharia.

As the white light dissipated, a black substance poured out of Zacharia's mouth and shaped itself into a head without a body, just a whispy trail. The face had glowing red eyes and sharp teeth.

"You think you can resist me now," the smoky head said with a strained voice. "But you are weak without me."

"No, Ergunus," said Zacharia, his skin all tan and his eyes brown. "I will be strongest when I master myself as I am now. You make me weak, like a drug, a venom I can't stand." He stood straight and took a deep breath, eyes fixed on the whispy demon with a fierce look. "Begone, Egunnus! I rebuke you!"

The black demon-head hissed and flew at Zacharia. At first, it appeared he had gone into the man again, but a few seconds after, the head was forced out of the man again and shot across the area. The black smoke trailed behind as

Ergunus' whispy form flew away.

"Thank you, Polaris," said Zacharia. Then he dropped to the ground, unconscious.

"Can we trust him enough to bring him back with us?" asked Rufius. "I still think we should leave him after his murder of our warriors."

"I saw him kill our men," said Emerald. "But he was Zargunn as he was possessed. I think Zacharia might be less malicious."

"The rising anger I felt around him is gone," said Opren. "It was like the Goldlight could sense—gave me the power to sense—when the demon was here, but the feeling left as soon as Ergunus flew away."

"That is an interesting discovery," said Polaris. "It lines up with what I have heard of the Goldlighter in stories. The warrior could sense evil and destroy it. I wonder how else that will be revealed."

"Do you trust him not to steal your Goldlight sphere?" asked Selios.

"I will have it with me as always," said Opren. "If I need to kill him with it, I will. But he said he can't use it, anyway. I don't fully trust him but, if he wants to help us, he will be a valuable ally. We are about to face the High King, after all."

"I'm holding onto hope High King Rykeron is not really behind the corruption," said Emerald. "But you are right. The more allies we have, the better. This could be an extremely dangerous mission."

"We will put him in prison, so we have a chance to question him before he is allowed out in our city," said Selios. "At least until the time comes for us to leave."

Barbosa volunteered to carry Zacharia's unconscious body, and the group made the rest of the trip back to Avarinnia. When they arrived, Selios led Barbosa and Opren to the dungeons of the palace while Emerald and Ruubi met with their parents and Athera to relay the news of what happened. Barbosa dropped Zacharia into a cell.

"I'm going to stay until he wakes up," said Opren. He wanted to be the first to question the man who had been aggressive about stealing his Goldlight orb.

Selios nodded and Barbosa followed the platinum-haired Elven warrior up the dungeon steps, while Opren took a seat outside of Zacharia's prison cell. It was late, but Opren did not feel like sleeping yet. He had too much on his mind.

23

Zacharia woke, body sweaty and head throbbing, but still better than when he first rebuked Ergunus. He lifted his hands, his blurred vision clearing up as he turned them over slowly and inspected them in the dim light; they were light brown as they should be—his true skin. There was not a speck of that abhorrent gray presence. There was not even a hint of Ergunus. He could be himself; cursed or not, he was at very least in full control of his own mind, decisions, and actions. He took a slow, deep breath. Unfortunately, the cleansing breath of relief turned out to bring a stench like men on a battlefield or working in a quarry, but without death or decay. But it was his first *free* breath in five years.

Zacharia sat up slowly and realized he was on the stone floor of a small room. He looked around and saw Opren Saphren seated on a chair outside of bars made of a light pink material—he was in a prison cell and it must have been in Avarinnia, due to the material with which the bars were formed. "Free" might have been a slight misjudgment, but he was certainly free in one way; this new trapping was only temporary and could not follow him to his sleep or even his grave, certainly not to another location the way that parasite had done.

Zacharia chuckled drily and said, "You do realize Avarinnium holds natural magic, spirit energy, and it can be enchanted, but it cannot hold supernatural power inside, right? It won't prevent me from breaking out of here, if I wish, any better than steel. It would not hold you, either, I suspect. Runaic magic is untamable by usual means."

"If you got out, I would use the Goldlight to kill you before you reached the door," said Opren, looking at Zacharia as if the latter were standing trial. Zacharia supposed it was only fair, considering his actions last he was in Avarinnia. "What is Runaic magic?"

"It is ironic how little you really know, Opren." Zacharia shifted his position and stood, slowly as not to provoke Opren further—it seemed the young man was on edge and ready for a fight without notice, especially after Zacharia's comment. "What I mean is," Zacharia said in a less condescending tone. "You have such potential and power, something that even runs in your blood—in your family history—yet you are barely aware of what it really seems to be, even as you take steps to wield it."

"Then enlighten me," said Opren. His tone was still forceful, but his eyes and brow eased a bit. He must have been genuinely curious, despite his false air of authority due to his anger.

"Runaic magic is old magic," said Zacharia. "It is the oldest form of categorized magic. Supernatural and Runaic magics were the first forms of magic, before anything had a name or designation. This was back when humans could wield magic just as well as any other being, before corruption, disbelief, imbalances of power, and lost teachings happened. Elves are the only race able to come close to using true Runaic magic today, but even they avoid most of it. Unity magic is the only Runaic magic used commonly, but that is even treated as advanced. Unity magic used to be the easiest magic, before any one person wanted to be all-powerful and harmony was lost."

"How does that apply to me?" asked Opren. "I'm not an elf, and I already know the basics of Unity magic as it exists now."

"It is not the Unity magic that matters," said Zacharia, grabbing the Avarinnium prison bars to get as close as he could. It might have been a mistake because Opren jumped up from his chair, but the young man did not draw his sword or summon a golden energy blade. "It is the Goldlight that does. I don't know what its original name was, but I do know through much research, and random memories that appeared while I was possessed by Ergunus, that the Goldlight has existed for thousands of years in some form. The kind of magic it comes from is Runaic, I think. It is *pure* magic. Runaic has sometimes been called 'true magic'."

"'True magic'," echoed Opren, looking at the wall for a moment instead of Zacharia. Once he finished his thought, he looked back at Zacharia and regained a stern-yet-inquisitive look. "I can produce pure magical blades from the Goldlight energy or even without a source as it powers me, for example, right?"

"Yes," said Zacharia. "And evidently, demons and corrupt beings cannot wield those blades. In fact, the Goldlight seems to have been used to fight against demons or 'monsters' throughout history. There has always been some 'glorious' or 'omnipotent' warrior who appeared in flashes or streaks or auras of golden light. Some called the man an angel or even thought he was a deity or not of this world. He would rid towns or kingdoms of corrupt creatures and evil."

"Obviously he knew more than I do about how the magic works if he accomplished all that and received all that praise," said Opren. He almost sounded like he was joking. But his brow furrowed again as he added, "But that doesn't mean I can't use it to kill you at my current level. I do have control now."

Zacharia quirked a half-smile. He did not allow Opren to see it before he dropped the corner of his mouth again, but he was satisfied with Opren's response. If he were still possessed, he would use the moment of vulnerability to break out and kill Opren, but he had little interest in harming anyone now. He needed to know what the oracle had told Opren, and he also intended to go with Opren if he were going toward the Royal Sect.

"You could kill me, yes," said Zacharia. "But I would actually prefer to help as a way to make amends for my attempts to kill you or harm your friends."

"Am I supposed to believe that's the only reason?" asked Opren.

"I also want information, as I mentioned before," said Zacharia. "Tell me what you learned from the oracle, since I could not observe you through scrying or any other means while you were inside her house."

"Oh, you don't have a way to zoom in on things to have read the notes on her scroll for me?" asked Opren. He was mocking this time, which was a good sign.

"The scroll is enchanted as well. Only those viewing it in person can read it, I suspect," said Zacharia.

"I don't remember the entire prophecy off the top of my head." Opren took out the oracle's scroll from his pocket, stepped forward, and extended it to Zacharia. "But you can read this." Zacharia reached through the bars for the scroll and Opren jerked it back and up. "Don't you dare betray us, or I will not hesitate to cut off your head. I'm sure you will die then no matter what magic you have. I have a goal and you are powerful to have as an ally. I appreciate your explanation. But you did try to hurt us, possessed or not."

"I understand." Zacharia gave a single nod. "That is a fair agreement. I will help you however I can until further notice and you should kill me if you suspect I mean to harm any of your allies."

"Good." Opren returned a firm nod. He re-extended his arm with the scroll and allowed Zacharia to take the scroll this time.

Zacharia opened the parchment and read:

"A boy turned man must find his way
The light he holds like Golden light of day
As it has been in past and present
It will be again in future however distant
The Dark with the Light
It cannot survive after Time
But the light in the dark
May not occur if not for a heart
One must surely seek
To find what he can be
A will beyond all alive
In where death should lie
While at that time unleash
To spark what can really be
Another will overcome
Tasks seemingly cumbersome
With a mind like no other
So worlds apart they can find the other
This Seeker traveling within light
Will come around at a proper time
Between the two a task will do
To satisfy their connection
When myth is truth there should be two
To manage a beautiful correction
But worsened still is the pain of worlds
If not for one with Silver holds
Together walking hand in hand
Against the evil forces planned"

As Zacharia looked over the scribbles and notes on the sheet his head was spinning, but it was difficult to know if the headache had simply turned to dizziness or if his hasty thoughts were the cause. The theory he had about more than one artifact holding power like the Goldlight might have been confirmed by a single document in this place, this dungeon of all things, right then. He did not know the power of the other—or others—but the sheer existence was fascinating.

"Do you intend to live out the prophecy or use it for a general direction of your next journey?" asked Zacharia, looking up from the page. Opren stood there, arms folded as he waited.

"I still intend to find the sleeskaxes, and to ask King Rykeron about the corruption in his sect," said Opren. "After that, I might. I have no other life to go back to, either way."

"I really am sorry about how your parents died, Opren," said Zacharia. His emotions had been twisted and hardened to a cold, power-oriented way of use for so long, he was not sure if he truly felt the sympathy, but he knew he should. He also hoped his tone sounded genuine outside of Ergunus' influence; he was not lying. Opren's parents were innocents who did nothing to provoke those who wanted the Goldlight power, and they did not deserve to die, especially brutally.

"Somehow, I believe you," said Opren. "I don't trust you fully, but I believe you feel something for me and my parents. The problem is you are not the one who killed them and can't atone for it or pay for it."

"True," said Zacharia. "I need to test my true abilities without Ergunus manipulating me." He stood straight and flexed a hand while looking at it again. Then at full volume and with as much sincerity as he could muster, "I would be glad to help you slay anyone who causes uundue harm. It will be my initial repentance for prior actions."

"Even if that means the High King of Humans?" asked Opren.

"I've never been fond of those born into rule, unless they earn it," said Zacharia, forcing a smile. "A corrupt king does not deserve his throne. As a cursed man, who better to take the blame for a king's death, if it must happen?"

"If you take the credit, I get to be free from the consequences if we have to kill him?" asked Opren. Zacharia nodded. "That would be the end of your redemption with me. You can choose what you want to do after that and, as long as we don't clash, I won't kill you."

"And I will never try to kill you again, Opren Saphren," said Zacharia. He reached a hand through the pink bars. Opren hesitated for a few seconds, then he firmly grasped Zacharia's hand. It was the first bond of any sort Zacharia had with another human—or in his case a Half-Demon or cursed person bonding with a human, if Opren Saphren, Keeper of the Goldlight, truly was only Human at this point himself. In any case, it felt good. It felt right.

Be damned, Ergunus.

Zacharia smiled to Opren and at the thought at once.

24

Opren found Emerald leaving the throne room of the Elven palace. He described to her his conversation with Zacharia and the details of his agreement with the formerly-possessed man. Emerald stated her distrust of Zacharia, but she agreed with Opren's decision as the best choice, especially if Zacharia did honestly want to make amends and could be of help.

"My mother wants him out of the city as soon as possible," said Emerald. "I was coming to tell you once I asked some guards to help with his release and escort from the city. I suppose the escort is no longer necessary; you are a better guard." She smiled.

"I hope so." Opren chuckled. "I am about to confront a king, even fight him if I have to."

"I still intend to approach this as if we don't have to go beyond civil conversation," said Emerald. She sighed. "But every bit of information about the Royal Sect makes the situation sound worse. He is either allowing it or cowering without action against it. Another problem came to light at Rhahkmant'e as well; Athera received word from Rutundo he cannot continue substitute instruction for her because a rabid, possibly possessed wyvern got into the city part of the mountain. He needs to bring it down before it kills anyone, and he is the only elite huntsman nearby for that kind of creature. Due to that and another regular assault, Athera must leave immediately, instead of joining us. She told me to send word if we need further assistance once we learn the truth of the Royal Sect. Vallot also chose to leave with her to begin personal contributions to the forces protecting the mountain, to find out why assaults have increased even after you left. He wished us well."

"I'm already grateful for their help to this point," said Opren. "I hate that I unknowingly made the mountain a target but at least they can protect it, I'm sure. Should we rest and leave as soon as we wake?"

He wanted to leave immediately, but he knew everyone should be at their best before a long journey. The Royal Sect was going to take two weeks to travel to; he missed motor vehicles when he learned of how far it would be. Up to a week was a good hike, but two weeks was a lot of travel time one way, especially while at least two nearly unbeatable, deadly creatures were killing and torturing to get to him. Now that he had the power and skill to confront them, waiting was not an acceptable luxury, and patience felt out of place while even somewhere like Rhahkmant'e was under threat.

Emerald nodded. "Are you ready for this, really? To encounter the sleeskaxes and the king? And be honest, Laleiy. Don't let your anger answer for you."

Opren looked into Emerald's violet eyes; it felt like her soul was seeing his, but without the weight of whatever the queen had done. He could not keep up a façade of strength or certainty with her. They were beginning to learn each other enough after the months living and training together she knew him, possibly even better than he knew her. On top of that, his affection for her had grown and her Elvish lure might be present as he stared into her eyes.

"I can't be false with you," said Opren. "I'm not sure if I am ready, not completely. But I *do* have to do this. Sometimes life doesn't wait for us to be ready and we have to hope and move forward and act. That is what I am going to do."

"I'm impressed." Emerald smiled. "Wise notion."

"My parents told me that."

Emerald stepped forward and embraced him. He put his arms around her, and they held each other. He was not keeping track of the time, but he wanted it to last long enough to feel thorough. It was likely the last chance to share such a peaceful moment, after all. If things went badly, he would need to fight to the death or leave her and his new friends to protect everyone by taking the target—himself—far away from the sect.

They released and allowed the bliss of the moment to linger before either moved, then Emerald went to gather Selios, Rufius, and Ruubi.

Opren returned to the dungeons to inform Zacharia of the update and expected time to leave. He found the formerly possessed man seated on the floor with his eyes closed, as though meditating or listening. It was strange to see the man who so recently gloated about being a Half-Demon and killed Elven warriors on a whim in such a calm, non-threatening state. The man's light-brown skin and black hair reminded Opren of someone from South Asia of his world, and Zacharia really was a man then, not a monster.

"Zacharia." Opren automatically held back from projecting his voice, as if Zacharia were sleeping.

"Opren," said Zacharia. He opened his eyes. "Do you have another question, or is this to be sure I haven't escaped after what I said?"

"Neither," said Opren. "I think Queen Bellavuu would be happy to let you leave even if you did escape. She wants you gone from the city as soon as possible."

"That is a fair response to the murder of her warriors," said Zacharia. He sounded almost sad.

"You know, it is getting difficult to hate you if you admit to everything with actual remorse," said Opren.

"Why do you feel the need to hate me?" asked Zacharia, getting to his feet.

"It makes it easier if I need to kill you."

"You are horrible at being intimidating, Opren," said Zacharia. "You are not supposed to allow the other to know if you are bluffing or unwilling."

"I'm not unwilling, and I am not bluffing," said Opren. "I just can't kill someone without thought or emotion like you did—like Zargunn you did."

"Being that you make the distinction, I suppose that means you see me differently now," said Zacharia.

"I recognize you are not just a monster or a demon," said Opren. "It will take a lot more to trust you, and that will not change in only twenty minutes or even twenty days without good reason."

"Well, I suspect you won't like the other side of me much," said Zacharia. "I still have my curse, the demon that is a real part of me.

"We'll find out," said Opren. "Were you meditating?"

"In a way," said Zacharia. "I center my spirit and mind and emotions whenever I am in control. It helps me keep a balance between my Human side and fused Demonic side."

"Your curse or whatever it is confuses me," said Opren. "But I'm glad you have a way to remain in control of yourself now. I am looking forward to seeing your abilities when they are toward someone who might deserve the aggression, instead of me or my friends."

"Hmm…I hope you enjoy the show when the time comes," said Zacharia.

"Queen Bellavuu won't allow me to let you out before it is time to escort you from the city, but I hope you get some rest with the uncomfortable sleeping arrangements. It seemed like the exorcism took its toll. We will start toward the Royal Sect tomorrow."

Opren was not sure if he felt sympathy for Zacharia, but he did believe the man was sincere and not trying to trick him. Zacharia was not quite Zargunn, and his personality did seem different. Opren intended to treat him like any new dangerous ally, rather than a guilty enemy.

The group consisting of Opren, Emerald, Rufius, Selios, Zacharia, Barbosa, and Ra'ze left shortly after the sun was up the next day. Polaris said he would meet them outside the walls of the central area of the Royal Sect before they were to speak with High King Rykeron. He had one piece of business to attend to before then.

Emerald left Shari in Avarinnia because the mare was not a battle-trained horse and had no natural combat ability, such as Ra'ze had, if they were to run into Demonics or larger dangerous creatures, like another groundwyrm. Sapphire had agreed to care for Shari the weeks Emerald would be gone. It was the first time Opren saw the sisters embrace each other without brevity or façade, and Sapphire had wished them all safety and good fortune and something in Elvish Emerald explained roughly meant "peace follow and find you".

Alcorn stayed behind after Selios convinced King Eeloneus the non-magical warrior would be more of a liability than a help where they were going due to lack of experience, which meant Ruubi was required to stay in the city as well. Ruubi chose to ignore her parents and snuck out in a commoner's cloak and hood to join the group a few hours after departure. Selios had spotted her first, so he silently snuck up to her and pulled off her hood.

"Go home, Ruubi," he said. "Before we get too far."

"I understand this will be dangerous," said Ruubi. "I might be able to help, and it won't hurt to have another princess when we request an audience with the High King, in case he tries to lie or dismiss just one of us. I want to see what Emerald does, and I want to be more than just secondary to Sofi at home. I know how serious this is, and parties won't distract me if I do nothing."

"Ruubi, this is not a trip for pleasure or education," said Emerald.

"I still might learn something or contribute something," said Ruubi. "You, of all people, should know what feeling stuck in Avarinnia is like."

"Fine," said Emerald. "Please be careful in any surprise circumstances."

"Eeloneus is not going to be happy I let you come," said Selios with a sigh. "He might actually discipline me, even if we are brothers, as he would as king with anyone else."

"Tell him I forced you," said Ruubi.

"Yes, that sounds believable," said Selios. They both laughed, and Selios shook his head. "As Emerald said, be careful and stay with the group at all times. If you do not follow my orders, I will bind you so you must remain close for everyone's safety."

Ruubi smiled and nodded.

For the first three nights, Opren requested some of them take shifts whenever they needed to stop, to keep watch over Zacharia. Selios took the first, then Opren. The next night Emerald and Rufius took their turns, then the last night Opren intended to take the whole night.

"It has been five hours," said Emerald, walking up behind him a while into the night. Opren had not been paying attention to the time, only his thoughts of whether he should trust Zacharia enough to get some rest, what he would do when he met the sleeskaxes that time, and how he would speak with the king. She put a hand on his shoulder. "Let me take the remaining time. I need less sleep on a normal night than you anyway. *We* are making this journey, and you need strength to wield the Goldlight if we run into any severe threats. Get some sleep."

"True," he agreed. "I never liked anyone taking on my responsibilities, so I wanted to push myself."

"I know." Emerald held a light smile. "That's why I came out to stop you from being foolish. We volunteered to take our turns. None of us will be good in battle if we are fatigued."

"Foolish? Hey, that's harsh. I was thinking driven." Opren chuckled and she smiled bigger. "All right, Liileiy. Good night."

"Good night, Laleiy." Emerald took his place on the log they had designated a "chair" as he stood. They had placed the log-chair by the fire with a straight line of sight to Zacharia's sleeping space.

Opren walked into his tent and lay down, thinking of how lucky he was to have been saved by someone like Emerald, not to mention everything that had come after. She might have kept him alive in multiple ways, such as forcing him to train before finding or fighting the sleeskaxes too soon and talking sense into him the way his mother would have done. He equally appreciated Emerald and missed his mother as he drifted into a dream that night.

The fifth night, Opren had chosen to forget about taking shifts to observe Zacharia. Selios even agreed it was unlikely the man would attempt to run, and it seemed Zacharia was not going to try to harm any of them. Ruubi even began to enjoy talking to him.

"Do you actually have any interest in what he is sharing, or are you trying to talk to him because he is reasonably good looking now that he is no longer gray and frightening?" asked Rufius as they walked through yet another group of trees the sixth afternoon.

"Just because I flirt with many people I meet doesn't mean I am not interested in the legitimate conversations," said Ruubi. "You all act as if I can't do both, flirt and learn. I am interested in him and his experiences. Believe it or not, I have not thought about trying to lie with him...or I hadn't, until now, but that's your fault."

"You all should really be sure who is within hearing range before talking, or it might give people the wrong idea," said Zacharia, increasing pace to be beside Rufius and Ruubi, just ahead of Opren as he had allowed Ra'ze to stop for cold water from a stream and had fallen behind. Selios continued to lead.

"Is that a tease?" asked Ruubi. "Have I finally opened you up to a sense of humor again?"

"I am not sure if humor touches me the same way yet," said Zacharia. "My emotional state was destabilized by the possession. But I suppose I do find that amusing."

"What about physical touch?" asked Ruubi.

"How shocking," said Rufius, rolling his eyes.

"Physical touch is normal," said Zacharia. "But intimate feelings are still skewed and doubtful. If you are curious whether I would lie with you, no, I don't expect it to be as enjoyable as you would hope."

"I'm sure I could fix that." Ruubi smiled and winked at Zacharia.

"Ruubi." Emerald turned to glare over her shoulder at her sister.

"I didn't say I *plan* to, just that I am sure I *could*." Ruubi stuck her tongue out at Emerald.

Emerald rolled her eyes and faced forward.

Opren almost laughed, but his mind was too focused on reaching their destination to give into a distraction fully. He and Ra'ze sped up to get close to Selios.

"It's eight more days, right?"

Selios nodded.

When Selios confirmed they were only three days from the Royal Sect, they reached a darker part of the woods where Selios had to cast a spell to create a glowing ball just to see the trees, then they came to a random opening in the trees where a small house sat alone. Opren walked up to the house and knocked. The door opened and nobody was there—it must have opened on its own the way Avarinnia's palace doors could do with magic. Everyone stepped inside and called out to whoever might be the owner.

Zacharia held his head suddenly and had to stabilize himself; he stood with his legs slightly apart, almost like a fighting stance.

"I almost forgot what this feels like," said Zacharia.

"What is it?" asked Opren.

"I have some sort of sense for demons and such," said Zacharia.

"So, your head hurts because there is a demon here?" asked Emerald.

"That is the basic sensation and concept, plus occasional vertigo," said Zacharia, hand still to his head. "Be alert."

"*Relista*," swore Selios. "I have read about these. Demons or not, they are dangerous. We need to ex—"

A cackling laugh cut off Selios' words. Opren began to feel his pulse and the anger he felt when Zacharia was around as Zargunn. Maybe it was not anger and he was experiencing some sort of sense of the demon too. It did only happen when there was someone or something considered a Demonic or monster around, not when danger was present otherwise, and not only when he had a reason to be angry. It was a bit different from his rage or spite toward the sleeskaxes, after all, but he had felt it in their presence along with the true pain and anger. Maybe it was something the Goldlight magic allowed him to do.

Opren shifted to Goldlighter form and felt the heated pulsing sensation more heavily, but he felt more stable. He suspected he was exactly right about what it meant. But *where* was the demon that laughed?

"Have you not heard the tales of the house in the woods?" a high voice echoed throughout the house. "Children go in and never come out. You are all inside the hungry mouth." It sounded gleeful, as if it were playing a game, but twisted with aggression.

"Who and what are you?" asked Opren. His voice sounded even louder than usual while in Goldlighter form due to the four walls in a small space. He looked around but, other than the glow he gave off, it was too dark to see much of anything.

"My pet is hungry," said the voice. A dim light turned on; it was enough to illuminate the group and the floor.

"Is the floor breathing, or am I hallucinating?" asked

Rufius.

"Don't look at the floor!" said Selios, grabbing Rufius' shoulder and shaking his son. "Everyone, eyes up!"

Opren stopped glancing back at the floor himself, but he wondered why it mattered. Then he saw Ruubi swaying back and forth in a sort of trance as she stared at the expanding and contracting floor. It must have been some sort of spell or hypnotic technique, and she had been caught by it more heavily than the others before the warning.

"Prey, prey, prey for us," said the voice, cackling again.

Opren felt a sharp pain across his back and spun. A short, dark figure dashed into a wall and...*merged* with the wall?

Ra'ze screeched, clawing at the wall after whatever struck Opren, but the thing was already elsewhere.

"These demons are able to change form and combine themselves to lure in prey and feed on anything and anyone," said Selios. "Craxevor is what they are called."

"Someone is smart, but it will not save you. A work of art, my pet shall eat you!"

The dark figure bubbled out of the wall and became an ugly face with charcoal skin and pointed teeth.

It smells like rotten beef to me, said Barbosa.

Then the ground and walls moved together, and the air felt moist. Opren thought the house really was breathing. Then it hit him.

"The *house* is the pet the thing keeps talking about! We need to get out now!"

The small demon cackled again and lunged forward to strike Emerald, but she had drawn her dagger and blocked its claw. It recoiled and leaped back into the wall-flesh of the larger demon-house. Then it moved through the wall, almost imperceptible as it did, and jumped from the floor to grab Selios' leg. Opren threw a Goldlight blade at it and it wailed and fell.

The demon writhed and shrieked as its leg deteriorated where Opren had struck it with the golden energy blade. Its skin seemed to flake off in pieces like golden ashes. Selios stabbed it directly through the chest, then removed his sword and sliced off its head.

The house around them began to feel humid and warm as it shook and creaked. Then a loud groan came from somewhere and what felt like raw meat fell onto Opren's shoulder. He knocked it off and everyone ran outside except Ruubi.

"Ruubi!" called Rufius. "Come to and get the hell out!"

Zacharia ran back in, staggering a bit but no longer holding his head. He grabbed Ruubi by both shoulders and stared into her eyes.

"Look at *me*," said Zacharia. "*I* am in control now."

Zacharia's skin changed from its light brown to a stone white while his eyes glowed red the way they had when he was Zargunn. It was not the same as Zargunn, but it still brought some apprehension to Opren—yet Opren did not feel the pseudo-anger or the pulsing heat. Ruubi snapped out of her daze.

"We need to go," said Zacharia. Ruubi nodded. He grabbed her hand and pulled her with him as they ran from the house. Zacharia returned to his normal state with light brown skin and a red tint to brown eyes and staggered but recovered his stance. "Are you all right, Ruubi?"

"Yes," said Ruubi. "Thank you, Zach."

Zacharia laughed twice. "I think I like that. I have never thought to shorten my name, but it makes me feel more like a friend than my former self."

"I like giving my own names to people," said Ruubi. "And you are my friend, as far as I am concerned. You just saved me."

"My pleasure," said Zacharia. He shook his head, then rubbed his temple.

The house morphed into a furry pile as it broke down behind them. Opren let out a breath as he shifted back to normal.

"Let's not enter any houses in the dark without a known owner again," said Rufius.

"You think?" said Opren. "At least I just learned something new."

"What is it?" asked Emerald.

"Did you see the demon when I threw my Goldlight blade at it?"

"No," said Emerald. "I saw it as Selios beheaded it."

"Its leg where I hit it began to disintegrate, like a completely burnt log lets off ashes on a fire," said Opren. "That has not happened to anything else so far, and Zacharia said demons can't wield the Goldlight properly."

"So, the legends about the Goldlighter slaying demonkind and monsters seem to be true," said Selios. "The Goldlight essence energy must be able to kill demons in a way normal blades or elemental magic cannot. It has been said even creatures that blades could not penetrate could be slain with a celestial golden sword."

We might need that if we run into more demons, said Barbosa. *I wasn't much good in there. This is not the sort of hunting and fighting I'm used to. I prefer the natural world.*

"At least you can smell and hear things that are amiss," said Rufius.

"Any ready warrior added is better than one missing," said Selios.

The group left the small clearing and walked through the trees to a spot they determined was far enough away from the demon-house to be comfortable. There, they set up camp and ate and rested for the night.

Two days before they would reach the Royal Sect, they came to a town with almost no people out and about. It seemed like the kind of town that should be busy, with several fresh fruit and vegetable stands—unoccupied at the time—and at least ten shops on each side of the street they walked through. It was a well-built town, with a lot of polished redwood around windows and doors but, no matter where they looked, no people were visible inside. They finally saw one woman hurry her son into a house and lock the door. On another street, one man swept the porch of a convenience store, but he did not respond to them when they called to him; he entered the shop and turned the sign to "Closed".

"Not very welcoming for such a place," said Rufius. "Why would they all not even want to do business?"

"Something is odd," said Emerald. "The air even feels wrong here, but I cannot place why." She looked around as if seeking the source of the feeling.

"I can feel the presence of magic, but not our sort of magic," said Selios. "The unease you feel is something I have experienced only once before. I hope—"

A shriek from their rear-left cut off Selios' words. Selios drew a blade, and everyone readied themselves for whatever might be next. They all turned toward the source of the sound, but there was silence again.

Footsteps, said Barbosa. *Not human or elf-like. And a stench from the building over there.*

Opren looked to his right, between the brick buildings Barbosa indicated, and a dark figure dashed by, then another. A snarl came from where the figures had run, then two strange person-shaped creatures, like faceless corpses covered in mud and bugs, dragged a clawing and weeping woman into the alleyway. A third dirt-zombie dropped from the roof to the right of the alley and slammed an arm through the woman as it landed, while the other two monsters pulled her apart as she screamed until the separation killed her. One creature began to eat the part of her it held—evidently possessing a mouth though it was missing eyes, but the other two noticed the group staring.

"What the hell are *those*?" Opren asked Selios.

"They are why everyone is hiding," said Selios. "They're called gruveks, unlife summons brought to form by decaying mass and sacrificial ritual. They are only possible if one possesses corrupt magic that is against Elven and Human laws. They lust for destruction and have no actual thoughts or source of life or soul. For them to be here, there is horrible magic at work. Knights and mages from the central Royal Sect should have come to deal with them this close, but either they failed or were never sent."

"How do we kill them, Father?" asked Rufius urgently, which Opren saw was due to the two who had noticed the group coming toward them.

"Locate their core, a pulsing sack of what looks like black blood, like a small beating heart," said Selios. "Breaking the core forces the magic created by sacrifice to go into another vessel but, if magic is used to destroy it, it fades and the decay returns to a natural cycle in Uundular."

Selios held up a hand and a loud gale knocked away the advancing gruveks. The monsters growled as they hit the ground twenty feet away.

This is a kind of enemy I can't help you with, said Barbosa. *Damn this foul magic! Again, I will only be the nose and ears for locating them.*

"That will be enough," said Emerald. "Thank you, Barbosa."

"All three this time," said Opren.

"Four," corrected Rufius, as another gruvek hopped off the building to the left of the alley.

"Five," further corrected Ruubi, as yet another of the creatures crawled from a broken window.

"They have no independent logic or reasoning," said Selios. "But they do hunt in groups, swarming prey and enemies like insects."

"No reasoning? So why attack us or even these people?" asked Rufius.

"We are alive," said Selios. "They are an antonym of life in magical terms and move toward the life they sense to end it."

"Why would anyone want that?" asked Emerald, shaking her head. "What reason would someone alive of any sort want that?"

"Such is the way of corrupt and cursed things," said Selios. "This is what violence, chaos, and tampering with death and unstable darkness can bring."

We have eight now, said Barbosa. *But why are they waiting?*

Opren looked around at the growing circle of gruveks, counting it reached ten at that moment. He realized they had stopped the second he reflexively shifted to Goldlighter form.

"It's me," said Opren. "I think they want to avoid the Goldlight. Maybe it hurts them worse than usual, like the demon in the house."

"That's fortunate for us, but how do we keep them occupied so they stop murdering the residents?" said Rufius.

"We can't for long," said Selios. "We will need to rid the city of all of them to prevent more destruction and death. Like a virus, even one left mobile can start a plague."

"So, let's make them come to us by providing the greatest source of life in the area, but without scaring them," said Opren.

"What do you mean?" asked Ruubi.

"I think he wants to shift back to normal, while we present life energy," said Emerald with a stern look. She turned to Opren. "More specifically, while *I* provide life energy in the form of my healing magic."

"Rufius and I will fight in the Unity," said Opren. "There is no chance of these things withstanding his lightning while enhanced. We can attract them, then kill—or whatever it is to end them—all of them."

"That is a good strategy," said Selios. "It will make us the only people in danger, but we can fight back, unlike most of the citizens here. The king's army is supposed to be their protection, but they have clearly left this area for reasons unknown."

"I can assist," said Zacharia.

"Oh, you are speaking again," said Rufius. "I thought you became too afraid or something."

"I was contemplating and waiting," said Zacharia. "I needed to know if I could do what I expected...I can sense their cores. I will pinpoint the cores and you can electrify them specifically, so as not to risk their dirt-body resisting or reforming. I will also set aflame any who pass you two."

"Ready, everyone?" asked Opren.

The group looked around at the gathering of what had reached about thirty gruveks. Zacharia and Barbosa confirmed there seemed to be no others roaming the city, all must have been alerted by the new lives out in the open, while Opren's Goldlight aura evidently held them at bay. It was time to switch to luring them like a moth to a light—in this case glowing life energy—so Rufius could be the living giant-bug-zapper.

Opren released the Goldlight essence and shifted to his normal self, while Emerald produced the soft green light of her healing aura. As soon as the golden aura faded, all the gruveks thumped the ground once and charged.

Opren and Rufius linked by the Unity magic while Zacharia located all the gruvek cores through intense concentration. Selios began to use his daggers covered by magic to stab the cores as Zacharia called out what bodyparts to pierce on the gruveks, then Rufius charged a massive field of lightning around himself as Opren provided double the *Nuuita*. Rufius shouted his spell-word, *Reiya*, as he unleashed the charged current and pierced or completely enveloped nearly every remaining gruvek with electricity. Opren blasted the final four monsters with sharp gusts in a pointed cone shape. The creatures that did not burst melted and became mud again as black liquid dripped to the ground.

"A-are they really dead?" asked a shaky man's voice. The group turned to see the shaggy-bearded man emerge from behind a fruit cart. "Is it safe again?"

"It should be," said Selios.

"Thank you so much!" exclaimed a blonde woman as she rushed over and knelt in front of the group with her hands together as if to pray. A very young blonde girl with curls in her hair rushed alongside the woman and followed the woman's example. The woman asked for the names of the city's "saviors", then invited them to rest at her family's home for the night before moving on.

The woman's name was Daria, and her eight-year-old daughter was Helena. Helena said she would make a cake for them for saving the place, which they assumed was a cute child's offer, until Helena actually brought a cake to hand to Zacharia as they were to leave the next day.

"You said you are part a demon," said Helena. "But you're too good, unless not all demons are bad. I will miss you, Sir Zach."

"I am not a knight," said Zacharia, kneeling and accepting a hug. "But thank you very much, Helena. I am glad your home is safe. I will enjoy thinking of you always."

As the group traveled to the next city, Zacharia commented several times on what Helena had said to him. He even smiled twice. The little girl seemed to lift his spirits all the way to the central Royal Sect.

Opren, on the other hand, only felt the intensity of his anticipation and drive grow, especially when the center capital, Ivorite Province, came into view.

25

Ivorite Province had people, especially near to where the palace stood, but its overall condition seemed worse than the previous towns.

Guards were gathering anyone who refused to follow orders. One man kept swearing and tried to punch a guard and the taller man in gold-trimmed armor with a lion on his pauldron grabbed the angry man by the neck, drew his sword, and stabbed the man; the guard's movements were mechanical and dull in effort despite the aggressive act. The man gasped, grunted, and the guard threw him to the ground as he withdrew his sword. The guard wiped the blade with a cloth and resheathed it. Something did not seem right about the guards, despite them being human, not apparently monsters, in identity. Were they possessed?

"Hey!" yelled Opren, brow furrowed. "Why did you kill him?"

"Opren, don't bring attention to us, yet," whispered Selios sharply.

"The circumstances here are stranger and worse than I expected," said a familiar voice. Opren and the others turned to see Polaris to their left. Polaris waved a hand as the guard who had killed the civilian approached them. The guard halted and turned around and walked away. "It's a good thing I know how to do that, or you would have gotten into trouble too soon. He won't remember the last two minutes until later."

A woman in armor approached and drew a pistol. Before she could cock the weapon, Opren shifted into Goldlighter form. He stepped in front of her—if anyone were going to be shot, it would be him, and he hoped the Goldlighter form might help dull the pain, but he also hoped he could prevent her from shooting at all. She made to pull the trigger, but Polaris cast a water spell around the weapon; it did not fire while in the big bubble. Opren disarmed her. Polaris waved his hand and she looked dazed.

A nearby male guard with a beard called out and drew a pistol. This time, Opren was faster than both Polaris and the guard, using the Goldlight sword in the shape of a katana to deflect the bullet. To his surprise, he not only deflected the bullet successfully, but the bullet was disintegrated by the golden blade. Opren smiled. He lost his smile as every guard in the area suddenly snapped their heads toward him.

"Release the Goldlighter form. *Now*," said Polaris. Opren shifted back to normal and pocketed the golden orb. Polaris took a deep breath. "I will take care of this."

Just as the group of over ten guards—and those were only the ones Opren could easily see in the area—made to come toward Opren and Polaris, the wizard chanted something and spread his hands apart, then brought them together on his staff. The spell caused every guard to pause and shake their heads as if they had been jarred suddenly from a drunken stupor. Then, they resumed their rounds as they were prior to the group's arrival.

"We could have used you in a demon's house the other day," said Opren. "Or against these things called gruveks the day before yesterday."

"I ran into some gruveks also. Glad you survived," said

Polaris. "I needed to find out something about High King Rykeron. It seems our formerly good king has been consorting with someone; I don't know who yet, but they are the reason for all this corruption. The king has gone mad or given up, according to the citizens. He is no longer the lauded 'Golden Lion King' who led armies that won many battles for his citizens to live well; it is as if he is an entirely different person. I'm curious if he is possessed."

"So much for a civil conversation," said Rufius.

"I met Lariat Rykeron once, before he was king," said Polaris. "I hope I can help you all talk some sense back into him if his conscious self knows me. He wants the Goldlight. He feels he deserves it, and he thinks it matches him as the Golden Lion King."

"He already has an entire kingdom and powerful army and mechanical weapons," said Selios. "What could he need a powerful magical weapon for now?"

"That is what concerns me the most," said Polaris. "Greed can cause men to do many things. If he intends to spread the kingdom or take over the lands of elves or Rhognomar, we will have war beyond what he prevented while he was good. If he is using corrupt magic—or ordering someone to—that would make it even worse."

The group walked through the main market area, which appeared to be the kind of place where exchanges for trinkets, fresh produce, fish, meats, and other possessions, such as books, would occur, on a normal day at least. The current state of the market included a few slow-moving merchants, only two actual customers, and a few guards scattered throughout. Some of the guards stood silently, while others questioned the citizens like those in the outer area of the city.

"Oy! Civilians!" called yet another male guard to their left as they walked by a fruit stand missing a merchant. The guard approached and kept a hand on his sword, but he did not draw the weapon. "What business have you here?" The guard looked over the group and his eyes widened as he landed on Zacharia.

"Is that Lord Zargunn in Human form?"

"We need to speak with High King Rykeron," said Opren, stepping slowly into a ready stance and prepared to shift into Goldlighter form if necessary.

Another guard had glanced over at the mention of Lord Zargunn. He joined the other and drew his sword. A third guard appeared on a second-story plateau and pointed a rifle at the group, likely aiming more specifically at Zacharia he assumed was still Zargunn.

"Leave this place," said the second guard in a deep voice.

"I am Princess Esmeraldi Avaria, and this is Princess Ruubi Avaria, of Avarinnia." Emerald inflected as she did when giving an official order. "We have a request from Queen Bellavuu and King Eeloneus for the High King of Humans."

"What business does *that* cursed man have here?" asked the first guard.

"Do you often make a practice of questioning royals about their business with other royals?" asked Ruubi. Her impersonation of Sapphire's attitude when finding herself in the right was spot on.

"Forgive us, Princess Ruubi, Princess Esmeraldi," said the two guards together. The deeper-voiced guard sheathed his sword and continued, "We have been given orders to prevent any and all resistance to the crown, and to investigate outsiders. But Light-Elves are not on the list of threats. We shall take you to the palace."

"You might want to hide yourself," said the first guard to Zacharia. "You are known here, and I will not stop my brothers from doing what they feel is right."

Zacharia pulled his hood up to somewhat conceal his face.

The group followed the two guards through the streets of the Royal Sect toward the middle of the city. They climbed steps or circular paths occasionally as they grew closer to the center. The massive white palace was at the highest point of the city once they reached the the exact center, which explained the climb.

The High King of Humans had a palace more like Opren would expect from stories than the palace in Avarinnia. It had high towers at three points, almost forming a triangular shape if one were to connect them from point to point. The wide walls were all polished white stone, with ballistas at each corner. From a distance it appeared like a large fairytale castle, but as they entered it felt like a combination of a battle fortress and a stark manor of a sort. The courtyard stretched on for over the length of a football field and was lined with guards atop the walls, and the doors to what the guard leading them said was the throne room were even taller than the doors to the palace in Avarinnia. Opren thought doors that massive were unnecessary, but they were impressive all the same. Each door had a huge golden lion engraved into it.

A short man in a hooded cloak came out of the throne room. His brown hood was still raised as he greeted them, so his face was hard to make out.

"Good day," said the man in a low voice. "High King Rykeron welcomes you to his palace. What business brings you here?"

Opren's pulse quickened and the feeling like hot anger rose in him. Was the man not Human?

"We need to speak to the king directly, please," said Opren. The urge to shift to Goldlighter form rose like a sudden flood as the hooded man rested his gaze on him. He stopped himself from impulsively pulling energy from the orb, in case it would draw more unwanted attention.

"What a coincidence," said the short man. Opren did not like the way he said it. The man reached up and pushed back the hood to reveal a face with mahogany skin and white hair, but a long, jester's nose and red eyes that were clearly not Human now that the light shone from them, instead of shining on them. "We have been waiting for you, Opren Saphren."

"*Relista*," swore Emerald quietly.

The guards stood behind the group, joined by six more in

full armor, forcing the allies forward whether they were going to walk or not. They all followed the small, red-eyed man with the long nose into the throne room. Atop a short final group of steps was a large, white marble throne with an equally large man in heavy all-gold armor with a lion's face embossed on his breastplate. The man wore a helmet, but his thick blonde hair stuck out enough from the back and sides, including where his short beard showed, to give the idea he had a mane of hair to suit his title.

"Approach, guests," said the man in a loud, deep voice. His voice filled the room like one might expect of a theater performer. Opren assumed he must be accustomed to announcements—or just loud, like Rutundo. But the volume had little to do with the presence; there was a charisma and intensity to his voice even Rutundo failed to project. "I am Lariat Rykeron, High King of Humans, Ruler of the Royal Sect and Head Royal of Everniot's Southland, Golden Lion King. What brings you?" King Rykeron stood as they approached.

"I am Princess Esmeraldi Avaria, with Princess Ruubi Avaria, of Avarinnia, Your Majesty," said Emerald with a tip of her head and gesture toward Ruubi, who also tipped her head. "We seek your responses to some questions so we might relay them to our parents, Queen Bellavuu and King Eeloneus of the Reiyal."

King Rykeron looked over the group silently as he stood atop the three steps to his throne. Then he stepped down slowly and his gaze held on Opren. Rykeron smiled and Opren's pulse quickened as he suddenly felt sick, angry, heavy. Something was extremely wrong, beyond what they had thought before—beyond what Opren expected anyway.

"It *is* you," said King Rykeron. "Heran was right." He indicated the short, long-nosed man. "Have you come to grant me the Goldlight weapon if I answer your questions?"

"Well, you have answered one already," said Opren. Heat was rushing through him, and he did not even care if he spoke informally or out of line. He held his eyes on King Rykeron and, had Emerald not placed her hand in his at that second, he might have shifted to Goldlighter form. "You cannot have the Goldlight sphere, King Rykeron."

"I could take it by force," said King Rykeron. He stepped toward Opren another few paces. Once within regular conversation distance, Opren realized the man must be broader than his father had been, but pure muscle, and nearly as tall as Rutundo, at least six feet-four inches. In a regular fight, the weight and size class would have been undeniably mismatched if Opren were to fight him. But that was before magic, before the Goldlight. That was before Opren's parents were murdered and he would no longer hold back even if it would get him killed.

"Should I call them, Majesty?" asked Heran with more enthusiasm than should fit the situation. "They will want to see the boy again after all this waiting."

Opren felt like a waterfall washed over him and like he was punched in the gut simultaneously. The heat was rising as he knew without a doubt that *them* meant the sleeskaxes. He hoped it was not true even as he knew it, but two silhouettes appeared in the doorway to a place behind the throne and the orange reptilian eyes were unmistakable.

"*You*," said Opren, almost unable to keep his voice stable. "You wanted the sleeskaxes to kill my parents because you want the Goldlight for a weapon!"

"You did take much longer than anticipated to come to find the sleeskaxes," said King Rykeron. "Most men do not have the patience for proper revenge, and the creatures made quite a stir of chaos to either lure you or locate you. When you met Jibna and removed his legs, he should have retrieved it, but I know now these creatures may not be able to hold the Goldlight sphere if it releases its energy, so it is better they lured you close. I did not expect you to deliver it to me directly. And the Goldlight *is* primarily a weapon, boy."

"At first, I only knew I wanted to kill the sleeskaxes," said Opren. Tears gathered under his eyes, but he blinked them away and kept his eyes on Rykeron's eyes. Rykeron removed his helmet, and his eyes were as gray as his emotion was apathetic toward Opren and his parents' murder.

"Do you plan to behead me now?" Rykeron gestured to his neck with a smirk.

"His eyes are gray," said Ruubi, as if they could not all see that.

"I noticed," said Opren. He had not meant to be rude to Ruubi, but he also had to figure out more important things than how to control his tone, like how to successfully kill the sleeskaxes, maybe even the king who permitted his parents' horrible death.

"High King Rykeron has rare yellow eyes," said Ruubi.

"Good observation, Ruubi," said Polaris. "I met you, King Rykeron, when you were about seventeen. Do you remember?"

"Polaris, the White Wizard," said the gold-armored king. "I do."

"What happened to your eyes?" asked Polaris. "What has gotten to you that has changed you? Did you lose your bloodline's power?"

"I have power I never had, goals I never realized were so valuable," said Rykeron.

"You never spoke this way in any of the stories I have heard, nor did you back then," said Polaris. "Something has poisoned you."

"That is not your concern at this time," said Rykeron. He seemed annoyed by the question, breaking the expectation of obvious authority in his voice. "Give me the Goldlight, Opren Saphren. I will not request something thrice."

"May I have some time to think it over?" asked Opren. "I've become attached to it. It was a gift from my late grandfather. You know how sentiment can be," he pushed his pain into his words as he allowed his voice to escalate, "especially once my parents were also dead because your fucking lizard mercenaries slaughtered and burned them!" He had no intention of giving the corrupt king the orb but, if there was no choice anyway, he wanted Rykeron to tell the sleeskaxes to attack. He wanted his chance to kill them for what they had done.

"Let me make your options clear, boy," said Rykeron, all hints of amusement gone from his face. "Heran, call the black dragon and finish the ritual." Heran ran from the room and Rykeron charged and grabbed Emerald before anyone could move. Opren expected him to be strong, but his speed matched Selios', so he must have been magically enhanced. Rykeron held a blade to Emerald's throat.

The sleeskaxes moved from their place in the shadows and each stabbed a claw into Ruubi and Zacharia. They laughed through their sharp teeth in their thin-skinned skulls and turned to Opren.

"Now, we mayyy kill you, boy," said one of the reptilian nightmares.

Opren shifted to Goldlighter form.

"Nobody else dies by your hand," said Opren. "Not around me. It's *your* turn."

"Not yet!" commanded Rykeron. "Do your other task."

The sleeskaxes whipped their heads toward the king, but they listened and dashed from the room. Opren turned to chase them, but Rykeron said, "I wouldn't leave, or she will die."

"What is their other task?" Opren turned back to the king.

Ra'ze glided toward Rykeron with a growl-shriek and outstretched claws. But Rykeron raised a hand at the wrist, not even releasing Emerald, and summoned ropes to bind the griffin's wings, causing her to stumble and be held to the stone floor. Then, Rykeron mouthed a spell that caused Ra'ze to slide back and become bound by the stone itself.

"Your pet will not save her," said Rykeron.

"Your mistake, King Rykeron, is thinking I would need to be saved," said Emerald. She dropped her weight and twisted from his grip while simultaneously knocking his knife-hand away from her enough to safely move. She ducked and rolled out of his reach and into a ready stance with her own dagger drawn. She then used a spell to change the dagger into a sword. Opren was impressed by her yet again.

"*Your* mistake, Princess, is the assumption you are any match for *me*," said Rykeron. His voice had no formal façade left, only a hateful drive to it. "I will kill you all if I must. The Goldlight *will* be mine to wield!"

"It will take much more to kill me," said Zacharia. "Did you not recognize who I am? Your guards did."

"You are not but a nuisance, especially without your other demon to make you truly a vicious threat," said Rykeron. "You should have taken the Goldlight yourself when you had the fleeting chance, if you wanted to stand against me."

"Conviction is much better a motivator than malice, King Rykeron," said Zacharia. He almost sounded like Zargunn, but he had more heart to his words and none of the other presence Ergunus had brought. "What you may not know is outside of possession, Demonic magic will not work on me if I don't allow it. Even my possession was originally willed by me, unknowingly at first, or it never would have worked."

"I do not need Demonic magic to kill you," said Rykeron. "And you may want to tend to your wounded who are less resilient." Rykeron lifted his chin in Ruubi's direction.

A bolt of lightning struck Rykeron's chest and sent the gold-armored king back into his throne. The marble seat cracked from the force of the impact. Rykeron shouted and flung his knife at Rufius as he stood again. Rufius caught the knife and threw it back. Rykeron deflected it with his armored forearm.

"I see you are a Reiycasteri," said Rykeron.

The sleeskaxes returned, nothing different about them, but what had been accomplished in the moments they were gone? There was no time to ask.

"Jibna, kill him." Rykeron gestured at one of the sleeskaxes, then toward Rufius.

The sleeskax sailed forward and produced a blade of

bone—by pulling it from his own forearm as it grew in seconds—clashing with Rufius' sword. The two locked in combat and Opren was unpleasantly surprised to see Jibna was as fast as Rufius. He could read their movements since he was in Goldlighter form, but they were like equals. And worse, none of Opren's group knew how to kill the sleeskaxes for certain yet, so only absolute victory and beheading them to burn the separated body parts was the current assumption.

"If you intend to kill my son, you will need to kill *me* first!" said Selios, charging Jibna. He never finished the dash because the other sleeskax zipped forward and struck him in the ribs with a bone blade of its own. Selios winced and turned on the second sleeskax.

"Your opponent isss Magva," hissed the sleeskax.

"I will kill you first, then," said Selios.

Opren wanted to kill the sleeskaxes himself, but the threat had grown from one to just his life to one that could impact a kingdom. He knew King Rykeron was who he needed to fight, while the sleeskaxes were occupied by Rufius and Selios. He turned back to the king to find Emerald had already begun to clash swords with the large gold-armored man.

"Opren, you need to make sure whatever dragon Heran was sent to summon does not get summoned," said Emerald as she flipped away from Rykeron for a few seconds, until the king charged. She rolled out of his path. "If it is what I think, it will cause destruction to entire cities, worse than gruveks. I can handle this."

"This can all end if you give me the Goldlight sphere and kneel, Opren," said Rykeron. Emerald took the opportunity while he paused to sweep Rykeron's legs to trip him. Rykeron growled as he fell on his back. He rolled back into a standing position and a smoky black aura began to come from him. "You foolish people will do as I command or die for treason!"

"Lariat Rykeron," said Polaris. "It is you who has been foolish. Demonic power is not meant for mortal men, and you have become a corrupt version of your previous self, weaker and a puppet shown an illusion of power, instead of the lion among men you once were."

Opren wanted to stay and help against any of the immediate danger to his friends, but he knew going after Heran as Emerald said was more important at that moment—her judgment and knowledge always bested his in that kind of situation. Polaris and Emerald could hold off the king until he did that—he hoped at least. He ran through the same door behind the throne Heran ran through a few moments before. When he reached the end of a long corridor, he entered a cracked door and found the small, long-nosed man chanting something while moving his hands, facing a cloud of black.

"No!" said Heran as he glanced back to see Opren. He frantically continued to chant and wave but Opren ran up to him, grabbed him and slammed his back into a wall.

"What are you summoning? Is it a dragon?" asked Opren, firmly pressing Heran's chest with his forearm to keep the small demon-man pinned.

"It's more than a dragon." Despite having to force the words under Opren's pressure, Heran had a sickening grin. "I am fusing a Black Ur-Dragon with cursed power to make it breathe black fire, the kind only Demonics use. This world's magic cannot stop black fire."

"Well, it's good I interrupted you," said Opren. He slammed Heran's head into the wall to knock the demon-man unconscious. Then he summoned two golden energy swords and threw them into the black cloud. They broke the cloud and huge holes were made as they flew through to the other wall. Whatever corrupt energy Heran had conjured seemed to have the same weakness to the Goldlight as the demon in the house in the woods. "Awesome."

Opren focused and pulled more Goldlight essence into himself, then thought of the biggest sword he could as he conjured another energy blade. It worked; floating in front of him was a massive sword, at least ten feet long and a foot wide. He grabbed the extra-long handle of the sword with both hands and sent the giant blade into the cloud of corrupt energy. The whole cloud imploded, and golden flecks rained down before nothing was there. Opren knew such a large sword would make no sense in a regular fight, but for the purpose which he just used it, it was impressive and fun he managed to summon one so enormous.

As Opren reached the throne room again, he arrived at the very moment Selios lost to Magva. Selios had cut the torso and leg of the sleeskax to shreds, then sliced off its hand and used a massive gale to slam it into the wall, but the creature just healed and got up to dash at Selios. The sleeskax sliced off Selios' sword hand and plunged a claw completely through Selios' chest at once. Magva removed his bloodied claw and Selios fell to his knees, coughing up blood that only added to the large amount pouring from his chest.

"NO!" yelled Opren. The sleeskax turned to him. "You killed my father and my mentor. I will *end* you!" He charged and summoned the longsword from the Goldlight orb itself. When he clashed blades with the sleeskax, Magva's bone blade broke with ease. Opren spun and sliced through the sleeskax's sword arm, then gashed the creature's body. He stabbed the sleeskax through the chest, removed the sword and beheaded Magva to guarantee there was no chance the monster could heal or consciously regenerate, unless sleeskaxes truly were unkillable. The body fell without further movement.

So they can *die. Finally.*

Rufius was still fighting Jibna with neither of them gaining the upper hand but, as Selios bled to death, Rufius made the mistake of chancing a glance. Jibna kneed him and disarmed him in that second. Opren was in front of his rival-partner before either the sleeskax or Rufius could register what was going on—in fact before Opren realized he himself had moved; pure instinct caused him to change positions and throw up his sword to block Jibna's clawed hand.

Jibna's hand met the golden blade and was sliced in half all the way to the elbow. Opren barely felt the resistance, more like cutting butter than flesh and bone. He kicked the sleeskax as hard as he could—which was clearly harder than he ever could have before, because Jibna flew back into the wall and cracked the polished white stone with his slender reptilian body. Opren summoned a Goldlight blade and waved his hand to cause the blade to slice off the sleeskax's skeletal head before the creature could retaliate.

"I'm so sorry, Rufius," said Opren. "This was meant to be my chance to avenge my parents' death, not an opportunity for these monsters to kill someone else's."

"He would not have stayed behind even if I begged," said Rufius. "And neither would I have. We are warriors and this threat could not be ignored."

"You are all dying gradually," said Rykeron. He body-checked Emerald which knocked her back and off-balance. "The rose-haired princess is barely holding on, your most experienced warrior will be dead without a doubt, and your cursed ally is fighting off a headache for the second time. What hope do you have? Princess, you will never beat me like this."

"I'm not done trying," said Emerald. She stood again and her body was glowing white. She was using Selios' technique to make her body stronger, more resilient, a weapon barehanded.

Emerald's clothes were torn in several places and there were spots of red scattered over her shirt and left pant-leg. She had been cut multiple times, but she was healing herself. As she lunged and managed to break the king's armor with her fist wrapped in spirit energy, the king cut her arm. The gash was so deep Opren was concerned she would not heal in time to move out of the way, but she *instantly* began to heal; the separated flesh stitched itself back together in only three seconds. Emerald was somehow able to heal herself without even moving or uttering a spell-word, just like the sleeskaxes!

"I am not easy to kill," said Emerald, her eyes on the king with an intensity Opren had yet to see. It was not simply anger or motivation. And then he noted her violet eyes were glowing.

"She has a Runaic bloodline trait," said Zacharia with

a forced grin. He appeared to be over his severe state of a headache, at least to the point he could function. "I don't know if she can kill Rykeron, but he won't likely kill her."

"I should... help," Ruubi strained between coughs and gasps of pain. "Emmi needs to heal...me." She still held her gut and her next cough brought up blood.

"Shit." Opren turned back to Emerald and Rykeron. "Ruubi needs to be healed before she is as bad as Selios! She's losing too much blood!"

"Relista!" swore Emerald. She dodged another of Rykeron's wide swings—this time with a summoned war ax. She rolled away from the king and turned to Ruubi. Rykeron threw a knife into her back but, after a yell in pain, she pulled it out and healed immediately. She knelt by Ruubi as Opren tossed a Goldlight blade into the next knife Rykeron threw, knocking the knife away and melting the spot where the blades collided. "Ruubi, you will be all right. I am sorry I made you wait." She continued talking to Ruubi in Elvish as she worked.

Opren put his body in front of Emerald and Ruubi as he held Rykeron's eyes, each man waiting for the other to move. Opren knew how to do this; he had many times in regular fights back home. Home: the place Rykeron had allowed to be burned down, maybe even ordered to be destroyed, along with the murder of his parents. Rykeron, who had charge over the monster that killed his mentor, Selios. Rykeron, already a king, who wanted to steal his most sentimental possession and use it for unnecessary gain or further dominance. Opren would *not* allow that to happen.

Rykeron turned his right hip enough to be noticed, especially with all the reflecting golden armor inside a white stone room. Opren intercepted the strike, blocked a kick —which still caused him to stagger back two steps with how much force Rykeron could generate—then countered by absorbing the Goldlight essence and mimicking Emerald and Selios when they enhanced themselves with magic. He cast the body-as-a-weapon spell his own way and the golden light coming from him solidified into a thick line of an aura that traced him. He punched Rykeron in the gut, cracking the armor further than Emerald had already done. Another punch cracked the gauntlet Rykeron used to block, then he kicked Rykeron to knock the king back a few paces, shattering and melting what was left of the armor around the king's forearms.

"What in the Realms of Hell is this?" growled Rykeron as he watched the armor fall and deteriorate. The "melting" was more like a *dissolving* from the magic, really, but since metal itself did not simply dissolve in air it was difficult to say what it did. It was like nothing he had ever seen—also true for Rykeron, evidently.

"It's the power you want to steal from me, didn't you know that?" said Opren. "Or did you only care that it was considered superior to all other weapons?"

"You don't deserve such power, butcher's boy!"

"But neither do you, High King. I was given the power and wish to use it for the good of others. You only want to use it for yourself."

"*Revenge* is a personal goal," said Rykeron.

"I would not have needed to care for revenge or any of this if not for your damn sleeskaxes and your actions now!"

Opren lunged forward again and pulled as much of the Goldlight into himself as he could. The rush was nearly overwhelming, but he held it. The two golden combatants clashed with a sound that reverberated throughout the stone throne-hall with such force it could be felt.

Opren wanted to check on Rufius and Ruubi, but he knew if he took his eyes off Rykeron, there was a chance the king would gain the upper hand or kill Emerald while she healed Ruubi. As if in response to his thoughts, he had his answer.

"Rufius and I have ensured the sleeskaxes are truly dead and burned the bodies," said Zacharia. "But I still feel the sensation of a sort of Demonic presence."

Rykeron let off the charcoal smoke of an aura once again and Opren realized his gray eyes and dark aura must mean he was possessed or not the real Rykeron. Emerald had mentioned magical shapeshifting was a concern for royals in Avarinnia, hence the enchanted tattoos. But this man in golden armor was too strong to be a fake, unless he was really some powerful demon posing as Rykeron. Rykeron might be himself, but his mind must be possessed the way Zacharia had become Zargunn, Opren thought.

"I have more power still," said Rykeron. "This earthly armor is nothing important."

The smoky aura poured out of Rykeron to form a cloud around him as he opened his arms wide, like one would to indicate or invite an embrace but, in what seemed like slow motion, he brought his hands together in a single clap which shook the room. Strangely, Opren could not hear the clap and moving while he watched was sluggish, so he never prevented it in time. Then, dizziness hit as he saw everyone else collapse. Everything was a blur and weight pulled down all of his senses before…nothing…

26

Opren opened his eyes and saw Rykeron approaching him. The king paused when he noticed Opren was conscious.

"Even though it forced you back to normal," said Rykeron. "You still woke in seconds. Impressive for another human, especially one not of this realm for your entire life."

Opren glanced down to see his aura was gone; he felt like he expended all his spirit energy so no surprise. But if Rykeron had used a Demonic ability to cause them all to pass out and drain their power, the Goldlight energy could not be removed the same way; Opren hoped, at least. He stood slowly, ready to defend any way he could.

Rykeron walked past Opren a few feet and crouched to reach the stone floor. Opren worried Rykeron was going to kill Emerald while she could not fight back, but he picked up something instead. It was the Goldlight orb.

No, no, no! Opren grew frantic. But what could he do without the Goldlight? Rykeron already stood a chance against him with all the power he could pull from the orb, but if Rykeron had the orb and he had only his wind, what could be done? Rufius was much more practiced, and lightning was a better offensive element to wield than wind or any of the others, and even Rufius had failed. If only Emerald was conscious, she could still fight. If she did not need to heal Ruubi, she might have been able to go on awhile.

Zacharia opened his eyes and began to stand. Rykeron snapped his head toward him. Zacharia was still in his alternate Demonic form. It was odd he still held the form, even after the spell Rykeron cast forced Opren out of Goldlighter form. Then again, did Demonic forms and Runaic magic forms work the same way? That would need to be a question for after they survived—if they survived. *Don't think that way. We must survive!* Zacharia spread his arms the way Rykeron had done, then he clapped the same way.

Everyone woke at once.

"*What* are you?" asked Rykeron, eyes wide.

"A cursed man and a demon in one body, even without my possessor," said Zacharia. "Truly, I do not know the extent of it. But I am able to copy anything a demon or Demonic magic can do—or reverse it, in this case. Now that I am in control of this spell, you cannot do it again or I will clap along with you."

"Damn you! You are becoming much more than a nuisance—a hindrance—and will need to die," said Rykeron. His voice contained something else this time, similarly to Ergunus being behind Zacharia's voice when Zacharia was Zargunn. The king was undoubtedly not controlling all his own actions with only his own intentions intact; something else was at work.

"Could you even use the Goldlight while you have a demon inside?" asked Opren.

Rykeron turned back to Opren and said, "I do not have a demon in me, boy."

"Then where do you get that smoke cloud of an aura? How could you do that clap spell to knock us out? Those seem demon-like to me," said Opren.

"He is still Rykeron," said Polaris. "I already attempted to exorcise him without notice while everyone else fought. It is why I have not fought as well. I wasted time and energy doing that because I also thought he is possessed in the way Zargunn was. I am at the ready to prevent corruption to you all."

"Good conclusion, old man," said Rykeron. "You are clearly a gifted wizard, but I must kill you for treason as well."

"I thought treason included going against the kingdom," said Opren. "Which you have done. We have only gone against you. That means you have also committed treason."

"I am the High King of Humans and Everniot," said Rykeron. "You are just a butcher's son! You do not tell me which decisions will be good for *my* kingdom!"

"But it *is* the right of other royals to challenge you," said Emerald. She stood and approached Opren, facing the king. "In the interim of our parents, Queen Bellavuu and King Eeloneus, taking your throne, I, Princess Esmeraldi Avaria, invoke the Right of Royals to unseat you due to being unfit for duty as the High King of Everniot. You may appoint an acting high king, or simply step down and allow us to choose. You know what the spelled contract will do if you refuse." She held her gaze on him sternly.

Rykeron laughed. "Let the butcher's boy be king then. It will only last until your death, at which time I will reclaim the title."

"Do you agree Opren Saphren should be acting High King of Humans and Everniot?" asked Emerald.

"To end this charade and your stalling… I do agree," said Rykeron. "With that complete…" Rykeron summoned another ax and threw it at Emerald. "Die."

Emerald dodged the ax with ease, evidently ready for Rykeron to do something like that. Emerald could now fight because Ruubi was healed and had begun to recover, though not enough to fight herself. A bit of morale rose in Opren, even some comfort as Barbosa sat with Ruubi. The granwolf had watched the whole time, unable to do much against armor and magic, but he could now at least keep an eye on Ruubi's condition and provide conversation as she recovered.

Rufius attempted to cast more lightning at Rykeron but his electricity fizzled out upon impact because Rykeron used his dark energy to resist it. Rufius must have used too much spirit energy against the sleeskax, so he gave up and sat with his father's lifeless body to recover and grieve.

"You better not die too," he directed to Emerald and Opren. Opren caught the desperation behind the sharp tone. Rufius intended to be flawless and strong, but Opren knew firsthand how much harder it was to feign strength or pride in the face of the death of a loved one.

"Fools!" Rykeron shook his head. "You are only still alive because I have not used all I have to kill you. Distractions and minions have brought your numbers down to half. Now, I will demonstrate why I am fated to remain above you."

Rykeron's aura grew until a black cloud shaped him like an armor made of thick smoke; it billowed and rippled around him. Opren could feel the energy in Rykeron, despite not being in Goldlighter form. Zacharia held his head again and appeared to experience brief vertigo, but he caught his balance. Opren hoped Zacharia would be stable enough if he needed to prevent any other spells Rykeron might attempt.

Emerald did not wait for Rykeron to finish whatever he was preparing to do. She enveloped her body in the white energy from Selios' technique, called her sword from the floor several feet away to her hand, and struck Rykeron between the places where his armor had split. Not much blood was drawn, but when she pulled back her sword and punched him, the remaining front of his breastplate broke away. She danced around to his back and struck again, removing every bit of the armor with another brutal punch.

Rykeron absorbed the black cloud around him as Emerald readied herself for another strike, then he caught her sword with his bare hand and snapped the blade. His hand bled for a few seconds, then healed as quickly as Emerald had. He grinned and kicked Emerald, knocking her back and into the wall to Opren's left. There was a frightening crack as she hit the white stone. Emerald stood, and her violet eyes glowed. Opren thought the impact might have cracked her skull or spine, but somehow her healing abilities—or the Runaic bloodline magic she had, according to Zacharia—must have saved her.

"I see I need to stop both of you at once," said Rykeron. "Alternating my attention has delayed this long enough."

Rykeron's black smoky aura poured out of him again as he held his hands apart, palms facing each other. It began to form a sphere of gaseous black energy. The ball of black smoke grew. Opren ran at Rykeron, but the larger man kicked Opren, knocking him back and to the ground. Zacharia tried to do something with his hands, but Rykeron only scoffed.

"Ha! You are not in a state to take my spell away, even if you could muster the strength," said Rykeron.

Emerald charged Rykeron and kicked the back of his knee, dropping him enough to reach his head. She summoned Rufius' sword to her hand and moved to behead the former king. Rykeron opened his hands quickly and a black shadow covered the room while some sort of force pushed against everyone. Ra'ze screeched and fell, Zacharia was thrown against the wall he was near, Emerald was blown back before she could follow through with her slice. Rufius, Barbosa, and Ruubi were pinned to the ground. Opren felt a sharp pain hit his chest as he flew back across the floor, no longer able to resist the push.

Opren looked around, desperately hoping no others were dead. Ra'ze had been struck with one of the weapons that lay on the ground. Opren winced. He realized the sharp pain in the right side of his chest was from Emerald's broken sword flying by him. He was not pierced like Ra'ze, but he had been cut as it struck him and fell at his side. It hurt, it bled, but it was not life-threatening. Opren staggered as he got to his feet. Ra'ze did not get to her feet.

"How do you keep getting up again?" asked Rykeron. "Your princess friend has more innate resilience than you, and I have taken her down finally, yet you are like a bug that won't remain squashed."

"I doubt she is dead," said Opren. *I hope. Please survive, Emerald. I can't lose you now too.*

"That may be wishful thinking," said Rykeron. "She was hit with the full force of my spell's blast and cut by the weapon she tried to use to behead me."

"I'll have to have faith," said Opren.

Rykeron scoffed, "Faith? What faith? Who gave you a naïve idea that faith could help someone?"

"I have faith in her ability to survive," said Opren. "And my mother who you had killed gave me that principle."

Rykeron walked toward Opren, still holding the Goldlight sphere. He looked at the golden orb, then at Opren and smiled.

"Looks like I still obtained what is better suited to me than you. Now, tell me the spell-word and bow to your king. End this foolishness."

Opren stared into Rykeron's eyes with all the hatred that had built in him for the man, the sleeskaxes, the actions that had caused his parents' death and the destruction of his home. He did his best to convey that and the emotions he had for Emerald and Selios and all of his allies through his eyes, his face.

"You are *not* my king. You made me acting High King of Humans, right? And I did not grow up in your kingdom, remember? So, you are just a corrupt ruler to me," said Opren. "I will not bow to you, Lariat Rykeron. My name is Opren Saphren, Keeper of the Goldlight by choice of my late grandfather. And the spell-word is…" Rykeron was then close enough for Opren to try his idea. "*Woffrumdus!*"

The orb flew from Rykeron's hand into Opren's as he rolled back to be sure to avoid any potential retaliatory strikes from Rykeron. Rykeron shouted as Opren shifted to Goldlighter form. The rush was more intense than the last few times he had changed, and he welcomed it. He took a ready stance and produced a Goldlight katana as he shifted the usual longsword that came from the orb into a katana as well.

Rykeron built up his aura as he charged toward Opren. He swung wildly, growling when he missed. Opren had brought him to the point of rage-fighting. Rykeron was no longer focusing on technique, only power and aggressive intent; that was when a fighter would always lose against an opponent who could control themselves and respond properly. Even without the immense power of the Goldlight, Opren had a slight upper hand by fighting to survive, not out of blind rage.

Opren dodged and deflected several attacks before he countered with a slash across Rykeron's unarmored chest. Rykeron responded by building more aura, but the slash seemed to have flecks of gold within the red of Rykeron's blood; the aura never reached the spot, as though it couldn't. Rykeron looked down to see he was not healing and swore.

Opren smiled. "The Goldlight doesn't like Demonic or corrupt energy."

Rykeron charged again, but Opren was more than ready for it and produced four energy daggers in the air while he blocked Rykeron's ax with the dual katanas. He disarmed Rykeron with a flick of his wrist and a pivot of his body, then dropped the second katana to grab a dagger and stabbed Rykeron in the thigh, then did the same for the other leg. Opren spun to get behind Rykeron and grabbed the other two daggers one at a time and stabbed Rykeron in the spine, one high and one low.

"How...is this possible?" asked Rykeron as he tried to fight against the pain and near paralysis, falling to his knees. He actually managed to move, but Opren was already in front of him. "I am the king, and you are only a butcher's boy. My master said you would be no hindrance."

"No matter who we are or where we come from," said Opren as he grabbed the golden energy katana. "We have a chance to do something great with hard work and persistence. My mother taught me that. She would also suggest I don't kill you, but she is dead because of you, so I am making my own choice."

Opren plunged the physical katana through Rykeron's gut, then impaled the man's central chest with the energy katana in his other hand, being sure to miss Rykeron's heart. Rykeron toppled backward with a groan and fell unconscious.

Opren was not sure if Rykeron was dead, but the former king would not get up again soon. For now, that was enough...maybe better. For now, he needed to check on Emerald. She would need to heal everyone she could, and he hoped more than anything she was still alive and not critically injured. He changed back to normal form and the golden katana transformed back into the orb, removing the sword from Rykeron's torso, and floated to his hand. Opren ran over to where Emerald lay and crouched down.

"Hey," he said. "Emerald. Wake up, Liileiy." He nudged her. She did not move, so he tried louder, "Emerald. Emerald! Wake up!" He pushed on her shoulders again and kissed her forehead. "Please, wake up." He waited a few more seconds before he opened his mouth again.

Then she opened her beautiful violet eyes and inhaled. She bolted up to a sitting position.

"What happened? Oh, did you kill Rykeron?" she asked as she looked around, her gaze landing on Rykeron's body. She looked back at Opren, part relief and part concern in her eyes. He expected the concern was for his emotions and actions, while the relief was due to the end of the fatal encounter. "Did you?"

A wheezing sound occurred and the two looked as a black billowing cloud suddenly rose from Rykeron's body and imploded. What was left was a shower of golden light that reminded Opren of tiny fireworks and glitter. Rykeron moved, but he did not speak or sit up; he was still not conscious, but he had survived.

"I suppose not," said Opren. "But he is finished. I beat him. And I'm finished with my retaliation for my parents' murder. Are you all right? Are you able to heal the others?"

"Yes," said Emerald. "I cannot bring back Shela Selios...or

Ra'ze." Her expression dropped once when she mentioned her uncle's death, then her brows creased in the middle as she took note of the griffin's fatal condition. "But I can heal any other problems."

"He is no longer possessed," said Zacharia, standing again. Opren was impressed at how many times Zacharia managed to get up again without assistance. Then again, Opren was surprised at how many times he had done so himself. "The headache is gone, and that cloud must have been the Demonic energy. My theory is the Goldlight destroys Demonic energy as well as it cuts through normal metals, maybe better. I might have killed myself by using it had I managed to steal it while possessed. Well done, Opren."

Emerald removed some shrapnel from Rufius' leg. Then she healed him and made sure Ruubi was in the condition needed to walk on her own. Even with magical healing it seemed severe wounds needed time to fully recover, but Ruubi was able to walk.

"The next person who puts something in me needs to start gently, and I want it to be more fun for us both," said Ruubi as she stood.

"I think you deserve that after going through this," said Emerald. Ruubi smiled.

Emerald checked on Polaris, but he had already healed himself and removed an apparent Demonic poison that came with being hit by the aura. Opren had not realized he felt sick due to something like that until Polaris also removed his infection; he had assumed it was just fatigue from the intense battle. He felt twice the energy and no nausea once Polaris had removed the corrupt energy.

"I suspect once you really master the Goldlight, corruption won't even touch you," said Polaris. "Be careful in the meantime, though."

Polaris made a bubble of translucent white energy to place around Selios' body, then another to carry Rykeron's unconscious body, and had the energy containers float behind them as they exited the throne room and walked down the white stone stairs and out of the palace. Something was different about the guards as they exited, as if the men in armor were confused why they had been so aggressive to civilians.

"What will you do now, acting High King of Everniot?" asked Rufius with a short laugh.

"I don't want to remain king of anything," said Opren. "I only ever wanted to help my family and be the best fighter. Other titles and authority aren't my thing, really."

"Well, you should keep the title for now, until you decide on a proper replacement," said Emerald. "I will help you. We will need to return here after we bring Shela Selios' back to Avarinnia. These people need help to rebuild and to be sure no other creatures are going to cause a problem."

"I will do my best," said Opren.

Rykeron woke two days later, but Polaris cast a sort of sleeping spell on the former king for the remainder of the journey to Avarinnia. Everyone was thankful there were no further encounters with any vicious creatures, dangerous people, or—especially—demons. They reached the Elven capital city in only a few hours longer than their trip took to reach the Royal Sect in haste. Once Rykeron was placed in a prison cell, they all gladly rested.

27

Lariat Rykeron regained consciousness somewhere he did not recognize. He looked around to see pink prison bars and stone walls. He attempted to rise to a seated position, but his back and legs ached so severely, he chose to wait. He turned his head toward the bars and noticed a young man with brown hair outside of the cell.

At first, the young man was blurry but after focusing for about ten seconds it became clear he was Opren Saphren.

"We made sure you would not die," said Opren. "But Queen Bellavuu thought it was safer to leave your pain and non-lethal damages. You are too powerful to risk your escape."

"Queen Bellavuu and pink materials for a prison cell," said Lariat. "You have brought me to Avarinnia."

"Right," said Opren with a single nod. "We needed to return the great warrior, father, brother, and uncle you had killed. It was convenient we could lock you here until a council of Elven royals and elders could decide your fate."

"I would argue my defense to be that I was possessed but, unlike usual possessions, I was completely conscious of all my words and actions," said Lariat. He felt weak, fatigued, useless.

He lay on the ground as he spoke to a boy who was not even a royal, instead of the other party bowing to him. Yet he knew his mistake. "A king should be the holder of such power. I never would have corrupted my own kingdom; I love my kingdom. But a small-town butcher's son has no claim when it comes to a power that has been said to start and end wars, shape kingdoms, and incite destinies."

"And attract violence and murder and loss, evidently," said Opren. "I recognize you were possessed, but I want to know why you care now or cared before that. Why do you, as yourself, want my family's orb and the Goldlight power?"

"Aside from fearing a power greater than my army's in the kingdom, unless I hold that power?" said Lariat. "I have been High King for over a decade, and I deserve the power more than you. That is the selfish reason you must be seeking. And I had hoped to protect other kingdoms, wanted to cripple enemies before much could happen during a battle."

"You let Demonic power or some other kind of chaos into the kingdom, Rykeron," said Opren. This lowborn commoner was actually judging Lariat Rykeron, the High King of Everniot, and Lariat's face felt tight and hot in that moment. "You already did exactly what you say you wanted to prevent. And you took my family from me. Then, you corrupted more of your sect of the kingdom, finally allowing it to spread just for this power."

"You have no ri–

"I have *every* right!" Opren slammed into the bars with his palms. His eyes welled with tears while his brow presented anger. "You took my parents and forced this path on me, which now can come to an end with your judgment by the king and queen here. You made me acting High King out of arrogance, but now I have every right to judge you, to break you down, to have beaten you. You deserve this. You never were my king, but I would have done the same thing even if I idolized you as I am sure some citizens did. Polaris told me stories of your past. You ruined yourself!"

"There is nothing I can do to restore what you have lost," said Lariat. "But I will do whatever I can to assist in restorations and setting things right, if allowed. I am sorry for the outcome of my actions and do not seek to dispute the guilt I should hold."

"I will consider requesting it because you admit the guilt," said Opren.

"The request need not be passed on," said the voice of a woman, and a youthful-yet-wise looking Elven woman stepped near to the cell to stand beside Opren. She had hair to her waist with blue streaks in golden blonde that gave off a sheen Lariat had never quite seen. He knew of Queen Bellavuu's description, but he had never officially met the Queen of Avarinnia in person. She had more presence than he had expected, and yet seemed so peaceful despite tales of hard choices and strength. "I am Queen Bellavuu, and I will consider the request tonight. Do not expect a light judgment because elves are generally people of balance and diplomacy." Her tone was even, controlled, but it held a stern adamancy.

"I suspect you will need to discuss the matter with the king as well," said Lariat.

"I do not need my husband to choose what to do with you," said Queen Bellavuu. "And he is too biased in his judgment, so he has suggested I make the choice alone; you are the overarching cause of his brother's death, after all."

"Ah, that would make his judgment severe," said Lariat. He struggled to sit up and managed to drag himself to a wall for support. Even leaning against the wall brought pressure and discomfort to his entire spine, but it was not more than he could handle. The new position allowed him to take in Opren's and Bellavuu's faces properly. Lariat could see the same eyes of the princess Opren called Emerald, Esmeraldi, but with less fire and eagerness within them. And the Elven queen had brilliant blue eyes, instead of the rare violet of the princess'. He coughed once, wincing from the pain, and said, "I hope your daughter who was injured by a sleeskax is in better health, at least. I am sincerely sorry for how far out of hand I allowed things to soar, particularly as it directly affected your family. Your other daughter, the one called Emerald, with the violet eyes, is something. She did well to invoke the Right of Royals."

"I do appreciate the respectful admission and apology," said Queen Bellavuu. Opren turned his head slightly, staring at the queen with the look of one who wants to say something contradictory but has not decided how to word it. "But what of your own people who reside in your immediate sect? You caused casualties of *your own* men and women. That is exactly the sort of needless violence we elves detest and prevent whenever possible."

"That," said Lariat, grunting as he attempted to shift his positon again—which only caused more discomfort and a pulse of pain. "That is something I neither expect nor deserve forgiveness for doing. But I do intend to fix the damage if I am allowed to leave alive."

"Elves do not sentence people to execution like you humans," said Queen Bellavuu. "We prefer you live, but live with your guilt or redeem yourself by cleaning up your own mess. As it stands, we will never restore your title and authority. The length of your sentence here or elsewhere prior to aiding the restoration and after is what I will contemplate with my council tonight. You will learn in the morning."

Opren and Queen Bellavuu exited the dungeon. Lariat remained against the wall for several minutes, then noticed a subtle change in the shadows, just enough to change the light through the windows. Had it been night and no light were shining through the cell windows, he would never have seen it. He was glad to retain his trained perceptions, even in such a useless state of physical disability.

"Who is there?" asked Lariat.

"How long did you know I was here?" asked a girlish voice. A young woman stepped into the light and her rose-petal red hair and porcelain skin revealed the princess who had nearly died facing Lariat's sleeskaxes. "You are more perceptive than most men I meet." She leaned on the bars of the cell, her position revealing much more cleavage than any princess should present, her white shirt sleeveless. Her eyes were a green Lariat had not noticed during the fighting. Then again, he was not himself and was not paying enough attention to take note while disregarding the group as fools and weaklings—which he now regretted and felt like a fool himself for having done. The princess had something in her eyes that reminded Lariat of himself the first time he had lost a fight in a humiliating way and hated the foe for it. But her eyes revealed something else he could not quite place as well.

"I only just noticed, Princess…?"

"Ruubi. Do you often forget the names of the women you try to have killed?"

"Princess Ruubi," said Lariat. She stared into his eyes with that combination of what he could not place and his own sort of resentment as she casually leaned on the bars. It was as if her body said "you want to bed me" while her eyes said "I will enjoy watching you suffer" yet…Lariat was growing frustrated by his lack of recognition of the other thing in her eyes. "I am glad to see you are well. What would you have the queen do with me?"

"'Well' is not the best way to describe me currently," said Ruubi. "You are the reason my sister's Laleiy's parents are dead, the reason I almost bled to death, and the reason my Shela—uncle, in your language—is dead. I am known to be promiscuous and have no problem enjoying myself, yet I tried to sleep with a man last night to let off some stress after the battle with you. Images of that monster under your command invaded my mind when the man tried to penetrate me. I imagined I was again impaled by the sleeskax, not penetrated in a pleasant way by a Human or Elven man. I nearly threw him from the bed, and he left in a bad state. I don't care what my mother does with you."

"I forgot to tell the queen of the one who was my master," said Lariat. "Please, relay the message for me. The whole kingdom might have a problem."

"I don't care about what you have to say," said Ruubi. She smiled. "But I see you have yellow eyes again."

Ruubi turned and silently left the dungeon before Lariat could say anything more. On top of being irritatingly unsure of how to read the red-haired Elven princess, he was already exhausted and forced his body to lie down once more. He allowed sleep to take him some long period of dull pain later.

28

The following morning, Opren received the Elven Nobility Seal tattoo, in deep green like Emerald's. King Eeloneus himself granted him the tattoo on his upper right arm, and Queen Bellavuu cast the enchantment on it as would have occurred for someone in the royal family. Opren felt honored and slightly out-of-place to be given such a high reward of respected symbolism.

"You helped the whole kingdom," said King Eeloneus. "You do deserve this. It is not simply for show."

"Ve harron, King Eeloneus," said Opren as the king finished the tattoo.

The queen finished her enchantment and added, "And you did not back down or give up against the unlikely odds you faced. Your dedication and persistence deserve their own rewards. You are a good man. Human or elf should respect you. You might even be able to find favor with dragons, as we have."

"Ve harron suuveiy, Queen Bellavuu," said Opren with a bow to both the queen and king. "I never expected such high praise when I chose this path."

"And that is all the more reason you deserve it," said

King Eeloneus. "Arrogance deserves nothing. Pride is usually misplaced. A goal of honor is not quite the same as doing something honorable to make the right decision, no matter the circumstances or lack of glory."

Opren had no further response, so he just smiled and nodded. Emerald brought him away as she noticed he was finished and probably seemed unsure what to do next during the short ceremony. A small crowd of attending elves, made up of high-ranking warriors, *Leiyuum Spewe*, Ruubi, Sapphire, Rufius, and a few nobles applauded as the two exited the throne room.

A few hours later, Queen Bellavuu had made her decision regarding Lariat Rykeron; she would allow him to return to the Royal Sect to aid in restoration plans as requested if Opren needed him, but until called upon he was to be indefinitely exiled outside of the borders of his former kingdom or her Elvish Sect, somewhere ruled by neither humans nor elves. He would be a free man, but nowhere he would have influence or the ability to gain power—to be sure, he would receive a facial marking to represent exile as a criminal. If he did anything suspicious or broke any further laws or ethical boundaries, she would have him immediately arrested and thrown into the deep dungeons of Luun Ellsmeria, the Luunal capital city, until his death.

Rykeron was given the news and agreed to the terms. He even preferred them, saying he was weak and should never have given in to such corrupt power as he had; he would earn his way back to any possible redemption.

Opren was not sure yet whether he believed the sentiment, but he appreciated the willingness on the former king's part. He was glad he had not killed Rykeron, because the man with a decade of experience would be a valuable help in fixing or running the Royal Sect if Opren had any questions. Then again, he hoped King Eeloneus, Queen Bellavuu, Emerald and her sisters would be enough help so he did not need the man who had caused him so much grief. But he also did not need the guilt of killing another human on his conscience.

Unfortunately, the last scheduled event of the day was not the happiest one, at least not entirely. Rufius took it upon himself to plan Selios' funeral with Sapphire and the king and queen. Opren learned Reiyal did not dress in black for funerals, but they wore white with light green make-up to represent balance and life as a cycle of pure nature, mostly focused on the life celebrations to follow the ceremony. Emerald had some tailors fit him for the events.

There were so many people at the funeral Opren assumed nearly every citizen of Avarinnia was in attendance. Selios had been a truly special warrior, a truly special person to many; King Eeloneus stated this thought aloud during his parting words about his brother. Opren had no idea what to say in such a circumstance among royal elves or even the warriors, so he remained silent throughout all the proceedings until the feast during the celebration of Selios' life (and all life), when Rufius approached him.

"Opren," said Rufius as he sat across from Opren and Emerald with a plate of food. "What do you intend to do next? I suspect I will need to take my father's place by default for now, unless you want to assign me to be a warrior for the Royal Sect."

"I don't plan to remain king." Opren gave a laugh. "I am sure you will make your father proud. You never mentioned taking his place before, but with your level of dedication and discipline, I see how it can suit you."

"Thank you, friend," said Rufius. "I do wish he could have seen us come together as friends after our tension."

"Maybe he's looking down," said Opren.

"What?" asked Rufius.

"Sorry, do you not have that expression? It means he is watching from the afterlife or Heaven or stars, which people in my realm assume is above us," said Opren.

"That is a nice thought," said Rufius. "Maybe. It would be like him to know more than we expect because he is always watching or listening. We call it listening from beyond."

"You know, lightning is a bit too blatant, even loud," said Opren. "The spying part might not suit you so well."

"How can one see me if they are already struck by lightning or unconscious?" asked Rufius, his smirk reaching the corners of his mouth.

Opren smiled. "True."

Opren walked through the gardens in Avarinnia with Emerald after they ate. It was the first instance he had taken the time to appreciate up close the huge flowering bushes, colorful vines, different-shaped fruits ranging from reds to yellows to something blue he had never seen before. The gardens were set up much like a maze but without the chaos, structured and organized with clear paths. Small trees lined the sides with the bushes where no flowers or fruits grew. It was peaceful. That must have been the calm and appreciation of nature the elves wanted to maintain regularly, and he was able to take it in without the need to move on to the next fight for the first time in a while. Emerald's presence made the peace turn to joy.

"Are you going to stay now that you have faced the sleeskaxes and Rykeron?" asked Emerald, halting between a tree with purple flowers that reminded Opren of large lilies and a bush with the blue oval fruits. She faced him and he was able to take in her violet eyes that suited the colors in this area of the gardens with the same slow attention as when they first met.

"Here in Avarinnia? Or in this world, you mean?"

"Either and both," said Emerald. "With me."

"I already had little reason to return to the other world," said Opren. "But now you are a huge reason to stay. So, I'm not going anywhere. I was born here and might as well make sure it is safe. While it's safe, I will spend time with you and Rufius and your sisters, without it being just for training. That said, I will need to use what I know now somehow."

"In that case, we will need to announce our official

courtship after we announce your kingship, both with silly ceremonial processes." She smiled. "Unless you think you won't want me as your partner in the future."

"I have never known anyone quite like you, Esmeraldi Avaria," said Opren. "I would be honored to court you officially, whether by label or just because we know we are committed to each other, and I am falling for you like nobody else."

Emerald had come closer and Opren subconsciously followed suit, so they were nearly touching. He embraced her, then kissed her. She stopped kissing him briefly and smiled widely, violet eyes glistening with genuine happiness, then kissed him again. After a long moment of mutual bliss, they finished the kiss, and she rested her head on his shoulder as she continued to hold him.

"I suppose if we want more peaceful private time like this, we should plan how to clean up the Royal Sect and figure out who is to replace you as High King of Everniot within the next six months, before it becomes a permanent duty," said Emerald, releasing him. "We obviously need someone who is able to prevent corruption to themselves or others. And someone who is going to be well-connected or able to learn quickly, otherwise you might as well remain in the position because you fit those criteria now. Any prospects, or should I join with Sapphire to make a list of nobility and warriors capable?"

Opren thought for a moment. Then the ground shook and the sky darkened in the direction of Rhahkmant'e.

Opren looked at Emerald and she looked at him in such a way they could both tell they had the same thought: *peaceful time together would have to wait longer; the problems were not yet over.*

"I feel my father calling. Let's see if he knows what that meant," said Emerald.

Opren followed her to the throne room and they were greeted by King Eeloneus.

"Somehow, you and Opren stopping Rykeron did not

stop everything," said King Eeloneus. "Rhahkmant'e has intercepted more assaults, and your mother is with the Elders who scryed a gathering of dark energy over the mountain just as the quake happened. Also, the Royal Sect spelled a letter to Polaris that other sleeskaxes have been spotted and a tower has been destroyed at the palace, but from what they do not know."

"Damn," said Opren. "You may have granted me the honor of this tattoo too soon, Your Majesty." He gestured to his right upper arm.

"We hold equal rank now, Opren," said King Eeloneus. "Whether you want the title or not, you can just refer to me as 'sir', or by name. And I still believe you deserve it, and these are extended problems we must now account for going forward that even Polaris and I did not predict. I cannot afford to send more of my people to die for a problem largely in Human areas, especially after my brother, but you have my support and resources yourself, whether you wish to live among us or continue to fight or take on your role as King of Humans."

"Thank you, sir," said Opren. "I will do what I can to help. I've never backed down from a fight."

"First, we need to investigate the palace, I think," said Emerald.

"Polaris is taking care of that," said Eeloneus.

"Good. I have another thing in mind," said Opren.

"What do you intend to do, Laleiy?" asked Emerald.

"You won't like it, but I'm not going to ask you to come or help, unless you want to," said Opren.

"What is it?" she asked.

"I need to use this power for more than just myself, and we have some time before I get stuck as king. The Goldlighter has always been known to kill demons and monsters," said Opren. "I'm going to stop the spread of them. I will hunt them like the sleeskaxes hunted me. If I must, I'll kill them all."

ACKNOWLEDGEMENT

Thank you so much for reading!

Please let me know your thoughts on my Instagram @rcozander or TikTok @CozanderBooks.

All official reviews are always greatly appreciated as well, and they help other readers find and choose indie books. If you truly enjoyed the adventure and want more, please leave a review where you got this book or your favorite review site.

I can't wait for the next part of this journey together!

Ve harron,
Cozander

Printed in Dunstable, United Kingdom

Imperial Russia

Also by John Paxton

CALENDAR OF WORLD HISTORY

ENCYCLOPEDIA OF RUSSIAN HISTORY
From the Christianization of Kiev to the Break-up of the USSR

EUROPEAN POLITICAL FACTS OF THE TWENTIETH CENTURY (*with Chris Cook*)

PENGUIN ENCYCLOPEDIA OF PLACES

Imperial Russia
A Reference Handbook

John Paxton

© John Paxton 2001

All rights reserved. No reproduction, copy or transmission of this publication may be made without written permission.

No paragraph of this publication may be reproduced, copied or transmitted save with written permission or in accordance with the provisions of the Copyright, Designs and Patents Act 1988, or under the terms of any licence permitting limited copying issued by the Copyright Licensing Agency, 90 Tottenham Court Road, London W1P 0LP.

Any person who does any unauthorised act in relation to this publication may be liable to criminal prosecution and civil claims for damages.

The author has asserted his right to be identified as the author of this work in accordance with the Copyright, Designs and Patents Act 1988.

First published 2001 by
PALGRAVE
Houndmills, Basingstoke, Hampshire RG21 6XS and
175 Fifth Avenue, New York, N.Y. 10010
Companies and representatives throughout the world

PALGRAVE is the new global academic imprint of
St. Martin's Press LLC Scholarly and Reference Division and
Palgrave Publishers Ltd (formerly Macmillan Press Ltd).

Outside North America
ISBN 0–333–76393–9

In North America
ISBN 0–312–23480–5

This book is printed on paper suitable for recycling and made from fully managed and sustained forest sources.

A catalogue record for this book is available from the British Library.

Library of Congress Cataloging-in-Publication Data
Paxton, John.
   Imperial Russia : a reference handbook / John Paxton.
     p. cm.
   Includes bibliographical references and index.
   ISBN 0–312–23480–5 (cloth)
    1. Russia—Handbooks, manuals, etc. I. Title.
DK14 .P39 2000
947—dc21
                                                  00–026867

10 9 8 7 6 5 4 3 2 1
10 09 08 07 06 05 04 03 02 01

Printed and bound in Great Britain by
Antony Rowe Ltd, Chippenham, Wiltshire

for
Cherrill, Elizabeth, George,
Joseph, Patrick, Samuel and Thomas

Contents

Preface	xiii
The Romanov Dynasty	xv
Maps	xvi
Introduction: Imperial Russia	1
1. Tsars and Important Advisers and Ministers (1533–1917)	5
2. The Regencies and the Problems of Dynastic Succession (1533–1917)	9
3. Political Chronologies	14
Ivan IV, Fedor I, Boris Godunov (1533–1605)	14
Time of Troubles (1605–1613)	15
Michael, Alexis, Fedor III (1613–1682)	16
Peter I (the Great) (1682–1725)	20
Catherine I, Peter II, Anne, Ivan VI, Elizabeth, Peter III (1725–1762)	23
Catherine II (the Great) (1762–1796)	24
Paul (1796–1801)	26
Alexander I (1801–1825)	27
Nicholas I (1825–1855)	29
Alexander II (1855–1881)	30
Alexander III (1881–1894)	32
Nicholas II and Revolution (1894–1917)	33
Nicholas II's inheritance	33
Chronology	34
4. The Influence of the West	41
The Westerner/Slavophile controversy	41
Peter I's visits to Western Europe	42
The Beard Tax	43
The founding of St Petersburg	44
Catherine II (the Great) and the Philosophes	44
5. Political and Administrative Changes in Imperial Russia	46
Ivan IV (the Terrible)	46
Zemskii Sobor is convened	46
Creation of the *Oprichnina*	46
The 'Forbidden Year'	46

Fedor I	46
Saint George's Day law	46
Michael	47
Emergency tax voted by *Zemskii Sobor*	47
Inventory of taxable land is taken	47
Alexis	47
New legal code (*Ulozhenie*)	47
'Copper Revolt'	47
Peter I (the Great)	47
Reform of government and administration	47
Reform of the army and navy	48
The Table of Ranks (1722)	50
Catherine I, Peter II, Anne, Elizabeth, Peter III	52
Creation of the Supreme Privy (Secret) Council	52
'Conditions of Mitau'	53
Catherine II (the Great)	53
Marshals of the Nobility (1766)	53
Legislative Commission (1767–68) and Catherine's *Nakaz*	54
The *Dvoryanstvo* Charter (1785)	55
Charter to the Towns (1785)	56
Alexander I	56
The State reforms of 1808–09	56
Nicholas I	57
The Creation of the Third Section or Department (the secret police)	57
Alexander II	58
Reform of military service (1863)	58
Zemstva (local self-government) in 1864	59
Alexander III	59
Counter-reforms	59
Nicholas II	60
Creation of the Duma	60
The Vyborg Manifesto	61
Political groupings in the *dumas*	62
6. Religion	**65**
Russia's conversion to Christianity	65
Chronology 1569–1918	65
Orthodox Church	76
Old Believers	76
Georgian Orthodox Church	77
Armenian Church	77

	Baptists	78
	Jews	79
	Islam	81
7.	Serfdom in Imperial Russia	82
	Chronology 1640s–1918	82
	The Pugachev Rebellion	84
	Number of serfs in 1762	85
	Peasant uprisings before emancipation	85
	The edict of Emancipation of the serfs (1861)	86
	Stolypin's agrarian reforms of 1911	89
	Agricultural production	90
8.	Social and Economic Progress	92
	Population	92
	Ethnic composition	93
	Changing status of women	93
	Government revenue and expenditure	97
	Money and banking	99
	Industrial growth	100
	Share capital of enterprises	101
	Decision on Employment of Minors	102
	Factory Regulations, 1886	102
	Operatives Working for Wages, 1804 and 1825	104
	Industrial Disputes 1895–1913	104
	Alcohol production	104
	Cotton industry	104
	Minerals	105
	Salt	105
	Petroleum production	106
	Exports and imports in 1901	106
	Customs and duties	107
	River and canal traffic	108
	Railways	108
	Weights and measures	110
9.	The Rise of Radicalism	111
	Monarchy and absolutism: an overview	111
	The Decembrists	112
	Petrashevsky Circle	113
	Liberation of Labour Group	114
	Land and Liberty Organisation	114
	People's Freedom or Will	114

Nihilism	115
Pan-Slavism	115
Bund	115
Constitutional Democratic Party	116
Bloody Sunday and the Revolution of 1905	116
Popular movements in 1905	118
Dashnaktsutyun	118
Anarchism	118
Menshevism	120
Bolshevism	121
February Revolution (1917)	121
Telegram of 27 February 1917 from Rodzyanko President of the State Duma to the tsar	121
Telegram of 28 February 1917 from General Alekseev Chief of Staff of the Supreme Commander to all the Commanders in Chief	122
Nicholas II abdicates	123
Provisional government	124
October Revolution (1917)	124
Murder of the ex-tsar	125
10. International Relations and the Expansion of Russia Overseas	**126**
Battles and Wars 1548–1918	126
Alliances, Congresses, Conferences and Treaties	130
Army	132
Navy	133
Russia and Sweden	133
Great Northern War	133
Russo–Swedish War 1788–90	134
Russia and the Ottoman Empire	134
Russo–Turkish War 1768–74	134
Russo–Turkish War 1787–92	134
Russo–Turkish War 1806–12	135
Treaty of (Edirne) Adrianople (1829)	135
Crimean War (1853–56)	135
Danubian Principalities	136
Russo–Turkish War 1877–78	136
Russia and Poland	136
Partitions of Poland	136
Russia and France	138
The War of the Second Coalition 1799–1802	138
The War of the Third Coalition 1803–07	138

	French invasion of Russia	139
	The Wars of Liberation 1813–14	140
	Congress of Vienna	140
	Russia and Japan	141
	Russo–Japanese War (1904–05)	141
	Russia and the First World War	142
	Russia and Persia	143
	Treaty of Turkmanchai	143
	Russia and Prussia	143
	Russia America (Alaska) 1741–1867	143
	Russian expansion overseas	144
	Russian Empire ethnic composition	147
11.	Education and the Arts	149
	Education	149
	Libraries	154
	Publishing	155
	Alphabet and Transliteration	155
	Literature	155
	Art	156
	Ballet	157
	Theatre	157
	Architecture	158
12.	Law, Crime and Punishment	160
	Law	160
	Chronology of punishments	162
	Third Section (Department)	163
	Okhrana	163
13.	Press and Censorship	165
	Newspapers and journals	165
	Censorship	168
14.	Biographies	171
15.	Glossary	221
16.	Bibliography	241
	Index	249

Preface

Imperial Russia: A Reference Handbook aims to provide an accessible reference tool for students, researchers, historians and Russian history enthusiasts. It covers the period from Ivan IV (the Terrible) to the death of Nicholas II.

There are many watersheds and turning points in Russian history, including Vladimir's conversion to Christianity in 988 AD, 'The Time of Troubles', the founding of St Petersburg by Peter I (the Great), the abolition of serfdom, the creation of the Third Section, in the twentieth century the establishment of the Duma, Lenin's return to Russia, the publication of the April Theses and the revolutions. The *Handbook* answers questions such as: Who were the Decembrists? What was the background of Aleksandr Kerensky and Grigory Rasputin? What is a *duma*? What was an *arshin, desyatin, pood* or *verst*? There are chronologies for each of the reigns and the *Handbook* explains important political and administrative changes, the influence of the West, religion, serfdom, and economic progress. Wars and international relations are succinctly explained as is the rise of radicalism and the revolutions of 1905 and 1917. Other sections deal with education, the arts, law, press and censorship. There are biographies which include the great, the eccentric, the wicked, the good and the talented, a glossary, a comprehensive bibliography, maps and an extended index.

As readers and writers know, transliteration problems arise in any book on Russia. I used the Library of Congress transliteration system, but it was necessary to break the rules from time to time. Certain forms, such as 'Alexei Sergeyevich' do not belong to the Library of Congress or to the British Standard schemes. Instead, they usually trace back to the idiosyncratic schemes of early translators who mixed equivalents, 'Alexis', with transliterations. Some idiosyncratic spellings, which as 'Tchaikovsky', are hallowed by tradition, and, of course, I have used English forms for such people as 'Catherine I (the Great)', and such places as 'Moscow'.

Dates also present confusion because until 1918, the Julian rather than the Gregorian calendar was used in Russia. Consequently, dates determined by the Julian calendar are twelve days behind the Gregorian calendar in the nineteenth century and thirteen days behind in the twentieth century. When Russia adopted the Gregorian systems, the Julian date 31 January became Gregorian date 14 February. In this *Handbook* I have used the old style, except for external events, where I have used new style throughout. The *Handbook* evolved over several years and the London Library was, as usual, extremely helpful and I have to thank once again my two friends Penny White and Dione Daffin for enormous help.

Thanks are due to Yale University Press for permission to reproduce from *A Source Book for Russian History to 1917* by George Vernadsky and Ralph T. Fisher and to HarperCollins for permission to quote from *Russia: People and Empire 1552–1917* by Geoffrey Hoskings.

Every effort has been made to trace all copyright holders but if any has been inadvertently overlooked, the author and publishers will be pleased to make the necessary arrangement at the first opportunity.

If errors are found they are my own and I shall be pleased, although sad at the time, to be alerted so that they can be corrected for future editions.

John Paxton
Bruton, Somerset
August 1999

THE ROMANOV DYNASTY

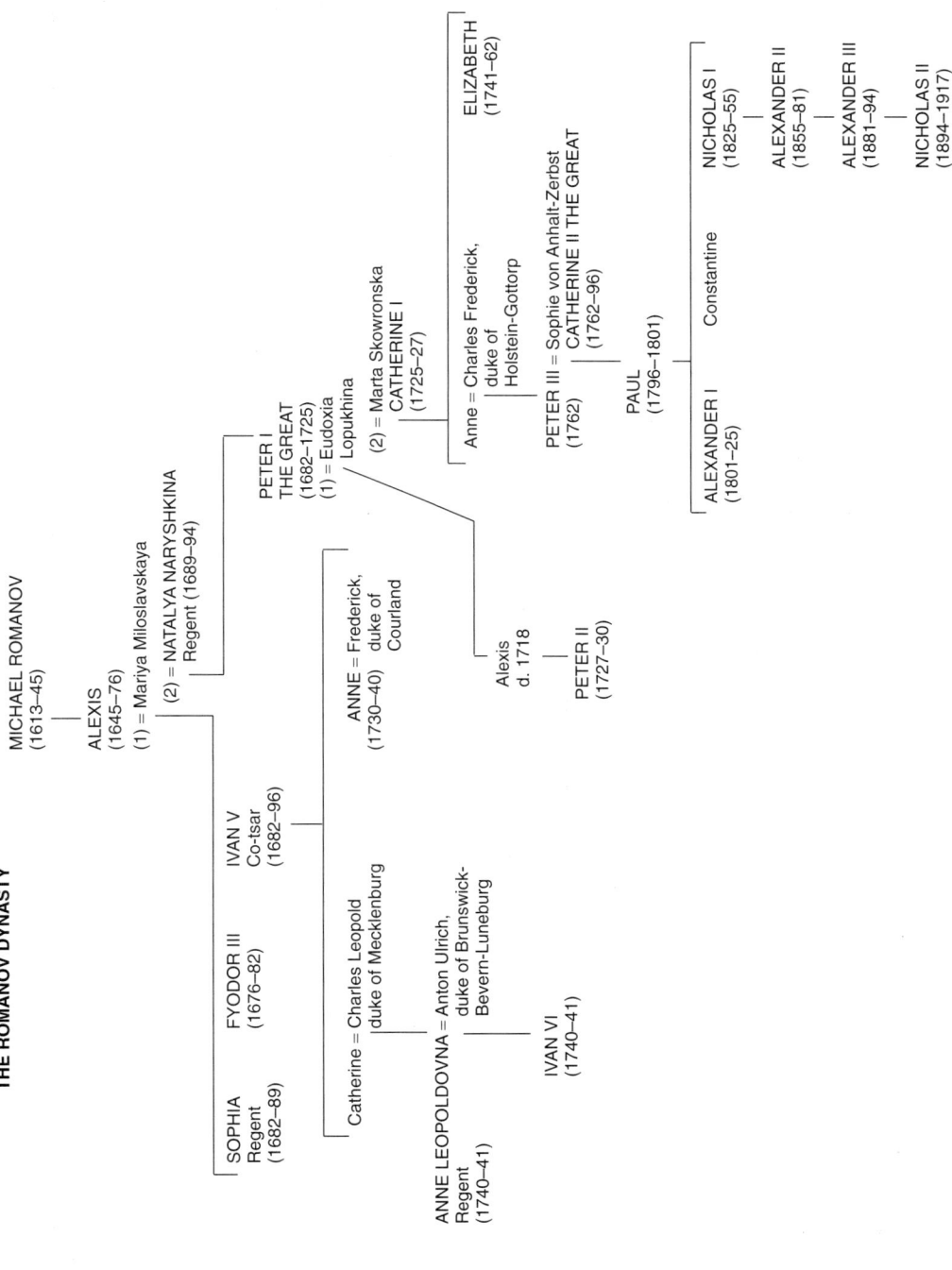

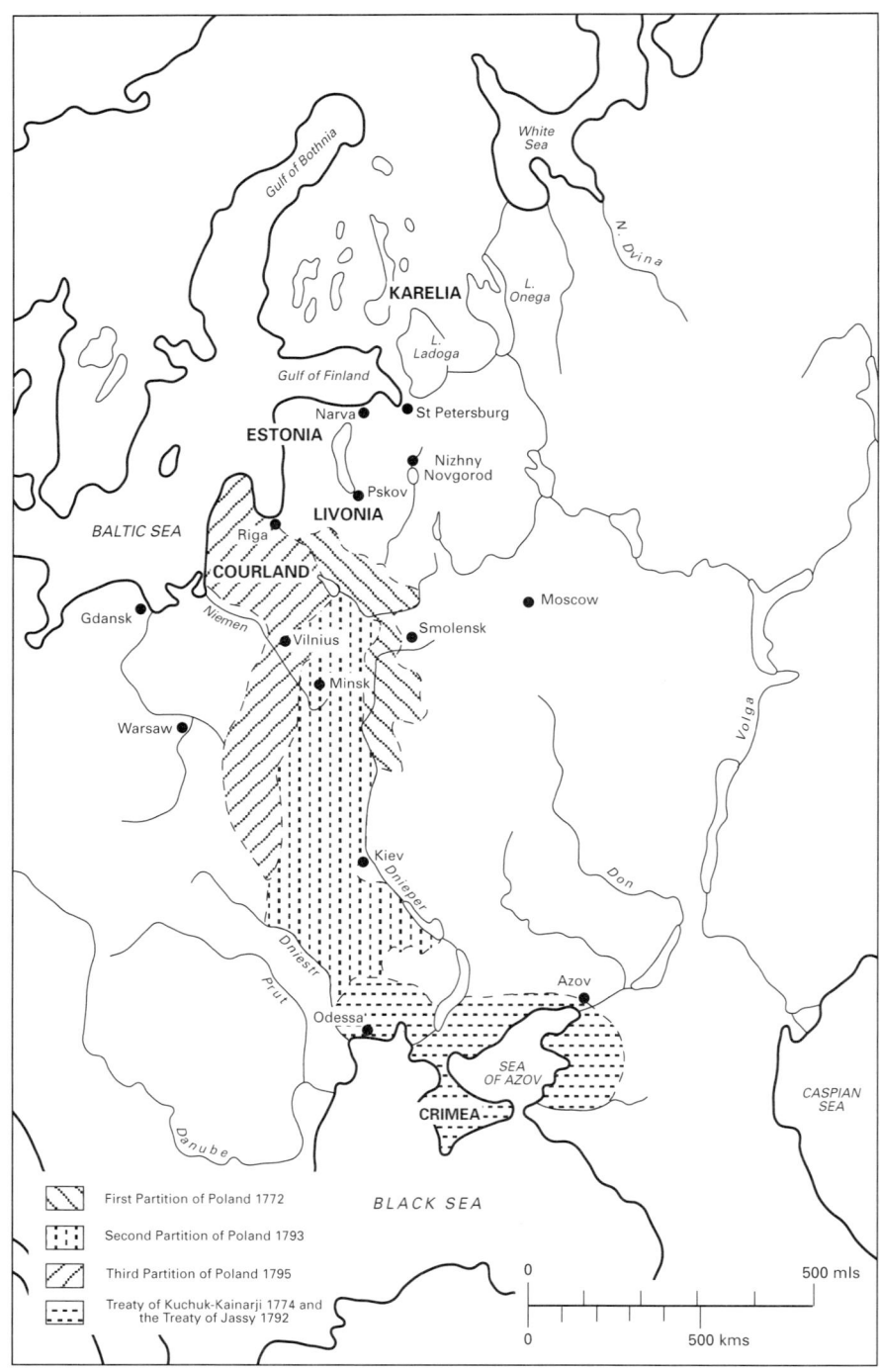

Map 1. Russian Expansion in the Reign of Catherine II (the Great) (1762–1796)

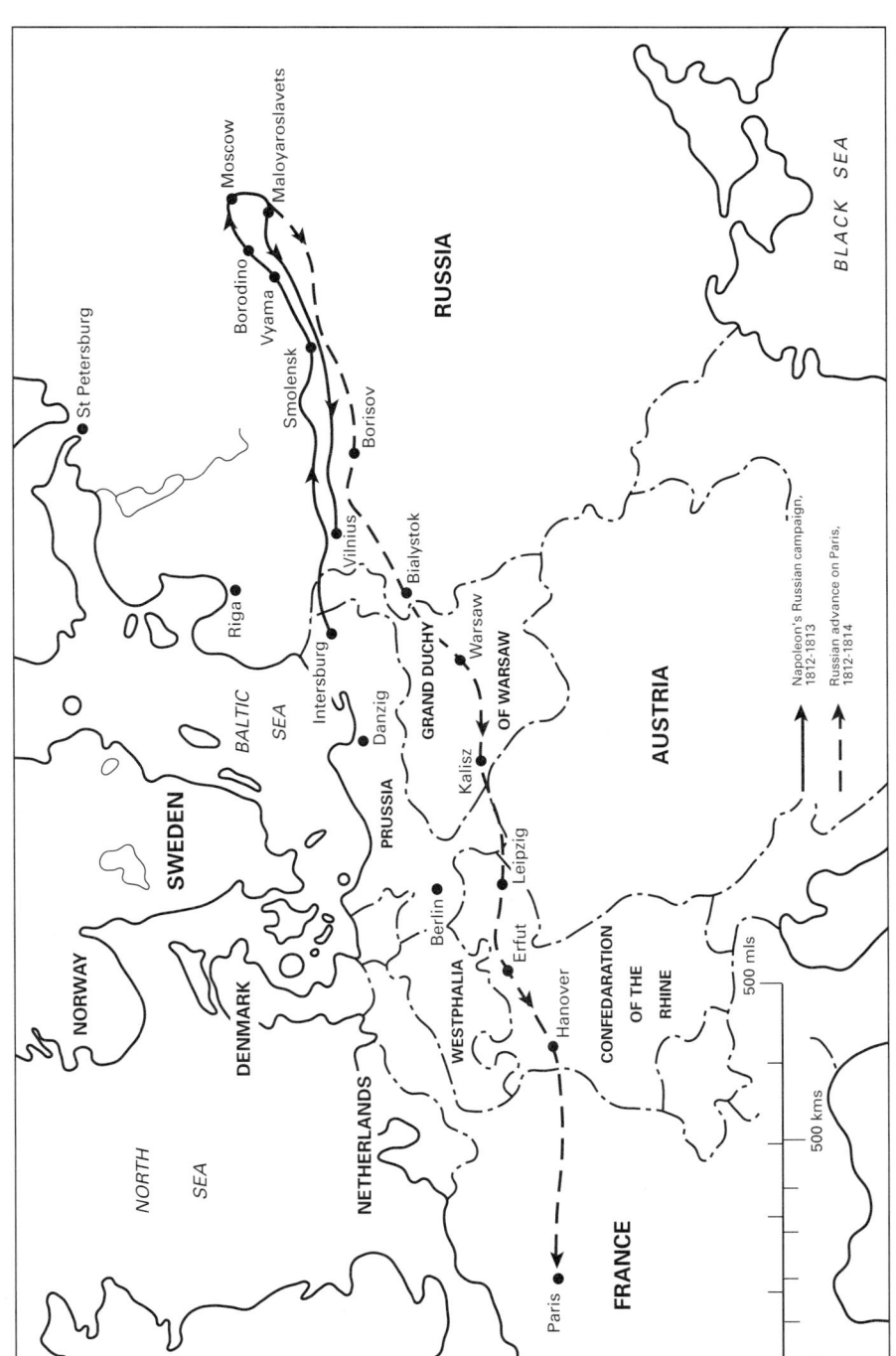

Map 2. The Napoleonic Wars

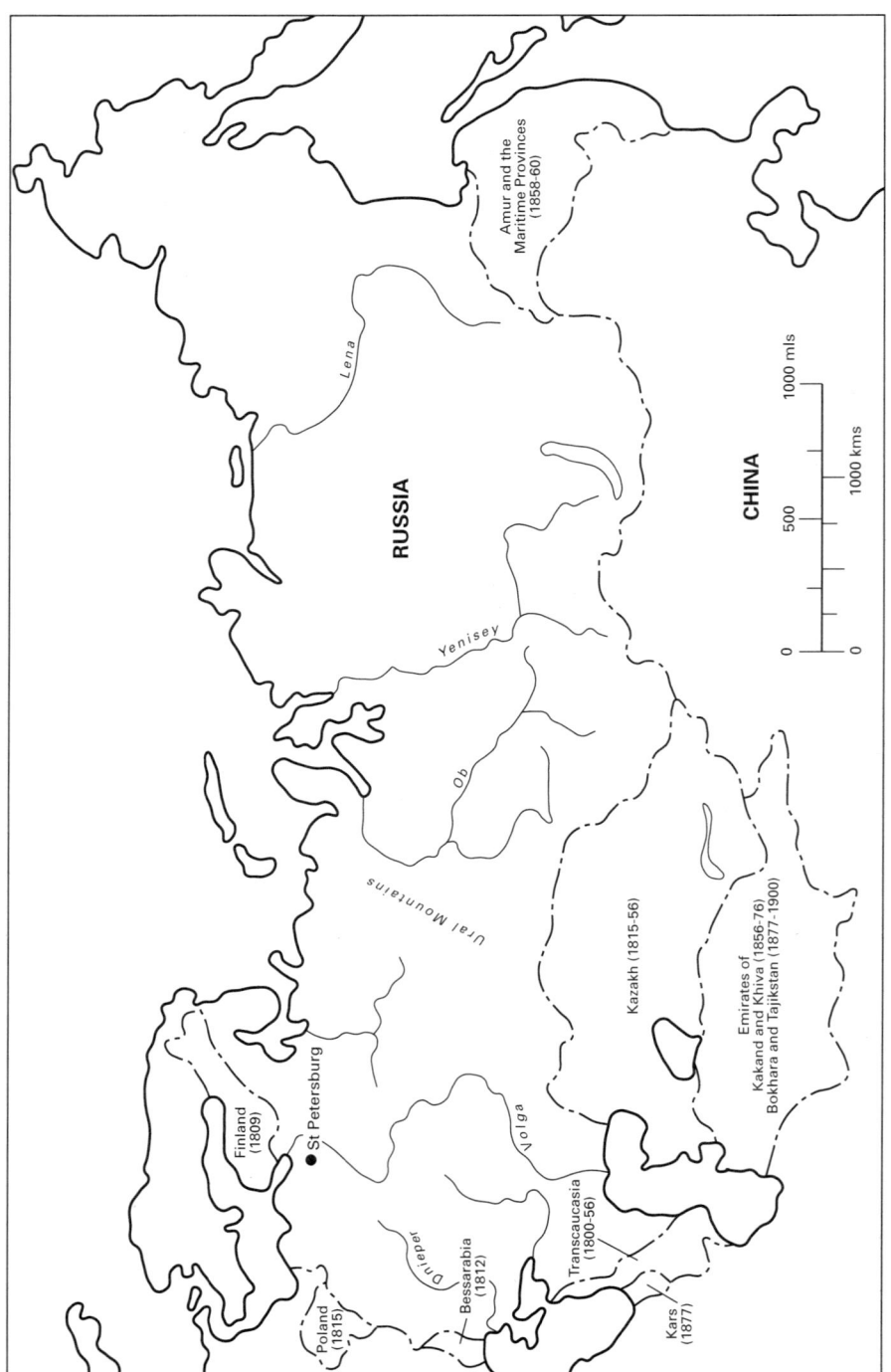

Map 3. Nineteenth-century Expansion of the Russian Empire

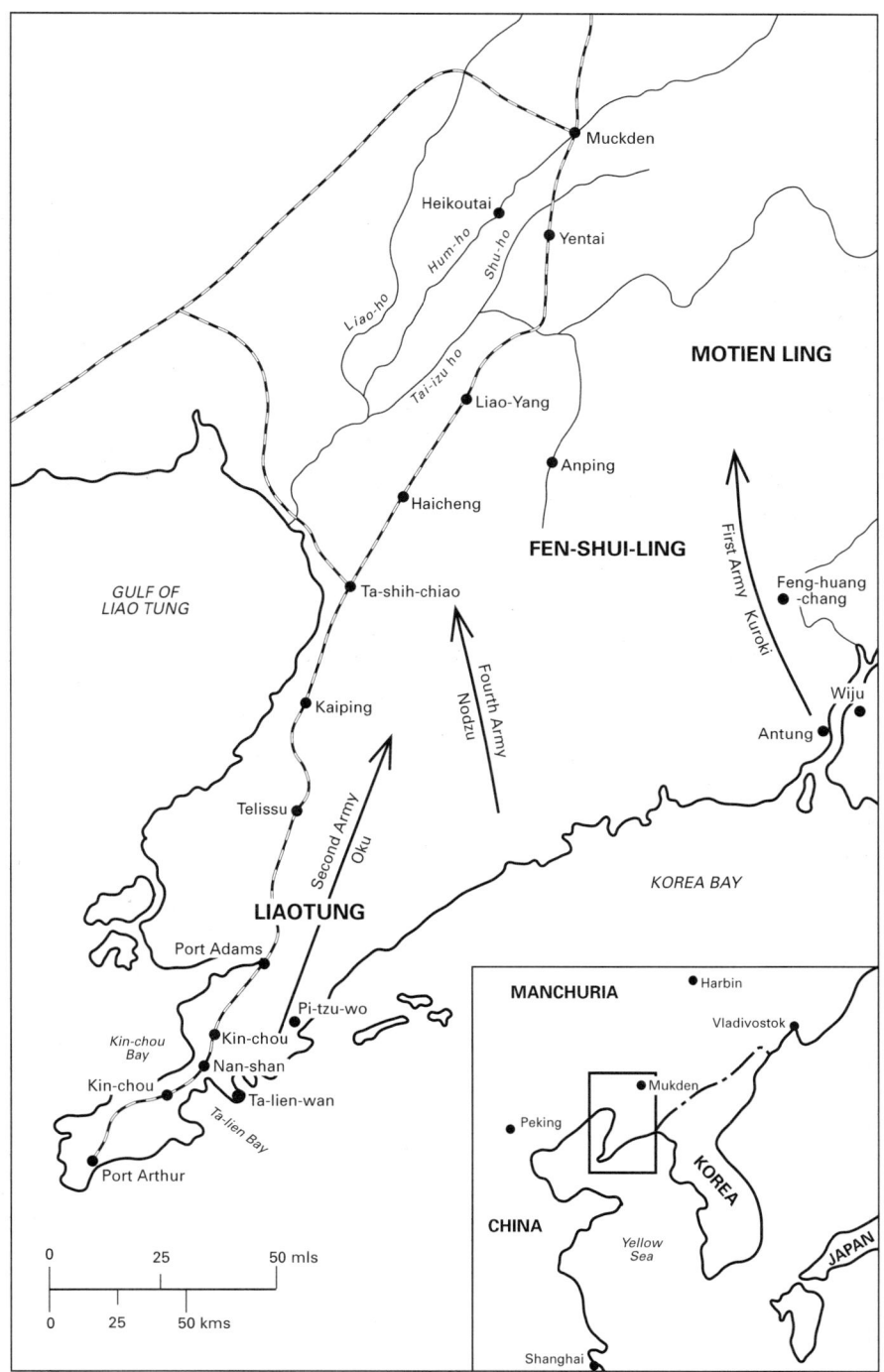

Map 4. Russo-Japanese War, 1904

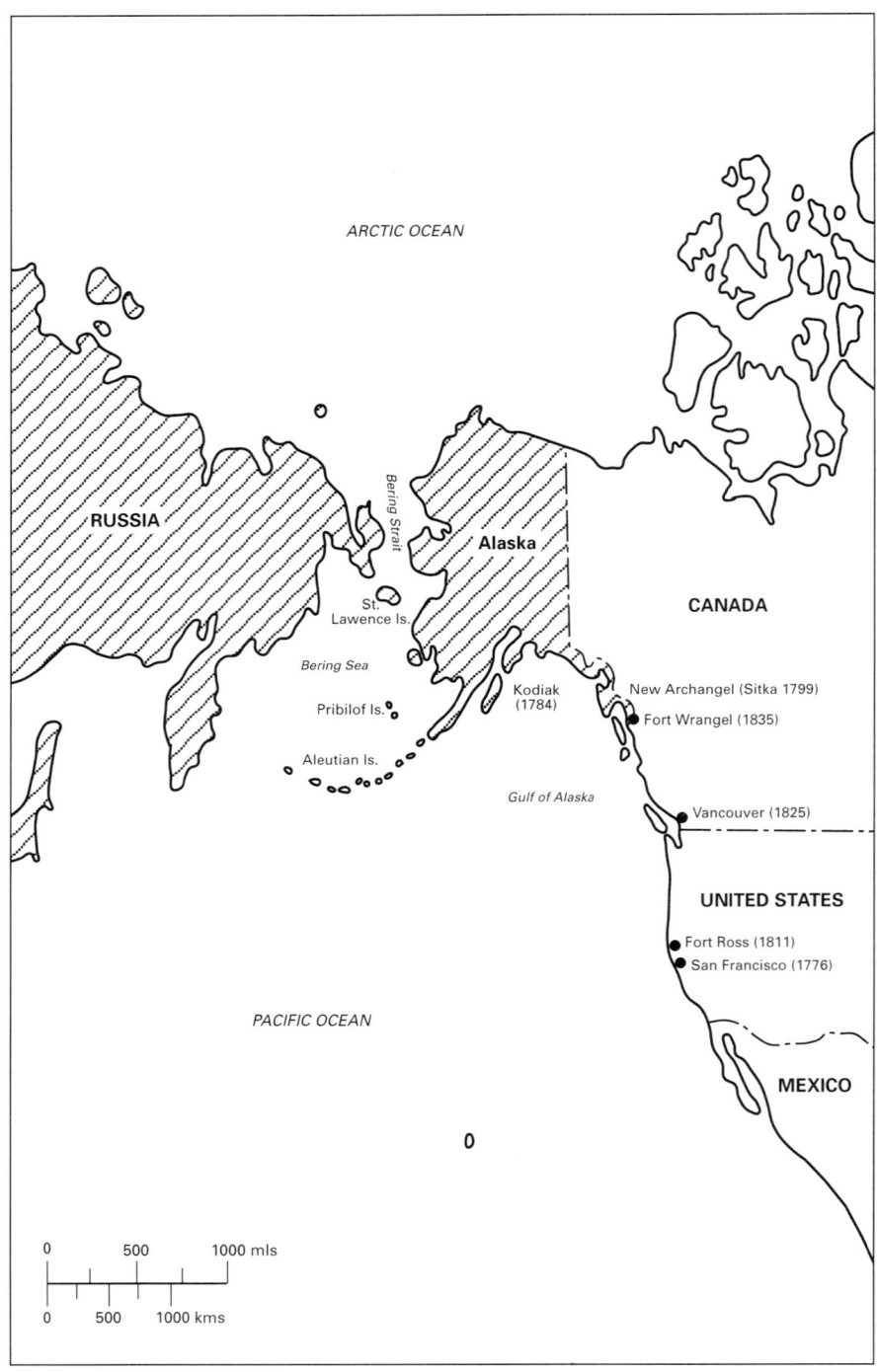

Map 5. Russia in America

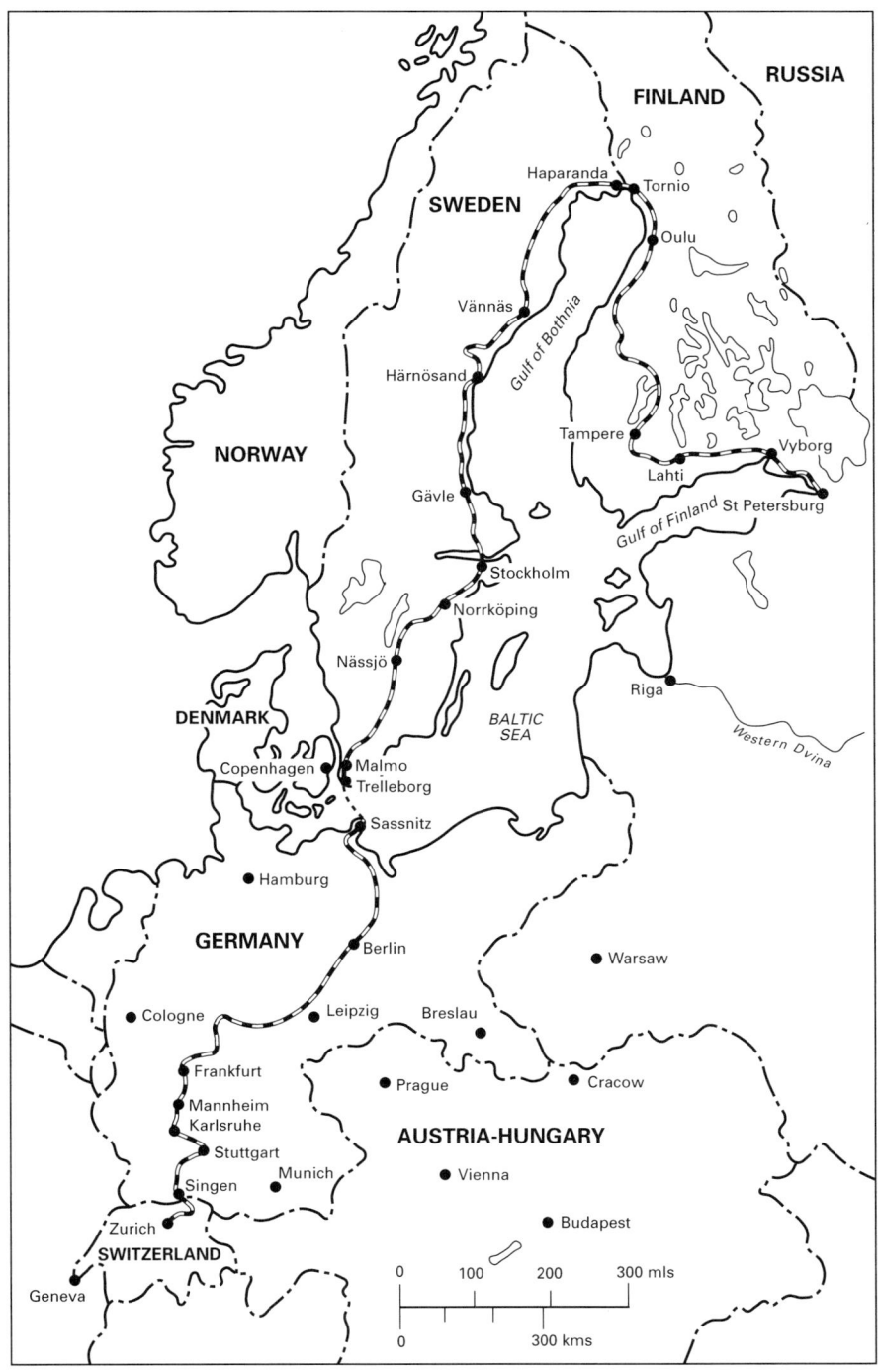

Map 6. Lenin's 'Sealed Train' Journey, 1917

Introduction: Imperial Russia

The official birth of the Russian Empire took place on 22 October 1721. After a thanksgiving service Peter I (the Great) proceeded to the senate and there was acclaimed 'Father of the Fatherland, Peter the Great, The Emperor of All Russia'. Imperial Russia ended with the abdication of Nicholas II in March 1917 and his eventual murder. The 'Empire' continued in a new form as the USSR, and even with its collapse continues in a milder form as the Commonwealth of Independent States (CIS). But when did Imperial Russia and the Empire begin?

Writers differ about a starting date. Some feel that Ivan III (the Great) (1462–1505) and Vasily III (1505–33) set the scene by dramatically enlarging the Princedom of Moscow and repudiating the Tatar yoke. This allowed Ivan IV (the Terrible) (1533–84) to expand eastwards. This *Handbook* begins with Ivan IV (the Terrible) although there are references to earlier years.

In 1547 Ivan IV (the Terrible) began the annexation of the Tatar kingdoms to the east; this opened the way to Siberia and to Russia's future as a multiracial empire.

Geoffrey Hosking quotes in his *Russia: People and Empire 1552–1917*

'With the aid of our Almighty Lord Jesus Christ and the prayers of the Mother of God . . . our pious Tsar and Grand Prince Ivan Vasilievich, crowned by God, Autocrat of all *Rus'*, fought against the infidels, defeated them finally and captured the Tsar of Kazan' Edigei-Mahmet. And the pious Tsar and Grand Prince ordered his regiment to sing an anthem under his banner, to give thanks to God for the victory; and at the same time ordered a life-giving cross to be placed and a church to be built, with the uncreated image of our Lord Jesus Christ, where the Tsar's colours had stood during the battle.'

Thus the official chronicle records Muscovy set out on its career of empire by conquering and annexing for the first time a non-Russian sovereign state, the Khanate of Kazan. Muscovite Rus was already a multi-national state, since it included within its borders some Tatars, as well as Finno-Ugrian tribes, but the conquest of Kazan signified a new approach to relations with its neighbours. Rus had embarked on a course of conquest and expansion which was to last for more than three centuries and create the largest and most diverse territorial empire the world has ever seen.

Reforms of Peter I (the Great) depended on the progress of the Great Northern War (1700–21). Sweden was eventually defeated and Russia gained the whole shore from Riga to Vyborg. St Petersburg was founded on the banks of the Gulf of Finland in 1703 and became the capital. Government organs were improved and included the creation of the Senate in 1711, the administrative colleges in 1718, and the procurator-general's office in 1722. Great changes were made in the church's administration. Provincial administration was reformed and the provinces (*guberniia*) were created in 1708, with further changes in 1718.

Other reforms took place, many were influenced by what was already established in Europe, particularly in the area of education with the founding of the Academy of Sciences, compulsory education for the children of nobility, the establishment of naval and engineering schools, the expansion of book publishing, the arrival of foreign specialists in Russia and Russian students studying abroad: all these added to the changes taking place.

Europe's political systems influenced Russia and in 1730, people who had not earlier doubted the tsar's supreme power demanded that the Empress Anne sign the Conditions of Mitau which would have deprived her of important royal prerogatives. It didn't work, but it showed that European political thought was active.

Peter gave control of the rural administrative and police powers to the landowners. During the reigns of empresses in the eighteenth century the landowners obtained the abolition of their state service obligations in the manifesto on the liberty of the nobility (1762) and the 'Charter of the Nobility' (1785). The eighteenth century saw good times for the Russian nobility, but it also experienced an uprising and slaughter of landowners (1773–75) under the leadership of Yemelyan Pugachov.

Under Elizabeth (1741–62) and Catherine II (the Great) (1762–96) the northern shore of the Black Sea was conquered and the Crimea was subdued in 1783. The legacy, however, was the Balkan wars which continued through most of the nineteenth century, and a struggle to subdue the Caucasus (although Georgia was incorporated in Russia in 1801) which lasted from the reign of Catherine II (the Great) into the 1860s. Between 1772 and 1795 the three partitions of Poland added substantially to Russian territory. The Russian eastward movement reached Alaska and America in the eighteenth century and in 1798 the 'Russian–American Company' was granted monopoly rights by Emperor Paul I to trade in and develop the lands on the American continent.

The Russian Empire, however, in contrast to the Moscow state, did not have its own clear foreign policy doctrines. Only the war of 1812 was Russia's war rather than purely the tsar's. From Ryurik to Nicholas II, ninety-nine per cent of the Russian people remained outside of politics and few could have understood why Russia was involved in many wars. But when Napoleon intruded into the depths of Russia, the whole nation rose to the danger. As soon as the enemy was driven out it lost its national character.

From the 'Time of Troubles' Russia failed to construct a Russian nation in order to establish and maintain an empire. This Russian national identity was lost, caused by the lack of a co-ordinated state administration.

An active revolutionary movement began in 1825. The movement displayed Jacobin tendencies from the very beginning, with proposals for the overthrow of the monarch and even the physical extermination of the ruling family. Two armed uprisings were staged in December 1825, one in St Petersburg on the 14th and the other on the 28th in the Vasilkov region in the south; hence the name 'Decembrists'.

Nicholas I began his reign with a revolt on the day of his succession to the throne. He regarded European revolutionary ideas as a product of education, and put restrictions on the schools and universities. Many new schools and higher institutions were opened during his reign, especially in technical fields, but teaching was severely hampered by the police supervision. Science and art laboured under similar difficulties and literature suffered greatly from censorship.

When Nicholas I's policies precipitated the Crimean War (1854–56), the army proved backward compared to the English and French armies in technical equipment and in military skill.

The first reactions to the defeats came from leading groups in the form of handwritten pamphlets calling for change.

Alexander II (1855–81) recognised the need for change and particularly the abolition of serfdom. Various schemes for the emancipation of the serfs were considered from the time of Catherine II (the Great). This institution had been extremely unjust since the liberation of the nobility from their obligations to the state in the second half of the eighteenth century.

However, the peasant and *zemstvo* reforms were not ideal and there were over a thousand peasant disturbances in the two years following the reforms.

Alexander III (1881–94) believed that his father's reforms had weakened the monarchy and in August 1881 issued the Temporary Regulation on Measures for the Safety of the State. This remained in force until 1917. The chief procurator of the Synod, Konstantin Pobedonostsev (1827–1907), became extremely influential. He was convinced that popular education, technical progress, and social evolution were dangerous. However, an industrial revolution took place and the machinery industry began to expand.

Nicholas II (1894–1917) had no experience in government and was led into a war with Japan in 1904. The government succeeded in averting a revolution with great difficulty, not a little assisted by the Peace of Portsmouth signed with Japan in 1905. The army, returned from Manchuria, was used to put down disturbances. Another important factor was a manifesto published in 1905, promising that civil liberties would be granted and that a *duma* would be called.

The Fundamental Laws of 1906 meant that the tsar retained much of his power; he appointed and dismissed ministers and he also appointed the majority of the State Council. Perhaps the most important factor was that he was the only person able to revise the Fundamental Laws. So it was only apparent democracy and the tsar's belief that the rural population would vote for monarchist candidates proved unfounded. The first Duma lasted two months.

World War I proved to be a turning-point and opposition parties strongly condemned the government for its incompetence in running the war. Nicholas I took a fatal step in taking supreme command of the army.

In February 1917 crowds formed in the streets of Petrograd, protesting against food shortages and demanding bread. The red flag appeared, and on 27 February the soldiers of the Petrograd garrison began to go over to the side of the insurgents. On the 28th the tsar was returning from general headquarters to Petrograd. On 2 March in Pskov, he signed his abdication and a provisional government was formed in Petrograd.

To quote from Geoffrey Hosking's *Russia: People and Empire 1552–1917* again,

> The Russian Empire fell apart in 1917 along fault-lines which were inherent in its situation as an empire with extensive vulnerable borders straddling Europe and Asia. For more than three centuries its structures had been those of a multi-ethnic service state, not those of an emerging nation.

1
Tsars and Important Advisers and Ministers 1533–1917

Ivan IV (the Terrible)	1533–1584	Son of Vasily III. In 1575 Ivan abdicated in favour of Simeon Bekbulatovich (see p. 177); Ivan resumed the tsardom in 1576.
Fedor I	1584–1598	Boris Godunov as regent
Boris Godunov	1598–1605	*Time of Troubles 1605–1613*

Fedor Godunov, son of Boris, succeeded as tsar, as Fedor II, for a few months in 1605 but was assassinated by the followers of the pretender Dmitry. False Dmitry I ruled for less than a year 1605–06 and was murdered by followers of Vasily Shuysky who was tsar 1606–10, who in turn was deposed. An interregnum followed 1610–13.

Michael	1613–1645	The first Romanov, elected tsar by the *Zemskii Sobor*
Alexis	1645–1676	Father of Peter I (the Great)
Fedor III	1676–1682	Half-brother of Peter I (the Great)
Ivan V	1682–1696	From 1682–1689 Sophia, eldest daughter of Alexis, was regent. After the overthrow of the regency Ivan V retained his title but never participated in government.
Peter I (the Great)	1682–1725	Sole tsar from 1696, but Natalia Naryshkina regent until 1694. Assumed the title of emperor from 1721.

Catherine I	1725–1727	Married Peter I (the Great) in 1712
Peter II	1727–1730	Grandson of Peter I (the Great). Son of Alexis, he was proclaimed emperor according to the will of Catherine I.
Anne	1730–1740	Daughter of Ivan V and niece of Peter I (the Great)
Ivan VI	1720–1741	Deposed
Elizabeth	1741–1762	
Peter III	1762	Probably murdered
Catherine II (the Great)	1762–1796	
Paul	1796–1801	Assassinated
Alexander I	1801–1825	
Nicholas I	1825–1855	
Alexander II	1855–1881	Assassinated
Alexander III	1881–1894	
Nicholas II	1894–1917	Abdicated and later assassinated

Important Advisers and Ministers

1696–1727	Prince Aleksandr Danilovich Menshikov, Chief Minister
1721–1741	Count Heinrich J. F. Ostermann, Foreign Minister
1730–1740	Ernst Johann Biron, Duke of Courland, Chief Minister
1732–1741	Count Burkhard Christoph von Munnich, Field Marshal
1742–1757	Count Betuzhev-Riumin, Foreign Minister
1762–1767	Count Burkhard Christoph von Munnich, Field Marshal
1762–1781	Count Nikita Ivanovich Panin, Chief Minister
1774–1791	Prince Grigory Aleksandrovich Potemkin, Chief Minister
1800–1802	Count Peter von der Pahlen, Foreign Minister
1802–1804	Count Alexander Voronzov, Foreign Minister
1804–1807	Prince Czartoyrski, Foreign Minister
1807–1812	Count Mikhail Mikhailovich, Administrative Secretary to Alexander I
1807–1814	Count Nikolai Rumyanzev, Foreign Minister
1808–1810	Count Alexey Andreyevich, War Minister
1810–1812	Prince Mikhail Andreyevich Barclay de Tolly, War Minister
1812–1816	Prince Nikolai Ivanovič Saltykov, Chief Minister
1816–1817	Count Anton Capodistrias, Foreign Minister
1817–1856	Count Karl Nesselrode, Foreign Minister
1823–1844	Count Yegor Frantsevich Kankrin, Finance Minister
1833–1849	Count Sergey Semoyonwich Uvarov, Education Minister

1834–1837 Count Nikolai Novosiliev, Chief Minister
1837–1847 Prince Hilarion Vasiltschikov, Chief Minister
1852–1855 Dimitry Gavrilovich Bibikov, Interior Minister
1848–1856 Prince Tschernyshchev, Chief Minister
1856–1861 Prince Aleksey Fyodorovich Orlov, Chief Minister
1856–1882 Prince Aleksandr Mikhailovich Gortchakov, Foreign Minister
1861–1864 Count Dimitry Bludov, Chief Minister
1862–1878 Count Mikhail Reutern, Finance Minister
1864–1872 Prince Paul Gagarin, Chief Minister
1872–1880 Count Nicholai Pavlovich Ignatiev, Chief Minister
1880–1881 Count Pyotr Aleksandrovich Valuyev, Chief Minister
1880–1881 Count Mikhail Taryelovich Loris-Melikov, Interior Minister
1881–1882 Count Nikolai Pavlovich, Interior Minister
1881–1887 Count Mikhail Reutern, Chief Minister
1882–1895 Nikolai Kristianovich Bunge, Chief Minister
1895–1899 Ivan Longinovich Goremykin, Interior Minister
1898–1901 Nikolai Pavlovich Bogolepov, Education Minister
1902–1904 Vyacheslav Konstantinovich Plehve, Interior Minister

Ministers in the Reign of Nicholas II

Date of taking office	Prime Minister	Foreign Minister	Finance Minister
16 Jun 1895	J. N. Durnovo		
Sep 1896		N. P. Shishkin	
		Count Muraviev	
22 Jun 1900		Count Lamsdorff	
29 Aug 1903	S. J. Witte		
31 Aug 1903			E. D. Pleske
10 Apr 1904			W. N. Kokovtsov
30 Oct 1905			I. P. Shipov
8 May 1906	I. L. Goremykin	A. P. Isvolsky	W. N. Kokovtsov
23 Jul 1906	P. A. Stolypin		
28 Sep 1910		S. Sazonov	
23 Sep 1911	W. N. Kokovtsov		
11 Nov 1914	I. L. Goremykin		P. L. Bark
2 Feb 1916	B. V. Stürmer		
23 Nov 1916	A. F. Trepov	N. N. Pokrovsky	
9 Jan 1917	N. D. Golitsin	P. N. Mikyukov	M. I. Tereshchenko
14 Mar 1917	G. J. Lvov[1]		
8 May 1917		M. I. Tereshchenko	

[1] Appointed by the provisional government.

Date of taking office	Prime Minister	Foreign Minister	Finance Minister
18 May 1917			A. I. Shingaryov
21 Jul 1917	A. F. Kerensky[1]		
6 Aug 1917			N. V. Nekrasov
27 Sep 1917			M. W. Bernatsky

[1] Appointed by the provisional government.

2
The Regencies and the Problems of Dynastic Succession (1533–1917)

Ivan IV (the Terrible)

Ivan IV succeeded to the Russian throne in 1533 at the age of three. His mother Grand Duchess Elena became regent. She died in 1538. In 1581 Ivan killed his eldest son Ivan, the tsarevich, in a fit of temper and in 1584, as he was dying, willed the tsardom to Fedor, his eldest surviving son.

Fedor I to The Time of Troubles

Giles Fletcher, the English diplomat, wrote of Fedor:

> The Emperour . . . is for his person of a meane stature, somewhat lowe and grosse, of a sallowe complexion, and inclining to the dropsie, hawk nosed, unsteady in his pase by reason of some weakness of his lims, heavie and inactive, yet commonly smiling almost to a laughter . . . simple and slowe witted, but verie gentle, and of an easie nature, quiet, mercifull, of no martiall disposition.

During Fedor's reign Boris Godunov acted as regent and at the time of Fedor's death (1598) there was still no law of succession. Boris Godunov was elected tsar. On his death (1605) the throne was occupied by Boris's son, Fedor Godunov, but he was assassinated within a few weeks and so began The Time of Troubles (see p. 15).

Michael, Alexis and Fedor III

The National Assembly elected Michael as tsar in 1613 and this ended The Time of Troubles. His son, the tsarevich Alexis, succeeded his father in 1645. By his two marriages Alexis had sixteen children; Fedor and Ivan were the only surviving sons of his first wife, Maria Miloslavskaya. His second wife, Natalia Naryshkina, left Peter who was only four at the time of Alexis death when Fedor III became tsar at the age of fourteen.

The Regency of Sophia

Sophia Alekseyana (1657–1704) was the eldest daughter of Tsar Alexis and Maria Miloslavskaya. After the death of her brother Tsar Fedor III in 1682 the successors to the throne were her mentally deficient brother Ivan and her half-brother Peter, son of Alexis's second wife Natalia Naryshkina (1651–94). Sophia was declared regent and ruled autocratically with her chief adviser and lover Prince Vasily Golitsyn, who became foreign minister. Two unsuccessful Crimean campaigns undermined their authority. In 1689 Sophia plotted to depose Peter. Peter was warned and fled to the Troisky Monastery, contacting the commanders of the army to inform them of the situation. Peter was supported by the Moscow Patriarch, by the majority of the nobles and part of the *streltsy*. Golitsyn was deported and Sophia was kept in a convent. Ivan died in 1696. During Peter's Grand Embassy in 1698 another attempt was made by Sophia's supporters to cause a rebellion. She was suspected of knowing about the plot and assuming the name Susanna; she was imprisoned in the Cloister of Intercession in Suzdal where she died. After Sophia had been deposed in 1689, Peter placed governing authority in the hands of his mother, Natalia Naryshkina, until 1694 when she died.

Alexis

Alexis (1690–1718), the son of Peter I (the Great) was the heir to the tsar but his unhappy relations with his father gradually worsened and Alexis left Russia in 1716. Peter encouraged him to return and then condemned him to death for treason; in fact he died before his execution. At Peter's death the succession problem was unsolved. Dying, he called for writing materials and wrote 'I leave all to . . .' but the rest was illegible. Following his death Russia had four emperors and empresses in a period of only sixteen years and a period of 'rule by favourites'.

Manifesto depriving Alexis of succession, 3 February 1718

> We saw that all our exertions for the upbringing and education of our son were vain, for he was never forthright in his obedience to us, paid no regard to what is appropriate for a good heir [to the throne], did not apply himself to study, and did not listen to the teachers we had appointed for him . . . Later we sent him abroad, in the hope that the sight of wellordered states would awaken his fervor and induce him to be upright and diligent. But all these efforts of ours availed nothing. The seeds of learning had fallen on stony ground: for not only did he fail to follow [good precepts], but he hated them and showed no inclination either for military or for civil affairs; instead, he constantly consorted with worthless and base people whose habits were coarse and disgusting . . . [There follows a lengthy account of

Alexis's misdeeds, culminating in his flight to the Habsburg lands, intrigues against Peter abroad, and of his return from Naples to Saint Petersburg. Although Alexis deserves to be put to death, the manifesto declares, Peter grants him full pardon and remission from all punishment.]

Nevertheless, in view of his unworthiness and his disreputable behavior described above, we cannot, in good conscience, leave him as our successor on the Russian throne, knowing that through his disgraceful actions he would forfeit all the glory of our people acquired by God's grace and our tireless toil and squander all the benefits we have gained for the state with so much labor – not only in restoring provinces torn away from our state by the enemy, but also in adding to it many notable cities and lands; it is also well known that we instructed our people in many military and civil sciences to the profit and glory of the state. Therefore, out of apprehension for our state and faithful subjects – lest they be brought by such a ruler into a worse condition than they had been in before – we, in virtue of our paternal power ... and as an autocratic sovereign, do, for the good of the state, deprive our son Alexis of the inheritance of our throne of all Russia on account of his faults and crimes, even if there be no person of our family left [to rule] after us. We proclaim as heir to the said throne our other son, Peter [Note: born in 1715, died in 1719], though he is still a minor, for we have no other heir who is of age. (Vernadsky and Fisher, 1972)

Catherine I (1725–27)

Peter I (the Great) having died intestate, his widow Catherine succeeded him, elected by a gathering not legally empowered to appoint a new monarch.

Peter II (1727–30)

Catherine I willed her throne to the grandson of Peter I (the Great), Peter Alekseyvich, in a document approved as valid at the time, though later regarded as a forgery.

Anne (1730–40)

The Supreme Privy Council offered the throne to Anne, daughter of Ivan V and niece of Peter I (the Great), conditional on her accepting less than autocratic power (see Conditions of Mitau p. 53). On becoming Empress she denounced the conditions on which she had accepted the throne.

Ivan VI (1740–41)

Great-nephew of Anne. Succeeded as nominal Emperor as an eight-week-old baby. Deposed (with regent Anna Leopoldovna) in the coup which brought Elizabeth to power.

Elizabeth (1741–61)

Daughter of Peter I (the Great) and Catherine I. Her claims to succeed Peter II in 1730 had arguably been greater than those of her cousin Anne, but had been passed over for the throne on earlier occasions.

Peter III (1761–62)

When Catherine II (the Great) seized power Peter III offered to share the throne with her as equal partner. She 'had a formula of unconditional abdication conveyed to him; he was to copy it and sign'. He was strangled in captivity a few days later.

Catherine II (the Great) (1762–96)

Catherine II usurped the throne and thrust her infant son Paul to one side instead of having him proclaimed Emperor with herself as regent during his minority.

Paul (1796–1801)

Tsar Paul inherited the throne from his mother Catherine II (the Great). He enacted a new law of succession in 1797 and this superseded the 1722 law of Peter I (the Great) that allowed each autocrat to nominate his own successor. The 1797 law was based on the principle of male primogeniture. The crown went first to the deceased tsar's sons and thereafter to his brothers. This law remained in force until the end of the dynasty, except for the 1825 crisis (see below). Paul was murdered in a coup which led to the succession of his son Alexander I.

The 1825 Crisis

Alexander I died in Taganrog on 19 November 1825 and news reached St Petersburg on 27 November. Grand Duke Constantine was considered by most to be heir presumptive but in 1822 he had sent Alexander a formal letter stating that he was unwilling to succeed to the throne. In 1823 Alexander signed a manifesto declaring Grand Duke Nicholas successor. However, Alexander decided to keep this information secret and Constantine continued to use the title Tsarevich. The news of Alexander's death did not reach Constantine until 7 December 1825 when he immediately proclaimed Nicholas as tsar. The same news reached Nicholas on 9 December and proclaimed Constantine as tsar. Constantine was Russian commander-in-chief of the Polish army at that time and refused to leave Warsaw. After an exchange of messages between Moscow and Warsaw Nicholas claimed the throne for himself. *The Times* said, 'The Empire is in the strange position of having two self denying Emperors and no active ruler.'

The End of the Dynasty

On 2 March 1917 Nicholas II abdicated in favour of his brother Grand Duke Mikhail Alexandrovich but on 3 March the Grand Duke refused the throne stating that he would only accept it if he was offered it by a democratically elected constituent assembly. This brought an end to the Romanov dynasty.

3
Political Chronologies

Ivan IV, Fedor I, Boris Godunov (1533–1605)

1533–1538	Regency of Ivan IV's mother, Elena.
1533–1586	Reign of Ivan IV (the Terrible).
1535	Edicts published against further monastic acquisitions of land.
1547	Ivan IV (the Terrible), adding to the title Grand Prince, assumes title 'Tsar'.
	Fire in Moscow destroys the arsenal, many churches and the palaces of the tsar and the metropolitan.
1549	First session of the *Zemskii Sobor* (Landed Assembly).
1550	Organisations of the *streltsy*; *Sudebnik* (Code of Laws) of Ivan IV.
	Tsarsky Sudebnik (Second of Laws Code): 1,064 'boyars' sons' given *pomestiya* in the environs of Moscow.
1550–1551	Council of *Stoglav* (Hundred Chapters).
	Stoglavy (Hundred headed) Synod.
1550s	First *prikazy* formed and reforms of local administration. Moscow constructs chain of stockades along the southern border and Russian colonisation of the steppe begins.
1552	Capture and annexation of Khanate of Kazan.
1553	Opening of the northern sea route to Russia by the English (Richard Chancellor).
1555	Formation of the Muscovy Company in London and extension of privileges to it for trade throughout the Moscow state.
1556	Conquest of Astrakhan.
1558–1583	The Livonian War of Ivan IV (the Terrible). A sustained but unsuccessful effort by Ivan IV to secure a Russian coastline on the Baltic at the expense of Poland and Sweden.
1561	The Livonian Order disbanded.
1564	First book printed in Moscow by Ivan Fedorov.

1564–1572	*Oprichnina* terror.
1565–1584	Ivan IV's reign of terror.
1566	*Zemskii Sobor* is convened to discuss Livonian War.
1569	Union of Lublin, resulting in the merger of Poland and Lithuania.
1570	Ivan IV's punishment of Novgorod.
	Novgorod razed on orders of Ivan IV: massacres of inhabitants.
1571–1572	Crimean Tatars raid and burn Moscow.
1572	*Oprichnina* abolished by Ivan IV.
1575	Simon Bekbulatovich installed in the Kremlin as tsar.
1577	Establishment of commercial ties with Holland.
1581	Ivan IV kills his eldest son, Ivan.
1581–1592	New cadaster books drawn up that serve as basis for serfdom.
1581–1587	Peasants forbidden to leave place on which they are tenants.
1582	Yermak conquers the Khanate of Sibir.
	Conquest of Siberia.
1584	Ivan IV (the Terrible) dies.
	Founding of the port of Archangel (Novokholmogory).
1584–1598	Rule of Tsar Fedor I.
	Zemskii Sobor convenes and crowns Fedor tsar.
1585	The principality of Tver becomes part of the Moscovite state; having been given to 'Tsar Simeon'.
1587–1598	Boris Godunov acts as regent.
1588	Giles Fletcher visits Moscow.
1589	Formation of the office of patriarch in Moscow.
	Metropolitan is raised to rank of patriarch.
1591	Death of Prince Dmitri at Uglich; Boris Godunov is accused of having him assassinated.
1594	Boris Godunov is named regent.
	Census taken of all cultivated land and registration of all peasant labourers is undertaken.
1596	Creation of Uniate Church in Poland-Lithuania.
1597	*Ukaz* grants nobles five years to claim their fugitive peasants.
	Death of Fedor I and end of the Ryurik dynasty.
1598	Boris Godunov is elected tsar by the *Zemskii Sobor*, and is crowned.
1601–1602	Edicts are published further restricting peasant mobility.
	Years of famine because of bad harvests (500,000 deaths).

Time of Troubles (1605–1613)

1605	Death of Boris Godunov and beginning of a period of unrest.
	Russia threatened with Polish and Swedish conquest.
1605–1606	Rule of first False Dimitry.
1606–1607	Bolotnikov's revolt.

1606–1610 Rule of Tsar Vasily Shuisky; he promises to govern with the Duma and the *Zemskii Sobor*.
1610–1612 Poles occupy Moscow.
1610–1613 Interregnum.
1610 Russians offer throne to Polish Prince Władysław.
The second False Dimitry is murdered by Tatars.
1611 Formation of popular militia to the north and east of Moscow.
1611–1612 National uprising against Poles.
1611–1617 Swedes occupy Novgorod.
1612 Militia relieves Moscow and drives out Poles.

Michael, Alexis, Fedor III (1613–1682)

1613 The *Zemskii Sobor* elect Michael Romanov as tsar and he is crowned by Metropolitan Cyril in Moscow.
Russian delegation is sent to Poland, but Sigismund III ignores its overtures. Philaret, father of the tsar, is taken prisoner.
Poland attacks Mozhaisk, Kaluga and Tula.
1614 Siege of Tula by the Swedes.
1615 New *Zemskii Sobor* is elected.
Gustavus Adolphus, king of Sweden, is defeated at Pskov. The German emperor Matthias offers to mediate the Russo-Swedish conflict.
1615–1616 Fiscal pressures increase. The Duma and the *Zemskii Sobor* vote for an emergency tax (20 per cent on property and 120 roubles per estate). The Stroganovs loan the state 56,000 roubles.
1617 Russia and Sweden sign the Peace of Stolbovo.
The Swedes return Novgorod but keep Ingria (Ingermanland) and Livonia, as well as fortifications along the border. Free trade is established between Sweden and Russia.
1618 Philaret Romanov, father of the tsar is freed by the Poles and is elected patriarch and shares power with his son. Under Philaret's influence, from 1622 to 1633, the role of the *Zemskii Sobor* is gradually reduced.
Poland and Russia sign a fourteen-year truce at Deulino. Russian prisoners are released and Russia abandons Smolensk without obtaining Ladislaus's renunciation of the Russian throne.
1619 The *Zemskii Sobor* makes an inventory of taxable land taken; peasants who had fled their land are encouraged to return; a special department is set up to deal with official abuses of power; a project to reform provincial administration, giving priority to elected assemblies, is put through and a national budget is established.

1621	The *Zemskii Sobor* issues a circular that encourages rural districts to resist the efforts of local officials to exact illegal taxes and corvées (unpaid labour).
1623	A French delegation comes to Moscow seeking an alliance against Poland and the Hapsburg Empire.
1624	Marriage of Michael Romanov to the princess Maria Dolgoruky. Maria dies within months and in 1625 he marries Eudoxia Streshniev.
1626	Gustavus Adolphus seeks to ally himself with Russia against Poland.
1626–1633	Military reforms are instituted: 5,000 foot soldiers, as well as cannon makers and instructors, are recruited from abroad, and arms are purchased from Holland and Germany.
1627	The powers and responsibilities of the magistrates and local tribunals are strengthened, usurping the prerogatives of the provincial governors (*voevoda*).
1628	Punishments are made more humane; a limitation is placed on the infliction of corporal punishment to recover debts.
1632	The tsar declares war on Poland following the death of Sigismund III.
1633	Philaret dies. Michael Romanov restores power to the *Zemskii Sobor* convoking it during crises.
1634	The Russians capitulate to the Poles. A permanent peace between Russia and Poland is established on the basis of the territorial status quo.
1637	The Don Cossacks seize Azov.
1645	Michael Romanov dies, and his eldest son (aged sixteen) Alexis I, succeeds him. The accession to the throne is confirmed by a vote of the *Zemskii Sobor*. Boris Morozov, Alexis's former tutor, exercises a de facto regency.
1646	Russian delegation travels to Poland and the tsar proposes that the Dnieper Cossacks and the Don Cossacks be combined, and that Russian and Polish troops join forces to invade the Crimea. The gradual elimination of the Boyar Duma, in favour of a council formed by the close advisers of the tsar (the 'Chamber Duma' or 'Privy Council of Boyars'). The Department of Secret Affairs is established. Initially a secret police and secret tribunal, the department will evolve into an administrative oversight agency. A census of households is conducted. Tax rates are increased, and a tax on salt is established.
1647	A code of military law is promulgated. The code is an adaptation

of Holy Roman Empire legislation (the 'Regulation of Charles V').

A Russian-Polish alliance begins military action against the Turks. The Poles battle the Turks in Turkey while the Russians fight them in the Crimea.

1648   The Poles are defeated by the Zaporozhian Cossacks, led by Bogdan Khmelnitsky, on the Dnieper River in the Ukraine and the Poles suffer another defeat at Piliavtsy.

1649   The *Zemskii Sobor* publishes a new legal code (*Ulozhenie*). Its nearly 1,000 articles reflect the essential content of the Mode of Ivan IV, with new elements borrowed from the Lithuanian and Byzantine codes. Under its terms, peasants are definitively attached to the land, privileges of foreigners are abolished, and the Church is subjected more firmly to state control.

Defeated at Zborov, Khmelnitsky signs a treaty with the Poles, but hostilities resume in 1650.

1651   Khmelnitsky suffers another defeat at the hands of the Poles, and he signs the Treaty of Belaia Tserkov.

1652   The first confrontation between Russians and Chinese on the Amur River takes place following the expedition of Khabarov (1649–1651).

1653   Alexis ceases to convoke the *Zemskii Sobor* on a regular basis.

With the intercession of Patriarch Nikon, Khmelnitsky asks for the assistance of the tsar.

Despite the treaty signed with Poland, the *Zemskii Sobor* accepts the idea of an intervention on the side of the cossacks. Alexis confirms the ancient rights of the cossacks to administrative autonomy and the free choice of their hetman.

1654   The campaign against Poland begins and Poland forms an alliance with the Crimean Tatars.

The Polish garrison at Smolensk capitulates. The *Rada* (the national assembly of the Ukraine) meets, on the initiative of Khmelnitsky, at Pereiaslavl. The Ukraine, under Khmelnitsky's control, recognises the sovereignty of the tsar.

1655   Russian and cossack forces lay siege to Lvov.

1656   Khmelnitsky dies. His successor, Vygovsky, is a partisan of Poland.

With imperial mediation, the Treaty of Vilna is signed. Alexis I will be offered the Polish throne on the death of Jan Casimir; in return, Alexis must abandon his conquests in Lithuania and the Ukraine and ally himself with Poland against Sweden.

Russia enters into its first negotiations with China.

1658   The Treaty of Gadiach is signed by the cossack hetman Vygovsky and Poland. Under its terms, one-third of the Ukraine is to be established as a west Russian grand duchy that will join the Polish Commonwealth with the same status as Lithuania. In addition, the Union of Brest-Litovsk is abrogated and freedom of Orthodoxy is guaranteed.

Russian troops invade the Ukraine and provoke an uprising against Vygovsky.

A three-year truce is signed by Sweden and Russia. Under its terms, Russian conquests in Livonia are guaranteed.

1659	Russian forces commanded by Prince Trubetskoi surrender to a coalition of Poles, cossacks and Tatars. Poland maintains its hold on the western bank of the Dnieper.
1661	Permanent peace is signed by Russia and Sweden.
	Alexis renounces his conquests in Livonia.
1667	Russia and Poland sign the Treaty of Andrusovo, a thirteen-year armistice. Poland retains possession of Vitebsk and Polotsk, and retains its rights in Livonia, but it cedes to Russia Smolensk and the surrounding region, as well as all of the eastern bank of the Dnieper. Although Kiev is on the western bank, Poland temporarily cedes the city to Russia.
1669	After the Peace of Andrusovo (1667), the Department of Foreign Affairs (directed by Afanasi Ordyn-Nashchokin) ceases to be responsible to the Duma and becomes autonomous.
1670–1671	Uprising of Stenka Razin who together with fugitive serfs and others savaged Ukraine and Southern Russia.
1671	Tsar Alexis marries Natalia Naryshkina.
	Execution of Stenka Razin.
	Artamon Matveev replaces Ordyn-Nashchokin as head of the Department of Foreign Affairs.
1672	Birth of Peter I (the Great).
	Russians establish embassies to all major European states.
1674	The tsarevich Alexis dies. His younger brother Fedor becomes the new heir to the throne.
1675	Using Jesuit intermediaries, Russia enters into new negotiations with China in Peking.
1676–1681	War with the Ottoman Empire and in the Crimea; confirming Russian possession of Ukrainian territories.
1676	Tsar Alexis I dies. Fedor III accedes to the throne. Actual power is exercised first by Artamon Matveev (until he is exiled to Siberia in July), and then by the clan of the tsar's late mother, Maria Miloslavsky (who died in 1669).
1678	An accord is reached between Poland and Russia, renewing the armistice of Andrusovo.
1679–1682	The penal code is revised and maiming is prohibited.

1681	Fedor III convokes the *Zemskii Sobor* to consult with him on the reorganisation of the army.
	The Peace of Bakhchirisai ends the Russo–Turkish conflict. Under its terms, all the lands between the Don and the Dniester rivers are to remain unoccupied, and no towns are to be established in the territory between Kiev and the lower Dnieper.
1682	Inspired by Basil Golitsyn, and with the consultation of the *Zemskii Sobor*, the council of boyars and the high clergy, Fedor III abolishes the mestnichestvo, the system of aristocratic precedence in the civil and military services.
	Death of Fedor III.

Peter I (the Great) (1682–1725)

1682	After *streltsy* attack on the Kremlin Ivan V and Peter I are established as co-tsars at a double coronation.
	Beginning of the Regency of Sophia with Prince Vasily Golitsyn as Foreign Minister.
	Execution of Archpriest Avvakum.
1682–1689	Sophia regent, with Peter I (the Great) as co-ruler and then as tsar.
1684	Institution of formal persecution of Old Believers.
1686	Russia enters the Holy League with the Holy Roman Emperor, Venice, and Poland.
1687	Slavo-Greek-Latin Academy in Moscow begins to function.
	Unsuccessful campaign against the Crimean Tatars.
1688	Peter I (the Great) begins experiments in shipbuilding on Lake Pleshcheyev.
1689	Peter I (the Great) marries Eudoxia Lopukhina.
	Treaty of Nerchinsk with China signed.
	Unsuccessful campaign against the Crimean Tatars.
	Sophia's regency overthrown, with Ivan's consent.
	Natalia Naryshkina becomes regent.
1690	Peter I (the Great) creates the first regiments of Preobrazhensky and Semenosky Guards.
1693	Peter I (the Great) visits Archangel and founds a shipyard.
1694	Natalia Naryshkina, the regent, dies.
1695–1697	Russian conquest of Kamchatka.
1696	Death of Ivan V, Peter I (the Great) becomes sole tsar.
	Capture of Azov, after an unsuccessful attack in the previous year. Building of a naval squadron begins there.
1697–1698	'Great Embassy' to Western Europe.
	Peter I (the Great) visits the Netherlands, England and Austria. He lives near a shipbuilding works at Zaandam where he works as

	an ordinary labourer. In London (1698) he meets William III and visits the Observatory and the Mint.
1698	*Streltsy* revolt breaks out and is savagely suppressed. Peter returns to Moscow. More than 200 are condemned to death.
	Sophia, the ex-Regent, is sent into exile to the Cloister of the Intercession in Suzdal.
	A permanent army is established.
	Peter I (the Great) orders the shaving of beards and the wearing of Western clothes.
	François Lefort, adviser to Peter I (the Great), dies.
1700	Peace is made with the Ottoman Empire.
	Outbreak of war with Sweden (Great Northern War) and Russian defeat at Narva.
	Patriarch Adrian dies but no successor is appointed and he is replaced by acting head of church.
	Julian calendar adopted.
1701	Foundation of navigation school at Moscow.
	Monasteries required to turn over revenues to state.
1703	St Petersburg is founded.
	Vedmosti, Russia's first newspaper, published in Moscow.
	Sophia, the ex-Regent, dies and is buried in the Novodevichy Convent.
1704	Reform of alphabet.
1705	The first systematic conscription for the armed forces in Europe is established.
	Beard tax introduced.
1705–1708	Outbreak of uprisings in Astrakhan, Bashkiria and the Don region against the tsar's policies.
1707	Great advance of Charles XII against Russia begins.
	Outbreak of Cossack rising in the Don area until 1708.
1708	Local administration by the creation of eight (later ten) *gubernii* (administrative provinces) and their subdivisions.
	The Swedes are defeated at the battle of Lesnaya but are joined by Mazepa.
1709	Decisive Russian victory over Sweden at Poltava, forcing Charles XII to take refuge in Turkey.
1710	Russians take Livonia and Estonia.
	Edict issued making official a simplified Cyrillic alphabet. Old Slavonic alphabet is retained only by the Church.
	Census of population.
1711	Outbreak of war with the Ottoman Empire and Russian defeat on the Prut, and loses Azov.

	Peter I (the Great) abolishes most trading monopolies and establishes monetary reform.
	Tsar's Council ('Boyar Duma') replaced by the Senate to supervise the administration.
1712	St Petersburg replaces Moscow as capital of Russia.
1713	Peace treaty with the Ottoman Empire.
1714	Decree forbids subdivision of estates among the heirs when the holder dies.
	Kormleniya (method of payment in kind paid by local population to administration, established in the fourteenth century) abolished and civil servants placed on a salary.
1715	Royal Naval Academy established at St Petersburg.
1716	Flight of the Tsarevich Alexis to Vienna and Naples.
	Russian occupation of Mecklenburg provokes the hostility of Britain and Emperor Charles VI.
	Ustav voinsky (Military Code) issued.
1716–1717	The second journey to Western Europe by Peter I (the Great). He visits the Netherlands and Paris.
	Alexis returns to Russia.
1718	Death of Alexis.
	Creation of the administrative colleges.
	Unsuccessful peace negotiations with Sweden in the Åland islands begin.
	Beginning of first 'soul' census.
	Colleges replace *prikazy* (Moscow government departments).
1719	Abolition of most state monopolies, excepting salt.
	Ladoga canal construction begun (completed 1731).
1720	*Morskoy ustav* (Naval Code) and *Generalny reglament* (General Regulation) issued; increasing efforts being made to systematise the machinery of government.
1721	War with Sweden is ended by the treaty of Nystad.
	Dukhovny reglament (Spiritual Regulation) issued and the Patriarchate abolished, replaced with Holy Synod.
	Merchants allowed to purchase villages in order to attach labouring force to industrial and mining enterprises.
	Senate proclaims Peter I (the Great) emperor.
	Peter I (the Great) acquires the right to nominate his own successor and assumes title of 'Emperor of all the Russias'.
1721–1723	Russo–Persian war.
1722	Table of Ranks promulgated.
1724	Catherine, the second wife of Peter I (the Great) married privately in 1707, is crowned as empress.

	Poll (Soul) tax introduced.
	First comprehensive protective tariff.
	Establishment of the Academy of Sciences in St Petersburg, later known as the Imperial Academy of Science.
1725	Death of Peter I (the Great) without having designated a successor.
	Accession of Catherine.

Catherine I, Peter II, Anne, Ivan VI, Elizabeth, Peter III (1725–1762)

1725–1727	Reign of Catherine I.
	Succession supported by Imperial Guards and most ministers.
1725	Vitus Bering's first expedition.
1726	A seven-member Supreme Privy Council, presided over by the Empress, established.
1727	Death of Catherine and accession of Peter II, grandson of Peter I (the Great) and son of the Tsarevich Alexis.
1727–1730	Rule of Peter II.
	Government by Supreme Privy Council during tsar's minority.
	Council dominated by Prince Aleksandr Menshikov.
1730	Death of Peter II from smallpox.
1730–1740	Rule of Empress Anne, daughter of Ivan V, and her favourite Biron (Bühren).
1730	Constitutional crisis; unsuccessful attempt by Supreme Privy Council to impose conditions on Anne.
	Supreme Privy Council abolished and Senate restored.
	Inheritance law of 1714 repealed.
1731	Establishment of Noble Cadet Corps and re-establishment of secret police, abolished by Peter I (the Great).
1733–1735	War of Polish Succession.
1733–1743	Bering's second expedition. He dies in Alaska.
1735	War with Turkey; Azov regained.
1736	Compulsory state service by nobles limited to twenty-five years and may begin at age twenty, but one son of each family may remain home to manage estates.
	Professional serfs attached in perpetuity to factories and mines.
1737	Serfs denied right to buy land.
c. 1740	Imperial Ballet School established at the Winter Palace.
1740	Death of Empress Anne.
1740–1741	Rule of Emperor Ivan VI, great-nephew of Anne, under regency of Count Biron.
1741	Emperor Ivan VI and his family imprisoned.

1741–1762	Rule of Empress Elizabeth, daughter of Peter I (the Great) and Catherine I.
1741–1743	War with Sweden.
1742	Elizabeth issues manifesto designating her nephew, the Duke of Holstein, as her successor.
1743	Treaty of Åbo gives Russia a portion of Finland.
1744	Death penalty abolished.
1745	Marriage of Peter, Duke of Holstein, nephew of Empress Elizabeth and heir to Russian throne, to Princess Sophia Augusta (later Catherine) of Anhalt-Zerbst.
1747–1762	Winter Palace, Smolny Convent and Peterhof Palace built by Rastrelli.
1749	First Russian oilfield discovered.
1753	Internal tariffs and tolls in Russian Empire abolished, and establishment of State Nobility Bank.
1754	University of Moscow founded and establishment of Commercial Bank in St Petersburg.
	Winter Palace in St Petersburg built.
1756	First permanent theatre opens in Russia.
	Academy of Fine Arts opens in St Petersburg.
1756–1762	Russia involved in Seven Years' War.
1762	Death of Empress Elizabeth.
	Peter III becomes tsar.
	'Manifesto of *Dvoryanstvo* Liberty' exempting the nobility, *dvoryanye*, from compulsory state service, allowing them to travel freely and to enter the service of foreign states.
	Secret police abolished and torture banned.
	Church and monastic properties sequestered; law effective in 1764.

Catherine II (the Great) (1762–1796)

1762	Catherine II (the Great) wife of Peter III gains throne by *coup d'état* (July 9).
	Peter III abdicates (July 10).
	Peter III murdered in mysterious circumstances (July 17).
	Senate ratifies *coup d'état* (August).
	Catherine II (the Great) crowned in Moscow (September 13).
1763	Senate divided into six departments, each with a Procurator General in charge.
1764	Automatic promotion for certain categories of civil servants.

Ivan VI murdered.
Church lands managed by the Economic College.
Most commercial and manufacturing monopolies abolished.
Law of 1721 allowing merchants to buy villages revoked.
Abolition of office of Hetman in the Ukraine.
First Hermitage is begun in St Petersburg.
Election of Stanislaw Poniatowski, former lover of Catherine II (the Great), as King of Poland, following Poland's occupation by Russian troops.
Russo–Prussian alliance and secret convention on Poland.
Regulation on the education of children is issued and the establishment of a school for young noble girls (the future Smolny Institute).
Diderot, the French encyclopedist, sells his library to Catherine II (the Great). She allows him to use it and also gives him a yearly pension of £1,000.

1765	Landowners allowed to punish serfs by sending them to penal servitude in Siberia.
	Free Economic Society founded in St Petersburg.
1766	Annexation of the Aleutian Islands.
1767	Automatic promotion rules for civil servants extended.
	Legislative Commission established to draft new code of laws. It met until December 1768 but failed to complete the work. It consisted of 564 deputies, 30 per cent nobles, 39 per cent city dwellers, 14 per cent state peasants, 12 per cent national minorities, 5 per cent state administration. One deputy was an ecclesiastic and serfs were not represented.
1768	War with Turkey.
1769	Advisory Council to Catherine II (the Great) formed.
	Russia's first satirical journals, *Vsyakaya vsyachina* and *Truten*, published.
1772	First Partition of Poland.
1773	Institute of Mines created.
1773–1775	Peasant and Cossack uprising under Yemelyan Pugachev. He declares himself Peter III and promises to liberate the serfs.
1774	Peace with Turkey concluded at Kuchuk-Kainardji.
1775	Provincial reform, increasing the number of provinces and making local government responsible to the Senate. Manufacturing activity open to all.
1781–1786	Ukraine and the Crimea incorporated into the empire.
1782	Pugachev executed in Moscow.

	The equestrian statue of Peter I (the Great) by Falconet is unveiled.
1782–1785	Hermitage built by Quarenghi.
1783	The Nobility, *Dvoryanye*, allowed to operate private printing presses.
	Count Grigory Orlov dies, Catherine II's lover who helped to put her on the throne.
1783–1784	Tanrida Palace built by Starov.
1785	Charter of Nobility (*Dvoryanstvo*) expanded aristocratic privilege by confirming nobles in hereditary tenure of estates and freedom from compulsory state service and set up local and regional corporations of nobles which chose officials subject to crown approval.
	Charter of Towns, which divided urban population into six groups, each of which elected representatives to town assembly; actual business of urban government carried out by executive board of six, one from each group, but police powers were left to officials appointed by crown.
1787–1791	War with the Ottoman Empire.
1788	War with Sweden, until 1790.
1790	Publication of Radishchev's *Journey from St Petersburg to Moscow*, a violent critique of autocracy and serfdom.
	He was arrested, condemned to death but sent into exile in Siberia.
	Treaty of Verala with Sweden.
1791	Catherine II (the Great) decrees Pale of Settlement, twenty-five western provinces where Jews are permitted permanent residence.
1792	Russia and Turkey sign Treaty of Jassy.
1793	Second Partition of Poland by Russia and Prussia.
1794	Catherine II (the Great) declares her intention to prevent Grand Duke Paul from surrendering to the throne.
1795	Third Partition of Poland by Russia, Prussia and Austria.
1796	Catherine II (the Great) dies.

Paul (1796–1801)

1796	All people detailed by the Secret Chancellory freed and a general amnesty declared for all officials facing prosecution.
	Treasury Ministry established.
	Article 15 of the Charter of 1785 is abolished. This exempts the nobility from corporal punishment.
	Forces sent to Persia by Catherine II (the Great) recalled.
1797	All unauthorised printing presses closed.

	Coronation of Tsar Paul.
	Decree issued on freedom of religion.
	Law on succession to the throne according to genealogical seniority.
1798	Russia joins Second Coalition against France.
	Importing of French books prohibited.
1799	Department of Appanages established, endowed with sufficient lands to provide for the needs of the Imperial family.
	Russian–American Company chartered Campaign in Northern Italy and Switzerland under Suvorov.
1800	Ministry of Commerce established.
	Importing of all foreign books prohibited.
	Paul forms alliance with Napoleon against England.
1801	Tsar Paul strangled.
	Georgia annexed by Russia.

Alexander I (1801–1825)

1801	Reform measures announced. Political prisoners are released and an amnesty declared.
	Foreign books again freely imported.
	Charter of Nobility reaffirmed.
	Secret (or Unofficial) Committee meets.
	A twelve-member permanent council established to study and prepare laws.
1802	Senate becomes the supreme institution of administration and justice.
	Eight ministries established: War, Navy, Foreign Affairs, Justice, Interior, Finance, Education and Commerce.
1803	Education is reorganised and Russia is divided into six educational districts.
1804	Kharkov and Kazan universities founded.
	Statute on Jews.
	Mild censorship law introduced.
	Report shows the superiority of paid over forced labour.
	Jews guaranteed freedom of religion as long as they reside in the Pale of Settlement.
1805	Russia joins the Third Coalition against France.
1806	War with Turkey following Russia's occupation of the Danubian principalities.
	Reconstruction of the Admiralty and the construction of the Institute of Mines and the Smolny Institute begin.
1807	Treaty of Tilsit with Napoleon.

	Russia joins the Continental System.
	Serfdom abolished in the Grand Duchy of Warsaw.
1807–1811	Speransky reforms.
1808	Plan to codify laws.
	Sale of serfs at markets forbidden.
1809	Abortive attempt to introduce civil service examinations.
	Abolition of owners' rights to deport serfs to Siberia.
	Conquest of Finland.
1810	State Council established to replace Permanent Council (1801) following the completion of Plan for State Reform (1809) which aimed at a move towards constitutional monarchy.
1811	Ninth ministry (of Police) created.
	Completion of the Marinsk and Tikhivin Canal Systems, connecting the Baltic to the Volga.
1812	French invade Russia and take Moscow.
1813	Grand Alliance against France.
1814	Paris taken and Alexander enters at the head of his troops.
	Congress of Vienna with Russia gaining the Grand Duchy of Warsaw.
	Formation of Kingdom of Poland under Russian control.
	Its constitutional charter provides for an elected Diet (or Sejin, a legislative assembly), a government and an army.
	First steamship in Russia constructed in St Petersburg.
	Peasant unrest in Poltava, Kursk and Orenburg.
1815	Holy Alliance and Quadruple Alliance.
	Russia acquires Duchy of Warsaw.
1816	Establishment of Union of Salvation (in 1817 renamed Union of Welfare), first secret organisation of the future Decembrists.
	Serfdom abolished in the Baltic provinces.
1817	State monopoly on alcohol.
1819	Ministry of Police combined with Ministry of Interior.
	University of St Petersburg founded.
1820	Jesuits expelled from Russia.
	Peasant uprising in the Don region.
1821	Union of Welfare dissolved and replaced by the Southern Society in the Ukraine and the Northern Society in St Petersburg.
	Patriotic Society founded in Warsaw.
1822	Right to deport serfs to Siberia reinstated.
1825	Death of Alexander I at Taganrog, and confusion over succession.
	Decembrist Revolt.
	Pushkin's *Boris Godunov*.
	Moscow Telegraph and *Northern Bee* founded.

Nicholas I (1825–1855)

1825	Constantine swears allegiance to Nicholas I.
1826	Execution of five Decembrist conspirators and over 100 deportations to Siberia.
	Second Section established with the task of codification of laws.
	Third Section established, secret police, which had been abolished by Alexander I.
	Censorship Code introduced.
1826–1828	War with Persia.
	Treaty of Turkmanchai and annexation of Armenia.
1827	State monopoly on alcohol abolished.
1828	Fourth Section responsible for women's education and public assistance established.
1828–1829	War with Turkey.
	Treaty of Adrianople.
1830	45-volume *Complete Collection of Laws of the Russian Empire* published.
	Cholera Riots.
	Literary Gazette founded.
1830–1831	Suppression of Polish revolt.
	Polish constitution abrogated.
1831	Pushkin completes *Yevgeny Onegin*.
1832	Polish constitution replaced by organic law and Poland integrated into Russia Empire.
1832–1833	Treaty of Unkiar–Skelessi.
1833	15-volume *Code of Laws* published.
	Made illegal to sell serfs without land at auction and also illegal to separate families.
	Münchengrätz agreement.
1834	Aleksandr Herzen banished to Vyatka.
	University of Kiev founded.
1835	Reform of University Statutes reduces their autonomy.
1836	Fifth Section responsible for administration of state peasants established.
	Paul A. Chaadayev declared insane by Nicholas for critique of Russian backwardness in his 'First Philosophical Letter' published in *Telescope*.
	First performance of Gogol's *Government Inspector* and Glinka's *A Life for the Tsar*.
1837	Pushkin killed in a duel.

	Ministry of State Domains established, replacing Fifth Section.
	First passenger railway – from St Petersburg to Tsarkoe Selo.
1840	Bakunin leaves Russia for Germany.
1841	Lermontov killed in a duel.
	Auction of serfs forbidden.
1842	Construction started on Moscow–St Petersburg railway.
	Gogol's *Dead Souls* appears.
1843	Sixth Section responsible for the administration of the Caucasus.
1845	Hereditary *dvoryanstvo* restricted to top five ranks.
	Revised version of Criminal Code.
	Petrashevsky Circle meets in St Petersburg.
	Russian Geographic Society founded.
1846	Dostoyevsky publishes *Poor Folk* and *The Double*.
	Aleksandr Herzen's *Who is to blame?*
1847	Turgenev publishes *A Sportsman's Sketches*.
	Aleksandr Herzen leaves Russia.
1848	Revolution in France, Austria, Italy and Germany.
	Publication of Marx's *Communist Manifesto*.
1849	Nicholas I intervenes to help Austria put down Hungarian revolt.
	Petrashevsky Cricle members arrested. Dostoyevsky and others sentenced to death but reprieved on scaffold and then deported to forced labour in Siberia.
1851	Opening of Moscow–St Petersburg Railway.
1852	Leo Tolstoy publishes *Childhood*.
	Death of Gogol.
1853	Aleksandr Herzen publishing from London as the Free Russian Press.
1853–1856	Crimean War.
1855	Death of Nicholas I.

Alexander II (1855–1881)

1855	Peasant agitation in the Ukraine.
1856	Treaty of Paris ends Crimean War.
	Hereditary nobility (*dvoryanstvo*) restricted to top four of the Table of Ranks.
	Alexander II advocates abolition of serfdom and appoints Select Committee. 'Better to begin to abolish serdom from above than to wait until it begins to abolish itself from below.'
1857	Herzen founds Kolokol (*The Bell*) in London.
	Introduction of protective tariffs.

1858–1860	Russian penetration in northeast Asia. Acquisition of Amur and Maritime provinces from China under terms of the Treaty of Aigun.
1858	Peasants working on the domains of the imperial family are emancipated.
1859	Shamil surrenders. Conquest of Caucasus complete except for Circassia (1864).
1860	Treaty of Peking. Foundation of City of Vladivostok. Rural courts introduced. State bank established.
1860–1873	First railway boom.
1861	Emancipation of serfs. *Zemlia i Volia* (Land and Freedom), a revolutionary secret society is established in St Petersburg. Army ceases to be used as punishment for criminals. Turgenev publishes *Fathers and Sons*. St Petersburg Conservatory of Music founded. Re-establishment of local government in Polish provinces.
1863	Polish rebellion.
1863–1864	Reforms of law, education, and local government (*zemstva*).
1864	Legal reform. Introduction of *zemstva* and city self-government.
1864–1868	Conquest of Central Asia.
1864–1880	Russia conquers Turkestan.
1865	Odessa University founded. Censorship relaxed.
1866	Prussia defeats Austria at Koniggratz. Attempt on Tsar Alexander's life by D. V. Karakozov. Moscow Conservatory founded. Dostoyevsky's *Crime and Punishment* published.
1867	Sale of Alaska and the Aleutian Islands to United States.
1868	Tolstoy's *War and Peace* finished (begun 1863).
1869	Tchaikovsky's first opera *The Voyevodye* performed.
1870	Aleksandr Herzen dies. Lenin born in Simbirsk. Formation of the Russian section of the First International. Compulsory military service introduced. Municipal *dumas* reorganised. First major strike in history at the Neva Cotton-spinning Mill, St Petersburg. Repudiation of Black Sea claims of the 1856 Treaty of Paris.

1871–1872	Education changes brought by Dmitri Tolstoy, Minister of Education, strengthens teaching of classical language.
1871	London Convention on the Straits.
	Bakunin's *Dieu et l'état*.
1872	Translation of Karl Marx's *Das Capital* published in Russia.
1873	Three Emperors' League.
	Attempt on Alexander II's life.
1873–1874	First 'Going to the People' movement.
	'Land and Liberty' secret society founded.
1874	Compulsory military service introduced.
1876	*Swan Lake* ballet by Tchaikovsky.
	Translation of Bible into modern Russian.
1877–1878	Russo–Turkish war ends with the Treaty of San Stefano.
	Mass trials of radicals, populists and revolutionaries (50 tried in March 1877 and 193 in January 1878).
1878	Bismarck presides over the Congress of Berlin.
	Vera Zasulich shoots St Petersburg police chief, but is acquitted by the jury.
	Terrorist assassinates Chief of Gendarmes (August).
	Temporary laws introducing courts-martial for terrorists.
	Secret circular authorising arrest and exile of persons suspected of seditious intent.
	Northern Union of Russian Workers formed in St Petersburg.
1878–1879	Mass strikes in St Petersburg.
1878–1881	Development of terrorist activity.
	Dynamiting of Winter Palace; wrecking of imperial trains.
1879	Electric lighting installed in St Petersburg.
	'Land and Freedom' split into 'People's Will' and 'Black Partition'.
	Stalin born.
	Attempt on life of Alexander II.
	'Temporary Governors General' created.
	Tchaikovsky's *Eugene Onegin*.
1880	Unsuccessful attempt on life of Alexander II by A. K. Solovev, terrorists succeeded in planting bomb in Winter Palace.
	Third Section abolishes former duties undertaken by Interior Ministry.
1881	Alexander II assassinated in St Petersburg by the National Freedom group, on the day he agrees to discuss political change.

Alexander III (1881–1894)

1881	Establishment of the Okhrana, Department for Safeguarding Public Security and Public Order.

	Institution of Emergency Powers, the tsar reaffirms his commitment to autocracy.
	Ascendancy of Konstantin Pobedonostsev.
	Major edict concerning 'Temporary Laws', i.e. rule of martial law.
	Pogroms against Jews occur in Elizavetgrad, Kiev and Odessa.
1882	*Communist Manifesto* by Marx and Engels is translated into Russian.
	Peasant Bank founded.
	Reduction of peasant redemption payments.
	Factory inspections established.
1883	Transcaucasus railway from Baku to Batum completed.
1884	*The Annals of the Fatherland* is suppressed.
	Holy Synod is given control over all primary schools.
	Universities lose their autonomy.
1885	Anglo–Russian crisis over Afghanistan.
	Land Bank for the Nobility founded.
	New edition of Criminal Code.
	Night work banned for women and children in textile mills.
1885–1887	Bulgarian crisis.
1886	Law requiring state peasants to buy out their land allotment.
	Abolition of soul tax (except in Siberia).
	Special rules governing forced labour.
1887	'Reinsurance Treaty' between Russia and Germany.
	Execution of Lenin's brother, and four others, for participating in attempt on the life of Alexander III.
1888	University of Tomsk opens.
1889	Restrictions on internal migrations is enacted.
1891	Construction of Trans-Siberian Railway begins.
	Secret Franco–Russian military convention against the Triple Alliance concluded.
	Many Jews evicted from Moscow and lose rights gained under Alexander II.
1891–1893	Severe famine in twenty-one provinces of European Russia.
1892	Sergie de Witte appointed Minister of Finance and Commerce.
	He revolutionises industry, commerce and transport.
1894	Death of Alexander III at Livadia in the Crimea.

Nicholas II and Revolution (1894–1917)

Nicholas II's inheritance

Although serfdom was abolished in 1861 by Alexander II the ex-serfs had to buy, by instalments, the land they had always worked. They became increasingly impoverished and still bound to their village communes. These became overcrowded and unrest became widespread, intensified by the Russian defeat in the Russo–Japanese War (1904–05), and led to the Revolution of 1905, which forced Nicholas II to authorise the establishment of a *duma*. The important agricultural reforms of Stolypin came too late to influence events. From the 1880s and up to the Revolution, there was a mass exodus from the Russian countryside into Siberia and to the towns and the commune lost its control of the peasants. The Russian industrial revolution began, based on plentiful and cheap labour. Railways and factories were built. St Petersburg and Moscow became textile and metal-working centres while the metallurgical industry developed in the Ukraine. Towns grew rapidly and the urban proletariat began to be established. The revolutionaries quickly exploited their troubles and hardships and paved the way for the February and October Revolutions.

Chronology

1894–1917	Reign of Nicholas II, son of Alexander III.
1895	Lenin founds the Union of Struggle for the Liberation of the Working Class in St Petersburg (November).
	Majority of members of the Union are arrested, including Lenin and Martov. Lenin's sentence was fifteen months in prison and exiled to Siberia for three years (December).
	Nicholas II condemns the 'insane dream' of elected assemblies.
1896	Expansion into Manchuria.
	Chinese Eastern Railway.
	One thousand people die in a stampede among crowds attending the coronation festivities of Nicholas II in Moscow.
	Tsar makes official visit to France.
1897	Foundation of Moscow Art Theatre.
	First census in Russia; total population 129,000,000 of which 13 per cent urban.
1898	Port Arthur leased by China.
	Foundation of Marxist Russian Social-Democratic Labour Party. Manifesto drafted by Pyotr Struve.
	Sergie Diaghilev publishes first edition of *Mir Isskustva* (*The World of Art*); continues until 1904.
1899	Student demonstrations and strikes occur at universities throughout the empire.
	Hague Convention.
1900	The newspaper *Iskra* (*Spark*) published in Leipzig and sold clandestinely in Russia.

	Lenin leaves Russia to live abroad.
	Russian is made the official language of Finland.
1901	Leo Tolstoy excommunicated.
1902	Trans-Siberian Railway opens. Journey from Moscow to Vladivostok takes fourteen days.
	Foundation of Socialist Revolutionary Party.
	Assassination of Dimitri S. Sipyagin (Minister of Interior).
	Lenin's *What is to be done?* is published.
1903	The Social-Democratic Labour Party meeting at their second congress in Brussels and later in London, splits into Bolshevik (led by Lenin) and Menshevik (led by Martov) wings; the Bund withdraws having been refused autonomy within the party.
	General strike in Baku; disturbances throughout Russia together with strikes.
1904–1905	Russo–Japanese war.
1904	Tsarevich Alexis is born (August).
	Assassination of Vyacheslav Plehve, Minister of Interior, who had carried on a systematic policy of repression.
	Zemstvo Conference demands a constitution and wider range of liberal reforms. An imperial *ukase* promises limited reforms.
	Dogger Bank incident.
1905	Surrender of Port Arthur (January).
	Bloody Sunday (January).
	Battle of Mukden (February–March).
	Destruction of Russian fleet at Tsushima by Japanese (May).
	Mutiny on the battleship *Potemkin* (June).
	Draft law on the establishment of a Consultative State Duma published (August).
	Treaty of Portsmouth, New Hampshire ends Russo–Japanese conflict. Russia cedes to Japan Port Arthur, the southern portion of the Manchurian railway and the southern half of Sakhalin Island (September).
	Assassination of Grand Duke Sergey.
	Abortive revolution and general strike.
	Establishment of Soviets of Workers' Deputies.
	Tsar issues manifesto promising a constitution and an elected parliament with genuine legislative power. The tsar also grants freedom of the press, free speech and religious toleration (October).
	The Constitutional Democratic Party (Cadets) is formed (October).
	Redemption payments are abolished for former serfs.

1906	Tsar issues Fundamental Law of the Empire by which the tsar retains most of his autocratic power.
	Legislative power is to be divided between the Duma and the upper house, half the members of which are to be appointed by the tsar. When the Duma is not in session the government may legislate by decree (May).
	First Duma assembles; votes no confidence in the government (May).
	Pytor Stolypin becomes prime minister.
	Deadlock over the constitutional issue leads to the dissolution of the Duma (July).
	New legislation enabling peasants to consolidate holdings and leave communes (November).
1907	The Second Duma meets; also known as the 'Red Duma' and 'Duma of Extremes' (March).
	The Third Duma meets; also known as 'The Duma of the Lords'.
	Hague Convention.
	Lenin emigrates and will not return to Russia for ten years.
1909	Women's access to universities is restricted and Jews are restricted by quotas.
	State Council refuses to let Old Believers form congregations.
1910	Death of Leo Tolstoy.
1911	Assassination of Pytor Stolypin by a double agent.
1912	Massacre of 270 mine workers in Lena goldfields after brutal repression.
	First issue of *Pravda* (Truth), the Bolshevik daily newspaper.
	Vyacheslav Molotov heads the editorial board and Joseph Stalin is also a member (May).
	Term of Third Duma ends (June).
	Elections to the Fourth Duma (November).
1914	General strike in St Petersburg (August).
	Germany declares war on Russia (August).
	Russia defeated at battle of Tannenberg (August).
	St Petersburg renamed Petrograd (August).
	Russians force Austrians from Galicia (September).
	Russia suffers severe losses at battle of the Masurian Lakes (September).
	Sale of alcohol forbidden for the duration of the war.
1915	Austro–German offensive in Galicia defeats Russians (May).
	Further Austro–German offensive leads by the autumn to over a million Russian casualties (July).

Duma meets to consider the way the war is being conducted (August).
Six parties in the Duma form the Progressive Block and demand a responsible ministry (August).
Tsar assumes supreme command of the armed forces (September).
Tsar rejects offer of resignation by his ministers to make way for a more popular administration (September).
Tsar prorogues Duma (September).
The number of strikes increases throughout the year.

1916 Duma meets (February).
Goremykin replaced as prime minister by Stürmer (February).
There are over 3,000,000 refugees in Russia because of military retreats (May).
Brusilov offensive gains some territory but fails to achieve decisive victory and costs over a million casualties (June–October).
Strikes and sporadic mutinies of soldiers at the front (September–October).
Rasputin murdered (December).

1917 Duma meets (February).
About 80,000 workers go on strike in Petrograd (February).
Tsar leaves Petrograd for army GHQ (March).
Large-scale demonstrations in Petrograd (March).
Queues at bakers' shops and crowds continue to demonstrate against the regime (March).
Police fire on crowds (March).
Strikes break out and soldiers join with the people; the tsar orders suppression of the trouble (March).
Police fire at demonstrators, but more soldiers join the protesters (March).
Tsar prorogues Duma (March).
Formation of Committee of State Duma to replace Tsarist government (March).
Formation of Petrograd Soviet of Workers' and Soldiers' Deputies (March).
First issue of *Izvestia* calls on people to take affairs into their own hands (March).
'Army Order No. 1' (*prikaz*) issued by Petrograd Soviet puts armed forces under its authority and urges rank and file to elect representatives to the Soviet (March).
Tsar Nicholas II, in Pskov, abdicates for himself and for his son, in favour of his brother, Grand Duke Michael, at the same time confirming the new ministry and asking the country to support

it. Grand Duke Michael chooses not to accept the throne unless he is asked by the Assembly (March).

The Provisional Government forbids the use of force against rioting peasants (March).

Constituent assembly meets; abdication of Grand Duke Michael (March).

Imperial family arrested (March).

Crown properties transferred to State (March).

Lenin arrives back in Petrograd (April).

'April Theses' published in *Pravda* having been read by Lenin on April 17.

Kornilov resigns command of forces in Petrograd, and Milyukov and Guchkov resign from the government (May).

Kerensky helps to reorganise provisional government (May).

State of renewed offensive on southern front (June).

Soldiers at front refuse to obey orders. Kornilov insists on offensive being called off and is appointed commander-in-chief (June).

State of northern offensive backed by Kerensky. Germans and Austrians drive Russians back after early successes (July).

Provisional government restores capital punishment and courts martial (July).

Bolsheviks organise demonstrations by sailors and Red Guards but the unrest is put down by loyal troops 'July Days'.

Fearing arrest, Lenin flees to Finland (July).

Lvov and Kadet ministers resign (July).

Formation of new government with Kerensky as prime minister (July).

Kornilov appointed commander-in-chief (August).

Kerensky resigns. Party leaders give him a free hand to form new government (August).

Kerensky holds Moscow State Conference to settle differences with Kornilov, but fails to reach agreement (August).

Riga falls to Germans (September).

Troops begin to move against Petrograd, and Kerensky denounces Kornilov 'plot' against the government. Collapse of movement followed by arrest of Kornilov and fellow generals (September).

Kerensky proclaims a republic (September).

Bolshevik majority in Moscow Soviet (September).

Trotsky becomes Chairman of Petrograd Soviet (October).

Lenin secretly returns to Petrograd from Finland (October).

Decision by Bolshevik Central Committee to organise an armed rising (October).

Formation of Military Revolutionary Committee by Bolsheviks (October).

Parliament refuses to give Kerensky powers to suppress the Bolsheviks (November).

Bolsheviks organise headquarters in Peter and Paul fortress and move on strategic points. Lenin takes command (November).

Bolsheviks seize power in Petrograd, taking key installations and services; the 'October Revolution' (November).

The Winter Palace cut off and ministers of provisional government arrested. Kerensky flees. Lenin announces the transfer of power to the Military Revolutionary Committee and the victory of the socialist revolution (November).

Lenin makes the Decree on Peace, an appeal for a just peace without annexations and indemnities, and the Decree on Land, affirming that all land is the property of the people (November).

A Bolshevik government is formed (November).

Counter-offensive by Kerensky against Petrograd fails (November).

Bolsheviks establish power in Moscow (November).

Metropolitan Tikhon elected patriarch in Moscow (November).

Left-wing social revolutionaries enter government after agreement with Bolsheviks (December).

Escape of Kornilov and fellow generals from prison in Bykhov (December).

Bolsheviks occupy Supreme Headquarters at Mogilev (December).

Finland declares itself independent from Russia (December).

Russia and Germany agree a ceasefire and start negotiations for a peace treaty in Brest–Litovsk (22 December).

Establishment of the *Cheka* (the All–Russian Extraordinary Commission for the Struggle against Counterrevolution, Sabotage and Speculation) headed by Felix Dzerzhinsky (December).

Banks are nationalised (December).

1918　Opening of Constituent Assembly (January).

Constituent Assembly dispersed (January).

Introduction of the Gregorian calendar (February).

Central Council of the Ukraine concludes separate peace with Central Powers, having declared its independence (February).

Brest–Litovsk negotiations broken off after German ultimatum (February).

Russians sign Treaty of Brest–Litovsk, giving up large areas of pre-Revolutionary Russia (March).

German troops continue to advance into central Russia and the Crimea (March).
Soviet government moves from Petrograd to Moscow (March).
Allied ships and troops arrive in Murmansk (April).
Execution of Imperial family at Ekaterinberg (July 16).

4
The Influence of the West

The Westerner/Slavophile controversy

The Slavophiles, who were most active in the 1840s and 1850s, represented an intellectual group that wanted the future of Russia to be based on its early history. They believed that Peter I (the Great) had corrupted Russia by looking to the West for inspiration. It was a philosophical and political movement that emphasised the rational individuality of Russia and idealised the Russian past, and particularly admired the pre-Petrine period. Basically the movement had liberal aims but was not democratic. The centre of the movement was Moscow and it attracted members of the old aristocracy whose interests included history, philosophy, theology, philology and folklore. Its members included Aleksei A. Khomyakov, Konstantin S. Aksakov, Ivan S. Aksakov, Ivan V. Kireyevsky, Pyotr V. Kireyevsky and Yury F. Samarin, and they were greatly influenced by Friedrich Schelling.

The Westerners believed in the superiority of Western Civilisation and maintained that Russian conditions were essentially similar to those in Western Europe, or Russia could easily imitate them and should Westernise as soon as possible. This included the development of capitalism and the introduction of constitutional governments. Both Slavophiles and the Westerners came from the same social and intellectual backgrounds and had in common disillusionment with the existing regime. Drawing distinctions between them is far from easy.

Slavophiles distrusted Western Europe with its Roman Catholic and Protestant religions, and considered constitutional government and capitalism as the outcome of a deficient society. The Russian Orthodox faith by contrast gave Russians a common faith so that the people were united in a 'Christian community'. Within this spiritual community an individual could find true freedom, therefore there was no need for Western state structures. The Slavophiles also believed in the peasant commune and an autocratic form of government. Some Slavophiles felt that once a truly Christian society was established Russia should reintroduce spiritual values in the West to replace rationalism, materialism and individualism.

Slavophiles urged extensive reforms to bring back autocracy and the church in their pure form and aimed at:

1 the emancipation of the serfs;
2 reducing bureaucracy;
3 freedom of speech;
4 freedom of the press;
5 freedom of conscience;
6 establishing of an institution representing the whole people similar to a *veche* or *zemskii sobor*.

Nicholas I objected to their criticism of his regime. His government censored their journals and generally tried to suppress the movement. After the Crimean War (1853–56), the death of many of its leaders and the reforms of Alexander II that achieved part of its aims, the movement declined. It then tended to merge with Panslavism.

Peter I's visits to Western Europe
In 1697 Peter I (the Great) organised an embassy of 250 to visit Western Europe. He was, in fact, the first tsar to travel west except on a military campaign and J. Bouvet in *The Present Condition of the Muscovite Empire* (1699) wrote

> the motive which could induce so great a prince to leave for some time his native country cannot be attributed to any other cause than his most ardent desire of improving his own knowledge and of his subjects, quite contrary to what has been practised by his predecessors, who looked upon the ignorance of their subjects as the main foundation stone of their absolute power.

The Grand Embassy consisted of three ambassadors headed by François Lefort and it left Moscow on 9 March 1697 and over a period of eighteen months travelled through Sweden, Holland and England and in the Hapsburg Empire. There were three main aims of the embassy, the first was to bring concerted action against Turkey by European states, the second was to obtain greater knowledge of shipbuilding, and the third was to recruit craftsmen and sailors. Peter travelled with the embassy incognito as Pëtr Mikhailov and spent many months working as a craftsman in the docks of Amsterdam and London, having left Holland for England in January 1698 with a squadron of the Royal Navy. He stayed in England for three and a half months.

John Evelyn (1620–1706), the English diarist, wrote in 1698 'The Czar of Muscovy being come to England, and having a mind to see the building of ships, hir'd my house at Sayes Court, and made it his Court and Palace, new furnished for him by the King.' Whilst Peter was in his house Mr Evelyn's servant writes to him:

> There is a house full of people, and right nasty. The Czar lies next your Library, and dines in the parlour next your study. He dines at 10 o'clock and 6 at night, is very seldom at home a whole day, very often in the King's Yard, or by water, dressed in several dresses. The King is expected there this day, the best parlour is pretty clean for him to be entertained in. The King pay for all he has.

During his stay he did so much damage, that Mr Evelyn had an allowance of £150 for it. He particularly regrets the mischief done to his famous holly hedge, which might have been thought beyond the reach of damage. It is said that one of Peter's favourite recreations was to demolish the hedges by riding through them in a wheelbarrow.

Later the tsar went on to Vienna and met Emperor Leopold I, but was unable to continue his journey to Venice and France because of the revolt of the *Streltsy* and was forced to return to Russia. By August 1698 he recruited over 750 foreigners to work in Russia.

In 1717 Peter I (the Great) made a second visit to Western Europe, visiting the Dutch Republic and France. In Paris Peter had meetings with the Regent and with Louis XV in the Tuileries. Visits were also made to the Sorbonne, the Observatory and the Opera. During this visit to Paris he recruited over sixty skilled technicians to work in Russia.

The Beard Tax

In Muscovy beards were 'essential to personal salvation' but the shaving of beards was begun by Peter I (the Great) after his return from the Grand Embassy. Wishing to modernise Russia, Peter ordered that beards be shaven and Western dress adopted. For Peter the beard represented all that was backward and uncivilised in Russia. For the majority of Orthodox believers, however, the beard had a special religious significance, and they considered it shameful to shave their beards. At first all Russians except the clergy were ordered to shave.

> In 1700 a boyar was sent to Kamyshin, a town on the Volga, to instruct the governor and town officials to shave off their beards and dress in the new style. They obeyed and the boyar returned to the capital. Their compliance enraged a nearby settlement of cossack Old Believers who promptly attacked the town and sacked it. The governor escaped and hid on a nearby island while the cossacks cut the heads off of anyone who had been so imprudent

as to shave. Persons found wearing Western dress had their pockets filled with stones and were dropped into the Volga. Others were tied to tree trunks and similarly cast into the river to be used for target practice. The cossacks stayed on the rampage for six weeks – until the governor was eventually handed over. Despite the fact that his beard had grown the cossacks still expressed a desire to kill him. They only spared his life when the entire population of Kamyshin interceded on his behalf. They finally withdrew under the threat of an advancing punitive force, having extracted from the townspeople an oath never to shave again.

Eventually those who wished to keep their beards could do so providing they paid an annual beard tax. The amount paid ranged from 2 kopeks for peasants to 900 roubles for wealthy merchants. The taxpayer then received a bronze medallion with a picture of a beard and the words 'tax paid' inscribed on it, which was to be worn on a chain around the neck.

The founding of St Petersburg

In 1703 Peter I (the Great) founded the city, having captured the Swedish fortress of Nöteborg, situated where the river Neva flows out of Lake Ladoga and enters the Gulf of Finland. He established a church dedicated to the Apostles Peter and Paul. This was situated on the island of Saiatschie; the Neva divides at this point into the main streams of the delta. The strategic delta had been contested by German and Swedish forces since the thirteenth century. Thousands of workers joined in the task of building, including prisoners of war and criminals released from prison. Masons had no alternative but to work in St Petersburg because of a decree which allowed only wooden buildings to be built elsewhere in Russia. Every nobleman who owned thirty families of serfs was compelled to build a house, at his own expense, in the new city.

The Admiralty and ship yards were the first constructions but there were elaborate plans for such roads as Nevsky Prospekt which was cut through the forests from the river Neva to a newly built monastery of St Alexander Nevsky. Alexander Nevsky defeated Sweden in 1240 and his bones are buried in the monastery. Government buildings were built and continuous expansion was achieved by bridging the many channels of the river Neva and building on the islands. Members of the government, trading and skilled classes, were obliged to live there. The city was proclaimed the capital of Russia in 1712.

Catherine II (the Great) and the Philosophes

Catherine II (the Great) was influenced by the literary men, scientists and thinkers in France known as the Philosophes who were convinced of the supremacy of human reason; among her friends were Voltaire and Diderot. They were inspired by René Descartes and were concerned for social, economic and political reforms. Initially the dominating figures were Voltaire and Montesquieu but in the second half of the eighteenth century the contributors to the *Encyclopédie*, Diderot, D'Alembert, Turgot, Condillac, Helvétius, Mably, Marmontel, Rousseau and Buffon, came to the fore. Publication of the *Encyclopédie* began in 1751 but in 1759 the Parlement ordered the burning of all volumes of the work published to that date, along with Voltaire's *Dictionaire philosophique*. The French Revolution of 1789 was held by many to be influenced by the writings of the Philosophes.

Although Catherine welcomed the Enlightenment she had no wish to give up her own privileges. Diderot was Catherine's guest in St Petersburg in 1773. He urged her to establish an English-style Parliament but Catherine replied that it was easy for him to reform on paper that did not answer back, but she had to deal with human beings with all their traditions and susceptibilities.

5
Political and Administrative Changes in Imperial Russia

Ivan IV (the Terrible)

The *Zemskii Sobor* was convened in 1550. The deputies reviewed with the tsar the outlines of new administration and judicial systems, and they set in motion the drafting of a new legal code. New governmental departments (*prikazy*) for finance, war and foreign affairs were established.

Limits are placed on the powers of provincial governors (*voevoda*), who were then made subject to the control of elected assemblies, and who will be gradually replaced by elected village mayors (*starosty*). The first census is taken to increase the accuracy of tax assessments.

Ivan IV issues a *ukase* organising the tsar's service. Land in the Moscow region was allocated to 1,000 boyar sons, who formed the nobility of the capital and served the sovereign.

The *oprichnina* was created in 1565 as a special political and police institution loyal to the tsar, and also as a separate jurisdictional zone within Russia. The country was divided into two zones, the first zone retained the former organisational structure, while the second zone, 'the special court territory', (the *oprichnina*) comprised a domain reserved for the service nobility. This reform was accompanied by a bloody repression and 3,500 boyars are executed. The *oprichnina* system was extended to cover more territory in 1566.

Rights of peasants to leave the domain on which they were tenants was suspended for one year in 1581. This measure was renewed each year until 1587 and was known as the 'Forbidden Year'.

Fedor I

The right of peasants to leave their landlord (the St George's Day law) was abrogated in 1592. In an effort to end the constant movements of the population, as well as to assure the exploitation of the land and to limit brigandage, peasants were bound to the land.

Michael

Zemskii Sobor vote for an emergency tax in 1615–16, 20 per cent on property and 120 roubles for each estate. The Stroganovs loan the state 56,000 roubles.

An inventory of taxable land is taken by the *Zemskii Sobor* in 1619. Peasants who had left their land are encouraged to return. A special department is established to deal with official abuses of power. Reform of provincial administration is envisaged, giving priority to elected assemblies and a national budget is established.

Zemskii Sobor (1621) encourages rural districts to resist the efforts of local officials to exact illegal taxes and *corvées* (unpaid labour).

Alexis

Zemskii Sobor (1648) approve a new legal code (*Ulozhenie*), enacted in 1649. The 1,000 articles provided the first comprehensive set of laws since 1550, but with new provisions taken from the Lithuanian and Byzantine codes. The aim was to give certainty to economic, social and political affairs after the Time of Troubles. Under the code, peasants were definitively attached to the land, and was the final establishment of serfdom (until 1835). Time limits for reclaiming runaways was removed, privileges of foreigners were abolished, and the Church was more firmly controlled by the state.

The government in 1656 decides to issue a copper rouble to replace the silver rouble on a one-for-one basis. The currency was debased to meet the cost of war. Inflation in 1662 caused by the circulation of copper roubles provokes the 'Copper Revolt'. In Moscow 7,000 people are killed in the revolt. In the provinces, agrarian troubles increase. A portion of the armed forces, under orders from Prince Kropotkin, joins the insurgents. *Ukase* of 1663 puts an end to the minting of copper coins, and coins are taken out of circulation.

Peter I (the Great)

Reform of government and administration

Peter I (the Great) reorganised and reformed central government and thereby increased his own power. His system remained in place in similar form until the end of the nineteenth century. Administration was carried out by ministerial colleges (agencies) which were established in 1717: foreign affairs, state revenue, justice, state control, army, admiralty, commerce, extractive industry and manufactures, and state expenditures. Each college had a specific responsibility and was managed by a director under a board. There was a Senate, replacing the Boyar *duma*, of appointed members whose function was to supervise the work of the colleges, but it had no real power to co-ordinate or plan. The Senate assumed many of the powers of the tsar when he was abroad and Peter I issued a *ukaz* listing the Senate's responsibilities.

1. To establish a just court, to deprive unjust judges of their offices and of all their property, and to administer the same treatment to all slanderers.
2. To supervise government expenditures throughout the country and cancel unnecessary and, above all, useless things.
3. To collect as much money as possible because money is the artery of war.
4. To recruit young noblemen for officer training, especially those who try to evade it; also to select about 1,000 educated boyars for the same purpose.
5. To reform letters of exchange and keep these in one place.
6. To take inventory of goods leased to offices or *gubernii*.
7. To farm out the salt trade in an effort to receive some profit for the state.
8. To organise a good company and assign to it the China trade.
9. To increase trade with Persia and by all possible means to attract to that trade, in great numbers, Armenians. To organise inspectors and inform them of their responsiblities.

In 1707 Peter I (the Great) divided the country into provinces (*gubernii*) under appointed governors. His later attempts, from 1718, at replacing provincial and town governments were not as successful, largely due to insufficient expertise and finance. The collection of the poll tax was all-important and a new local unit, the regimental district, was created and the poll tax was collected by military units. The poll tax (soul or head tax) was a capitation tax paid by every male peasant and by urban artisans and burghers introduced by decree in 1723. It became an important element of state revenue; the household tax and tax on cultivated land was abolished. Although this placed a considerable burden on the peasants it resulted in an increase in the area of land cultivated, since it was in the peasant's interest to cultivate as much as possible in order to pay the tax. The accumulation of arrears of the tax forced the government to lower the rate of tax in 1725, in 1742 and again in 1750–58. Later it was increased again, reaching one rouble in 1794. It was finally abolished in 1887.

Reform of the army and navy

The Russian army was formed in medieval times from feudal levies of nobles. These levies were called out when needed. Such armies had serious disadvantages in that the soldiers were only partially trained and generally they only served for one campaign. Ivan IV created the *Streltsy*, a small number of professional soldiers, who by 1600 numbered 12,000. Peter I (the Great) set about establishing a Russian army in modern form. He disbanded the *Streltsy* in 1698 after a bloody mutiny. His 'play regiments', which he had formed for his childhood games of war, became the Preobrazhensky and Semyonovsky Guards and are regarded as the first units of the Russian regular army. In November 1699 Peter I ordered that there should be an enlistment of volunteers and peasant conscripts. Commissions were established in Moscow, Novgorod, Pskov and Smolensk. Better conditions were provided for the recruits and volunteers were paid eleven roubles a year. Landowners provided one foot soldier for every fifty peasant households and a cavalryman for each hundred households. Those in civil administration had to provide an infantryman for every thirty peasant households and monasteries and church servants had to provide one for every twenty-five households. From the 32,000–33,000 men recruited, twenty-seven new infantry regiments and two of dragoons were formed. There were levies for recruits in 1702, two in 1705, five in 1706 (two for infantrymen and three for cavalry) plus one of 1,000 for the navy. Peasant recruitment continued throughout Peter's reign. Recruiting and training officers proved more difficult and many were recruited from abroad; some proved to be unpopular and in a proclamation of 1702 the tsar stressed that he wanted competent and skilled officers. About 10 per cent of the officers in Peter's new army were foreigners. Peter also sent young Russians abroad, particularly to France, to study military tactics.

The need for specialised training saw the establishment of the first of the Schools of Artillery in 1701, an Engineering School in Moscow in 1709 and in St Petersburg in 1719. The War College was established 1718–19. Units of infantry, cavalry, and artillery used the tactics of Western armies to good effect against the Swedes in the Northern War and won the battle of Poltava in 1709. The Peace of Nystadt in 1721 made Russia a Baltic power. Irregular forces of Cossacks and Bashkir tribesmen were also used, but it was the regular army founded by Peter that made Russia powerful throughout the eighteenth century.

Peter I (the Great) was also the architect of the modern Russian navy. A School of Navigation was opened at Azov and the Navy Department in 1698. In 1701 the Admiralty Prikaz was established to supervise the building of the new fleet. The Naval Academy was established in St Petersburg in 1715 for 300 students (500 by 1718).

Expenditure on the navy:

	roubles
1701	81,000
1706	204,000
1715	700,000
1724	1,200,000

By the end of Peter's reign there were thirty-four ships of the line and fifteen frigates manned by 28,000 men. Many British officers served in the Russian navy in the eighteenth century and Russian officers trained with the British navy.

Russia had the third largest navy in the world until the Russo–Japanese War, after which she came sixth as a world naval power. Russia was rebuilding her navy when World War I broke out. There were several mutinies in the 1905 Revolution, and the navy played an important part in both the February and October Revolutions.

The Table of Ranks (1722)

The Table of Ranks was a system devised by Peter I (the Great) in 1722 that assigned military, court and civilian service to fourteen parallel grades. Each rank in one section had a corresponding rank in the other two. All those entering service began on the bottom rung, and promotion was to be dependent on ability and length of service, rather than on birth. Membership of the *dvoryanstvo* or nobility was automatically granted to those who had succeeded in climbing the first eight ranks of the civil or court ladder, and the first fourteen of the military ladder. Theoretically, therefore, even those not of noble birth could become hereditary noblemen with the right to possess serfs. The traditional way of providing service to the state was for noblemen to serve in the army or administration, the merchants and peasants to pay their taxes, and for the clergy to pray. The Table of Ranks simultaneously consolidated the rights and the obligations and duties of the nobility.

The Ranks were:

	Civil	*Navy*	*Army*
1	Chancellor	General-Admiral	Generalissimo
			Field Marshal
2	Actual Privy Councillor	Admiral	General of Artillery
			General of Cavalry
			General of Infantry
3	Privy Councillor	Vice-Admiral	Lieutenant General
4	Actual State Councillor	Rear Admiral	Major General
5	State Councillor	Captain-Commander	Brigadier
6	Collegiate Councillor	First Captain	Colonel
7	Court Councillor	Second Captain	Lieutenant Colonel
8	Collegiate Assessor	Lieutenant-Captain of the Fleet	Major
		Third Captain of Artillery	
9	Titular Councillor	Lieutenant of the Fleet	Captain or Cavalry Captain
10	Collegiate Secretary	Lieutenant-Captain of Artillery	
11	Ship's Secretary	Lieutenant of Artillery	Staff Captain or Staff Cavalry Captain

	Civil	Navy	Army
12	Secretary in Superior Courts and in *guberniia* administration	Midshipman	Lieutenant
13	Provincial Secretary	Artillery Constable	Sublieutenant
14	Collegiate Registrar		Guidon Bearer

The Table of Ranks was used until 1917 although adaptions were made from time to time, particularly in 1845. The following Table of Ranks was published in 1901:

	Civil	Navy	Army
1	Chancellor	Admiral General	Field Marshal General
2	Actual (or Right) Privy Councillor	Admiral	General of Cavalry General of Infantry General of Artillery
3	Privy Councillor	Vice-Admiral	Lieutenant General
4	Actual (or Right) State Councillor High Procurator Master Herald	Rear Admiral	Major General
5	State Councillor		
6	Collegiate Councillor	Captain, 1st Grade	Colonel
7	Court Councillor	Captain, 2nd Grade	Lieutenant Colonel
8	Collegiate Assessor	–	Captain
9	Titular Councillor	Lieutenant	Staff Captain
10	Collegiate Secretary	Warrant Officer	Lieutenant
11	–	–	–
12	*Guberniia* Secretary	–	Sublieutenant
13	–	–	Ensign
14	Collegiate Registrar	–	–

Classes 1 and 2 were addressed as 'Your Supreme Excellency', 3, 4 and 5 as 'Your Excellent', and 6–14 as 'Your Honour'.

Peter I (the Great) added rules to the Table of Ranks to show how they should be interpreted. Important ones included:

> Those princes who are related to Us by blood or those who are married to Our princesses always take precedence and rank over all other princes and high servants of the Russian state.
>
> Naval and land commanding officers are to be determined in the following manner: if they both are of the same rank, the naval officer is superior at sea to the land officer; and on land, the land officer is superior to the

naval officer, regardless of the length of service each may have in his respective rank.

Whoever shall demand respect higher than is due his rank, or shall illegally assume a higher rank, shall lose two months of his salary; if he serves without salary then he shall pay a fine equal to the salary of his rank; one third of that fine shall be given to the individual who reported on him, and the remainder will be given to a hospital fund. The observance of this rank procedure does not apply on such occasions as meetings among friends or neighbours or at social gatherings, but only to churches, the Mass, Court ceremonies, ambassadorial audiences, official banquets, official meetings, christenings, marriages, funerals, and similar public gatherings. An individual will also be fined if he should make room for a person of lower rank. Tax collectors should watch carefully [for any signs of violations of these procedures] in order to encourage service [to the state] and to honour those already in service, and [at the same time] to collect fines from impudent individuals and parasites. The above prescribed fines are applicable to male and female transgressors.

An identical penalty will be given to anyone who will demand a rank without having an appropriate patent for his grade.

Equally, no one may assume a rank that has been acquired in the service of foreign state until We approve it, an action which We shall do gladly in accordance with his service.

No one may be given a new rank without a release patent, unless We personally have signed that release.

All married women advance in ranks with their husbands, and if they should violate the order of procedure they must pay the same fines as would their husbands if they had violated it.

Although We allow free entry to public assemblies, whereever the Court is present, to the sons of princes, counts, barons, distinguished nobles, and high servants of the Russian state, either because of their births or because of the positions of their fathers, and although We wish to see that they are distinguished in every way from other [people], We nevertheless do not grant any rank to anyone until he performs a useful service to Us or to the state . . .

Catherine I, Peter II, Anne, Elizabeth, Peter III

Creation of the Supreme Privy (Secret) Council

On 8 February 1726 the Supreme Privy (Secret) Council was established, presided over by Empress Catherine I. It reduced the powers of the Senate and had seven members including Alexander Menshikov and Peter Tolstoy. Alexander Menshikov had repeatedly urged her to form a small exclusive group of ministers to stand between her and the governing Senate. The Council met twice a week, dealing with home affairs on Wednesdays and foreign policy on Friday. Initially Catherine I attended sessions but subsequently she was content with signing the Council's decisions into law. When Catherine I died in 1727 the Council ruled in the name of Peter II. After his death it elected Anne Ivanovna empress on condition that she remained subject to the Council. On ascending the throne she declined to have her power curtailed and became an autocrat. The Council was abolished in 1730.

'Conditions of Mitau'

The conditions that the Supreme Council aimed to place on Anne, sometimes known as the 'Conditions of Mitau' were:

1   that she did not marry;
2   that she did not appoint a successor;
3   that the Supreme Council controlled State affairs;
4   that the Council's membership should remain eight;
5   that the Empress could not declare war;
6   that the Empress could not make peace;
7   that she could not levy taxes;
8   that she could not commit state funds;
9   that she could not confiscate estates, neither could she grant estates;
10 that she could not appoint anyone to a rank higher than that of a colonel;
11 all armed forces, including the guards, to be under the control of the Supreme Council.

Thus, for a very short period, constitutional rule was established in Russia. Anne had exchanged an absolute monarchy for an absolute oligarchy in the form of the Council. Although the agreement suited the Dolgorkys and Golitsyns it was not welcomed generally by the gentry. On 25 February 1730 Anne destroyed the agreement and on 4 March she dissolved the Council by a manifesto when the lower nobility and guards regiments supported her assumption of absolute power.

Catherine II (the Great)

Marshals of the Nobility (1766)

Elected representatives of the nobility, a system initiated under Catherine II in 1766. Organised locally, there were both provincial and district marshals, elected by assemblies of deputies every three years.

Legislative Commission (1767–68) and Catherine's Nakaz

Commission set up by Catherine II (the Great) in order to introduce fundamental changes of policy based on the ideas of the Enlightenment. Catherine prepared 'The Instruction' (*Nakaz*) for the commission, which was to undertake the codification of laws and work toward the modernisation of Russian law and life. The *Nakaz* together with its two supplements consisted of 655 articles and was the most important writing of Catherine II (the Great). It represented Catherine's ideas on how Russia's laws could be remodelled on Western lines. At its first session in 1767, the commission consisted of 564 deputies; 28 had been appointed and 536 elected; 30 per cent were nobles, 39 per cent city dwellers, 14 per cent state peasants, 12 per cent for national minorities, 5 per cent representatives of state administration, 1 representative an ecclesiastic and serfs not represented. The commission received 1,441 registers of grievances and despite its 203 sessions, the commission bore little fruit and divided into different factions. It did, however, provide Catherine with a large source of information about Russia, which influenced her later reforms. She disbanded the commission in 1768.

Catherine's account of the Legislative Commission, 1765–68:

> I decided in my own mind [c. 1765] that the general attitude and the civil law could only be improved by the adoption of useful rules, which would have to be written and ratified by me, for all the inhabitants of the Empire and for all circumstances.
>
> And to this end I began to read and then to write the Instruction for the law-making Commission.
>
> I read and wrote two years and said not a word for a year and a half, but followed my own judgment and feelings, with a sincere striving for the service, the honor, and the happiness of the empire, and with the desire to bring about in all respects the highest welfare of people and of things, of all in general and each individual in particular. When in my opinion I had pretty well arrived at my goal, I began to show parts of the subjects I had worked out to different persons, laying before each that which would be of interest to him, among others Prince Orlov and Count Nikita Panin. The latter said to me: 'Those are principles to cast down walls.' Prince Orlov thought very highly of my work and often wished to show it to this person or that; but I never showed more than one or two pages at a time. At last I composed the manifesto concerning the calling of delegates from the whole empire, in order to learn more about the conditions of each district. The delegates then assembled in Moscow in the year 1767. I summoned several persons of quite different ways of thinking to the Kolomensky Palace, where I was living at the time, in order to have them listen to the finished Instruction for the Commission on Laws. At every section there was a dif-

ference of opinion. I permitted them to cross out and efface whatever they liked. They crossed out more than a half of what I had written, and the Instruction remained as it was printed . . .

The Commission on Laws assembled and brought me light and knowledge from the whole empire, with which we had to deal and which we had to care for.

(Vernadsky and Fisher, 1972)

The Dvoryanstvo *Charter (1785)*

In the seventeenth century, military service for the Russian nobility, *dvoryanstvo*, was hereditary. In 1642 and 1649 it was established that only the *dvoryanstvo* could own land worked by serfs. Peter I (the Great) extensively reformed the rights and position of the *dvoryanstvo*; although from then on the *dvoryanstvo* were virtually forced to serve either in the army, navy or bureaucracy. In 1785, a Charter issued by Catherine II (the Great) recognised the privileged position of the nobility as the ruling class and implicitly recognised the peasants' status as chattel slaves. It also provided for the creation of autonomous corporations of the nobility, with legal powers. The *dvoryanstvo* enjoyed such privileges as exemption from poll tax and the fact that they could not be stripped of estates, title, or status without trial by their peers.

Extracts from the Charter:

> The title of the nobility is hereditary and stems from the quality and virtue of leading men of antiquity who distinguished themselves by their service – which they turned into merit and acquired for their posterity the title of the nobility.
>
> It is to the advantage of both the Empire and the Crown, as it is also just, that the respectful title of the nobility be maintained and approved firmly and inviolably; and therefore, as formerly, now and in the future the title of the nobility is irrevocable, hereditary, and belongs to those honourable families who use it; and accordingly:
>
> A nobleman transmits his noble title to his wife;
>
> A nobleman transmits his noble title to his children hereditarily.
>
> The following acts are contrary to the standards of noble dignity and can deprive one of the title: (i) violation of an oath; (ii) treason; (iii) robbery; (iv) thefts of all sorts; (v) deceitful acts; (vi) violations which call for either corporal punishment or a deprivation of honour; (vii) incitement of others to commit violations – if this be established.
>
> A nobleman cannot be deprived of his title without due process of law.
>
> A nobleman cannot be deprived of his life without due process of law.
>
> A nobleman cannot be deprived of his property without due process of law.

A nobleman can be judged by his peers only.

All criminal acts of a nobleman which for ten years went either unnoticed or had no action taken on them we decree be henceforth forgotten forever.

A nobleman cannot be subjected to corporal punishment.

Noblemen who serve as junior officers in Our armed forces should be punished according to regulations applicable to senior officers.

A nobleman has the power and the authority to give away to whomever he wishes the property which he acquired legally as first owner, to bequeath this property in his will, to confer it as dowry, or to sell or give it away for his livelihood. He may, however, dispose of inherited property only in conformity with the provisions of the law.

The inheritable property of a nobleman who may be convicted of a serious crime should pass on to his legal heirs.

The nobles have the right to purchase villages.

The nobles may have factories and mills in their villages.

The homes of the nobility in villages are to be free from quartering of soldiers.

A nobleman is personally freed from the poll tax.

Charter to the Towns (1785)

Under the terms of the Charter, issued by Catherine II (the Great) in 1785, residents of cities were divided into six classes:

1 land proprietors;
2 merchants (divided into three guilds);
3 artisans (organised into occupational associations (*tekhi*);
4 independent artisans;
5 eminent citizens of the liberal professions;
6 foreign and temporary residents.

City dwellers were allowed to elect a city *duma*, composed of six municipal councillors, one for each class, and a mayor. According to the terms of the charter the burghers were still liable for soul tax and were unable to own peasants or estates.

Alexander I

The State reforms of 1808–09

Early in his reign, Alexander I seemed willing to study the problem of administrative reforms and worked with a small group of friends known as the 'Unofficial Committee of 1801–1803'. The Committee was formed on 6 July 1801 and consisted of Nikolai Novosiltsev, Pavel Stroganov, Viktor Kochubey and Adam Czartoryski. It discussed reforms and questions of the day, but its only real achievement was to establish ministries as the basis of administration instead of the earlier colleges.

Mikhail Mikhailovich Speransky (1772–1839) was Minister of State and a political reformer. As Alexander I's adviser he devised a liberal constitutional system for Russia. He drafted several proposals including that a Council of State be established to advise on legislation. He also planned for elected representative assemblies in central and local administration; their task to be advisory.

He proposed a gradual transition from the autocratic oligarchical constitution to what he termed the 'monarchical government' of the West.

He also planned a reform of the taxation system based on the agricultural wealth of the country and the establishment of an annual budget which would be approved by the tsar and the Council of State.

In addition he planned a review of the mass of Russian law.

In March 1812 he was summoned by the tsar and dismissed. Intrigues by his opponents, who, among other things, accused him of being a French spy, led to his fall. It is to be noted that the *duma* in 1905 mirrors plans produced and established by Speransky.

Nicholas I

The creation of the Third Section or Department (the secret police)

Formed by Tsar Nicholas I in 1826, six months after the Decembrist uprising, as one of the six departments of His Majesty's Own Chancery. It was a secret police force responsible for political security and was the tsar's chief weapon against subversion; it symbolised his reign. Designed by Count Aleksandr Benckendorff, head of the department (1826–44), its chief functions were surveillance, the gathering of information on undesirables such as political dissidents and foreigners, the running of state prisons, prosecution of forgers, banishment of political criminals, and censorship. The department had a vast network of spies and informers and the co-operation of the military corps of gendarmes, established in 1836.

The actual decree establishing the Third Section published on 3 July 1826:

> Deeming it necessary to establish a Third Section in my own chancery, to be headed by Adjutant General Benkendorf, I command that the Special Chancery of the Ministry of Internal Affairs be abolished.
>
> The matters to occupy this Third Section of my own chancery shall be as follows:
>
> 1. All instructions and announcements of the higher police on all matters.
> 2. Intelligence concerning the number of various sections and schismatic [religious] groups existing with the state.

3. Information concerning the discovery of counterfeit banknotes, coins, stamps, documents, and so on, the investigation and further prosecution of which remains under the jurisdiction of the Ministries of Finance and Internal Affairs.
4. Detailed intelligence concerning all persons under police surveillance, as well as all orders bearing on this matter.
5. The exile and placement of suspicious and harmful persons.
6. Supervisory and economic management of all places of internment where state criminals are kept.
7. All edicts and instructions concerning foreigners residing in Russia, arriving within its borders, and leaving it.
8. Reports on all events, without exception.
9. Statistical information relevant to the police.

The department, although supposed to protect the proletariat, became increasingly repressive, causing the arrest of many populists (*narodniki*, see Populism, p. 235). This led to the assassination of the then head of the Third Section, General N. V. Mezentsov, in 1878.

The failure of the department to achieve much, largely due to the proliferation of false reports brought in by informers, resulted in its closure in 1880 by General Mikhail Loris-Melikov. Its functions were transferred to the Ministry of the Interior.

Alexander II

In 1857 Alexander II appointed commissions to study the possibility of reforms in five main areas:

1 serfdom (see p. 82);
2 local government (see p. 59);
3 justice (see p. 160);
4 education (see p. 149);
5 military (see below).

These liberal reforms met with fierce opposition from both Conservatives and the Revolutionaries. Assassinated in 1881 he was unable to implement reforms for the police or the civil service. Unsuccessful assassination attempts were made on his life in 1866, 1879 and 1880.

Reform of military service (1863)

Prior to the Great Reforms of Alexander II, there was no standardised recruiting system for the army. Those to whom the lot of military service fell had to serve for twenty-five years, although this was reduced to sixteen years in 1861, and mass recruitment had been from the serfs, and it also recruited from criminals. Although the conditions were appalling many peasants joined to escape serfdom. Alexander II's reform was introduced in 1863. There was a need for modernisation as had been shown in the Crimean war and his reforms made the army the most democratic institution in Russia. It provided for:

(a) universal military service for all men over twenty years for six years rather than twenty-five;
(b) shorter period of service for those with elementary or higher education;
(c) call-up geared to family obligations;
(d) humanisation of discipline;
(e) basic education for illiterate conscripts;
(f) elimination of class differences as method of advancement.

Zemstva (local self-government) in 1864

Name for local self-government institutions for European Russia and Ukraine, established in 1864 during the period of the Great Reforms. The aim of the *zemstva* was to provide social and economic services. Although they were limited from time to time in their authority and revenues and were dominated by the nobility, their existence and liberal influence achieved much in the field of education, communications, agriculture and health. The authority of the *zemstva* was increased after the February Revolution of 1917, but they were replaced by Soviets after the Bolshevik seizure of power.

Alexander III

Counter-reforms

Alexander III's aim was to achieve a political ideal of a nation containing one nationality, one language and one religion. He wished to curb the reforms brought about by his father, Alexander II, and immediately on ascending the throne issued the Temporary Regulations of 1881 and these and other measures included:

(a) the power of officials to (i) search, (ii) exile, (iii) try by courts martial anyone considered to be a threat to the state;
(b) the post of Land Captain (*zemsky nachalnik*) was introduced so that peasants were under more restrictions;
(c) the State Gentry Bank was established (1885);
(d) town government (1892) and the *zemstvo* system (1890) were reorganised and the electorate decreased. The electorate of St Petersburg decreased from 21,000 to 8,000 and Moscow from 20,000 to 7,000;

(e) university autonomy abolished (1884);
(f) higher education for women abolished;
(g) russification of minorities such as Poles, Georgians, Armenians and Finns;
(h) restrictions of Jews – from 1881 pogroms occur;
(i) pressure brought on all those not of the Orthodox faith;
(j) press regulation made it impossible for radical journals to be published.

Nicholas II

Creation of the Duma

The manifesto of Nicholas II dated 30 October 1905 (see p. 61) aimed to establish as an unbreakable rule that no law should become effective without the confirmation by the State Duma, and that the elected representatives of the people should be guaranteed an opportunity of real participation in the supervision of the legality of the acts by authorities that the tsar would appoint.

Duma was the name of a Kievan political institution consisting of a council of boyars, but is better known as the elected legislative assemblies, which, with the Council of the Empire, comprised the Russian legislature from 1906 to 1917, and which were established in response to the 1905 Revolution. The tsar could rule absolutely when the *duma* was not in session and he could dissolve it at will. The First State 442-member Duma, elected by universal male suffrage met for 73 days in 1906 and the second met in 1907 for 102 days. The First and Second Dumas were unsuccessful in that, although it was expected that the representatives would be conservative, they were mainly liberal and socialist, and their demands for reform were totally unacceptable to the government. In 1906 the Council of the Empire was attached to the *duma* as an upper house with 196 members, 98 of them nominated by the tsar and 98 elected by the clergy, the corporations of nobles and other academic, civic and commercial bodies. Both houses had the same powers. The *duma* had limited competence and could not consider the army or navy; all laws must be proposed to a minister who would consider them and prepare his own draft, and ministers were responsible to the tsar. A preliminary report of all measures must be submitted to the Council of the Empire and the tsar for approval. A majority vote of the *duma* was submitted to the upper house, and in case of disagreement the tsar could intervene. The Third Duma ran its full five-year term (1907–12) and gave support to the government's agrarian reforms and military reorganisation. The Fourth Duma sat from 1912 to 1917, but it gradually became opposed to the government's war policy and increasingly critical of the imperial regime. On the abdication of Tsar Nicholas II the provisional committee established by the *duma* asked Prince Lvov to form a provisional government.

October Manifesto, 30 October, 1905:

By the Grace of God, We Nicholas II, Emperor and Autocrat of all Russia, Tsar of Poland, Grand Duke of Finland, etc.

Make known to all Our loyal subjects: Rioting and disturbances in the capitals and in many localities of Our Empire fill Our heart with great and heavy grief. The well-being of the Russian Sovereign is inseparable from the national well-being; and the national sorrow is His sorrow. The disturbances which have appeared may cause a grave national tension that may endanger the integrity and unity of Our state.

By the great vow of Tsarist service We are obligated to use every resource of wisdom and Our authority to bring a speedy end to an unrest dangerous to Our state. We have [already] ordered the responsible authorities to take measures to terminate direct manifestations of disorder, lawlessness, and violence, and to protect peaceful people who quietly seek to fulfil the duties incumbent upon them. To successfully fulfil general measures which We have designed for the pacification of state life, We feel it is essential to coordinate the activity of the higher government.

We impose upon the government the duty to execute Our inflexible will:

1. To grant the population the inviolable foundations of civic freedom based on the principles of genuine personal inviolability, freedom of conscience, speech, assemblies and associations.

2. Without postponing the scheduled elections to the State Duma, to admit in the participation of the Duma insofar as possible in the short time that remains before its scheduled meeting all those classes of the population which presently are completely deprived of voting rights, and to leave further development of general elective law to the future legislative order;

3. To establish as an unbreakable rule that no law shall become effective without the confirmation by the State Duma, and that the elected representatives of the people shall be guaranteed an opportunity of real participation in the supervision of the legality of the acts by authorities whom We shall appoint.

We summon all loyal sons of Russia to remember their duties towards their country, to assist in terminating this unprecedented unrest, and together with Us to make very effort to restore peace and tranquility in Our native land.

Given in Peterhof, 30 October, the year of Our Lord 1905, and eleventh of Our reign.

Nicholas

The Vyborg manifesto

In July 1906 about 180 deputies met in Vyborg to protest the dissolution of the First Duma by Nicholas II. The largest majority were Kadets (Constitutional Democratic Party), and the manifesto urged the people not to pay taxes and to avoid military service when conscripted. The plan failed and the deputies were arrested, given three months' imprisonment, and, probably more important for Russia, deprived of their right to stand for election to the Second Duma.

Political groupings in the dumas

The predominance of the large landowners and upper-middle class was made certain by the electoral law of 11 December 1905. The actual elections (in February–March 1906) took place in an atmosphere of active police repression. The Bolsheviks boycotted the election (with obvious success in St Petersburg, Poland and the Baltic). The Kadets (Constitutional Democrats) easily emerged as the largest single party.

Composition of the First Duma

The Right (Monarchists, Octobrists, Industrialists, etc.)	44
The Autonomists (Polish League, Lithuanian Circle, Ukrainian Democrats, etc.)	44
Party for Democratic Reform	6
Kadets	179
Labour Group	94
Social Democratic Group	18
Cossack Group	1
Non-party	100
	486

Composition of the Second Duma

The Reactionary Right	10
Octobrists	42
Polish League	46
Muslim Group	30
Party for Democratic Reform	1
Kadets	98
Labour Group	104
Popular Socialists	16
Socialist Revolutionaries	37
Social Democrats	65
Cossack Group	17
Non-party	50
	516

Composition of the Third Duma (First Session)

The Reactionary Right	49
Moderate Right Wing	69
Russian National Group	26
Alliance of 17 October	148
Polish/Lithuanian Group	7
Polish League	11
Progressives	25
Muslim Group	8
Kadets	53
Labour Group	14
Social Democrats	20
Non-party	16
	446

Composition of the Fourth Duma (First Session)

The Reactionary Right	64
Moderate Right	88
Centre Party	32
Alliance of 17 October	99
Polish/Lithuanian Group	6
Polish League	9
Progressives	47
Muslim Group	6
Kadets	58
Labour Group	10
Social Democrats	14
Non-party	5
	438

After the elections to the Fourth Duma, no further elections occurred until after the fall of the tsarist regime. During 1917, the provisional government had been organising elections to establish a constituent assembly. The Bolsheviks allowed these elections to take place on 25 November 1917. With universal suffrage, the electorate numbered 41,700,000. No reliable figures exist for the results, but the following table gives approximate figures.

Party	Votes cast	Delegates returned
	17,100,000 (Total)	429 (Total)
Bolsheviks	9,600,000	168
Mensheviks	1,400,000	18
Kadets	2,000,000	17
Monarchists	300,000	..
National Minorities	1,700,000	..

At the end of 1917, the Kadets were proscribed. The constituent assembly met on 18 January 1918. It was dissolved by the Bolsheviks a day later after rejecting (237 votes to 136) a Bolshevik motion to recognise the Congress of Soviets as the supreme government authority.

6
Religion

Russia's conversion to Christianity

The origins of Christianity in Russia date back to the ninth century. In 944 Russian Christians signed a Byzantine–Russian treaty and c. 955 Princess Olga, regent of Kiev, was baptised. However, subsequent rulers, Svyatoslav (942–72) and Vladimir (died 1015), preferred paganism. Vladimir, however, realised that since Kiev was surrounded by powerful countries, each of which had accepted either Islam, Judaism or Christianity, it was necessary for the security of Kiev to accept one of these faiths. He chose Byzantine Christianity, was baptised in 988, and married the emperor of Constantinople's sister in 989. Personal conversion was judged necessary only for the upper echelons of society, who enforced Christianity on the masses.

Chronology 1569–1918

1569	Lublin Union of Poland and Lithuania strengthens Roman Catholicism and poses threat to Russian Church.
1589	Moscow Patriarchate established.
1640	Zealots of Piety, led by the tsar's confessors, formed to purge Church of impurities.
1652	Nikon becomes Patriarch and receives full authority to reform Church.
1658	Alexis I breaks with Nikon, who resigns.
1666	Nikon exiled by Church Council but his reforms are implemented. Avvakum leads Old Believers against reform and subjection of Church to state.
c. 1670	*The Life of Archpriest Avvakum by Himself.*
1681	Avvakum burnt at the stake.
1684	Decree issued by the Regent Sophia, threatening all impenitent Old Believers with death by fire.

1696	Peter I (the Great) limits rights of parish and monastic clergy to dispose freely of their income.
1700	On the death of Patriarch Adrian the patriarchate is left vacant. Authority over church properties, income and secular responsibilities placed under monastery *prikaz*, charged with administering, judging and taxing inhabitants of ecclesiastical lands. A community of Old Believers settles in Karelia.
1701	Principle established that monasteries forward all revenues to state treasury in return for fixed salaries.
1705	Russian missionaries reach Kamchatka.
1710	The Old Slavonic alphabet is retained only by the Church.
1716	Census of Old Believers and they are charged double soul tax.
1719	'Spiritual Regulations' rules governing Church affairs are promulgated.
1721	Peter I (the Great's) Ecclesiastical Regulation. Formal abolition of the patriarchate of Moscow, and replaced it with an Ecclesiastical College (Most Holy All-Ruling Synod). Church formally merged with state administration. The tsars, their wives and heirs, were required by law to be Orthodox. As the tsar's power over the Church increased, the Church lost political and social influence in the social and political field.
1730	Anne issues manifesto ordering clergy to follow ritual practices and condemns reforming tendencies.
1733	Action against Old Believers. Baptism of children becomes obligatory and those convicted by proselytisation are sentenced to forced labour.
1739	Seminaries established in every diocese.
1743	Instruction in the catechism made obligatory in schools.
1762	Peter III ordered that all Church lands be incorporated into state properties.
1763	Catherine II (the Great) gives lands and funds to the Moravian Brothers, a religious community. She also gives them the right to practise their religion and thirty years dispensation from taxes and military service.
1764	Catherine II (the Great) confirmed the 1762 edict and closed 569 of 954 active monasteries. Of 385 monasteries remaining, only 161 supported by the state; 224 others disendowed and left to support themselves.
1771	Group of Old Believers allowed by Catherine II (the Great) to establish themselves in Moscow.
1784	Pejorative term 'schismatic' abandoned; double taxation of religious dissenters removed.

1791	Pale of Settlement established consisting of twenty-five western provinces where Jews are permitted permanent residence.
1797	Decree proclaiming freedom of religion (except for Catholic propaganda in Poland).
1798	Old Believers allowed to build churches in all dioceses.
1800	Paul I declares himself in favour of a reunion of the Roman Catholic and Eastern Orthodox Churches.
1804	Freedom of religion is guaranteed to the Jews.
1811	Alexander I, who was friendly with Quakers, tolerant towards other denominations and towards his Moslem subjects, stopped the Holy Synod persecuting those who did not profess the Orthodox faith. Alexander was at first friendly towards the Jesuits, who had been welcomed in Russia by Catherine II (the Great) when their society was abolished in 1773 and they were expelled from Catholic countries. They were allowed to work in Russia, chiefly as teachers. This was an embarrassment to the Pope, as canonically the Jesuits were rebels.
1814	Prince Alexander Golitsyn, the Procurator, accused the Jesuits of proselytising.
	Jesuits were ordered to close their schools in Moscow and St Petersburg and were exiled to the provinces.
	The Bible Society of Russia is founded.
1815	Pact of the Holy Alliance signed between the Emperor Francis I of Austria, King William I of Prussia and Tsar Alexander I. According to the pact they were henceforth brothers of one faith which, according to Holy Scripture, looked to Jesus Christ as the only true sovereign.
1817	The Ministry of Education combined with the Ministry of Spiritual Affairs.
	All religions, including the Russian Orthodox faith, to be treated equally.
1818	Concordat between Russia and the Holy See establishing the canonical position of Catholics in Poland.
1819–1821	The policy of religious toleration was denounced by the monk, Photius, as an insult to pure Orthodoxy and as a sin against the Holy Ghost.
	Photius's campaign was successful and repressive measures were introduced.
	Professors at the new universities were removed, textbooks on natural law, morals and logic were banned, because they were not based on the Bible.
	Golitsyn was dismissed.

1820	Jesuits expelled from the Russian Empire for continuing to proselytise.
1822	Imperial decree, banning secret societies.
	The 'Decembrists', originally freemasons, had already broken away to form their own secret society.
1830	Polish rising, powerfully supported by the Catholic clergy.
	Nicholas I demanded that Pope Gregory XVI should condemn all the clergy who had taken part, and the Pope did so, reminding them that they should respect 'the legitimate authority of princes'. But the conversion of Orthodox believers in Poland was forbidden, mixed marriages were declared null and void, and 200 monasteries closed.
1832	Encyclical *Cum primum* in which Pope Gregory XVI directed Polish Catholics to 'obey their mighty Emperor who would show them every kindness'.
	This was published in Poland just as the Russian occupying forces were persecuting the Catholic Church. At the same time the Pope wrote to the tsar denouncing the 'wicked chicanery' of the government in Poland and asking that a papal *chargé d'affaires* be sent to Poland. This letter was not published and there was no reply.
1835	Cardinal Bernetti pressed the tsar for a reply to the Pope's protest and request. The reply was that the deplorable events in Poland were the fault of the Catholics and particularly the clergy.
1839	Nicholas I proposed uniting the Polish Catholic Church with the Catholic Church of Russia, under one archbishop and a college of bishops.
1840	Dispute over Holy Places.
	Proposed marriage between the Grand Duchess Olga, third child of Nicholas I (Orthodox), and Archduke Stephen of Austria (Catholic) failed because of the opposition of the Catholic Church.
	State grants to augment clerical salaries.
1841	Dispute over Holy Places.
	France suggested making Jerusalem a free city.
1842	Gregory XVI published a denunciation of Russian persecution of Catholics in Poland.
1843	Nicholas tried again to arrange the marriage of the Grand Duchess Olga and Archduke Stephen, and sought the consent of the Pope. The Pope agreed on condition that Nicholas I ceased the persecution of the Catholic Church. Nicholas I denied that he was persecuting the Church.
1845	Visit of Nicholas I to Rome. The Pope reminded Nicholas I that

he had taught people to render unto Caesar that which is Caesar's. 'I remind Caesar of what belongs to God.' The Pope protested against laws which prevented Catholics from practising their religion.

Nicholas I asserted that the Catholic clergy in Russia were undisciplined and wore religion as a mask to hide rebellion.

1846 Dispute over the Holy Places.

Bishop of Bethlehem assaulted.

1847 Concordat between Russia and the Holy See arranging a method of appointing Roman Catholic bishops in Russia, and defines the position of the Catholic Church in Russia.

First Russian Ecclesiastical Mission established in Palestine.

1850 Dispute over the Holy Places between France and Russia.

1853 Dispute over Holy Places. Nicholas I intervened to protect Christians in Turkey and to confirm Russian rights over the Holy Places.

Because of British intervention Russia failed to obtain a treaty with Turkey giving Russia a protectorate over Christians in the Ottoman Empire.

Russia was suspected of imperialism behind a religious pretext and the Western European powers allied themselves with Turkey.

Russia declared war on Turkey (November).

1858 The Church owned about 3,000,000 serfs attached to its monastic estates and so was opposed to the proposed emancipation of serfs. Most of the bishops were against reform but Bishop Gregory of Kaluga preached that Christianity and slavery were incompatible.

Metropolitan Philaret of St Petersburg believed that the serfs belonged to God and to free them would mean giving them to a Satan-dominated world.

1863 Catholic rising in Poland.

Priests executed.

Catholics deported, churches and religious houses sacked. Bismarck handed back to the tsar Polish refugees who had escaped to Prussia.

Pope Pius IX denounced the persecution.

The concordat between Russia and the Holy See repudiated by the tsar.

1864 Church and *zemstvos* jointly in charge of supervising education.
1866 Diplomatic relations between Russia and the Holy See broken off.
1869 Hereditary priesthood abolished in Russia.
1875 Last Apostolic See of the Roman Catholic Church in Russia suppressed.

1877	Holy War against Turkey to 'liberate Balkan Christians', to make the Church of Santa Sofia Orthodox again and to re-establish Constantinople as a great Christian centre.
	In Europe these aims were seen as a cloak to hide Russian ambitions.
	Russia won the war against Turkey but she was not allowed by Britain to occupy Constantinople and thus control the Straits.
1880	Constantine Petrovich Pobedonostsev (1827–1907) appointed Procurator of the Holy Synod in April.
	He was tutor to the future Alexander III in 1861; an isolationist and devout believer in Orthodox Christianity.
	Pobedonostsev petitioned the tsar to raise the office of Procurator to ministerial status, and was appointed to the Council of Ministers. Though in a minority he successfully opposed the programme of constitutional reform of Count Loris-Melikov (1825–1888).
1881	Alexander II assassinated.
	Anti-Jewish pogrom.
	Pope Leo XIII attempted to improve the situation for Catholics in Russia.
	The tsar insisted that Catholics must remain out of politics.
	First pogroms against the Jews in Elisavetgrad, Kiev and Odessa.
1882	Orthodox Palestine Society founded.
	Diplomatic relations between Russia and the Holy See resumed.
	Decrees to restrict Jews to the south-west of Russia (May).
	No Jew could hold an administrative post, become a lawyer, appeal against a court sentence, own land, or marry a Christian unless converted to Christianity. Jewish schools were closed and books in Hebrew banned. An estimated 225,000 Jewish families left Russia for Western Europe because of these decrees.
1883	The ban on conversions from Orthodoxy is tightened.
	Pobedonostsev launched a programme to establish parish schools throughout European Russia.
	Non-Orthodox given freedom to worship but activities strictly limited.
	When Tolstoy supported student disorders Pobedonostsev accepts that Tolstoy should be officially removed from membership of the Russian Orthodox Church.
	Act allowing schismatics to hold religious services at home, to work, and to hold internal passports, but not to build new places of worship, not to worship publicly, nor to proselytise.
1884	Lord Radstock and Russian supporters exiled again for circulating

	Bunyan's *Pilgrim's Progress* without permission.
	He had been expelled first in 1880.
	Decree establishing many more parish schools, with emphasis on Christian doctrine, literacy and singing.
	1880 4,348 church schools with 108,900 students.
	1905 43,407 church schools with 1,900,000 students.
	Half the primary schools in Russia were under the Synod.
1885	Synod forbade mixed marriages in Estonia and Latvia unless the children were raised in the Orthodox faith.
	Protests by Lutheran clergy and gentry and by the Evangelical Alliance who complained to the tsar.
	It was denied that there was a persecution of religion, only of proselytising, and that the survival of Russia depended on religious unity.
1887	Quotas are placed on the number of Jews attending universities (10 per cent of students at universities in the Pale, 3 per cent at Moscow and St Petersburg and 5 per cent elsewhere).
1889	Dalton, a clergyman, published an open letter to Pobodonostsev in Russia, German and English, accusing him of fabricating charges against the Lutheran clergy and asserting that there was no basis in law for his policies.
	Russian Ecclesiastical Mission merged with the Palestine Commission, bringing it under government control.
	It worked closely with Russian consuls, produced scholarly publications, arranged tours for pilgrims, protecting them from harassment, and built schools in Palestine and Syria.
1891	20,000 Jews expelled from Moscow.
1892	Alexander III granted 250,000 roubles towards raising the salaries of the clergy.
	Number of clergy increased by reducing training and increasing salaries.
	Anti-Jewish pogroms in Moscow.
	Thousands sent to the Pale in south-west Russia.
	Alexander III wrote in the margin of a report: 'We must never forget that it was the Jews who crucified the Lord and spilled his precious blood.'
1894	Papal encyclical states that Polish Catholic clergy would no longer oppose Russia.
	Izvolski appointed minister to the Vatican.
	Pobedonostsev successfully opposed appointment of papal nuncio to St Petersburg and rejected Church of England efforts to establish relationship with the Orthodox Church.

Persecution of Evangelical sects.

Stundists declared dangerous and their schools and chapels closed.

1897 Bishops to be moved every few years to prevent them becoming too powerful.

1898 Antoni Vadkovsky made Metropolitan of St Petersburg.

1900 Revolts in seminaries.

Rift between Orthodox and Russian intelligentsia.

1901 Founding of the Religious Philosophical Society.

Meetings in St Petersburg 1901–03.

Attempt to work with intelligentsia on problems.

1903 Several hundred Jews killed or injured in massive pogrom which began in Kishinev.

1904 Official membership of Russian Orthodox Church put at 88,000,000, 66 dioceses, 40,000 parishes, 106,620 clergy (47,743 priests, 14,701 deacons, 44,176 cantors). 27,000 parish churches received 11,500,000 roubles from state funds.

Committee set up to review church matters and recommend legislation.

1905 Bloody Sunday. St Petersburg Union of Factory Workers led by the priest Father George Gapon (1870–1906) demonstrated, carrying ikons and church banners. About 100,000 demonstrators petitioned the tsar for freedom of the press, a constitutional parliament, and 8-hour day and distribution of land to peasants. They were met by armed resistance by the Palace Guard and an unknown number killed or wounded.

Group of Thirty-two (St Petersburg priests) founded. Petitioned for church reform. Spokesman of group, Father Gregori Petrov, elected as Constitutional Democrat deputy, to Second Duma. Sentenced by Synod to three months' confinement in a monastery and later unfrocked.

Declaration by thirty-two clergy, approved by Metropolitan Antoni, calling for freedom of church from state control so that it could be involved in social problems. Asked for restoration of the patriarchate, abolished 1700, and local councils. The group saw riots as 'just judgement of God' but did not question Tsarist rule or social structure.

Religious Tolerance Law. It became possible to leave the state Church and join another denomination.

The Evangelical sects founded the League of Freedom, whose platform included schooling, equal rights for denominations, constitutional monarchy and equal suffrage.

Religion 73

> The political programme of the Old Believers embraced constitutional monarchy, suspension of class privileges, distribution of land to the peasants. This led to persecution by the Minister of the Interior.
>
> By May, 301,450 people had left the Orthodox Church mainly to become Roman Catholic, but some Muslims and Lutherans. Conference of Ministers wished to consider new regulations of Church.
>
> Metropolitan Antoni officially proposed 'over-control by the secular authority to be removed or relieved'. Witte said that the Church had been paralysed since the time of Peter the Great. The tsar refused to permit the discussion of these problems by the Committee of Ministers but referred them to the Synod.
>
> The Synod asked the tsar for permission to elect a Patriarch and carry out reforms. The tsar refused to discuss the matter 'in the present time of unrest'. A committee was set up to prepare for a council of the Orthodox Church but this was suspended by the tsar a year later.
>
> Konstantin Pobedonostsev dismissed and replaced as Procurator of the Holy Synod by Lukyanov (October).
>
> Anti-semitic violence in Odessa instigated by militant nationals was known as the 'Black Hundreds'.

1905–1908   During this period the *staretz* (holy man) Grigory Rasputin (c. 1870–1916) was introduced to the royal family and credited with having helped the Tsarevich back to health.

1906   Metropolitan Antoni refuses contact with the right-wing League of Russian People, but other dioceses and clergy supported the League actively.

Father George Gapon assassinated.

1907   Synod declared that it was incompatible with priestly office to belong to parties which strove to overthrow the state, the social order or the authority of the tsar. Electoral law prevented left-wing clergy being members of the Duma.

Archimandite Mikhail published *How I became a People's Socialist*. He lost priesthood and joined the Old Believers.

1908   Seminaries not allowed independence but should make the rebellious students 'submissive to the throne and fatherland'. Parish reform was blocked by the hierarchy of the Church, which became increasingly identified with political reaction. The Synod told the bishops to permit and bless participation of the Orthodox clergy in the work of the League of the Russian People and other monarchist patriotic societies. Fourth Missionary

Conference in Kiev concerned with socialism. Courses at seminaries and academies on the 'true nature of socialism'.

Church apologists attacked German, French and English socialist thinkers and defended the existing social order. Poverty was rooted in the sinful nature of man. The hard life of the poor and secure well-being of the rich were the will of God.

Socialism appealed for class struggle and enmity, Christianity for unity and love. Therefore Christian socialism was impossible. Russian Evangelical League founded, calling for moral regeneration to replace class struggle.

Rasputin claimed that he averted a war with Austria over Bosnia and Herzegovina by telling the tsar that a war with Austria would be the end of Russia and that the Balkans were not worth the life of a single Russian.

1909 State Council refuses legalisation of congregation of Old Believers.

Signposts published an attempt to reconcile Christian convictions with political and social involvement. Bulgakov and Berdyaev, former Marxists, led the movement. Bulgakov founded League of Christian Politics.

1910 Synod calculated that a yearly grant of 75 million roubles was necessary for the renunciation of church land and congregational gifts.

Every Baptist and Evangelical conference had to be vetted by the Minister of the Interior with a police agent present. Stolypin becomes alarmed at Rasputin's influence with the tsar.

1911 Rasputin made a pilgrimage to the Holy Land (May).

Stolypin assassinated.

Rasputin returned to St Petersburg.

Metropolitan Antoni and Procurator Lukyanov failed to remove Rasputin from the court.

The new president of the Duma, Rodzianko, persuaded Rasputin to leave St Petersburg (August).

1912 Kholm, part of Poland united with Russia, considered to be Russian and Orthodox.

Tsarevich again ill, but recovered after Rasputin had prayed for him. Rasputin back in favour with the royal family. Rasputin told the tsar 'While I live your throne is secure. If I die you will lose your throne and your life.' Lukyanov replaced as Procurator by Sabler who was under the influence of the Rasputin group.

State Church put forward clergy as conservative candidates for the

	Fourth Duma. Forty-six entered, two of them Progressives, two Octobrists and forty right-wingers.
	Rasputin denounced as a member of the Khlysty sect.
1914	Metropolitan Antoni died, succeeded by Metropolitan Vladimir.
	Attempted assassination of Rasputin (November).
	Protestants suspected of German affiliations, persecuted.
1915	Second Law of Tolerance. Procurator Sabler opposed canonical self-government.
	Sabler succeeded by A. D. Samarin who tried to resist Rasputin and was dismissed.
1916	Ivan Goremykin, Prime Minister, dismissed; replaced by Boris Stürmer, a puppet of Rasputin (February).
	Stürmer dismissed. Rasputin denounced in Duma.
	Rasputin assassinated (December).
1917	Synod refused to condemn the Revolution.
	Provisional Government withdraws church schools from church administration and puts them under the Ministry of Education.
	V. N. Lvov appointed Procurator. Reforms led to the formation of an All Russian Council of the Church which had not been convened for 200 years. It included bishops, clergy and laymen. The council rejected the separation of church and state. The Patriarch was restored.
	Bolshevik Revolution. Provisional Government overthrown (October).
	Metropolitan Tikhon elected Patriarch of the Orthodox Church. The Patriarch and Council were anti-Soviet.
	The remainder of the Group of Thirty-two formed a league of democratic Orthodox clergy and laity. It supported the socialist revolution (November).
	Civil marriages instituted and a decree on divorce issued (December).
1918	Separation of church and state formally proclaimed (January). Abolition of religious teaching, censorship of sermons, ban on religious youth groups, confiscation and ban on the sale of religious objects. Council of People's Commissars stated that 'Church and religious societies do not have a right to property . . .'
	The All Russian Council of the Church dissolved (September). The new society based on the negation of God and of all religion. According to Marx the extinction of religion would be accomplished by the forward march of society, but meanwhile, because religion is an ally of capitalism, it is to be annihilated.

Orthodox Church

The Orthodox Church is the most important church in Russia and one of the three main forces of Christianity in the world. It has played an important role in the history of Russia since Kievan times, in its culture, and in the shaping of the Russian national character. In 1448, the Russian Church became autocephalous, in that it was placed under the jurisdiction of an independent metropolitan of Moscow and was thus no longer under the authority of Rome. In 1458, however, Rome appointed another 'metropolitan of Kiev and all Russia'. This metropolitanate, controlled by Roman Catholic Poland, accepted union with Rome in 1596. In 1686, however, the metropolitanate of Kiev was attached to the patriarchate of Moscow. Muscovite Russians came to regard themselves as the last true Orthodox believers, considering Moscow to be the 'Third Rome'. Patriarch Nikon's liturgical reforms resulted in a major schism in the Russian Church. Millions of clergy and laity refused to accept a reformed Russian liturgy closely modelled on the Greek. Peter I (the Great) rejected the Byzantine heritage and abolished the patriarchate in 1721, replacing it by a state department. Because of the Church's reluctance to involve itself in social issues, the radicals of the nineteenth century grew increasingly disillusioned with it. In June 1918 the Bolshevik government published a decree depriving the Church of all legal rights. Following the imprisonment for opposing the regime's religious policy, Patriarch Tikhon decided to conform.

Russian Orthodox Church (1914)

Baptised Orthodox	87,123,604
Dioceses	73
Active bishops	163
Parochial clergy	51,105
Churches	54,174
Chapels	25,593
Monasteries	1,025
Monks and nuns	94,629
Theological academies	4
Seminaries	57
Minor seminaries	185
Parochial schools	37,528
Hospitals	291
Hospices	1,123
Parochial libraries	34,497

Old Believers

Patriarch Nikon introduced reforms into religious texts and rituals of the Orthodox Church to correct errors that had crept in since the translation from the original Greek. His reforms were opposed by a section of the Church led by Archpriest Avvakum Stephen Vonifatiyev and Ivan Neronov, who in 1653 accused him of heresy. Nikon was vindicated, and his opponents withdrew as a separate sect known as the Old Believers. They were persecuted severely, and some, believing the reforms to be an indication of the end of the world, committed self-immolation.

They rejected the sign of the cross made with three fingers (used in the Greek Church), the return to the pure Greek texts, the new spelling of 'Jesus', and other small innovations. They had no theological basis for dissent, but simply refused to recognise any departure from Muscovite custom, regarding their own Muscovite culture as the true Russian tradition, to be copied by others and to be above compromise.

The movement split during the eighteenth century into two sects. The *popovtsy* (priestly ones) continued to have priests, although they obtained them with difficulty. Some *popovtsy* eventually set up their own episcopate; others were reconciled to the Orthodox Church, keeping their own rites. The *bespopovtsy*, as their name indicates in Russian, had no priesthood, and developed a new religious life with no sacraments except baptism and confession.

They carried their conservatism into political life, denouncing the reforms of Peter I (the Great), whom they saw as the Antichrist. They suffered periodic persecution until an edict of toleration was passed in 1905.

Georgian Orthodox Church

The Georgian Church began in 330 after St Nino was martyred for his faith. By the twelfth century Georgia was a great Christian kingdom. Despite pressure from the Golden Horde and from Persia and Turkey over the centuries, independence was retained until the nineteenth century. In 1801, having been annexed by Russia, Georgia lost its independence; the Catholicos, Anthony II, was deposed and the Georgian Church was incorporated into the Russian Orthodox Church. It regained its independence in 1918 (but this was not recognised by the Moscow patriarchate until 1943).

Armenian Church

The Armenian Apostolic (Orthodox) Church was, according to tradition, founded at Caesarea by the apostles Bartholomew and Thaddaeus in the fourth century. It is not the same communion as the Russian Orthodox Church and was at first dependent on Syrian traditions for its liturgy; after being adopted as the national Armenian church in A.D. 300, it gradually developed a national liturgy, stimulated by St Mashtots, who established Armenian as a literary language fit for use by the Church. In 506 at the Council of Dvin the Church broke from the other Orthodox churches in its Monophysitism (insistence that

Christ had only one nature); in this respect it followed St Cyril of Alexandria, as did the Coptic Church.

The primate is the Catholicos of all Armenians; he resides at Echmiadzin. The Catholicos of Sis owes him spiritual allegiance but enjoys administrative autonomy. The patriarchate of Jerusalem dates from 1307, that of Constantinople was created in 1461 by the Ottoman Sultan, Mehmed II.

Baptists

The Baptist Movement appeared in continental Europe in 1834 in Hamburg, Germany, where Johann Gerhard Oncken, the Father of Continental Baptists, set up a church.

In 1864 he visited St Petersburg. One of his colleagues named Niemetz, obtained an interview with the Minister of the Interior, and openly declared Baptist intentions to undertake missionary work all over Europe. In 1867 the first known believer's baptism of a Russian took place in Tbilisi, Georgia. Modern Russian Baptists regard that date as the beginning of their denomination.

Three main streams of Baptist life flowed into Imperial Russia:

Among German settlers, leading to the Union of German Baptists in Russia, Operative in the Black Sea area, the Volga River region, Caucasus, Siberia, and linked with Latvia and Estonia. This movement grew out of Lutheran and Reformed revival movements in the 1830s and 1840s, which led to diligent study of the Scriptures and the practice of believer's baptism – their first baptisms were in 1864.

Among Slavs, largely the result of German Baptist initiatives, in some cases through groups of German settlers, but primarily through the efforts of Oncken and his colleagues from Hamburg. There was strong pioneering work in Kiev and Ukraine and they achieved rapid growth. This aroused severe opposition from the Orthodox Church and the Czarist State, but wherever leaders were exiled they formed churches there. In 1884 the All-Russian Baptist Union formed and by 1914 their membership was almost 100,000 (that represented baptised believers only, so their community strength would be considerably larger). Another significant person in the Baptist Movement was William Fetler, a Latvian, who had trained at Spurgeon's College in London. In 1908 he founded a large church in St Petersburg.

Also among the Slavs, many baptised believers belonged to a body of Evangelical Christians, developed from the aristocratic family of Countess Chertkova in St Petersburg who came under the influence of the preaching of the English Lord Radstock, an evangelical Anglican. She invited him to Russia in 1870, his preaching led to the conversion of Count Bobinsky (a former State Minister), Count Korff and Colonel Pashkoff, they in turn took the gospel to their workers and began Christian social work and tract distribution. Evangelical Christian Churches began to be formed – they invited other evangelical groups in Southern Russia to join them, including some Baptists and 'Stundists' – planned to form a Union. This led to fierce persecution and the exile of Korff and Pashkoff. A new leader emerged, Ivan Prokhanoff (from Caucasus), studied in German and French universities and at Bristol Baptist College, returned to work as an engineer and professor, but spent much of his time preaching and organising churches – began Christian publishing and produced a hymn-book. When a Decree of Toleration was passed in 1905 opposition was reduced. In 1909 the All-Russian Union of Evangelical Christians was formed and held their first Conference in 1909, with Government approval, a Bible School for the training of ministers opened in 1913 in St Petersburg, but closed by the 1914 war.

In 1911 the Baptist World Alliance held its Congress in Philadelphia, USA. A strong Russian delegation attended it, and Prokhanoff was elected one of the Alliance's vice-presidents. The 1917 Revolution led to greater religious freedom, though it was short-lived. At first, separation of Church and State robbed the Orthodox of its power, while supporting the stance taken by Baptists. However, Baptists and Evangelicals were soon under suspicion because of their German, British and American links.

Jews

There were very few Jews in Russia until the partitions of Poland in 1772, 1793 and 1795. In 1791 Catherine II (the Great) instituted the Pale of Settlement, a vast territory in the western provinces to which the majority of Jews were confined. The attitude of the Russian authorities was basically hostile, though it fluctuated with the general political atmosphere and was particularly acute in the reigns of both Alexander III and Nicholas II. The authority of the Jewish communal organisations (*kahal*) was officially recognised; no direct attempts were made to convert the Jews except in the time of Nicholas I, with the conscription of about 100,000 Jewish boys for a period of twenty-five years beginning at twelve, who came under very strong pressure to be baptised. Although Alexander II was more liberal, there were violent pogroms under Alexander III and these, in turn, led to the large-scale emigration of Jews to Western Europe and the United States. Russia was the home of the largest number of Jews in the nineteenth century, and all the main cultural and political developments in Jewish life took place there including the rise of Hassidism, the development of modern literature in both Hebrew and Yiddish, the spread of Zionism and the growth of the Jewish socialist movement. Jews played an active part in the general cultural and political life of the country, being prominent from the late ninteenth century in both the liberal and the revolutionary movements. Many former restrictions were removed after the revolution of 1905, and after the February revolution of 1917 the Provisional Government established complete legal equality for Jews.

In 1897 there were 5,200,000 Jews in the Russian Empire (4,800,000 living in the Pale); this represented 4.2 per cent of total population (11.6 per cent in the Pale).

Occupation	% non-Jewish work force 1897	% Jewish work force 1897
Agriculture	61	3
Professions	3	5
Personal service		
Liquor trade and related fields	16	19
Commerce	2	32
Transportation	2	3
Manufacturing and mechanical pursuits	15	38

Important dates in Russian Jewish life:

1791 Catherine II (the Great) creates the Pale of Settlements where Jews are permitted permanent residence.
1804 Freedom of religion is guaranteed if resident in Pale of Settlement.
1827 Jewish boys conscripted at the age of twelve for period of twenty-five years.
1844 The Kahal, the autonomous organisation of Jewish communities, is abolished.
1856 Military mobilisation of Jewish children abolished. Dispensations granted allowing Jews to live outside the Pale of Settlement.
1881 First large-scale pogroms in Elisavetgrad, Kiev and Odessa.
1882 Jews banned from owning land.
1887 Quotas placed on Jews permitted to attend universities.
1891 Over 20,000 Jews expelled form Moscow.
1892 Jews lose right to vote for Duma representations.
1897 'The Bund', Union of Jewish Workers in Lithuania, Russia and Poland founded.
1903 Pogrom in Kishinev; several hundred Jews killed and injured.
1905 Pogrom in Odessa. Anti-Semitic violence in western provinces instigated by the 'Black Hundreds'.
1906 Pogrom in Bialystok.
1909 Rigid quotas placed on enrolment of Jews at universities.
1912 Jews banned from the re-established office of Justice of the Peace.

Islam

Islam came with the Arab conquests of Transcaucasia and Central Asia in the seventh to eighth centuries and further extended to the Turkic people of Eastern Russia at the time of the Golden Horde. Muslims in Russia were Caucasian-, Turkic-, and Iranian-speaking people and the Adzhars of Georgia. They were mainly Sunni-Muslims although Shi-ites were found in Azerbaijan. Some Tadzhiks were Ismailites. There were attempts at forcible baptism of the Tatars immediately after the Russian conquest of the Kazan khanate; again in the eighteenth century; at the time of the Caucasian wars of the mid-nineteenth century and during the uprising in Central Asia in 1916 holy wars were proclaimed against the Russian infidels. However the relationships between the Muslims and the Russian authorities were generally good. A modernist movement among Muslims in Russia, largely led by Tatars, developed in the late nineteenth and early twentieth centuries. During the revolution of 1905 the modernists formed, at Nizhny Novgorod, an All-Russian Muslim League which urged regional autonomy, and they subsequently dominated the Muslim faction in the Duma, which associated itself with the Constitutional Democratic Party. There was also a number of regional Muslim parties of a more radical character, the most important of which was the Mussavat in Azerbaijan. The Council of the Muslim Union supported the Provisional Government in 1917; but it was suppressed when the Bolsheviks seized power.

7
Serfdom in Imperial Russia

Chronology 1640s–1918

1649	New legal code, *Ulozhenie*, introduced and serfdom fully established. The code included the removal of time limits for reclaiming runaway peasants.
1699	Peter I (the Great) forms a permanent army comprising serfs and enlisted men.
1760	A decree is issued limiting the rights of masters over their serfs in criminal matters.
1764	Church deprived of extensive land holdings and over 900,000 serfs become state peasants with more favourable living conditions.
1766	Catherine II suggests to the Free Society of Political Economy, which she founded, that it sponsor an essay competition on the abolition of serfdom and its consequences. The Society receives 120 submissions.
1773	The Pugachev Rebellion begins (September).
1785	Under the Charter of Nobility masters are given sole authority over their serfs.
1801	Serfs cannot be sold unless land is also sold.
	Commoners can purchase land without serfs.
1803	A *ukase* provides for voluntary emancipation of serfs. These freed serfs received some land. Only 47,000 serfs were freed during Alexander I's reign.
1804	A report by the Free Economic Society claims the superiority of paid labour.
1807	Grand Duchy of Warsaw abolishes serfdom.
1808	The sale of serfs at markets and fairs is forbidden.
1809	The right of landowners to deport serfs to Siberia is abolished. (The right will be re-established in 1822.)

1812	Believing that the elimination of serfdom is imminent, peasants riot in Penza (December).
1816	Serfs in Estonia are freed, but they are not provided with land.
1817	Courland serfs are given their freedom.
1818	Arakcheev's plans for freeing the serfs are put forward, to no effect.
1819	The serfs are freed in Livonia.
1824	A law is passed authorising manufacturers to free their serfs with the permission of the Committee of Ministers.
1833	Prohibitions are imposed on the selling of serfs without land at auction in order to pay off private debts, and also on sales that would result in the separation of family members.
1840	A law is promulgated authorising the liberation of factory serfs (June).
1844	Landowners are authorised to liberate their house serfs without land by means of bilateral contracts (June).
1844–1848	'Inventories' are gradually introduced into the western provinces. They strictly establish the obligations of serfs.
1846	The Brotherhood of Cyril and Methodius is founded in Kiev by the historian Nikolai Kostomarov and the poet Taras Shevchenko. They recommend the abolition of serfdom (January).
1847	Serfs are authorised to buy their freedom from their masters, in the event that the estate is put up for sale to cover debts.
1848	Serfs are granted the right to acquire unpopulated land and buildings, with the consent of their masters (March).
1854	A *ukase* calls for volunteers for the Baltic Fleet and large numbers of serfs migrate from central provinces towards Moscow.
1856	Peasant uprisings increase. Proposals for emancipation increase and details appear in *The Contemporary* and in Herzen's publications in London. Alexander II states that it is better to abolish serfdom from above than to wait until it begins to abolish itself from below.
1857	A secret committee is created to study the possible emancipation of the serfs (January). An imperial decree mandates that provincial committees of the nobility be created to work out proposals for the emancipation of the serfs (November).
1858	Peasants who work on the domains of the imperial family are emancipated.
1860	The drafting commissions reviewing proposals for emancipating the serfs complete their work. An emancipating statute is submitted to an oversight committee (October).
1861	Statute abolishing serfdom is enacted.

	Twenty million serfs on private domains are emancipated. A period of forty-nine years 'temporary obligation' is established during which the former serfs must compensate the state for land transferred to them. Land transferred to peasants in many cases is insufficient to support them.
1881	Redemption of land obligatory for all former serfs, including those peasants still under 'temporary obligation'.
1905	Redemption payments are abolished for ex-serfs.
1906	Stolypin puts forward an agrarian reform programme.
1910	Law allows peasants to leave the commune (June).
1911	Law enacted to allow the dissolution of peasant communes.

The Pugachev Rebellion

Rumours of emancipation led to the peasant revolt of 1773–74. The leader was Don Cossack Yemelyan Ivanovich Pugachev (1726–75). He served in the Seven Years' War against Prussia, the Polish campaign of 1764 and the Russo–Turkish War in 1768–74. Declaring himself Emperor Peter III in 1773 the rebellion started in the Urals and it soon spread over a vast area and his troops captured Kazan, Penza, Saratov and other cities. On 31 July 1774 Pugachev issued his emancipation decree:

> We, Peter III, by the Grace of God Emperor and Autocrat of All-Russia, etc. This is given for nationwide information.
>
> By this personal decree, with our monarchial and fatherly love, we grant freedom to everyone who formerly was in serfdom or in any other obligation to the nobility; and we transfer these to be faithful personal subjects of our crown; to the Old Believers we grant the right to use the ancient sign of the Cross, and to pray, and to wear beards; while to the Cossacks we restore for eternity their freedoms and liberties; we hereby terminate the recruiting system, cancel personal and other monetary taxes, abolish without compensation the ownership of land, forest, pastures, fisheries and salt deposits; and finally we free everyone from all taxes and obligations which the thievish nobles and extortionist city judges have imposed on the peasantry and the rest of the population. We pray for the salvation of your souls and wish you a happy and peaceful life here on earth where we have suffered and experienced much from the above-mentioned thievish nobles. Now since our name, thanks to the hand of Providence, flourishes throughout Russia, we make hereby known by this personal decree the following: all nobles who have owned either estates granted by the state or inherited estates, who have opposed our rule, who have rebelled against the empire, and who have ruined the peasantry, should be seized, arrested, and hanged;

that is, treated in the same manner as these unchristians have treated you, the peasantry. After the extermination of these opponents and thievish nobles everyone will live in a peace and happiness that shall continue to eternity.

The insurrection finally collapsed, but it caused Catherine II (the Great) to consider seriously problems of law and order in the countryside and the role of the gentry.

1774 Pugachev captured (September).
       Brought to trial in Moscow (December).
1775 Pugachev executed in Moscow (January).

Number of serfs in 1762

Number of Serfs	Percentage of Proprietors
Less than 20	51
21 to 100	31
101 to 500	15
501 to 1,000	2
More than 1,000	1

Peasant uprisings before emancipation

The most successful and highly organised uprising was the Pugachev rebellion in 1773–74, but there were over 500 other uprisings in the years before emancipation and they increased in frequency, length and in seriousness in the 1840s and 1850s.

1828	17
1829	13
1830	13
1831	9
1832	10
1833	11
1834	20
1838	15
1839	14
1840	15
1841	17
1842	21

1843	19
1844	34
1845	31
1846	16
1847	31
1848	64
1849	25
1850	21
1851	28
1852	44
1853	33
1854	23

Source: *Brockhouse Encyclopedia* Vol. 32

The Edict of Emancipation of the serfs (1861)

This was the edict of 1861, by which some serfs, hitherto regarded as chattels of the landowner, were liberated. Although a landmark in the history of Russia – the serf could marry, take legal action, own property in his name, and engage in business or trade – he was in fact economically dependent on the landlord. The serf had to buy the land from his previous owner; the amount and type of land often depended on the individual landowner's whim. The land could be redeemed by thirty to forty days' labour annually, or by *obrok*, a 6 per cent tax paid to the landowner. In many cases the serfs were worse off following the 1861 edict.

The Manifesto of His Majesty the Emperor:

> By the grace of God, we, Alexander II, Emperor and Autocrat of all the Russias, King of Poland, grand Duke of Finland, etc., to all our faithful subjects make known:
>
> Called by Divine Providence and by the sacred right of inheritance to the throne of our ancestors, we took a vow in our innermost heart so to respond to the mission which is intrusted to us as to surround with our affection and our Imperial solicitude all our faithful subjects of every rank and of every condition from the warrior who nobly bears arms for the defence of the country to the humble artisan devoted to the works of industry ...
>
> We thus came to the conviction that the work of a serious improvement of the condition of the peasants was a sacred inheritance, bequeathed to us by our ancestors – a mission which, in the course of events, Divine Providence called upon us to fulfil.
>
> We have commenced this work by an expression of our Imperial confi-

dence towards the nobility of Russia, which has given us so many proofs of its devotion to the Throne and of its constant readiness to make sacrifices for the welfare of the country...

Having invoked the Divine assistance, we have resolved to carry this work into execution.

In virtue of the new dispositions above mentioned, the peasants attached to the soil (*attaches à la glebe*) will be invested within a term fixed by the law with all the rights of free cultivators.

The proprietors retaining their rights of property on all the land belonging to them, grant to the peasants for a fixed regulated rental the full enjoyment of their close (*enclos*); and, moreover, to assure their livelihood and to guarantee the fulfilment of their obligations towards the Government, the quantity of arable land is fixed by the said dispositions as well as other rural appurtenances (*ougodie*).

But, in the enjoyment of these territorial allotments, the peasants are obliged, in return, to acquit the rentals fixed by the same dispositions to the profit of the proprietors. In this state, which must be a transitory one, the peasants shall be designated as 'temporarily bound' (*temporairement obligés*).

At the same time they are granted the right of purchasing their close (*enclos*) and, with the consent of the proprietors, they may acquire in full property the arable lands and other appurtenances which are allotted to them as a permanent holding (*jouissance*). By the acquisition in full property of the quantity of land fixed the peasants are free from their obligations towards the proprietors for land thus purchased, and they enter definitively into the condition of free peasants – landholders (*paysans libres – proprietaires*).

By a special disposition concerning the domestics (*gens de la domesticite – dvorovye*) a transitory state is fixed for them adapted to their occupations and the exigencies of their position. On the expiration of a term of two years, dating from the day of the promulgation of these dispositions, they shall receive their full enfranchisement and some temporary immunities...

We also count upon the generous devotion of our faithful nobility, and we are happy to testify to that body the gratitude it has deserved from us, as well as from the country, for the disinterested support it has given to the accomplishment of our designs. Russia will not forget that the nobility, acting solely upon its respect for the dignity of man and its love for its neighbour, has spontaneously renounced rights given to it by serfdom actually abolished, and laid the foundation of a new future, which is thrown open to the peasants...

And now, pious and faithful people, make upon the forehead the sacred sign of the cross and join thy prayers to ours to call down the blessings of the Most High upon the first free labours, the sure pledge of thy personal wellbeing and of the public prosperity.

Given at St Petersburg, the 19th day of February [March 3] of the Year of Grace 1861, and the seventh of our reign.

ALEXANDER

Prince Peter Kropotkin (see p. 195) was a student in the Corps of Pages in 1861 when a statute abolishing serfdom was enacted. This extract from his *Memoirs of a Revolutionist* (1899) recalls the reaction to emancipation in St Petersburg and on a family estate at Nikolskoye, Kaluga:

On 21 February 1861 we went on parade; and when all the military performances were over, Alexander II, remaining on horseback, loudly called out, 'The officers to me!' They gathered round him, and he began, in a loud voice, a speech about the great event of the day.

'The officers ... the representatives of the nobility in the army' – these scraps of sentences reached our ears – 'an end has been put to centuries of injustice ... I expect sacrifices from the nobility ... the loyal nobility will gather round the throne' ... and so on. Enthusiastic hurrahs resounded amongst the officers as he ended.

We ran rather than marched back on our way to the corps, – hurrying to be in time for the Italian opera, of which the last performance in the season was to be given that afternoon; some manifestation was sure to take place then. Our military attire was flung off with great haste, and several of us dashed, lightfooted, to the sixth-story gallery. The house was crowded.

During the first entr'acte the smoking-room of the opera filled with excited young men, who all talked to one another, whether acquainted or not. We planned at once to return to the hall, and to sing, with the whole public in a mass choir, the hymn 'God Save the Tsar'.

However, sounds of music reached our ears, and we all hurried back to the hall. The band of the opera was already playing the hymn, which was drowned immediately in enthusiastic hurrahs coming from all parts of the hall. I saw Bavéri, the conductor of the band, waving his stick, but not a sound could be heard from the powerful band. Then Bavéri stopped, but the hurrahs continued. I saw the stick wave again in the air; I saw the fiddle-bows moving, and musicians blowing the brass instruments, but again the sound of voices overwhelmed the band. Bavéri began conducting the hymn once more, and it was only by the end of that third repetition that isolated sounds of the brass instruments pierced through the clamour of human voices.

The same enthusiasm was in the streets. Crowds of peasants and educated men stood in front of the palace, shouting hurrahs, and the tsar could not appear without being followed by demonstrative crowds running after his carriage. Herzen was right when, two years later, as Alexander was drowning the Polish insurrection in blood, and 'Muravioff the Hanger' was strangling it on the scaffold, he wrote, 'Alexander Nikolaevich, why did you not die on that day? Your name would have been transmitted in history as that of a hero.'

Where were the uprisings which had been predicted by the champions of slavery? Conditions more indefinite than those which had been created by the Polozhenie (the emancipation law) could not have been invented. If anything could have provoked revolts, it was precisely the perplexing vagueness of the conditions created by the new law. And yet, except in two places where there were insurrections, and a very few other spots where small disturbances entirely due to misunderstandings and immediately appeased took place, Russia remained quiet, – more quiet than ever. With their usual good sense, the peasants had understood that serfdom was done away with, that 'freedom had come', and they accepted the conditions imposed upon them, although these conditions were very heavy.

I was in Nikolskoye in August 1861, and again in the summer of 1862, and I was struck with the quiet, intelligent way in which the peasants had accepted the new conditions. They knew perfectly well how difficult it would be to pay the redemption tax for the land, which was in reality an indemnity to the nobles in lieu of the obligations of serfdom. But they so much valued the abolition of their personal enslavement that they accepted the ruinous charges – not without murmuring, but as a hard necessity – the moment that personal freedom was obtained . . .

When I saw our Nikolskoye peasants, fifteen months after the liberation, I could not but admire them. Their inborn good nature and softness remained with them, but all traces of servility had disappeared. They talked to their masters as equals talk to equals, as if they never had stood in different relations. Besides, such men came out from among them as could make a stand for their rights.

Stolypin's agrarian reforms of 1911

The first great agrarian reform was the abolition of serfdom in 1861. The outcome was not without difficulties and some of the seeds of the 1905 revolution lay with the impoverishment of ex-serfs who drifted to the towns. The Stolypin government enacted the second major agrarian reform in November 1906 and this was revised and extended in 1911.

It (a) ended the power of the commune;
   (b) introduced individual land ownership by peasants;

(c) title of the land could be claimed by the property being in one allotment rather than divided into strips;
(d) in 1911 the partitions into private holdings were extended from arable to grazing land with the exception of traditional common land;
(e) land held by the peasant household was vested in the head of the household;
(f) the government extended the power and increased the resources of the Peasants' Land Bank i.e. peasants were able to borrow to extend their holdings and the Bank was given the power to buy large estates and to subdivide and sell them in smaller lots;
(g) the Peasants' Land Bank lowered its interest rate to $4\frac{1}{2}$ per cent as a further incentive;
(h) the government also gave assistance to those who desired to migrate to the Eastern provinces of the Empire;
(i) reduced by 50 per cent from 1 January 1906 and terminated completely after 1 January 1907 payments from peasants for land which prior to 1861 was the property of nobles, state and crown.

Stolypin had also a political aim in that he hoped to create a strong conservative peasant class.

In the period 1906–17 over 25,000,000 acres of land in European Russia had been transferred to the peasants. In 1905 there were 12,300,000 peasant households in European Russia of which 9,500,000 were on communal tenure. Statistics on the changes brought about by the Stolypin reforms vary. The largest number of those to leave the commune took place 1907–09 and by 1915 about 23 per cent of households had filed for separation and about 25 per cent had completed the process. Losing the human and material assistance of the commune was a deterrent to leaving it.

It is felt that the timescales for the reforms were too short, the numbers affected too small and the gains too far into the future.

Agricultural production

The emancipation of serfs in 1861 failed to raise the economic standards of farming. The ex-serfs became increasingly impoverished and still bound to their village communes. The three main reasons for this failure were:

(a) the smallness of the holding given to the ex-serfs. Holdings averaged 35.6 acres (14.4 hectares) for each family in 1877. This was far smaller than the peasant holding worked before the emancipation;
(b) the burden of redemption payment, payable by instalments, which very often exceeded the market value of the land;
(c) the institution of the village commune.

With adequate investment and modern cultivation methods it could well have provided full employment and fair income. Land had been allotted to communes which, in turn, assigned it to member households. Under this system, a peasant household owned individually only its home with the adjoining small garden plot. Pastures and woodland were used in common. Cropland was divided into three fields, one of which lay fallow each year. Each family received its land allotment in numerous scattered strips. Land was periodically repartitioned among commune members, but this system deprived the individual farmer of any incentive to improve this land. Strip farming with compulsory rotation minimised the scope for initiative and innovation and involved enormous waste of land and labour. With the land reform of 1906 redemption payments were abolished and the government withdrew its support of the commune. Peasants formed individually owned farms consolidating their scattered strips and enclosing them. Government credit was provided to finance purchase of estate and stand land by peasants. By 1916, more than 50 per cent of peasant households held their land in individual, hereditary tenure. Peasants purchased over 10,500,000 hectares of additional land in European Russia alone and some 2,500,000 colonists were settled in Siberia in 1905–15. By the time of the 1917 Revolution peasants held some 75 per cent of all privately owned land in European Russia; nobility about 17 per cent; churches and monasteries, over 1 per cent, townsmen the remainder. The huge holdings of the state and imperial family (157 million hectares) consisted overwhelmingly of forests and cultivable land. Landed estates, while still accounting for 12 per cent of grain output and 5–6 per cent of livestock herds had lost some 40 per cent of their land since 1877, a process intensified by the Stolypin reforms.

| | Wheat | Rye | Barley | Oats | Potatoes | Sugar Beet |
		(in millions of hectolitres)				(million tons)
1870	99	278	58	263	135	1.4
1879	60	202	44	179	122	2.7
1885	78	309	44	171	107	5.5
1890	94	197	72	238	146	4.9
		(in millions of metric tons)				
1900	9.2	22.7	4.5	11.5	25.3	6.4
1910	22.8	22.2	10.6	15.5	36.6	13.2
1913	28.8	25.7	13.1	18.2	35.9	12.4

8
Social and Economic Progress

Population

Year	Total Population
1796	36,000,000
1811	41,000,000
1815	45,000,000
1835	59,000,000
1846	65,900,000
1859	74,000,000
1870	86,000,000
1887	98,000,000
1897[1]	106,000,000
1908	155,000,000
1915	131,000,000

[1] First modern census.

Population of major cities (in thousands of residents)

	1811	1840	1863	1897	1914	1917
Baku	–	–	14.0	112	218	232
Ekaterinberg	–	–	20.0	118	–	211
Ivanovo	–	–	1.5	54	–	146
Kiev	23	47	68	248	520	365
Moscow	270	349	462	1,039	1,763	1,050
Odessa	11	60	119	404	500	425
Riga	32	60	78	282	588	690
St Petersburg	220	470	540	1,265	2,119	722

Emigration

1871–1880	58,000
1881–1890	288,000
1891–1900	481,000
1901–1910	911,000
1911–1920	420,000

Ethnic composition

The ethnic composition of Russia at the end of the nineteenth century:

	percentage
Slav	73[1]
Finns	5
Turko-Tatars	9
Jews	4

Economically Active Population (1897[2])

Agriculture, forestry and fishing	15,077,000
Mining and extractive industry	155,000
Manufacturing	2,920,000
Commerce, finance, etc.	1,051,000
Transport and communications	649,000
Services, including armed services	3,207,000
Others occupied	227,000

Changing status of women

Only after the Revolution of 1905 did any real shift in the status of women take place in Russia. Women who, apart from housework, undertook hours of work in the fields, were considered second-class members of the peasant household. *Domostroi*, Russia's first book of manners published in the sixteenth century, which concerns itself with 'the management of the household' said that wife-beating was a necessity and a virtue.

Women played a significant part in the revolutionary movements in the first half of the nineteenth century and are mainly remembered as the wives of Decembrists who joined their husbands in Siberia.

In the 1870s and 1880s names such as Sofia Perovskaya (who was in charge of operations to assassinate Alexander I), Vera Figner and Vera Zasulich are well known. A new generation of revolutionaries arose in the period 1905–07 with

---

[1] of which Russian 66, Poles 7.
[2] Excluding Poland.

the appearance of suffragette movements but few of these movements survived for long. The 1905 reforms brought about no real improvement for women. They had no right to vote and divorce and inheritance laws remained unaltered, so that they were, in fact, disenfranchised.

Open discussion of political issues was not possible before 1905, but with the October Manifesto many more political parties were established and some of their aims demanded improvements in the status of women.

In 1903 the Russian Social Democratic Workers' party (Bolshevik) aimed for:

> Universal, equal, and direct suffrage for all male and female citizens, twenty years old or over, at all elections to the legislative assembly and to the various local organs of self-government.
>
> A law providing a weekly uninterrupted forty-two-hour respite for all hired labour, of both sexes, in all branches of the national economy.
>
> Prohibition of female labour in those branches of industry which are injurious to women's health; relief from work four weeks before and six weeks after childbirth, with regular wages paid during all this period.
>
> Establishment of nurseries for infants and children in all shops, factories, and other enterprises that employ women; permission for freedom of at least a half-hour's duration to be granted at three-hour intervals to all nursing mothers.
>
> Appointment of an adequate number of factory inspectors in all branches of the national economy and extension of their supervision to all enterprises employing hired labour, including government enterprises (domestic service also to be within the sphere of their supervision); appointment of special women inspectors in those industries where female labour is employed; participation of representatives, elected by the workers and paid by the state in supervising the enforcement of the factory laws, the fixing of wage scales, and in accepting or rejecting the finished products and other results of labour.

In 1905 the Socialist Revolutionary Party demanded:

> Prohibition of women and child labour in some branches of industry.

In 1905 the Russian Constitutional Democratic Party (Cadets) demanded:

> People's representatives to be elected by general, equal, direct and secret ballot irrespective of their religion, nationality or sex.
>
> Protection of female and child labour and an eight-hour working day.

Any real change in status for 50 per cent of Russia's population only came after the October revolution.

There is a Russian peasant saying 'A crab isn't a fish and a woman isn't a person.'

1762	Catherine II (the Great) is proclaimed empress.
1764	A general regulation on the education of children is issued; it is inspired by Catherine II (the Great) and based on the Rousseauist principle of segregated education according to sex. An institute dedicated to the education of young noble girls (the future Smolny Institute) is established.
1772	A society to aid widows and orphans is established.
1783	Princess Catherine Dashkova is named director of the Russian Academy, which is modelled after the French Academy. She seeks to establish uniform rules of Russian spelling and grammar, to begin work on a dictionary and to 'encourage the study of national history'.
1796	Catherine II (the Great) dies.
	Princess Catherine Dashkova is exiled to her estate at Troitskoe.
1828	The Fourth Section of the Chancellery responsible for women's education and public assistance is created.
1870–1873	The populist Chaikovsky circle forms in St Petersburg.
	The circle includes Nikolai Chaikovsky, Mark Natanson, Sofia Perovskaya, Peter Kropotkin and Sergei Kravchinsky.
1876	A new *Zemlia i Volia* (Land and Freedom) society is formed by populists, including George Plekhanov, Alexander Mikhailov, M. Natanson and Vera Figner.
1878	Vera Zasulich makes an attempt on the life of General Fedor Trepov, the police chief of St Petersburg. She is acquitted by a jury on 31 March, and, with the complicity of the crowd, she is able to escape the police, who are waiting to rearrest her.
	The Bestuzhev courses, which provide higher education for women, are established in St Petersburg.
1879	*Zemlia i Volia* holds congresses in Lipetsk and Voronezh at which differences among members over terrorism come into the open. As a result of these differences, the society splits into two groups: one group, *Narodnaia Volia* (Will of the People), whose members include Sophia Perovskaya, favours terrorist methods; whereas the other, *Chernyi Peredel* (Black Repartition), whose members include Vera Zasulich, favours propaganda.
1871	N. Nekrasov: Russian Women (1871–1872).
1881	The five individuals responsible for the assassination of Alexander II are hanged, including Andrei Zheliabov and Sofia Perovskaya.
1882	The *Communist Manifesto*, by Karl Marx and Friedrich Engels, is translated into Russian by George Plekhanov and Vera Zasulich.

1884	A new statute on universities is issued: the autonomy previously enjoyed by universities is eliminated, the trustees' powers are strengthened, and higher education for women is restricted. The mathematician Sofia Kovalevskaia departs for the University of Stockholm.
1885	Nighttime work is prohibited for women and children.
1887	Ivan Delianov, the minister of public instruction issues a circular (June), limiting access to gymnasiums (excluded are the sons of 'coachmen, servants, laundresses and cooks').
1899	New currents in Russian Marxism appear: the 'economism' of the Union of Struggle in St Petersburg, which gives priority to the everyday demands of workers . . . ; the economism of the Union of Russian Social Democrats Abroad (Workers' Cause and Ekaterina Kuskova's manifesto, Credo); and 'legal' Marxism . . .
1900	The first issue of *Iskra* (the 'Spark'), a journal expressing the views of the group made up of Lenin, Martov, Alexander Potresov, Plekhanov, Pavel Axelrod and Vera Zasulich, is published in Leipzig.
1901	The Socialist Revolutionary Party (SR) is founded in Berlin at a meeting of the Russian Socialist Revolutionaries, the Union of Socialist Revolutionaries living abroad, and the Agrarian Socialist League, which maintains its autonomous existence. The party membership included Ekaterina Breshkovskaia . . .
1908	A law makes ten years of primary education obligatory. The number of enrolled primary-school students will increase from 4 million in 1900 to 7.2 million (including 2.3 million girls) in 1914.
1909	The University of Saratov is founded. Women's access to universities is restricted, and the enrolment of Jews is subject to rigid quotas.
1910	In Paris Sergei Diaghilev presents Igor Stravinsky's *The Firebird*. Russian ballet begins to receive huge acclaim, thanks to the choreography of Mikhail Fokin, the set designs of Lev Bakst and Alexander Benois, and the dancing of Anna Pavlova and Vaslav Njinsky.
1912	The 'Poets' Atelier' is founded by Anna Akhmatova, Nikolai Gumilev and Osip Mandelstam. This marks the birth of the 'acmeist' movement, which is formed in reaction to symbolism.
1913	The principles of rayonism are formulated by M. Larionov and Natalia Goncharova.
1917	On International Women's Day in February a large demonstration takes place in Petrograd to protest the scarcity of food.

Government revenue and expenditure

	Revenue	Expenditure
1803	102	109
1810	178	279
1820	447	500
1830	393[1]	428
1839	–	628[2]
1840	155	188
1850	202	287
1860	278	438
1870	460	564
1880	629	793
1890	944	1,057
1900	1,704	1,883
1910	2,781	2,597
1914	2,898	4,865

[1] Millions of paper roubles until 1830 then silver.
[2] Millions of paper roubles until 1839 then silver.
The silver rouble was worth roughly four times the paper rouble.

State revenue (1902)

		millions roubles
Direct taxes:		133
including Land and forest	49	
Trade licences	66	
Indirect taxes:		429
including Spirits	39	
Tobacco	45	
Sugar	81	
Naphtha, matches	38	
Customs duties	225	
Duties:		101
including Stamp duties	45	
Transfer duties	24	
Passports, railway tax	32	
State monopolies:		545
including Mining	3	
Mint	4	
Post	34	

		millions roubles
Telegraphs and telephone	20	
Spirits	485	
State domains:		524
including Rent	25	
Forests	58	
Mines	14	
Railways	408	
Banking	17	
Redemption of land:		90
including Liberated serfs	39	
Crown peasants	51	
Miscellaneous		75
Extraordinary revenue:		202
Total		2,167

State expenditure (1902)

		millions roubles
Ordinary expenditure:		1,802
including State debt	290	
Holy synod	28	
Imperial house	18	
Foreign affairs	6	
War	343	
Navy	100	
Treasury	334	
Agriculture and state domains	43	
Interior	94	
Public instruction	37	
Ways of communication	446	
Justice	47	
Audit	8	
State studs	2	
Extraordinary expenditure:		365
including Building new railways	161	
Cost of loan (1902) anticipating Chinese indemnity	172	
Famine	19	
Total		2,167

Local Finance (1900)[1]

	Receipts	Expenditure
	(in millions roubles)	
34 provincial assemblies (*zemstvos*)	89	88
14 provinces of European Russia not represented in the *zemstvos*	8	10
Transcaucasus	3	3
Siberia	3	3
Steppes and Turkestan	2	2
Livonica and Estonia	.1	.5
Total	105	107

[1] Not including Poland.

Of the expenditure of the *zemstvos* 9.9 per cent was spent on administration; 27.6 on medical help; 17.4 on education; 11.2 on debt and 11.1 on roads.

Debt of all *zemstvos* (1899) 39,370,131 roubles.

Money and banking

The history of the rouble, which is divided into 100 kopecks, dates back to the thirteenth century as a silver or copper coin. Throughout its history the rouble has been debased by reducing its metal content. There were attempts in 1667 and 1689 to establish by statute the worth of the rouble in terms of silver. In 1768 Catherine II (the Great) introduced paper currency. The rouble became inconvertible in 1777 and remained so until 1897 when the gold standard was introduced. In the years in between Russia lived with a system of inconvertible and depreciated paper currency. The gold standard was suspended in 1914 when World War I began.

The first banks were founded in 1754; one for the landed nobility and one for commerce. In 1860 the government also established a central bank, known as the Bank of Russia; it acted as the state bank and also undertook commercial banking. In 1903 it had 113 branches.

Bank of Russia: Assets and Liabilities in 1903

Assets	millions roubles	Liabilities	millions roubles
Cash and credit notes	995	Capital and reserve	55
Portfolio	236	Note circulation	630
Advances and loans	223	Deposit and current accounts	450
Bonds and stock	54	Treasury	305
Accounts at branches	362	Accounts at branches	418

In 1864, the first private joint-stock bank was founded and by 1914 47 commercial banks with 743 branches existed, as well as a state-owned savings bank, co-operative banks, and mutual credit societies. A considerable share of the banks' resources consisted of foreign capital.

Industrial growth

The beginnings of industrial development on any scale began in the sixteenth and seventeenth centuries but when Peter I (the Great) came to the throne Russia was still a medieval country with a primitive, backward economy. Peter's reign marks a watershed in Russia's political and economic history; the changes brought about by the creation of a navy, the modernisation of the army and other Petrine reforms made great demands on imports and existing industries. Some very large industries existed, particularly for the manufacture of armaments and stores for both the army and navy. But much of the production of other consumer goods such as silks and woollens was the result of cottage industries. When Peter I (the Great) died there were only about 200 large industrial enterprises.

The labour force in c. 1800 was about 200,000; in 1860 c. 800,000 and represented about 1 per cent of the total population. Other changes taking place in this period were the decline of the White Sea port of Archangel and foreign trade being diverted to ports in the Baltic and the Black Sea.

The emancipation of the serfs was another turning-point in Russian history without which the subsequent economic progress could not have been achieved. The Stolypin land reforms of 1906–11 were a major step toward the removal of the legal and economic disabilities of the peasants.

From 1890 industrial employment grew steadily and in 1913 reached some 3,000,000 which however was still only about 2 per cent of the total population. The value of industrial production rose from 1,500 million roubles in 1890 to 5,700 million in 1913. The largest gains were made by the cotton, coal, iron and steel industries. Beginning in the 1890s rapid expansion took place in the development of the Donets basin, a region in the south of European Russia rich in coal and iron ore. Between 1890 and 1913 the population increased by 37 per cent, of which 69 per cent was urban. Per capita output of grain was 35 per cent and per capita industrial output 124 per cent. A programme of railway building, financed by foreign capital, and by an aggressive protectionism which reached exorbitant heights by the end of the nineteenth and early twentieth century fostered industrial growth. The railway construction stimulated industries such as the manufacture of rails, rolling stock and coal. A comprehensive system of private banks was created and in 1897 Russia introduced the gold standard which was maintained until 1914. In 1914 nearly four-fifths of the state revenue was still derived from indirect taxation and more than 25 per cent came from tax on the state monopoly of spirits.

World War I caused the loss of foreign markets, enemy occupation of the industrial western provinces, mobilisation of millions of men, breakdown of the transport system and vast war expenditures. The consequences were an imbalance of international accounts, inflation, decline in productivity, shortage of supplies, especially in the larger cities, rising prices, general impoverishment and the suspension of the gold standard.

The 1917 February revolution by the citizens of Petrograd originated in a bread shortage, and this had been brought about by the conscription of farm workers resulting in a food supply crisis. The process of economic disintegration had begun and aided by revolutionary ideals there was occupation of factories by workers and the seizure of large estates. So much industrial progress had been made since 1890 with increased technical skill, industrial organisation and know-how. Following the October Revolution this was the base on which Soviet Russia was to base its economic development programmes.

	Number of Factories or Workshops	Workmen	Annual Output in Roubles
1850	9,483	317,700	166,000
1863	16,659	419,600	351,800
1870	26,377	435,800	500,100
1879	34,774	861,000	1,290,300
1890	32,254	1,424,800	1,502,600
1900	38,141	2,373,400	3,438,900
1908	39,866	2,679,600	4,908,600
1912	29,965	2,931,300	5,738,100

Share capital of enterprises

The share capital of various financial, manufacturing, industrial, steamship, and other enterprises in operation in 1898, numbering 1181, was estimated at 1,736,856,000 roubles. Nearly 20 per cent represented the capital of foreign companies. Below is a list of the most important industrial enterprises:

Enterprises	Number	Share capital £ Sterling
Manufacturing	177	29,853,168
Metallurgical	101	26,527,703
Coal mining	17	4,596,640
Naphtha	19	5,302,406
Chemicals	36	3,814,320
Breweries, distilleries, etc.	44	3,103,363
Paper mills	24	2,153,156
Saw mills and wood-working companies	15	1,205,937

Decision of the State Council on the Employment of Minors, 1 June 1882 confirmed by the emperor.

1. Children under the age of twelve are not permitted to work.
2. Minors between the ages of twelve and fifteen cannot be employed at work for more than eight hours a day . . .
3. Minors under the age of fifteen cannot be employed at work between nine o'clock in the evening and five o'clock in the morning, or on Sundays and high holidays.
4. Minors referred to in article 3 are forbidden to be employed in industries, or at particular jobs in such industries, which by their nature are harmful to the health of minors or must be regarded as exhausting for them . . .
5. Owners of mills, plants, and factories are obliged to afford those minors working in their establishments, who do not have a certificate of course completion from at least a one-grade primary school or another equivalent school, the opportunity to attend the aforesaid educational institutions for no less than three hours daily, or eighteen hours a week.

For supervising the observance of the ordinances on labor and education for underage workers, a special inspectorate is instituted.

(Vernadsky and Fisher, 1972)

Factory regulations of 3 June 1886

Decision of the State Council, confirmed by the emperor. Some of the points include:

It is forbidden to lower the wages of workers before the expiration of a term contract negotiated with them, or without giving two-weeks' notice to workers hired for an indefinite term . . . Workers likewise have no right, to demand any changes in its conditions . . .

A worker who has failed to receive the wages due to him on time has the right to demand the legal dissolution of the contract negotiated with him . . .

It is forbidden to pay workers in coupons, promissory notes, bread, merchandise, or other articles in place of money . . .

It is forbidden to charge workers for . . . medical assistance . . .

A hiring contract may be cancelled by the manager of a mill or factory:

a. In consequence of the absence from work of a worker for more than three consecutive days without a satisfactory reason . . .

c. In consequence of insolence or bad behavior on the part of a worker, if it threatens the property interest of the factory or the personal safety of any member of the factory administration . . .

A worker is also permitted to demand the cancellation of a contract:

a. In consequence of beatings, severe insults, and mistreatment in general on the part of the owner, his family, or persons entrusted with supervision of workers.

b. In consequence of the violation of conditions relating to the furnishing of food and living quarters to the workers.

c. In consequence of work detrimental to his health... For stopping work in a mill or factory through a strike among workers, with the aim of forcing mill or factory owners to raise wages or change other conditions of the hiring contract before the expiration date of the latter, those guilty are subject to: imprisonment for a term of four to eight months, for instigating the beginning or continuation of a strike; imprisonment for a term of two to four months, for otherwise participating.

Those participants in a strike who discontinue the same and commence work upon the first demand of the police authorities, are freed from imprisonment...

For an arbitrary refusal to work before the expiration date of the hiring contract, guilty mill or factory workers are subject to arrest for not more than one month... Rules for supervision over industrial factory establishments and for mutual relations between factory owners and workers.

Supervision over the observance of proper organization and order in mills and factories is entrusted to the local guberniia authorities and is carried out by them with the assistance of guberniia bureaus for factory affairs, officials of the factory inspectorate, and the police.

Guberniia bureaus for factory affairs, under the chairmanship of the governor, are composed of the vice-governor, the prosecutor of the district or his assistant, the head of the guberniia department of gendarmes, the district factory inspector or his assistant, the chairman or a member of the guberniia zemstvo executive board (who shall be elected by this executive board), and the mayor of the capital city of the guberniia or a member of the local municipal executive board (who shall be elected by the latter body)...

Every worker... must be issued a pay book...

The manager of a mill or factory is subject to a monetary fine of from fifty to three hundred rubles:

a. For charging workers for articles the use of which should be accorded them free of charge...

c. For paying workers in promissory notes, bread, goods, or other articles including coupons, instead of in money.

(Vernadsky and Fisher, 1972)

Operatives Working for Wages in Russian Industries in 1804 and 1825

	Enterprises		% of wage workers	
	1804	1825	1804	1825
Cotton	196	484	83	95
Iron and steel	28	170	28	22
Leather	843	1,784	97	93
Linen	285	196	60	71
Ropemaking	58	98	85	92
Silk	328	184	73	83
Wool	157	324	10	18

Industrial disputes 1895–1913

	Number of Strikes	Number of Strikers	Number of Working Days Lost
1895	68	31,100	156,800
1900	125	29,300	119,500
1905	13,995	2,863,100	23,609,300
1910	222	46,600	256,300
1911	466	105,100	791,000
1912	2,032	725,500	2,375,600
1913	2,404	887,000	3,863,200

Alcohol production

In 1894 the Crown undertook the retailing of spirits. The monopoly was limited to the sale of spirits and did not include fermented beverages such as wine, beer, etc. The manufacture of spirits remained in the hands of private persons, and the distilleries were subject to the same regulations as under the excise.

The production of alcohol in the Russian Empire in 1900 was 86,052,000 gallons. In 1903 there were 2,358 distilleries in the Russian Empire (2,328 in European Russia).

Cotton Industry

	Production (in millions of roubles)				
	Spinning	Weaving	Printing and dyeing	Finishing	Total
1880	74	100	61	6	241
1885	97	98	59	3	257
1893	135	161	99	3	398

Import of raw cotton and yarn

	Raw cotton (in thousand tons)	Cotton yarn (in thousand tons)
1824–1826	0.9	5.4
1826–1836	4.6	10.1
1842–1844	8.4	9.5
1848–1850	21.4	4.5
1889–1891	117.4	3.4
1899–1903	180.0	2.9

In 1900 there were 227 cotton factories with 6 million spindles with 146,000 looms. Moscow had 56 factories, Vladimir 67 and St Petersburg 24.

Mineral production (1900)

	(kilogrammes)
Gold	38,699
Platinum	6,223
Silver	325

	(tons)
Lead	323
Zinc	6,000
Copper	8,000
Pig Iron	2,849,000
Iron and steel	1,816,000
Coal	16,170,000
Naphtha	9,697,000
Salt	1,928,000

Salt production

Salt production in Russian Empire in 1901 (in pouds):

Rock Salt	30,082,514
From salt-marshes	51,378,065
From brine by evaporation	24,528,089
Total	105,988,668

Of the salt extracted in 1901, 52,941,401 pouds were from South Russia; 20,835,092 from Astrakhan; 18,008,484 from Perm; 5,623,983 from Siberia;

3,106,085 from Caucasia, 1,896,534 from Orenburg; 1,114,134 from Transcaspian Province; the remainder came from Turkestan, North Russia, Poland and Kwang-Tung province.

Petroleum production of the Baku district

Production of the oil fields of Balakhany, Sabunchi, Romany, Bibi-Eybat, and Binagadin, for five years, in millions of pouds:

	1897	1898	1899	1900	1901
Illuminating oil	90	92	110	128	121
Lubricating oil	9	11	12	14	14
Various naphtha products	1	1	1	3	1
Residuum	224	239	231	287	322
Crude oil exported	24	44	25	39	35
Total	348	387	379	471	493
Waste	80	101	119	131	149
Total naphtha production	428	488	498	602	642

Exports and imports in 1901

Total Russian exports in 1901:
        761,683,000 gold roubles

Percentage of exports to:

Germany	23
Great Britain	20
Holland	11
France	8
Austria	4
United States	0.5

Total Russian imports in 1901:
        593,425,000 gold roubles

Percentage of imports from:

Germany	36
Great Britain	17
United States	6
France	5
Austria	4

Customs duties as percentage of the total value of imports

Year	Percentage
1851–56	24
1857–68	18
1869–76	13
1877–80	16
1881–84	19
1885–90	28
1891–1900	33
1902	40

Duties on various categories of imports

	Foods	Raw Materials and semi-manufactured	Manufactured goods	All goods
	%	%	%	%
1894	73	24	27	31
1896	72	27	25	32
1898	80	33	28	37
1900	81	25	25	33
1902	96	31	28	40

Gross national product *per capita* (in roubles)

	1897	1913
USA	346	682
Great Britain	273	461
France	233	–
Germany	184	300
Russia	63	101

Merchant ships

	Sailing ships	Steamers	Sailing ships	Steamers
	(number)		(thousand tons)	
1859	1,416		173	
1866	2,045	87	181	
1869	2,534	114	230	
1880	4,276	326	379	89
1895	2,135	522	323	206
1900	2,293	745	269	364
1910	2,504	943	260	463
1913	2,597	1,103	257	526

River and canal traffic

In 1900 European Russia there were 76,500 miles of rivers, canals and lakes, 16,680 miles being navigable for steamers, 8,105 for small sailing vessels and 26,800 for rafts. About 32,711,100 tons of goods were carried, of which 17,073,000 tons on the Volga Canals were developed in the 18th and 19th centuries. As the elevations within the European part of Russia are rather low, the sources of rivers flowing in opposite directions are in many instances very close to each other. Several canals were built to connect the headwaters of rivers in central European Russia, especially the Mariinsky system joining the Volga via several connections to the Neva. The Volga-Don canal was a Peter I (the Great) project and was only completed after World War II by forced labour.

Railways

The first Russian railway line was opened from St Petersburg to Tsarskoye-Selo in 1836. This was for horse traction because the locomotive had not arrived from England and so exactly a year later it was opened with a locomotive. By order of the tsar a set of musical instruments, consisting of eleven trumpets and a trombone, were on the locomotive so that warning could be given of the approaching train. Locomotives were used only when forty or more passengers were to be carried; platform wagons were open for the transport of passengers seated in their own carriages. In 1851 the St Petersburg–Moscow line was completed, and when Alexander II (1855) came to the throne this was the main railway. A decree of 26 January 1857 started the building of 12,000 miles of railway during Alexander's reign:

> Raiways, the need for which has been doubted by many over the last ten years, have now been recognized by all strata as a necessity for the empire and have become a national need and a common and insistent desire.
>
> In this profound conviction we gave orders immediately after the first cessation of hostilities for funds to be arranged so that this urgent need might be satisfied in the best way. Thorough discussion showed that it was best for the sake of convenience and speed to turn, following the example of all other countries, to private enterprise, both domestic and foreign, so as in the latter case to profit from the experience gained in the building of many thousands of miles of railway lines in western Europe.
>
> On this basis various offers were invited, presented, and examined, and after the matter had received due consideration by the Committee of Ministers and been discussed in our presence, the terms offered by the Society of Russian and Foreign Capitalists, at the head of which is our banker, Baron Stieglitz, were unanimously considered the best and were approved by us.

Under these terms the society undertakes: to build at its own expense within ten years and to maintain for eighty-five years the indicated network of about four thousands versts of railway, with the government guaranteeing to pay 5 percent interest on the amount calculated for the construction, and with the entire network becoming the property of the treasury when the time limit expires.

The network will extend from Saint Petersburg to Warsaw and the Prussian frontier; from Moscow to Nizhnii-Novgorod; from Moscow through Kursk and the lower reaches of the Dnieper to Feodosiia [in the Crimea]; and from Kursk, or Orel, through Dinaburg [Duenaburg, Dvinsk] to Libava [Liepaja, Libau] – and thereby through twenty-six guberniias it will, by an uninterrupted stretch of railway, link together three capitals, our main navigable rivers, our richest grain regions, and two ports on the Black Sea and Baltic that are open almost all year round. Thus it will facilitate our exports abroad and will ensure the transportation and supply of food at home.

(Vernadsky and Fisher, 1972)

It was in the 1860s–1870s that the basic network was constructed, and in 1891 work on the Trans-Siberian Railway was started, serving as an economic link between European Russia and the Far East; the single-track all-Russian rail route to Vladivostok *via* Harbin was completed in 1917. About a million passengers used the line to migrate to Siberia between 1903 and 1913; the journey took thirteen days.

Length of railway line open (in kilometres)

1838	27
1845	144
1850	501
1860	1,626
1865	3,842
1870	10,731
1875	19,029
1880	22,865
1885	26,024
1890	30,596
1895	37,058
1900	53,234
1905	61,085
1910	66,581
1915	65,100
1917	70,300

Weights and measures

The metric system of weights and measures was introduced into Russia in 1899 and was made obligatory in 1918.

Traditional forms of weights and measurements were:

Linear measure

1 *versta* = 500 *sazhens* = 0.66 mile = 1.0668 km.
1 *sazhen* = 3 *arshins* = 7 feet = 2.13 m.
1 *arshin* = 16 *vershoks* = 28 *dyuims* (inches) = 71.12 cm.
1 *fut* = 12 dyuims = 1 foot = 30.48 cm.
1 *vershok* = 1.75 inches = 4.445 cm.
1 *dyuim* = 1 inch = 2.54 cm.

Square measure

Desyatina = 2,400 square *sazhens* = 217 acres = 1.0925 hectare.

Liquid measure

Vedro = 12.3 litres
Chetvert = 3.075 litres

Weights

1 *pud* (*poud, pood*) = 40 *funts* = 36.11 lb.
1 *funt* = 96 *zolotniks* = 0.903 lb

9
The Rise of Radicalism

Monarchy and absolutism: an overview

Peter I (the Great) set about the reform of the state and to extend the power of the tsars built up in previous reigns. The boyar class was abolished and the church came under the control of the tsar. The absolutism of the monarchy changed under Catherine I and Peter II, with actual power being exercised by the Supreme Privy Council. With the abolition of the Council in 1730 Anne restored autocracy. In the latter part of the eighteenth century Catherine II (the Great) did attempt certain liberalisation of the absolute monarchy. Catherine believed that absolute monarchy was the only form of government suited to Russia, but that it must be based on strict observance of the law, of which the Crown was the sole source. This concept of 'legal paternalism' was continued by Paul. Alexander I, however, brought a vacillating liberalism to the throne in 1801. The reign began with liberal experiments and there were plans for constitutional reform. Later in the reign Alexander I became more conservative and liberal ideas and plans were abandoned.

Under Nicholas I the tsar was the source of all law and the actual head of the administration and absolutism reached its high point between 1825 and 1855. Although Alexander II introduced many reforms, he would not agree to any curtailment of the powers of the monarchy. Alexander III's short reign brought a conservative reaction to the reforms of his predecessor.

Nicholas II was forced to grant constitutional concessions in 1905 following 'Bloody Sunday' and the Russo-Japanese conflict. With the establishment of the *duma* Russia formally became a limited constitutional monarchy. The tsar was never reconciled to the status of a constitutional monarch and his inability to compromise and come to terms with a changed situation eventually led to the end of the monarchy in 1917.

The Decembrists

The origins of the Decembrist insurrection arose from the many secret societies that had sprung up after the war with Napoleon of 1812–15.

1816 Union of Salvation, St Petersburg
    leading members: Prince Sergey Trubetskoy
                Matvey and Sergey Muravyov-Apostol
                Aleksandr and Mikhail Muravyov
                Pavel Pestel
1818 Union of Public Good
    re-established as
1822 Northern Society (Society of the North)
    leading members: Nikita Muravyov
                Prince Sergey Trubetskoy
                Prince Yevgeny Obelensky
                Nikolai Turgenev
                Kondraty Ryleyev
1821 Southern Society
1823 Society of United Slavs founded by Pyotr Borisov
1825 Merged with the Southern Society

The Northern Society advocated a British-style constitutional monarchy, the abolition of serfdom and equality before the law.

The Southern Society was republican and aimed at the abolition of the monarchy. It also aimed at devolution, giving areas such as the Ukraine far more power over their own affairs. It was also advocated that 50 per cent of the land should be taken into state ownership and the balance be divided among the peasants. It wanted a federal union with Poland and their ideas and ideals were dominated by Panslavism.

There were several moves to bridge the gap between the ambitions of the two societies but this had not been achieved by the time of the death of Alexander I and the confusion concerning the succession.

The date fixed for the insurrection was 14 [26] December 1825 and it proved to be a fiasco. It was arranged for the day soldiers were to take the oath of loyalty to Nicholas I. It was hoped that the soldiers would refuse. In fact only 3,000 soldiers and sailors refused to take the oath. The rebellious regiments went to Senate Square but were without effective leadership and unprepared for action. The rebels found themselves surrounded and surrendered, but not before they had killed the Governor-General Miloradovich; Pyotr Kakhovsky fired the shot.

The St Petersburg insurrection was followed by the rebellion of the Chernigov regiment on 29 December 1825, which was put down at Kovalevka in the Ukraine on 3 January 1826.

About 579 individuals were investigated for being involved in the uprising; 79 per cent were army personnel and 121 were brought to trial.

Five were hanged: Pestel, Muravyov-Apostol, Bestuzhev-Ryumin, Kakhovsky and Ryleyev. Thirty-one went into penal servitude. The rest were deported. Many of the soldiers were forced to run the gauntlet and the Chernigov regiment was sent to the war in Caucasia.

This was the first rebellion against the tsar in modern times and paved the way for future revolutionary movements.

Only when Alexander II came to the throne in 1855 were the surviving Decembrists released from imprisonment.

Court Report on the punishment of the Decembrists, 13 July 1826

This is an excerpt from the report of the Supreme Criminal Court to the tsar. The effect of the sentences on the public was heightened because capital punishment had not been used as a legal penalty in Russia for fifty years, since the time of Pugachev.

> Your Imperial Majesty will graciously observe:
> That, of the 121 defendants sentenced by the Supreme Criminal Court, 5 persons designated outside the categories are condemned to death by quartering; 31 persons, in the first category, are condemned to death by beheading; 17 persons, in the second category, are sentenced to civil death, exiled for life at hard labor; 2 persons, in the third category, are exiled to hard labor for life; 38 persons, in the fourth, fifth, sixth, and seventh categories, are sentenced to hard labor for specified terms, and then to penal settlement; 15 persons, in the eighth category, upon divestment of their rank and nobility, are sentenced to penal settlement for life; 3 persons, in the ninth category, upon divestment of their rank and nobility, are sentenced to banishment to Siberia for life; 1 person, in the tenth category, upon divestment of his rank and nobility, is sentenced to service as a common soldier until he earns promotion; 8 persons, in the eleventh category, upon divestment of their rank, are sentenced to service as soldiers with the right to earn promotion.

Petrashevsky Circle

A group of several hundred people met in secret every Friday, from 1845, at the house of Mikhail Butashevich-Petrashevsky to discuss economic and sociopolitical thought. Influenced by Blanc, Proudhon and Leroux, the general philosophy of the group eventually combined elements of Feuerbachian and Fourierist thought; great emphasis was placed on the natural sciences and on the need to build a socialist utopia. Petrashevsky himself favoured legal struggle in order to achieve partial reforms; the radicals, on the other hand, under the leadership of Nicholas Speshnev (1821–1882), favoured armed revolt. In 1845 and 1846 the Petrashevsky published their ideas in the celebrated *Pocket Dictionary of Foreign Terms*. In 1849, twenty-one of the Petrashevsky were charged with plotting to overthrow the state and fifteen were condemned to death, but the death sentence was commuted at the last minute; one of the condemned was the writer Fedor Mikhailovich Dostoyevsky. The Petrashevsky did, however, make a valuable contribution in pioneering socialist ideas that were to be discussed by radical groups later in the century.

Liberation of Labour Group

The Liberation of Labour Group was an early Russian Marxist organisation founded in 1883 by the former populists Georgy Plekhanov and Pavel Axelrod, who were living in exile in Western Europe. They translated the works of Marx and Engels and smuggled them into Russia. In 1888 the Liberation of Labour Group organised a Russian Social Democratic Union abroad, but they left it in 1900. Having worked with Lenin on *Iskra* in 1903, they joined the Russian Social Democratic Workers' Party at the Brussels–London Congress, and with this action the group dissolved.

Land and Liberty Organisation

In 1861, *The Bell* (kolokol), asked the question 'What do the people need?' and answered this by saying 'It is very simple, the people need land and liberty.' This became the name of a movement operating between 1861 and 1863. However, the formal populist organisation, *Zemlya i Volya*, was founded in 1876. It consisted of a highly organised group of 200 intellectuals, who believed that the land should be given to the serfs and that the state as it existed should be destroyed. In seeking to promote expressions of popular discontent they staged a mass demonstration in front of Kazan Cathedral in St Petersburg, at which Georgy Plekhanov delivered a speech on populism. Acts of terrorism occurred more and more frequently; Vera Zasulich fatally shot the governor of St Petersburg, General Trepov; Sergey Stepnyak shot General Nikolai Vladimirovich Mezentsov, chief of the Third Section; and attempts were made on the tsar's life. In 1879, owing to differences of opinion on the use of vigilance, Land and Liberty was dissolved and was replaced by the People's Freedom, *Narodnaya Volya*, group.

People's Freedom or Will

The revolutionary organisation, Narodnaya Volya, came into being after the split of the *Zemlya i Volya* organisation in 1879. It believed in the seizure of power, and in practice concentrated on the killing of high government officials. It was responsible for the assassination of Alexander II (1811). Led by

Aleksandr Ulyanov, Lenin's older brother, the St Petersburg group attempted the assassination of Alexander III in 1887. Although some members later joined the Social Democrats and became Bolsheviks, by 1902 a large proportion had become members of the Socialist Revolutionary Party.

Nihilism

A radical intellectual movement of the 1860s, Nihilism grew up largely as a result of the rejection of the historical and aesthetic idealism of the 1830s and 1840s. Nihilism represented a revolt against the established social order and it negated the authority of the state, family and Church. Social sciences and classical philosophical systems were rejected. In place of these structures and values were scientific materialism and positivism. The existence of the soul and spiritual world was denied utterly. The concept of nihilism was popularised by Ivan Turgenev in his novel *Fathers and Children* (1862), with its depiction of Bazarov, the nihilist. The liberal Chernyshevsky in his novel *What Is To Be Done?* (1863) concentrated on the positive aspects of nihilism and ascribed their excesses to the lack of opportunities to fight for social reform.

Pan-Slavism

Pan-Slavism was a nineteenth-century movement to unite all Slavic peoples for cultural and political ends. It was formed in the early nineteenth century by intellectuals among western and southern Slavs seeking cultural identity for emerging national groups. In 1848 it became a political movement for Slavic emancipation from the Austrian empire. In the 1860s in Russia it developed an idealistic campaign whereby Holy Russia was to save a spiritually bankrupt Europe; Russian liberation of other Slavs from Austrian or Turkish rule was seen as a prerequisite. In this respect the movement influenced Russian foreign policy in the Russo–Turkish war of 1877–78.

Bund

A Jewish Social Democratic Party in Russia and Poland, this was a socialist political movement founded in Vilna in 1897 and was active in the formation of the Russian Social Democratic Labour Party. Its aims were an end to anti-Jewish discrimination and a reorganised, federal, Russian empire. It was recognised as the most powerful socialist body by 1900. It was in conflict with Lenin over its emphasis on Jewish interest, and it left the Russian Social Democratic Party in 1903. It demanded that the Bundists be recognised as the sole representatives of Jewish workers and that it should have autonomy within the Russian Social Democratic Labour Party. After 1906 it supported the Mensheviks and supported the Provisional Government in 1917.

Constitutional Democratic Party

The Constitutional Democratic Party, known as the Party of People's Freedom or Kadets, based on the two initial letters in the Russian name, was a party formed in October 1905 under the leadership of Paul Milyukov, an amalgamation of the Union of Liberation and the Zemstvo Militants. The party wished to establish the English governmental system of a ministry responsible to an elected legislature, elected by universal suffrage and these reforms were advocated at the first two Congresses in 1905 and 1906. It also advocated an eight-hour working day and redistribution of land with compensation for landowners. The party was a focus for liberalism and had strong support from some of the landowners and the business and professional classes. Membership reached 70,000 and in addition to Milyukov other leaders were: Prince P. D. Dolgorukov, I. V. Gessen, F. D. Kokoshkin, V. A. Maklakov, S. A. Muromtsev, V. Nabokov, N. V. Nekrasov, F. Rodichev, A. I. Shingaryev, P. Struve, Prince Ye, N. Trubetskoy and M. Vinaver. At the election for the First Duma they won 179 seats, sufficient to dominate the legislature. In the Second Duma their representation was reduced to 98 because many of their former members had been disenfranchised and made ineligible for elective office following their involvement in the Vyborg Appeal. In the Third Duma they had 53 members and in the fourth 58. By 1917 they had become one of the most conservative groups and they showed little interest in re-establishing the Constituent Assembly and were eventually outlawed by the Bolsheviks.

Bloody Sunday and the Revolution of 1905

On 9 January 1905 many innocent, peaceful demonstrators were fired upon by troops in St Petersburg and marked the beginning of the 1905 Revolution. The employees of the Putilov factory who were members of Father Georgii Gapon's organisation of workers felt that some of their members had been victimised and had gone on strike. The employers decided upon a lockout, whereupon the workers decided to present their grievances to the tsar in the form of a petition (see below); a certain number of political demands were also included by intellectuals. Having told the authorities of this planned march the demonstrators were fired on by troops; as a result 96 people were killed and 339 wounded.

The petition read:

> We working men of St Petersburg, our wives and children, and our parents, helpless and aged men and women, have come to you, our ruler, in quest of justice and protection... We have no strength at all, 0 Sovereign. Our patience is at an end. We are approaching that terrible moment when death is better than the continuance of intolerable sufferings...
>
> Our first wish was to discuss our needs with our employers, but this was

refused to us; we were told that we have no legal right to discuss our conditions...

Every worker and peasant is at the mercy of our officials, who accept bribes, rob the Treasury and do not care at all for the people's interests. The bureaucracy of the government has ruined the country, involved it in a shameful war and is leading Russia nearer and nearer to utter ruin. We, the Russian workers and people, have no voice at all in the expenditure of the huge sums collected in taxes from the impoverished population. We do not even know how our money is spent. The people are deprived of any right to discuss taxes and their expenditure. The workers have no right to organize their own labour unions for the defence of their own interests.

Is this, 0 Sovereign, in accordance with the laws of God, by whose grace you reign? And how can we live under such laws? Break down the wall between yourself and your people... The people must be represented in the control of their country's affairs. Only the people themselves know their own needs. So not reject their help, accept it, command forthwith that representatives of all classes, groups, professions and trades shall come together. Let captialists and workers, bureaucrats and priests, doctors and teachers meet together and choose their representatives. Let all be equal and free. And to this end let the election of members to the Constitutional Assembly take place in conditions of universal, secret and equal suffrage.

This is our chief request; upon it all else depends; this is the only balm for our sore wounds; without it our wounds will never heal, and we shall be borne swiftly on to our death.

The Bloody Sunday massacre precipitated nationwide strikes, uprisings, and mutinies (most notably the mutiny on the cruiser *Potemkin*). The situation created a serious threat to the regime. By October Russia was gripped by a general strike, and the establishment of the St Petersburg Soviet (workers' council) which was dominated by the Mensheviks. In August the tsar promised to create an elected national institution, the Duma. The insurrection continued until October. Nicholas II issued his October manifesto promising a constitutional monarchy. The revolution was substantially crushed by the end of December.

The October manifesto main clauses were:

We impose upon the government the duty to execute Our inflexible will:

To grant the population the inviolable foundations of civic freedom based on the principles of genuine personal inviolability, freedom of conscience, speech, assemblies and associations.

Without postponing the scheduled elections to the State Duma, to admit in the participation of the Duma insofar as possible in the short time that remains before its scheduled meeting all those classes of the population which presently are completely deprived of voting rights, and to leave further development of general elective law to the future legislative order;

To establish as an unbreakable rule that no law shall become effective without the confirmation by the State Duma, and that the elected representatives of the people shall be guaranteed an opportunity of real participation in the supervision of the legality of the acts by authorities whom We shall appoint.

Popular movements in 1905

	Number of peasant uprisings	Number of striking workers
January	17	443,929
February	109	293,152
March	103	73,081
April	144	104,646
May	299	220,523
June	492	155,741
July	248	152,474
August	155	104,133
September	71	37,851
October	219	518,752
November	796	325,534
December	575	433,357
Total	3,228	2,863,173

Dashnaktsutyun

The Confederacy Party, commonly called Dashnaks, was a national revolutionary grouping founded in Turkish Armenia in 1890. The party started to recruit Russian Armenians with the aim of establishing an independent state of Great Armenia. When Nicholas II closed many Armenian schools, libraries and newspaper offices in 1903 and took over the property of the Armenian Church, the Dashnaks carried out a policy of civil disobedience in Russian in 1903–05. They supported the provisional government but were opposed to the Bolshevik Revolution Party in the independent Armenian republic of 1918–20.

Anarchism

Central to all anarchist logic is the emphasis on individual freedom and the denial of any authority, and that this can only be achieved by the abolition of the state. Anarchism is of particular emotional appeal whenever an agrarian society is undergoing the upheavals caused by industrialisation. In Russia anarchism was influential in the late nineteenth and early twentieth centuries; its chief theorists were Michael Bakunin (1814–1876) and Prince Peter Kropotkin (1842–1921), both of whom also influenced populism. Leo Trotsky (1828–1910) advocated a form of Christian anarchism.

Bakunin believed that the social instinct within man rather than laws enforced by state or church was sufficient to make man behave in a socially acceptable manner. He was active in the international workers' movement, travelled abroad, and met Karl Marx and P. J. Proudhon. Kropotkin believed that animal and primitive communities were based on mutual aid and asserted that war was not a basic instinct of savage man. His ideals were published in his book *Mutual Aid* (1902).

Anarchists divided into individualists, syndicalists, and communists late in the nineteenth century. Numerous anarchist groups existed during the period of the first and second revolutions (1905 and 1917). With the exception of the followers of Kropotkin, of the 'Makhayevists', and Tolstoy, all used terroristic methods in their activities. The principal centres of anarchist activity in Russia were Belostock (1903–04), Odessa, Warsaw and Yekaterinoslav. After 1905 groups of Anarchists were also formed in St Petersburg, Moscow, Kiev and Riga, as well as in the Caucasus and in the Urals. In 1906 and 1907, a wave of anarchistic 'expropriations' (armed robberies) took place in many places in Russia. In 1917 a federation of anarchists was established.

The Russian Revolution was the first occasion when anarchists attempted to put their theories into practice on a wide scale. By means of 'direct action' they sought to build a new, libertarian society and to make their stateless vision a reality.

Masalsky wrote in *Burevestnik* in December 1917:

Worker!

What were you under Nicholas the Bloody? You were a slave. You were locked up in sweltering workshops as in a prison. For a few pitiful copecks you gave your labour – not gave but were forced to give – so that the fat, ugly, detestable manufacturer, who himself did nothing, could enjoy all the good things of life and satisfy his animal lusts in wild drunken orgies. He compelled you to work so that he, the capitalist, your eternal enemy, could gleefully squander on wild orgies what you yourself made with your sweat and blood, your dreamless, cheerless nights; your slave labour.

That is what you toiled for, worker! So that you would not die of hunger. Nor were you alone. You had a wife and children. Yet what you earned was not enough for yourself or your family. In order to have even the bare necessities, your wife too had to go to work for the manufacturer. She had to go to work to help you, so that you wouldn't go to the grave before your time, so that your children would not be left as homeless orphans to wander the streets.

But even that was not enough, worker! The capitalist fleecer paid you and your wife only enough to keep you from your starving to death. But there was not enough for your children, so you had to take your ten-year-old son and put him to work too, in order to earn a piece of bread.

Forward then to battle. Forward without stopping, without losing an hour, not a minute. Let your battle-cry be:

All production to the workers!

Down with the compromise of control!

Down with the Constituent Assembly!

Down with all authority!

Down with private property!

Long live the Anarchist Commune, and with it Peace, Liberty, Equality and Brotherhood!

Menshevism

Democratic faction of Marxist socialism coming into being as the result of a split at the Second Congress of the Russian Social Democratic Labour Party, which opened in Brussels and was concluded in London (1903). At this Congress the followers of Lenin received a majority of the votes for the directing organs of the party, and hence were called Bolsheviks (majority). The opposing group, which was in the minority, came to be known as the Mensheviks (minority).

The Mensheviks stood for an open democratic labour movement. From 1912 it became a separate political party and before the Revolution was the Bolsheviks' major rival for working-class support and throughout 1917 was dominant in the Soviets. They saw that Lenin's 'organisational centralism' ran the risk of putting control of the party in the hands of individuals, anxious for power, who were likely to be adverse to the wishes of the working masses. Leading Mensheviks such as Fedor Dan, Pavel Axelrod, Alexandr Potresov, Vera Zasulich, Yuly Martov and Georgy Plekhanov argued for participation by all who shared the political ideas of the party and who were willing to work towards those aims.

Splits in the party came in World War I and one group, led by Potresov, believed in 'my country first' but the Menshevik internationalists saw the war as the beginning of a long-awaited socialist revolution.

After the October 1917 revolution Mensheviks were persecuted and their leaders arrested. Their publication *Socialist Courier* was published in Berlin from 1921 and later from Paris and New York.

Bolshevism

The Bolshevist party comprised the radical faction of the Russian Social Democratic Workers' Party when it split in 1903. The Bolsheviks, meaning those in the majority (Mensheviks were the minority), were headed by Lenin who believed that the revolution must be led by a single centralised party of professional revolutionaries. Lenin had already worked out the main principles of Bolshevism in the 1890s and these had been incorporated in the Iskra organisation established by Lenin in 1900. At an All-Russian Party Conference, called by Lenin, without authorisation, held in Prague in January 1912, it elected an all-Bolshevik Central Committee replacing the multi-factional one elected at the Fifth Party Congress. This Conference marked a watershed between the Bolshevik and Menshevik factions. Many attempts were made to solve the dispute and it was agreed that it should be put to arbitration at the Congress of the Second International convened for August 1914; it never met because of World War I. The name Social Democratic Labour Party (Bolsheviks) was retained until 1918 when it was replaced by Communist Party (Bolsheviks).

February Revolution (1917)

Revolution during which the monarchy fell and the provisional government and the Soviets of workers' and soldiers' deputies were established. Over 14,000,000 peasants were engaged in military service, which in turn led to acute food shortages; this proved to be one of the factors that triggered the revolution. Having taken command of the army in 1915, Nicholas II was at the front, and the tsarina, with advice from Rasputin, was responsible for much of the decision making on domestic matters. In February 1917 there were widespread bread riots, strikes and demonstrations in Petrograd and the troops, summoned to restore order, mutinied. This caused the abdication of the tsar, and a provisional government led by Prince Lvov and later Aleksandr Kerensky, assumed power. The provisional government and the Soviets vied with one another for power, and the government proved to be incapable of dealing with the rising power of the Bolsheviks.

Telegram of 27 February 1917 from Rodzyanko President of the State Duma to the tsar

> The session of the State Duma has been suspended until April by Your Majesty's Ukaz. The last bulwark of order has been eliminated. The Government is absolutely powerless to suppress disorders. Nothing can be hoped from the troops of the garrison. The reserve battalions of the guard regiments are in rebellion. Officers are being killed. Having joined the crowds and the popular movement they are proceeding to the Ministry of the Interior and the State Duma. Civil war has started and is spreading rapidly.

Order the immediate calling of a new government according to the principles reported by me to Your Majesty in my telegram of yesterday. Cancel Your Imperial Ukaz, and order the reconvening of the legislative chambers. Make these measures known without delay through an Imperial manifesto. Your Majesty, do not delay. If the movement spreads to the army, the Germans will triumph, and the ruin of Russia, and with her the Dynasty, will become inevitable. In the name of all Russia I beg Your Majesty to fulfil the foregoing. The hour which will decide the fate of Yourself and of the motherland has come. Tomorrow it may already be too late.

RODZYANKO
President of the State Duma

Krasnii Arkhiv (Moscow–Leningrad 1927), Vol. 21, pp. 6–7.

Telegram of 28 February 1917 from General Alekseev Chief of Staff of the Supreme Commander to all the Commanders in Chief

... On February 27 about midday, the President of the State Duma reported that the troops were going over to the side of the population and killing their officers.

General Khabalov around midday on the 27th reported to His Majesty that one company of the Pavlovsky Regiment's reserve battalion had declared on February 26 that it would not fire on the people. The Commander of a battalion of this regiment was wounded by the crowd. On February 27 training detachments of the Volynsky Regiment refused to proceed against the rebels, and its commander shot himself. Then this detachment together with a company of the same regiment proceeded to the quarters of other reserve battalions, and men from these units began to join them ...

On the 27th, after 7 p.m. The Minister of War reported that the situation in Petrograd had become very serious. The few units which have remained faithful to their duty cannot suppress the rebellion, and troop units have gradually joined the rebels. Fires have started. Petrograd has been placed under martial law ...

On February 28 at 1 a.m. His Majesty received a telegram from General Khabalov stating that he could not restore order in the capital. The majority of the units have betrayed their duty and many have passed over to the side of the rebels. The troops which have remained faithful to their duty, after fighting the whole day, have suffered many casualties.

Towards evening the rebels seized the greater part of the capital, and the small units, which have remained faithful to their oath, have been rallied in the vicinity of the Winter Palace.

On February 28 at 2 a.m. the Minister of War reported that the rebels had occupied the Mariinsky Palace and that the members of the revolutionary government were there. On February 28 at 8.25 a.m., General Khabalov reported that the number of those who had remained faithful had dropped to 600 infantrymen and 500 cavalrymen with 15 machine guns and 12 guns having only 80 cartridges and that the situation was extremely difficult . . .

We have just received a telegram from the Minister of War, stating that the rebels have seized the most important building in all parts of the city. Due to fatigue and propaganda the troops have laid down their arms, passed to the side of the rebels, or become neutral. In the streets disorderly shooting is going on all the time; all the traffic has stopped; officers and soldiers who appear in the streets are being disarmed.

The ministers are all safe, but apparently the work of the Ministry has stopped.

According to private information, the President of the State Council Shcheglovitov, has been arrested. In the State Duma, a council of party leaders has been formed to establish contact for the revolutionary government with institutions and individuals. Supplementary elections to the Petrograd Soviet of Workers' and Soldiers' Deputies from the workers and the rebel troops have been announced.

We have just received a telegram from General Khabalov which shows that actually he cannot any longer influence events. Communicating to you the foregoing, I should add that we, the active army, all have the sacred duty before the Tsar and the motherland to remain true to our duty and to our oath, and to maintain railway traffic and the flow of food. ALEKSEEV. February 28.

Arkhiv Russkoi Revolyutsii (Berlin 1922), Vol. 3, pp. 250–1.

Nicholas II abdicates

In the days of great struggle with an external foe, who has been striving for almost three years to enslave our native land, it has been God's will to visit upon Russia a new grievous trial. The internal disturbances which have begun among the people threaten to have a calamitous effect on the future conduct of a hard-fought war. The destiny of Russia, the honour of our heroic army, the welfare of the people, the whole future of our beloved fatherland demand that the war be carried to a victorious conclusion no matter what the cost. The cruel foe is straining his last resources and the time is already close at hand when our valiant army, together with our glorious allies, will be able to crush the foe completely. In these decisive days in the life of Russia, We have deemed it Our duty in conscience to help Our people to draw closer together and to unite all the forces of the nation for a speedier attainment of victory, and, in agreement with the State Duma, We have judged it right to abdicate the Throne of the Russian State and to lay down the Supreme Power. Not wishing to be parted from Our beloved Son, We hand over Our succession to Our Brother, the Grand Duke Mikhail Alexandrovich, and bless Him on his accession to the Throne of the Russian State[1]. We enjoin Our Brother to conduct the affairs of the state in complete and inviolable union with the representatives of the people in the legislative bodies on the principles to be established by them, and to take an inviolable oath to this effect. In the name of the dearly beloved native land, We call upon all true sons of the Fatherland to fulfil their sacred duty to It by their obedience to the Tsar at this time of national trial and to help Him, together with the people's representatives, to lead the Russian State onto the path of victory, prosperity, and glory. May the Lord God help Russia!

NICHOLAS

Pskov, March 2, 1917, 3.0 p.m.
N. de Basily, *Diplomat of Imperial Russia 1903–1917 Memoirs* (Stanford, California 1973), pp. 187–8.

Provisional government

Government formed by the *duma* in February 1917 in Petrograd upon the collapse of the autocracy. The provisional government promised to form a constitutional assembly and to hold free elections. It abolished the secret police and granted religious freedom. Many of its leaders were of a conservative outlook, although Aleksandr Kerensky was a moderate socialist. Because of the war effort, grave problems, such as redistribution of land and the rights of non-Russian people to self-government, could not be resolved. As a result, discontent continued to grow. At the same time as the provisional government, the Soviet of workers' deputies had been established; this had the support of industrial workers and socialists and in October 1917 they overthrew the provisional government.

October Revolution (1917)

The second revolution of 1917, which came about by the failure of the provisional government, under Prince Georgy Lvov and then Aleksandr Kerensky, to end Russia's participation in World War I and to deal with food shortages, led to the demand of the Bolsheviks under Lenin for 'all power to the Soviets'. The Bolsheviks, who had gained a majority in the Soviet by September, staged the October (or Bolshevik) Revolution, seizing power and establishing the

---

[1] Grand Duke Michael Alexandrovich (1878–1918) brother of Nicholas II refused the throne on 3 March 1917.

Soviet of people's commissars. The new government made peace with Germany in early 1918 but almost immediately faced opposition at home. In the subsequent Civil War (1918–21) the Red Army was ultimately victorious against the anti-Communist Whites but with the loss of some 100,000 lives. In addition, some 2,000,000 Russians emigrated.

Murder of the ex–tsar

With the Whites on the edge of Ekaterinberg where the royal family was housed, the Ural Soviet took action and sent the following message by direct wire to the Chairman of the All-Russian Executive Committee:

> In view of the fact that Czechoslovak bands are threatening the red capital of the Urals, Ekaterinburg, and bearing in mind that the crowned executioner, if he goes into hiding, may escape the people's court, the executive committee executing the will of the people, had decided: shoot the ex–Tsar, Nikolai Romanov, guilty of innumerable bloody crimes.
>
> The decision of the executive committee was carried out during the night of 16/17 July (1918).
>
> The Romanov family has been transferred from Ekaterinburg to another, safer place.
>
> Presidium of the Ural Soviet of Workers'
Peasants' and Red Army Deputies

P. Gilliard, *Tragicheskaya Sudba Russkoi Imperatorskoi Familii*. Tallinn, 1921.

10
International Relations and the Expansion of Russia Overseas

Battles and Wars 1548–1918

1548–1552	Campaign to conquer Kazan. Ivan IV (the Terrible) with 150,000 men and 150 canon sets out from Moscow and Kazan falls in October 1552.
1556	Khanate of Astrakhan is annexed to Moscow after being defeated.
1557	Tatars invade Livonia. War continues until 1582.
1570	Novgorod is razed by Ivan IV (the Terrible); massacres of inhabitants.
1571	Tatars of the Crimea sack Moscow.
1582	Yermak conquers the Khanate of Sibir. Conquest of Siberia.
1610–1612	Poles occupy Moscow.
1612	Militia drive out the Poles and relieve Moscow.
1639	Cossacks reach the Pacific.
1648	Ukrainian Cossack uprising against Poland.
1654–1667	War with Poland ending in the Treaty of Andrusovo; Muscovy gained Eastern Ukraine, Kiev and Smolensk.
1669	Led by Stenka Razin Cossacks attack Persian flotilla on the East coast of Caspian Sea.
1670	Major peasant rebellion. Stenka Razin takes Astrakhan (June) but is defeated at Simbirsk (October). Insurrection collapses.
1671	Stenka Razin executed in Moscow (June).
1681	War with the Ottoman Empire and in the Crimea.
1687	Unsuccessful campaign by Prince Vasily Golitsyn against the Crimean Tatars.
1695	Defeat at Azov against the Crimean Tatars and Turks.
1696	Recapture of Azov after an unsuccessful attack in the previous year against the Turks and Tatars.

1698	*Streltsy* revolt breaks out and is savagely suppressed.
1700	Beginning of war with Sweden (the Great Northern War) and Russia defeated at Narva.
1701	Russo–Polish army defeated at Riga (July).
	Russia defeat Swedes at Erestfer (December).
1702	Russian victories at Hummelshof (July), Volmar (July). Peter I (the Great) takes Nöteborg and renames it Schlüssellburg.
1703	Russian naval victory at mouth of Neva (May).
1704	Narva retaken by Russians.
1705	Outbreak of uprising in Astrakhan (until 1706).
1708	Great advance of Swedes against Russia begins. Charles XII advances on Grodno (January).
	Outbreak of Cossack rising in the Don area led by Ivan Mazepa.
1709	Decisive Russian victory over Sweden at Poltava (July).
1710	Russians take Livonia and Estonia.
1711	Outbreak of war with the Ottoman Empire and Russian defeat on the Prut.
1718	Charles XII, King of Sweden, dies in Norway.
1722	War with Persia begins with a campaign along the Caspian Sea.
1734	In War of Polish Succession fighting breaks out between Russia and France. Anne sends a fleet to the Baltic where it defeats the French (June).
1736	War starts between Turks and allied Russo–Austrian armies (October).
1748	Russia sends troops to the Rhine, the first intervention by Russia in a conflict in Western Europe.
1757	Russian army defeats Prussian army at Gross–Jägersdorf (August).
	Russian army occupies Königsberg (January).
1758	Prussians encircle Russians at Zorndorf (August).
1759	Russian forces defeat Prussians at Palzig (July).
	Prussian forces defeated at Kunersdorf (August).
	Russian forces enter Berlin (October).
1768	Turkey declares war on Russia (October).
1770	Count Aleksey Orlov destroys Turkish fleet at Chesme (July).
1771	Russian troops occupy Crimea.
1772	First partition of Poland (August).
1773	Peasant and Cossack uprising under Yemelyan Ivanovich Pugachev until 1775.
1787	Turkey declares war on Russia.
1788	Gustavus III declares war on Russia.
1792	Russians invade Poland (May).

1793	Second partition of Poland (January).
1794	Polish insurrection against Russian occupation begins (March).
1795	Third partition of Poland (October).
1799	Russian campaigns in northern Italy and Switzerland.
1805	Russia conquers Karebakh and Shirvan in the Caucasus.
1806	Russia conquers Baku and Derbent. Turkey declares war on Russia.
1808	War with Sweden; Russia occupies Finland.
1809	Creation of Grand Duchy of Finland whose Grand Duke is the Emperor of Russia. War with Turkey.
1810	Russia conquers Abkhazia.
1812	Russians found Fort Ross in California. Russian ultimatum to Napoleon. *Grand Armée* crosses the Niemen at Kovno, Russians withdraw (June). French attack Smolensk, Russians withdraw (August). Inconclusive battle of Borodino, Russians withdraw again (September). French enter Moscow; fire destroys two-thirds of city (September). French evacuate Moscow but the battle of Maloyaroslavets prevented a southward escape and caused the French to retreat along the same route by which they had invaded (October). Napoleon returns to Paris and the remnants of the *Grand Armée* (18,000) cross the Niemen (December).
1813	Russians occupy Warsaw. Napoleon's army defeated by Russian, Prussian and Austrian forces at Leipzig at 'Battle of the Nations' (October).
1814	Allied invasion of France (January–February). Paris taken and Alexander I enters at head of Russian troops (March).
1815	Paris occupied by Allies for second time (July).
1821	Outbreak of the Greek uprising against Ottoman domination.
1826	War with Persia continues until 1828.
1827	Destruction of the Turkish fleet at Navarino Bay (October).
1828	Russia declares war on Turkey (April).
1830–1831	Suppression of Polish revolt.
1832–1833	First Mohammed Ali crisis.
1839–1840	Second Mohammed Ali crisis.
1848	Revolutions in France, Austria, Italy and Germany.
1849	Nicholas I intervenes to help Austria put down Hungarian revolt (June).
1853	Crimean War begins.
1854	Russians defeated at Alma (September). Seige of Sevastopol begins (September). Battle of Balaklava (October). Battle of Inkerman (November).

1855	End of seige of Sevastopol (September), having held out for 349 days.
1859	Conquest of Caucasus complete except for Circassia (1864).
1863	Polish revolt suppressed.
1864	Russians advance in Turkestan and take Chimkent.
1865	Russians take Tashkent.
1868	Russians take Samarkand (May).
	Emirate of Bokhara becomes a Russian protectorate (June).
1876	Russia annexes Khanate of Koland.
1877	Russia declares war on Turkey (April).
	Russians take Shipka Pass (July).
	Russians take Kars (November).
	Russians take Plevna (December).
1878	Russians take Adrianople (January).
1881	Russians invade Turmena and take Geok Tepe.
1884	Merv in Turkistan is annexed.
1885	Bulgarian crisis; Russia objecting to the unification of Eastern Rumelia and Bulgaria.
1900	Military occupation of Manchuria.
1904	The Russo–Japanese war breaks out (February) at Port Arthur after surprise attack by Japanese fleet.
	Japanese beseiged Port Arthur (July).
	Battle of Liao-Yang (August–September).
	Russian forces retreat to Mukden (September).
1905	Russians surrender Port Arthur (January).
	Russian defeated at Mukden (March).
	Russian Baltic fleet destroyed in the Tsushima Strait (May).
	'Bloody Sunday'. Father Gapon leads a peaceful protest of thousands of people to the Winter Palace in St Petersburg with a Petition for the tsar; troops open fire, killing many protesters. Russian defeats in Japanese War add to the crisis (January).
1912	First Balkan War (October).
1913	End of First Balkan War (May).
	Second Balkan War (June).
	End of Second Balkan War (August).
1914	Germany declared war on Russia (August).
	Austria–Hungary declared war against Russia (August).
	Austrians invade southern Russian Poland (August).
	Russian armies invade East Prussia and Galicia (August).
	German victory over Russian Second Army in the battle of Tannenberg (August).
	Austrian defeat in Galicia in the battle of Rawa Ruska (September).

	Russian First Army decisively defeated in Masurian Lakes campaign, and driven from East Prussia (September).
	Offensive by Austro–German forces, which withdrew after coming within nineteen km (twelve miles) of Warsaw (September–November).
	Russia declared war on Turkey (November).
	Germans almost succeed in enveloping the Russian Second Army in the battle of Lodz and the Russians fall back (November).
1915	Winter battle of Masuria and Germans encircle Russian Tenth Army (February).
	German–Austrian offensive breaks Russian line between Gorlice and Tarnow (May).
	Russians defeated in battle of Krasnotav (July).
	Germans enter Warsaw (August).
	Russia declared war on Bulgaria (October).
1916	Massive Russian offensive south of the Pripet Marshes led by General Brusilov; over a million casualties (June–September).
1917	Russian Revolution begins. Tsar abdicates. Prelude to disintegration of Russian armies (March).
	Start of renewed offensive on southern front (June).
	Start of northern offensive backed by Kerensky, Minister of War. Germans and Austrians drive Russians back after early successes (July).
	Suspension of hostilities (December).
1918	Bolsheviks accept peace terms at Brest-Litovsk (March).
	Death penalty reinstated at the front (July).
	Kornilov named commander-in-chief (July).
	Kerensky proclaims himself commander-in-chief (September).

Alliances, Congresses, Conferences and Treaties

1681	Treaty of Bakhchisarai with Turkey ends Russo–Turkish conflict (started 1676). Land between the rivers Don and Dniester to remain unoccupied.
1686	Poland renounces claim to Kiev and Russia promises Poland military assistance against Tatars in a treaty of 'eternal peace'.
1689	Treaty of Nerchinsk with China signed and gains rights to trade with China.
1700	Peace of Constantinople signed between Russia and the Ottoman Empire (July).
1709	Quadruple alliance formed with Russia, Poland, Denmark and Prussia against Sweden.
1717	Commercial treaty signed by Russia and France.

1721	The Great Northern War with Sweden is ended by the treaty of Nystad.
1724	Russia signs treaty with Turkey dividing the Caspian territories between themselves.
1726	Russia adheres to the Treaty of Vienna, originally signed in 1725 between Charles VI, the Hapsburg Emperor and Spain.
1739	Treaty of Belgrade ends wars between Turkey and Russo–Austrian alliance. Russia recovers Azov.
1743	Treaty of Abö agreed between Sweden and Russia.
1760	Agreement that Austria will gain western Prussia and Russia gains the western bank of the Dnieper from Poland.
1762	Peter III signs peace treaty with Prussia (April).
1764	Alliance between Russia, Denmark and England agreed; known as the Northern System.
1774	Peace with Turkey concluded at Kutchuk-Kainardji (July).
1790	Peace of Wereloe between Sweden and Russia.
1792	Russia and Turkey sign Treaty of Jassy.
1793	Catherine II (the Great) annuls all treaties with France following execution of Louis XVI (February).
1798	Quadruple defensive alliance proposed between Russia, Austria, Prussia and England.
1800	Franco–Russian alliance signed in Paris (October).
1807	Creation of the Grand Duchy of Warsaw and Treaty of Tilsit signed by Napoleon and Alexander I (June).
1808	Treaty of Erfurt; Napoleon and Alexander meet again (October).
1809	Russo–Swedish conflict ends with the Treaty of Frederikshamn; Sweden recognises annexation of Finland and Åland Islands by Russia.
1812	Russo–Turkish war ends with the treaty of Bucharest; Russia retains Bessarabia (May).
1813	Anti-French alliance enlarged to include Russia, Prussia, Sweden, England and Austria (June–August).
1815	Congress of Vienna.
	Holy Alliance of Russia, Prussia and Austria created at the initiation of Alexander I (September).
	Quadruple Alliance of England, Austria, Prussia and Russia formed (November).
1818	Congress of Aix-la-Chapelle.
1822	Congress of Verona.
1824	Russia and USA sign treaty dealing with Alaska.
1828	Peace of Turkmanchai signed by Russia and Prussia (February).
1829	Treaty of Adrianople signed by Russia and Turkey (September).

1833	Treaty of Unkiar Skelessi between Russia and Turkey contains secret clause allowing for the closure of the Dardanelles to foreign warships (July). Münchengrätz agreement between Russia and Austria concerning Polish territories.
1856	Treaty of Paris ends Crimean War.
1860	Treaty of Peking between China and Russia.
1867	Russia sells Alaska and the Aleutian Islands to the US (March).
1871	Convention of London.
1873	Formation of an alliance between Germany, Austria–Hungary is established, 'The League of the three Emperors'.
1875	Treaty of St Petersburg between Russia and Japan (May).
1878	Russo–Turkish war ended by the Treaty of San Stefano (March). Treaty of Berlin concerning Bulgaria signed.
1885	An accord with Britain is signed establishing Afghanistan borders.
1893	France and Russia sign commercial and military treaties.
1896	Russo–Chinese treaty and concessions granted for Trans-Siberia railway through Manchuria (June).
1905	Treaty of Bjorko, a defensive alliance signed by Wilhelm II of Germany and Nicholas II of Russia. Treaty of Portsmouth, New Hampshire ends Russo–Japanese war (September).
1907	Anglo–Russian accords clear way to Triple Entente between France, Britain and Russia (August).
1913	Treaty of London ends First Balkan War (May). Treaty of Bucharest ends Second Balkan War (August).
1918	Central Council of Ukraine concludes separate peace with Central Powers, having declared its independence (February). Russians sign Treaty of Brest-Litovsk (March).

Army

The Russian army was formed in medieval times. The nobility and gentry provided the officers and the common soldier was recruited by an annual levy and served for twenty-five years. Ivan IV created the *Streltsy*, a small number of professional soldiers, who by 1600 numbered 12,000. Peter I (the Great) set about establishing a Russian army in modern form. He disbanded the *Streltsy* in 1698 after a mutiny and formed the Preobrazhensky and Semyonovsky Guards which are regarded as the first units of the Russian regular Army. Units of infantry, cavalry and artillery used the tactics of Western armies to good effect against the Swedes in the Northern War to win the battle of Poltava in 1709 and the Peace of Nystadt in 1721, making Russia a Baltic power. Irregular forces of Cossacks and Bashkir tribesmen were also used (the Don Cossacks had sixty cavalry regiments in 1812), but it was the regular army founded by Peter I (the Great) that made Russia powerful throughout the eighteenth century.

Additional levies were called in an emergency. In 1812 there were three, recruiting 420,000 men, increasing the army to 600,000, but only about 200,000 were available to fight Napoleon because of the threat from the Turks.

Russia's hold on the Caucasus was consolidated in the middle of the 1860s and in Central Asia Russia took Tashkent, Samarkand and Khiva. The army was reformed in 1874 by Alexander II.

Russia's devastating defeat in the Russo–Japanese war (1904–05) see p. 141, showed up the shortcomings of Russian strategy and errors of the senior commanders. These deficiencies were still not fully corrected at the beginning of the First World War; the result was the disaster at Tannenberg in East Prussia, 26–30 August 1914.

Navy

Peter I (the Great) was the architect of the modern Russian navy. The Naval Academy was established in St Petersburg in 1715 for 300 students, and the ship yards on the river Neva built a fleet of Western-style warships. Many British officers served in the Russian navy in the eighteenth century and Russian officers trained with the British navy. In 1805 there was a Baltic fleet of thirty-two ships of the line and twelve frigates, and a Black Sea fleet of twelve ships of the line and four frigates. Russia had the third largest navy in the world until the Russo–Japanese War (1904–05) see p. 141, after which she came sixth as a world naval power. Russia was rebuilding her navy when World War I broke out. There were several mutinies in the 1905 Revolution, and they played an important part in both the February and October Revolutions.

Russia and Sweden

Great Northern War

The Great Northern War (1700–21) was fought by Russia, Denmark/Norway, and Saxony/Poland against Sweden because they objected to Swedish domination in the Baltic. The Treaty of Preobrazhenskoe was signed by Peter I (the Great), Augustus II of Saxony (also Elector of Saxony) and Frederick IV of Denmark in 1699. The following year the war began. Charles XII of Sweden defeated Russia at Narva (1700), resulting in the withdrawal of Norway from the Anti-Swedish alliance. In 1706, after six years' fighting, he defeated Poland and it too was forced to leave the alliance. Peter I (the Great) meanwhile increased his military strength in the Baltic and finally beat the Swedish forces at Poltava in 1709. Turkey attempted to intervene in 1710, but from then on the Swedes lost ground and initiated peace negotiations. A peace congress was held on the Åland Islands in the Gulf of Bothnia between Russia and Sweden in 1718. The Russian delegation was led by Bruce and Osterman, the Swedish delegation by Goertz and Count Gyllenborg. Sweden wished to regain some of its territories from Peter I (the Great). While Goertz eventually agreed with some of the Russian proposals, Charles XII of Sweden disapproved of them. After several months of abortive negotiations, Goertz was told that Peter would terminate the conference if a treaty was not concluded in December. Goertz set off to consult with Charles but was arrested, and Charles himself was killed in battle. The Treaties of Stockholm (1719–20) and the Treaty of Nystad (1721) established the peace and also Russia emerged as a great European state.

Under the Treaty of Nystad Sweden ceded to Russia Ingria, part of Karelia, Livonia (including Estonia), and several islands in the Baltic. Russia retained Vyborg but returned the rest of Finland to Sweden and paid Sweden an indemnity. Peter I (the Great) formally assumed the title of emperor after the ratification of the treaty, thus officially inaugurating the imperial period of Russian history, and Russia's predominant power in the Baltic.

Russo–Swedish War 1788–90

In June 1788 Gustavus III of Sweden took advantage of the Turkish War to declare war on Russia, but a mutiny in his army and a Danish invasion prevented the advances he had planned for 1788. Gustavus defeated the Danes and internal opposition, and in 1790 routed the Russian fleet at Svenskund, but he agreed to make peace with Russia soon afterwards on the basis of the pre-war situation.

Russia and the Ottoman Empire

As a result of wars between Russia and the Ottoman Turkish Empire, Russian territory was extended to include the Prut River and the land beyond the Caucasus. The first Russo–Turkish war was fought from 1676 to 1681. Subsequent wars occurred in 1735–39, 1768–74, 1787–91, 1806–12, 1828–29, 1853–56, and 1877–78.

Russo–Turkish War 1768–74

Turkey declared war on 6 October 1768 after Russian troops burnt the Turkish town of Balta. By 1771 the Russians had occupied Moldavia, Wallachia and the Crimea, but the Pugachev Revolt at home forced them to end the war by the Treaty of Kutchuk Kainardji in 1774, before Turkey was completely defeated.

Russo–Turkish War 1787–92

Turkey declared war on Russia in August 1787 but Austria joined the Russians in February 1788 and Turkey soon faced major setbacks. In 1788 Austria overran Moldavia and Russia defeated Turkey at sea and in 1789 the scale of the Austro–Russian advance seemed to point to the collapse of Turkey. The

Russians, however, were diverted by war with Sweden, and Austria faced diplomatic pressure from Prussia and Britain to make peace. In 1791 Austria agreed to the Treaty of Sistova with Turkey and Russia made peace at Jassy in 1792.

Russo–Turkish War 1806–12

Turkey declared war due to Russian claims on her territory, but again the Russians proved the dominant power. The imminent danger of war with France induced Russia to sign the Treaty of Bucharest in 1812 in which Turkey lost Bessarabia.

Treaty of (Edirne) Adrianople (1829)

The Treaty of Adrianople (also called the Treaty of Edirne) was signed by Russia and the Ottoman Empire on 14 September 1829.

It gave Russia, as the victors:

(a) control of the mouth of the Danube by the annexation of various islands;
(b) control of the Caucasus coastal strip by annexation of considerable territory in the Caucasus;
(c) Moldavia and Wallachia, the Danubian principalities, to have autonomous status under a Russian protectorate;
(d) heavy indemnities against Turkey;
(e) guaranteed Russian merchant ships free passage through the Straits of the Dardanelles and the Bosporus;
(f) the Ottoman Empire recognised Russia's rights in Georgia.

Crimean War (1853–56)

War fought by Turkey, Great Britain, and France against Russia. France and Turkey disputed over rival claims to control the Holy Places in Palestine. Tsar Nicholas I demanded that the Turkish government recognise the Orthodox Church and population in Turkey. Despite Nicholas's desire for a peaceful settlement, Turkey declared war on Russia in October 1853; the Turkish fleet was destroyed at Sinope in November. Fearing a Russian success Great Britain and France joined Turkey in March 1854. Russia was defeated and at the Treaty of Paris (1856) ceded Bessarabia to Moldavia and agreed to the neutralisation of the Black Sea area. Its influence in Europe was by then considerably diminished.

Important battles:

Alma	20 September 1854
	First engagement of the war. Russians defeated.
Balaklava	25 October 1854
	Indecisive military engagement in the Crimean war. The

	Russians retained the town but the British lost their best supply route, the Woronzoff road, connecting Balaklava with the heights above Sevastopol, then under siege. Noted for 'The Charge of the Light Brigade'.
Inkerman	5 November 1854
	Began as a sortie by Russian troops. After heavy fighting the Russians withdrew with losses of about 12,000 men. British losses about 2,500 and French losses about 1,000.
Sebastopol	8 September 1855
	The city held out for 349 days against British, French, Turkish and Sardinian forces in 1884–85. In June 1855 the assault on the city was begun and the final onslaught was made in September.

Danubian Principalities

In 1812 Napoleon objected to Russian control of the Danubian principalities of Moldavia and Walachia as they were a threat to the growth of French influence in the Near East. By the Treaty of Adrianople (1829) Turkey recognised a Russian protectorate over the principalities, which were, however, to enjoy an autonomous existence. In 1848 Russia intervened to suppress a revolution by the Romanian national movement. Russian occupation of the Danubian principalities in 1853, in an attempt to force the Turks to come to terms in the so-called Holy Land controversy, precipitated the Crimean War, which began in the same year. Moldavia and Walachia were occupied by Austria to separate the Russians from the Turks in the Balkans; eventually peace was established in 1856. Under the Treaty of Paris (1856) the Danubian principalities were placed under the joint guarantee of the signatory powers.

Russo–Turkish War 1877–78

In 1875–76 revolts had broken out against Ottoman rule in Bosnia and Bulgaria, and the Turks responded ruthlessly. On 24 April 1877 the Russians declared war on Turkey but their invasion stalled with the siege of Plevna, which did not fall until December. By the time the Turks made peace at San Stefano, in March 1878, the great powers were ready to oppose large-scale Russian gains and forced a new settlement in the Balkans at the Congress of Berlin in July.

Russia and Poland

Partitions of Poland

There were Polish uprisings in 1768, 1794, 1830–31 and 1863. The first uprising was known as the Bar Confederation (1768–72) and was brought about by the policy and interference in Polish affairs by the Russian ambassador, Prince Nikolai Repnin. The rebellion was defeated and brought about the First Partition (August 1772) and it accordingly divided one-third of Poland between Russia, Prussia and Austria. The proclamation of a reasonably democratic new Constitution in 1791 was opposed by Russia and led to the Second Partition (January 1793) which was mostly to the advantage of Russia. In 1794 a Polish Rising under Kosciuszko led to the occupation of the rest of Poland, which was divided between the three autocracies in the Third Partition (October 1795) and Poland completely lost her independence, and by this act the country was broken up as follows:

	Sq. miles	Population
To Prussia	52,000	3,500,000
To Austria	64,000	4,800,000
To Russia	168,000	6,700,000

After the defeat of Napoleon and the collapse of the Grand Duchy of Warsaw (1807–14), there was a Fourth Partition under the provisions of the Treaty of Vienna (1815) by which the Russians extended their region westwards, and by the establishment of a Kingdom of Poland under the suzerainty of the Russian tsars.

The whole ancient territory of the Polish nation was redistributed as follows:

	Sq. miles	Population
To Prussia	29,000	1,800,000
To Austria	30,000	3,500,000
To Russia	178,000	6,900,000
To Kingdom of Poland	47,000	2,800,000

Alexander I granted a liberal Constitution but it was never completely implemented and on the accession of Nicholas I the mood changed and tension grew leading to the Polish revolt of 1830. The Poles were defeated and the 1815 Constitution abandoned and the Russians then governed with great ruthlessness. The last uprising (also known as the January Insurrection) was an attempt to overthrow this Kingdom. In the early 1860s a variety of conspiratorial groups organised nationalistic demonstrations. The Agricultural Society, headed by Andrew Zamoyski, won the support of many sections of the population, and other groups more interested in open revolt and protest formed in Warsaw, affiliating themselves with the Military Academy. Faced with growing anti-Russian feeling, Marquis Alexander Wielopolski, virtual leader of the government of the Congress Kingdom, decided to draft the radical youths into the army. The conscripts, however, escaped, and on 22 January 1863, with the aid of the revolutionary committee, issued a manifesto calling for a nationwide insurrection. The rebels won widespread support. There were peasant revolts in other areas of Poland, and an underground government was set up in Warsaw. The ill-equipped and untrained rebel army waged guerrilla warfare against the Russian army. Without strong leadership and military assistance, however, the insurrection lost momentum by October. In 1864 those leaders who had not escaped the country were executed.

Russia and France

The War of the Second Coalition 1799–1802

By early 1799 British diplomacy had brought together the second coalition against France with Russia, Austria, Portugal and Naples. A series of Allied victories in 1799 in Italy and Germany were soon reversed, however, and on 14 June 1800 Bonaparte, now First Consul of France, won a great victory over the Austrians at Marengo. Russia left the coalition in 1800, Austria made peace at Lunéville in 1801, and Britain came to terms with France in 1802 at Amiens.

The War of the Third Coalition 1803–07

In 1803 war again broke out between Britain and France and in 1804 a new anti-French coalition was formed by Britain, Russia, Austria and Sweden. But whilst the British fleet was triumphant at Trafalgar (21 October 1805), the Austrians and Russians were defeated by Bonaparte, who had crowned himself Emperor of France, at Austerlitz (2 December 1805). Austria was forced to make peace, and when Prussia joined the coalition in 1806 she in turn was defeated at Jena-Auerstadt (14 October). Napoleon proved unable to defeat the Russians at Eylau, on 8 February 1807 but had greater success at Friedland on 14 June, after which Russia and Prussia made the peace of Tilsit. Treaties of Tilsit were signed in July 1807 establishing an alliance between Russia and France and ending the Franco–Prussian War. As there was no neutral territory where Alexander I and Napoleon could meet to discuss and agree the Franco–Russian Treaty, it was arranged that meetings should take place midstream on the River Niemen. The first treaty was signed between France and Russia on 7 July. France agreed to restore to Prussia the province of Silesia and land between the Elbe and the Niemen, but Polish lands seized by Prussia in the Second and Third Partitions (1793 and 1795) were to form the new Duchy of Warsaw. Danzig became a free city while Oldenburg, Mecklenburg-Schwerin and Saxe-Coburg were returned to their dukes; French garrisons were to remain in the first three. Russia recognised the changes made by Napoleon in Naples, Holland and Germany – in particular the creation of the Kingdom of Westphalia to be ruled by Jerome Bonaparte. The second was signed between France and Prussia on 9 July. Prussia was to pay an indemnity and to suffer military occupation until this was complete; she was to limit her army to 42,000 men and should close her ports to British shipping and join the Continental System.

A conference was held at Erfurt, Germany, in March 1808 between Napoleon I and Tsar Alexander I in the presence of German princes. The meeting was intended to consolidate agreements reached at Tilsit (1807), but mutual resentment and suspicion prevented a lasting alliance. Relations deteriorated after the conference and Napoleon attacked Russia in 1812.

French invasion of Russia

1811 April	Russia protests at French annexation of the Duchy of Oldenburg.
1812 April	Alexander I issues an ultimatum to Napoleon: (1) Russia is to be allowed to trade with neutrals; (2) French troops are to evacuate Prussia. Following Napoleon's acceptance of these terms, Alexander is prepared to negotiate an indemnity for his brother-in-law (the Duke of Oldenburg, whose lands had been taken by Napoleon) and a reduction of the Russian customs dues on French goods. This ultimatum was issued following fears of Napoleon's development of the Duchy of Warsaw and the effect on Russian trade brought about by the Continental System.
24 June	Invasion of Russia began with the first units of the *Grand Armée*, 600,000 strong, crossing the River Niemen at Kovno. The Russians withdraw before them; probably at this stage they withdraw because they are reluctant to face Napoleon rather than because they are following any scorched earth policy.
28 June	Napoleon crosses River Vilna after Russian retreat.
16 August	The French attack Smolensk.
17 August	The Russians defeated at Smolensk; but following this the Russian government orders Kutusov to block the French advance on Moscow.
7 September	Inconclusive battle of Borodino fought between Napoleon and Kutusov; the Russians withdraw again.
14 September	After a 12-week campaign the French enter Moscow, which had been evacuated by Russian forces, to find it in flames and after five days 75 per cent of the city had been destroyed. Alexander refused to negotiate with the French.
19 October	The French evacuate Moscow intending to withdraw south to winter quarters.

24 October	At the battle of Maloyaroslavets, Kutusov forces Napoleon to retake the route his army devastated on its way into Russia.
27 October	Earlier than usual the first frost of the winter.
9 November	The French reach Smolensk where they rest.
16 November	The French withdraw from Smolensk. The temperature falls to −20°C, sometimes to −30°C.
27–29 November	The French cross the River Berezina, on pontoon bridges under attack from the Russians.
5 December	Napoleon leaves the army in charge of Joachim Murat at Smogorni and travels to Paris (arriving on 18th).
18 December	Remnant of the *Grand Armée*, about 18,000 strong, crosses the River Niemen, of which only about 1,000 were fit to fight.

The Wars of Liberation 1813–14

In March Prussia joined Russia in the war against France, and Sweden soon followed. In May Napoleon won two victories at Lutzen and Bautzen but in August Austria joined the Allies and, despite another French victory at Dresden, Napoleon was finally decisively defeated at Leipzig (16–19 October). The war was carried into France, and despite gallant resistance by Napoleon, Paris was taken on 31 March 1814. Napoleon was exiled to Elba.

Congress of Vienna

The Congress met from October 1814 to June 1815. Its aim was the reconstruction of the internal boundaries of Europe following twenty-two years of war and revolutionary upheaval, and to establish the conditions which would best enable these boundaries and the whole reconstructed European order to survive. There were forty-one sittings of the congress after the Final Act was signed on 9 June 1815. Much of the work was done in a series of specialist committees, staffed by diplomats from a variety of European states big and small, which considered issues as varied as diplomatic precedence, the slave trade and population statistics. The principal representatives of the four great powers allied against Napoleon (Austria, Britain, Prussia and Russia), subsequently joined by France, reserved for themselves the major task of redistributing territory.

Between November 1814 and January 1815 the proceedings were dominated by the problem of the Polish and Saxon territories. There were sharp divisions between Prussia and Russia on the one hand (who proposed that Poland be taken over by Russia and Saxony by Prussia) and Britain and Austria on the other. The friction led to a secret defensive alliance being signed in the first week of January 1815 between Britain, Austria and France. The content of the alliance was deliberately leaked to Russia with the desired effect of achieving a compromise: the tsar became king of a reduced, semi-independent Poland ('Congress Poland') with other Polish territories divided between Austria and Prussia; Prussia got only 40 per cent of Saxony, but considerable new territory on the left bank of the Rhine. Austria became the dominant power in Germany, and was put at the head of a new German Confederation; she was also re-established in Lombardy and Venetia thus becoming the dominant great power on the Italian peninsula.

In different ways the leading diplomats in Europe (Tsar Alexander, Castlereagh, Metternich and Talleyrand) saw the congress as the first act of a permanent system of diplomacy, a 'Concert of Europe'; and Vienna was indeed the first of a series of congresses (Aix-la-Chapelle, Laibach, Troppau, and Verona) which met in an endeavour to resolve European problems in the decade following Napoleon's overthrow.

The main provisions for Russia were:

(a) In Poland, Russia received the greater part of the grand duchy of Warsaw which was to be made into a separate kingdom of Poland. Cracow became a free city state under the protection of Russia, Austria and Prussia.
(b) Russia retained Finland, conquered from Sweden in 1808.
(c) Russia retained Bessarabia, taken from Turkey in 1812.

Russia and Japan

Russo–Japanese War (1904–05)

Russia, in order to become a great Pacific naval power needed an ice-free port in the Far East. In 1896 it obtained a lease for Port Arthur from China and connected this port with St Petersburg by means of the Trans-Siberian Railway. In 1900 Russia assumed power over the Chinese province of Amur but this was opposed by Japan and Britain. Russia eventually agreed to evacuate the area it had occupied but, in fact, failed to keep the agreement. In 1903 suggestions were made to clarify the integrity of China, Manchuria and Korea. Russia failed to respond to these overtures and Japan withdrew its minister from St Petersburg. Two days later Japan landed troops at Chemulpo and on 8 February 1904 there was a surprise attack on the Russian Far Eastern Fleet in the harbour of Port Arthur. The Japanese did not declare war until six says later and subsequently they besieged the city, finally taking it on 19 December 1904. The Japanese army captured Korea and much of Manchuria and decisively defeated the Russian army at Mukden in March 1905. In October 1904 the Russian Baltic Fleet sailed to the Far East under Admiral Zinovi Rozhestvenskii and created an international incident (known as the Dogger Bank Incident) when the Russian vessels fired on some English fishing trawlers on the Dogger Bank, an extensive sandbank in the North Sea, and inflicted casualties. Russia claimed by way of excuse that there were Japanese torpedo boats with the fishing boats. Russian poorly maintained and obsolete naval fleets were destroyed by the Japanese on 27 May 1905 at the battle of Tsushima. Losses to the Russians: eight battleships, several cruisers, five destroyers; five ships were captured and only three returned to Vladivostok; Japanese losses, three torpedo boats. Japan lost about 170,000 men and Russia 400,000. The war ended with the Treaty of Portsmouth (New Hampshire) and was mediated by US President Theodore Roosevelt. Japan gained Port Arthur, half of Sakhalin Island and an important role in Korea, and Russia and Japan left Manchuria and Chinese exclusive administration was resumed.

Russia and the First World War

International conferences known as the Hague Conventions were convened by Nicholas II and met 18 May to 19 July 1899 and 15 June to 18 October 1907, with the aim of 'a possible reduction of the excessive armaments which weigh upon all nations' by 'putting a limit on the progressive development of the present armaments'. Twenty-six countries were represented. The first convention's achievements were limited but did include agreement on the use of gas, expanding bullets, and banning of explosives launched from balloons, and the creation of a court of arbitration (the International Court of Justice). The second convention reached agreement on a number of naval matters and on the employment of force to recover debts but failed to reach any consensus on major issues. A further convention was planned for 1915 but because of World War I did not meet. The two conventions did influence the planning for the League of Nations.

The Russian army had a war strength of 5,500,000 by August 1914, having recovered from the Russo–Japanese war. It was, however, much inferior to the German army in artillery, machine guns, planes and communications, although stronger than the Austrians. To relieve the French the army invaded East Prussia, suffering defeats at Tannenberg and the Masurian Lakes. It also overran Galicia, although by early 1915 its ammunition was spent. In May the Germans attacked with overwhelming artillery and drove the Russians back with frightful losses to a line from Riga to Galicia. When the offensive halted in October the Russians rebuilt the army, which had lost 3,400,000 men since August 1914, and by June 1916 it was stronger than ever. Under General Aleksey Alekseyevich Brusilov the Russians overran the Austrians and by September had taken 400,000 prisoners. But the Russian losses of almost 2,500,000 men during 1916 demoralised the soldiers, who were already deserting in large numbers. On the Turkish front the Russians also achieved considerable but indecisive successes. By early 1917 the Russian army was close to collapse.

See Chronology p. 129.

Russia and Persia

Treaty of Turkmanchai (1828)

The Russian Caucasus region was attacked by the Shah of Persia's armies and the war lasted from June 1826 to February 1828. The Persians were defeated. At the subsequent talks peace and commercial settlements were signed by the Treaty of Turkmanchai on 22 February 1828. These provided a legal framework for future Russo–Persian commercial relations. As a result:

(a) a definitive frontier was established;
(b) Russia annexed the Persian provinces of Erivan and Nackhichevan;
(c) Russia had rights to have a navy in the Caspian Sea;
(d) heavy war indemnity (20,000,000 silver roubles) to be paid to Russia;
(e) various commercial concessions including Persian rights to levy customs duties limited to 5 per cent *ad valorem*.

Russia and Prussia

The Seven Years' War 1756–63 (or Third Silesian War and also known as the Austro–Prussian War) was fought in Europe by Frederick II (the Great) of Prussia with troops provided by Great Britain against a coalition of Austria, Russia, France, Sweden and Saxony, and by Great Britain against France. Russia fought Prussia until the beginning of 1762 when the two countries made a separate peace. The Treaty of Itubertusburg (Hubertsburg) between Austria, Prussia and Saxony was signed in 1763. Russia succeeded in eliminating French influence from Poland. It also established Prussia in Pomerania and Silesia and laid the foundations of modern Germany.

Russia America (Alaska) 1741–1867

1741 Russian navigators Vitus Bering and Aleksandr Chirikov explore coast of north–east corner of North America.
1778 Capt. James Cook undertook first survey of the coast between Sitka and Bering Strait.
1784 First Russian settlement established on Kodial Island by the Shelekhov-Golikov company in order to exploit the fur trade. It moved to a better site at Kodia in 1792.
1799 Mikhailovsk, a Russian settlement, founded. Later destroyed (1802) by Aleuts. The Russian–American Company granted a monopoly.
1804 New Archangel founded, later renamed Sitka.

1811   Fort Ross founded to counter Spanish control of San Francisco. It was sold to an American trading company in 1841.
1821   Russian claim to exclusive navigational rights above 50° North rebutted by the US and Britain and the boundary fixed at 54°40′N. The tsar also claimed the whole of the US Pacific coast north of the 51st parallel, including part of Oregon territory.
1834   Fort Wrangel built to prevent growing British influence on Pacific Coast.
1835   Russian claim to exclusive rights above 54°40′N ignored by whalers and traders.
1867   Alaska, including Aleutian, St Lawrence, and Pribilof Islands sold by Russia to the United States for US$7,200,000.

Russian expansion overseas

Peter I (the Great) assumed the title of Emperor in 1721 but the acquisition of new territories by Russia had been taking place throughout the sixteenth and seventeenth centuries. The Empire reached its largest extent in the period 1885–95 and in 1905 it started to decline. The Empire continued in being after the October Revolution (1917) right up to the break-up of the Soviet Union, long after other European countries had lost their colonial possessions; it continues in a looser form as the Commonwealth of Independent States.

Abkhazia.   In 1810 the area of Sukhumi was annexed by Russia from Turkey, and the Russians established a protectorate over all Abkhazia. The entire region was not formally annexed by Russia until 1864.

Alaska.   See p. 143.

Amur river.   Left bank of Amur river ceded to Russia by the Treaty of Aigun in 1859.

Armenia.   The territory was acquired from Persia in 1828.

Ashkhabad (Askahabad).   Founded by Russians in 1881.

Azerbaijan.   The region, known as Albania, was disputed between Turkey and Persia until it was ceded to Russia by Persia in 1813 (Treaty of Gulistan) and 1828 (Treaty of Turkmanchai). Elizavetpol has been taken in 1804, and Baku was annexed in 1806.

Bessarabia.   The annexation of Georgia (completed 1810) gave rise to the Russo–Turkish war (1806–12). At the Treaty of Bucharest Russia was granted Bessarabia, additional areas on the east coast of the Black Sea, and extensive rights in Moldavia and Wallachia on the Danube. Under the Treaty of Adrianople (1829) these Danubian principalities were guaranteed autonomy under a Russian protectorate.

Bokhara.   Bokhara conquered and made a Russian protectorate in 1862.

Caucasus.   Pacification of the Caucasus complete in 1859.

Crimea.   The Crimea was annexed by the Tatars in the thirteenth century and became a vassal of Turkey in the late fifteenth century and in 1783 was annexed by Russia. In 1787 the Turks issued an ultimatum on the evacuation of the area, and the second Turkish War (1787–92) resulted. By the Treaty of Jassy (1792) Russia acquired Ochakov fortress and the Black Sea shore as far as the Dniester River, and Turkey recognised Russia's annexation of the Crimea.

Daghestan.   The region of Daghestan was ceded to Russia by Persia by the Treaty of Gulistan (1813).

Finland.   Finland was a dependency of Sweden from the thirteenth century, but the country was always under threat from Russia. By the Peace of Nystad the province of Vyborg was ceded to Russia in 1721, and in 1743 the Russian frontier was extended to the Kymmene by the Peace of Turku. A further extension occurred in 1809 when Sweden ceded the remainder of Finland with the Åland Islands at the Peace of Hamina. Finland, however, retained its autonomy and the tsars became grand dukes of Finland. The government was headed by a governor-general who was the personal representative of the tsar. In 1899 Russia declared its right to legislate on the Finnish affairs and in 1900 undertook the first stage of incorporating the Finnish army into the Russian army. The governor-general was assassinated and his successor made some concessions. In 1910 the Imperial Legislation Law deprived the Finnish parliament of the right to legislate on taxes, maintain law and order, and control prices. In 1917, following the collapse of the monarchy, Finland declared itself independent.

Decree limiting Finnish autonomy issued by Nicholas II, 20 March 1903.

From 1898 Finnish autonomy was progressively reduced and the decree was issued to preserve 'public tranquility':

The governor general is authorized:

   a. To order the temporary closure of hotel, wholesale and retail bookstores, and any commercial and industrial establishments whatsoever.
   b. To forbid any kind of public or private gatherings.
   c. To dissolve private associations and their branches.

d. To forbid persons regarded by him as detrimental to political order and public tranquility from residing in Finland . . .

Municipal magistracies, as well as municipal and rural communal administrations, are subject to the supreme authority of the governor general and to the direct authority of the governors, on the following basis:

a. The names of persons elected as mayors and aldermen, as chairmen and vice-chairmen of municipal councils, and to other offices in the municipal and rural communal administrations shall be submitted to the local governor for confirmation. Should he twice refuse to confirm the person elected the office shall be filled through appointment by the Economic Department of the Senate in agreement with the governor general.

b. Mayors and municipal aldermen, chairmen and vice-chairmen of municipal councils, and other persons holding office in municipal and rural communal administrations can, by administrative process, be removed from office by the Economic Department of the Senate in agreement with the governor general . . .

c. The governors are authorized to suspend the execution of decisions adopted by communal authorities subordinate to them, if such decisions do not conform to the general national interests or the needs of the local population, or if they violate the requirements of the law.

(Vernadsky and Fisher 1972)

Georgia. Held by Persia and Turkey, east Georgia (Kartlia and Kakhetia) and west Georgia were acquired by Russia, the former in 1800–01 and the latter between 1803 and 1810. Kars was annexed in 1829.

Kars region. The Kars region was attacked by Russia in 1807, 1828 and 1855. Ceded to Russia at the Congress of Berlin in 1878.

Khabarovsk. Founded as a city in 1858.

Khiva. The Khiva Khanate fell to the Russians in 1873 and became a Russian protectorate.

Merv. Merv was conquered in 1884.

Nikolaevsk. Nikolaevsk on the Amur founded as a city in 1853.

Ossetia. From the early eighteenth century the region was strongly influenced by Russia, and by 1806 the Russians had annexed the entire territory.

Poland. By the partition of 1772 Russia had gained Latgale and Byelorussia east of the Dvina and Dnepr rivers. Russia again invaded Poland in 1792, and by 1793, after a second partition, only central Poland remained independent – and even this was under some Russian control.

A third partition in 1795 enabled Russia to annex Courland and Lithuania. Boundary changes in Russia's favour were also made at the Congress of Vienna (1815).

Russia America (Alaska). See p. 143 above.

Sakhalin. The southern half of the island of Sakhalin passed from Japan in exchange for the Kurile islands in 1875.

Samarkand. Samarkand fell to the Russians in 1868.

Ussuri. The Ussuri region of China ceded to Russia by the Treaty of Peking in 1860.

Vladivostok. Founded as a city in 1860.

Russian Empire ethnic composition (percentage of population in brackets)

	1719 (in thousands)	1914/17 (in thousands)
Russian	11,127 (70.7)	76,672 (44.6)
Ukrainian	2,026 (12.9)	31,032 (18.1)
Belorussians	383 (2.4)	6,768 (4.8)
Poles	–	11,208 (6.5)
Lithuanians	–	1,786
Latvians	162	1,635
Moldavians	–	1,216
Jews	–	7,253 (4.2)
Germans	31	2,448
Tadjiks	–	488
Ossetians	–	237
Armenians	–	1,989
Greeks	–	261
Georgians	–	1,748
Kabardians	–	103
Cherkes	–	59
Chechens	–	253
Peoples of Dagestan	–	772
Finns	164	2,697
Udmurts	48	535
Estonians	309	1,154
Mordva	107	1,188
Tatars	293	3,010
Bashkirs	172	1,733

	1719 (in thousands)	1914/17 (in thousands)
Chuvash	218	1,124
Azeri Turks	–	1,996
Nogai	114	57
Turkmen	–	361
Kazakhs	–	4,698
Kirghiz	–	737
Uzbeks	–	1,964
Iakuts	–	227
Kalmyks	200	169
Buriats	48	279

S. I. Bruk and V. M. Zabuzan 'Etnicheskii sostav naseleniia Rossii (1717–1971)' *Sovetskaia etnografia*, N. 6 (1980).

11
Education and the Arts

Education

Schools were established in Kiev (988) and Novgorod (1028) according to the Nestor Chronicle. Education was mainly confined to the clergy, but the first attempts at popular education came from the Church. In the sixteenth and seventeenth centuries the Catholic Church gave the lead and this was followed by the Orthodox, who opened a school at Lvov in 1586. In Muscovy, the church and monastery schools taught reading, writing and arithmetic in addition to religious subjects. The language of instruction was Church Slavonic, the counterpart in the Russian Orthodox Church to Latin in the West.

Peter I (the Great) was the great influence on education in the eighteenth century, and a modernised Russian alphabet replaced Church Slavonic. The School of Mathematics and Navigation was founded in Moscow in 1699 and was soon followed by schools of Engineering, Artillery, and Surgery. The Naval Academy at St Petersburg was created in 1715 and the Academy of Sciences was founded in 1724 (see p. 152). Education for the sons of the nobility (see pp. 154 and 233) was provided through the Corps of Pages, Cadets, and Midshipmen.

Due to the efforts of the scientist Mikhail Vasilyevich Lomonosov, Moscow University was founded in 1755. The Smolny in Moscow and the Yekaterininsky in St Petersburg, both boarding schools, were for women and established in 1764. The School Act of 1786 established two types of national schools, with five- and two-year courses, respectively. By the beginning of the nineteenth century there were 315 of these schools with 19,915 pupils, including 1,787 girls.

The School Act of 1804 established four levels of schools: Parish schools (one year); county schools (two years); secondary schools (four years), extended to seven years in 1811; universities (four years).

	1830	1840	1850
Parish schools	718	983	1,106
County schools	416	439	439
Secondary schools	62	73	76
Universities	6	6	6

University Foundations (generally with four faculties: History and philology, physics and mathematics, law, and medicine).

1602	Derpt (now Tartu)
1755	Moscow
1804	Kazan
1804	Kharkov
1819	St Petersburg
1833	Kiev
1864	Odessa
1869	Warsaw
1888	Tomsk

The universities were reformed in 1863, and in 1864 two acts were passed to improve elementary and secondary education. With the exception of the church schools, all the elementary schools were brought under the supervision of the Ministry of Education, and three types of secondary schools were created: classical, with Greek and Latin; classical, with Latin only; and modern. Education for women was made more available, and adult education saw the opening of 200 evening and Sunday schools. These liberal improvements were undermined by the minister of education, Count Dmitry Tolstoy, when, in 1871, a decree made schools revert to classical curricula in order to distract students from the issues of the day. Thousands of students were excluded from the universities for political reasons. Secondary education became more expensive, and access to it was restricted, with quotas established for Jewish pupils. As a result, thousands of Russians studied in Western Europe and many returned with radical views.

The 1897 census shows that 21 per cent of the population was literate (34 per cent male, 12 per cent female), and with far higher rates in the cities and in European Russia than in the countryside and in the Asian parts of the empire. The majority of the people were illiterate until the second half of the nineteenth century. By 1917 about 40 per cent of the population over ten years of age was literate.

From 1895 to 1904, the number of technical schools rose from 51 to 93, vocational schools from 91 to 237, and commercial schools from 6 to 139. Emphasis on classicism was largely abandoned in 1902 and a law providing for compulsory school attendance was enacted in 1908.

By 1915 there were about 122,000 schools with 8,122,000 pupils. The number of children in elementary schools of all kinds was estimated at 7,260,000. Secondary schools had 764,000 pupils, and professional and technical schools had 93,200 on the elementary level and 35,000 on the secondary level. Higher educational institutions numbered 39, including 10 universities, and had 62,225 students. The 19 technical institutes had 22,379 students, and 9 agricultural institutes had about 6,000.

In an address to Nicholas II the First Imperial Duma stated that one of its aims was 'to use every effort for the promotion of national education, and, first of all, to draft a law for universal free education'. Neither the First nor the Second Dumas achieved this but some progress was made by the third. Advance in education came from the *Zemstvos* and the town councils. Educational spending by *Zemstvos* 1871–1911:

	roubles
1871	767,000
1881	3,684,000
1891	5,334,000
1901	16,544,000
1911	52,278,000

Development of Primary Education, 1856–1911

	1856	1878	1896	1911
Number of pupils	450,002	1,065,889	3,804,262	6,629,978
Number of girl pupils	36,900	188,662	810,308	2,134,856
Number of primary schools	8,227	24,853	87,080	100,749
Ratio of pupils to population	1:143	1:77	1:33	1:24
Ratio of primary schools to population	1:7,762	1:3,299	1:1,443	1:1,499
Pupils as a % of population	0.70	1.20	3.02	4.04

Number of Children Denied Admission to First Grade, for every 100 admitted, 1911

	Boys	Girls
Russian Empire		
Urban schools	30.0	28.7
Village schools	30.5	33.6
All schools	30.4	32.6
Zemstvo schools	25.4	24.8
Church parish schools	34.9	31.4

Moscow Province (1910). Number out of 100 able to read and write:

		Men	Women
Aged 55–60	29.4	45.6	1.9
35–40	43.1	70.8	9.6
20–25	56.1	85.2	33.4
12–15	82.4	93.4	74.5

Extracts from the Decree on the Founding of the Academy of Sciences, 28 January 1724:

His Imperial Majesty has ordained the establishment of an academy where it would be possible to study languages as well as other sciences and fine arts, and where books would be translated.

Two types of establishments were normally used for the development of arts and sciences: one is called a university, and the other, an academy, or society of arts and sciences.

1. A univeristy is an association of learned men who teach young men high sciences, like theology, jurisprudence, medicine, and philosophy up to the limit to which these sciences have been developed. An academy is an association of learned and skilled men who not only know their respective sciences to the extent to which they are developed but also seek to perfect and to develop them further through new discoveries (and publications), while taking no pains to teach others.

2. Though academy and university both comprise the same sciences and the same qualified members, there is no connection between them in some countries, where the large number of learned men makes it possible to set up several learned assemblies. This is done so that teaching duties would not interfere with the speculations and research of the academy, whose sole purpose is to improve arts and sciences – from which both university professors and students benefit; at the same time the university should not be distracted from teaching by various ingenious investigations and speculations, which would leave the young men unattended to.

5. The most appropriate type of an association for Russia would be one consisting of the very best men of learning who would:

a. develop and perfect the sciences, but in such a way that they would at the same time
b. teach young men publicly (those who are found fit for it) and
c. give special instruction to several men who would then be able to teach the fundamentals of all the sciences to young men . . .

7. ... The sciences to be represented in this academy can generally be divided into three classes: the first class to comprise the mathematical sciences and all that depends on them; the second class – all parts of physics; and the third class – the humanities, history, and law ...

11. The duties of the academicians are as follows:

a. To seek out everything that has already been achieved in the sciences; to perform the tasks necessary for their correction and expansion; to make reports on all their discoveries in this connection, and to give them to the secretary, who must then edit and publish them at the appropriate time.
b. Every academician must read the good authors in this field who publish their works abroad; it will thus be easy for him to draw up a summary of such works; these summaries shall be published by the academy at designated times, together with other findings and deliberations.
c. Since the academy is nothing but a society of persons who must cooperate with one another in the development of sciences, it is highly important that they should meet together for several hours every week. Each member could then present his own opinions, benefit from the advice and opinions of others and check in the presence of all the members experiments that he had performed alone; this last feature is especially necessary, for very often in the conduct of such experiments one member will hold another to a perfect demonstration – for instance, the anatomist might do it with the mechanist, and so forth.
d. The academy must also:
   i. Examine all the discoveries that will be made from time to time in the above-mentioned sciences, and give its candid appraisal as to whether they are correct.
   ii. Determine whether they are of great or of little use.
   iii. Determine whether they were known before nor not.
e. Should his Imperial Majesty demand from an academician an investigation of some matter within the sphere of his science, he must perform it with the utmost application and report on it after a reasonable lapse of time (for there are many matters that appear to be simple, but demand time-consuming research).
f. Each academician must draw up a system or an exposition of his science for the benefit of students, which shall then be published in Latin at the expense of the imperial government. And since it would redound not only to the great benefit but also to the glory of the Russian people to have such books published in Russian, let each class of the academy have

a translator attached to it; likewise, one translator shall be attached to the secretary.

h. It is necessary to organize a library and a natural science collection, so that the academicians will not suffer from any lack of materials they need. The librarian shall have control over this and shall be empowered to order the books and instruments needed by the academy or to have the instruments made here ... the treasury shall pay for the things that an academician needs for his experiments, both private and public.

(Vernadsky and Fisher, 1972)

Decrees on Compulsory Education of the Russian Nobility, 12 January and 28 February 1714:

Send to every *gubernia* some persons from mathematical schools to teach the children of the nobility – except those of freeholders and government clerks – mathematics and geometry; as a penalty [for evasion] establish a rule that no one will be allowed to marry unless he learns these [subjects]. Inform all prelates to issue no marriage certificates to those who are ordered to go to schools ...

The Great Sovereign has decreed: in all *gubernias* children between the ages of ten and fifteen of the nobility, of government clerks, and of lesser officials, except those of freeholders, must be taught mathematics and some geometry. Toward the end, students should be sent from mathematical schools [as teachers], several into each *gubernia*, to prelates and to renowned monasteries to establish schools. During their instruction these teachers should be given food and financial remuneration of three *altyns* and two *dengas* per day from *gubernia* revenues set aside for that purpose by personal orders of His Imperial Majesty. No fees should be collected from students. When they have mastered the material, they should then be given certificates written in their own handwriting. When the students are released they ought to pay one ruble each for their training. Without these certificates they should not be allowed to marry nor receive marriage certificates.

Libraries

The first libraries in Russia were the collections of manuscripts held by Orthodox monasteries. The monasteries of Vilnius and Lvov have libraries dating from 1570 and 1608. In 1714 the Academy of Sciences accepted books of Peter I (the Great) and in 1755 the Moscow University Library was founded. In 1814 the Imperial Public Library opened in St Petersburg. The total number of libraries in 1914 was 13,400.

Publishing

The first dated Russian printed book (*Apostle*) was printed by Ivan Fedorov and Peter Mstislavets at the Imperial Printing House in 1563–64. The printers, because of the activity of the *oprichnina*, were soon obliged to go to Lithuania, but they continued their publishing in Lvov and Ostrog. The reforms of Peter I (the Great) encouraged publishing, which was a government monopoly until 1783. Publishing flourished under enlightened scholar-entrepreneurs like Nikolai I. Novikov but, inspired by reaction to the French Revolution, Catherine II (the Great) curbed the press in 1796. In the eighteenth century 9,500 titles were published.

The nineteenth century saw the growth of capitalist publishing, mainly by enlightened aristocrats or booksellers. In 1860, 2,085 titles were published; in 1880 10,562. Throughout the century there were various decrees on censorship varying in severity, and to escape these some publishers set up abroad, for example, Aleksandr Herzen published in London. A breakdown of types of literature at the end of the nineteenth century shows a predominance of religious literature followed by light fiction 'for the people' published by various 'improvement' societies. In 1913, 30,079 titles were published, 2,737 in languages other than Russian.

Alphabet and Transliteration

Russian uses the Cyrillic alphabet, traditionally attributed to Saints Cyril and Methodious, ninth-century Greek Orthodox missionaries who reduced Old Slavonic to writing in order to spread the Gospel. It bears a marked resemblance to Greek.

Literature

The great period for Russian literature began in the nineteenth century starting with Pushkin's *Eugene Onegin* and the end of this era came with the death of Chekhov in 1904. The beginning and end of this period saw attempts to bring about political change by attempts to overthrow the autocracy.

Important novels of the period are:

1825–1831	*Eugene Onegin*	Pushkin
1839–1840	*Hero of Our Time*	Lermontov
1842	*Dead Souls*	Gogol
1847	*Oblomov*	Goncharov
1850	*A Thousand Souls*	Pisemsky
1856	*Rudin*	Turgenev
1860	*On the Eve*	Turgenev
1862	*Fathers and Children*	Turgenev

1866	*Crime and Punishment*	Dostoyevsky
1867	*Smoke*	Turgenev
1868	*The Idiot*	Dostoyevsky
1868–1869	*War and Peace*	Tolstoy
1869	*Precipice*	Goncharov
1872	*The Possessed (Devils)*	Dostoyevsky
1872	*Cathedral Folk*	Leskov
1872–1876	*Golovlyov Family*	Saltykov-Shchedrin
1873–1877	*Anna Karenina*	Tolstoy
1877	*Virgin Soil*	Turgenev
1879–1880	*The Brothers Karamanzov*	Dostoyevsky
1896	*Shadows*	Sologub
1899	*Resurrection*	Tolstoy

Art

During the reign of Peter I (the Great) all native, Byzantine, and Oriental schools were rejected in favour of Western European models. Russian artists began to follow European trends, with no particular distinction until the emergence of a realist school in the nineteenth century. The first Russian Academy of Fine Arts was founded in St Petersburg in 1757. It had an impact on the development of Russian art and was the centre of artistic life and professional education. In the nineteenth century in the St Petersburg Academy there arose a conflict between conservative officials who adhered to the academic tradition and painters aspiring to realism. The conflict became particularly acute when a group of students withdrew in 1863 from the Academy as a protest against academism. Nevertheless the Academy maintained its importance as a school for training artists. In 1918 the Academy was abolished and its work was carried on by other schools. The genre paintings of Alexey Venetsiyanov (1779–1847) and Pavel Feodotov (1815–1852) were popular, the former with his lyrical treatment of peasant scenes and Russian landscape, the latter imbued with satire or sentiment drawn from everyday bourgeois life. The first vigorous painter of peasant life was Ilya Repin (1844–1930), inspirer of the later Socialist Realism.

The first modern movements developed under the influence of the painter Michael Vrubel (1856–1891) and of the circle of designers surrounding Serge Diaghilev, Aleksandr Benois and Leon Bakst. Three later schools were of international importance: Rayonism was a style of abstract painting that flourished from 1911, the mass of an object being projected into space by radiating lines of colour. The Donkey's Tail Exhibition was held in Moscow in 1912. It was organised by Vladimir Tatlin, Michael Larionov, Natalya Goncharovo, Kazimir Malevich and others. Bright colour combinations derived from Russian folk art were a feature of the exhibition. Constructivism was a type of abstract sculpture practised by the brothers Naum Gabo and Anton Pevsner from 1917, using movement and transparency as well as mass; Suprematism was a school of abstract painting founded by Kazimir Malevich in 1913, using only the geometric shapes of rectangle, triangle, circle and cross.

Ballet

The empresses Anna and Elizabeth established Russian ballet; they engaged German and Italian directors to train Russian dancers. By 1740 the Imperial School of Ballet was established at the Winter Palace. Many of the dancers were serfs attached to the royal household and already trained in folk traditions; this introduced a virility into Russian ballet that ensured its ultimate victory over increasingly effete French and English styles of dancing. Productions were spectacular owing to the patronage of the tsar.

Charles Didelot arrived in St Petersburg in 1811. He was a French teacher and choreographer and an outstanding representative of the classical tradition who laid the foundations for the St Petersburg school and the company's greatness. Jules Perrot, Didelot's successor as ballet master in 1851, continued his work until he was replaced by Marius Petipa, another french dancer, in 1862. Petipa combined the romantic style in vogue in Western Europe with the spectacle and formal approach that the tsar demanded.

In 1825 the Moscow Ballet, now the Bolshoi Ballet Company, had been founded and by this time the ballet in Russia was firmly established as a serious art. Productions were of a high quality in spite of a growing tendency for the dancing to become no more than a mechanical display of technique and stagecraft.

It was in 1890 that Tchaikovsky's ballet *The Sleeping Beauty* brought about a revival of direct emotional appeal to the audience while retaining the spectacle.

The first season of Serge Pavlovich Diaghilev's Ballets Russes in Paris in 1909 was a landmark in the art and he used dancers trained at the Maryinsky Theatre, and avant-garde Russian composers and designers; Michael Fokine was chief choreographer and Igor Fedorovich Stravinsky principal composer, while its most notable designers were Aleksandr Nikolayevich Benois and Leon Bakst. The company's principal dancers were Tamara Karsavina and Vaslav Nijinsky. Through the Ballets Russes, the influence of Russian ballet reached England with Alicia Markova, France with Serge Lifar, and the United States with George Balanchine.

Theatre

Michael, the first Romanov tsar, ordered the construction of the first known theatre in Russia in 1613. The actors were probably German. Apart from court performances by foreign actors and fairground shows, there was little interest in drama in Russia until Empress Elizabeth established the first public theatre in 1756 at St Petersburg, directed by Aleksandr Sumarokov. Theatre became more popular under Catherine II (the Great); she founded the Imperial Theatre School in 1779 and authorised the construction of the Petrovsky (Bolshoi) Theatre. This was also known as the Kamenny (stone) theatre and performances were first held there in 1783. Until the appearance of the first Russian playwright, Denis Fonvizin, plays consisted of translations and imitations of French neoclassical plays. The best known of the chief Russian theatres is the Bolshoi Theatre in Moscow. It was founded in 1776, but a theatre was not built on the present site until 1821–24. It was rebuilt and altered considerably in 1856 by Alberto Kavos after it had suffered extensive damage in a fire in 1853. Opera and ballet have been performed at the Bolshoi Theatre since 1825. In 1824 the Maly (small) theatre was opened with a company originally formed in 1806; it is the oldest Moscow theatre. In 1832 the Alexandrinsky Theatre was built in St Petersburg on the orders of Nicholas I. The tsar used the theatre for political ends and is considered to have virtually invented the patriotic play, a form of drama through which playwrights flattered him. The number of theatres increased under Alexander I and Nicholas I, but many of the best plays were banned by censorship; Aleksandr Griboyedov's *Woe from Wit* (1823) was not staged in its full version until 1869. Similarly Pushkin's *Boris Godunov* (1825) was not performed until 1870. Under Alexander II, censorship was relaxed, and the plays of Aleksandr Ostrovsky were popular. In 1883 all Yiddish plays were forbidden as a part of the anti-semitic measures taken after the tsar was assassinated. Many dramatists left Russia to settle in the United States, making New York the new centre of Yiddish drama. In 1898 Konstantin Stanislavsky and Vladimir Nemirovich-Danchenko founded the Moscow Art Theatre, which achieved worldwide acclaim for its theatrical naturalism. Stanislavsky, who was in charge of stage direction, strove to strip the theatre of commercialism and stereotyped mannerisms by concentrating on inner moods and emotions; in this he was influenced by the German Meiningen Company. The original ensemble was composed of amateur actors from the Society of Art and Literature. The theatre performed plays by Gorky, Andreyev, Maeterlinch, and Hauptmann, and in particular the works of Chekhov.

Architecture

Buildings in Russia were traditionally based on a wooden structure (*klet*) with walls made of horizontally stacked timbers and a steep roof. In pre-Kievan Russia the *klet* formed the nucleus of all buildings; large buildings were made from a cluster of *klety* joined by short passages. More important buildings were carved with decorative designs from folk art.

With the conversion of Kievan Russia to Christianity, the influence of Byzantium predominated; the wooden structures were sometimes translated into stone, which was scarce, and always adapted to strict Byzantine rules, as nearly all important buildings were religious. The Byzantine convention of a cube (the earth) surmounted by a dome or cupola (heaven) was adapted to custom, climate and resources. Russian churches had smaller, darker interior spaces, greater verticality, and decoration on the outside. The Byzantine cupola became elongated into an onion dome on a cylindrical drum.

In the sixteenth century Italian architects were brought to Moscow to build in stone for Ivan III (the Great). Their main work was the Cathedral of St Basil the Blessed in the Kremlin (1555–60), in which they used their expertise with stone to produce a traditional Russian design consisting of nine separate units on one foundation, each octagonal in shape.

The decorative baroque European style was popular in Russia before the deliberate Westernisation of Russian art under Peter I (the Great). From then on Russian architects, notably Andreyan Zakharov (Admiralty, St Petersburg, from 1805), worked in successive fashionable Western styles. In the early years of the twentieth century the school of Constructivism produced outstanding modern buildings.

12
Law, Crime and Punishment

Law

The code (*Ulozhenie*) of 1649 covered the laws of the previous hundred years, with special emphasis on consolidation of those laws and decrees enacted since the establishment of the Romanov dynasty. Implied in its provisions was the complete subordination of the individual to the state. Its attempted definition of the law on serfs reflected this general orientation, guaranteeing the landlord the labour of his peasants while making him responsible for the collection of peasant taxes. Thus hereditary serfdom received formal recognition. In this and other respects, the Code of 1649 remained the framework of the Russian legal system until 1833.

Not being satisfied with the Code, Peter I (the Great) proposed a revision of the Code in 1700 and 1718, as did the Empress Elizabeth, but nothing came of this. Catherine II (the Great) envisioned an entirely new code and she established a legislative commission in 1766 and, though knowing little of Russian law herself, published an *Instruction* for their benefit, a restatement of the ideas of such Western thinkers as Montesquieu and Beccaria. Catherine urged modest improvement in the legal and economic status of the peasantry, but there were to be no changes in the position of the nobility.

The commission started work in 1767 and continued in existence until 1774, but achieved nothing. In 1826 Nicholas I appointed Count Mikhail Speransky to lead Section II of His Majesty's Own Chancery charged with the task of compiling a new code. In 1833 Speransky's group published:

1. a complete collection of the laws of the Russian Empire, from those in the Code of 1649 to those issued prior to 1 January 1830;
2. a code of laws of the Russian Empire covering all the laws in effect.

Speransky was also responsible for a new criminal code in 1845 and several collections in such specialised areas as army and navy regulations and taxation laws. The Code of 1833 was extended to the west and south-west provinces of the Empire in 1840, another stage in the process of unification and Russification characteristic of this period. In 1850 a committee was appointed to draft reform legislation. It was led first by Count D. N. Bludov and, after 1861, by S. I. Zarudny and D. N. Zamyatin.

The law as published in November 1864 provided:

(a) for equality of all before the law;
(b) the right to be heard by impartial tribunals;
(c) implementation of the principle, *nullum crimen, nulla poena sine lege*;
(d) a uniform and simplified judicial procedure;
(e) separation of the judicial from the legislative and executive arms of government;
(f) irremovability of all judges except those found guilty of misconduct;
(g) open proceedings;
(h) trial by jury;
(i) representation by qualified members of the bar;
(j) election of lower court judges;
(k) exclusion of police from preliminary investigations, which were now to be carried out by magistrates.

Justices of the peace were to be elected by the *zemstvos* in the country districts, and by the city councils in Moscow and St Petersburg. As a further step toward ensuring justice where previously the landowner had supreme sway as local magistrate, the decisions of justices of the peace could now be appealed to county sessions. More important cases went to district courts and appeals to local higher courts. Both latter sets of judges were to be appointed by the Crown from candidates nominated by the judiciary.

A law of April 1863 abolished capital punishment in its worst forms, revised the penal system but allowed flogging to continue under certain circumstances. This system never became general throughout the empire. The examining magistrates, who ought on principle to have been irremovable, were very rarely confirmed in their office, and the investigation of criminal cases was entrusted to magistrates temporarily appointed. By a law of May 1885 the principle of irremovability was restricted; by laws of May 1878 and July 1889 the assistance of a jury in certain cases was suppressed. A law of 12 July 1889 abolished elective justices of peace, putting in their places in the country districts the country chiefs, and in the town the urban justices; in both cases the appointments being made by the Minister of Justice. Justices of peace had been retained only in St Petersburg and Moscow and in six of the largest towns of the empire.

Reformed tribunals, but without juries, were introduced in

1875	Poland
1889	Baltic Provinces
1894	Astrakhan
1894	Olenets
1894	Orenburg
1894	Ufa
1897	Siberia
1898–1899	Turkestan
1898–1899	Provinces of the Steppes
1898–1899	NE District of Vologda
1898–1899	Transcaspian Provinces

Chronology of punishments

from

- 1648 Criminals were sent to Siberia after branding or amputation
- 1729 Political prisoners sent to Siberia
- 1762 Exile for recalcitrant serfs
- 1763 Exile for convicted prostitutes
- 1800 Exile for Jews who failed to pay taxes for three consecutive years

The peak years for those going into exile were 1825 Decembrists, 1831 and 1863 mainly Polish insurgents and from 1880 Revolutionaries including Anarchists, Populists and Bolsheviks. In 1891 there were in exile an estimated 100,000 Polish rebels, 40,000 Russian criminals, 50,000 Russian political exiles, and 5,000 wives and children who had voluntarily joined their husbands. About 3,400 exiles left weekly wearing leg-fetters on the 1,000-mile journey on foot to Irkutsk, taking three months.

In 1896 there were 888 prisons of which 125 were in Poland.

Prison population

	Male	Female
Under judgment	20,804	1,456
Condemned to imprisonment	40,916	4,231
exile	9,628	540
Waiting transport to Siberia	5,144	507
Detained by order of Admin	811	24
Voluntarily following their parents or husbands	744	871
Total	78,047	7,629

Third Section (Department)

The Third Section was established by Nicholas I in 1826 as one of the six departments of His Majesty's Own Chancery. It was a secret police force responsible for political security and was the tsar's chief weapon against subversion, and it symbolised his reign. Designed by Count Aleksandr Benckendorff, head of the department (1826–44), its chief functions were surveillance, the gathering of information on undesirables such as political dissidents and foreigners, the running of state prisons, prosecution of forgers, banishment of political criminals, and censorship. The department had a vast network of spies and informers and the co-operation of the military corps of gendarmes, established in 1836.

The department, although supposed to protect the proletariat, became increasingly repressive, causing the arrest of many populists (*narodniki*). This led to the assassination of the then head of the Third Section, General Nikilai Vladimirovich Mezentsov, in 1878.

The failure of the department to achieve much, largely due to the proliferation of false reports brought in by informers, resulted in its closure in 1880 by General Mikhail Loris-Melikov. Its functions were transferred to the Ministry of the Interior.

Okhrana

The Okhrannye otdeleniia, or Okhrana for short, was the department for defence of public security and order (security police), which existed from 1881 until it was abolished by the provisional government in 1917. It was particularly active after the 1905 revolution. The Okhrana enjoyed considerable independence from other government agencies. They were explicitly exempt from the authority of governors and governors-general, and were even known to ignore the minister of the interior. They undertook the interception of mail and checked the credibility of people entering St Petersburg. They employed agents for shadowing suspects, reporting suspicious organisations and individuals and, probably most important of all, infiltrated organisations believed to be subversive.

An example of infiltration was the foundation in 1901 of a society for mutual self-help for engineering workers by Sergey Zubatov, the chief of the Moscow Okhrana. Under police protection the society flourished and other legal trade unions were established in Minsk, Odessa and St Petersburg. Zubatov maintained control in Moscow but in other centres the unions became increasingly revolutionary. It was Zubatov's ideas that led Father Gapon, who had been an Okhrana agent, to organise a march of factory workers taking a petition to the tsar on 9 January 1905 which led to Bloody Sunday and the beginning of the first Russian revolution.

There was also infiltration into political parties and newspapers. Police agents were editors of two Marxist journals, *Nachalo* in 1899 and *Pravda* in 1912–13.

13
Press and Censorship

Newspapers and journals

1621	*Kuranty* (The Chimes)
	Earliest publication in Russia.
1702	*Vedomosti Moskovskogo Gosudarstva* (Gazette of the Moskovite State)
	Founded by Peter I (the Great). Circulation *c.* 1,000 of 2–7 pp. Published by the Academy of Sciences from 1728 as *Saukt Peterburgskie Vedomosti* (St Petersburg Gazette) and became a daily newspaper in 1815.
1728	*St Petersburg News*
	Inspired by English publications and included popular science.
1756	*Moskovskie Vedomosti* (Moscow Gazette)
	Founded by Mikhail Kheraskov. Published until 1917.
1782	*Pochta Dukhov* (The Courier of the Spirits)
	Edited by I. A. Krylov.
1791	*Moscow Journal*
	Founded by Nikolai Karamzin. He published literary criticism, translations and his own work.
1792	*Zritel* (The Spectator)
1796	(Paul I ordered the closing of private printing presses in 1796 and this led to a decrease in the number of publications.)
*c.*1800	(About 70 periodicals were published regularly.)
1802	*Messenger of Europe*
1802	*Moskovsky Merkury* (The Moscow Mercury)
1802	*Vestnik Evropy* (Herald of Europe)
	Magazine expressing conservative ideas, founded in Moscow, and until 1804 edited by Nikolai Karamzin. Publication ceased in 1830.
1804	*Severny Vestnik* (The Northern Messenger)

1805 *Zhurnal Rossiyskoy Slovestnosti* (Journal of Russian Literature)
1813 *Russky Invalid* (The Russian Veteran)
Published only military communiques and became the official publication of the Ministry of War in 1847.
1818 *Annals of the Fatherland*
Literary and political journal of progressive socialist persuasion, first published in St Petersburg. From 1820, it was published monthly, and at this stage was not yet of particular political significance and publication ceased in 1830. In 1839 Krayevsky revived the *Annals* in the so-called thick journals. Contributors included Vissarion Belinsky, Aleksandr Herzen, T. N. Granovsky, and Nicholas Ogarev. Works by Ivan Turgenev, Nicholas Nekrasov, and Michael Lermontov, were also published. Because of its political views, the *Annals* was attacked by the censor but its influence was wide. Publication ceased in April 1884.
1820 *Vestni Yevropy* (European Messenger)
1821 *Dukh Zhurnalov* (Review of Reviews)
Banned in 1821 following publication of the US Constitution and articles on representative government.
1823 *Polyarnaya zvezda* (Polar Star)
Published 1823–1825 in Russia. The manuscript of the final edition confiscated after the Decembrist revolt. Published 1855–1862 by Aleksandr Herzen in London and in 1869 in Geneva.
1823 *Polyarnaya Zvezda* (The Northern Star)
Sympathised with the Decembrist movement and Aleksandr Herzen.
1825 *Severnaya Pehela* (The Northern Bee)
Published the works of Pushkin and others. Closed 1864.
1827 *Moscow Herald*
Founded by Mikhail Pogodin.
1830 (Censorship increased following the revolution in France.)
1830 *Literaturnaya Gazeta* (Literary Gazette)
Literary publication banned from publishing political news. Appeared in 1830–1831 and 1840–1849. A publication with this title resumed publication in 1929.
1831 *Telescop* (Telescope)
Founded as a bi-weekly by N. T. Nadezhdin and became a weekly in 1836. The publication of P. Ya Chaadaev's 'Philosophical Letter' forced it to close in 1836. Nadezhdin was exiled and the censor dismissed.
1836 *Sovremennik* (The Contemporary)
Founded by Aleksandr Pushkin. Closed down by the authorities in 1866.

1839   *Otechestvennye Zapiski* (National Annals)
        Declined in importance in the 1860s but was revitalised in 1868 by the joint editorship of Nikolai Nekrasov and M. Saltykov-Shchedrin, and it became the leading publication of the populists. Closed in 1884 for political reasons.
1841   *Moskvityanin* (The Muscovite)
        Slavophile organ founded by M. P. Pogodin. Lack of support caused publication to cease in 1856.
1852   *Moskovsky Sbornik* (Moscow Articles)
        Expressed slavophile ideas and was suspended after its second issue.
1857   *Kolokol* (The Bell)
        Published in London by Aleksandr Herzen and smuggled into Russia in large numbers. Later published in Geneva. Publication ceased in 1867 with the 245 number. A French version was published in 1868 but abandoned and a further attempt to revive it in 1870 was made but abandoned after six issues.
1861   *Den* (The Day)
        Expressed slavophile thought and closed in 1865.
1863   *Russkie Vedomosti*
        Organ of the liberal intelligentsia. Closed in 1918.
1866   *Vestnik Evropy* (Herald of Europe)
        Magazine expressing liberal views and contributors included Ivan Turgenev and Ivan Goncharov. Publication ceased in 1918.
1868   *Novoye Vremya* (The New Times)
        Had by this year two daily editions and a circulation of 60,000. Closed in 1917.
1868   *Narodnoye Delo* (The Peoples' Cause)
        Published in Geneva aimed at a popular revolution of the peasants.
1873   *Vpered* (Onward)
        A legal journal published in Zurich by Kievan social democrats.
1875   *Nabat* (Alarm)
        Published in Geneva aiming at radical revolution.
1880   *Rus* (Russia)
        Slavophile daily – closed 1887.
1885   *Rabochaya Zarya* (The Worker's Dawn)
        Unsuccessful attempt at printing in Russia.
1885   *Rabochy* (The Worker)
        Unsuccessful attempt at printing in Russia.
1897   *Russkoye Bogatstvo* (Russian Wealth)
        Edited on populist lines.
1897   *Zhizn* (Life)
        Semi-Marxist publication published abroad after 1901.

1898	*The World of Art* Published by Diaghilev, Benois, Bakst and Vrubel. Helped to establish modern art in Russia. Closed 1904.
1900	*Iskra* (The Spark) First issue published in Leipzig with Lenin as contributor. The publication provided Lenin with his first position of influence.
1901	*Revolyutsionnaya Rossiya* (Revolutionary Russia) Journal of the Social Revolutionaries published in Finland.
1902	*Osvobozhdenie* (Liberation) Review of Russian Liberals living abroad published by P. B. Struve.
1904	*Russkoye Slovo* (Russian Word) Daily newspaper founded with a circulation by 1916 of 700,000 serving lower-middle class.
1904	*Syn Otechestva* (Son of the Fatherland)
1908	*Rech* (The Speech) Organ of the Constitutional Democratic Party. Closed.
1908	*Utro Rossii* (The Moving of Russia) Financial journal. Closed 1918.
1910	*Zvezda* (The Star)
1911	*Mysl* (The Thought)
1911	*Prosveshchenie* (Enlightenment)
1912	(Nearly every aspect of political thought was catered for by 2,167 periodicals in 33 languages in 246 cities.)
1912	*Pravda* (Truth) First issue of Bolshevik daily newspaper in St Petersburg (5 May). Circulation (1913) 40,000. Joseph Stalin on editorial board.
1917	*Izvestia* First issue of the organ of the Petrograd Soviet (13 March).

Censorship

Censorship was first officially introduced by Peter I (the Great). In order to suppress religious dissent the Senate decreed in October 1720 that because of 'irregularities' the monastery presses of Kiev and Chernigov were to print only 'church books' which had previously been published with church authority.

> And prior to printing these old church books are to be corrected in accordance with the church books used in Great Russia, and made to agree with them perfectly, so that all differences and local idioms should be eliminated.
> And no other books, whether old or new publications, are to be printed in these monasteries without prior notification to the Ecclesiastical College

and without its permission, in order that books adverse to the Eastern church and not in Great Russian print should not appear.

(Vernadsky and Fisher, 1972)

The Synod confirmed the Senate's decree and two copies of all books and reprints were sent to the censor's office. The title page was printed with

> By the most gracious permission of the Great Sovereign Tsar and Great Prince Peter the First, All-Russian Emperor, and with the consent of the most Holy All-Ruling Synod, this book [title] is printed in the town of [name] at the [name] monastery.

(Vernadsky and Fisher, 1972)

General censorship was established in 1803, although the first comprehensive laws on censorship were not drawn up until 1828.

Duties and principal divisions of the censorship were incorporated in the Statute of Censorship, 22 April 1828:

1. It is the duty of the censorship to examine works of literature, science, and art intended for publication within the country by printing, engraving, or lithography, as well as those works brought in from abroad, and to permit the publication or sale of only those works that are not at variance, either wholly or in part, with general rules stated in section 3 below.
2. The expression 'works of literature, science, and art' is understood to include books of every kind and in all languages, prints, drawings, sketches, plans, maps, and also music with lyrics.
3. Works of literature, science, and art are to be banned by the censorship: (a) if they contain anything that tends to undermine the teachings of the Orthodox Greco–Russian church, its traditions and rituals, or in general the truths and dogmas of the Christian faith; (b) if they contain anything infringing upon the inviolability of the supreme autocratic power or upon the respect of the imperial house, or anything contradicting basic government legislation; (c) if they offend the honor of any person especially by slander and by indecent expressions or injurious dissemination of that which concerns his morals or domestic life.
4. The censorship is set up under the Ministry of Public Education and is divided into internal and foreign sections. The former examines works of literature, science, and art intended for publication inside the country. The latter permits or forbids the sale of books, prints, and so forth, brought from abroad.
5. A Chief Censorship Administration is to be formed for general supervision over the activities of the censorship, both internal and foreign, and

over the accurate execution of everything that is contained in the present statute.

(Vernadsky and Fisher, 1972)

Censorship was abolished for newspapers and certain books in 1865, but the revolutionary movement prompted stricter measures to be taken. Preliminary censorship of journals and periodicals was abolished 1905–06 and only foreign books were subject to censorship. Some editions of journals thought to be contravening the law could be brought before the courts. Such offences could be 'spreading of false information concerning state agencies and officials' or 'favourable comments on criminal acts'. The period 1906–14 was one of comparative freedom for the press. Censorship of the press disappeared after the February Revolution of 1917 but was soon reinstated following the October Revolution.

The penalties imposed by the authorities included deleting words, phrases or paragraphs or confiscations of editions. Also detention in the local police station with warnings, fines, exile and surveillance by the police were other forms of punishment.

Aleksandr Pushkin (1799–1837) was probably the best-known victim of the censor, twice exiled, once in 1820 and again in 1824, but after his release in 1826 Nicholas I agreed to act as his personal censor and Pushkin hoped that this arrangement would release him from normal censorship; it didn't.

14
Biographies

ADRIAN, PATRIARCH (1627–1700). The archimandrite of Chudov Monastery and metropolitan of Kazan, Adrian was chosen as the new patriarch in 1690 and was the tenth and last of the original line of patriarchs. The co-tsars formally ratified his election although Peter would have preferred another candidate. A devout and godly man who held extremely conservative views, he opposed Peter the Great's plans to reform the Church and strove to prevent the tsar from interfering with the life of the Church. A number of Adrian's religious writings have been preserved. After his death, the patriarchate was abolished, and the Church was brought under the jurisdiction of the state and the new holy governing synod.

AEURENTHAL, COUNT ALOIS LEXA VON (1854–1912). Politician and diplomat of the Austro-Hungarian Empire, he was ambassador to St Petersburg from 1898–1906. He then became foreign minister (1906–12), and while he occupied this post, Austria-Hungary, with German approval, annexed Bosnia and Herzegovina (1908). This action, which raised the threat that Russia would make war, was one of the incidents leading to World War I.

AKHMATOVA, ANNA (1888–1966). Russian poet. Born near Odessa. She began publishing poetry in 1907 and with Nikolai Gumilev, whom she married in 1910, launched the neo-classicist Acmeist movement. The style is represented in her early collections *Evening* (1912), *Beads* (1914) and *The White Flock* (1917).

ALEKSEYEV, MIKHAIL VASILYEVICH (1857–1918). General who was chief of staff to Tsar Nicholas II (1915–17) during World War I and commander-in-chief on the western front (1915). He was chief of staff to Kerensky for a brief period after the overthrow of the tsar. In 1918 he took the initiative to organise the White (anti-Bolshevik) forces in the Civil War and later that year died of pneumonia.

ALEXANDER I (1777–1825). Tsar of Russia 1801–25, who came to the throne after the murder of his father, Paul I. Alexander received a progressive humanitarian education planned by his grandmother Catherine II (the Great), and his policies were at first liberal in outlook, but later the so-called enigmatic tsar was influenced by Metternich and gave way to reactionary policy. In the first part of his reign the council of state and ministeries were established as were a state school system and several universities and censorship was relaxed and restrictions on travel abroad were lifted. The serfs were liberated without land in the Baltic, torture was abolished, and Poland was granted a constitution. Alexander planned to transform Russia with the help of the 'unofficial committee', but he became disillusioned and abandoned his plans to abolish serfdom and the autocracy, and the plans of Count Mikhail Speransky for a constitution were not implemented. Under the influence of General Arakcheyev and Prince Aleksandr Golitsyn, Alexander carried out a number of increasingly reactionary policies, particularly in the field of education. At the time of his death a group of revolutionary liberals, later known as the Decembrists, infuriated by the tsar's policies, were planning an uprising. Abroad, Alexander formed the Holy Alliance with Austria and Prussia, gained part of the Caucasus, Finland and Bessarabia, and alternated between alliances with England and France. He fought the patriotic war of 1812 against Napoleon and played a key role at the Congress of Vienna (1814–15). Toward the end of his life he withdrew into seclusion. He was succeeded by his brother, Nicholas I.

ALEXANDER I, GRAND PRINCE OF BULGARIA (1857–1893). Son of Prince Henry of Hesse (Battenberg), Alexander was elected constitutional prince in 1879. He served with the Russian forces in the Russo–Turkish War (1877–78), the result of which was the autonomy of Bulgaria. In 1883 he restored the constitution to combat Russian influence. He was forced to abdicate in 1886 after the war with Serbia.

ALEXANDER II (1818–1881). Tsar of Russia 1855–81. Although conservative in outlook, Alexander implemented a series of great reforms in many spheres of life and was known as the Liberator. After much discussion, 10 million serfs and their families were emancipated in 1861, 1863, and 1866 (hence his nickname). The *zemstvo* system of local government was reformed in 1864, and the various *zemstva* made a valuable contribution to public health and education. The municipal government was also reformed in 1864, with the judiciary becoming a separate part of the government and losing its air of secrecy, and he encouraged railway construction and banking. In 1874 military service was reorganised and the length of service reduced. There were a number of peasant revolts, however, and a series of mysterious fires in St Petersburg and in towns by the Volga, while the radical populist group grew and increased its activity.

Abroad, Alexander dealt with the Polish uprising of 1863, finally conquered the North Caucasus, liberated Bulgaria from Turkey in 1878, and presided over the Russian expansion in Central Asia. Before being able to implement a new constitution, he was assassinated in St Petersburg in 1881 by a terrorist bomb thrown at his coach.

ALEXANDER III (1845–1894). Tsar of Russia 1881–94, Alexander III wished above all to curb changes introduced by Alexander II and to suppress revolts and strengthen the autocracy. His repressive policies were influenced by Constantine Pobedonostsev, and to a lesser extent by Dmitry Tolstoy and Ivan Delyanov. As a result of the Temporary Regulations of 1881, officials had the power to search, exile, and try by courts-martial any who were considered to be a threat to state security. National minorities such as Poles, Georgians, Armenians and Finns were russified, while restrictions were placed on the Jews; from 1881 pogroms occurred, and pressure was applied to all who were not of the Orthodox faith. Restrictions on the peasants were introduced; the post of *zemstvo* chief was created in 1880; the *zemstvo* chief, a member of the gentry, had direct bureaucratic and judicial power over his group of peasants. The State Gentry Bank, founded in 1885, further consolidated the position of the gentry. Counter reforms were also implemented in town government and in the *zemstvo* system, and the electorate decreased. University autonomy was abolished, as was higher education for women. A protectionist economic policy encouraged the rapid growth of industrialisation; he consolidated Russian colonisation in Central Asia, authorising the building of the Trans-Siberian Railway, and formed an alliance with France. He died a natural death although there were several assassination attempts. He was succeeded by his son, Nicholas II.

ALEXANDRA FEDOROVNA (1872–1918). Tsaritsa of Russia. Alexandra was born a princess of Hesse-Darmstadt and was a granddaughter of Queen Victoria. She married Nicholas II of Russia in 1894. She was deeply pious and her belief in the powers of Rasputin to cure the young tsarevich of haemophilia brought her under Rasputin's disastrous domination and encouraged her to exert a nefarious political influence, much resented by the tsar's ministers and the population at large. After the 1917 Revolution she was shot at Ekaterinberg along with her husband and children.

ALEXIS (1690–1718). Russian prince. The son and heir of Tsar Peter I (the Great). He took part in the siege of Narva (1704) and married Princess Sophia Charlotte of Brunswick-Wolfenbüttel in 1711. Alexis opposed the reforms of his father. Their relationship progressively worsened and he fled to Vienna (1716) and later to Naples. Peter induced him to return, promising a full pardon, but condemned him to death for treason. He died from the effects of torture in the Peter-Paul Fortress while awaiting execution. His son became tsar as Peter II.

ALEXIS I MIKHAILOVICH (1629–1676). Tsar (1645–76), known as the Quiet One and as The Most Gentle Tsar. Alexis succeeded Michael Romanov, the first Romanov tsar. Viewed by some as the epitome of Muscovite culture and as a pioneer of interest in the West, he relied heavily on advisers, in particular on Boris Morisov and Prince Elijah Miloslavsky. Alexis debased the coinage in 1656 in an attempt to solve financial problems, but this led to inflation and a number of revolts, including the copper coin riot of 1662. Among other revolts during his reign were the Cossack and peasant rebellion in Ukraine (1624–38) and the celebrated uprising led by Stenka Razin in 1670. Other important events in Alexis's reign were the granting of the new legal code (*Ulozheniye*) of 1649, which remained in force until the early nineteenth century and which favoured the landowners and confirmed peasant serfdom, and a permanent schism in the Orthodox Church. He fought Poland (1654–67) and Sweden (1656–61) and won Ukraine for Russia. By his second wife he was the father of Peter I (the Great).

ANASTASIA (ANASTASIYA NIKOLAYEVNA) (1901–1918). Grand duchess and youngest daughter of Tsar Nicholas II. It was assumed that she had been murdered with the rest of the Russian royal family at Ekaterinberg (1918) until a German citizen named Anna Anderson claimed to be Anastasia (1929). Anderson died in 1984, but in 1994 scientists were trying to solve this mystery after nine skeletons were exhumed near Ekaterinberg in 1990.

ANDREYEV, LEONID NIKOLAEVICH (1871–1919). Novelist, short-story writer and playwright. Born in Orel, he studied law in St Petersburg and Moscow and graduated as a lawyer. To support himself he painted portraits, having given up the law when he lost his first case. In the first ten years of the twentieth century he became one of the most popular writers in Russia and for the first five years was close to Gorky and his literary milieu. During World War I he was violently anti-German and pro-war. He was against the October Revolution and died in exile in Finland. All his major works, and a great many secondary ones, have been translated into English, including *The Seven that were Hanged* (1909) and *The Red Laugh* (1905).

ANNA LEOPOLDOVNA (KARLOVNA) (1718–1746). Duchess of Brunswick-Wolfenbüttel and regent of Russia (1740–41). She was the granddaughter of Ivan V and the daughter of Charles Leopold, duke of Mecklenburg-Schwerin, and of Catherine, sister of Tsarina Anne Ivanovna. She married the prince of Brunswick-Wolfenbüttel, and their son Tsar Ivan VI succeeded Anne.

ANNE IVANOVNA (1693–1740). Empress of Russia (1730–40). The youngest daughter of Ivan V and the niece of Peter I (the Great), Anne married (1710) Frederich William, duke of Courland, who died the following year. She was elected to become empress by the Supreme Privy Council on the condition that she accept a number of provisions curtailing her powers. In practice, on ascending the throne she abolished the Supreme Privy Council and became an autocrat, establishing a reign of terror; at least 20,000 people were banished to Siberia. Her administration was run by her German favourite, Ernst Johann Biron. Azov was recaptured in the Russo–Turkish War (1736–39) during her reign.

APRAKSIN, COUNT FEDOR MATVEYEVICH (1671–1728). Naval commander and creator of the Russian navy, he was a life-long friend of Peter I (the Great). In 1700 he was made governor of Azov and was also put in charge of shipbuilding and the construction of naval installations. He defeated the Swedish attempt on St Petersburg in 1708 and was created a count in 1709 for his services. In 1713 he won Russia's first naval victory against Sweden at Hangö, and in 1721 he concluded the Treaty of Nystad with Sweden. He was tried three times for embezzlement and each time was punished with heavy fines.

APRAKSIN, COUNT STEPAN FEDOROVICH (1702–1758). General, and nephew of Count Fedor Matveyevich Apraksin. He was commander-in-chief of the Russian army during the Seven Years' War and defeated the Prussians at the battle of Gross Jagersdorf in 1757. He died in prison, having fallen out of favour.

ARAKCHEYEV, COUNT ALEXEY ANDREYEVICH (1769–1834). Soldier and statesman. He was a stern and conservative adviser to Tsar Paul I and Tsar Alexander I and minister of war (1808–10). He virtually ruled Russia during Alexander's frequent absences abroad. This period of Russian history was known as the *Arakcheyevshchina*.

AUGUSTUS II THE STRONG (1670–1733). King of Poland and elector of Saxony (known as Frederick Augustus I of Saxony). He succeeded to the electorship in 1697 having renounced Protestantism and become a Roman Catholic in the previous year. He regained Poland's former provinces of Podolia and Ukraine. He joined with Russia and Denmark against Sweden and began the Great Northern War (1700–21). Russia defeated Sweden but Augustus was defeated, and deposed by the Polish Diet. He was restored to the throne by Peter I (the Great) in 1710. In 1716–17 Russia once again intervened between Augustus and the Polish nobles and in 1720 annexed Livonia. Augustus at last acknowledged

Russia's influence in Poland. However, he was unable to re-establish a strong monarchy, and the court was known as the most dissolute in Europe. At his death, Poland was no longer a major European power and had become a protectorate of Russia.

AXELROD, PAVEL BORISOVICH (1850–1928). Leader of the Mensheviks together with Yuly Martov and Fedor Dan. Axelrod's two-part essay in *Iskra* (1903–04), which expounded the differences between the two factions within a Marxist party, incurred the anger of Lenin.

BAGRATION, PRINCE PETER IVANOVICH (1765–1812). Russian soldier of Georgian and Armenian extraction, descended from the Bagratids, a noble Georgian family. He entered the Russian army in 1783 and served against the French revolutionary and Napoleonic armies in Italy, Switzerland, and Austria, and against Turkey in 1809. He commanded the second Russian army against Napoleon during the advance on Moscow in 1812 and was killed at the Battle of Borodino. Nicholas I erected a monument to his memory on the site of the battle. The town of Bagrationovsk is named in his honour.

BAKUNIN, MICHAEL ALEKSANDROVICH (1814–1876). Anarchist. An aristocrat who, for a short time, served in the army; he left Russia in 1840. In 1848 he was sentenced to death after taking part in a rising at Dresden, and was handed over to the Russian authorities and imprisoned. He was exiled to Siberia in 1857 but escaped and reached England in 1861 and worked with Aleksandr Herzen. He was involved in the uprisings in Lyons (1870) and in Spain (1873). His life was then spent in a struggle with Karl Marx to decide upon the form that socialist doctrine should take. The anarchists were defeated and Bakunin was expelled from the International at the Hague Congress in 1872. His book *God and the State* (1882) called for militant atheism and the destruction of the state.

BARCLAY DE TOLLY, PRINCE MIKHAIL BOGDANOVICH (1761–1818). Field marshal of Scottish descent. He entered the Russian army in 1786 and was commander in Finland (1808–09) and is famous for his march across the ice of the Gulf of Bothnia and his capture of Umeo. He was minister of war (1810–13), and commanded one of the two armies operating against Napoleon in 1812, but his strategy of retreat and his defeat at Smolensk (17–18 August 1812) caused dissatisfaction in the country. He was replaced as commander by Kutuzov, but after Kutuzov's death in 1813 he again took command and achieved distinction at Leipzig and at the capture of Paris. He is described by some as the real architect of Napoleon's defeat in the 1812 campaign. He was created prince and field marshal in 1815.

BARYATINSKY, PRINCE ALEKSANDR IVANOVICH (1814–1879). Commander of Russian troops who distinguished himself in the Caucasus campaigns beginning in 1857. He defeated and captured Shamil at Gunib in 1859, thus completing the Russian conquest of the northern mountain peoples.

BEKBULATOVICH, SIMEON (16th century). A Tatar, and a descendant of Genghis Khan. He was appointed Tsar and Great Prince of All Rus by Ivan IV (the Terrible). He ruled from 1575 to 1576, signing documents under his own name and seal while Ivan lived as a boyar. He was subsequently dethroned when Ivan, tired of obscurity, resumed the tsardom. Simeon was pensioned off and made Grand Prince of Tver.

BEKOVICH-CHERKASSY, PRINCE ALEKSANDR (?–1717). In 1711 he was sent as a diplomat to Karbada by Peter I (the Great). He later worked to bring together the peoples of the Caucasus with the Russian people and then forged links with Persia. After exploring the Caspian Sea, he drew the first map of it in 1715. He was fatally wounded en route to Khin, where he had intended to search for gold and subjugate the khan.

BELL, JOHN (1691–1780). Scottish traveller and physician. Bell set out for St Petersburg in 1714, joining an embassy there before going to Persia. He returned to St Petersburg four years later, then spent the following four years in an embassy to China, passing through Siberia and Mongolia. Peter I (the Great) summoned Bell in 1722 to accompany him on his voyage to Derbent and the Caspian Gates. He visited Constantinople on a mission, after which he settled there before returning to his estate in Antermony. Bell's *Travels from St Petersburg in Russia to Various Parts of Asia* (1763) provided a vivid picture of life in Russia.

BENCKENDORFF, COUNT ALEKSANDR KHRISTOFOROVICH (1783–1844). General, statesman, chief of police, and suppressor of liberal thought, Benckendorff was a member of the band of officers who murdered Emperor Paul in 1801. He then directed his attention to a predominantly military career and was commandant of Moscow after Napoleon's retreat, distinguishing himself time and time again. In 1819 Benckendorff was aide-de-camp to Tsar Alexander I, and in 1825 commanded the troops that put down the Decembrists. He then took measures against any Russian noble families that had been connected with the Decembrists. In 1826 he was chief of the gendarmerie and the Third Section of the Imperial Chancery.

BENNIGSEN, COUNT LEVIN AUGUST VON (1745–1826). German soldier. Joining the Russian army in 1773 he played a part in the assassination of Paul I in 1801. During the Napoleonic war he commanded the Russian centre at the battle of Borodino (1812) and defeated Joachim Murat at Tarutino (1812). He also fought at the battle of Leipzig (1813), leading one of the victorious columns. Tsar Alexander I made Bennigsen a count in the field.

BERING, VITUS JONASSEN (1681–1741). Danish navigator who joined the newly formed fleet of Peter I (the Great) in 1703. In 1724 he was appointed by the tsar to direct the first Kamchatka expedition, which was to investigate whether there was a land connection between America and Asia. After building the ship, Bering set sail and named the Diomede Islands in the middle of the strait. In 1741 he again set sail, with 600 others, and eventually landed in the Gulf of Alaska. Worn out and suffering from scurvy, he went ashore on Bering Island, where he died, together with 19 of his crew. Capt. Cook confirmed his discoveries.

BESTUZHEV, ALEKSANDR ALEKSANDROVICH (1797–1837). Writer and Decembrist. He was co-editor with Ryleyev of the *Polar Star*. In 1829 Bestuzhev was transferred to the Caucasus as a private soldier, where he was recommended for the St George's Cross and where he wrote his best novels. He was charged with the murder of his mistress and, although the inquest could not prove his guilt, lost all interest in life. In 1837 he was savagely killed by the Circassians at the storming of Adler on the Black Sea coast.

BESTUZHEV-RYUMIN, COUNT ALEKSEY PETROVICH (1693–1766). Grand chancellor of Russia. Bestuzhev-Ryumin was sent to Copenhagen as Russian minister in 1721 and it was not until 1740 that he was summoned back to Russia by Ernst Johann Biron. Appointed vice-chancellor by the empress, Elizabeth, for the following sixteen years, he was in charge of the foreign policy of Russia. Despite his successful handling of the war of the Austrian succession, he was arrested and condemned to death, accused of engaging in treasonous activities. The sentence was commuted to banishment to his estates. When Catherine II (the Great) came to the throne (1762) she recalled him and appointed him as a field marshal, but he never had any further leading role in public affairs.

BIBIKOV, DMITRY GAVRILOVICH (1792–1870). Bibikov was appointed military governor of Kiev in 1837 and was minister of internal affairs from 1852 to 1855. He pursued a policy designed to strengthen the autocracy, and, wishing to russify Ukraine, replaced local clerks with Russians and altered the laws regarding the Polish gentry.

BIRON (BÜHREN), ERNST JOHANN, DUKE OF COURLAND (1690–1772). German favourite of Tsaritsa Anne Ivanovna (1730–40). Having been expelled from the Academy of Königsberg for misbehaviour in 1714, Biron went to Russia, and his influence over Anne grew steadily. In 1727 he became her lover and was made grand chamberlain and count; indeed was the real ruler of Russia. He was extremely unpopular owing to his vindictive and corrupt character but did, in fact, reform the country's administration. He was regent for three weeks after Anne's death, but was deposed and banished to Siberia. Peter III, however, permitted him to return to St Petersburg.

BLUDOV, DMITRY NIKOLAYEVICH (1785–1864). Civil servant under Nicholas I and a minor writer. In 1832 Bludov was minister of foreign affairs, from 1837 to 1839 minister of justice, in 1855 president of the St Petersburg Academy of Science, and in 1862 president of the state council and committee of ministers.

BRESHKO-BRESHKOVSKAYA, EKATERINA KONSTANTINOVNA (1844–1934). Revolutionary, often called the Grandmother of the Russian Revolution. As a result of her work as a member of the Socialist Revolutionary Party, Breshko-Breshkovskaya spent years in prison and in exile. After the Bolshevik Revolution she emigrated to Prague.

CATHERINE I (YEKATERINA ALEXEYEVNA) (1684–1727). Empress of Russia and consort and successor to Peter I (the Great). After the death of her mother, a Lithuanian peasant, Marta Skowronska (as she was then called), worked as a servant for Pastor Glück before marrying a Swedish dragoon. She was captured as a Russian prisoner of war and sold to Prince A. D. Menshikov, at whose house she became the lover of Tsar Peter I (the Great). Marta was received into the Orthodox Church in 1703 and rechristened Yekaterina Alexeyevna. Catherine was officially married to Peter in 1712 as his second wife, and she was crowned empress-consort in the Uspensky cathedral in 1724. She was declared empress regent in 1725 after Peter's death, and established the Supreme Privy Council the following year. She was succeeded by Peter's grandson, Peter II.

CATHERINE II (THE GREAT) (1729–1796). Empress of Russia from 1762. The daughter of Prince Christian of Anhalt-Zerbst (in Prussia), she was born in Stettin and was originally named Sophie Augusta Frederika of Anhalt-Zerbst. She entered the Orthodox Church in 1744, and married the future tsar, Peter III, in 1745. Although she hated her degenerate and feeble-minded husband, Catherine realised that her marriage to him could be a path to power. Their only child was the future Paul I (born 1754). Peter became tsar in 1762, but six months later a military coup led by Grigory Orlov and Prince Grigory Potemkin deposed him, and he was murdered some days later. Intelligent and ambitious, Catherine took the throne. Rather than acting as regent for her son she proclaimed herself ruler. In her zeal for self-education she read and corresponded with Voltaire and the Encyclopedists and practised and patronised art and literature. However, she ruled as an enlightened despot, but a despot nonetheless, never forgetting her political dependence on the nobility and gentry who had set her on the throne. She abolished capital punishment, except for political crimes, and prepared comprehensive schemes of administrative, legal and educational reform, but little was actually accomplished during her reign. The military and economic burdens on the peasantry grew worse and the number of serfs increased. Her domestic policy became increasingly repressive following the revolt (1773–75) led by Yemelyan Pugachev, a pretender who claimed to be her dead husband Peter III. She pursued an imperialist foreign policy and, in two wars with Turkey (1768–72 and 1787–92), expanded her territories near the Black Sea and annexed the Crimea. Ukraine was fully absorbed, and when Poland was obliterated by the three partitions of 1772, 1793, and 1795, Russia took the largest share.

CATHERINE IVANOVNA (1684–1727). Duchess of Mecklenburg. She was the daughter of Tsar Ivan V, but was considered ineligible to ascend the throne because she had married an alien.

CHARLES XII (1682–1718). King of Sweden (1697–1718), son of Charles XI. In the Great (Second) Northern War Charles defeated the Russians at Narva in 1700. In 1707 his troops left Saxony to invade Russia. Although Sweden won the Battle of Holowczyn the following year, Charles was forced to march on Ukraine instead of Moscow, as had been planned. By 1709 Charles had the choice of withdrawing to Poland or fighting the Russians. The Swedes attacked the Russian fortified camp at Poltava and were forced to surrender. This marked the birth of the great expansion of the Russian Empire. Charles spent the following five years in exile in Turkey, returning to Swedish Pomerania in 1714. He was killed by a sniper's bullet at the beginning of an invasion of Norway in 1718.

CHEKHOV, ANTON PAVLOVICH (1860–1904). Dramatist and short-story writer. He was born at Taganrog on the Sea of Azov, grandson of a liberated serf and son of a shopkeeper. He was educated at the gymnasium there, then went to Moscow to study medicine. Chekhov began writing for comic newspapers while a student in order to supplement his family's meagre income. His collected stories, published in 1886, were warmly received by the public, and also by the editor of the daily paper *Novoye Vremya*, Aleksey Suvorin, who invited him to contribute stories for publication. In 1890 Chekhov visited the penal colony of Sakhalin Island, and his report on it, *Sakhalin Island* (1891), is alleged to have influenced reforms in prisons, which were introduced in 1892.

Having settled with his family at Melikhovo in 1891 he wrote many of his finest stories there. He also spent time and money on local improvements, including working as head of a sanitary district during the cholera epidemic, 1892–93. Consumption forced him to spend the rest of his life on the southern coast of the Crimea and at foreign health resorts. Owing to his left-wing political views he broke with Suvorin. His short stories are rich in suggestion, evoking moods in an economical way, and often contain a poignant blend of humour with sadder aspects of life.

CONSTANTINE NIKOLAEVICH, GRAND DUKE (1827–1892). Second son of Nicholas I. He served in the navy, becoming an admiral (1851) and minister of marine (1855). He commanded the Baltic fleet during the Crimean War, and the Russian navy changed from sail to steam during his period of office. He cooperated with the reforms of his brother Alexander II; but retired from public life on the accession of Alexander III.

DAGMAR, PRINCESS MARY (MARIA FEDOROVNA) (1847–1928). Daughter of King Christian IX of Denmark and sister of Queen Alexandra of Great Britain. She was bethrothed to Nicholas, heir of Tsar Alexander II, but Nicholas died at the age of twenty-two before succeeding to the throne. His brother, the future Tsar Alexander III, married her in his stead in 1866. Later, as dowager empress, she retained considerable influence over her son, Tsar Nicholas II.

DASHKOVA, PRINCESS CATHERINE ROMANOVNA VORONTSOVA (1743–1810). Princess, author and patron of literary arts in Russia during the eighteenth century, she belonged to an influential family, her uncle being chancellor under Tsaritsa Elizabeth and her sister the mistress of Peter III, husband of Catherine II (the Great). In 1759 she married Prince Mikhail Ivanovich Dashkov. After Tsaritsa Elizabeth's death in 1762 Princess Dashkova was associated with the plans to overthrow Peter III and to make Catherine regent for her son Paul. She also took part in the plans to place Catherine on the throne in 1762.

Princess Dashkova travelled and lived much in Europe, but in 1783 she was appointed by Catherine the Great to direct the St Petersburg Academy of Arts and Sciences. In September 1783 she became first president of the Russian Academy, which compiled a Russian dictionary under her supervision and influence. Her other literary activities included editing a journal and writing plays.

Following the death of Catherine and the accession of Paul, Princess Dashkova was forced to retire and was banished to her estates near Novgorod. When Alexander I became tsar she was allowed to live just outside Moscow. Her memoirs were published in England in 1840 and in Russia in 1859.

DELYANOV, IVAN (1818–1897). He was appointed head of the Ministry of Education by Alexander III in 1882. A supporter of autocracy and opposed to revolutionaries, he nonetheless continued Dmitry Tolstoy's education policies, keeping a tight control on education and exercising discipline. In 1887 he issued a circular which appealed to his subordinates to keep socially undesirable elements or 'children of coachmen, servants, cooks, washerwomen, small shopkeepers, and persons of similar type' out of the classical gymnasiums, which were the only places of secondary education from which one could advance to a university.

DIDEROT, DENIS (1713–1784). French man of letters and philosopher, chief editor of the French *Encyclopédie*. After publication, the first three volumes of his monumental work were very quickly translated into Russian, with the work supervised by the Director of Moscow University. The completion in 1772 left Diderot without any source of income; on learning of this, Catherine II (the Great) bought his library and appointed him librarian on an annual salary for the duration of his life, asking him to keep the books until she needed them. Diderot went to St Petersburg in 1773 to thank her, staying five months and being received with honour and warmth. He wrote *Plan d'une université pour le gouvernement de Russie* (published 1813–14) for Catherine. However, he soon became disillusioned with Russia's enlightened despotism, as can be gleaned from his *Observations sur les instructions de sa majesté impériale au députés* (1774).

DIEBITSCH, COUNT HANS FRIEDRICH ANTON (IVAN TVANOVICH DIBICH ZABALKANSKIY) (1785–1831). Field marshal. German-born and educated in Berlin, he joined the Russian army in 1801 and was chiefly responsible for the Russian victory in the Russo–Turkish War (1828–29), owing to his Balkan campaigns. He fought in the Napoleonic Wars, acquiring the rank of major general, and in 1815 he was present at the Congress of Vienna and subsequently became adjutant general to Alexander I. Diebitsch was appointed chief of the Russian general staff in 1824, helped to suppress the Decembrist uprising (1825), and from 1826 to 1832 served on a secret committee formed by Nicholas I to examine programmes for administrative and social reform.

He was made commander of the Russian forces in Europe in 1829 and inflicted three serious defeats on the Turks (at Silistria, at the Kamchyk River near Varna, and at Burgas). A fourth battle at Sliven ensued and Adrianople was forced to capitulate, precipitating the conclusion of the peace treaty of Adrianople. For his successful campaigning Diebitsch was made a field marshal and given the name Zabalkanskiy ('crosser of the Balkans') to commemorate his march across the Balkans. He died of cholera while leading the Russian army suppressing the Polish insurrection of 1830–31.

DMITRIEVA, ELIZABETH (1851–1910). Russian-French socialist. The daughter of a Russian nobleman, she married an army officer in order to attend university in Switzerland. There she met other Russian radicals. She went to London and as a member of the Socialist International became a friend of Karl Marx. When she left England for Paris she sent him detailed analyses and descriptions of events in 1870. During the Commune of 1871 she organised the Women's Union for the Defence of Paris as a branch of the Socialist International. When the communards were defeated, she escaped and returned to Russia, where she married a political prisoner who had been condemned to exile in Siberia, and lived there until her death.

DMITRY, FALSE. Name of three pretenders to the Muscovite throne during the Time of Troubles. All three claimed to be Dmitry, son of Ivan IV (the Terrible, ruled 1533–84), who had died under mysterious circumstances in 1591 while still a boy.

Fedor I (ruled 1584–98) was the last of the Rurik dynasty and was succeeded by his brother-in-law, Boris Godunov, during whose rule the first False Dmitry appeared and claimed the throne. Thought by many historians to have been Gregory Otrepev, one of the Russian gentry who had been a friend of the Romanovs before becoming a monk, the first False Dmitry seems to have believed that he was who he claimed to be. He pursued his claim in Moscow (1601–02) but fled to Lithuania when threatened with exile. In 1603 he sought armed assistance from Lithuanian and Polish nobles and from the Jesuits, and in 1604 he marched on Russia. Although he was defeated, when Boris died (1605) the government decided to support the pretender and he was proclaimed tsar. Dmitry enjoyed considerable support until he began to favour Polish friends, disregarding the traditions and customs of the Muscovite court. When he planned a Christian alliance to drive the Turks from Europe, Vasily Shuysky, one of the boyars, led a coup against him in 1606, murdered him, and became tsar himself.

In August 1607 a second pretender appeared claiming to be the recently murdered tsar; although quite unlike the first Dmitry in appearance, he attracted a large body of supporters and gained control of southern Russia. In spring 1608, he established a base, including a full court and government administration, at Tushino (hence his nickname, Thief of Tushino). His troops ravaged northern Russia, and his authority soon rivalled that of Shuysky, who, in 1610, forced the pretender to flee to Kaluga. While there the second Dmitry continued to press his claims until fatally wounded (October 1610) by one of his own followers.

In March 1611 a third False Dmitry, identified as a deacon named Sidorka, laid claims to the throne; he gained the support of the Cossacks (1612), who were laying waste to the environs of Moscow, and of the people of Pskov (from which he is called Thief of Pskov), but was betrayed and executed.

DOLGORUKIY, PRINCE VASILIY LUKICH (1670–1739). Diplomat. He was ambassador to Denmark (1707–20) and later minister in Paris (1720–22). He was also a member of the Supreme Privy Council and on the death of Peter II he was in favour of the conditions that would have transferred much of the monarch's power to the nobles. He was beheaded, together with others of his family, for forging Peter II's will.

DOLGORUKIY, PRINCE VASILIY VLADIMORIVCH (1667–1746). Field marshal. Dolgorukiy was responsible for the suppression of the mutiny of Bulavin and for this he gained the confidence of Peter I (the Great). Later he opposed many of the tsar's reforms and was deprived of his rank and title by Peter because of intrigue, but was subsequently reinstated. Dolgorukiy supported the accession of Ivanovna and helped to compile the conditions for her to gain the throne. He was again deprived of his rank and title, but in 1741 Empress Elizabeth restored these and he was made president of the War College.

DOSTOYEVSKY, FEDOR MIKHAILOVICH (1821–1881). Russian novelist and one of the most influential writers in European literature. In 1839 his father, a Moscow doctor, was murdered by his serfs at his country home, and this event haunted Dostoyevsky all his life. He studied at the Military Engineering College at St Petersburg but resigned (1844) to take up a literary career. His first novel, *Poor Folk* (1846), achieved considerable success. Disaster overtook him when he was arrested in 1849 on a charge of sedition (on the flimsiest of grounds) and condemned to be shot; he was already facing a firing squad when a reprieve arrived. He had to endure four years as a convict and two years of exile in Siberia, an experience that undermined his health and that he described in his *Memoirs from the House of the Dead* (1861). While in Siberia he contracted an unhappy marriage, which ended in 1863 on the death of his wife. On his return from his exile in 1855 he engaged for some years in journalistic enterprises that failed and left him deeply in debt, a state aggravated by his passion for gambling. In 1865 he travelled to Germany with a young woman, Polina Suslova, to retrieve his fortune by a supposedly infallible method of winning at roulette. This, of course, failed, so on his return he set about writing a potboiler to satisfy his creditors (*The Gambler*). He hired a stenographer, Anna Snitkina, and shortly afterward married her. They again had to go abroad to avoid creditors, a humiliating time for Dostoyevsky, but his wife gradually restored order to his finances and they returned to Russia. In his later years he evolved a peculiar Slavophilism compounded of hatred for aristocrats and socialists alike, and of religious obsessions. Passionately interested in religion, he shows in his work a preoccupation with good and evil and the search for God. A naturalistic writer, acclaimed by Vissarion Belinsky, he was particularly interested in the psychology of the abnormal because he believed that through a study of abnormality he would come to understand the true nature of man. His attitude toward his characters is one of great compassion. Even in his lifetime he won recognition both inside and outside Russia as a great novelist.

DUBBELT, GENERAL LEONTIY VASILYEVICH (1792–1862). Soldier and police chief under Nicholas I. He was in charge of the Third Section and created the renowned Gendarmerie. Dubbelt fought at the Battle of Borodino and survived being under suspicion during the investigations following the Decembrist conspiracy. On retiring from the army he was appointed to the new Corps of Gendarmes, the executive arm of the Third Section.

DURNOVO, PYOTR NIKOLAYEVICH (1844–1915). Politician. Minister of the interior under Nicholas II, he replaced General Dmitry Trepov and was largely responsible for the downfall of Sergey Witte, to whom he owed his post. His measures to quash the 1905 Revolution were ruthless and harsh. His successor as minister of the interior was Pyotr Stolypin.

ELIZABETH PETROVNA (1709–1762). Empress of Russia (1741–62). Daughter of Peter I (the Great) by his second wife, Catherine I. She acceded to the throne having overthrown the infant emperor Ivan VI and his regent Empress Anne, with the assistance of the Preobrazhenskiy Guards. Elizabeth never married; she took the duties of government seriously and attempted to carry on the policies of her father. She abolished the death penalty, was one of the founders of Moscow University (1755), built the Winter Palace in St Petersburg, and introduced French culture to the court. The Treaty of Abo concluded the war she started with Sweden (1741–43), but her dislike of Frederick II (the Great) caused her to join the Franco-Austrian alliance and plunged Russia into the Seven Years' War. She was succeeded by her nephew, Peter III, who was an admirer of Frederick and withdrew Russia from the war.

EUDOXIA (EVDOKHIYA FEDOROVNA LOPUKHINA) (1669–1731). Tsaritsa and first wife of Peter I (the Great). She and Peter were married when they were both seventeen, Peter's mother hoping that the marriage would make the youthful tsar abandon his wild and libertine behaviour. The marriage was not a success; the tsaritsa was unintelligent and had little in common with Peter. In 1698 he forced her to take the veil and sent her to a monastery for having sympathised with the *streltsy* rebellion that year. Although she had taken vows, she later reversed her decision and left the monastery soon afterward. She entered into a liaison with Stepan Glebov, but did not assist her son, the tsarevich Alexis, with his flight to Austria in 1716. Alexis was tried for treason in 1718 and Eudoxia was imprisoned in a fortress on Lake Ladoga. In 1727 she was freed and officially rehabilitated by her grandson, Peter II, on his accession and installed in the Uspensky convent. Following his death in 1730 she made a half-hearted and unsuccessful attempt for the throne.

FALCONET, ÉTIENNE MAURICE (1716–1791). French sculptor who worked under the patronage of Madame de Pompadour at Bellevue. Through the influence of Denis Diderot he was employed by Catherine II (the Great) in St Petersburg (1766–78), where he executed the bronze equestrian statue of Peter I (the Great) situated in Decembrists' Square. The plaster cast was completed in 1779 and the finished statue weighed 16 tons. The block of granite weighing 1,600 tons on which the statue stands came from the village of Lasht, and was manœuvred the seven miles to St Petersburg by 500 men taking five weeks. The statue was unveiled in August 1782. Nicknamed 'The Bronze Horseman', it shows Peter reining-in his horse on the brink of a rock, and was the subject of a poem by Pushkin in 1832. The pedestal bears the inscription PETRO PRIMO CATHARINA SECUNDA MDCCLXXXII on one side and the same in Russian on the opposite side.

FEDOR I (1557–1598). Tsar of Russia from 1584, and third son of Ivan IV (the Terrible). Somewhat feebleminded, he was tsar in name only; Russia was at this time governed by Boris Godunov. Fedor was the last member of the house of Rurik to be tsar.

FEDOR II (1589–1605). Tsar of Russia April–June 1605. The son of Boris Godunov, Fedor was proclaimed tsar on his father's death. His mother, however, attempted to take charge of matters, and aroused the fury of the boyars, the powerful Russian aristocracy, who murdered both Fedor and his mother.

FEDOR III (1661–1682). Educated by Simeon of Potolsk, and tsar of Russia 1676–82. I. M. Yazykov and Alexis Likhachev virtually ruled on his behalf, because of his health and youth, and from 1681 Vasily Vasilyevich Golitsyn was highly influential. *Mestnichestvo*, the system by which appointments of court officials, ambassadors and army officials depended on inherited rank and status, was finally abolished during Fedor's reign.

GAPON, FATHER GEORGI APOLLONOVICH (1870–1906). Priest and police-agent. He believed in police socialism and in 1903 founded the Assembly of Russian Factory and Mill Workers in St Petersburg, which was financed by police funds. A strike at the Putilov works in St Petersburg, which began because of alleged victimisation of assembly members, soon spread. Gapon decided to make an appeal to the tsar. He promoted a petition that was revolutionary in its demands and organised an illegal march to the Winter Palace. After giving warning to disperse, the police fired on the 200,000 demonstrators, killing at least 200 of them; 9 January 1905 became known as Bloody Sunday and was the beginning of a year of revolutionary unrest. Gapon, however, was not trusted by his fellow revolutionaries and was murdered.

GODUNOV, BORIS FEDOROVICH (1551–1605). Tsar of Russia (from 1598). He rose to importance under Ivan IV (the Terrible); his sister, Irene, married Ivan's heir, the feebleminded Fedor. During Fedor's reign (1584–98) Boris acted as regent, and after his death, which ended the established dynasty, the *Zemskii Sobor* elected Godunov tsar. His reign inaugurated the Time of Troubles, but he was an able if tyrannical ruler. He was suspected of the murder of the rightful heir, Fedor's younger brother, Dmitry, who had died mysteriously (1591). Boris was killed in suppressing a revolt during the advance on Moscow of a false claimant to the throne. His life is the theme of Mussorgsky's opera *Boris Godunov* and a play by Pushkin.

GOLITSYN, PRINCE ALEKSANDR NIKOLAYEVICH (1773–1844). Minister of education under Alexander I, his considerable influence at court continued into the days of Tsar Nicholas I. From 1813 he was president of the Russian Bible Association.

GOLITSYN, BORIS ALEKSEYEVICH (1654–1713). Russian statesman and tutor of Peter I (the Great). In 1683 Golitsyn was appointed head of the government department for the administration of the lower Volga region by the regent, Sophia Alekseyevna. In 1689 he directed the Naryshkin faction, which brought Peter to power. He helped with many of Peter's undertakings, although in 1697–98 he remained at home during Peter's trip abroad and acted as one of the triumvirate in charge. After taking harsh measures against the *streltsy* Golitsyn directed his attention to the lower Volga, ruling it despotically. He took monastic vows shortly before dying.

GOLITSYN, PRINCE DMITRY MIKHAILOVICH (1665–1737). Russian statesman. In 1704 Golitsyn commanded the auxiliary troops in Poland against Charles XII. He was governor-general of Kiev from 1715 to 1719, was made senator in 1719, and from 1719 to 1722 was president of the Kamer-Killegiia, a finance ministry created in 1718 by Peter I (the Great) to manage the state's income and estimate its expense. Golitsyn developed the concept of limiting the autocracy and drew up a constitution that Empress Anne Ivanovna was forced to sign. His career was marred by involvement in the disgrace of Vice-

Chancellor P. P. Shafirov. Golitsyn was arrested in 1736 and sentenced to death, ostensibly for his part in a conspiracy, but actually for his anti-monarchial views. The sentence was commuted to life imprisonment, but he died the following year.

GOLITSYN, PRINCE MIKHAIL MIKHAILOVICH (1675–1730). Soldier. An accomplished strategist, he was made a field marshal under Peter I (the Great). He fought in many battles against Sweden including the battle of Poltava. Later he was president of the War College (ministry), a senator, and member of the Supreme Privy Council.

GOLITSYN, PRINCE VASILY VASILYEVICH (1643–1714). Russian statesman in charge of foreign affairs prior to 1689. In 1682, under the rule of Tsar Fedor III, Golitsyn assisted in the reorganisation of military service and the abolition of *mestnichestvo*. Under the regent Sophia Aleksyevna, Golitsyn was principal minister and head of the foreign office. The outcome of his negotiations with Poland was successful, but his expeditions against the Crimean Tatars met with failure, as a result of which he was stripped of his rank and wealth and banished by Peter I (the Great).

GOLOVKIN, GAVRIL IVANOVICH (1660–1734). The first state chancellor of the Russian Empire. Golovkin accompanied Peter I (the Great) on his first tour of Western Europe. He was in charge of foreign affairs from 1706 and was made state chancellor at Poltava in 1709 and a count of the Russian Empire in 1710. Under Catherine I, Golovkin was a member of the Supreme Privy Council, and under Anne a member of the first Russian cabinet, which opposed suggestions for the limitation of the rights of the autocracy. However, illness prevented him from being politically active in Anne's reign.

GOLOVNIN, ALEKSANDR VASILYEVICH (1821–1886). Minister for education (1862–66). He had a relatively liberal outlook, and was responsible for the University Statute of 1863, which gave universities greater autonomy than before. He also introduced a statute for secondary education, which was officially accepted in 1864.

GOLOVNIN, VASILY MIKHAILOVICH (1776–1831). Navigator who explored the coasts of Kamchatka and Russian America (Alaska). He served in the British navy (1801–06), was captured by the Japanese (1811–13), and circumnavigated the world (1817–19). As vice-admiral, he was responsible for the construction of ships, including the first ten Russian steamships. His writings included *Journey Round the World* (1822) and *Narrative of My Captivity in Japan* (1816, trans. 1824).

GORCHAKOV, PRINCE ALEKSANDR MIKHAILOVICH (1798–1883). Statesman. Gorchakov's diplomatic career started in 1817. He was made an ambassador in 1854 after serving in embassies in various European capitals, and succeeded Count Nesselrode as foreign minister in 1856. As a result of his great success in this post, he was made chancellor in 1866 and was the most powerful minister in Europe until Bismarck. In the face of Bismarckian Germany, however, his popularity lessened in the 1870s, although in 1873 he played an important part in forming the Three Emperors' League. Although his influence in Russia's policy in the Balkan crisis (1875–78) was less considerable, he remains one of the most noteworthy diplomats of nineteenth-century Europe.

GORCHAKOV, PRINCE MIKHAIL (1793–1861). Military officer and statesman. Cousin of Prince Aleksandr Gorchakov. He served with distinction in the Napoleonic campaigns of 1812–14 and in 1853 became chief of staff of the army. He gained fame by his skilful and gallant defence of Sevastopol (1854–55) and was military governor of Poland from 1856 to 1861.

GORDON, PATRICK (1635–1699). Scottish soldier. He served in the Swedish-Polish wars (1655–60) fighting for each side in turn, then joined the Russian army in 1661. He became a friend of Peter I (the Great), helped the tsar to overthrow the regent, Sophia, in 1689 and to suppress the *streltsy* revolt of 1698, and rose to the rank of general. *Passages from the Diary of General Patrick Gordon of Auchleuchries* was published in 1859.

GOREMYKIN, IVAN LONGINOVICH (1839–1917). Minister of the interior under Nicholas II 1895–99, and chairman of the council of ministers 1906 and 1914–16. He was considered not to have taken enough action against Rasputin and was forced to resign.

GORKY, MAXIM (pen name of Aleksei Maksimovich Peshkov) (1868–1936). Novelist, playwright, and critic. His pen name is Russian for bitter. Gorky was orphaned as a child and wandered about Russia, receiving no formal education and holding various jobs. This period of his life is described by him in *Childhood* (1913), *My Apprenticeship* (1918), and *My Universities* (1923). Gorky first achieved fame in 1898 with his collected tales. His early writings tended toward romanticism, but later stories were often Chekhovian, and finally his work is a denunciation of capitalist society, *Mother* (1907) and *Klim Samgin* (1927–36) being examples of this. A supporter of the Bolsheviks, he lived the life of an émigré on Capri (1906–13) and established the Vpered faction with Aleksandr Alexandrovich Bogdanov. Following the February Revolution of 1917, Gorky set up the New Life group, a non-Bolshevik Left Social Democratic group. Opposed to the Bolshevik seizure of power, he nevertheless co-operated with them from 1919, although he lived in Italy from 1921 to 1928. After his return to the USSR he was a firm supporter of the Soviet régime and headed the Writers' Union from 1932. He was a close friend of Stalin and was proclaimed the founder of Socialist Realism. It is uncertain whether Gorky died from natural causes or whether his death was engineered by the anti-Soviet Bloc of Rightists and Trotskyists.

GRINEVITSKY, IVAN (1857–1881). He assassinated Alexander II on 13 March 1881 near the Winter Palace in St Petersburg. A group of Nihilists agreed to make an attempt on the tsar's life, but the first of their bombs was not successful. Grinevitsky's bomb achieved its aim but he himself was also killed.

GUCHKOV, ALEKSANDR IVANOVICH (1862–1936). Leader of the moderate liberals in Russia (1905–17). Founder and chairman of the Octobrists' party and president of the Third State Duma. In World War I he was chairman of the *duma* committee on military and naval affairs, and subsequently chairman of the non-governmental central war industries committee. He became the minister for war and navy in the provisional government. A critic of the imperial regime, in March 1917 he went to Pskov and formally received the abdication of Nicholas II. After the October Revolution he lived in Paris, engaging in anti-Communist activities.

GURKO, IOSIF VLADIMIROVICH (1829–1901). Field marshal who took a major part in the Russo–Turkish War of 1877–78. Having fought in the Crimean War (1854–56) and the suppression of the Polish uprising in 1863, he defeated the Turkish armies and occupied Sofia, Plovdiv, and Erdine, thus bringing the war to an end in 1878. From 1882 to 1883 Gurko was governor-general and military commander in Odessa. He then served in similar posts in Warsaw (1883–94), where he repressed Polish nationalistic tendencies and implemented a policy of russification in Poland. He was made a member of the imperial council in 1884.

HERZEN, ALEKSANDR IVANOVICH (1812–1870). Radical journalist and political thinker. An illegitimate child of an aristocrat, he disliked the social order of Russia and as a result of his association with a radical discussion group he was exiled (1834–42). His father, who died in 1846, left him a fortune and Herzen left Russia in 1847, never to return. He was much influenced by the Revolution of 1848 and set up the Free Russian Press in London, where he lived mainly, publishing *Kolokol* (The Bell 1857–67), the first Russian émigré journal, which had considerable influence inside Russia. His works include *Childhood, Youth and Exile*.

HUGHES, JOHN (1814–1889). A Welshman who in 1869 succeeded in obtaining a concession for a company to be called the New Russia Company. It produced coal, iron and rails. The mining settlement of Yuzovka, which was to become one of the great metallurgical cities in the world, is named after him.

HUMBOLDT, BARON VON (FRIEDRICH HEINRICH) ALEXANDER (1769–1859). German naturalist and traveller, known primarily for his work on the current off the west coast of South America now named after him. In 1829 Tsar Nicholas I of Russia invited him to journey to Central Asia, during which meteorological data and other information were tabulated and diamonds discovered in the gold mines of the Urals. As a result of Humboldt's efforts, the Russian government allowed a line of magnetic and meteorological stations to be established across northern Asia. He is considered a great representative of German scientific culture.

IGNATIEV, COUNT NIKOLAI PAVLOVICH (1832–1908). Diplomat and conservative politician. As envoy to China from 1859, he secured the Ussuri region for Russia by the Treaty of Peking (1860). In 1864 he became ambassador to Turkey, where his encouragement of nationalistic and Pan-Slavic feeling against the Ottoman Empire was partly responsible for the Bulgarian rebellion.

Having urged Russia to declare war on Turkey in 1877, he negotiated the concluding Treaty of San Stefano (1878); this would so greatly have strengthened Russian influence in the Balkans that it was immediately challenged by Great Britain and Austria–Hungary, and its terms were not implemented. As minister of the interior from 1881, he was active in promoting ultraconservative and Slavic nationalist policies. He was dismissed in June 1882.

IVAN IV, VASILYEVICH (THE TERRIBLE) (1530–1584). Tsar of Muscovy from 1533, he was crowned at the age of seventeen. His youth was dominated by the threats and conspiracies of the boyars. The early years of his reign, influenced by the good advice of the church and loyal boyars, and of his first wife Anastasia Romanova, were constructive and progressive. He called the first *Zemskii Sobor* in 1549, and this body approved reforms in the law and in local administration. In 1551 a church council took place that regulated and improved the church's position in the state. In 1550 and 1556 reforms were made in the army and in the military service owed by the gentry.

With improved forces Ivan succeeded in conquering the most important of Muscovy's traditional enemies, Kazan, Astrakhan, and the Livonian Order. He had by 1560 established the authority of the tsar, greatly strengthened the state, and established commercial relations with England.

The second half of his reign was characterised by extreme behaviour – uncontrollable rages, suspicion of the whole boyar class, and a harsh personal despotism. His deterioration was exacerbated by the death of Anastasia (1560) and his belief that she had been murdered. His withdrawal from the boyars and the church, and his insistence on personal control, found its most extreme form in the creation of the *oprichnina* parts of the state that were separately governed by officials directly under his control, *oprichniki*, who acted as his personal police and whose function it was to kill those whom he considered his enemies. The internal disintegration of the state coincided with pressure from its enemies in the Crimea and in the northwest where the Livonian war was revived, with Poland and Sweden joining forces against Muscovy.

In 1581 the tsar killed his son and heir Ivan in a fit of rage; the event appeared to finally destroy his mental balance. He was succeeded in 1584 by his surviving son Fedor.

IVAN V, ALEKSEYEVICH (1666–1696). Tsar of Russia (1682–96). Ivan was the younger son of Tsar Alexis by his first wife, and succeeded his brother Fedor III. Because he was an invalid and mentally retarded, it was agreed that Ivan should rule under the regency of his sister Sophia together with his half-brother Peter I (the Great). In 1689 the regency was overthrown; Ivan retained his title but never participated in government, and Peter became the effective ruler.

IVAN VI, ANTONOVICH (1740–1764). Tsar when still an infant, Ivan was the great-grandson of Ivan V and the son of Anne Leopoldovna and Prince Anthony of Brunswick-Bevern-Lüneburg. He succeeded his great-aunt, Tsaritsa Anne, under the regency of the Duke of Courland and then of his mother; she was an unpopular regent and was overthrown in favour of Elizabeth, daughter of Peter I (the Great), who became tsaritsa in 1741. Ivan's youth was spent in confinement and his psychological development remained that of a child. Vasily Mirovich, an army officer, tried to liberate him in 1764, but this threat to the new empress Catherine II (the Great) led to Ivan's murder by his guards.

IZVOLSKY, COUNT ALEKSANDR PETROVICH (1856–1919). Diplomat and minister. As foreign minister he concluded a treaty with Britain resolving Anglo–Russian disagreements in the Middle East, and in 1908 sought Austria's help in asserting Russia's right to use the Dardanelles. The resulting agreement strengthened Austria in the Balkans at Russia's expense and no aid was given in the Dardenelles question. Following this unsuccessful agreement, Izvolsky was dismissed in 1910 and transferred to Paris. He served there as the Russian Ambassador from 1910 to 1917, during which period he strengthened the military alliance between Russia and France.

JOHN OF KRONSTADT, FATHER (IVAN ILIYCH SERGEYEV) (1829–1909). Russian Orthodox priest. After his ordination he went to Kronstadt, where his sermons attracted large congregations from all classes of society and in his lifetime admirers started a cult of divine worship. He opposed the teachings of Lev Tolstoy and rejected all radical political reform, concentrating his work on the unskilled poor and establishing a centre for training in industrial skills.

JOHN III SOBIESKI (1624–1696). King of Poland (1674–96). A member of the nobility Sobieski was appointed field commander of the Polish army in 1666 and came to prominence through his victories against the Cossacks and Tatars. He was confirmed in popularity after a victory over the Turks in 1673; indeed his whole reign was spent campaigning against Turks and Tatar invaders. He was elected king in 1674. In 1686 he concluded a treaty (The Eternal Peace) with Russia, the traditional enemy of Poland, in order to secure Russian aid against Turkey.

JOSEPH II, HOLY ROMAN EMPEROR (1741–1790). German emperor. Son of Francis I and Maria Theresa he was elected Holy Roman Emperor after his father's death in 1765 but his mother limited his power until her death in 1780. Ally of Catherine II (the Great). He visited her twice and made two important agreements with her, the first of which was the tripartite partition of Poland in 1772 among Austria, Russia and Prussia. The second was an alliance sharing power in Eastern and South-eastern Europe between Austria and Russia. When Catherine declared war on Turkey in 1787 Joseph raised an army in support. His policy, however, was unpopular at home, and Austria withdrew from the war.

KAKHOVSKY, PYOTR GRIGOREVICH (1797–1826). Decembrist. He was active in all the preparations for the unsuccessful uprising of December 1825 and was responsible for killing Governor-General Mikhail Andreyevich Miloradovich. Kakhovsky was sentenced to death and hanged in July 1826.

KALEDIN, ALEKSEY MAKSIMOVICH (1861–1918). Cossack leader and soldier. He served from 1914 in command of a cavalry division, but opposed the military reforms of the provisional government and was forced to resign in 1917. He then returned to the Don region and was elected hetman of the Cossacks. He organised an anti-Bolshevik campaign, but suffered many defeats, including Taganrog, resigned and shot himself in February 1918.

KERENSKY, ALEXANDER FEDOROVICH (1881–1970). Statesman and lawyer. A moderate socialist, he was elected to the Fourth Duma in 1912–17 and there led the Labour group of socialist peasant members. He was a brave opponent of the tsarist government, and later joined the Socialist Revoutionary Party. During 1917 he held many government posts: minister of justice (February), minister of war and navy (May), and in July prime minister. As prime minister his aim was to continue the war against Germany, but this undermined his popularity. In November 1917 he was ousted by the Bolsheviks and thereafter lived in exile, first in France and then in Australia, and finally, from 1946, in the United States.

KNIPPER-CHEKOVA, OLGA (1870–1959). Russian actress. Born in Glazov, she made her debut in 1898 at the Moscow Art Theatre. She appeared in Chekov's plays as Arkadina in *The Seagull* (1898), Helena Andreyevna in *Uncle Vanya* (1899), Anna Petrovna in *Ivanov* (1901), and made a particular impact as Masha in *Three Sisters* (1901). She married Chekhov in 1901, and after his death, three years later, she remained one of the principals at the Moscow Art Theatre.

KOLCHAK, ADMIRAL ALEKSANDR VASILYEVICH (1873–1920). Naval commander and explorer. Kolchak served with distinction in the Russo–Japanese War and later with the Black Sea fleet where he was the commander during World War I. He was leader of the anti-Bolshevik troops in Siberia (1918–20). He overthrew the Ufa Directory and was recognised by anti-Bolshevik organisations as representing the provisional government. His early successes were followed by withdrawals, and after the fall of Omsk in 1919 he retreated to Irkutsk and was betrayed, taken prisoner, tried and shot.

KOLLONTAI, ALEXANDRA MIKHAYLOVA (1872–1952). Feminist and revolutionary. Born in St Petersburg and although of an upper-class family (her father was a general in the Imperial army), she joined the Russian Social Democratic Party. At first she was a Bolshevik but became a Menshevik, rejoining the Bolshevik party in 1915. She was exiled to Germany in 1908 for her revolutionary activity but returned to Russia in 1917 following the Revolution, becoming commissar for social reforms. Later she became the world's first female ambassador.

KONSTANTIN PAVLOVICH (1779–1831). Russian grand duke, second son of Emperor Paul I, and brother of Alexander I and Nicholas I. Educated under the supervision of his grandmother, Catherine II (the Great). He began his military career in 1799 in Italy against Napoleon. In 1805 he was in command of the guards and was partially responsible for the Russian defeat at Austerlitz. After the Congress of Vienna (1815) he was made commander-in-chief of the Polish armed forces. Preferring Poland to Russia, Konstantin renounced any claim to the throne; the Decembrists, on the other hand, unsuccessfully demanded that Konstantin should rule. He was, however, most unpopular in Poland, incompetent, and taken by surprise at the 1830 insurrection in Warsaw, having thought that his army was loyal. He died of cholera.

KORNILOV, GENERAL LAVR GEORGEVICH (1870–1918). Soldier. He served in the Russo–Japanese War (1904–05) and in World War I. He was captured by the Germans but made a spectacular escape. He was Petrograd military district commander in 1917 and was responsible for the arrest of Nicholas II and his family. As commander-in-chief of all Russian forces in August 1917, he believed that the provisional government was incapable of dealing with any threat from the Bolsheviks. Mistakenly believing that Alexander Kerensky was in agreement, he organised his troops to march on Petrograd but was arrested on Kerensky's orders. This action strengthened the Bolsheviks, and, after the fall of Kerensky, Kornilov escaped to join the anti-Bolshevik forces of Anton Denikin on the Don, where he was killed in action.

KROPOTKIN, PRINCE PETER ALEKSEYEVICH (1842–1921). Geographer, explorer and anarchist. He was secretary of the Russian Geographical Society and explored parts of Manchuria, Siberia and Scandinavia. From 1872 he was associated with the most revolutionary wing of the International and was arrested in 1874. He spent two years in prison, but escaped to England in 1876 and later went to Switzerland and then France, where he was imprisoned (1883–86). From 1886 until 1917 he lived in England, twice visiting the United States during this time. He was opposed to communism but returned to Russia after the Revolution and was held in great esteem. His literary output was great and he wrote many popular books and pamphlets in which he advocated complete social reorganisation based on mutual aid, sympathy, individual liberty through free co-operation and solidarity. The basis of his views on anarchism was given in *Ethics: Origin and Development* (1924).

KRUPSKAYA, NADEZHDA KONSTANTINOVNA (1869–1939). Revolutionary and wife of Lenin. Educated at the Women's College in St Petersburg, she aided Lenin in his revolutionary work and married him in Siberia in 1898, having accompanied him in his exile. After their return to Russia from Switzerland Krupskaya was a member of the commissariat of education and developed and expounded the party's plans for education. She was later to become vice-commissar of education and a member of the central committee of the Communist party and the presidium of the USSR. She died in the Kremlin on 27 February 1939.

KUSMICH, FEDOR (?–1864). Siberian holy man, or *starets*. There are no facts about his age or background. He spent his life in prayer and meditation, settling in a village near Tomsk. A belief developed that Alexander I had not died in 1825 at Taganrog, but had gone into voluntary exile in Siberia under the name Kusmich. Certainly Kusmich's knowledge of court life was quite great and it is possible that he had connections with the imperial family.

KUTUZOV, PRINCE MIKHAIL ILARIONOVICH (1745–1813). Soldier. He served with distinction against the Turks (1768–74, 1787–92) and was commander of the Russian troops at Austerlitz (1805), a battle that was fought against his advice. He replaced Barclay de Tolly as commander-in-chief against Napoleon in 1812, and at first he continued de Tolly's strategy of avoiding a pitched battle. However, he revised tactics at Borodino, where, after great losses on both sides, the Russians withdrew. Kutuzov then reverted to de Tolly's tactics and Napoleon occupied Moscow. The advent of the winter and the Russian military forces caused Napoleon to begin his disastrous retreat. Kutuzov won a victory at Smolensk and harassed the Grand Army continuously on its homeward route, through Poland and Prussia, where he died.

LACY, COUNT PETER (1678–1751). Irish soldier and Russian field marshal. He joined the Russian army of Peter I (the Great) in 1697 and in 1725 was appointed commander-in-chief for St Petersburg, Ingria, and Novgorod. He fought in the 1733–35 war to put Augustus of Saxony on the Polish throne and in 1736 was made a field marshal. Lacy is also noted for having captured Azov from the Turks and the Swedish port of Wilmanstränd, and was responsible for many reforms within the Russian army.

LA HARPE, FRÉDÉRICK-CÉSAR DE (1754–1838). Swiss political leader and tutor to the future tsar Alexander I from 1784. Having left Switzerland because of his opposition to the Bernese government, La Harpe plotted a Vaudois rebellion from St Petersburg. In 1794 he obtained French assistance in freeing Vaud from Bern, and in 1798 he and Ochs formed a unitary government for Switzerland. Having deposed Ochs in 1799, La Harpe was deposed in a coup the following year. In 1815 he represented his canton and Switzerland at the Congress of Vienna. La Harpe is important in Russian history because of his attempt to instil democratic and liberal ideas in Alexander. It is sometimes felt that his teaching had little in common with Russian reality, and that this was partly responsible for the contrast between the theory and the practice of Alexander I's reign.

LAVROV, PYOTR LAVROVICH (1823–1900). Socialist philosopher, mathematician, and populist leader. Lavrov advocated that the intelligentsia should strive to educate the peasants in the hope that ultimately this would produce a socialist society. He emigrated in 1868 and settled in Paris, where he was a leader of the Russian revolutionary movement abroad. Influenced by Comte and Feuerbach, he described his philosophy of history in his *Historical Letters* (1868–69), which stressed the significance of the individual in history. This had considerable impact on followers of Nadrodniki (Populist) thought, who made use of the ideas expressed in his writings to justify political violence. He was editor of the revolutionary journal *Forward* until 1872 when he joined the First International.

LEFORT, FRANÇOIS JACOB (1653–1699). Swiss soldier who fought for the Russian army. He was a close friend of Peter I (the Great), and had a considerable influence over him. It is thought that he suggested to Peter that he undertake foreign travels. Lefort assisted in the reorganisation of the army and the navy and was appointed a general and an admiral. In 1697–98 he headed the Grand Embassy of which Peter I (the Great) was a member.

LENIN (VLADIMIR ILYICH ULYANOV) (1870–1924). Russian revolutionary, leader of the Bolsheviks, and chief theoretician of Russian Marxism. He was born at Simbirsk into a middle-class family. His brother Aleksandr (see Ulyanov, Aleksandr) was hanged in 1887 for planning an attempt on Tsar Alexander III's life, and this greatly influenced Lenin's early life. Lenin studied law at Kazan University, but was expelled for subversive activity. Having studied Marx extensively, he went to St Petersburg and organised the League for the Liberation of the Working Class. As a result he was arrested in 1897 and exiled for three years to Siberia, where he married Nadezhda Krupskaya. He continued his revolutionary activities abroad, and in 1903, in London, became the leader of the Bolshevik faction of the Russian Social Democratic Labour Party. Lenin returned to Russia for the 1905 Revolution, but in 1907 fled to Switzerland where, by means of underground organisations, he continued to mastermind the Russian revolutionary movement. He was living in Switzerland during World War I, and in March 1917 the Germans clandestinely arranged for him to return home in a sealed train. Once in Petrograd, Lenin turned his attention to the overthrowing of Aleksandr Kerensky's provisional government and was appointed chairman of the council of people's commissars. The April Theses were published, and during the summer of 1917 he took refuge in Finland before returning to organise the October Revolution together with Trotsky. He secured peace with Germany by the Treaty of Brest-Litovsk and in 1919 set up the Comintern to work toward world revolution. Lenin and the Red Army fought until 1921 before defeating the Whites. His position as chairman was strengthened, and he became a virtual dictator. Lenin instituted the New Economic Policy in 1921 to restore the economy. His health, which had been failing since an assassination attempt in 1918, grew worse. Although Lenin warned that Stalin should not be allowed to continue as secretary general of the Communist party his warning went unheeded. He died in 1924, and his body, which was embalmed, lay in a mausoleum in Red Square.

LIPRANDI, GENERAL P. P. (1796–1864). Commander of the artillery during the Crimean War. Having captured positions held by Turkish troops, Liprandi advanced to Balaklava and destroyed the legendary Light Brigade of the British army.

LORIS-MELIKOV, GENERAL COUNT MIKHAIL TARYELOVICH (1826–1888). General and statesman. He joined the army in 1843, and from 1863 to 1875 was governor of the Terek region. Having distinguished himself during the Russo–Turkish War, he was made a count. After a period as governor-general of the lower Volga region, he was transferred to Central Russia. He advocated a number of modest reforms of the administration, economy, and educational system and was appointed chairman of a commission whose task was the suppression of the revolutionary movement. As minister of the interior Loris-Melikov devised a plan for a representative assembly and a cabinet government. He resigned his post when this plan was rejected by Alexander III.

MAKLAKOV, VASILY ALEKSANDROVICH (1870–1957). Statesman and lawyer. A member of the Second, Third and Fourth Dumas, he acted as counsel for the defence for political cases during the 1905 Revolution. A member of the Constitutional Democratic party, he was appointed ambassador to France after the February Revolution by the provisional government in 1917, and subsequently was active in relief work for Russian émigrés in Paris.

MARTOV, YULY OSIPOVICH (1873–1923). Leader of the Mensheviks. Martov joined the Social Democrats in 1892. After working with Lenin on the union for the struggle of the working class, he dropped his links with him at the Russian Social Democratic party in Brussels in 1903. He was appointed official leader of the Menshevik party from 1905 to 1907. In 1920 he settled in Berlin and edited the *Socialist Courier*.

MARX, KARL HEINRICH (1818–1883). German political philosopher and social theorist. His main thesis was that humankind developed politically through three stages, leading to the dictatorship of the proletariat, the withering away of the state, and the emergence of a classless society. Born in Trier, Germany, of Jewish parents, Marx studied at the universities of Bonn, Berlin, and Jena. In 1842 he was editor of the *Rheinische Zeitung*, but this was suppressed by the Prussian government in 1843. In the same year he married Jenny von Westphalen (1814–1881). He met Friedrich Engels in Paris and in Brussels in 1847 produced his *Misère de la Philosophie* and the *Manifest der Kommunistischen Partei* (1848). Exiled in London, and although helped financially by Friedrich Engels, Marx lived a life of poverty. He worked in the British Museum (now the British Library) and wrote his best-known work *Das Kapital*. Volume I appeared in 1867 and the second and third volumes were published posthumously in 1885 and 1894, edited by Engels. *Das Kapital* was published in Russia in 1872 and was the first translation into a foreign language. He died in 1883 and was buried at Highgate Cemetery, London. His works are often quoted, although generally inaccurately, but the influence of these writings has been immense.

MATVEYEV, ARTAMON SERGEYEVICH (1625–1682). Diplomat and statesman. Matveyev was chief of the *streltsy* in 1654 and head of the foreign department in 1671. In the following year he played a leading role in concluding an agreement with Poland concerning Turkey. His influence on Tsar Alexis was considerable, and in 1674 he was appointed privy councillor. He was responsible, in part, for introducing Western culture to Russia. Exiled by Tsar Fedor III, he was pardoned in 1682. Recalled to Moscow by Peter I (the Great), Matveyev was killed by the *streltsy*.

MAZEPA, IVAN STEPANOVICH (c. 1645–1709). Hetman of the Cossacks. He conspired with the Polish king, Stanisław Leszczyński, and Charles II of Sweden with the aim of overthrowing Peter I (the Great). Mazepa and the Zaporozhian Cossacks supported Charles XII's invasion of the Ukraine. They were defeated at the Battle of Poltava in 1709 and fled with Charles XII to Turkey.

MENSHIKOV, PRINCE ALEKSANDR DANILOVICH (1673–1729). Statesman and field marshal. He distinguished himself at the siege of Azov. A friend of Peter I (the Great), whose reforms he influenced and helped. He accompanied Peter on his travels to Holland and England. Menshikov ruled Russia with almost absolute authority during the reign of Catherine I and the minority of Peter II. Eventually, because of intrigue at court, when he was about to marry his daughter to the tsar, he was banished to Siberia and his property confiscated.

MENSHIKOV, ALEKSANDR SERGEYEVICH (1787–1869). General and grandson of Aleksandr Danilovich Menshikov. During the Crimean War Menshikov was ambassador to Constantinople and unsuccessfully led the Russian army at Alma, Inkerman and Sevastopol.

MICHAEL ALEKSANDROVICH, GRAND DUKE (1878–1918). Brother of Nicholas II. Following the abdication of Nicholas II in 1917 Michael was offered the crown. He refused it, consenting to accept it only if it was offered to him by a democratically elected constituent assembly. Although Pavel Milyukov and Aleksandr Guchkov of the provisional government implored Michael to accept the throne, he declined, thus bringing the Romanov dynasty to an end.

MICHAEL FEDOROVICH ROMANOV (1596–1645). Son of the Patriarch Philaret. Elected tsar in 1613 at the end of the Time of Troubles. In order to restore internal order Michael expelled the Swedes and Poles from Moscow and tried to restore the country's ailing economy. Under his rule, Russia continued to expand westward.

MILYUKOV, PAVEL NIKOLAYEVICH (1859–1943). Political leader and historian. He was a founder of the Constitutional Democratic Party established in 1905, and a member of the *duma*. As foreign minister in the Provisional Government he argued for continuing the war and respecting Russia's military obligations. He was anti-Bolshevik and left Russia, settling in Paris after a period in London. His works include the three-volume *Outlines of Russian Culture* (1942). During World War II he advocated support for the Soviet Union against Germany.

MOROZOV FAMILY. Family of Old Believers, of serf origin, who became industrial entrepreneurs. Even before the emancipation of 1861, they had amassed considerable wealth from their textile business at Orekhovo-Zuevo and from their potash business. One of the most prominent members of the family, Savva Timofeyevich Morozov (1862–1905), was a patron of the arts. He founded the Moscow Art Theatre, befriended artists and writers, such as Gorky, and collected post-Impressionist works. He also helped finance the Russian Social Democratic Party. The strike at the Morozov textile mill in 1885, organised by the populists, attracted attention to the plight of the working class and involved 8,000 workers. It was a turning-point in the history of the revolutionary movement. From 1882 to 1884 workers' wages were decreased five times and fines constituted 25 per cent of their wages.

MURAVEV–APOSTOL, SERGEY IVANOVICH (1796–1826). Decembrist. Colonel of the Chernigov regiment who successfully led a military uprising from 11–15 January 1826. He started his military service in 1810, was a member of one of the first Decembrist groups, the Union of Salvation, in 1816 and one of the three directors of the Southern Society in 1825. He led the Chernigov regimental uprising on 29 December 1825 but was not supported in this by other regiments. He was hanged in 1826 in St Petersburg.

NAKHIMOV, ADMIRAL PAVEL STEPANOVICH (1802–1855). Naval commander. In 1822–24 he circumnavigated the world in the frigate *Cruiser* and participated in the sea battle of Navarino in 1827. He commanded the Russian navy in the Black Sea during the Crimean War and in 1853 destroyed the Turkish squadron at Sinop, capturing its commander. He was killed during the siege of Sevastopol, which he led after the death of Admiral Vladimir Kornilov.

NARYSHKIN, NATALYA KIRILLOVNA (1651–1694). Second wife of Tsar Alexis and mother of Peter I (the Great).

NECHAYEV, SERGEY GENNADIYEVICH (1847–1882). Revolutionary. After the failure of the Narodniki to incite the peasants to rebel, Nechayev became a ruthless advocate of terrorism in order to obtain the reforms he felt necessary for Russia. He established the secret Society of the Axe in the late 1860s and wished to create a professional revolutionary cadre linked with a conspiratorial organisation that would cover all Europe. Having won the approval of Michael Bakunin and Nikolai Ogarev, he set up groups of 'revolutionary fives', all unknown to each other. In order to obtain absolute obedience, Nechayev deliberately involved his fellow revolutionaries in a common crime. His theories on revolution are outlined in his *Revolutionary Catechism*. He was imprisoned and spent ten years in a dungeon in the Peter and Paul fortress in St Petersburg. A legendary figure, he had considerable influence on his contemporaries and was Dostoyevsky's model for Pyotr Verkhovensky in *The Possessed*.

NESSELRODE, COUNT KARL ROBERT (1780–1862). Statesman and foreign minister. Born in Lisbon, he was a Protestant and was educated in Germany. He was naval aide-de-camp to Paul I for a period, but soon chose to enter the diplomatic service instead. As a result of his friendship with Metternich, he favoured Russo–Austrian co-operation with Metternich's anti-revolutionary policies. Diplomatic secretary to the Russian generals during the 1806–07 war against France, he subsequently served as an intermediary between Talleyrand and Alexander I in Paris. He unsuccessfully implored Alexander I to negotiate with Napoleon rather than fight, but went with the Russian army to Paris and signed the Treaty of Chaumont in 1814. Appointed director of the college of foreign affairs in 1816, Nesselrode accompanied Alexander I to the congresses of Aix-la-Chapelle, Troppau, Laibach and Vienna. He saw disadvantages in exploiting Balkan nationalism and in territorial expansion in Asia.

NICHOLAS I (1796–1855). Emperor of Russia (1825–55) and third son of Paul. Commander of a brigade of the guard and inspector general of the engineering branch, Nicholas came to the throne in 1825 following the assassination of his brother Alexander I, Grand Duke of Constantine having resigned his claim to the throne in 1822. Nicholas began his reign by suppressing the Decembrist movement. Aware of his country's need for reform, he appointed a committee to investigate the state of the country, and the codification of existing laws as undertaken. Alarmed by the revolutionary movement sweeping Western Europe in 1830, Nicholas became increasingly dictatorial; his motto was 'Autocracy, Orthodoxy, and Nationality'. Accordingly, discipline in the army, civil service, and universities was tightened, travel abroad restricted, and the dreaded Third Section (secret police) was established. He did, however, improve the lot of the serf and encourage the development of industry. The 'iron tsar' suppressed the Polish rising of 1830–31 with great cruelty and in 1849 assisted the emperor of Austria to quell the Hungarian revolt. Eager to support Turkey's Christian subjects against the sultan, Nicholas's policies led to the opposition of both Britain and France, and brought on the Crimean War, during which he died.

NICHOLAS II (1868–1918). Last tsar of Russia (1894–1917) and the eldest son of Alexander III. In his accession speech to the Tver Zemstvo he declared that he intended to preserve the autocracy. However, in 1905 he granted a constitution providing for the establishment of a legislative assembly (*duma*), following the humiliating defeat of Russia in the war with Japan (1904–05). After the outbreak of World War I, Nicholas acted as commander-in-chief of the armed forces. His wife, Tsaritsa Alexandra, had come under the influence of Rasputin, and she in turn influenced the tsar. This lost Nicholas the support of the aristocracy, his natural allies. He abdicated at the beginning of the February Revolution and was later banished to Siberia, where he was shot by the *Cheka* on Lenin's orders, together with his family.

NICHOLAS, GRAND DUKE (1843–1865). Son and heir of Alexander II and brother of Alexander III. It was hoped that Nicholas would prove to be an enlightened monarch. However, he contracted meningitis at his betrothal to the Danish Princess Dagmar (Maria Fedorovna) and died.

NICHOLAS, GRAND DUKE (1856–1929). Grandson of Tsar Nicholas I and nephew of Alexander II. He was an army officer. Commissioned in 1872, he introduced major military reforms while serving in the Russo–Turkish war of 1877–78 and as inspector general of the cavalry (1895–1905). In 1905 he was appointed commander of the military district of St Petersburg and first president of the imperial committee for national defence. He was commander-in-chief at the beginning of World War I and was then sent to the Caucasus as viceroy of Nicholas II, remaining there until 1917. He was then reappointed commander-in-chief by the tsar, but Prince Georgy Lvov, head of the provisional government, cancelled the appointment. Nicholas escaped abroad and settled in France.

NIKON (NIKITA MININ) (1605–1681). Patriarch of Moscow (1652–66). His reforms created a schism in the Orthodox Church and alienated a section of the clergy and of laymen (the Old Believers). These reforms included the standardisation of the ritual and the introduction of a new prayer book (1654). He aroused considerable opposition and was condemned by a church council in 1666–67 and deposed and confined to a monastery. His reforms, however, were continued after his fall.

NOVOSILTSEV, COUNT NIKOLAI NIKOLAEVICH (1761–1836). Statesman. A confidant of Tsar Alexander I, he was a member of the unofficial committee (1801–03) that was established to investigate reforms. He wrote *Constitutional Charter of the Russian Empire* in which he saw the empire divided into twelve large administrative areas enjoying limited autonomy. In 1820 the plan was presented to Alexander I, who accepted it and began to implement it, but the scheme was abandoned on the death of the tsar in 1825.

OBOLENSKY, PRINCE YEVGENY PETROVICH (1796–1865). Soldier and member of one of the oldest families in Russia. A leader of the Northern Society, he took part in the Decembrist revolt in December 1825 on the accession of Nicholas I. He was condemned to death, but his sentence was changed to banishment to Siberia.

ODOYEVSKY, PRINCE ALEKSANDR IVANOVICH (1802–1839). Romantic poet. He participated in the 1825 Decembrist revolt and was condemned to exile in Siberia for eight years hard labour. In 1837 he was sent to the Caucasus as a private solider and there met Mikhail Lermontov. He died there in an epidemic. Freedom and patriotism provide the main themes of his poetry, which was heavily influenced by contemporary idealism.

ORLOV, PRINCE ALEKSEY FYODOROVICH (1786–1861). Army officer and statesman. He was an adviser to Nicholas I (1825–55) and Alexander II. Orlov joined the army in 1804, and in 1825 was appointed commander of a cavalry regiment and made a count as a result of his part in the suppression of the Decembrist revolt. During the war with Turkey Orlov was appointed lieutenant general and played a leading part in the conclusion of the Treaty of Adrianople (1829). In 1833 he was made ambassador to Turkey and commander-in-chief of Russia's Black Sea fleet; he enhanced Russia's defences by means of the alliance with Turkey at Hünkâ Iskelesi. Orlov served from 1839 to 1842 on the secret committee that examined the possibility of limited improvements for the peasantry. In 1844 he was head of the Third Department, and also of the chancellery. In 1854 he was dispatched on an unsuccessful trip to persuade Austria to refrain from taking sides during the Crimean War. After helping negotiate the Treaty of Paris (1856), he was made prince and also president of the state council and the council of ministers. In 1858 he was appointed chairman of a committee established to examine the question of the emancipation of the serfs. His attempts to prevent the emancipation were unsuccessful.

ORLOV, COUNT ALEKSEY GRIGORYEVICH (1737–1808). Russian nobleman and a leader of the conspiracy to put Catherine II (the Great) on the throne. Having joined the cadet corps in 1749, Orlov later became an officer in the Russian guards. After his brother had become Catherine's lover, Orlov helped him plan the overthrow of Tsar Peter III. When Catherine had been proclaimed empress Orlov received Peter's abdication and took him into custody. Since the latter was killed shortly afterward while still in Orlov's hands, it is alleged that Orlov murdered him. Appointed as a major general and commander of the Russian fleet, he succeeded in destroying the much larger Turkish fleet at Chesme. After imprisoning a possible rival to the throne, Yelizaveta Aleksyevna Tarakanova, Orlov retired from the army.

ORLOV, COUNT GRIGORY GRIGORYEVICH (1734–1783). Military officer and lover of Catherine II (the Great). Having put her on the throne, he remained her close adviser. Orlov joined the cadet corps in 1749 and fought in the battle of Zorndorf during the Seven Years' War. He became Catherine's lover c. 1760; in 1762 he succeeded in overthrowing Tsar Peter III and in putting Peter's wife, Catherine, on the throne. He was then made count, director-general of engineers, and general-in-chief. Motivated by the desire to update Russia's agricultural system, Orlov was one of the founders of the Free Economic Society; Catherine, however, disregarded his schemes for the emancipation of the serfs. In 1722 he was chief delegate to the peace conference that was to end the Russo–Turkish War, but peace was not concluded until two years later. He ceased to be Catherine's lover c. 1772, left Russia in 1775, and married in 1777. In 1782 he lost his sanity.

OSTERMANN, COUNT ANDREY IVANOVICH (HEINRICH JOHANN FRIEDRICH OSTERMANN) (1686–1747). Statesman. Born in Westphalia, he went to Russia in 1704 and was appointed interpreter at the foreign office in 1708 and secretary in 1710. He took part in the congresses at Aland (1718–19) and Nystad (1721) and his success in negotiations with Sweden and Persia gained him the rank of baron and the vice-presidency of the foreign office. His period of greatest influence began in 1725 with the accession of Catherine I, when he became vice-chancellor, a member of the supreme privy council, and president of the commission on commerce. The dominant influence on foreign policy until 1740, he cultivated Austria as an ally and this brought him the hostility of France. He was overthrown by French-inspired intrigue after the death of the Empress Anne in 1740 and sentenced to death, but was reprieved and banished to Siberia.

PANIN, COUNT NIKITA IVANOVICH (1718–1783). Statesman and diplomatic adviser to Catherine II (the Great), he adopted an anti-French policy as Russian minister to Stockholm. He was appointed to supervise Grand Duke Paul's education in 1760, and during the 1762 Revolution he supported Catherine. Panin was head of the foreign college in 1763 and instigated the Northern Accord but was taken by surprise by the Confederation of the Bar and the Turkish War. He also advocated a permanent 'Imperial Council' that would advise the tsar. From then on his influence waned, and he was dismissed in 1781.

PASKEVICH, IVAN FEDOROVICH (1782–1856). Army officer who suppressed the Polish insurrection of 1820–31. Paskevich served in the army in wars with Turkey, France and Persia. He took part in the prosecution at the trial of the Decembrists, and in 1829 he was appointed field marshal. He was commander-in-chief of the Russian forces against Polish insurgents. Paskevich was made prince of Warsaw and viceroy of Poland, which he ruled harshly from 1832 to 1856.

PAUL I (PAUL PETROVICH) (1754–1801). Tsar of Russia from 1796 to 1801. Second son of Peter III and Catherine II (the Great). Paul was taken from her as a child by Elizabeth Petrovna. Catherine's coup d'état in 1762 against his father, Peter III, and his belief later that Catherine had instigated the murder of his father, both shocked Paul greatly. In 1783, Catherine gave Paul and his second wife an estate at Gatchina, where he planned various reforms, including the liberalisation of laws on serfdom (1797). He ruled in a mostly despotic manner, hoping to save Russia from a revolution such as France had seen. In 1798 he joined the second coalition against France, but eventually turned against Great Britain. Guards officers, who had grown tired of his incompetence and his harsh treatment of them, conspired to compel him to abdicate, and in 1801 he was murdered in a scuffle.

PESTEL, COLONEL PAUL I (1799–1826). Decembrist leader. Pestel graduated from the Corps of Pages in 1811 and took part in the Franco–Russian war of 1812. A former aide-de-camp to General Wittgenstein and a colonel of a regiment, Pestel joined the Union of Salvation and maintained a secret group (the Southern Society) in Tulchin after the Union had been dissolved. He was the author of *Russian Truth* and was arrested on the eve of the Decembrist uprising and condemned to death.

PETER I (THE GREAT) (1672–1725). Tsar of Russia (1682–1721) and Emperor of Russia (1721–25). He was co-tsar with his half-brother Ivan V (1666–96) on the death of their elder brother, Fedor III, under the regency of their sister, Sophia. He began the Westernisation and modernisation of Russia by a number of *ad hoc* reforms and with tireless energy established Russia as an important European power. Peter was interested in the army and in shipbuilding from an early age, and in the 1690s undertook a tour of Western Europe, studied foreign countries, and worked as a shipwright. He returned home with many skilled technicians, he reformed trade, industry and the army, set up schools and arranged for textbooks to be translated, brought the church under state control by abolishing the patriarchate and establishing the Holy Synod, and introduced a poll tax. He also established the Table of Ranks, by which state service was made compulsory for the nobility. Disregarding the extreme unsuitability of the swampy site given to flooding and the massive cost in human lives, Peter built a new capital of Russia on land conquered from Sweden, the city of St Petersburg, thereby creating the 'window on the West'. He defeated Charles XII at Poltava after initial defeats in the war with Sweden (1700–21) and annexed parts of Finland, Estonia and Livonia, thus gaining access to the Baltic. Peter's campaign against the Turks (1700–13) met with less success, but he gained extra land in the Caspian region in the war with Persia (1722–23). Peter died in 1725 and was succeeded by his consort, Catherine I, having imprisoned his son Alexis for suspected treason and who died after torture (1718).

Samuel Collins MD (1619–1670) lived in Russia for nine years and was physician to Peter I (the Great). He wrote *The Present State of Russia* which was published in 1671. There are many portraits of the tsar and these give us some idea of the man, but the following two extracts from *The Present State of Russia* add further dimensions:

> I shall now give you a further description of the Czar. He is a goodly person, about six foot high, well set, inclin'd to fat, of a clear complexion, lightish hair, somewhat a low forehead, of a stern countenance, severe in his chastisements, but very careful of his Subjects love. Being urged by a Stranger to make it death for any man to desert his Colours; he answer'd, it was a hard case to do that, for God has not given courage to all men alike. He never appears to the people but in magnificence, and on Festivals with wonderful splendour of Jewels and Attendants. He never went to any Subjects house but his Governours when he was thought past all recovery. His Centinels and Guards placed round about his Court, stand like silent and immoveable Statues. No noise is heard in his Pallace, non more than if uninhabited. None but his Domesticks are suffer'd to approach the inward Court, except the Lords that are in Office. He never dines publickly but on Festivals, and then his Nobilitys dine in his presence. At *Easter* all the Nobility and Gentry, and Courtiers kiss the Emperours hand, and receive Eggs. Every meal he sends dishes of meat to his Favourites from his own Table. His stores of Corn,

and dry'd flesh are very considerable, with these he pays his *Strelsies* or *Janzaries*, giving them some cloth, but very little money; for they have all Trades, and great Priviledges.

As to the *Czars* Religion, he is of the Greek Faith, and very strict in the observation thereof. He never misses divine Service, if he be well he goes to it, if sick it comes to him in his chamber. On Fast-dayes he frequents midnight prayers (the old vigils of the Church) standing four, five or six hours together, and prostrating himself to the ground sometimes a thousand times, and on great Festivals fifteen hundred. In the great Fast he eats but three meals a week, *viz.* on *Thursday*, *Saturday*, *Sunday*; for the rest he takes a piece of brown bread and salt, a pickled Mushroom or Cucumber, and drinks a cup of small beer. He eats Fish but twice in the great Lent, and observes it seven weeks together, besides *Maslinets* (or cleansing) week, wherein they eat milk and eggs. Out of the Fast he observes *Mondays*, *Wednesdayus* and *Fridays* and will not then eat any thing that comes of flesh. In fine, no Monk is more observant of Canonical hours, then he is of Fasts. We may reckon he fasts almost eight months in twelve, with the six weeks fast before *Christmas* and two other small fasts.

PETER II (1715–1730). Emperor of Russia from 1727 to 1730. The grandson of Peter I (the Great), and son of Alexis, he was proclaimed emperor according to the will of the late Empress Catherine I. The will was considered valid at the time, but later regarded as a forgery. Peter dismissed Menshikov, the leader of the Supreme Privy Council, in 1727 and banished him to Siberia. Peter II was taken to Moscow from St Petersburg by the Dolgorukiy family. He was crowned in 1728 and led a pleasure-seeking life, but died of smallpox on the day arranged for his wedding to Princess Dolgorukaya. He was succeeded by the Empress Anne Ivanova, daughter of Peter I's (the Great) half-brother and co-tsar, Ivan V.

PETER III (1728–1762). Emperor of Russia (1761–62) and Duke of Holstein. He returned the Prussian provinces conquered during the Seven Years' War and released the nobility from obligatory state service, thus reversing a principle laid down by Peter I (the Great) that compulsory service was for all. Somewhat weak-minded and ineffective as a ruler, he was overthrown by a guards' plot. It is alleged that he was killed by Orlov, his wife's lover. She was later crowned empress and ruled as Catherine II (the Great).

PHILARET (VASILY MIKHAYLOVICH DROZOLOV) (1782–1867). Russian Orthodox metropolitan. He was a great orator and the most influential Russian churchman of the nineteenth century. He was bishop of Reval (1817), archbishop of Tver (1819) and Metropolitan of Moscow in 1821. His *Christian Catechism of the Orthodox Catholic Eastern Greco–Russian Church* (1823) greatly influenced the theology of the nineteenth century.

PHILARET, PATRIARCH (1553?–1633). In secular circles, Philaret was known as Fedor Nikitich Romanov, a successful soldier and diplomat. Compelled to take monastic vows by Boris Godunov, he was released by the first False Dmitry and made metropolitan of Rostov in 1606. In 1609 the second False Dmitry made him patriarch of All Russia. He was arrested and sent to Poland in 1611. After his son Michael was elected tsar he returned to Moscow and was enthroned as patriarch in 1619. From that time on he ruled Russia jointly with Tsar Michael.

PLATER, EMILIJA (1806–1831). Lithuanian soldier. She was born in Vilnius. She took Joan of Arc as her model, and studied military subjects, learning the use of weapons. When an insurrection broke out she and a group of cadets at the military academy of Daugavpils (Latvia) began plotting to seize that strategically important garrison town. She helped organise an insurgent unit from the area around their estate, consisting of 60 mounted nobles, 280 mounted riflemen and several hundred peasants armed with scythes. When they approached Daugavpils they were met and routed by the Russians. She then joined another rebel unit and participated in the capture of Ukmerge. A subsequent attempt to dislodge the Russians from Vilnius failed. Later, when the insurgents were organised into regular military units, Emilija was appointed company commander with the rank of Captain.

After the battle of Kaunas, where she was nearly captured, her regiment was compelled to retreat and laid down their arms in Prussia. Emilija refused to give up and attempted to reach Poland, where the fighting was still continuing. She fell ill en route and died near Kapčiamiestis.

PLEHVE, VYACHESLAV KONSTANTINOVICH (1846–1904). Russian statesman and one of the most reactionary figures of the reign of Nicholas II. Plehve served in the department of justice from 1867, and in 1881 was appointed director of the police department. As a result of his harsh suppression of terrorism, he was made deputy minister of the interior in 1884 and head of the imperial chancellery in 1894. In 1902 he was appointed minister of the interior. He was assassinated in 1904 by the Socialist Revolutionary, Yegor Sozonov.

POBEDONOSTSEV, KONSTANTIN PETROVICH (1827–1907). Statesman and jurist. He was a professor of civil law at Moscow University 1859–65 and was appointed procurator of the Holy Synod of the Russian Orthodox Church in

1880. Pobedonostsev was tutor to both Alexander III and Nicholas II. He was reactionary and was responsible for the illiberal schemes of Alexander III, fighting against a constitution, freedom of the press and trial by jury.

POTEMKIN, PRINCE GRIGORY ALEKSANDROVICH (1739–1791). Statesman and soldier, and favourite of Catherine II (the Great). He joined the Russian Horse Guards in 1755. Potemkin was the viceroy of New Russia from 1774, and president of the war department and field marshal from 1784. Crimea was annexed to Russia after he had persuaded the khan of Crimea to abdicate. In 1787 Potemkin erected fake villages in New Russia, so that Catherine, visiting the area, would believe it to be more populated than it actually was; hence the term 'Potemkin village'.

PROKOPOVICH, FEOFAN (1681–1736). Ukrainian theologian and archbishop of Novgorod. Prokopovich studied at Rome, then taught at the theological academy in Kiev and later became rector of the Kiev-Mogilyansk Academy there. In 1716 Peter I (the Great) summoned Prokopovich to St Petersburg, where he assisted Peter with his reforms, both ecclesiastical and secular. In 1705 he produced a tragicomedy in which the hero is a thinly disguised portrait of Peter I (the Great).

PUGACHEV, YEMELYAN IVANOVICH (1726–1775). Cossack leader of a revolt during the reign of Catherine II (the Great). Declaring himself Emperor Peter III in 1773, he issued a manifesto promising to liberate the serfs. Pugachev won widespread support in the Volga area and in the Urals, but the revolt was eventually crushed, and he was executed.

PUSHKIN, ALEXANDER SERGEYEVICH (1799–1837). One of the great figures of world literature and Russia's greatest poet. He came from a poor but noble family. His maternal great-grandfather was an Ethiopian who became a general under Peter I (the Great). Pushkin was influenced by the Enlightenment and the French Revolution, and was a personal friend of many of the Decembrists. He was twice exiled for his views, once to New Russia in 1820 and once to the family estate in 1824. Nicholas I freed him from the ordinary censorship by undertaking to be censor himself. He was killed in a duel with a French nobleman whom he suspected of being his wife's lover.

Pushkin's first poem was published when he was fifteen. Early in his writing career he was influenced by Anacreon, Parny and Voltaire; later Byron was his main inspiration, and even later he adopted Realism. He was fully conversant with all Western literary forms, but he assimilated them and used them to create an entirely Russian literature. His materspiece is the novel in verse *Eugene Onegin* (1823–31). Other works include *Ruslan and Lyudmila* (1819), *Caucasian*

Prisoner (1821), *Poltava* (1828), *The Bronze Horseman* (1833), and the play *Boris Godunov* (1825).

RADISHCHEV, ALEKSANDR NIKOLAYEVICH (1749–1802). Writer and revolutionary thinker. His *Journey from St Petersburg to Moscow* (1790), exposing the injustices of serfdom, earned him the death sentence. This was commuted to ten years' exile in Siberia, where Radishchev continued his literary activity. He was permitted to return following the death of Catherine II (the Great), and in 1801 served on the commission for the codification of laws. In 1802, despairing that he had been unable to alleviate the lot of the serf, he committed suicide.

RASPUTIN, GRIGORY YEFIMOVICH (1872–1916). Peasant and mystic, born in Tobolsk, who had considerable influence at court and in political affairs. As a youth Rasputin had been influenced by the Khlysty (Flagellants) sect. Although without education, he allegedly possessed hypnotic powers, which he did not hesitate to exploit, preached that physical contact with himself had a healing effect and claimed to be able to work miracles. Rasputin arrived in St Petersburg in 1903 as a *starets* (holy man) and as such gained access to the highest circles of society. His views were that there was a need to sin in order to achieve humility and as a result, salvation. By using hypnotism to stop the haemophiliac tsarevich's bleeding, he exercised virtually unlimited influence on Tsaritsa Alexandra, who viewed him as a divine missionary sent to save the dynasty. The Church, however, denounced Rasputin as an imposter, and he was sent back to Siberia in 1912. He returned to St Petersburg in 1914, and in 1915, when Nicholas II was at army headquarters, and the tsaritsa was left in charge of domestic affairs, his influence was vast, and many of the more capable ministers were dismissed. His dissolute habits continued until his assassination at the Yusapov Palace in 1916.

RASTRELLI, COUNT BARTOLOMEO (1700–1771). Italian architect. Restrelli served as court architect to Elizabeth and designed the Winter Palace (1754–62), and the palaces of Peterhof and Tsarskoye-Selo (1783, later altered by Charles Cameron). He also built St Andrew's Cathedral in Kiev (1747), which exemplifies the mature baroque style in Russia, and the Smolny Convent (1748).

REPIN, ILYA YEFIMOVICH (1844–1903). Painter of the naturalistic school. Repin was trained as an icon painter, and later studied at the Society for the Encouragement of Art in 1863, and from 1864 to 1871 at the Academy of Arts. His work became gradually more impressionistic in style after his second visit to Paris in 1863. Repin was a leading member of the Wanderers, a group of non-academic painters who sought to bring art to a mass audience through social realism. In his later years he turned to religious paintings. His best-known paintings include *The Volga Boatmen, The Religious Procession in Kursk Province*, and *Ivan the Terrible with the Body of his Son*. From 1893–1907 he was professor of painting at St Petersburg Academy and lived in Finland after the Revolution.

REUTERN, COUNT MIKHAIL (1820–1890). Minister of finance from 1862 to 1878. Reutern worked toward the stabilisation of the paper rouble and the improvement of his country's balance of payments through the strengthening of Russia's export position, and he sought to encourage railway construction and private banking. Although he argued that war would harm the country's economic position, Reutern was unsuccessful in preventing the war with Turkey of 1877–78. He was also in favour of the sale of Alaska to the United States.

RODZYANKO, MIKHAIL VLADIMIROVICH (1859–1924). Statesman. He was leader of the Union of October (Octobrist Party) and president of the Third and Fourth Dumas. Having supported the autocracy's suppression of the 1905 Revolution, he unsuccessfully opposed the idea that Tsar Nicholas II should take command of the army. After the defeat of the anti-Bolshevik armies in 1919–20, he emigrated to Yugoslavia where he died.

ROMANOV, PRINCE KONSTANTIN NIKOLAYEVICH (1827–1892). General, admiral, and son of Tsar Nicholas I. Romanov was made a member of the state council in 1850, a member of the secret committee in 1857, and the leader of the committee for peasant affairs in 1860. He carried out reforms in the army and navy, and in 1862–63 was governor-general of Poland.

ROMODANOVSKY, PRINCE FEDOR (1640–1717). Companion of Peter I (the Great) and member of the Most Drunken Sobor (council) of Fools and Jesters. He was later appointed head of the secret police.

ROSSI, KARL IVANOVICH (1775–1849). Architect of Italian descent. Rossi acted as the chief architect to Alexander I and was in charge of the building of the ensembles of the Mikhail Palace, the Alexandra (Pushkin) Theatre, Palace Square, and the Admiralty and Senate Squares. The replanning of St Petersburg was in the style and on the scale of imperial Rome.

ROSTOPCHIN, COUNT FEDOR VASILYEVICH (1763–1826). Statesman and close adviser to Paul I. He was appointed military governor and chief commander of Moscow in May 1812, and was held responsible for the burning of the city. Although the fire was a major factor in Napoleon's withdrawal from

Moscow and his disastrous retreat, Rostopchin was dismissed and exiled in 1814. He defended himself in *The Truth Concerning the Fire of Moscow* (1823). He went with Alexander I to the Congress of Vienna.

ROSTOVTSEV, GENERAL YAKOB IVANOVICH (1803–1860). Having warned the government of the impending Decembrist revolt, Rostovtsev was appointed chief of the military schools. He became a member of the secret committee in 1857 and chairman of the editing commission in 1859. Having played a leading part in preparations of the emancipation of the serfs, he died from over-exertion.

ROZHESTVENSKI, ZINOVI PETROVICH (1848–1909). Admiral and commander of the Baltic fleet. His fleet sailed to the Far East in the Russo–Japanese War of 1904–05; the fleet was destroyed and this led to the armistice with Japan.

RUMYANTSEV, COUNT PYOTR ALEKSANDROVICH (1725–1796). Statesman, army officer and founder of the Royal School of Military Art. He achieved fame during the Seven Years' War (1756–63) and the Russo–Turkish War of 1768–74, after the peace of Kuchuk-Kainarji (1774), was made field marshal and given the title Count Zadunaysky. Having enjoyed favour under Peter III, he was appointed governor-general of the Ukraine by Catherine II (the Great), who in 1794 enlisted his help to pacify the Poles.

RYLEYEV, KONDRATY FEDOROVICH (1795–1826). Decembrist and poet. In 1823, Ryleyev and Aleksandr Bestuzhev began publishing a yearly almanac, the *Polar Star*. Much of Ryleyev's narrative verse is similar to that of Byron, but his best poems are those inspired with revolutionary zeal, such as 'The Citizen' (1826). After the suppression of the Decembrist revolt he was arrested and hanged in the Peter and Paul fortress.

RYSAKOV, NIKOLAI IVANOVICH (1861–1881). Terrorist. In 1881 he threw a bomb at Alexander II's carriage in St Petersburg, but the tsar was unharmed. Later on the same day another attempt was made which achieved the desired result. Rysakov was arrested and executed.

SAMOILOVA, KONKORDIYA (1876–1921). Russian socialist. Born in Siberia, the daughter of a priest, she became a student in St Petersburg. In 1897 she organised a demonstration after the suicide of Maria Vetrovna, who set fire to herself in her cell in Peter-Paul prison in protest at her treatment. She became a political activist, participating in the great demonstrations of 1901, and working under cover as 'Natasha' from 1903. She was imprisoned in 1903–04 and then worked in the Caucasus, attempting to win workers' wives to the radical movement.

Samoilova was an editor of *Pravda* from its foundation in 1912, and in 1913 was one of the six editors of the new journal *Rabotnitsa* (*Woman Worker*); she was arrested with the whole editorial board on the eve of International Woman's Day in 1914. In 1917 the journal was revived as part of the attempt to mobilise women in the Bolshevik revolution.

SAMSONOV, ALEKSANDR VASILYEVICH (1859–1914). Soldier. General Samsonov commanded the army that invaded eastern Prussia in August 1914 and was defeated at the battle of Tannenberg (1914), where two Russian corps were destroyed and three others reduced to half size. Samsonov committed suicide.

SAZONOV, SERGEY DMITRIYEVICH (1861–1927). Diplomat and statesman. Sazonov began working for the foreign ministry in 1883 and was appointed foreign minister in 1910. He attempted to ease relations with Germany, but relations with Great Britain deteriorated. He eventually forced the Germans to relinquish command of Turkish troops in Constantinople. After the assassination of Archduke Francis Ferdinand, Sazonov pressured the tsar to agree to complete mobilisation. As a result of his view that an autonomous Poland should be created, he was dismissed in 1916. He was appointed ambassador to London in 1917, but the revolution prevented him from taking up the post and he then acted as foreign minister for Admiral A. V. Kolchak.

SERGIUS ALEXANDROVICH, GRAND DUKE (1864–1905). Governor-general of Moscow, the grand duke succeeded in alienating virtually every sector of society. He was assassinated in 1905 in the Kremlin by a bomb thrown by Ivan Kalyayev, the Socialist Revolutionary.

SHUVALOV, COUNT IVAN (1727–1797). Shuvalov suggested in 1755 that Peter I (the Great) found the first university in Russia, at Moscow, and the first state-controlled secondary schools. He also proposed that *gimnazii* (high schools) be set up in all large cities, although this did not happen. He was responsible for the creation of the Academy of Arts in 1757.

SHUVALOV, COUNT PYOTR ANDREYEVICH (1827–1889). Russian government official and ambassador. A member of an old noble family, Shuvalov began his military career in 1845 and his diplomatic career in 1856 at the Paris Peace Conference. After being in charge of the St Petersburg police, he was made director of the political police (1861–64), and in 1866 he was chief of staff of the gendarmerie corps and head of the Third Section. He then became an influential adviser of Alexander II and was opposed to liberal reform. In 1874 he was sent to London as ambassador and because of a diplomatic failure following the Russo–Turkish war (1877–78), in which he was involved, he was recalled to St Petersburg.

SHUYSKY, PRINCE VASILY (fl. early seventeenth century). After the False Dmitry's accession to the throne in 1605, it was announced that Vasily Shuysky had denounced him as an impostor. The general assembly of land (*Zemskii Sobor*) found Vasily guilty and sentenced him to death. The pretender, however, reprieved him. Vasily continued to conspire against Dmitry, and in 1606 he charged into the Kremlin and the pretender was killed. In 1606 he was made tsar. Though Vasily was popular with the upper classes, the majority of people supported the new pretender. Eventually, representatives of every class deposed him on 17 July 1610; he was seized and forced to become a monk.

SOPHIA ALEKSEYEVNA (1657–1704). Regent of Russia (1682–89). The eldest daughter of Tsar Alexis by his first wife and sister of Tsar Fedor III. Seizing power shortly after Fedor's death in 1682 with the help of the *streltsy*, she was proclaimed regent during the minority of her handicapped brother, Ivan V, and of her half-brother Peter I (the Great), who reigned jointly. She disposed of her opponents in a brutal fashion and ruled autocratically with her chief adviser and lover Prince Vasily Vasilyevich Golitsyn. Sophia aimed to be tsarina in her own right, but she had insufficient support among the nobility and clergy, and two unsuccessful campaigns against the Turks of Crimea helped undermine her power. When it was rumoured that Sophia intended to assassinate Peter and become sole ruler, Peter overthrew the regency and confined her in a convent, deposed Ivan and exiled Golitsyn. After an attempted revolt of the *streltsy* in 1698, Sophia was obliged to take the veil and assumed the name of Susanna. She was imprisoned in Novodevichy convent where she died.

SPERANSKY, COUNT MIKHAIL MIKHAILOVICH (1772–1839). Russian minister of state and political reformer. As Alexander I's adviser he devised a liberal constitutional system for Russia based on the Napoleonic plan, but, after the invasion of Russia by Napoleon, the intrigues of his opponents drove him from office and nullified his work. Under Nicholas I he returned to power and took a prominent part in the proceedings against the Decembrist conspiracy and also codified Russian law in 1832.

STOLYPIN, PYOTR ARKADYEVICH (1862–1911). Statesman. As a liberal conservative he failed to win the approval of either the extreme right or the radicals. He once said, 'Give the state 20 years of internal and external peace, and you will not recognise Russia.' From 1906 Stolypin was minister of the interior and chairman of the council of ministers. While firmly suppressing the 1905 Revolution he wished to carry out liberal reforms. Under his agrarian reforms of 1906–11, peasants were permitted to leave village communities, settle on separate farms, buy land and were encouraged to settle in less populated areas. In 1907 Stolypin altered the electoral system by imperial decree, by restricting the franchise and reducing the representation of nationalities. He was assassinated by a Socialist Revolutionary terrorist in 1911 at the Kiev Opera, in full view of the tsar.

STÜRMER, BORIS VLADIMIROVICH (1848–1917). Prime minister. A previous master of ceremonies at court, Stürmer was appointed prime minister in 1916. He was also in charge of the ministry of foreign affairs. It was considered that he mishandled the war effort and was a puppet of Rasputin. He was not liked and was dismissed from the *duma* on 23 November 1916.

SUVOROV, COUNT ALEKSANDR VASILYEVICH (1730–1800). Military commander. Suvorov enlisted at the age of twelve and first saw action in the Seven Years' War of 1756–63, taking part in the battle of Kunersdorf (1759). He was promoted to lieutenant colonel, and fought in the Russo–Turkish War of 1768–74. Suvorov brilliantly commanded the Russian armies in the Russo–Turkish War of 1787–91 and was created Count Rymnitsky by Catherine II (the Great) and a count of the Reich by the Holy Roman Emperor. In 1794 he successfully but harshly suppressed an insurrection in Poland. Out of favour during Paul I's reign, he went into exile in Novgorod, but was recalled when Russia joined the coalition against France. He expelled most of the French from Italy and in 1799 was appointed generalissimo of the Russian forces. His most famous exploit was the 1799 Swiss expedition. Suvorov's *The Science of Conquering* strongly influenced Russian military thought.

SVERDLOV, YAKOV MIKHAILOVICH (1885–1919). Politician and close collaborator of Lenin. He joined the Social Democratic Labour Party in 1901, and from 1902 to 1917 acted as a professional revolutionary for the Bolsheviks. In 1913 he was made part of the central committee. Following the February 1917 Revolution Sverdlov was the chief organiser of the party and acted as a one-man Secretariat for the party throughout 1917. After the Bolshevik revolution he became chairman of the All-Russian Central Executive Committee of the Soviets.

TATISHCHEV, VASILY NIKITICH (1686–1750). Historian, administrator and geographer. Tatishchev aided Peter I (the Great) by studying Peter's reforms and carrying them out, particularly in the Urals, where he was chief of the mining administration. His five-volume *History of Russia from the Earliest Times* is considered by many the foundation of modern Russian historiography.

TKACHEV, PYOTR NIKITICH (1844–1885). Publicist and leader of the revolutionary 'Jacobins'. Tkachev was a contributor to radical journals and a member of various underground revolutionary groups in the 1860s and early 1870s. As a result of the Sergey Nechayev affair he emigrated and published the journal *Alarm Bell* in Geneva. In this, Tkachev developed his ideas of a seizure of power in order that socialist reforms could be carried out by the state. This influenced the populist *Narodnaya Volya* organisation, The Fokin organisation and Lenin.

TOLSTOY, COUNT DMITRY (1823–1889). *Oberprokuror* of the Holy Synod in 1864, Tolstoy continued his career as a reactionary minister of education. Assuming office in 1866, he argued that much greater importance was accorded to classical languages in order to distract students' attentions from the issues of the day. In 1882 Tolstoy was appointed head of the Ministry of the Interior.

TOLSTOY, COUNT LEV NIKOLAYEVICH (1828–1910). Novelist and philosopher. Born into a family of the Russian nobility at the family estate of Yasnaya Polyana, Tolstoy was an orphan by the age of nine. He studied oriental languages and law at Kazan University. He joined an artillery unit in the Caucasus and took part in the siege of Silistria, and in the defence of the Fourth Bastion during the Crimean War. Some of his experiences are recorded in his *Sevastopol Stories* (1855). Tolstoy spent the years from 1856–61 in St Petersburg and Moscow, and at Yasnaya Polyana. During this time he grew increasingly disgusted with European civilisation, egotism, and materialism in general and began to turn to the Russian peasants as the repository of all virtues. In 1862 he married Sofia Andreyevna Behrs and for a time was absorbed in the pleasures of family life. It was at this period in his life that he wrote *War and Peace* (1862–69), considered by some to be the greatest novel in the world, which gives a panoramic view of Russian society during the Napoleonic wars. While writing *Anna Karenina* (1873–77) Tolstoy underwent a spiritual crisis, described with powerful sincerity in *A Confession*. He became estranged from his wife, renounced art and literature, and lived a life of asceticism while evolving an ethical theory of non-resistance to evil, largely based on a rational interpretation of the Sermon on the Mount. He was tormented by the question of how one should conduct one's life; this obsession prompted the writing of the masterpiece *The Death of Ivan Ilyich* (1886). Having denied the deity and resurrection of Christ, and the deity of the Holy Spirit, he was excommunicated in 1901. He died in 1910 at Astapovo railway junction.

TROTSKY, LEV DAVIDOVICH (BRONSHTEYN) (1879–1940). Politician. Trotsky joined the Social Democrats in 1896. He was banished to Siberia, but escaped and became a member of the Iskra Group. When the party split in 1903, he became a Menshevik, prophesying that Leninist theory would result in a one-man dictatorship. He was again banished as a result of his role in the 1905 Revolution, when he held the position of chairman of the St Petersburg Soviet. While trying to reunite the factions of the Russian Social Democrats, Trotsky led the internationalist wing of the Mensheviks during World War I. Expelled from France as a result of his pacifist propaganda, he settled in the United States. Back in Russia following the February 1917 Revolution, Trotsky became a Bolshevik and the chief supporter of Lenin, playing a leading role in organising and carrying out the October Revolution. He was head of the St Petersburg Soviet and its military revolutionary committee, commissar of war (1918–25), leader of the Red Army during the Civil War, and from 1919 to 1927 was a member of the Politburo. Trotsky became a frequent opponent of Lenin and was expelled from the party in 1927. The 'combined opposition' of Trotsky, Grigory Zinoviev, and Lev Kamenev was unsuccessful, and in 1929 Trotsky was expelled from the Soviet Union. He was accused of espionage during the Great Purge and was murdered in Mexico City by Soviet agents, which was admitted by the USSR in 1989. In 1930 he wrote *My Life: An Attempt at an Autobiography*.

TRUBETSKOY, PRINCE SERGEY NIKOLAYEVICH (1790–1860). Decembrist. In 1823 he was appointed leader of the Northern Society. He wished to abolish serfdom while retaining the administrative apparatus of the government. In 1826 he was charged with high treason, but his death sentence was commuted to hard labour in Siberia.

ULYANOV, ALEKSANDR ILYICH (1866–1887). Elder brother of Vladimir Ilyich Ulyanov (Lenin). A member of the People's Will and the manufacturer of the bombs intended for the assassination of Alexander III, Ulyanov was executed on 8 May 1887 for planning the attempt. His involvement in the revolutionary movement and his execution made a great impact on Lenin's subsequent development.

USHAKOV, ADMIRAL FEDOR FEDOROVICH (1744–1817). Naval commander and one of the founders of the Russian navy. When Russia became a member of the second coalition against France, Ushakov won a victory against the

French in the Mediterranean and the Adriatic by seizing the Ionian Islands in 1798.

VALUYEV, COUNT PYOTR ALEKSANDROVICH (1814–1890). Minister of the interior (1861–68) and president of the committee of ministers (1877–81). He helped to establish the *zemstva* and was active in planning the Great Reforms. In 1863 he produced a constitutional plan that would have established a consultative assembly combining elected and appointed ministers. The scheme was not implemented, but was however, re-examined in 1880.

VOLKONSKY, PRINCE SERGEY GRIGORYEVICH (1788–1865). Decembrist and major general. He fought in the Napoleonic Wars (1806–12) and in the Patriotic War (1812). Volkonsky was sentenced to death after the failure of the Decembrists' uprising, but served twenty years in the Nerchinsky mines. After the amnesty of 1856 he returned home.

VOLTAIRE, FRANÇOIS MARIE AROUET (1694–1778). French philosopher and writer whose influence extended to Russia. He was elected an honorary member of the Academy of Sciences during Elizabeth's reign and was commissioned by the government to serve as a historian of Peter I (the Great). Catherine II (the Great), desirous of strengthening ties with France, corresponded with Voltaire (1768–78). French ideas, particularly educational theory, came to inform part of Russian life among the upper echelons of society.

VORONTSOV, MIKHAIL ILLARIONOVICH (1714–1767). Statesman. Page at Elizabeth Petrovna's court, he assisted her in the coup d'état that made her empress. In 1744 Vorontsov was appointed vice-chancellor of the empire, and after the Seven Years' War he was made imperial chancellor, replacing Aleksey Bestuzhev-Ryumin. Vorontsov at first refusing to serve under Catherine II (the Great) and was put under house arrest, but he swore allegiance to her after learning of the death of Peter III. He was then reinstated and remained chancellor until his resignation in 1763.

WITTE, COUNT SERGEY YULYEVICH (1849–1915). Statesman born in Tbilisi. Witte was appointed minister of transport in 1892 and was minister of finance from 1892 to 1903. He encouraged industrial growth in Russia by protectionist tariffs, large foreign loans, and the large-scale building of railways. From 1903 to 1906 Witte was prime minister, and was in charge of negotiating the peace treaty with Japan at Portsmouth, New Hampshire. As a moderate conservative who attempted to establish a constitutional government, Witte was attacked by both liberals and the extreme right. He was disliked by both the Emperor and Empress and just before the convocation of the new Parliament he resigned but he continued as an independent member of the council of state and was a strong critic of World War I.

WRANGEL, BARON FERDINAND PETROVICH (1796–1870). Admiral and explorer. Having travelled around the world from 1817 to 1819, Wrangel then explored extensively in the Arctic, mapping the shores of north-eastern Siberia. He sighted, but failed to reach, Wrangel Island which was named after him, and he was a critic of the sale of Alaska. His diaries, entitled *Polar Expedition* were published in translation in 1840.

YAGUZHINSKY, PAVEL IVANOVICH (1683–1736). Army commander and an assistant of Peter I (the Great). Said to have originally been a swineherd in Lithuania, he was one of the able men taken by Peter from the lower classes when the tsar found the nobility hostile to reform. In 1722 Yaguzhinsky became the first procurator-general of the senate.

YANKOVICH DE MIRIEVO, THEODORE (*c.* 1740–1814). Serbian educator brought to Russia by Catherine II (the Great) in 1782. Catherine admired the educational system that the Austrian empire had instituted in 1774. She formed a commission for the establishment of popular schools to carry out plans recommended by Yankovich de Mirievo. He devised a three-tier school system, laid down an educational programme, and supervised the training of teachers. He also translated a number of Austrian textbooks into Russian.

YEROPKIN, PYOTR MIKHAILOVICH (1690–1740). Architect and town planner. Peter I (the Great) sent him to Italy to study architecture. In 1737 Yeropkin was appointed a member of the committee for the building of St Petersburg and played a leading role in the planning of the city, in particular designing the Admiraltyeska part of St Petersburg. The first Russian treatise on architecture was produced under his leadership. A loyal patriot, Yeropkin was a member of A. P. Volynsky's group, for which he was arrested and executed in 1740.

YUROVSKY, YANKEL (*fl.* early twentieth century). Grand commander and regional commissar for justice who, on behalf of the local Soviet, it is claimed, shot Nicholas II and his family in Ekaterinberg.

ZHELYABOV, ANDREY IVANOVICH (1850–1881). Revolutionary leader. The son of an ex-serf from Odessa, he was among those on the executive committee of the revolutionary Peoples' Will organisation, which was founded in 1879. Zhelyabov was a leader in the plan to assassinate Tsar Alexander II; the final arrangements were made by his accomplice and lover, Sofya Perovskaya, as he and Mikhail Mikhailov were arrested before the assassination took place, but he volunteered a confession and was hanged.

ZUBATOV, SERGEY VASILYEVICH (1864–1917). Chief of the Moscow *Okhrana* from 1890 to 1903. In 1901 Zubatov, with others, founded the society of mutual help for workers in mechanical production. Under police protection this society flourished, and such legal trade unions were established in Minsk, Odessa and St Petersburg. Zubatov was able to maintain control of the movement in Moscow, but elsewhere the unions got out of control and were used for revolutionary purposes. In 1903 the government withdrew its protection and he was dismissed.

ZUBOV, PRINCE PLATON ALEXANDROVICH (1767–1822). Lover and favourite of Catherine II (the Great). The last in a long line of her lovers, he was the only one of Potemkin's successors who had any political importance, and there is some evidence to suggest that he and Catherine were secretly married. Zubov had plans for the revival and extension of Potemkin's 'Greek Project', and advance toward India as well as toward Constantinople, but they were abandoned at Catherine's death in 1796. He was involved in the plot to murder Catherine's son, Paul I.

15
Glossary

Abramtsevo colony. Village and farmstead in the Moscow region, bought by the industrialist and railway tycoon Mamantov in the nineteenth century. It became an important centre of Russian folk culture and art, visited by Turgenev. Gogol had been a frequent visitor when the previous owner, Sergey Aksakov lived there, and while there he wrote part of *Dead Souls*. It also has several picturesque churches. After 1917, Abramtsevo became a museum and a small town for artists including Vasily Polenov, Ilya Ye, Repin, the Serovs, the Vasneknovs, the Mamontovs and Michael Vrubel.

Acmeists. Group of poets based in St Petersburg who founded the Poets' Guild in 1912. The most outstanding members were Anna Akhmatova and Osip Mandelstam. Other members included Nicholas Stepanovich Gumilev, Michael Kuzmin and Sergey Gorodetsky. They published a journal *Apollon* (1909–17), under the editorship of Sergey Makovsky. Their poetry is generally individualistic with a strong emphasis on aesthetics and form. The group disbanded in 1917.

Adrianople, Treaty of. Treaty signed 14 September 1829 between Russia and Turkey concluding the war of 1828–29. Russia obtained the right of unlimited transit of commercial ships through the Dardanelles, and of free trade without the Turkish empire. The European border with Turkey was established along the Prut and Danube rivers. Turkey handed over to Russia the east coast of the Black Sea from the mouth of the Kuban River to the port of St Nicholas and acknowledged the transfer to Russia of Georgia and other Transcaucasian lands. Autonomy was given to Serbia, and the independence of Greece was recognised. Moldavia and Wallachia were to be occupied until Turkey paid an indemnity.

Aix-la-Chapelle, Congress of (1818). Meeting of the Quadruple Alliance (Great Britain, Austria, Prussia and Russia) and France at Aix-la-Chapelle (now Aachen), attended by Tsar Alexander I. The Alliance reaffirmed the political reorganisation of Europe established by the Congress of Vienna (1814–15) and restored France's status as an independent power. It withdrew its occupying forces and admitted France into what thus became the Quintuple Alliance.

All-Russian Congress of Soviets. The first congress met in Petrograd in June 1917 with representatives from more than 350 units from all over Russia. It appointed a central executive committee, which sat permanently in Petrograd. Some of the leaders of this committee were also leaders of the executive committee of the Petrograd Soviet, having attended the congress as delegates.

All-Russian Period. The reign of Peter the Great (1682–1725), also known as the Imperial Age and the St Petersburg Era.

April Theses. On his return to Petrograd in April 1917, Lenin published a policy statement that defined his own position and was intended to direct the Bolsheviks toward the seizure of power. The theses contributed to the October uprising because in effect they were asking the Bolsheviks to withdraw support from the provisional government. In the theses, Lenin opposed continuation of the war; proposed that power be handed over to the Soviets, including control of banks, production, and distribution of goods; advocated abolition of the existing police force, army, and bureaucracy and the confiscation of all private land; and suggested that the Social Democratic Party be called the Communist Party and that the Socialist International be reconstructed.

The theses met with considerable opposition even from within the Bolshevik Party and the Petrograd and Moscow Bolshevik committees voted against them, but within a few weeks they were adopted by the Bolsheviks.

Archimandrite. Highest rank for monastic superiors.

Arestantskaia Rota. Convict detachment, a form of organisation for prisoners in Imperial Russia.

Arshin. Linear measure equal to 28 inches (71 cm), applied particularly to cloth production in industrial statistics in Imperial Russia.

Artel. An association of work people in Imperial Russia. A traditional form of industrial co-operative working and living together and sharing the profits of each job. They generally existed among workers in seasonal trades.

Assignat. Form of unconvertible paper currency issued by the Russian government during the late eighteenth and early nineteenth centuries.

Ataman. Commander of Cossack combat units. In the Ukraine initially an elected official but after 1723 the appointed head of the civil or military administration. Stenka Razin also had this title.

August Bloc. An organisation of Russian socialist factions which met in Vienna in August 1912. Its desire was to keep the Russian Socialist Democratic Labour Party from being fragmented by Lenin and others. However, so many factions boycotted the August Bloc that any chance of success was virtually precluded from the outset. The dominant figure of the August Bloc was Lev Trotsky, who was supported by the Mensheviks and the Bundists. The August Bloc failed in its ostensible goal of unity and succeeded only in establishing several short-lived periodicals. By 1914 even Trotsky disowned the group and it faded into oblivion.

Aurora. In August 1917 the sailors of the cruiser *Aurora* guarded the Winter Palace against Kornilov. On the morning of 7 November, *Aurora*, on the orders of the Military Revolutionary Committee, entered Neva and anchored near the Nikolayevsky Bridge. In the evening the *Aurora* opened fire on the Winter Palace. The fire did very little damage and lasted only one hour because the Winter Palace was quick to surrender.

Autocrat and Autocracy. Total power exercised by Russian tsars. Ivan III (the Great) modelled his court on that of the Byzantine emperors and used the titles tsar and autocrat (*samoderzhets*). The latter, as used in Moscow, originally referred to the complete independence of the Muscovite sovereign from any overlord after the withdrawal of the Tatars. Originally the title implied independence from any other ruler, but it came to mean an absolute monarch, particularly under Peter I (the Great). Even when the power of the tsar was limited by that of the state *duma* and state council following the 1905 Revolution, the title autocrat was retained in the constitution.

Bagratids. Royal Armenian and Georgian dynasty. It ruled Armenia from 885 to 1045, keeping the country free from the influence of the Byzantine Empire, and ruled Georgia from 1045 until its annexation in 1800 by Russia.

Baltic Germans. The descendants of the Teutonic Knights and their followers who settled in the Baltic provinces. In the eighteenth century the provinces became part of Russia.

Baltic Provinces. Name given in pre-revolutionary times to the provinces of Estland, Livland and Kurland. Once belonging to the Teutonic Knights, they later belonged to Sweden and Poland and were annexed by Russia in the eighteenth century, after which russification measures were instigated.

Baltic Sea. Sea surrounded by Sweden, Denmark, Germany and Poland and the republics of Lithuania, Latvia and Estonia. It is connected to the North Sea by a channel between Denmark and the south of Sweden. The Baltic has been the principal maritime trade route between Russia and Western Europe since the Middle Ages.

Baraba Steppe. Wooded steppe in south-western Siberia between the Irtysh and Ob rivers colonised since the eighteenth century by Russians and Ukrainians.

Barin. Russian landlord, usually one with large land holdings.

Barshchina. Unpaid labour that serfs were obliged to render to a landlord. Under the *barshchina* system one part of an estate was divided into allotments and farmed by the peasants on their own account. The majority of the estate was managed directly by the owner and was cultivated by the labour of the same peasants. The peasants' obligations were discharged by work and no monetary payment was made, but the landlord paid the poll tax. Generally three days a week were spent on the estate of the landlord. After the emancipation of 1861 this system survived in a modified form.

Beard Tax. (See p. 43.)

Bednyak. Impoverished peasant, owning some land but usually not enough to support a family.

Belorussians. An east Slavic people living in Belorussia and surrounding areas, for 77 per cent of whom Belorussian is the mother tongue. They first developed a national identity when the Lithuanians were outnumbered by Russians during the thirteenth and fourteenth centuries; this continued to grow, and by the late seventeenth century a Belorussian literature and press had appeared. There are Belorussian communities in Lithuania, Latvia, and the Białystok district of Poland.

Bezpopovtsy. Priestless faction of the Old Believers who in the early nineteenth century controlled industries, particularly in Moscow.

Birzha. Commercial stock exchange, a place for business transactions in tsarist Russia.

Black Earth. *Chernozem* or fertile black soil which stretches from the Carpathians and the Black Sea to the Altay mountains. Normally about one foot deep but in places over three feet. It is neutral chemically (neither alkaline nor acid) and has a calcareous layer under the humus. In this last respect it differs from similar soils in the United States.

Black Hundreds. Reactionary extreme right groups particularly active during Stolypin's premiership, 1906–11. While endorsing national representation and the need to improve the life of peasants and workers, they also supported absolutism and anti-Semitism. The least harmful activity was the staging of popular demonstrations at which the crowds would carry icons and portraits of the royal family, accompanied by patriotic and religious songs. More sinister was the hatred of the Jews, which was encouraged. They organised pogroms against Jews and general terror against university students, members of the free professions and revolutionaries. The authorities tended to ignore the pogroms, and Nicholas II thanked the Black Hundreds for their support.

Bloody Sunday. (See p. 116.)

Blue Rose Arts Society. Radical arts society founded in 1907. It consisted of a group of Symbolist Impressionists, many of whom tended toward a lyric mysticism in their art; blue and lavender frequently dominated their work.

Bobyl. Tenant farmer or landless peasant.

Bochka. Measure of capacity of a cask or barrel and equivalent to 4.92 hectolitres or 108.28 gallons. There were 40 *vedro* to a *bochka* and 10 *krushka* to a *vedro*.

Bolsheviks. Radical faction of the Russian Social Democratic Workers' Party when it split in 1903. The Bolsheviks, meaning those in the majority (Mensheviks were the minority), were headed by Lenin, who believed that the revolution must be led by a single centralised party of professional revolutionaries.

Bosporus. Strait uniting the Black Sea with the Sea of Marmara, dividing Europe from Asia. Securing open passage for Russian naval and commercial shipping through the warm waters of the Bosporus has been a touchstone of Russian diplomacy from the mid-seventeenth century to the present. After 1841 no warships could pass through the strait without permission from Turkey.

Boyar. A member of the medieval Russian aristocracy in the sixteenth century, as distinguished from the *pomeshchik* (service noble). Boyars received their titles from the tsars, headed important offices, and participated in the deliberation of the *boyarskaya duma*. This was an advisory council to the Russian grand princes and tsars, consisting of important boyars, nobles, and high church dignitaries.

Bund. (See p. 115.)

Burlak. Human hauler of barges on Russian rivers.

Cadets (Kadets). (See p. 116.)

Cadets, Corp of. Military school founded in 1732 at St Petersburg to prepare children of commissioned officers for military careers. It was abolished in 1918.

Calendar. Until 1700 Russia had its own national calendar which reckoned the years from an estimated beginning of the world and not from the birth of Christ. The year ran from September. In 1700 Peter I (the Great) adopted the Julian calendar, which had been or was about to be abandoned by Western Europe in favour of the Gregorian system. The Julian calendar was ten days behind the Gregorian calendar in the seventeenth century, eleven in the eighteenth and twelve in the nineteenth, and by 1900 thirteen days behind. The Gregorian calendar was adopted by decree on 26 January 1918 fixing 1 February 1918 as 14 February 1918. The anniversary of the Revolution of 25 October now became 7 November although it was still known as the 'October' Revolution.

Peter I (the Great) issued a decree on a New Calendar on 20 December 1699.

> All Greeks from whom we accepted our Orthodox faith number their years from eight days after the birth of Christ, that is from 1 January, and not from the creation of the world. There is a great difference in those two calendars. This year is 1699 since the birth of Christ, and on 1 January it will be 1700 as well as a new century. To celebrate this happy and opportune occasion, the Great Sovereign has ordered that henceforth all government administrative departments and fortresses in all their official business use the new calendar beginning 1 January 1700. To commemorate this happy beginning and the new century in the capital city of Moscow, after a solemn prayer in churches and private dwellings, all major streets, homes of important people, and homes of distinguished religious and civil servants should be decorated with trees, pine, and fir branches similar to the decoration of the Merchant Palace or the Pharmacy Building – or as best as one knows how to decorate his place and gates. Poor people should put up at least one tree, or a branch on their gates at the entrance of their homes. These decorations are to remain from 1 January to 7 January 1700.

Charter of the Towns. (See p. 56.)

Charter of the Nobility. Charter issued under Catherine II (the Great) in 1785, which recognised the privileged position of the nobility as the ruling class and implictly recognised the peasants' status as chattel slaves. It also provided for the creation of autonomous corporations of the nobility, with legal powers (see p. 56).

Cheka. Extraordinary Commission, organised as a network to combat counter-revolutionaries and saboteurs established by the Bolsheviks on 7 December 1917.

Chetvert. Dry measure equal to about 5.9 bushels (2.099 hectolitres).

Collegiate System. Administrative system introduced by Peter I (the Great) in 1718. The system was borrowed from Sweden and the old central administrative offices were abolished and nine colleges established. The system was abolished by Alexander I in 1802.

Commissar. Title of various high-ranking officials. Commissars were first appointed by the provisional government after the February 1917 Revolution.

Communism. Basic aims of communism were first expounded in the *Communist Manifesto* of Marx and Engels. Its main characteristics are the absence of social classes, private property, and the state.

Conditions of Mitau. (See p. 53.)

Constituent Assembly. Democratically elected assembly that met in Petrograd on 18 January 1918 and was dissolved by the Bolsheviks after one session.

Cossacks. People of southern and south-western Russia descended from independent Tatar groups and escaped serfs from Poland, Lithuania and Muscovy. They established a number of independent self-governing communities, which were given special privileges by Russian or Polish rulers in return for military services. Known for their horsemanship, each Cossack community provided a separate army. The Cossacks slowly lost their autonomy as Russia expanded in the seventeenth and eighteenth centuries, and there were occasional rebellions. Many fled Russia after the Revolution (1918–21), and collectivisation subsumed remaining Cossack communities. Originally frontiersmen; the name coming from a Turkic world meaning 'Adventurer'.

Council of State. Advisory body formed in 1810 by Alexander I, its members being appointed by the emperor. It was not a legislative body and the emperor was not obliged to follow its advice. In 1906 Count Witte redefined its role; only half of its members were to be appointed; the rest were to be elected.

Danubian Principalities. In 1812 Napoleon objected to Russian control of the Danubian principalities of Moldavia and Walachia as they were a threat to the growth of French influence in the Near East. By the Treaty of Adrianople (1829) Turkey recognised a Russian protectorate over the principalities, which were, however, to enjoy an autonomous existence. In 1848 Russia intervened to suppress a revolution by the Romanian national movement. Russian occupation of the Danubian Principalities in 1853, in an attempt to force the Turks to come to terms in the so-called Holy Land controversy, precipitated the Crimean War, which began in the same year. Moldavia and Walachia were occupied by Austria to separate the Russians from the Turks in the Balkans; eventually peace was established in 1856. Under the Treaty of Paris (1856) the Danubian Principalities were placed under the joint guarantee of the signatory powers.

Desyatina. Measure of land approximately equivalent to 2.7 acres or 1,092 hectares.

Desyatovskiy's Report. A. P. Zablotskiy-Desyatovskiy, a government official under Alexander II, produced a report in 1841 on the condition of the serfs, mainly in central European Russia, which gave a horrifying account of the lives of peasant serfs and the callousness of the average landlord.

Dokhod. Tsarist state revenue, largely rents and also proceeds from the sale of liquor produced in government distilleries and of precious metals from government mines.

Dual Entente. Alliance between Russia and France 1893–1917.

Dual Power. Situation whereby the authority of the provisional government established 2 March 1917 was constantly undermined by the rival influence of the Soviet of the workers' and soldiers' deputies, thus enabling the Bolshevik takeover at the October Revolution.

Dukhobory. Peasant religious sect, also known as the Spirit Wrestlers, founded in the eighteenth century. They called themselves Christians of the Universal Brotherhood until 1839 and then the Union of Spiritual Communities of Christ. The sect preached equality and opposed all authority that conflicted with their conscience. They were opposed to the priesthood and the sacraments, and their approach to religious matters resembled that of the Quakers. They were persecuted under Catherine II (the Great). Alexander I persuaded them to settle near the Sea of Azov, where about 4,000 farmed and flourished. They were forcibly moved from their farms and shifted eastward in 1840–41 when they refused to accept military conscription. In 1887 they again resisted conscription and their leader, Peter Verigin, was exiled to Siberia. Leo Tolstoy petitioned the tsar to let the sect emigrate. English Quakers provided funds and 7,500 reached Canada in 1899 while 12,000 remained in Russia.

Duma. Legislative assembly at the end of the tsarist period (1905–17). It criticised the conduct of World War I and was suspended, but met in November 1916 to warn of the possibility of revolution (see p. 60).

Dusha. Peasant under poll tax obligation, a soul.

Dvoryanstvo. A member of the Russian nobility. In the seventeenth century, military service for the *dvoryanstvo* was hereditary. In 1642 and 1649 it was established that only the *dvoryanstvo* could own land worked by serfs. Peter I (the Great) extensively reformed the rights and position of the *dvoryanstvo*; although from then on the *dvoryanstvo* were virtually forced to serve either in the army, navy or bureaucracy. In 1785, a charter reaffirmed and consolidated their status, and the *dvoryanstvo* enjoyed such privileges as exemption from poll tax and the fact that they could not be stripped of estates, title or status without trial by their peers. Their rights over the serfs were also reaffirmed, and so by this time the *dvoryanstvo* was a full-fledged class of nobles.

Dvorovye Liudi. Landless serfs who worked in the household of their lord before the 1861 emancipation. In the early nineteenth century, some serfs attached to the town houses of the nobility undertook factory work.

Eastern Question. Historian's name for the problems created in the nineteenth century by Turkey's decline to the position of Sick Man of Europe. Manifestations included the Greek War of Independence, the Crimean War, Balkan rivalries, and disputes about the status of the Dardanelles; they usually involved clashes between Russian and European aims.

Electoral System. Prior to 1906 the electorate was restricted to the selection of local officials and was based on a narrow franchise, with the majority of population having no voice.

An electoral system was created for the election of the State Duma in 1906. Suffrage was not universal. The minimum age to gain the vote was twenty-five, and women, soldiers, sailors and students were not enfranchised.

Emancipation. Edict of emancipation of 1861 by which some serfs, hitherto regarded a chattels of the landowner, were liberated. Although a landmark in the history of

Russia – the serf could marry, take legal action, own property in his name, and engage in business or trade – he was in fact economically dependent on the landlord.

Entente. Agreement involving Russia, Britain and France, the Entente came into existence gradually after the Franco-Russian Dual Alliance of 1894.

In 1904 Britain concluded an 'understanding' with France on outstanding colonial problems which had divided the two countries for many years. With French encouragement, Russia, defeated by Japan and anxious for new allies, and Britain, alarmed by the growing strength of Germany, signed a 'convention' in 1907 settling their differences, chiefly with regard to Persia. But this series of agreements did not become a formal military alliance until 5 September 1914, when the three powers vowed not to make a separate peace and to refrain from offering peace terms without prior agreement.

February Revolution. (See p. 121.)

Field of Mars. An open space in St Petersburg that was used for military parades, festivities, and fireworks and was begun by Peter I (the Great). Its name is taken from the god of war and the monument in the grounds of a Russian leader, Count Suvorov, who is portrayed as Mars. Originally known as the Field of Amusement, it was, in the eighteenth century, also known as the Tsarina's Meadow.

Finland Station. Railway station in (Petrograd) St Petersburg where Lenin arrived back in Russia from Switzerland in April 1917 in a sealed train.

Fires of 1862. Series of outbreaks, the cause of which was unknown but suspected to be arson, in St Petersburg and in towns on the Volga River. They formed part of a general unrest that was otherwise marked by peasant riots, student actions, and revolutionary propaganda.

First International. Formed by Marx in London in 1864, the First International Workingmen's Association aimed to co-ordinate efforts by the working classes in different countries to establish Socialism and was the earliest attempt to form a world organisation. Disputes between the anarchists and Marxists culminated in the final break between Marx and Bakunin in 1872. The First International moved its headquarters to New York. It was finally dissolved in 1876.

Freemasonry. Freemasonry was introduced into Russia in the 1730s and gained strength later in that century with lodges founded in St Petersburg, Moscow and Riga. Catherine II (the Great) was at first in favour of freemasonry, but withdrew her approval in 1794 fearing the spread of revolutionary ideas from France. Tsars Paul and Alexander I continued the interdict, but by 1803 Alexander I allowed meetings of the lodges. The lodges attracted the membership of some officers who would lead the Decembrist uprising of 1825. All Masonic lodges were closed in 1822 and attempts to revive freemasonry after the 1905 Revolution failed.

Gorod. City or larger town.

Gramota. Written document.

Great Embassy. (See p. 42.)

Great Northern War. War, also known as the Second Northern War, fought by Russia, Denmark/Norway, and Saxony/Poland against Sweden. The Treaties of Stockholm (1719–20) and the Treaty of Nystad (1721) established the peace and also made Russia a powerful state in the Baltic (see p. 133).

Guberniia. Administrative unit introduced by Peter I (the Great).

Haemophilia. The Tsarevich, Grand Duke Alexis Nicolayevich, the fourth child and first son of Tsar Nicholas II and Tsaritsa Alexandra Fyodorovna, suffered from haemophilia, a hereditary condition characterised by excessive bleeding. Usually only affecting males and a minor wound may result in fatal bleeding. The Tsaritsa was a granddaughter of Queen Victoria, several of whose descendants suffered from it. His apparently successful treatment of Alexis gave Rasputin ascendancy over Alexandra.

Hague Conventions. International conferences convened by Nicholas II that met 18 May to 19 July 1899 and 15 June to 18 October 1907, with the aim of 'a possible reduction of the excessive armaments which weigh upon all nations' by 'putting a limit on the progressive development of the present armaments'. Twenty-six countries were represented. The first convention's achievements were limited but did include agreement on the use of gas, expanding bullets, the banning of explosives launched from balloons, and the creation of a court of arbitration (the International Court of Justice). The second convention reached agreement on a number of naval matters and on the employment of force to recover debts, but failed to reach any consensus on major issues. A further convention was planned for 1915, but because of World War I did not meet. The two conventions did influence the planning for the League of Nations.

Hermitage. The Hermitage was originally constructed in order to house the art collection of Catherine I, and under Catherine II (the Great) it was a centre of musical and theatrical activity. The Old Hermitage (1755–84), the New Hermitage (1839–50), and the Hermitage Theatre (1787), and known as the Winter Palace it was the seat of the Provisional Government in 1917. Lenin gave the order to fire on the Palace on 25 October 1917, and within a few hours the Palace had fallen to the Bolsheviks.

Hetman. Cossack leader; see Ataman.

Holy Alliance. An agreement signed between the monarchs of Austria, Prussia and Russia in September 1815 (published the following January) to preserve the peace in Europe and to support each other in achieving the end. The document was originally drafted by Tsar Alexander and was profoundly religious in its language, insisting that Christian principles should guide princes and that the government and peoples of Europe should all regard themselves as members of the same Christian nation. The document was dismissed by Castlereagh as 'a piece of sublime mysticism and nonsense'; Metternich had little time for many of the ideas in it, but used it nevertheless to maintain the status quo in Restoration Europe. The alliance was subsequently signed by most of the European monarchs, though not by the British king.

'The Holy Alliance' was also the term used pejoratively by some contemporary liberals, and by later historians, to describe the reactionary attitudes and acts of the conservative monarchies in Restoration Europe.

Holy Synod. Council created by Peter I (the Great) in 1720 to exercise state control over the Orthodox Church. It was based on the Lutheran model (see p. 76).

Imperial Academy of Sciences. Founded in St Petersburg in 1724 by Peter I (the Great). Originally known as the Russian Academy of Sciences, the St Petersburg Academy of Sciences, and until 1917 the Imperial Academy of Sciences.

Imperiya Vserossyskaya. Designation of the Russian state from an act passed by Peter I (the Great) in October 1721 until the abdication of Nicholas II in March 1917.

Iskra (The Spark). Marxist newspaper founded by Lenin published abroad after 1900, first in Germany, then London, and from 1903 in Switzerland. Also a satirical journal published in St Petersburg (1859–73).

Izgoy. Feudal serf, bounded to his/her owner and to the soil.

Jacobins. Minor revolutionary organisation in Russia in the early nineteenth century. The Jacobins were led by Jacobin Frédéric-César La Harpe, the former chief tutor of Alexander I. Influenced by the French radicals, they advocated republicanism, although La Harpe himself extolled the merits of both radical ideas and enlightened absolutism to Alexander I.

July Days. Period from 16 to 18 July 1917, when servicemen and civilians, in sympathy with the Bolsheviks, tried to seize power from Kerensky's provisional government in Petrograd. Lenin considered their uprising inopportune; they received no significant support and the attempt failed. Bolshevik involvement was ascribed to pro-German sympathies and Bolsheviks in general were accused of treason. Lenin fled to Finland.

Kadets. See Cadets.

Kantonists. In 1721 Peter I (the Great) founded schools for sons of soldiers destined for military service from birth. From 1798 they were known as War Orphan Institutions and in 1805 the pupils of these schools were named Kantonists and later were included in the 'military colonies'. Most Kantonists became soldiers at the age of twenty. Kantonists were abolished in 1856 when there were about 380,000.

Katorga. Hard labour.

Kazennaya. Treasury office.

Khodynka Field Disaster. Celebrations for the coronation of Nicholas II in 1896 ended in disaster when too large a crowd, numbering 500,000 gathered at Khodynskoye Field. There was inadequate organisation, and panic led to a stampede that caused the deaths of over 2,000 people with many more injured.

Khozain. Head of household in the Russian Mir.

Kitai Gorod. Commercial centre of Old Moscow, located near the Kremlin.

Kopek. One hundredth of a rouble.

Kreditnyi Bilet. Note of credit, a form of tsarist paper money which succeeded the *assignat* in the 1840s.

Kremlin. The main fortress in a medieval Russian city, usually built on the high bank of a river, or rivers in the case of a confluence, and separated from the rest of the city by a wall with ramparts, a moat, and towers and battlements. The kremlin itself contained the palaces for the bishop and prince, their offices, a cathedral, and stores and weapons in case of siege. The best-known kremlin is the Moscow Kremlin, built according to a triangular design at the confluence of the Moskva and Neglinnaya rivers. The rampart and red-brick towers were built by Italian architects in the days of Ivan III (the Great). The ornate spires were added in the seventeenth century. The Kremlin contains the Cathedral of the Dormition, the Cathedral of the Archangel Michael, and the Cathedral of the Annunciation, as well as the Palace of the Pacets and Terem Palace. The present Great Kremlin Palace was built in 1839–40 by Konstantin Thon, in the Russo-Byzantine style.

Kulak. Wealthy peasant in later imperial and early Soviet Russia.

Kustar. Peasant engaged in cottage industry.

Kvas. Fermented beverage.

Land Captain (zemskii nachalnik). Office of chief of the *zemstvo*, established in 1889. He was appointed by the minister of the interior; the land captain was under the authority of the minister, and as such he represented the immediate bureaucratic supervision of the peasants. He exercised complete control over the peasant officials and could fine or imprison them. He was responsible for confirming the decisions made at peasant meetings. The land captain therefore replaced independent elected justices of the peace. Since they had to be appointed from members of the local gentry with a certain property qualification, the position of land captain emphasised the role of the gentry in the countryside. Their powers were diminished by the reforms of Stolypin in the early 1900s.

League of Armed Neutrality. League based on doctrine of armed neutrality at sea, advanced by Russia in 1780 in order to protect the trade of neutral states against the British. A number of European countries accepted the proposals of Catherine II (the Great), which became part of international maritime law. Neutral ships were not to be interfered with, even when trading with combatants; combatants' goods in neutral ships were not to be seized, and blockades were not to be legal until they were enforced.

Lena Goldfield Massacre. In 1912 workers in the Lena goldfield went on strike in order to obtain better living and working conditions and higher wages. About 5,000 protesters were confronted by troops, who fired on them, killing approximately 200 and wounding many others. As a result, the Russian work force became incensed, and during that year some 725,000 workers went on strike. The *duma*, also angered, called for an investigation of the massacre, which resulted in heavy criticism of the way in which the goldfield was managed.

Liberation of Labour Group. Russian Marxist organisation founded in Switzerland in 1883 by the former populists Georgy Plekhanov and Pavel Axelrod, who were living in exile in Western Europe. They translated the works of Marx and Engels and smuggled them into Russia.

Malozemlie. Land hunger. Lack of land suffered, in particular, by peasants after the 1861 agrarian reform.

Marxism. The main thesis of Marxism was that humankind developed politically through three stages, leading to the dictatorship of the proletariat, the withering away of the state, and the emergence of a classless society.

Marxism-Leninism. Theories arising from the adaptation of nineteenth-century Marxism to twentieth-century facts, and in particular to the problems of governing Russia; it includes belief in 'Socialism in one country' and peaceful co-existence with countries under different social systems.

Maximalists. Small terrorist group of populists that split off from the Socialist Revolutionaries in 1904. Having taken an active part in the Revolution of 1905, they continued to organise violence, and in 1906 blew up Pyotr Stolypin's summer residence. As a result, many Maximalists were executed and others escaped abroad. They worked with the Bolsheviks after the latter's seizure of power in 1917 and were represented in the central executive committee.

Mensheviks. Political party established in August 1917 (see p. 120).

Meshchanin. Urban inhabitant of lower-class origin in the nineteenth century, not enrolled in the merchants guilds but permitted limited commercial rights and subject to the head tax and to military service. The registered urban lower class collectively, as distinguished from peasants, merchants and nobles.

Mestechko. Small town, larger than a village.

Mestnichestvo. System by which appointment of court officials, ambassadors and army officials depended upon inherited rank and status. Records of genealogical tables were burned in 1682, thus abolishing *mestnichestvo*.

Metropolitan. Primate of the Orthodox Church. In the nineteenth century, a metropolitan resided in each of the historic capitals of the Russian Empire: Kiev, Moscow and St Petersburg.

Military Settlements (Colonies). The first military settlement was established in 1810. Crown peasants were turned into hereditary soldiers, often bringing great hardship. Between 1816 and 1812 about 33 per cent of the peacetime army was located in military settlements. There were several rebellions including Chuguevin in the Ukraine (1819).

Mir. Rural assembly that administered an agricultural community. This did not always correspond to one village and generally it refers to the rural community and its inhabitants. After the emancipation in 1861 the mir was retained for administrative reasons, but was abolished after the Stolypin reforms of 1906–11.

Monjik. Peasant.

Muscovy. State from the fourteenth to the eighteenth century. The grand princes of Vladimir were the first princes to rule Muscovy. As Moscow became more powerful it took over as capital of the grand principality. The last tsar of Muscovy was Peter I (the Great), the first emperor of Russia.

Names. Before the October Revolution in 1917, first names were limited to saints' names. Name days of the saints were celebrated more commonly than birthdays. Other limitations on names were imposed, some relating to social status and occupation. Each person has at least three names: a first name, a patronymic, and a surname. The patronymic is formed by adding the endings -ovich, -evich, or -ich to the father's first name in the case of a man, or by adding -ovna, -evna, -inichna, or -ichna to the father's name in the case of a woman. In addition, a wide number of diminutive forms of the first name are also used, including Kolya for Nikolai, Mash for Mariya, Sasha for Alexander(a), Vanya for Ivan.

According to B. O. Unbegaun, in *Russian Surnames* (1972), the twelve most popular surnames in St Petersburg in 1910 were: Ivanov, Vasilyev, Petrov, Smirnov, Mikhailov, Fedorov, Sokolov, Yakovlev, Popov, Andreyev, Alekseyev and Aleksandrov.

Namestnik. Administrator, or Viceroy, of a large administrative unit, usually a highborn nobleman appointed by the tsar.

Narodniki. Populists, revolutionaries who turned 'to the people', the *narod*, in the years 1860–90.

Nemets. Literally, one who is dumb, unable to speak. Originally used to describe any foreigner, it became more specifically used to mean a German.

Nihilsm. Radical intellectual movement of the 1860s. Nihilism grew up largely as a result of the rejection of the historical and aesthetic idealism of the 1830s and 1840s. Nihilism represented a revolt against the established social order and it negated the authority of the state, family and Church.

Nobility. In Muscovite Russia, the government promoted the interests of the gentry by passing laws that limited the peasants' movements. From 1475 boyar families in state service were entered in a state genealogical book; many squabbles ensued as the boyars fought to maintain their rank. In 1722 Peter I (the Great) introduced compulsory state service, and with his Table of Ranks advancement was open to all. Titles of nobility were conferred on those who deserved it, regardless of social standing. In 1785, during what is considered the Golden Age of Nobles, Catherine II (the Great) issued a Charter to the Nobility; this recognised the gentry of each district and province as a legal body, headed by an elected district or regional marshal of nobility. Members of the gentry were also exempt from tax obligations and personal service. The position of the nobility began to decline considerably under Alexander I and Nicholas I. According to the 1877 census, the nobility owned 73,100,000 desyatin of land, but by 1911, it owned only 43,200,000 desyatin.

Obrok. Annual payment by serfs to their masters. Most of the land of an estate was farmed by peasants on their own account and they paid the owner an annual amount known as *obrok*. Sometimes payments were made in kind or by performing services. About 44 per cent of peasants worked under this system in the eighteenth century and those working under *obrok* generally enjoyed greater freedom than those working under *barshchina*.

Obrok is also a term used for the consolidation of taxes and for the owner being responsible for collecting taxes and delivering them to the authorities; thus the tenants were relieved of dealing directly with tax officials.

October Revolution. (See p. 124.)

Octobrists. Right-wing liberals who supported the October Manifesto of 1905.

Okhrana. Political security police existing from 1881 until abolished by the provisional government in 1917. From the Russian word *okhrana*, meaning 'protection'.

Old Believers. Russian dissenters who in the seventeenth century refused to accept the patriarch Nikon's reform of the services of the Russian Orthodox Church (see p. 76).

Old Church Slavonic. Slavic language based on Macedonian dialects spoken around Thessalonika. Its once relatively widespread usage is attributed to the fact that this is the language used by Saints Cyril and Methodius when translating the Bible and when preaching to the Moravian Slavs. The language as used after the twelfth century is referred to as Church Slavonic.

Pacification. The policy of suppressing revolutionary terrorist activity and restoring order, carried out by Stolypin's government after 1905. Widespread terrorism was countered by placing different areas of Russia under different centres of control, censoring the press, organising infiltration of revolutionary movements by police spies, and summary court-martial.

Pale of Settlement. Russian Jews were required to live in a defined area called the Pale of Settlement, and it was only in exceptional circumstances that a Jew could move out of the Pale (Pale meaning a fenced area).

Pan-Slavism. A nineteenth-century movement to unite all Slavic people for cultural and political ends. It was formed in the early nineteenth century by intellectuals among western and southern Slavs seeking cultural identity for emerging national groups. In 1848 it became a political movement for Slavic emancipation from the Austrian empire. In the 1860s in Russia it developed as an idealistic campaign whereby Holy Russia was to save a spiritually bankrupt Europe; Russian liberation of other Slavs from Austrian or Turkish rule was seen as a prerequisite. In this respect the movement influenced Russian foreign policy in the Russo–Turkish War of 1877–78.

Paris, Treaties of. The major treaties signed in Paris concerning Russia are the treaties of 1814–15 and the treaty of 1856. In the former, Austria, Britain, Portugal, Prussia, Russia and Sweden met to discuss the fate of France following Napoleon's defeat. At the latter, the influence of Russia in the Ottoman Empire following the Crimean War was discussed, and Russia ceded Bessarabia to Moldavia and agreed to the neutralisation of the Black Sea area.

Partitions of Poland. The first partition in 1772 divided Poland between Russia, Prussia and Austria, the second in 1793 was mainly to Russia's advantage and in the third in

1795 Poland lost her independence. In the fourth partition under the Treaty of Vienna (1815) the Kingdom of Poland was established under the suzerainty of the Russian tsars.

Patriarch. Title conferred on the head of the Russian Orthodox Church from 1589 until the era of Peter I (the Great). It was re-established in November 1917.

Pauper's allotment. The pauper's allotment was an additional provision of the emancipation reform law of 1861. There were variants on the application of the land settlement in different areas of the country, but the basic plan was that the peasants would receive that part of the land that they had cultivated for themselves, which was roughly half of the total. They had to pay the landlords for the land they acquired, or, alternatively, they could take a quarter of their normal parcel of land, the pauper's allotment, without payment.

Peasants' Union. Organisation established in 1905 as a result of populist activity. The union demanded that land be nationalised and that it be used only by those who tilled it. Its members disagreed as to whether to use peaceful or violent methods to achieve their aims, and the union disintegrated in 1906.

Peter and Paul Fortress. Built on Hare Island, St Petersburg, in 1703 by Peter I (the Great), from 1718 onward the hexagonal fortress served as a prison for political offenders. It was built according to the designs of Lambert, a pupil of Vauban. Within the fortress is the Cathedral of St Peter and St Paul, by Domenicko Andrea Trezzini, the golden spire of which is a focal point of St Petersburg.

Petrashevsky Circle. Group of several hundred people who met to discuss the need to build a socialist utopia. In 1849 twenty-one members were charged with plotting to overthrow the state. Fifteen were condemned to death but this was commuted at the last moment; one of the condemned was the writer Dostoyevsky.

Pochtovyi Trakt. Postal road.

Pogrom. Term, meaning 'destruction', used to denote anti-Jewish violence, first used to describe attacks on the Jews authorised by the Tsarist authorities in 1881. Pogroms in Eastern Europe forced many Jews to emigrate in the late nineteenth and early twentieth centuries.

Pomeshchik. Landed proprietor; from the Russian word *pomestie*, meaning an estate granted in reward for service rendered to the tsar, from 1478 until the seventeenth century.

Populism (Narodnost). Socialist movement of intellectuals which emerged in the 1860s. The populists sought to transform society by basing it on the traditional peasant *mir* (community). Inspired by Michael Bakunin, in 1873–74 the *narodniki* (populists) adopted the tactic of 'going to the people' (*khozhdeniye v narod*) with the main aim of educating the masses with revolutionary ideas. This having failed, the more secretive Land and Liberty (*Zemlya i Volya*) group was formed in 1876. Three years later, those members advocating more violent methods formed the People's Will (*Narodnaya Volya*) terrorist group. It was this group that was responsible for the assassination of Alexander II in 1881. The moderates, the Black Repartition (*Cherny Peredel*), continued to employ more peaceful means.

Poud (Pud). Measure of weight equivalent to 36 pounds avoirdupois.

Posad. Small town, usually commercial or suburban, inhabited by members of the urban lower and middle classes.

Potomstvennyi Potochnyi Grazhdanin. Title of hereditary honourable citizen, created in the early nineteenth century and granted to merchants for service or distinction, also to military and civil servants not promoted to hereditary or personal nobility.

Preobrazhenskoye. Village near Moscow from which the senior guards infantry regiment of the Imperial Russian Army derived its name.

Provisional Government. (See p. 124.)

Pud. see Poud.

Pugachevshchina. Peasant rising led by Yemelyan Pugachev in 1773–74 (see p. 84).

Quadruple Alliance. Alliance first formed in 1813 between Russia, Austria, Britain and Prussia and officially renewed in 1815. The four powers agreed to maintain the Second Peace of Paris (signed the same day) and to prevent the return of Napoleon. They also agreed to hold periodic conferences of sovereigns or chief ministers to maintain the stability of Europe and discuss matters of common interest. There were four such meetings: in Aix-la-Chapelle (1818), Troppau, Laibach (1820–21), and Verona (1822); by then, differences had emerged between Great Britain, which was opposed to direct intervention in the internal affairs of sovereign states, and the others, which were prepared to intervene directly to suppress revolution. Further differences emerged (between Russia and Austria) in 1825 and the system was abandoned. At the meeting in Aix-la-Chapelle in 1818 France was reacknowledged as one of the great powers of Europe and the Quadruple Alliance became the Quintuple Alliance.

Rada. Ukrainian council. Term used in the seventeenth and twentieth centuries.

Raznochintsy. Term used in the nineteenth century for those who neither belonged to the peasantry nor the nobility. Many of this intermediate class wrote or taught for a living; the *raznochintsy* were to become one of the main sources of the intelligentsia.

Redemption Payments. Fixed amount of money paid annually to the government by peasants who were former serfs for the land they received from the landlord at the time of the emancipation of the serfs. The government had immediately compensated the landowners, and redemption payments were to last for forty-nine years, but the government reduced the amount of debt and in 1906 they were remitted.

Reinsurance Treaty. Secret treaty concluded between Germany and Russia in 1887 after the Three Emperors' League had expired. Each country was to remain neutral if the other engaged in warfare, with the exception of an aggressive war of Germany against France or Russia against Austria–Hungary. After Bismarck's resignation in 1890, Germany abrogated the treaty.

Riad.   Stall or small shop where goods were sold, or a row of similar structures offering the same products within a large market place.

Romanovs.   The last ruling dynasty of Russia reigning from 1613–1917, noted for their absolutism and for transforming Russia into a large empire. The first Romanov tsar was Michael, whose election ended the Time of Troubles. Peter I (the Great) was succeeded by his second wife, Catherine, the daughter of a Livonian peasant, and she by Peter II, the grandson of Peter, with whom the male line of Romanovs terminated in the year 1730. The reign of the next three sovereigns of Russia – Anne, Ivan VI, and Elizabeth – of the female line of Romanovs, formed a transitional period, which came to an end with the accession of Peter III of the house of Holstein-Gottorp. All the subsequent emperors, without exception, connected themselves by marriage with German families. The wife and successor of Peter III, Catherine II (the Great), daughter of the prince of Anhalt Zerbst, general in the Prussian army, left the crown to her only son, Paul I, who became the father of two emperors, Alexander I and Nicholas I, and the grandfather of a third, Alexander II. All these sovereigns married German princesses, creating intimate family alliances, among others, with the reigning houses at Württemberg, Baden and Prussia.

Russian Social Democratic Labour Party.   Founded in Minsk in 1898, it split into Mensheviks and Bolsheviks after 1903.

Russification.   To make Russian in culture, language and customs. Attempts were made at russifying the national minorities of the Russian empire to prevent regionalism and a break-up of the state.

Sakhalin.   Russian island penal colony from 1851 in the Pacific Ocean just north of Japan. Anton Chekhov visited in 1890 and in his *Ostrov Sakhalin* (1893–95) gave graphic details of the appalling conditions under which prisoners lived. On 1 January 1896 there were, on the island, 6,703 convicts serving hard labour and 8,433 released convicts and exiles. In addition there were 1,323 women who had followed their husbands, with about 4,800 children. There were also free settlers totalling 2,838.

Samizdat.   Writings critical of the state written by dissidents in great secrecy, and circulated by hand from one person to another. Samizdat can be traced back to the 1820s to the poet Pushkin and it continued to flourish in the second half of the nineteenth century among revolutionary groups. The authorities strongly disapproved of circulating uncensored material and strict penalties were imposed on those who were caught.

Sealed Train.   Train that took Lenin, and thirty of his comrades, after years in exile, from Zurich, Switzerland, to the Finland Station, St Petersburg, in April 1917. The journey through Germany, Sweden and Finland was arranged by the German government with the aim of helping to bring to an end the fighting on the Eastern Front and so free a million troops to reinforce their armies in France. (See Map).

Second International.   Formed in Paris in 1889. A decentralised organisation, with no formal secretariat established until 1900. From an early date the Second International was preoccupied with the issue of revisionism, with Kautsky a central figure. The main congresses of the Second International were:

1905	Amsterdam
1907	Stuttgart
1910	Copenhagen

Seriously weakened by divisions over the war, the movement collapsed. In March 1919 the Russian Bolsheviks established the Third International (the Comintern).

Serfs. Peasants who could be bought, sold and generally treated as chattels by their owners. Various schemes for emancipation were considered from the time of Catherine II (the Great), but serfdom was finally abolished in 1861.

Shidlovsky Commission. Appointed on 29 January 1905 for the purpose of 'investigating the causes of discontent among the workers in the St Petersburg area'. It was established following the shooting of workers during a peaceful demonstration led by Father Gapon on 9 January. The Commission was denounced by the Bolsheviks as an attempt to divert the workers from the revolutionary class struggle but was supported by some of the moderate leftist groups. The Commission lasted only a month and was dissolved in February 1905.

Skoptsi. Religious sect whose members practised self-mutilation.

Slavophile. Adherent of the groups that opposed the Westernisation of Russia (see p. 41).

Sloboda. Village or settlement inhabited by free peasants.

Soul Tax (Poll or Head Tax). Capitation tax paid by every male peasant and by urban artisans and burghers introduced by Peter I (the Great) in 1723. It became an important element of state revenue; the household tax and tax on cultivated land was abolished. Although this placed a considerable burden on the peasants it resulted in an increase in the area of land cultivated, since it was in the peasant's interest to cultivate as much as possible in order to pay the tax. The accumulation of arrears of the tax forced the government to lower the rate of tax in 1725, in 1742 and again in 1750–58. Later it was increased again, reaching one rouble in 1794. It was finally abolished in 1887.

Southern Society. Society led by Colonel Paul Pestel, which had as its goal the forcible establishment of a republic. In 1825 it merged with the Northern Society led by Nikita Muravev and staged the abortive Decembrist uprising of 14 December 1825.

Soviet. Political council of the masses during the Revolution of 1905, and then from February 1917 onward.

Spirit Wrestlers. See Dukhobory.

Streltsy. The *Streltsy* were Russian infantrymen, the first to carry firearms, established by Ivan IV in 1550. They formed a large proportion of the Russian army for a century and also provided the tsar's bodyguard. At the end of the seventeenth century they started to exercise political influence, having become discontented by their conditions of service. They became involved in the struggle for succession to the Russian throne begun in 1682, between the half-brothers Peter I and Ivan V. Supporting Ivan, in 1682 they staged a revolt against Peter's mother's family, the Naryshkins. They named both Ivan and Peter tsars, and made Ivan's sister Sophia Alekseyevna the regent. In 1698, then 50,000 strong, they were unsuccessful in an attempt to unseat Peter I and restore Sophia. Peter I was on his Western European expedition but the revolt had been rigorously dealt with before he reached Moscow. However this did not stop him launching bloody reprisals against the *Streltsy* in which he took an active personal part. The *Streltsy* was then disbanded.

Stundists. Puritan religious sect, not unlike the German Baptists, living in southern Ukraine and said to be descendants of Russian soldiers converted from the Orthodox Church by German missionaries. They broke from the Russian Orthodox Church in 1870. They were persecuted in Kherson in 1879 and from 1891 strong repressive measures were taken against the sect and Stundist meetings were forbidden in 1894. They were again granted freedom to worship in 1905 by the tsar when religious disabilities were removed.

Table of Ranks. System that assigned military, court and civilian service into fourteen parallel grades. It was devised by Peter I (the Great) in 1722 (see p. 50).

Taiga. Siberian forests.

Third Section. Secret police force, also known as the Third Department, formed by Nicholas I in 1826 and responsible for political security. It was closed down in 1880 (see p. 57).

Tsar. Title of the Russian rulers first used by Ivan IV in 1547. Peter I (the Great) adopted the title of Emperor of All Russia. It has remained in popular usage until the abdication and execution of Tsar Nicholas II in 1918. The tsar's wife was known as tsarina or tsaritsa and his eldest son as the tsarevich.

Ukase. Decree or edict; it was first used in medieval times and continued until 1917.

Union of the Russian People. Reactionary organisation founded in 1905 by the secret police, which directed most action against the revolutionaries. For the most part, the Union of the Russian People blamed the Jews for the granting of civil liberties, and hence the Union encouraged the street mobs' anger against the Jews.

Vedomosti (News). The first Russian newspaper, published irregularly from 1703. The first edition was edited by Peter I (the Great).

Verst. Unit of distance equivalent to approximately two-thirds of a mile.

Voevoda. Military governor.

Volost. Smallest administrative division in rural Russia comprising several villages.

Westerners (Westernisers). Intellectuals who felt that the future of Russia lay with the West (see p. 41).

Winter Palace. Palace built in St Petersburg by Bartolomeo Rastrelli in the mid-eighteenth century on the left bank of the Great Neva. It and several buildings now house the Hermitage Museum of Art.

Yassak. Tax in furs paid by non-Orthodox subjects to the tsar.

Zemstvo. Local self-government institutions established in 1864, during the period of Great Reforms, in every district and province in the Russian empire. The aim of the *zemstva* was to provide social and economic services. Although they were limited from time to time in their authority and revenues and were dominated by the nobility, their existence and liberal influence achieved much in the field of education, communications, agriculture and health.

16
Bibliography

Atlases

The Times Atlas of World History
Channon, J. *The Penguin Historical Atlas of Russia* (1995)
Gilbert, M. *Imperial Russian History Atlas* (1978)
Milner-Gulland, R. *Atlas of Russia and the Soviet Union* (1989)

Encyclopedias

Brown, A. et al., *The Cambridge Encyclopedia of Russia and the Soviet Union* (1982)
Florinsky, M. T. *McGraw-Hill Encyclopedia of Russia and the Soviet Union* (1961)
Paxton, J. *Encyclopedia of Russian History, From the Christianization of Kiev to the Break-Up of the USSR* (1993)
Utechin, S. V. *Everyman's Concise Encyclopaedia of Russia* (1961)

Chronologies

Conte, F. *Great Dates in Russian and Soviet History* (1994)
Paxton, J. and E. W. Knappman, *Calendar of World History* (1999)

General histories

Acton, E. *Russia* (2nd ed., 1995)
Auty, R. and D. Obolensky, *Introduction to Russian History* (1976)
Billington, J. *The Icon and the Axe* (1970)
Cracraft, J. *Major Problems in the History of Imperial Russia* (1994)
Dmytryshyn, B. *Imperial Russia: A Source Book* (1967)
Dukes, P. *The Making of Russian Absolutism 1613–1801* (2nd ed., 1990)
Florinsky, M. *Russia* (1953)
Freeze, G. *From Supplication to Revolution: A Documentary Social History of Imperial Russia* (1988)
Hosking, G. *Russia: People and Empire* (1977)
Kaiser, D. and G. Marker, *Reinterpreting Russian History* (1994)
Kochan, L. and R. Abraham, *The Making of Modern Russia* (1983)
Mendelsohn, E. and M. Shatz, *Imperial Russia 1700–1917* (1988)
Pipes, R. *Russia under the Old Regime* (1974)
Raeff, M. *Russian Intellectual History: An Anthology* (1966)

Raeff, M. *Understanding Imperial Russia* (1984)
Riasanovsky, N. *History of Russia* (5th ed., 1993)
Rogger, H. *Russia in the Age of Modernisation and Revolution 1881–1917* (1983)
Saunders, D. *Russia in the Age of Reaction and Reform 1801–1881* (1992)
Seton-Watson, H. *The Russian Empire 1801–1917* (1967)
Vernadsky, G. and R. T. Fisher, *A Source Book for Russian History from Early Times to 1917* 3 vols (1972)

Russian monarchs, regents and heirs

Tsar, title from Latin *Caesar*, was used by the rulers of Muscovy from the fifteenth century to Peter I (the Great), who adopted the title Emperor of All Russia. The title Tsar, however, remained in popular usage during the imperial period.

Alexander, J. T. *Catherine the Great: Life and Legend* (1989)
Anderson, M. S. *Peter the Great* (1978)
Anisimov, E. *The Reforms of Peter the Great* (1993)
Anisimov, E. V. *Empress Elizabeth: Her Reign and Her Russia* (1995)
Bing, E. J. *Letters of Nicholas II and his Mother* (1937)
Bobrick, B. *Ivan the Terrible* (1990)
Brennan, J. *Enlightened Despotism in Russia: The Reign of Elizabeth 1741–1762* (1987)
Empress Catherine II, *Memoirs* (1955)
Cronin, V. *Catherine: Empress of All the Russias* (1978)
Curtiss, M. *A Forgotten Empress: Anna Ivanovna and Her Era* (1974)
Daniels, R. V. *N. Tatishchev: Guardian of the Petrine Revolution* (1973)
De Jonge, A. *Fire and Water: A Life of Peter the Great* (1979)
Dukes, P. *Russia under Catherine the Great* (2 vols, 1977–78)
Fennell, J. L. I. *Ivan the Great of Moscow* (1961)
Feodorovna, A. *A Czarina's Story* (1948)
Fuhrmann, J. *Tsar Alexis, His Reign and His Russia* (1981)
Gibbes, C. S. *Tutor to the Tsarevich* (1975)
Golovine, A. *Russia under the Autocrat Nicholas I* (1846)
Grey, I. *Boris Godunov: The Tragic Tsar* (1973)
Hartley, J. *Alexander I* (1994)
Hughes, L. *Sophia: Regent of Russia 1657–1704* (1990)
Hughes, L. *Russia in the Age of Peter the Great* (1998)
Jackman, S. W. *Romanov Relations: The Private Correspondence between Tsars Alexander I, Nicholas I and the Grand Dukes Constantine and Michael and their Sister Queen Anna Pavlovna* (1969)
Kliuchevskii, V. *Peter the Great* (1958)
Leonard, C. S. *Reform and Regicide: The Reign of Peter III of Russia* (1993)
Lieven, D. *Nicholas II* (1993)
Lincoln, W. B. *Nicholas I Emperor and Autocrat of All the Russias* (1978)
Lincoln, W. B. *The Romanovs* (1981)
Longworth, O. *Alexis Tsar of All the Russias* (1984)
Longworth, P. *The Three Empresses* (1982)
de Madariaga, I. *Russia in the Age of Catherine the Great* (1981)
de Madariaga, I. *Catherine the Great: A Short History* (1990)
Massie, R. K. *Peter the Great. His Life and World* (1981)
McConnell, A. *Tsar Alexander I* (1970)
McGrew, E. R. *Paul I of Russia* (1992)

O'Brien, C. B. *Russia under Two Tsars – The Regency of Sophia* (1952)
Oliva, L. *Russia in the Era of Peter the Great* (1969)
Palmer, A. *Alexander I: Tsar of War and Peace* (1974)
Presniakov, A. E. *Emperor Nicholas I of Russia* (1974)
Raeff, M. *Catherine the Great: A Profile* (1972)
Raeff, M. *Peter the Great Changes Russia* (1972)
Ragsdale, H. *Tsar Paul and the Question of Madness* (1988)
Soloviev, S. M. *Empress Anna* (1984)
Sumner, B. *Peter the Great and the Emergence of Russia* (1951)
Talbot Rice, T. *Elizabeth Empress of Russia* (1970)
Troyat, H. *Ivan the Terrible* (1984)
Troyat, H. *Peter the Great* (1988)

Nobility

Becker, S. *Nobility and Privilege in Late Imperial Russia* (1985)
Crummey, R. *Aristocrats and Servitors* (1983)
Dukes, P. *Catherine the Great and the Russian Nobility* (1967)
Edmondson, L. and P. Waldron, *Economy and Society in Russia and the Soviet Union, 1860–1930* (1992)
Emmons, T. *The Russian Landed Gentry and the Peasant Emancipation of 1861* (1968)
Hamburg, G. M. *Portrait of an Elite: Russian Marshals of the Nobility, 1861–1917* (1981)
Hamburg, G. M. *Politics of the Russian Nobility 1881–1905* (1984)
Jones, R. *The Emancipation of the Russian Nobility* (1973)
Le Donne, P. *Absolutism and Ruling Class* (1991)
Lieven, D. *Russia's Rulers under the Old Regime* (1989)
Lieven, D. *The Aristocracy in Europe 1815–1914* (1992)
Manning, T. *The Crisis of the Old Order in Russia: Gentry and Government* (1982)
Meehan-Waters, B. *Autocracy and Aristocracy: The Russian Service Elite of 1730* (1982)
Raeff, M. *Origins of the Russian Intelligentsia* (1966)

Slavophiles

Christoff, P. *An Introduction to Nineteenth-Century Russian Slavophilism* (4 vols, 1961–91)
Gleason, A. *European and Muscovite: Ivan Kireevsky and the Origins of Slavophilism* (1972)
Walicki, A. *The Slavophile Controversy* (1975)

Government and towns

Alexander, J. *Bubonic Plague in Early Modern Russia* (1980)
Bater, J. *St Petersburg* (1976)
Bradley, J. *Muzhik and Muscovite: Urbanization in Late Imperial Russia* (1985)
Emmons, T. and W. Vucinich, *The Zemstvo in Russia* (1982)
Hamm, M. *The City in Russian History* (1976)
Hamm, M. *The City in Late Imperial Russia* (1986)
Hamm, M. *Kiev: A Portrait, 1800–1917* (1993)
Herlihy, P. *Odessa: A History 1794–1914* (1986)
Hittle, J. *The Service City: State and Townsmen in Russia, 1600–1800* (1979)
Johnson, R. *Peasant and Proletarian: The Working Class of Moscow in the Late 19th Century* (1979)
Lincoln, W. *The Great Reforms* (1990)
Mosse, W. *Alexander II and the Modernization of Russia* (2nd ed. 1992)

Pearson, T. *Russian Officialdom in Crisis: Autocracy and Local Self-Government, 1861–1900* (1989)
Pereira, N. *Tsar-Liberator* (1983)
Pintner, W. and D. Rowney, *Russian Officialdom* (1980)
Schmidt, A. *The Architecture and Planning of Classical Moscow* (1989)
Starr, S. *Decentralization and Self-Government in Russia, 1830–1870* (1972)
Yaney, G. *The Systematization of Russian Government* (1973)

Religion

Beeson, T. *Discretion and Valour* (1974)
Bennigsen, G. and C. Lemercier-Quelquejay, *Islam in the Soviet Union* (1968)
Bourdeaux, M. *Religious Ferment in Russia* (1968)
Bushkovitch, P. *Religion and Society in Russia: The Sixteenth and Seventeenth Centuries* (1992)
Cracraft, J. *The Church Reform of Peter the Great* (1971)
Crummey, R. *The Old Believers and the World of Antichrist* (1970)
Curtiss, J. *Church and State in Russia: The Last Years of the Empire 1900–1917* (repr. 1965)
Fedotov, G. P. *The Russian Religious Mind* 2 vols (1946–66)
Fennell, J. *A History of the Russian Church to 1448* (1995)
Freeze, G. *The Russian Levites: Parish Clergy in the Eighteenth Century* (1977)
Freeze, G. *The Parish Clergy in Nineteenth-Century Russia* (1983)
Hackel, S. A. *The Orthodox Church* (1971)
Hosking, G. A. *Church, Nation and State in Russia and Ukraine* (1991)
Nichols, R. and T. Stavrou, *Russian Orthodoxy under the Old Regime* (1978)

Serfdom

Avrich, P. *Russian Rebels 1600–1800* (1972)
Bartlett, R. *Land Commune and Peasant Community in Russia* (1990)
Blum, J. *Lord and Peasant in Russia from the Ninth to the Nineteenth Century* (1961)
Eklof, B. and S. Frank, *The World of the Russian Peasant* (1990)
Emmons, T. *The Russian Landed Gentry and the Peasant Emancipation of 1861* (1968)
Field, D. *The End of Serfdom: Nobility and Bureaucracy in Russia, 1851–1861* (1976)
Gill, G. *Peasants and Government in the Russian Revolution* (1979)
Hoch, S. *Serfdom and Social Control in Russia: Petrovskoe, a Village in Tambov* (1986)
Kolchin, P. *Unfree Labor: American Slavery and Russian Serfdom* (1987)
Koslow, J. *The Despised and the Dammed: the Russian Peasant Through the Ages* (1972)
Kravchinskii, S. M. *The Russian Peasantry: their Agrarian Condition, Social Life and Religion* (1888)
Moon, D. *Russian Peasants and Tsarist Legislation on the Eve of Reform* (1992)
Robinson, G. *Rural Russia under the Old Regime* (1932)
Semenova-Tian-Shanskaia, O. *Life in the Russian Village* (1993)
Smith, R. E. F. *The Enserfment of the Russian Peasantry* (1968)
Vucinich, W. S. *The Peasant in Nineteenth-Century Russia* (1968)
Worobec, C. D. *Peasant Russia: Family and Community in the Post-Emancipation Period* (1991)
Zaionchkovsky, P. *The Abolition of Serfdom in Russia* (1978)

Economic activity

Blackwell, W. L. *The Beginnings of Russian Industrialization 1800–1860* (1968)
Blanchard, I. *Russia's 'Age of Silver': Precious Metal Production and Economic Growth in the Eighteenth Century* (1989)

Christian, D. *'Living Water': Vodka and Russian Society on the Eve of Emancipation* (1990)
Dmitriev-Mámonov, A. I. *Guide to the Great Siberian Railway* (1900)
Kahan, A. *The Plow, the Hammer, and the Knout: An Economic History of Eighteenth-Century Russia* (1985)
Kaiser, D. *The Workers' Revolution in Russia, 1917* (1987)
Reading, D. *The Anglo-Russian Commercial Treaty of 1734* (1938)
Rieber, A. *Merchants and Entrepreneurs in Imperial Russia* (1982)

Women

Engel, B. *Mothers and Daughters: Women of the Intelligentsia in Nineteenth-Century Russia* (1983)
Engel, B. *Between the Fields and the City: Women, Work and Family in Russia, 1861–1914* (1994)
Farnsworth, B. and L. Viola, *Russian Peasant Women* (1992)
Glickman, R. *Russian Factory Women* (1984)
Ransel, D. *The Family in Imperial Russia* (1978)
Ransel, D. *Mothers of Misery: Child Abandonment in Russia* (1988)
Stites, R. *The Women's Liberation Movement in Russia* (1978)

Rebellions

Alexander, J. *Autocratic Politics in a National Crisis: The Imperial Russian Government and Pugachev's Revolt 1773–1775* (1969)
Barratt, G. *The Rebel on the Bridge: A Life of the Decembrist Baron Andrey Rozen 1800–84* (1975)
Mazour, A. G. *The First Russian Revolution, 1825* (1961)

1917 Revolutions

Acton, E. *Rethinking the Russian Revolution* (1990)
Bone, A. *The Bolsheviks and the October Revolution* (1974)
Browder, R. and A. Kerensky, *The Russian Provisional Government* (1961)
Bunyan, J. and H. Fisher, *The Bolshevik Revolution 1917–1918* (1934)
Burbank, J. *Intelligentsia and Revolution* (1986)
Ferro, M. *The Bolshevik Revolution: A Social History of the Russian Revolution* (1980)
Figes, O. *Peasant Russia, Civil War: The Volga Countryside in Revolution, 1917–21* (1989)
Figes, O. *A People's Tragedy* (1996)
Fitzpatrick, S. *The Russian Revolution* (1982)
Frankel, E. *Revolution in Russia* (1992)
Geyer, D. *The Russian Revolution* (1987)
Hunczak, T. *The Ukraine 1917–1921* (1977)
Kaiser, D. *The Workers' Revolution in Russia, 1917* (1987)
Katkov, G. *Russia 1917: The Kornilov Affair* (1980)
Keep, J. *The Russian Revolution: A Study in Mass Mobilization* (1976)
Keep, J. *The Debate on Soviet Power* (1979)
Koenker, D. *Moscow Workers and the 1917 Revolution* (1981)
McCauley, M. *The Russian Revolution and the Soviet State* (1975)
Mohrenschildt, D. *The Russian Revolution of 1917* (1971)
Munck, J. *The Kornilov Revolt* (1987)
Pethybridge, R. *The Spread of the Russian Revolution* (1972)
Pipes, R. *Revolutionary Russia* (1968)
Pipes, R. *The Russian Revolution 1899–1919* (1990)

Pipes, R. *Russia under the Bolshevik Regime 1919–1924* (1994)
Rabinowitch, A. *Prelude to Revolution* (1968)
Raleigh, D. *Revolution on the Volga: 1917 in Saratov* (1986)
Raskolnikov, F. *Kronstadt and Petrograd in 1917* (1982)
Read, C. *Culture and Power in Revolutionary Russia* (1990)
Rosenberg, W. *Liberals in the Russian Revolution* (1974)
Schapiro, L. *1917* (1984)
Service, R. *The Bolshevik Party in Revolution 1917–1923* (1979)
Service, R. *The Russian Revolution 1900–1927* (1986)
Service, R. *Society and Politics in the Russian Revolution* (1992)
Shkliarevsky, G. *Labour in the Russian Revolution* (1993)
Shukman, H. *The Blackwell Encyclopedia of the Russian Revolution* (2 vols, 1935)
Sukhanov, N. *The Russian Revolution* (1955)
Trotsky, L. D. *The History of the Russian Revolution* (trans. 1977)
White, J. *The Russian Revolution 1917–1921* (1994)
Williams, B. *The Russian Revolution 1917–1921* (1987)
Wood, A. *The Russian Revolution* (1979)

War and military

Baumgart, W. *The Peace of Paris 1856* (1981)
Bourgogne, A. J. B. F. *Memoirs of Sergeant Bourgogne* (1930)
Brett-James, A. *1812* (1966)
Bushnell, J. *Mutiny and Repression: Russian Soldiers in the Revolution of 1905–1906* (1985)
Curtiss, J. *The Russian Army under Nicholas I* (1965)
Curtiss, J. *Russia's Crimean War* (1979)
Daly, J. *Russian Seapower and 'The Eastern Question', 1827–41* (1991)
Deane, J. *History of the Russian Fleet during the Reign of Peter the Great* (1899)
Englund, P. *The Battle of Poltava* (1992)
Getzler, I. *Kronstadt 1917–1921* (1983)
Goldfrank, D. *The Origins of the Crimean War* (1994)
Hellie, R. *Enserfment and Military Change in Muscovy* (1971)
Josselson, M. and D. *The Commander: A Life of Barclay de Tolly* (1980)
Kagan, F. W. *The Military Reforms of Nicholas I* (1999)
Keep, J. H. L. *Soldiers of the Tsar: Army and Society in Russia* (1971)
Mawdsley, E. *The Russian Revolution and the Baltic Fleet* (1978)
Menning, B. W. *Bayonets Before Bullets: The Imperial Russian Army 1861–1914* (1992)
Phillips, E. J. *The Founding of Russia's Navy. Peter the Great and the Azov Fleet 1688–1714* (1995)
Puryear, V. *England, Russia, and the Straits Question 1844–1856* (1931)
Rich, N. *Why the Crimean War?* (1985)
Rothstein, A. *Peter the Great and Marlborough. Politics and Diplomacy in Converging Wars* (1986)
Saab, A. *The Origins of the Crimean Alliance* (1977)
Saul, N. *Russia and the Mediterranean 1797–1807* (1970)
Saul, N. *Sailors in Revolt: The Russian Baltic Fleet in 1917* (1978)
von Hagen, M. *Soldiers in the Proletarian Dictatorship 1917–30* (1991)
Wetzel, D. *The Crimean War: A Diplomatic History* (1985)
Wildman, A. *The End of the Russian Imperial Army: The Old Army and the Soldiers' Revolt (March–April 1917)* (1980)

Wirtschafter, E. *From Serf to Russian Soldier* (1990)
Woodward, D. *The Russians at Sea* (1965)

Foreign policy and the expansion of Russia

Allworth, E. *Central Asia: 120 Years of Russian Rule* (1989)
Anderson, M. S. *The Eastern Question 1774–1923* (1966)
Anderson, M. S. *The Great Powers and the Near East 1774–1923* (1970)
Aronson, I. *Troubled Waters: The Origins of the 1881 Anti-Jewish Pogroms in Russia* (1990)
Atkin, M. *Russia and Iran, 1780–1828* (1980)
Barratt, G. *Russia in Pacific Waters, 1715–1825* (1981)
Bartlett, R. *Human Capital: The Settlement of Foreigners in Russia, 1762–1804* (1979)
Becker, S. *Russia's Protectorates in Central Asia* (1968)
Broxup, M. *The North Caucasus Barrier* (1992)
Davies, N. *God's Playground: A History of Poland* (1981)
Donnelly, A. *The Russian Conquest of Bashkiria 1552–1740* (1968)
Ezergailis, A. *The Latvian Impact on the Bolshevik Revolution* (1983)
Fisher, A. *The Russian Annexation of the Crimea 1772–1783* (1970)
Fisher, R. *The Russian Fur Trade 1550–1700* (1943)
Forsyth, J. *A History of the Peoples of Siberia* (1992)
Gibson, J. *Imperial Russia in Frontier America; The Changing Geography of Supply of Russian America, 1784–1867* (1976)
Gillard, D. *The Struggle for Asia 1828–1914* (1977)
Grimsted, P. *The Foreign Ministers of Alexander I* (1969)
Henriksson, A. *The Tsar's Loyal Germans: The Riga German Community 1855–1905* (1983)
Jelavich, B. *Russia's Balkan Entanglements 1806–1914* (1991)
Jewsbury, G. *The Russian Annexation of Bessarabia, 1774–1828* (1976)
Judge, E. *Easter in Kishinev: Anatomy of a Pogrom* (1993)
Kaplan, H. *The First Partition of Poland* (1962)
Khodarkovsky, M. *Where Two Worlds Met: The Russian State and the Kalmyk Nomads 1600–1771* (1992)
Klier, J. and S. Lamboza, *Pogroms* (1992)
Kohut, Z. *Russian Centralism and Ukrainian Autonomy: Imperial Absorption of the Hetmanate 1760s–1830s* (1988)
Lantzeff, G. *Siberia in the Seventeenth Century* (1943)
Lantzeff, G. and R. Pierce, *Eastward to Empire* (1973)
Leslie, R. *Reform and Insurrection in Russian Poland 1856–65* (1969)
Lord, R. *The Second Partition of Poland* (1915)
Löwe, H-D. *The Tsars and the Jews* (1992)
Marks, S. *Road to Power: The Trans-Siberian Railroad and the Colonization of Asiatic Russia, 1850–1917* (1991)
Pallot, J. and D. Shaw, *Landscape and Settlement in Romanov Russia* (1990)
Pienkos, A. *The Imperfect Autocrat: Grand Duke Constantine Pavlovich and the Polish Congress Kingdom* (1987)
Ragsdale, H. *Imperial Russian Foreign Policy* (1993)
Roberts, I. *Nicholas I and the Russian Intervention in Hungary* (1991)
Rywkin, M. *Russian Colonial Expansion to 1917* (1988)
Saunders, D. *The Ukrainian Impact on Russian Culture 1750–1850* (1985)
Subtelny, O. *The Mazepists* (1981)
Subtelny, O. *Ukraine: A History* (1988)

Sumner, B. H. *Peter the Great and the Ottoman Empire* (1949)
Suny, R. *The Making of the Georgian Nation* (1989)
Thackeray, F. *Antecedents of Revolution: Alexander I and the Polish Kingdom, 1815–1825* (1980)
Thaden, E. *Russification in the Baltic Provinces and Finland 1855–1914* (1981)
Thaden, E. *Russia's Western Borderlands 1710–1870* (1984)
Treadgold, D. *The Great Siberian Migration* (1957)
Wood, A. *The History of Siberia* (1991)

Education

Alston, P. *Education and the State in Tsarist Russia* (1969)
Black, J. L. *Citizens for the Fatherland* (1979)
Brooks, J. *When Russia Learned to Read: Literacy and Popular Literature, 1861–1917* (1985)
Brower, D. *Training the Nihilists: Education and Radicalism in Tsarist Russia* (1975)
Eklof, B. *Russian Peasant Schools: Officialdom, Village culture, and Popular Pedagogy, 1861–1914* (1986)
Flynn, J. *The University Reform of Alexander I* (1988)
Kassow, S. *Students, Professors and the State in Tsarist Russia* (1989)
Seregny, S. *Russian Teachers and Peasant Revolution: The Politics of Education in 1905* (1989)
Sinel, A. *The Classroom and the Chancellery: State Educational Reform in Russia under Count Dmitry Tolstoy* (1973)
Whittaker, C. *The Origins of Modern Russian Education: An Intellectual Biography of Count Sergei Uvarov, 1786–1855* (1984)

Intellectual activity

Acton, E. *Alexander Herzen and the Role of the Intellectual Revolutionary* (1979)
Black, J. L. *G. F. Müller and the Imperial Russian Academy* (1986)
Christoff, P. *The Third Heart: Some Intellectual-Ideological Currents and Cross-Currents in Russia 1800–1830* (1970)
Gleason, W. J. *Moral Idealists, Bureaucracy, and Catherine the Great* (1981)
Jones, W. G. *Nikolay Novikov* (1984)
Kelly, A. *Mikhail Bakunin* (1987)
Marker, G. *Publishing, Printing, and the Origins of Intellectual Life in Russia, 1700–1800* (1985)
McConnell, A. *A Russian Philosophe: Alexander Radishchev* (1964)
Miller, M. *Kropotkin* (1976)
Nahirny, V. *The Russian Intelligentsia* (1983)
Pomper, P. *Peter Lavrov and the Russian Revolutionary Movement* (1972)
Riasanovsky, N. *A Parting of Ways: Government and the Educated Public in Russia 1801–1855* (1976)

Law, crime and punishment

Orlovsky, D. *The Limits of Reform: The Ministry of Internal Affairs in Imperial Russia, 1802–1881* (1981)
Squire, P. *The Third Department* (1968)
Wortman, R. *The Development of a Russian Legal Consciousness* (1976)

Index

Abdication of Nicholas II   4, 123–4
Abkhasia   144
Åbo, Treaty of   24
Abramtsevo colony   221
Absolutism   111
Academy of Sciences   2, 152–4
Acmeists   221
Administrative changes from 1550   46–64
Adrian, Patriarch (1627–1700)   21, 171
Adrianople, Treaty of (Edirne)   135, 221
Aeurenthal, Count Alois Lexa von (1854–1912)   171
Agrarian reforms   89–90
Agricultural production   90–1
Aix-la-Chapelle, Congress of (1818)   221
Akhmatova, Anna (1888–1966)   171
Alaska   2, 143–4
Alcohol production   104
Alekseyev, Mikhail Vasilyevich (1857–1918)   171
Alexander I (1777–1825)   12, 172
Alexander I, Grand Prince of Bulgaria (1857–1893)   6, 172
Alexander II (1818–1881)   6, 32, 172–3
Alexander III (1845–1894)   3, 6, 173
Alexander III's counter reforms   59–60
Alexandra Fedorovna (1872–1918)   173
Alexis (1690–1718)   10, 173
Alexis I Mikhailovich (1629–1676)   5, 9, 47, 174
Alliances, Congresses, Conferences and Treaties, 1681–1918   130–2
All-Russian Congress of Soviets   221–2
All-Russian Period   222
Alma   135
Alphabet and transliteration   155
Amur river   144
Anarchism   118–20
Anastasia (Anastasiya Nikolayevna) (1901–1918)   174
Andreyev, Leonid Nikolaevich (1871–1919)   174
Anna Karenina   156
Anna Leopoldovna (Karlovna) (1718–1746)   174

Annals of the Fatherland   166
Anne Ivanovna (1693–1740)   6, 11, 175
Apraksin, Count Fedor Matveyevich (1671–1728)   175
Apraksin, Count Stepan Fedorovich (1702–1758)   175
April Theses   222
Arackcheyev, Count Alexey Andreyevich (1769–1834)   175
Archimandrite   222
Architecture   158–9
Arestantskaia Rota   222
Armenia   144
Armenian Church   77–8
Army   132–3
Arshin   222
Art   156–7
Artel   222
Ashkhabad   144
Assignat   222
Ataman   222
August Bloc   222
Augustus II the Strong (1670–1733)   133, 175–6
Aurora   222
Autocrat and Autocracy   223
Awakum   65
Axelrod, Pavel Borisovich (1850–1928)   176
Azerbaijan   144

Bagratids   223
Bagration, Prince Peter Ivanovich (1765–1812)   176
Bakunin, Michael Aleksandrovich (1814–1876)   176
Balaklava   135
Ballet   157
Baltic Germans   223
Baltic Provinces   223
Baltic Sea   223
Banking   99–100
Baptists   78–9
Baraba Steppe   223
Barclay de Tolly, Prince Mikhail Bogdanovich (1761–1818)   6, 176

249

Barin 223
Barshchina 223
Baryatinsky, Prince Aleksandr Ivanovich (1814–1879) 177
Battles and Wars 1548–1918 126–30
Beard Tax 21, 43–4
Bednyak 223
Bekbulatovich, Simeon (16th century) 5, 15, 177
Bekovich-Cherkassy, Prince Aleksandr (?–1717) 177
Bell, John (1691–1780) 177
Belorussians 223
Benckendorff, Count Aleksandr Khristoforovich (1783–1844) 177
Bennigsen, Count Levin August von (1745–1826) 177–8
Bering, Vitus Jonassen (1681–1741) 23, 143, 178
Bessarabia 144–5
Bestuzhev, Aleksandr Aleksandrovich (1797–1837) 178
Bestuzhev-Ryumin, Count Aleksey Petrovich (1693–1766) 178
Bezpopovtsy 223
Bibikov, Dmitry Gavrilovich (1792–1870) 7, 178
Biron (Bühren), Ernst Johann, Duke of Courland (1690–1772) 6, 178–9
Birzha 224
Black Earth 224
Black Hundreds 224
Bloody Sunday 35, 116–17
Bludov, Dmitry Nikolayevich (1785–1864) 7, 179
Blue Rose Arts Society 224
Bobyl 224
Bochka 224
Bokhara 145
Bolshevism 121, 224
Bosporus 224
Boyar 224
Breshko-Breshkovskaya, Ekaterina Konstantinovna (1844–1934) 179
Brest-Litovsk, Treaty of 39
Brothers Karamanzov, The 156
Bund 115
Burlak 224

Cadets (Kadets) 35
Cadets, Corp of 225
Calendar 225
Canal traffic 108

Cathedral Folk 156
Catherine I (Yekaterina Alexeyevna) (1684–1727) 6, 10, 23, 179
Catherine II (the Great) (1729–1796) 2, 6, 12, 24, 179–80
Catherine Ivanovna (1684–1727) 180
Caucasus 2, 145
Censorship 168–70
Census (1594) 15, (1646) 17, (1710) 21, (1897) 34
Charles XII of Sweden (1682–1718) 133, 180
Charter of the Nobility 2, 55
Charter of the Towns 56
Cheka 225
Chekhov, Anton Pavlovich (1860–1904) 180–1
Chetvert 225
Chirikov, Aleksandr 143
Christianity, conversion to 65
Cities, population 92
Code of Laws (1833) 29
Collegiate System 225
Commissar 225
Communism 226
Conditions of Mitau 2, 53
Confederacy party 118
Conferences, 1681–1918 130–2
Congresses, 1681–1918 130–2
Constantine Nikolaevich, Grand Duke (1827–1892) 181
Constituent Assembly 226
Constitutional Democratic Party (Kadets) 116
Cossacks 226
Cotton production 104–5
Council of State 226
Crime 162
Crime and Punishment 31, 156
Crimea 2, 145
Crimean wars 3, 10, 30, 135–6
Cyrillic alphabet 155

Daghestan 145
Dagmar, Princess Mary (Maria Fedorovna) (1847–1928) 181
Danubian Principalities 136, 226
Dashkova, Princess Catherine Romanovna Vorontsova (1743–1810) 181
Dashnaktsutyun 118
Dead Souls 30, 155
Decembrists 3, 28, 112–13

Delyanov, Ivan (1818–1897) 182
Den 167
Desyatina 226
Desyatovskiy's Report 226
Diderot, Denis (1713–1784) 25, 44–5, 182
Diebitsch, Count Hans Friedrich Anton (Ivan Ivanovich Dibich Zabalkanskiy) (1785–1831) 182
Dmitrieva, Elizabeth (1851–1910) 183
Dmitry, False 5, 183
Dogger Bank incident 35
Dokhod 226
Dolgorukiy, Prince Vasiliy Lukich (1670–1739) 184
Dolgorukiy, Prince Vasiliy Vladimorivch (1667–1746) 184
Dostoyevsky, Fedor Mikhailovich (1821–1881) 184–5
Dual Entente 226
Dual Power 226–7
Dubbelt, General Leontiy Vasilyevich (1792–1862) 185
Dukh Zhurnalov 166
Dukhobory 227
Duma 4, 36, 60, 227
Duma, political groupings 62–3
Durnovo, Pyotr Nikolayevich (1844–1915) 185
Dusha 227
Dvoryanstvo 227
Dvoryanstvo Charter 55
Dvorovye Liudi 225
Dynastic succession, problems of 9–13

Eastern Question 227
Edirne, Treaty of 135
Education and the arts 149–59
Electoral System 227
Elena, Grand Duchess 9, 14
Elizabeth Petrovna (1709–1762) 2, 6, 12, 185
Emancipation 86–9, 227–8
Emigration 93
Entente 228
Ethnic composition 93, 147–8
Eudoxia (Evdokhiya Fedorovna Lopukhina) (1669–1731) 185–6
Eugene Onegin 32, 155
Exports 106

Factory regulations 102–4
Falconet, Etienne Maurice (1716–1791) 186

Fathers and Children 155
February Revolution (1917) 121
Fedor I (1557–1598) 5, 46, 186
Fedor II (1589–1605) 5, 186
Fedor III (1661–1682) 5, 9, 186
Field of Mars 228
Finance, local 99
Finland 145–6
Finland Station 228
Fires of 1862 228
First International 228
First World War 142–3
Fletcher, Giles 9
France invades Russia 28, 139–40
Freemasonry 228
Fundamental laws 4

Gapon, Father Georgi Apollonovich (1870–1906) 186
Georgia 2, 27, 146
Georgian Orthodox Church 77
Godunov, Boris Fedorovich (1551–1605) 5, 9, 187
Golitsyn, Prince Aleksandr Nikolayevich (1773–1844) 187
Golitsyn, Boris Alekseyevich (1654–1713) 187
Golitsyn, Prince Dmitry Mikhailovich (1665–1737) 187–8
Golitsyn, Prince Mikhail Mikhailovich (1675–1730) 188
Golitsyn, Prince Vasily Vasilyevich (1643–1714) 10, 188
Golovkin, Gavril Ivanovich (1660–1734) 188
Golovlyov Family 156
Golovnin, Aleksandr Vasilyevich (1821–1886) 188
Golovnin, Vasily Mikhailovich (1776–1831) 188
Gorchakov, Prince Aleksandr Mikhailovich (1798–1883) 189
Gorchakov, Prince Mikhail (1793–1861) 189
Gordon, Patrick (1635–1699) 189
Goremykin, Ivan Longinovich (1839–1917) 7, 189
Gorky, Maxim (pen name of Aleksei Maksimovich Peshkov) (1868–1936) 189–90
Gorod 228
Government revenue and expenditure 97–8

Gramota 228
Great Embassy 10, 20–1, 42–3
Great Northern War 2, 133–4, 229
Grinevitsky, Ivan (1857–1881) 190
Gross national product 107
Guberniia 2, 48, 229
Guchkov, Aleksandr Ivanovich (1862–1936) 190
Gurko, Iosif Vladimirovich (1829–1901) 190
Gustavus III of Sweden 134

Haemophilia 229
Hague Conventions 229
Hermitage 229
Hero of Our Time 155
Herzen, Aleksandr Ivanovich (1812–1870) 190
Hetman *see* Ataman 222
Holy Alliance 229
Holy Synod 230
Hughes, John (1814–1889) 191
Humboldt, Baron von (Friedrich Heinrich) Alexander (1769–1859) 191

Idiot, The 156
Ignatiev, Count Nikolai Pavlovich (1832–1908) 7, 191
Imperial Academy of Sciences 230
Imperiya Vserossyskaya 230
Imports 106–7
Industrial disputes 104
Industrial growth 100–1
Inkerman 136
Iskra (The Spark) 34, 168, 230
Islam 81
Ivan III (The Great) (1462–1505) 1
Ivan IV, Vasilyevich (The Terrible) (1530–1584) 1, 5, 9, 46, 191–2
Ivan, V, Alekseyevich (1666–1696) 5, 192
Ivan VI, Antonovich (1740–1764) 6, 11, 192
Izgoy 230
Izvestia 168
Izvolsky, Count Aleksandr Petrovich (1856–1919) 192

Jacobins 230
Jews 79
John of Kronstadt, Father (Ivan Iliych Sergeyev) (1829–1909) 192–3

John III Sobieski (1624–1696) 193
Joseph II, Holy Roman Emperor (1741–1790) 193
Journals 165–8
July Days 230

Kadets 115
Kakhovsky, Pyotr Grigorevich (1797–1826) 193
Kaledin, Aleksey Maksimovich (1861–1918) 193
Kantonists 230
Kars region 146
Katorga 230
Kazan, Khanate of 14
Kazennaya 230
Kerensky, Alexander Fedorovich (1881–1970) 8, 38, 193–4
Khabarovsk 146
Khiva 146
Khodynka Field Disaster 230
Khozain 230
Kitai Gorod 230
Knipper-Chekova, Olga (1870–1959) 194
Kolchak, Admiral Aleksandr Vasilyevich (1873–1920) 194
Kollontai, Alexandra Mikhavlova (1872–1952) 194
Kolokol 167
Konstantin Pavlovich (1779–1831) 194
Kopek 230
Kornilov, General Lavr Georgevich (1870–1918) 195
Kreditnyi Bilet 231
Kremlin 231
Kropotkin, Prince Peter Alekseyevich (1842–1921) 195
Krupskaya, Nadezhda Konstantinovna (1869–1939) 195
Kulak 231
Kuranty 165
Kusmich, Fedor (?–1864) 195
Kustar 231
Kutuzov, Prince Mikhail Ilarionovich (1745–1813) 196
Kvas 231

Lacy, Count Peter (1678–1751) 196
La Harpe, Frédérick-César de (1754–1838) 196
Land and Liberty Organization 114
Land Captain (*zemskii nachalnik*) 231

Lavrov, Pyotr Lavrovich (1823–1900) 196–7
Law 160–2
League of Armed Neutrality 231
Lefort, François Jacob (1653–1699) 197
Legal code, new 47
Legislative Commission 25, 54
Lena Goldfield Massacre 231
Lenin (Vladimir Ilyich Ulyanov (1870–1924) 38, 197
Liberation of Labour Group 114, 231–2
Liberation, Wars of (1813–14) 140
Libraries 154
Liprandi, General P. P. (1796–1864) 197–8
Literature 155–6
Literaturnaya Gazeta 166
Lomonosov, Mikhail Vasilyevich (1711–1765) 149
Loris-Melikov, General Count Mikhail Taryelovich (1826–1888) 7, 198
Lublin, Union of 15
Lvov, Prince Georgy Yevgenevich (1861–1925) 7

Maklakov, Vasily Aleksandrovich (1870–1957) 198
Malozemlie 232
Manchuria 4
Marshals of the Nobility 53
Martov, Yuly Osipovich (1873–1923) 198
Marx, Karl Heinrich (1818–1883) 198–9
Marxism 232
Marxism-Leninism 232
Matveyev, Artamon Sergeyevich (1625–1682) 199
Maximalists 232
Mazepa, Ivan Stepanovich (c. 1645–1709) 199
Menshevism 120, 232
Menshikov, Prince Aleksandr Danilovich (1673–1729) 6, 199
Menshikov, Aleksandr Sergeyevich (1787–1869) 199
Merchant ships 107
Merv 146
Meshchanin 232
Messenger of Europe 165
Mestechko 232
Mestnichestvo 232
Metropolitan 232

Michael Aleksandrovich, Grand Duke (1878–1918) 13, 199
Michael Fedorovich Romanov (1596–1645) 5, 9, 47, 200
Military service reforms (1863) 58–9
Military Settlements (Colonies) 232
Miloslavskaya, Maria 9
Milyukov, Pavel Nikolayevich (1859–1943) 200
Mineral production 105–6
Minors, employment of 102
Mir 232
Money and banking 99–100
Monjik 232
Morozov Family 200
Moscow 22
Moscow, Occupation by Poles 16
Moscow Herald 166
Moscow Journal 165
Moscow University 24
Moskovskie Vedomosti 165
Moskovsky Merkury 165
Moskovsky Sbornik 167
Moskvityanin 167
Muravev-Apostol, Sergey Ivanovich (1796–1826) 200
Muscovy 233
Mysl 168

Nabat 167
Nakhimov, Admiral Pavel Stepanovich (1802–1855) 200
Names 233
Namestnik 233
Napoleon 136
Narodniki 233
Narodnoye Delo 167
Naryshkin, Natalia Kirillovna (1651–1694) 5, 9, 201
Naval Academy 133
Navy 49–50, 133
Nechayev, Sergey Gennadiyevich (1847–1882) 201
Nemets 233
Nesselrode, Count Karl Robert (1780–1862) 6, 201
Newspapers 165–8
Nicholas I (1796–1855) 3, 6, 12, 201–2
Nicholas II (1868–1918) 4, 6, 38, 40, 123, 124, 202
Nicholas, Grand Duke (1843–1865) 202
Nicholas, Grand Duke (1856–1929) 202

Nicolaevsk   146
Nihilism   115, 233
Nikon (Nikita Minin) (1605–1681)   65, 202–3
Nobility   233
Nobility, decrees on compulsory education (1714)   154
Novgorod, Swedes occupy   16
Novosiltsev, Count Nikolai Nikolaevich (1761–1836)   7, 203
Novoye Vremya   167
Nystad, Treaty of   134

Oblomov   155
Obolensky, Prince Yevgeny Petrovich (1796–1865)   203
Obrok   233–4
October Revolution (1917)   124–5
Octobrists   234
Odoyevsky, Prince Aleksandr Ivanovich (1802–1839)   203
Okhrana   32, 163
Old Believers   65, 76
Old Church Slavonic   234
On the Eve   155
Oprichnina   46
Orlov, Prince Aleksey Fyodorovich (1786–1861)   7, 203
Orlov, Count Aleksey Grigoryevich (1737–1808)   204
Orlov, Count Grigory Grigoryevich (1734–1783)   204
Orthodox Church   76
Ossetia   146
Ostermann, Count Andrey Ivanovich (Heinrich Johann Friedrich Ostermann) (1686–1747)   6, 205
Osvobozhdenie   168
Otechestvennye Zapiski   167
Ottoman Empire   134

Pacification   234
Pale of Settlement   234
Panin, Count Nikita Ivanovich (1718–1783)   6, 205
Pan-Slavism   115, 234
Paris, Treaties of   234
Paskevich, Ivan Fedorovich (1782–1856)   205
Patriarch   235
Paul I (Paul Petrovich) (1754–1801)   2, 6, 12, 205

Pauper's allotment   235
Peasants' Union   235
People's Freedom (Will)   114
Persia, Russia and   143
Pestel, Colonel Paul I (1799–1826)   205
Peter and Paul Fortress   235
Peter I (the Great) (1672–1725)   2, 5, 47, 205–7
Peter II (1715–1730)   6, 11, 207
Peter III (1728–1762)   6, 12, 24, 207
Petrashevsky Circle   30, 113–14, 235
Petrograd   4
Petroleum production   106
Philaret (Vasily Mikhaylovich Drozolov) (1782–1867)   207–8
Philaret, Patriarch (1553?–1633)   208
Philosophes and Catherine II (the Great)   44
Plater, Emilija (1806–1831)   208
Plehve, Vyacheslav Konstantinovich (1846–1904)   7, 208
Pobedonostsev, Konstantin Petrovich (1827–1907)   3, 208–9
Pochta Dukhov   165
Pochtovyi Trakt   235
Pogrom   235
Poland   146–7
Poland, partitions of   136–8, 234–5
Political changes from Ivan IV   46–64
Polyarnaya Zvezda   166
Pomeshchik   235
Pood   235
Popular movements of 1905   118
Population   92
Populism (*Narodnost*)   235–6
Port Arthur, surrender of   35
Portsmouth, Peace of   4
Posad   236
Possessed, The   156
Potemkin, Prince Grigory Aleksandrovich (1739–1791)   6, 209
Potomstvennyi Potochnyi Grazhdanin   236
Poud   235
Pravda   36, 168
Precipice   156
Preobrazhenskoye, Treaty of   133
Procurator-General   2
Prokopovich, Feofan (1681–1736)   209
Prosveshchenie   168
Provisional Government   4, 124
Prussia, Russia and   143

Publishing 155
Pud 236
Pugachev, Yemelyan Ivanovich (1726–1775) 2, 209
Pugachevshchina 236
Punishment 162
Pushkin, Aleksandr Sergeyevich (1799–1837) 29, 170, 209–10

Quadruple Alliance 236

Rabochaya Zarya 167
Rabochy 167
Rada 236
Radicalism, rise of 111–25
Radishchev, Aleksandr Nikolayevich (1749–1802) 210
Railways 108–9
Rasputin, Grigory Yefimovich (1872–1916) 37, 210
Rastrelli, Count Bartolomeo (1700–1771) 210
Raznochintsy 236
Rech 168
Redemption Payments 236
Regencies 9–13
Reinsurance Treaty 236
Religion 65–81
Repin, Ilya Yefimovich (1844–1930) 210–11
Resurrection 156
Reutern, Count Mikhail (1820–1890) 7, 211
Revolution of 1905 116–18
Revolyutsionnaya Rossiya 168
Riad 237
River traffic 108
Rodzyanko, Mikhail Vladimirovich (1859–1924) 211
Romanov, Prince Konstantin Nikolayevich (1827–1892) 211
Romanovs 5, 237
Romodanovsky, Prince Fedor (1640–1717) 211
Rossi, Karl Ivanovich (1775–1849) 211
Rostopchin, Count Fedor Vasilyevich (1763–1826) 211–12
Rostovtsev, General Yakob Ivanovich (1803–1860) 212
Rozhestvenski, Zinovi Petrovich (1848–1909) 212
Rudin 155

Rumyantsev, Count Pyotr Aleksandrovich (1725–1796) 212
Rus 167
Russia America (Alaska) 1741–1867 143–4
Russian American Company 2
Russian Social Democratic Labour Party 237
Russification 237
Russkie Vedomosti 167
Russkoye Bogatstvo 167
Russkoye Slovo 168
Russky Invalid 166
Russo-Japanese War 4, 141–2
Russo-Swedish War 1788–90 134
Russo-Turkish War 1768–74 134
Russo-Turkish War 1787–92 134
Russo-Turkish War 1806–12 135
Russo-Trukish War 1877–78 136
Ryleyev, Kondraty Fedorovich (1795–1826) 212
Rysakov, Nikolai Ivanovich (1861–1881) 212

St George's Day law 46
St Petersburg 2, 21, 22, 36, 44
St Petersburg News 165
Sakhalin 147, 237
Samizdat 237
Samoilova, Konkordiya (1876–1921) 212–13
Samsonov, Aleksandr Vasilyevich (1859–1914) 213
Sazonov, Sergey Dmitriyevich (1861–1927) 213
Sealed Train 237
Sebastopol 136
Second Coalition, War of the 138
Second International 237–8
Senate 2
Serfdom 31, 82–91, 238
Serfs, emancipation of 86–9
Sergius Alexandrovich, Grand Duke (1864–1905) 213
Severnaya Pchela 166
Severny Vestnik 165
Shadows 156
Shidlovsky Commission 238
Shuvalov, Count Ivan (1727–1797) 213
Shuvalov, Count Pyotr Andreyevich (1827–1889) 213–14

Shuysky, Prince Vasily (fl. early 17th century) 5, 214
Siberia, Conquest of 15
Skoptsi 238
Slavophile 41
Sloboda 238
Smoke 156
Sophia Alekseyevna (1657–1704) 5, 10, 214
Soul Tax (Poll or Head Tax) 238
Southern Society 238
Soviet 238
Sovremennik 166
Speransky, Count Mikhail Mikhailovich (1772–1839) 214
Spirit Wrestlers see *Dukhobory* 227
State reforms of 1808–09 56–7
Stenka Razin (?–1671) 19
Stolypin, Pyotr Arkadyevich (1862–1911) 7, 89–90, 214–15
Streltsy 20, 21, 48, 238–9
Stundists 239
Stürmer, Boris Vladimirovich (1848–1917) 7, 215
Supreme Privy (Secret) Council 52
Suvorov, Count Aleksandr Vasilyevich (1730–1800) 215
Sverdlov, Yakov Mikhailovich (1885–1919) 215
Syn Otechestva 168

Table of Rank 22, 50–2
Taiga 239
Tatishchev, Vasily Nikitich (1686–1750) 215–16
Telescop 166
Theatre 157–8
Third Coalition, War of 138–9
Third Section (Department) 57–8, 163, 239
Thousand Souls, A 155
Tilsit, Treaty of 27
Time of Troubles 5, 9
Tkachev, Pyotr Nikitich (1844–1885) 216
Tolstoy, Count Dmitry (1823–1889) 216
Tolstoy, Count Lev Nikolayevich (1828–1910) 216–17
Trans-Siberian Railway 35
Treaties 1681–1918 130–2
Trotsky, Lev Davidovich (Bronshteyn) (1879–1940) 217

Trubetskoy, Prince Sergey Nikolayevich (1790–1860) 217
Tsar 239
Turkmanchai, Treaty of (1828) 143

Ukase 239
Ulozhenie 47, 160
Ulyanov, Aleksandr Ilyich (1866–1887) 217
Union of the Russian People 239
Uprisings, peasant 85–6
Ushakov, Admiral Fedor Fedorovich (1744–1817) 217–18
Ussuri 147
Utro Rossii 168

Valuyev, Count Pyotr Aleksandrovich (1814–1890) 7, 218
Vasily III (1505–1533) 1
Vedomosti (News) 21, 239
Vedomosti Moskovskogo Gosudarstva 165
Verst 239
Vestni Yevropy 166
Vestnik Evropy (1805) 165, (1866) 167
Vienna, Congress of 140–1
Virgin Soil 156
Vladivostok 147
Voevoda 239
Volkonsky, Prince Sergey Grigoryevich (1788–1865) 218
Volost 239
Voltaire, François Marie Arouet (1694–1778) 44, 218
Vorontsov, Mikhail Illarionovich (1714–1767) 218
Vpered 167
Vyborg Manifesto 61–2

War and Peace 31, 156
Wars 1548–1918 126–30
Weights and measures 110
West, influence of the 41–5
Westerner/Slavophile controversy 41–2
Westernisers 41–2
Winter Palace 239
Witte, Count Sergey Yulyevich (1849–1915) 7, 218–19
Women, changing status of 93–6
World of Art, The 168
World War I 4, 142–3
Wrangel, Baron Ferdinand Petrovich (1796–1870) 219

Yaguzhinsky, Pavel Ivanovich
  (1683–1736) 219
Yankovich de Mirievo, Theodore
  (*c*. 1740–1814) 219
Yassak 240
Yeropkin, Pyotr Mikhailovich
  (1690–1740) 219
Yurovsky, Yankel (*fl.* early 20th century)
  219

Zemskii Sobor 5, 14, 16, 46, 47

Zemstvo 240
Zhelyabov, Andrey Ivanovich
  (1850–1881) 219–20
Zhizn 167
Zhurnal Rossiyskoy Slovestnosti 166
Zritel 165
Zubatov, Sergey Vasilyevich (1864–1917)
  220
Zubov, Prince Platon Alexandrovich
  (1767–1822) 220
Zvezda 168